Oracle Press™

# Oracle Business Intelligence Discoverer 11*g* Handbook

Michael Armstrong-Smith
Darlene Armstrong-Smith

New York Chicago San Francisco Athens
London Madrid Mexico City Milan
New Delhi Singapore Sydney Toronto

**Cataloging-in-Publication Data is on file with the Library of Congress**

McGraw-Hill Education books are available at special quantity discounts to use as premiums and sales promotions, or for use in corporate training programs. To contact a representative, please visit the Contact Us pages at www.mhprofessional.com.

**Oracle Business Intelligence Discoverer 11*g* Handbook**



1 2 3 4 5 6 7 8 9 0 DOC DOC 1 0 9 8 7 6 5 4 3

ISBN 978-0-07-180430-1
MHID 0-07-180430-7

**Sponsoring Editor**
Paul Carlstroem

**Editorial Supervisor**
Jody McKenzie

**Project Manager**
Sheena Uprety, Cenveo® Publisher Services

**Acquisitions Coordinator**
Amanda Russell

**Technical Editor**
Steve Fitzgerald

**Copy Editor**
Kim Wimpsett

**Proofreader**
Claire Splan

**Indexer**
Claire Splan

**Production Supervisor**
James Kussow

**Composition**
Cenveo Publisher Services

**Illustration**
Cenveo Publisher Services

**Art Director, Cover**
Jeff Weeks

*We dedicate this book to the power of love and perseverance. We were married less than a year when we wrote the first Discoverer Handbook. Twelve years and two editions later, we are more in love and the dearest of friends. If our marriage can survive this, it can survive anything.*

# About the Authors

**Michael Armstrong-Smith** is the principal consultant for Armstrong-Smith Consulting, specializing in data warehousing, E-Business Suite, and Oracle Discoverer training and implementation. A fellow of the Institute of Analysts and Programmers and an Oracle Ace in business intelligence, he has more than 30 years of systems development experience. Michael is a leader in the field of business intelligence, with specialist knowledge of data warehouses and, of course, Oracle Discoverer. He is also a conference speaker and has spoken on Discoverer at conferences throughout the United States and Canada. Armstrong-Smith Consulting has a weblog and forum on all things Discoverer at http://ascbi.com and http://learndiscoverer.blogspot.com.

Michael's real passions are giving service to God by serving others and exploring model railroading. He gives countless hours counseling and supporting the Young Single Adults in his local Stake of The Church of Jesus Christ of Latter-Day Saints. He is also a tireless missionary and loves to organize service projects to spruce up towns and clean up and care for the homes of the elderly, handicapped, and widowed.

Michael's model railroad takes up one-third of a very large basement and is a true masterpiece of tiny railroad engineering. Darlene loves his hobby because she knows that when he is not out doing God's work, he is happily puttering in his basement.

**Darlene Armstrong-Smith** has 20 years of experience in curriculum development, training, and system design. She learned almost everything she knows from amazing mentors who were generous with their knowledge and time. She began her IT career at Custom Computers in Anchorage, Alaska, working as the repair-bench technician. Her mentor was a crusty, former 20-year employee of IBM named Arty. He was wonderfully kind to someone who knew absolutely nothing but who was willing to try. Her greatest mentor has been her husband, Michael Armstrong-Smith, a true genius and tireless worker.

When Darlene is not busy solving IT-related problems, she is cooking gourmet meals and poring over magazines to get decorating ideas for her home. She is an avid homemaker, gardener, and goat herder. She is also active in The Church of Jesus Christ of Latter-Day Saints and has served in a variety of callings from leading the music for the children's Primary to Relief Society President to Stake Director of Public Affairs.

# About the Technical Editor

**Steve Fitzgerald** joined Oracle in 1997 after obtaining a bachelor's degree in business administration in 1992 and working in several business and finance-oriented roles, gaining experience in data extraction, warehouse, report writing, and analytic analysis. During his time at Oracle, he has worked with several product teams and products including Data Browser, Data Query, Reports, Forms, Discoverer, OBIEE, and BI Publisher. He also obtained a master's degree in information security/project management and additionally a WebLogic Administrator certification. He is fluent with several operating systems and experienced in related BI technology integration points including application servers, HTTP servers, single sign-on, security, LDAP, exalytics, and portals, and he is technically adept with databases, E-Business Suite, virtualization, and other technologies.

Currently, in his role on an Oracle BI Enterprise Edition (OBIEE) advanced resolution technical team, he is focused on engaging with strategic customers to ensure their BI implementations, configuration, usage, and performance are successful. He also contributes to internal BI, process improvement, and knowledge projects. His BI interests include topology/architecture, systems management, life cycle, infrastructure, optimization, performance, and integration.

# Contents at a Glance

## PART I
## Getting Started with Discoverer



## PART II
## Editing the Query



## PART III
## Advanced Discoverer Techniques

PART IV

## Using the Discoverer Administration Edition Chapter



PART V

## Appendixes

Contents

## PART II
## Editing the Query

## PART III
## Advanced Discoverer Techniques

# Acknowledgments

When you write a book, you develop a "love-hate" relationship with just about everyone working on the project. A husband and wife team working on a book together could cause all kinds of problems, but we are crazy in love enough to get through it without coming to blows. Everyone in our family will be so happy when we can stop saying, "I can't, I have to work on the book." We want to acknowledge our children for their sensitivity and patience. We also want to acknowledge each other for demonstrating genuine kindness under difficult conditions.

So far, it sounds like a whole lot of love. Where is the hate? The real "love-hate" relationships are between the authors and their editors. In retrospect, we could easily say that we loved Paul Carlstroem, our sponsoring editor, and Amanda Russell, our acquisitions coordinator, throughout the entire project, but that would be a lie, and you know where liars go! Some mornings opening our e-mail was the hardest thing to do because we knew that we were going to be hounded for delinquent chapters or missing screen shots. But the end result is a book we are proud of and that was not drastically overdue. Paul was truly good to us and treated us with respect and sensitivity. We appreciate his hard work more than we can say.

We would also like to acknowledge our editorial supervisor Jody McKenzie and copy editor Kim Wimpsett, without whom we would sound like idiots. Michael uses too many words, which Kim gently removed without hurting his feelings. Darlene, on the other hand, does not use enough words, and Jody was diplomatic in stating that something could use a better explanation.

Sheena Uprety was the soft and quiet voice that urged us on to the finish line.

We also acknowledge the work of Steve Fitzgerald, our technical editor from Oracle. His insight and knowledge were so important to this work, and we thank him for sharing his expertise.

# Introduction

The first step in writing the third edition of the *Oracle Discoverer Handbook* was to determine who our audience was. In the first edition, we limited the content to the end-user edition of Discoverer, with the focus primarily on Desktop. In the second and this, the third, edition, we changed our target audience to cover not only end users but administrators as well. The focus for end users has switched to Discoverer Plus. However, Desktop is still covered, and we have also included information on Discoverer Viewer.

It has always been a challenge to know whether we should stick with Discoverer Plus and Desktop only, but we cannot leave our Discoverer administrators out in the cold. It is difficult to write one book that should be two, but we cannot find a way to uncouple the admin tool from the end user tool and so they remain between the same covers.

We also knew that users of Discoverer at all levels were in need of a tutorial on this powerful and very complex piece of software. We made the decision to reach out to all users—from the novice end user to the true power user.

We believe there is something in this book for every Discoverer end user and administrator. Novices will be taken from the very first step of each task through to its successful completion. Power users will find information they may have otherwise needed to look for elsewhere. We have organized the steps for every task into useful and easy-to-follow workflows and have tried to provide as much detail as possible. Administrators will find help and support to release the power of Discoverer to their end users. We have shared with you skills and methods that have taken us years to develop.

When we took on the challenge of writing this tutorial, our desire was to bring all of Discoverer's powerful features into one source. You will find many hitherto undocumented Discoverer features in this book as well as dozens of tips and tricks.

## How This Book Is Organized

This book is divided into five sections, including four appendixes.

- **Part I, Getting Started with Discoverer** Part I covers the basic history and philosophy of Discoverer. It also contains an extensive description of the types of databases with which Discoverer can interface. Following this introductory material, we deal with the login sequence and all steps of the Discoverer Workbook Wizard.
- **Part II, Editing the Query** Part II focuses on turning a basic Discoverer query into much more. We begin with formatting issues, such as font, colors, headings, and numbers. We then move on to graphing in Discoverer and turning a query into a well-formatted and ready-to-deliver report. Chapter 9 is all about analyzing data. This is a powerful tutorial on the elements of analysis as well as how to use Discoverer's various tools to analyze your data. Chapter 10 covers using Discoverer Viewer. There is enough power in this tool that it deserved its own chapter. Don't overlook the advantages of using this tool in your organization.
- **Part III, Advanced Discoverer Techniques** The first three chapters of Part III take all of the Discoverer tools and give detailed instructions on how to use them effectively, including refining items, drilling, and building effective conditions, along with refining parameters, calculations, sorting, and percentages. The next two chapters of Part III deal with query management, user preferences, the toolbar, and how to interact with the Discoverer administrator.
- **Part IV, Using the Discoverer Administration Edition** In this section, we have attempted to pass on as much of our knowledge and experience in building and managing great business areas as we could in the pages allowed. We could have easily written a 1,000-page book on administering Discoverer, but we surely would have killed each other had we tried. Chapters 19 and 20 cover managing WebLogic and configuring Discoverer. These are highly technical chapters and are a must-read for anyone wanting to know how to manage Discoverer on an application server. Chapter 21 will introduce you to Oracle's analytic functions and show you how to make use of these very powerful objects within Discoverer.
- **Part V, Appendixes** Part V contains four appendixes. Appendix A is "Michael's Gold Mine of Answers to FAQs." As you can imagine, questions come in to us at what is sometimes an alarming rate, but Michael tries to answer them all. We have attempted to include as many of the questions he has answered over the years as possible. Appendix B contains a detailed list of all of Discoverer's functions, including syntax, descriptions, and examples. It also contains a detailed list of format masks. Appendix C describes the various types of databases you can use with Discoverer. This appendix also covers views and in particular focuses on Oracle's business views in E-Business Suite and NoetixViews. Appendix D describes the tutorial database we used throughout this book.

# PART I

# Getting Started with Discoverer

# CHAPTER 1

# An Overview of Discoverer

This chapter will introduce you to Oracle Business Intelligence Discoverer 11*g* (11.1.1.6), henceforth referred to as Discoverer, the time-tested reporting and analysis tool from Oracle Corporation. We will discuss business intelligence and show how Discoverer is perfectly suited to be your company's tool of choice. We also will discuss some of the recent business intelligence trends and how Discoverer fits in with these trends.

The 11.1.1.6 release of Discoverer came out in 2009 and continues to demonstrate Oracle's grip on excellence in information delivery. This release maintains its status with two powerful and flexible web-based products, Oracle Business Intelligence Discoverer Plus and Oracle Business Intelligence Discoverer Viewer, henceforth referred to as Plus and Viewer. Plus and Viewer still access online analytical processing (OLAP) data, but we have been disappointed with the performance and usability of the OLAP feature. For this reason, we have chosen to remove the OLAP chapter from this edition of the Discoverer Handbook. Also, since the last release of this book, Oracle has introduced Oracle BI Enterprise Edition (OBIEE), where the real power of OLAP is in full force. If your organization is ready for OLAP, it is time for you to consider the move to OBIEE.

We continue the overview of some of the more general aspects of query writing by showing you the differences between ad hoc and predefined queries. We are also eager to discuss the things we have learned, important lessons that we want to share regarding the development of a true business intelligence solution using Discoverer. The final section in this overview tells you how to use various sources of help to find out more about Oracle Discoverer.

# Business Intelligence and Your Organization

Oh, how far we have come since writing the first edition of the Discoverer Handbook 12 years ago; it was obvious that we were sold on Discoverer back then, and we are even more so now. It might surprise you to find that it is still our bread and butter, but not perhaps in the way you might think. Using it in connection with an Oracle database, the world's finest and most commonly used database system, you have tremendous reporting power at your disposal. However, we no longer think of Discoverer as the end-all and be-all of our business intelligence (BI) strategy. We have shifted our focus to the database and having done so are able to do things with Discoverer that most BI shops never get close to doing. We will demonstrate some of our discoveries in later chapters. As the majority of our work is with organizations utilizing Oracle E-Business Suite (also known as Oracle Applications), we have found that the best way to assist them is by implementing embedded data warehouses. This way, we are able to capitalize on the seeded views provided with Discoverer and custom views that cross E-Business Suite module boundaries and overcome performance issues related to the use of the Oracle views. In addition to the improvement in Discoverer reporting that goes along with an embedded data warehouse, the true benefit is that it makes you ready to move to a new tool such as OBIEE. We now do 80 percent of our work at the database level. This creates a much more flexible environment for our clients' long-term needs.

As one of the leading providers of both traditional and web-based business intelligence, Oracle Corporation has gone to great lengths to try to understand the links and interactions between databases (and database technologies) and delivery of information. Anyone interested in delivering information within their business should look to Oracle. The terms *information delivery*, *business intelligence*, and *decision support* are all included under the same umbrella. In fact, these terms are often used interchangeably. While the definitions remain vague, an organization's need is clear. Companies are investing billions of dollars, pounds, euros, yen, and so forth, into information technology. The goal for all of these companies is to gather data and make use of it, enabling faster and better-informed business decisions.

Companies can no longer be satisfied with knowing how many sales were made today. They want to know how many sales were made last week, last month, or last year. They want to know whether their company's bottom line is improving and want to be able to forecast trends with better accuracy. As a company executive once said to one of us, "Tell me something about my company that I don't already know." By harnessing the power of Discoverer, users can gain insights into their businesses that would be simply difficult or even impossible without writing hundreds of sophisticated SQL queries. Put Discoverer in the hands of an expert data analyst, and you will surprise even the most seasoned users of other products. Another executive recently said, "Show me those things that are within my area of control that are not within normal limits or... appear to be heading away from normal...you know, those things that I should be aware of."

If you are reading this book, you have Discoverer. You might not be sure how your company came to adopt it, but you have it and don't know what to do next. We often hear from our customers that "we got Discoverer for free when we bought E-Business Suite." We assure them that they did not get it for free. Instead, they bought is as part of the larger purchase. Unfortunately, when they believe that it was free, they tend to think of it as a "throwaway" and do not give it the time or consideration that it deserves. We have learned over time that Discoverer is powerful, is flexible, and can be your enterprise-wide reporting system.

## Your Discoverer Investment

Oracle Corporation's statement of direction implies that it will not force you off Discoverer and on to another tool. It is important for you to understand, however, that like all software, Discoverer will one day be phased out in order to make way for more modern BI solutions. You currently have three options:

- Protect your investment by staying with Discoverer, continuing to receive Oracle's outstanding support.
- Extend your investment by continuing to use Discoverer while integrating with other Oracle BI tools such as Oracle BI Enterprise Edition.
- Evolve your investment by formulating a strategy to fully migrate to one of Oracle's other BI tools, more than likely OBIEE.

As we were completing this chapter of the book, in February 2013, we were informed by Oracle that the latest version of the Discoverer Metadata Migration Assistant (DOMA for short) had just been released. DOMA translates the metadata from an Oracle BI Discoverer system to that which can be used by OBIEE. Oracle tells us that this version of DOMA will be able to migrate both the End User Layer (EUL) metadata and the metadata associated with Discoverer Workbooks. Please refer to Chapter 20 for more detail.

In summary, therefore, your choices are to protect your investment, to extend and integrate, or to evolve to another platform (that is a coined phrase of a product manager).

## Connecting to Other Databases

For some time now, Discoverer has not supported the use of native ODBC drivers to connect to non-Oracle databases. Instead, you must use generic connectivity to retrieve data from any non-Oracle database. In other words, the EUL must be stored in an Oracle database. Generic connectivity is done via Heterogeneous Services, a set of common architecture and administration mechanisms provided with the Oracle database to enable you to connect non-Oracle databases. Discoverer users can use generic connectivity to access ODBC (Open Database Connectivity) or OLE DB (object linking and embedding database) databases.

The non-Oracle database must comply sufficiently with the ODBC standard (for more information about ODBC and OLE DB connectivity requirements, see the Oracle Database Heterogeneous Connectivity Administrator's Guide).

In previous versions of Discoverer, users could connect to non-Oracle databases using ODBC drivers. The major difference between using ODBC drivers to connect to a non-Oracle database using the Oracle database generic connectivity feature is the location of the EUL, as follows:

- With ODBC drivers, the EUL is stored in the non-Oracle database.
- With generic connectivity, the EUL is stored in the Oracle database.

So, if you have not yet switched to using Oracle databases, you can still benefit from the power and ease of use built into the Discoverer product. Organizations today are generating unprecedented amounts of data to support their day-to-day functions—but collecting and collating data is no longer enough. An organization must have a means of turning that data into that most precious of business commodities, information. Anyone with decision-making power needs the ability to view and manipulate company data. Oracle Discoverer does just that. It can unleash your data, turning it into a true asset for your business. We will present a more in-depth discussion on the concept of generic connectivity from a Discoverer perspective in Chapter 19.

# Business Intelligence and Trends

You have seen us use the term *business intelligence* several times so far in this book. But what is business intelligence? According to the Data Warehousing Institute (TDWI), www.tdwi.org, the definition of business intelligence is as follows:

> Business intelligence (BI) unites data, technology, analytics, and human knowledge to optimize business decisions and ultimately drive an enterprise's success. BI programs usually combine an enterprise data warehouse and a BI platform or tool set to transform data into usable, actionable business information.

The term *business intelligence* has been around for some time and was first used in a Gartner Group report in 1996, but the principles have been around a lot longer than that. In their time, these principles have been called management information systems (MIS), business support systems (BSS), and now BI. Whatever the name, the principles remain the same. However, recently there have been some exciting new trends, trends that Discoverer will ideally help you with.

You will also have heard the term *data warehousing* many times, and we will use it in several places within this book. Once again a definition might help. The Data Warehousing Institute states the following:

> Data warehousing incorporates data stores and conceptual, logical, and physical models to support business goals and end-user information needs. A data warehouse (DW) is the foundation for a successful BI program.
>
> Creating a DW requires mapping data between sources and targets [and] then capturing the details of the transformation in a metadata repository. The data warehouse provides a single, comprehensive source of current and historical information.

# Recent Business Intelligence Trends and Discoverer

We have noticed that there is a trend to shift away from departmental to enterprise-wide reporting systems. When you add to this the fact that IT management is being pressured to make more and more data available in near real time, you can see that the need for data is increasing. As the need for data increases, the need for better reporting tools also increases. Oracle Business Intelligence Discoverer 11*g* (11.1.1.6) can help you.

## Data Mining

Data mining continues to be the essence of BI. Oracle's own version of this, called Oracle Data Mining, has been available since 2004. The following is according to Oracle:

Oracle Data Mining enables users to discover new insights hidden in data and to leverage investments in Oracle Database technology. With Oracle Data Mining, you can build and apply predictive models that help you target your best customers, develop detailed customer profiles, and find and prevent fraud. Data analysts can find patterns and insights hidden in their data. Application developers can quickly automate the extraction and distribution of new business intelligence—predictions, patterns, and discoveries—throughout the organization. The end result of a data mining algorithm is data in a table. If you use Discoverer Administrator to build a business area on this data, you can then use one of the Discoverer end-user tools to query the data mining results. An interesting new development is Oracle Data Miner 11g Release 2, which is a free extension to Oracle SQL Developer 3.1 that "enables analysts to work directly with data inside the database, [to] explore the data graphically, and to build and evaluate multiple data mining models.

## Data Federation

Another trend we have noticed is data federation. Using this approach, the software enables an organization to aggregate data from disparate sources into a virtual database in order to be used for BI purposes. One very important element of federated data is that the virtual database contains information only about the data and its location. The data itself remains in its original database and as such is left *in situ*. Think for a moment about a SQL view that leaves the data where it is but allows the pulling together of information from multiple sources into a single object. By extending this to multiple objects, you begin to see how federated data could be very useful. Many different federated methods are available, among which we would like to mention the following:

- **Horizontal federation** In this method, the data is at the same level of granularity so that you join cubes to cubes, summaries to summaries, or detail to detail. In other words, the data is all using the same dimension. For example, you can join back from a summary table to the original relational E-Business Suite database. The number of rows should not change, but you can build queries that "add in" data from the source.
- **Vertical federation** In this method, the data has different levels of granularity so that this time you can join summaries to detail, in essence allowing a drill-through technology to expand the data to see more information. The number of rows will probably change as you drill through. You can think of this as hyper-drilling through from a sales summary report to the sales details. Discoverer hyper-drills very well, and we will show you how to do this in a future chapter.

### Self-Service

The trend for self-service is where the information is put in the hands of more frontline users, such as business analysts, for faster decision support. In essence, you are looking to get the right information to the right person at the right time. Using a self-service, Discoverer users can access their own personal information. These are two ways in which Discoverer users can access their own data:

- By integrating Discoverer with E-Business Suite so that Discoverer understands the user responsibilities, thus ensuring that the same report delivers different information depending upon which user is logged in.
- By employing a virtual private database (VPD) wherein the database filters the content rather than the application. A VPD when properly configured and installed will actually improve the performance of many queries.

### Democratization of Data

Another trend is what is called the *democratization of data*. Put in its simplest form, this means making data available to the masses. The Internet is perhaps the greatest expression of this trend, where one can find information on just about any subject in the world, all without leaving home. According to a report published by professors Hal Varian and Peter Lyman of the School of Information Management and Systems, "A century ago, the average person could only create and access a small amount of information. Now, ordinary people not only have access to huge amounts of data, but are also able to create gigabytes of data themselves and, potentially, publish it to the world via the Internet." The logical extensions of this democratization are web services being used with a Common Information Model (CIM). This "design once, use anywhere" approach uses an open-systems methodology where the user interacts with a web interface but has no idea where the data is coming from. The underlying data objects should be able to be swapped in and swapped out without impacting the end user. The front-end user interface is developed independently from both the system and the underlying platform. If you think about some of the modern Internet tools that we are so used to working with, tools such as Facebook, the Weather Channel, or Google, the user has no idea of the complexities of the underlying objects. So long as the front end remains unchanged, the software vendor can switch applications, operating systems, and platforms at any time and as many times as are needed without impacting the end user.

### Analytic Applications

We see a continuing trend toward using analytic applications. Analytics are the logical progression for modern BI applications. They look at historical data and use it to predict future activity in order to enable the business to make better informed decisions. A report in the MIT Sloan Management Review in November 2011 (http://sloanreview.mit.edu/feature/achieving-competitive-advantage-through-analytics/) determined that "organizations using analytics are more than twice as likely to substantially outperform their competitive peers."

Analytics allow companies to differentiate themselves from their competitors. After all, if every company was to use the same piece of software as their competitors, how could one gain a greater market share from the next? Companies that use analytics run more efficiently, make the most of their customers, and, important to the shareholders, become more profitable.

According to TDWI, www.tdwi.org, the business intelligence market can be broken down into the following two types of analytic application:

- Packaged
- Custom

**Packaged Analytic Applications** This is generally referred to as the "buy" option. You buy a vendor-supplied package that provides out-of-the-box analytics. According to TDWI, this type of package "contains an integrated set of analytic tools, data models, ETL mappings, business metrics, predefined reports, and 'best practice' processes that accelerate the deployment of an analytic application in a given domain."

When we wrote the second edition of this book in 2004, we expected to see more in the way of third-party applications developed to use with E-Business Suite. We had anticipated the development of better views, more creative uses of the Oracle tables, and effective leveraging of the vast quantities of data. Nope, did not happen. From time to time we were invited to look at a "wonderful" new tool that would mine for Oracle data gold, rewrite your Discoverer queries, and make it ever so easy to migrate to OBIEE. Until February 2013, we had not seen one that was anything but clunky and confusing or actually worked on anything but a superficial level. With the release of the newest version of DOMA during the first quarter of 2013, we are hopeful that the wait is over. Please see Chapter 20 for more details.

**Custom Analytic Applications** This is generally referred to as the "build" option. You build your own analytics using tools provided by a vendor. According to TDWI, this solution "is primarily built using tools, code, or customizable templates to provide the exact look-and-feel functionality desired by an organization for its analytic environment."

Because packaged applications generally do not cover everything that an organization wants, many IT managers are wary of using them. Customizing a packaged application can be expensive and subsequently difficult to upgrade. We have seen a large uptake in custom applications where organizations build their own data warehouse. Using Oracle's flagship Oracle Data Integrator (ODI) or Oracle Warehouse Builder (OWB), or even native PL/SQL and Discoverer, you can create such an environment. To date, we have not seen any significant movement away from the custom to the packaged approach, and we believe there is still significant demand for the "build" approach.

Custom applications can themselves be further broken down into two categories:

- Shrink-wrapped products, like Discoverer and OBIEE, which can also include prebuilt embedded functionality
- Building-block products that allow you to create your own BI applications and products

As you can see, whichever method you choose for obtaining your information, Discoverer is ideal for helping you with your data reporting. We hope the preceding discussion on the trends of business intelligence helps you understand that Discoverer remains a key component in Oracle's BI offerings.

# Discoverer's Role in Business Intelligence

As stated earlier, Oracle has firmly positioned Discoverer right at the heart of its business intelligence strategy. But Discoverer is more than just a component of a suite of tools (albeit an extremely powerful suite). It has the ability to stand on its own two feet, to make a place for itself within your company, and to be your analysis tool of choice. This book, therefore, will now concentrate on Discoverer. So, just where does this tool come from, and how can it fit in with your company's business intelligence strategy?

## The Nine Parts of Discoverer

Discoverer consists of nine components:

- Oracle Business Intelligence Discoverer Plus
- Oracle Business Intelligence Discoverer Viewer
- Oracle Business Intelligence Discoverer Desktop
- Oracle Business Intelligence Discoverer Administrator
- EUL Command Line utility for Java
- Oracle Discoverer Portlet Provider
- Oracle Fusion Middleware Control
- Oracle WebLogic Server Administration Control
- Oracle BI Spreadsheet Add-In

### Oracle Business Intelligence Discoverer Plus

This version, one of the two web-based end-user query tools, uses a downloadable Java applet to enable the user to interact with the database. This applet uses a set of reusable Java components that are the building blocks for many of Oracle's web-based tools. Born out of Desktop in the late 1990s, Plus has been progressively improved over the years such that now it has almost all of the Desktop features, with additional features that are not available in Desktop.

As with Discoverer 10*g*, Discoverer 11*g* can also be used both stand-alone and as part of a full-blown application server environment. By full-blown we mean that it was installed with Oracle Identity Management and possibly Single Sign-On. Please refer to Chapter 19 for more information about the differences between the stand-alone and full-blown Discoverer installs.

What you will notice about 11*g* is that it is highly modularized. You just choose which components you want to use and install them.

### Oracle Business Intelligence Discoverer Viewer

This version, utilizing Hypertext Markup Language (HTML) technology, is the product of choice for executing and running workbooks. It is the second of the web-based end-user tools and allows the user to view and execute an existing query. While you cannot create new workbooks in Viewer, if you have been granted the appropriate privileges by your Discoverer manager, you can, for the first time, save changes. The changes you can save are those made by drilling, pivoting, changing page items, and changing graph types and sizes. Formatting or stoplight format changes are not saved. Viewer is licensed in the same way as Plus, and the two come bundled for the purchase of one license. You cannot purchase just Plus or just Viewer, though; they come hand in hand. You can think of them as being two peas in a pod. If you have one product, you have both. Of course, it is your choice whether you actually use them both or restrict your users to one or the other. Many organizations today are making use of Viewer as their tool of choice for delivering end-user reports, and if you have not used it, we strongly recommend you take a look.

### Oracle Business Intelligence Discoverer Desktop

This version is the end-user query tool that you would use if you are not using the Web. It is available only for Windows. However, it is Oracle's original flagship product and as such is very stable. We have used this tool for many years, and it is an excellent product. As mentioned earlier, there are some features of Desktop that are not available in any of the other end-user components. In addition to being able to save to the file system and create workbooks that use subqueries, Desktop also has 3-D graph rotation and the ability to embed images into titles and into the background of your report. Desktop is licensed separately from the web components and will usually be the first tool employed by your organization. It is cheaper and easier to install and therefore lends itself ideally for evaluation. Unfortunately, Oracle has not continued development of Desktop as it has for Plus. This means there are several pieces of added functionality that you will find in Plus but not in Desktop. At one time, we suspected that Oracle's intention was to drop Desktop at some point in the future. However, 11*g* has been released and Desktop remains, so we no longer have that fear. However, do not worry, because even if Oracle did decide to drop Desktop, it will continue to support it and provide run-time compatibility between all components of Discoverer and Desktop for as long as Desktop ships. For now it remains a core component of the Oracle Business Intelligence family of products. We can say quite honestly as folks who are in and out of Discoverer daily, we use Desktop only rarely and mostly for administrative functions, such as migrating workbooks from one environment to another.

### Oracle Business Intelligence Discoverer Administrator

This version, like Desktop available on Windows only, is client based and allows you to create and maintain the relational End User Layer. All of the background work that is needed to prepare relational data for the end user is done here. In the original handbook, we did not cover Discoverer Administrator at all; however, there was such an outcry that we decided it could not be left out of the second edition. We will, therefore, cover Discoverer Administrator in quite some detail in this, the third edition. For those of you who are employed as Discoverer managers, there is no change to the tried and tested interface that you have come to love. The 11*g* Administrator tool is the same as the 10*g* tool, which itself, apart from a few additional features, had a very similar look and feel to the 3.1, 4.1, and 9.0.2 versions.

Oracle did not introduce a new End User Layer for 11*g*, so if you are already using 10*g*, then you can simply install the 11*g* Administrator tool and point it at the same one. This makes any upgrade much easier.

Of all the metadata preparation tools on the market, we believe that Discoverer Administrator, while being extremely powerful, is also the easiest of all to use. Normally, more power means more complexity and hence less ease of use, but not in this case. Discoverer Administrator can make data available to end users in a fraction of the time that it would take in other relational metadata preparation tools. Add to this the fact that Discoverer Administrator works with and understands Oracle Applications better than any other metadata tool, bar none, and you have a win-win situation.

### EUL Command Line Utility for Java

This, the new incarnation for the EUL Command Line utility, is one of the Oracle BI Discoverer command-line tools. It is not an end-user tool but a utility that allows Discoverer managers to perform relational, End User Layer maintenance tasks, tasks that hitherto have been the domain of the Discoverer Administrator tool. There are still some tasks, such as adding new folders or editing custom folder properties, that cannot be done using the Java command-line utility. We were, however, pleasantly surprised at the utility's ease of use in managing the tasks that it can maintain. If you can master this interface, you can avoid ever having to log into Discoverer Administrator. We say "perhaps" because, in our opinion, there are just too many occasions when it is more cost-effective to use Discoverer Administrator to warrant not using it.

### Oracle Discoverer Portlet Provider

This component is web based and is available only if you have installed the Oracle Portal repository user and Oracle Portal components, including the Discoverer Portlet Provider. Using a portal, your organization can create a front end or dashboard for its business intelligence needs. For executives and senior management, these dashboards will be your interface of choice. Placing Discoverer portlets onto a dashboard enables you to make worksheet data available without the need for the executive to have to log in to Plus or Viewer. For more detailed data analysis, your executives can drill through from a Discoverer portlet back into Viewer. There are three types of Discoverer portlet: a list of workbooks portlet, a worksheet portlet, and a gauges portlet.

A new feature added to Discoverer 11*g* is the ability for Discoverer to now publish JSR 168–compliant portlets. This therefore means that Discoverer also supports integration with Oracle Web Center Spaces.

### Oracle Fusion Middleware Control

This component is also web based but is definitely not an end-user tool. In 10*g* you would have known that the tool used to manage the behind-the-scenes web controls was called Oracle Application Server Control. This has been replaced in 11*g* by a much more powerful version called Fusion Middleware Control. This tool, also known as Oracle Enterprise Manager 11*g* (OEM), allows the Discoverer manager to maintain settings that control how Plus, Viewer, and the Discoverer Portlet Provider function. OEM is also the tool that is used to make OLAP data available for querying inside Discoverer, as well as to manage your application deployments, WebLogic domain, and the web tier. Should you want to take advantage of the Identity Management (IM) or Metadata Repository (MR) control, the OEM interface is the place to go. As you will see in Chapter 19, even though OEM sounds complicated, it really is a joy to use.

### Oracle WebLogic Server Administration Console

This is another of the web-based, administrative tools. This is the tool that allows you to manage the WebLogic application server. In it you can configure your applications and manage your domain configurations. For Discoverer, you will use this tool to start the Discoverer service. According to the Oracle WebLogic Server Administration Console Guide, a WebLogic Server domain is a logically related group of WebLogic Server resources that you manage as a unit. A domain includes one or more WebLogic Servers and may also include WebLogic Server clusters. Clusters are groups of WebLogic Servers that work together to provide scalability and high availability for applications. You deploy and manage your applications as part of a domain. We will discuss this console more in Chapter 19.

### Oracle BI Spreadsheet Add-In

This is a client-based tool that adds Discoverer BI functionality to Microsoft Excel. Like Plus, this tool is built using BI Beans. The Oracle BI Spreadsheet Add-In is available only for accessing OLAP data. It cannot be used to access relational data that has been made available via an End User Layer. We will not discuss the Spreadsheet Add-In in this book. The Add-In can be found on the same CD that you used to install Desktop and Discoverer Administrator.

## How to Use This Book

This book focuses on the Oracle Business Intelligence 11*g* (11.1.1.6) release of Discoverer. The first part of the book is primarily aimed at end users and will be invaluable to beginners as well as to experienced report writers. The second part of the book is for administrators and as such will concentrate on the more technical aspects of the product. We hope that this book will therefore become known as your one-stop shopping place for everything to do with Discoverer. In the end-user part of this book, reference will be made to many administrative functions that, when utilized, will improve the user's awareness of what features are available within the product. This will enable end users to know what their administrators can do for them.

Discoverer managers will find much useful information for optimizing the product for maximum performance. By seeing and understanding how end users will use the tool, they will also learn how to provide a better service. Working together as a team, the Discoverer manager, report writers, and end users will thus be able to use this product to its maximum effectiveness. In the part of this book on administration, we will show you how to take requests from end users, analyze those requests, and then use one of the administrative tools to improve the effectiveness of the End User Layer. We firmly believe that Discoverer administration is an art, not a science, something to be enjoyed and not seen as a chore.

Your organization has most likely already purchased Discoverer, so you may be wondering what it can do for your company. You have probably heard about its easy-to-use interface and its ability to link to just about any database you can name, or maybe you're just caught up in the business intelligence revolution that is shaping our modern world. Whatever your reason for purchasing this book and whatever your level of expertise with Discoverer, there is something here for everyone.

## Example Database

Throughout this book we have used an Oracle 11*g* database and created sales records for a fictitious company called Global Widgets. This database has been used to demonstrate the creation of useful and meaningful business areas and queries. We have also added a mix of examples, showing both Discoverer Desktop and Discoverer Plus functionality. When there is a functional difference between the two end-user products, we will show both. When the difference is cosmetic only, we will give the description but not necessarily add a figure or illustration.

In the example database, our fictional company, Global Widgets, uses a fiscal year that begins on the Saturday following the last Friday in September. Thus, quarter one (Q1) runs from October to December, Q2 from January to March, and so on. We have done this to demonstrate Discoverer's ability to deal with fiscal years, because we are aware that not all companies base their fiscal year on the calendar year. Global Widgets used to deal exclusively with orders received and processed using traditional channels, but during 2007 it started using e-commerce. We have done this so that we can show you examples of queries where we analyze sales performance of the two channels.

You will also be shown how to analyze data from various sales districts and regions as a means of demonstrating Discoverer's drilling and filtering capabilities. The fiscal date hierarchy also allows us to demonstrate drilling, but this time from year to quarter to month to day. As a Discoverer manager, you will see how to create these hierarchies.

Appendix D provides an entity-relationship diagram (ERD) of the example database and a list of tables and indexes. The database is also available for download on both the Oracle Press and Learn Discoverer web sites.

# A New Direction in Reporting

In the past, it was the job of the developer to take the requirements of the business unit and turn them into queries and reports. Often, this was accomplished with the use of a middle layer of people: the analyst and the database administrator (DBA).

The business unit representative explained to the analyst what information was needed in the report. The analyst, in conjunction with the DBA, looked at the information available in the database and determined the best way to extract it and how it should be presented. This information was conveyed to the developer, who wrote the programming code for the report.

The developer passed the programming code on to the DBA, who implemented the new programming into the system.

The final step gave the report to the business unit, who would usually say it was all wrong—and the process would begin again.

This example may seem a bit extreme, but the truth is that this type of organizational setup can sometimes resemble the children's game "telephone." Of course, there are many companies with excellent communications in the links between the users, analysts, developers, and DBAs. However, even under the best of circumstances this can be a time-consuming and labor-intensive way for queries and reports to be created.

No one knows better what information is needed and how it should be organized than the person who will be using it. With Discoverer, the end user is now able to do the following:

- Create queries
- Analyze data in seconds rather than days or weeks
- Create custom reports

## The Discoverer Interface

Oracle has developed an interface in Oracle Discoverer that is a natural to use for those well acquainted with standard spreadsheets, databases, web browsers, and Microsoft Windows.

Figures 1-1 and 1-2 show the startup screens for Discoverer Desktop and Plus.

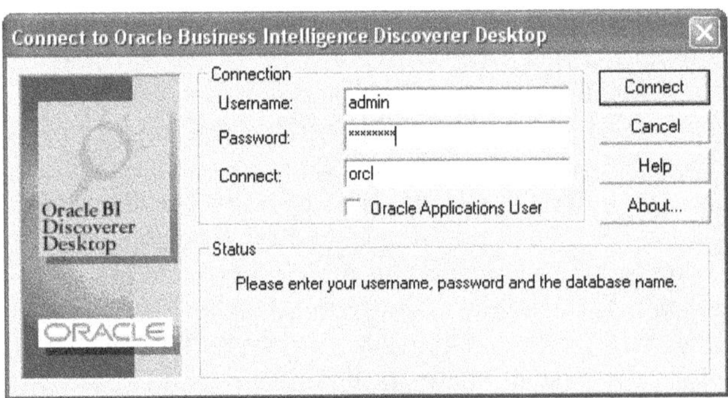


**FIGURE 1-1.** *The Discoverer Desktop startup screen*

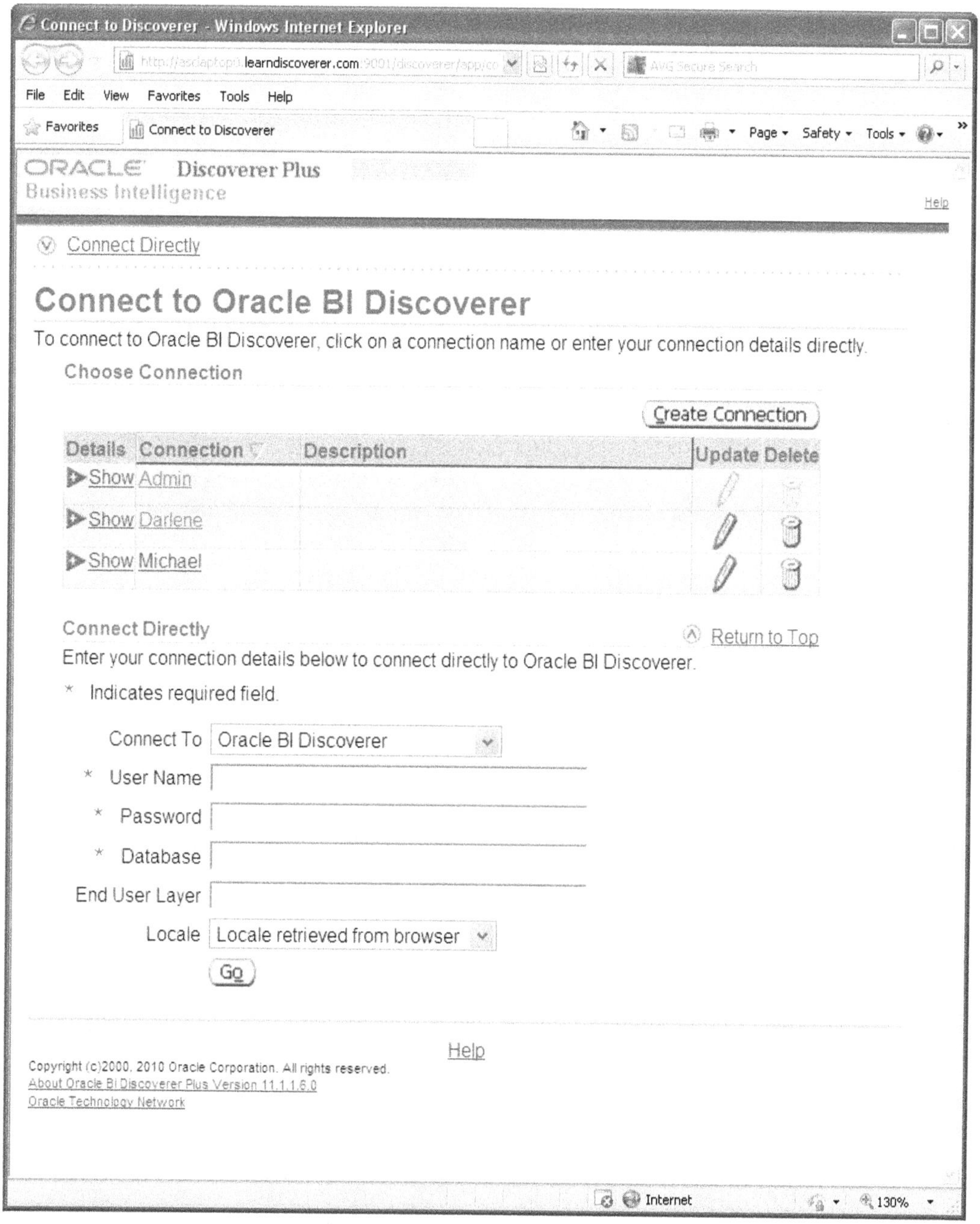

FIGURE 1-2. *The Discoverer Plus startup screen*

## Ad Hoc Queries vs. Predefined Queries

Predefined reports and queries are at the heart of most information systems. Companies invest millions in development. Most database systems come with a myriad of predefined reports. You either use the same reports everyone else uses or spend a great deal of money and time having them modified to meet your company's needs.

Ad hoc queries are a relatively new concept, one that can be difficult to come to terms with. Given they have had some education in how it is done, users can build queries. With a good foundation in the principles of query writing, the end user can produce queries and reports almost instantly. However, a person without an understanding of these principles may spend hours on a query and end up with data that is completely useless. You will begin learning to create queries and reports that will give you the information you need in Chapter 4. You will also learn how to avoid writing "the query from the Twilight Zone." Later, in Chapter 8, you will be shown how to turn a Discoverer query into a report.

### Nonpredictability vs. Predictability

Prewritten reports and queries are predictable—predictable in their output, predictable in their formatting, and predictable in their internal processing. Every time you run them, they will give you the same data, same formatting, same font, and same sort order. Predictability is fine to a point, but in the twenty-first century more and more companies are realizing that they need to think outside of the box to compete in today's market. You probably need to know something today that you did not need to know yesterday. To wait two or three weeks for a programmer to define a new report might be too late, and the opportunity will be lost.

Ad hoc reports, by their very nature, are unpredictable. The same data can be output and formatted in a seemingly endless variety of ways. When you, as a report writer, start the Query Wizard and begin to select the bits of information you think you need, you don't know what the return will be. When the query has been run, the real fun begins.

As the Discoverer manager, it is your job to ensure that the data is made available to your report writers in a way that makes their job as easy as possible. You will use the Administrator tool to give the data meaningful business names, preformatted and aggregated to enable users to use your definitions without the need of extensive data dictionaries.

### Easy to Change vs. Fixed Queries

In an ad hoc query, the data can be rearranged, unneeded information removed or masked, crosstabs created, and drill-downs formed to dig deeper and deeper. Oracle Discoverer performs these tasks with one click of the mouse.

A *fixed* query is virtually impossible for a user to change. Most users can see a better way to do it but don't have the power to make the change. It would be great if the MIS department could have programmers poised in the aisles waiting for a user to raise their hand. They could then rush to the user's side, find out what was needed, and make the programming change before lunch. This is of course impossible, unless you use Armstrong-Smith Consulting, so ad hoc queries are the answer.

Until the most recent release of Discoverer, end users using Discoverer Viewer could, to all intents and purposes, work with only fixed queries. This is because they were unable to save any changes that they had made. Providing the user has the correct privileges, as granted by the Discoverer manager, the new Viewer interface now allows a user to save a query that they have just modified.

### The Benefits of Both Types of Queries

It may sound as though there is no place in the modern organization for a fixed query or report. This is not the reality. In many cases, the report is so complex and the amount of knowledge required about the database structure is so vast that there is no choice but to have a fixed report that has been created by a skilled programmer or report writer. Another benefit to the fixed report is that some reports will never change. A Total Quantity Shipped report will be the same quarter after quarter, year after year.

Some benefits of the ad hoc query and report are as follows:

- Instantaneously accessing data
- Creating crosstabs (pivot tables)
- Drilling (slicing and dicing)
- Sorting
- Adding calculations and percentages

Some of these terms may be familiar to you, some not. We will cover these various concepts and more as we teach you to use this powerful tool.

**NOTE**

*There needs to be a balance between the fixed report and the ad hoc report. It is impractical for an organization to rely solely on one type or the other. Some companies may see the use of Oracle Discoverer as a means of downsizing their business intelligence departments with a "users can do it all" mentality. This would be folly, and we are not suggesting it. Discoverer should be seen as a complement to the fixed report and a means of seeing "what you don't already know." Indeed, in the right hands, Discoverer can be used to create both report types.*

## Oracle Applications Standard Reports vs. Discoverer Reports

Now that you are familiar with the generic terms of fixed and ad hoc queries and reports, let's be specific. Oracle Applications is probably being used by most of the readers of this book. You might be using Discoverer already, or you may be considering whether to add it to your list of tools. This section may help you in your decision and should help you correctly position Discoverer in your suite of reporting tools.

If you have implemented all of the modules of Oracle Applications, you may be aware that Oracle provides more than 700 prewritten standard reports. Getting to know these reports is a mammoth undertaking and not to be underestimated. These reports are an excellent resource to your organization, and it is to your benefit to take full advantage of them. It is a sad waste of time and effort to use Discoverer to create reports that already exist in Oracle Apps. In other words, *don't reinvent the wheel.*

A consulting company with expertise in Oracle Apps can help you sift through the standard reports and find the ones best suited to your needs. Some companies have a great enough demand for reporting that a full-time reports analyst should be employed. This analyst is responsible for taking the users' requirements and finding the reports that fill them. They can then make recommendations to either use a standard report "as is," rework an existing report, or say that no standard report fulfills the requirements.

This is where Discoverer comes into the picture. Discoverer should not be seen as the replacement for Oracle standard reports. It is an enhancement to give you greater power to access your data—and wow, what power!

### Library Reports vs. Requirements

Having decided that you have no other choice but to use Discoverer, you should take a look at your organization's Discoverer library documentation. Perhaps you will find that a Discoverer report already exists that covers your requirements. Wouldn't that be nice? Perhaps you will find a report that is so close to meeting your requirements that a small tweak would solve your problem too. Should you find that either of these scenarios exist, you should approach your library manager to see whether access to the report can be granted or whether the report can be modified.

If all else has now failed, you have no choice but to build the report yourself or, if you are lucky enough to have report writers, request that the report be built for you. You will find that Discoverer is a joy to work with, so dive right in—the water is warm and there are no undercurrents to sweep you out to sea. Should you find yourself getting out of your depth, there are plenty of places to get help.

## Getting Help with Discoverer

Oracle and the Oracle community have provided comprehensive resources for getting help about Discoverer.

The very first place to look for help is within the product itself by selecting Help from the menu bar. For those readers familiar with standard Windows applications, this will be second nature.

To access the Help menu, click Help on the menu bar.

From the Help menu you can select the following:

- **Help Topics** An Oracle-provided index of help topics (see Figure 1-3)
- **Using Help** Instructions from Microsoft on how to use the Windows help features
- **Quick Tour** A brief overview of the main features of the Discoverer End-User Edition
- **Cue Cards** A set of crib sheets to step you through some common topics
- **Manual** The online end-user manual provided by Oracle

Figure 1-3 shows the Discoverer Desktop help window.

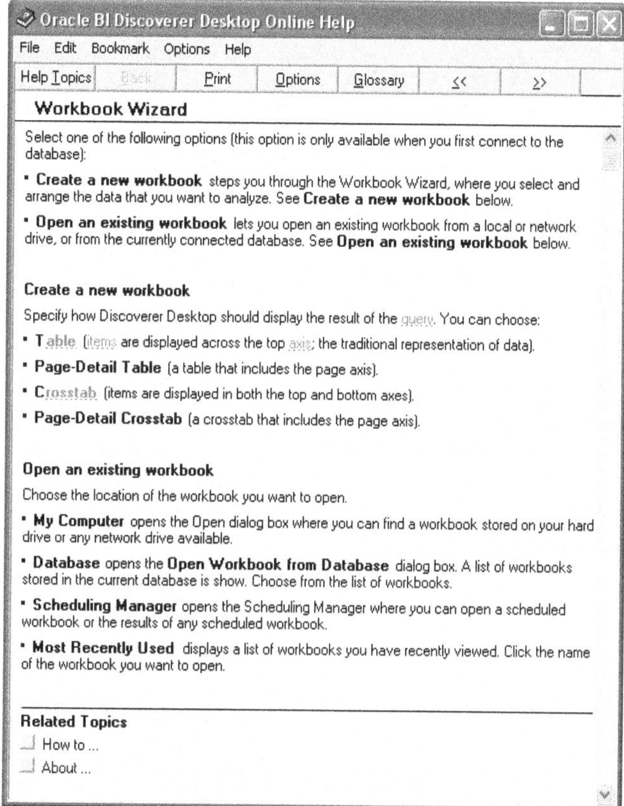


**FIGURE 1-3.** *The Discoverer Desktop help window*

Other sources of help can be found on the Web. Some of the most useful help sites are listed here:

| Source of Help | Web Site | Contents and Features |
|---|---|---|
| Oracle's main documentation web site | http://docs.oracle.com | Here you will find all of the documentation relating to Discoverer and WebLogic. |
| Oracle Technology Network (OTN) | www.oracle.com/technetwork/developer-tools/discoverer/overview/index.html | Here you will find white papers, FAQs, Quick Tours, demos, etc. |

| Source of Help | Web Site | Contents and Features |
|---|---|---|
| My Oracle Support | https://support.oracle.com<br>https://communities.oracle.com | These sites are available to companies that have purchased support from Oracle. You will be required to register. To register, you will need to know your company's customer support identifier (CSI) number. The support site contains technical libraries, a Discoverer forum, and even a means of creating service requests (SRs), formerly known as technical service requests or TARs, online.<br>We also recommend you take a look at the community link on the Oracle web site. It is a great place to get more help. |
| Oracle's Discoverer Forums | https://forums.oracle.com/community/developer/english/business_intelligence/business_intelligence_foundation/discoverer_2 | This site is another Oracle Discoverer forum run by Oracle and is also dedicated to providing help on Discoverer. Unlike when using My Oracle Support, you do not need a CSI number to use this forum, although you will need to register if you want to place new forum messages or provide answers to help other users. |
| Oracle University On-Line Library | http://ilearning.oracle.com/ilearn/en/learner/jsp/login.jsp | This site is available to companies or individuals who have purchased an online learning agreement. The library that you will find here contains more than 30 self-paced courses for Discoverer and an equal number for maintaining WebLogic. An annual subscription is required to access this library. If you attend an Oracle University training course on Discoverer, you may well find that a one-year subscription is included in the price. |
| Oracle University's Online Library | http://education.oracle.com/pls/web_prod-plq-dad/ou_product_category.getPage?p_cat_id=257 | This site is available to everyone to purchase classroom-based training and live virtual classes on Oracle Discoverer. |
| ODTUG web site | www.odtug.com/ | This is a members-only site for the Oracle Development Tools User Group. You can join by completing the online registration form. The site contains case studies, feature articles, links to related material in the ODTUG Technical Journal, and a technical journal online. |

| Source of Help | Web Site | Contents and Features |
|---|---|---|
| IOUG web site | www.ioug.org/ | This site belongs to the International Oracle Users Group. It contains technical information on discussion forums and even has a technical repository. It is not the place to go if you are an end user, but if you are a Discoverer administrator, you will find plenty of interesting technical subjects to use as bedtime reading. |
| Armstrong-Smith Consulting, Business Intelligence | http://ascbi.com | This site belongs to us. It contains information about training courses and consulting services, as well as general information concerning Discoverer. You will also find white papers and presentations available for download free of charge. |

# Summary

Oracle Business Intelligence Discoverer 11*g* (11.1.0.6) is slick, easy to use, and intuitive. From the introduction of the Desktop (aka Windows) version in the 1990s through to the latest 2013 Plus and Viewer (Web) releases, Discoverer has played an ever-increasing role in business intelligence. With the release of Discoverer Plus, the product has brought a full release of the Desktop edition to the Internet.

In this chapter, you learned that this book is aimed at both end users and Discoverer managers. Throughout the book you will be shown examples of queries and reports taken from a fictitious company database. We are sure that the examples accurately reflect "real-world" situations that will be useful in teaching you good query design using Discoverer.

In the section "A New Direction in Reporting," we described how things used to be in many companies and how Discoverer can overcome many obstacles in reporting. The Discoverer interface makes Discoverer intuitive and user friendly. You also learned how ad hoc queries differ from predefined queries and the benefits of both.

Finally, we gave you a table showing the variety of help resources available to end users and Discoverer administrators alike.

# CHAPTER 2

# Users and Databases

Everybody is familiar with the terms *hardware* and *software*. When something goes wrong with a system, it is to these that people usually look when seeking the reason why. Because of this, not all companies invest as much as they should into the other (and probably more important) resource, which is the user. That said, users can do a lot to help themselves when they are required to start working with Discoverer.

This chapter will deal with the general responsibilities of the end user and then discuss the tasks of setting up, using, and managing Discoverer libraries. We will introduce you to the Discoverer manager, the library manager, Discoverer report writers (formerly known as *superusers* in our original 10*g* Discoverer Handbook), and report viewers. You can use the terms Discoverer *query builders* and Discoverer *business analysts* instead of Discoverer *report writers*. Throughout this chapter we will make reference to other staff members, such as DBAs and Discoverer administrators, but we will leave the discussion of these people for the next chapter.

# What Starts Right Stays Right

Managing Discoverer is an art—not a science—and is not something you can just throw a resource at and expect to see a successful, efficient, smooth-running environment. Without adequate training and guidance, you will not get the most out of Discoverer.

A colleague of ours coined the saying "What starts right stays right." This advice, while applicable to all computer-based systems, is of paramount importance when used in the context of business intelligence. Let's say you want to get from A to B but don't have a road map or plan that tells you how to get to B from A. In this situation you could start out by taking a first step in any number of directions. No matter which direction you start, so long as you take the correct turns and twists along the way, you might eventually end up at B. It is these twists and turns that cost your company time and money, which are valuable resources that you cannot afford to waste.

The benefit of doing it correctly—the first time—is peace of mind and credibility with your customers, whoever they may be. Success in many respects has more to do with delivering reliably on organizational expectations than with simply installing the technical software environment. Quite possibly, the risk and political exposure on your project may be such that it should warrant investment in the development and implementation of a formal plan—addressing critical aspects of structure, process, and discipline. Time and time again we see companies that have not gone all the way and subsequently complain that they are not getting the most out of their investment in business intelligence. To successfully set up a Discoverer environment, you need to invest time, money, and the right resources.

So, wouldn't it be nice if someone were to lay out a road map in front of you and tell you which direction to start in? In this and the next chapter, we will do just that. We will lay out the basic concepts and direction that you need to take in order to get going so that you can get to a fully working, well-managed Discoverer environment in the shortest possible time. If you do not set up the basics, you face a major chance of failure or costly rework. Our experience with similar projects indicates that what starts right stays right.

# The Responsibility of the End User

If you don't understand your responsibilities as a Discoverer end user, you are lost. Queries cannot be defined if you are not aware of the data available to you, if you don't know which folders contain the data, and if you are unclear on what end result you are after. Therefore, before you begin to explore the power of Discoverer, you will need to understand the following:

- Your business
- Your reporting requirements
- Your database, or at least your EUL

**NOTE**

*As a business analyst or end user, it is important to remember that by definition Oracle Business Intelligence Discoverer provides a business view, the EUL, to hide the complexity of the underlying data structures, enabling you to focus on solving business problems. The Discoverer administrator, by definition, must know the actual database, whereas you, as the end user, quite often do not need to know it. However, in an ideal world, even the business analyst will find it greatly beneficial to also know the database and the table structures.*

## Your Business

The most important question you can ask yourself is "What is my business?" Are you the CEO of your own small company? Perhaps you are an analyst in the accounting department of a large manufacturing firm. Whatever your business, the first step in viewing company data is to understand what it is you need to know about your business and get a feeling for what it is that you don't already know.

If you don't know about your company—what it does and how you fit into the scheme of things—how can you begin to create reports that can have a meaningful impact upon your business? You need to at least understand your company's objectives and then get someone to explain how your role fits in to the overall plan. Once you have ascertained exactly how important you are to your company, you can begin making some headway into the area of query creation for your department. But where do you start?

The best way to begin is by looking at any predefined queries and reports that already exist. These may arrive on your desk in the form of a weekly or monthly report. Perhaps a clever programmer developed this report to meet some long-forgotten request. That request may have come from your department, perhaps even from your predecessor. It may also have come from another department; perhaps someone in your unit felt it would be useful.

If that report was designed and created more than a year ago, chances are that no one remembers why it was built in the first place. You may be lucky and find that someone actually documented the report and what it does. More likely, you will have nothing other than the query itself, a query that probably means very little to you today.

Each time the report is found in your inbox, you read it with some frustration because it does not really answer the questions you have. Sure, it answers questions A, B, and C, but what you really *need* to know is D and what you *want* to know is E. Because you know your business, you know the answers that are missing from your existing reports. More important, you know the questions to pose in order to get the answers you need.

## Your Reporting Requirements

Now that you know how to look for what is missing, it is time to brainstorm. Write down everything you want to know about your business. Be as detailed as you can, but bear in mind that you will not likely get everything you want. It is something like a Christmas wish list. Don't write down just what you need to know; also write what you would like to know. The following story illustrates how understanding what you want to know leads to more questions.

A successful commercial real estate firm realized the need to automate and centralize information, so it built a database. The database contained the names of building owners, building information, building tenants and all of their lease information, maintenance companies, and other information. Not understanding the kinds of questions to ask, users approached the database timidly at first. The DBA was asked questions like, "Can you tell me which tenants' leases expire in the next six months?" Then the DBA was asked, "Which tenants have an increase in their rent in the next three months?" Soon, the users asked more and more questions, and the DBA responded by creating more queries and more reports.

The people in this company had come to realize the power of the information in the database and were asking the right questions. It is your responsibility to do the same. Once you have ascertained what is missing, you need to formulate a plan to aid you in getting what you need.

### Determining End-User Requirements

Your best resource for defining end-user requirements is your current pool of end users, your business unit managers, and your database administrators. These people can be a great source of help and inspiration when all seems lost. Remember to find out whether anyone else is using Discoverer, and see whether they know how to get the data that you need for your report. Your Discoverer manager and library manager (the concept of the library will be explained later in this chapter) are also great sources of help, and you should use them as well.

### Employing an Incremental Approach

Don't try to answer every question by using one query, and don't try to answer all your questions in one session. You also don't want to have one query for every question. Take your time, and remember that whatever fit the bill perfectly last year may not do so now. Requirements change, business direction changes, and people change. Try to remember this when you are analyzing requirements.

Flexibility is a great asset to have, and using a "develop, demonstrate, and revise" approach will work wonders. Develop a report that will handle the current needs, demonstrate that it works and satisfies requirements, and then be prepared to revise it when the time arises. This iterative process will help you manage your requirements. Discoverer is a powerful tool and will allow you to change your query at any time. When your manager realizes that you have that power under control, they will naturally see other ways to harness your Discoverer talents.

### Documenting Your Requirements

Perhaps one of the hardest and most unenvied of all tasks is documentation. We all try to avoid creating documentation as if it were some terminal disease from which there was no hope of recovery. Yet, when trying to remember why a query was designed in a specific way, the first thing we all go looking for is the documentation. How pleased we are when we find that we did in fact write down the reason why management wanted our query to pull in data from only four of the five sales regions.

So, what should you document? Well, you at least need to identify who told you that something had to be done this way rather than that way. You need to give examples of report layouts and specify any special requirements (which will later become conditions) that need to be applied in order to make the query do what you want.

This may all seem like overkill, and in some cases this may be so. But we can tell you that not documenting is usually far worse than over-documenting. Remembering that requirements change is itself a reason to write down why you have done something. Developing, demonstrating, and revising will become a whole lot easier when you have documentation. Assuming that you will always be the one modifying a query is bad practice too. Having documented what your query is supposed to do, you need to be aware of the data that is available to you and where you can find help about that data.

# Your Database

Perhaps the most daunting responsibility anyone tasked with creating queries can have is to understand the database they are working with. You cannot know what questions to ask of the database if you don't know what data is available to you. It is in this step that you must become a partner with your Discoverer administrator. The Discoverer administrator can familiarize you with the database structure you are using and the data that is available to you.

**NOTE**

*Just because there is data in the database does not mean it will be available to you. Security issues and "need to know" are important parts of access. If there is some part of the database that you have not been granted access to and want, you will need to make a case for why you should have access.*

It is also important for you to know what type of database system you are using. Is it a live production system, a copy of production, or a data warehouse? Each system has different characteristics and parameters that you need to familiarize yourself with if you are to become an expert in Discoverer.

## OLTP Systems

The "live" databases, otherwise known as *online transaction processing* (OLTP) systems, are where the work is being done. Until a few years ago there were a myriad of OLTP systems to choose from. Each of these had their own niche market, and each had different characteristics, strengths, and weaknesses. Recently there has been a consolidation by the major players in the marketplace, with large vendors acquiring smaller vendors such that Oracle now offers E-Business Suite, PeopleSoft, and J.D. Edwards.

Another OLTP system that we have come across is the Banner system produced by Ellucian, formerly known as SunGard Higher Education (SGHE). This system is extensively used in higher education and can be found in thousands of educational institutions across the world. The Discoverer End User Layer provided with its operational data store (ODS) was in fact designed by us and as such incorporates many of the features of a good reporting system that we will outline throughout the book.

OLTP systems are where invoices are entered, orders are taken, payments are recorded, inventory is counted, and all of the other tasks are performed in order to run the organization. It is in "production" that the data is the freshest because it is all happening now. So, the question might be asked, "Why don't we just do all of our querying and reporting from the production database and forget about those other systems?" The answer is simple.

An OLTP system has been designed and built for entering and storing transactions quickly. It is not built for querying or reporting. You may ask, "What is the difference?" There are several reasons that the transaction systems and reporting systems are different:

- The database structures are different.
- Reporting from an OLTP system is slow.
- The data is volatile.
- OLTP table names are not easy to understand.
- OLTP systems are frequently purged of their data.

By their very nature, OLTP systems need to be tuned in order to perform well. This tuning ensures that transactions can be entered and stored efficiently. Running large reporting queries will slow down the transactions. This is not acceptable to users of the OLTP system.

Interesting to us is how different vendors treat the thought of having end users querying their OLTP databases. Some positively encourage it and go to great lengths to make database views available to the users. Some, on the other hand, strongly discourage reporting against the OLTP system. Oracle is among the former, whereas Ellucian is firmly in the other camp. Its approach is to use another database, called an *operational data store*, updated in near real time from the OLTP system. Another approach, and one that is gaining momentum, is the concept of an embedded data warehouse. We will discuss some of these approaches more in detail in Appendix C when we discuss databases and views.

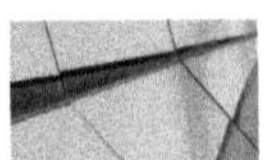

**NOTE**

*The comment about table names being not easy to understand is a moot point if your Discoverer manager renames the folders. If your Discoverer system does not have user-friendly table names, you should speak with your Discoverer manager and ask whether it is possible to change them.*

**The Database Structures Are Different** If you are familiar with database design, you will have heard of *normalization*. This technique uses many tables and never repeats an item of data. It uses small indexed tables to hold everything. On your transaction tables, an OLTP system stores ID numbers or codes as cross-references (foreign keys or lookups) to other tables. For example, in the OLTP system, the city San Francisco is listed in the City lookup table only with a code of 430. Every customer in San Francisco is listed in the Customer table with the code 430.

In a data warehouse, data mart, or operational data store we generally use denormalized table structures. Continuing the present example, where the code 430 is used to reference San Francisco, we will replace the code with the name. This means the word *San Francisco* will be repeated many times. Using this technique speeds up reporting, but you can see how it would slow down a transactional system. To create a report that displays descriptions instead of key values (e.g., San Francisco instead of the value 430), the SQL behind the report has to join multiple tables to get the results.

**Reporting from an OLTP System Is Sloooooooow** Because an OLTP system is optimized for entering transactions, it is not optimized for reporting. The database that can do both quickly and efficiently has not yet been invented. However, Oracle is making great strides in this direction. One day this will no doubt be possible. Until then, the reality is that when you use your OLTP system for reporting, it can be deadly slow. We first made this statement in our original Discoverer Handbook and at the time assumed that it would be not far into the future when we saw this being realized. Well, here we are several years later and find that OLTP systems are still slow to report from. Indeed, because of their complexity and the large volumes of data being stored, we find that OLTP systems have become more difficult to query from.

You might find yourself beginning to run your query, getting a cup of coffee, visiting a friend, calling to make a vet appointment for Muffy to get her teeth cleaned, and then coming back to find that your query has timed out. To make matters worse, you will have impacted your online colleagues, who will already have been complaining that the database is running slow. You may even find that the DBA terminated your query because it was drawing too many system resources. How wonderful it would be if the company built a database just for you!

Before we move on, we would like to comment on the approach taken by some organizations to solve the slowness of reporting against an OLTP. The approach adopted here is to add new *reporting* indexes to the OLTP tables. The purpose of these reporting indexes is to allow queries to run faster. This approach is very commendable and with an experienced DBA at the helm has been known to be very effective. We know because we have done it ourselves many times. Unfortunately, the approach is also fraught with danger, and in many cases we have seen the online system performance deteriorate dramatically. Our recommendation is not to do this unless you have a very experienced DBA who fully understands the implications of adding reporting indexes to OLTP database tables.

**The Data Is Volatile** In an OLTP system, the data is changing constantly. If you run a report at 9 a.m. and your co-worker runs the same report at 11 a.m. and you both bring the report to the 3 p.m. staff meeting, the reports will be different. In the two hours between the reports, new orders will have been placed, invoices paid, shipments made, and so on.

To further compound the problem, your supervisor will see the difference in your reports and may decide to check the figures for herself at 3:30 p.m. Guess what? Her answers will be completely different, so maybe she decides you are both incompetent and the two of you get fired! Of course, this is an extreme example, but it does illustrate one problem with using an OLTP system for reporting.

**OLTP Table Names Are Not Easy to Understand** When you are selecting the criteria for your query, you need to know where the data comes from. In an OLTP system, the table names are not obvious. You might think that the City table would be called City. You will probably be wrong. It might have a simple, but still difficult to decipher, name like hz_locations, or it might be called table_19975. Just imagine the nightmare in trying to build reports using these names. This may sound far-fetched, but the truth of the matter is that system designers frequently don't take the needs of end users into account when designing databases. In reality, these system designers should not be expected to do so. Hybrid systems that attempt to do this have a tendency to be the proverbial jack of all trades and master of none.

If you have Oracle E-Business Suite, sometimes referred to as Oracle Applications or just Apps for short, and want to build a report showing all invoices, did you know that the main tables you need are oe_order_headers_all, oe_order_lines_all, ra_customer_trx_lines_all, ra_customer_trx_all, hz_cust_accounts, hz_cust_site_uses_all, hz_cust_acct_sites_all, hz_party_sites, and the previously mentioned hz_locations? Not only do you need to know the names of all these tables, you need to know how to link them and also which schema owns them, assuming of course that you have access to those schemas.

Here, the tables that begin with the characters *oe* are owned by the ONT user, the *ra* tables are owned by the AR user, and the tables that begin with *hz* are also owned by the RA user. Confusing, isn't it? The typical end user would have no idea where to begin because the system was built for storing transactions—not reporting.

To add even more confusion, which tables do you think contain the Customer Name and Address? It is certainly not obvious from the table names. Which tables were they? Oh yes, the table that contains the Customer Name and Address is hz_parties. But is that the Ship To Customer or the Bill To Customer? To determine this, you will have to look at the SITE_TYPE flag in the hz_cust_site_uses_all table.

This book is not intended to be a lesson in how to understand the inner workings of E-Business Suite. We simply include these examples to demonstrate how difficult it is for an end user to understand the inner workings of this particular OLTP database.

If your company has decided not to invest in another alternative, you have no choice but to report from the OLTP system. Perhaps your company is small and has only one person in MIS, or perhaps you simply cannot afford one of the alternative systems. Whatever the reason, you should work with your Discoverer manager, who is able to at least change the names of the tables to something more meaningful. They may even be able to build some views of the database for you, bringing together common tables for your reporting needs. A view, by the way, is a means of hiding the logic that goes into joining tables. Not only do they look like tables, but you can query from them as if they were tables.

If you are using Oracle E-Business Suite, your company may have purchased a product called NoetixViews or be using Oracle's Business Views, formerly known as BIS. In both of these instances, Oracle and Noetix have analyzed the most common end-user requirements and have put together sets of views for most of the modules. We will discuss both Oracle's business views and NoetixViews in greater detail in Appendix C.

**NOTE**
*Oracle BIS is deprecated, but we know that many of you still have it. Oracle is still shipping the business views and pre-seeded EUL contents, so we still consider it worthy of mention in this book.*

**OLTP Systems Are Frequently Purged of Their Data** Most OLTP systems do not store large amounts of history, or at least they should not. Since these systems are designed for immediate response, their data is often purged, many times within a few months of capture. Therefore, you typically will not be able to get any significant historical information from an OLTP system.

**Snapshot Databases** These are copies of your data. They can be one of the following two types:

- A complete copy of your OLTP system
- A partial copy of the database saved to a local server

**Complete Copy of the OLTP System** The preceding section outlined the drawbacks of reporting from an OLTP system. Many companies minimize these drawbacks by making a complete copy of their OLTP database for use in reporting. The benefits of a complete copy are as follows:

- The data is constant. If you run your report at 9 a.m. and your colleague runs the same report at 11 a.m., you will both have the same information for your 3 p.m. meeting—and ideally keep your jobs.
- There is no impact on the OLTP system. You will not have unhappy co-workers complaining about your query mucking up the system.

Some companies take a full copy of their OLTP system every night following the close of the working day, placing that copy on a different machine from the OLTP system.

The disadvantages to the complete copy are as follows:

- You could still have the problems over database structure and table names (see the accompanying note).
- It is still inherently an OLTP system, so it is not designed for reporting.
- The data is not up to date—in some cases, it may be 24 hours or more old. This may not be seen as a disadvantage, depending on what you will use the data for. If you want to analyze shipments made yesterday, the snapshot is to your advantage. If you want to analyze today's shipments, you must wait until the next refresh cycle.
- Because it is a copy of the OLTP system, you cannot do historical reporting.

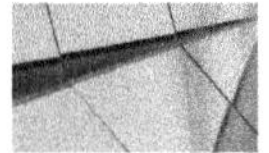

**NOTE**

*One of the tasks of a database administrator is to present the data to you in a meaningful way. This includes simplifying the view of the database, although this should be transparent to the end user.*

Complete snapshot copies are becoming increasingly popular. They overcome some of the disadvantages of reporting from an OLTP system, as long as you are aware of your company's refresh cycle.

**A Partial Copy of the Database Saved to a Local Server** If your company uses a centralized database, it could be located many thousands of miles (or kilometers) from your office. To improve performance, you can make local copies of some of the tables you need for your reports. Snapshots can be used to copy all or part of a table. If your database is in Paris and your office is in Denver and you are interested in reporting only on North American data, your DBA can arrange to copy only the data you need.

The simplest forms of partial copy take the tables in their entirety, rather than the more complex forms, which use queries to extract just the portions you need. The advantages of this approach are as follows:

- The data is constant.
- There is no impact on the OLTP system.
- The performance in relation to speed is increased.
- The DBA can define some indexes specifically designed for your reporting needs.

The disadvantages are as follows:

- You still have the problems over database structure and table names.
- It is still inherently an OLTP system, so it is not designed for reporting.
- The data is not up to date—in some cases, it may be 24 hours or more old.
- If you have copied only parts of the database and you now need to report on something outside of the copied data, you cannot.
- Because the data is a copy of the OLTP system, you cannot do historical reporting.

### Data Mart, Data Warehouse, or Operational Data Store

Data marts and data warehouses are commonly discussed together, and some industry experts will tell you that the two cannot exist side by side. We will not involve ourselves in that debate. We will simply tell you what they are.

**Data Warehouses** According to Bill Inmon, commonly regarded as the father of data warehousing, a *data warehouse* is a "subject-oriented, integrated, non-volatile, time-variant collection of data used in support of management decisions." What the heck does that mean?

Quite simply, a data warehouse is a business-relevant (subject-oriented) collection of data from various sources. The data can come from the OLTP system, from spreadsheets, from word processor documents, and even from your customers. In essence, the data warehouse will contain all of the items needed to satisfy the reporting requirements for your business area.

Because the data can come from various sources, it has to be manipulated into a common format (integrated). For example, your customers may all provide you with information about their sales of your products, but they probably will send you that data using their own in-house codes and ID numbers. It is necessary to convert these numbers into your codes. This is accomplished by the integration process.

Once the data has been collected into the data warehouse, it will not change and cannot be deleted (being nonvolatile), implying that you will have historical data. Because a data warehouse is a read-only database, users cannot change it. The only way the data can change is during the refresh cycle when new data is added.

Because the data is collected periodically, you will be able to report trends over time according to the refresh cycle. What this means is that if you collect your data every day, you can analyze your daily sales. If you refresh your data only weekly, you can analyze weekly sales, and so forth (time-variant). You need to specify what your requirements are so that the data warehouse is built accordingly. If you are working from an existing data warehouse, you might not have the necessary clout to change the refresh cycle, but you certainly need to know what it is.

The advantages of a data warehouse are as follows:

- It is optimized for reporting.
- It contains historical data.
- It does not impact the OLTP system.
- It has meaningful table names.
- It is not subject to change.
- You can perform data mining ("tell me something I don't already know").
- It contains data from multiple sources, not just your OLTP system.

The disadvantages of a data warehouse are as follows:

- It can be extremely expensive to build and maintain. You may need to have buy-in from senior management to get approval for a data warehouse.
- You need large amounts of storage space, potentially 1TB or more.
- Because there is a huge amount of data, it is possible to write queries that seem to run forever and never come back with an answer (the query from the Twilight Zone).
- The data is not up to date—in some cases, it may be 24 hours or more old.
- Data warehouses are not easily changed. If you spot an error in the data warehouse, you will have to correct it in the source system. If that system cannot be changed, the data warehouse cannot be changed and you will have to live with incorrect data. For example, company ABC Widgets could be stored in the database as A.B.C. Widgets, AB and C Widgets, or AB&C. Unless you know about these possible irregularities, you will get incomplete results. You may have a difficult time persuading your company to change its procedures to satisfy the data warehouse.

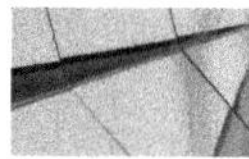

**NOTE**
*The data cleansing procedures available in extract/transform/load (ETL) tools address the issue of inconsistent naming to some extent.*

- Because the data is coming from different sources, you may not be able to get the same answer from your OLTP system as you do from the data warehouse. It will be difficult, if not impossible, to identify whether any OLTP transactions are missing from the data warehouse.

You may find it interesting that some very large companies such as Amazon, Wal-Mart, and France Telecom have data warehouses with fact tables containing hundreds of millions of records, some even running into the billions.

**Data Mart** A *data mart* is a table or set of tables that has been created for a specific reporting requirement. Data marts provide a subject-oriented view of the data in your system and contain significantly smaller amounts of data than in your OLTP or data warehouse systems. Where they exist, they will be the prime focus of the online analytical processing (OLAP) by the end users. The table structure(s) will be simple, the table names will correspond to folders within business areas, and the data items should have user-friendly, meaningful names.

**NOTE**
*The names of the data items should not be an issue if your DBA has created user-friendly, meaningful names. In the vast majority of cases, this will be true; however, sometimes you may need to speak with the DBA and request that the names be changed.*

Data marts are like snapshots in that they are refreshed periodically. In fact, most data marts are actually refreshed from a data warehouse if you have one, making your data marts a subset of your data warehouse. When you don't have a data warehouse, they are refreshed from the OLTP system. Unlike snapshots—but like data warehouses—they have been optimized for reporting purposes. In fact, their sole purpose in life is reporting.

Typically, one data mart contains all of the data you need to satisfy the reporting requirements for a single business area. Using the Oracle example highlighted in the previous section, where you had to pull from at least seven tables to obtain a complete invoicing report, all of this data is now found in a single invoicing table. It also has been given the delightful name Invoices.

The advantages of a data mart are as follows:

- It is a single source of data for a business area.
- It has no impact on the OLTP system.
- It is optimized for reporting.
- It is fast, because it has special indexes created to enable you to extract the data quickly.
- When sourced directly from an OLTP system, it can be quick to build and less expensive than a data warehouse. It could even be used as a prototype for a future data warehouse.

As with all things, there are disadvantages, namely the following:

- It usually contains data to satisfy predefined reports. If you suddenly decide you need more data in a report, you can't have it easily. You will need to submit a request to your administrator to have the data mart structure, and possibly the data warehouse, changed. This can be a difficult and time-consuming process.
- Data marts are not typically built to cross-link one business area to another. This is not a Discoverer limitation but a business rule implementation. For example, your company may have sales regions across the world and have built a data mart for each region. If your company has decided to prevent users in one region from querying the sales data from another, your Discoverer administrator will not be prevented from cross-linking the data marts.
- If they are pulling from an OLTP system, they are not historical.
- Because the data is usually a subset of another system, you may not be able to get the same answer from your OLTP system as you do from the data mart. In fact, if your data mart is sourced from a data warehouse, you are two steps away from the source.

For a more detailed explanation of data warehouses and data marts, we recommend you read *Oracle8 Data Warehousing: A Practical Guide to Successful Data Warehouse Analysis, Build, and Roll-Out*, by Michael J. Corey, Michael Abbey, Ian Abramson, and Ben Taub (Oracle Press, 1998). A more up-to-date warehousing reference book is *Oracle 10g Data Warehousing*, by Lilian Hobbs, Susan Hillson, Shilpa Lawande, and Pete Smith (Digital Press, 2004).

**Operational Data Stores** An *operational data store* is a database that has been designed to combine data from multiple sources for additional operations on the data. The data is then fed back to the OLTP system for further processing or passed on to a full-blown data warehouse for reporting.

Because the data comes from multiple sources, the integration usually involves some form of cleansing that resolves redundancy and checks business rules for integrity. An ODS will usually be designed to contain low-level, detail data such as transactions and prices. It will typically have limited history and have the data captured in real time or as near to real time as possible.

Not all organizations adhere to this definition, but those that do have very efficient operations. For example, in a master data management (MDM) system, you may have multiple in-house systems that all refer to products, with each having a slightly different definition for the life cycle of the same product. You may have multiple item numbers in use, with, for example, one system handling components and another handling finished goods.

The ODS system will take the data from both of these disparate systems and collate it into a product master record. In time, this system may well become what is commonly known as the *system of record* and be used as the master definition. Managing customer data like this is another very common use of an ODS.

While it is not common to build a reporting layer on top of an ODS, it is certainly feasible and, when done correctly, can be a very valuable asset to the company. As mentioned earlier, we in fact designed the Discoverer End User Layer that sits on top of the Ellucian (formerly known as SunGard) ODS.

The advantages of an ODS are as follows:

- It can be used as a single source of data for a business area.
- It has no impact on the OLTP system.
- You have access to the system of record.
- Real-time or near-real-time reporting can be achieved.
- The data has been cleansed to remove idiosyncrasies and data integrity issues.
- The data structures are easier to understand than in the original systems.

There are also disadvantages of an ODS, namely the following:

- Most operational data stores are not built for reporting and will typically not have indexes designed for reporting. There are exceptions to this rule.
- The data structures cannot be easily tied back to the various multiple source systems, making validation of the data difficult.
- ODS data is not summarized.
- Any reporting done off an ODS system will usually satisfy strictly predefined reports, typically returning a master ID along with all of the disparate IDs that link to it.
- Only those OLTP fields needed to resolve ODS issues are brought through into the ODS.
- There is little leeway to alter the tables in an ODS. If you decide you need more data in a report, you will usually be out of luck unless your administrator can join your table to another table in the ODS. You cannot submit a request to your administrator to have the structure changed like you can with a data mart or data warehouse.

As with a data mart, an ODS will not be designed to cross-link one business area to another. Again, this is not a Discoverer limitation but a business rule implementation.

# The Discoverer Library Concept

The concept of a Discoverer library is relatively new and was developed by us as a way to help our clients save money, time, and resources. Although it is not an integral part of Discoverer, we got the idea from the libraries in Oracle E-Business Suite and expanded on that concept. We have gone into companies where we have seen multiple administrators and business analysts creating views, materialized views, End User Layers, business areas, workbooks, and worksheets that are virtually identical. Imagine the number of wasted man-hours and the effect on your bottom line when one department does not know what the other department is doing. The end result is that the wheel is reinvented over and over again and chaos reigns. To make matters worse, now imagine what happens when the original developer leaves the company.

Implementing Discoverer libraries in your company will end the chaos.

## The Definition of a Library

So, what is a Discoverer library? In its simplest form, a Discoverer library is

- A collection of reports based upon a common theme or a collection of reports for a single business segment
- A collection of reports that have been validated for accuracy and adherence to corporate standards and are guaranteed to work
- Controlled by a library manager

A well-defined Discoverer library will contain reports that are documented, with that documentation available to all users. This documentation will allow users to read a description of the report as well as to see where the data comes from, what algorithms are being used, and perhaps even a screenshot or two. Such a practice will help alleviate bottlenecks in your system by eliminating the need for users to run or create reports unnecessarily. It also allows users to see reports that have already been created but have not yet been added to their personal report list. Users can then submit a request to the library manager for access. The users should feel confident that, after reviewing the documentation, they are opening or requesting access to reports that will satisfy their needs. They will also know that the reports have been validated and that the information will be correct and up to date.

## The Definition of a Library Manager

A library manager is defined as being a responsible person who

- Is a subject-matter expert with knowledge of the business segment for which they are responsible
- Has a separate username and password for managing the library
- Has the power to accept or deny changes from report writers
- Has the power to accept or deny requests for access to reports in their library
- Ensures that corporate standards are being adhered to
- Could be given some Discoverer administrator rights in order to undertake some tasks normally performed by the Discoverer manager

Only the library manager should have the power to add, update, or delete reports from the library. End users should have the ability to use a library report, but they should not be able to change it. The library manager should also have a very good working knowledge of the end-user versions of Discoverer.

# The Report Writer Concept

The concept of a report writer (formerly known as a *superuser* in our previous edition) has been around for some time, so the principles proposed here will probably not come as a surprise to you. On the other hand, you may find them to be a new idea.

**NOTE**
*You can use the terms Discoverer query builder and Discoverer business analyst instead of Discoverer report writer.*

## The Definition of a Report Writer

A report writer is defined as being a subject-matter expert with

- An expert knowledge of the functionality of Discoverer
- A sense of business acumen—basically a pretty good idea of what their part of the business does
- A good grounding in needed formulas, definitions, and so forth
- A sense of the business unit's strategic goals and objectives
- A temperament suited to helping others
- A very good understanding of the database(s) used by the business unit

From this list you can see why the terms *business analyst* and *query builder* are equally acceptable alternatives to the term *report writer*. Most companies have one or two Discoverer users who stand out from the rest because they possess these qualities. Pooling these staff persons as an additional resource can have great benefits for a company, as we will show. Some companies choose to increase their IT department by employing Discoverer experts as report writers.

## The Benefits of Having Report Writers

There are a number of reasons for having report writers in your organization. The following list is not exhaustive but is given as a means to show how beneficial it might be to designate report writers within your company:

- They are a first line of support for Discoverer-related issues to other end users.
- They will have additional know-how about solving problems with queries and reports.
- They will be able to give at least some introductory Discoverer training to other end users.
- They will be responsible for producing your company's standard reports.
- They have an excellent working relationship with both the library manager and the Discoverer manager.

In smaller companies, report writers can also be the library managers.

## The Benefits of Being a Report Writer

It may seem at first that becoming a report writer would simply mean more work. There are, however, a number of benefits:

- You would receive additional Discoverer training, thus becoming an expert in this growing field (not a bad addition to your résumé, but don't tell that to your boss when you ask for additional training).
- You will have a direct line to the library and Discoverer managers for help and guidance in solving problems.
- You will have greater database access rights than a normal end user.
- You should be included in strategic planning for your business unit when Discoverer issues are discussed.
- You will have the ability to help other end users by being their first line of support for Discoverer-related issues.

## Choosing Your Report Writers

You may not be in a position to become a report writer, but you might be the person who will choose your company's or department's report writers. When first choosing a report writer, there are a number of questions you should ask yourself about the person under consideration:

- Is the person a subject-matter expert in the business area that they will be serving?
- Does the person have an expert knowledge of Discoverer or the ability to become an expert?
- Does the person have the respect of their fellow users?
- Does the person have the ability to act as a first line of support to other end users?

You may find that some managers resist the idea of designating report writers, because they fear the IT department will see them as a pretext for reducing its level of support. After all, IT members are supposed to be the experts in everything to do with computers, aren't they? Well, this used to be true in the days of mainframe computers, when the IT staff were locked away behind glass walls. But ask most modern users about computers and they nearly all have one at home. They know how to use the Internet, they know how to use spreadsheets and word processors, and they no longer need to have their hands held by the IT department.

Companies are looking to employ computer-literate staff, the same staff who will soon become experts in Discoverer. Whether your company chooses to embrace this pool of knowledge at this time is an internal matter. What we can say is that Discoverer is a powerful tool, it has been designated by Oracle as being a key component of its business intelligence strategy, and the ability to master this product will be a much sought-after commodity. The IT department, not being fully aware of business issues, will not be in a position to fill this role.

## Summary

In this chapter, we discussed in detail the roles and responsibilities of the end user in connection with Discoverer. It is important for you to understand your business, your reporting needs, and how your data is stored. Once you understand these things, you are ready to determine exactly what your reporting requirements are.

You also learned how things change in business and how your reporting needs will change with those things. An incremental approach will lead to a need for documentation as you build queries and reports.

How your data is stored and the differences between OLTP systems, snapshots, data warehouses, data marts, and operational data stores were discussed in detail. You learned the benefits and drawbacks of each type of system and how you will need to interact with them.

Next, we discussed the library concept and how to implement this in your company. You learned the definitions of both libraries and library managers. Finally, we discussed the report writer/business analyst/query builder concept and how to implement this in your company. You learned the benefits of having report writers, what it is to be a report writer, and the attributes of a good report writer. We also discussed why the IT department is not always a good replacement for report writers.

# CHAPTER 3

# Getting Started in Discoverer

In this chapter, you will learn about the importance of some key members of your Discoverer team. Depending upon the complexity of your environment, you will have one or more of the following: a Discoverer manager, a library manager, a DBA, an Apps administrator, and a report writer. Developing good relationships with these key personnel can be very beneficial in your successful use of Discoverer.

We will introduce you to some important terms that will be useful to your success in using Discoverer, and we will extend the concept of the Discoverer library. You will also learn how Discoverer manages SQL queries and their interaction with your source database. You will come to understand the process that must be followed prior to gaining access to the system, and you will gain some insight into what happens behind the scenes.

We will introduce you to Discoverer's *memory*, referred to by Oracle as its "Sticky Feature." Just before we show you how to launch Discoverer, we give you a list of cool things it can do. Then, at last, you will be launching and logging in to Discoverer.

# Key Personnel

In all companies, no matter what you call them, there are a number of key personnel with whom you should become familiar. If the size of your organization gets in the way of knowing these people personally, you should at least have a basic understanding of their job function. The key personnel with whom you need to form a relationship are as follows:

- Your Discoverer manager
- Your library manager
- Your database administrator
- Your E-Business Suite administrator (only when using E-Business Suite)
- Your report writer(s)

In some smaller organizations or where Discoverer has not yet gained significant inroads into your company, you may not have separate roles for these job functions. In this case, you may well find that the roles are handled by just one or two people. For the purposes of clarity, we will describe the basic functions of each role separately.

## Discoverer Manager

The Discoverer manager is probably the most important member of the support staff with whom you need to maintain contact. The Discoverer manager is responsible for the following:

- Maintaining the End User Layer (EUL)
- Maintaining user access to the EUL
- Defining Discoverer strategy and monitoring Discoverer performance
- Setting the default item names and table characteristics (essential for Plus)
- Being a source of help for all Discoverer-related matters

The Discoverer manager works with the individual business unit and library managers to identify the data required for each business area (sometimes called *business functions*). Oracle has provided two separate tools: Discoverer Administrator and the Discoverer EUL Command Line for Java. The Discoverer manager works with these tools to create the seamless interface that you will encounter. These tools provide a highly secure, centralized link to the EUL.

**NOTE**
*The EUL is the interface between you and the database. What you see when you log in to Discoverer is the EUL. It maintains all of the links between you and the underlying database. Whenever you create a Discoverer query, it is converted into a Structured Query Language (SQL) statement by the EUL. When you submit your query, Discoverer converts it into efficient SQL code and sends it to the database, keeping you from needing to know the underlying database or SQL. In other words, thank goodness for the EUL!*

For more information about the roles and responsibilities of the Discoverer manager, including what the Discoverer manager can do for you, please refer to Chapter 19.

## Library Manager

The library manager is another very important member of the support staff with whom you need to maintain contact. The library manager is responsible for the following:

- Maintaining the approved list of reports within the library
- Accepting or denying requests for new reports
- Accepting or denying requests for access to reports
- Being a source of help to management for report availability

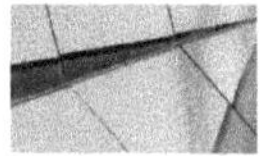

**NOTE**
*Library manager is a term that we have created; it is not a tool or component in the Discoverer product family.*

The library manager works closely with the Discoverer manager and the report writers within their business unit to identify the reports that are required. Having identified that a new report is required, the library manager then works with one of their department's report writers to create the report. Once a report has been written and has passed acceptance testing by the users, the manager should take an objective look at the report to make sure that corporate standards have been adhered to and that the report documentation effectively describes what information the report does and how it should be used. Assuming that all standards and documentation are correct, the library manager should take control of the report and make it available within the library. We give an extended definition of a library later in this chapter.

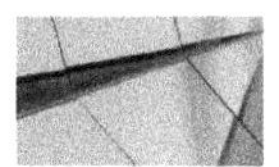

**NOTE**
*The library manager does not write the reports. They are working on a higher plane and have more responsibility for report availability and accuracy than for the inner workings of the report.*

## Database Administrator

Besides being the person we all love to hate, the DBA is a crucial piece of the Discoverer jigsaw puzzle. Without DBAs, the databases would cease to function. Their main responsibilities are as follows:

- Maintaining the databases
- Maintaining user access to the databases
- Defining database strategy and monitoring database performance
- Being yet another source of help

DBAs are a much-maligned group of people and are misunderstood by many. They have an unenviable role in the organization and bear the brunt of everyone's frustrations whenever the system goes down. The fact of the matter is that systems go down by their very complex nature, and it is the DBA for the most part who gets the system going again.

We are so used to having our systems up and running for 100 percent of the time that a break in service of even 15 minutes seems like a lifetime. The DBA has to find where in this complex system the breakdown is and repair it. Most of the time you don't even know that a problem existed, because the DBA monitors the system constantly and corrects many problems before they even affect the uptime. So, the next time your system goes down and you feel like venting at your DBA, just get them a pack of cookies from the vending machine instead and go answer some e-mails.

## E-Business Suite Administrator

If your company is using Discoverer against E-Business Suite, in other words in Apps mode, this person is key to your successful interaction with the applications. The main responsibilities of the E-Business Suite administrator, as they relate to Discoverer, are as follows:

- Maintain user access to the applications
- Maintain the E-Business Suite responsibilities
- Maintain the E-Business Suite flex field definitions (user-defined data fields available within EBS that organizations can use as required in order to add new data to the system)

Like our beloved DBAs, the E-Business Suite administrators are also much maligned and overworked. As a senior manager once quipped to one of us, "If all the E-Business Suite administrators in the world were laid end to end, they would still not reach a conclusion." We think the poor, unfortunate administrators he was describing simply had far too much on their plates. So, before you go bending the ear of your administrator, ask yourself whether your request is urgent or whether perhaps it could wait until tomorrow. We are sure you will get a better response, and if this does not work, bribery does!

## Report Writers

Within your company, you may be lucky to find that your department or business unit has designated report writers. It is your responsibility to locate and pick the brains of these "superusers." Report writers are users just like you, but they have been given added responsibilities and extra training. Their responsibilities may include the following:

- Being your primary source of help for all Discoverer workbook- and worksheet-related issues
- Being a subject-matter expert in Discoverer
- Knowing your business unit's goals and objectives
- Being the link between the user community and both the Discoverer and library managers
- Being able to submit reports for inclusion in the library

For more information about the roles and responsibilities of report writers, please refer to Chapter 2.

Having learned about the key personnel within your organization, you are now ready to turn to Discoverer itself, but first you will need to have everything set up.

# Gaining Access to Discoverer

Before you can even begin to think about logging in to Discoverer, the following steps will need to have been completed:

**NOTE**

*This section assumes that Discoverer is part of a corporate installation. You may want to install Discoverer for testing or trial purposes. You can do that by downloading Discoverer for free from OTN under a developer's license. Discoverer is easy enough to install that release 11g can be up and running in as little as 20 minutes.*

1. If your company is installing Discoverer directly on to your PC, a request will have to be submitted for this to be done. Perhaps your company has decided not to install Discoverer this way and to use a terminal server instead (see the following note explaining terminal servers). In this case, a request will have to be made for that software to be installed. If your access to Discoverer is to be via the Web, your IT department should ensure that you have your company's standard browser correctly installed and configured. Whichever method your company uses to provide access to Discoverer, we would hope that you will be provided with an icon on your desktop that can be double-clicked to launch the login sequence. This step may sound elementary, but it is amazing how many times these basic requirements are overlooked.
2. You or your manager will need to request that access to Discoverer be made available to you. In the request, you will need to specify which database you need and to which business areas you should be granted access. The request should also contain your telephone number, your position, and whether you need to have full Discoverer access (report writer) or just the ability to run prewritten queries (report viewer).

   If you are new to the company, your manager should complete this on your behalf and send it to your library manager or to your Discoverer manager if libraries are not in use.

Perhaps your manager can name another person within your department who has the same access you need and ask for that access to be duplicated. The more information you can give to your Discoverer or library manager, the easier the setup will be.

3. Your library manager will take your request and coordinate it with the DBA, E-Business Suite administrator, and Discoverer manager. If your company is using Discoverer in standard mode, the DBA will create a database account for you, assigning a username and password as determined by your company's standards. However, if your company is using Discoverer in Apps mode, your Apps system administrator will create an account for you, assigning a username, a password, and one or more responsibilities as determined by your company's standards.
4. After your DBA or E-Business Suite administrator has created the user account, your Discoverer manager will complete their tasks by granting you access to the required business areas or responsibilities and possibly arranging for you to attend a training course. This course either could be an official Oracle-given course at one of their many training centers or could be given internally if your company has a training department. You might even be in training right now using this book as your text!
5. After your Discoverer manager has completed their tasks, they will pass the request back to the library manager for completion. The library manager will ensure that all relevant reports to which you need access have been shared with you.
6. Finally, when all of the preceding steps have been completed, you will receive notification from your library manager or, if you do not have a library manager, your Discoverer administrator that your account has been set up and has been activated. In this notification, you will be informed of any usernames, passwords, and database connect strings that you may need to use. We say "may" because Discoverer Plus has what are known as public connections. These connections hide the complexity of the login requirements from you. Depending upon the setup within your organization, you may or may not have public connections. If these are in use, the security requirements that are in force within your organization may require you to enter a password. In addition, if you are using Oracle Applications, your Applications responsibility will be made known to you. You will also be informed what user level you have been assigned (report writer or report viewer) as well as having any appropriate reports shared with you. If you are going to be connecting to Discoverer via the Web, you will also be given the appropriate URL.

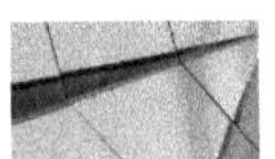

**NOTE**
*If your main database is not located at your work site, your company may well have decided to use one or more terminal servers. These powerful PCs are used as a link between you and the database and have a full working copy of Discoverer 11g Desktop on them. They are usually installed in your data center with a direct connection to the database. You connect to a terminal server from your PC using your network, and then you can use it just as if it were your own PC. The benefits of this approach are reduced network traffic and improved performance. Anyone who has tried running Discoverer from their own PC connected to a database more than 1,000 miles away will know what we mean.*

Having had the correct setups completed, you are now ready to use Discoverer.

# Key Definitions

Before we get into the Discoverer login sequence, we will explain four key definitions that you need to know.

## Workbooks and Worksheets

Discoverer uses workbooks. Anyone familiar with spreadsheets should understand the concept of workbooks. A *workbook* is a group of worksheets. Each workbook can be thought of as being like an Excel document. Every *worksheet* in a workbook is a single query (a SQL statement that returns data from the database—see the next section). You can think of worksheets as being like individual Excel spreadsheets. Every worksheet in a workbook will usually be related in some way to the other worksheets, but it does not need to be that way. We recommend, however, that you not keep unrelated worksheets in the same workbook. This makes for sloppy design and difficulties in both maintenance and security.

For example, you may have a workbook that pulls in the data for the sales in your eastern region. One worksheet may have sales broken down by salesperson, another may have sales sorted showing highest sales to lowest by customer, and yet another may show the regional sales compared to last year. The worksheets are related, but each one puts a different spin on the data and answers a different business question. Let's say you now add a worksheet that shows fixed assets. Any subsequent requests for access to your sales reports cannot be done without also granting access to the fixed asset report. Believe us when we say that this causes problems. We have been there and done that, and it does not work well.

**NOTE**

*Multiple worksheets should be used cautiously at first, and perhaps you should not use them at all in your first few workbooks. The idea behind Discoverer is its ease of use. Getting bogged down in worksheet maintenance is not always to your advantage. Also, having too many worksheets can cause issues with performance and memory, so please do not get carried away. Each worksheet in a workbook is related to its own query.*

## Queries

We have already used the term *query* a number of times in this book. However, you may not know what a query is. A *query* is simply a question that is posed of the database. When you tell Discoverer to run a worksheet, it generates a SQL query and sends the code to the database. Ideally, the answer you expect comes back. An example of a query is "How many blue widgets did we sell in the southwest region last week?" If the query was created correctly, the answer will come back to you in a matter of seconds. Some queries will take a long time, though, especially if you are not careful with your worksheet design. In Chapter 4 we introduce you to the query from the Twilight Zone, the query that seems to run forever, and show you how to construct Discoverer worksheets that avoid this issue.

## Reports

As with queries, we have already used the term *report* several times, and we think it is important that you understand what we mean by a report as opposed to a query, worksheet, or workbook.

A *report* is a worksheet that has been formatted to a level acceptable for delivery to a department, to the entire company, or even to external customers. Reports use headers and footers, company logos, company colors, fonts, and layout characteristics that adhere to your corporate standards. Finally, we recommend that reports be centrally maintained and administered as a library.

## Libraries

A Discoverer *library* is a collection of reports based around a common theme or business unit. The reports in a library differ from the normal workbooks and reports that are owned by individual report writers. Library reports are

- **Owned by a library manager** The manager will not normally be a real user but a role or responsibility that can be granted to a user. Adopting this method of working ensures the continued existence of the library following the departure of the manager either from the company or from that position. By default, the Discoverer manager also has the library manager role for all libraries.
- **Guaranteed to be accurate and perform efficiently** Candidate reports will have stringent user testing to confirm that they do what they are supposed to do. Before being put forward as candidates for the library, new reports will require user sign-off and documentation.
- **Guaranteed to adhere to corporate standards** These standards will dictate the layout, style, and naming conventions that are to be used. There should be an agreed list of abbreviations to which all library reports will conform. Standard headers and footers will be employed, and the data will be displayed in your corporate colors. A confidentiality statement will be used where necessary. The adoption of these standards ensures that your reports display a corporate image. The library manager is responsible for checking that the standards are being correctly used. Reports that do not conform will be rejected and sent back to the report writer.
- **Centrally documented** Library documents will have meaningful descriptions for the report requirements, column names, and function definitions. Any special requirements such as parameter usage will be explained in detail. There should also be a set of example screenshots from the report. Users will be able to use this documentation to understand what the report does and thus decide whether it satisfies the need they have.
- **Secure with access being strictly controlled** Access to a library report will require a request from either an end user or the end user's manager. No user will be allowed to change a library report. Following the approval of a request, the library manager will liaise with the Discoverer manager to ensure that the user has access to the relevant business area. When this confirmation has been received, the library manager will share the report with the user. Finally, the user will be informed that their request has been accepted and that the report is now available to them.
- **Maintained centrally** Following a request for a change to a library document, the library manager will consult with the requesting end user or department head and that department's report writer. The end result of this consultation will be either acceptance or rejection of the request. When a change request is accepted, the library manager will release the workbook containing the report and assign it to a report writer. Following a change, the report will need user testing, sign-off, and updated documentation prior to acceptance back into the library.

## Sticky Features

Discoverer has a memory. From time to time, Discoverer will make a note of "last used" options. The next time you are given a choice for one of these options, Discoverer will remember what you last did and default to that setting. These are called Discoverer's Sticky Features.

## Main Features of Discoverer

We have told you how great Discoverer is and how easy it is to use. According to *PC Week*, "Oracle's Discoverer breaks new ground with its high-performance mix of dynamic and precomputed queries, while its usable interface ensures its power can be put to immediate use."

We have not told you all of the terrific things Discoverer does. It might be in your mind that all you can do is view data and create queries. This is far from the truth. If you are used to working with spreadsheets or even DOS-based systems, you may not be aware of some of the features that Discoverer has available. The following table shows a list, though not exhaustive, of some of these features.

| **Folders based on tables and views** | **Items based on columns** |
|---|---|
| Descriptions of folders and items | Lists of values |
| Joins based on primary- and foreign-key definitions | Default date hierarchies (year-quarter-month) |
| Drills to related items, other workbooks, or even hyperlinks | Complex objects (pivots, filters, calculations, functions) |
| Complex joins (folders joined to other folders) | Derived items (items based on other items) |
| Graphing | Percentages |
| Exceptions | Exporting to other applications |
| Sorting (simple, group sorting, sort within sort) | Totaling (grand totals and subtotals) |
| Formatting (fonts, colors, justification, italics, bold, numeric) | Adding bitmaps to reports (Desktop only) |
| Applying titles | Adding page breaks and pagination |
| Queries based upon other queries (subqueries, but only in Desktop) | Printing and print preview |
| Scheduling | Sharing queries with other users |
| Shortcuts | Right mouse button support (context menus) |
| Templates for complex calculations | Report parameters |

This table by no means includes all of the features of Discoverer but is meant to give you a flavor of what to expect in the coming chapters. Okay, now the bit you have been waiting for. In the next section, you will learn to log in and get started in Discoverer.

# Discoverer Login Sequence

From this point forward in the book, we will be describing step-by-step instructions for using Discoverer. We suggest you perform these steps for yourself as a way of reinforcing the skills you are learning. Imagine you are in a classroom and the book is your instructor. We will first of all show you how to connect using Discoverer Desktop, and then we will show you how to connect using 11*g* Plus and Viewer.

## Connecting Using Discoverer Desktop

You launch Discoverer Desktop using the same process you use for all of your Windows applications. You can either use the Start menu or double-click an icon on your desktop.

If your company uses a terminal server for the connection to Discoverer, you should first connect to the terminal server and then launch Discoverer from the Start menu of that machine. Whichever approach your company has adopted, follow the procedures that are the standard in your company. If you are not sure how to log in, you should contact your library manager, report writer, or Discoverer manager.

Having successfully launched Discoverer Desktop, you will be presented with the following login screen.

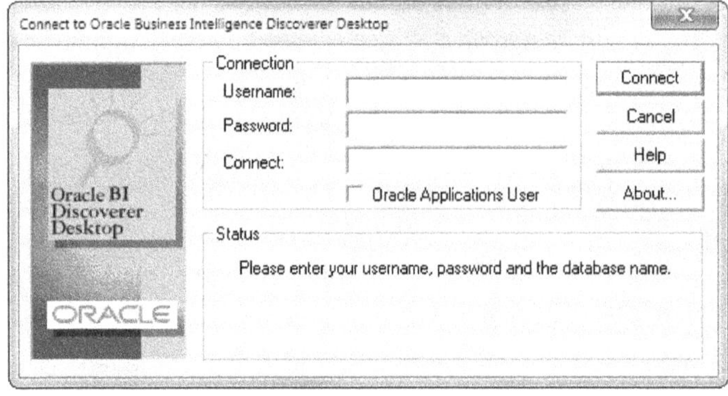


Enter your username and password in the appropriate fields in the startup screen. You will also need to know and enter the name of the database you want to access. This takes us back to the earlier part of this chapter, on your Discoverer manager and the DBA. Since each company will address these issues uniquely, we can give you only generic instructions.

When you have entered your username, password, and database, click Connect. You will be allowed three attempts to get this right before Discoverer terminates your connection. However, don't worry, because Discoverer does not lock you out; it only closes and makes you start again.

If you are using Discoverer in Apps mode, you can either type a colon following your username or check the Oracle Applications Userbox. If you successfully connect, you will next be presented with the Choose A Responsibility dialog box. Here you should select the Oracle responsibility that you want to connect using and then click OK.

**NOTE**
*Entering a colon after your username is a trick that tells Discoverer you want to connect using Apps mode. If you know your Apps responsibility, you can type it following the colon.*

# Launching 11*g* Discoverer Plus or Viewer

Logging in to Discoverer Plus or Viewer is done via your web browser. Your Discoverer manager will give you a uniform resource locater (URL) for the application as it is stored on your company's web server. This may sound complicated, but it really isn't. Just remember to ask for the instructions for launching, and then follow those instructions.

**TIP**
*Don't forget to add the URL to your bookmarks or web favorites.*

Unlike in previous versions of Discoverer Plus where to launch Discoverer you needed to click the large Start button, when you first launch the URL to start Discoverer 11*g* Plus, the URL that you use will take you straight to the connection screen. The same is true for the 11*g* Discoverer Viewer. The items presented to you on the connection screen differ depending whether your organization is using Discoverer stand-alone or as part of an application server.

## Connecting to a Stand-Alone Instance

When you connect to a stand-alone instance of Discoverer Plus or Viewer, you will see a Connect To Oracle BI Discoverer screen, with a subheading of Connect Directly.

Connect to OracleBI Discoverer
Welcome to OracleBI Discoverer.
Connect Directly
Enter your connection details below to connect directly to OracleBI Discoverer.
* Indicates required field.
Connect To: OracleBI Discoverer
* User Name
* Password
* Database
End User Layer
Locale: Locale retrieved from browser
Go

In this illustration you can see that Discoverer offers you a set of connection boxes. Depending upon the type of connection you choose, you will be offered either five or six of the following boxes:

- **Connect To** This is a mandatory drop-down box. Use this box to select the type of connection you want to make. You have three choices. They are
  - **OracleBI Discoverer** Use this option to connect to standard End User Layers.

- **Oracle Applications** Use this option to connect to Oracle Apps End User Layers.
- **Oracle BI Discoverer for OLAP** Use this option to connect to the OLAP catalog, which in turn accesses OracleOLAP cubes.

- **User Name** This is a mandatory box; you must enter your username.
- **Password** This is a mandatory box; you must enter your password.
- **Database** This is also a mandatory box, and you must enter the database that you want to connect to. If you are unsure as to what you should enter here, you should contact your Discoverer manager.

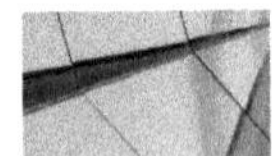

**NOTE**
*The connection information is different when you are connecting to a relational or Apps data source and when you are connecting to an OLAP data source.*

- **End User Layer** This is an optional box and will be displayed only if you are connecting to a standard or Apps EUL. If you find that you cannot connect, try entering the name in uppercase.
- **Locale or Responsibility** This box changes its context depending upon the connection you are trying to make. When you are connecting to a standard EUL or to an OLAP database, this box will allow you to set your language locale. Change this to the language you desire to work in. When you are connecting to an Apps-mode EUL, this box will allow you to type your Oracle responsibility.

After you have entered or selected the information, click Go. Provided that you entered the correct information, Discoverer will open a connection to the selected database. If Discoverer fails to make the connection, you should look at whatever error message is displayed and then take corrective action. In our experience, the most usual connection errors are either that you entered an incorrect username/password combination or that you failed to type the EUL name in uppercase.

## Using Public and/or Private Connections

When your system is associated with a metadata repository in which you have installed the necessary schemas, via the Repository Creation Utility (RCU), you will be presented not only with the Connect Directly set of connection information as shown in the illustration in the preceding section but also the Choose Connection dialog.

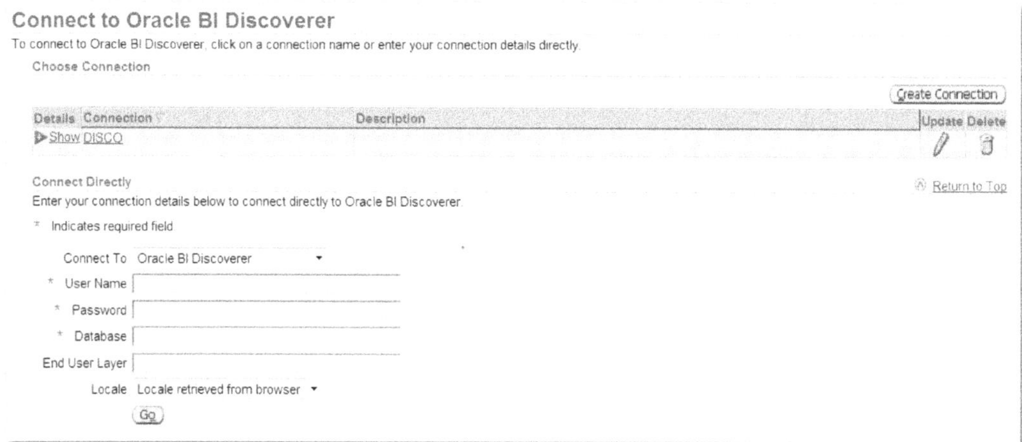

**NOTE**

*Unlike 10g, where you needed to have an infrastructure database, public and private connections do not rely on an "application server" to be available. In 11g they rely on the connection schemas and the connections having been enabled.*

There are two types of connection, public and private. These are described as follows:

- **Public connection** This type of connection uses a set of predefined connection criteria that have been provided for you by your Discoverer manager. All you need to do is click the connection you want to use. Depending on whether the Discoverer manager has previously set the password for the connection, when you click the connection, you will either be connected directly into Plus or Viewer or be prompted for the password. Not all organizations use public connections, and if you have the correct privileges, you may need to create your own private connection. The information about public connections is stored in the infrastructure database of the application server.
- **Private connection** This type of connection is predefined by you, or at least by someone who had access to your computer. Because the information about private connections is stored as cookies within the computer, you should use private connections only when you are confident that you will be the only person using the computer. If you are not the only person having access to the computer and you still want to use a private connection, we recommend you create it minus the password. This way, anyone using your computer, including yourself, will always be prompted for the password.

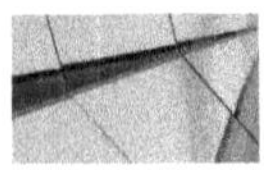

**NOTE**

*Private connections in a stand-alone Discoverer environment use cookies to store details about the connection you create. Therefore, these private connections are available to someone who uses your computer, logs in as you, and uses the same browser; for example, if you create the connection using Internet Explorer and someone else uses Firefox, that user will not see the private connection you created. However, if your company is using single sign-on (SSO), where Discoverer is attached to an infrastructure database, your private connection will be stored within the database and thus be available to you no matter which machine you use.*

Public and private connections display identically to one another onscreen. To identify which type of connection is in use, click the Show button alongside the connection name. Clicking Show displays the following additional detailed information about the connection.

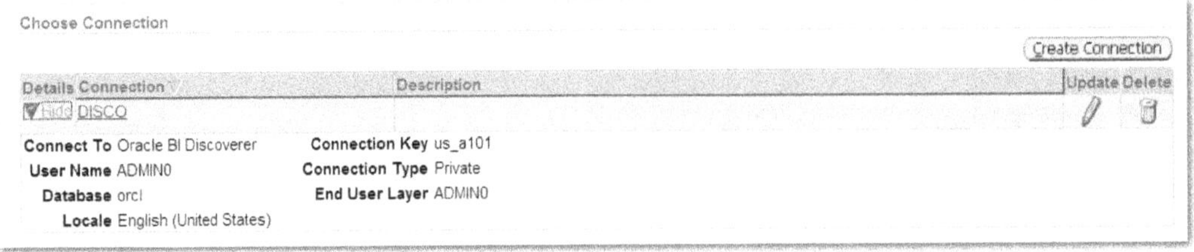


As you can see, clicking the Show button displays information about the connection type and the user being used for the login, as well as the database and EUL that are being used in the connection.

As previously stated, public connections are created and maintained by your Discoverer manager. You therefore cannot change these types of connection. However, providing that you have the necessary privileges, you are able to create and work with your own private connections.

**NOTE**

*If your organization is using SSO, you will see an SSO login screen before the Discoverer connection screen. You can see this login screen in the following illustration. You must enter your SSO username and password. This extra level of security is used to authenticate valid users of the system.*

Sign In

Enter your Single Sign-On user name and password to login

User Name

Password

Login Cancel

**Creating a Private Connection** If you can see a Create Connection button, you have the privilege to create your own private connection. If the "create private connection" privilege has not been switched on, then the button is still visible on the Discoverer Plus/Viewer connections page but is grayed out so that it cannot be clicked.

To create your own private connection, follow this workflow:

1. Click the Create Connection button to open the Create Connection dialog box.

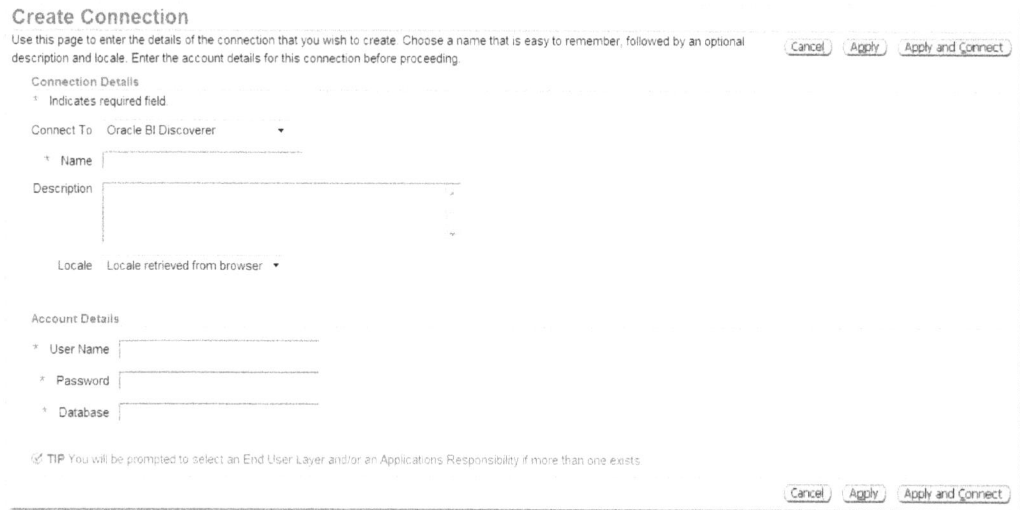


2. In the Create Connection dialog box you will notice two sections, Connection Details and Account Details.
3. In the Connection Details section, enter the following:
   a. **Connect To** Supply the connection type using the drop-down box provided.
   b. **Name** Enter a meaningful name for the connection. It is possible to create a private connection using the same name that exists for a public connection, because connections are stored and identified by their connection ID; however, we do not recommend it. We suggest you always use unique names for your connections.
   c. **Description** Enter an optional description for this connection. While this step is optional, should you decide to create a private connection using the same name as already exists for a public connection, we recommend using the description to differentiate your connection from the public one.
   d. **Locale** Set the default language for this connection. Unless you want to pick a specific language, we recommend you stick with the default of Locale Retrieved From Browser.
4. In the Account Details section, enter the following:
   a. **User Name** Enter the name of the user to connect by.
   b. **Password** Enter the password for the user. If you leave this blank, you will be prompted for the password when you run the connection.

c. **Database** Enter the name of the database you want to use for this connection. The name provided here must equate with a name that exists within the TNSNAMES.ORA file on the server. If you do not know the name of the database, you should ask your Discoverer manager.

5. After you have provided all of the preceding information, click either Apply or Apply And Connect. Discoverer will attempt to connect to the database using the criteria that you provided. If you provided valid criteria, the connection will be created, and if you clicked Apply And Connect, the connection will be executed and you will be connected to the database. However, if you entered any invalid criteria, the connection creation will fail, with a message displayed at the top-left corner of the screen.

**NOTE**
*There are two common reasons for a failed connection: you entered invalid username/password combination or you entered an invalid database name. An invalid username/password combination will result in a"ORA-01017: Invalid username/password; logon denied" message, whereas an invalid database name will result in a"ORA-02154: TNS could not resolve the connect identifier specified" message.*

6. If the connection criteria that you provided were correct, you may see a further End User Layer dialog box. This box is displayed only when there is more than one EUL available to the user in the database specified. A list of the available EULs will be given. You should select one of them from the drop-down list provided and then click Continue.
7. If you are using E-Business Suite, you may also see an additional Responsibility dialog box. This box is displayed only when you are using Apps mode and you have more than one responsibility available to you. A list of the available responsibilities will be given. You should select one of them from the drop-down list provided and then click Continue.

**NOTE**
*If you see a message saying "You must upgrade your EUL tables to use this software release," this means you are attempting to connect to a non-11g EUL. This is not allowed.*

**Editing a Private Connection** If you have previously created a private connection, you have the ability to change its definition. To edit an existing private connection, follow this workflow:

1. Locate the private connection that you want to edit.
2. Click the Update button alongside the connection (it looks like a pencil). This opens a new Update Connection screen.

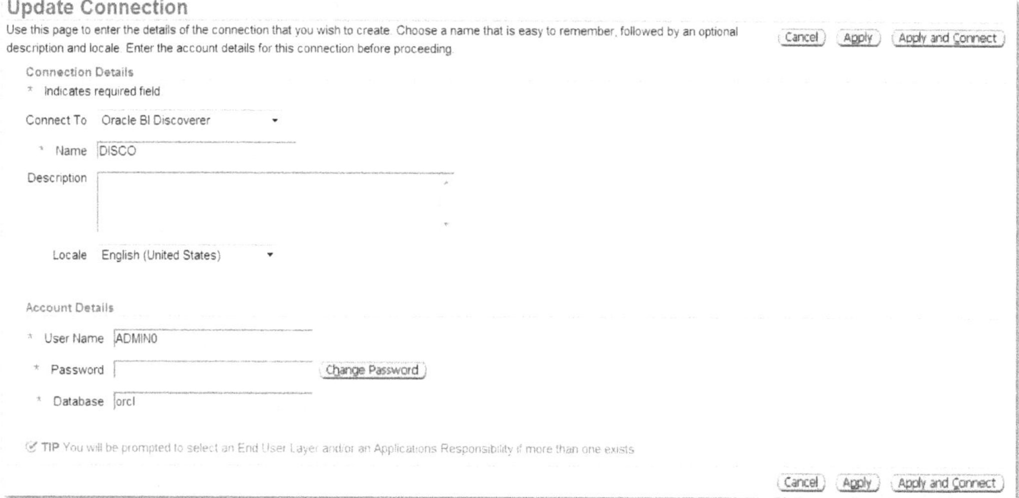


3. This screen has three components. These are
   a. An area called Connection Details
   b. An area called Account Details
   c. A Change Password button
4. Make the required changes to the Connection Details and Account Details sections.
5. In addition to the changes you can make to the Connection Details and Account Details sections, you will notice that there is an additional, optional button called Change Password. Click this if you want to change the account password. You will need to know the old password to make this change. Having entered a new password, click Apply; you will be returned to the Update Connection screen.

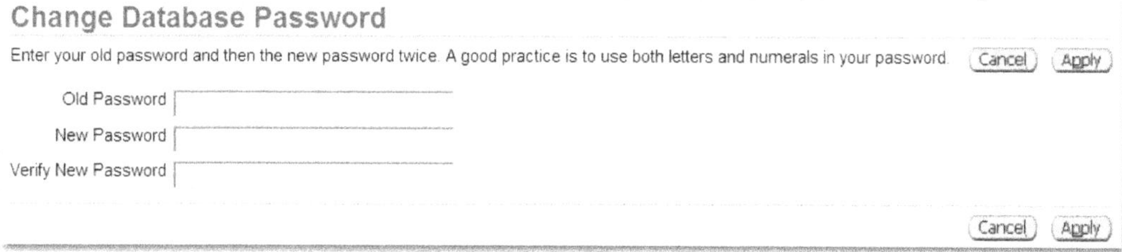

Change Database Password
Enter your old password and then the new password twice. A good practice is to use both letters and numerals in your password.
Cancel
Apply
Old Password
New Password
Verify New Password
Cancel
Apply


6. Having made all of the updates, click Apply or Apply And Connect.
7. Once again the connection criteria will be validated. If they are valid, the connection information will be changed. If not, you will need to rework the criteria until you have a valid connection.

**Deleting a Private Connection** If you have previously created a private connection, you have the ability to delete it. To delete an existing private connection, follow this workflow:

1. Locate the private connection that you want to delete.
2. Click the Delete button alongside the connection (it looks like a trash can). This opens a new Warning screen.

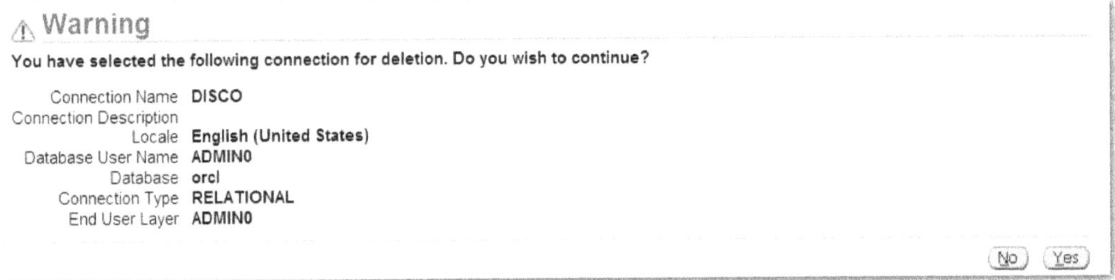

Warning
You have selected the following connection for deletion. Do you wish to continue?
Connection Name DISCO
Connection Description
Locale English (United States)
Database User Name ADMIN0
Database orcl
Connection Type RELATIONAL
End User Layer ADMIN0
No
Yes


3. This screen has three components. These are
   a. The basic information about the connection
   b. The message "You have selected the following connection for deletion. Do you wish to continue?"
   c. No and Yes buttons
4. To delete the connection, click Yes; otherwise, click No or use the back button in your browser to return to the previous screen.

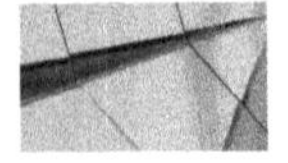

**TIP**
*Unlike Discoverer Desktop, Discoverer Plus is not "sticky" when it comes to logging you in. If you close your browser, it will not remember who you are or where you were last connected. You will have to type these again. This is part of Oracle's security guidelines.*

# Starting a Workbook

Assuming you have successfully logged in to either Discoverer Desktop or Plus, you are now on the first screen of the Discoverer Workbook Wizard. In Discoverer Desktop, this wizard has the following six workflow steps:

1. Choose whether to open an existing workbook or to create a new one. If you elect to create a new workbook, you will also be prompted to choose the display type. If you open an existing workbook, the workbook opens and the wizard will close.
2. Select items for your worksheet.
3. Define the screen layout.
4. Define any conditions.
5. Define any sort criteria.
6. Define any calculations.

However, in Plus, Oracle has reduced the number of steps in the wizard to five. These are

1. Choose the worksheet type.
2. Choose items and define conditions and calculations.
3. Define the initial layout.
4. Define an initial sort order.
5. Define parameters.

The steps that you will find in the Plus edition are far more logical than in any of the prior versions of Discoverer. To be honest with you, we never could see the reason for defining the screen layout before defining calculations. This is because you would have to adjust the screen layout again following the addition of any calculations. The new logical ordering of the steps is a big improvement and one that you will surely find easy to work with.

By following the step-by-step instructions, you can start creating queries quickly.

**NOTE**

*It may seem simple enough to use the Workbook Wizard, and you might be asking yourself, "Why do I need this book?" The answer is that using the wizard is easy, but creating an effective query is not. Chapters 11, 12, and 13 will focus on advanced query techniques to help you create better and more complex queries.*

# Summary

You learned the importance of your Discoverer team: the Discoverer manager, the library manager, the DBA, the Apps administrator, and the report writer. Forging a good relationship with each of these important contacts will be of benefit as you become an expert in Discoverer.

We introduced you to some important terms and features of Discoverer, including managing your workbooks with libraries. You also learned about SQL queries and how Discoverer manages them. We explained about Discoverer's Sticky Feature. In addition, we gave you a step-by-step procedure for gaining access to the system. Finally, we showed you how to launch Desktop and Plus in preparation to begin using the Workbook Wizard.

In the next chapter, the fun begins! You will be taken through the first steps of the Workbook Wizard to create what might be your first Discoverer query. In Chapter 5, we will cover the remaining steps of the Workbook Wizard, showing how more complex criteria can be added to your queries using the wizard.

# CHAPTER 4

# The Workbook Wizard: The Essential Steps

In Chapter 3, you learned how to launch Discoverer and log in to your database. In this chapter, you will learn about the Workbook Wizard and how to create your first query. We call the first four steps the essential steps, in that these are the basic steps you need to use in order to produce a working query.

We will teach you a simple workflow that you should follow to build your queries. If you follow this workflow, you will find that this is the quickest way to get a new query up and running. We will also teach you how to use constraints in order to avoid creating "the query from the Twilight Zone," the dreaded query that seems to run forever.

Finally, we will show you how to make Discoverer run your query and then teach you how to save it using a meaningful name. We know you will enjoy coming to grips with this brilliant tool, so let's begin.

# The Workbook Wizard

As discussed in Chapter 3, the Discoverer Desktop Workbook Wizard has six steps, while Discoverer Plus has only five steps but all of the functionality. However, the quickest way to build a new query is to use only four of the steps. These steps form a simple workflow and will be covered in this chapter.

## The Workbook Wizard Steps

As previously stated, depending upon which version of Discoverer you are using, the number of steps in the wizard will change. In the following sections, we tell you the ordering of the steps in both versions. We also tell you at a glance which steps are essential and which are optional.

### Desktop Steps

In Discoverer Desktop, there are six steps to the Workbook Wizard. These are

- Choose worksheet type—essential
- Choose items—essential
- Define the initial layout—essential
- Define conditions—essential
- Define an initial sort order—optional
- Define calculations—optional

### Plus Steps

In Discoverer Plus, there are five steps to the Workbook Wizard. These are

- Choose worksheet type—essential
- Choose items, define conditions and calculations—first two essential; calculations are optional
- Define the initial layout—essential
- Define an initial sort order—optional
- Define parameters—optional

As you can see, the overall number of steps in Plus has been reduced. The sequencing of the steps has also been changed, which, in our opinion, is a great step forward. We never could understand why you would ever want to define the initial layout before having created calculations. As soon as you created a calculation, you would need to revisit the layout to determine where to place that calculation.

## A Simple Workflow

In this chapter, we will take you through the essential steps by applying the following workflow:

1. Choose a worksheet type.
2. Choose the items.
3. Arrange the layout of the data.
4. Define conditions to avoid "the query from the Twilight Zone."
5. Finish.

If you follow the preceding workflow, omitting the optional steps of the Workbook Wizard, you can quickly generate a new query.

## The Workbook Wizard Options

When you first open the Desktop Workbook Wizard, as shown in Figure 4-1, or the Plus Wizard, as shown in Figure 4-2, you are prompted to create a new workbook or open an existing workbook. As you can see, Discoverer displays a graphic on the left side. As you move through

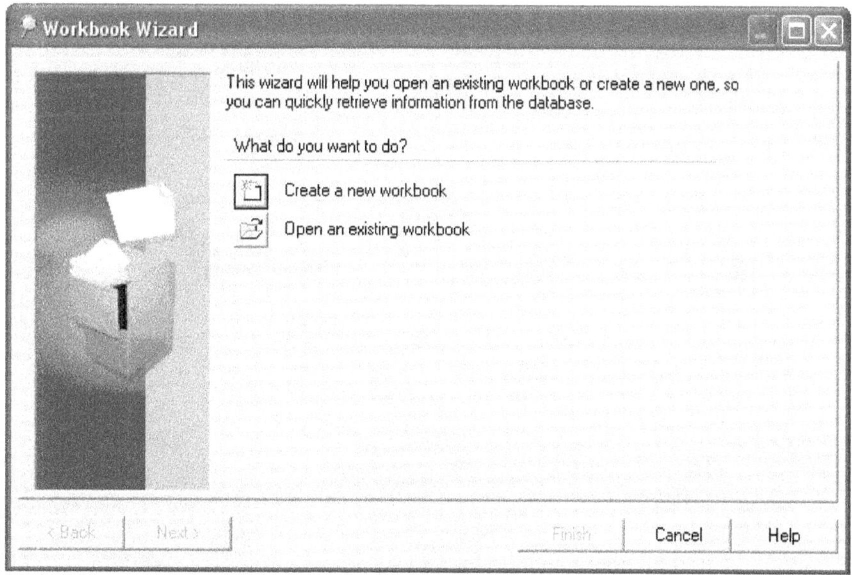


**FIGURE 4-1.** *The Desktop Workbook Wizard, screen 1*

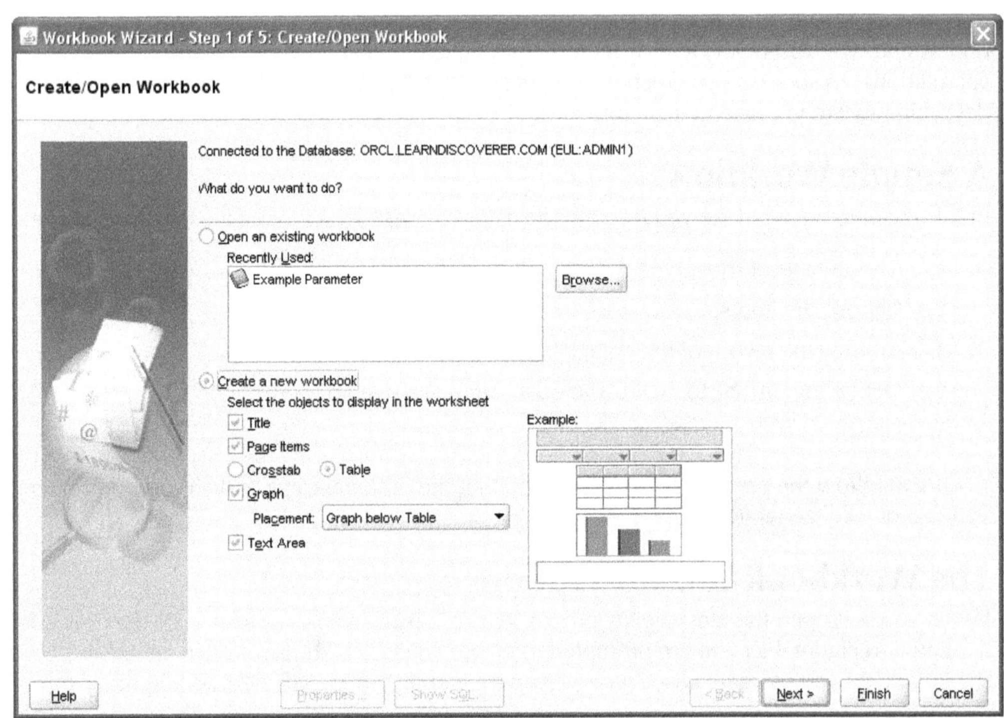


**FIGURE 4-2.** *The 11.1.1.6 Plus Workbook Wizard, screen 1*

the steps of the Workbook Wizard, the graphic changes to represent the step that you are currently working in. In Discoverer Plus you will see some cool new features in the background. Just ignore them for now (if you can).

At the bottom of each Workbook Wizard screen are buttons. The order of the buttons varies, but the functionality is the same.

The illustration that follows shows the buttons on the Desktop Workbook Wizard:

< Back | Next > | Options... | Finish | Cancel | Help

The next illustration shows the buttons on the Discoverer 11.1.1.6 Plus Workbook Wizard. As you can see, this version has one additional button.

Help | Properties... | Show SQL... | < Back | Next > | Finish | Cancel

## Back

Use this button to move back to the previous screen. When you are on screen 1 of the Workbook Wizard, this button is inactive (gray).

### Next

Use this button to move to the next screen. On screen 1, this button is inactive until you tell Discoverer to create a new workbook or open an existing workbook. When you are on the final screen of the Workbook Wizard, this button is inactive (because there is no next screen!).

### Options/Properties

In Desktop this button is called Options, while in Plus the button has been renamed to Properties. Whatever name you see, use this button to set up defaults for query formats and display settings. These will be covered in detail in Chapter 14. When you are on screen 1 of the Workbook Wizard, this button is grayed out until you get to screen 2. Should you want to set any of these attributes, you should do so when you get to screen 2.

### Finish

Use this button to tell Discoverer that you have finished creating the query. This is not available on the first screen unless you have moved to screen 2 and then come back. It is possible to create a query that does not select anything from the database. This is not a bug, and there may be good reasons to do just this. For example, you could create a query that returns the current fiscal month, using functions only. This query could be saved as a template for future queries that may need to use the fiscal month.

**NOTE**

*You can click Finish at any time; however, clicking Finish too soon can result in "the query from the Twilight Zone" (this will be covered later in this chapter).*

### Cancel

Use this button to tell Discoverer that you don't want to continue with the current query.

### Help

In Desktop, this button opens a standard Windows help file on using the Workbook Wizard. In Plus, it opens a second browser and displays the Discoverer Plus online help (in HTML format). The help that has been provided by Oracle is excellent and highly recommended. It is very detailed and informative and will help you through most workbook creation issues.

### Show SQL (Discoverer Plus Only)

This button opens the SQL Inspector dialog box, which allows you to view and copy the SQL for the items you select for the query. The dialog box also has a Plan tab that allows you to look at the explain plan for the SQL that Discoverer is generating. Please be aware that the explain plan you see here is not necessarily the explain plan for the final query that will be submitted to the database. This is because the Oracle database has a feature called *optimization*. This feature grants the database permission to look at any query that gets submitted to it and adjust the SQL to the form that is the most efficient. The dialog box will remain empty, and the button grayed out, until you select at least one item.

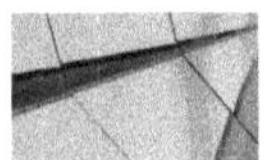

**NOTE**

*If you are familiar with other Windows applications, you might be in the habit of using keyboard hot keys or shortcut keys instead of your mouse. Both versions of Discoverer make these keys available throughout, although there are some minor differences between the versions. If you have not used hot keys or shortcut keys before, they are a combination of either the* ALT *or* CTRL *key with another key. For example, on screen 1 of the Workbook Wizard, pressing* ALT-N *selects Next. You can tell which key to press by looking for the letter that has the underscore.*

## Workbook Wizard Step 1: Creating a New Workbook or Opening an Existing Workbook

Upon successfully getting past the login screen, you will be taken to the first screen of the Workbook Wizard. This window has buttons to create a new workbook or open an existing workbook. You have the option to make additional choices at this point in Discoverer Plus. For now we will not select them, but how to use them will become apparent as we go on. We will begin by creating a new workbook.

### Create a New Workbook

While both versions intrinsically do the same thing, the mode of operation is sufficiently different to warrant separate explanations for Plus and Desktop.

**Desktop** From the initial screen of the Workbook Wizard, select Create A New Workbook. This brings up the second part of the initial screen of the Workbook Wizard. In Desktop, Discoverer now asks you "How do you want to display the results" and then displays four buttons for Table, Page-Detail Table, Crosstab, and Page-Detail Crosstab, as shown in Figure 4-3.

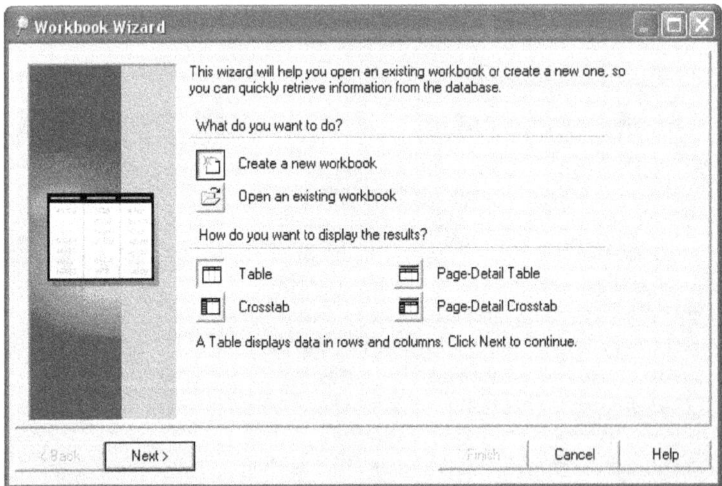


**FIGURE 4-3.** *Workbook Wizard, step 1, with display type buttons*

**Discoverer Plus** Screen 1 of the Discoverer Plus Workbook Wizard contains all the choices that are available on the first two screens of the Desktop Workbook Wizard. However, your options are now displayed as check boxes and radio buttons instead of buttons, but their functionality is the same. You will also note that on this page you can add a graph, add a title, and add a text area to your workbook. As these are not essential to building a query, we will not show these features in this chapter, but we will show them to you in subsequent chapters.

These are the check boxes and radio buttons for the various objects that can be displayed in your worksheet:

- **Title** Check this box if you want to display a title for your worksheet. As this is not essential to building a query, we recommend you uncheck this at this time. You can enable it later, when you have finished creating your query and are getting ready to turn it into a report. Please see Chapter 6 for more information.
- **Page Items** Uncheck this box if you do not want to create a worksheet with page items. By default this is enabled.
- **Crosstab/Table** Use these radio buttons to tell Discoverer that you want to create a crosstab (pivot table) or table. The default is Table.
- **Graph** Uncheck this box if you do not want to create and display a graph during worksheet creation. Unless you are an expert worksheet creator (and because this is not essential to creating a query), we do not recommend creating graphs at this time. The time to add a graph is after you have converted your query into a report. Chapter 7 discusses graphing in detail. If you decide that you do want to create your graph now, check the box and then use the Placement drop-down to tell Discoverer where to place the graph. By default, graphing is enabled, and the placement will be below the crosstab or table.
- **Text Area** Check this box to enable a text area that will display at the bottom of the worksheet. In this text area you will place additional information, hints, and suggestions that will help the user execute your worksheet. Once again, as this is not essential to creating a query, we recommend you uncheck this box at this time. The use of the text area is discussed in Chapter 5.

**NOTE**

*You can change the default settings for the Title and Text Area options using Tools | Options. Please refer to Plus Options in the "Sheet Format" section of Chapter 15 for more information. Unfortunately, the defaults for Page Items, Crosstab, Table, and Graph are not under your control.*

Select the objects to display in the worksheet
Title
Page Items
Crosstab Table
Graph
Placement: Graph below Table
Text Area
Example:

There are four display choices for a query.

- Table

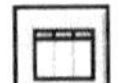

- Crosstab

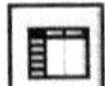

- Page-Detail Table

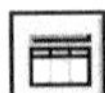

- Page-Detail Crosstab

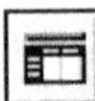

**NOTE**
*Discoverer Desktop remembers the type of display you used last and offers it as the default for your next worksheet.*

## Table

For anyone experienced with spreadsheets, the table is a familiar sight. In the table, data is organized in rows (across) and columns (down). By default, Discoverer numbers the output rows down the left side and assigns names to the column headings as defined by your Discoverer manager. Typically, these names come from the source database. Tables are essentially data organized in a list. In Discoverer, you can rename the column headings to make them more meaningful. You can even turn off the row numbers. This will be covered later in the chapter.

## Crosstab (Pivot Table)

The Crosstab option, short for cross-tabulation, will be less familiar to some end users than the standard table. In a crosstab, the interrelationship of two or more sets of data is viewed. This multidimensional view of data is one of the most exciting features of Discoverer. Crosstabs can look at data from various sources and allow the user to view the interrelationships of the data "on the fly." For those familiar with the Excel pivot table, the functionality is similar. However, the Discoverer crosstab is far easier to use and the data much easier to access.

**NOTE**
*You might hear the output of a crosstab referred to as multidimensional. That is because a crosstab consists of at least two dimensions of data: one item for the column edge (at the right) and one for the data points or row edge (the data you actually see in the table). You can also add a row edge axis (at the top) and a page axis (in the Page Items area); these are nice to have but are not essential. In Discoverer, you can have multiple items in the top and side axes, giving you greater power in your analysis of the data. We will look more closely at multidimensional data in Chapter 9, when we discuss analysis.*

In Figure 4-4, the data from the Products folder is shown as a table.

Oracle Business Intelligence Discoverer Desktop - [First Workbook]

Double-click here to edit this title.

| Prodid | Product | Size | Unit Cost Price | Unit Selling Price | Prod Line |
|---|---|---|---|---|---|
| 67 | AVR-800 | LARGE | 15.94 | 34.65 | SUPER-WIDGET |
| 68 | AVR-900 | LARGE | 15.94 | 34.65 | SUPER-WIDGET |
| 23 | AB-3000 | SMALL | 9.88 | 21.25 | SUPER-WIDGET |
| 47 | AVR-550 | MEDIUM | 11.48 | 26.95 | SUPER-WIDGET |
| 46 | AVR-500 | MEDIUM | 11.48 | 26.95 | SUPER-WIDGET |
| 61 | QB-1000 | LARGE | 12.42 | 23.45 | WONDER-WIDGET |
| 62 | QB-2008 | LARGE | 12.42 | 23.45 | WONDER-WIDGET |
| 63 | QB-3000 | LARGE | 12.42 | 23.45 | WONDER-WIDGET |
| 21 | AB-2008 | SMALL | 7.22 | 13.50 | WONDER-WIDGET |
| 43 | QB-6000 | MEDIUM | 8.33 | 17.66 | WONDER-WIDGET |
| 42 | QB-5500 | MEDIUM | 8.33 | 17.66 | WONDER-WIDGET |
| 41 | QB-5000 | MEDIUM | 8.33 | 17.66 | WONDER-WIDGET |
| 65 | CD-550 | LARGE | 10.62 | 22.18 | MEGA-WIDGET |
| 66 | CD-625 | LARGE | 10.62 | 22.18 | MEGA-WIDGET |
| 64 | CD-500 | LARGE | 10.62 | 22.18 | MEGA-WIDGET |
| 22 | AB-2500 | SMALL | 5.99 | 12.75 | MEGA-WIDGET |
| 44 | CD-100 | MEDIUM | 6.21 | 15.25 | MEGA-WIDGET |
| 45 | CD-200 | MEDIUM | 6.21 | 15.25 | MEGA-WIDGET |
| 12 | MS-1200 | MINI | 3.95 | 5.55 | MINI-WIDGET |
| 11 | DS-1200 | MINI | 3.85 | 5.35 | MINI-WIDGET |
| 14 | DS-1300 | MINI | 4.02 | 5.95 | MINI-WIDGET |
| 13 | MS-1300 | MINI | 4.10 | 6.00 | MINI-WIDGET |

Table | Crosstab

For Help, press F1 NUM

**FIGURE 4-4.** *Standard Discoverer table*

In the standard table, you see the data as a list of related items. This is fine for most types of output, but where more analysis is needed, or where the list is pages long, the crosstab can be a better choice. In Figure 4-5, the same data is shown as a crosstab.

## Page-Detail Tables and Page-Detail Crosstabs

A page detail is used when there is a large amount of data to display. In this type of worksheet, an element or elements of the data are moved to the page axis. Page items are ideal when you want to view your data one slice at a time.

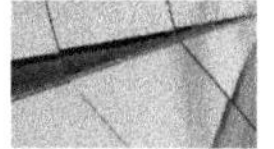

**NOTE**

*Page detail refers to the overall concept of opening up the page axis and is the final result that you see in your query. The page axis is the space at the top of the worksheet labeled Page Items. It is into this area that you place data items from the table or crosstab.*

Oracle Business Intelligence Discoverer Desktop - [First Workbook]

Double-click here to edit this title.

| | | Unit Selling Price | Unit Cost Price |
|---|---|---|---|
| MINI | | 22.85 | 15.92 |
| | DS-1200 | 5.35 | 3.85 |
| | DS-1300 | 5.95 | 4.02 |
| | MS-1200 | 5.55 | 3.95 |
| | MS-1300 | 6.00 | 4.10 |
| SMALL | | 47.50 | 23.09 |
| | AB-2008 | 13.50 | 7.22 |
| | AB-2500 | 12.75 | 5.99 |
| | AB-3000 | 21.25 | 9.88 |
| MEDIUM | | 137.38 | 60.37 |
| | AVR-500 | 26.95 | 11.48 |
| | AVR-550 | 26.95 | 11.48 |
| | CD-100 | 15.25 | 6.21 |
| | CD-200 | 15.25 | 6.21 |
| | QB-5000 | 17.66 | 8.33 |
| | QB-5500 | 17.66 | 8.33 |
| | QB-6000 | 17.66 | 8.33 |
| LARGE | | 206.19 | 101.00 |
| | AVR-800 | 34.65 | 15.94 |
| | AVR-900 | 34.65 | 15.94 |
| | CD-500 | 22.18 | 10.62 |

**FIGURE 4-5.** *Products folder shown as a crosstab*

There are two reasons for using a page detail.

- When you have a large amount of data to display and you want to use drop-down lists. This will, in essence, give you multiple sheets, one behind the other.

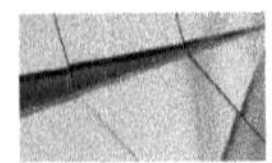

**NOTE**
*Page detail worksheets should be used sparingly, as they consume a lot of memory. The most efficient type of worksheet is the table.*

- When you have a unique constraint (applied as a condition). For example, take a look at Figure 4-5. If we had opted to place a condition on the product size so that only medium sizes were selected, we would be wasting a column by leaving the size item in the main body of the table. We should move the product size to the page axis.

Figure 4-4 shows all sizes of widgets and widget model numbers. In a real business database there might be thousands of part numbers or even millions. By moving one or more items from the body of the table to the page axis, you can choose to see only one part of the table at a time. In Figures 4-6 and 4-7, you can see that we have moved the product size to the page axis. Size becomes a drop-down list, and you can view each size individually.

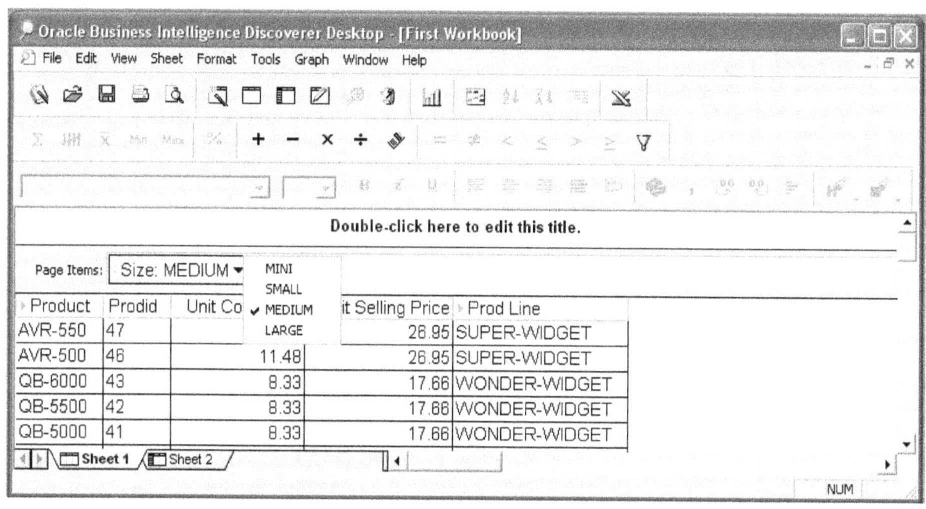


**FIGURE 4-6.** *The Products folder shown as a table with page detail*

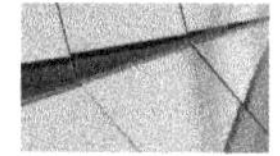

**TIP**

*After you have selected your data and run the query, look to see whether you have a single item being selected in a column. If you have, turn on the page-detail feature and move the item to the top of the page. To turn on page items, from the menu bar select View | Page Items.*

**FIGURE 4-7.** *The Products folder shown as a crosstab with page detail*

### Open an Existing Workbook

Whenever you open an existing workbook, Discoverer does one of three things, depending upon your preferred options. The three alternatives are as follows:

- Ask for confirmation (the default)
- Run the query automatically
- Don't run the query and leave the sheet empty

The mechanism for setting these options is explained in Chapter 14.

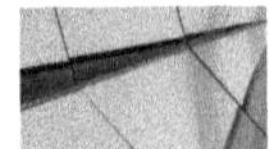

**NOTE**

*If your preference is to be prompted and you have multiple worksheets, then one of the Discoverer Sticky Features remembers which worksheet you had open last. Discoverer calls this the active worksheet. This is the one that is prompted. As you navigate into each of the other worksheets, Discoverer will prompt you again. However, if your preference is for the worksheets to run automatically and you have multiple worksheets, Discoverer runs the last one you had open. As you navigate to the other worksheets, Discoverer runs them automatically.*

## Workbook Wizard Step 2: Selecting the Data

The next step in creating a query is to select the data you want. After selecting the display type, click Next. This brings up the second step of the Workbook Wizard, shown in Figures 4-8 and 4-9.

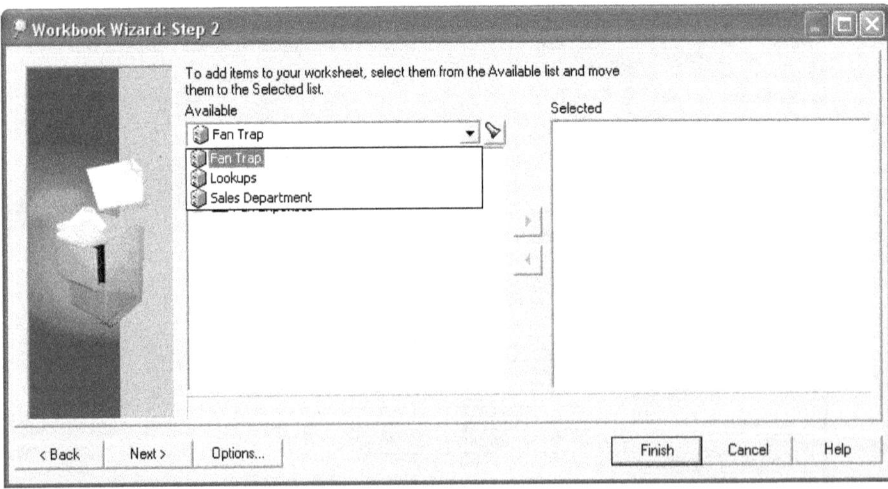


**FIGURE 4-8.** *The Desktop Workbook Wizard, step 2*

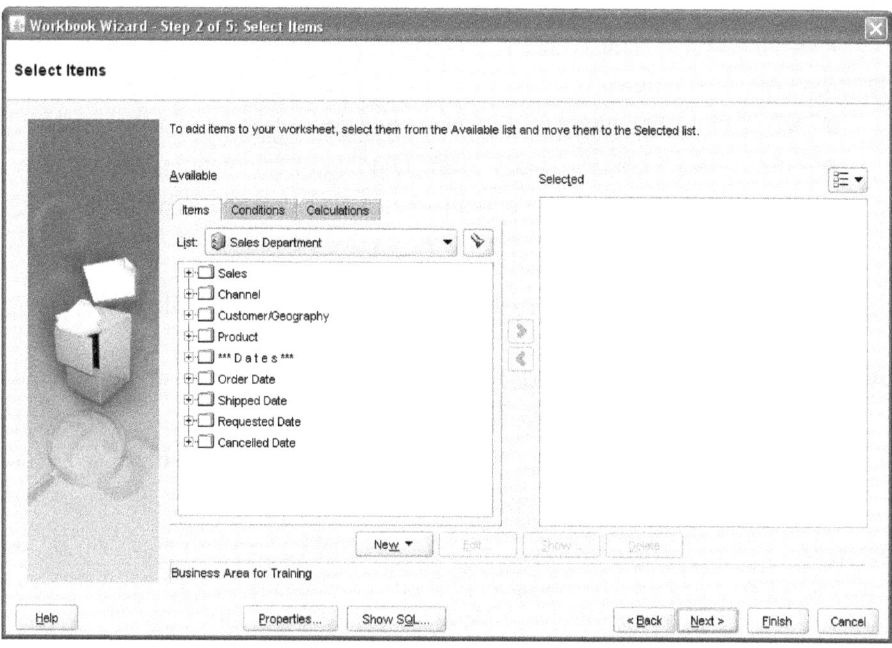


**FIGURE 4-9.** *The Plus Workbook Wizard, step 2*

## The Desktop Window

The Desktop window, as shown in Figure 4-8, has the following three areas:

- A folders, items, and business area selection box with the heading Available.
- A box with the heading Selected where you place your choices.
- A Find button, with the icon of a flashlight. Clicking this button opens the Find dialog box.

The Find dialog boxes are described later in this chapter.

## The Plus Step 2 Window

The Plus window, as shown in Figure 4-9, has the following five areas:

- A selection box, with the heading Available, that has three tabs: an Items tab, a Conditions tab, and a Calculations tab. Inside the Items tab you will see the business areas, folders, and items that are available for selection within the worksheet. Items that are being used within the worksheet have a tick mark alongside them. This will help you easily identify what is in use and what is not. If you see an unchecked item and decide that you would like to use it, right-click the item and from the pop-up menu select Add To Worksheet. Similarly, you can remove an existing item from the worksheet by selecting Remove From Worksheet from the same menu.
- A box with the heading Selected where you place your choices.

- A Views drop-down, located immediately above the Selected box. This drop-down allows you to alter the display in the Selected box. By default, the folder names are hidden. Clicking Views pops up a box from where you can choose either Show Folders or Hide Folders.
- A set of four additional buttons:
  - **New** Use this button to create new conditions, calculations, percentages, and totals.
  - **Edit** Use this button to edit existing conditions, calculations, percentages, and totals.
  - **Show** Use this button to show the details about predefined conditions. You will not be allowed to edit the condition, but you will be able to see the criteria that your Discoverer manager used to create it.
  - **Delete** Use this button to delete a user-defined condition, calculation, percentage, or total.
- A Find button, with the icon of a flashlight. Clicking this button opens the Find dialog box. The Find dialog boxes are described later in this chapter.

You can select from a business area to which you have access. Each business area contains folders, and within the folders are the items you will select to create your query.

**NOTE**
*You will notice that there are two additional tabs available in step 2 of the Plus Workbook Wizard. These tabs, titled Conditions and Calculations, allow you to create and apply conditions and calculations. You can add conditions at this point, or you can come back to this tab before running the query. Remember, we always recommend adding conditions before running a new query. We do not suggest you add calculations at this point. We will show you how to do this later.*

## Choosing a Business Area

The first thing you must do is choose the business area you want to work with from the Available list. If the one you want is not shown, press the down arrow and select the business area from the drop-down list, as shown here.

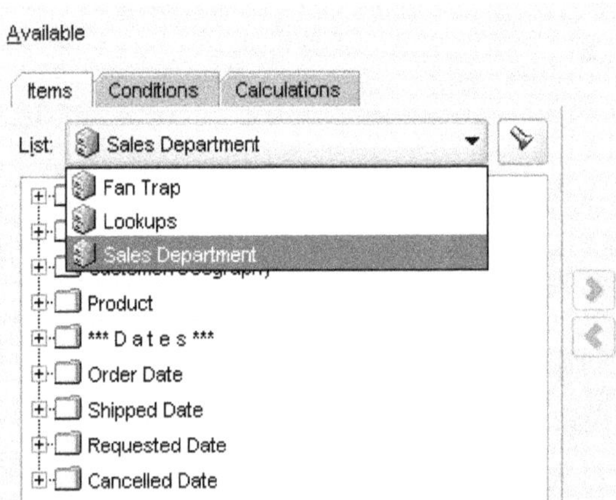

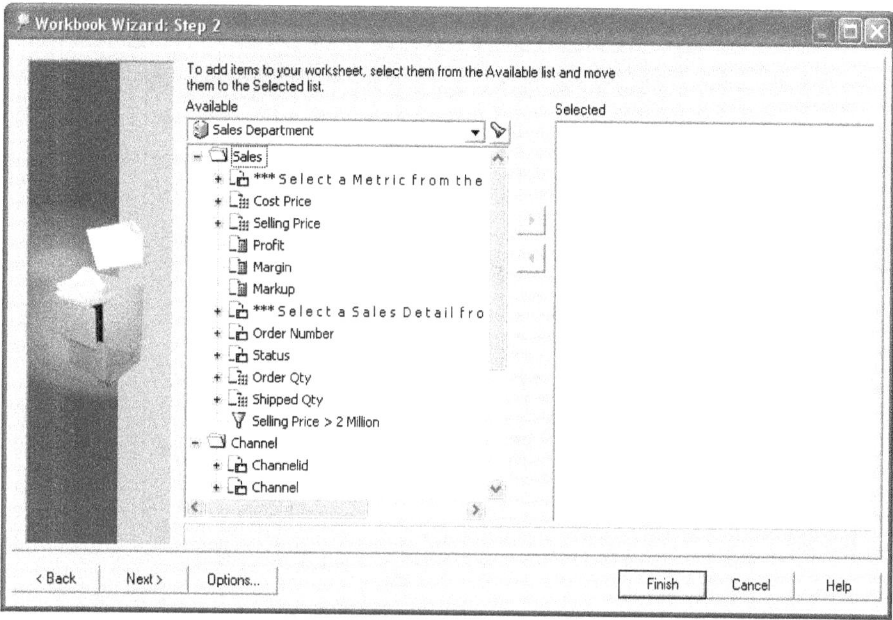


**FIGURE 4-10.** *Folders open, showing the items*

## Choosing a Folder

Once you have selected the business area you want, Discoverer displays a list of all the folders that are available to you from that business area, as shown in Figure 4-10. Open a folder you want to use by clicking the plus sign to the left of the folder. Each folder contains a list of items. These items form the basis of your query.

## Choosing an Item

Having chosen a folder to work with, you are ready to select the item(s) from that folder. There are three ways to do this.

- **Point and click** Point to the item you want, click it to highlight it, and then click the selection arrow as shown here.
- **Drag and drop** Click the item you want and drag it over into the Selected box.

- **Add to worksheet** In Plus only, right-click the item you want and from the pop-up box select Add To Worksheet.

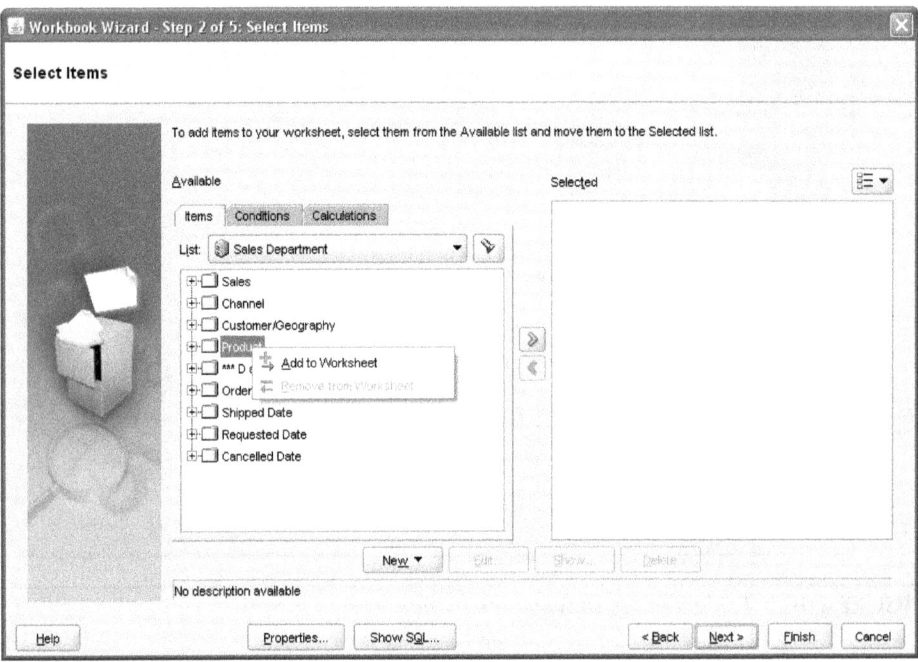


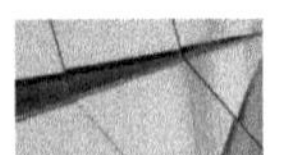

**TIP**

*If you have decided to include more than one item from the same folder, you can select multiple items by holding down the* CTRL *key and clicking each of the items you want to select. As you click them, they will be highlighted. When you have them all selected, click the selection arrow, or click one of the highlighted items and drag it (and the others) into the Selected box, as shown in Figure 4-11.*

When an item is selected, the selection arrow becomes active. When there are one or more items in the Selected box and you highlight one of them, the de-selection arrow is activated. Use the de-selection arrow to remove unwanted items from the selected box.

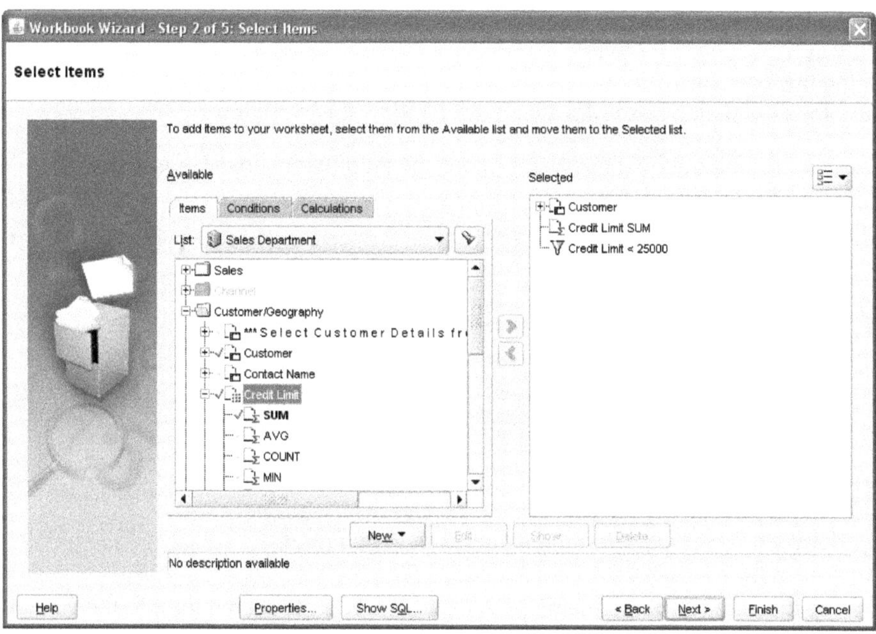


**FIGURE 4-11.** *Items selected for the query*

In Discoverer Plus you can view the selected items with the folders shown or hidden.

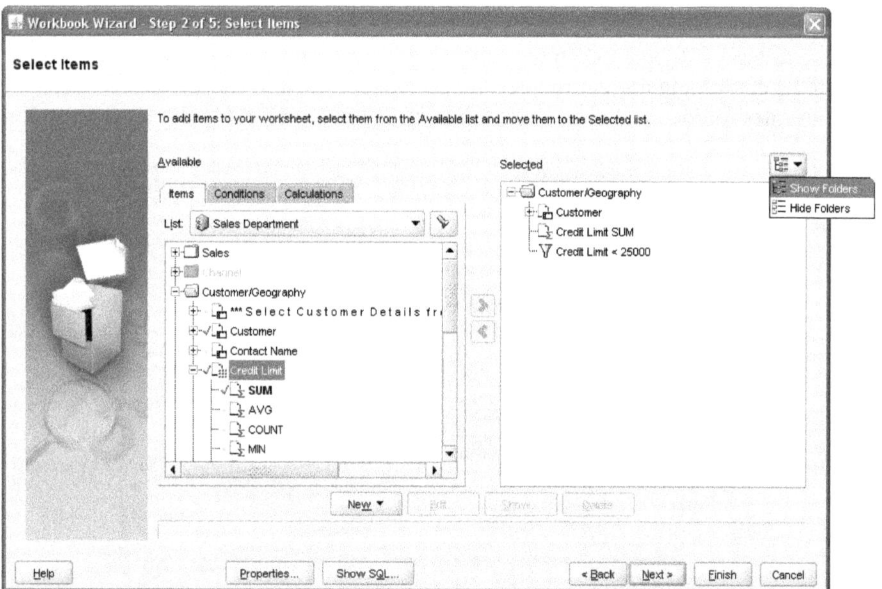

### Finding an Item in Desktop

When using Discoverer Desktop, if you are not sure whether an item exists within the business area that you have selected, use the Find dialog box. This dialog box allows you to search for items in the business area, producing a list of all items that match the search criteria.

To use the Find dialog box to locate an item, follow this workflow:

1. Click the Find button. Discoverer opens the Find dialog box shown here:

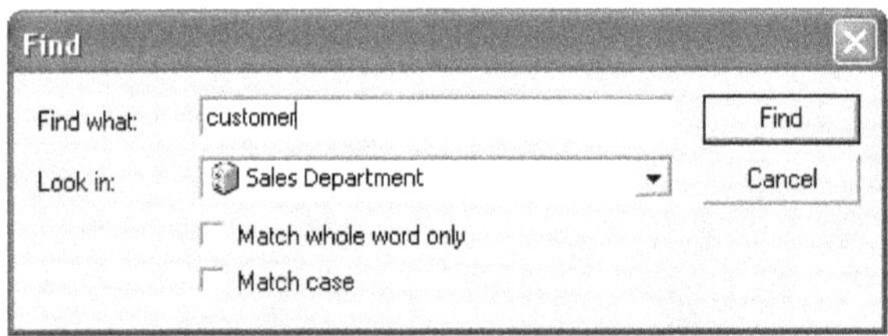

**NOTE**
*The Find button is located to the right of the Discoverer business area drop-down list. This button has the icon of a flashlight on it.*

2. Type the name or partial name of the item you want to search for into the Find What box.
3. In the Look In box, select the business area you want Discoverer to use for the search. Click the arrow to obtain a drop-down list of your available business areas. To tell Discoverer to search all business areas, select the All Business Areas item.
4. Check Match Whole Word Only if you want Discoverer to find an exact match.
5. Check Match Case if you want Discoverer to match the case.
6. Click Find. Discoverer searches the business area and displays a list of all items matching the criteria you entered. In the following illustration, we asked Discoverer to search for items containing the word *cost*. As you can see, Discoverer located a Cost Price item in the sales folder, as well as a second item called Unit Cost in the products folder.

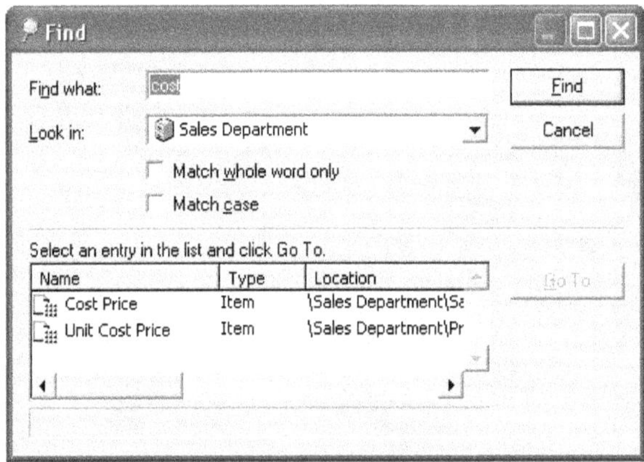


7. From the list of items, highlight the one you want to use.

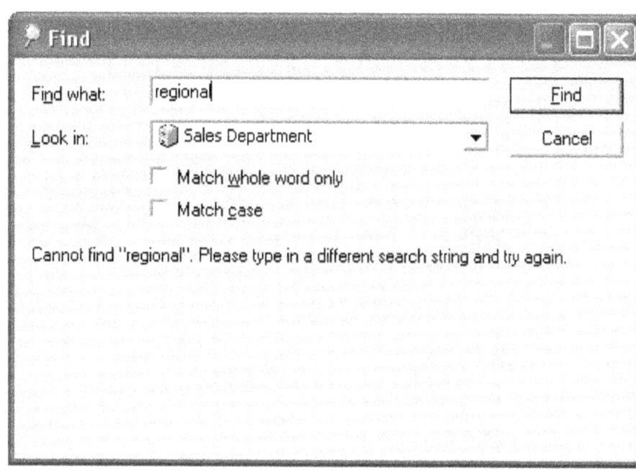


8. Click Go To. Discoverer closes the Find dialog box and returns you to step 2 of the Workbook Wizard. The folder containing the item is automatically opened; the item you found will be highlighted and available for selection.
9. If Discoverer could not find an item matching the search criteria, this dialog box is displayed. As you can see, Discoverer informs you that the search has failed and prompts you to try again. To abandon the search at this point, click Cancel.

In our opinion, this ability of Discoverer to locate items in business areas is excellent. We recommend that you use the preceding workflow frequently, especially when you are not sure whether the item exists.

## Finding an Item in Plus

Just as you did for Desktop, when using Discoverer Plus, you can use a Find button to search for items in the business area, producing a list of all items that match the search criteria.

To use the Find dialog box in Plus to locate an item, follow this workflow:

1. Click the Find button. Discoverer opens the Find dialog box shown here:

**NOTE**
*As in Desktop, the Find button is located to the right of the Discoverer business area drop-down list. This button has the icon of a flashlight on it.*

2. Use the Search In box to select the business area you want Discoverer to use for the search. Click the arrow to obtain a drop-down list of your available business areas. To tell Discoverer to search all business areas, select the All Business Areas item.
3. Use the Search By box to tell Discoverer what search action to take. The available search actions are
   - Contains
   - Starts with
   - Ends with
   - Exactly matches
4. In the Search For box, you should type the name or partial name of the item you want to search for.
5. Check the Case-sensitive button if you want Discoverer to match the case.
6. Click Go. Discoverer searches the business area and displays a list of all items matching the criteria you entered. In the following illustration, we asked Discoverer to search for items containing the word *cost*. As you can see, Discoverer located an item called Cost Price in the sales folder and a second item called Unit Cost in the products folder.

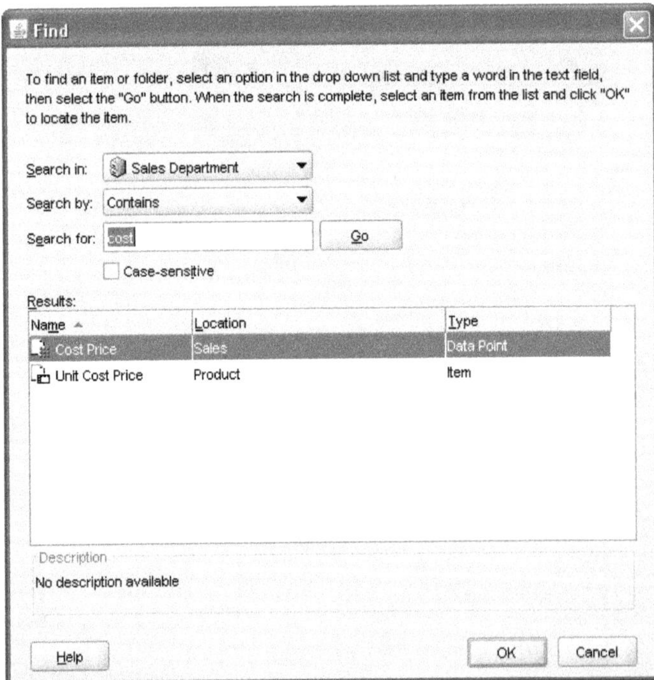

7. From the list of items, highlight the one you want to use.
8. Click OK. Discoverer closes the Find dialog box and returns you to step 2 of the Workbook Wizard. The folder containing the item is automatically opened; the item you found will be highlighted and available for selection.
9. If Discoverer could not find an item matching the search criteria, the following message is displayed: "No values were found matching your request. Try typing a different word or phrase, or selecting a different option from the dropdown list in the search area above." As you can see, Discoverer informs you that the search has failed and prompts you to try again. To abandon the search at this point, click Cancel.

### Item Types

Discoverer uses icons to represent different types of data and the options you have to choose from when making your selections. These types of data and options are as follows:

- Strings and dates
- Numbers
- Predefined conditions

**Strings and Dates** The icon to the left is the one you will see most often. It represents either strings (names, cities, customers, and so on) or dates. If the item has a plus sign to the left of it, you have some options for placing constraints on the data. This is called a *list of values* (LOV).

Plus sign indicating a list of values → + Status

For example, if the Customer folder contains an item called postcode and this item has a plus sign, clicking the plus sign gives you a list of customer postcodes. If you are interested in seeing the data for only selected postcodes, you can choose only those Zip codes you want to see, thus applying a constraint.

**NOTE**
*If you cannot see a plus sign next to a data item and you believe that a list of values would help you create your queries more efficiently, you should speak with your Discoverer manager. They have the ability to create these lists for you.*

**Numbers** The data represented by this icon (it is supposed to look like a numeric keypad) is numeric, such as selling and cost prices. When you click the plus sign next to an item with this icon, you have at least six subitems to choose from. If you don't choose, the choice is made for you and defaults to whatever the Discoverer manager has set up. Most often this will be SUM (the default will be in bold, as shown in Figure 4-12).

The following is the list of available choices and their definitions. You will not always see all of these options, because the type of data and how your Discoverer manager has set it up determines

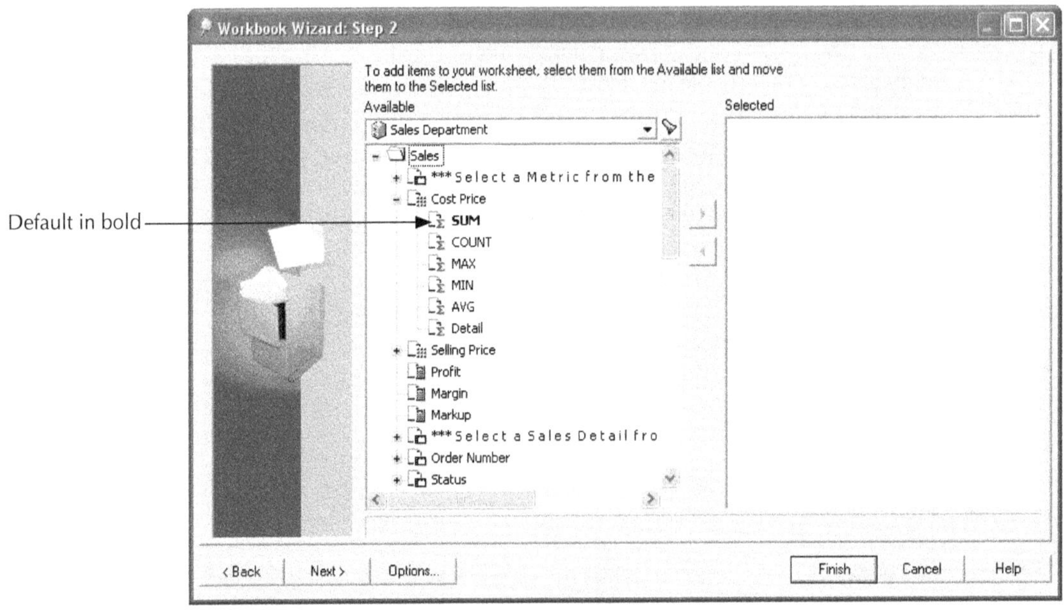


**FIGURE 4-12.** *Numeric item with default in bold*

what is available. It is also possible to have an LOV with numeric items. When such a list exists, it will appear before the other available functions.

Cost Price
**SUM**
COUNT
MAX
MIN
AVG
Detail

- **SUM** This returns a sum of all the values.
- **COUNT** This returns the number of values in the query where the expression is not null.
- **MAX** This finds the maximum value of the expression.
- **MIN** This finds the minimum value of the expression.
- **AVG** This computes the mathematical average.
- **Detail** This does not apply any aggregation. For example, if you have a line-detail table that is showing shipments for the same line over several days, select Detail if you want to see one row per shipment. If you select SUM, you will see a single row with all of the shipment details totaled (including the line number!).

**NOTE**
*If you forget what each of the items does, simply click the item and the Workbook Wizard status bar gives the description.*

Channel IN ('EXTERNAL')

**Predefined Conditions** If you are familiar with Microsoft Excel and Access, you will recognize this as the Filter by Item icon. In Discoverer, it serves a similar function. Your Discoverer manager can set predefined conditions and add them to the business area.

For example, assume you don't give credit to some of your customers. You need a report showing which of your customers have a credit limit and what the amounts are. It makes sense to ask your Discoverer manager to create a predefined condition on the item Credit Limit, which will include only those customers with a credit limit greater than zero. The condition appears in the folder like any of the other items and can be identified by the Predefined Condition icon (the filter). You can select the condition for your query, but if you don't want to use it, you don't have to.

By selecting a predefined condition, you won't need to create one of your own when setting up your queries. Predefined conditions can be applied or deactivated at any time by right-clicking the condition and from the drop-down list selecting Remove From Worksheet (see Figure 4-13). You will be shown in Chapter 13 how to use predefined conditions and apply other conditions to your queries.

**NOTE**
*Predefined conditions can be optional or mandatory. Mandatory conditions are always applied and not visible to the end user.*

**NOTE**
*Predefined conditions are created by the Discoverer manager. They cannot be modified except by the Discoverer manager. However, the end user can combine two or more conditions defined by the manager to create a complex condition. If the condition you want is not covered by any predefined condition or combination of conditions, you will need to create one of your own. Complex conditions are explained in Chapter 12.*

## Selecting Items for Your Query

The order in which the chosen items are displayed in the Selected box is governed by the following:

- The folder in which the item resides.
- The ordering of the items in that folder. If your Discoverer manager listed the folders alphabetically, then the order of the folders in the Selected box will be alphabetical—no matter in what order you made your selections.

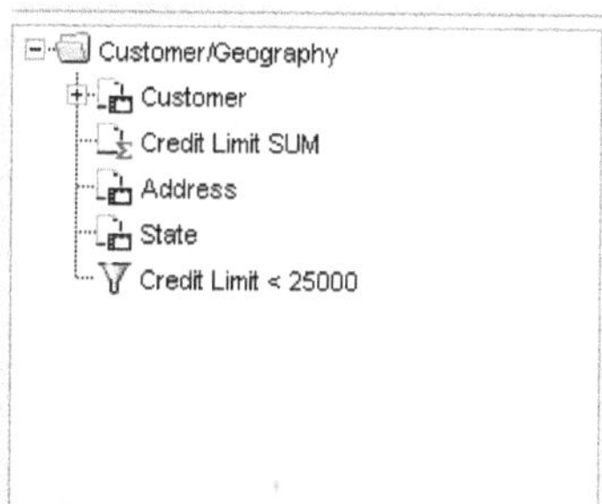


**FIGURE 4-13.** *Query using a predefined condition*

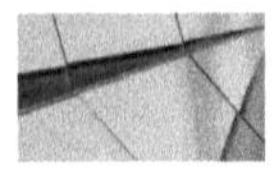

**NOTE**
*This note is for managers who may be reading this section. If you arrange the folders in the order in which your users will most likely need them, this will speed up the selection process. Similarly, you might order the items within a folder by placing the most commonly used items near the top of the list. Both of these tips will help your users make their selections more quickly.*

A useful feature of the product is that when an item has been selected, only the folders that have links to the chosen item remain active. This helps you to know where the links are and what data is available to use in the query. When folders are not available to you for selection, they will be grayed out. However, you can still see the items inside the folder by clicking the PLUS key.

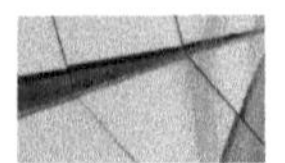

**NOTE**
*Your Discoverer manager can set the ordering of the folders and items in the most logical order for you to select. If you believe that the ordering is not correct, you can ask them to change it.*

Discoverer knows about the links between the folders, and you should make a point to read your company's documentation in order to know which folders link together. You will have to select from the folders in a logical sequence.

**NOTE**
*If you are using NoetixViews, we recommend that you have the NoetixViews help file open when you are making your selections. The help provided by Noetix is probably one of the best online help manuals around. Not only does the help file describe the folders and the items in them, but it also tells you which folders can be joined to the current folder. For more details on using NoetixViews, refer to Appendix C.*

## Workbook Wizard Step 3: Arranging the Order of the Output

The next step in creating a query is to arrange the order of the output. After selecting the data you want to view, click Next.

**NOTE**
*Don't worry about conditions just yet; we will get to them in the next section.*

This brings up the third screen of the Workbook Wizard, in which you specify the order in which you want the data displayed. No matter which order you selected the items, Discoverer will always display them in the order of their listing within the business area. The wizard step 3 screen, shown in Figure 4-14, is the place where Discoverer gives you a chance to change that order and make two other choices.

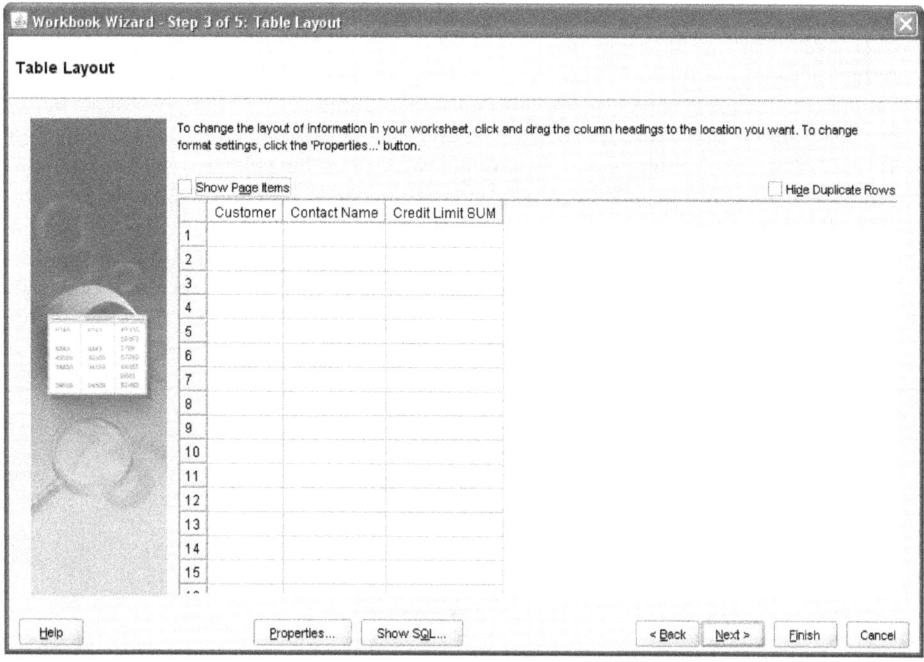


**FIGURE 4-14.** *Workbook Wizard, step 3: arranging the order of the output*

You can choose one of the following:

- Show Page Items

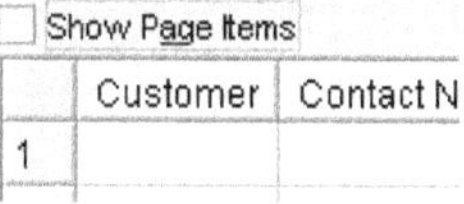


- Hide Duplicate Rows

## Show Page Items

Check this box if you want to turn the table or crosstab into a page-detail table or crosstab (we will show more examples of page-detail tables and crosstabs in Chapter 9).

**NOTE**

*If you did not select Page Items in step 1 of the Workbook Wizard, you can choose it now. This will cause Discoverer to open a new Page Items box. This new box will be located above the column headings.*

### Hide Duplicate Rows

Depending upon the data you have selected, you may find that your query has two or more identical rows. If you want to see only one of these, you should check this box.

In the following example, Global Widgets sells products to 39 customers in 17 countries. We want a report that shows only a distinct listing of the countries that Global Widgets has customers in. The Customer/Geography folder has information about customers. In this table there are items called City Name and Country Code. Building a worksheet that selects only the Country Code item from the Customer/Geography folder, without checking the Hide Duplicate Rows box, will produce a list with 39 country codes, some of which are duplicates.

In Figure 4-15, you will notice that the US and GB are listed several times, while BR, MX, and PT are listed twice. For the sake of the preceding example, we want to see each country listed only once.

| Country Code |
|---|
| PH |
| US |
| US |
| US |
| US |
| US |
| US |
| GB |
| GB |
| PT |
| PT |
| BR |
| GB |
| GB |
| FR |
| IT |
| ES |
| US |
| US |
| US |
| US |
| CA |
| MX |
| MX |
| BR |
| JP |
| HK |
| KR |
| CH |
| US |
| US |
| US |
| US |
| PE |
| PL |
| US |
| US |
| CL |
| US |

**FIGURE 4-15.** *Country code from Customer/Geography with duplicates*

With the Hide Duplicate Rows box checked, the list now contains only the 17 countries in which we have customers. Looking at the list in Figure 4-16, you will see that BR, GB, MX, PT, and US are listed only once. This satisfies the requirement to see what countries have customers.

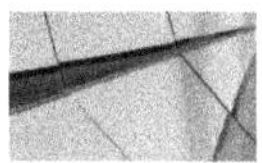

**NOTE**
*You won't always want to hide duplicate rows; in fact, your report might be inaccurate if you do. You can use duplicate rows for a more complex view of the data.*

## Arranging the Order of the Columns

To change the order of the columns, simply click the column you want to move and drag it to the desired location. If you have selected a large number of items for the query, you may not be able to see them all onscreen. You should start by locating the item you want to display in column 1 and move it first, following with each of the other items in turn. The best practice recommended by Oracle is to limit the number of columns to 16.

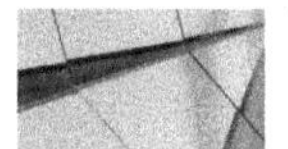

**TIP**
*If you cannot see column 1 onscreen and you need to move the current column to that position, you should click the column you want to move, hold down the mouse button, and drag the item off the active screen (which will reset). Now move the item to the desired position and then release the mouse button. This now works in Plus as well as in Desktop. In previous versions of Plus you had to move the item over as far as you could and then scroll over and move it again.*

| Country Code |
|---|
| US |
| PH |
| ES |
| CA |
| CH |
| FR |
| IT |
| MX |
| PE |
| KR |
| PT |
| CL |
| GB |
| HK |
| BR |
| JP |
| PL |

**FIGURE 4-16.** *Country code from Customer/Geography without duplicates*

## Workbook Wizard Step 4: Setting User-Defined Conditions

The next step in creating a query is to set the conditions. After arranging the table layout in Desktop, click Next. In Discoverer Plus, conditions are set on the previous screen, so you need to click the Back button to return to step 2 and then select the Conditions tab.

### What Are Conditions?

*Conditions* are constraints, criteria, or filters that you apply to your query. All of these terms can be used interchangeably. If you have used other products such as Microsoft Access, you are used to the terms *criteria* and *filters* in query writing. In terms of SQL, a condition is a `WHERE` clause.

A condition is a set of criteria that filters data in a worksheet. You use a condition when you want to limit the amount of data or refine the level of detail in the sheet. You are essentially eliminating data that you do not want to view or analyze.

The following three examples illustrate the concept of conditions in queries:

- You know that fiscal quarter 2 is always the best for sales and you want to analyze sales data from that quarter in order to produce a presentation for your shareholders. You can set a condition that will return only the numbers for quarter 2 and filter out everything else. The condition quarter=Q2 will satisfy this example.
- Your company has one salesperson per district and rewards them by giving a vacation to all who have generated sales in excess of $10 million. By setting a condition that reports district sales revenue in excess of $10 million, you can tell at a glance who gets the all-expense-paid trip to the Bahamas for two. The condition Revenue>10000000 will meet the requirement for this query.
- You have decided to create a report analyzing the margin between sales and costs. To do this correctly, you need to exclude zero-cost items from the query. Setting a condition Cost<>0 will give you the numbers you need.

You are not restricted in the number of conditions you may create. However, there is a trade-off between applying conditions and query performance. Ideally, you should attempt to apply your conditions to items that are indexed. If you do this, you will improve the performance of the query. Applying conditions to nonindexed items could have a negative impact on performance. The more nonindexed conditions you apply, the longer your query could take to run. Check with your Discoverer manager or system documentation to see which database items are indexed.

**NOTE**

*If you have NoetixViews, you should look inside the NoetixViews help file. Open the folder containing the item you want to apply the condition to and look to see whether the item name begins with A$. Noetix uses this prefix to indicate which items are indexed. It is strongly recommended that you always apply conditions to these items, if at all possible. For more information concerning NoetixViews, see Appendix C.*

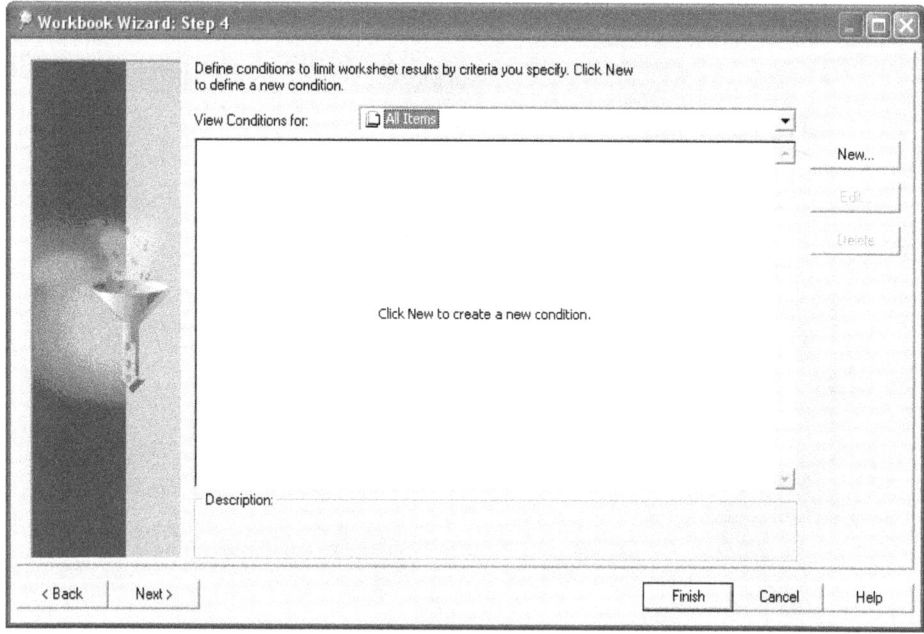


**FIGURE 4-17.** *Desktop Workbook Wizard, step 4: setting up user-defined conditions*

## Creating Conditions in Desktop

Having clicked Next on the previous screen, you will now be in the fourth screen of the Workbook Wizard, as shown in Figure 4-17. This window contains three boxes.

- **View Conditions For** A drop-down box where you can choose to view conditions for all items, the active items, or a specific item only
- **Conditions** A list box showing all of the conditions based upon the selection made in the View Conditions For drop-down box
- **Description** A box showing the description of the condition highlighted in the Conditions box

The screen also contains three new buttons.

- **New** This button is used to create a new condition.
- **Edit/Show** This button toggles between Edit, for conditions that you can edit, and Show, for predefined conditions that you cannot edit but can view in the Show Conditions window.
- **Delete** Be careful using this one. It does just what it says and without prompting! You can use the Undo feature to undo the delete operation, but it is best not to delete the condition in the first place.

**View Conditions for Drop-Down Box** You will need to select one of the items from the View Conditions For drop-down box. The choices are described here:

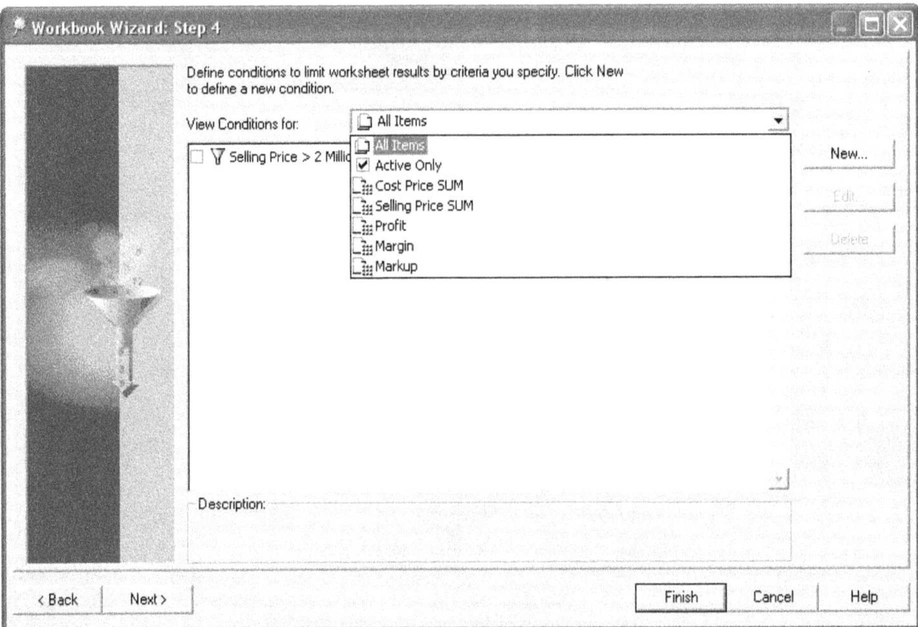


- **All Items** This is the default and will show all conditions used within the entire workbook. If you have more than one worksheet in the workbook, viewing conditions for all items will list those conditions from the other worksheets as well as the one you are working on. This could be confusing, and you might delete a condition by accident because you believed you did not need it. You might have a workbook with worksheets from different business areas. If you try to select a condition that applies to an item that is not used in the current worksheet's business area, you will get the following error message in Desktop:

This issue does not arise in Plus because Plus will not allow you to select incompatible conditions or items.

- **Active Only** This option allows you to view only those conditions that are being used in the current worksheet. If you have multiple worksheets in the workbook and they use completely different sets of items, perhaps even from different business areas, you may want to select this option. It will, in some situations, help reduce confusion to use the

Active Only option; however, *use this option with care*. You might already have the exact condition created, but you will not know it if you select Active Only.

- **Specific Items** Discoverer maintains a list of all the items in your query, whether or not they have conditions. Clicking the down arrow not only lists the options already referred to but also includes all the items in the query. You may choose to view the conditions for just one of these items. If you have multiple conditions on the same item and your query is producing unexpected results, you will probably find that you have a wrongly defined condition. Selecting to view the conditions for just the item concerned will allow you to ascertain where the error lies.

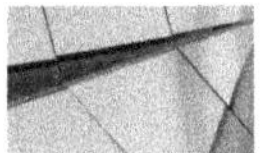

**NOTE**
*After you have finished debugging your conditions, don't forget to switch the view back to All Items or Active Only. If you save the query and exit, then when you come back into the worksheet, Discoverer will reset the view to All Items.*

**Conditions** The large box in the middle of the window shown in Figure 4-18 contains the conditions (predefined and user defined) available for use in this workbook. When you have more than one condition, Discoverer will highlight by default the first condition in the box.

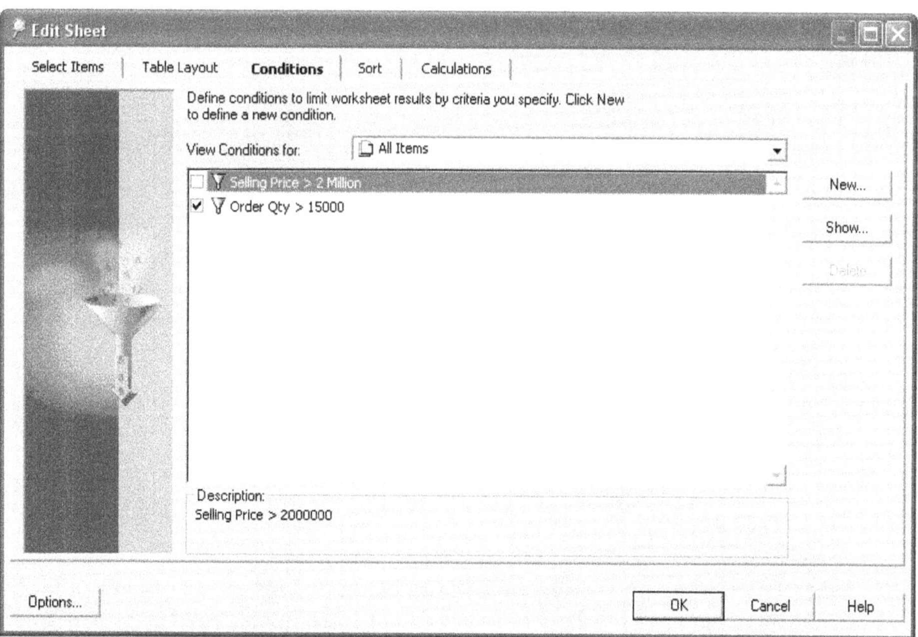


**FIGURE 4-18.** *Workbook Wizard, step 4*

**NOTE**
*There is a Sticky Feature that will remember the last condition you selected, and that will be the one highlighted when you return to the conditions step of the Workbook Wizard.*

**Description** The gray box below the list of conditions contains a description of the selected condition in the box shown earlier in Figure 4-18.

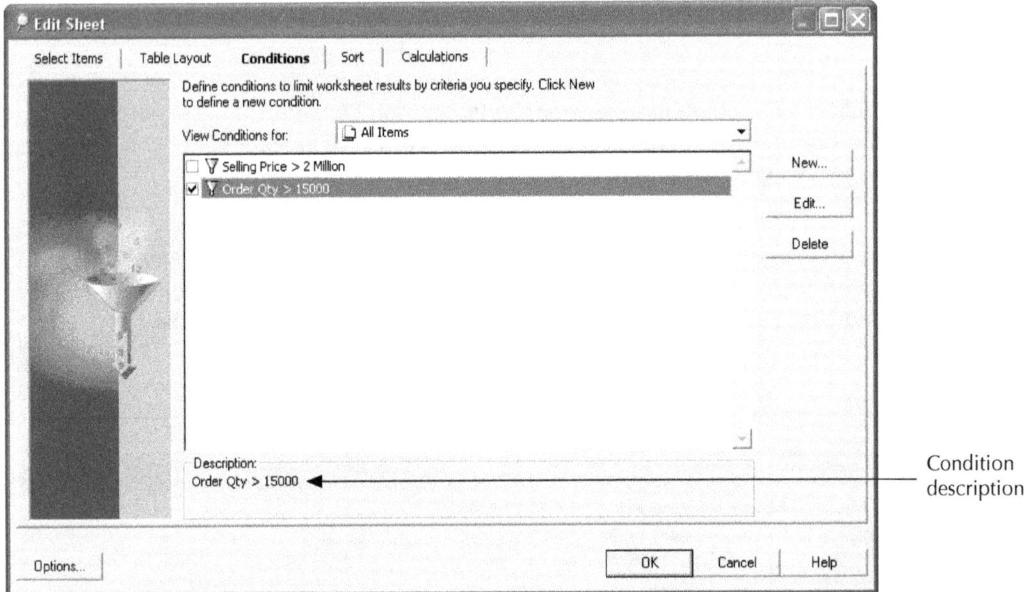


In this box, Discoverer will display a description of the highlighted condition. You can use this "at-a-glance" feature to get help on the condition. Many conditions are short and sweet, and you can view the entire condition without even looking in the Description box. However, some conditions are complex, and the Description box can display the user- or manager-defined description of the condition. If no description has been provided, Discoverer will display the condition itself.

**The New, Edit, and Show Buttons** These buttons open three windows that appear to be identical but function in slightly different ways. The only evidence you have of which window you are in is the title bar.

- **New** Use this button to open the New Condition dialog box, shown in Figure 4-19, to create a condition to use in your query.
- **Edit** Use this button to open the Edit Condition dialog box. This button is visible only when you have selected a condition that you can edit. An example of an editable condition is one you or another user has defined or a constraint you applied in step 2 of the Workbook Wizard.

- **Show** Use this button to open the Show Conditions dialog box. This button is visible only when you have selected a condition that cannot be edited. Predefined conditions cannot be edited, but you can view how the condition was created.

These dialog boxes will be shown in greater detail in Chapter 7, along with how to create useful and meaningful conditions.

## Creating Conditions in Plus

Having clicked the Back button on the previous screen, you will now be returned to the second screen of the Workbook Wizard. As already mentioned, this screen has three tabs. To get to the section of the screen that handles conditions, click the Conditions tab, as shown in Figure 4-20. This window contains five areas.

- A selection box, with the heading Available, that has three tabs: Items, Conditions, and Calculations. Inside the Conditions tab you will see the predefined and user-defined conditions that are available for selection within the worksheet. Conditions that are being used within the worksheet have a tick mark alongside them. This will help you easily identify what is in use and what is not. If you see an unchecked condition and decide that you would like to use it, right-click the condition and, from the pop-up menu, select Add To Worksheet. Similarly, you can unhook an existing condition from the worksheet by selecting Remove From Worksheet. This does not delete the condition but simply disconnects it from use.
- A box with the heading Selected where you place your choices. You will already see the items that you selected in step 2.

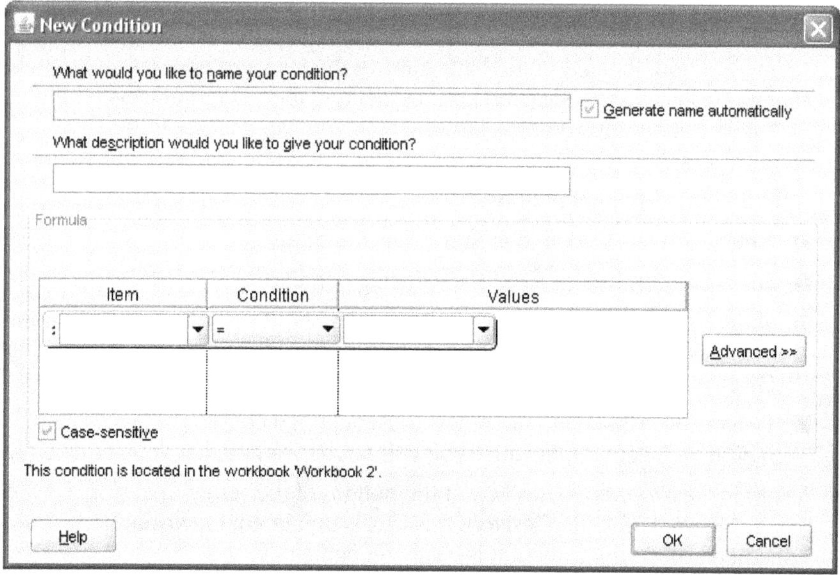


**FIGURE 4-19.** *The Desktop New Condition dialog box*

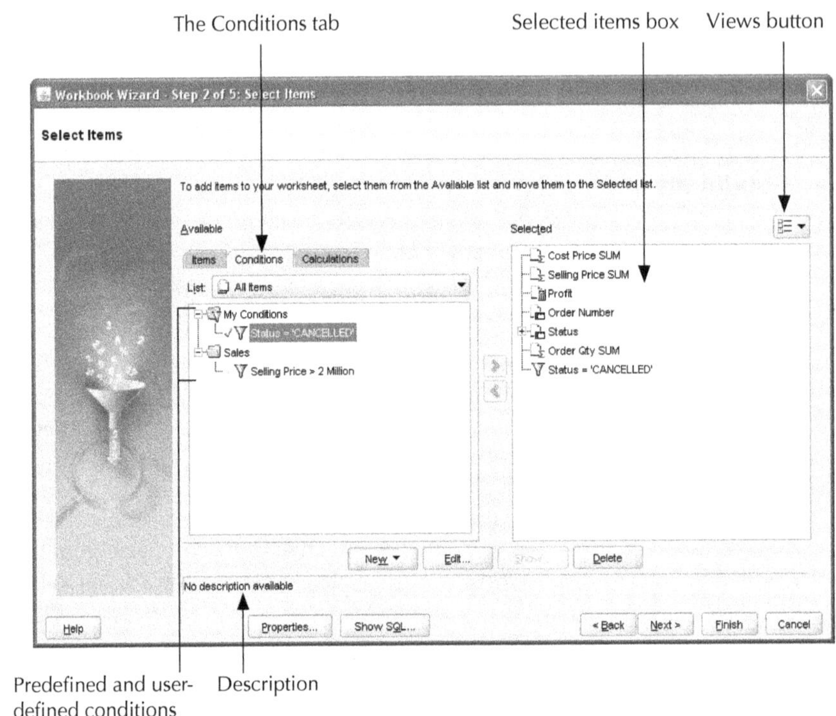


**FIGURE 4-20.** *Plus workbook methodology, step4: setting up user-defined conditions*

- A Views button, located immediately above the Selected box. This button allows you to alter the display in the Selected box. By default, the folder names are hidden. Clicking the Views button pops up a box from which you can choose either Show Folders or Hide Folders.
- A set of four additional buttons:
  - **New** Use this button to create a new condition.
  - **Edit** Use this button to edit an existing condition.
  - **Show** Use this button to show the details about a predefined condition. You will not be allowed to edit the condition, but you will be able to see the criteria that your Discoverer manager used to create it.
  - **Delete** Use this button to delete a user-defined condition. Once again, use this button with caution, because you will not be warned that you are deleting a condition.
- Just as in Desktop, there is a box at the bottom of the screen that displays a description of the condition. Unlike in Desktop, this box is unnamed. However, because it is the only unnamed box on the screen, it is easily recognizable.

Creating a new condition in Plus is very easy because you simply click the New button and, from the pop-up menu, select New Condition. This opens the Plus New Condition dialog box, as shown here:

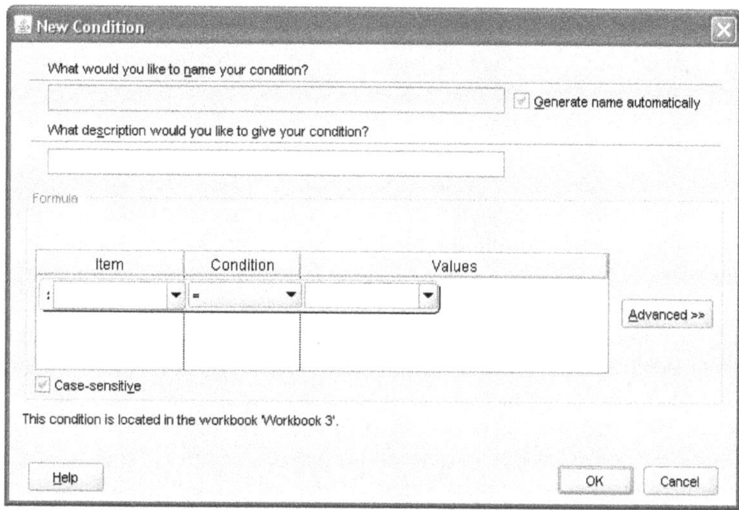


This dialog box is similar to the Desktop dialog box shown earlier in this chapter and works in the same way. Here is a simple workflow for creating a condition using this box:

1. Choose whether to give the condition a name by checking/unchecking the Generate name automatically box.
2. If you uncheck the Generate name automatically box, you must give the condition a name.
3. While the box for the description is optional, we recommend using it. Here you should place a meaningful description for your condition, in a language that most novice users would understand. This is useful for documentation.
4. In the Formula area, create the condition. Please refer to Chapter 14 to gain a full understanding of creating effective conditions.
5. Click OK. You will now see the condition displayed in both the Available and Selected boxes. Note the tick mark alongside the condition in the Available box. As mentioned earlier, this is a really cool way of knowing which conditions are in use.

## The Query from the Twilight Zone and How to Avoid It

The phrase "the query from the Twilight Zone" was first introduced to one of us by an Oracle trainer during a course on data warehousing several years ago. Since then it has become an intrinsic part of the Armstrong-Smith methodology because it describes perfectly the type of query that users should avoid writing.

So, what is it? Well, to put it simply, it is a query that never—or seemingly never—returns any information. Once submitted, the query just appears to run forever, apparently having been submitted to that "big database in the sky" from whence nothing ever returns. Somewhere out there in the bowels of data land are millions of queries still searching for their elusive data, and we hope the users are not still sitting at their desks waiting for the results!

Having all the data from your company available to you, coupled with the newly unleashed power of Discoverer, makes it tempting to query everything.

For example, let's say you work for a company that produces widgets and you currently have 10,000 finished products. Your bill of materials defines what components make up those widgets and the current monthly cost of each of those components. So, let's say each of your widgets has 50 components and that you are a fairly large company with 20 manufacturing plants worldwide. We are sure this sounds familiar to many of you. At this point, you therefore have to maintain monthly costs for 10 million (10,000 × 50 × 20) different components.

If you were trying to build a query to analyze your current costs, you would not want to let your first attempt run against all of those records, would you? To further compound the issue, imagine trying to compare the current month's costs against those during the past year. This query would compare the current 10 million with the 110 million from the previous 11 months. This example may seem somewhat extreme, but it isn't. There are thousands of companies like this, many of which are actually bigger and more complex.

The query just described that analyzes 10 million records may, depending upon what kind of hardware your company has, actually produce a result in four or five hours. Realistically, though, your Discoverer manager will probably have set a limit for the maximum length of time they will allow you to run your query, and your query will have timed out. We therefore have to explore ways of reducing the length of time required to build your query.

There are many ways to reduce the length of time when building a query. Six of these are as follows:

- Using data marts and summary tables
- Applying constraints to avoid creating long-running queries
- Applying Discoverer query governors to reduce the time allowed or the maximum number of rows of data returned
- Applying a sort order after the query results have been ascertained
- Creating totals and subtotals on a subset of the data
- Applying calculations after the query has run

**NOTE**
*These are Discoverer-specific methods, not to be confused with database optimizations, which are different.*

The first three will be covered in this chapter, and the last three will be covered in Chapter 5.

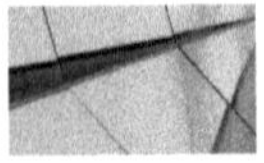

**NOTE**
*You may want to look at the preceding list as a workflow. By applying the steps listed, you should be able to effectively manage large data selections without creating "the query from the Twilight Zone."*

## Using Data Marts and Summary Tables

Data marts and summary tables can greatly reduce the time taken to produce reports that require large amounts of data. Therefore, whenever you have to create a query that needs to report a large amount of data, you should consult with your Discoverer manager and inquire whether there are any data marts in existence. As described earlier, a data mart is basically a table that has been specially created for reporting and has indexes specially built for reporting. Summary tables can be created by your Discoverer manager. Where these exist, Discoverer will analyze your query and, if all the items you want can be found within a summary table, redirect your query to use that table. In an Oracle database, these tables are called *materialized views*. The great advantage of these is that they can be preaggregated and have indexes defined on the items that you choose to place conditions on.

While you yourself cannot point your query to a summary table, discussing your requirements with your Discoverer manager may well reveal that such a table exists. Where these do exist, you may want to consider amending your requirements so that you include only those items that are contained within the summary table. If this is not possible, your Discoverer manager may well be the friendly sort of person who would not mind either changing the existing summary or creating a new one for you.

If there are no data marts or summary tables in existence, you may want to discuss your requirements with your report writer or Discoverer manager. These people may be able to help you start the process for having one of these objects created for you. Do not feel that you need to give up on any queries that you want to create. There is always something you can do, and there is always something that can be done for you. You should therefore stay close to and make use of the resources available.

### Applying Constraints to Avoid Creating Long-Running Queries

The first thing every good query writer learns is how to apply constraints. Discoverer calls these *conditions*. You need to work with your Discoverer manager and possibly your DBA to find out as much as you can about the nature of the data you will be working with.

You need to know which tables contain large numbers of items and what the values are within your main indexes so that you can define suitable conditions. Very large tables need to be constrained on their index items. If you attempt to create your conditions on nonindexed items, then this will hardly make any impression on the time taken to run your query because the system will still have to search all of the items in order to decide whether each of those items meets your condition.

In the example query we are using, where we have 10 million current cost records, you would need to find out what code your system uses to define the current month's costs (Oracle Applications calls the current cost the *frozen cost*, and usually it has the code value 1). This will at least reduce the number of items being searched to those 10 million records.

**Applying Temporary Constraints to Quickly View Preliminary Output** If you get to work closely with your Discoverer manager and spend some time learning about the data in your system, you will soon become aware that querying from some tables will take a very long time. This experience, coupled with some common sense, will tell you to look for ways to minimize the time it takes to at least get some preliminary output. You don't want to wait several hours to see the column ordering or wait that long only to discover you left something out or included something you didn't need.

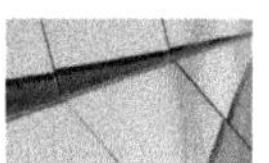

**NOTE**

*Setting temporary constraints in order to get preliminary output is an essential tool in your armory and will result in a rapid building process.*

Returning to our example query, we have already ascertained what the code value is for the current month, but this would still result in a query of 10 million records. While the end result may be that we do in fact want to produce a report of that magnitude, during the construction of the query we do not want to be running against that volume of data. We would therefore look to reduce the number of items being queried. This is done by limiting the query to search only one manufacturing facility (reducing the query to 500,000 items) and by limiting it further by restricting the query to, say, only ten finished products (reducing it to a manageable 500 items). This query will run very quickly, and you can now concentrate on defining your sort criteria, totals, and subtotals, along with the final data formatting characteristics.

## Using Discoverer's Query Governor

Discoverer has a rather clever way to artificially cut down the length of time it takes to run a query. This is called the *query governor*. No matter which version of Discoverer you are using, the way you access the query governor is via the toolbar. From the toolbar, select Tools | Options and select the Query Governor tab. This opens the Query Governor dialog box shown here.

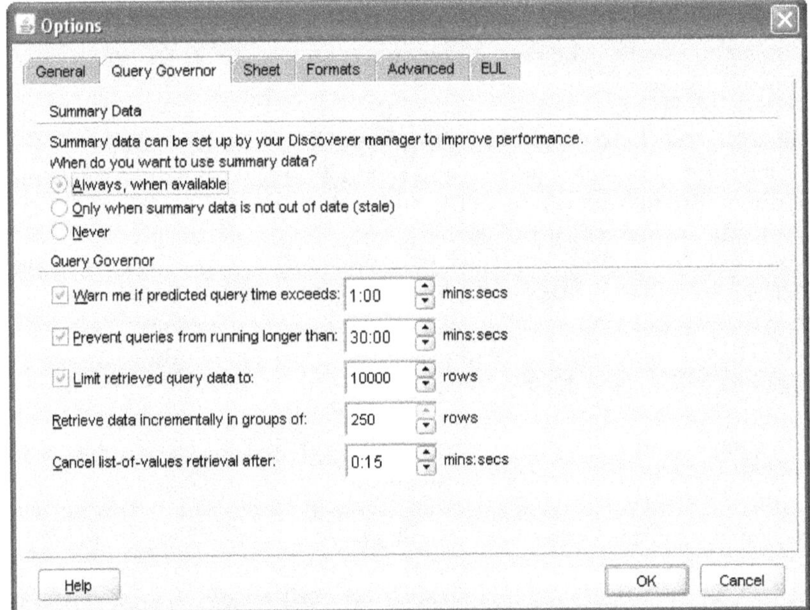


The Query Governor dialog box has two important settings that you can apply.

- Prevent Queries From Running Longer Than
- Limit Data Retrieved To

The usage of both of these is detailed next.

**NOTE**

*Using the query governor can slow things down a little because when it is switched on, Discoverer needs to gather statistics.*

**Prevent Queries from Running Longer Than** Use this setting to set a time limit for how long you are prepared to wait for your results. We recommend you initially set this really low, to something like one minute. You will then get some idea as to how much data is returned in that time.

**Limit Data Retrieved To** Use this setting to set a row limit for how many rows of data you are prepared to work with in your initial query. We recommend you initially set this low to something like 50. Again, you will get a great idea as to how long it will take to pull back that much data.

**NOTE**
*Your Discoverer manager will have set maximums for these settings. As an end user, you have the ability to reduce those settings at will, but you cannot set them higher than the preset maximum.*

# Viewing the Results

Although there are more steps to the Workbook Wizard, we feel the best way to proceed is to leave the wizard now and run the query. Don't worry—the remaining steps of the wizard will still be available to you after running the query. There is a good reason for this. We feel that people new to creating queries should keep them simple to begin with and build them up by steps. If you continue through the remainder of the wizard, you could find that after all of your work, you have created a query that will return either no data or so much data that you are timed out of the system before it can finish running. Build the foundation of the query and see the basic data, and then go on from there.

To view the results of the query, click Finish. Discoverer closes the Workbook Wizard, runs the query, and displays the results. Figure 4-21 shows the results from a typical Desktop query.

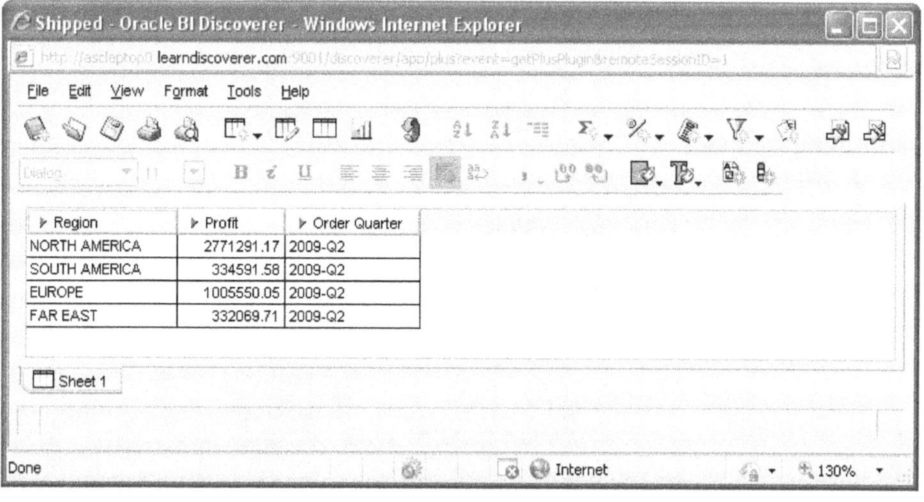


**FIGURE 4-21.** *A basic query in Desktop*

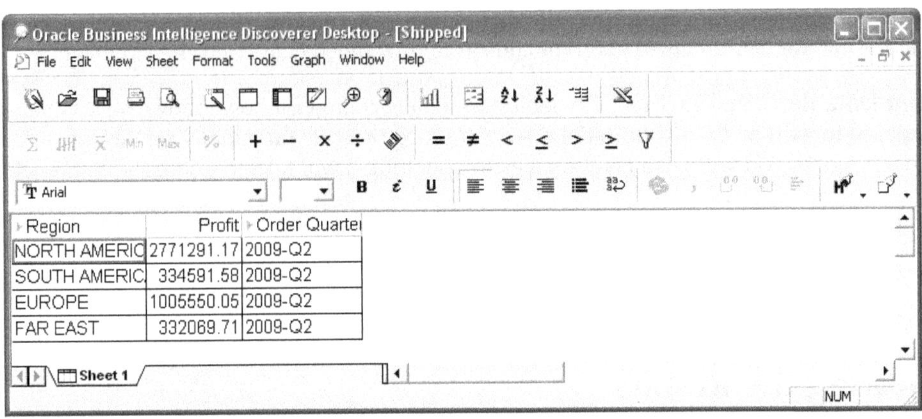


**FIGURE 4-22.** *The Discoverer Plus default view*

In Figure 4-22 you can see the same results displayed in Discoverer Plus. The Available Items pane and the Selected Items pane are available to the left of the query. We think these are very useful features, and we will show you how to use them in Chapter 5.

## Interrogating the Results of a Query

When viewing the results of a query that has been run in Discoverer, you may want to check whether a certain piece of data has been retrieved. The long, laborious way of doing this is to use the mouse to page through the results until you find the item that you want. In Discoverer, the quickest way to check whether an item has been retrieved is to use the Find Results dialog box.

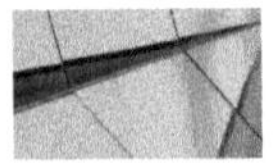

**NOTE**
*The Find feature looks only within the current page item combination.*

**Interrogating the Results in Desktop** To check whether an item has been returned among the results of a Desktop query, use the following workflow:

1. With the results of the query visible onscreen, from the menu bar select Edit | Find, or from the keyboard press CTRL-F. Either way, Discoverer opens the Find dialog box shown in Figure 4-23.
2. In the Find Text That box, use the drop-down list to select the type of search you want to do. The options are
   - Contains
   - Exactly Matches
   - Begins With
   - Ends With
   - Is NULL

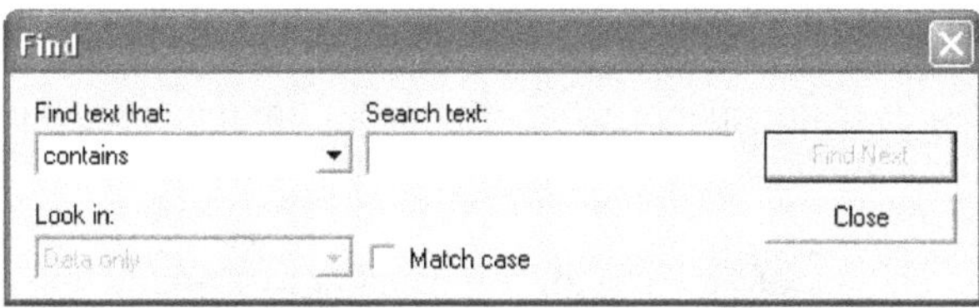


**FIGURE 4-23.** *Desktop Find dialog box*

3. In the Look Inbox, use the drop-down list to indicate whether you want Discoverer to search in the data and headings or the data only. When working with a table, you have the option of searching in the data only. It is only when you are in a crosstab that you can look at the data and headings also.
4. In the Search Text box, type the item you want Discoverer to search for.
5. Check the Match Case box if you want Discoverer to search for results that match the case of the item you entered in step 4.

**NOTE**
*If you are certain that the item can be in only the case you have specified, checking Match Case will increase the efficiency of the find and perform the search faster.*

6. Click Find Next. Discoverer will now search for the item you entered.
7. If the item is found, Discoverer displays, in the background, the first row containing that item. In this illustration, you can see that we searched for cebu and Discoverer has located the first instance of CEBU WIDGET CO in our results.
8. Repeat steps 6 and 7 as many times as required, viewing all rows that contain a match of the search criteria.
9. If the item you are looking for is not located within the results or there are no more items matching the search criteria, Discoverer will display an error message.

| | | |
|---|---|---|
| 09-FEB-2011 | ABC WIDGET CO | 62,511 |
| 11-FEB-2011 | YAMATA WIDGET LTD. | 6,328 |
| 15-FEB-2011 | ABC WIDGET CO | 1,547 |
| 24-FEB-2011 | CEBU WIDGET CO | 2,206 |
| 24-FEB-2011 | HONG KONG WIDGETS | 552 |
| 07-FEB-2011 | CEBU WIDGET CO | 37,128 |
| 15-FEB-2011 | HONG KONG WIDGETS | 14,851 |
| 25-FEB-2011 | CEBU WIDGET CO | 1,600 |
| 08-FEB-2011 | YAMATA WIDGET LTD. | 1,800 |
| 21-FEB-2011 | ABC WIDGET CO | 18,564 |
| 03-FEB-2011 | YAMATA WIDGET LTD. | 1,800 |
| 22-FEB-2011 | YAMATA WIDGET LTD. | 7,484 |
| 15-FEB-2011 | CEBU WIDGET CO | 75 |
| 01-FEB-2011 | CEBU WIDGET CO | 11,196 |
| 21-FEB-2011 | CEBU WIDGET CO | 150 |
| 22-FEB-2011 | HONG KONG WIDGETS | 22,195 |

Find
Search in: Data only
Search by: Contains
Search for: cebu
Case-sensitive
Find Previous | Find Next
Help | Close

**Interrogating the Results in Plus** To check whether an item has been returned among the results of a Plus query, use the following workflow:

1. With the results of the query visible onscreen, from the menu bar select Edit | Find, or from the keyboard press CTRL-F. Either way, Discoverer opens the Find dialog box shown in Figure 4-24.
2. Use the Search Inbox to tell Discoverer whether to search in the data only or both the data and headings. The option to search by both data and headings is available only in crosstab queries and will be grayed out in a table. When that option is available, click the down arrow to obtain a drop-down list of the available options.
3. Use the Search By box to tell Discoverer what search action to take. The available search actions are
   - Contains
   - Starts with
   - Ends with
   - Exactly matches
   - Is Null
4. In the Search For box, type the name or partial name of the item you want to find.
5. Check the Case-sensitive button if you want Discoverer to match the case.
6. Click Find Next or Find Previous. Discoverer searches the results and highlights, in the background, the next or previous item that matches the criteria you entered.

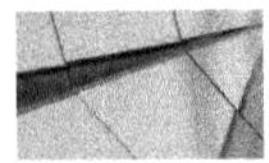

**NOTE**
*Discoverer will search from whichever cell currently contains the focus. If your active cell is near the end of the results, Discoverer may not find anything between there and the end of the data. What happens now is that Discoverer begins searching from the top of the data.*

**FIGURE 4-24.** *Plus Find dialog box*

7. In the following illustration, we asked Discoverer to search for something containing the word *small*. As you can see, Discoverer located an item called SMALL in the column called Product Size.

| SOUTH AMERICA | 32,796 | 2011-Q2 | SUPER-WIDGET | AVR-500 | MEDIUM |
|---|---|---|---|---|---|
| FAR EAST | 11,030 | 2011-Q2 | WONDER-WIDGET | QB-1000 | LARGE |
| FAR EAST | 191,828 | 2011-Q2 | SUPER-WIDGET | AVR-550 | MEDIUM |
| FAR EAST | 27,744 | 2011-Q2 | MEGA-WIDGET | CD-550 | LARGE |
| NORTH AMERICA | 143,778 | 2011-Q2 | MEGA-WIDGET | AB-2500 | SMALL |
| FAR EAST | 120,047 | 2011-Q2 | SUPER-WIDGET | AVR-500 | MEDIUM |
| EUROPE | 374,200 | 2011-Q2 | SUPER-WIDGET | AVR-900 | LARGE |
| EUROPE | 2,217 | 2011-Q2 | WONDER-WIDGET | QB-2008 | LARGE |
| FAR EAST | 2,206 | 2011-Q2 | WONDER-WIDGET | QB-2008 | LARGE |
| FAR EAST | 21,696 | 2012-Q2 | MEGA-WIDGET | CD-100 | MEDIUM |

Find
Find text that: contains
Search text: small
Look in:
Match case
Find Next
Close

8. When you have completed your search, click Close.
9. If the item you are looking for is not located within the results, Discoverer displays this error message:

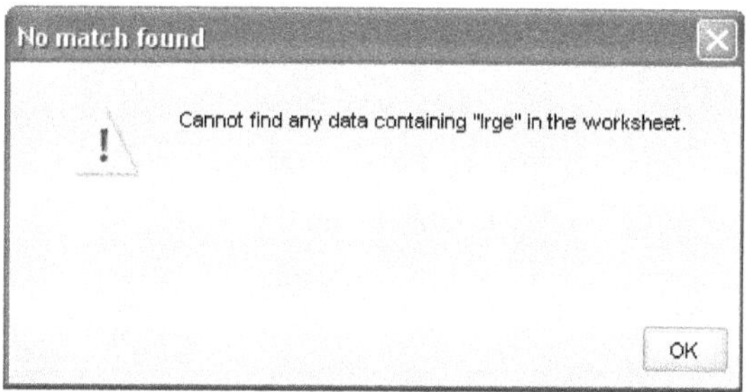

No match found
Cannot find any data containing "lrge" in the worksheet.
OK


## Saving the Query

Computers never crash, do they? One of the quirky things about computers is that they sometimes appear to have minds of their own. They know when you're busy, they know when you have an important document or query onscreen that you haven't yet saved, and they know that you're taking a risk by not saving your work! Of course, if you save your work regularly, guess what? The system never crashes—but hold off on saving and you know what will happen. Yes, the evil elf inside the system decides to teach you a lesson and crashes your computer, so you lose everything. We don't know which chip on the motherboard has been programmed to do this, but if we did, we wouldn't need to write this section because we would be rich and famous.

The truth of the matter is that computer systems do crash, network connections fail at the most awkward of times, and laptops run out of battery power. What we are trying to instill into you is the discipline to save your work regularly.

Therefore, before doing anything else, save the query, and do it now. Don't take a coffee break, don't admire the output of your first query, and don't tempt fate! There is nothing more frustrating than creating the best query anyone has ever built and then losing it before you get a chance to save it or show it to your boss. And how is it that the second attempt never produces the same result? We don't know, but with the foundation of your query built and saved, you can refine it by formatting it and applying sort orders, calculations, totals, and so on, or you can use it as the basis for creating more complex queries.

**NOTE**
*Discoverer saves your query, the items, the layout, and the formatting characteristics, along with any calculations or conditions you may have applied. It does not save the output of your query. This subject will be dealt with in Chapter 8.*

These are the six ways to make Discoverer save a new query:

- Press CTRL-S.
- Click the Save icon on the toolbar.
- Click File | Save.
- Click File | Save As.
- Click File | Close.
- Click File | Exit.

When you take the last option, Discoverer asks whether you would like to save changes to Workbook1, as shown here.

- **Yes** Displays the Save Workbook dialog box (see Figure 4-25)
- **No** Closes the workbook without saving
- **Cancel** Exits the Close dialog box and keeps the workbook open without saving it

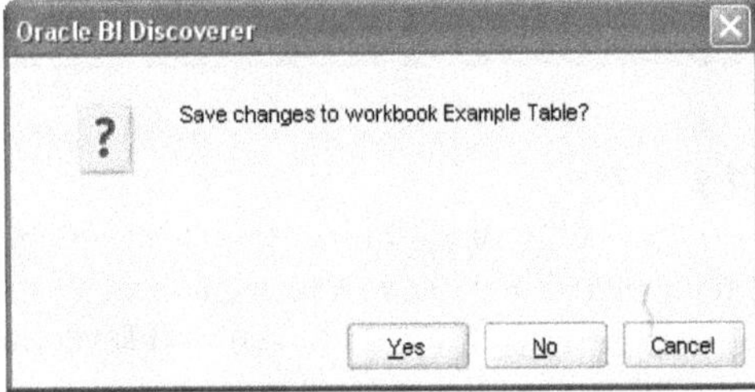


Whichever way you decide to save your query, Discoverer displays the Save Workbook dialog box shown in Figure 4-25.

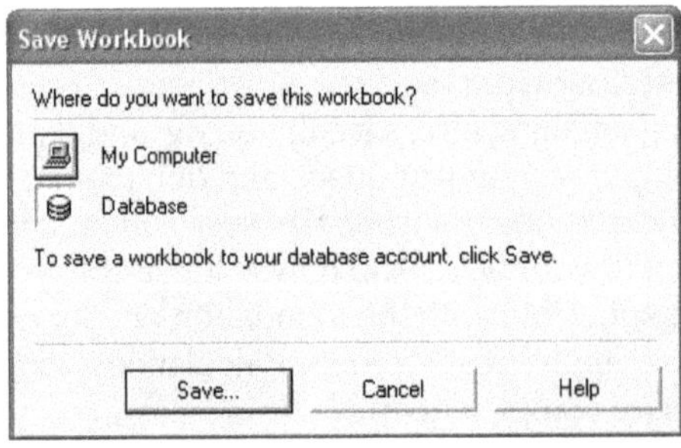


**FIGURE 4-25.** *Save Workbook dialog box*

**NOTE**

*If you are working in Plus, Discoverer cannot save to My Computer. Therefore, you will not be prompted to choose where to save the workbook. Discoverer Plus takes you straight to the Save Workbook to Database dialog box (see Figure 4-28, later in the chapter).*

Discoverer prompts you with "Where Do You Want to Save This Workbook?" and gives you the following two options:

- **My Computer** This allows you to save your workbook on your computer, to a floppy drive, or to a network account on your server. When you first create a new query, we recommend you take this option, unless you are working in Plus, in which case you have no choice and will be saving to the database server.
- **Database** This allows you to save your workbook to your database server. When you are working in Desktop, you should save only fully completed and working queries to the database, saving test and uncompleted work to the file system.

## My Computer

Choosing this option will allow you to save your worksheet to either your hard disk, your flash drive, or your network account, by default with the extension .DIS. If you are going to save your workbooks on either your hard disk or a network account, we recommend you create a special area where you can safely save them. This way, you can store all your queries in the same place, categorize them, and organize them into folders.

**NOTE**

*If you are on a terminal server, remember that the hard disk you see is not on your PC but on the terminal server. Your company will probably have defined a folder or folders on the server for your use. Make sure you always save your files into your assigned area. If you want to see your work after logging off the terminal server, copy it back to your PC hard disk or network account before you exit.*

Having opted to save your workbook, click Save.

Discoverer now opens the Save As dialog box shown in Figure 4-26. This box has four main areas.

- Save in
- Available Workbooks
- File name
- Save as type

**Save In** This area displays the current folder into which your worksheet will be saved. If you do not want to save your worksheet in this folder, you should switch to another folder or create a new folder by clicking the New Folder icon.

**Available Workbooks** This area lists all the workbooks that you currently have saved in the folder highlighted.

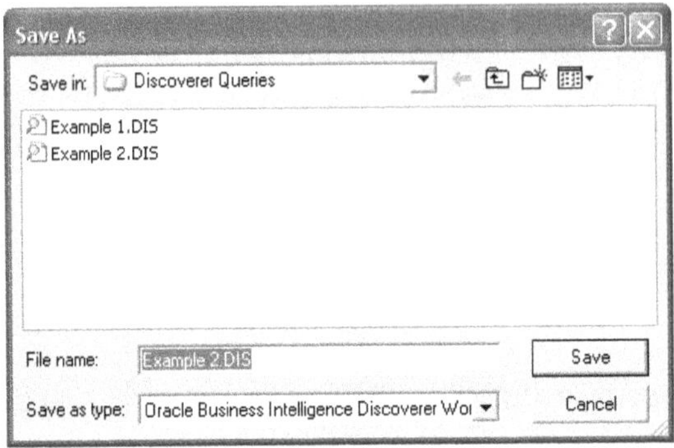


**FIGURE 4-26.** *The Save As dialog box*

**File Name** This area enables you to type in a meaningful name for your workbook. By default, Discoverer will name your query Worksheet1.DIS.

**NOTE**
*We don't recommend saving workbooks using the default name; instead, you should give your query a meaningful name (see the following section).*

**Save as Type** This area allows you to change the file format you can save your query in. By default, Discoverer will give your workbook the extension .DIS and save it as an Oracle Discoverer workbook. If you do not want to save your query using this extension, you can click the down arrow and select All Files (*.*). You can now save your query using any extension of your choosing. However, the file type is still an Oracle Discoverer workbook and can only be used as such.

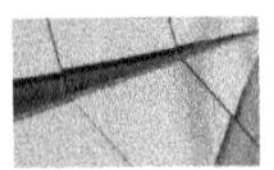

**NOTE**
*We don't recommend saving workbooks using any extension other than the default. If you do decide to save your workbooks using different extensions, you will make it more difficult for yourself to later locate and maintain your workbooks.*

Having given your query a name and chosen where to save it, click Save. Your query is now safe, and if your system decides to crash, it will make no difference.

## Database

Choosing this option will save your workbook to your Discoverer account on the database server. Workbooks typically do not take up a lot of space—on average less than 100KB for a moderately complex workbook. The other advantage of saving it to the database is that it is secure, is available from anywhere you can access the database, and gets backed up along with the rest of the data in your database.

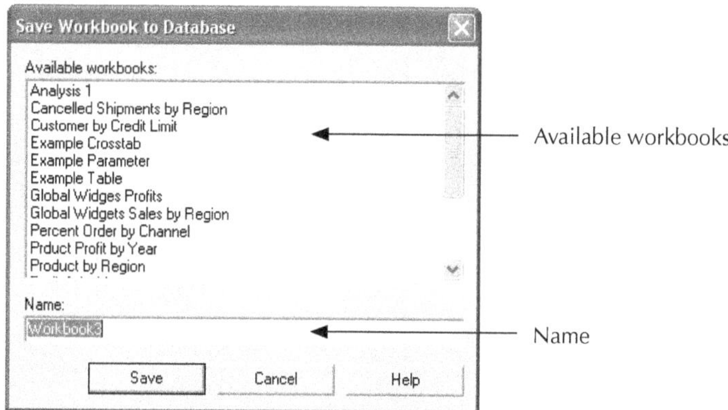


**FIGURE 4-27.** *The Desktop Save Workbook to Database dialog box*

Having opted to save your workbook to the database, click Save. Discoverer now opens the Save Workbook to Database dialog box, as shown in Figure 4-27.

**Saving to the Database from Within Desktop** Once you have clicked Save to save to the database from within Desktop, Discoverer displays the dialog box shown in Figure 4-27. This box has five areas.

- Available workbooks
- Name in Desktop, New Name in Plus
- Save
- Cancel
- Help

**Available Workbooks** This area lists all of the workbooks you currently have saved under your account in the database.

**Name (New Name in Plus)** This area enables you to type in a meaningful name for your workbook.

**Save** Clicking Save saves the workbook. If you choose to save using the same name as an existing workbook, Discoverer warns you that a workbook already exists by that name and asks whether you would like to overwrite it, as shown here.

You have the following three options:

- **Yes** This overwrites the file.
- **No** This exits the Warning dialog box and allows you to type in a new name for the workbook.
- **Cancel** This also exits the Warning dialog box and allows you to type in a new name for the workbook.

**Cancel** Clicking this cancels the save and returns you to your results.

**Help** Clicking this calls up the Discoverer Help screen.

**NOTE**
*In Discoverer Desktop, if you do not see the option to save to the database, this is because your Discoverer manager has disabled this option. You may need to speak with them if you think you should be able to do this.*

**Saving to the Database from Within Plus** Once you have clicked Save to save to the database from within Plus, Discoverer displays the dialog box shown in Figure 4-28. This box has nine areas.

- View
- View Style
- Name Contains
- Clear
- Workbooks
- New Name
- Help
- Save
- Cancel

**View** Clicking this allows you to select all workbooks that you have access to or just the workbooks you own.

**View As** This button, alongside the words *Name Contains*, allows you to choose a style for displaying the workbooks that you have access to. When you click it, you are offered the following three choices:

- **Workbook Tree** This displays in alphabetical order.
- **User Tree** This displays in alphabetical order of owner and then in alphabetical order of the workbooks.
- **Table** This option also displays in alphabetical order, and except for the absence of the lines to the left of the workbook names, it is the same as Workbook Tree.

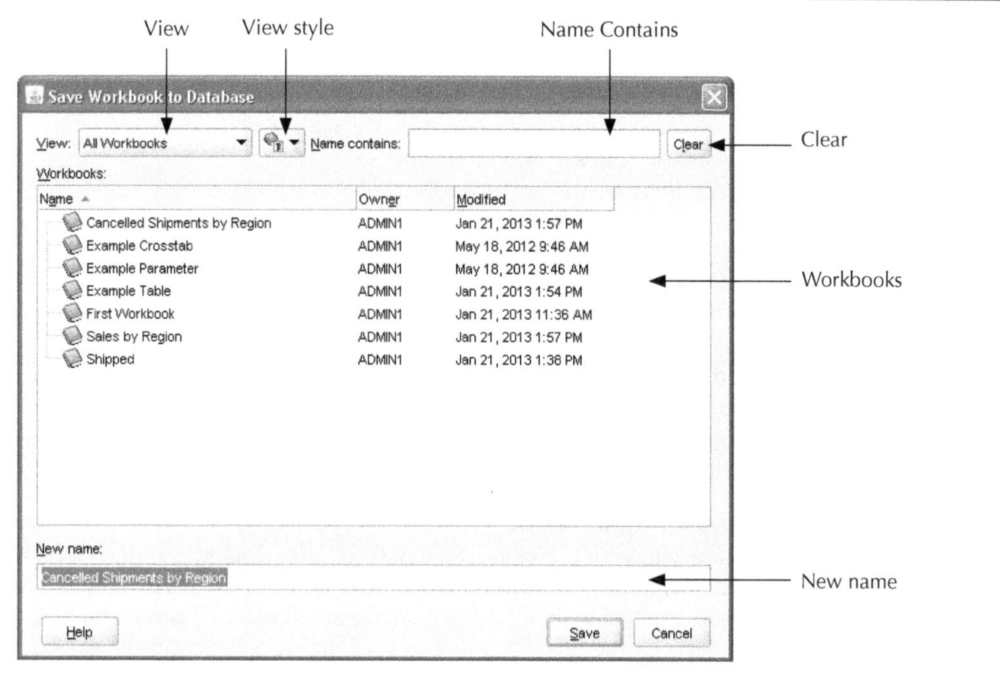


**FIGURE 4-28.** *The Plus Save Workbook to Database dialog box*

**Name Contains** If you have a lot of workbooks that you have access to, use this box to filter the workbook list. As you begin typing characters into this box, Discoverer automatically filters by those characters. We like this feature and would like to see it used in other Discoverer filter boxes.

**Clear** If you have already begun typing something into the Name Contains box, clicking this button instantly clears the box and stops filtering the workbook list.

**Workbooks** This box displays the workbooks you have access to after applying the style and filters. The workbooks are displayed by Name, Owner, and Date Modified. You can sort on each of these by clicking the appropriate heading. Clicking a heading once will sort the list in ascending order, while clicking the same heading a second time will sort the list in descending order.

**New Name** As you click an existing workbook in the Workbooks box, the name of the workbook will be displayed here. You can either save over and replace an existing workbook that you own or type in your own name for the new workbook.

**Help** Click this button to get context-sensitive help about saving workbooks.

**Save** Click this button to save the workbook. If there is already a workbook saved by the name you are trying to use, you will be warned and asked whether you want to overwrite the existing workbook. Your options are Yes, No, and Cancel. Clicking No or Cancel returns you to the dialog box without saving the workbook.

**Cancel** Click this button if you want to cancel saving the workbook.

**NOTE**

*If your Discoverer manager has disabled the option to save to the database, you are up the river without a paddle! Obviously, if you cannot save to My Computer and you are barred from saving to the database, you have nowhere to save your query. Run, do not walk, to your Discoverer manager and ask them to enable saving to the database. But seriously, there may be good reason why some users are barred from saving queries to the database. Perhaps they are novices to Discoverer, or perhaps your company restricts creation of queries to staff working in-house. If this applies to your company, you will only be able to run queries, not create them.*

If you are working in Discoverer Plus and have created a new query but your Discoverer manager has barred you from saving to the database, the accompanying note has explained that you will not be able to save the query at all. Any attempt to leave the query will display a warning that you have insufficient privileges.

### Giving the Query a Meaningful Name

As with all files that you save to your computer, especially to a networked computer, you should get into the good habit of giving your Discoverer workbooks and worksheets meaningful names. There can be nothing more frustrating than having a database full of workbooks with meaningless names when you are looking for the one that will give your manager your end-of-year results.

Avoid giving your queries names like "Bob's first query,""Bob's test query," or "My query." This will only end up frustrating you and your colleagues. Describe what the query is referencing, such as "Q2 sales by region 2010" or "Gross Margin by Product Feb 2010." These names tell you exactly what the query is about and will not leave you guessing. They will also keep you from saving queries that you don't use (because the name does not tell you what it is for, and you are afraid to delete it) and will prevent you and your colleagues from reinventing the wheel. The authors have seen the same queries duplicated many times simply because they were not given meaningful names and were therefore not reused but re-created.

The age of the eight-character DOS naming convention is long gone. Let it die and give your files meaningful names!

## Summary

In this chapter, you learned a simple workflow for creating new queries. We explained that in Discoverer Desktop, there are six steps to the Workbook Wizard, while in Discoverer Plus, there are five steps with more functionality included in each step.

By following the first four steps of the Workbook Wizard, you learned to create a working query and to avoid "the query from the Twilight Zone." Feels good, doesn't it? You also learned to view the results and save your work. As a novice in Discoverer, this is a good approach and should be used until you become more experienced in creating queries. In fact, even seasoned Discoverer users adopt this approach, and they rarely use the remaining steps of the wizard before viewing the initial output.

However, it would be remiss of us to not explain the remaining steps of the Workbook Wizard. These will be covered in the next chapter.

# CHAPTER 5

# The Workbook Wizard: The Optional Steps

In Chapter 4, you saw the essential steps in using the Workbook Wizard to create a working query. In this chapter, you will explore the remaining steps of the Workbook Wizard: sorting, calculations, percentages, totals, and parameters. We say that these steps are optional because they can be added after you have a functional query.

Because the steps of the Workbook Wizard covered in this chapter are optional, it is necessary to learn how to reopen the Workbook Wizard to add them to your query. In the second part of this chapter, you will learn how to create a text area to add context, tips, hints, notes, or userhelp to your worksheets. You will also learn to open the Edit Sheet dialog box in Desktop and the Edit Worksheet dialog box in Plus to edit an existing query. Even though they are named differently, they are essentially the same box. This form contains all the steps of the Workbook Wizard in a multitabbed configuration, thus making the functionality of Discoverer easy to access. We will also introduce you to the Available Items pane and the Selected Items pane in Plus, features that make Discoverer even easier to use.

# The Text Area in Plus

Before moving into the optional steps of the Workbook Wizard, we will introduce you to a feature of Plus called the *text area*. We like this feature very much because it can be a great help to end users. When you create a workbook to be used by others, this text area will help your users understand how to use the worksheets. You can add helpful hints about the conditions, calculations, parameters, and so on, in use in the worksheet. This illustration shows the text area in use in a query.

This report shows a ranking of revenue against Product Size and Product Name.
There are no parameters in this report.

The use and formatting of the text area will be described in detail in Chapter 14.

# The Optional Steps of the Workbook Wizard

The following steps occur in both the Plus and Desktop Workbook Wizards. Although they are not accessed the same way, they are functionally the same.

- Creating a sort order
- Creating user-defined calculations
- Creating user-defined percentages
- Creating user-defined totals
- Creating user-defined parameters

**NOTE**
*Throughout the final steps of the Workbook Wizard, you can run your query at any time by clicking Finish. You can even skip a step if you want, simply by clicking Next. As long as you stay in the Workbook Wizard, you can return to a previous step by clicking Back.*

# Workbook Wizard Step 5: Creating a Sort Order (Tables Only)

Let's assume you have not run and saved your query. For a table query, the next step after creating user-defined conditions is creating a sort order. For crosstab queries, this step is omitted, and you should continue with the setting of calculations. While it is possible to add sort criteria to crosstab queries, the Workbook Wizard does not allow you to do this. If you are using a crosstab, you need to complete your query, display the results onscreen, and then apply or refine your sort.

This section therefore applies only to table queries. From here until the end of this section on sorting, we will assume that you are working with a table query. After applying conditions, in Desktop click Next. In Plus you need to navigate to step 4 of the wizard.

This brings up the sort screen of the Workbook Wizard. Figure 5-1 shows the Desktop screen, while Figure 5-2 shows the Plus screen. These screens consist of the following features:

- **Sorting box** This box will be empty until you add a sort order. As you apply sorts to your items, Discoverer will display them in here in the order in which you defined the sort.
- **Add** Click this to add an item to sort.
- **Delete** Click this to delete a sort.
- **Move Up** Click this to promote a sort.

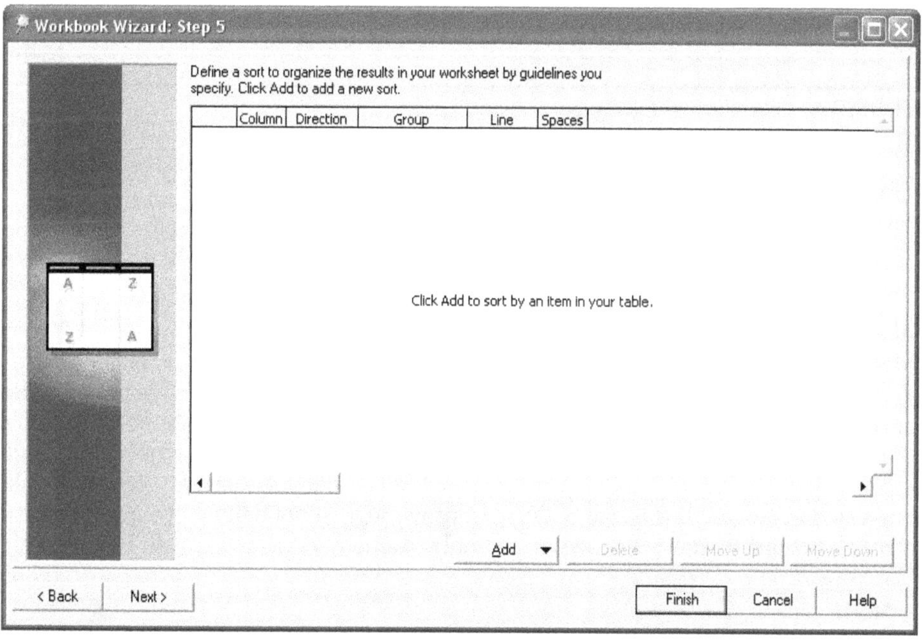


**FIGURE 5-1.** *The Desktop sort screen*

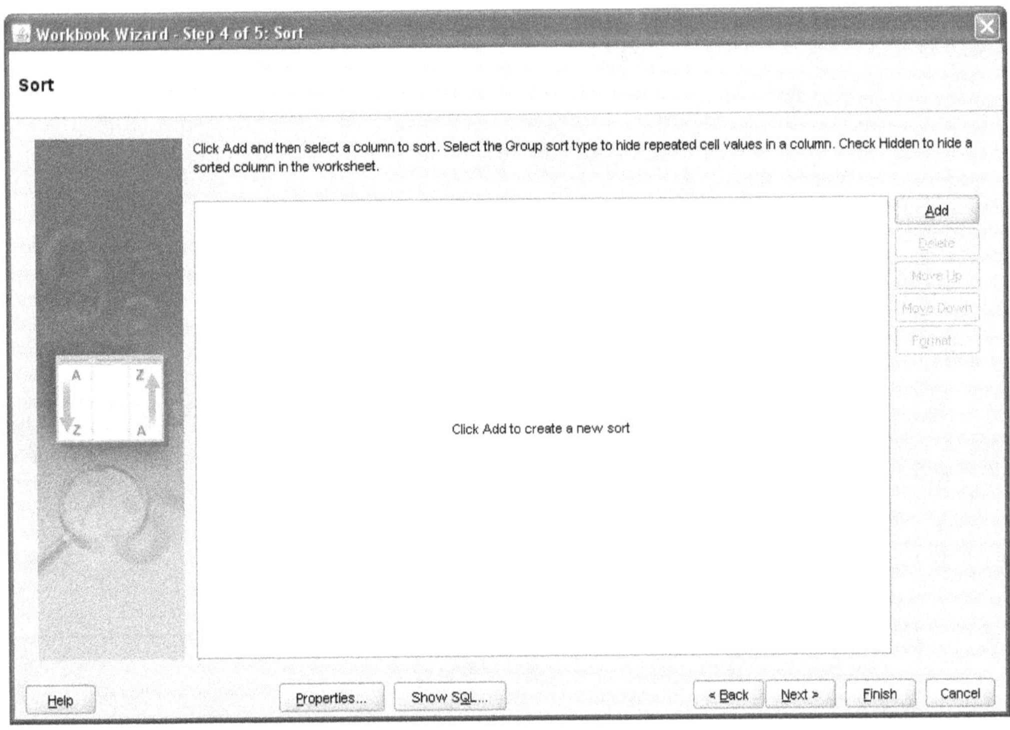


**FIGURE 5-2.** *The Plus sort screen*

- **Move Down** Click this to demote a sort.
- **Format (Plus Only)** Click this to apply formats to your data and to control how page breaks are controlled. As you can see in Figure 5-2, this button is available only in Plus.

## Sorting: What Is It?

Sorting arranges text in alphabetical order or numbers in numerical order in either Low to High (ascending, a–z, 1–10) or High to Low (descending, z–a, 10–1) order. This creates an orderly means of viewing data, such as employees alphabetically or customer sales from highest to lowest. Anyone familiar with Excel has used sorting before and will probably be looking for a Sort button. Discoverer has these also but not in the Workbook Wizard. In the wizard, you need to take a more complicated approach. This is one of the reasons we suggest not defining your sort orders in the Workbook Wizard. Figure 5-3 shows an example of a numeric sort in Low to High order.

**NOTE**

*There is one important problem with sorting that you must watch out for. When sorting in a crosstab, you cannot sort on calculated items. You can sort only on items that came directly from the data source. It is necessary to duplicate the crosstab as a table, where you can sort on calculated items. This is a known bug.*

| Customer | Credit Limit SUM | Address | State |
|---|---|---|---|
| OXFORD WIDGETS | .00 | 27 OXFORD STREET | LONDON |
| MUM'S WIDGET CO. | .00 | 750 THE CRESCENT | MERSEYSIDE |
| WIDGETS SA | .00 | 1550, CHEMIN DU LAC | QUEBEC |
| WIDGETS DE MEXIC | 10000.00 | 2716 CINCO DE MAYO | NULL |
| WIDGETS OESTE | 15000.00 | CASILLA 114 | NULL |
| WILD WEST WIDGET | 25000.00 | 1428 NORTHWOOD ROAD | MISSOURI |
| WALKING HORSE W | 45000.00 | 2000 WILLOW | TENNESSEE |
| GATOR WIDGETS | 45000.00 | 6732 WEST PALMETTO | FLORIDA |
| MOUNTAIN WIDGET | 50000.00 | 9594 COLFAX | COLORADO |
| LOTS OF WIDGETS | 50000.00 | 7870 AMSTERDAM | NEW YORK |
| WIDGETS R US | 50000.00 | 1711 LOMBARD | CALIFORNIA |
| TRICOLOR WIDGETS | 50000.00 | RUE DE MADELINE, 52 | CENTRALE |
| WIDGET AIR | 50000.00 | SFO INTERNATIONAL | CALIFORNIA |
| WE'VE GOT WIDGET | 50000.00 | 90 S. BROAD ST | PENN |
| LONDON WIDGETS | 50000.00 | 5 MIDDLE AVENUE | LONDON |
| THING'S | 50000.00 | 112 AVENIDA VERDE | NULL |
| WONDER WIDGETS | 50000.00 | 1594 BUSH ST | CALIFORNIA |
| WIDGET O THE MER | 50000.00 | 1532 DAVIS LN | MERSEYSIDE |
| WIDGET SUPPLY C | 50000.00 | 5002 RIVINGTON | NEW YORK |
| WIDGETS BY THE B | 50000.00 | 21100 MARKET ST | CALIFORNIA |
| WARSAW WIDGETS | 75000.00 | PRUSA 15 | NULL |
| HONG KONG WIDGE | 80000.00 | 98 HIGH STREET | VICTORIA |
| PALMELA WIDGETS | 80000.00 | PARQUE DE PALMELA | NULL |
| YAMATA WIDGET L | 80000.00 | 10-3 NAGATA | NULL |

**FIGURE 5-3.** *Simple Low to High sort (credit limit sorted, unsorted customer name)*

Discoverer also allows for group sorting. If you are not familiar with group sorting, think of a group sort as a more specialized form of Low to High or High to Low sort. When you select this type of sort, Discoverer leaves blank all repeating items, thus making your reports much easier to read and more aesthetically pleasing.

Figure 5-4 shows the same data used in Figure 5-3, sorted as a group sort.

## Creating a New Sort

When creating a new sort, you should use the following workflow:

1. Open the Edit Sheet/Worksheet dialog box.
2. Select the Sort tab.
3. Click Add.

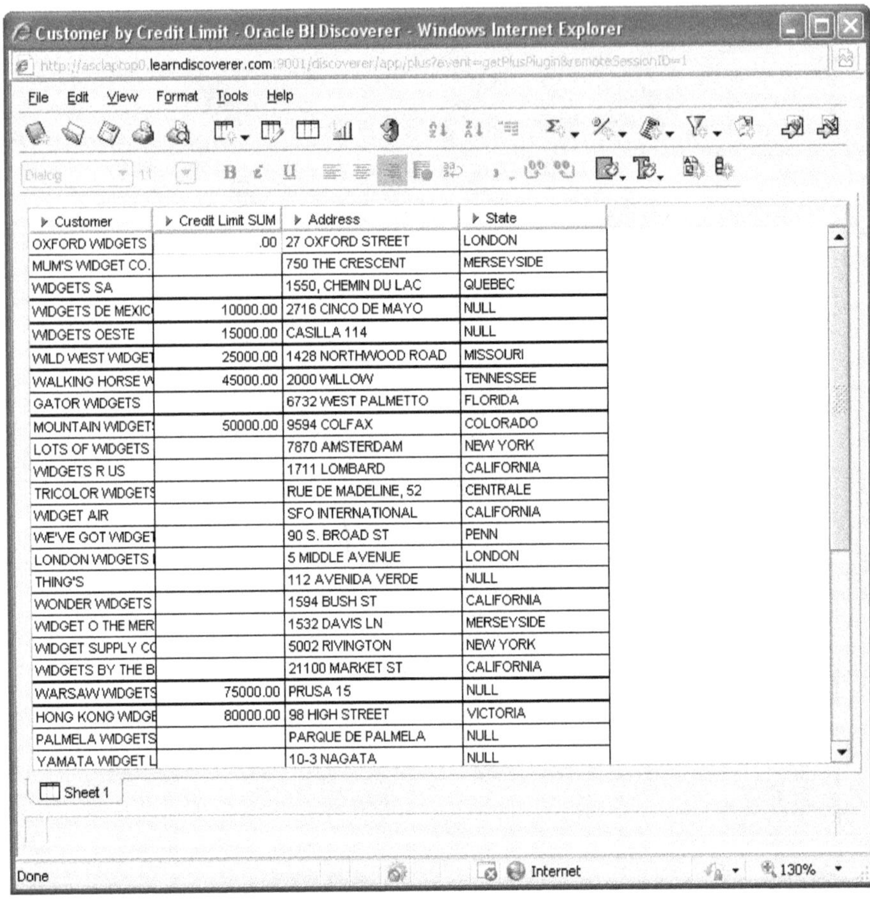


| Customer | Credit Limit SUM | Address | State |
|---|---|---|---|
| OXFORD WIDGETS | .00 | 27 OXFORD STREET | LONDON |
| MUM'S WIDGET CO. | | 750 THE CRESCENT | MERSEYSIDE |
| WIDGETS SA | | 1550, CHEMIN DU LAC | QUEBEC |
| WIDGETS DE MEXIC | 10000.00 | 2716 CINCO DE MAYO | NULL |
| WIDGETS OESTE | 15000.00 | CASILLA 114 | NULL |
| WILD WEST WIDGET | 25000.00 | 1428 NORTHWOOD ROAD | MISSOURI |
| WALKING HORSE W | 45000.00 | 2000 WILLOW | TENNESSEE |
| GATOR WIDGETS | | 6732 WEST PALMETTO | FLORIDA |
| MOUNTAIN WIDGET | 50000.00 | 9594 COLFAX | COLORADO |
| LOTS OF WIDGETS | | 7870 AMSTERDAM | NEW YORK |
| WIDGETS R US | | 1711 LOMBARD | CALIFORNIA |
| TRICOLOR WIDGETS | | RUE DE MADELINE, 52 | CENTRALE |
| WIDGET AIR | | SFO INTERNATIONAL | CALIFORNIA |
| WE'VE GOT WIDGET | | 90 S. BROAD ST | PENN |
| LONDON WIDGETS | | 5 MIDDLE AVENUE | LONDON |
| THING'S | | 112 AVENIDA VERDE | NULL |
| WONDER WIDGETS | | 1594 BUSH ST | CALIFORNIA |
| WIDGET O THE MER | | 1532 DAVIS LN | MERSEYSIDE |
| WIDGET SUPPLY C | | 5002 RIVINGTON | NEW YORK |
| WIDGETS BY THE B | | 21100 MARKET ST | CALIFORNIA |
| WARSAW WIDGETS | 75000.00 | PRUSA 15 | NULL |
| HONG KONG WIDGE | 80000.00 | 98 HIGH STREET | VICTORIA |
| PALMELA WIDGETS | | PARQUE DE PALMELA | NULL |
| YAMATA WIDGET L | | 10-3 NAGATA | NULL |

**FIGURE 5-4.** *Simple Low to High group sort (credit limit as a group sort, customer name unsorted)*

4. Select the item you want to sort on. In Plus, Discoverer automatically selects the first named column, in alphabetical order, and creates a normal, Low to High sort. In Desktop, you will be offered a drop-down of all available items.
5. Define the sort parameters.
6. Click OK to finish.

When you first enter step 5 of the wizard, the main box in the center of the screen will be empty (see Figures 5-1 and 5-2). You need to think about what item or items you want to apply a sort on. Unfortunately, unlike conditions, there are no administrator-created sorts, so it is all up to you.

Because you can create multiple sorts in your query, you should try to create them in a logical sequence, defining the primary sort first. If you cannot define the logical sequence at this time, do not worry, because you can change the sequence later. The important thing is to get the items sorted. There is no limit on the number of sorts you can define, other than the number of items in your query, but we recommend you restrict your choices to a maximum of two or three within the Workbook Wizard. Creating complex sort sequences greater than this is very difficult to visualize, and we strongly advise you to create these later.

**NOTE**
*Adding complex sorts on numerous columns, while possible and tempting to do, should be done with caution. Every sort you ask Discoverer to do will cause your query to take longer and consume more memory. We recommend you apply sorts only when necessary, using the minimum number of sort sequences to produce the desired result.*

When you have decided what column(s) needs to be sorted, click Add.

### Sorting in Desktop

As mentioned earlier, after you click Add, Desktop displays a drop-down list of all the items in your query.

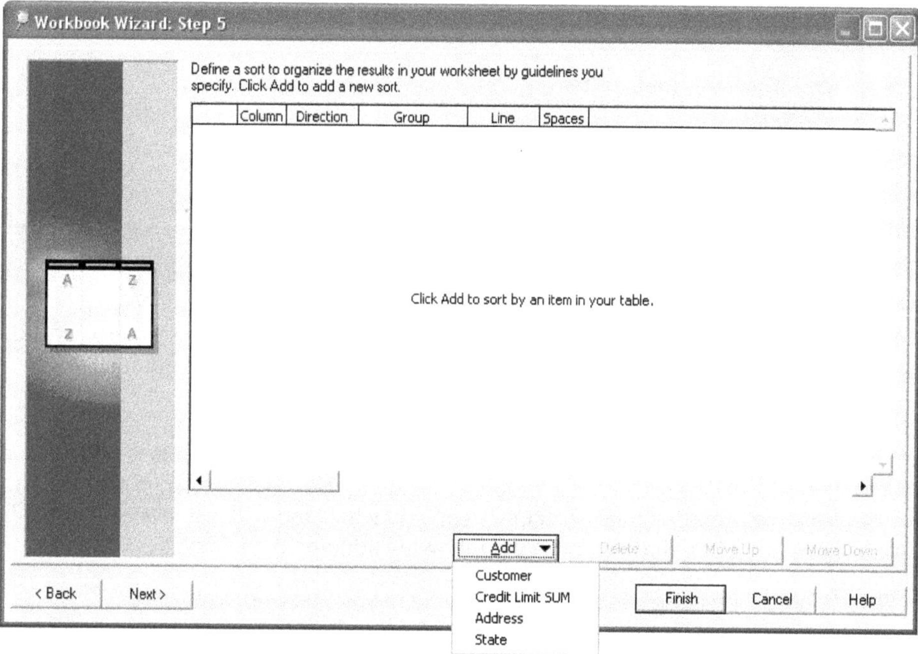


From the list, pick the item you have decided to use for the primary sort item. Discoverer will create your first sort and add its definition to the box. You now have the following additional choices:

- **Column** This displays the name of the item you chose for your sort.
- **Direction** Click this to set the sort order (defaults Low To High) for the item. The available options are Low To High and High To Low.

- **Group** Click this for a drop-down list of group sort options. The available options are None, Group Sort, Page Break, and Hidden.
- **Line** Click this if you want to change the width of the line between group-sorted items.
- **Spaces** Click this if you want to add extra line spacing between group-sorted items.

The Desktop sort criteria are shown in the following illustration:

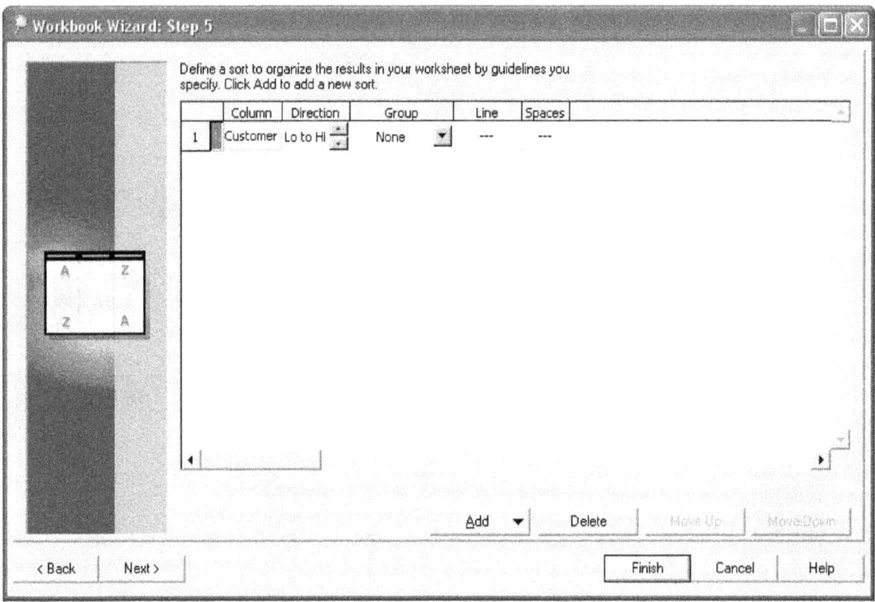


At this point, you will notice that the Delete button is activated. If you have made a mistake and selected the wrong item for your sort, click Delete, and it will be removed.

Assuming you have chosen the correct item, Discoverer defaults the sort into ascending order; it is not a group sort (as indicated by the word *None* under the Group heading).

## Sorting in Plus

After you click Add, Plus inserts the first available item, in alphabetical order, into the sorted items box automatically. If this is not the item that you want to use, click the down arrow alongside the item and from the drop-down list select the item you want. You will also notice that the Delete button is now active and that you have the following additional choices:

- **Column** This displays the name of the item you chose for your sort.
- **Direction** Click this to set the sort order for the item. The available options are Low To High and High To Low.
- **Sort Type** Click this for a drop-down list of the two available sort types, Normal and Group Sort. Discoverer defaults to Normal.
- **Hidden** Check this check box if you want the sorted column to be hidden.

The Plus sort criteria are shown in the following illustration.

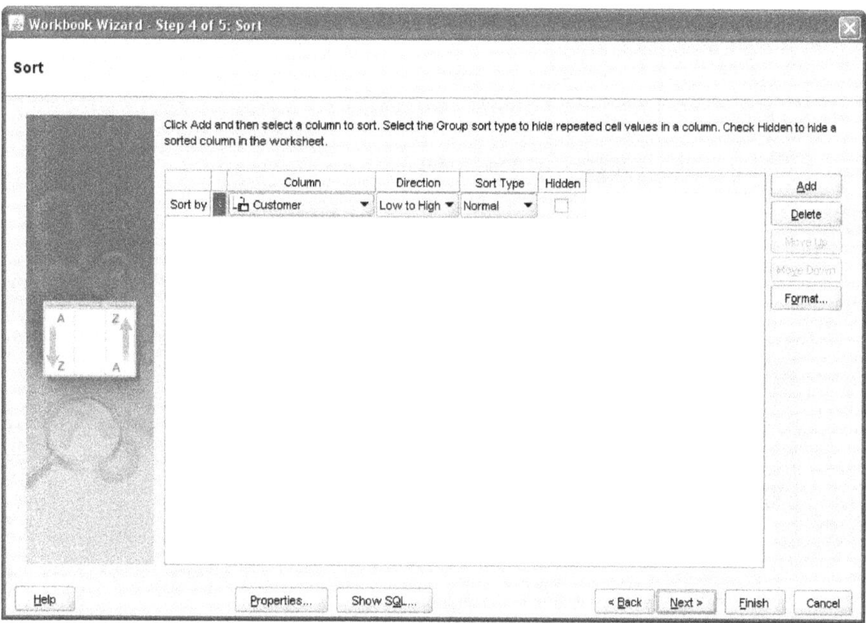


We showed you how to add lines, blank spaces, and page breaks in group sorts in Desktop. You can also add these items in Plus using the Format Data dialog box, which is a multitabbed form that is used for formatting the data in a worksheet. You will learn about this dialog box in detail in Chapter 6. However, we think this is the right place to show you the Breaks tab of this dialog box.

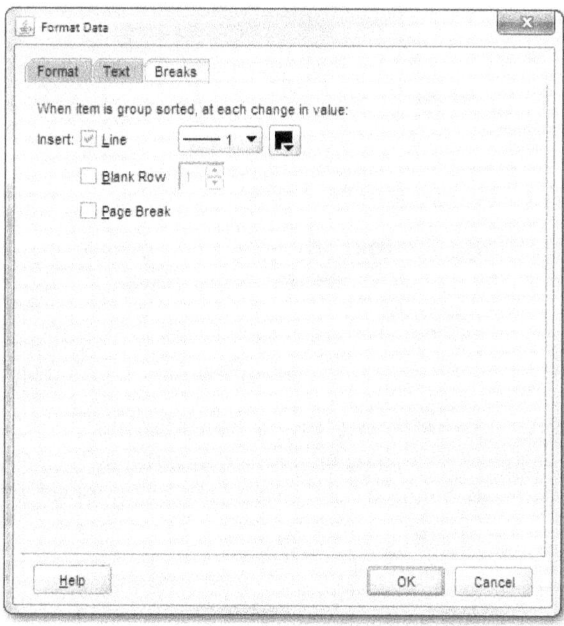

## Quick Sorting

Sometimes sorting is a simple matter of adding one group sort and perhaps one additional sort ascending. These can be accomplished using drop-down menus, right-click menus, or toolbar buttons. Also, sorts that you create using any method can be deleted using a drop-down list that appears with a right-click.

### Adding a Quick Sort from a Drop-Down List

To add a quick sort, use the following workflow:

1. Right-click in the column upon which you want to base your sort.
2. From the drop-down, select Group Sort, Sort Low To High, or Sort High To Low.

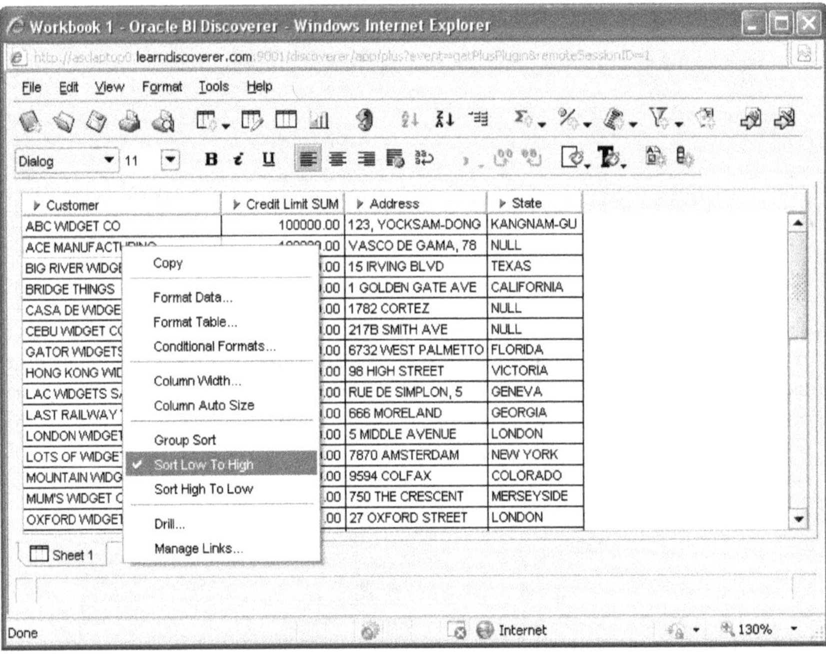


### Adding a Quick Sort from the Toolbar

To add a quick sort from the toolbar, use the following workflow:

1. Click in the column upon which you want to base your sort.
2. On the toolbar click the button for Group Sort, Sort Low to High, or Sort High to Low.

### Quickly Removing a Normal Sort Using a Drop-Down

A normal sort, no matter how it was created, can be deleted by right-clicking and using a drop-down list or by using the toolbar. To remove a normal sort using a drop-down, use the following workflow:

1. Right-click in the column with the sort you want to remove.
2. From the drop-down select Sort Low to High or Sort High to Low. This will remove the check mark and delete the sort.

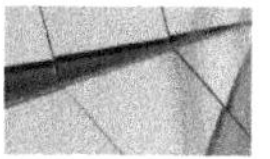

**NOTE**
*Clicking the Group Sort button on a previously unsorted item will sort it ascending and also place a group sort.*

### Quickly Removing a Group Sort Using a Drop-Down

A group sort, no matter how it was created, can be deleted by right-clicking and using a drop-down list. To remove a group sort using a drop-down, use the following workflow:

1. Right-click in the column with the group sort you want to remove.
2. From the drop-down list select Group Sort. This will remove the group sort and change it to a Low to High or High to Low sort, depending on how you had the original group sort defined.
3. Right-click again and select Sort Low to High or High to Low. The sort has now been completely deleted.

### Quickly Removing a Normal Sort Using the Toolbar

To remove a normal sort from the toolbar, use the following workflow:

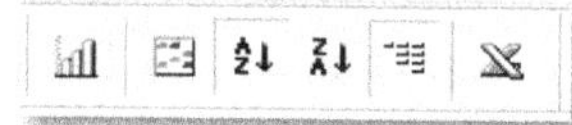

1. Click in the column with the sort you want to remove.
2. From the toolbar deselect Sort Low to High or Sort High to Low. This will change the button from indented to normal and delete the sort.

### Quickly Removing a Group Sort Using the Toolbar (Desktop Only)

To remove a group sort in Desktop from the toolbar, use the following workflow:

1. Right-click in the column with the group sort you want to remove.
2. From the toolbar click the Group Sort button. This will change it from indented to normal and will remove the group sort and change it to a Low to High or High to Low sort, depending on how you had the original group sort defined.
3. From the toolbar click Sort Low to High or Sort High to Low. This will change it from indented to normal, and the sort will be completely deleted.

## Refining a Sort

Having created your first sort, you may find that it needs refining. Perhaps you want to have the data sorted High to Low or to change the sort type in order to apply a group sort.

### Refining a Sort in Desktop

These are the methods for changing the sort order or sort type in Desktop:

- To toggle between a Low to High sort and a High to Low sort, click the up or down arrow beneath the heading Direction. You will see the direction indicator change accordingly.
- To change the sort type, click the down arrow beneath the Group heading, and from the drop-down list select Group Sort, Page Break, or Hidden.

### Refining a Sort in Plus

These are the methods for changing the sort order or sort type in Plus:

- To switch between a Low to High sort and a High to Low sort, click the down arrow alongside the current setting and select the new option from the drop-down list.
- To change the sort type, click the down arrow beneath the Sort Type heading and from the drop-down list select Group Sort.

## Building a Group Sort

We will now explain in detail how you can add and refine your own group sort. Because the method used is sufficiently different between Desktop and Plus, we will describe each separately.

### Building a Group Sort in Desktop

To build a group sort in Desktop, follow this workflow:

1. Determine what type of group sort to employ.
2. Define the line width.
3. Define the line spacing.

When building a group sort in Desktop, you first need to decide what type of sort to use. Click the down arrow beneath the Group heading. Discoverer produces a drop-down list of the available group sort types.

- **None** Select this option if you do not want to use a group sort.
- **Group Sort** Select this option to convert your existing sort into a group sort. This automatically opens the Line and Spaces options, both of which are explained under the headings that follow.
- **Page Break** Select this option if you want Discoverer to insert a page break into the final output every time the group sort encounters a new value. In the final display onscreen, Discoverer indicates that there is a page break by inserting a broken line between the groups of sorted items. Whenever you print a report containing a page break, Discoverer will begin each group on a new page.
- **Hidden** Select this option if you do not want to display any of the data values for that item onscreen. You should apply this type of sort with great care, because it may not be obvious to someone looking at your report that the query is applying a sort on a hidden item. You can also add a comment in the text area noting the sort order being applied.

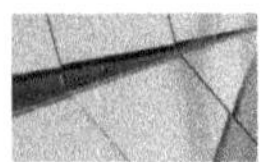

**NOTE**
*The Hidden option can be very powerful, and the following are good examples of its usage. First, suppose HR wants to produce a report, by department, of the employees based on their salaries but does not want to print the actual salary amounts. Applying a sort on the salary figures and then hiding those items from the report will print the employees in order of salary. Second, suppose you want a report showing your best-performing departments in terms of sales, without printing the actual sales figures. You would simply create a sort on the sales figures and hide them.*

Having selected the type of group sort to use, you now have two final options that you can set.

**Line Width** By default, Discoverer sets this to 1. If you want to change the width of the line separator, click the down arrow alongside the number 1 under the Line heading. This displays the following drop-down list:

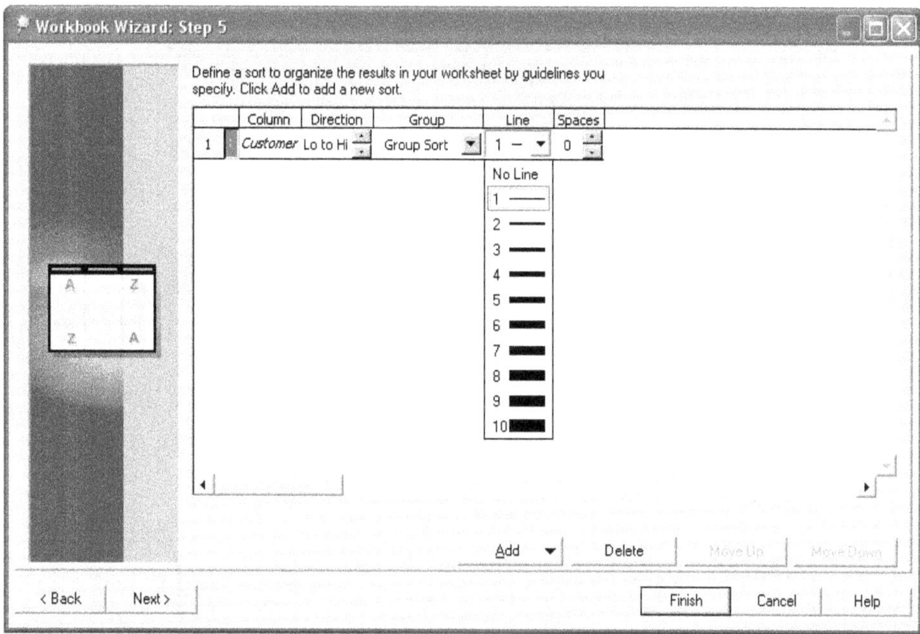


As you can see, you can choose to use no lines or you can choose a line width of between 1 and 10.

**Line Spacing** By default, Discoverer sets this to 0. If you want to change the spacing between the groups of sorted items, click the down arrow alongside the 0 under the Space heading.

Use the up and down arrows to set the number of spaces you want to appear between each group of sorted items.

## Building a Group Sort in Plus

To build a group sort in Plus, use this workflow:

1. Define the sort type.
2. Determine whether the sort item should be hidden.
3. Apply the remaining sort options.

To change the sort type, click the down arrow beneath the Sort Type heading. Discoverer produces a drop-down list of the available sort types. These are

- **Normal** Select this option if you do not want to use a group sort.
- **Group Sort** Select this option to convert your existing sort into a group sort.

If you do not want to display any of the data values for the item that is being used for the sort, you can hide it from the final display. As with Desktop, you should apply this option with great care, because it may not be obvious to someone looking at your report that the query is applying a sort on a hidden item. Having determined that you want to hide the item, check the Hidden box.

You can now set additional options to further refine the group sort. These options are available from the Breaks tab of the Format Data dialog box, as shown in the following illustration:

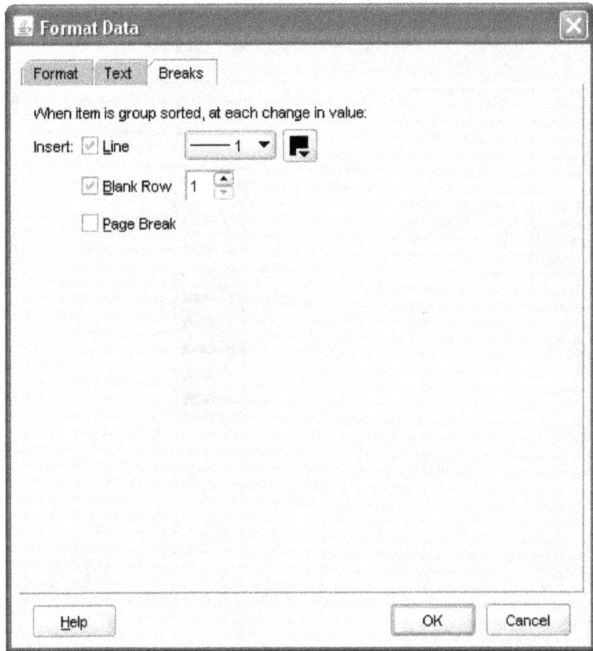


To open the Format Data dialog box, click the Format button. It is located to the right of the sort you just created. The options on the Breaks tab are available only when you are formatting a group-sorted item. All of these options are grayed out for items that are not part of a group sort. The options that you can set are

- **Line** Check this box if you want to insert a solid line between the groups of sorted items. By default this box is checked.
- **Line Width** Until Line is checked, this box is grayed out. By default, the line width is set to 1. Use the drop-down list to change the width to anything from 1 to 10.
- **Line Color** Until Line is checked, this box is grayed out. By default, the line color is set to black. Click the button to pop up a palette of available colors. If you do not see the color you want to use, on the palette click Edit. This opens the Color Palette Editor. In Plus, you can even create your own custom colors.
- **Blank Row** Check this box if you want to insert blank rows between the groups of sorted items. By default, this box is unchecked.
- **Number of Blank Rows** Until Blank Row is checked, this box is grayed out. By default, the number of blank rows is set to 1. Use the up and down arrows to increase or decrease the number of blank rows that you want Discoverer to insert.

- **Page Break** Check this box if you want Discoverer to insert a page break into the final output between the groups of sorted items. By default, this box is unchecked. When it is selected, in the final display onscreen, Discoverer indicates that there is a page break by inserting a broken line between the groups of sorted items. Whenever you print a report containing a page break, Discoverer will begin each group of sorted items on a new page.

## Adding Another Sort

Having created one sort, you may decide to add a second, third, and so on. This will cause items to sort within other items.

For example, in our original sort shown in Figure 5-4, we have a group sort by credit limit. However, the customers are not sorted. It would be a better report to have the customers also sorted alphabetically. We therefore need to add a second sort to our query. To do this, click Add. You will once again go through the steps outlined earlier in this chapter in the section "Creating a New Sort."

**NOTE**
*Any item that has already been selected for sorting will not appear in the drop-down list again. You can apply only one sort to an item. When there are no more items available for sorting, the Add button is deactivated.*

Figure 5-5 shows a Discoverer Plus example of a multiple-sort sequence. We have taken the previously group-sorted list (see Figure 5-4) and applied a second sort on the Customer column.

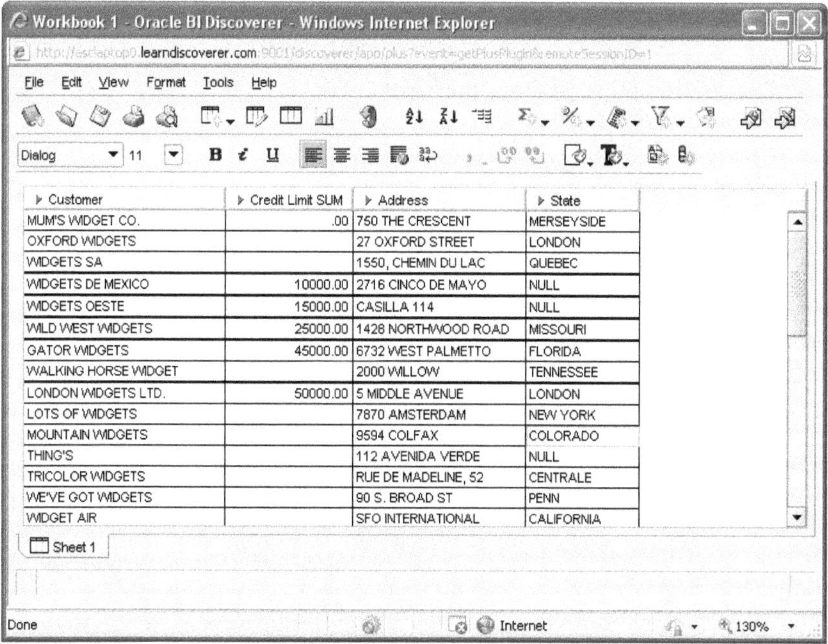



| Customer | Credit Limit SUM | Address | State |
|---|---|---|---|
| MUM'S WIDGET CO. | .00 | 750 THE CRESCENT | MERSEYSIDE |
| OXFORD WIDGETS | | 27 OXFORD STREET | LONDON |
| WIDGETS SA | | 1550, CHEMIN DU LAC | QUEBEC |
| WIDGETS DE MEXICO | 10000.00 | 2716 CINCO DE MAYO | NULL |
| WIDGETS OESTE | 15000.00 | CASILLA 114 | NULL |
| WILD WEST WIDGETS | 25000.00 | 1428 NORTHWOOD ROAD | MISSOURI |
| GATOR WIDGETS | 45000.00 | 6732 WEST PALMETTO | FLORIDA |
| WALKING HORSE WIDGET | | 2000 WILLOW | TENNESSEE |
| LONDON WIDGETS LTD. | 50000.00 | 5 MIDDLE AVENUE | LONDON |
| LOTS OF WIDGETS | | 7870 AMSTERDAM | NEW YORK |
| MOUNTAIN WIDGETS | | 9594 COLFAX | COLORADO |
| THING'S | | 112 AVENIDA VERDE | NULL |
| TRICOLOR WIDGETS | | RUE DE MADELINE, 52 | CENTRALE |
| WE'VE GOT WIDGETS | | 90 S. BROAD ST | PENN |
| WIDGET AIR | | SFO INTERNATIONAL | CALIFORNIA |

**FIGURE 5-5.** *Credit limit/customer group sorted by Credit Limit and Customer ascending*

## Rearranging the Sort Order

Whenever you have two or more sorts in use, you should look carefully at the relationship between the items and determine whether the sort sequence is correct. Earlier, we suggested you should try to create your sorts in the order that you want to see them in the final report. However, with even the best design or analysis, sometimes you may have created them in the wrong order.

If you decide you have a sort in the wrong place, you can use the Move Up and Move Down buttons to promote or demote items. These buttons become active only when you have created two or more sorts. You can also use your mouse to click and drag the items to change their position within the sort sequence. To drag, click the drag zone provided next to each sort.

For example, suppose we had created a query with the items' ship date, product number, and quantity shipped. We want to have our final display in date order with the products in alphabetical order by date. However, by mistake we created the sort on the products before we created the sort on the dates. The result will appear as in Figure 5-6. By promoting the ship date above the product, our display will be correct as shown in Figure 5-7.

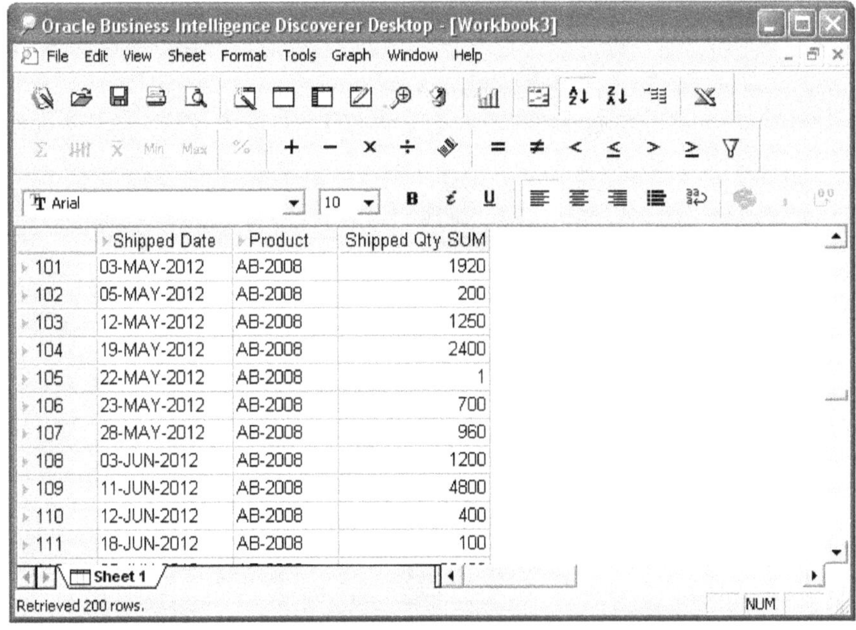


**FIGURE 5-6.** *Ship date, product, and ship quantity, sorted by product and then date*

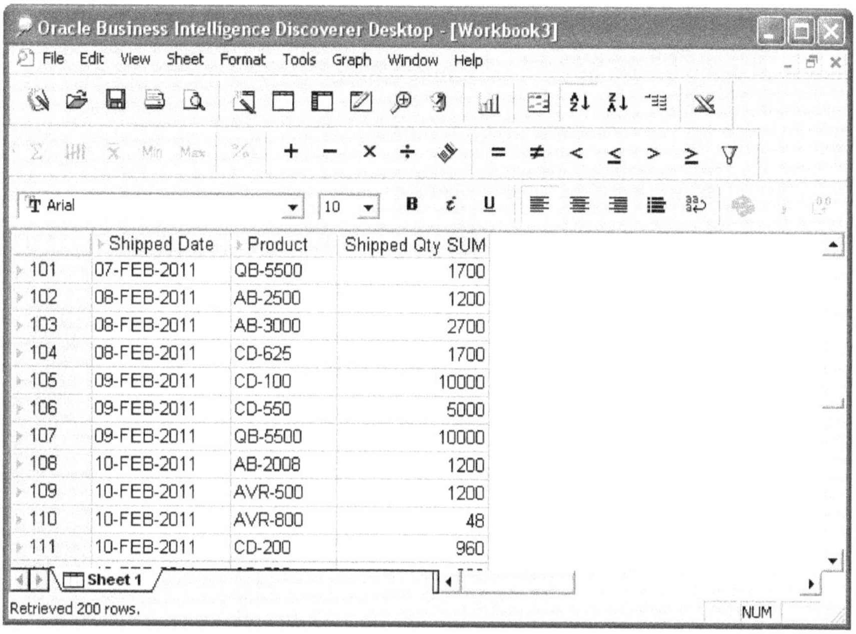
Oracle Business Intelligence Discoverer Desktop - [Workbook3]
File Edit View Sheet Format Tools Graph Window Help
Arial
10
Shipped Date
Product
Shipped Qty SUM
101 07-FEB-2011 QB-5500 1700
102 08-FEB-2011 AB-2500 1200
103 08-FEB-2011 AB-3000 2700
104 08-FEB-2011 CD-625 1700
105 09-FEB-2011 CD-100 10000
106 09-FEB-2011 CD-550 5000
107 09-FEB-2011 QB-5500 10000
108 10-FEB-2011 AB-2008 1200
109 10-FEB-2011 AVR-500 1200
110 10-FEB-2011 AVR-800 48
111 10-FEB-2011 CD-200 960
Sheet 1
Retrieved 200 rows.
NUM

**FIGURE 5-7.** *Ship date, product, and ship quantity, sorted by date and then product*

# Why Not Sort in the Wizard?

When you are working with queries that need to pull a large amount of data, we recommend you not attempt to create your sort sequences inside the Workbook Wizard. We recommend against this because sorting increases the amount of time it takes to run a query and consumes memory. If you have defined complicated sorts, you will add unnecessary overhead to your query. This overhead could actually cause your query to exceed the maximum query time set by your Discoverer manager, and your query could time out.

When you have a working copy of your query, you can concentrate on the sort criteria. You should look at the data that your query has brought in and try to define the best way to display that data. Presenting your data using appropriate and meaningful sort criteria should be done only after you have some data onscreen as a result of a reduced set of constraints.

In Chapter 9, you will learn how the different types of sort affect your report and how to create a useful sort order. Even though there is no step in the Crosstab Wizard for sorting, you can do this, but only after you have created the initial query. We will show you how to add sorts to crosstab worksheets in Chapter 9 also.

After applying crosstab conditions or adding sort orders to a table, in Desktop click Next. This brings up the sixth screen of the Workbook Wizard. In Plus, we recommend you click the Back button twice to return to the second screen of the Workbook Wizard and then click the Calculations tab.

**NOTE**
*The hierarchy of sorts can affect the appearance of your data in ways that may not be obvious at first. For example, if you have a group-sorted item and you then add a sort on another item, the new sort applies only at the group level.*

# Workbook Wizard Step 6: Creating User-Defined Calculations

The ability to add your own calculations is, along with conditions and parameters, one of the features that make Discoverer a powerful analysis tool. Master calculations and you are on your way to mastering Discoverer. Because Desktop and Plus are sufficiently different, we will describe the wizard screens separately.

## Desktop Calculations Screen

As shown in Figure 5-8, step 6 of the Desktop Workbook Wizard contains three boxes and three buttons.

- **View Calculations For box** This is a drop-down box where you can choose to view calculations for all items or a specific item only. In Discoverer Desktop, you also get an option to view active-only calculations.

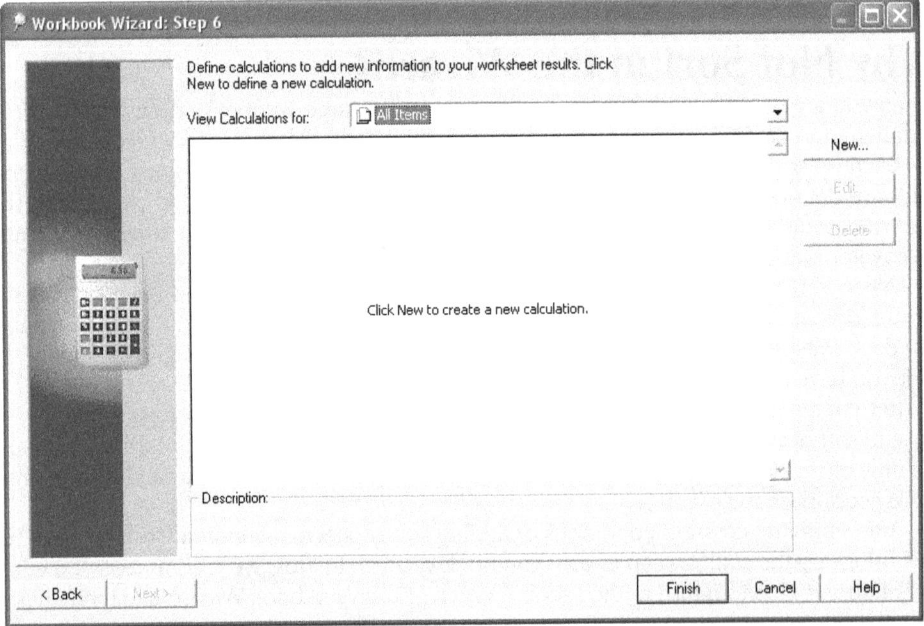


**FIGURE 5-8.** *Desktop Workbook Wizard, step 6*

- **Available Calculations box** This box will be empty until you add a calculation. As you add calculations to your query, Discoverer will display them here in the order in which you create them.
- **Description box** This box shows the description of the calculation highlighted in the Calculations box.
- **New button** Click this to add a new calculation.
- **Edit button** When it is active, click this to edit an existing calculation.
- **Delete button** Click this to delete a calculation. As with conditions, be careful using this one because it does just what it says and without prompting!

## Plus Calculations Tab

As shown in Figure 5-9, the Plus Calculations tab has the standard buttons available throughout the wizard, with three additional default settings. These are

- **My Calculations** Displays a list of the calculations you have defined
- **My Percentages** Displays a list of the percentages you have defined
- **My Totals** Displays a list of the totals that you have defined

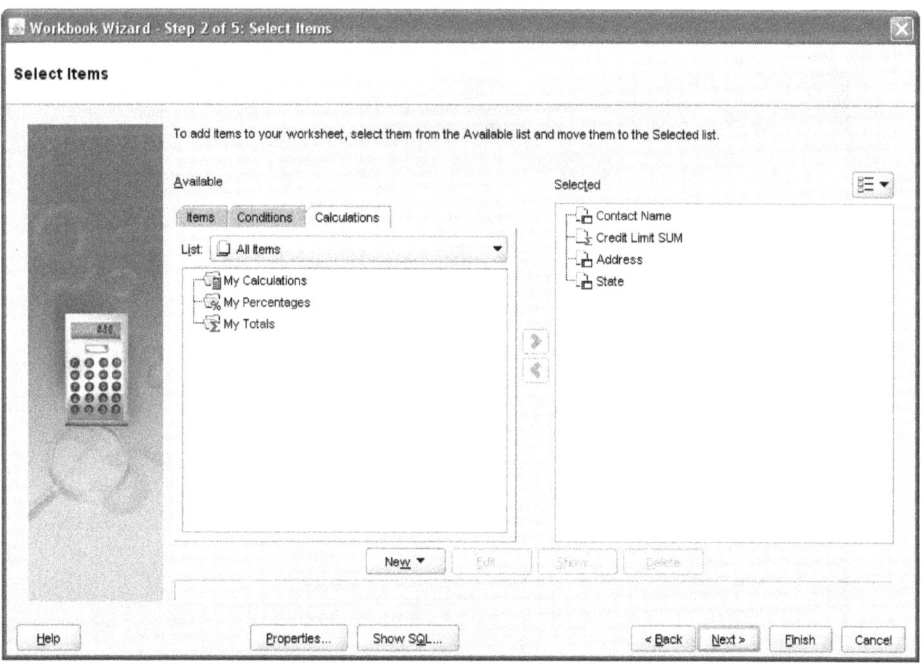


**FIGURE 5-9.** *The Plus Calculations tab*

## Calculations: What Are They?

The word *calculate* means to compute mathematically, to ascertain by computation, to reckon, to estimate, or to plan. Calculations have been with us almost from the dawn of time, and throughout the ages man has been trying to devise new and quicker ways to perform them. The computer you are working on right now has the capability to perform millions of calculations per second (MIPS). In a business environment, you will most likely want to use calculations to aid you in estimating, trending, and forecasting.

Calculations give you more power in ad hoc reporting. When no underlying item in the database contains the data you want, Discoverer allows you to create new items. The formulas used to create these items can be very simple, or they can be complex mathematical or statistical expressions.

When using calculations, you can use existing items from the database, such as the operators multiply (*), divide (/), add (+), and subtract (-); literals such as 1, 100, and 65.5; and functions. You can also use calculations that have been created for you by your Discoverer manager.

It is possible to see profits, costs, and margins calculated and grouped in a matter of minutes. Using mathematical formulas, calculations enable you to produce more complex queries. They usually apply some sort of algorithm or equation to the query results. A simple example of a calculation in a query is subtracting a product's cost price from its selling price to see the profit. A more complex calculation would be to see the profit margin, which is the sum of the profit (itself a calculation) divided by the sum of the selling price.

Figure 5-10 shows a simple calculation used in a query. You can see that the selling price minus the cost price is shown as the profit Calculation0.

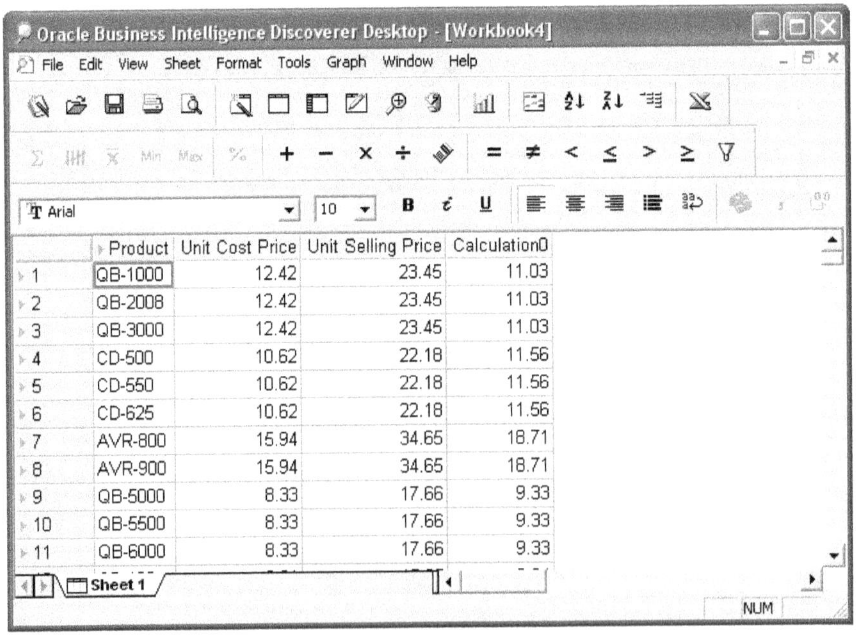
Oracle Business Intelligence Discoverer Desktop - [Workbook4]
File Edit View Sheet Format Tools Graph Window Help
Arial
10
B
U
Product Unit Cost Price Unit Selling Price Calculation0
1 QB-1000 12.42 23.45 11.03
2 QB-2008 12.42 23.45 11.03
3 QB-3000 12.42 23.45 11.03
4 CD-500 10.62 22.18 11.56
5 CD-550 10.62 22.18 11.56
6 CD-625 10.62 22.18 11.56
7 AVR-800 15.94 34.65 18.71
8 AVR-900 15.94 34.65 18.71
9 QB-5000 8.33 17.66 9.33
10 QB-5500 8.33 17.66 9.33
11 QB-6000 8.33 17.66 9.33
Sheet 1
NUM

**FIGURE 5-10.** *A simple calculation in Desktop*

**NOTE**
*Discoverer makes available calculations grouped by categories such as Analytical, Conversion, Database, Date, Group, Numeric, String, and Others.*

## Creating a Calculation in Desktop

When creating a new calculation in Desktop, use the following workflow:

1. Click New. This opens the Edit Calculation dialog box (see Figure 5-11).
2. Give a meaningful name for your calculation. This name will appear as the column heading. By default, Discoverer inserts the word *calculation* followed by an integer.
3. Alongside the heading Show are two radio buttons. These are
   - **Items** These are items that exist within folders that are linked to your query, whether in use or not.
   - **Functions** These are predefined functions that exist within the database. Please refer to Appendix B for a full list of available functions. This appendix describes the syntax for every function and also gives meaningful examples of their use.
4. Build your calculation using a combination of expressions and operators.
5. Click OK to finish.

**NOTE**
*Unlike Plus (see the next section), Desktop does not provide templates for creating analytic functions. You need to create calculations based on these functions yourself.*

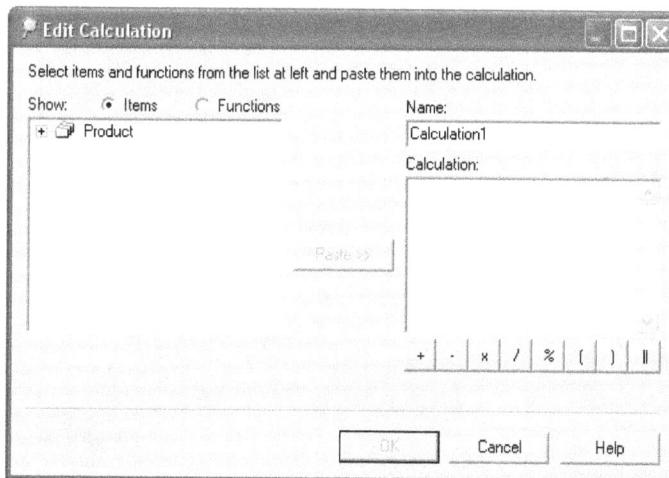

**FIGURE 5-11.** *Desktop Edit Calculation dialog box*

## Creating a Calculation in Plus

When creating a new calculation in Plus, use the following workflow:

1. Launch the New Calculation dialog box (see Figure 5-12).

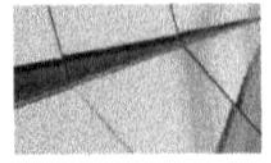

**NOTE**
*There are two ways to launch the New Calculation dialog box. The first way is to click New and then from the drop-down box select New Calculation. The second way is to right-click My Calculations and from the pop-up box select New Calculation.*

2. Give a meaningful name for your calculation. This name will appear as the column heading. By default, Discoverer inserts the word *calculation* followed by an integer.
3. Click Show to see a list of available expressions. These are
   - **Functions** These are predefined functions that exist within the database. Please refer to Appendix B for a full list of available functions. This appendix describes the syntax for every function and also gives meaningful examples of their use.
   - **Selected Items** These are the items that are in use in your query.
   - **Available Items** These are items that exist within folders that are linked to your query but are not yet in use.

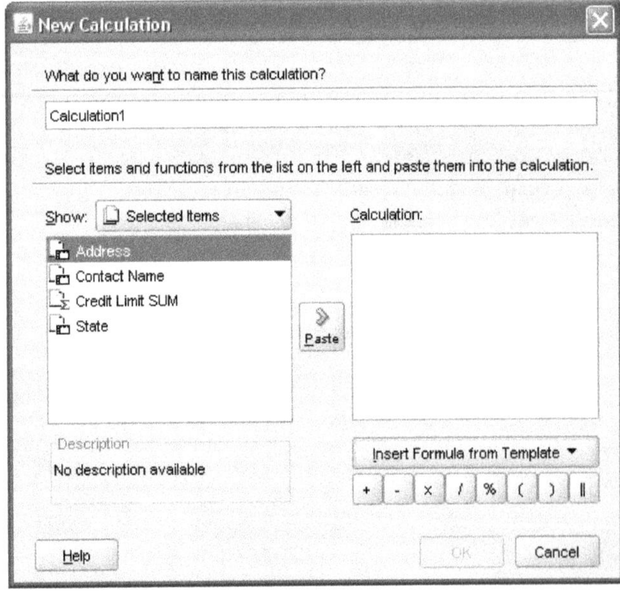


**FIGURE 5-12.** *Plus New Calculation dialog box*

- **Calculations** These are calculations that you have previously created. Yes, you can create calculations based on other calculations!
- **Parameters** These are parameters that you have previously created. Obviously, at this point we have not created any parameters, so for now ignore this option.

4. Build your calculation using a combination of expressions and operators.
5. To use an analytic function, click the Insert Formula from Template button. Discoverer now displays a list of the available analytic functions. We will describe how to access and use these functions in Appendix B.
6. Click OK to finish.

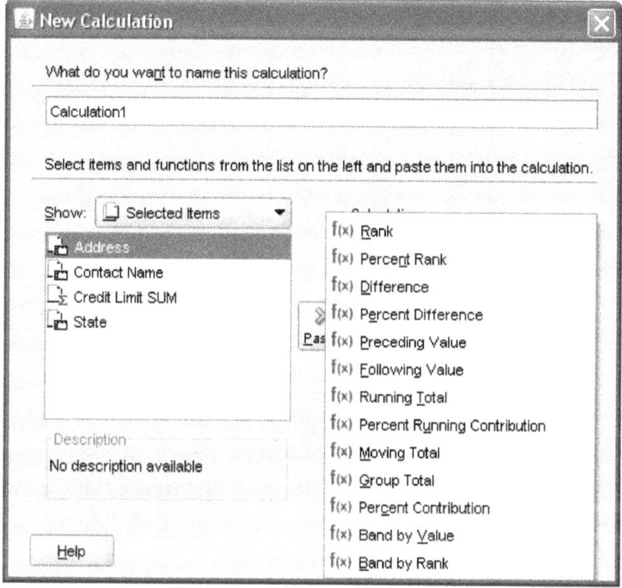


# Understanding Calculations

When you first enter step 6 of the Desktop Wizard (see Figure 5-8) or first enter the Calculations tab in Plus (see Figure 5-9), the main box in the center of the screen will be empty. You need to think about what item or items you want to use in your calculations. Like conditions, there are administrator-created calculations for you to choose from. You select these predefined calculations in the same way as you select the items in your query. In Chapter 4, you were shown the different icons for the types of items you could select. Simple predefined calculations appear as a numeric item, and aggregate calculations appear as a calculator.

In the example that follows, the Discoverer manager has created simple calculations for standard margin, markup, and profit. There is also an administrator-defined aggregate calculation called *profit margin*. The first three appear as normal items, and you can use the usual mathematical functions of SUM, AVG, and so forth on these. The item called profit margin, however, is an aggregate item. These are items that have been created by either dividing the SUM of one item into another or preapplying SUM to a calculation. This type of aggregated calculation stands alone in that it cannot have any other function applied to it, which is why it does not have any (+) character.

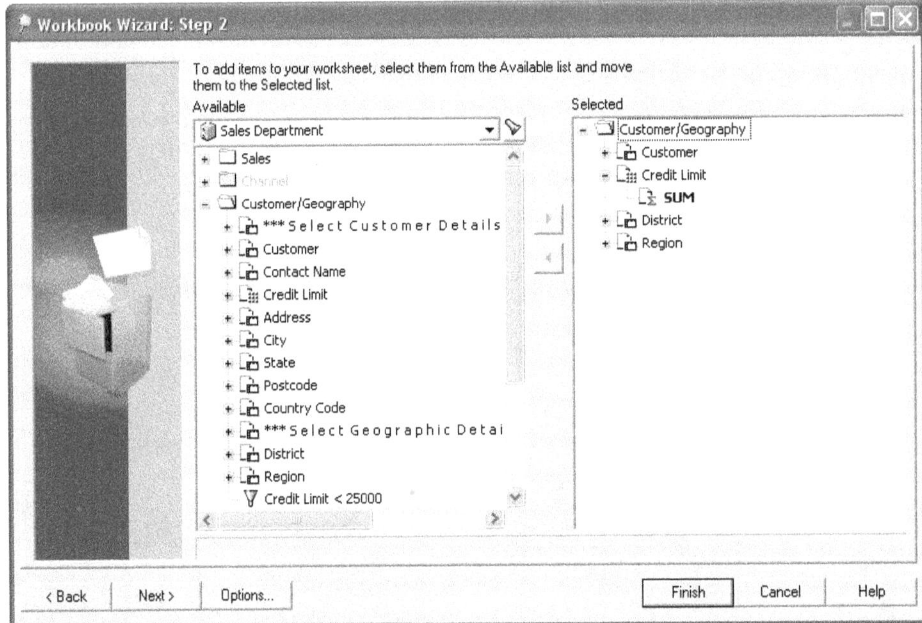


Because you can create multiple calculations in your query, you should try to create them in a logical sequence, defining simple calculations first. There is no limit on the number of calculations you can define. Creating complex calculations requires a great deal of preplanning, perhaps working out your calculations on paper before you begin to define them in the Workbook Wizard. One of the most common mistakes made by end users is defining or attempting to define extremely complex calculations in the Workbook Wizard.

**NOTE**

*It is always worthwhile to try complex calculations on small data sets, where it is easy to verify the results before trying them on large data sets. Calculations will run faster on small data sets than large ones.*

When you have decided what columns you need for a calculation, click New.

The previous Figure 5-11 shows the Edit Calculation dialog box used in Discoverer Desktop, and Figure 5-12 shows the New Calculation dialog box used in Discoverer Plus. These dialog boxes consist of the following sections:

- **Name** The name given here will appear as the column heading.
- **Calculation box** Type or paste the components for your calculation here.
- **Available box** This box displays a list of the items that are available for selection within the calculation.
- **Paste** Click this button to add an item, function, parameter, or other calculation to the Calculation box.

- **Operators** This is a set of buttons for standard mathematical operators. Clicking one of these pastes the operator into the calculation.
- **Description** This displays a description of an item, calculation, or function.
- **Show drop-down box** This is a drop-down list of the items, functions, parameters, or other calculations available to use in this calculation. This box is available only in Plus.
- **Items** Click this radio button to display a list of the items available to create your calculation. This button is available only in Desktop.
- **Functions** Click this radio button to display a list of functions available to create your calculation. This button is available only in Desktop.
- **Insert Formula from Template** Click this button to see a list of the analytic functions that are available for use within the calculation. This button is available in Plus. When a function is selected for use, a template dialog box opens. In this dialog box, Discoverer preselects the most suitable options. Appendix B contains a full description of this dialog box.

When you have created a calculation, click OK. This causes Discoverer to test the mathematical properties of your calculation. If you have defined an incorrect calculation, Discoverer will warn you, and you will have to correct your formula before continuing. Discoverer also tests the syntax of the calculation to ensure that basic errors in your calculation are caught at the first step itself.

Assuming you have created a valid calculation, Discoverer inserts it into the box for calculations and ticks the check box automatically. Also at this point, you will notice that the Edit and Delete buttons that were inactive are now activated, and in Desktop, Discoverer has inserted the formula into the Description box. In Plus, this shows only for predefined functions or custom calculations. These descriptions will display in the box after you have created them and go back and select them from the list. If you have made an error in your formula, use the Edit button to reopen the Calculation dialog box and change it. If you decide you no longer need this calculation, click Delete and it will be removed. In Plus you can also right-click the calculation. When you do this, a drop-down box is displayed, from which you can select Edit or Delete. You can also opt to remove a calculation from the worksheet. This does not delete the calculation but merely deactivates it.

Discoverer adds the calculations into the box in the order you create them. You can use your calculations or the administrator-predefined calculations to create more complex algorithms.

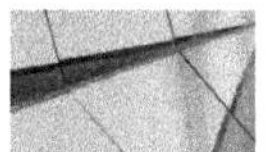

**NOTE**

*Be very careful creating calculations that employ division. You need to ensure that the divisor column does not contain any zero values; otherwise, you will encounter the dreaded divide-by-zero error, which will cause your query to fail. You will have to either apply a condition on the column that is being used as the divisor (Column<>0) or create your calculation using a DECODE or CASE function to tell Discoverer what to do when it encounters this situation. A DECODE calculation can be thought of as an IF . . . THEN clause. This will be explained fully in Chapter 13. If you are debugging a query that contains division, the first step is to check for the required nonzero condition and implement one of the two solutions outlined here. This is probably the single most common reason why calculations fail.*

## Why Not Calculate in the Wizard?

Applying calculations is one of the most challenging and complicated aspects of query design. It is recommended that you not attempt to create calculations using the Workbook Wizard until you have become proficient in the use of Discoverer. The authors have spoken with numerous expert Discoverer users, and none of them said they attempt to add calculations in the wizard. They wait until they have a working query with the data needed and then begin to create their calculations.

As with all querying tools, the more complicated the query, the higher the risk becomes that you will make an error—usually with no data being returned. This becomes even riskier when adding calculations, especially calculations using division. One expression in the wrong place and you could wait several minutes for a query to run, only to come back with a message that no data was found. The best way around this type of frustration is to build yourself a basic working query and then add your calculations.

**NOTE**
*If your Discoverer manager has predefined calculations for your use, you will probably be safe adding these by using the Workbook Wizard.*

If you are working in Desktop, you have now completed all the steps of the Workbook Wizard and you should click Finish. In Plus, there are three more steps.

# Discoverer Plus Workbook Wizard Remaining Steps

This section is applicable only to Discoverer Plus. If you are using Desktop and have no interest in Plus, you may want to skip this section. However, most companies are moving toward web-based analysis, and we recommend you continue reading.

Having completed calculations, the Discoverer Plus Workbook Wizard additionally allows you to create

- User-defined percentages
- User-defined totals
- User-defined parameters

All of these options are available in Desktop but not as part of the Workbook Wizard. We will show you later in the chapter how to access them in Desktop.

# Creating User-Defined Percentages in the Plus Workbook Wizard

As shown earlier in Figure 5-9, the Plus Calculations tab has the standard buttons available throughout the wizard, with three additional default settings. These are

- **My Calculations** Displays a list of the calculations you have defined
- **My Percentages** Displays a list of the percentages you have defined
- **My Totals** Displays a list of the totals that you have defined

Thus, because we just completed adding our first calculations, there is no need to navigate away from the Calculations tab. In fact, we stay right here throughout both of the next two steps as we create percentages and totals.

## Percentages: What Are They?

The word *percent* comes from the Latin words *per* (meaning by) and *centum* (meaning hundred). A percentage is quite simply the rate of an item per hundred, or in accounting terms, a commission, duty, or interest based on 100. Most countries in the world use a currency based on 100 parts: 100 cents in a dollar, 100 centimes in a franc, 100 pennies in a pound. These allow for very simple percentage calculations, but it wasn't always this way. As recently as 1970, England had 240 pennies in one pound, but to make it worse they had 12 pennies in a shilling and 20 shillings in a pound (incidentally, the guinea that is still used in race horse trades is 21 shillings).

Calculating percentages of numbers with the answer being part of 100 is a typical data analysis task. Discoverer allows you to choose the data to use both for the percentage calculation itself and for the value used to represent the percentage (grand total, subtotal, and so on). Don't worry about the terms used at this stage, as these will all be fully covered.

**NOTE**

*Because percentages are just a specialized form of calculation, many of the comments that were given in the preceding section on calculations are valid for percentages as well.*

Percentages are mathematical formulas that enable you to analyze your data more effectively. They apply standard mathematical algorithms to the item you have chosen. A simple example of a percentage in a query is "Show me the percentage of my sales by channel for the month of January 2010." A more complex percentage would be to see the same query extended for the whole of fiscal quarter Q2, with the percentages being applied over the whole quarter's profit margin—which is the sum of the profit (itself a percentage) divided by the sum of the selling price.

Figure 5-13 shows a simple percentage being applied in a query. You can see that the selling price has been totaled by channel and that the percentage of sales is shown by channel and by total. Because the month is used only to define a condition, it has been moved to the Page Items box.

**NOTE**

*Because of rounding in percentages, don't expect your percentage totals to always add up to 100 percent. This is a common phenomenon, and anyone familiar with spreadsheet programs such as Excel has encountered this situation.*

## Creating a New Percentage

When creating a new percentage, you should use the following workflow:

1. Launch the New Percentage dialog box (see Figure 5-14).

**NOTE**

*There are two ways to launch the New Percentage dialog box. The first way is to click New and then from the drop-down box select New Percentage. The second way is to right-click My Percentages and from the pop-up box select New Percentage.*

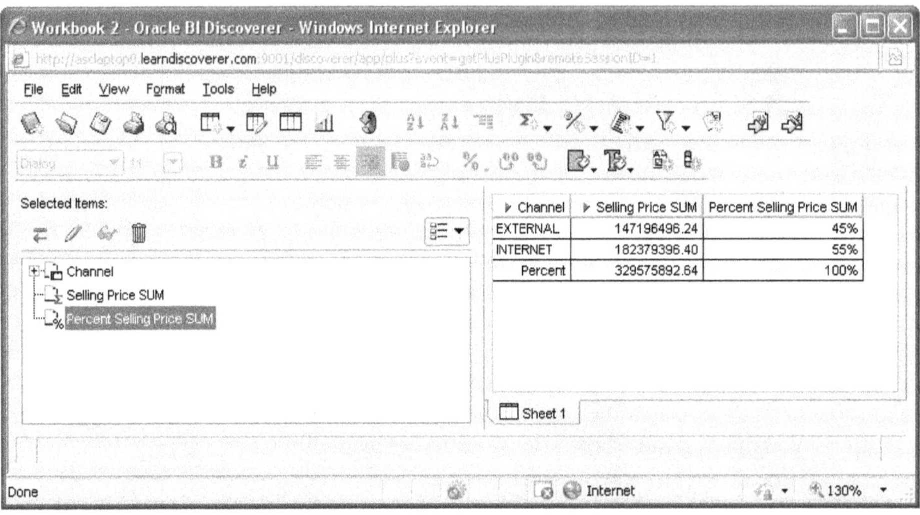


**FIGURE 5-13.** *Selling price as percentage by channel for January 2010*

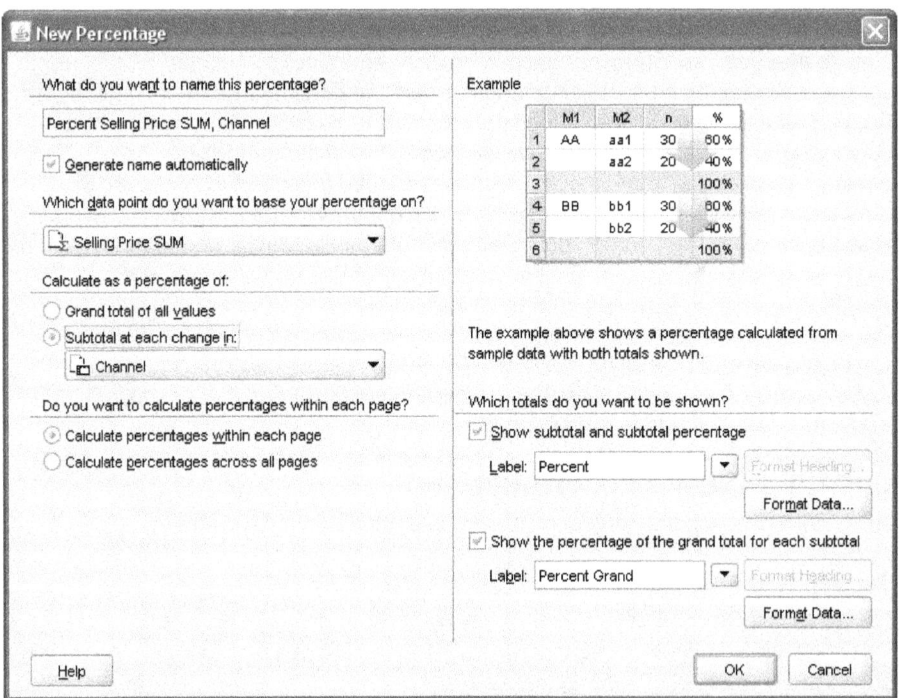


**FIGURE 5-14.** *New Percentage dialog box*

2. Uncheck the Generate name automatically box, and give a meaningful name to your percentage. This name will appear as the column heading. If you leave this blank, the percentage column will have no label. By default, Discoverer prefixes the column heading with the word *Percent*. This is not good practice; Discoverer only does this to help you just in case you forget to name the percentage yourself.
3. Click the Data Point drop-down box to see the list of available data points, and select the data item you want to apply the percentage on from the list. If you have only one item that can be used, Discoverer inserts that item by default and disables the drop-down.
4. Choose whether you want your percentage to be based on a grand total of all values or on a subtotal, and then check the appropriate radio button. If you opt to create a percentage based on a subtotal, you will also need to tell Discoverer which item it should use to create the subtotal.
5. Next you need to determine whether you want Discoverer to calculate the percentages according to only values in the current page or values across all pages. If you are not using page items or have only one page item, then the choice makes no difference. The only time you really need to make a decision is when page items are in use and you have multiple pages. We advise you to be careful when calculating percentages across multiple pages because it may not be evident to the casual observer that this is what you have done.
6. Choose whether to include totals in your percentages. If you do so, you may also give a label for the percentage. This is not mandatory, and you may leave it either with the default or nothing at all.
7. If you want to use a different color of font for your percentage, click the Format Data button.
8. Click OK to finish.

You need to think about what item or items you want to use in your percentages. Unlike calculations, there are no administrator-created percentages for you to choose from. However, you can have calculations that give the answer as a percentage, but they cannot be edited as percentages.

Because percentages usually stand alone as data items, it doesn't really matter in what order you create them. Although you probably wouldn't have more than one or two in your query, there is no limit on the number of percentages you can define. Creating valid and meaningful percentages can be somewhat taxing at first, but don't worry, because most of the fun of working with Discoverer lies in examining and trying things for yourself.

When you have decided what data item you need for a percentage, launch the New Percentage dialog box. This dialog box contains the following sections:

- **What do you want to name this percentage?** The name given here will appear as the column heading. Discoverer will create a name for you if you don't specify one. Figure 5-14 shows Discoverer inserting default names. We recommend you review the Discoverer names and change them to something more meaningful.
- **Generate name automatically** Check this box if you want Discoverer to name percentages for you (not a good idea).
- **Which data point do you want to base your percentage on?** This section contains a drop-down list of the data points that you can use to base percentages on. If there is only one data point, the drop-down will be inactive.

- **Grand total of all values** Click this radio button if you want your percentages to be based on the grand total of all values.
- **Subtotal at each change in** Click this radio button if you want your percentages to be based on a subtotal. Having clicked this button, select the item on which you want to create the subtotal from the drop-down list.
- **Calculate percentages within each page** Click this radio button if you want percentages to be based only on the items displayed onscreen.
- **Calculate percentages across all pages** Click this radio button if you want percentages to be based on all page items.
- **Show grand total and grand total percentage** Check this box if you want to show the grand total percentages onscreen. You can also then use the drop-down list to select items for labeling the grand total (see the later section "Labeling Percentages and Totals"). This box will be available only when you previously checked the Grand total of all values button. When in use, a Format Data button situated immediately to the right of the box will activate. Click this Format Data button if you want to set a format for the percentage that is different from the normal data.
- **Show subtotal and subtotal percentage** Check this box if you want to show the subtotals and their percentages onscreen. You can use the drop-down list to select items for labeling the subtotal (see the later section "Labeling Percentages and Totals"). By default the label will be Percent Grand. This box will be available only when you previously checked the Subtotal at each change in button. When in use, a Format Data button situated immediately to the right of the main box will activate. Click this Format Data button if you want to set a format for the percentage that is different from the normal data.
- **Show the percentage of the grand total for each subtotal** Check this box if you want to show the grand total percentages onscreen. You can also then use the drop-down list to select items for labeling the grand total (see the section "Labeling Percentages and Totals" later in this chapter). By default the label will be Percent. This box will be available only when you previously checked the Subtotal at each change in button. When in use, a Format Data button situated immediately to the right of the box will activate. Click this Format Data button if you want to set a format for the percentage that is different from the normal data.

When you have created a percentage, click OK. Unlike calculations, where Discoverer has to test the mathematical properties of the calculation, percentages always work. There is no such thing as having defined an incorrect percentage, although the results you see onscreen may not be that obvious at first—as we will show you in a moment.

Assuming you have created a valid percentage, Discoverer inserts it into the box under the My Percentages subheading and places a tick mark alongside. Percentages are added into the box in the order you create them.

Also at this point, you will notice that the Edit and Delete buttons are activated and Discoverer has inserted the formula into the Description box. If you have made an error in your formula, open the Edit Percentage dialog box and correct it. To open the Edit Percentage dialog box, click the Edit button (looks like a pencil) or right-click the percentage and select Edit from the drop-down list. If you decide you no longer need this percentage, click Delete, or right-click the percentage and from the drop-down list select Delete. The percentage will be removed.

**NOTE**
*You will not be warned when deleting percentages, so take care.*

When you have completed adding percentages to your query, you can either click Finish, which causes Discoverer to run the query, or move to step 8 of the Workbook Wizard by clicking Next.

# Examples of Percentages

Because there are many options available to you within the Workbook Wizard, we will show you examples of each type. For the purpose of these examples, we have specified a query that pulls in the selling price SUM, the sales channel, and the fiscal quarter. We have created a condition to constrain the report to only fiscal years 2007 and 2008. We will start by using a very simple percentage calculation and progress through all of the options so that you can see at a glance what each option does. In all of these examples, the only data point open to us is the selling price SUM.

## Example 1: A Simple Percentage

In this example, we will apply the following options:

- Calculate as a percentage of the grand total
- Calculate percentages for current page items only
- Do not show any totals

This is by far the easiest type of percentage to create and apply within your query and probably the easiest for anyone viewing your output to understand. When you set the options and then click OK, Discoverer will create the percentage calculation. As you can see, Discoverer has sorted the query by channel and quarter. You can see at a glance that Global Widgets' best quarter was the second quarter of 2008 in the External channel, with 50 percent of sales for the year. You may also spot that there were no sales from the Internet in the first quarter of 2007; this is because the company didn't start its e-business until the beginning of Q2.

You can also see that Discoverer has inserted the default name Percent Selling Price SUM. Again, we recommend you review these default names and change them to something more meaningful. We have not done so here in order to highlight how Discoverer inserts default names.

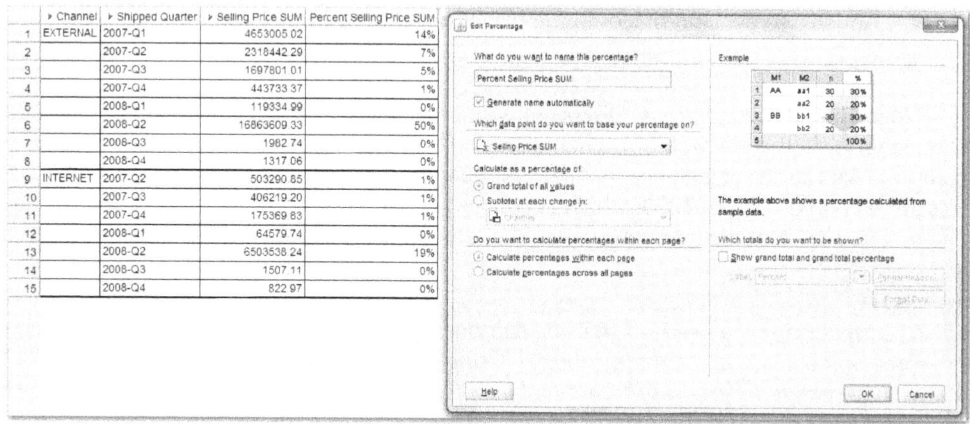

| | ▸ Channel | ▸ Shipped Quarter | ▸ Selling Price SUM | Percent Selling Price SUM |
|---|---|---|---|---|
| 1 | EXTERNAL | 2007-Q1 | 4653005.02 | 14% |
| 2 | | 2007-Q2 | 2318442.29 | 7% |
| 3 | | 2007-Q3 | 1697801.01 | 5% |
| 4 | | 2007-Q4 | 443733.37 | 1% |
| 5 | | 2008-Q1 | 119334.99 | 0% |
| 6 | | 2008-Q2 | 16863609.33 | 50% |
| 7 | | 2008-Q3 | 1982.74 | 0% |
| 8 | | 2008-Q4 | 1317.06 | 0% |
| 9 | INTERNET | 2007-Q2 | 503290.65 | 1% |
| 10 | | 2007-Q3 | 406219.20 | 1% |
| 11 | | 2007-Q4 | 175369.83 | 1% |
| 12 | | 2008-Q1 | 64579.74 | 0% |
| 13 | | 2008-Q2 | 6503538.24 | 19% |
| 14 | | 2008-Q3 | 1507.11 | 0% |
| 15 | | 2008-Q4 | 822.97 | 0% |

### Example 2: Showing the Grand Total

In the next example, we have edited the previous percentage and redefined it as follows:

- Calculate as a percentage of the grand total
- Calculate percentages for current page items only
- Show grand total and grand total percentage and use the label *Percent*

When you set these options, Discoverer will refine the percentage calculation. As you can see, Discoverer shows grand totals for both the Selling Price SUM and the Percentage columns.

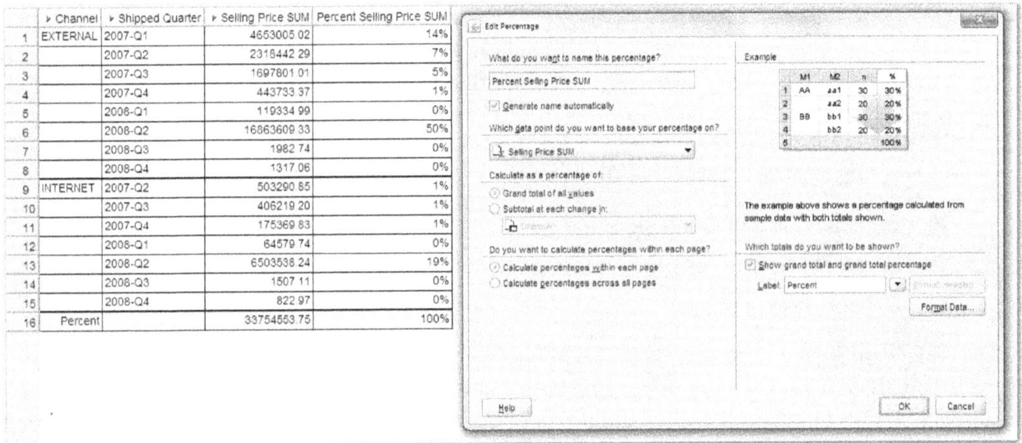

| | Channel | Shipped Quarter | Selling Price SUM | Percent Selling Price SUM |
|---|---|---|---|---|
| 1 | EXTERNAL | 2007-Q1 | 4653005.02 | 14% |
| 2 | | 2007-Q2 | 2318442.29 | 7% |
| 3 | | 2007-Q3 | 1697801.01 | 5% |
| 4 | | 2007-Q4 | 443733.37 | 1% |
| 5 | | 2008-Q1 | 119334.99 | 0% |
| 6 | | 2008-Q2 | 16863609.33 | 50% |
| 7 | | 2008-Q3 | 1982.74 | 0% |
| 8 | | 2008-Q4 | 1317.06 | 0% |
| 9 | INTERNET | 2007-Q2 | 503290.85 | 1% |
| 10 | | 2007-Q3 | 406219.20 | 1% |
| 11 | | 2007-Q4 | 175369.83 | 1% |
| 12 | | 2008-Q1 | 64579.74 | 0% |
| 13 | | 2008-Q2 | 6503538.24 | 19% |
| 14 | | 2008-Q3 | 1507.11 | 0% |
| 15 | | 2008-Q4 | 822.97 | 0% |
| 16 | Percent | | 33754553.75 | 100% |



### Example 3: Showing Subtotals

In the next example, we have further edited the percentage and redefined it as follows:

- Calculate as a percentage of the subtotal based on the channel
- Calculate percentages for current page items only
- Added two decimal places to the data
- Show subtotals and subtotal percentages, using the label *Percent*

When you set these options, Discoverer will refine the percentage calculation. As you can see, Discoverer is showing subtotals by channel for both the Selling Price SUM and Percentage columns. We can see at a glance that the best quarter for Global Widgets via its external channel was the second quarter of 2008, which accounted for 64.61 percent of that channel's annual sales. The best quarter from the Internet came in the same quarter, with 84.95 percent of annual sales.

**NOTE**

*To correctly apply a percentage using subtotals, you need to define sorts on the items you want to subtotal. Using the preceding example, we have created a group sort on the channel and applied a normal ascending order sort on the fiscal month.*

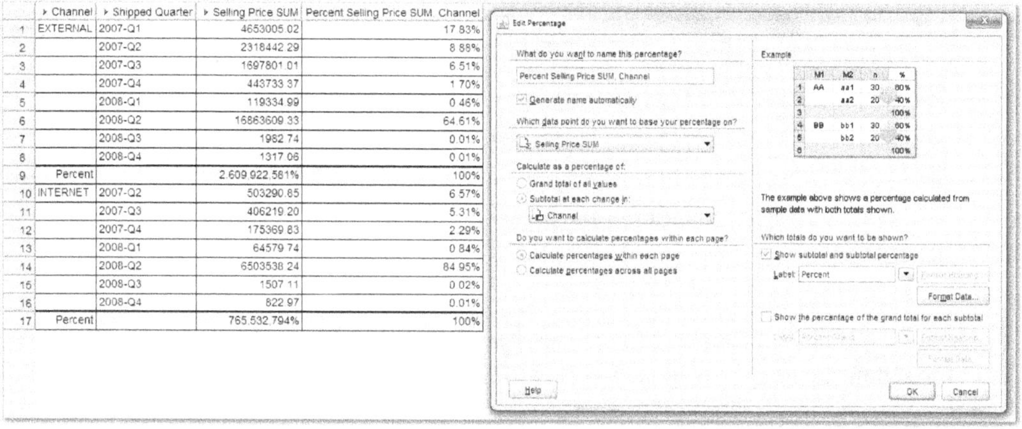

| | Channel | Shipped Quarter | Selling Price SUM | Percent Selling Price SUM, Channel |
|---|---|---|---|---|
| 1 | EXTERNAL | 2007-Q1 | 4653005.02 | 17.83% |
| 2 | | 2007-Q2 | 2318442.29 | 8.88% |
| 3 | | 2007-Q3 | 1697801.01 | 6.51% |
| 4 | | 2007-Q4 | 443733.37 | 1.70% |
| 5 | | 2008-Q1 | 119334.99 | 0.46% |
| 6 | | 2008-Q2 | 16863609.33 | 64.61% |
| 7 | | 2008-Q3 | 1982.74 | 0.01% |
| 8 | | 2008-Q4 | 1317.06 | 0.01% |
| 9 | Percent | | 2,609,922.581% | 100% |
| 10 | INTERNET | 2007-Q2 | 503290.85 | 6.57% |
| 11 | | 2007-Q3 | 406219.20 | 5.31% |
| 12 | | 2007-Q4 | 175369.83 | 2.29% |
| 13 | | 2008-Q1 | 64579.74 | 0.84% |
| 14 | | 2008-Q2 | 6503538.24 | 84.95% |
| 15 | | 2008-Q3 | 1507.11 | 0.02% |
| 16 | | 2008-Q4 | 822.97 | 0.01% |
| 17 | Percent | | 765,532.794% | 100% |



## Example 4: Showing Subtotals and a Grand Total

In the next example, we have further edited the percentage and redefined it as follows:

- Calculate as a percentage of the subtotal based on the channel
- Calculate percentages for current page items only
- Show subtotals and subtotal percentages, using the label *Percent*
- Show grand totals and grand total percentages, using the label *Percent Grand*

By setting these options, Discoverer will refine the percentage calculation. As you can see, Discoverer is now showing not only the subtotals by channel for both the Selling Price SUM and Percentage columns but also the percentage of each as compared to the grand total. We can now see that the external channel accounted for 77 percent of all sales for the two years covered by the report, with the Internet accounting for just 23 percent.

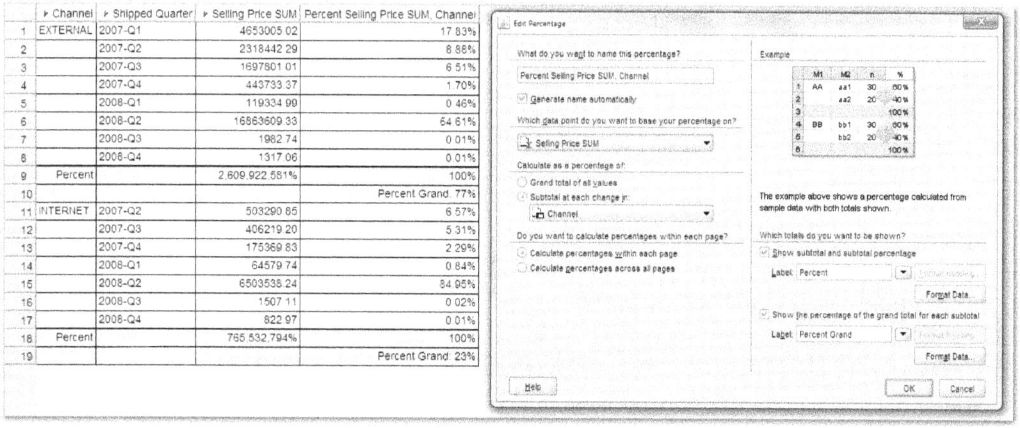

| | Channel | Shipped Quarter | Selling Price SUM | Percent Selling Price SUM, Channel |
|---|---|---|---|---|
| 1 | EXTERNAL | 2007-Q1 | 4653005.02 | 17.83% |
| 2 | | 2007-Q2 | 2318442.29 | 8.88% |
| 3 | | 2007-Q3 | 1697801.01 | 6.51% |
| 4 | | 2007-Q4 | 443733.37 | 1.70% |
| 5 | | 2008-Q1 | 119334.99 | 0.46% |
| 6 | | 2008-Q2 | 16863609.33 | 64.61% |
| 7 | | 2008-Q3 | 1982.74 | 0.01% |
| 8 | | 2008-Q4 | 1317.06 | 0.01% |
| 9 | Percent | | 2,609,922.581% | 100% |
| 10 | | | | Percent Grand: 77% |
| 11 | INTERNET | 2007-Q2 | 503290.85 | 6.57% |
| 12 | | 2007-Q3 | 406219.20 | 5.31% |
| 13 | | 2007-Q4 | 175369.83 | 2.29% |
| 14 | | 2008-Q1 | 64579.74 | 0.84% |
| 15 | | 2008-Q2 | 6503538.24 | 84.95% |
| 16 | | 2008-Q3 | 1507.11 | 0.02% |
| 17 | | 2008-Q4 | 822.97 | 0.01% |
| 18 | Percent | | 765,532.794% | 100% |
| 19 | | | | Percent Grand: 23% |

### Example 5: Showing Subtotals and a Grand Total Using Page Items

In the next example, we have further edited the percentage and redefined it as follows:

- Added the fiscal year and placed it in the page items
- Calculate as a percentage of the subtotal based on the channel
- Calculate percentages for all page items
- Show subtotals and subtotal percentages, using the label *Percent*
- Show grand totals and grand total percentages, using the label *Percent Grand*

As you can see, Discoverer is still showing subtotals by channel and a grand total. We have chosen to look at the sales for 2007. At first glance, the results may appear to be incorrect; however, they are not. If you look closely at the percentage totals for the external channel in 2007, you will see that Discoverer has inserted values of 35 percent for the subtotal and 27 percent for the grand total. What this means is that in FY 2007, Global Widgets had external sales that accounted for 35 percent of all the external sales in the two-year period and that this same amount equated to 27 percent of *all* sales in the same period. Looking at the Internet channel, you can see that *only* 14 percent of their sales came in 2007 and that this accounted for just 3 percent of the total sales in the same period.

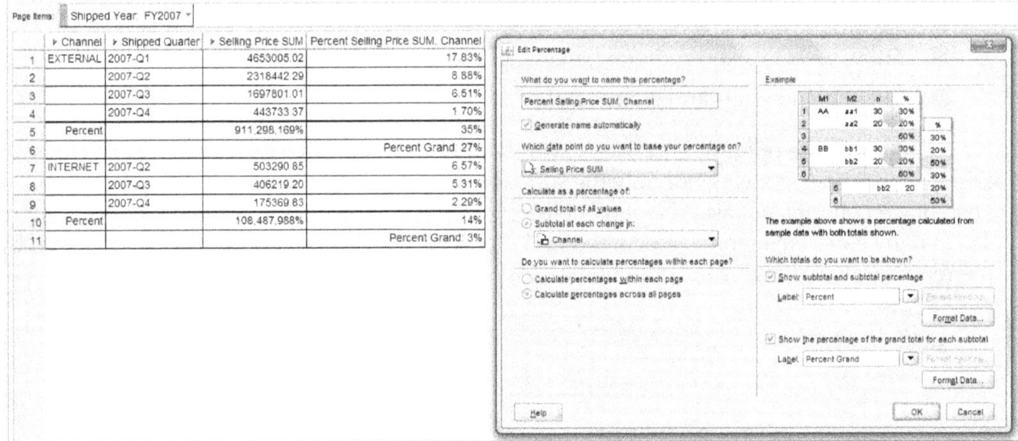

**NOTE**

*Oracle added the capability to create percentages based on page items when it introduced its web version of Discoverer. The preceding example can therefore be created only in Plus.*

## Why Not Perform Percentages in the Wizard?

As the preceding examples have shown, applying percentages and understanding what the various Discoverer options mean can be quite daunting, even to a seasoned query writer. Percentages can also take some time to compute, and it may not be the best use of your time to worry about percentages until after you have a working version of your query. For this reason, we again recommend that you not attempt to create percentages using the Workbook Wizard until you have become proficient in the use of Discoverer.

You have now completed step 7 of the Desktop Workbook Wizard. Click Next to move to step 8.

# Creating User-Defined Totals in the Plus Workbook Wizard

As shown earlier in Figure 5-9, the Plus Calculations tab has the standard buttons available throughout the wizard, with three additional default settings. These are

- **My Calculations** Displays a list of the calculations you have defined
- **My Percentages** Displays a list of the percentages you have defined
- **My Totals** Displays a list of the totals that you have defined

Thus, because we just completed adding our first calculations and percentages, there is no need to navigate away from the Calculations tab. We stay right here while we create totals.

## Totals: What Are They?

Discoverer Desktop defines a *total* as follows: "The result of a calculation that summarizes data in a sheet. Examples of totals are minimum, maximum, average, and sum." The definition within Plus states: "When working with numeric information, you often need to see various summations of the data. Totals can sum rows and columns of numbers, find averages and standard deviation, compute subtotals and grand totals, and so on. When you add a total to a worksheet, Discoverer automatically adds a column or row to the worksheet for the totals data."

If you read both definitions closely, there is a clue in the Plus definition that Oracle has enhanced the totaling capabilities of Discoverer in its web version. This is absolutely true, and Plus has more options for totaling than are available in the Windows version.

Calculating totals of numbers is again a typical data analysis task. Discoverer allows you to choose the data to use both for the total itself and for the value used to represent the total (grand total, subtotal, and so on). Don't worry about the terms used at this stage, as these will all be fully covered.

**NOTE**

*If in the previous step you created a percentage based on either a grand total or a subtotal, you would not want to create it again here. If you have decided not to create totals based on percentages, you now have the option of creating them in this step of the Workbook Wizard.*

Like percentages, totals are mathematical formulas that enable you to analyze your data more effectively. They apply standard mathematical algorithms to the item you have chosen. A simple example of a total in a query is "Show me the grand total of product ordered for the month of January 2010." A more complex total would be to see the same query extended to include subtotals for each change of product.

Figure 5-15 shows a simple total being applied in a query. You can see the total amount of product sold. Again, because the month is used to define only a condition, it has been moved to the page item.

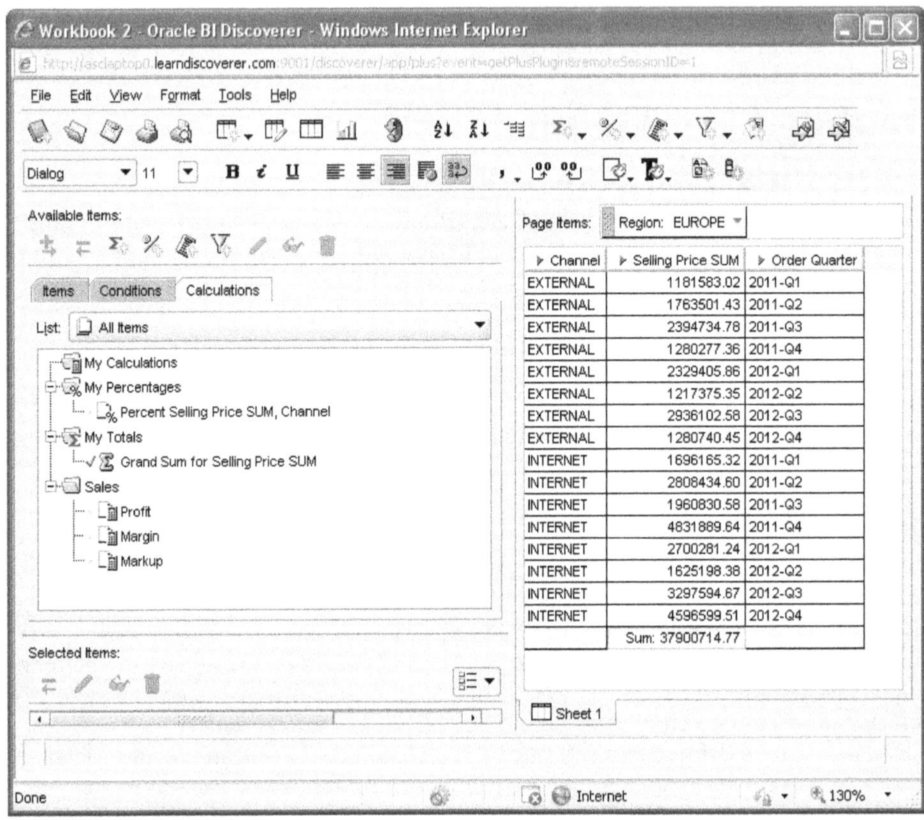


**FIGURE 5-15.** *Grand total of products for 2011 to 2012*

## Creating a New Total

Before you launch the New Total dialog box, you need to think about what item or items you want to use in your totals. Unlike calculations, there are no administrator-created totals for you to choose from. However, you can have totals that are based on percentages, but they cannot be edited as totals.

Because totals usually stand alone as data items, it doesn't really matter in which order you create them. Although you probably wouldn't have more than one or two in your query, there is no limit on the number of totals you can define.

When creating a new total, you should use the following workflow:

1. Launch the New Total dialog box (see Figure 5-16).

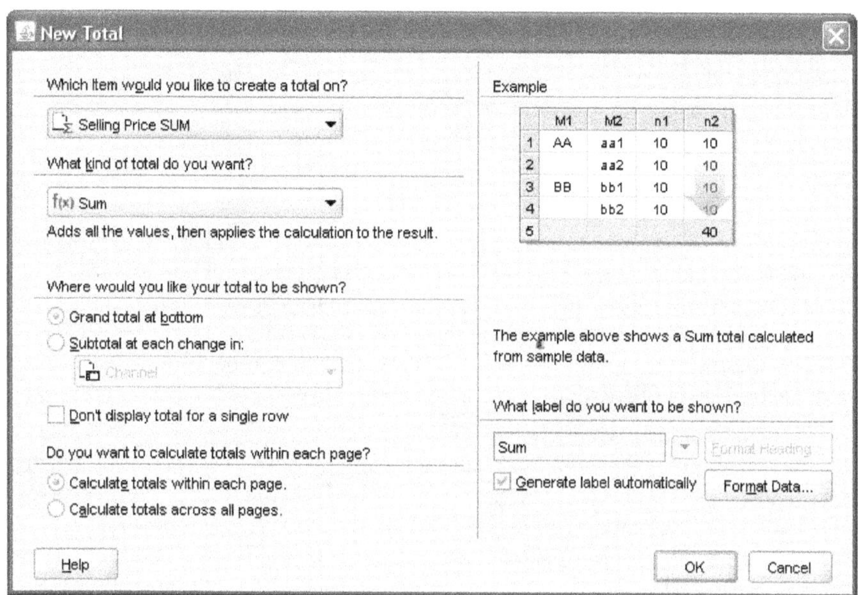


**FIGURE 5-16.** *The New Total dialog box*

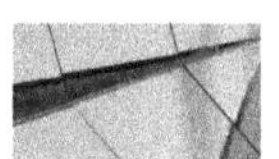

**NOTE**
*There are two ways to launch the New Total dialog box. The first way is to click New and then from the drop-down box select New Total. The second way is to right-click My Totals on the Calculations tab and from the pop-up box select New Total.*

2. The first thing to do is to choose which data point or points you want the total to be on. Click the drop-down button and from the list pick the item you want to use. You have the option of selecting a single item or all items. Unfortunately, there is no option to select combinations of items for totaling. To make Discoverer add a total for all items, from the drop-down box select the All Data Points item.
3. Choose the type of total you want to apply by clicking the drop-down button and selecting the total from the list. After you have selected the total, Discoverer inserts a brief description, in your language, of what that total will produce.
4. Choose whether you want to see a grand total of all values or subtotals, and then check the appropriate radio button. If you opt to create subtotals, you will also need to tell Discoverer which item it should use to create the subtotal. Discoverer will automatically create a group sort in Low to High order for the item being subtotaled.

**NOTE**
*If you start with a subtotal and then change your mind and alter it to being a grand total, whatever group sort was created for handling the subtotal will remain in place. If you do not want the group sort, you will need to navigate to the Sort window of the wizard to remove it.*

5. Choose whether to display totals for a single row. This is a very useful check box and one that we make extensive use of. We recommend you do likewise.
6. Next you need to determine whether you want Discoverer to calculate the totals only according to the values in the current page or across all pages. If you are not using page items or have only one page item, then the choice makes no difference. The only time you really need to decide is when page items are in use and you have multiple pages. We advise you to be careful when creating totals across multiple pages because it may not be evident to the casual observer that this is what you have done.
7. You next need to decide what label you want Discoverer to use for the total. You can allow Discoverer to insert a label automatically by checking the Generate Label Automatically box. Should you choose not to allow Discoverer to do this, uncheck this box and add your own label. You can either type the label yourself or select one of the predefined labels from the drop-down list provided (see the section "Labeling Percentages and Totals," later in this chapter). You can even use labels that combine your own label with a predefined label from the drop-down list.
8. Finally, click the Format Data button to set a format that is different from the normal data. We recommend you adopt the habit of applying different colors to totals because this draws the recipient's eyes to the subtotal or total.
9. Click OK to finish.

Unlike calculations, where Discoverer has to test the mathematical properties of the calculation, totals always work. There is no such thing as having defined an incorrect total, although the results you see onscreen may not be that obvious at first, especially if your totals are being computed across multiple pages! Assuming you have created a valid total, Discoverer inserts it under the My Totals heading. It also places a tick mark alongside the total to indicate that it is in use within the query. Totals are added and displayed in the order you create them.

Also at this point, you will notice that the Edit and Delete buttons are activated and Discoverer has inserted the formula for the total into the Description box. If you have made an error in your total, use the Edit button to reopen the Total dialog box and change it. If you decide you no longer need this total, click Delete, and it will be removed.

When you have completed adding totals to your query, either you can click Finish, which causes Discoverer to execute the query, or you can move on to the final step of the Workbook Wizard, parameters, by clicking Next three times.

## Labeling Percentages and Totals

In the preceding two sections of this chapter, for percentages and totals, we told you that Discoverer has a set of predefined label options that you can use to help you create your own labels. The three predefined labels that are available to you are

- **Insert Item Name** When you select this option, Discoverer inserts the name of the item on which you are subtotaling. If you are subtotaling by Sales Channel, for example, and the heading for the data item is Channel, then Discoverer will insert the word *Channel* into the label. However, if you select this label option when the item has only a grand total, Discoverer inserts the label *All Items*.
- **Insert Data Point Name** When you select this option, Discoverer inserts the column name of the sorted item into the label. If you are sorting on the Selling Price, for example, and the heading for the data item is Price, then Discoverer will insert the word *Price* into the label.
- **Insert Value** When you select this option, Discoverer inserts the actual value for the item on which you are subtotaling. If you are subtotaling by Sales Channel, for example, and you have two channels, EXTERNAL and INTERNAL, then Discoverer will insert the channel names into the appropriate subtotal. However, if you select this label option when the item has only a grand total, Discoverer inserts the label *All Values*.

**NOTE**
*The codes &Item, &Date, and &Value, corresponding to the labels in the preceding list, tell Discoverer to insert the item name, data point name, or value, respectively. These codes can either be selected from the drop-down list or be typed in. The format used always begins with the & character followed by a word, with the first letter of that word in uppercase.*

# Creating User-Defined Parameters in the Plus Workbook Wizard

Figure 5-17 shows the final step of the Discoverer Plus Workbook Wizard. This step in the Workbook Wizard has a dialog box containing the following two boxes and five buttons:

- **Available Parameters box** This box will be empty until you add a parameter. As you add parameters to your query, Discoverer will display them here in the order in which you create them.
- **Description box** This box shows the description of the parameter highlighted in the Available Parameters box.
- **New button** Click this to add a new parameter.
- **Edit button** When this is active, click it to edit an existing parameter.
- **Delete button** Click this to delete a parameter. As with conditions, again, be careful because it does just what it says and without prompting!
- **Move Up button** If you have multiple parameters, click this to promote the highlighted parameter. The order controls the sequence in which the parameters are prompted when the query is run.
- **Move Down button** If you have multiple parameters, click this to demote the highlighted parameter.

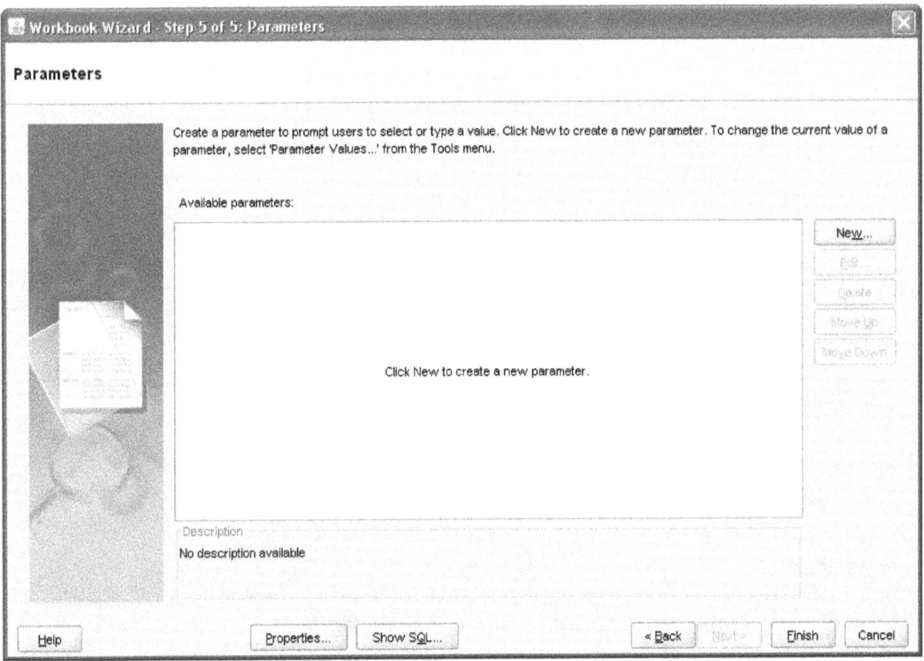


**FIGURE 5-17.** *Parameters step of the Plus Workbook Wizard*

# Parameters: What Are They?

Parameters offer choices each time the query runs. They are placeholders that accept dynamic input values either from the keyboard or from another workbook. Parameters are typically used in two situations.

- To provide input to a condition
- To provide input to a calculation

## Parameter Input to a Condition

This is the most usual usage for a parameter. In this usage, Discoverer will associate a parameter with a condition and then, when executed, pass the received dynamic value to the condition for filtering. Whenever you create a parameter that is to be associated with a condition and no such condition yet exists, Discoverer will also create the condition.

## Parameter Input to a Calculation

This is the more complex, yet probably the cleverer, usage for parameters. In this usage, Discoverer will not associate the parameter with a condition but will make the input that it receives available for use in calculations. For example, we could accept from the user an upper number and a lower number for use in a statistical calculation. We will cover this method of parameterization in Chapter 13 when we discuss advanced handling of parameters.

For the remainder of this section, we will be working with parameters that are associated with conditions.

As previously stated, whenever you create a parameter where no condition currently exists, Discoverer will create a condition and will link the parameter to that condition. Parameters are unlike regular conditions in that they allow you to use different criteria each time the query is run. For example, say you have created a query that shows total sales for the past seven years with a condition Year>=2005. Every time you run this query, you see all of the sales from 2005 until today. If you want to run the query for just the last five years, you would need to edit the condition and save the query. If you add a parameter to the condition, Year>=[Year Entered], you will be prompted before the query runs to add the value for the earliest year you want to see. This avoids the need to edit and resave the query.

Figure 5-18 shows the prompt you will see before the query runs.

As you can see, Discoverer displays a dialog box allowing you to enter the exact filter you want to apply to your query in terms of a certain condition. This capability allows the same query to be used by many people with different reporting needs.

## Differences Between Conditions and Parameters

One of the things that new Discoverer users find difficult to understand is the difference between a condition and a parameter and when to apply them. Both are filters, and both are used to constrain your query.

Conditions are fixed filters, and you will see the same results every time you run the query. The only way to change the output is to edit the query and change the condition. However, some users don't have the ability to edit queries because a constraint has been applied to their profiles by the Discoverer manager. This constraint is primarily used for new Discoverer end users who haven't yet taken training and learned how to edit correctly. Another reason all end users don't have editing rights is system integrity. You would not want to have a query you spent many hours creating edited by a novice end user and find that it no longer works.

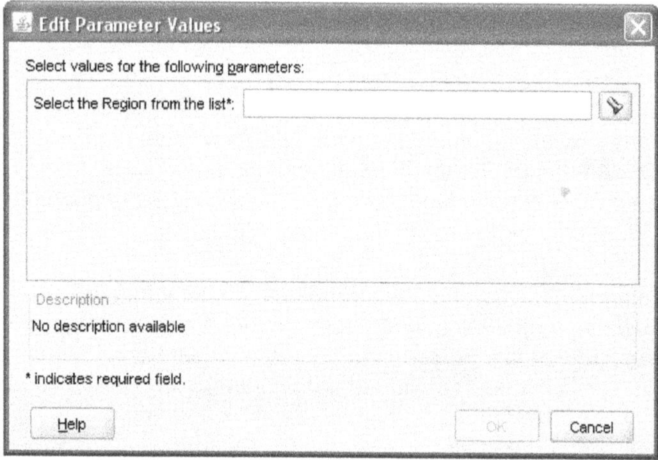


**FIGURE 5-18.** *Edit Parameter Values dialog box*

Parameters are variable filters, so you don't see the same results every time you run the query. A well-written parameterized query can satisfy dozens of different user requests without the need to edit the query or jeopardize its integrity. This is an excellent reason for having report writers. It allows queries to be built by them on behalf of your department. Other end users and report viewers can then be granted access rights to run the query. They would simply fill in the parameters that fit their needs without having to rebuild or create a new query. In other words, there is no need to reinvent the wheel. We have heard of Discoverer users who have, in extreme cases, used only 10 to 15 worksheets to satisfy requirements that at one point required more than 100 different worksheets, all by using effective parameters.

Another difference between conditions and parameters is that parameters help you open a workbook quickly to see only the data you need. Your day-to-day mission-critical queries need to be parameterized, allowing them to be used by many people time and time again. Conditions, being designed more for ad hoc analysis, are aimed at helping you find very specific data. For example, suppose you are puzzled because the sales from Europe for a particular product are lower than expected. You could not have anticipated this, and therefore you will not have a prewritten query. You will need to create an ad hoc query using conditions to isolate by both Europe and the product in question. This query will probably be used only once and will never need to be parameterized. Parameters and conditions can be mixed for creating more sophisticated filtering procedures.

The rule of thumb on parameters and conditions is that parameters should always be utilized in queries that are used more than once and by multiple users, whereas conditions should be created in queries that are more for analysis or ad hoc reporting needs.

## Creating a New Parameter

When you first enter this step of the wizard, the main box in the center of the screen will be empty (see Figure 5-19). You need to think about what item or items you want to use in your parameters. Unlike calculations, there are no administrator-created parameters for you to choose from.

It does not make any difference to Discoverer in what order you create your parameters. In fact, in most cases, it makes no difference in what order they are run. However, you will probably want to present them to the user in a logical sequence. This sequence could simply be alphabetical, or you may want to offer the parameters in their sort order. Whatever method you choose, you should always do it the same way—thus creating query standardization.

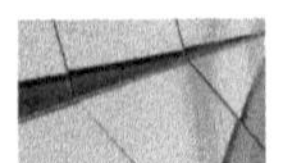

**NOTE**
*If you are using cascading parameters, where the input from one parameter is used to filter the available items in subsequent parameters, the order is important. We discuss cascading parameters in Chapter 13.*

If your company already has reporting standards, you should follow them. For example, if your company always prompts for a date before a customer, so should you. Similarly, if your company has standards for naming prompts, you should use these—thus making your queries look professional. The last thing you want to do is create a wonderful query that does not adhere to your company standards.

When creating a new parameter, you should use the following workflow:

1. Click New. This opens the New Parameter dialog box, as shown in Figure 5-19.

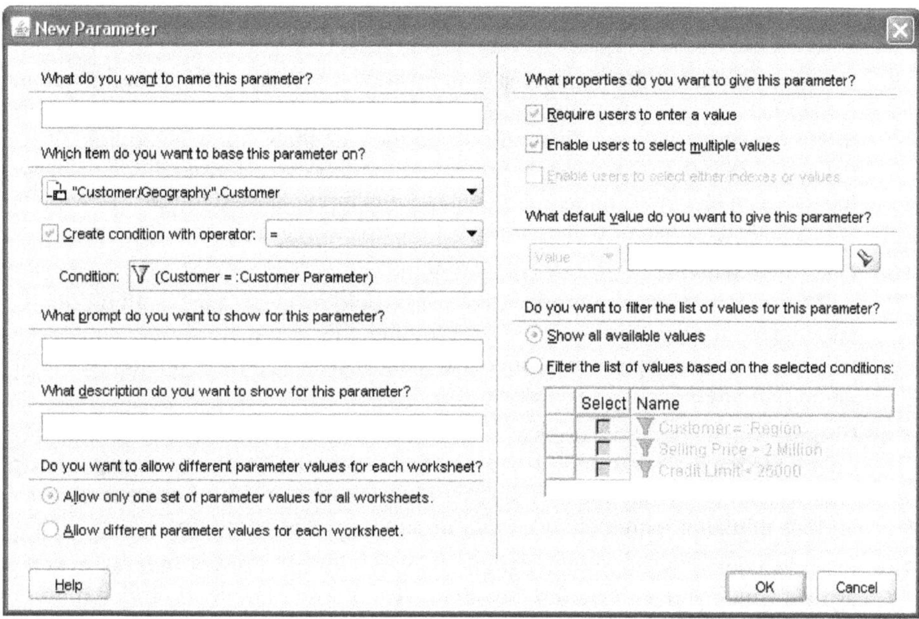


**FIGURE 5-19.** *New Parameter dialog box*

2. Give a name for your parameter. This is only an internal name used by the system; however, you should still give it a short, meaningful name. If you leave this blank, Discoverer will insert a name for you.
3. Click the Item drop-down box to see the list of available items, and select the data item you want to apply the parameter on from the list.
4. Determine whether you want this new parameter to be associated with a condition. If you do decide that this is what you want, Discoverer will create the condition for you at the same time that it creates the parameter.
5. If the parameter is being used in a condition, click the Operator drop-down box to see a list of the available operators. From this list you need to select one operator. You will notice that the Condition box has been updated to give you a visual interpretation of the condition that Discoverer will now create.
6. Enter the text you want to prompt the user with. For example, **Enter the year**. Leaving this blank causes Discoverer to generate a prompt for you.
7. Enter a description of the parameter that is easy to understand. Discoverer will display this to the user as context-sensitive help. Unlike in the previous steps, if you leave this blank, Discoverer will not create a description for you. The user will therefore get no context-sensitive help.
8. Next you need to determine whether you want Discoverer to use the same parameter value for all worksheets in the workbook or whether to allow users to key in a different

parameter value for each worksheet. We like the idea of restricting parameter values to all worksheets. This way, when a user navigates from worksheet to worksheet, Discoverer will automatically use the same parameter value, thus ensuring that the data is consistent.

9. Determine whether the parameter is mandatory. If you determine that the parameter is mandatory, at run time Discoverer will display an asterisk alongside the parameter prompt, even in Desktop. This indicates to the user that a value is required. If you determine that the parameter is optional, at run time no asterisk will be displayed, and the user can elect to run the query without any input. Should the user provide no input whatsoever, Discoverer will assume that the user wants to query *all* values.
10. Determine whether users can select multiple values. For example, if you check this box and the prompt was for a product, the user would be given a list of all products and allowed to check the ones they want. We think this is a really clever feature, as you will see later. Leaving this box unchecked allows users to enter single values only when prompted.
11. Choose whether to allow users to select either indexes or values. This box will be active only if the database has an index on the table and the Discoverer manager has created a cross-reference to that index in the properties of the item. This feature is new in 11.1.1.6, and we think it is extremely useful for improving system performance.
12. Provide a default value for the parameter or, if a list of values or indexes exist for the item against which you are creating the parameter, choose from the drop-down list of values. Discoverer does not require a default value to be entered.
13. Choose whether you want to employ cascading parameters. A cascading parameter is where the value from one parameter is taken to filter the list on subsequent parameters. For example, let's say we have two parameters: Region and District. If the user selects a region, we can use the region as a filter to the district. This restricts the District list of values to only those districts within the selected region. We will cover this usage of parameters in Chapter 13.
14. Click OK to finish.

Unlike calculations, where Discoverer has to test the mathematical properties of the calculation, parameters always work. There is no such thing as having defined an incorrect parameter, although the results you see onscreen may not be that obvious at first.

Assuming you have created a valid parameter, Discoverer inserts it into the box for parameters. If you checked the box to create a condition, Discoverer will insert a number alongside the parameter. Parameters are initially added into the box in the order you create them. If you go back to the second step of the wizard and click the Conditions tab, you will see that Discoverer has created a new condition. If the name that Discoverer has given this condition does not follow your naming convention, change it now.

Back in step 5 of the wizard, you will notice that the Edit and Delete buttons are activated, and Discoverer has inserted the description you created into the Description box. If you have made an error, use the Edit button to reopen the Parameter dialog box and change it. At this stage, you will no longer be allowed to change the operator being used for the condition. If you need to change this, you will have to edit the condition itself. If you did not create a condition, editing the parameter will not allow you to do this either. The only way to do this now is to create a new condition by going back to step 2 of the Workbook Wizard. If you decide you no longer need this parameter, click Delete and it will be removed.

## Rearranging the Parameter Order

Whenever you have two or more active parameters, you should look carefully at the list and determine whether the parameter sequence is logical. If you decide you have a parameter in the wrong place, you can use the Move Up and Move Down buttons to promote or demote items. These buttons become active only when you have created two or more active parameters. The sequence determines the order in which parameters are offered to the end user. If you are using cascading parameters, make sure you offer the unconstrained parameters first before you invite input to the filtered parameters. If you attempt to move the dependent parameter above the primary parameter, Discoverer will prompt you with a warning. However, it does not allow you to cancel the action, but we will tell you how to handle this warning in Chapter 13.

**NOTE**

*An active parameter is a parameter that either has been associated with a condition or is being used as input to a calculation. Only these parameters will be used as prompts.*

## Why Not Create Parameters in the Wizard?

Although parameters do not add an overhead to your query in the same way that calculations, sorting, totaling, and percentages do, we still recommend that, when working with new queries, you do not create them inside the Workbook Wizard. We do strongly recommend that you create conditions, which should suffice for getting the query up and running.

When you have a working copy of your query, you should concentrate on the conditions and look to see which ones can be parameterized. You are also in a better position to ascertain whether you need any new conditions and have the choice whether to do this as a parameter. Finally, taking the time in the Workbook Wizard to create parameters, when your query may not even work, can be very frustrating and time-consuming.

When you have completed adding parameters to your query, you have finished with the Workbook Wizard. Either you can click Finish, which causes Discoverer to run the query, or you can click Back to go back to validate previous steps.

# Editing the Sheet After the Query Has Run

Because we recommend that you use the Workbook Wizard only for the first four steps of a query, we need to show you how to reopen the Workbook Wizard after you have a working query.

In Desktop, from the menu, select Sheet | Edit Sheet or click the Edit Sheet icon on the toolbar. This opens a multi-tabbed form in Desktop and a sidebar in Plus with one step of the Workbook Wizard per tab/selection. In Plus, the form has a slightly different layout. The Plus form is shown in Figure 5-20.

**NOTE**

*Throughout the rest of the book we will refer often to the Edit Sheet dialog box in Desktop and the Edit Worksheet dialog box in Plus. These two dialog boxes function in almost identical ways. For the sake of simplicity, when we refer to these two dialog boxes, we will call them the Edit Sheet/Worksheet dialog box.*

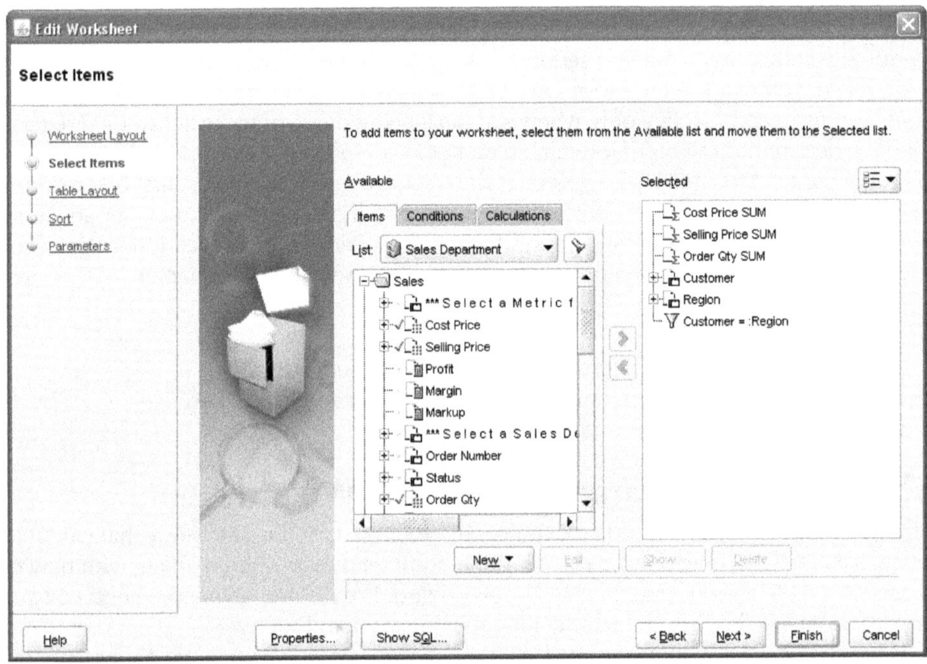


**FIGURE 5-20.** *The Plus Edit Worksheet dialog box*

The forms in both Desktop and Plus function in the exact manner of their respective Workbook Wizards, but you do not have the Back and Next buttons. You can click randomly from tab to tab or sidebar selection, adding the criteria you want to your query. When you are done adding criteria, click OK, and your query will run with the changes you have made.

In addition to the Edit Sheet/Worksheet dialog box, each of the forms from the Workbook Wizard can be accessed directly from the menu bar. In both versions of Discoverer, the Tools menu option gives you a drop-down list of available forms. In addition, Desktop offers an analysis bar, while Plus has an analysis area on the toolbar containing buttons to access the tools. For more detail on the analysis bar and the analysis area, see Chapter 9. For more instruction on using all of the tools offered in the Workbook Wizard, see Chapters 10, 11, and 12.

In Plus you have more options for making changes after the query has run. You can reopen the wizard using the Edit menu. Here you can choose which of the tabs/sidebar selections on the wizard to open. After it is open, you can make changes to any of the available options. You can also open the Edit Worksheet dialog box by clicking the Edit Worksheet button on the toolbar. The Edit Worksheet dialog box functions just like the wizard. You can also edit the query directly from the Plus window. The panes to the left allow you to add or delete items on the fly or modify calculations and conditions.

## The Available Items Pane

The top pane is the Available Items pane. It contains many features of the Workbook Wizard. At the top is a toolbar with tools to help you edit your query. Next is a list box with business areas available to you as well as the search button. The box at the bottom of the Available Items pane contains the actual folders from the business area you selected. There are also two other tabs, Conditions and Calculations. All of these items are used in the same way as in the Workbook Wizard. In the illustration at right, you can see the features of the Available Items pane.

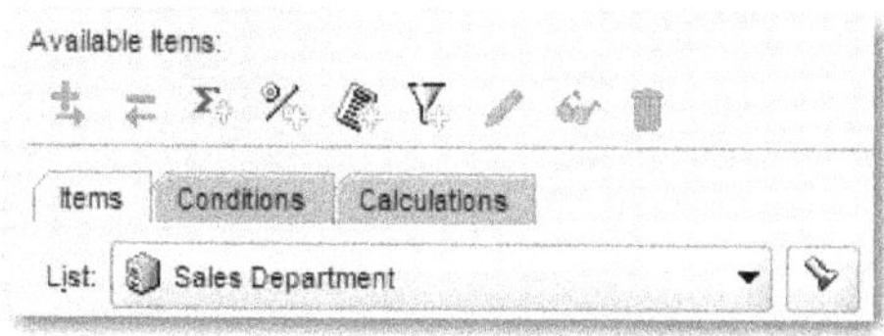


### The Available Items Toolbar

The toolbar contains the following buttons:

- **Add to Worksheet** Use this button to move a selected item to the worksheet.
- **Remove from Worksheet** Use this button to remove a selected item from the worksheet. If the item is a total, percentage, calculation, or condition, the item's definition will remain; however, the item will no longer be used within the worksheet. If you look in the Available Items pane, these items will be unchecked.
- **New Total** Use this button to open the New Total dialog box.
- **New Percentage** Use this button to open the New Percentage dialog box.
- **New Calculation** Use this button to open the New Calculation dialog box.
- **New Condition** Use this button to open the New Condition dialog box.
- **Edit** Use this button to open the edit dialog box associated with the selected total, percentage, calculation, or condition.
- **Show** Use this button to display the Show Condition (see Figure 5-21) dialog box. This box displays information about the selected administrator-created calculation. Because the information being displayed is for information purposes only, all of the features of the box are grayed out. Clicking OK or Cancel removes the box.
- **Delete** Use this button to delete the selected total, percentage, calculation, or condition. There is no dialog box associated with this button. Clicking it deletes the item without warning. If you delete an item by mistake, before making any other change, you need to immediately select Undo Edit Sheet from the Edit menu.

**NOTE**

*You can use the Add to Worksheet and Remove from Worksheet buttons to move items in and out of your query, or you can simply drag and drop. You can even right-click an item and, from the drop-down, select Add To Worksheet or Remove From Worksheet.*

### The Selected Items Pane

The bottom pane is the Selected Items pane. It contains the items you selected for use in your query. At the top is a toolbar with tools to help you edit your query. Below this is a list box showing all of the items in use in the worksheet. To the right of the toolbar is a Views button that allows you to switch the display to either show folders or hide folders. The following two

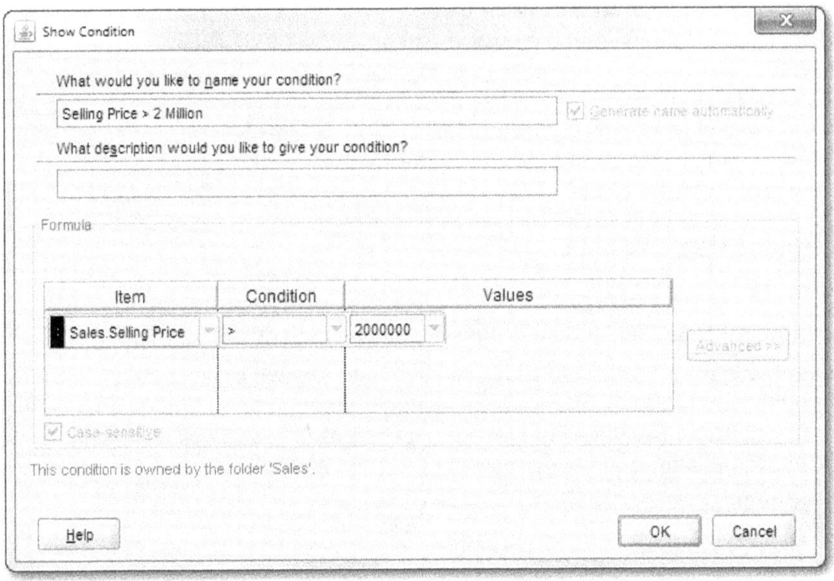


**FIGURE 5-21.** *The Show Condition dialog box*

illustrations show the Selected Items pane first with the folders hidden and then with the folders visible:

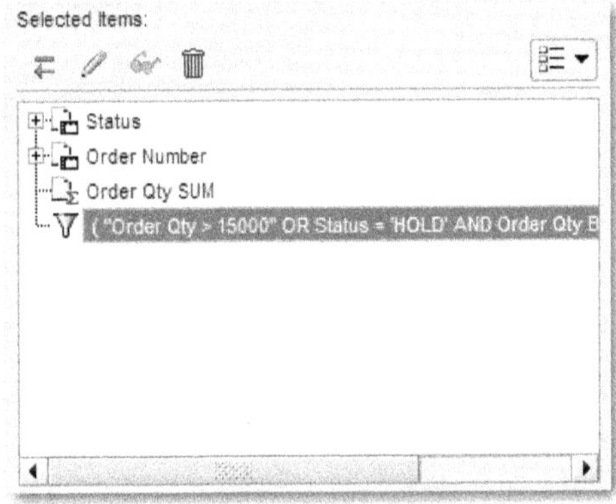


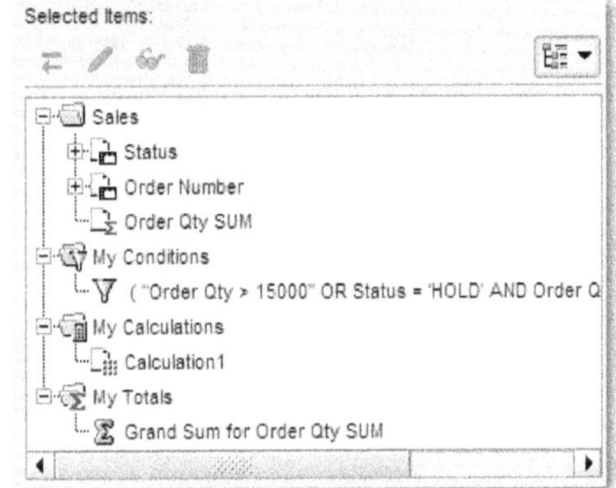


As we refer to the Edit Worksheet dialog box, you will see that the Available Items pane and the Selected Items pane share the same features. Use the panes as often as possible to save time. These are effective tools and will simplify the editing process.

### The Selected Items Toolbar

The toolbar contains the following buttons:

- **Remove From Worksheet** Use this button to remove a selected item from the worksheet. If the item is a total, percentage, calculation, or condition, the item's definition will remain; however, the item will no longer be used within the worksheet. If you look in the Available Items pane, these items will be unchecked.
- **Edit** Use this button to open the edit dialog box associated with the selected total, percentage, calculation, or condition.
- **Show** Use this button to display the Show Condition (see Figure 5-21) dialog box. This box displays information about the selected administrator-created calculation. Because the information being displayed is for information purposes only, all of the features of the box are grayed out. Clicking OK or Cancel removes the box.
- **Delete** Use this button to delete the selected total, percentage, calculation, or condition. There is no dialog box associated with this button. Clicking it deletes the item without warning. If you delete an item by mistake, before making any other change, you need to immediately select Undo Edit Sheet from the Edit menu.

## Summary

In this chapter, you learned the optional steps of the Workbook Wizard as well as how to reopen the Workbook Wizard with the Edit Sheet and Edit Worksheet forms. We defined sorts, calculations, percentages, totals, and parameters and how they can be used in a query. You also saw the steps used to add these functions to a query.

In each section we explained why it is recommended to complete the first four essential steps and run your query prior to adding sorts, calculations, percentages, totals, and parameters.

These topics and those in Chapter 4 defined the Workbook Wizard steps and gave an overview of each function. This will get you started creating simple queries. More in-depth examples will be given and skills taught in Chapters 11 and 12.

# PART II

# Editing the Query

# CHAPTER 6

# Formatting the Output in Discoverer Desktop and Plus

As we have already explained, Discoverer can be used to produce both ad hoc queries, which answer a specific one-off question, and queries that will be used by multiple users. Both can remain as queries, but as soon as you decide that the output needs to be viewed by somebody else, it becomes a report. This is especially true if you are planning on giving the results to senior management.

When you have a fully working query of this type, it needs to be formatted. Put in its simplest form, formatting is the shape, size, typeface, and general appearance of a document. Formatting is an important step in turning your query into an easy-to-read, attractive, and well-organized report. This is true whether or not you intend the output to be viewed onscreen, printed, or exported. The latter two possibilities will be dealt with in Chapter 8.

In this chapter, you will learn how to rename and reposition column headings in order to fit your needs. You will be shown how to rearrange the order and position of the output.

Another way to use formatting to improve a query is to change fonts and font sizes, font and background colors, and text justification. This chapter will show you in detail how to perform these functions. You will also be taught how to format numbers as currency, with commas, and with the correct number of decimal places.

You will be taught to add titles to your query and how to format them with fonts, sizes, and colors, as well as how to add bitmaps to the title. Finally, you will be shown how to add graphics to the background of a query to add interest and flair.

**NOTE**

*If you use an older release of Plus, you might be frustrated with the limitations in formatting. These limitations were nearly all eliminated with release 9.0.4 (10g release 1), and with 10.1.2 the formatting issues are gone. Now that the 10.1.2 release and higher use the table/crosstab BI Beans, it is possible to do in-context formatting. Discoverer Plus OLAP goes one step further and allows users to also perform individual cell-level formatting.*

# Giving Your Headings Meaningful Names (Desktop and Plus)

As discussed in Chapter 2, your Discoverer administrator can give items in business areas meaningful names. However, one business area could be used by a variety of departments, and what is meaningful to one department might not be to you.

Throughout the book, whenever you have had an opportunity to create new items, such as calculations, percentages, parameters, and totals, we recommend giving these meaningful names as well. Even though in many cases Discoverer will insert a name for you, this is not a good habit. What is meaningful and obvious to Discoverer, and even to you at the time, may not be so obvious to you later. Therefore, as soon as you have a working query, the first thing you should do is look at the column names and decide whether they are meaningful. If they are not, you need to change them.

Discoverer adds the word *SUM*, *AVG*, or the like to each numeric heading. While this may be okay for an ad hoc query, you should change this on your report by removing it from each heading. You must change each heading individually.

As you change column names, Discoverer resizes the width of the column to match the name, even if that means you won't be able to see all of your data. If Discoverer has resized the column to be too small, see the "Resizing" section later in this chapter to correct it.

**NOTE**
*You cannot rename columns in Viewer.*

## How to Rename Columns in Desktop

To change the name of a column, use the following workflow:

1. Place your cursor on the column heading.
2. Right-click. This displays the following pop-up list of options:

3. Select Item Properties. This displays the following Item Properties dialog box:

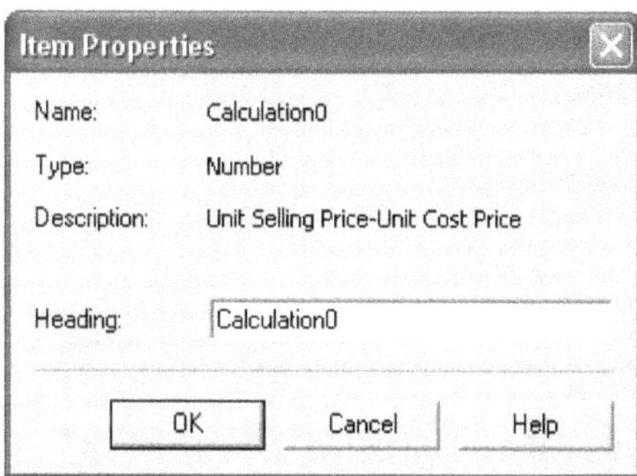


4. Change the heading name in the ItemProperties dialog box.
5. Click OK or press ENTER to finish.

## How to Rename Columns in Plus

To change the name of a column, use the following workflow:

1. Place your cursor on the column heading.
2. Right-click. This displays the following pop-up list of options:

3. Select Edit Heading. This displays the following dialog box:

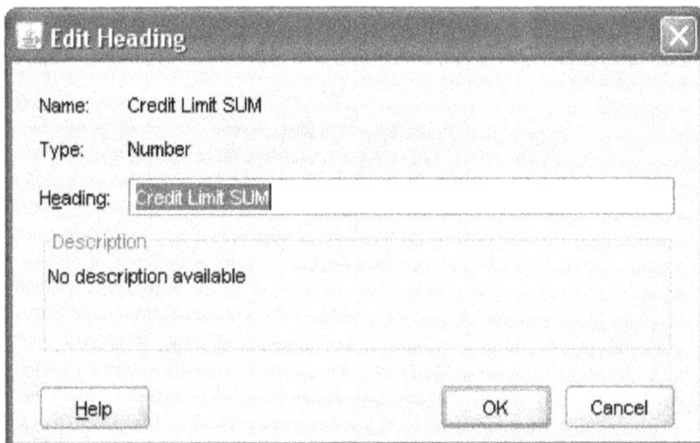


4. Change the heading name in the Edit Heading dialog box.
5. Click OK or press ENTER to finish.

# Rearranging the Order of the Output

After you have renamed your columns, the next step is to make sure the columns are really in the order you want them. When you were in the Workbook Wizard, you arranged the order of the columns. After running the query, you may find that the order just does not look right, and you can see how rearranging them will make your report easier to read.

## How to Rearrange Columns

There are two ways to rearrange columns in Desktop and three ways in Plus, and you can rearrange them in the worksheet or in the Edit Sheet/Worksheet dialog box. We will show you all the methods, but we always suggest you use the simplest. For rearranging single columns, we recommended using the worksheet. When rearranging multiple columns, you can use either method. If you are certain of the order you desire, do it in the worksheet. If you are not sure how you want the columns arranged, use the Edit Sheet/Worksheet dialog box. This option allows you to "sample" an arrangement; however, you can click Cancel if you want to return the order to its original configuration.

### Moving a Single Column in Desktop and Plus Using Drag and Drop

To move a single column using drag and drop, use the following workflow:

1. Click and hold on the column heading you want to move.
2. Drag the column heading to the desired location and then release the mouse button.

Figure 6-1 shows a column being moved to the left. In Desktop the mouse pointer changes to a double-headed arrow. In Plus the mouse pointer changes to a hand.

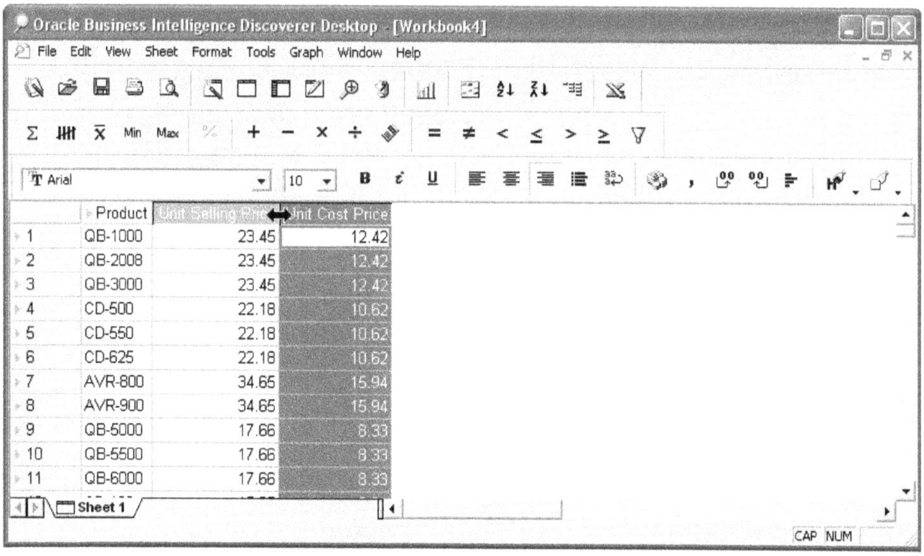

**FIGURE 6-1.** *Moving a column using drag and drop*

## Moving a Single Column in Plus from a Drop-Down List

To move a single column in Plus from a drop-down list, use the following workflow:

1. Click the column heading you want to move.
2. Right-click and from the following drop-down list select Move To.

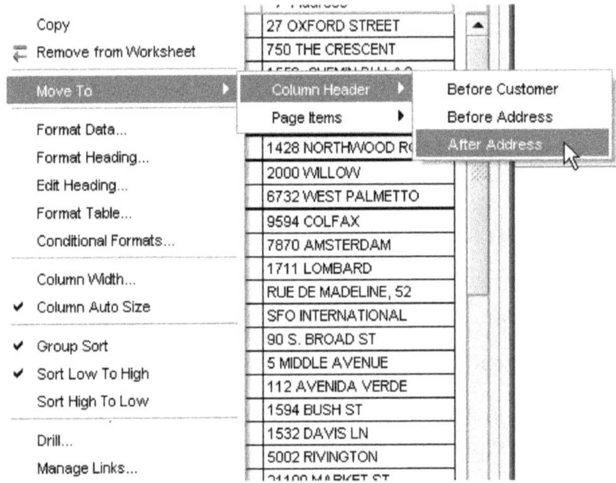


3. Select Column Header to move the column before or after another column, or select Page Items to move the column to the page items.

## Moving Multiple Columns

To move multiple columns, or to "sample" a configuration, use the following workflow:

1. From the menu bar, in Desktop select Sheet | Edit Sheet, or in Plus select Edit | worksheet; or from the toolbar in Desktop or Plus, click the Edit Sheet/Worksheet icon—either of these methods displays the Edit Sheet/Worksheet dialog box (Figure 5-20 in the preceding chapter).
2. Click the Table/Crosstab Layout tab. Drag and drop the columns into their desired locations, as seen on the next page.
3. Click OK or press ENTER to finish.

**NOTE**
*If you have started to reorder the columns and want to abort the changes you have made, do not click OK or press ENTER. Click Cancel to have Discoverer abandon all column moves and reinstate the ordering as it was before you started.*

We don't recommend using this method for moving a single column because it involves unnecessary keystrokes.

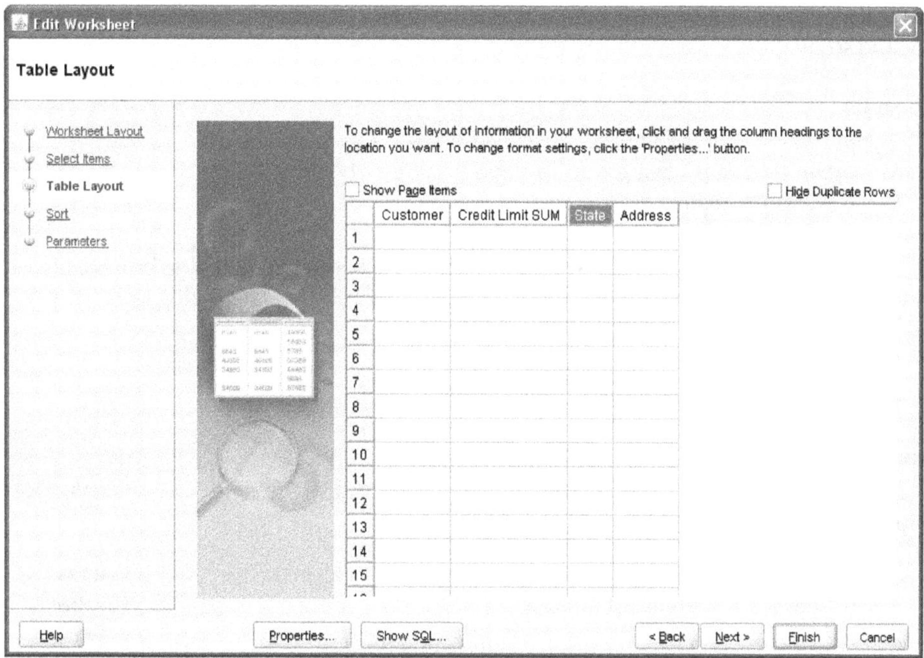


# Formatting Data

After you have changed your column names, you should look at the data items in each column and decide whether they need formatting. Discoverer recognizes three types of data— text, dates, and numbers—and each can be formatted in a variety of ways.

## Formatting Tools

Discoverer provides tools on the toolbar for formatting data. These buttons perform many of the standard formatting functions. We will explain what each button does later in the appropriate section of this chapter.

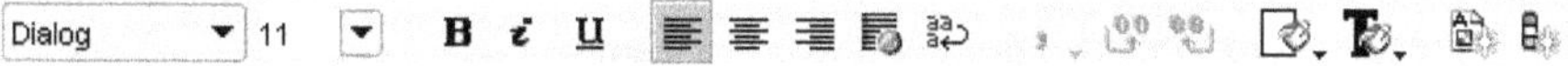


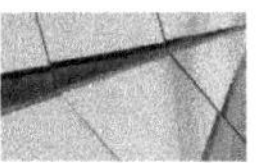

**NOTE**

*If you cannot see the formatting bar in Desktop, click View | Formatting Bar to make it appear. In Plus, click View | Toolbars and then click Formatting Bar.*

## Format Data Dialog Box

Discoverer provides a Format Data dialog box in Desktop that has three tabs, one each for formatting fonts, setting the alignment, and changing the background color. In Plus the tabs for formatting font alignment and background color have been consolidated into one Format tab. There is one additional tab that changes depending on the type of data in the column. For example, a column for text will have a Text tab, while a column for numbers will have a Number tab, and so on.

**NOTE**
*In Plus, there is one additional tab, called Breaks. This tab is for formatting the breaks in a group sort and was described in Chapter 5 in the section "Creating a New Sort."*

Many of the functions that are available within the Format Data dialog box are also available on the formatting bar. There are two ways to access the Format Data dialog box.

- From a pop-up list
- From the menu bar

## From a Pop-up List

To access the Format Data dialog box from a pop-up list, use the following workflow:

1. Right-click anywhere in the column you want to format. This displays a pop-up list of options.
2. Select Format Data. This displays the dialog box.

**NOTE**
*To apply the same format to multiple columns, hold down the* CTRL *key and select the columns you require. If you select columns of different types, only the Font, Alignment, and Background Color tabs will be available. Selecting multiple columns of the same data type with the same formatting characteristics causes all tabs to be active.*

## From the Menu Bar

To access the Format Data dialog box from the menu bar, use the following workflow:

1. Click anywhere in the column you want to format.
2. From the menu bar, select Format | Data, as shown in this illustration.
3. Discoverer opens the Format Data dialog box.

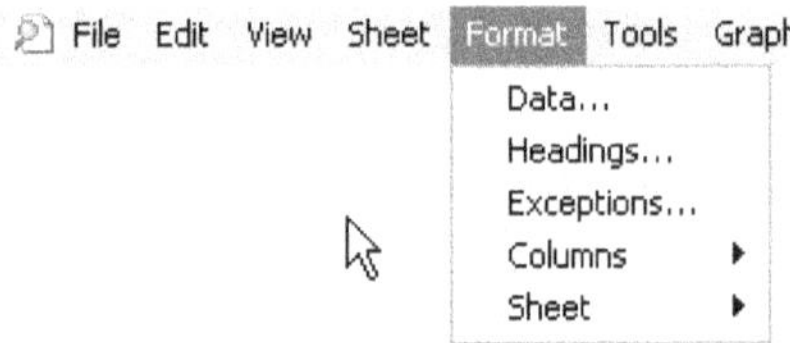

## The Format Data Dialog Box

As you can see in the next illustration, there are four tabs to the Desktop dialog box. These are

- **Font** Select this tab to change the font, style, size, color, and effect.
- **Alignment** Select this tab to change the horizontal and vertical alignment.
- **Background Color** Select this tab to change the background color of your data.
- **Date, Text, or Number** Select this tab to set specific formatting requirements for the data type of the column. The heading will change according to the data type.

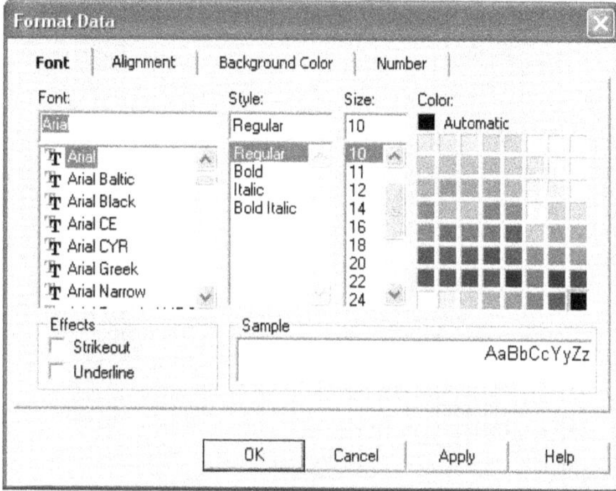


In Plus the first three tabs have been consolidated into the Format tab shown here.

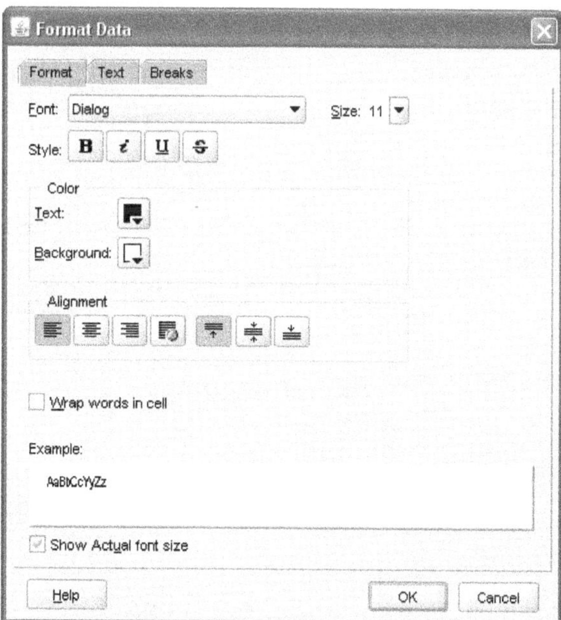

### The Font Tab (Part of the Format Tab in Plus)

Clicking the Font tab displays the Font dialog box, as shown here:

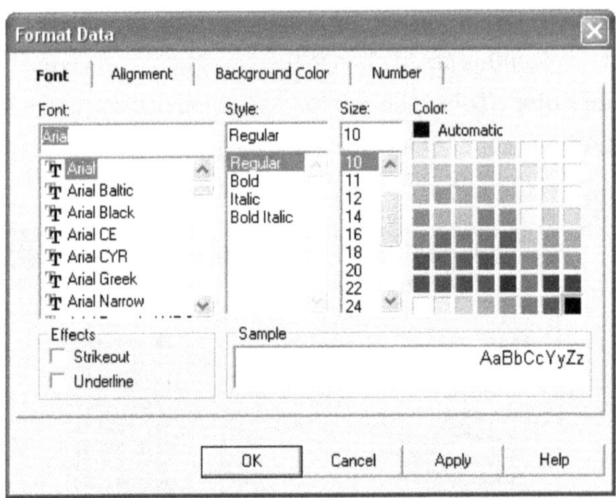


- **Font** Select the font you require from the list provided.
- **Style** Select Regular, Bold, Italic, or Bold Italic.
- **Size** Select the font size you require.
- **Color** Select the foreground color for the data.
- **Effects** Select Strikeout or Underline.
- **Sample** This shows you how your selections will look. As you move from tab to tab, this will show whatever effect you have applied so far.

If you have no more formatting to do, click OK. This will apply your changes to the data and close the dialog box. If you have more formatting to do, click one of the other tab headings and proceed.

Apart from the strikeout effect, all of the preceding font characteristics can also be applied directly from the formatting bar.

The formatting bar has several buttons that provide shortcuts to the most popular formatting functions, as shown here:

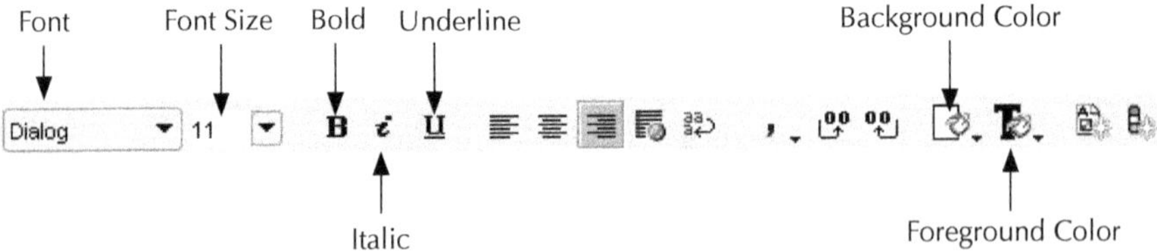


- **Font** Select the font you require from the list provided.
- **Font Size** Select the font size you require.
- **Bold** Click this button to display your data in bold.

- **Italic** Click this button to display your data in italics.
- **Underline** Click this button to display your data underlined.
- **Foreground Color** Click this button to change the foreground color.
- **Background Color** Click this button to change the background color.

### The Alignment Tab (Part of the Format Tab in Plus)

Clicking the Alignment tab displays the Alignment dialog box.

- **Horizontal** Select Left, Center, or Right alignment, and also choose whether to allow your data to wrap within the column.
- **Vertical** Select whether to display the data in the top, center, or bottom of the cell.
- **Sample** This shows you how your selections will look.

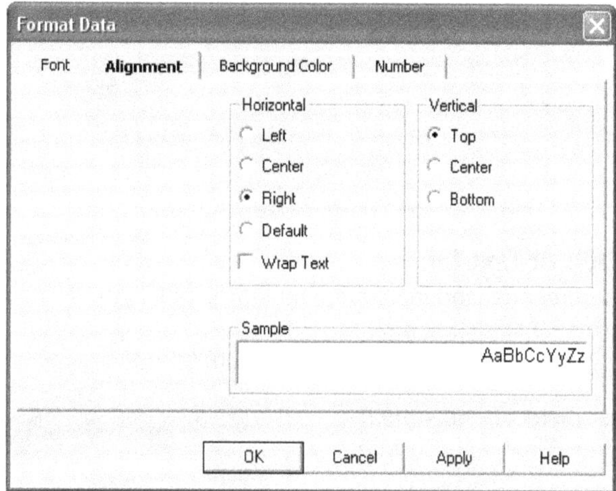


Only the following horizontal alignment characteristics can be applied directly from the formatting bar:

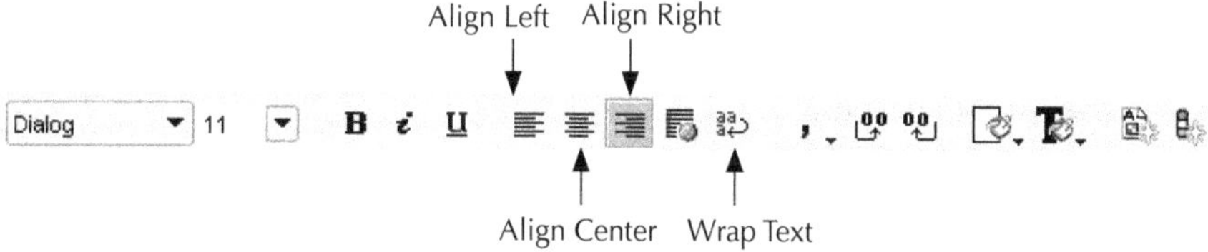


- **Align Left** Click this button to align the data to the left.
- **Align Center** Click this button to align the data to the center.
- **Align Right** Click this button to align the data to the right.
- **Wrap Text** Click this button to wrap the text in the column. You cannot wrap text in the headings, and text will wrap only when there is a space in the data.

### The Background Color Tab

Clicking the Background tab displays the Background Color dialog box.

- **Background Color** Select the color you want for the background. Check No Fill to display no background color.
- **Sample** This shows you how your selections will look.

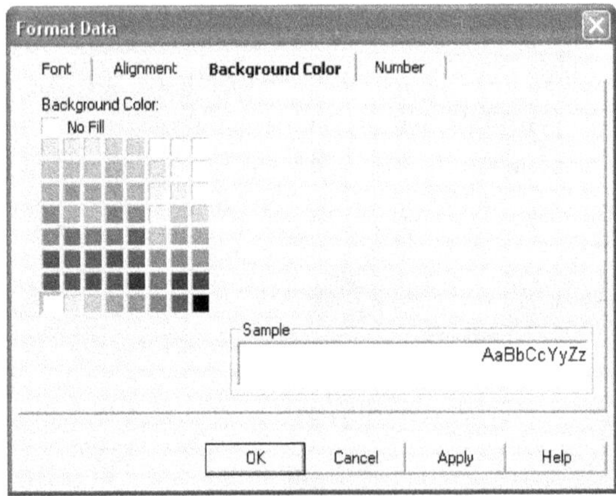


### The Date, Number, or Text Tab

We often use dates in reports, and there are a multitude of ways to format them. Clicking the Date tab displays the Format Date dialog box.

The Date tab gives you five controls to choose from.

- **Categories** Select from None, Default, Date, Time, and Custom.
- **Type** This selection list appears if you have selected a category other than None or Default. It is a list of all types available. If you are working with the category Custom, an edit box will open allowing you to create custom types.
- **Add** This button is displayed when you select the category Custom. If you have created a custom type, click this button to add it to the list.
- **Delete** This button will remove a custom type.
- **Sample** This shows you how your selection or custom type will look.

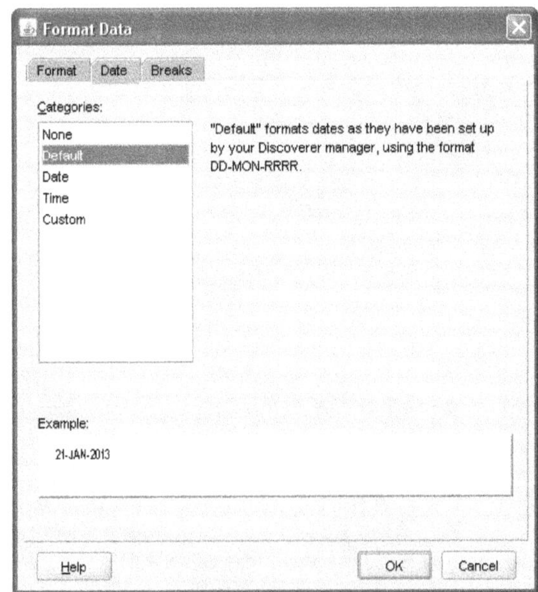

**None** This displays the date in the format exactly as it is stored in the database. If you are unsure what the format is for your database, click Custom. The top item on the custom list is the date format used on your database.

**Default** This is the default selection and displays dates using the format mask set up by your Discoverer administrator. The most common format mask in use within Oracle is DD-MON-YYYY, which would display March 4, 2012, as 04-MAR-2012. If you are unsure what format has been set by your Discoverer administrator, click Custom. The second item on the custom list is the date format specified by your Discoverer administrator and is labeled Default.

**Date/Time/Custom** The Date selection gives you a list of the most common date formats available. Discoverer displays the list using the actual format as it would appear in your query.

The Time selection gives you a list of the most common time formats available. Discoverer displays the list using the actual format as it would appear in your query.

The Custom selection gives you an opportunity to create a customized date and/or time. Discoverer lists the most common types, this time using standard masks. For example, instead of showing a format of 04-Mar-2012, the mask would display as DD-Mon-YYYY.

When you view the custom list, the top two items on the list are given the names None and Default. None means that no special date format was set by your Discoverer administrator and that the format used by the database is being applied. Default means that a special date format was set by your Discoverer administrator.

The following table displays the relationships between the formatted dates and times and their format masks:

| Date | Time | Custom Mask |
|---|---|---|
| 03/04 | | MM/DD |
| 03/04/12 | | MM/DD/YY |
| 03/04/2012 | | MM/DD/YYYY |
| 03-04 | | MM-DD |
| 03-04-12 | | MM-DD-YY |
| 03-04-2012 | | MM-DD-YYYY |
| 04-Mar | | DD-Mon |
| 04-Mar-12 | | DD-Mon-YY |
| 04-Mar-2012 | | DD-Mon-YYYY |
| 04 March 2012 | | DD fmMonth YYYY |
| March 4, 2012 | | fmMonth DD, YYYY |
| Monday, March 04,2012 | | fmDay, fmMonth DD, YYYY |
| 04-Mar-12 12:15 PM | 04-Mar-12 12:15 PM | DD-Mon-YY HH:MI AM |
| 04-Mar-12 12:15:30 | 04-Mar-12 12:15:30 | DD-Mon-YY HH24:MI:SS |
| | 12:15 | HH:MM |
| | 12:15 PM | HH:MM AM |

| Date | Time | Custom Mask |
|---|---|---|
| 12:15:30 | HH:MM:SS | |
| 12:15:30 PM | HH:MM:SS AM | |
| 12:15 | HH24:MM | |
| 12:15:30 | HH24:MM:SS | |

In this table, you see various format masks. By combining uppercase and lowercase characters, you can create additional masks.

For example, the table includes a mask for DD-Mon-YYYY that would display October 14, 1958, as 14-Oct-1958. If you wanted to display this date as 14-OCT-1958, you would simply create a new type using the mask DD-MON-YYYY.

For a full list of all date and time format masks, please see Appendix B.

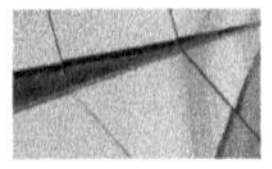

**NOTE**
*If you are not sure about the relationship between dates, times, and their format masks, select a date or time from the date or time list. You can see its mask by clicking Custom. This can be very helpful when creating complex calculations that use date functions.*

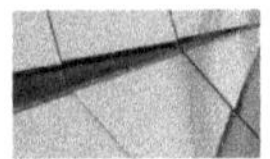

**NOTE**
*No date formatting features are available from the formatting bar.*

**Adding a New Date or Time Mask** To add a new date or time format to the list available, you must follow this workflow:

1. Open or create a query containing a date.
2. Place your cursor in any column containing a date.
3. Right-click. This displays a pop-up list of options.
4. Select Format Data. This opens the Format Data dialog box.
5. Select the Date tab.
6. Select the Custom category.
7. In the Type box, enter the mask for the format you require. As you type, Discoverer will convert that mask into a date or time and display this in the Sample box. See Appendix A for a list of available masks.
8. When you have entered the new type, click Add. The new type will be added to the bottom of the list.
9. If you want the new format to be applied to the column, click OK or Apply. If you want to only create the new format but do not want to use it, click Cancel.

### The Number Tab

By default, Discoverer formats numbers with no decimal places, no comma separator, and negative numbers displayed using a minus sign in front of the number—for example, –1234.

The Number tab is quite a busy little box and changes depending upon the category you choose. It has three areas that are common to all of the number categories: a list of categories, a check box for showing graphic bars, and a Sample window.

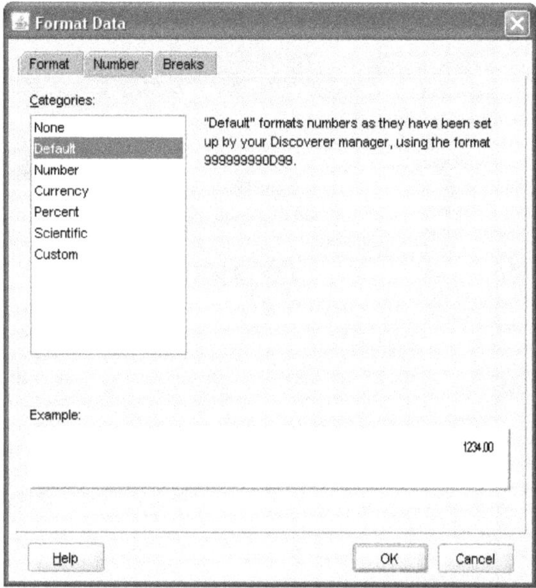


- **Categories** This is always present. Select from None, Default, Number, Currency, Percent, Scientific, and Custom.
- **Show Graphic Bars** In Desktop, check this to add a graphic bar indicating the size of your numbers in relation to each other. This is not available in Plus.
- **Example** This is always present. This shows you how your selection or custom type will look.
- **Description** This is displayed only for None and Default. This area displays a brief description of the current setting.

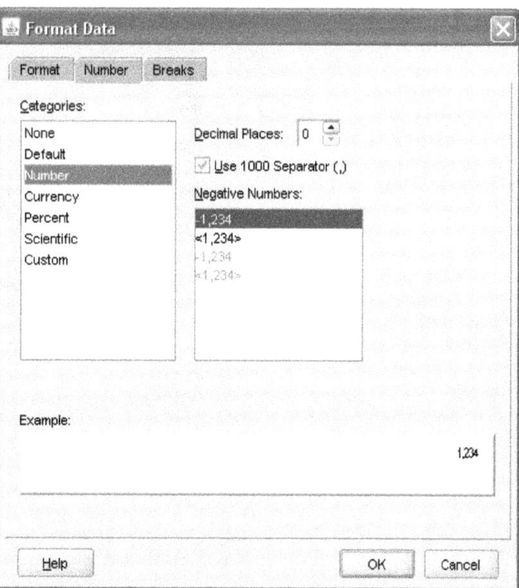


The categories Number, Percent, and Scientific, in addition to the areas we've just detailed, contain three additional areas.

- **Decimal Places** Increase or decrease the number of decimal places to display.
- **Use 1000 Separator** Check this to display a comma separator in large numbers. It is not available for percentages or scientific.

- **Negative Numbers** Choose from the list how you want Discoverer to display negative numbers. It is not available for scientific numbers.

As shown next, the Currency category has a drop-down for determining whether to use a currency symbol. Use the Display Symbol drop-down to select from a list of available currencies.

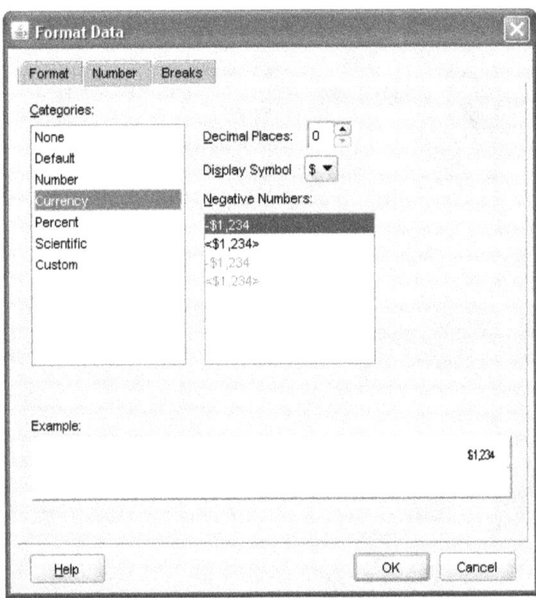


The final number category is for adding custom number formats, as shown here:

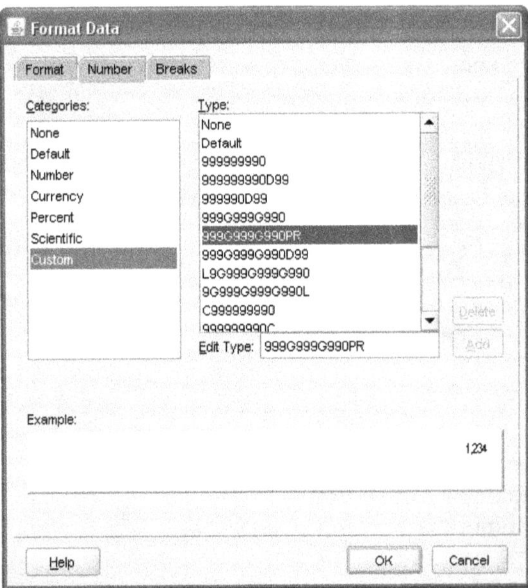

- **Type** This selection list appears if you have selected the category of Custom. It is a list of all types available. An edit box will allow you to create custom types.
- **Add** This button is displayed when you select the category Custom. If you have created a custom type, click this button to add it to the list.
- **Delete** This button will remove a custom type.

The following table displays the standard number formats and how they will appear onscreen:

| Format Mask | Will Display 1234 As |
|---|---|
| 999999990 | 1234 |
| 999999990D99 | 1234.00 |
| 999990D99 | 1234.00 |
| 999G990 | 1,234 |
| 999G990PR | 1,234 |
| 999G9990D99 | 1,234.00 |
| 9990V99 | 123400 |
| 9.99EEEE | 1.23E+03 |
| HH:MI:SS | 20:34 (20 minutes 34 seconds) |
| 0HH:MI:SS | 00:20:34 |
| 9EEEE | 1E+03 |
| 9D99EEEE | 1.23E+03 |
| 99G999G990D99 | 1,234.00 |
| 99999999990 | 1234 |
| 99G999G999G990 | 1,234 |

For a full list of all number format masks, please see Appendix B.

The following illustration shows the numeric buttons of the Desktop formatting bar:

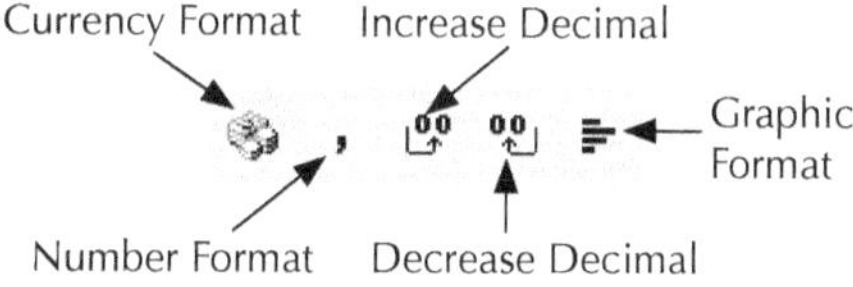


- **Currency Format** Click this to apply standard currency formatting that places a dollar sign, two decimal places, and comma separators.
- **Number Format** Click this to apply standard number formatting, that is, two decimal places and no comma separators. In Plus, the Currency Format and Number Format options appear together on a drop-down list.
- **Increase Decimal** Click this to add one decimal place to your number.
- **Decrease Decimal** Click this to remove one decimal place from your number.
- **Graphic Format** This is not available in Plus; in Desktop, click this to display a graphic bar.

**Adding a New Number Mask** To add a new number format to the list available, you must follow this workflow:

1. Open or create a query containing a number.
2. Place your cursor in any column containing a number.
3. Right-click. This displays a pop-up list of options.
4. Select Format Data. This opens the Format Data dialog box.
5. Select the Number tab.
6. Select the Custom category.
7. In the Type box, enter the mask for the format you require. See Appendix A for a list of available masks.
8. When you have entered the new type, click Add. The new type will be added to the bottom of the list and an example displayed in the Sample box.
9. If you want the new format to be applied to the column, click OK or Apply. If you want to only create the new format but do not want to use it, click Cancel.

### The Text Tab

Clicking the Text tab opens the Text dialog box, as shown here:

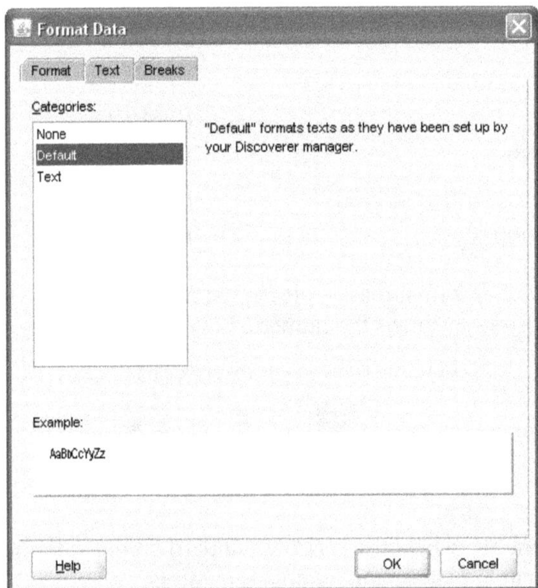


- **Categories** Select from None, Default, or Text.
- **Type** When you select the category Text, you can choose from None, Default, Uppercase, Lowercase, or Capitalized.
- **Sample** This shows you how your selection or custom type will look.

These features are not available from the formatting bar.

**NOTE**
*Throughout the preceding section, whenever we have referred to a category of None, this means that the data will be displayed in the format as defined on the database. Whenever we refer to the Default category, the data will be displayed as formatted by the Discoverer administrator.*

# Formatting Columns

After you have formatted your data, you should look at the columns and decide whether any formatting is required. This includes formatting column headings, deleting columns, and resizing columns.

## Formatting Column Headings

As when you are formatting data, Discoverer provides a Format Heading dialog box. There are two ways to access the Format Heading dialog box.

- From a pop-up list
- From the menu bar

**From a Pop-up List** To access the Format Heading dialog box from a pop-up list, use the following workflow:

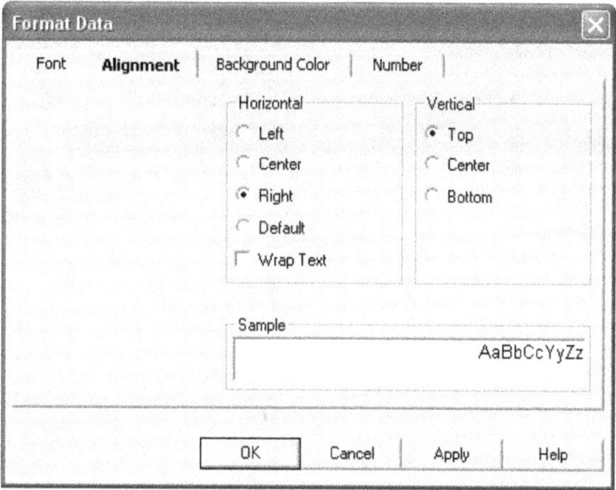


1. Click the heading you want to format.
2. Right-click the heading. This displays a pop-up list of options.
3. Select Format Heading. This displays the following dialog box in Desktop.

This box has the same functionality as the Format Data dialog box that was explained in the section "Formatting Data." The only difference is that the Format Heading dialog box has only the first three tabs, for font, alignment, and background color. In Plus the tabs are consolidated into one tab called Format.

**NOTE**
*To apply the same format to multiple headings, hold down the* CTRL *key and select the columns you require.*

### From the Menu Bar

To access the Format Heading dialog box from the menu bar, use the following workflow:

1. Click the heading you want to format.
2. From the menu bar, select Format | Headings. This displays the Format Heading dialog box.

## Formatting Multiple Headings and Columns in Plus

In Plus you can set all of your heading and column formats in one place. To format multiple headings and columns, use the following workflow:

1. From the menu bar, click Format | Item Formats. This opens the Format dialog box with a list of all of the items in the worksheet, as shown here:

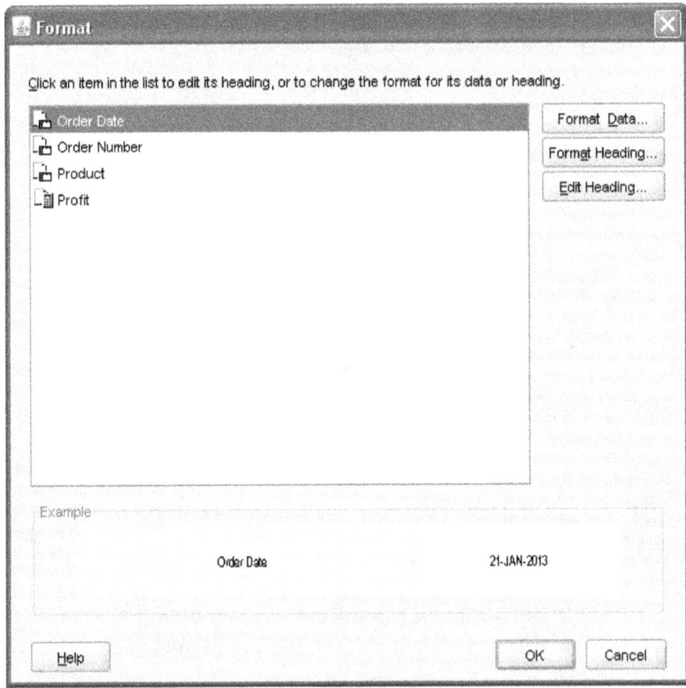

2. Select the item you want to format. You can format the data and the heading, as well as edit the heading name. These dialog boxes should be familiar to you, as their functionality was described to you earlier in this chapter.
3. When you have completed all of the formatting you require, click OK.

# Deleting Columns from a Worksheet

While you were rearranging and formatting the column headings, you may have spotted a column that is unnecessary. You may have included something that has no bearing on the desired final result. For example, Global Widgets always ships what is ordered. Including Order Qty and Ship Qty in the same query would be redundant, so you could remove one of them.

Another reason for removing a column is when the sole purpose for including it was to enable the column to be used in a calculation or condition. Now is the time to get rid of these columns. Do not worry about your calculations or conditions, as Discoverer will remember which columns were used and will continue using them after you have deleted them from the output. This holds true even when the item being deleted was the only item being selected from a folder. We think this is a really clever feature. This will be explained in detail in Chapter 12.

## How to Delete a Column

There are three ways to delete a column from the output of your query in Desktop.

- From the keyboard
- From a pop-up list
- From the Edit Sheet/Worksheet dialog box
- And one additional way in Plus: drag and drop

Always use the simplest method, which in this case is by using the keyboard.

### From the Keyboard

To delete a column using the keyboard, use the following workflow:

1. Click the column heading for the column you want to delete.
2. Press DELETE.

### From a Pop-up List

To delete a column from a pop-up list, use the following workflow:

1. Right-click the heading of the column you want to delete. This displays a pop-up list of options.
2. In Desktop, select Delete. In Plus, select Remove From Worksheet.

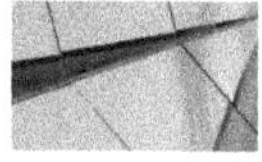

**NOTE**

*For both of the preceding workflows, you can delete multiple columns by holding down the CTRL key as you make your selections.*

### From the Edit Sheet/Worksheet Dialog Box

If you are not sure which columns you want to delete and simply want to see how the worksheet will look without some of the columns, you should use this method.

To delete columns from the Edit Sheet/Worksheet dialog box, use the following workflow:

1. From the menu bar, select Sheet | Edit Sheet/Worksheet, or from the toolbar, click the Edit Sheet/Worksheet icon. Either of these displays the Edit Sheet/Worksheet dialog box (see Figure 5-20 in the preceding chapter).
2. Click the Table Layout tab.
3. Highlight the column you want to delete.
4. Press DELETE on your keyboard.
5. Click OK or press ENTER to finish.

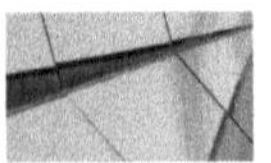

**NOTE**
*If you have deleted the wrong column, do not click OK or press ENTER.*

Clicking Cancel causes Discoverer to abandon the delete and reinstate the column.

### Drag and Drop in Plus

To delete a column by drag and drop, use the following workflow:

1. Click the column heading of the column you want to remove from the worksheet.
2. Drag it to the Available Items pane and release your mouse.

## Resizing Columns

There are four ways to resize columns in Discoverer. Some of these are very precise, while others are free-format and simply resize to whatever manual width setting you apply to the column.

The four ways you can resize a column are as follows:

- Drag the column edge to the required width.
- Double-click a column edge (precise).
- Manually resize a single column using the Format menu.
- Autosize using the Format menu (precise).

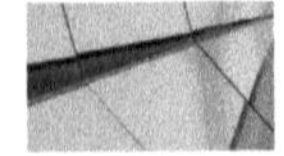

**NOTE**
*To view the current width of a column in Desktop, place the cursor on the right edge of the column and then click and hold the left mouse button. This causes Discoverer to embolden all of the column's right edge and to display the current width at the bottom of the screen (see Figure 6-2).*

### Resizing by Dragging the Column Edge to a Required Width

Resizing a column using this method is quick but imprecise and comes down to user preference. This method is sufficient for working on the screen but not usually accurate enough for printing or

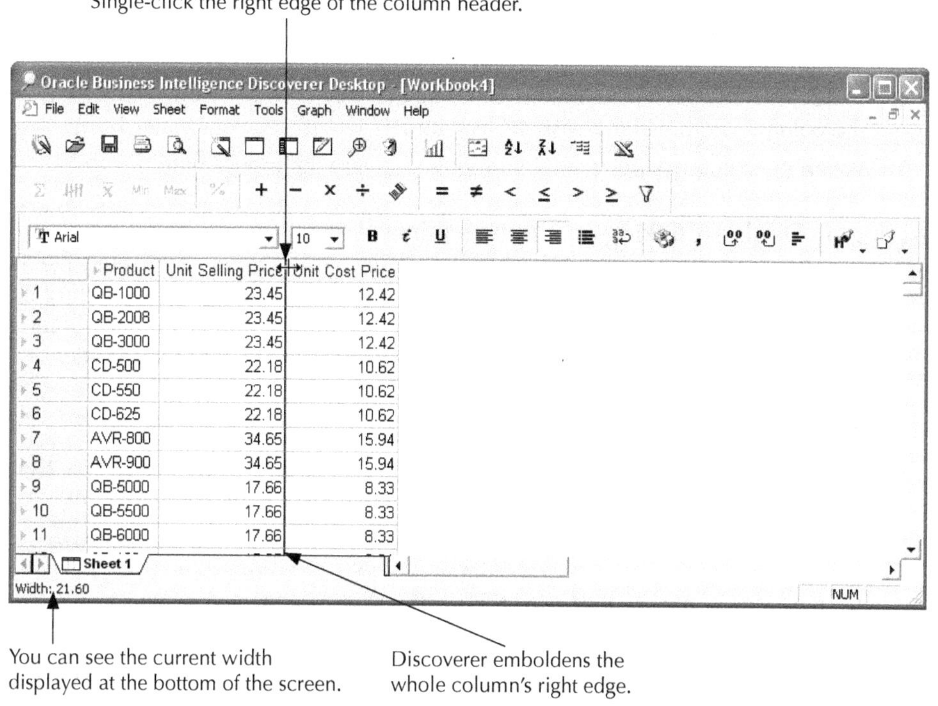


**FIGURE 6-2.** *Displaying the column width in Desktop*

creating a report. Discoverer will resize a column to any width you choose, even if that means being unable to see all of the data. There are valid occasions when you may want to do this. For example, a company using long product names may decide that the first 20 characters in the name are sufficient for the purpose of displaying on reports.

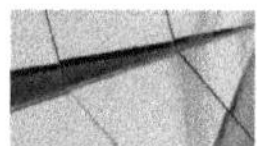

**NOTE**
*We don't understand why Oracle has done this, but the only way to resize a column in a Plus crosstab is by using this dragging method. This is a real problem when the columns going down the left side of the crosstab have more than about 40 characters. We recently encountered this issue in a crosstab we were designing. The second left-side column of our crosstab was a varchar with more than 100 characters. Because the column went beyond the width of the screen, we could not scroll to get to the edge of the column to resize it, but no other method of resizing is available. In the end we had to go into the Oracle Discoverer 11g Administration edition and restrict the number of characters allowed in the field. According to Oracle this has been fixed, and the fix will become available in a patch.*

To resize a column by dragging its edge, follow this workflow:

1. Place the mouse pointer on the right edge of the column header you want to resize. This causes the pointer to change to the resize pointer.
2. Hold down the left mouse button and drag the pointer to the left or right. As you do this, the column width will increase or decrease.
3. When the column is the width you require, release the mouse button.

### Resizing by Double-Clicking a Column's Edge

Resizing a column using this method is very precise and causes Discoverer to autosize the width of the column. Autosizing means that Discoverer automatically works out the width of the column from the width of the header and the width of the longest data item in the column. It will resize the column to make it one character bigger than either the width of the header or the width of the longest data item.

To autosize a column by double-clicking its edge, follow this workflow:

1. Place the mouse pointer on the right edge of the column you want to resize. This causes the pointer to change to the resize cursor.
2. Double-click the left mouse button. This causes the column width to autosize.

### Manually Resizing a Single Column Using the Format Menu

This method of resizing a column is again imprecise and somewhat hit-and-miss. You will probably repeat the resizing several times before you get the column to the width that appears correct. If you want to resize a number of columns, you will have to repeat the method for each column.

**NOTE**
*This method is not available in crosstabs.*

To manually resize a single column using the Format menu, follow this workflow:

1. Click anywhere in the column you want to resize. This causes Discoverer to highlight the column.
2. From the menu, select Format | Columns | Width. This displays the following Column Width dialog box:

   Column Width
   Column width: 19.20
   OK
   Cancel

3. Enter a number for the width of the column. The number you enter is the number of characters that will display, based on an 8-point font. You can enter decimal places if you want.
4. Click OK.

### Autosizing Using the Format Menu

This method of resizing columns is very precise and should be used when creating a report or printing or when you want to resize multiple columns. There is nothing hit-and-miss about this method because the columns are autosized.

**NOTE**
*This method is not available in crosstabs.*

To autosize a column or columns using the Format menu, follow this workflow:

1. Highlight the column or columns to be autosized. You do this by clicking in a column, holding down the CTRL key, and then clicking any other desired columns. To select all columns, click the blank item immediately to the left of the first data item. The following illustration shows where to click:

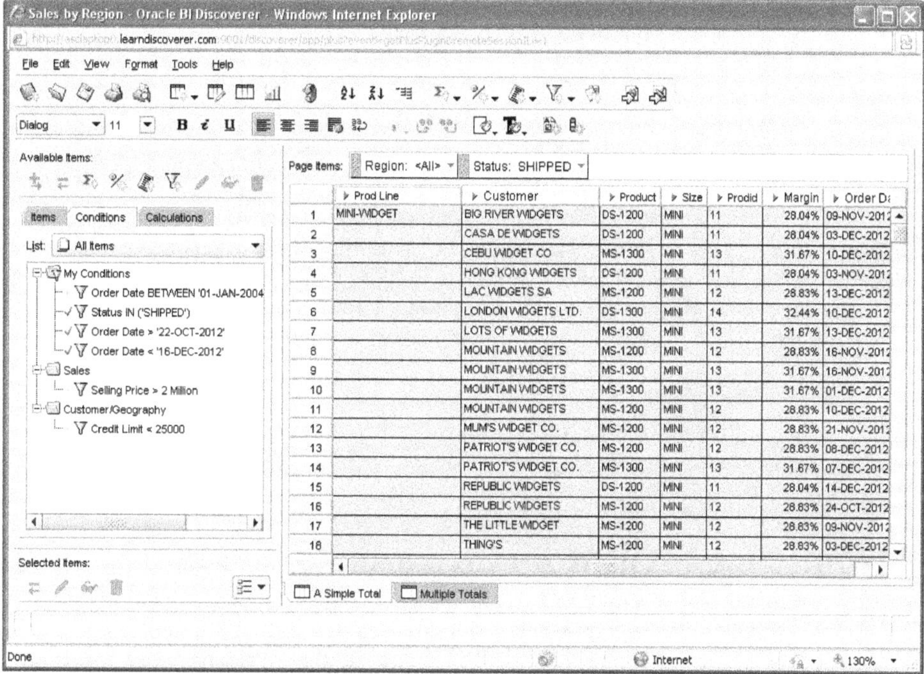


2. When you have selected a column or columns, from the menu select Format | Columns | Auto Size. This causes Discoverer to automatically resize all of the highlighted columns.

# Formatting Totals

If you have added totals to your query, you can format them. Discoverer uses the Format Data dialog box to let you format totals. You can also use some of the toolbar buttons when working with totals.

## Formatting Totals Using the Format Data Dialog Box

The Format Data dialog box is accessible in two ways.

- From the menu bar
- From the Total pop-up list

### From the Menu Bar

To access the Format Data dialog box from the menu bar, use the following workflow:

1. From the menu bar, select Tools | Totals.
2. Highlight the total you want to format.
3. Click the Edit button. This opens the Edit Total dialog box.
4. Click the Format Data button. This opens the Format Data dialog box.

### From the Total Pop-up List

To access the Format Data dialog box from the Total pop-up list, use the following workflow:

1. Right-click the row containing the total.
2. From the pop-up menu, select Edit Total. This opens the Edit Total dialog box.
3. Click the Format Data button. This opens the Format Data dialog box.

If you have only one total in your worksheet, clicking any cell in the row containing the total displays the Edit box for that total. When you apply the format to a single total, Discoverer applies the format to the complete row. If you have multiple totals in your worksheet, clicking the cell containing a total displays the Edit box for that total. Clicking any other cell in the Totals row displays the Edit Totals dialog box, from which you will have to select the total you want to format.

**NOTE**

*There is no way to format all totals at once. When you have multiple totals in your worksheet, you can apply a format only to those cells that are totals.*

## Formatting Totals from the Formatting Bar

After you have created a total or totals in your worksheet, rather than calling up a dialog box, Discoverer allows you to format totals directly from the formatting bar.

To format from the formatting bar, you should do the following:

1. Click the row containing the total. Discoverer then activates some of the formatting buttons on the formatting bar.
2. Click any of the buttons: Font, Font Size, Bold, Italic, Underline, Wrap Text, Foreground, and/or Background Colors. This applies that format setting to the total.

If you have only one total in your worksheet, clicking any cell in the row containing the total activates the formatting bar. When you click one of the formatting buttons, Discoverer applies that format to the whole row. If you have multiple totals in your worksheet, the formatting bar is activated only when you click one of the cells containing a total. In this situation, Discoverer applies the format only to that total. Clicking any cell that does not contain a total disables the formatting bar.

# Formatting Exceptions

One of the analysis features of Discoverer is the ability to format data exceptions. We will explain how to create and format these in Chapter 8 when we discuss using Discoverer to analyze data.

# Adding a Title to Your Query

Discoverer handles titles by offering the Edit Title dialog box. The box has two tabs in Desktop, one for formatting the text and one for adding bitmaps to the title. The Bitmaps tab also serves the purpose of allowing you to preview the title. In Plus there is only one tab, for formatting. A bitmap cannot be added to a workbook in Plus; however, using the OEM of Discoverer, a logo can be added to the top of the browser environment. This will be shown to you in Chapter 20. You can also insert text codes into the title, such as workbook name or any conditions present in the query.

**NOTE**
*You can give an individual name to each worksheet in a workbook.*

## Editing the Title

To edit the title of a query, use one of the following three methods:

- Double-click the title bar. The title bar is directly above the column headings and page details.
- Right-click the title bar, and from the drop-down menu select Edit Title.

**NOTE**
*If you cannot see the title bar, you can activate it from the Tools | Options menu. Click the Crosstab or Table tab and check the box Title. In Plus, use View | Title.*

- From the Plus menu bar, use Edit| Title. From Desktop, use Sheet | Edit Title.

If you haven't created a default title, Discoverer will display "Double-click here to edit this title" as the title. This doubles for the instructions, so don't be confused when the Edit Title dialog box opens and still seems to be giving instructions to double-click.

**NOTE**
*You can create your own default title from the Crosstab or Table tab on the Options menu. This default is created in the same way as you create a normal title, so all that you read in this section equally applies to creating a default title. This illustration shows the Table Options tab in Desktop.*

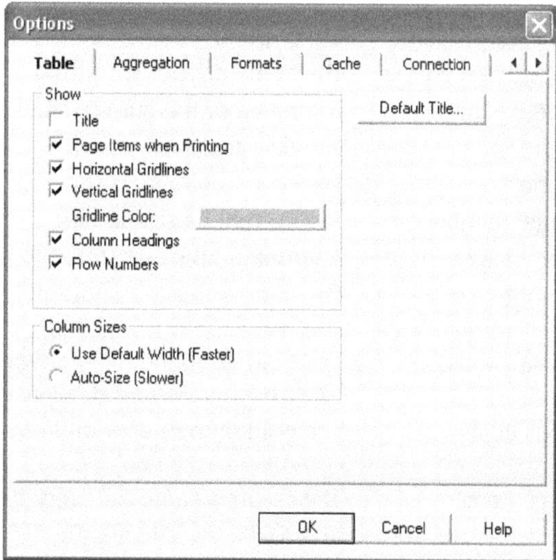


Whichever method you chose to edit the title, Discoverer now displays the Edit Title dialog box. This box has two tabs in Desktop: a Text tab and a Bitmap tab. In Plus there is no tab.

### The Edit Title/Text Tab

Using the Text tab, you can change the font, font size, font properties, and alignment, as well as foreground and background color. You are also given a drop-down list of special text codes that you can add to the title, as shown here:

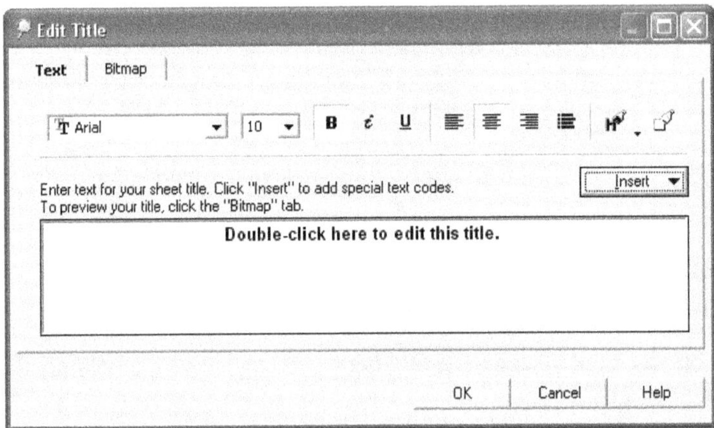


- **Formatting toolbar** These buttons work in the same way as on the main Discoverer formatting bar.
- **Insert** Select from a list of special text codes. See the following table.
- **Title box** As you select options for your title, Discoverer inserts the options here. You can also type text into the box.

The following table explains the special text codes available:

| Text Code Name | Description |
|---|---|
| Workbook Name | The name of your workbook. |
| Sheet Name | The name of the current sheet. |
| Date | The date the query is run. |
| Time | The time the query is run. |
| Page Number | The current page number. |
| Total Pages | A count of all pages in the worksheet. |
| Conditions | The name of each condition in the worksheet is displayed, separated by a comma. |
| Data Points | The column name for each data point (mathematical expression) in the worksheet is displayed, separated by a comma. |
| Axis Items | The column name for all items in the worksheet is displayed, separated by a comma. |
| Page Items | The column name for every page item in the worksheet is displayed, separated by a comma. You can edit the list and remove any that you don't want to display. |
| Conditional Formats | The description for every exception in the worksheet is displayed, separated by a comma. In Desktop, the code is called Exceptions. |

**NOTE**

*The preceding text codes display on the Text tab with an ampersand (&) as the first character. This character is programming code and will not display as part of the title. You can force Discoverer to show an individual page item by typing its name into the Title box preceded by an ampersand.*

To create a new title, select the text "Double-click here to edit this title" and type in your new workbook title. You might want to make the worksheet name the title, in which case select Worksheet from the Insert drop-down list.

With the text of the new title selected, use the formatting tools at the top of the dialog box to format the text. If you want more than one line for the title, press ENTER to go to the next line. There are no tabs or multiple areas for the title as there are in the header and footer, so creating a complex and well-formatted title is not easy. We recommend you use the Header and Footer options of Page Setup to create a better title and stick to a simple one- or two-line title with a graphic here.

**NOTE**

*Headers and footers will be covered in detail in Chapter 8.*

### The Bitmap Tab (Desktop Only)

Using the Bitmap tab, you can insert bitmaps into the background of your title. For example, perhaps you want to insert your company's logo.

The Bitmap tab consists of the following three sections:

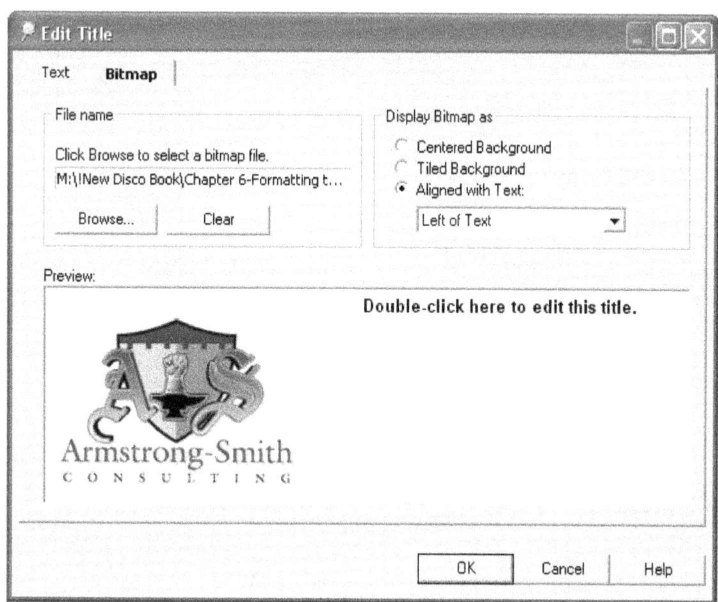

- **File Name box** Use the Browse button to locate a bitmap, and use the Clear button to delete it. When a bitmap is selected, Discoverer displays the path and name of the file.
- **Display Bitmap As box** Check the radio buttons to center the bitmap in the background, to tile the bitmap in the background, or to display the bitmap aligned with the text. You can align a bitmap above, below, to the left of, or to the right of the text.
- **Preview box** Discoverer displays how the bitmap will look when combined with the options selected from the Text tab.

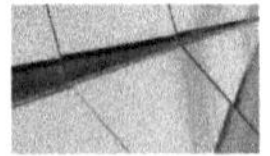

**NOTE**
*You can create a bitmap of your company's logo by scanning it from a piece of stationery. Let us give you a word of warning about scanned images. These images are rarely as good as original artwork and certainly not good enough for printing onto reports that will be sent externally. It is likely that your company has standard artwork, and you should speak with your Discoverer administrator to find out where the images are stored.*

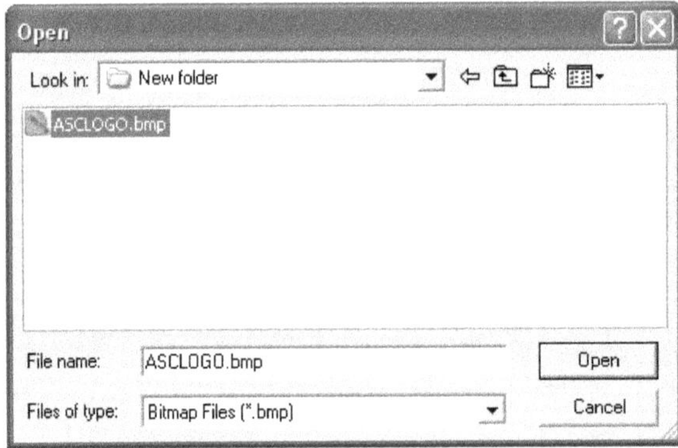


To add a bitmap to a title, use the following workflow:

1. Click the Bitmap tab on the Edit Title dialog box.
2. Click the Browse button. This causes Discoverer to display the Open dialog box.
3. Find the bitmap you want to insert.
4. Click Open. Discoverer displays the full path and name of the bitmap and also shows you how the bitmap will look.
5. Select an option for displaying the bitmap. You can choose from Centered Background, Tiled Background, or Aligned With Text. If you choose Aligned With Text, you will need to select how it will be aligned. You can choose from Left Of Text, Right Of Text, Above Text, or Below Text.
6. When you are satisfied that you have the correct bitmap and that it is displayed correctly, click OK. This will display the title in your query.

7. The following example shows a title with a bitmap aligned to the left:

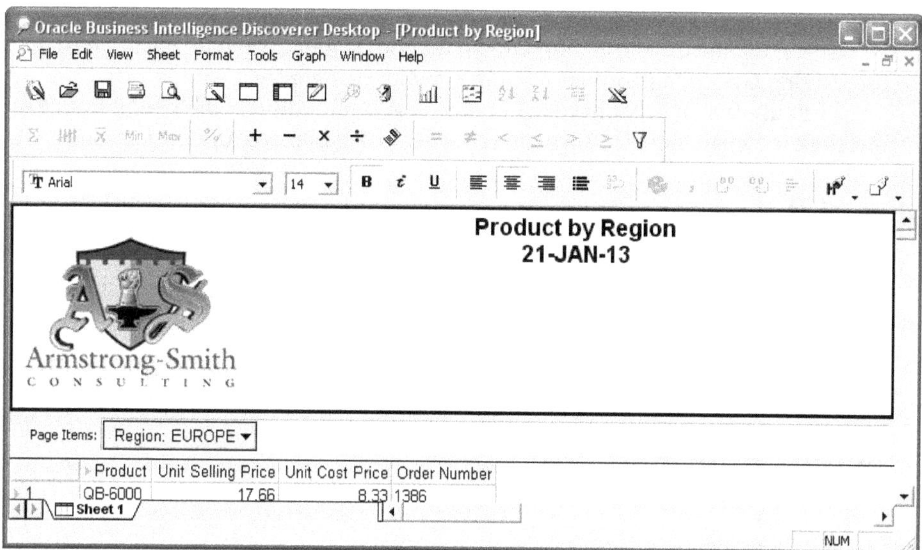

**NOTE**
*If you do not want to use the selected bitmap, you can remove it and start again by clicking Clear.*

**TIP**
*Discoverer remembers the way you last displayed a bitmap and offers this as the default the next time you insert a bitmap.*

## Suppressing a Title from Displaying

To suppress a title from displaying in Plus, use View | Title. To suppress a title in Desktop, use the following workflow:

1. From the menu bar, select Tools | Options.
2. Select the Crosstab or Table tab.
3. Uncheck the Title check box.

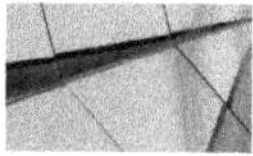

**NOTE**
*Suppressing a title from displaying does not delete the title. It still exists and can be reactivated by rechecking the Title check box.*

# Adding a Background Bitmap (Desktop Only)

This final section on formatting shows you how to add a bitmap as a background to your whole worksheet. Again, as we explained in the section dealing with bitmaps in titles, you should try to use existing artwork rather than scanning in your own image.

Try to use bitmaps that have light colors and do not distract the reader from the report. We therefore recommend exercising caution when using bitmaps as a background.

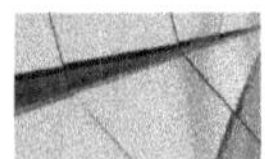

**NOTE**
*When using any form of bitmap, you should ensure that you are not infringing on any copyright or proprietary rights. If you are not sure whether you can use a bitmap, you should consult your company's legal department for advice. The best advice we can give you is, if in doubt, don't use it. You don't want to invoke a lawsuit on your company because you infringed on a copyrighted image.*

## Setting a Background

There are two ways to set a background:

- From a pop-up list
- From the menu bar

### From a Pop-up List

To set a background from a pop-up list, use the following workflow:

1. Right-click anywhere on the worksheet that you want to add a background to. This displays a pop-up list of options.
2. Select Set Background. This causes Discoverer to display the Open dialog box.
3. Find the bitmap you want to insert.
4. Click Open. Discoverer displays the bitmap tiled in the background.

### From the Menu Bar

To set a background from the menu bar, use the following workflow:

1. From the menu bar, select Format | Sheet | Set Background. This displays the Open dialog box.
2. Find the bitmap you want to insert.
3. Click Open. Discoverer displays the bitmap tiled in the background.

## Clearing a Background

If you already have an existing background and now want to remove it, you must use the Clear Background command. There are two ways to clear a background.

- From a pop-up list
- From the menu bar

### From a Pop-up List

To clear a background from a pop-up list, use the following workflow:

1. Right-click anywhere on the worksheet that you want to clear a background from. This displays a pop-up list of options.
2. Select Clear Background.

### From the Menu Bar

To clear a background from the menu bar, use the following workflow:

- From the menu bar, select Format | Sheet | Clear Background.

## Summary

In this chapter, you learned why you should give meaningful names to query column headings and any item that might become a heading. You saw how to rearrange the order of the columns and rename the headings.

You saw how formatting can improve a query by changing fonts and font sizes, font and background colors, and text justification.

This chapter also showed you how to format numbers as currency, with commas, and with the correct number of decimal places.

Finally, you learned to format totals and add titles to your query. You also learned how to add graphics to a query by placing bitmaps into the title as well as adding graphics to the background.

By adding formatting to a query, you will add interest and make the query easier to read and more pleasing to view. Formatting the query gives you an excellent beginning in turning a query into a report. In Chapter 8, you will learn more about reporting in Discoverer.

# CHAPTER 7

# Using Graphs to Present Data

Saying that a picture tells a thousand words refers to the notion that a complex idea can be conveyed with just a single image, in our case a graph. It also aptly portrays one of the main goals of reporting, namely, making it possible for the recipient to absorb large amounts of data quickly.

Graphs are a powerful, visual representation of the data from your database. Discoverer uses a Graph Wizard to take you through the steps of creating a graph. Since the first edition of this book, Oracle has brought graphing forward dramatically in Discoverer. Graphing has been available in both Desktop and Plus since release 4, and it is featured prominently in Plus today.

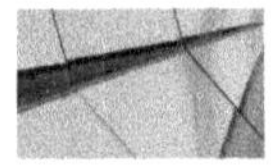

**NOTE**
*Any graph created in Desktop cannot be displayed in Plus or Viewer. Equally, you cannot display a graph created in Plus in Desktop; however, if you create a graph in Plus, it will display in Viewer.*

You can use both tables and crosstabs to create a graph, but you cannot select certain parts of the data to use in the graph. Discoverer uses all of the data points to create the graph and decides for you what it is you want. You are left with only the power to format it.

If you want to use only some of the data points of a table or crosstab, Discoverer will allow you to move those unwanted data points to the page items. However, it takes practice and experimentation to learn how to create a graph that represents the way you want to display your data in a meaningful way.

If you want to use only some data points of a table or crosstab, it is necessary to turn on the page item feature and move the data points you don't want included in the graph to the page axis. Later, when you have finished graphing, you will need to return the columns to the body of the worksheet. What we normally do when a graph is wanted for a report is to create a separate *graph tab* in the workbook and have only the data items wanted in the graph in this special worksheet.

If you want only data that meet certain conditions, you will have to create those conditions. This will be a big change for those used to creating graphs in Excel, where you can select only the data you want to use in the graph from your table. The upside is that once the graph has been created, it is easy to tweak until you get it right. If you make a change to the worksheet, the changes are made to the graph instantly with no intervention from the user. The graph will also be automatically updated each time the query is run.

**NOTE**
*Because Discoverer will create graphs only based on data points, you need to create calculations that change the desired items into data points. This is the trick to getting graphs on non-data-point items.*

There are enough different types of graph styles to choose from, including 3-D models, that you should be able to find a format that meets your needs. There are also bountiful formatting options, including a nifty little paint can to pour your color selection in place. More than 50 graph types and subtypes are available. You can also unlink the layout from the graph, which gives you some amount of freedom over your display. There is also a trend line plotting capability exposed in Plus that you can apply to your graphs.

Discoverer allows graphing options that even Excel does not provide, such as split dual Y graphs. Even dual Y and combination graphs require an incredible amount of manual work to get working in Excel.

In this chapter, you will learn to create, modify, and format graphs. You will be shown how to begin with the Graph Wizard and then use the graph toolbar as well as the Modify Graph dialog box to make changes to the graph. You will learn about the various types of graphs available and how to create titles and add legends.

In our experience, the ability to create business-oriented, powerful, and meaningful graphs is a skill that is sorely lacking in many analysts. We therefore strongly recommend that you spend some time working through this chapter and mastering how to create graphs.

# The Available Graph Styles

Eleven graph types are available, and each graph type has one or more subtypes available. Here are the main graph types in the order they appear within Plus:

- **Bar** Used to show trends or compare values. Some subtypes can be used to show trends and relationships at the same time. Others show changes in percentage over time. There are seven bar subtypes.
- **Horizontal Bar** Used in the same way as line graphs except the results are presented horizontally instead of vertically. There are seven horizontal bar subtypes.
- **Pie** Used to show percentages of a total. Some subtypes show a stacked bar alongside that further displays information about the slice clicked. There are six pie subtypes.
- **Line** Used in the same way as line graphs except the results are presented as lines. There are seven line subtypes.
- **Area** Used to show values via overlapping areas. These are used to show spikes in the data. There are five area subtypes.
- **Combination** Combines bars and lines, bars and areas, lines and areas, or all three. There are two combination subtypes.
- **Scatter/Bubble** The location of each data point shows two or three values, depending upon the chosen subtype. Scatter graphs compare two measures, whereas bubble graphs compare three measures. There are two scatter subtypes and two bubbles subtypes.
- **Stock** Used to show high, low, and closing values. Some subtypes show trading volume as well. There are eight stock subtypes.
- **Circular** Used to show data that is directional or cyclical in nature, such as monthly sales for the past two years. There are two circular subtypes.
- **Pareto** Used to identify sources or the causes of defects. There are no Pareto subtypes.
- **3-D** Used to show trends or compare values. There are five 3-D subtypes, one each for area, bar, cube, ribbon, and surface.

In this section, we will show you the same query via the most popular types of graphs. The query used to show the graphs is a comparison of sales for Global Widget's four regions in the second quarter of 2010 and 2011.

| | Region | Profit | Shipped Quarter |
|---|---|---|---|
| 1 | EUROPE | 1501009.67 | 2010-Q2 |
| 2 | EUROPE | 1936482.56 | 2011-Q2 |
| 3 | FAR EAST | 227788.60 | 2010-Q2 |
| 4 | FAR EAST | 1072527.78 | 2011-Q2 |
| 5 | NORTH AMERICA | 1626797.84 | 2010-Q2 |
| 6 | NORTH AMERICA | 3251026.81 | 2011-Q2 |
| 7 | SOUTH AMERICA | 405500.34 | 2010-Q2 |
| 8 | SOUTH AMERICA | 245317.41 | 2011-Q2 |

## Bar (Desktop and Plus)

The bar graph shows values in comparison to beginning and ending values. This is useful in graphing financial data and stock prices. The Y axis shows the values, and the X axis shows the categories.

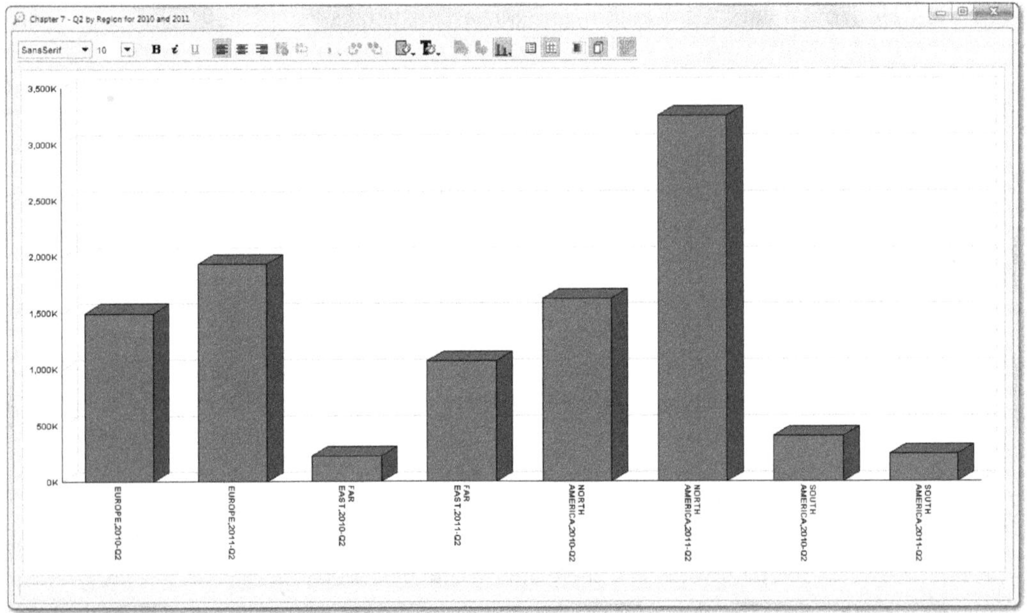


## Combination (Plus Only)

The combination graph shows bars and lines, bars and areas, lines and areas, or all three if you choose. We found this type of graph so complicated that it was hard to make sense of at first. If you are an experienced grapher, try it, but it is not for the faint of heart. For this example, we needed more data to compare, so we added the quantity shipped to the worksheet.

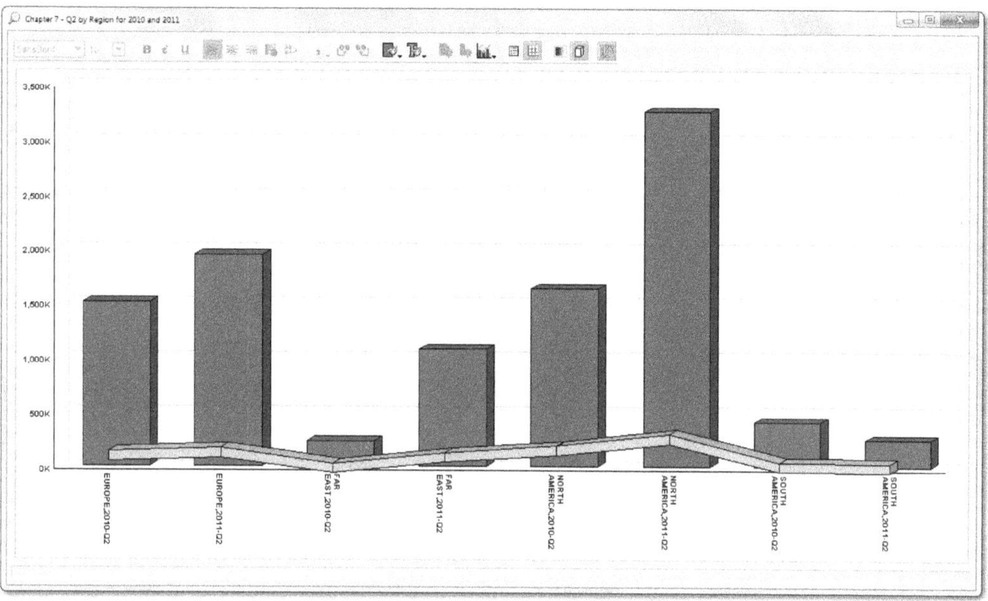


## Cube (Grouped with 3-D Options in Plus)

The cube graph shows trends in values across categories, separated by category. The top of the cube represents the value. The Y axis shows the values, and the X axis shows the categories.

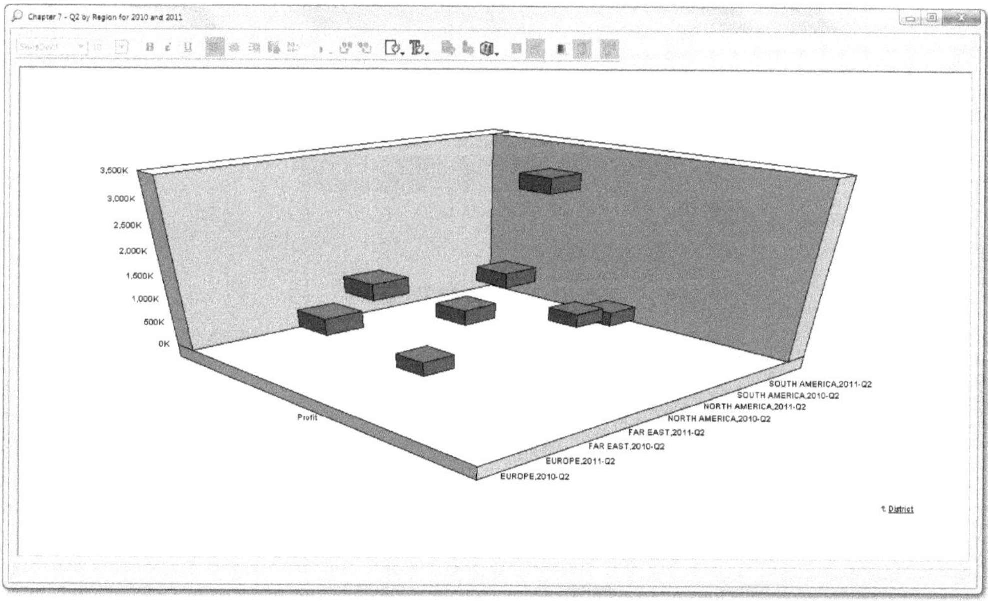

## Doughnut (Desktop), Ring (Grouped with Pie in Plus)

The doughnut graph shows values across categories. Each value is shown as a portion of the whole.

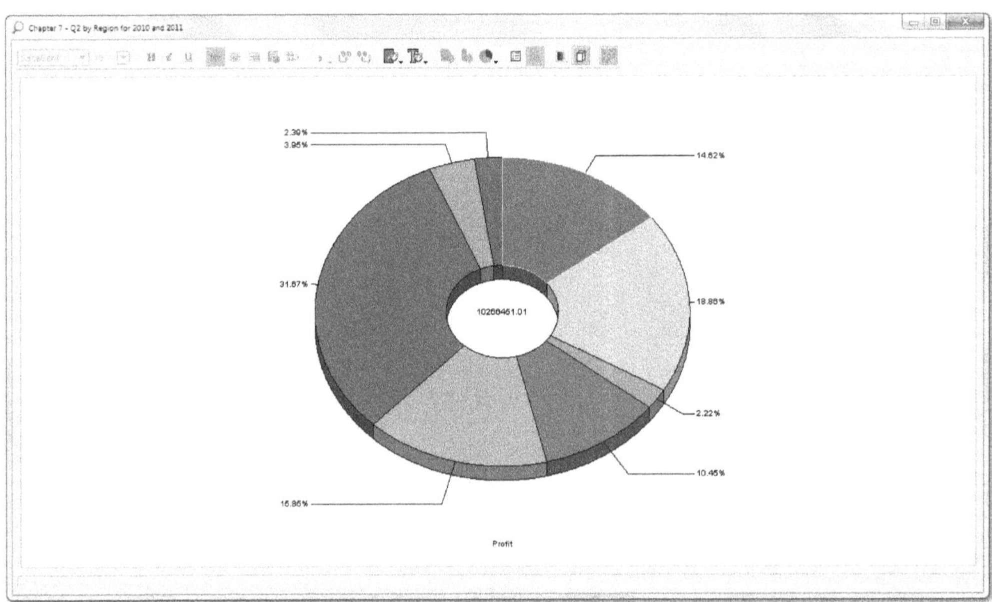


## Horizontal Bar (Desktop and Plus)

The horizontal bar graph shows trends in values across categories. It is a regular bar graph turned on its side and presented horizontally instead of vertically.

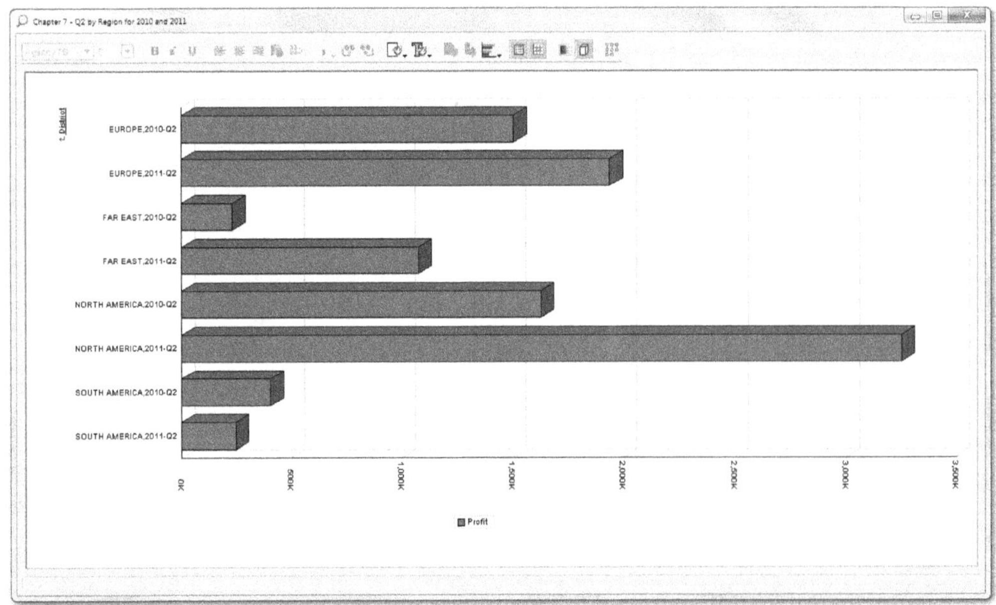

## Line (Desktop and Plus)

The line graph shows trends in values across categories. The values are shown as dots separated by categories, and a line is drawn to emphasize the trend.

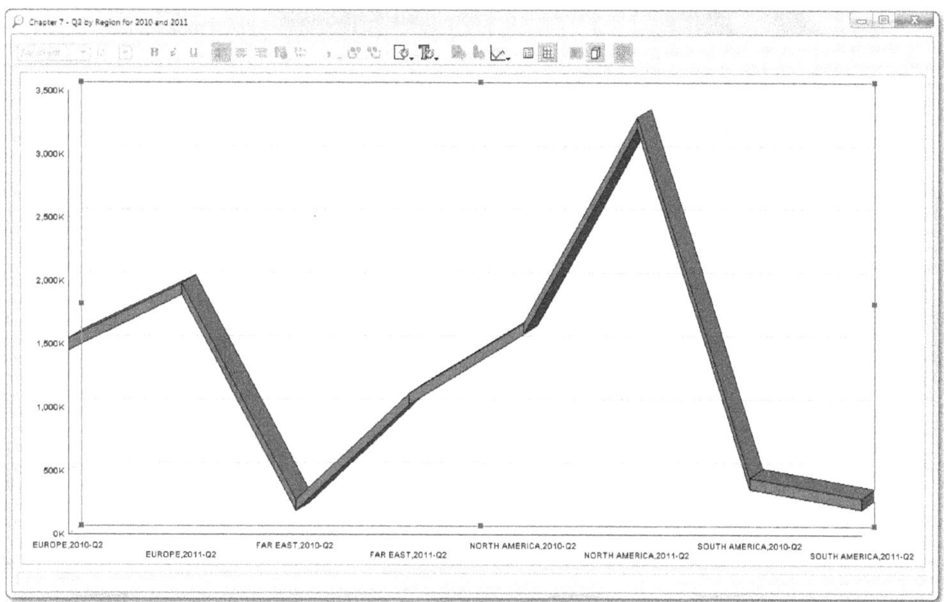


## Pie (Desktop and Plus)

The pie graph shows values across categories. Each value is shown as a portion of the whole pie. To show this, we had to select Series By Row.

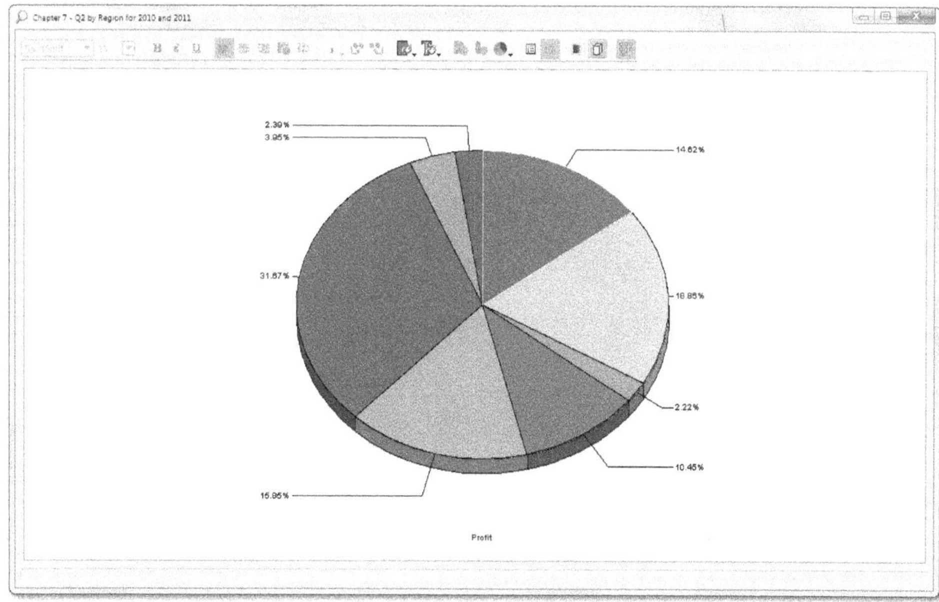

# The Discoverer Desktop Graph Window

Discoverer displays graphs in the Graph window. The first time you open the window, Graph Wizard will assist you in creating the graph. After you have created a graph in Discoverer, it becomes a permanent part of the worksheet it is based on.

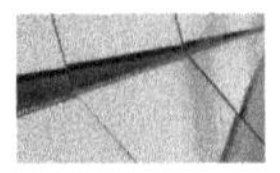

**NOTE**
*In Plus, a graph is always part of any worksheet you create; the only option you have is whether to display it. Also, the first time you choose to display the graph, you are taken through the wizard.*

Figure 7-1 shows a simple query, and Figure 7-2 shows the graph based upon the query.

## The Features of the Discoverer Desktop Graph Window

Unlike Excel, Discoverer does not embed the graph into the worksheet. Instead, the graph is created in its own sheet that can be opened for viewing as the associated worksheet is changed or updated. This is a nice feature, and we especially like the way the graph automatically refreshes itself with the changing data.

Figure 7-3 shows the features of the Discoverer Graph window.

Oracle Business Intelligence Discoverer Desktop - [Chapter 7D]

File Edit View Sheet Format Tools Graph Window Help

| | Shipped Quarter | Region | Profit |
|---|---|---|---|
| 1 | 2010-Q2 | EUROPE | 1501009.67 |
| 2 | | FAR EAST | 227788.60 |
| 3 | | NORTH AMERICA | 1626797.84 |
| 4 | | SOUTH AMERICA | 405500.34 |
| 5 | 2011-Q2 | EUROPE | 1936482.56 |
| 6 | | FAR EAST | 1072527.78 |
| 7 | | NORTH AMERICA | 3251026.81 |
| 8 | | SOUTH AMERICA | 245317.41 |

Q2 by Region for 2010 and 2011

NUM

**FIGURE 7-1.** *A simple query*

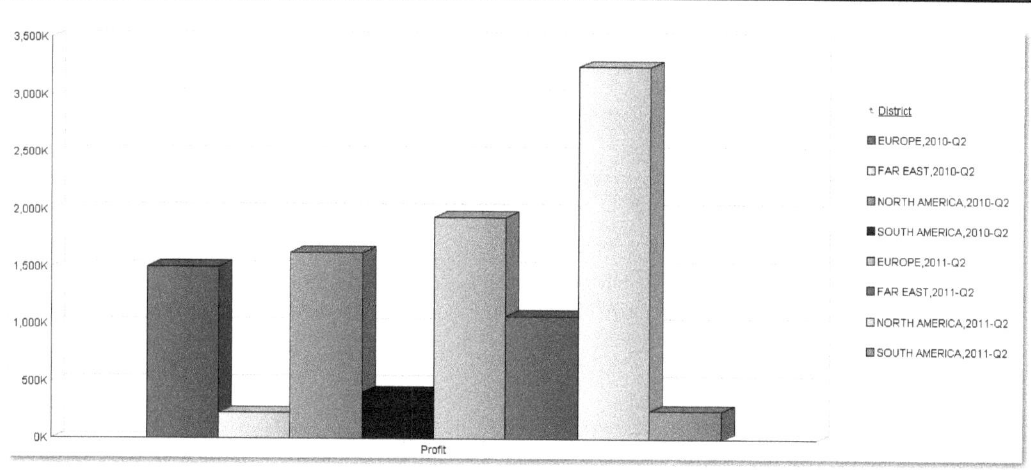


**FIGURE 7-2.** *A graph based on a simple query*

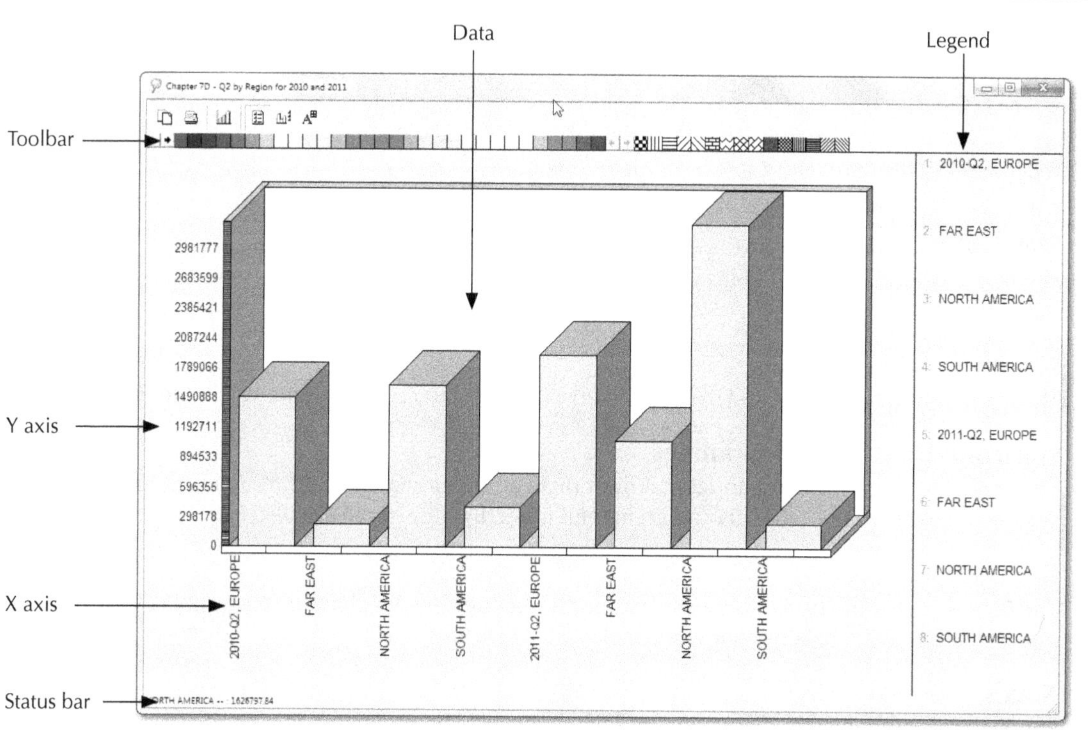


**FIGURE 7-3.** *The Discoverer Graph window*

### Toolbar

The Discoverer Graph window has a toolbar used to work with the graph details, as shown here:

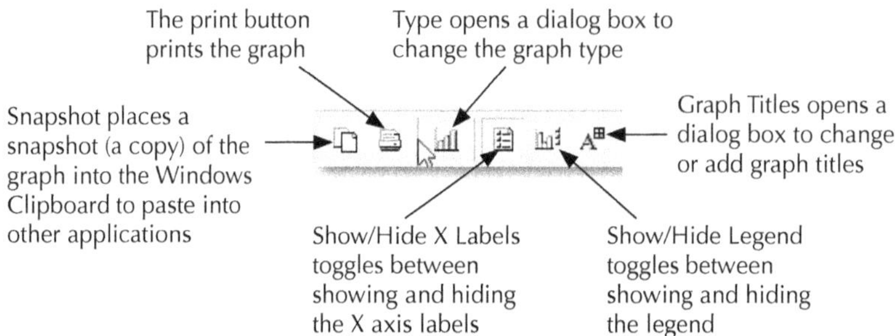
The print button prints the graph
Type opens a dialog box to change the graph type
Snapshot places a snapshot (a copy) of the graph into the Windows Clipboard to paste into other applications
Graph Titles opens a dialog box to change or add graph titles
Show/Hide X Labels toggles between showing and hiding the X axis labels
Show/Hide Legend toggles between showing and hiding the legend

### Y Axis

Discoverer creates a scale appropriate to the data of the original worksheet. This is shown in the Y axis (along the left side of the graph). For example, if the worksheet is based on sales for the first quarter by region and the highest sales were $534,109, Discoverer would create a scale in increments from $0 to $535,000. You can format the scale yourself as well as add decimal points.

### Scroll Bar

Some types of graphs, such as bar charts, contain a large number of bars. You might need to use the scroll bar to see all of the data items of the graph.

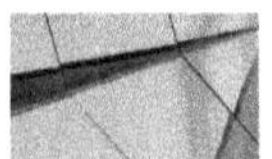

**NOTE**
*You can also use the Auto-Fit option to make sure that the entire graph fits within the confines of the Graph window.*

### Status Bar

As you point to various data items on the graph, Discoverer will display the associated data in the status bar.

### Legend

The legend shows the color and the label used to display the corresponding worksheet data.

### Horizontal and Vertical Gridlines

The gridlines are vertical and horizontal lines that can be turned on or off. You can choose to use vertical, horizontal, or both. This can be helpful in reading the graph details.

### Data

The data is simply the bars of the bar chart or the slices of the pie chart. It is a graphical representation of the data in your worksheet.

### X Axis

The X axis shows the labels used to identify the data. When your data has long names, they will be replaced by numbers. If you have short names, they will be shown below the associated data and will eliminate the need to show the legend.

**NOTE**
*You can add up to three reference lines per Y axis. This is available on the Plot Area tab of the Graph Wizard.*

# Creating a Graph in Desktop

To create a graph, you can use the Graph button on the main Discoverer toolbar or use the menu bar.

To begin using the Discoverer graphing tool, select Graph | Edit Graph from the menu bar or click the Graph button on the toolbar.

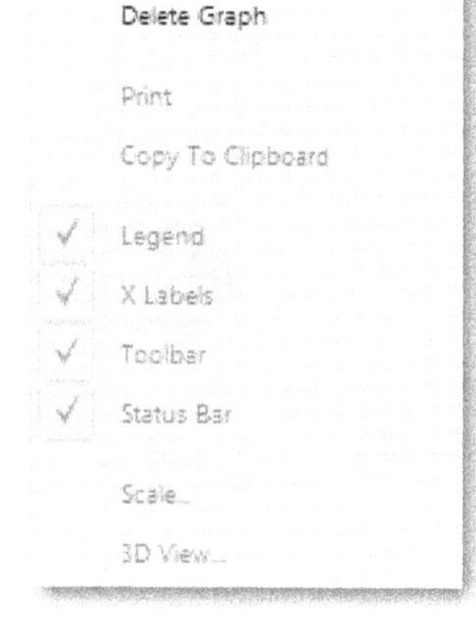


## The Desktop Graph Wizard

Following one of the two methods previously described will open the Graph Wizard. There are four steps to the Graph Wizard that take you through the process of building your graph. The four steps are as follows:

- Selecting the graph type
- Formatting the graph type
- Adding titles and legends
- Adding special graph options

Don't worry if you are not sure how your graph will turn out. If you are not satisfied with the results, it is easy to edit the graph until you are. You can also click Back at any time to return to the previous steps.

### Graph Wizard Step 1: Selecting the Graph Type

The first step in creating your graph is to select the graph type. The features of step 1 of the Graph Wizard are as follows:

- **Graph types** Select the type of graph you want to use to best represent your data.
- **Graph example** See an example of the graph type.
- **Description box** See a description of the graph type. If the description is too long for all of it to be seen, click the Description box, and the box will expand to show the complete description.

Figure 7-4 shows the first step of the Discoverer Desktop Graph Wizard. To select the graph type, use the following workflow:

1. Click the graph type you want to use.

**NOTE**
*If you change your mind about what type of graph you want, you can change it later.*

2. Click Next.

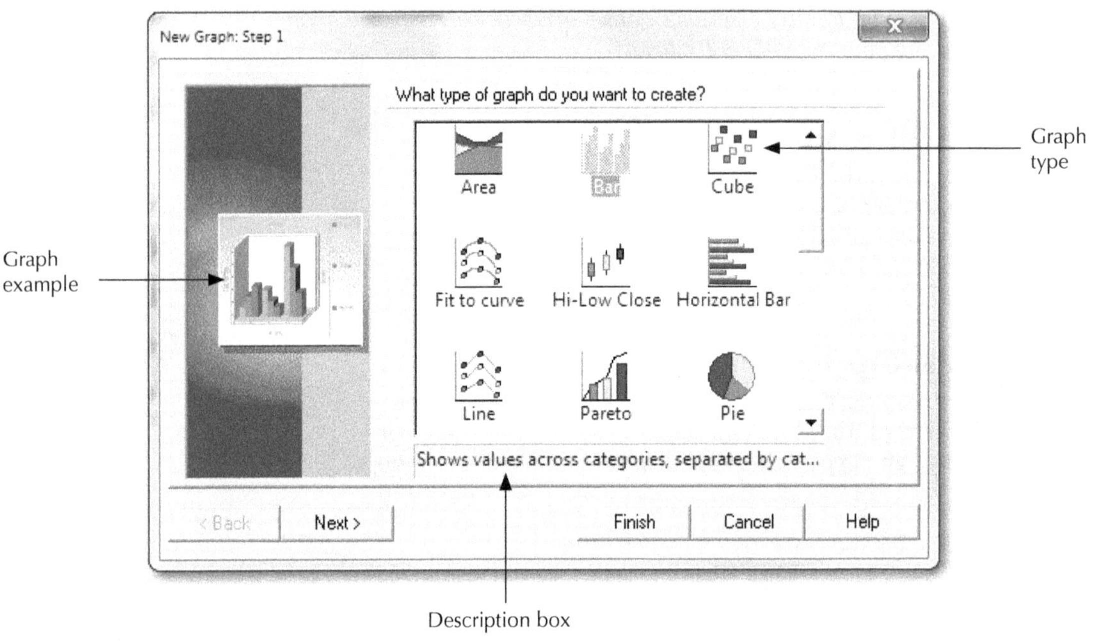


**FIGURE 7-4.** *Graph Wizard, step 1*

## Graph Wizard Step 2: Selecting the Graph Format

After selecting the graph type, Discoverer will advance you to step 2 of the Graph Wizard—selecting the graph format. Discoverer gives you, in most cases, several format choices for the graph type you have selected. The features of step 2 of the Graph Wizard are as follows:

- **Graph format style** Select the type of graph you want to use to best represent your data.
- **Graph format style example** See an example of the graph with the format selected.
- **Description box** See a description of the graph format style. If the description is too long for all of it to be seen, click the Description box, and the box will expand to show the complete description.

Figure 7-5 shows the second step of the Discoverer Desktop Graph Wizard. To select the graph type, use the following workflow:

1. Click the graph format style you want to use.
2. Click Next.

## Graph Wizard Step 3: Titles and Legends

The next step is to add titles to your graph. You can have titles on the top, the bottom, and both sides. You can also format the font type, style, size, and color, as well as use underline or strikeout effects.

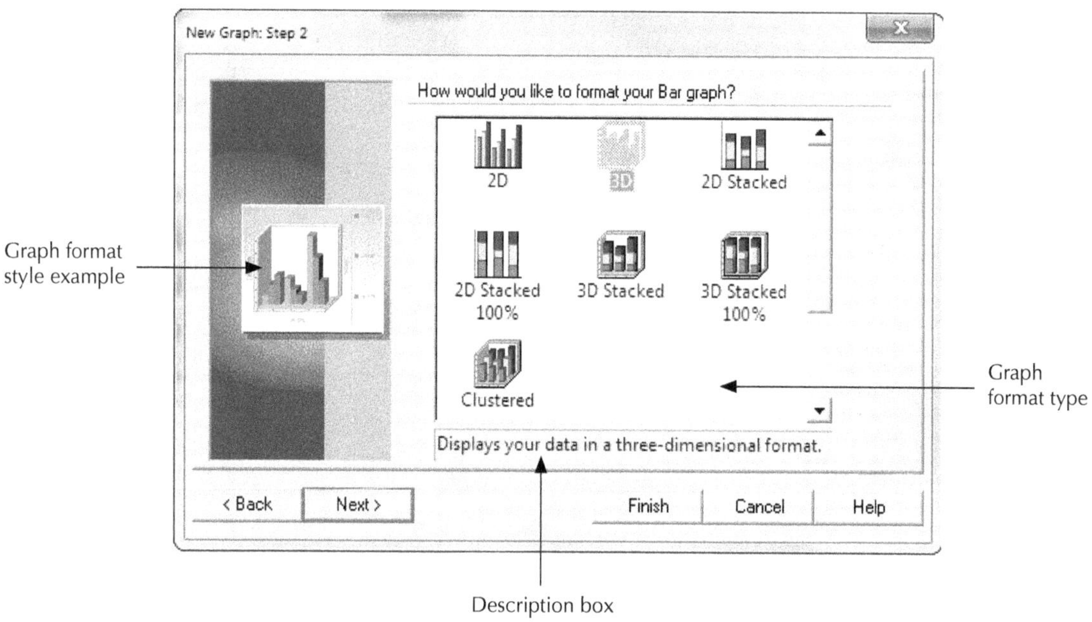


**FIGURE 7-5.** *Graph Wizard, step 2*

Step 3 also gives you an opportunity to show and format the graph legend and to format the fonts for the X and Y axes. The features of step 3 of the Graph Wizard are as follows:

- **Titles** Add titles for top, left, bottom, and right of the graph.
- **Legend** Select to show and format the font of the legend.
- **Axis** Format the fonts of the X and Y axes.

Figure 7-6 shows the third step of the Discoverer Desktop Graph Wizard.

To add titles, add a legend, and format the font of the X and Y axes of your graph, use the following workflow:

1. Decide where you want to add titles to your graph.
2. Click in the field for the title you want to add and format.
3. Type in the title.
4. Click the Legend Font button to the right of the title.

5. Select the font type, style, size, color, and effect.
6. Click OK.
7. Decide whether you want to show the graph legend.
8. Format the legend using the same method described in steps 5 and 6.
9. Format the X and Y axes.
10. Click Next.

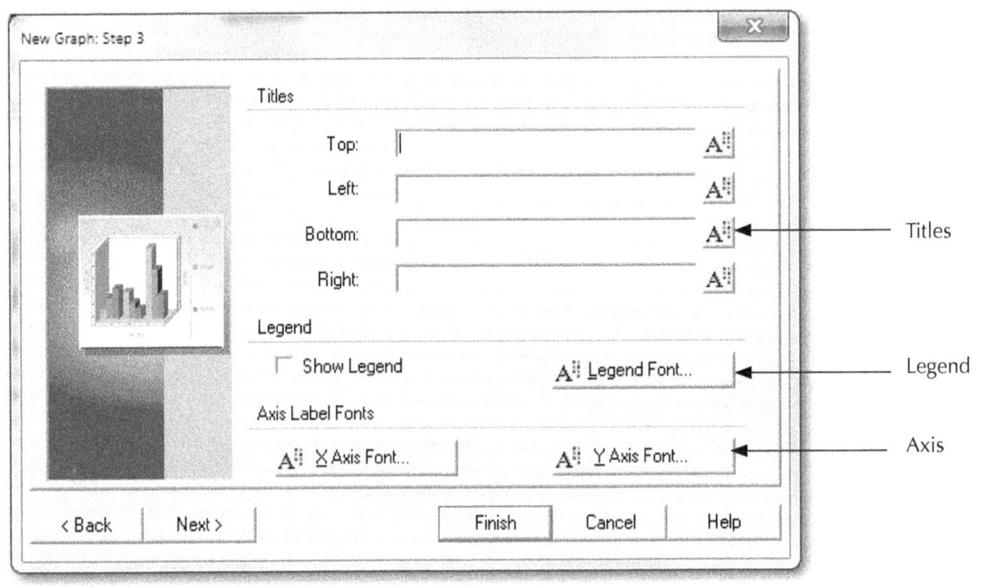


**FIGURE 7-6.** *Graph Wizard, step 3*

## Graph Wizard Step 4: Adding Special Graph Options

Step 4 of the Graph Wizard allows you to change some options of the graph. This is where you can either accept the default scale Discoverer chooses or create your own. You can also add decimal places to the scale. The features of step 3 of the Graph Wizard are as follows:

- **Y Axis Scale** Use the scale created by Discoverer, or type in the scale of your choice.
- **Decimals** Use this to determine how many decimal places will be displayed.
- **Show Gridlines** Click to show horizontal or vertical gridlines.
- **Graph Series By** Select to use the data in the columns or rows of the workbook to be the X axis for the graph.

Figure 7-7 shows the fourth step of the Discoverer Desktop Graph Wizard. To format the options of your graph, use the following workflow:

1. Decide whether you want to create your own scale or use the default set by Discoverer.
2. If you choose to change the scale, click in the Maximum field and type the highest number you want to use for the scale.
3. Click in the Minimum field and type the lowest number you want to use for the scale.
4. To add decimal places to the scale, click in the Decimal field and type the number of decimal places you want to use for the scale.
5. Decide whether you want to add gridlines to your graph and click the check box for the gridlines you want to use—vertical, horizontal, or both.

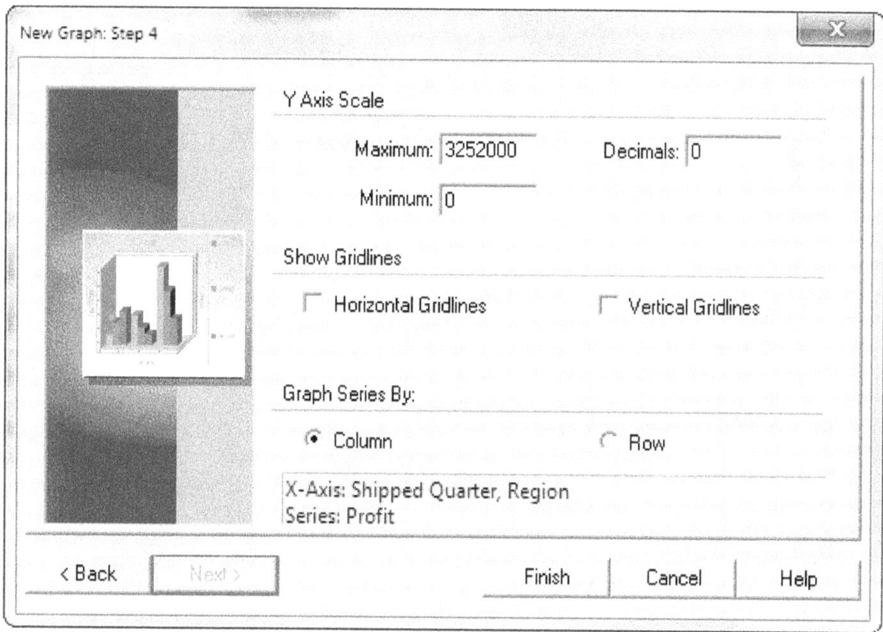


**FIGURE 7-7.** *Graph Wizard, step 4*

6. Decide whether you want to use the data from the worksheet's rows or columns for the X axis and select the corresponding radio button. If you are not sure which series you want to use, a hint is displayed below the radio buttons.
7. Click Finish.

You have completed creating your graph, and Discoverer will close the Graph Wizard and open the Graph window (shown earlier in Figure 7-3).

# Graphing in Discoverer Plus

Graphing in Plus has some of the same basic limitations of Desktop and has fewer available graph types. However, there is definitely power in formatting graph information on the X and Y axes. The graphs in Plus are not as flexible as in Desktop, and all of the 3-D options are grouped together instead of being with their graph type. We find this easier because all of the 3-D graphs are in the same place.

You also approach graphing differently in Plus. You are presented with graphing options in step 1 of the Workbook Wizard. If you choose not to add a graph at the beginning, don't worry; you can add one later. There is no Graph Wizard in Plus. Instead, it uses a workflow-style Edit Graph dialog box. This is changed from 10*g* when the box used to be multitabbed.

**NOTE**
*Graphing in Plus is a Sticky Feature. Discoverer will remember the graph type you chose and will default to it the next time you create one.*

## Creating a Graph in the Plus Workbook Wizard

To create a graph in conjunction with a new query in step 1 of the Plus Workbook Wizard, use the following workflow:

1. From the menu bar, select File | New.
2. Click the Graph box shown here:

   Graph
   Placement: Graph below Table

3. Select the location of the graph from the Placement drop-down list. The options for graph placement are
   - Graph Right Of Table
   - Graph Left of Table Above
   - Graph Above Table
   - Graph Below Table (the default)
   - Graph In Separate Window

You will want to try different locations on the screen for your graph. We recommend that if you have a small amount of data—for example, total sales year—showing the graph in the same window is fine, as shown here:

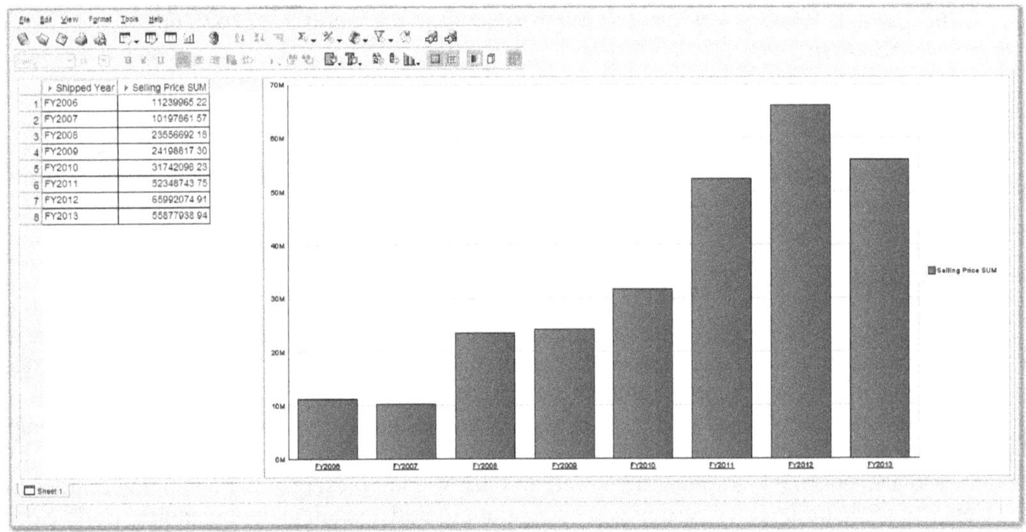


If you have a large amount of data, such as sales by customer, the graph might be too small to display correctly in the same screen. For this example, try putting the graph in a separate window, as shown here:

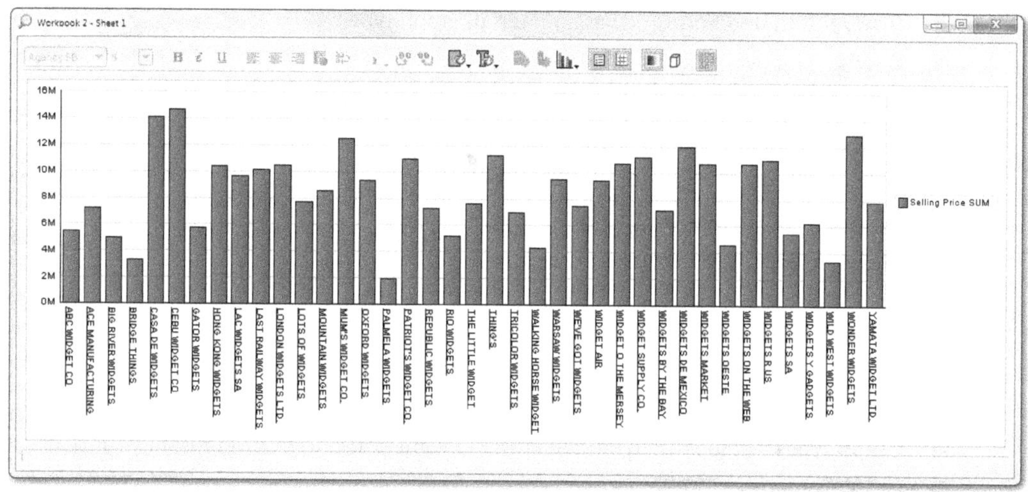


The graphic to the right of the Placement drop-down list shows you how the graph will appear in your query. Complete the steps of the Workbook Wizard. Your graph will be generated when the query runs.

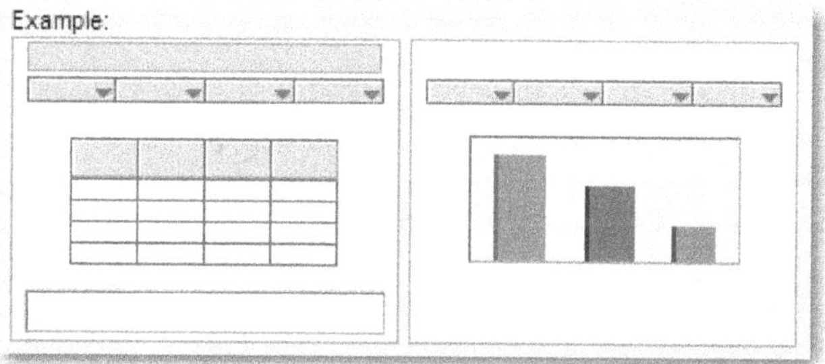


## Creating a Graph in Plus after a Query Has Been Generated

If you decide to add a graph to an existing query, select Edit | Graph or click the Graph button on the toolbar shown here. The Edit Graph dialog box will open.

If you are used to working with graphs in Discoverer 10*g*, the first thing you will notice is that there are no longer any tabs in the Edit Graph dialog box. Instead, in Discoverer 11*g*, Oracle has replaced the tabs with a workflow on the left side. You can choose which graph element you want to work with by either clicking the appropriate workflow link or using the Next and Back buttons to move from page to page.

There are various links in the workflow, each corresponding to a different page in the graphing dialog. The graph type determines which pages are available. Here is a full listing of all the possible graph pages:

- **Type** Available for all graph types
- **Style** Available for all graph types

- **Titles, Totals, and Series** Available for all graph types
- **X-Axis** Not available for pie graphs
- **Y-Axis** Not available for pie or Pareto graphs
- **Y1-Axis** Available for only Pareto graphs
- **Y2-Axis** Available for only Pareto graphs
- **Plot Area** Available for all graph types
- **Legend** Available for all graph types

## Edit Graph Dialog Box—Type Page

The first step in creating your graph is to select the graph type. The features of the Edit Graph Wizard Type page are as follows:

- **Graph types** Select the type of graph you want to use to best represent your data.
- **Graph subtypes** This shows an example of the graph type.
- **Description box** This describes the graph type. Figure 7-8 shows the first step of the Discoverer Plus Edit Graph dialog box.

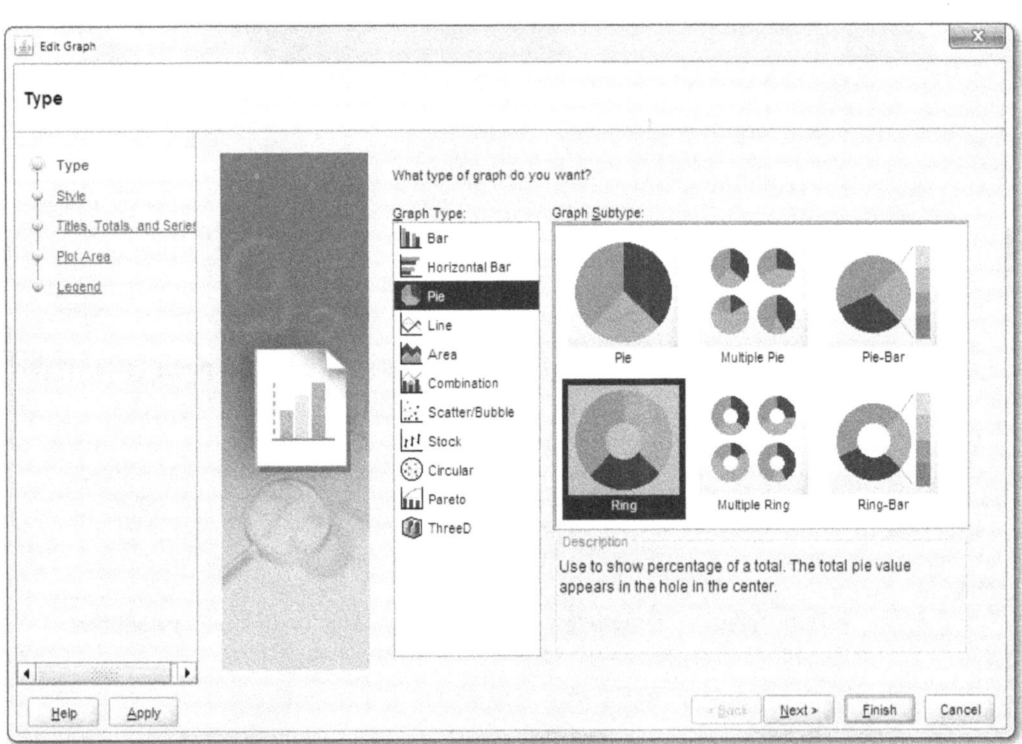


**FIGURE 7-8.** *Choosing a graph type*

To select the graph type, use the following workflow:

1. Click the graph type you want to use.

**NOTE**
*If you change your mind about the type of graph you want, you can change it later.*

2. Click Next to move on to the Style page.
3. If you are done, click Finish.

## Edit Graph Dialog Box—Style Page

This is a very cool feature of Discoverer graphing in Plus—one whose value will immediately be apparent to most users. No longer do you have to muck around to get that "nice and correct" look and feel for your graphs: fonts, foreground color, background color, text size, series color, and so on. Discoverer does all that for you!

After selecting the graph type, you will move on to the Style page. Discoverer gives you, in most cases, several style choices for the graph type you have selected. The features of the Edit Graph Style page are as follows:

- **Style** Oracle has preset a variety of color options.
- **Sample** This shows an example of the graph with the style options selected.
- **Gradient Effect** Click here to show gradients in your colors or deselect if you want the colors to be flat.
- **3D Effect** Click here to turn on or off 3-D effects.

Figure 7-9 shows the Style page of the Discoverer Plus Edit Graph dialog box. To select the graph style, use the following workflow:

1. Click the graph style you want to use.
2. Select or deselect Gradient Effect.
3. Select or deselect 3D Effect.
4. Click Next to move on to the Titles, Totals, and Series page.
5. If you are done, click Finish.

## Edit Graph Dialog Box—Titles, Totals, and Series Page

The next step is to add titles to your graph. In Plus you can have titles only on the top of the graph. You can also format the font type, style, size, color, and alignment. The Titles, Totals, and Series page also gives you an opportunity to decide what you want to display in the graph. You can choose whether to graph data and/or totals and whether to graph the rows or columns in your report.

The features of the Edit Graph dialog box Titles, Totals, and Series page are as follows:

- **Show Title** Add a title to the graph.
- **What would you like to display in your graph?** Decide whether to show totals only, data only, or both totals and data in the graph.
- **Show Null Values As Zero** Click this box to show null values as zero.

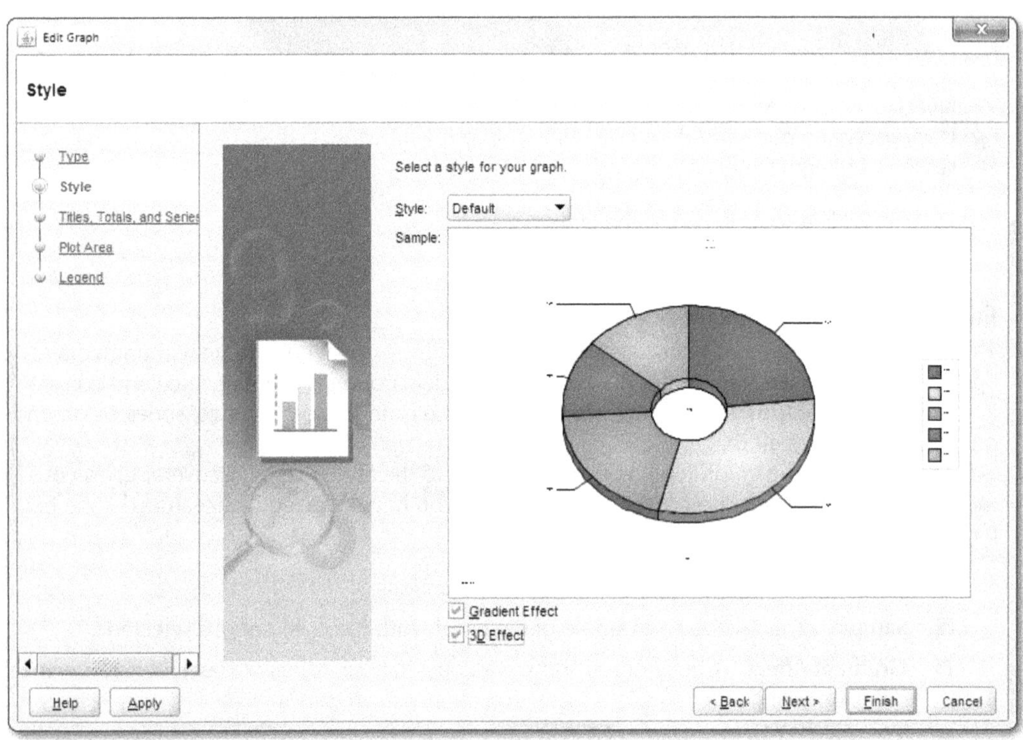


**FIGURE 7-9.** *Choosing a graph style*

- **Graph series by** Here you choose to graph by columns or by rows.
- **Pie Chart Options** Click this button to show additional options for pie charts.

Figure 7-10 shows the Titles, Totals, and Series page of the Edit Graph dialog box. To add titles, totals, and series to your graph, use the following workflow:

1. Type in the title of your graph, or click the Insert button and select from the drop-down list if you want to use any of the predefined title elements. You can choose any combination of the following with text of your own:
   - Sheet Name
   - Workbook Name
   - Date
   - Time
   - Page Items
   - Axis Items
   - Data Points

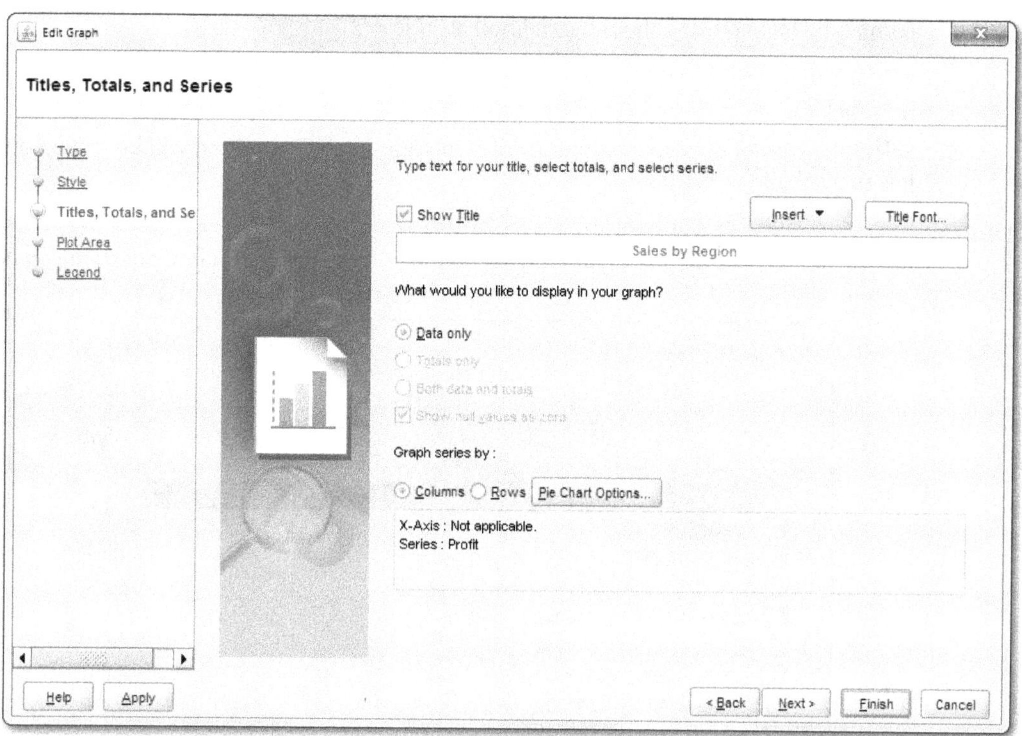


**FIGURE 7-10.** *Entering a title; choosing totals and series*

2. Click the Title Font button to the right of the title.

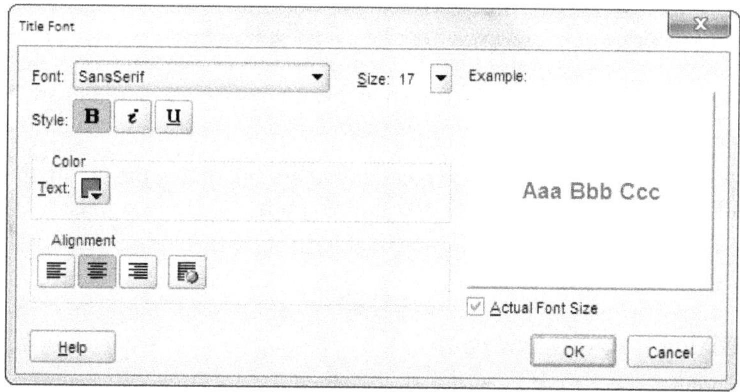


   a. Select the font type, style, size, color, and alignment.
   b. Click OK to close the Title Font dialog.

3. Decide whether you want to show the graph legend.
4. Format the legend using the same method as in step 2.
   a. Format the X and Y axes.
   b. Click OK.
5. Select the type of data you want to display in your graph. The option will be grayed out if it is unavailable in the query.
6. Choose whether to graph by column or by row.
7. For pie charts, click the Pie Chart Options button to open the Pie Chart Options dialog box.

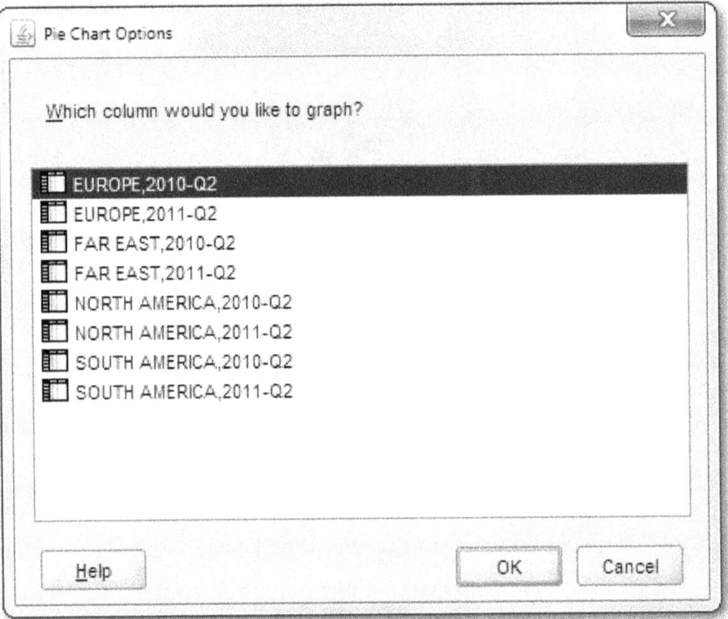


   a. Select the column or row on which you want to graph your pie chart.
   b. Click OK.
8. Click Next to move on to the next page. If you are building a pie graph, the next page you will see will be Plot Area. For all other graph types, the next page you will see is the X-Axis page.
9. If you are done, click Finish.

## Edit Graph Dialog Box—X-Axis Page

The Edit Graph dialog box X-Axis page shown in Figures 7-11 through 7-15 allows you to format how the X axis of your graph will look. This page is not available if you are creating a pie graph. The type of graph you are building determines which variant of X-Axis page is available to you.

The five variants of X-Axis pages are as follows:

- **Variant 1** This is the most common X-Axis page and is the one used for all graphs except circular, scatter/bubble, 3-D, and pie, the latter of which never has an X-Axis. Figure 7-11 shows variant 1 of the X-Axis page.
- **Variant 2** This is used only for scatter/bubble graphs. Figure 7-12 shows this variant of the X-Axis page.
- **Variant 3** This is used only for circular graphs of the Polar type. Figure 7-13 shows this variant of the X-Axis page.
- **Variant 4** This is used only for circular graphs of the Radar type. Figure 7-14 shows this variant of the X-Axis page.
- **Variant 5** This is used only for 3-D graphs. Figure 7-15 shows this variant of the X-Axis page.

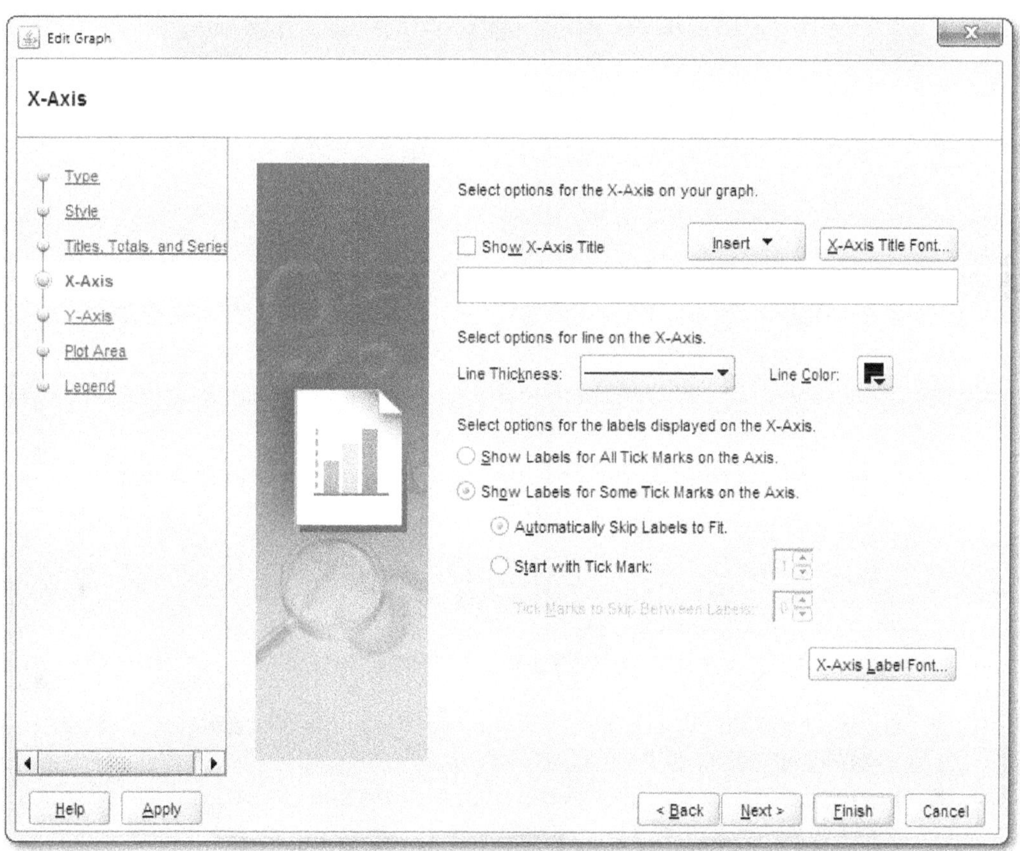


**FIGURE 7-11.** *X-Axis Variant 1 page of the Edit Graph dialog box, used for most graphs*

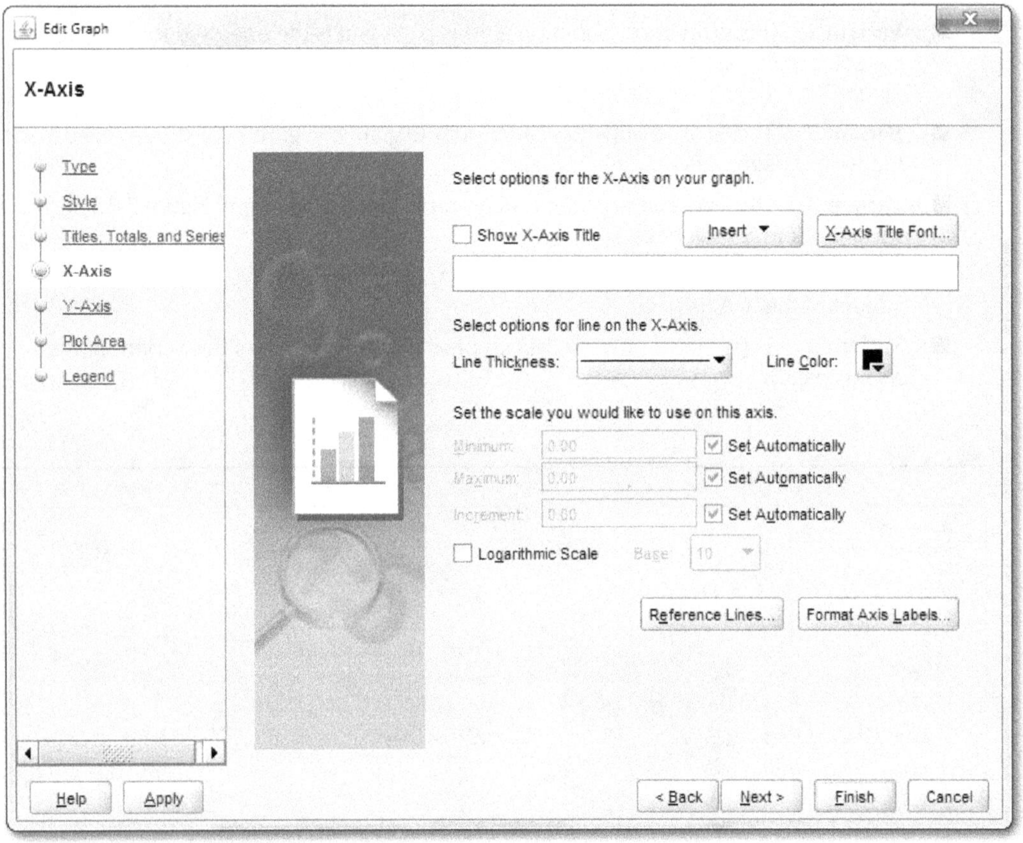

**FIGURE 7-12.** *X-Axis Variant 2 page of the Edit Graph dialog box, used for scatter/bubble only*

The X axis is the axis going across the bottom of the graph and has the following features:

**NOTE**
*Many of the features of the X-Axis page are common to all of the variants of the page. While all of the features are described here, not all will be available on every variant. We will let you know when a feature is not available on a certain page.*

- **Show X-Axis Title** Check this box if you want the X-axis title to display. This feature is not available on any of the circular graphs.
- **Insert** Use this button in the same way you added a title to the graph. This feature is not available on any of the circular graphs.
- **X-Axis Title Font** This opens the Format Font dialog box to format the X-axis title. This feature is not available on any of the circular graphs.

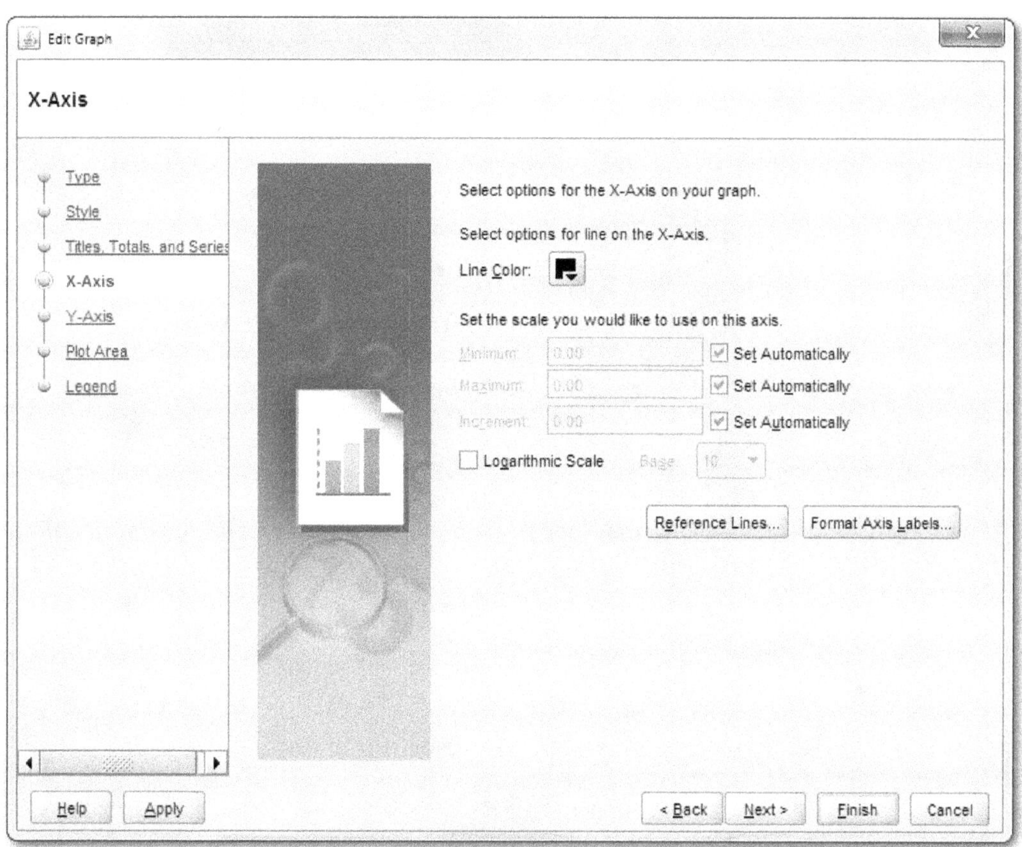


**FIGURE 7-13.** *X-Axis Variant 3 page of the Edit Graph dialog box, used for circular Polar only*

- **X-Axis Title** Add a title that will go across the bottom of the graph. You can use the Insert button to insert a common element into the title, or you can simply type in your own title. Typically, we find a combination of the two to be very effective. After you have created a title, if you deselect the Show X-Axis Title box, the title will not show. This feature is not available on any of the circular graphs.
- **Line Thickness** Use this drop-down list to select the weight of the line of the X axis. This feature is not available on circular and 3-D graphs.
- **Line Color** Use this drop-down to change the color of the X-axis line. This feature is not available on 3-D graphs.
- **Show Labels For All Tick Marks On The Axis** Check this radio button to show all tick marks along the X axis (every data item). This feature is not available on any of the scatter/bubble graphs and available only on circular graphs of type Radar.

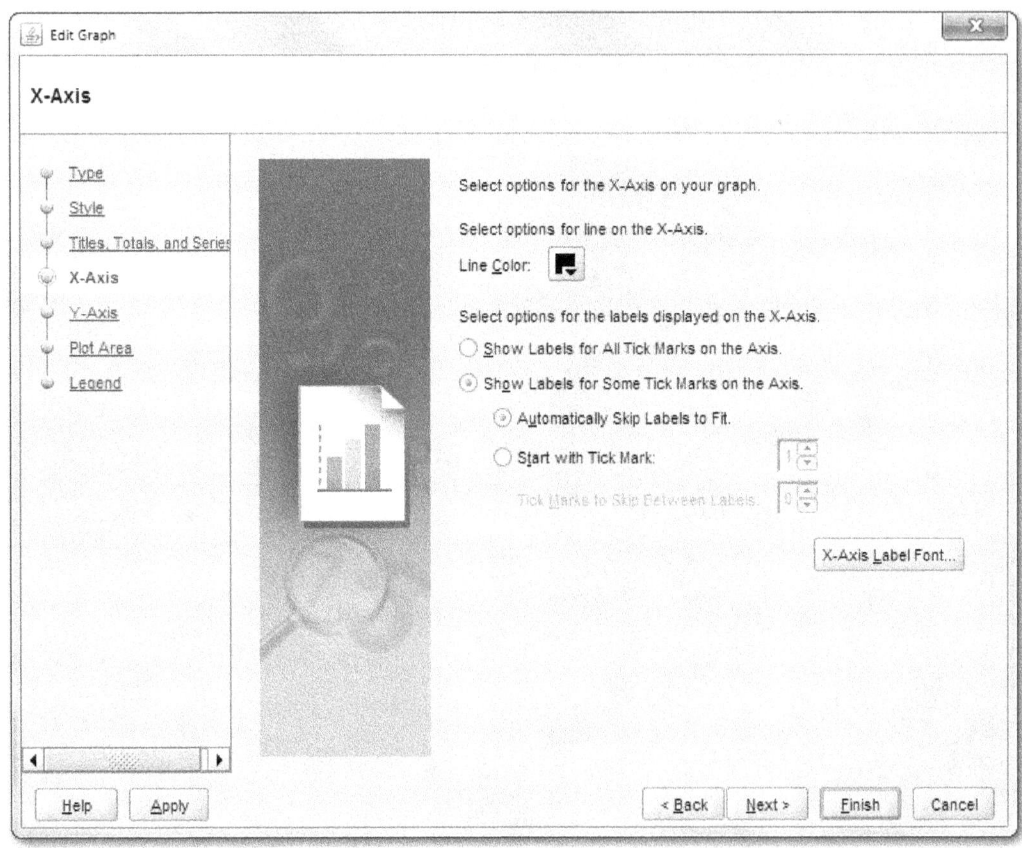


**FIGURE 7-14.** *X-Axis Variant 4 page of the Edit Graph dialog box, used for circular Radar only*

- **Show Labels For Some Tick Marks On The Axis** Check this box to show only some of the tick marks on the axis. This feature is not available on any of the scatter/bubble graphs and available only on circular graphs of type Radar. When you select this radio button, you will be given three more options:
  - **Automatically Skip Labels To Fit** Check this radio button if you want Discoverer to determine for itself what X-axis labels to show.
  - **Start With Tick Mark** This allows you to choose which tick mark to start with. It seems to us that the first tick mark is the place to start with as a benchmark. This option is good to use if don't need to see each data item but want to show the data incrementally.

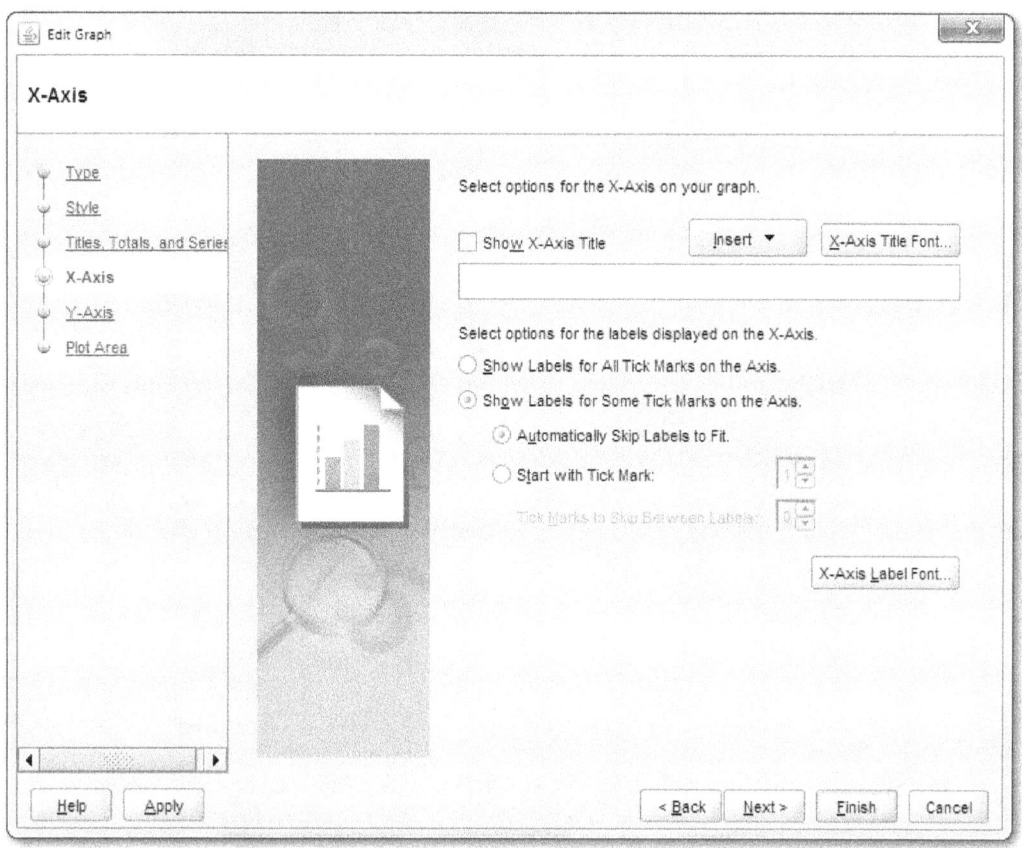


**FIGURE 7-15.** *X-Axis Variant 5 page of the Edit Graph dialog box, used for 3-D graphs only*

- **Tick Marks To Skip Between Labels** If you have 30 data items and don't need to see each one, skipping every three would leave you with fewer labels on the axis and give you a cleaner graph. However, don't use this option when you need to see everything, such as customer names or quarters in years.

- **X-Axis Label Font** Use this button to open the Format X1Axis Labels dialog box shown in the following illustration. This button works like the other Format Font dialog boxes with one exception: you can change the orientation of the text. This is helpful if labels are long, such as city names or customer names. You can choose

  - **Automatic** This is the default and will display the labels in normal left-to-right text orientation.
  - **0** This also displays the text in normal orientation.
  - **90** This will put the text in bottom-to-top orientation.

- **270** This will put the text in top-to-bottom orientation.

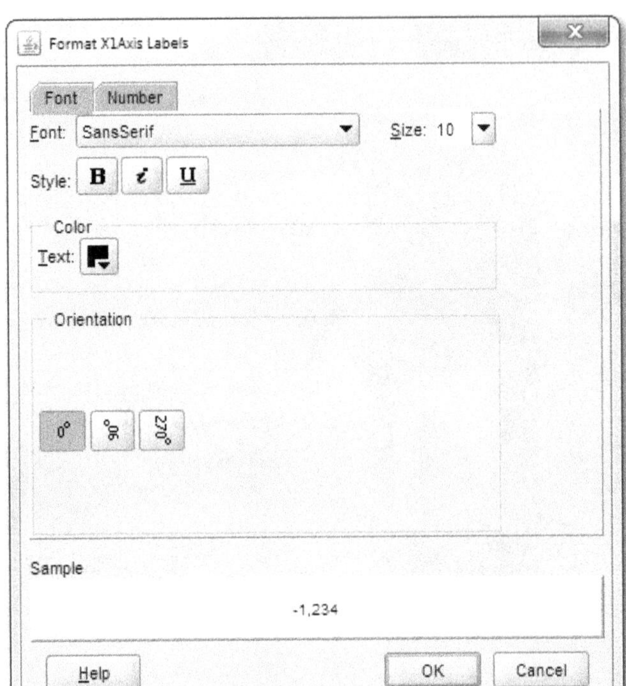


- **Set The Scale You Would Like To Use On This Axis** This area of the X-Axis page is available only for scatter/bubble graphs and circular graphs of type Polar. It has the following three features:
  - **Minimum** Use this field to change the lower axis range. Select the Set Automatically check box if you want Discoverer to select the best range for you.
  - **Maximum** Use this field to change the higher axis range. Select the Set Automatically check box if you want Discoverer to select the best range for you.
  - **Increment** Use this field to change the incremental axis range, or the granularity of the graph. Select the Set Automatically check box if you want Discoverer to select the best range for you.
- **Logarithmic Scale** This feature of the X-Axis page is available only for scatter/bubble graphs and circular graphs of type Polar. Use this check box to change the default linear scale of the X axis to a logarithmic scale. When you select this check box, the adjacent Base drop-down list becomes active, which enables you to change the default logarithmic base value. You might use a logarithmic scale when you have numeric data that is widely spaced and you want to maintain the visibility of the smaller values. For example, if you had data ranging in value from 10 to 100,000 and you use the default linear scale, smaller values might not register on the graph. If you changed to a logarithmic scale of base 10, the smaller values would register on the graph.

**NOTE**
*The Evalue in the Base drop-down list equals 2.71 (sometimes referred to as a natural logarithm).*

- **Reference Lines** This feature of the X-Axis page is available only for scatter/bubble and circular graphs of type Polar. It is most commonly used with the latter. Use this button to display the Reference Lines dialog, shown here, which enables you to define up to three lines on a graph to emphasize particular data values on a graph. For example, you might add a reference line showing the target sales value to emphasize which regions achieved a target.

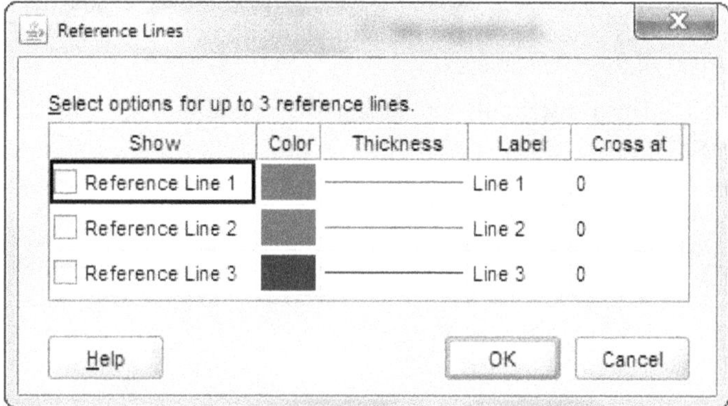


- **Format Axis Labels** This feature of the X-Axis page is available only for scatter/bubble and circular graphs of type Polar. This button works like the other Format Font dialog boxes with one exception: you can change the orientation of the text. This is helpful if labels are long, such as city names or customer names. You can choose
  - **Automatic** This is the default and will display the labels in normal left-to-right text orientation.
  - **0** This also displays the text in normal orientation.
  - **90** This will put the text in bottom-to-top orientation.
  - **270** This will put the text in top-to-bottom orientation.

To format the X axis of your graph, use the following workflow:

1. Add a title for the X axis and format the font.
2. Modify the line color and thickness if desired.
3. Make changes to the frequency of tick marks.
4. Set the scaling, if available.
5. Format the labels.
6. Click Next to move on to the next page. If you are building a Pareto graph, the next page you will see will be the Y2-Axis page. For all other graph types that have an X-Axis, the next page you will see is the Y-Axis page.
7. If you are done, click Finish.

## Edit Graph Dialog Box—Y-Axis Page

The Edit Graph dialog box X-Axis page shown in Figures 7-16 through 7-19 allows you to format how the Y axis (the data shown on the left side of the graph) will look. This page is not available if you are creating a pie graph. If you are working with a Pareto graph or a dual stacked bar, there will be two Y-Axis pages. These are described in the next section. The type of graph you are building determines which variant of Y-Axis page is available to you.

The four variants of Y-Axis pages are as follows:

- **Variant 1** This is the most common X-Axis page and is the one used for all graphs except circular, scatter/bubble, stock, Pareto, 3-D, and pie, the latter of which never has a Y-Axis. Figure 7-16 shows variant 1 of the Y-Axis page.
- **Variant 2** This is used only for scatter/bubble and circular graphs. Figure 7-17 shows this variant of the Y-Axis page.
- **Variant 3** This is used only for stock and 3-D graphs. Figure 7-18 shows this variant of the Y-Axis page.
- **Variant 4** This is used only for area graphs of type Percent. Figure 7-19 shows this variant of the Y-Axis page.

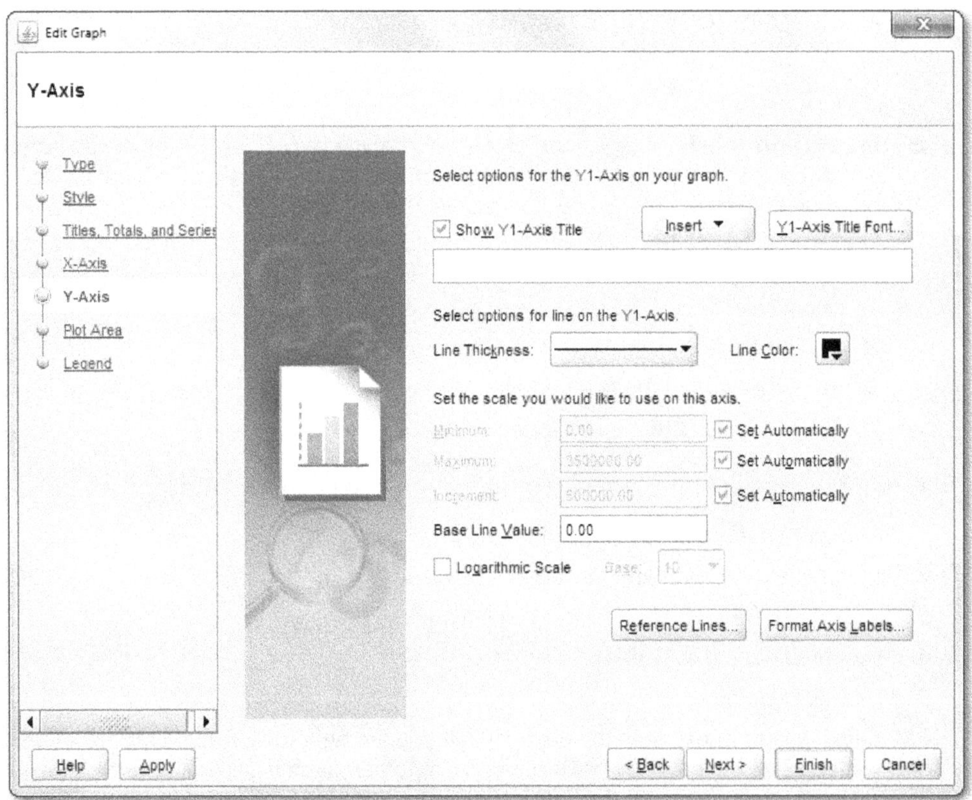


**FIGURE 7-16.** *Y-Axis Variant 1 page of the Edit Graph dialog box, used for most graphs*

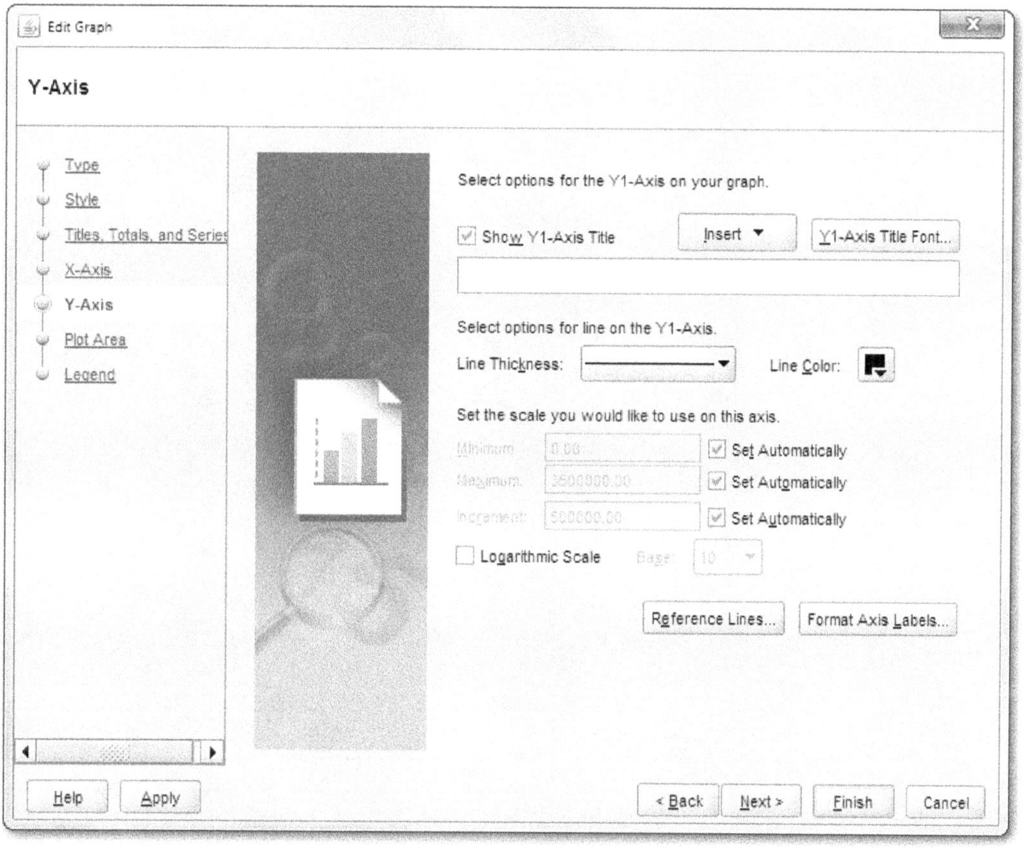

**FIGURE 7-17.** *Y-Axis Variant 2 page of the Edit Graph dialog box, used for scatter/bubble and circular only*

The Y axis is the axis going along the left side of the graph and has the following features:

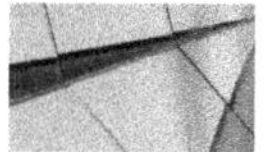

**NOTE**

*Many of the features of the Y-Axis page are common to all the variants of the page. While all the features are described here, not all will be available on every variant. We will let you know when a feature is not available on a certain page.*

- **Show Y1-Axis Title** Check this box if you want the Y-Axis title to display. This feature is available on all the graphs.
- **Insert** Use this button in the same way you added a title to the graph. This feature is available on all the graphs.

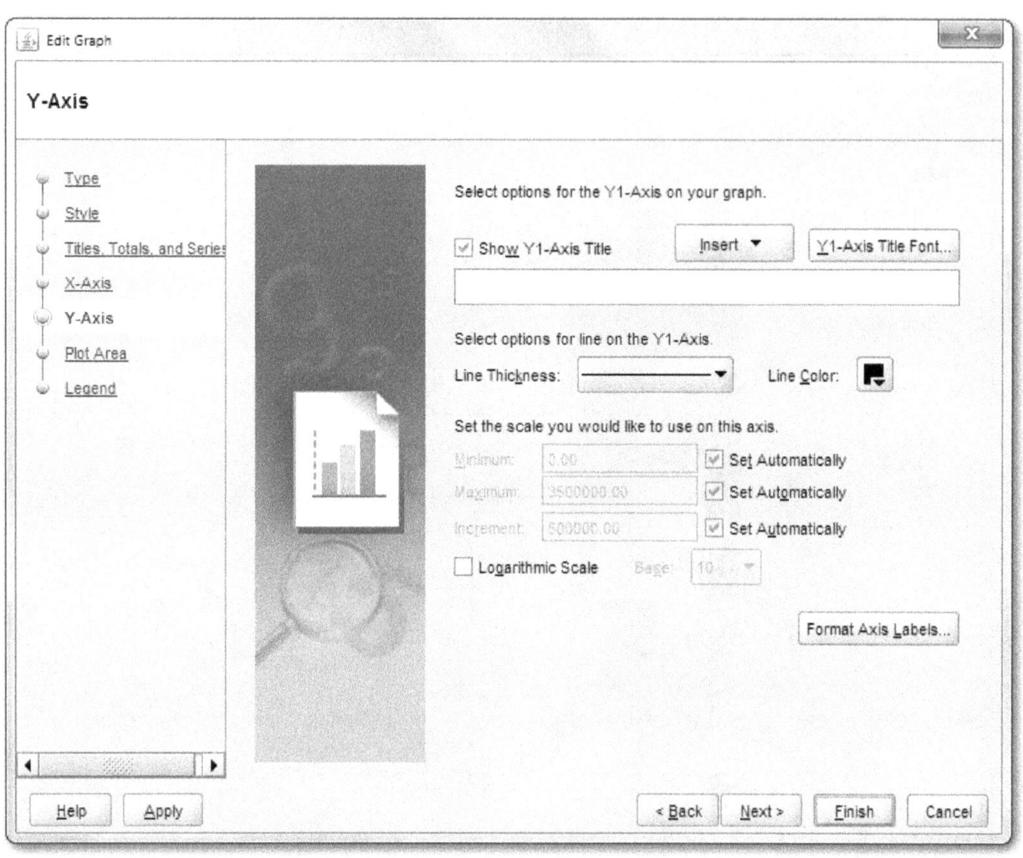


**FIGURE 7-18.** *Y-Axis Variant 3 page of the Edit Graph dialog box, used for stock and 3-D only*

- **Y-Axis Title Font** This opens the Format Font dialog box to format the Y-axis title. This feature is available on all the graphs.
- **Y-Axis Title** Add a title that will go across the left side of the graph. Either you can use the Insert button to insert a common element into the title or you can simply type in your own title. Typically, we find a combination of the two to be very effective. After you have created a title, if you deselect the Show Y1-Axis Title box, the title will not show. This feature is available on all of the graphs.
- **Line Thickness** Use this drop-down list to select the weight of the line of the Y axis. This feature is available on all the graphs.
- **Line Color** Use this drop-down to change the color of the Y axis line. This feature is available on all the graphs.
- **Set the scale you would like to use on this axis** This area of the Y-Axis page is available on all graph types except Percent. It has the following three features:

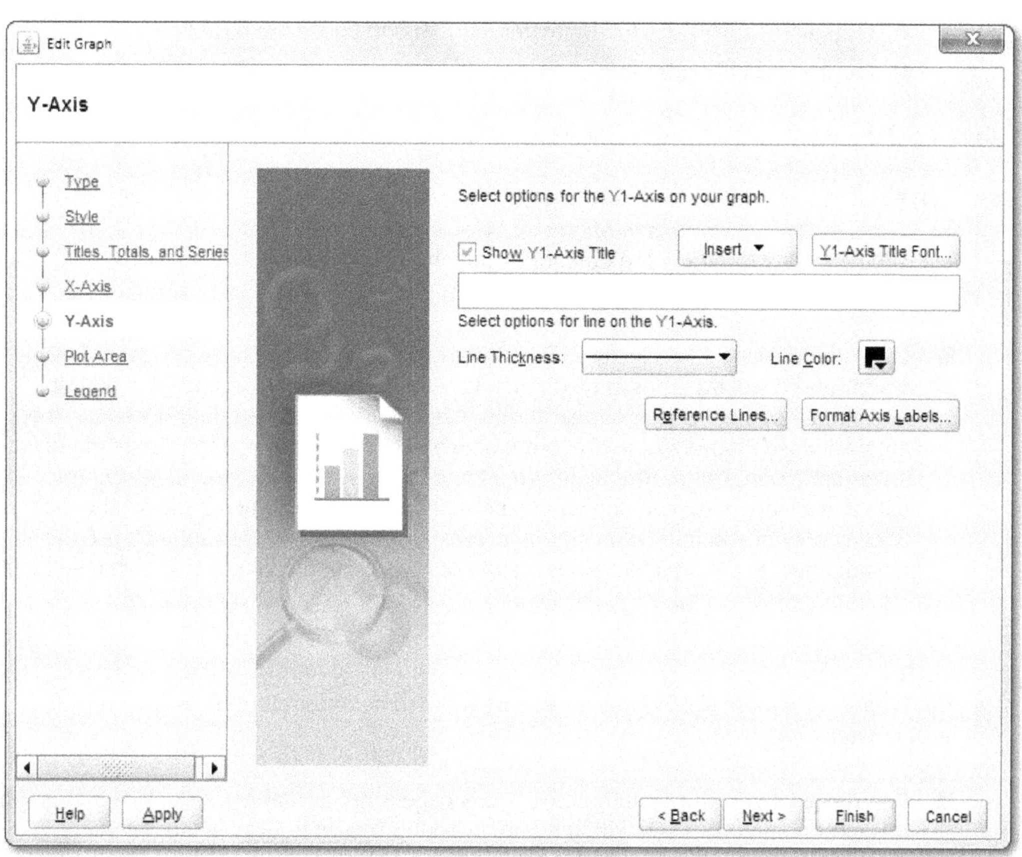


**FIGURE 7-19.** *Y-Axis Variant 4 page of the Edit Graph dialog box, used for percent only*

- **Minimum** Use this field to change the lower axis range. Select the Set Automatically check box if you want Discoverer to select the best range for you.
- **Maximum** Use this field to change the higher axis range. Select the Set Automatically check box if you want Discoverer to select the best range for you.
- **Increment** Use this field to change the incremental axis range or the granularity of the graph. Select the Set Automatically check box if you want Discoverer to select the best range for you.

- **Base Line Value** This feature of the Y-Axis page is available for all graphs except circular, scatter/bubble, stock, 3-D, and any of the stacked (such as bar graphs of subtype Dual Y-Stacked) or percent graphs (such as bar graphs of subtype Percent). Use this field to specify a starting value for the Y axis. For example, you might have a monthly sales target of 10,000 units and want to emphasize how total sales for each month relate to the 10,000 target.

In other words, on a vertical bar graph, you might want to do the following:

- Display monthly sales totals greater than 10,000 above the base line
- Display monthly sales totals less than 10,000 below the base line

To achieve this graph layout, you set Base Line Value to 10,000.

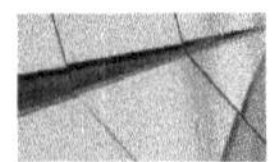

**NOTE**
*If you are familiar with graphs in Microsoft Excel, changing the base line value is similar to setting the Category value in Microsoft Excel graphs.*

- **Logarithmic Scale** This feature of the Y-Axis page is available only for scatter/bubble graphs and circular graphs of type Polar. Use this check box to change the default linear scale of the Y axis to a logarithmic scale. When you select this check box, the adjacent Base drop-down list becomes active, which enables you to change the default logarithmic base value. You might use a logarithmic scale when you have numeric data that is widely spaced and you want to maintain the visibility of the smaller values. For example, if you had data ranging in value from 10 to 100,000 and you use the default linear scale, smaller values might not register on the graph. If you changed to a logarithmic scale of base 10, the smaller values would register on the graph.

**NOTE**
*The Evalue in the Base drop-down list equals 2.71 (sometimes referred to as a natural logarithm).*

- **Reference Lines** This feature of the Y-Axis page is not available for stock or 3-D graphs. It is most commonly used with the latter. Use this button to display the Reference Lines dialog, shown here, which enables you to define up to three lines on a graph to emphasize particular data values on a graph. For example, you require customers to exceed sales orders of $25,000 per quarter to receive a 10 percent discount and to exceed sales orders of $50,000 to receive a 15 percent discount. Your graph can have reference lines set at $25,000 and $50,000 to see which customers fall in the required sales to keep their discounts.

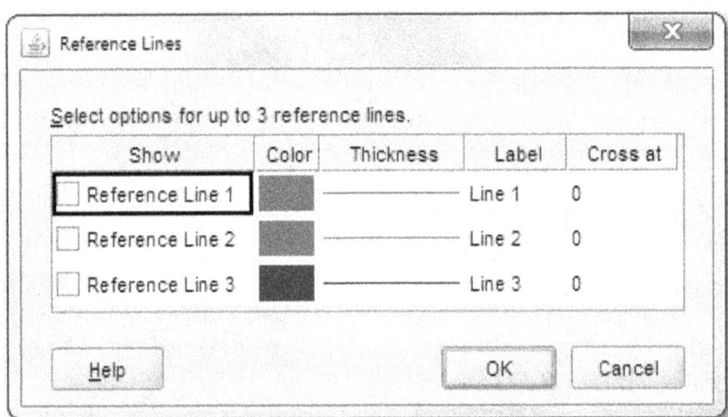

- **Format Axis Labels** This feature of the Y-Axis page is available for all graphs. This button works like the other Format Font dialog boxes with one exception: you can change the orientation of the text. This is helpful if labels are long, such as city names or customer names. You can choose
  - **Automatic** This is the default and will display the labels in normal left-to-right text orientation.
  - **0** This also displays the text in normal orientation.
  - **90** This will put the text in bottom-to-top orientation.
  - **270** This will put the text in top-to-bottom orientation.

To format the Y axis of your graph, use the following workflow:

1. Add a title for the Y axis and format the font.
2. Modify the line color and thickness if desired.
3. Format the Y axis label font.
4. Decide whether you want to create your own scale or use the default set by Discoverer.
5. If you choose to change the scale, click in the Maximum field and type the highest number you want to use for the scale.
6. Click in the Minimum field and type the lowest number you want to use for the scale.
7. Decide whether you want to use an alternate logarithm and base to your scale.
8. If reference lines are available, set them using the Reference Lines dialog box.
9. Format the Y axis label font.
10. Click Next to move on to the Plot Area page.
11. If you are done, click Finish.

### Edit Graph Dialog Box—Y1-Axis and Y2-Axis Tabs

When using a Pareto graph or a graph that has a dual Y axis, you will have two Y axes, Y1 and Y2. The pages are identical, and instead of setting up scales, you set up the increments in which you want to see the data displayed. You can also set up reference lines. Refer to the previous section to see the features of the Y axis.

### Edit Graph Dialog Box—Plot Area Page

The next step is to specify how worksheet items are plotted on the graph. For example, you might want to set the background color of a graph or specify the color of bars on a bar graph. The Edit Graph dialog box Plot Area page shown in Figures 7-20 through 7-23 allows you to specify how the items are plotted. The type of graph you are building determines which variant of Plot Area page is available to you.

The four variants of Plot Area pages are as follows:

- **Variant 1** This is the most common Plot Area page and is the one used for all graphs except pie, Pareto, and 3-D. Figure 7-20 shows the variant 1 of the Plot Area page.
- **Variant 2** This is used only for pie graphs. Figure 7-21 shows this variant of the Plot Area page.

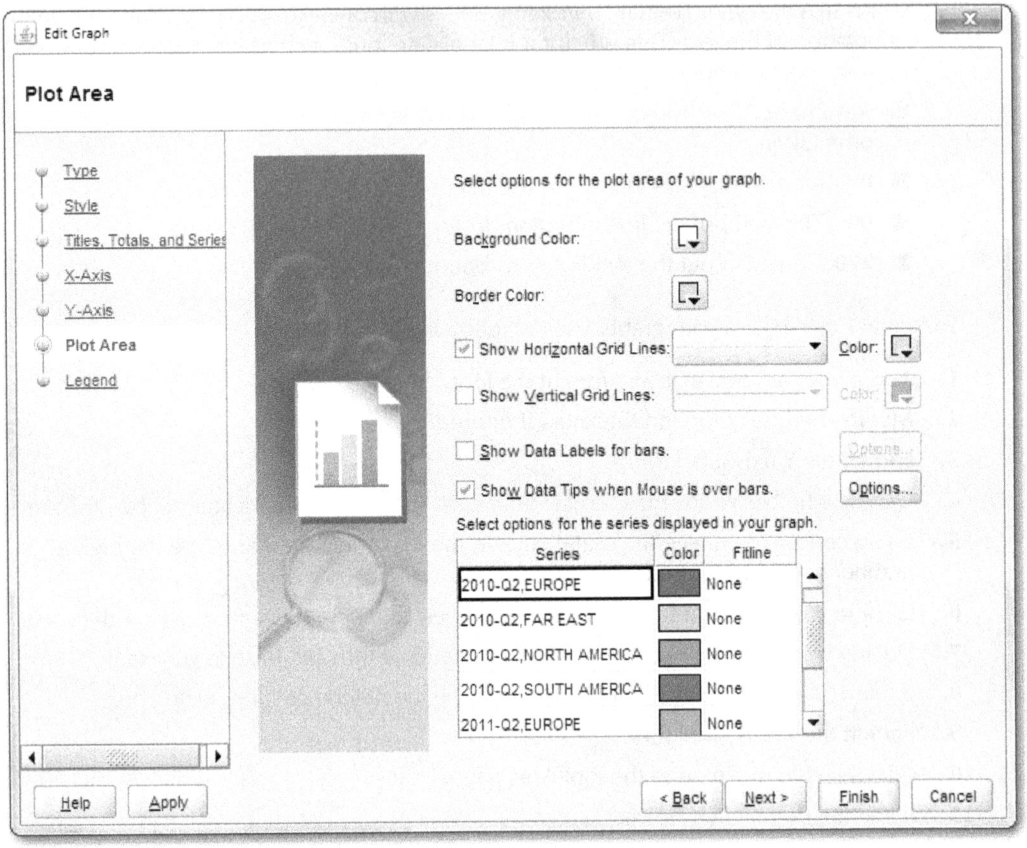

**FIGURE 7-20.** *Plot Area Variant 1 page of the Edit Graph dialog box, used for most graphs*

- **Variant 3** This is used only for Pareto graphs. Figure 7-22 shows this variant of the Plot Area page.
- **Variant 4** This is used only for 3-D graphs. Figure 7-23 shows this variant of the Plot Area page.

The Plot Area page has the following features:

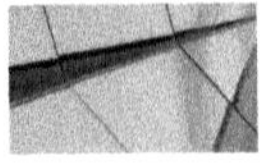

**NOTE**
*Many of the features of the Plot Area page are common to all the variants of the page. While all the features are described here, not all will be available on every variant. We will let you know when a feature is not available on a certain page.*

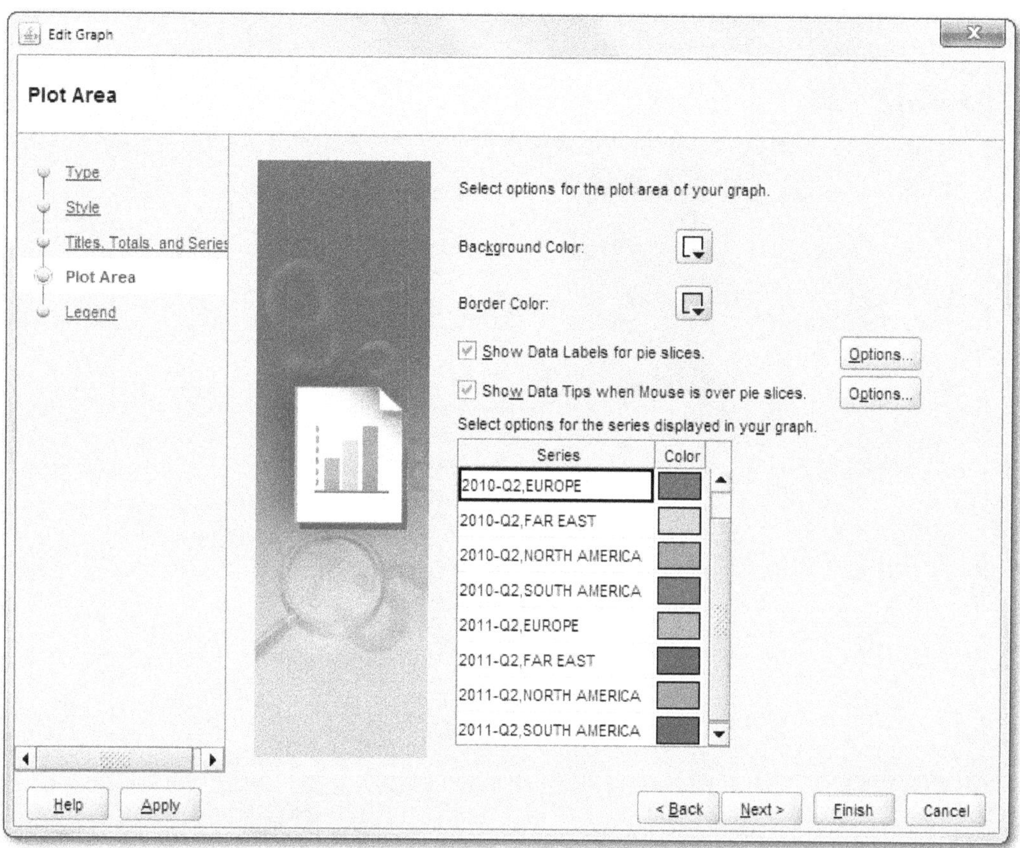


**FIGURE 7-21.** *Plot Area Variant 2 page of the Edit Graph dialog box, used for pie only*

- **Background Color** Use this drop-down to display a color palette from which to select the background color of the graph. This feature is available on all the graphs.
- **Border Color** Use this drop-down to display a color palette from which to select the border color of the graph. This feature is available on all of the graphs.
- **Show Horizontal Gridlines** Check this box if you want the horizontal gridlines to display on the plot area of the graph. This feature is not available on pie or 3-D graphs. When it's checked, the following additional features are available:
  - **Line Thickness** Use this drop-down list to select the weight of the gridline.
  - **Line Color** Use this drop-down to display a color palette from which to select the color of the gridline.

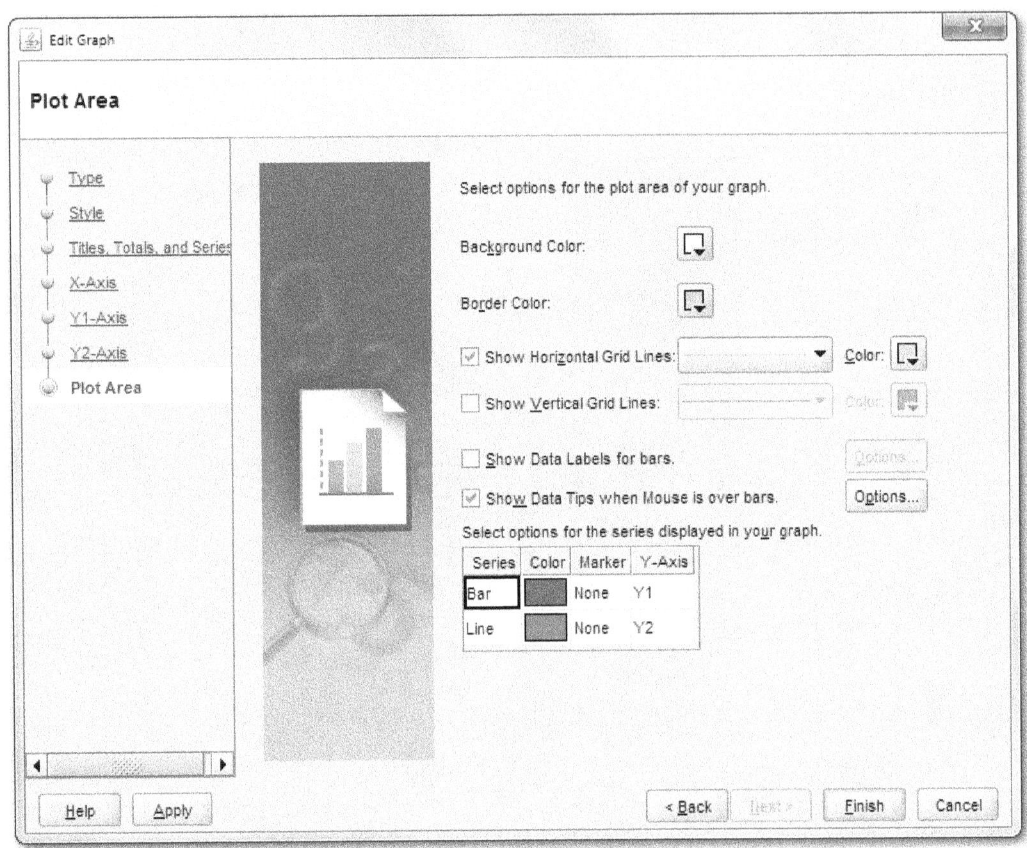


**FIGURE 7-22.** *Plot Area Variant 3 page of the Edit Graph dialog box, used for Pareto only*

- **Show Vertical Gridlines** Check this box if you want the vertical gridlines to display. This feature is not available on pie or 3-D graphs. When it's checked, the following additional features are available:
  - **Line Thickness** Use this drop-down list to select the weight of the gridline.
  - **Line Color** Use this drop-down to display a color palette from which to select the color of the gridline.
- **Show Data Labels For *graph type*** Click this box to enable the display of data labels. This feature is not available for 3-D graphs, and the wording changes to Show Data Labels Above Lines when a line graph is being created (shown here). The words *graph type* will change depending upon what type of graph is being created. When checked,

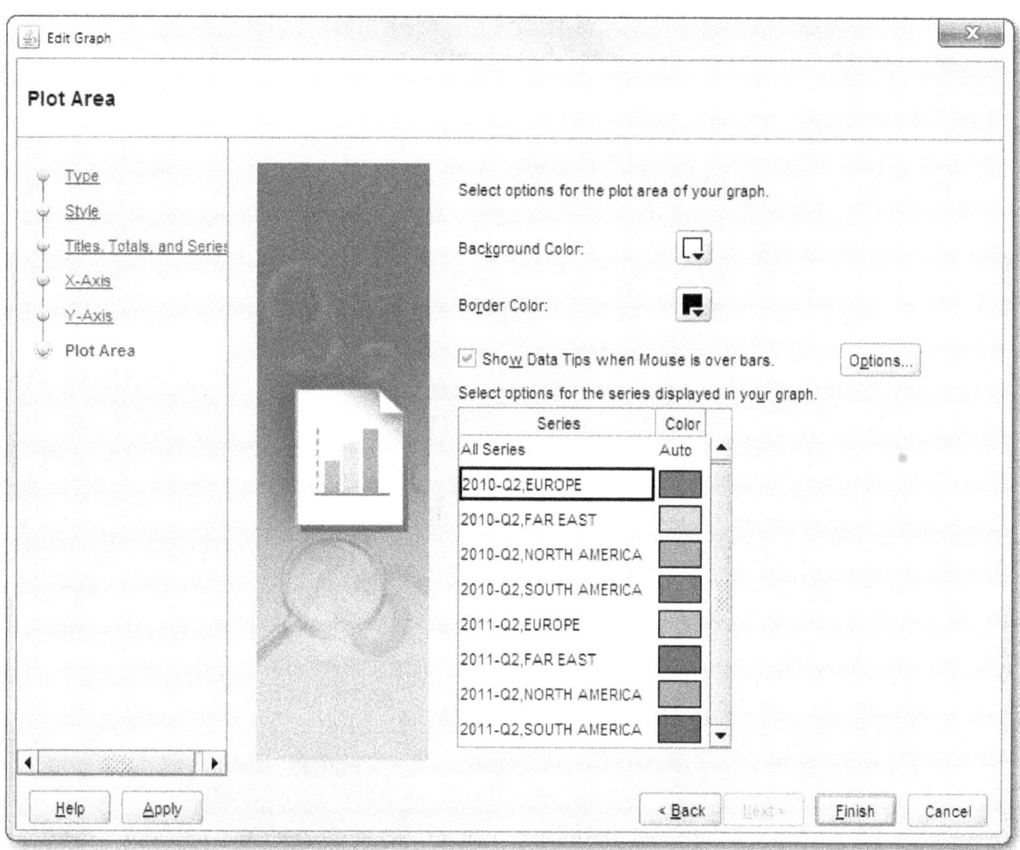


**FIGURE 7-23.** *Plot Area Variant 4 page of the Edit Graph dialog box, used for 3-D only*

the Options button will also become enabled. When the Options button is clicked, a Data Label Options dialog box displays. The Data Label Options dialog box for a bar graph is shown here:

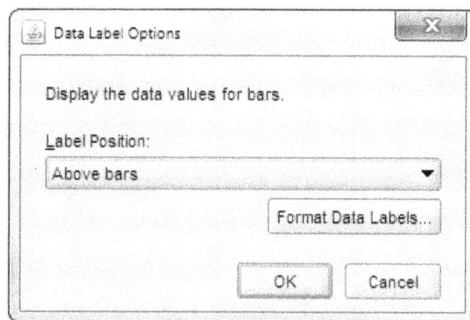

Data Label Options
Display the data values for bars.
Label Position:
Above bars
Format Data Labels...
OK
Cancel

The options are completed by choosing whether to position the data labels above or centered upon the graph and by formatting the label.

- **Show Data Labels Above Lines** This appears instead of Show Data Labels For whenever the graph is a line. Check the box to enable the display of the label. When you select this check box, the Format Data Labels button becomes active, which enables you to determine the font for the label.
- **Show Data Tips When Mouse Is Over ...** Check this box to display mouse tips when your mouse hovers over areas of the graph. This feature is available for all graph types. Pop-up labels help identify areas of the graph. When you select this check box, the Options button becomes active, which enables you to change the label settings. For example, you might want to display the series name (for example, Sales SUM) and the value (for example, 30,000) when you move the cursor over plotted values.

  The actual options that are available depend upon the type of graph being created and are as follows:

  - **Series Label** When checked, this will display series information as the mouse is hovered over the label. This is checked by default and is available for all graph types.
  - **Group Label** When checked, this will display group information as the mouse is hovered over the label. This is checked by default and is available for all graph types.
  - **Value** When checked, this will display the value as the mouse is hovered over the label. This is checked by default and is available for all graph types.
  - **Percent** When checked, this will display the percentage as the mouse is hovered over the label. This is not checked by default and is available only on a pie graph.
- **Select options for the series displayed in your graph** Use this table to specify how the worksheet items are displayed on the graph. This feature is available for all graphs.
  - **Series** This column displays the names of worksheet items that are being plotted on the graph. Depending on the type of graph being created, you can select options for each series for some of the following features. Look back at Figures 7-21 through 7-23 to see the different options and series available.
  - **Color** Clicking the current color allows you to select a different color.
  - **Line** Clicking the current line setting allows you to select a different line thickness for changing the plot line weight (for example, for the plot line on line graphs).
  - **Marker** Clicking in the Marker cell allows you to change the graphical symbol for a series (for example, for the plot area on scatter graphs). The drop-down is shown in the illustration at right.
  - **Y-Axis** Clicking in the Y axis offers you a drop-down list of axes for specifying which worksheet items are displayed on which series (for example, on Dual-Y type graphs).
  - **Fitline** These show trends or provide a simplified explanation of the data. The drop-down is shown in the illustration at right.

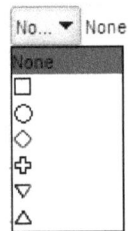

- **Graph** This is used in a combination graph to indicate what type of graph type to use for a particular data value. For example, you might have a Volume row for specifying how the Volume worksheet item is displayed. Use the All Series row to specify how all worksheet items are displayed on the graph. Select Automatic in the Color column or Auto in the Marker column if you want Discoverer to format these attributes for you. The Options part of the page from a combination graph is shown here:

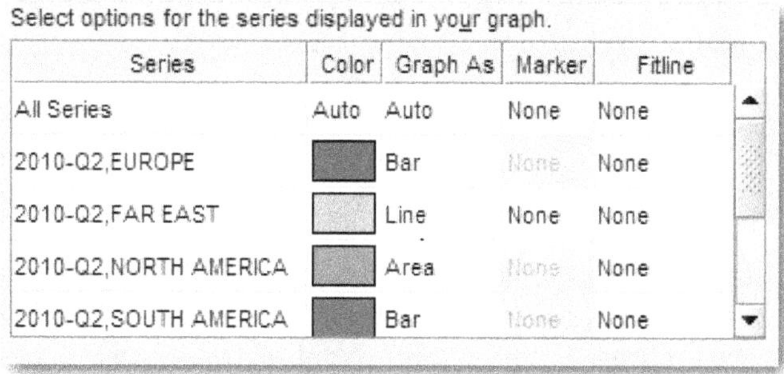

Select options for the series displayed in your graph.
Series
Color
Graph As
Marker
Fitline
All Series
Auto
Auto
None
None
2010-Q2,EUROPE
Bar
None
2010-Q2,FAR EAST
Line
None
None
2010-Q2,NORTH AMERICA
Area
None
2010-Q2,SOUTH AMERICA
Bar
None


To complete the plot area of your graph, use the following workflow:

1. Select the background and border colors.
2. Modify the horizontal and vertical line colors and thicknesses if desired.
3. Determine whether to show data labels, and if they are displayed, determine the position and color of the labels.
4. Determine whether to show data tips, and if they are displayed, determine what will appear when the mouse hovers over parts of the graph.
5. Complete the Options area of the page.
6. Click Next to move on to the Legend page (not available for Pareto or 3-D graphs).
7. If you are done, click Finish.

## Edit Graph Dialog Legend Page

The final step is to add a legend to your graph. The graph legend (sometimes called a *key*) explains how worksheet data is represented on a graph. For example, you might want to display a legend to explain which colors represent which worksheet items plotted on a graph. Figure 7-24 shows the Legend page of the Edit Graph dialog box.

The features of the Legend page are as follows:

- **Show Legend** Check this box if you want a legend to display on the graph.
- **Location** Use this drop-down list to change the position of the legend (for example, above the graph or to the right of the graph). Select Automatic if you want Discoverer to choose the best legend position for you.

Automatic
Top
Bottom
Right
Left

- **Background Color** Use this drop-down to display a color palette from which to select the background color of the legend.
- **Border Color** Use this drop-down to display a color palette from which to select the border color of the legend.

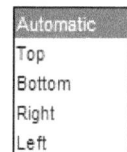

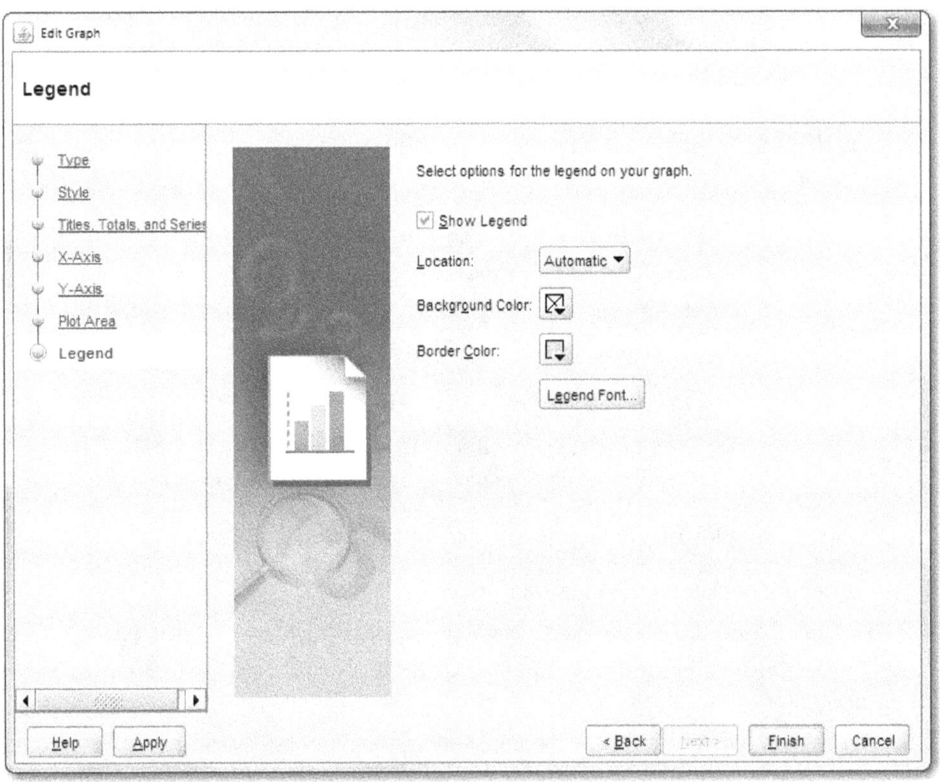


**FIGURE 7-24.** *Entering a graph legend*

- **Legend Font** Click this button to show additional options for pie charts.

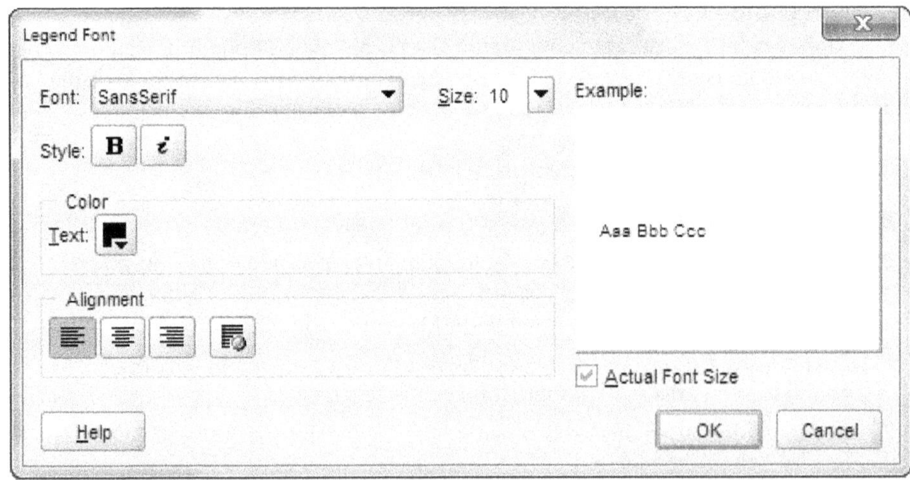

To add a legend to your graph, use the following workflow:

1. Determine whether the legend should be displayed.
2. Determine the location where the legend will be displayed.
3. Select the background and border colors for the legend.
4. Determine the font to use for the legend.
5. When done, click Finish

# Modifying a Graph in Plus

Because you are not using a wizard in Plus, it is easy to modify your graph. Simply reopen the graph using the Graph button, or from the menu bar select Edit | Graph. Select the link from the workflow on the left side and make your modification.

# Modifying a Graph in Desktop

After the graph has been created, it is again easily modified. The Modify Graph dialog box is viewed in one of two ways. If you open it from the worksheet, it is displayed in the same format as the Graph Wizard. If, however, you open it from the graph itself, it opens as a four-tab form with the same steps as the Graph Wizard. Each of the tabbed dialog boxes is used in the same way as the four steps of the wizard.

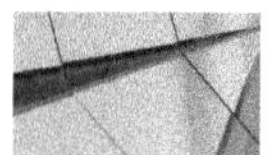

**NOTE**
*Remember that you do not need to do anything for the data to be updated with changes to the query. Discoverer does this for you automatically.*

## To Modify the Graph from the Worksheet

When the graph is closed, you can either use the Graph button on the toolbar or use the menu bar. If you use the menu bar, you will notice that only two options are available to you in Desktop: Graph | Show and Graph | Edit Graph. The rest of the items are available only when the graph is open and the Graph window is maximized. After you modify the graph, the Graph window will open.

To open the Modify Graph dialog box from the worksheet, use the following workflow:

1. Select Graph | Edit Graph.
2. Follow the instructions in the "The Desktop Graph Wizard" section earlier in this chapter.
3. After making the desired modifications, click OK.

## To Modify the Graph from the Graph Window

It is easier to modify the graph with the Graph window open because you have the toolbar available. Many of the changes you will want to make can be made from the toolbar. With the Graph window open, you can also access all of the options on the Graph drop-down list on the menu bar. Unless the Graph window is maximized, it seems as though the menu bar is not available to you, but it is. Click the menu bar of the worksheet, and it will become active, leaving the Graph window open in the front in an inactive state.

You can also access all of the same options by right-clicking in the Graph window. This opens a pop-up list of options for working with the graph.

To open the Modify Graph dialog box from the Graph window, use the following workflow:

1. From the menu bar select Graph | Edit Graph, or right-click in the Graph window and select Edit Graph.
2. Select the tab you want to use.
3. Follow the instructions in the "The Desktop Graph Wizard" section earlier in the chapter.
4. After making the desired modifications, click OK.

### Resizing the Graph

You will, in most cases, need to resize the graph or some of its components. Most of the graph elements can be resized. Figure 7-25 shows the resizable elements of a graph.

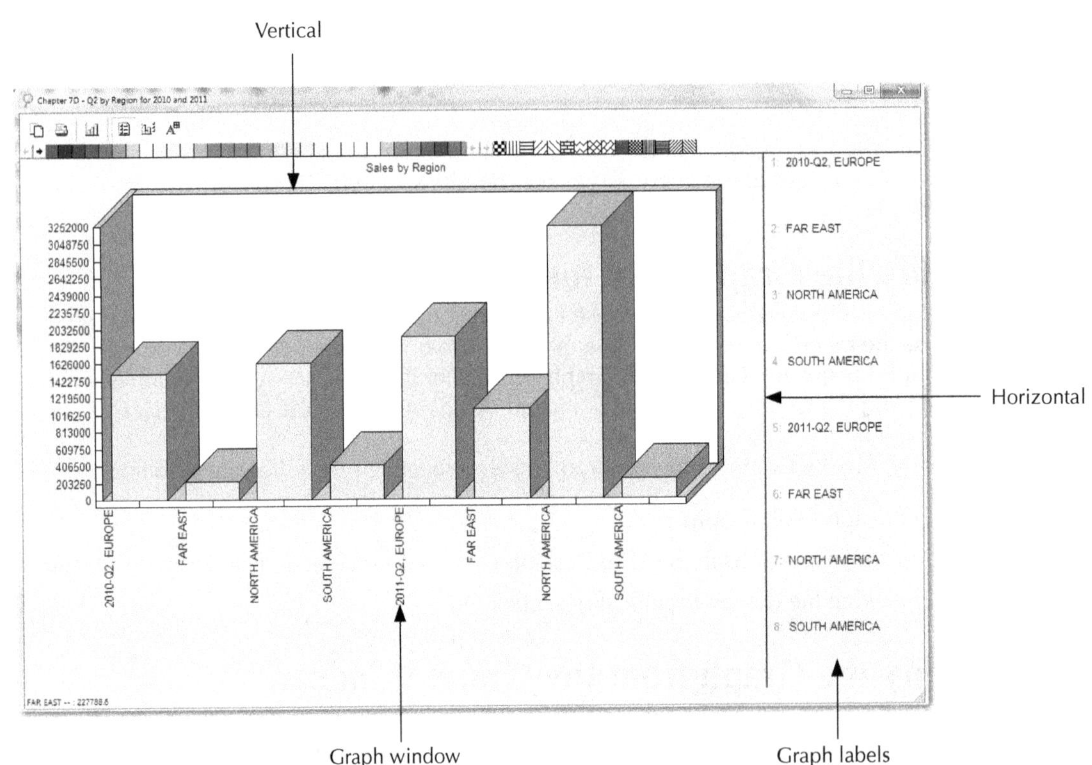


**FIGURE 7-25.** *The resizable elements of a graph*

To resize a graph element, use the following workflow:

1. Click the resizable element until the mouse pointer changes to a double-headed arrow.
2. Drag until you obtain the desired size.

### Modifying the Scale

Although you set the scale in the Modify Graph dialog box, there is a separate dialog box that allows for the setting of more options. Along with the minimum and maximum of the data, you can also set the scale unit. For example, if you are analyzing sales in terms of units sold and you want a graph that shows sales in thousands of units, you should set the scale unit to 1,000. This is equally effective for showing dollar values in the millions. Simply set the scale unit to 1 million, and you will reduce the size of the numbers on the Y axis, while still showing the relationship of the data. The number on the scale is shown in the upper-left corner of the Graph window as a fraction, such as 1/1000 for setting the scale unit to one per thousand.

Discoverer sets the increments between the numbers on the Y axis in terms of the lowest and highest numbers being analyzed. The increments are divided equally and will change automatically when the query updates. By choosing Fixed instead and selecting a number, you can create smaller or larger increments. Be careful when choosing, however; if you choose too large a number, the gaps between increments may be so small you might not be able to see them all. If you make the increment too small, it may be difficult to effectively analyze the data.

One other thing you can do in the Scale And Numbers dialog box is to change the scale from linear to logarithmic. We recommend leaving the setting at linear unless you are analyzing scientific or complex mathematical formulas.

To open the Scale And Numbers dialog box from the Graph window, use the following workflow:

1. From the menu bar, select Graph | Scale, or right-click in the Graph window and select Scale.
2. Make the modifications desired.
3. Click OK.

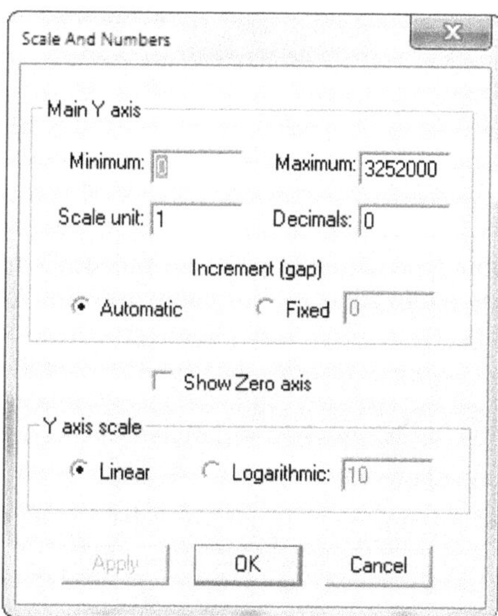

## Changing Colors

After the graph is created, use the Color and Pattern section of the toolbar to change colors. Discoverer uses a drag-and-drop system for changing colors and patterns.

To change a color or pattern on the graph, use the following workflow:

1. Click the color or pattern you want to use.
2. Hold down the mouse button until the mouse pointer changes to a paint can.
3. Drag the paint can (mouse pointer) to the data on the graph you want to change.
4. Release the mouse button.

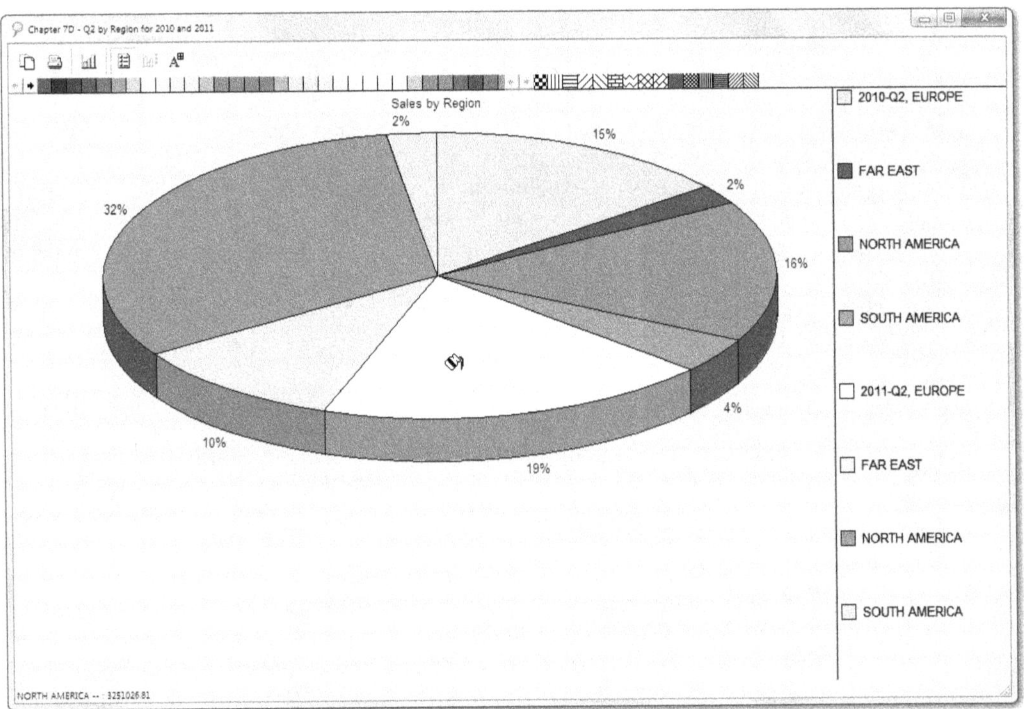


## Using Pull-Outs

When using a pie or doughnut type of graph, you can "pull out" one or more sections of the graph. Do this to emphasize certain data, such as the highest and lowest sales regions or the first quarter of the past three years.

To pull out an element on a pie or doughnut graph, use the following workflow:

1. Click the data section of the pie you want to pull out.
2. Drag it away from the center of the graph.
3. Continue the preceding steps until you have pulled out all of the data you want to emphasize. This is shown in the following illustration:

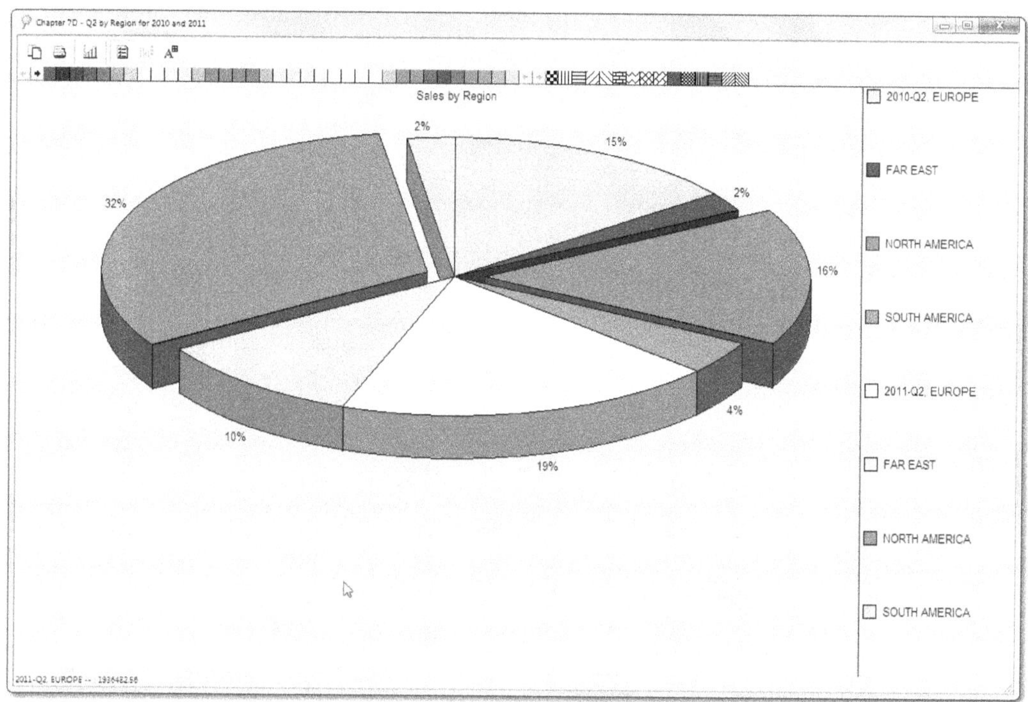


## Modifying 3-D Effects

When you select the type and format for the graph in the wizard, you have limited control over the formatting. Some of the graph types have one or more 3-D formatting options. Using 3-D formatting can add interest and character to a graph, and most graph types default to a 3-D format. If you choose to use a 3-D format, you can modify it after you have finished creating the graph with the 3D View Properties dialog box. The options available include changing the angle of the graph, applying a full 3-D view, and making the graph deeper or shallower.

To open the 3D View Properties dialog box, select Graph | 3D View, or right-click the graph and select 3D View. The box contains the following features:

- **3D check box** Applies standard 3-D effects
- **Full 3D View check box** Adds full 3-D effects
- **Shadows check box** Adds or removes shadows in the graph
- **X Angle box** Changes the X axis angle
- **Y Angle box** Changes the Y axis angle
- **Depth sliding scale** Increases or decreases the depth of the 3-D effects
- **X and Y axes diagram** Changes the angle of the X and Y axes

Figure 7-26 shows the 3D View Properties dialog box.

Oracle makes an excellent recommendation when working with the 3D View Properties dialog box: write down all of the settings before you begin to modify the 3-D effect so that you

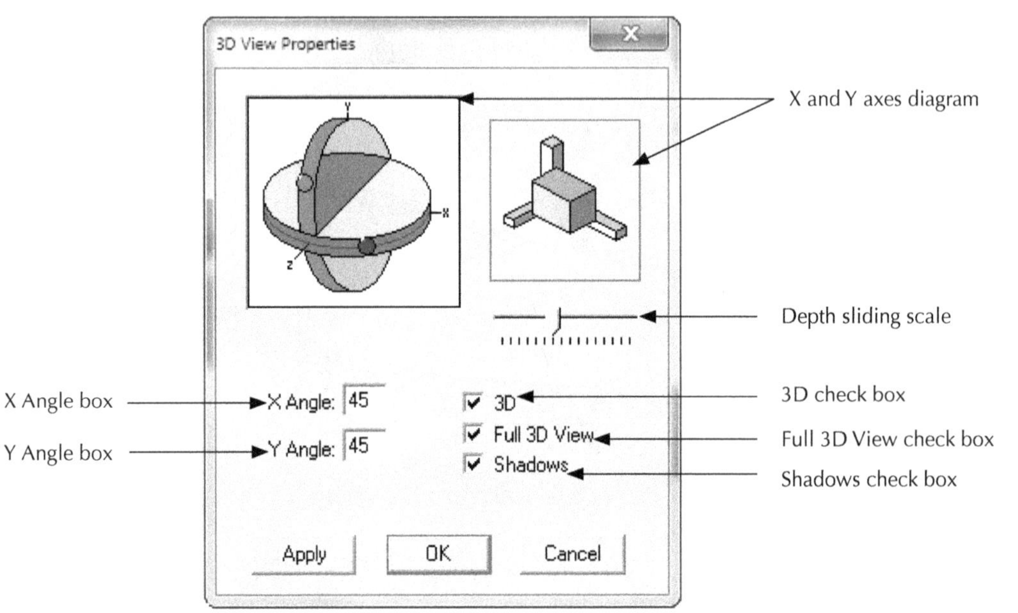


**FIGURE 7-26.** *3D View Properties dialog box*

can return them to the defaults if you want. Then you are free to experiment with different rotations and angles.

To change the 3-D effects of a graph, use the following workflow:

1. Check the Full 3D View check box.
2. Click and drag the dots on the X and Y axes diagram; the numbers in the X Angle and Y Angle boxes will change as you do this.
3. Move the depth sliding scale to increase or decrease the depth of the graph.
4. Click Apply to view the changes to the graph.
5. When done with the modifications, click OK.

# Summary

In this chapter, you learned how to use the Graph Wizard to create graphs in Desktop or the Edit Graph dialog box in Plus based on your queries. You learned to add interest and detail by adding titles, changing fonts, and adding legends and labels. You also saw how to modify your graphs in a variety of ways, including using pull-outs, adding 3-D effects, and changing the scale of the Y axis.

Graphs are an excellent way to represent your data visually. By using the Discoverer graph tool, you will add a new dimension to your queries.

# CHAPTER 8

# Turning a Discoverer Query into a Report

It may seem premature at this point to show you how to create a report. However, we think that once you have a working query, you should know how to turn it into a report. In the coming chapters, you will learn more advanced Discoverer techniques for building bigger and better queries. As you do, the lessons you learn here will enable you to create reports based upon those queries.

A Discoverer report is simply a well-formatted query. There is no wizard to guide you, or button to click, that will magically turn your query into a stunning printable report. You have a bit of work to do, but we think it is fun to format reports!

Report aesthetics are all-important. If you present your report in a logical order, using meaningful, business-friendly column names and fonts that are pleasing to the eye, you are well on the way toward having your report accepted by those who will read it. Sloppy reports with bad formatting, misspelled column names, and illogical ordering invite criticism such as "If they can't even give me a report with a good layout, maybe I should get someone to double-check the figures."

A well-written report induces confidence in the creator.

Many companies have a standard for reporting. If your company does have a standard, it is important to learn it and use it in your reports. It is possible, however, that there is no established standard. If this is the case, you may be the one who introduces such a standard to your company.

Avoid using frilly or unusual fonts. Times New Roman and Arial are the default fonts for a reason. They are easy to read and pleasing to the eye. Also, adding too much detail to headers and footers and using too many colors can distract from the data. The old adage "Keep it simple, stupid" is a good one to adopt in reporting. Another reason to stick with normal fonts is how they will appear on the Web. You can't assume that everyone has the same font sets as you do. Even though virtual font mapping takes place, which maps Java fonts to the physical fonts installed on a user's computer, you cannot always be guaranteed of the results when using esoteric fonts.

We have already covered the steps for creating and formatting titles, column headings, widths, and colors, as well as changing fonts in the data, so we will not repeat them here. These formatting steps have been added to the workflow to give you an idea of where to do them if they were not done while the query was created. Many queries are around for a long time just waiting to become a report and so have a good deal of the formatting already done. We call these *wish queries* because they are queries that wish they were reports, or more likely, there is someone who is saying, "I wish I had a report that did this or answered that" when there is already a query that does. It simply needs to be turned into a printable report.

In this chapter, you will learn a workflow that will prepare your queries to be turned into reports. You will learn how to format the report for printing, including how to format the sheet, headers, footers, and margins; how to format the table options to determine whether the printable report will have gridlines; and how to insert page breaks. We will show you how to use the Page Setup feature to give you greater flexibility in how your pages will print. We will also teach you to use the Print Preview feature of Discoverer as a tool for fine-tuning the report.

Discoverer has the ability to export reports into other applications. You will be shown the steps to follow for exporting your reports as spreadsheets, HTML, and text files.

# A Workflow for Building Reports

Although you have already learned about the basic concepts included in the report workflow, we offer them here to help you save time and unneeded effort in report building. The workflow ensures that you perform your formatting in the right order so you don't need to do the same thing twice.

For example, if you format the width of your columns and then rename them, the column might not be wide enough to accommodate the new name and you will need to format the width again. This is a waste of time. Thus, by following the workflow, you can avoid duplication of effort.

Included in the workflow are reminders on when to save your query. It may seem elementary, but we think there are good times to save in terms of changes you have made to your report. It might also be a good idea for you to save your query by some other name as a backup in case you get carried away and want to begin again from the base query.

# Report Workflow

Use the following workflow to begin turning a query into a report:

1. Create a working query that avoids the Twilight Zone.
2. Rearrange the columns in the query and move to the page items those columns that have the same data repeated in every row.
3. Decide whether any columns could be better displayed on their own sheet and move these also to the page items (using page items will be discussed in more detail when we explain analysis in Chapter 9).
4. Rename any item that does not have a meaningful name.
5. Adjust column widths.
6. Save the query.
7. Refine temporary conditions and create new ones to select only the data from the database that you want to use in the final report—if you make a mistake, you can always reload from the saved copy. Conditions should be refined, honed, and so forth, as many times as needed. This step is also included in the analysis workflow that will be covered in detail in the next chapter.
8. Create any calculations that you need. This step adds or replaces data items that cannot be pulled in directly from the database. You may want to concatenate some items, create new items based on values in other columns, or even replace difficult-to-understand codes with more meaningful values. This step is also included in the analysis workflow that will be covered in detail in the next chapter.
9. Save the query again.

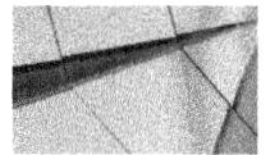

**NOTE**

*When working with Plus, it is even more advisable to save often, because network connections can be unreliable—it is better to save and undo your steps if needed than not to save and lose a lot of work.*

10. Upon completion of your calculations, you should review the final arrangement of the columns. Even though you may have done an initial column order during step 2, now that you have added calculations, you should make sure these new items are also in the right place. In particular, you should place all items that will be sorted in the first columns, with the primary sort item in column 1 and so on.
11. Delete unwanted columns. Yes, you can delete columns that have been used in calculations and in conditions, and the calculation or condition will still work. This step will be covered in Chapter 11, when we cover advanced queries.

12. Apply any sorting that you need. By this stage, your query should contain all of the database and calculated items that will be used to produce the final result, with all items in their correct order. You should now apply all of the sort criteria that will be used to make an understandable and presentable report.
13. Save the unfinished report.
14. Create subtotals and totals that you need. Having created a sort order, you should decide whether you need to include any subtotals and totals. These are an essential element if your report will be used for analysis. This step is also included in the analysis workflow that will be covered in detail in the next chapter.
15. Save the report.
16. Create and format a report title.
17. Format headings.
18. Format data.

If you have followed the preceding workflow, you are ready to do the following:

1. Format the report for printing.
2. Format the sheet, headers, footers, and margins.
3. Format the table options to determine whether the printable report will have gridlines.

# Formatting the Report for Printing

It may seem premature to begin with the print setup, but we have a good reason to start here. There is no place in the Page Setup dialog box to format the paper size, so you must do it in the Print Setup dialog box. Since you will be using Print Preview as a tool for fine-tuning the report before printing, it is essential that the paper size be set before moving on. We have also discovered that in the Print Setup dialog box, there are some performance issues in Desktop that need to be covered to save you some frustration.

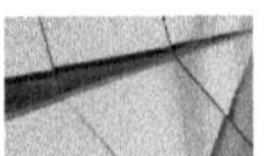

**NOTE**
*Print Setup and Page Setup are sufficiently different in Desktop and Plus to describe them separately.*

## Print Setup in Desktop

To prepare your report for printing in Desktop, use the following workflow:

1. Select File | Print, and the Windows Print dialog box will open. Here, you have a standard print setup.

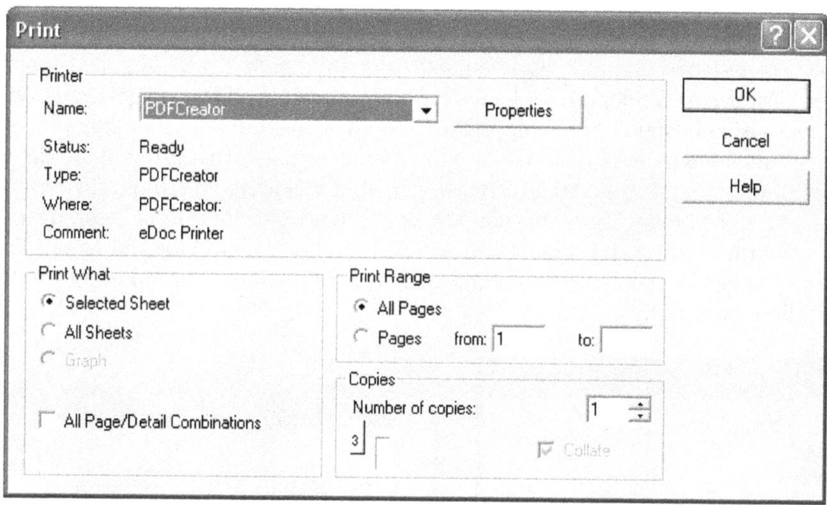

**NOTE**
*When you click the Print button in Desktop, be prepared for your report to print, because you will not be prompted in any way.*

2. Select the printer that will be used to print the report. It is important to use the correct printer because they all print differently.
3. Set the print range.
4. Select the number of copies.
5. Click the Properties button. This opens the Printer Setup window. Depending upon the printer you have, you will have different setup options. There are usually several tabs. The ones we are concerned with here are the orientation and paper size.
6. Set the paper size you think will best display your report.
7. Set the orientation that will best suit the layout of your report.
8. Click OK, and the Properties dialog box closes, taking you back to the Print dialog box.
9. This is where it becomes a little tricky. You have set up your paper size and orientation, but you are not ready to print your report. If you are like us, you will expect that your property selections have been saved after you click OK. This is not the case. If you click Cancel at this point, the paper size and orientation, as well as any other changes you made, will return to what they were before you started. You must click OK in the Print dialog box as well as the Properties box to save your print setup, thus causing your print job to run.
10. Your report is not ready to print, so you might want to do what we did and turn off the printer if possible. If your computer is slow enough, you might be able to hit the Cancel button in time. Or if your printer is slow, you can open the Print Queue window and cancel it there. Of course, another possibility is to simply let it print and see what your preliminary output is.
11. Click OK.

## Print Setup in Plus

Discoverer is designed primarily as an analytic tool and not as a print engine. For simple report printouts, Discoverer is fine, but for heavy report printing needs, we suggest you consider advancing to BI Publisher. Print Setup in Plus still gives us a little bit of heartburn. Each time you open the Print Setup dialog box, it is set to the default settings. That is fine if the default is what you want but not fine if you want to deviate from it. If you are going to use the report workflow we gave you at the beginning of this chapter, you will need to reset Print Setup every time you want to use Print Preview. It is not as bad as it sounds, because in Plus you have a Print Preview button in Print Setup. This is a definite improvement. To prepare your report for printing in Plus, use the following workflow:

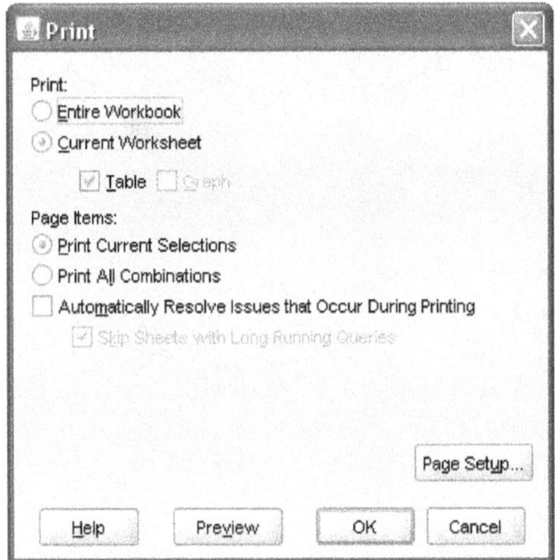


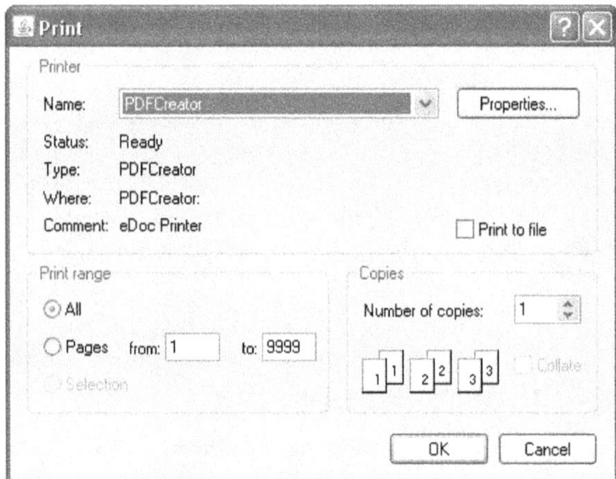


1. Select File | Print, and the Print dialog box will open.
2. Choose to print the entire workbook or the current worksheet.
3. Select the view to print. By selecting the check boxes, you can print the table or crosstab only, you can print the graph only, or you can print both.
4. Select how to print the page items. You can print only the selected page item that is currently showing or all combinations. Choosing All Combinations will print all of the items in the page details.
5. Select the number of copies.
6. Click OK. This will open the standard Windows Print dialog box.
7. Click Properties and go through the tabs for your printer to set up the paper size and orientation. You can also set the orientation in the Page Setup dialog box, which we will show you later in the chapter.
8. Set the paper size you think will best display your report.
9. Set the orientation that will best suit the layout of your report.
10. Click OK, and the Properties dialog box closes, taking you back to the Print dialog box.

11. As with Desktop, this is where it becomes a little tricky. You have set up your paper size and orientation but are not ready to print your report. If you are like us, you expect that your property selections are saved after you click OK. This is not the case. If you click Cancel at this point, the paper size and orientation, as well as any other changes you made, will return to what they were before you started. You must click OK in the Print dialog box as well as the Properties box to save your print setup, thus causing your print job to run.
12. Your report is not ready to print, so you might want to do what we did and turn off the printer if possible. If your computer is slow enough, you might be able to hit the Cancel button in time. Or if your printer is slow, you can open the Print Queue window and cancel it there. Of course, another possibility is to simply let it print and see what your preliminary output is.
13. Click OK.

# Page Setup

When creating a report in Discoverer, you have many of the same page setup options as when working in some familiar word processors and spreadsheets. You can set page margins, add headers and footers, change the orientation from portrait to landscape, and set up print features.

**NOTE**
*The functions of the Page Setup dialog box are not available on the formatting bar.*

To open the Page Setup dialog box, click File | Page Setup.

# The Sheet Tab in Desktop

The Sheet tab is divided into four sections.

- **Print What** In this area, you can select whether to print only the selected sheet (the sheet you are working on), all sheets in the workbook, and any graphs you have included in the workbook.
  There is also an All Page Detail/Combinations selection box. If your worksheet includes page detail, selecting this will print all combinations available. For example, say the page detail is Year with 2010, 2011, and 2012 in the drop-down list but only 2010 is showing in the worksheet. If you check this box, all three years will print.
- **Page Order** This area allows you to determine the order the pages will print when the data on the worksheet is too large to print on one page. For example, if the worksheet is twelve columns wide but only eight columns will fit on a page, use the default, Down. Then Across will print all pages with the first eight columns first and then the pages with the remaining four columns.
  The second option is Across, Then Down. We prefer this option, because it prints each page with the first eight columns followed immediately by a page with the remaining four columns, thus keeping all the items together.

- **Orientation** Here, you will select whether to print in portrait or landscape orientation (select the same orientation used in the print setup).
- **Scale** In this area, you can select to scale the report so that it will fit better on a page. This feature is available only if you are using a PostScript printer.

# The Worksheet Tab in Plus

The Worksheet tab is divided into five areas.

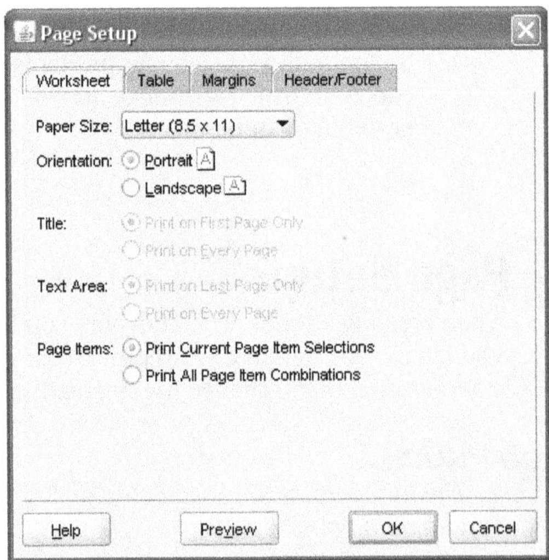


- **Paper Size** This area shows the paper size you chose in the Print Setup dialog box. You cannot change it here. It is just a display.
- **Orientation** This area shows the page orientation you chose in the Print Setup dialog box. You can change it here if you want.
- **Title** Choose whether to print the title on only the first page of the report or on all pages.
- **Text Area** If you have chosen to put a text area in your report, you can choose whether to print the text area on only the last page of the report or on all pages.
- **Page Items** Choose to print only the page items showing or all combinations of page items.

# The Table/Crosstab Tab in Plus

In Plus you have a Table or Crosstab tab, depending on which type of layout you have chosen.

- **Table/Crosstab Page Order** This area allows you to determine the order the pages will print when the data on the worksheet is too large to print on one page. For example, if the worksheet is twelve columns wide but only eight columns will fit on a page, using the default—Down, Then Across—will print all pages with the first eight columns first and then the pages with the remaining four columns.
  The second option is Across, Then Down. We prefer this option, because it prints each page with the first eight columns followed immediately by a page with the remaining four columns, thus keeping all of the items together.
- **Repeat** Check this box if you want row, column, and page item headers on every page.
- **Table/Crosstab Scaling** In this area, you can choose to scale the report so that it will fit better on a page. This feature is available only if you are using a PostScript printer.

## Headers and Footers

Headers and footers are a great way to add to a report detail that will repeat on each page, such as page numbers, the date the report was printed, or even the name of the report's author. In Desktop, the Header and Footer tabs of the Page Setup dialog box function in the same way. In

Plus, the Header and Footer tabs have been combined into one. We will demonstrate the steps for creating a header and a footer at the same time.

The first time you use these screens, the Available Headers or Available Footers list will show None. As you create headers and footers, you can add them to the list of available headers and footers. Thus, you can use the same ones each time to create continuity and consistency in your report writing.

There is also an Insert button. Use this button to insert codes for items such as date, time, filename, and location. It is a good idea to place these codes in the same locations each time you use them. Those who read your reports will appreciate the continuity and find your reports easier to navigate than if you use a variety of formats. You can also add a line between your header and the body of the report. The Line button allows you to select from predefined line widths. Play with these options, look at other reports that you find attractive and easy to read, and then adapt them to your own reports. Headers and footers are an excellent way to add distinction to your reporting.

The Header and Footer tabs contain

- **Available Headers or Available Footers** A drop-down list of available headers or footers. These are headers and footers that are user defined and saved for use in other reports. These are not available in Plus.
- **Add** A button used to add saved headers and footers to the Available drop-down list. This button does not exist in Plus.
- **Remove** A button used to remove saved headers and footers from the Available drop-down list. This button does not exist in Plus.
- **Line Width** A drop-down box to set the line width that separates the header or footer from the body of the report.
- **Insert** A drop-down button used to insert predefined codes.
- **Font** Opens the Fonts dialog box to allow you to format the header or footer.
- **Left section, Center section, Right section** Sections where you create the header or footer.
- **Preview** A button to see a print preview of the report.

The next illustration shows the Header tab of the Page Setup dialog box in Desktop.

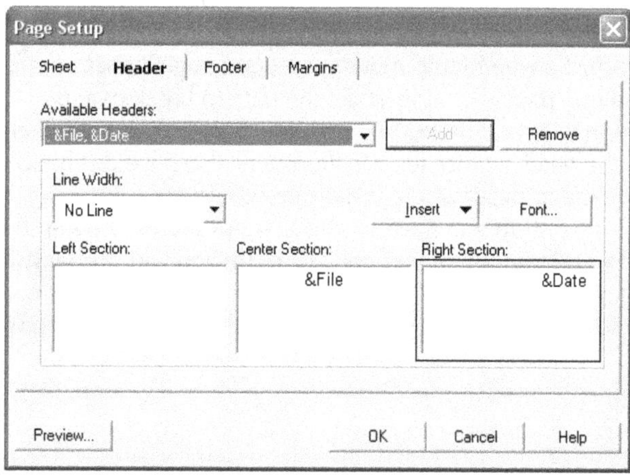

To create a header or footer, use the following workflow:

1. Click the Header or Footer tab.
2. Select an available header or footer in Desktop or create your own in Desktop or Plus.
3. To create your own header or footer, click in the Left, Center, or Right section.
4. Type in the text you want, or use the Insert drop-down button as shown in the preceding illustration to select from predefined codes. These codes can insert
   - Workbook name
   - Sheet name
   - Date
   - Time
   - Page number
   - Conditions
   - Data points
   - Axis items
   - Page items

You can even add parameter names and values. We demonstrate how this is done in Chapter 13, in the section called "Using Parameters in the Title, Header, or Footer."

1. Format the font type, size, and color.
2. Select a line width, if desired.
3. Click Preview to see the report as it will print.
4. Make any adjustments to the header or footer.
5. When you are satisfied with the header or footer, click OK.

### Margins

Adjusting margins is a good way to gain added control over how your report will print. The default margins are 1 inch for the top and bottom margins and 0.75 inch for the side margins. This might work for you if you have a small report, but for larger reports, some fudging may be in order. There are times the data is just a wee bit too much for a good page layout, and by adjusting the margins you can get it all on one page—or at least get the data to break better.

Use some caution when adjusting margins. It is possible to make them so small that data will actually print over the header or footer. Most printers also have a printable area, and you could lose some data from the printout where the printer could not print.

Another formatting option you have on the Margins tab is whether to center the report on the page. You can select horizontally or vertically or both. You will probably always want to center the report horizontally. This will give a nice look to the report; however, vertical centering should be used sparingly. Sometimes the report is small, and vertical centering will bring the report too far down the page.

The Margins tab has the following sections:

- **Units** This option is available in Plus only. Select from Inches, Pixels, or Centimeters.
- **Margins** These four up/down boxes are used to adjust the margins.
- **From Edge** These two up/down boxes are used to adjust how far from the edge of the page the header or footer will print.
- **Center on Page** This option is available in Desktop only. Two check boxes are used to center the report on the page horizontally or vertically.
- **Preview** This button shows a print preview of the report.

To set the margins, use the following workflow:

1. In the Page Setup dialog box, click the Margins tab.
2. In Plus only, select the units of measure you want to use.
3. Use the up/down buttons in the Margins section to set the margins, or type in the margin you want.
4. Use the up/down buttons in the From Edge section to determine how far from the edge of the paper you want the margins to print. Be careful to not set these larger or the same as the margins, and do not set them outside your printer's printable area.
5. In Desktop only, center the report on the page horizontally, vertically, or both.
6. Click Preview to see the report as it will print.
7. Make any adjustments to the margins.
8. When you are satisfied with the margins, click OK.

Before moving on to the next section, you might want to revisit column widths at this time. It is possible that by slightly widening or narrowing the column widths, your report will fit better on the page. By going back and forth between column widths and margin sizes, you can fine-tune the report layout. You might even want to take another look at font sizes to see whether your report will fit better on the page. Use Print Preview often as you prepare your report to print.

# Table and Crosstab Gridlines

Remember that Discoverer is WYSIWYG—you will need to format the table if you don't want to see gridlines printed in your report. You do this through the Options dialog box. In Desktop the Options dialog box defaults to the Table or Crosstab tab, depending upon the type of query you are working with. In Plus you will need to select the Sheet tab.

We are disappointed that the gridlines cannot be turned off for printing only, because you can turn them off in Excel. We like to work on a table with the gridlines showing but turned off for a final report. It is a nuisance to have to change back and forth. We hope this functionality will be incorporated into a future release of Discoverer.

If you chose to leave the gridlines on for your report, you might want to change the gridline color. Be careful with this type of formatting and be sure that it is not just pretty but actually helps display the data in a meaningful way.

## Table Gridlines

The following illustration shows the Table tab of the Options dialog box in Desktop.

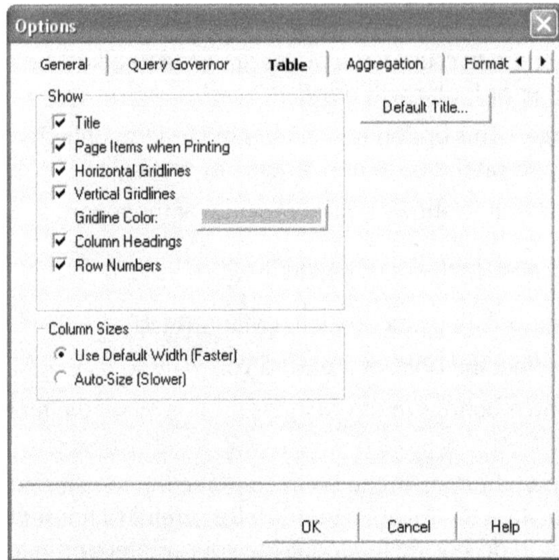


The next illustration shows the Sheet tab of the Options dialog box in Plus.

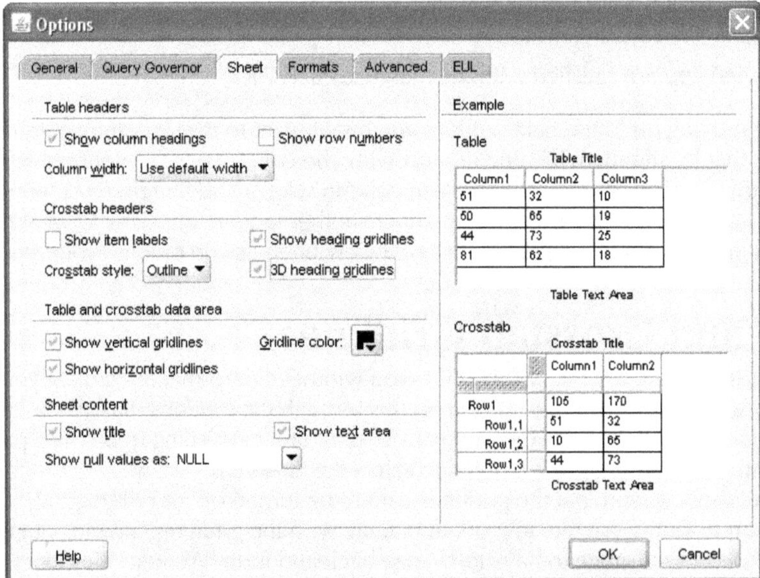


To change the gridline properties of a table, use the following workflow:

1. From the menu bar, select Tools | Options. In Plus you will need to select the Sheet tab.
2. Deselect the horizontal and vertical gridlines as desired.

3. If leaving the gridlines on but changing the gridline color, click the box to the right of Gridline Color.
4. Select a new color from the color selection box.
5. Click OK.

## Crosstab Gridlines

Crosstabs have two more choices associated with the crosstab. You can also choose whether to show the axis item labels and whether to show axis gridlines in 3-D. Additionally, you can choose the style of your crosstab here. You can choose to show crosstab labels inline (labels stacked on top of each other) or in an outline format (staggered labels and data items). The latter of the two requires more space, so if the size of the report is a concern, you might try inline. Work with it until you have it in a format that is easy to read and aesthetically pleasing. The illustrations that follow show an inline crosstab and an outline one:

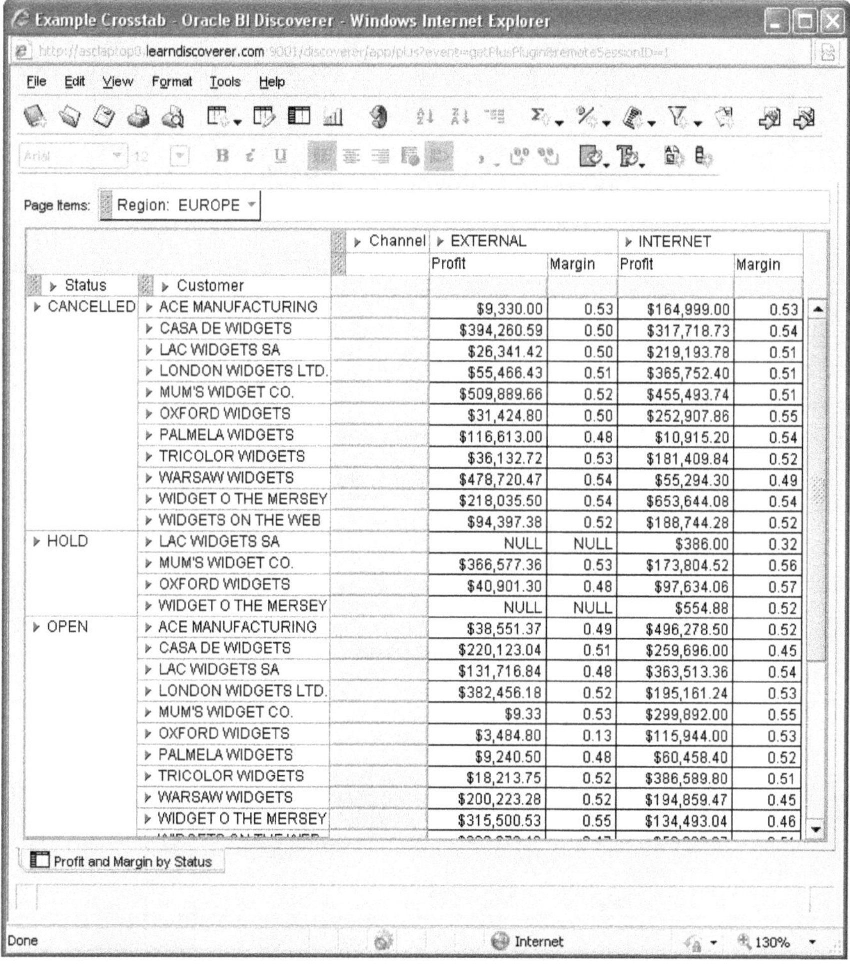


| Status | Customer | EXTERNAL Profit | EXTERNAL Margin | INTERNET Profit | INTERNET Margin |
|---|---|---|---|---|---|
| CANCELLED | ACE MANUFACTURING | $9,330.00 | 0.53 | $164,999.00 | 0.53 |
| | CASA DE WIDGETS | $394,260.59 | 0.50 | $317,718.73 | 0.54 |
| | LAC WIDGETS SA | $26,341.42 | 0.50 | $219,193.78 | 0.51 |
| | LONDON WIDGETS LTD. | $55,466.43 | 0.51 | $365,752.40 | 0.51 |
| | MUM'S WIDGET CO. | $509,889.66 | 0.52 | $455,493.74 | 0.51 |
| | OXFORD WIDGETS | $31,424.80 | 0.50 | $252,907.86 | 0.55 |
| | PALMELA WIDGETS | $116,613.00 | 0.48 | $10,915.20 | 0.54 |
| | TRICOLOR WIDGETS | $36,132.72 | 0.53 | $181,409.84 | 0.52 |
| | WARSAW WIDGETS | $478,720.47 | 0.54 | $55,294.30 | 0.49 |
| | WIDGET O THE MERSEY | $218,035.50 | 0.54 | $653,644.08 | 0.54 |
| | WIDGETS ON THE WEB | $94,397.38 | 0.52 | $188,744.28 | 0.52 |
| HOLD | LAC WIDGETS SA | NULL | NULL | $386.00 | 0.32 |
| | MUM'S WIDGET CO. | $366,577.36 | 0.53 | $173,804.52 | 0.56 |
| | OXFORD WIDGETS | $40,901.30 | 0.48 | $97,634.06 | 0.57 |
| | WIDGET O THE MERSEY | NULL | NULL | $554.88 | 0.52 |
| OPEN | ACE MANUFACTURING | $38,551.37 | 0.49 | $496,278.50 | 0.52 |
| | CASA DE WIDGETS | $220,123.04 | 0.51 | $259,696.00 | 0.45 |
| | LAC WIDGETS SA | $131,716.84 | 0.48 | $363,513.36 | 0.54 |
| | LONDON WIDGETS LTD. | $382,456.18 | 0.52 | $195,161.24 | 0.53 |
| | MUM'S WIDGET CO. | $9.33 | 0.53 | $299,892.00 | 0.55 |
| | OXFORD WIDGETS | $3,484.80 | 0.13 | $115,944.00 | 0.53 |
| | PALMELA WIDGETS | $9,240.50 | 0.48 | $60,458.40 | 0.52 |
| | TRICOLOR WIDGETS | $18,213.75 | 0.52 | $386,589.80 | 0.51 |
| | WARSAW WIDGETS | $200,223.28 | 0.52 | $194,859.47 | 0.45 |
| | WIDGET O THE MERSEY | $315,500.53 | 0.55 | $134,493.04 | 0.46 |

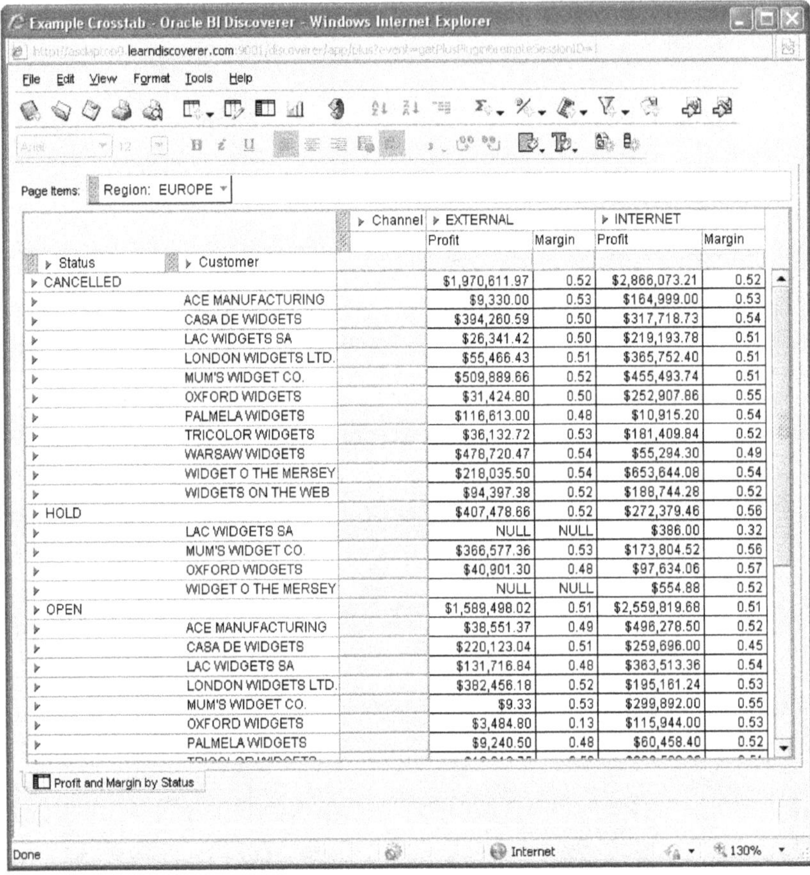


| Status | Customer | EXTERNAL Profit | EXTERNAL Margin | INTERNET Profit | INTERNET Margin |
|---|---|---|---|---|---|
| CANCELLED | | $1,970,611.97 | 0.52 | $2,866,073.21 | 0.52 |
| | ACE MANUFACTURING | $9,330.00 | 0.53 | $164,999.00 | 0.53 |
| | CASA DE WIDGETS | $394,260.59 | 0.50 | $317,718.73 | 0.54 |
| | LAC WIDGETS SA | $26,341.42 | 0.50 | $219,193.78 | 0.51 |
| | LONDON WIDGETS LTD. | $55,466.43 | 0.51 | $365,752.40 | 0.51 |
| | MUM'S WIDGET CO. | $509,889.66 | 0.52 | $455,493.74 | 0.51 |
| | OXFORD WIDGETS | $31,424.80 | 0.50 | $252,907.86 | 0.55 |
| | PALMELA WIDGETS | $116,613.00 | 0.48 | $10,915.20 | 0.54 |
| | TRICOLOR WIDGETS | $36,132.72 | 0.53 | $181,409.84 | 0.52 |
| | WARSAW WIDGETS | $478,720.47 | 0.54 | $55,294.30 | 0.49 |
| | WIDGET O THE MERSEY | $218,035.50 | 0.54 | $653,644.08 | 0.54 |
| | WIDGETS ON THE WEB | $94,397.38 | 0.52 | $188,744.28 | 0.52 |
| HOLD | | $407,478.66 | 0.52 | $272,379.46 | 0.56 |
| | LAC WIDGETS SA | NULL | NULL | $386.00 | 0.32 |
| | MUM'S WIDGET CO. | $366,577.36 | 0.53 | $173,804.52 | 0.56 |
| | OXFORD WIDGETS | $40,901.30 | 0.48 | $97,634.06 | 0.57 |
| | WIDGET O THE MERSEY | NULL | NULL | $554.88 | 0.52 |
| OPEN | | $1,589,498.02 | 0.51 | $2,559,819.68 | 0.51 |
| | ACE MANUFACTURING | $38,551.37 | 0.49 | $496,278.50 | 0.52 |
| | CASA DE WIDGETS | $220,123.04 | 0.51 | $259,696.00 | 0.45 |
| | LAC WIDGETS SA | $131,716.84 | 0.48 | $363,513.36 | 0.54 |
| | LONDON WIDGETS LTD. | $382,456.18 | 0.52 | $195,161.24 | 0.53 |
| | MUM'S WIDGET CO. | $9.33 | 0.53 | $299,892.00 | 0.55 |
| | OXFORD WIDGETS | $3,484.80 | 0.13 | $115,944.00 | 0.53 |
| | PALMELA WIDGETS | $9,240.50 | 0.48 | $60,458.40 | 0.52 |

The following illustration shows the Crosstab tab of the Options dialog box in Desktop:

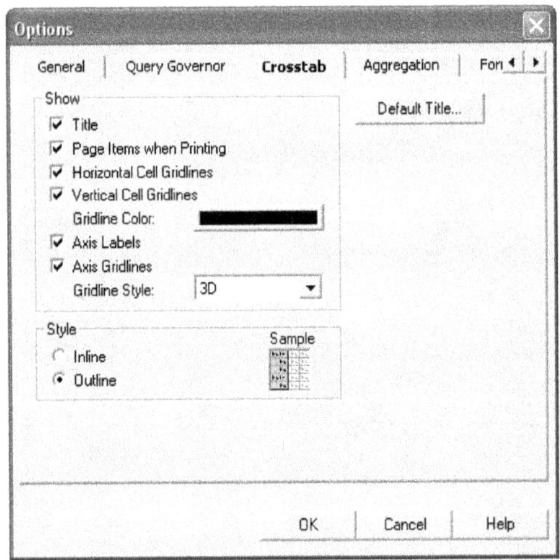

To change the gridline properties of a crosstab, use the following workflow:

1. From the menu bar, select Tools | Options.
2. Deselect the horizontal and vertical gridlines as desired.
3. If leaving the gridlines on but changing the gridline color, click the box to the right of Gridline Color.
4. Select a new color from the color selection box.
5. Check the Axis Labels box if you want the names of the axis items to appear in your report.
6. Check Axis Gridlines if you want gridlines to appear around the axis items in Desktop.
7. Select the crosstab style.
8. Click OK.

# Inserting Page Breaks in Tables (Sorry, No Page Breaks in Crosstabs)

Page breaks are useful when you want to add logical breaks between data items. For example, your reports show the sales for all of your regions. You want a page break between each of the regions. By group sorting by region in your report, you can also add a page break between them. When you add a page break to items that cover more than one page, the column headings repeat as do the item names at the top of each column.

To create a page break, follow this workflow:

1. Click Tools | Sort.
2. Click the item you want to group sort and create a page break on.
3. From the Group drop-down list, select Page Break.
4. Click OK.

# Exporting Your Report to Another Application

Once you have a great report formatted and ready for printing, you might also want to send the file to someone who does not have Discoverer. Discoverer files can be exported in many different formats, the most common being Excel, HTML, Comma Separator Delimited (CSV), and Tab Delimited (Text). In addition to these, there is also PDF in Plus and Viewer.

Excel is an excellent spreadsheet program, and many companies use it. However, with some experimentation, we have discovered that exporting to Excel can be time-consuming, but these are usually configuration or system issues such as low memory, temp space, or CPU utilization. It is recommended that instead of exporting into an Excel format, you use CSV, which Excel imports easily. This method will save you time and frustration, but you will lose your formatting, so you should experiment and see what works best for your system and requirements.

HTML is also a popular format and creates files that anyone with a browser can view. The downside, of course, is that the data can be viewed only in HTML and not worked with. Discoverer Viewer result sets are displayed as HTML and allow users to open predefined queries and perform some limited analysis, such as drilling down a hierarchy. HTML data can, however, be copied and pasted into a spreadsheet or word processor. The data will have to be reformatted, but it can be worked with.

To export a Discoverer report to another application, use the following workflow:

1. Click File | Export. This opens the Export dialog box shown here:

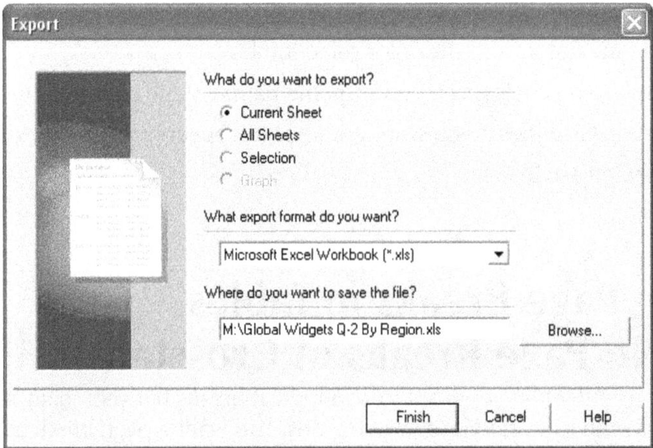


2. Select the part of the workbook you want to export. If you want to export a graph, the graph needs to be the active window and will export as a WMF file.
3. From the drop-down list, select the format you want to export the file in.
4. Give the location you want to save the file to.
5. Click Finish. The file is now ready to be used in another application.

# Summary

In this chapter, you learned a workflow to use in preparing your queries to be turned into reports. You saw how to format the report for printing and how to format the sheet, headers, footers, and margins. We also showed you how to format the table options to determine whether the printable report will have gridlines and how to insert page breaks.

We showed you how to use the Page Setup feature to give you greater flexibility in how your pages will print, as well as how to use the Print Preview feature of Discoverer as a tool for fine-tuning the report. You also learned how to export reports into other applications such as spreadsheets, HTML, and text files.

# CHAPTER 9

# Using Discoverer to Analyze Data

There is an almost endless variety of possible combinations of facts in table and crosstab design, and it would be impossible for us to describe them all to you in this book. In fact, as we have explored the various permutations that Discoverer allows, we have come to the conclusion that we could write an entire book on just table layouts and their relationship with analysis.

Therefore, in this chapter, we will teach you how we analyze data in Discoverer using basic and clear-cut methods. As you become more skilled in the use of the product, you should begin experimenting and see how it will work for you.

In this chapter, you will learn the meaning of analysis and the five basic types of analysis—statistical, classification, deviation, trend, and aging—that we will describe using Discoverer. You will learn how to perform these types of analysis, using both Desktop and Plus. We will introduce an analysis workflow that we hope will help you analyze your data more effectively.

We will show you more ways to access the tools that were introduced to you in Chapters 4 and 5. We will introduce you to the tools available on the toolbars and show how to cut your analysis time by using the terrific features of Discoverer. Throughout the chapter, we will talk about analysis and statistics and describe some of the fundamentals and pitfalls involved.

# What Is Analysis?

*Analysis* provides the capability to discover new and meaningful information by using existing data. Analysis techniques massage the data in some way, either by constraining the initial selection to just a subset of what is available or by reducing the final output to make it more meaningful. Facts are taken and then dissected, compared, rearranged, put back together, and finally reported.

Having decided upon the data items you need for your query and having ordered those items into columns and rows and formatted them, you have completed the first part of your task. However, before you can turn your query into a report, you need to decide whether any analysis of the data is required.

Think about what it is that your analysis is trying to do. Throughout this chapter on analysis, you must stay focused and remember to always keep in mind what question it is that you are trying to answer. If you do this, you will be visualizing at least part of the final display and already be anticipating what to do if the figures do not in fact produce the result you wanted.

# Types of Analysis

The world of analysis is full of different methodologies. Also, many types of analysis techniques are available to you, and we want to give you an understanding of five of them that can be used in Discoverer. We hope you will find these useful. They are as follows:

- Statistical analysis
- Classification analysis
- Deviation analysis
- Trend analysis
- Aging analysis

We will also include some ideas and examples from our own database to show you the results that can be obtained from these different analysis techniques. You can find full details on how to build these examples in the section called "How to Build the Example Queries."

## Statistical Analysis

The *statistical* approach uses rules or conditions and is based on data relationships. Usually what you will end up with are statistics, but how are statistics derived? An example of a statistical application may determine that all sales orders beginning with a 5 are regular sales orders, while orders beginning with a 7 are returns. By analyzing only the returns and determining that 18 percent of the sales orders begin with a 7, you can accurately state that 82 percent of sales orders are regular orders—without ever querying those orders that begin with 5. Of course, this statement is true only if all the other sales orders begin with a 5. If you have another class of orders that begin with a different number, then the statement is untrue, so you need to be careful about making statements from statistics.

Common sense can really cloud statistical results. For instance, we heard about a technology firm that had determined that 40 percent of all sick days were taken on a Friday or a Monday. Armed with this information but before realizing its mistake, the company immediately began clamping down on its employees. You see, the company had overlooked the fact that 40 percent represents two days out of a five-day working week and therefore the data result was a perfectly normal spread, rather than a reflection of opportunist employees trying to extend their weekends.

There is a popular saying in England that "one can drive a bus through statistics." While this may sound somewhat exaggerated, in fact there is more than a grain of truth to this statement. One of the authors went to school with a professor of mathematics who in later life became a professional witness at trials. Depending on which side he was hired for, he would find statistics to prove the case either for the prosecution or for the defense. We often wonder what would have happened if another professor of mathematics had been hired for the other side! In a saying made popular by Mark Twain, "There are three kinds of lies: lies, damned lies, and statistics."

So, now that we have shown you the pitfalls, let's talk about creating statistics. Many statistics are produced to satisfy corporate or personal objectives. Perhaps someone is looking for data to prove that a particular product has sold exceptionally well, and otherwise overlooks the fact that the product also had an exceptional number of returns. The end result of that analysis may have produced a set of statistics that do not tell the complete story.

For example, suppose you were asked to write a query that analyzed all the sales for the past year, showing how each region had fared when compared to the other regions. It should be evident that your query needs to be constrained to just one year, so adding a condition on this item will be the first technique you apply. Having constrained or filtered your query to include only the year in question, you would run the query and take a look at the output to decide what other analysis tools need to be applied. These rules are the building blocks for further analysis.

We will therefore show how to build the preceding query using our database. As the specification states, we need to include the year, the region, and the sales amount (the selling price). If we build this as a crosstab, we can place the region on the side axis and the year on the page axis. Finally, adding a percentage on the selling price makes the query look like what is shown in Figure 9-1.

As you can see in the example, the percentage of sales for Europe was almost 28 percent, which means that the sales for all other regions must be just over 72 percent. There is no need to add them up because by deduction this statistic must be true.

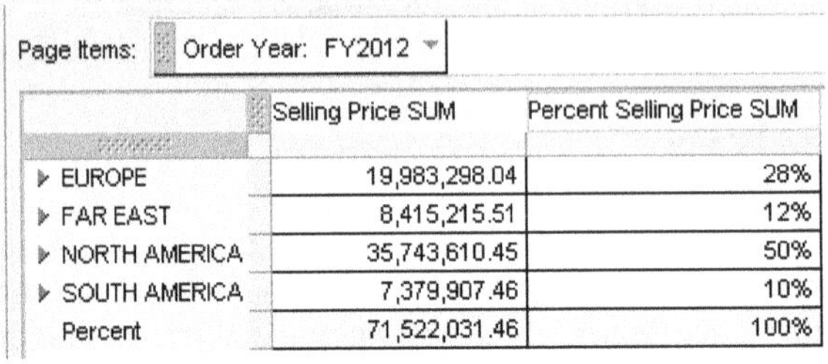

Page Items: Order Year: FY2012

| | Selling Price SUM | Percent Selling Price SUM |
|---|---|---|
| EUROPE | 19,983,298.04 | 28% |
| FAR EAST | 8,415,215.51 | 12% |
| NORTH AMERICA | 35,743,610.45 | 50% |
| SOUTH AMERICA | 7,379,907.46 | 10% |
| Percent | 71,522,031.46 | 100% |

**FIGURE 9-1.** *Statistical example: sales for 2012 based on region*

We know this example is simple, but it demonstrates how you can take one figure that you do know to derive another statistic that you do not.

Discoverer provides many statistical functions that the typical business analyst understands. Among these statistical functions are mean, median, variance, standard deviation, covariance, percentiles, and so on. Please take a look at Appendix B for a full listing of the functions available to you in Discoverer.

## A Discussion about Averages

Many people think that the term *mean* means the same thing as *average*. It doesn't. The term *mean* is a mathematical term, whereas the term *average* is often used loosely as a description for a person or a data item. In mathematics, average is "a number that typifies a set of numbers of which it is a function." In other words, average can stand for mean, median, or mode. So, what is the difference between these three terms?

- **Median** This is the middle value in a distribution or set of numbers, above and below which lie an equal number of other values.
- **Mean** This is a number that typifies a set of numbers, such as a geometric or arithmetic mean; it is what most people think of as being the average value of a set of numbers.
- **Mode** This is the value or item that occurs most frequently in a set or series of statistical data.

Look at the following two sets of data:

Example set: 1 15 16 17 17 17 18 19

Analyzing this first set of data, representing the ages of the seven students in a school who enjoy drama, we get the following:

- **Mean** 17
- **Median** 17
- **Mode** 17

Example set: 2 15 17 17 17 21 29 52

Analyzing this second set of data, representing the ages of the seven night-school students who enjoy drama, we get the following:

- **Mean** 24
- **Median** 17
- **Mode** 17

As you can see, the median age and the modal age for both sets of students are the same, whereas the mean age is completely different. Which *average* you choose will determine whether you consider the average age for students who enjoy drama to be the same for both normal schools and night schools. If statistics teach us nothing else, they show us that there is no such thing as an average.

We hope this discussion helps you understand why people have difficulty interpreting statistical averages. Many people try to make their statistics fit the normal distribution, but there are *non-normal* distributions too. The statistics that are used for normal distributions are often inappropriate when the distribution is patently non-normal.

## Classification Analysis

The *classification* approach groups data according to some similarity in the data or some derived commonality. Knowledge of your company—and more to the point, the database—can be important in this scenario. This background knowledge of how your data is being used can be a tremendous asset in helping you understand whether the classifications you have determined are valid.

What we are implying is that you should use sorting and paging to manipulate your data. Moving the data around onscreen like this is another function Discoverer does very well. Unless you change the selections or conditions, you can manipulate the data onscreen without impacting the system. This is because once Discoverer has completed the base query, it stores all of the resulting data in memory, allowing you the pleasure of manipulating it to your heart's content.

If you use Discoverer Viewer, you will instantly recognize that this scenario is exactly what Viewer is designed to do. By allowing you to manipulate the data onscreen without changing the base query, Viewer is the perfect tool for undergoing classification analysis.

Let's show you what we mean by using Viewer. Figure 9-2 shows the cost price, selling price, and total amount of profit made in each quarter of 2012, by each product, with the query grouping the products by their respective product lines.

By moving around some of the items, we can display the same data using a completely different classification. In Figure 9-3, the same query has been manipulated to show the profit only for all products in all product lines.

See the section "How to Build the Example Queries" near the end of this chapter for full instructions on how to construct and manipulate this query.

**NOTE**

*If you are unsure as to what we did, we moved the data points out into the page items so that each data point became a drop-down. This allows us to look at the data for cost price, selling price, and profit independently.*

Page Items: Prod Line: MEGA-WIDGET

| | Cost Price | Selling Price | Profit |
|---|---|---|---|
| AB-2500 | 1,008,536.30 | 2,146,717.50 | 1,138,181.20 |
| 2012-Q1 | 216,107.22 | 459,994.50 | 243,887.28 |
| 2012-Q2 | 278,121.69 | 591,995.25 | 313,873.56 |
| 2012-Q3 | 328,491.60 | 699,210.00 | 370,718.40 |
| 2012-Q4 | 185,815.79 | 395,517.75 | 209,701.96 |
| CD-100 | 1,308,974.85 | 3,214,471.25 | 1,905,496.40 |
| 2012-Q1 | 249,070.68 | 611,647.00 | 362,576.32 |
| 2012-Q2 | 335,992.05 | 825,101.25 | 489,109.20 |
| 2012-Q3 | 466,072.92 | 1,144,543.00 | 678,470.08 |
| 2012-Q4 | 257,839.20 | 633,180.00 | 375,340.80 |
| CD-200 | 1,262,132.82 | 3,099,440.50 | 1,837,307.68 |
| 2012-Q1 | 434,817.99 | 1,067,789.75 | 632,971.76 |
| 2012-Q2 | 185,977.08 | 456,707.00 | 270,729.92 |
| 2012-Q3 | 344,108.52 | 845,033.00 | 500,924.48 |
| 2012-Q4 | 297,229.23 | 729,910.75 | 432,681.52 |
| CD-500 | 1,590,132.60 | 3,321,011.40 | 1,730,878.80 |
| 2012-Q1 | 478,123.02 | 998,565.78 | 520,442.76 |
| 2012-Q2 | 258,915.60 | 540,748.40 | 281,832.80 |
| 2012-Q3 | 538,009.20 | 1,123,638.80 | 585,629.60 |
| 2012-Q4 | 315,084.78 | 658,058.42 | 342,973.64 |
| CD-550 | 983,093.40 | 2,053,202.60 | 1,070,109.20 |
| 2012-Q1 | 242,560.80 | 506,591.20 | 264,030.40 |
| 2012-Q2 | 387,630.00 | 809,570.00 | 421,940.00 |
| 2012-Q3 | 213,249.60 | 445,374.40 | 232,124.80 |
| 2012-Q4 | 139,653.00 | 291,667.00 | 152,014.00 |
| CD-625 | 4,080,618.18 | 8,522,421.02 | 4,441,802.84 |
| 2012-Q1 | 843,535.98 | 1,761,735.22 | 918,199.24 |
| 2012-Q2 | 808,808.58 | 1,689,206.62 | 880,398.04 |
| 2012-Q3 | 1,287,451.98 | 2,688,859.22 | 1,401,407.24 |
| 2012-Q4 | 1,140,821.64 | 2,382,619.96 | 1,241,798.32 |

**FIGURE 9-2.** *Classification example: profit for 2012 by product*

# Deviation Analysis

In its simplest form, *deviation* analysis uses percentages and exceptions to the rule to identify areas for improvement. A series of numbers such as sales figures, electrical consumption, and attendance records are excellent types of data for this kind of analysis. To perform this analysis, you work out a percentage of each item when compared to the total. Then you apply an exception to identify those items that are deviating too high or too low.

Having worked out the percentage deviations, you will want to highlight those items whose deviation is beyond what you consider to be the norm. The use of conditional and stoplight formatting comes into its own, bringing out the anomalies even more.

In Figure 9-4, we have analyzed the sales for all of Global Widgets products that begin with *QB* by status and channel. We wanted to know whether there was any difference between the channels. In particular, we wanted to analyze the percentage of orders shipped and cancelled and

Page Items: Data Point: Profit

| | 2012-Q1 | 2012-Q2 | 2012-Q3 | 2012-Q4 |
|---|---|---|---|---|
| MINI-WIDGET | 329,132.68 | 124,203.30 | 353,129.24 | 271,291.89 |
| DS-1200 | 40,788.00 | 58,741.50 | 43,191.00 | 67,081.50 |
| DS-1300 | 77,346.68 | 18,875.40 | 63,165.04 | 105,943.49 |
| MS-1200 | 132,436.80 | 12,614.40 | 170,355.20 | 74,496.00 |
| MS-1300 | 78,561.20 | 33,972.00 | 76,418.00 | 23,770.90 |
| SUPER-WIDGET | 2,991,350.33 | 2,292,927.77 | 4,898,309.16 | 3,899,671.91 |
| AB-3000 | 779,663.64 | 367,103.19 | 647,566.98 | 848,315.70 |
| AVR-500 | 1,074,035.69 | 886,585.70 | 1,572,123.28 | 1,343,832.49 |
| AVR-550 | 544,544.00 | 380,871.40 | 1,515,193.68 | 937,420.12 |
| AVR-800 | 197,577.60 | 204,649.98 | 414,258.11 | 148,557.40 |
| AVR-900 | 395,529.40 | 453,717.50 | 749,167.11 | 621,546.20 |
| MEGA-WIDGET | 2,942,107.76 | 2,657,883.52 | 3,769,274.60 | 2,754,510.24 |
| AB-2500 | 243,887.28 | 313,873.56 | 370,718.40 | 209,701.96 |
| CD-100 | 362,576.32 | 489,109.20 | 678,470.08 | 375,340.80 |
| CD-200 | 632,971.76 | 270,729.92 | 500,924.48 | 432,681.52 |
| CD-500 | 520,442.76 | 281,832.80 | 585,629.60 | 342,973.64 |
| CD-550 | 264,030.40 | 421,940.00 | 232,124.80 | 152,014.00 |
| CD-625 | 918,199.24 | 880,398.04 | 1,401,407.24 | 1,241,798.32 |
| WONDER-WIDGET | 3,002,602.50 | 1,502,515.56 | 2,838,812.19 | 2,762,755.93 |
| AB-2008 | 321,787.20 | 191,470.92 | 376,680.68 | 484,439.20 |
| QB-1000 | 206,349.24 | 277,967.03 | 336,525.30 | 220,390.43 |
| QB-2008 | 551,941.20 | 174,726.23 | 390,991.44 | 303,325.00 |
| QB-3000 | 484,669.23 | 102,490.76 | 408,551.20 | 287,552.10 |
| QB-5000 | 460,080.96 | 218,508.60 | 445,992.66 | 417,051.00 |
| QB-5500 | 431,979.00 | 281,448.78 | 278,006.01 | 631,454.40 |
| QB-6000 | 545,795.67 | 255,903.24 | 602,064.90 | 418,543.80 |

**FIGURE 9-3.** *Classification example: profit for 2012 for all product lines*

to see whether there was anything for us to report. For us, a percentage shipped of 90 percent or more is considered acceptable, while cancellations greater than 10 percent are considered unacceptable. We know from experience that products that begin with *QB* are the highest sellers.

In Figure 9-4, we have taken the percentage of the order quantity for each status, by product and channel for 2013. The results surprised us and only went to underline the benefit of doing this type of analysis. As you can see, only three of our *QB* products in the External channel—that is, our normal non-Internet channel—have a percentage shipped of 90 percent or greater. Looking at the Internet channel, we were amazed to see that only two products made the cut.

If you look at the report in more detail, you can see that we have a high percentage of open, non-shipped orders for product QB-2008 in the External channel, whereas the same product in the Internet channel has little in the way of backlog. Looking further, you can see that we also have a very high percentage of cancellations for QB-1000 (coincidentally for the External channel). These figures will make for an interesting discussion the next time we have a board meeting with the vice president of external sales!

See the section "How to Build the Example Queries" near the end of this chapter for full instructions on how to construct and manipulate this query.

Page Items: Order Year: FY2013

| | | Percent Order Qty SUM | | | |
|---|---|---|---|---|---|
| Channel | Product | CANCELLED | HOLD | OPEN | SHIPPED |
| EXTERNAL | QB-1000 | 28% | 3% | 11% | 57% |
| | QB-2008 | 3% | 0% | 55% | 42% |
| | QB-3000 | 3% | 4% | 1% | 92% |
| | QB-5000 | 4% | | 11% | 86% |
| | QB-5500 | | | 5% | 95% |
| | QB-6000 | 6% | | 4% | 91% |
| INTERNET | QB-1000 | 0% | | 5% | 95% |
| | QB-2008 | | | 1% | 99% |
| | QB-3000 | 11% | | 12% | 76% |
| | QB-5000 | 9% | | 6% | 85% |
| | QB-5500 | 12% | | 20% | 67% |
| | QB-6000 | 19% | | 12% | 69% |

**FIGURE 9-4.** *Deviation example: status percentage by product and channel*

# Trend Analysis

*Trend* analysis, as the name suggests, looks for trends and makes assumptions or forecasts based on those trends. Many people today, through either lack of understanding or lack of available time, focus their reporting mainly on showing status and identifying problems. An example of a status report could be a list of orders shipped yesterday or the number of employees who came into work on time, while a problem report could be the list of orders that did not ship or the employees who did not get in on time. These reports are based on facts and figures within the database and are obtained by constraining the data to look at a particular flag or status.

An organization that concentrates on status or problem reports will typically be in "fire-fighting" mode, reacting after the event to something that has already happened. By its very nature, this reactive form of reporting does not offer much in the way of trending or performance reporting—the latter being required if the organization is to establish guidelines to determine whether performance expectations are being met.

Let's look at one of the preceding examples and see whether we can use trending to give us a better type of report. We will take the example of the late employees. While it is important to know how many were late, wouldn't it also be useful to know who was habitually late or whether a particular day—perhaps the Monday following a holiday—was more likely to have a higher rate of latecomers or absenteeism? By knowing these figures, you could easily extrapolate; that is, you could infer or estimate other values by projecting outward from a known value or values.

If your company is in the business of selling products, one of the hardest things to do is to try to forecast how many of these products will be required each quarter. Traditionally, the company will turn to its sales force and ask each salesperson to submit a forecast, based on discussions with each person's customers. If you are in the manufacturing business with an army of salespeople, you know only too well what happens next: the predictions are too high. But just how do you reign in an overly enthusiastic salesperson who insists that the projections are correct?

| | Order Year | Percentage | | | | | | | |
|---|---|---|---|---|---|---|---|---|---|
| Region | | FY2006 | FY2007 | FY2008 | FY2009 | FY2010 | FY2011 | FY2012 | FY2013 |
| EUROPE | | 37% | 30% | 31% | 36% | 34% | 33% | 32% | 31% |
| FAR EAST | | 17% | 14% | 10% | 12% | 7% | 10% | 9% | 13% |
| NORTH AMERICA | | 45% | 49% | 51% | 45% | 54% | 51% | 51% | 47% |
| SOUTH AMERICA | | 1% | 6% | 9% | 8% | 4% | 6% | 8% | 8% |

**FIGURE 9-5.** *Trend example: yearly sales by region*

The answer is, by looking back over time and comparing how products have actually sold and then comparing those actuals with the forecasts received from the sales force. Perhaps you can see a trend that will allow you to predict a better, more accurate forecast this time.

Now we'll show an example we built in Discoverer. Using a crosstab, we created a query to find total sales by region for each of our past years. We then added a percentage and obtained the results shown in Figure 9-5, shown graphically in Figure 9-6. As you can see, the trend shows that, on average, the North American region has about 50 percent of sales in any one year, whereas the Far East started out well in 2006 but then continually lost percentage points to the other regions until 2012, when it regained some of the lost ground of earlier years.

See the section "How to Build the Example Queries" near the end of this chapter for full instructions on how to construct and manipulate this query.

Using this information, we will take whatever sales have been forecast for these districts and extrapolate total quantities required for our factory for the next quarter. Therefore, if the North American region sales force forecasts 58,400 for the next quarter, because they average 50 percent of all sales, we can estimate that we will need to have 116,800 products available altogether. Let's say that the South American region forecasts 10,000. Based on their 8.6 percent

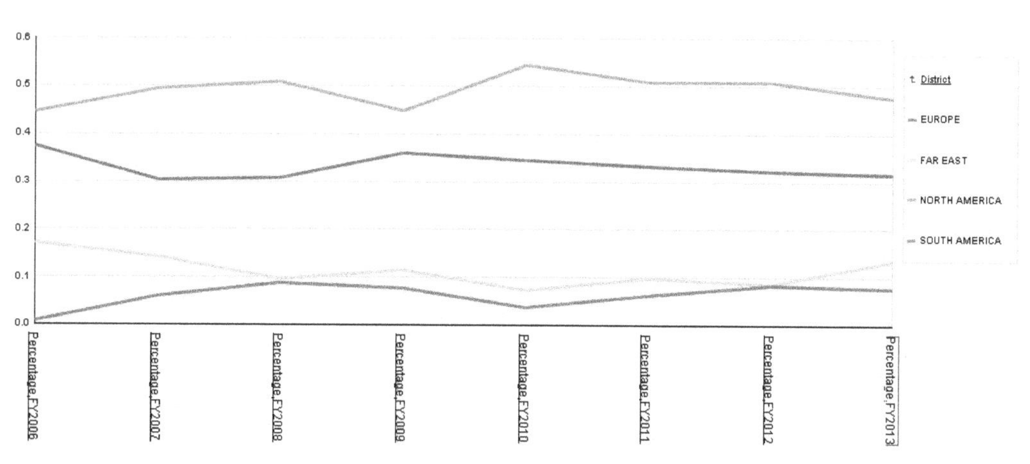


**FIGURE 9-6.** *Trend graph example: yearly sales by region*

in 2005, this would produce a total demand of 116,280 units. Finally, if Europe forecasts 35,000, this equates to 116,665 units. You can see that these three forecasts validate each other, and we will probably be safe issuing an order for our factories to build 120,000 units.

Let's now assume that our Far East region comes in with a forecast of 115,000 units, a not unreasonable number, you might think. However, based on their average sales of 12.4 percent, this would require us to build a total of 927,420 units, an amount that is way off when compared to the other three regions. In this situation, we will ask our Far East sales department to recheck their forecast and come back with a reason why the sales should be that high. We would not just accept the forecast, because if we did, we would almost certainly end up with excess inventory at the end of the quarter.

**NOTE**
*Perhaps someone transcribed the number for the Far East wrong, because if we compute 15,000 instead of 115,000, we end up with a total forecast of 120,000, much more in line with what we expect.*

## Aging Analysis

*Aging* analysis, as the name suggests, looks at data from the past and gives an analysis as to how well the company has performed over time. This is very similar to trending but not quite the same. For example, suppose you were a manufacturing company and were keen to show how well you were making shipments to your customers. You, and your shareholders, might be interested in knowing how many sales orders you managed to deliver on time. As with all statistics, the key to making this work is to accurately determine your definitions. You need to carefully define what you mean by an on-time delivery.

However, before you can define and measure what makes an on-time delivery, you need to define what constitutes a delivery. Is this the date you shipped the item from your factory or the date that the item arrived at the customer? If you are building a ship, is it the date it slipped into the water, the date it was delivered to your customer, or the date it completed its sea trials? Statistics again, you see. We can drive a bus through them, depending which date you pick.

Having defined what constitutes the delivery date, you now need to determine what other date you will compare this date to in order to work out how long it took to ship the item. Are you going to take the customer's original request date, or are you going to take the date your system said that you would ship the item? After you have determined how many days, months, or years it took you to ship the item, you now need to determine what defines an on-time shipment.

For some companies, shipping to the customer later than two days after the customer wanted it might classify this shipment as being a late delivery. However, if you are in the business of constructing an oil tanker that takes years to build, you might consider delivering the ship within two months of the requested date as being on time.

In our fictional company, because it is a global company with shipments over long distances, we define an on-time shipment as being within three days. However, not only do we want to know how many orders ship on time, but we also want to know the percentage of our product that does not ship within the required three days. In our case we have decided that we want to create the following four aging buckets:

- Orders that ship within three days of their requested date (considered on time)
- Orders that ship within seven days

Page Items: Shipped Year: FY2012

| | On Time Percentage | | | |
|---|---|---|---|---|
| | a. On Time | b. Within 1 week | c. Within 2 weeks | d. Over 2 weeks |
| EUROPE | 66% | 17% | 14% | 3% |
| FAR EAST | 68% | 16% | 12% | 4% |
| NORTH AMERICA | 66% | 17% | 14% | 3% |
| SOUTH AMERICA | 59% | 22% | 15% | 4% |

**FIGURE 9-7.** *Aging example: on-time deliveries by year*

- Orders that ship within fourteen days
- Orders that take longer than fourteen days

Figure 9-7 displays the final result.

As you can see, in 2012 three of our four regions managed to get an on-time delivery rate of 65 percent or more. We are not trying to say that this is good by any means. However, our vice president insisted that these numbers were too low and asked us to recalculate, removing the second category (orders that ship within seven days) and redefine on time as being up to seven days. When we did that, we got the answer shown in Figure 9-8.

The answer we now get is amazing and shows that we have an on-time percentage of more than 81 percent in all regions. This is what we will report to our shareholders. Remember how earlier we commented that you can drive a bus through statistics? We just did! We changed the formula to satisfy our internal politics. Of course, if someone asks how many shipped within three days, we will have to give the previous answer, but if we don't offer that information voluntarily, we haven't lied, and we haven't done anything wrong; we simply altered our reporting criteria. The bottom line didn't change, and the amount of profit we made is unaffected.

We hope that, having seen how powerful an aging report can be, you will take the time to learn how to create them for yourself. See the section "How to Build the Example Queries" near the end of this chapter for full instructions on how to construct this query.

Page Items: Shipped Year: FY2012

| | On Time Percentage | | |
|---|---|---|---|
| | a. On Time | b. Within 2 weeks | c. Over 2 weeks |
| EUROPE | 82% | 15% | 3% |
| FAR EAST | 85% | 12% | 4% |
| NORTH AMERICA | 83% | 15% | 3% |
| SOUTH AMERICA | 81% | 16% | 4% |

**FIGURE 9-8.** *Aging example: on-time redefined*

# Fundamentals of Analysis

Here is another quote that we think captures the essence of business intelligence: "The greatest value lies in getting information out of the database, not so much putting it in." Unfortunately, we do not know where this comes from; otherwise, we would give the necessary credit.

Knowledge discovery is what most enterprises strive for yet mostly dream about. In our opinion, not enough resources are being dedicated to finding out what information is available. Vast amounts of money are being spent on transactional systems, with super-fast servers and dedicated data lines, yet reporting databases are frequently relegated to secondary, and sometimes outdated, machines.

The amount of data being collected and stored in databases today far exceeds the capability of humans to reduce and analyze that data with any accuracy. What we need is some sort of methodology to overcome the difficulties involved in accurately transforming the raw data into knowledge. Therefore, getting the most from your stored data depends on the following:

- Your understanding of discovery techniques
- Your understanding of how to apply those techniques
- Your ability to use all of the features of Oracle Discoverer

Many OLTP business databases are growing at an unparalleled rate. Yet, it is the very fact that we have this large amount of data available to us that makes it possible to analyze with any accuracy in the first place. The irony of this situation is that the more data we have, the longer our queries take to run—yet the more accurate our analysis becomes.

Therefore, in order to effectively analyze data from large databases, you need to understand the following fundamentals:

- Good analysis is based on large amounts of data (a data warehouse, for example).
- Accuracy is essential (filtering out unwanted data).
- Some form of methodology or workflow is required.
- A query tool is required (Discoverer, of course).
- Analysis sometimes produces interesting or unexpected results.
- The results should be presented in a manner that is understandable to humans.

This book has tried to address all of these fundamentals. We have used workflows wherever we can, and the preceding chapter explained how to turn your query into a report that is capable of being understood by human beings.

Uncontrolled queries can very quickly exceed the capacity of the system. Therefore, before you begin to analyze anything, you need to ask these questions:

- Do you want to include detail or summary data?
- Do you want to work from the top down or from the bottom up?
- Do you want to focus on one piece of your organization or the complete entity?
- Do you want to export the information to a spreadsheet tool to do more complex analysis?
- Do you want your users to be able to slice the data? If so, use page items.
- Do you want your users to be able to dice the data? If so, teach the users how to use pivoting.

Before you take any more steps in the analysis of your data, answer these questions. It will save you time and keep you from "spinning your wheels." After you have answered these questions, you are ready to proceed to the analysis workflow.

# An Analysis Workflow

While this book is not designed to teach analysis, it would be deficient of us not to include some basic tips on how to analyze data. We understand that you may already be an experienced analyst who does not need another lesson in analysis. On the other hand, you may be employed as an analyst for the first time and be wondering how Discoverer can help you achieve your objectives.

Throughout an early career in the field of analysis, one of us was employed to analyze data for a large company that specialized in the leasing and management of vehicles to corporate clients. Being asked to analyze any form of data for the first time is a daunting task, but when the results of the analysis will be sent to customers who will then take actions based upon that report, the task can become frightening. So, just where does one start, and how does one analyze something?

During those early days with the company just referred to, the author spent many hours with senior analysts defining and refining the best way to use the tools available. While the tools may have improved, the fundamental steps to analyze data have not. We will share with you those same steps, and we believe that, by following this workflow, you will quickly be able to achieve at least a rudimentary understanding of how to analyze data.

In the preceding chapter, we gave you a reporting workflow. Within that workflow were several analysis steps. These steps have been extracted to form the following analysis workflow:

1. Revisit any existing conditions and create new conditions to select only the data from the database that you want to use in the final report.
2. Create calculations.
3. Create percentages.
4. Create subtotals and totals.
5. Apply sorting.
6. Create conditional formats (formerly known as *exceptions*).
7. Use the information and produce a report.

Not all of these steps will be used in all cases. However, we recommend that as you analyze your data, you follow the preceding workflow; omitting unneeded steps will benefit you.

# Core Examples Used in This Chapter

After many hours of experimentation, we have concluded that analyzing data in a crosstab is slicker and more user-friendly when compared to a standard table.

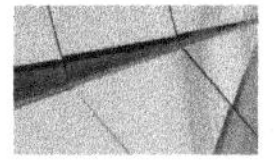

**NOTE**

*The use of crosstabs does come at a cost where performance is concerned. It might be better to use parameters in your workbooks rather than using crosstabs when you are analyzing more than a few hundred rows of data.*

Using Plus against our database, we created two identical queries, a table and a crosstab. These queries will form the basis for most of the analysis examples in the rest of this chapter. Throughout this chapter we will show you examples of these queries being executed in Desktop and Plus. This first illustration is a table, while the second is a crosstab. Both queries produced the same basic result by selecting the quantity shipped and the selling price for all products sold in financial year 2013. We have moved the product to the page axis and opted to view the results for just the product AB-2500.

Page Items: Product: AB-2500

| Order Quarter | Shipped Qty SUM | Selling Price SUM |
|---|---|---|
| 2013-Q2 | 51,810 | 663,127.50 |
| 2013-Q3 | 40,527 | 662,694.00 |
| 2013-Q1 | 56,752 | 942,888.00 |

Page Items: Product: AB-2500

| Order Quarter | Shipped Qty SUM | Selling Price SUM |
|---|---|---|
| 2013-Q1 | 56,752 | 942,888.00 |
| 2013-Q2 | 51,810 | 663,127.50 |
| 2013-Q3 | 40,527 | 662,694.00 |

While most of the analysis techniques in this chapter can be demonstrated using these two queries, some cannot. Whenever we encounter a technique that cannot be shown with the preceding queries, we will include a more suitable example.

**NOTE**

*Did you remember the two reasons for using page items (moving items to the page axis)? You place items there either when you want to see multiple pages of data or when you have items that would display the same data in every row. In the preceding two queries, you can see that we have moved the product to the page axis. This is because we didn't define any condition on the product and wanted to be able to see the quarterly results for other products by clicking the drop-down arrow.*

# Description of the Analysis Tools Available

In Chapters 4 and 5, you saw the Discoverer tools available to you as part of the Workbook Wizard. We also showed you how to access these tools through the Edit Sheet/Worksheet dialog box. But you will recall that in Desktop, the Edit Sheet dialog box gives you access to only some of the tools and should be used only when you want to edit several worksheet definitions at once. All of the tools are available in the Edit Worksheet dialog box of Plus, so you can use it if you want.

Anyone familiar with computer software knows that there are at least three ways to do anything! Discoverer is no exception. There are two more ways to access the Discoverer tools: from the menu bar and through smart menus. When you access the tools using these methods in Desktop, they open as stand-alone dialog boxes, not as the multitabbed Edit Worksheet dialog box that you will see in Plus; therefore, you can edit only a particular tool. In Plus, when you select one tool, you actually open the Edit Worksheet dialog box, and it dynamically places the focus into the tab for the tool that you want to work with. This is yet another of those wonderful little features of Discoverer Plus.

The process you follow for using these tools is virtually identical in every case. You can decide to turn on a tool to analyze the data, turn off the tool to return the data to its previous state, edit the definition to change the analysis being performed, create additional definitions, and apply the analysis tool to one or more data items. All of these options are under your control (refer to Chapters 4 and 5 for instructions on using these tools and to Chapters 11, 12, and 13 for advanced techniques).

One additional tool is available, and that is the tool to find exceptions. Exceptions highlight data that fall outside of an established norm. For example, maybe you want to highlight in red any product that has a markup of less than 33 percent. You can create an exception that will do just that. Exceptions (or to give them their correct Discoverer Plus name, *conditional formats*) are a terrific weapon in the analyst's armory. In versions of Discoverer prior to 10*g* you could add only a single exception. *Stoplighting* is a type of three-in-one conditional format that allows you to set upper and lower limits to a single definition. Creating conditional formats and stoplighting will be covered later in the chapter.

## Turning a Tool On and Off

In both versions of Discoverer, you can activate a tool from the menu bar. Clicking Tools displays a drop-down menu (this one is from Discoverer Plus).

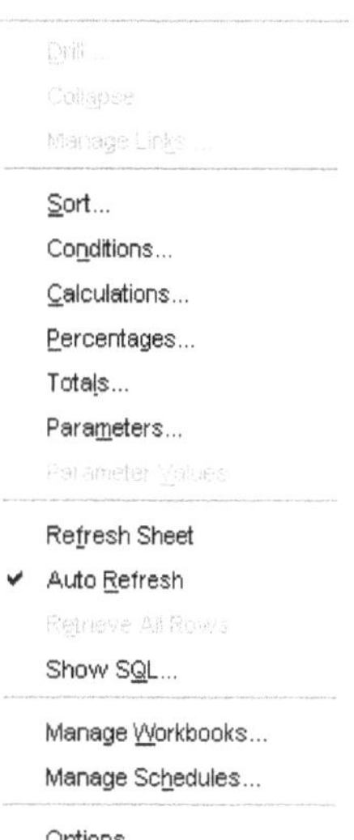


You can see that this menu has several options. The Desktop version has only seven of these options: Conditions, Sort, Totals, Percentages, Calculations, Parameters, and Options. In this chapter, we are concerned only with the following:

- Conditions
- Sort
- Totals
- Percentages
- Calculations

We have excluded the Parameters option because parameters are a specialized form of condition that will be covered in Chapters 12 and 13. The final menu item, Options, also has nothing to do with analysis and so is not discussed here. This menu item is explained in detail in Chapter 15.

The final way to access the tools is through smart menus. After a tool has been used to create an analysis definition, right-clicking in the column where it has been used will give you a smart menu offering a selection to edit the item definition.

In Plus, you can also access conditions, calculations, percentages, and totals from within the Available Items pane. You locate the areas called My Conditions, My Calculations, My Percentages, and My Totals. Right-clicking these headings brings up a pop-up menu that allows you to create a new item of the type on which you clicked. Items that are in use are shown with a check mark in the Available Items pane. You can turn a definition on and off by right-clicking the definition and selecting either Add to Worksheet or Remove from Worksheet.

In Desktop, whichever method you choose to launch an analysis tool, a dialog box appears. This box shows any analysis definitions that you have already created and whether they are currently in use. In front of each definition is a check box. You can turn a definition on and off by checking and unchecking this box.

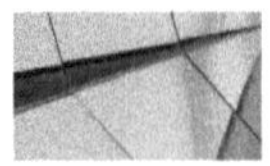

**NOTE**
*After you have created analysis definitions, do not be too hasty to delete them. If you have decided that a definition is no longer required, in Desktop simply uncheck it for now, or in Plus right-click the definition and select Remove from Worksheet from the pop-up menu. This leaves the definition intact but does not apply that definition to the current query. Adopting this method of working will allow you to come back later and reuse the definition if required.*

# The Analysis Toolbar Buttons

Do you remember, in Chapters 4 and 5, that we recommended you not create calculations, percentages, or totals in the Workbook Wizard? In this section we will show you another good reason why. The real power of GUI applications is toolbar buttons, and Discoverer has many very useful ones. Learn the buttons and you are a mouse click away from opening another powerful tool. As you will see, these toolbar buttons provide shortcuts that allow you to create calculations, percentages, and totals by a single click of your mouse.

**NOTE**
*If you cannot see the analysis bar on your Desktop screen, activate it from the menu bar by clicking View | Analysis Bar. In Plus it is part of the standard toolbar. Activate it by clicking View | Toolbars | Standard.*

The Desktop analysis bar, shown here, has a number of buttons and is broken up into four main areas, each divided from the next by a line:

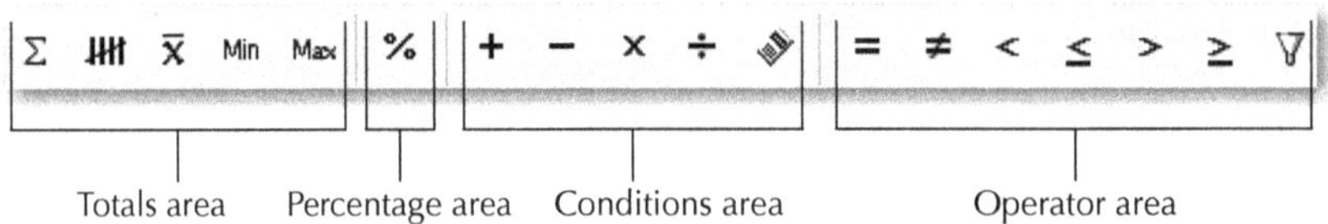


The Plus approach to these tools is slightly different. Instead of a large toolbar with lots of buttons, each main button when clicked opens the dialog box for that operation. Each main button has drop-downs containing buttons for the associated functions. This illustration shows the Totals button and its associated drop-down tools. Together, we call this the Totals area. There are similar "areas" for Percentages, Calculations (referred to as the Operator area in this list), Conditions, and Parameters.

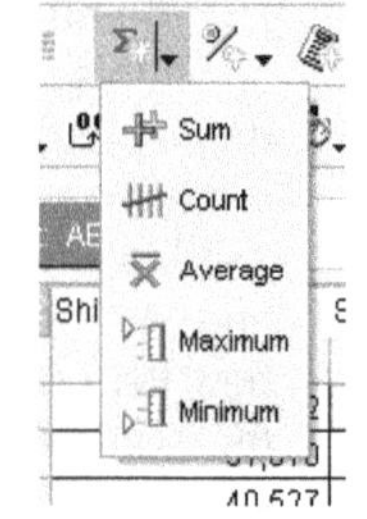


- **Totals area** This area contains five buttons, one each for the functions sum, count, average, minimum, and maximum.
- **Percentage area** In Desktop this area contains a single button. In Plus this area contains a New Percentage button with a drop-down alongside, although the drop-down has a single entry that performs exactly as if you had clicked the New Percentage button. After you have highlighted a column of data, click this button to create a percentage. In Desktop, the percentage is automatically created for you. In most cases, because the

default selected by Discoverer is not always quite right, you will usually end up having to edit the percentage that has just been created. In Plus, the New Percentage dialog box opens, thus allowing us to set up the percentage in advance of executing it. We like this feature very much.

- **Operators area** This part of the bar contains buttons for the four basic mathematical operators (add, subtract, multiply, and divide). Both versions have a New Calculation button to launch the New Calculations dialog box. Here is the Plus area.

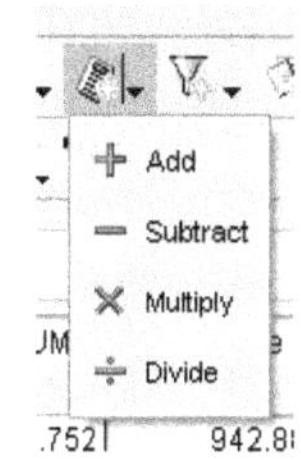


- **Conditions area** This area contains six buttons that allow you to create conditions based on testing whether values are equal, nonequal, less than, less than or equal to, greater than, and greater than or equal to. There is also a New Condition button to launch the New Condition dialog box. Here is the Plus area.

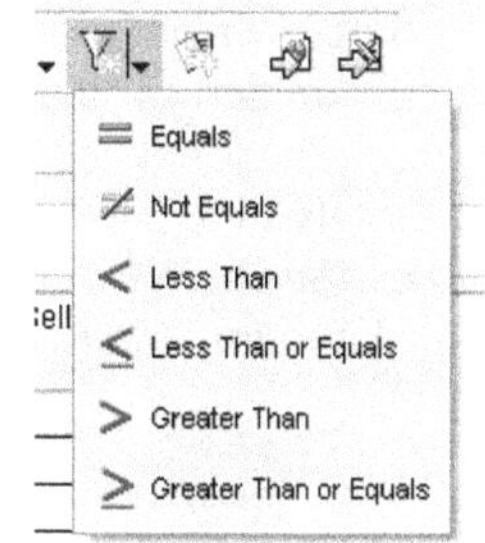


- **Parameters area** This area exists in Plus only and consists of a single New Parameter button that launches the New Parameter dialog box.

We will describe each area in turn and tell you what each button does. Many of the buttons on the toolbars are mathematical and will work only if you include numerical data in your query. Having created a query, you now simply highlight the column or columns containing the data you want to analyze and click the button for the operation you want Discoverer to perform. It really is that easy!

**NOTE**

*After you highlight a column, moving the cursor along the analysis bar causes Desktop to highlight, in a bigger font, those analysis features that are available to you. Any function that does not display in this bigger font cannot be applied to the data you have selected. In Plus, Discoverer places an outline around the active buttons as you move the cursor along the bars.*

## Totals Area

The first part of the analysis bar, which we call the Totals area, provides five buttons, one each for the functions sum, count, average, minimum, and maximum. Unless you highlight a column of data (remember, to highlight a column of data, place your cursor on the column heading and click the mouse button), these buttons will be inactive.

You can also select a single cell and have a total created for that column or item. If you are using group-sorted items, Discoverer is smart enough to recognize this and will insert subtotals.

You cannot highlight multiple data points and expect Discoverer to insert totals for all of these columns. You may think that it should, and to be fair to you, so did we. In Plus, if you select multiple data points and create a total, in a table the total will be created on the first item that you selected, but in a crosstab the total will be created on the last item that you selected. In Desktop, when you select multiple data points, all of the buttons in the Totals area will be inactive, thus preventing you from creating any erroneous totals.

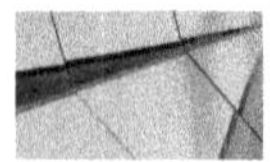

**NOTE**
*In Plus, if you select any nondata point in a crosstab and then click one of the drop-down buttons, Discoverer always launches the New Total dialog box. However, if you select a data point and repeat this exercise, Discoverer dynamically creates the total. In Desktop, Discoverer assumes you want to calculate the total on all data points and dynamically creates the total.*

## Tables Are Complicated to Analyze

Before we get too far into this section, we will remind you one more time that we strongly recommend you analyze using crosstabs whenever possible.

The following example may help convince you that analyzing in a table, especially from the Totals area, can be unpredictable. First we clicked the heading for the quarter. In Desktop, you can see here that Discoverer has highlighted all of the quarters and enabled only the Count, Minimum, and Maximum buttons in the Totals area:

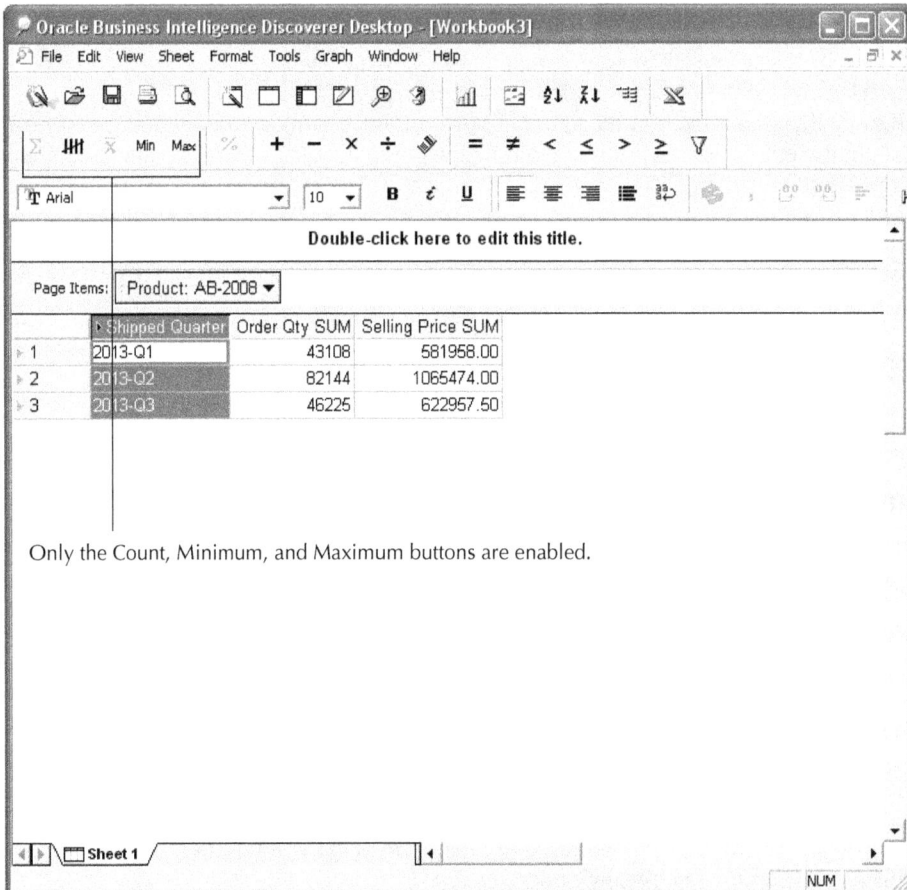



Only the Count, Minimum, and Maximum buttons are enabled.

Let's repeat this in Plus. We again clicked the heading for the quarter. When we went to the Totals area, we clicked Sum because we saw that all of the drop-down buttons were still active. Rather than create a total, as is the normal behavior when we do this, Discoverer opened the following New Total dialog box:

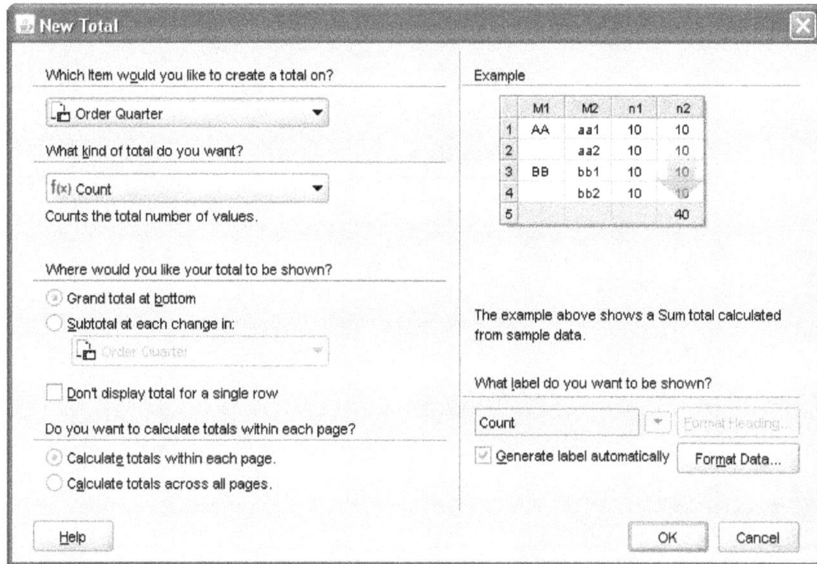


As you can see, Discoverer has changed the total to being a Count. While we understand why this is happening, we are sure it could be confusing to the novice user. You therefore need to be careful when clicking the Totals buttons in the Totals area when in Plus to make sure that you are on the correct column. As previously mentioned, in Desktop there is no such issue, because Desktop grays out the options that do not apply.

## Crosstabs Are Great to Analyze

Before we explain what the different buttons can do, we want to show you why analyzing a crosstab is simpler and easier to understand when compared to a table. The biggest advantage is that you can apply any of the functions in the Totals area to all of the data points at the same time. You do this by clicking the heading for one of the side axis items and then clicking one of the buttons in the Totals area of the analysis bar.

For example, here we have highlighted the quarter heading. As expected, in Desktop all of the buttons in the Totals area are now active.

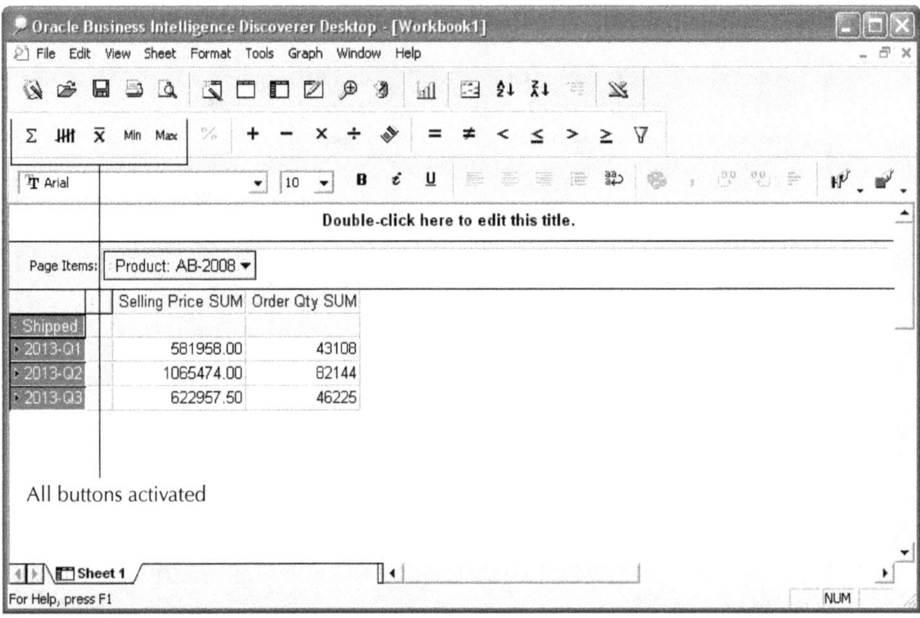


The illustration that follows shows the result of applying the sum function. You can see that Discoverer inserted a grand total for all of the data points.

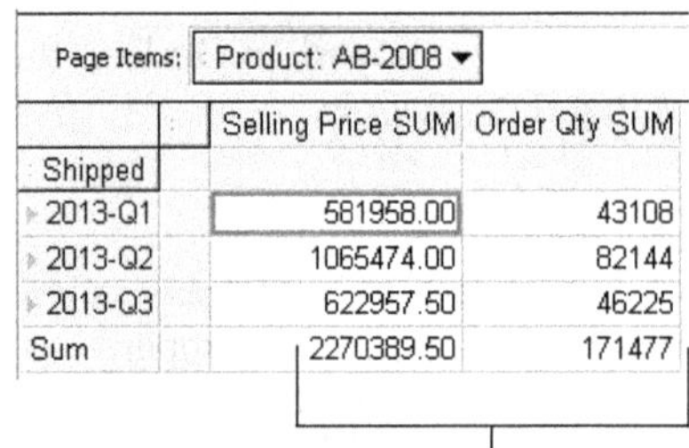

Page Items: Product: AB-2008

| Shipped | Selling Price SUM | Order Qty SUM |
|---|---|---|
| 2013-Q1 | 581958.00 | 43108 |
| 2013-Q2 | 1065474.00 | 82144 |
| 2013-Q3 | 622957.50 | 46225 |
| Sum | 2270389.50 | 171477 |

Grand total for all of the data points

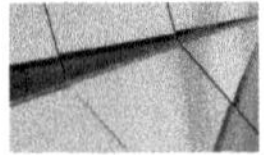

**NOTE**
*The format applied to any of the functions in the Totals area is the default format as specified on the Format tab of the Tools | Options dialog box. Also note that you can apply a total only to a numeric column of data.*

## Using Totals with Sorts

As we said earlier, Discoverer offers increased flexibility when you are using group sorts, especially in a crosstab. In the examples shown next, we have taken our base queries and moved the product out of the Page Items area, thereby allowing us to see all of the data for each product grouped together.

For the following table, the product has been placed in front of the quarter. We then defined a group sort on the product and placed a standard Low to High sort on the quarter.

| | Product | Shipped Quarter | Selling Price SUM | Order Qty SUM |
|---|---|---|---|---|
| 1 | AB-2008 | 2012-Q4 | 1013040.00 | 75040 |
| 2 | | 2012-Q3 | 777343.50 | 57581 |
| 3 | | 2012-Q2 | 562153.50 | 41641 |
| 4 | | 2012-Q1 | 474390.00 | 35140 |
| 5 | AB-2500 | 2012-Q4 | 392878.50 | 30814 |
| 6 | | 2012-Q3 | 721127.25 | 56559 |
| 7 | | 2012-Q1 | 544144.50 | 42678 |
| 8 | | 2012-Q2 | 533345.25 | 41831 |
| 9 | AB-3000 | 2012-Q4 | 1217412.50 | 57290 |
| 10 | | 2012-Q3 | 1141422.50 | 53714 |
| 11 | | 2012-Q2 | 847386.25 | 39877 |
| 12 | | 2012-Q1 | 1255280.00 | 59072 |
| 13 | AVR-500 | 2012-Q4 | 2341011.75 | 86865 |
| 14 | | 2012-Q3 | 2622666.20 | 97316 |
| 15 | | 2012-Q2 | 1576844.50 | 58510 |
| 16 | | 2012-Q1 | 1499147.65 | 55627 |
| 17 | AVR-550 | 2012-Q3 | 1998180.80 | 74144 |
| 18 | | 2012-Q1 | 878570.00 | 32600 |
| 19 | | 2012-Q4 | 1937597.20 | 71896 |
| 20 | | 2012-Q2 | 631169.00 | 23420 |

For the crosstab shown here, the product and quarter have been moved to become side axis points. As you can see, Discoverer automatically created a group sort and, because our crosstab is defined as being Outline, also inserted a subtotal by product.

| Product | Shipped ( | Selling Price SUM | Order Qty SUM |
|---|---|---|---|
| AB-2008 | | 2,826,927 | 209,402 |
| | 2012-Q1 | 474,390 | 35,140 |
| | 2012-Q2 | 562,154 | 41,641 |
| | 2012-Q3 | 777,344 | 57,581 |
| | 2012-Q4 | 1,013,040 | 75,040 |
| AB-2500 | | 2,191,496 | 171,882 |
| | 2012-Q1 | 544,145 | 42,678 |
| | 2012-Q2 | 533,345 | 41,831 |
| | 2012-Q3 | 721,127 | 56,559 |
| | 2012-Q4 | 392,879 | 30,814 |
| AB-3000 | | 4,461,501 | 209,953 |
| | 2012-Q1 | 1,255,280 | 59,072 |
| | 2012-Q2 | 847,386 | 39,877 |
| | 2012-Q3 | 1,141,423 | 53,714 |
| | 2012-Q4 | 1,217,413 | 57,290 |
| AVR-500 | | 8,039,670 | 298,318 |
| | 2012-Q1 | 1,499,148 | 55,627 |
| | 2012-Q2 | 1,576,845 | 58,510 |
| | 2012-Q3 | 2,622,666 | 97,316 |
| | 2012-Q4 | 2,341,012 | 86,865 |

Subtotal by product

No matter which of the two queries we now work on, clicking the heading for any of the data points and then clicking any of the buttons in the Totals area works the same as for a non-sorted query. Discoverer simply inserts a grand total on that item. However, clicking one of the sorted items causes Discoverer to insert a subtotal.

### Sum Button

To show you how easy it is to create a sum using the analysis bar, we highlighted the Quantity Shipped column and clicked the Sum button. As you can see, Discoverer automatically inserted a grand total of the quantity shipped. Defining a total this way produces the same result as creating a total in the Totals dialog box, based on the sum function.

The illustration that follows shows a grand total applied to a table:

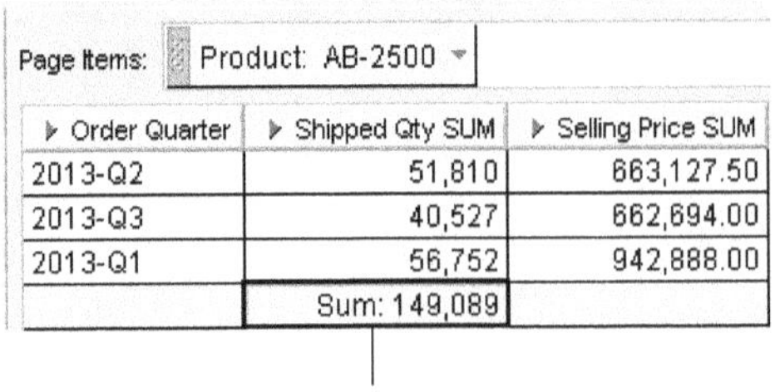

Page Items: Product: AB-2500

| Order Quarter | Shipped Qty SUM | Selling Price SUM |
|---|---|---|
| 2013-Q2 | 51,810 | 663,127.50 |
| 2013-Q3 | 40,527 | 662,694.00 |
| 2013-Q1 | 56,752 | 942,888.00 |
| | Sum: 149,089 | |

Grand total applied to a table

The next illustration shows a grand total applied to a crosstab:

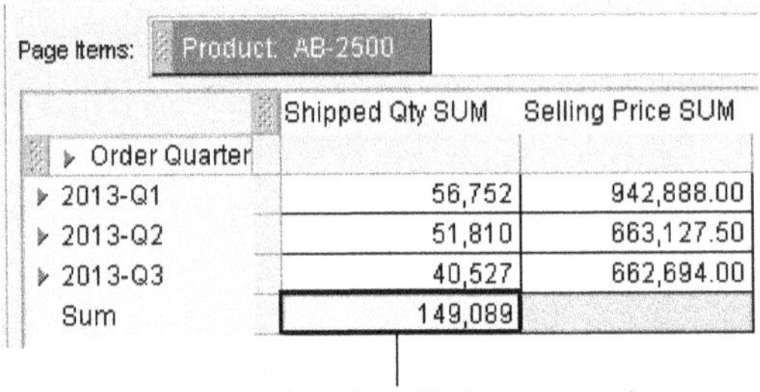

Page Items: Product: AB-2500

| Order Quarter | Shipped Qty SUM | Selling Price SUM |
|---|---|---|
| 2013-Q1 | 56,752 | 942,888.00 |
| 2013-Q2 | 51,810 | 663,127.50 |
| 2013-Q3 | 40,527 | 662,694.00 |
| Sum | 149,089 | |

Grand total applied to a crosstab

If you are working with a crosstab and you want to insert a grand total for all data points, there are three ways to correct the situation.

### Edit the Existing Total Definition

To insert a grand total by editing the definition for the existing total, use the following workflow:

1. Right-click the axis label for the total. This displays a drop-down list of options.
2. Select Edit Total from the list. This opens the following Edit Total dialog box.

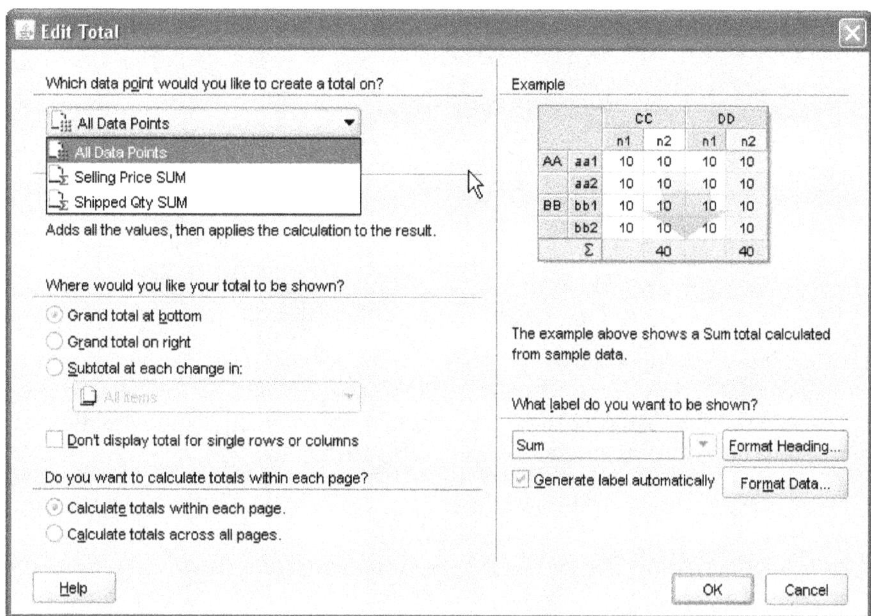


3. Click the down arrow beside the item currently being totaled, and change the drop-down selection to All Data Points.
4. Click OK. The results are shown next.

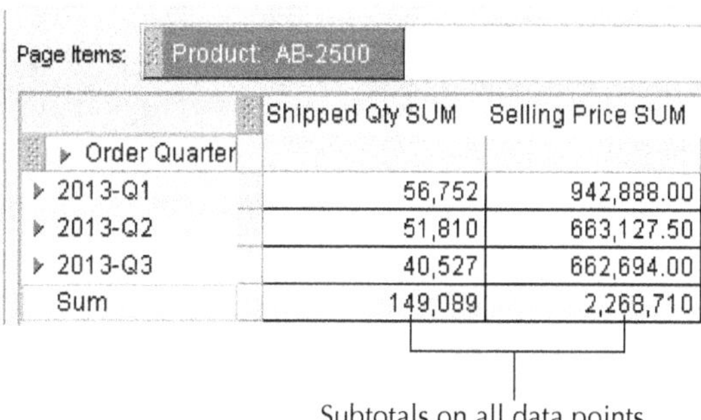
Page Items: Product: AB-2500

| Order Quarter | Shipped Qty SUM | Selling Price SUM |
|---|---|---|
| 2013-Q1 | 56,752 | 942,888.00 |
| 2013-Q2 | 51,810 | 663,127.50 |
| 2013-Q3 | 40,527 | 662,694.00 |
| Sum | 149,089 | 2,268,710 |

Subtotals on all data points

**Create a Grand Total for All Data Points** To create a grand total for all data points, use the following workflow:

Page Items: Product: AB-2008

| Shipped | Selling Price SUM | Order Qty SUM |
|---|---|---|
| 2013-Q1 | 581958.00 | 43108 |
| 2013-Q2 | 1065474.00 | 82144 |
| 2013-Q3 | 622957.50 | 46225 |
| Sum | 2270389.50 | 171477 |

1. Click the axis label. In Desktop, this highlights all of the time periods in the axis. In Plus, as you can see, only the label is highlighted.

Page Items: Product: AB-2500

| Order Quarter | Shipped Qty SUM | Selling Price SUM |
|---|---|---|
| 2013-Q1 | 56,752 | 942,888.00 |
| 2013-Q2 | 51,810 | 663,127.50 |
| 2013-Q3 | 40,527 | 662,694.00 |
| Sum | 149,089 | 2,268,710 |

2. Click the Total button on the analysis bar. Discoverer Desktop automatically inserts a grand total at the bottom. Discoverer Plus launches the New Total dialog box. In either case, when the total is created, Discoverer is not smart enough to use the existing definition but inserts a new row, as shown next in Plus.

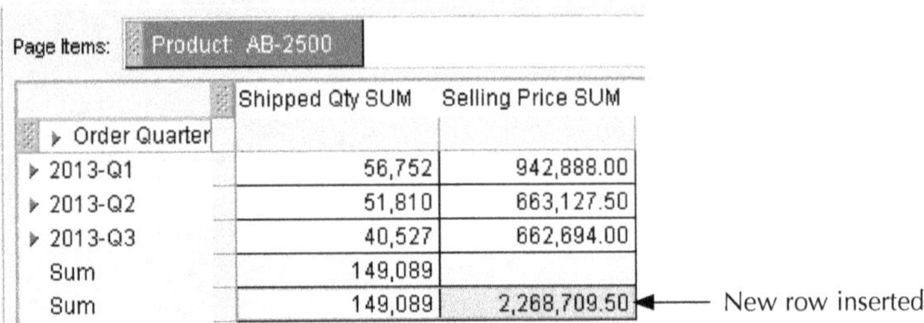

Page Items: Product: AB-2500

| Order Quarter | Shipped Qty SUM | Selling Price SUM |
|---|---|---|
| 2013-Q1 | 56,752 | 942,888.00 |
| 2013-Q2 | 51,810 | 663,127.50 |
| 2013-Q3 | 40,527 | 662,694.00 |
| Sum | 149,089 | |
| Sum | 149,089 | 2,268,709.50 |



3. Click the axis label for the old total. This highlights the label.
4. In Desktop only, press DELETE on your keyboard. The row and the definition will be removed. The total will not be deleted, however, but only suppressed from being displayed in the report.
5. In Plus, right-click the total in the Available Items pane, and from the pop-up menu select Remove from Worksheet.

**Create New Definitions for the Other Data Points** The third way to correct the situation is to add individual totals to the data points that are currently not totaled. Highlight, in turn, each data point label you want to be totaled, and click the Total button. When we did that in our example, Discoverer added the word *Sum* in front of each total, as shown next.

Page Items: Product: AB-2500

| | Shipped Qty SUM | Selling Price SUM |
|---|---|---|
| 2013-Q1 | 56,752 | 942,888 |
| 2013-Q2 | 51,810 | 663,128 |
| 2013-Q3 | 40,527 | 662,694 |
| Sum | 149,089 | 2,268,710 |

**NOTE**

*If you decide that you want to have the word Sum appear only once, you should create a new total using the axis label, as described earlier. However, in Desktop, when you now press the* DELETE *key, Discoverer does nothing. You will have to use the Totals dialog box if you want to disable or delete these two totals. In Plus, as in the previous section, right-click the total in the Available Items pane and from the pop-up menu select Remove from Worksheet.*

**Count Button** Highlighting a column of data and clicking this button inserts a count of the number of rows in the query. Let's assume we want to know how many sales orders shipped in January 2000. Using our example query, highlighting the Sales Order column and clicking Count caused Discoverer to insert the count.

| | | |
|---|---|---|
| DEC-12 | 10986 | 1200 |
| OCT-12 | 10670 | 200 |
| FEB-13 | 11202 | 1920 |
| NOV-12 | 10708 | 1200 |
| DEC-12 | 10918 | 8400 |
| JAN-13 | 11087 | 600 |
| MAR-13 | 11477 | 1200 |
| MAR-13 | 11542 | 1200 |
| MAR-13 | 11548 | 48 |
| MAY-13 | 12255 | 2400 |
| MAR-13 | 11648 | 50 |
| APR-13 | 11883 | 200 |
| | Count: 1561 | Sum: 2972326 |

Count

**NOTE**

*You will notice that Discoverer has placed the count of sales orders on the same row as the total number of items shipped. Older versions of Discoverer do not do this but will display the two figures on separate rows.*

**Average Button** Highlighting a column of data and clicking the Average button inserts a calculation of the average of the data items in the row or rows highlighted. Let's assume we want to know the average number of items shipped on each sales order. Using our example query again, highlighting the Shipped Quantity column and clicking Average caused Discoverer to insert the average of 1904.

| | | |
|---|---|---|
| JAN-13 | 11087 | 600 |
| MAR-13 | 11477 | 1200 |
| MAR-13 | 11542 | 1200 |
| MAR-13 | 11548 | 48 |
| MAY-13 | 12255 | 2400 |
| MAR-13 | 11648 | 50 |
| APR-13 | 11883 | 200 |
| | Count: 1561 | Sum: 2972326 |
| | | Average: 1904 |

**Minimum Button** Highlighting a column or columns of data and clicking the Minimum button inserts a calculation of the lowest-valued item in the column or columns. For example, assume we want to know the minimum number of items that we shipped on any one sales order. Using our query, highlighting the Shipped Quantity column and clicking Minimum caused Discoverer to insert the minimum value in the column.

| | | |
|---|---|---|
| JAN-13 | 11087 | 600 |
| MAR-13 | 11477 | 1200 |
| MAR-13 | 11542 | 1200 |
| MAR-13 | 11548 | 48 |
| MAY-13 | 12255 | 2400 |
| MAR-13 | 11648 | 50 |
| APR-13 | 11883 | 200 |
| | Count: 1561 | Sum: 2972326 |
| | | Average: 1904 |
| | | Minimum: 1 |

**Maximum Button** Highlighting a column or columns of data and clicking the Maximum button inserts a calculation of the highest-valued item in the column or columns. For example, assume we want to know the maximum number of items that we shipped on any one sales order. Using our query, highlighting the Shipped Quantity column and clicking Maximum causes Discoverer to insert the maximum value in the column.

| | | |
|---|---|---|
| DEC-12 | 10918 | 8400 |
| JAN-13 | 11087 | 600 |
| MAR-13 | 11477 | 1200 |
| MAR-13 | 11542 | 1200 |
| MAR-13 | 11548 | 48 |
| MAY-13 | 12255 | 2400 |
| MAR-13 | 11648 | 50 |
| APR-13 | 11883 | 200 |
| | Count: 1561 | Sum: 2972326 |
| | | Average: 1904 |
| | | Minimum: 1 |
| | | Maximum: 15000 |

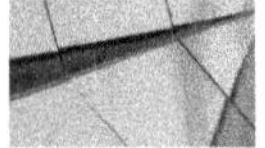

**NOTE**

*Minimum and Maximum can be applied to dates and strings just as easily as to numbers. If we had highlighted the Date Shipped column and clicked first Minimum and then Maximum, Discoverer would have inserted the first and last dates in January that we shipped the displayed product.*

# Percentage Area

The second part of the analysis bar, which we call the Percentage area, provides a single button for creating percentages. Highlighting any column of numeric data activates this button. When you create a percentage this way, Discoverer creates a new column displaying a percentage based on the grand total, for each row. It names the column by prefixing the word *Percent* in front of the source column name. For example, if the source column is named Selling Price, the new column will be called Percent Selling Price.

To change the percentage definition, use the following workflow:

1. Right-click the column heading and select Edit Percentage from the drop-down list, or from the menu bar select Tools | Percentages.
2. Change the percentage definition (refer to Chapter 5 for an explanation of percentage definitions, and see Chapter 13 for more advanced techniques).
3. Click OK.

# Operators Area

The third part of the analysis bar contains buttons for the four main mathematical operators add (+), subtract (-), multiply (*), and divide (/), along with a button to launch the Calculations dialog box.

## Add (+), Subtract (-), Multiply (*), and Divide (/) Buttons

These four buttons work in the same way and usually require you to highlight two columns of numeric data before you click one of the buttons. We say "usually" because Discoverer will allow you to highlight non-numerical columns before clicking the Add button. Doing this causes Discoverer to concatenate the two columns of data.

Follow this simple workflow to create new calculations based on these four operators:

1. Highlight a column of data.
2. Hold down the CTRL key and highlight a second column of data.
3. Click one of the four operators.

In Desktop, Discoverer launches the appropriate dialog box. In Plus, Discoverer dynamically creates and executes the calculation, generating a default name of Calculation1. Because all of the Desktop dialog boxes look the same, we will describe only the Subtract dialog box.

As you can see in the following bullet points, the Subtract dialog box contains the following six areas:

- **Name** The name typed here will appear as the column heading for the calculation.
- **Defined as** These two boxes contain the names of the two columns upon which the calculation is based.
- **Advanced** Click this to launch an advanced dialog box for the appropriate calculation.
- **OK** Clicking OK completes the calculation, closes the dialog box, and displays the results in a column named by whatever name you gave the calculation.
- **Cancel** Clicking Cancel abandons the calculation and returns you to the original query.
- **Help** Clicking Help launches the standard Discoverer help system.

When you use the add and multiply functions, it makes no difference which column you highlight first. However, when you use the subtract and divide functions, the order is vitally important. The data in the second column will be subtracted from or divided into the data in the first column.

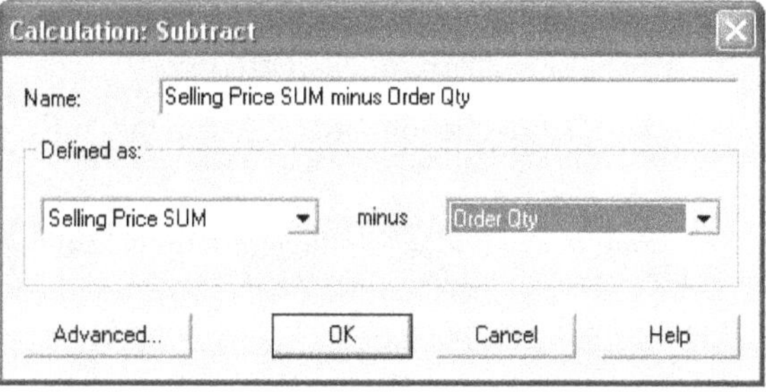


If you are working in Plus and you have highlighted the columns in the wrong order, you will need to use the Edit Calculation dialog box to remedy the situation. The issue is easier to correct in Desktop because you can click the down arrow beside each of the columns in the dialog box to change the columns being used.

### Calculation Button

Clicking this button launches the Edit Calculations dialog box. This button is always active.

## Conditions Area

The final part of the analysis bar is the Conditions area. This area contains seven buttons, which allow you to create conditions based on values being equal (=), nonequal (<>), less than (<), less than or equal to (<=), greater than (>), and greater than or equal to (>=), as well as a button to launch the New Condition dialog box. This final button is always active.

The first six buttons can save you time and effort in creating conditions based on the data that has been returned by your query. For example, assume you have a query that has returned the total quantity sold by product. If you want to see the query conditioned to display only the quantity from product CD-100 and greater, use the following workflow:

1. Click in the cell containing the data item CD-100.
2. Click the >= button. This opens the New Condition dialog box, with the item, condition, and value prefilled.
3. Click OK. This completes and applies the condition to the query. Discoverer does not rerun the query because the condition specified constrains the data to a subset of the data that you originally selected.

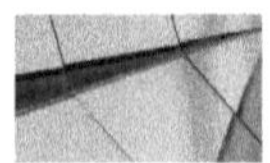

**NOTE**
*Just as with calculations, you can select a dimension and filter on it with a simple click. To do this, you click in the cell that you want to use for the filter and then click the appropriate condition button. Discoverer will dynamically create the condition for you and re-execute the query to apply the new filter.*

## Finding Exceptions Using Formatting

As we mentioned earlier in the chapter, exceptions highlight data that falls outside of an established norm. You can create many exceptions concerning the same data items. If you have overlapping exceptions, be careful not to turn both on at the same time. Let's say you have two exceptions for Profit SUM, one for all values greater than 10,000 and the other for values between 40,000 and 60,000. If you inadvertently select two or more conflicting exceptions, a message asks you to reselect the exception so that they don't conflict.

To use exceptions effectively, you need to bear in mind the following criteria:

- Define the exception itself, such as "is greater than 10,000" or "is less than 25%" or "is between 10,000 and 50,000."
- Define the format of the data that the exception will be applied to so that you can see it easily among the rest of the data.

Desktop and Plus handle exceptions in different ways. Desktop uses the term *exception*, whereas Plus calls it *conditional formatting*. Even though the differences are minimal, we will show you how to perform this operation by version.

### Using Desktop to Highlight Exceptions

To create exceptions, use the following workflow:

1. Select Format | Exceptions from the toolbar, or right-click a column of data and select Format Exception from the drop-down menu displayed. This opens the Exceptions dialog box shown next. The functionality of this dialog box is the same as the other tools.

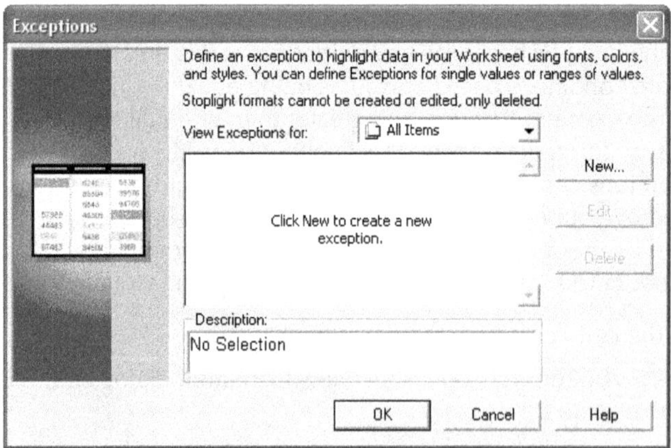

2. Click New. This opens the Exception dialog box. We will not explain its use until later in this section.

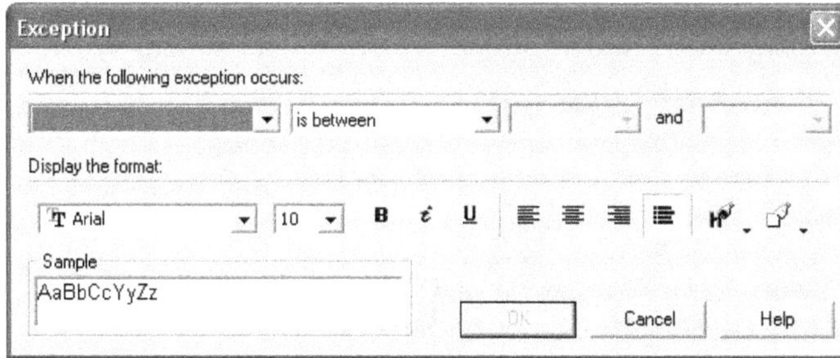


3. Define the exception.
4. Click OK. This will close the Exception dialog box.
5. Click OK in the Exceptions dialog box (yes, we know the names of the boxes are the same except for the *s* on the end).

It is quite easy and intuitive to create an exception in Discoverer.

## Using Plus to Create Conditional Formatting

To create conditional formatting, use the following workflow:

1. Select Format | Conditional Formats from the toolbar, or right-click a column of data and select Conditional Formats from the drop-down menu displayed. This opens the Conditional Formats dialog box shown next.

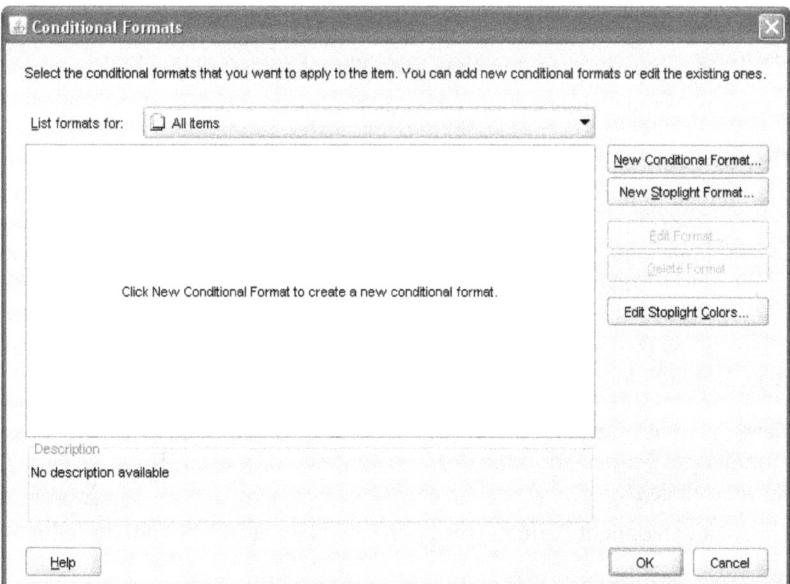

2. Click New Conditional Format. This opens the New Conditional Format dialog box. We will not explain its use until later in this section.

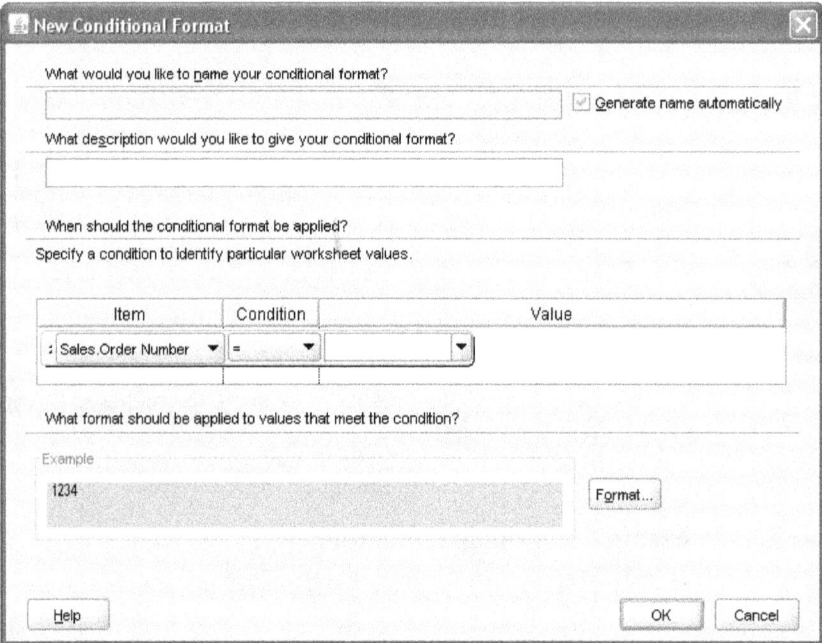


3. Name and define the conditional format. We generally allow Discoverer to autoname the conditional formats because it uses the syntax of the conditional formatting and it is quite clear what it is.
4. Click OK. This will close the New Conditional Format dialog box.
5. Click OK in the Conditional Formats dialog box.

## Using Plus to Create Stoplight Formatting

Another useful feature of Plus is stoplight formatting. *Stoplighting* takes conditional formatting to the next level. For example, you want to see at a glance the sales categories that each customer falls into. Customers with sales of less than $10,000 per year are unacceptable, while customers with sales exceeding $60,000 are desirable. You can use stoplighting to highlight in red customers who fall into the unacceptable sales category, in green those customers who are in the desired range, and in yellow everyone in between.

To create stoplight formatting, use the following workflow:

1. Select Format | Conditional Formats from the toolbar, or click a column of data and select Conditional Formats from the drop-down menu displayed. This opens the Conditional Formats dialog.
2. Click New Stoplight Format. This opens the New Stoplight Format dialog box.

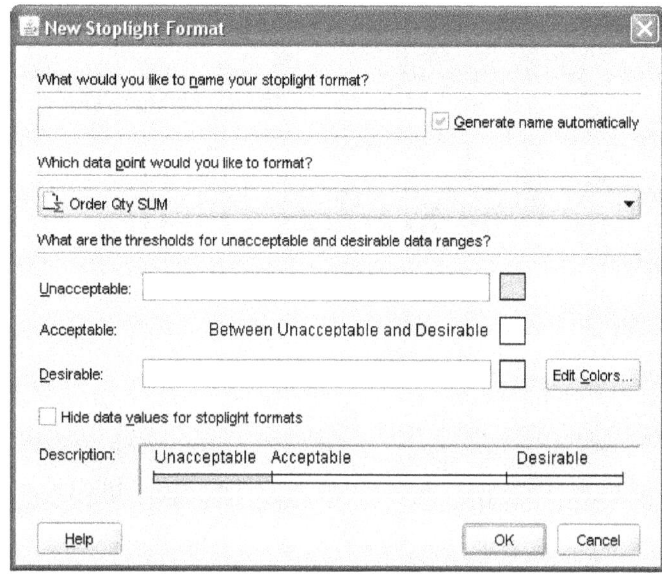


3. Name the stoplight format. Remember to give it a meaningful name or let Discoverer name it automatically.
4. Select the data point upon which you want the stoplighting.
5. Enter your unacceptable and desirable thresholds. You do not select the middle range; it is quite simply everything that falls in between the other two.
6. Edit the colors of the stoplight by clicking the Edit Colors button; then use the drop-down to change the colors, and click OK.
7. Select whether you want to show the actual data point values or just the stoplight colors in the cells.
8. Click OK. This will close the New Stoplight Format dialog box.
9. Click OK in the Conditional Formats dialog box.

Here is a sample stoplight, shown at right.

Another extremely useful feature of stoplight formats allows you to hide the data values for a column that has had stoplight formatting applied to it. If you look back to the New Stoplight Format dialog box, at the bottom left of the dialog box is a Hide data values for stoplight formats check box. If you check this, Discoverer will display the stoplight cell colors for the column but will suppress the data values.

Page Items: Product: AB-2500

| Order Quarter | Shipped Qty SUM | Selling Price SUM |
|---|---|---|
| 2011-Q1 | 22,479 | 286,607.25 |
| 2011-Q2 | 15,841 | 330,747.75 |
| 2011-Q3 | 38,879 | 624,227.25 |
| 2011-Q4 | 81,382 | 1,140,130.50 |
| 2012-Q1 | 35,878 | 459,994.50 |
| 2012-Q2 | 43,751 | 591,995.25 |
| 2012-Q3 | 54,740 | 699,210.00 |
| 2012-Q4 | 30,713 | 395,517.75 |
| 2013-Q1 | 56,752 | 942,888.00 |
| 2013-Q2 | 51,810 | 663,127.50 |
| 2013-Q3 | 40,527 | 662,694.00 |
| Sum | 472,752 | 6,797,139.75 |

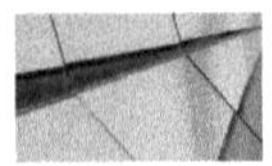

**NOTE**
*You can still see the values by clicking the small cell underneath the column heading and the data itself. Discoverer will redisplay the values but in a very faint color. To re-hide the values, click anywhere inside the data that has been stoplight formatted.*

# How to Build the Example Queries

When explaining the different types of analysis, we showed you the results of queries to display examples of the five types. This section shows you how we went about building those queries and highlights which analysis tools were used.

## Statistical Analysis

If you recall, this query was quite simple and was a crosstab built using the year, region, and selling price sum. The year was placed on the top axis because we didn't want to display the same data item in every row. The region was placed in the side axis, while the selling price sum was left on the top axis.

To complete the query, in Desktop we clicked the Selling Price SUM label and then the Percentage button on the analysis bar. In Plus, we clicked the drop-down alongside the New Percentage button and selected % Percentage. In both cases we created the new percentage, as shown next:

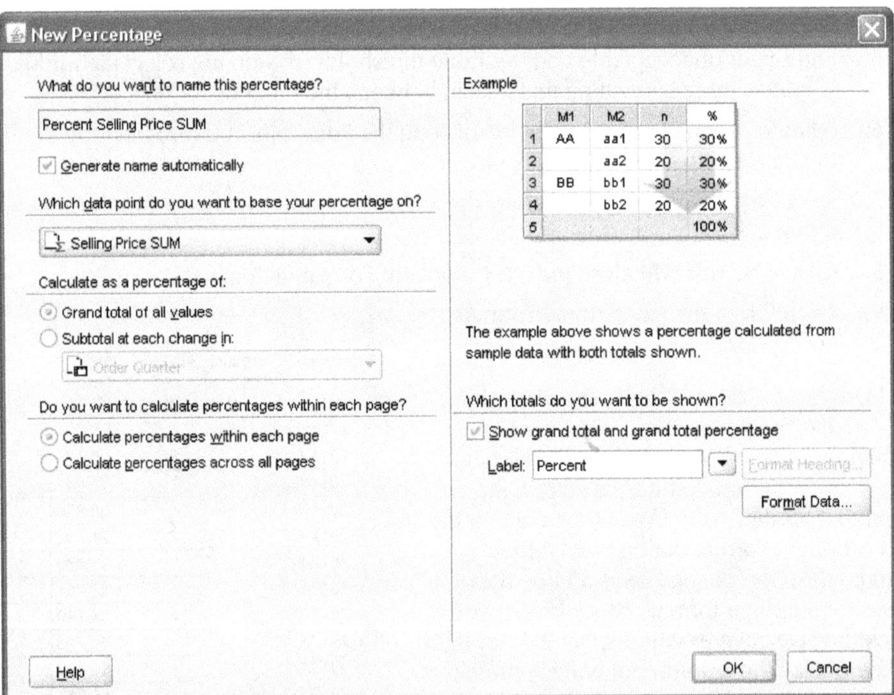


You can see the completed query earlier in Figure 9-1.

# Classification Analysis

This query is, once again, a crosstab. This one selects the cost price, selling price, profit, product name, product line, and quarter, with a condition that the quarters are all for 2012. We did not apply a condition on the product line, but we did move it to the page axis in order to be able to select one product line at a time. After moving the product name and quarter to the side axis, the resulting output is as it was shown in Figure 9-2.

So far, so good. But just how did we end up with the result that was shown in Figure 9-3? First, despite how it may look, we have to tell you that it really is the same query. We did not edit any of the selections, and we did not change any of the conditions. Moving the items between the various axes did everything.

If you remember, we told you that we would be showing you how to do all of this manipulation in Viewer. We will also show you how to do the same thing in both Desktop and Plus.

## Manipulating in Viewer

In Viewer, before you can move the data points from their traditional axis to the page axis, you need to move another item into the data point axis first. This is because the data point axis in a crosstab in Viewer must contain something.

The first thing we did was to expand the Layout link on the Tools menu, which you will find just above the page items. Next we moved Quarter to below Cost Price using these settings:

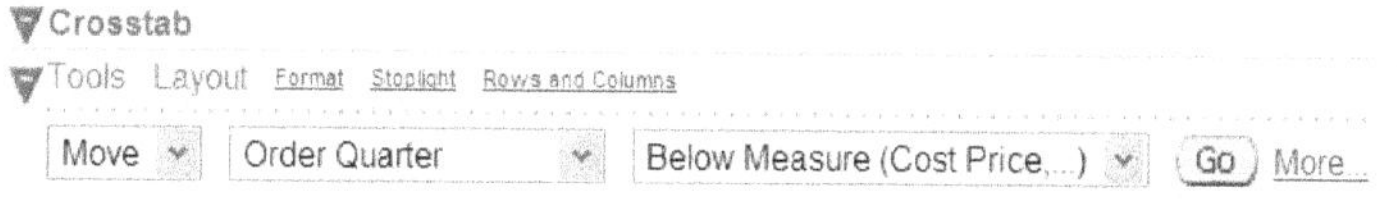


Next we moved Cost Price to the page items, using these settings:

The intermediate result now looks like this:

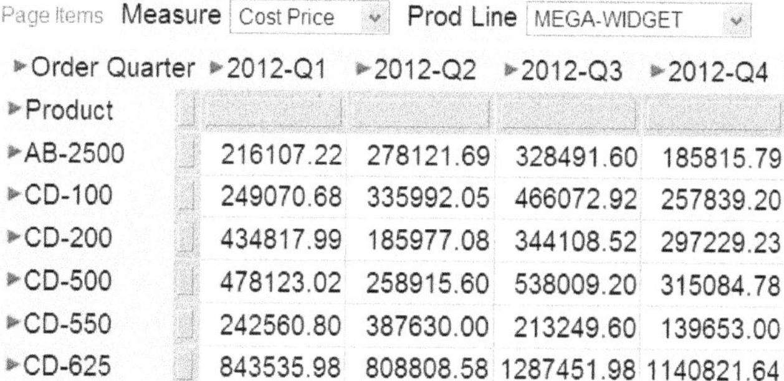

Page Items Measure Cost Price Prod Line MEGA-WIDGET

| Order Quarter | 2012-Q1 | 2012-Q2 | 2012-Q3 | 2012-Q4 |
|---|---|---|---|---|
| Product | | | | |
| AB-2500 | 216107.22 | 278121.69 | 328491.60 | 185815.79 |
| CD-100 | 249070.68 | 335992.05 | 466072.92 | 257839.20 |
| CD-200 | 434817.99 | 185977.08 | 344108.52 | 297229.23 |
| CD-500 | 478123.02 | 258915.60 | 538009.20 | 315084.78 |
| CD-550 | 242560.80 | 387630.00 | 213249.60 | 139653.00 |
| CD-625 | 843535.98 | 808808.58 | 1287451.98 | 1140821.64 |

To complete the pivoting, we moved the line name from the page items and placed it on the side axis immediately before the product name. Finally, we minimized the Tools menu so that the final result was what you saw previously, in Figure 9-3.

### Manipulating in Desktop and Plus

Unlike in Viewer, in both Desktop and Plus you can move the items around without the need for something to be in the data points axis. Of course, as you will see, until you put something into the data points, you will not see results.

The first thing we did was to move the data point items from the top axis to the page axis. It doesn't matter which data point you pick because, if you select and move one, Discoverer actually moves them all. For the record, we clicked the cost price and dragged it to the page axis. When we released the mouse button, Discoverer moved all three items and built a drop-down box, as you can see next.

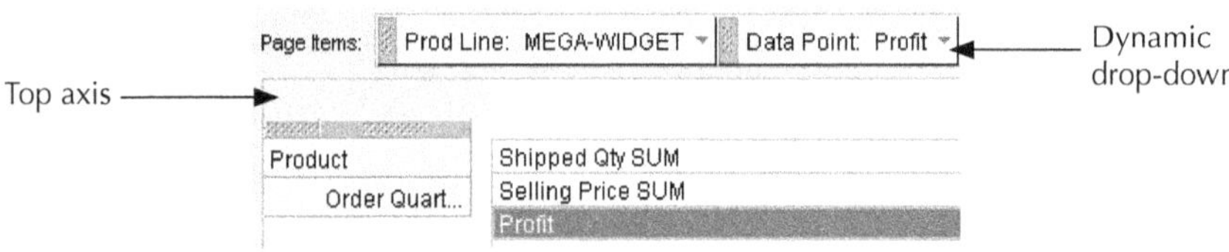


To make some costs display, we have to move something to the top axis. So, we dragged the quarter there, which immediately caused Discoverer to display the price for each quarter, as shown here:

Page Items: Prod Line: MEGA-WIDGET | Data Point: Selling Price

| Product | Order Quarter | 2012-Q1 | 2012-Q2 | 2012-Q3 | 2012-Q4 |
|---|---|---|---|---|---|
| AB-2500 | | 459,994.50 | 591,995.25 | 699,210.00 | 395,517.75 |
| CD-100 | | 611,647.00 | 825,101.25 | 1,144,543.00 | 633,180.00 |
| CD-200 | | 1,067,789.75 | 456,707.00 | 845,033.00 | 729,910.75 |
| CD-500 | | 998,565.78 | 540,748.40 | 1,123,638.80 | 658,058.42 |
| CD-550 | | 506,591.20 | 809,570.00 | 445,374.40 | 291,667.00 |
| CD-625 | | 1,761,735.22 | 1,689,206.62 | 2,688,859.22 | 2,382,619.96 |

**NOTE**

*There are no costs displayed in the main body of the uppermost report previously shown because there is no item in the top axis. This is one of the most common reasons why users complain that they can see no output from a query of this type. In any query, you must have at least one item in the top axis.*

You can see from the preceding illustrations that the output has changed, yet we can assure you that Discoverer did not requery the database. This is one of the wonderful features of Discoverer that will be covered in more depth when we discuss advanced queries in Chapter 11.

Having moved the quarter to the top axis, the next thing we did was to click the product line and move it to the side axis. The next illustration shows this step completed, with the product line having been placed before the product name. You can see that Discoverer automatically does a group sort in this situation.

Page Items: Data Point: Selling Price

| Prod Line | Product | Order Quarter: 2012-Q1 | 2012-Q2 | 2012-Q3 | 2012-Q4 |
|---|---|---|---|---|---|
| MINI-WIDGET | | 1,091,407.55 | 418,738.55 | 1,181,019.10 | 899,344.70 |
| | DS-1200 | 145,477.20 | 209,511.35 | 154,047.90 | 239,257.35 |
| | DS-1300 | 238,452.20 | 58,191.00 | 194,731.60 | 326,613.35 |
| | MS-1200 | 459,390.15 | 43,756.20 | 590,919.60 | 258,408.00 |
| | MS-1300 | 248,088.00 | 107,280.00 | 241,320.00 | 75,066.00 |
| SUPER-WIDGET | | 5,375,257.65 | 4,113,376.45 | 8,743,236.40 | 6,985,784.35 |
| | AB-3000 | 1,457,155.00 | 686,098.75 | 1,210,272.50 | 1,585,462.50 |
| | AVR-500 | 1,871,057.65 | 1,544,504.50 | 2,738,766.80 | 2,341,065.65 |
| | AVR-550 | 948,640.00 | 663,509.00 | 2,639,590.80 | 1,633,062.20 |
| | AVR-800 | 365,904.00 | 379,001.70 | 767,185.65 | 275,121.00 |
| | AVR-900 | 732,501.00 | 840,262.50 | 1,387,420.65 | 1,151,073.00 |
| MEGA-WIDGET | | 5,406,323.45 | 4,913,328.52 | 6,946,658.42 | 5,090,953.88 |
| | AB-2500 | 459,994.50 | 591,995.25 | 699,210.00 | 395,517.75 |
| | CD-100 | 611,647.00 | 825,101.25 | 1,144,543.00 | 633,180.00 |
| | CD-200 | 1,067,789.75 | 456,707.00 | 845,033.00 | 729,910.75 |
| | CD-500 | 998,565.78 | 540,748.40 | 1,123,638.80 | 658,058.42 |
| | CD-550 | 506,591.20 | 809,570.00 | 445,374.40 | 291,667.00 |
| | CD-625 | 1,761,735.22 | 1,689,206.62 | 2,688,859.22 | 2,382,619.96 |
| WONDER-WIDGET | | 6,055,897.31 | 3,022,641.04 | 5,735,044.74 | 5,543,019.35 |
| | AB-2008 | 691,740.00 | 411,601.50 | 809,743.50 | 1,041,390.00 |
| | QB-1000 | 438,702.60 | 590,963.45 | 715,459.50 | 468,554.45 |
| | QB-2008 | 1,173,438.00 | 371,471.45 | 831,255.60 | 644,875.00 |
| | QB-3000 | 1,030,416.45 | 217,897.40 | 868,588.00 | 611,341.50 |
| | QB-5000 | 870,849.92 | 413,597.20 | 844,183.32 | 789,402.00 |
| | QB-5500 | 817,658.00 | 532,731.56 | 526,215.02 | 1,195,228.80 |
| | QB-6000 | 1,033,092.34 | 484,378.48 | 1,139,599.80 | 792,227.60 |

Automatic group sort

Finally, as you can see here, we clicked the drop-down arrow alongside the Data Point:

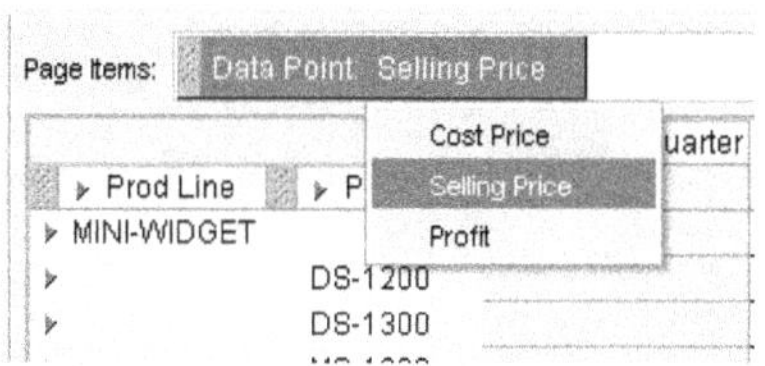


From the drop-down list provided, we selected the profit, which resulted in the output you saw previously in Figure 9-3.

**NOTE**

*By the way, if you are wondering how we got the side axis items to line up as they do, you can do this in Plus by right-clicking anywhere in the crosstab and from the pop-up menu selecting Format Crosstab. In the Format Crosstab dialog box we made sure the Crosstab style was set to Inline. In Desktop, you do this using Tools | Options off the menu bar. Select the Crosstab tab and then make sure that Axis Labels and Axis Gridlines are checked, with Gridline Style set to 3D and Style set to Inline.*

## Deviation Analysis

This query is a little more complex than the other examples, but you should be able to easily follow how we did it. We used a crosstab, of course, because we couldn't have performed the manipulations that we wanted had we chosen a table.

The selections were very easy. We took the order quantity and the status from the sales folder, the product name from the product folder, and the channel. Before we left the Workbook Wizard, we moved the channel and product name to the side axis and then defined the following condition on the product name: Product Name like 'QB%'. This condition will constrain our selection to just those products that begin with *QB*. After running the query, the result is as shown next. Notice how Discoverer has automatically built a group sort on the channel.

| | | Order Qty SUM | | | |
|---|---|---|---|---|---|
| | Status | CANCELLED | HOLD | OPEN | SHIPPED |
| Channel | Product | | | | |
| EXTERNAL | | 15161 | 2500 | 30162 | 168850 |
| | QB-1000 | 10000 | 1200 | 3801 | 20206 |
| | QB-2008 | 960 | 100 | 19040 | 14424 |
| | QB-3000 | 1000 | 1200 | 160 | 28600 |
| | QB-5000 | 1200 | | 3560 | 28788 |
| | QB-5500 | | | 2400 | 46248 |
| | QB-6000 | 2001 | | 1201 | 30584 |
| INTERNET | | 79371 | | 79026 | 528518 |
| | QB-1000 | 100 | | 3812 | 69114 |
| | QB-2008 | | | 600 | 47067 |
| | QB-3000 | 11160 | | 12020 | 75200 |
| | QB-5000 | 8960 | | 6368 | 88300 |
| | QB-5500 | 18970 | | 31210 | 102278 |
| | QB-6000 | 40181 | | 25016 | 146559 |

The next part is straightforward, just requiring us to create percentages. We clicked the label for the top axis item called Order Qty SUM, and then we clicked the Percentage button. This simple task opened the following New Percentage dialog box:

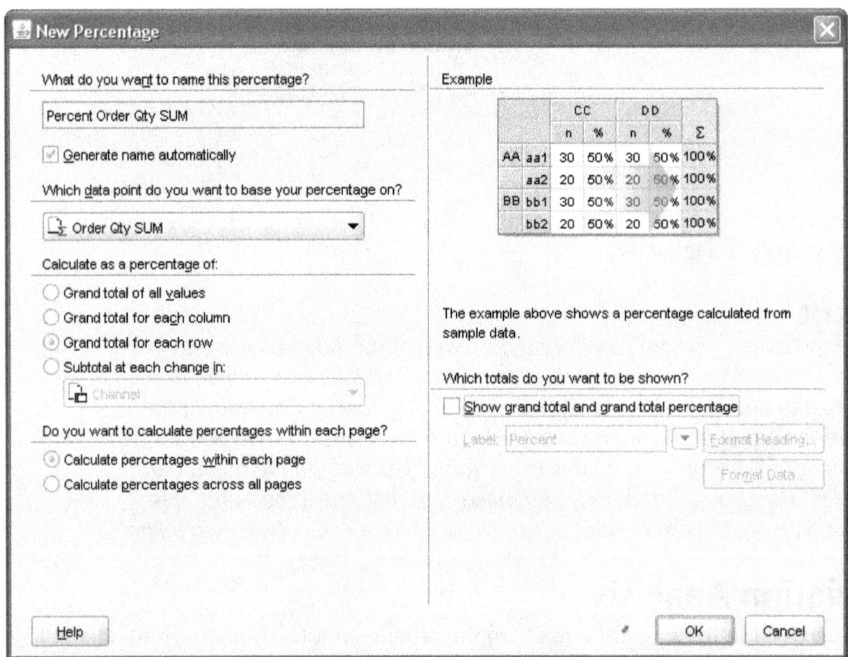

To set up the percentage as we want it, we changed the percentage to Grand total for each row and unchecked Show grand total and grand total percentage. After clicking OK to close the dialog box, we clicked in any of the percentage cells and increased the decimals to three places. Next, we opened the page items and added the Order year to the page items, displaying the data for 2013, our last complete year. To complete the setting up of the query, we clicked the Order Qty SUM heading and removed it from the worksheet, leaving just the percentage, as you can see here:

Page Items: Order Year: FY2013

| | | Percent Order Qty SUM | | | |
|---|---|---|---|---|---|
| | Status | CANCELLED | HOLD | OPEN | SHIPPED |
| Channel | Product | | | | |
| EXTERNAL | | 6.997% | 1.154% | 13.921% | 77.928% |
| | QB-1000 | 28.403% | 3.408% | 10.796% | 57.392% |
| | QB-2008 | 2.781% | 0.290% | 55.150% | 41.780% |
| | QB-3000 | 3.230% | 3.876% | 0.517% | 92.377% |
| | QB-5000 | 3.577% | | 10.612% | 85.811% |
| | QB-5500 | | | 4.933% | 95.067% |
| | QB-6000 | 5.923% | | 3.555% | 90.523% |
| INTERNET | | 11.555% | | 11.504% | 76.941% |
| | QB-1000 | 0.137% | | 5.220% | 94.643% |
| | QB-2008 | | | 1.259% | 98.741% |
| | QB-3000 | 11.344% | | 12.218% | 76.438% |
| | QB-5000 | 8.646% | | 6.145% | 85.209% |
| | QB-5500 | 12.443% | | 20.471% | 67.086% |
| | QB-6000 | 18.975% | | 11.814% | 69.211% |

We're almost done, apart from adding five conditional formats based on the percentage so that we can easily view the deviation. To do this, we right-clicked anywhere inside our worksheet and from the pop-up menu selected Conditional Formats. In the Conditional Formats dialog box that was displayed, we clicked the New Conditional Format button, one by one adding the following five conditional formats:

- Percentage less than 10 percent colored in a light gray background
- Percentage between 10 percent and 20 percent colored in a light blue background
- Percentage between 60 percent and 79.9 percent colored in a red background
- Percentage between 80 percent and 90 percent colored in an amber background

- Percentage greater than 90 percent colored in a green background

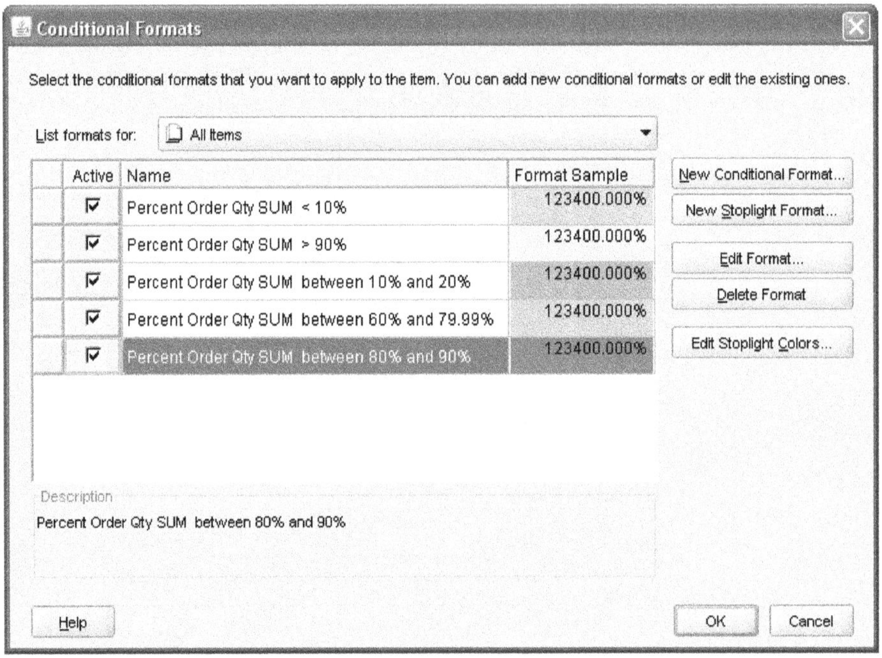

The final result with the NULL values displayed as blanks was illustrated in Figure 9-4.

## Trend Analysis

Yet another crosstab. Now there's a trend for you!

If you recall, this query displays the percentage of sales for each region for all the years that the company has been in operation. We started by selecting the ship quantity, the year, and the region. As in the example for statistical analysis, we need to use the region without displaying the customer or the city.

Having selected our data, we placed the region in the side axis and the year in the top axis, moving the year below the ship quantity. The following illustration shows the query after we executed it with the items in their correct positions:

| | | Shipped Qty SUM | | | | | | | |
|---|---|---|---|---|---|---|---|---|---|
| | Order Year | FY2006 | FY2007 | FY2008 | FY2009 | FY2010 | FY2011 | FY2012 | FY2013 |
| Region | | | | | | | | | |
| EUROPE | | 68,608 | 38,404 | 158,638 | 136,083 | 140,201 | 226,970 | 257,680 | 219,511 |
| FAR EAST | | 31,560 | 18,085 | 49,613 | 43,474 | 30,209 | 66,959 | 69,060 | 93,017 |
| NORTH AMERICA | | 81,760 | 62,602 | 261,788 | 168,999 | 221,393 | 346,334 | 406,699 | 330,572 |
| SOUTH AMERICA | | 1,650 | 7,802 | 45,028 | 29,358 | 15,506 | 42,138 | 67,014 | 54,218 |

To complete the query, we clicked the top axis label called Ship Qty SUM and then clicked the Percentage button on the analysis bar. We completed the New Percentage dialog box as follows:

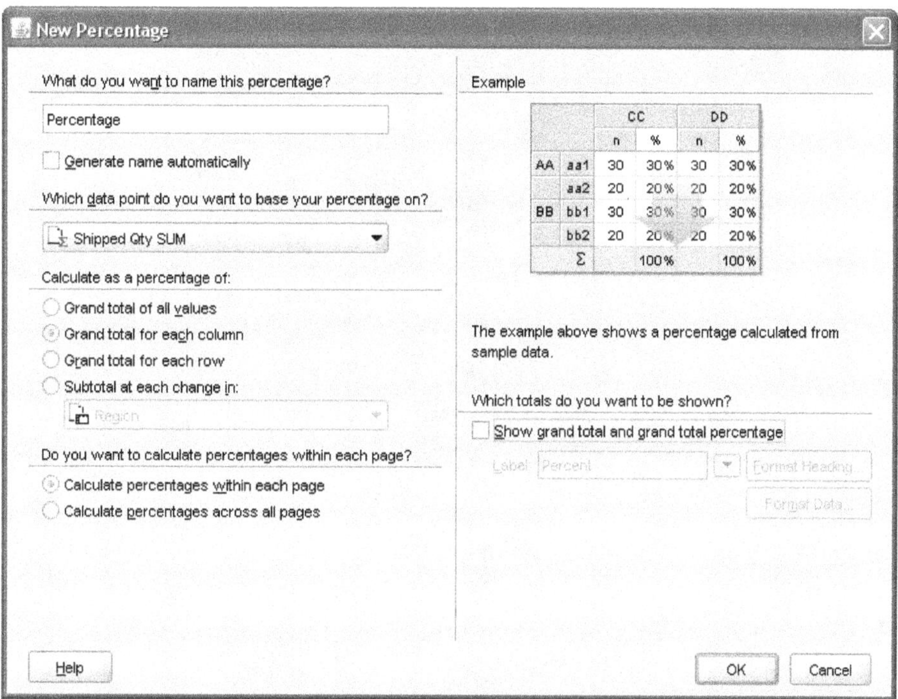


As you can see, this time we named the percentage to be Percent, setting it to calculate on Grand total for each column. We also unchecked Show grand total and grand total percentage. Next, just as we did with the deviation worksheet, we deleted the Ship Qty SUM column, leaving just the percentage itself. The final result was shown in Figure 9-5, with the corresponding line graph shown in Figure 9-6.

## Aging Analysis

Guess what kind of worksheet we are going to build? Yes, once again, if you said crosstab, you are correct. This query displays the number of sales orders that shipped on time by region.

We started by selecting the count of the order number, the shipped date, the order date, and the region. To make sure we really only count sales orders that have shipped, we created a condition on the status, limiting it to shipped only. Having chosen our base items, we created a new calculation called Diff that simply subtracts Order Date from Ship Date. We cannot include any NULL dates in our query, because these will give a completely invalid answer. Therefore, we have to place a condition on Diff such that this is not NULL. Because we want to see only the number of days that an item took to ship, we no longer need these two dates, so they need to be removed from the query. However, this cannot be done until after we have created the initial query; otherwise, we will end up summing the total number of days, which is not what we want to see.

To set up our initial worksheet, we place the region and both dates on the side axis. The initial results looked like this:

| Region | Order Date | Shipped Date | Diff |
|---|---|---|---|
| EUROPE | 01-OCT-2011 | 02-OCT-2011 | 1.00 |
| | | 03-OCT-2011 | 2.00 |
| | 04-OCT-2011 | 05-OCT-2011 | 1.00 |
| | | 06-OCT-2011 | 2.00 |
| | | 09-OCT-2011 | 5.00 |
| | | 11-OCT-2011 | 7.00 |
| | | 16-OCT-2011 | 12.00 |
| | 07-OCT-2011 | 08-OCT-2011 | 1.00 |
| | 08-OCT-2011 | 11-OCT-2011 | 3.00 |
| | | 13-OCT-2011 | 5.00 |
| | | 14-OCT-2011 | 6.00 |
| | | 15-OCT-2011 | 7.00 |
| | 10-OCT-2011 | 10-OCT-2011 | 0.00 |
| | | 17-OCT-2011 | 7.00 |
| | 11-OCT-2011 | 16-OCT-2011 | 5.00 |
| | | 18-OCT-2011 | 7.00 |
| | 16-OCT-2011 | 26-OCT-2011 | 10.00 |
| | 17-OCT-2011 | 20-OCT-2011 | 3.00 |
| | 21-OCT-2011 | 25-OCT-2011 | 4.00 |

Next, we created another calculation called Order Count as the count of the order number. We also removed both of the dates from the worksheet and then placed Diff on the side axis in front of Region so that the intermediate result now looks like this:

| Diff | Region | Order Count |
|---|---|---|
| 0.00 | EUROPE | 65.00 |
| | FAR EAST | 24.00 |
| | NORTH AMERICA | 123.00 |
| | SOUTH AMERICA | 14.00 |
| 1.00 | EUROPE | 146.00 |
| | FAR EAST | 84.00 |
| | NORTH AMERICA | 284.00 |
| | SOUTH AMERICA | 53.00 |
| 2.00 | EUROPE | 53.00 |
| | FAR EAST | 26.00 |
| | NORTH AMERICA | 112.00 |
| | SOUTH AMERICA | 25.00 |
| 3.00 | EUROPE | 69.00 |
| | FAR EAST | 20.00 |
| | NORTH AMERICA | 116.00 |
| | SOUTH AMERICA | 17.00 |
| 4.00 | EUROPE | 29.00 |
| | FAR EAST | 10.00 |
| | NORTH AMERICA | 58.00 |
| | SOUTH AMERICA | 13.00 |

Next, we created a new calculation that works out the on-time category. We used the following `CASE` statement:

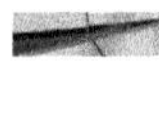

```
CASE WHEN Diff <= 3 THEN 'a. On Time'
WHEN Diff <= 7 THEN 'b. Within 1 week'
WHEN Diff <= 14 THEN 'c. Within 2 weeks'
ELSE'd. Over 2 weeks' END
```

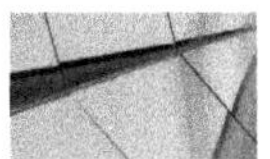

**NOTE**

*The leading characters, such as* `a.` *and* `b.` *in the preceding calculation, are needed to make sure that the categories display in the desired order.*

We then removed Diff from the worksheet and placed the new category on the top axis. To make the query more meaningful, we added Ship Year and placed it in the page items. We also started looking at year 2012, as you can see here:

Page Items: Shipped Year: FY2012

| | Order Count | | | |
|---|---|---|---|---|
| | a. On Time | b. Within 1 week | c. Within 2 weeks | d. Over 2 weeks |
| EUROPE | 334 | 88 | 75 | 17 |
| FAR EAST | 154 | 37 | 26 | 8 |
| NORTH AMERICA | 635 | 165 | 143 | 25 |
| SOUTH AMERICA | 109 | 40 | 29 | 7 |

To complete the query, we clicked the top axis label called Order Count and then clicked the Percentage button on the analysis bar. We completed the New Percentage dialog box as follows:

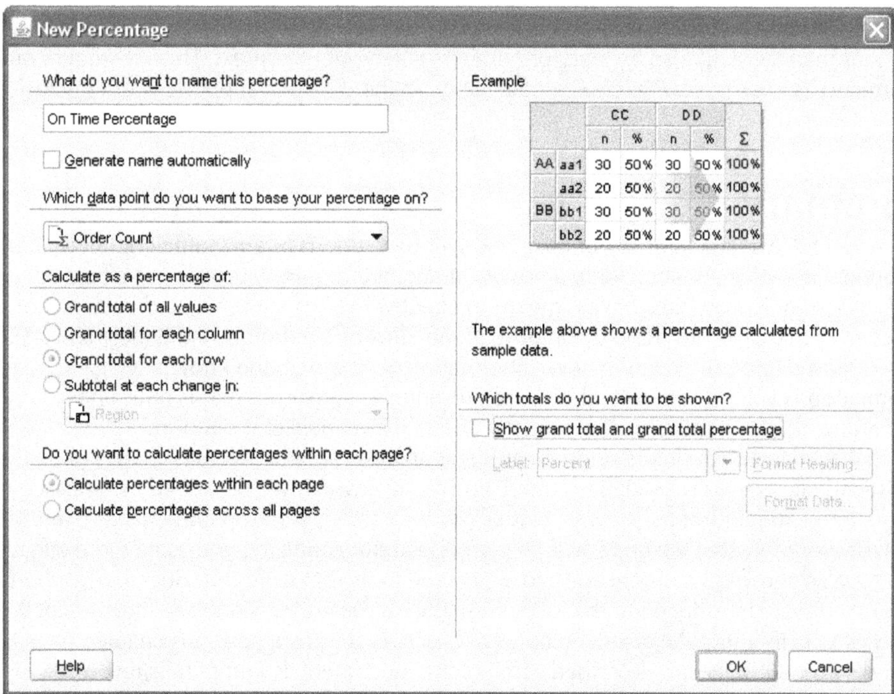

As you can see, this time we named the percentage to be On Time Percentage, setting it to calculate on Grand total for each row. We also unchecked Show grand total and grand total percentage. Next, just as we did with the deviation worksheet, we deleted the Order Count column, leaving just the percentage itself. The final result was shown in Figure 9-7.

# Overcoming the Manager Who Is Wary of Your Analysis

Do you have a manager who is suspicious of analysis? Whenever you present that person with a page full of your analysis results, does that manager start asking questions? This is good. A good manager should not take your analysis results at face value but will need to have some further background information on hand before presenting the findings to the board.

Therefore, before you show your great analysis report to your manager, make sure you can answer the following questions:

- Where did the data come from?
- Who ran the survey?
- Is there an ulterior motive for having the results go one way?
- How was the data collected?
- What questions were asked, who asked them, and who was asked?

Your manager will be wary of comparisons. Remember that two events happening at the same time are not necessarily related, so be careful not to produce statistics to show that they are unless you have additional information to back you up.

Your manager will also be wary of numbers taken out of context. This technique, often referred to as *cherry picking*, concentrates only on the data that supports your conclusion and ignores everything else.

# Summary

Once you have a large amount of data, you will have the basis and sufficient information to seek additional knowledge. Since large amounts of data are required, processing efficiency is essential—that is, you must have a means to effectively filter out unwanted data. A tool such as Discoverer that provides these techniques at the click of a button is highly desirable. Accuracy is then required to ensure that whatever information is obtained, the knowledge gleaned from that information is valid. The results should be presented in a manner that is both understandable and interesting; that is, it must have potential value to the readers of the report.

In this chapter, you learned the meaning of analysis and the five basic types of analysis—statistical, classification, deviation, trend, and aging—which we described using Discoverer. You learned how to perform these types of analysis, using both Desktop and Plus. We introduced an analysis workflow that we hope will help you go about analyzing your data more effectively.

We also showed you more ways to access the tools that were introduced to you in Chapters 4 and 5. You were introduced to the tools available on the toolbars and saw how to cut your analysis time by using the terrific features of Discoverer. Throughout this chapter, we talked about analysis and statistics and described some of the fundamentals and pitfalls involved.

# CHAPTER 10

# Using Discoverer Viewer to See Your Data

In this chapter you will learn about Discoverer Viewer 11*g*, another part of Oracle Business Intelligence. We highly encourage the use of Viewer and think it is a really terrific tool.

Viewer is a thin-client HTML-based version of Discoverer Plus. It is packaged with the Fusion Middleware Application Server and installed along with Plus, so if you are using Desktop only, you will not have access to Viewer. It allows you to view reports that were created in both Desktop and Plus, but there are limitations to Viewer's ability to see everything created in Desktop. In other words, it is fully integrated with Plus features but not Desktop features. This release has many cool features that make it much more than just a viewer. We think it should be called "Viewer on steroids."

# Why Use Viewer?

You might be wondering why you should even consider using Viewer. You can't create new workbooks with it, but you can apply parameters, and you can slice and dice data. You can use the advanced drilling features of Plus, including drilling in graphs. Lots of formatting options are available, including what we think are really important features, namely, conditional formatting and stoplighting. We don't recommend using it for report formatting. Leave the big jobs to Plus and Desktop. They are your workhorses. If you are not a library manager or a report writer, Viewer might be the best tool for you. It requires only a browser and not an additional JRE, so that is a great feature as well.

If you have not yet considered using Viewer, read on. We went to one client to do some training to explain all the available features of Discoverer. When we began to prepare the course, most of the decision makers told us not to bother demonstrating Viewer. We suggested that we add a half-hour segment to introduce Viewer, and they agreed. By the time we finished the class, those same decision makers exclaimed that 75 percent of their Discoverer users would be using Viewer exclusively. It really is that good, and since it is licensed with Plus, we think you should give it a closer look.

## The Benefits of Viewer

The following are some of Viewer's top selling points:

- **A user-friendly browser interface with all the features you expect from a web-based application** You can use your Back and Forward buttons and bookmark your favorite reports. We like the look and feel of Viewer and think most end users will find it a comfortable and friendly environment for report viewing.
- **Consistency with Discoverer Desktop and Plus** The EUL and business areas that have already been built are immediately accessible in Viewer, and all reports created in Desktop or Plus can be analyzed in Viewer.
- **Full customization** You can make your Viewer look like a page from your company intranet by adding a company logo and company colors.
- **Database security** Viewer uses the same security that is set up by the Discoverer manager for use in Desktop and Plus.

- **National language support** Viewer supports many different languages, which you choose from the Connect or Options page.
- **The ability to publish to Oracle Portal** Discoverer workbooks can be published quickly and easily to Portal.
- **Better integration with the Discoverer Portlet Provider** This allows for a single-worksheet Viewer mode when analyzing Discoverer worksheets from Portal.
- **The ability to perform at the individual cell level** This includes selections, formatting, and conditional formatting all within an individual cell, thanks to Discoverer's leveraging of the thin-client BI Beans in Viewer, and all within the confines of standard DHTML, CSS, and JavaScript—standard browser technologies.
- **The graph toolbar** It allows changes to the graph type and subtype, size, 3-D effects, and gradient colors.
- **The ability to drill from graphs** Drilling is an important feature of Discoverer, and you are able to leverage this feature directly within your graphs. When viewing a graph, you will see a small "drill" label. The label describes where the drill path will take you; for example, if the graph gives a representation of sales by quarter, the drill path will be to the next level up in the hierarchy, in most cases month.
- **An improved worksheet navigator** It allows you to select the worksheet to run. Also, the ability to "zoom in" to a workbook means improved usability and improved performance, especially if you have a large number of workbooks in your catalog.

## Extra Viewer Features

The features of Viewer are many, and some of them are so good that we continue to endorse it as part of an enterprise-wide business intelligence plan. The extra features of Viewer are

- Single sign-on support
- E-mail support
- Save to database capability
- Customization of Viewer's look and feel
- Drilling into related data, even in graphs
- Slicing and dicing for improved analysis
- Improved printing by converting worksheets to PDF format
- Export to Excel, Excel Web Query, and PDF
- Worksheet formatting, including conditional formatting and stoplight formatting
- Handling of parameters and selecting from list of values
- Graph handling

## The Connect Page

It is necessary for you to gain specific instructions from your Discoverer administrator on how you will access and log in to Viewer. Your organization can choose whether to enable Viewer. There is additional information on access procedures in Chapter 3, in the section called "Gaining Access to Discoverer." This is the Viewer Connect page:

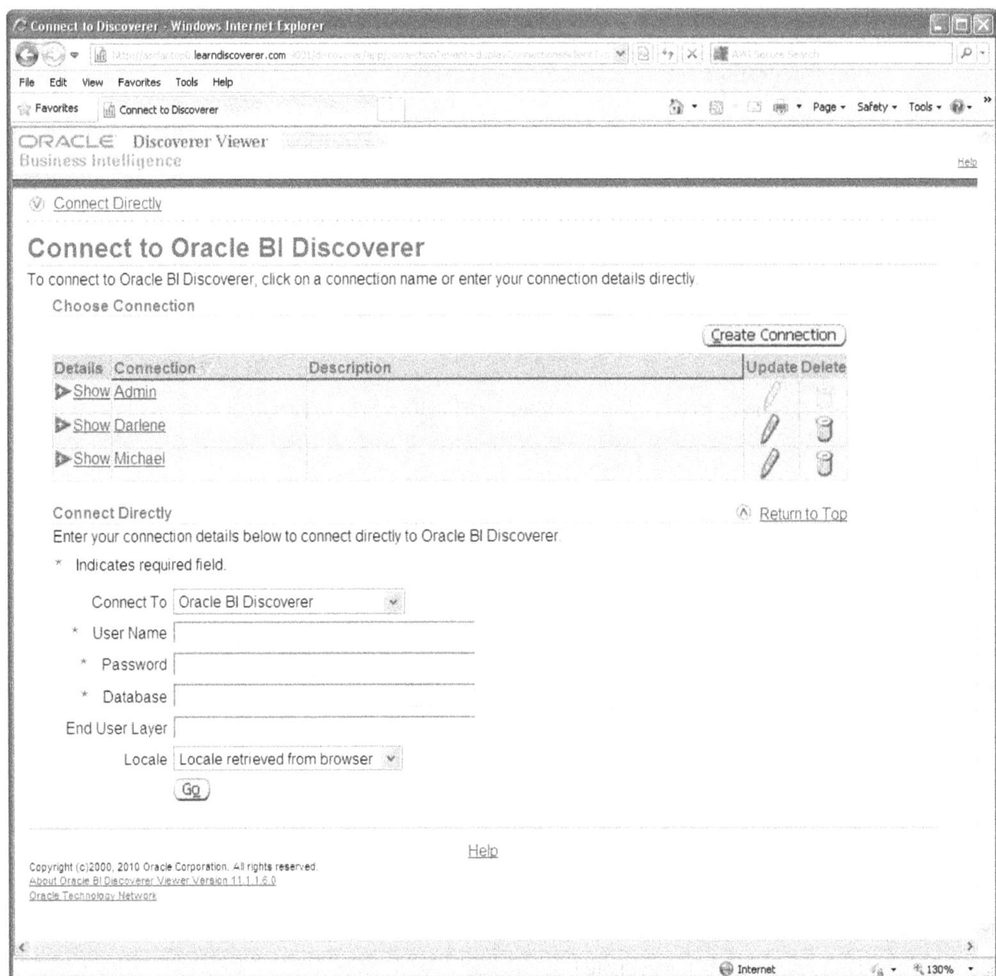


## The Worksheet List

After logging in, the first Viewer page is the Worksheet List. In Viewer you select a single worksheet from a workbook. If you want to work with multiple worksheets within a workbook, Viewer makes it easy with links. Remember, this is HTML, and navigating from workbooks and worksheets is as easy as navigating any web site.

Figure 10-1 shows the Worksheet List in Viewer. As you can see, the layout is clean and simple to understand. The only limitations are how well workbooks and worksheets have been named, if no library system is in place, and if meaningful descriptions have not been added to the workbooks.

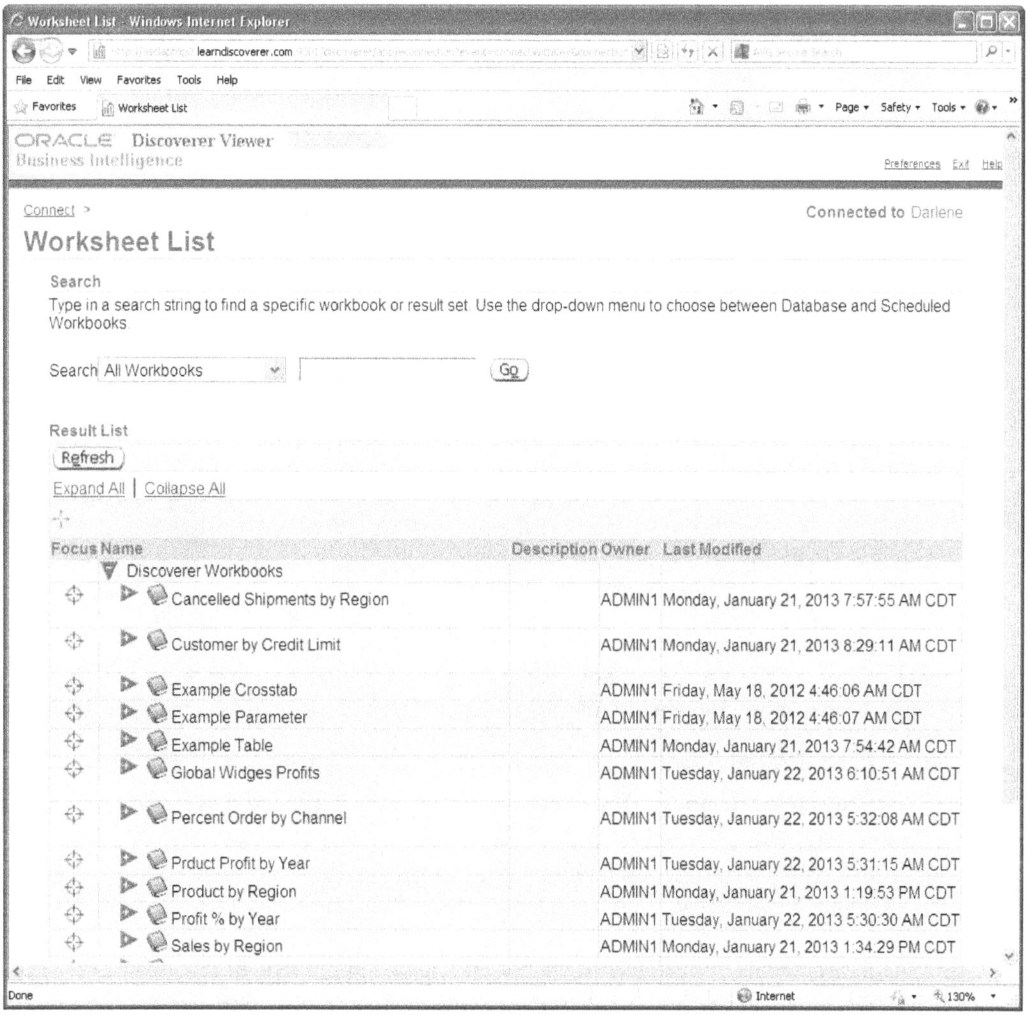

**FIGURE 10-1.** *The Worksheet List*

**NOTE**

*Discoverer always names workbooks and worksheets by default using names such as Workbook1 and Sheet1. Leaving these defaults in place causes problems understanding what the report does, which is why we say you will have problems if these have not been named well. Discoverer also does not add descriptions by default. Descriptions can be very useful.*

Starting at the top left of the screen, you can see how a corporate identity can be added to Viewer in the form of a company logo. The default is the Oracle logo, but this is easily changed by your Discoverer manager.

To the right of the logo are three helpful links:

- **Preferences** Set up your own performance preferences. This can be compared to the Tools | Options menu in Desktop and Plus. We will show you these choices later in the chapter, in the section "Setting Up User Preferences in Viewer."
- **Exit** Use this link to log out. It is important to get into the habit of logging out this way because it is how you close your Discoverer connection. Clicking the *X* in the upper-right corner of the browser only closes the browser, and you are left with an open connection to the database, as well as an active session on your middle tier, which will continue to use memory until the session is terminated after a period of inactivity.
- **Help** This takes you to the Oracle BI Discoverer help system. It is context-sensitive and will take you to help depending on where you are when you click the link.

Below the top banner you see where you are. The path on the Worksheet List page is back to Connect. Click this link, and you are back at the connection page. Below the path is the name of the page: Worksheet List. On the far right you can see the name of the EUL that you are connected to. If you want to change the EUL, click the Connect link, and you will be taken back to the connection page to make the change.

## Searching for a Worksheet

The next area of the Worksheet List page is the Search area. You can search for a specific workbook or worksheet. You can choose from a search of

- **Database Workbooks** The query will run and display the most current data.
- **Scheduled Workbooks** The query has already run at a scheduled time, and the results are stored in the database.
- **All Workbooks** The search will include all workbooks from the database and from the scheduled workbooks.

**Using the Search Feature of the Worksheet List Page** Simply type in all or part of the name of the workbook you want to display. Wildcards are not necessary. In the next illustration, we have used the search string *profit*. As you can see, there is a mix of workbooks containing the words *Profit* and *Profits*.

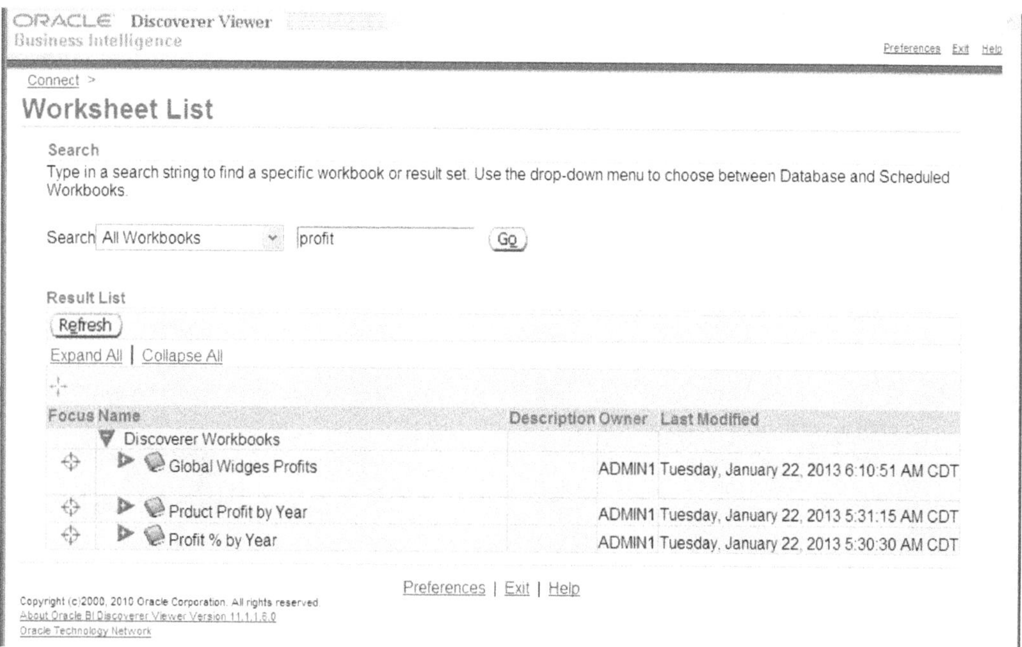


If you don't perform any type of search, the Result List area will contain all workbooks you have been granted permission to view. You could have dozens of workbooks available to you, so getting in the habit of using some simple searches to limit the list is a good idea.

## Result List

The area called Result List is the list of available workbooks corresponding to your search. It has the following features, as shown in Figure 10-2:

- **Refresh** Clicking the Refresh button will make sure that the list is up to date. This is important if new workbooks are being created and added to the library. If, for instance, you click the Back link from another worksheet and forget to click Refresh, this will keep you from seeing whether a new workbook has been added to the database or whether a scheduled workbook has run.
- **Expand All/Collapse All** Clicking Expand All will expand the list of worksheets within the list of workbooks from the current search. Clicking Collapse All will close the list of worksheets and show only the workbook names.
- **Focus** Clicking the focus icon next to a workbook name will limit the list to that workbook and the worksheets it contains.
- **Name** In the Name column you will see a small triangle. When the list is collapsed, the triangle displays a plus sign. Click the triangle, and the list will expand to display the worksheet in the workbook and the icon will change to a minus sign.

Result List

Refresh

Expand All | Collapse All

| Focus | Name | Description | Owner | Last Modified |
|---|---|---|---|---|
| | Discoverer Workbooks | | | |
| | Cancelled Shipments by Region | | ADMIN1 | Monday, January 21, 2013 7:57:55 AM CDT |
| | A Simple Total | | | |
| | Multiple Totals | | | |
| | Customer by Credit Limit | | ADMIN1 | Monday, January 21, 2013 8:29:11 AM CDT |
| | Sheet 1 | | | |
| | Example Crosstab | | ADMIN1 | Friday, May 18, 2012 4:46:06 AM CDT |
| | Profit and Margin by Status | | | |
| | Example Parameter | | ADMIN1 | Friday, May 18, 2012 4:46:07 AM CDT |
| | Prod Line Details | | | |
| | Example Table | | ADMIN1 | Monday, January 21, 2013 7:54:42 AM CDT |
| | A Simple Total | | | |
| | Multiple Totals | | | |
| | Global Widges Profits | | ADMIN1 | Tuesday, January 22, 2013 6:10:51 AM CDT |

Internet 130%

**FIGURE 10-2.** *The Result List*

- **Description** If your report writers are in the habit of giving meaningful descriptions to their workbooks, you will see them in this column. Descriptions are a great way of reducing the time you spend opening the wrong worksheets. If your organization has not implemented a policy of adding meaningful descriptions, you might suggest they begin doing so.

**NOTE**

*Only workbook descriptions are available in Viewer. Worksheet descriptions that you may have added in Plus are not visible in Viewer.*

- **Owner** The owner is the person who created the workbook and saved it to the database. If your organization is using a library, the owner is the library manager.
- **Last Modified** This column shows the last date and time that the workbook was modified.

## Opening a Worksheet from the Results List

To open a worksheet in Viewer, use the following workflow:

1. Expand the workbook from which you want to select a worksheet.
2. Click the name of the worksheet you want to open.
3. The query will run and open in the browser.

## The Main Viewer Page

After selecting the worksheet to open, you will see the main Viewer page. Figure 10-3 shows a sample workbook opened in Viewer.

**NOTE**

*The banner at the top of the screen has not changed. This is the banner you will see on all Viewer pages. Also, each page will display the connection you are using.*

Beneath the banner you can see that the path has grown. As you can see in the next illustration, we now have links back to Connect and Workbooks.

Below the links are the workbook name and the current worksheet. The area directly below the names shows the last time this worksheet was run.

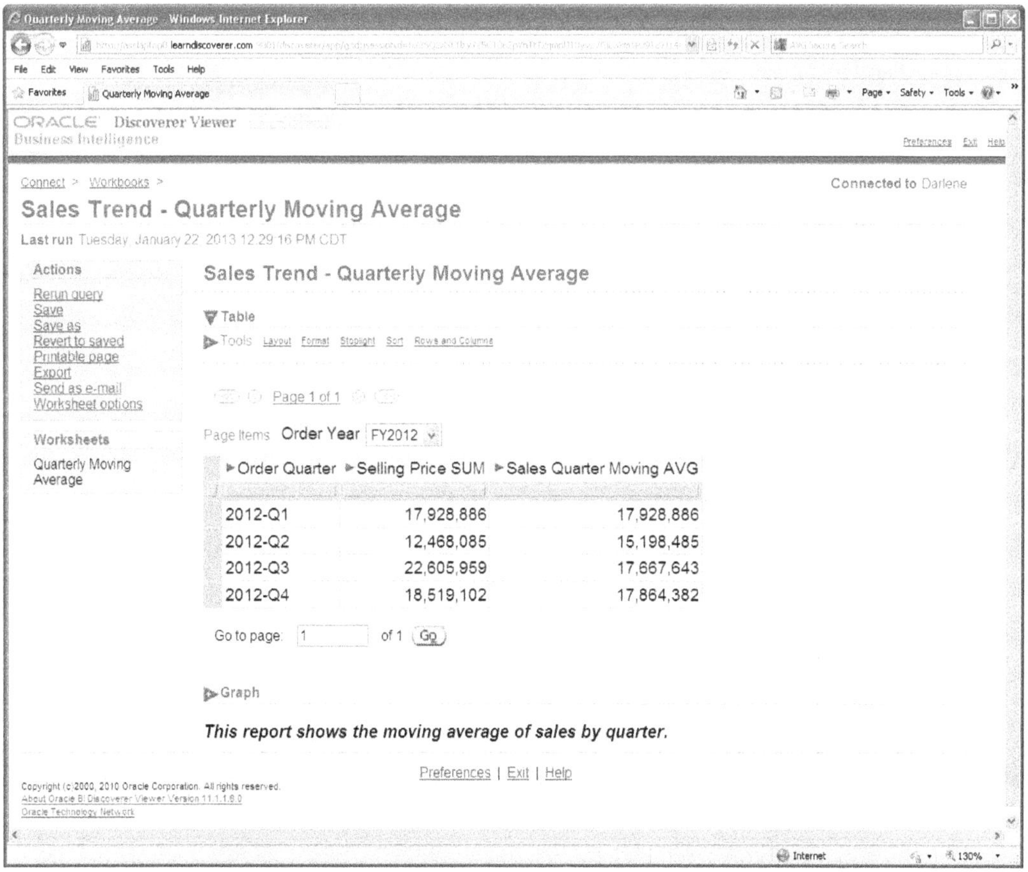

**FIGURE 10-3.** *A sample workbook in Viewer*

## Actions

The Actions area shown in this illustration gives you useful links to perform a variety of functions, as described here:

Actions
Rerun query
Save
Save as
Revert to saved
Printable page
Export
Send as e-mail
Worksheet options

- **Rerun query** Use this link to rerun the query. This is useful when you are reporting against live data and need to check for updates.
- **Save** If you own the workbook that you currently have open and you make a change to it you have the option to save those changes.
- **Save as** Yes, you heard right. You can now make changes to a worksheet in Viewer and save them to the database. This is a right that your Discoverer administrator can give or deny, so if the link is not there, it means you don't have that privilege.
- **Revert to saved** If you make changes to the worksheet but want to see it in its original layout and formatting, click this link.
- **Printable page** This link takes you to a setup page to prepare the worksheet to print to PDF format.
- **Export** This link takes you to a page to select from a variety of export options, such as Excel, PDF, comma or tab delimited, and HTML.
- **Send as e-mail** This link takes you to a page where you choose the file type (these are the same as the Export options) to e-mail and then go on to an e-mail form. E-mailing must be set up by your Discoverer administrator, so if it does not work, you will need to check with her to see whether it can be made available to you.
- **Worksheet options** This takes you to a page where you can set up how to view the worksheet.

**Printable Page** To set up the worksheet for printing, use the following workflow:

1. Click the Printable page link. This opens the Printable page screen Content tab shown in Figure 10-4.
2. Under General Options, select how you want to print the page items.
   - Print the current selection of page items
   - Print all combinations of page items
3. Under General Options, select how you want to show the page items.
   - On the first page
   - Never
4. Under General Options, select how you want to show the title. This option is only displayed if the worksheet was created with the title enabled.
   - On the first page
   - Never
5. Under General Options, select how you want to show the text area. This option is only displayed if the worksheet was created with the text area enabled.
   - Always, when available
   - Never

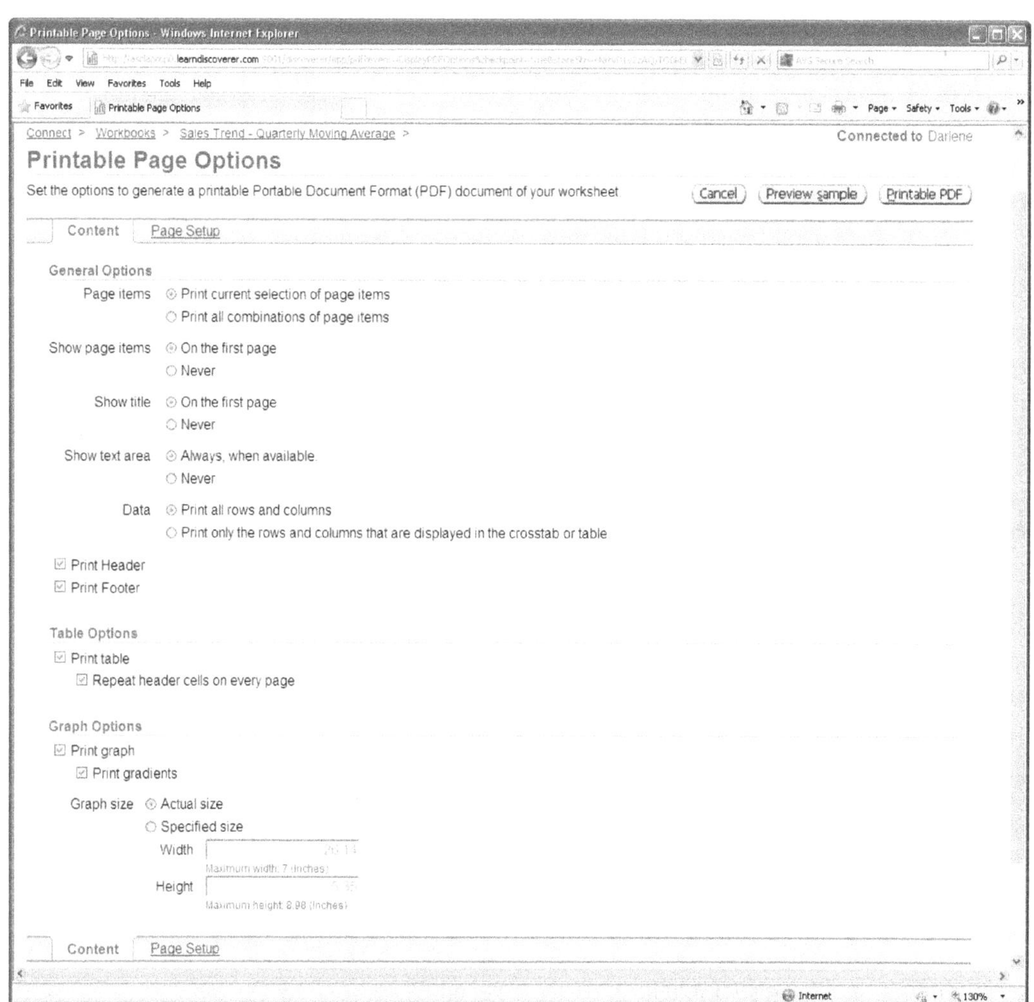


**FIGURE 10-4.** *The Printable Page options Content tab*

6. Under General Options, select how to print the data.
   - Print all rows and columns
   - Print only the rows and columns that are displayed in the crosstab or table
7. Under General Options, choose to print headers and footers by leaving the boxes checked, or uncheck them to suppress them from printing.
8. Under Table or Crosstab Options, use the check box to print the table or crosstab. Deselect the box if you do not want the table or crosstab to print. This option is useful if you want to print only the graph. The heading for this show Table or Crosstab to reflect the type of worksheet you are managing.

9. Under Table or Crosstab Options, use the check box Repeat header cells on every page. If you are printing a table or crosstab, you will want to keep this one checked. We can't think of an instance when you would not want to see header cells on each page.
10. Under Graph Options, use the check box to print the graph. Deselect the box if you do not want the graph to print.
11. Under Graph Options, use the check box Print Gradients if you want the gradient colors shown onscreen to print.
12. Under Graph Options, use the radio buttons to determine the size of the graph in the printout. You can select Actual Size, or you can determine the exact size of the graph.
13. Click the Page Setup tab.
14. Under Paper Setup, choose the paper size and orientation.
15. Under Margins, define the Top, Bottom, Left and Right margins.
16. Under Scaling, use the drop-down to select the scale to use for the printed worksheet. You can choose anywhere between 10% and 200% but you cannot type in your own choice. This is useful when you have a large worksheet that is wider than one page and you want to try to get it all on one page.
17. Under Column Sizes you set the width of the printed columns and determine whether you want to always wrap text when the size exceeds the column width. These are useful features because you cannot resize columns in Viewer but might want to change the widths for printing. Don't get too excited about this feature, though, because you will have to reset these options every time you open the worksheet for printing. Discoverer Viewer does not retain the settings.
18. Leave the Wrap text box checked or the data will be clipped off.
19. Click Printable PDF to print the PDF, or click Preview Sample to view a sample PDF.

**NOTE**
*The difference between Printable PDF and Preview Sample is that the Preview Sample generates a PDF of the worksheet based on the first 50 (or maybe 100) rows of data and the graph. The thinking is that 50 rows should be sufficient for the user to get an idea as to how the printed worksheet will appear, while the preview generation process will not be too resource-intensive. PDF generation is a CPU- and memory-intensive operation on the middle tier.*

20. When the PDF has been created, you will get a link to open the PDF. Click the link and determine whether the PDF is as you like it and ready to print or if it needs more work.

**Export** You can export your Discoverer Viewer worksheets to any of the following file types:

- CSV (comma delimited)
- DIF (data interchange format)
- Formatted text (space delimited)

- GIF image
- Hyper-Text Markup Language (HTML)—saved in a zip file
- Microsoft Excel workbook
- Microsoft Excel Workbook with Pivot Table (when exporting a Crosstab)
- Oracle Reports XML
- PNG image
- Portable Document Format (PDF)
- SYLK (symbolic link)
- Text (tab delimited)
- Web Query for Microsoft Excel 2000+
- WKS (Lotus 1-2-3)

To set up the worksheet for export, use the following workflow:

1. From an open worksheet, click the Export link.
2. From the Choose Export Type screen, select the format you want to use from the drop-down list shown in the following illustration:

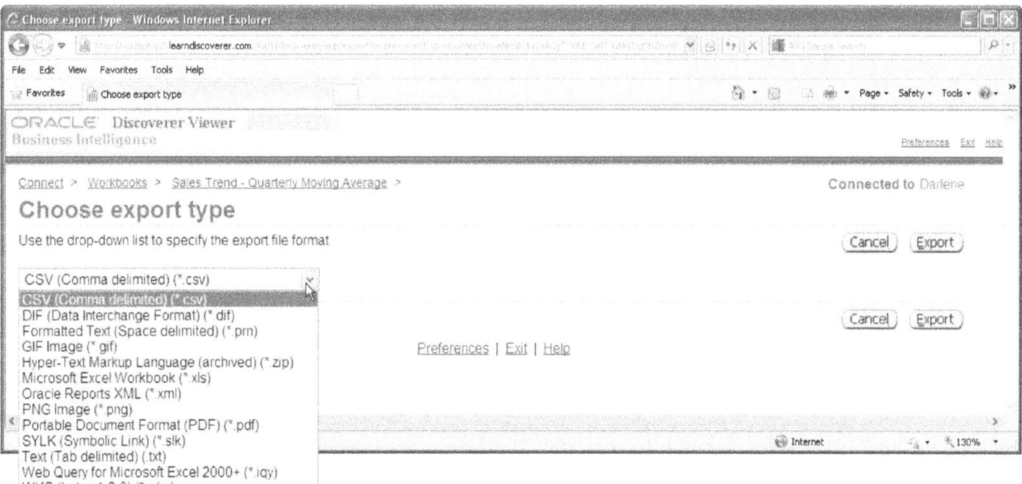


3. Click the Export button. The page will change, and you now see *Export Ready* at the top of the page and the following message: "The export you requested is ready. Please click the button below to open the exported document to view or save it."
4. Click the Click to view or save button.
5. Click Open to view the file or Save to save it.

6. When you are finished with the export file, use the links at the top of the browser to get back to the worksheet or to open another worksheet.

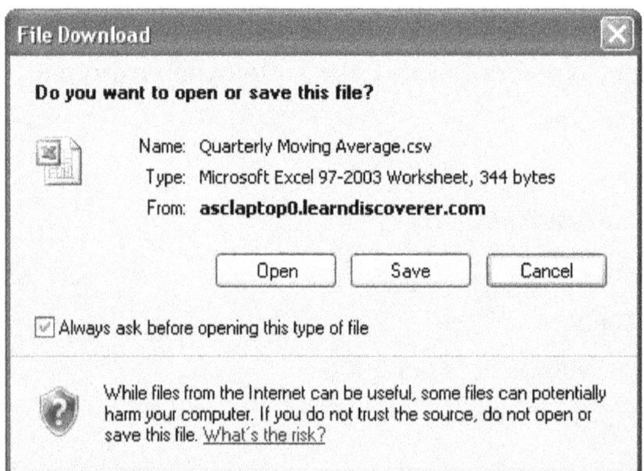


**Send as E-mail** Another very nice feature of Discoverer Viewer is the power to e-mail reports. The worksheet goes through the Export process to prepare it as an attachment first. Then you are presented with a simple e-mail utility to enter the sender and recipient information, a subject line, and a message.

This is a feature that must be set up by your Discoverer administrator, so check to see whether e-mailing is available to you.

To send a Discoverer Viewer report by e-mail, use the following workflow:

1. From an open worksheet, click Send as e-mail.
2. From the Choose Attachment Type page, select the export type from the drop-down list.
3. Click Next. This opens the Send Email page shown here:

Send e-mail

The worksheet was exported successfully. The e-mail will contain the document as an attachment.

* Indicates required field.

* Sender
john.doe@company.com
* Recipient
john.doe@company.com, jane.doe@company.com
CC
john.doe@company.com, jane.doe@company.com
Bcc
john.doe@company.com, jane.doe@company.com
Subject
Enter any text
Body
Enter any text
View Attachment

4. Fill out the e-mail form. You can review the file before sending by clicking the View Attachment button. As you can see above, you are required to provide a Sender and a Recipient. It is also good e-mail practice to add a Subject.
5. Click Finish.
6. When you are finished with the e-mail, use the links at the top of the browser to get back to the worksheet or to open another worksheet.

**Worksheet Options** Use the Worksheet options link to set up the item you want to display in the current worksheet. You can select from the following:

- **Title** Select this check box to show the title. This box is only displayed if the worksheet was created with the title enabled.
- **Table/Crosstab** Select this check box to show the table or crosstab.
- **Graph** Select this check box to show the graph associated with the worksheet.
- **Both** Select this radio button to display the graph and the table/crosstab data.
- **Text Area** Select this check box to show the text area in the worksheet. This box is only displayed if the worksheet was created with the text area enabled.
- **Show null values as** If no data is returned for a field in a worksheet, you can determine how you want the null value to appear. If you want the word *NULL* to appear, leave the setting as it is. If you want 0 to appear, type **0**, and if you want the field to be blank, clear it.
- **Show values that cannot be aggregated as** When a worksheet tries to aggregate an item that cannot be aggregated (for example, Rank), you can define here how the data is displayed. For example, if you enter **N/A** in this field, worksheets will display the text *N/A* where the data cannot be aggregated.

### Worksheets

The Worksheet area (below the Actions area) has links to all of the worksheets contained in the current workbook. Using these links is similar to using the tabs in Desktop or Plus. When you click a link to another worksheet in the workbook, the new query will run and display. Remember that this is HTML. You can use your browser buttons to go back and forth between the worksheets. The queries won't rerun; instead, the pages are cached. If you need to see up-to-the-minute data, you will need to use the Rerun Query link from the Actions area.

## The Table or Crosstab Display Area

In this area, the table or crosstab is displayed; however, there is the ever-present triangle to the left of the word *table* or *crosstab*. When the table or crosstab is displayed, the triangle will have a minus sign on it. If you don't want to see the table or crosstab and want to see only the graph, for example, click the triangle, and the table will close. The triangle icon will now show a plus sign, and to reopen the table/crosstab, click it again.

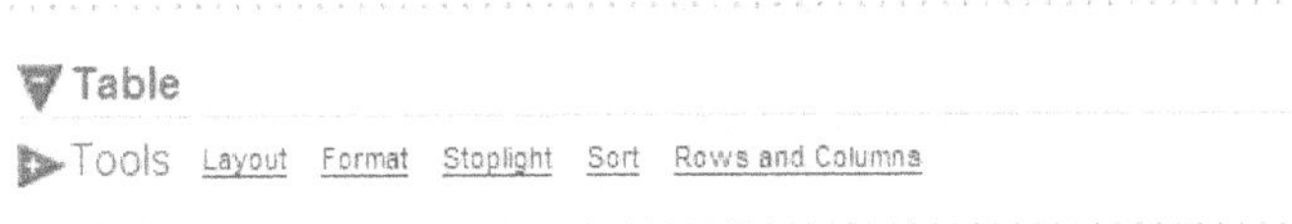


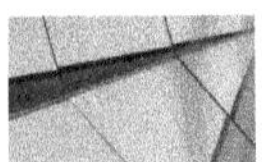

**NOTE**
*You are basically collapsing and expanding the table/crosstab using the triangle icon. When you want to expand it, the query does not rerun, but the cached data is displayed.*

## Tools

Five tools are available in Discoverer Viewer that you can use to slice and dice the data. You can reorder the columns, move columns into page items, add formatting (even conditional formatting and stoplighting), and sort. You can also decide how many rows and columns you want to display per page. You no longer have to worry about very wide crosstabs scrolling off to the right—you simply decide how many columns you want to view. You can view the 40th column while still being able to view the edge axis labels and values.

**NOTE**
*Best practice is not to use wide columns because it is resource intensive. Sixteen is ideal with cross-tabs, exporting, and printing.*

In Figure 10-5 you can see a worksheet open in Viewer. The tools are listed below the table type. You can make the following format changes:

- **Layout** Use this feature to change the arrangement of the columns.
- **Format** Use this feature to change the font formatting as well as background and foreground colors. You can also use this feature to add conditional formatting.
- **Stoplight** Use this feature to add exception formatting.
- **Sort** Use this feature to sort the data. This tool is not available if you are working with a Crosstab. The items on the side axis always determine the sorting in these reports, even if you defined a different sort order using Plus.
- **Rows and Columns** Use this feature to change the number of rows and columns to display per page of the browser.

### Layout

You can completely change the layout of a table or crosstab in Viewer. You can move or swap columns, and you can move items into page items or out of page items. Any rearranging of rows and columns you can do in Desktop or Plus you can do in Viewer. It is not drag and drop, but it is

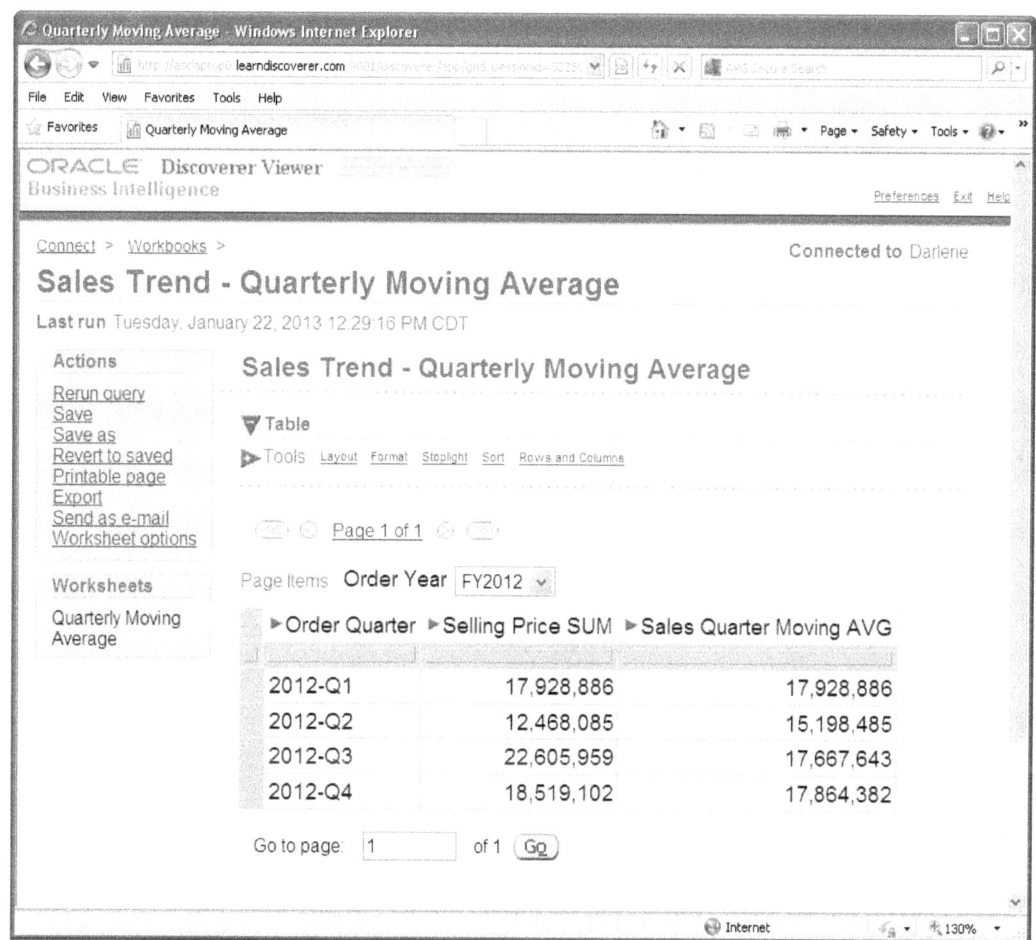


**FIGURE 10-5.** *A worksheet with Viewer tools*

still quite simple. If you get the layout completely messed up, don't worry, just click the Revert to saved link and start over.

There is no toolbar in Viewer, only the Tools menu shown in the following illustration:

Sales Trend - Quarterly Moving Average

Table

Tools Layout Format Stoplight Sort Rows and Columns

Move | Order Quarter | Left of Sales Quarter Moving AVG | Go | More...

### Moving or Swapping Columns

To move or swap columns in a table or crosstab, use the following workflow:

1. Click Layout from the Tools menu.
2. Select Move or Swap from the drop-down list shown here:

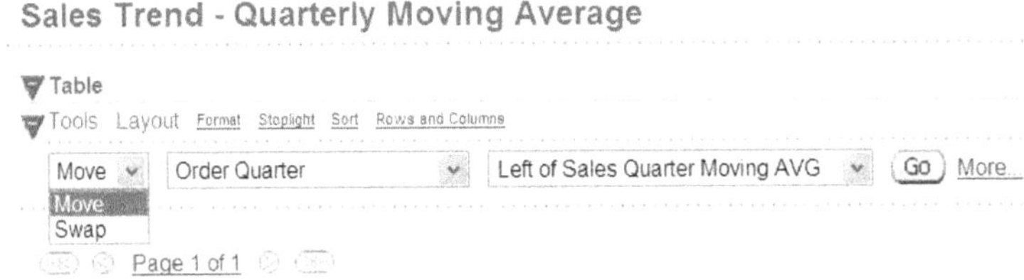


3. Select the column you want to move from the drop-down shown here:

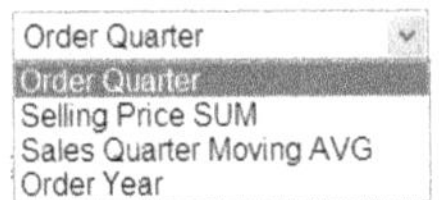


4. Select where you want to move it from the following drop-down:

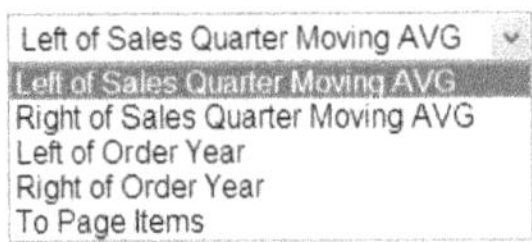


5. Click Go.

**Adding or Moving Page Items** There is also a More link. This takes you to a Table or Crosstab Layout page shown next that gives you more layout options, including adding and moving page items:

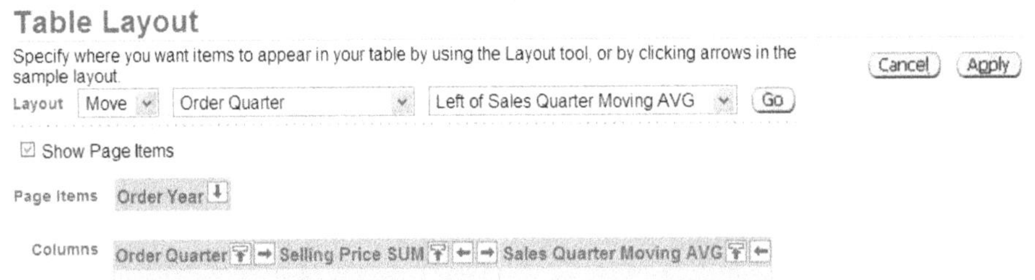

To add or move page items, use the following workflow:

1. Select the Show Page Items check box.
2. Next to each column name in the worksheet is an icon with an up arrow. Click this icon on the column or columns you want to add to page items.
3. The item or items have been added to the Page Items area and have an icon with a down arrow next to each page item name. To move them back out of page items, click the down arrow.
4. When you are editing a Crosstab worksheet, additional arrows allow you to horizontally move items in the left axis or to move items between the page axis, side axis, and top axis.
5. When you are done rearranging the columns, click Apply.
6. You are taken back to the table/crosstab page.

## Format

Many formatting options are available to the Viewer user. It makes the tool much more useful for end users who want to prepare a worksheet for printing. The only thing missing as far as formatting is concerned is the ability to format numbers. If, for example, dollar signs and decimal places were not formatted during the creation of the worksheet, you are stuck with the unformatted numbers.

When you click the Format tool, what looks like a toolbar appears below the Tools menu. Simply select the column you want formatted and then click the format button you want to apply. You can

- Bold fonts
- Italicize fonts
- Underline fonts
- Change the background color
- Change the font color

There is also a More link following the buttons. Clicking this link takes you to a page where you can perform all of the same functions. We think it is simpler to use the buttons.

**Conditional Formatting** The Format tool also has a link to create conditional formatting. Conditional formatting is used to color ranges of data within a column, for example, customers with sales exceeding $20,000. When conditional formatting (called *exception formatting* in Desktop) has been added to a worksheet during its creation, you will see it in Discoverer Viewer. You can also create additional conditional formats in Viewer.

To create conditional formatting, use the following workflow:

1. Click Format from the Tools menu, and then click the Create Conditional Format link from the Format menu.

2. This opens one of the Create Conditional Cell Format pages shown below. The page with the Dimension area is displayed when you are editing the formats for a crosstab.

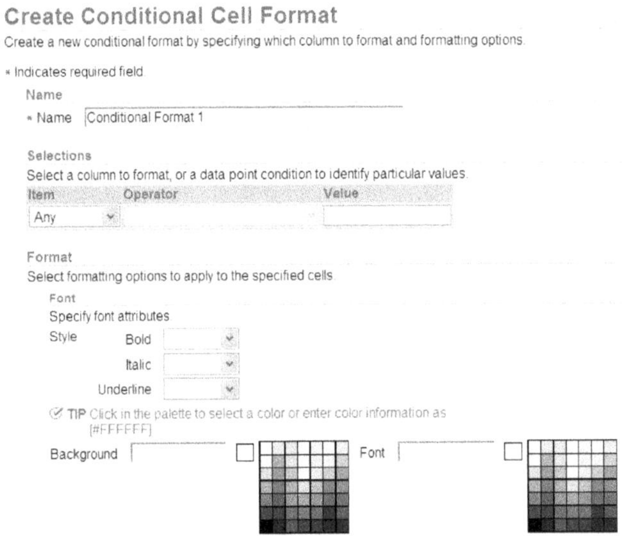

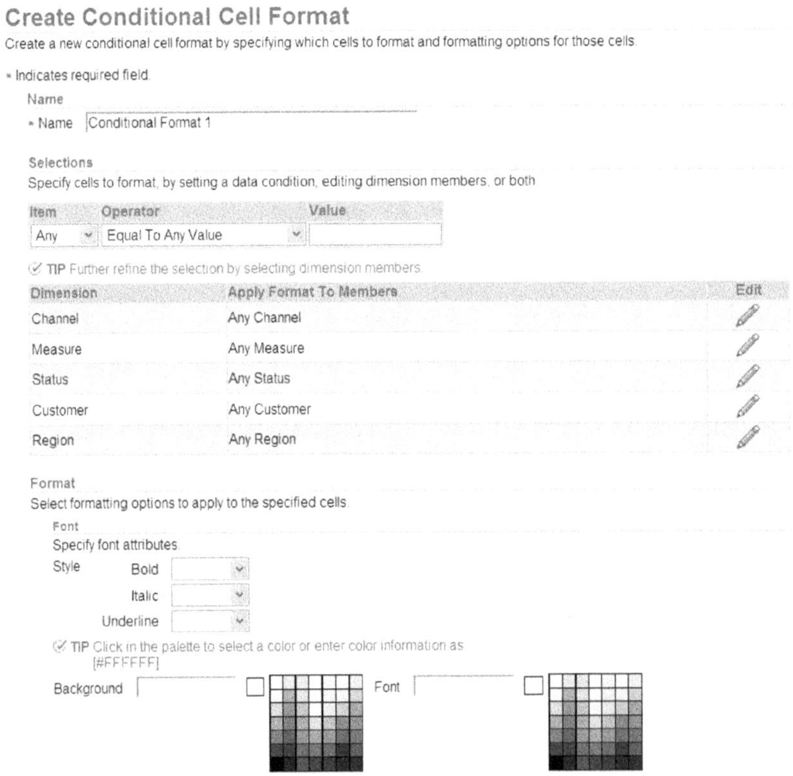

**Create Conditional Cell Format**

Create a new conditional format by specifying which column to format and formatting options.

* Indicates required field

Name

* Name Conditional Format 1

Selections

Select a column to format, or a data point condition to identify particular values.

| Item | Operator | Value |
|---|---|---|
| Any | | |

Format

Select formatting options to apply to the specified cells.

Font

Specify font attributes.

Style Bold

Italic

Underline

TIP Click in the palette to select a color or enter color information as [#FFFFFF]

Background Font

**Create Conditional Cell Format**

Create a new conditional cell format by specifying which cells to format and formatting options for those cells.

* Indicates required field.

Name

* Name Conditional Format 1

Selections

Specify cells to format, by setting a data condition, editing dimension members, or both

| Item | Operator | Value |
|---|---|---|
| Any | Equal To Any Value | |

TIP Further refine the selection by selecting dimension members.

| Dimension | Apply Format To Members | Edit |
|---|---|---|
| Channel | Any Channel | |
| Measure | Any Measure | |
| Status | Any Status | |
| Customer | Any Customer | |
| Region | Any Region | |

Format

Select formatting options to apply to the specified cells.

Font

Specify font attributes.

Style Bold

Italic

Underline

TIP Click in the palette to select a color or enter color information as [#FFFFFF]

Background Font

3. Give your conditional format a meaningful name.
4. Select the numeric column to which you want to add the conditional format from the Item drop-down list.
5. Select the operator from the Operator drop-down list.
6. Enter the value in the Value field.
7. Select the formatting you want to apply from the Format area.
8. If you are editing the formats for a crosstab, you can optionally choose which dimension(s) you want the conditional format to apply to. This gives Viewer much more flexibility than Plus or Desktop and is a great feature.

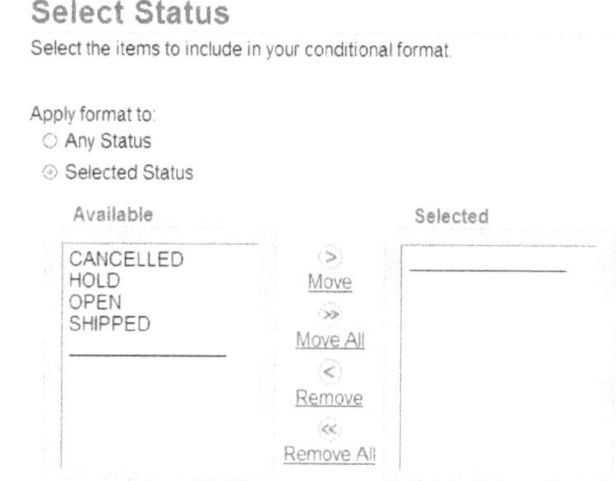


9. Click Apply.

**NOTE**
*Conditional formats defined in Viewer are only available within the session. Even if the user opts to save the workbook, the formats will not be saved.*

**Conditional Formats** The final link in the Format menu is Conditional Formats. Clicking this link takes you to a page where you can manage all of your conditional formatting, stoplight formatting, and header (column name) formats. We will describe the use of this page at the end of the next section.

## Stoplight

The next link in the Tools menu is Stoplight. Stoplight formatting is similar to conditional formatting. It formats data in a column using three ranges: Unacceptable, Acceptable, and Desirable. As with conditional formatting, if stoplight formatting is created in Plus (stoplighting is not available in Desktop), it will display in Discoverer Viewer. Because they use ranges, stoplight formats are always based on numeric fields, for example: all customers with sales less than $10,000 in red, all customers with sales between $10,000 and $40,000 in yellow, and all customers with sales exceeding $40,000 in green.

To apply stoplights, use the following workflow:

1. From the Tools menu select Stoplight. This opens the stoplight bar below the Tools menu.



2. Select the column upon which you want to base your stoplight from the Format drop-down list.
3. In the Unacceptable field, type in the highest number of the low range.
4. In the Desirable field, type in the lowest number of the high range. Notice how the Acceptable range is calculated for you using all values between the low and high ranges.
5. If you don't want to use the default colors, click the palette icon to the right of each range and select a color from the color palette.
6. Click Go. The stoplight format is applied as shown here.

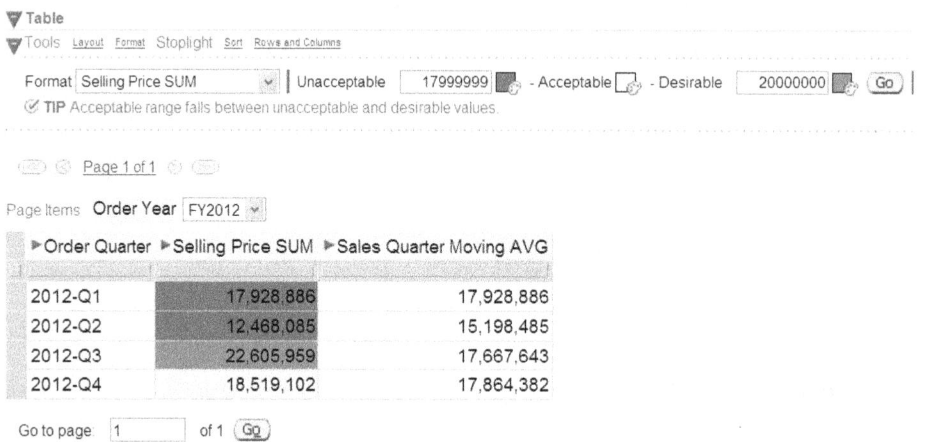


## The Conditional Formats Link

In both the Formats and Stoplight menus is a Conditional Formats link. This link takes you to a page where you can manage the formats you have created in Discoverer Viewer. It does not, however, manage the conditional formats that were created using Desktop or Plus. Those are a fixed part of the worksheet, and you have no control over them in Viewer. You can, however, create a new conditional format overriding the settings made in Plus. Again, this only applies for the session as you cannot save any conditional formats created within Viewer.

If you have created stoplights or conditional formatting in the current worksheet using Discoverer Viewer, you will see them here. You can also use this utility to create, edit, or delete new stoplights and conditional formatting. You cannot format column headers using the Format menu; instead, you must use this utility.

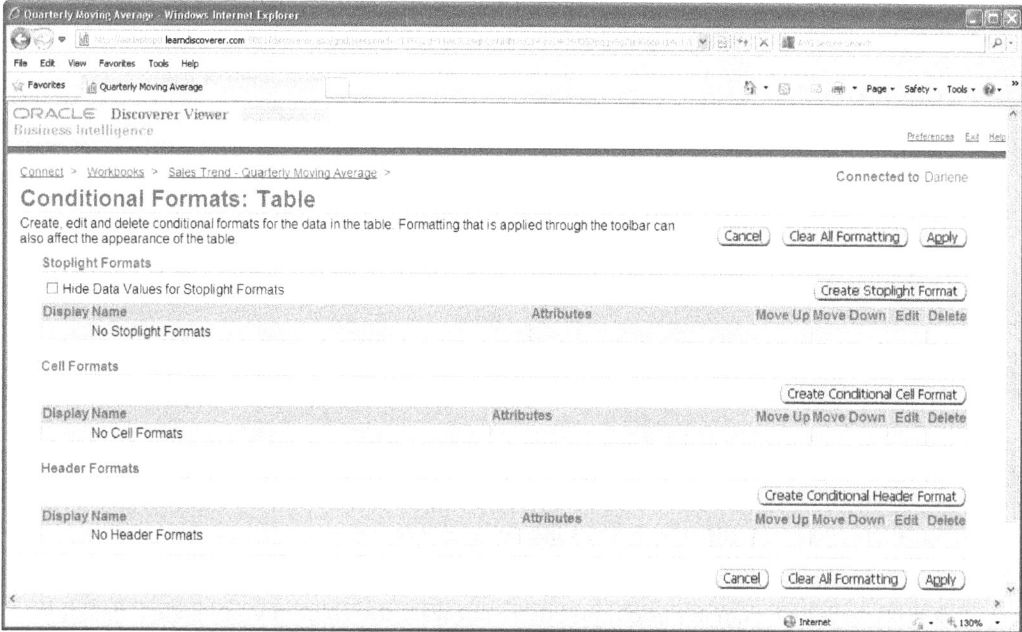


The Conditional Formats page is divided into three sections.

- **Stoplight Formats** Use this area to manage stoplights you have created in Discoverer Viewer.
- **Cell Formats** Use this area to manage conditional formats you have created in Discoverer Viewer.
- **Header Formats** Use this area to format the column headers.

If you want to deactivate the formatting, simply click the check box next to the format name to remove the check mark.

# Sort

You can add both normal and group sorts in Discoverer Viewer, but you can only do this to a Table. Unlike conditional formatting, if you add or alter a sort inside Viewer and save the workbook the revised sort options will be saved. The Sort link on the Tools menu opens the sort menu.

To apply a normal sort in Discoverer Viewer, use the following workflow:

1. Select the column you want to sort from the Sort drop-down list.
2. Select A-Z or Z-A from the Order drop-down list.
3. Click Go.

To apply multiple and group sorts, use the following workflow:

1. Click More from the Sort menu. This opens the Multiple Sort page.

**Multiple Sort**

Specify a column, sort order, sort type and whether the column is visible in your table

| | Column Header | Sort Order | Sort Type | Hide Column |
|---|---|---|---|---|
| First Sort | Region | A to Z | Group | ☐ |
| Second Sort | District | A to Z | Group | ☐ |
| Third Sort | State | A to Z | Group | ☐ |
| | City | A to Z | Group | ☐ |
| | | Ascending | Normal | ☐ |
| | | Ascending | Normal | ☐ |
| | | Ascending | Normal | ☐ |
| | | Ascending | Normal | ☐ |
| | | Ascending | Normal | ☐ |
| | | Ascending | Normal | ☐ |

2. From the Column Header drop-down list, select the column you want to sort.
3. From the Sort Order drop-down list, select the order.
4. From the Sort Type drop-down list, select Normal or Group.
5. If you want to sort on a column but do not want the column visible, click the Hide Column check box next to the sort.
6. Click Apply.

To remove a sort, use the following workflow:

1. Click More from the Sort menu. This opens the Multiple Sort page.
2. From the Sort Order drop-down list in the row you want to remove the sort from, select No Sort Order.

## Rows and Columns

The final link on the Tools menu is Rows and Columns. Here you select how many rows and columns you want to appear on a page. You can limit the number so that you do not need to scroll down; instead, you will use the down link to go to the next page. You can also set up a default in your preferences that will limit the number of rows and columns for all worksheets.

# Hyper-Drilling

Hyper-drills that have been created using Plus are available for use in Discoverer Viewer. This is another great feature of this tool. Hyper-drilling allows you to go deeper into the data; for example, say you are looking at sales for the CEBU WIDGET CO and see that the margin was particularly low for order number 10947, so you want to examine the sales for that sales order in more detail. When a hyper-drill is available, with a simple click of the mouse, another worksheet, or even another workbook, will open with the detailed information you seek. You can also drill to higher-level detail.

**NOTE**
*For information on hyper-drilling and its uses, please refer to Chapter 11.*

You know when a hyper-drill is available by the small, triangle-shaped Drill to Link icon to the left of the drill item. The illustration that follows shows a hyper-drill on the Order Number:

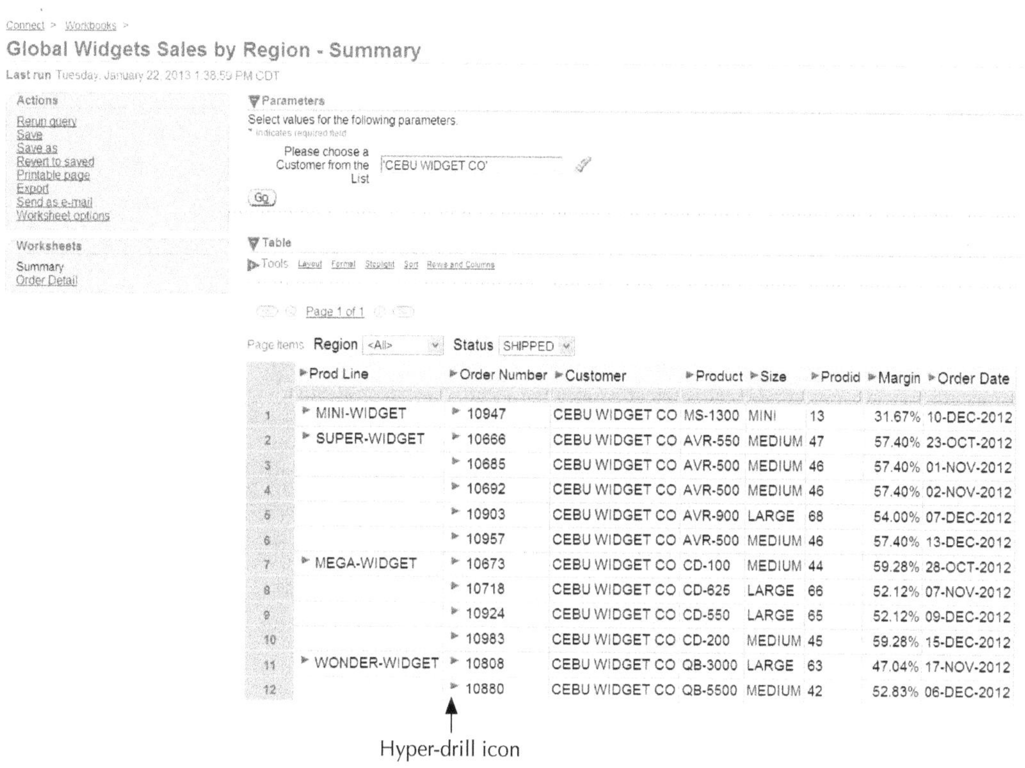

Clicking the icon gives you a pop-up list of available hyper-drills, because an item can have multiple drill links.

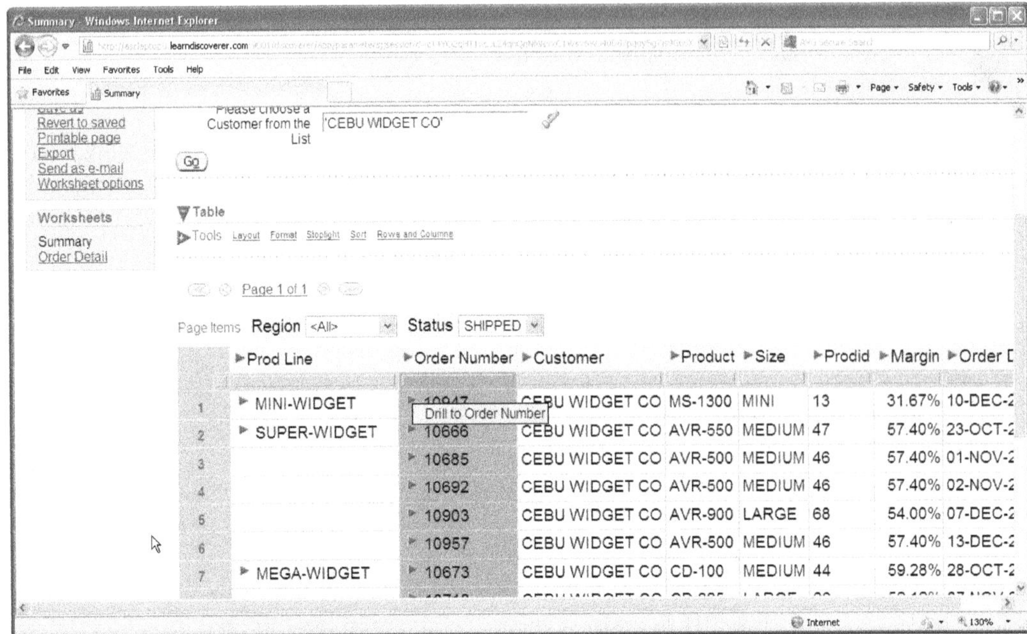

Click the link you want to follow; the current worksheet will close, and the hyper-link will open.

# Graphs

When a graph has been created using Plus, you will be able to work with it in Discoverer Viewer. You even have tools that will allow you to change the graph type, the size of the graph, and the graph's 3-D and gradient effects.

**NOTE**
*Graphs created in Desktop are not available in Discoverer Viewer.*

To hide the graph, click the plus sign alongside the word *Graph* in the graph area of the worksheet.

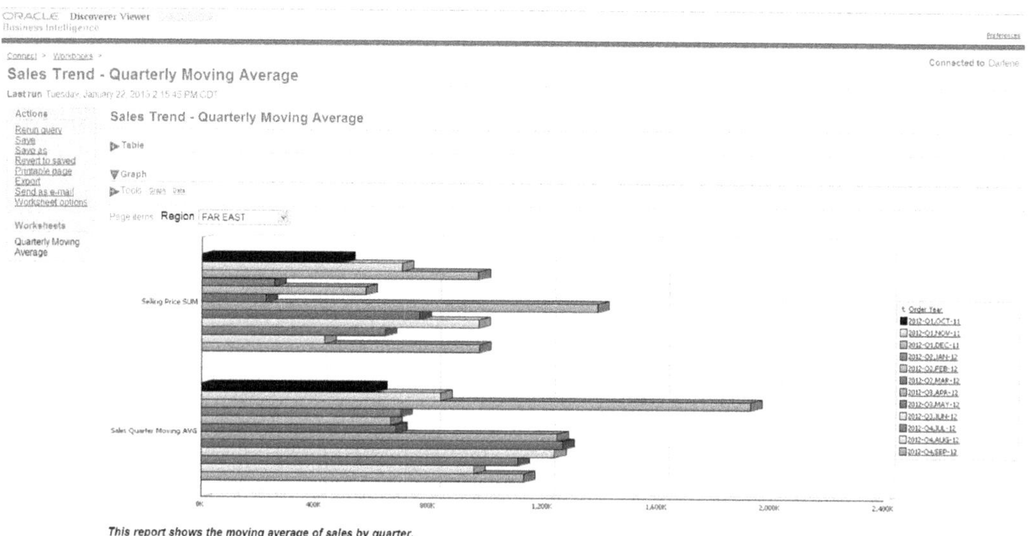


To open the graph, click the minus sign alongside the word *Graph* in the graph area of the worksheet.

To modify the graph, use the following workflow:

1. With the graph open, click the minus sign on the icon alongside the word *Tools* in the graph area of the worksheet. The graph tools will open.

2. Click on the Graph link.
3. Change the graph type by selecting from the two Type drop-down menus.
4. After you make your choice, click Go directly to the right of the type menus.
5. To change the size of the graph display, experiment typing in numbers between 300 and 800 in the width and height boxes. Keeping the numbers close will help maintain good width-to-height ratios.
6. After typing in the width and height, click Go directly to the right of the boxes.
7. Use the check boxes to the right to turn on and off 3-D effects and color gradient effects.
8. Click the Data link.
9. Change the data being graphed by selecting between All data and Displayed data.
10. After you make your choice, click Go directly to the right.
11. If page items are enabled you can choose which page item to graph or whether to graph all items.
12. When done, click the plus sign on the icon alongside the word *Tools*. The tools menu will be removed.

## Drilling in Graphs

Using graphs to drill in Discoverer Viewer is great way to use the tool for your data analysis. If a graph is based on an item that is part of a hierarchy, you can drill to another level in the graph. In the next illustration, the graph is based on regions and shows the total revenue for years 2012 and 2013. In the graph legend, there is an up arrow. This indicates a drill hierarchy exists. In this case, the drill will go from Region to District.

**NOTE**
*A new option available only in Viewer allows you to specify whether the graph should be for the entire worksheet or only for the subset of data that is currently displayed in the table/crosstab.*

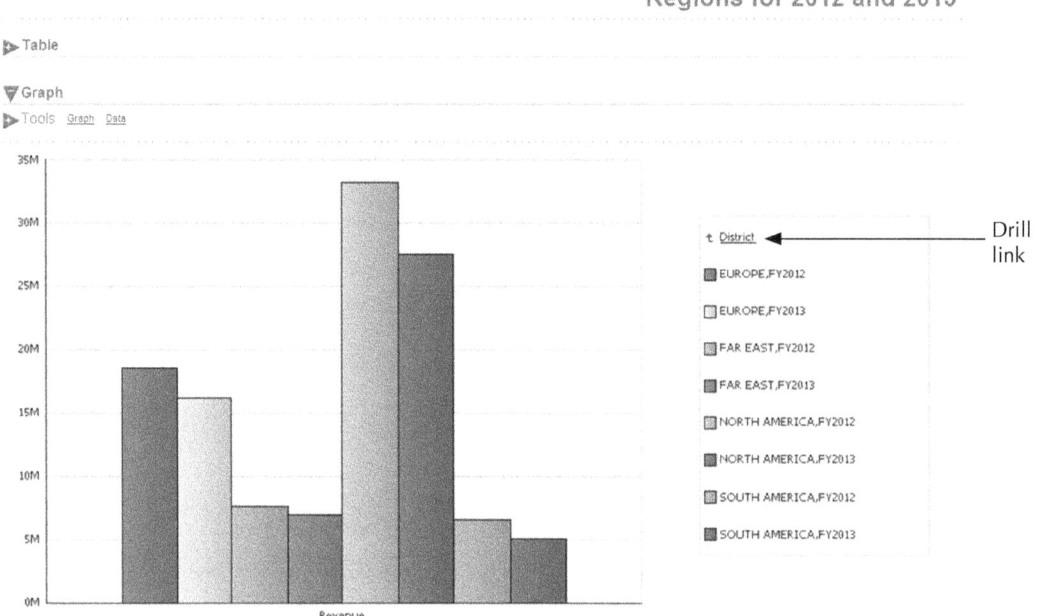


Clicking the up arrow will take you deeper into the data, now showing a new graph displaying the districts. Also notice that the worksheet has changed to reflect the district, and looking at the graph legend, you see that there is a new drill available to City.

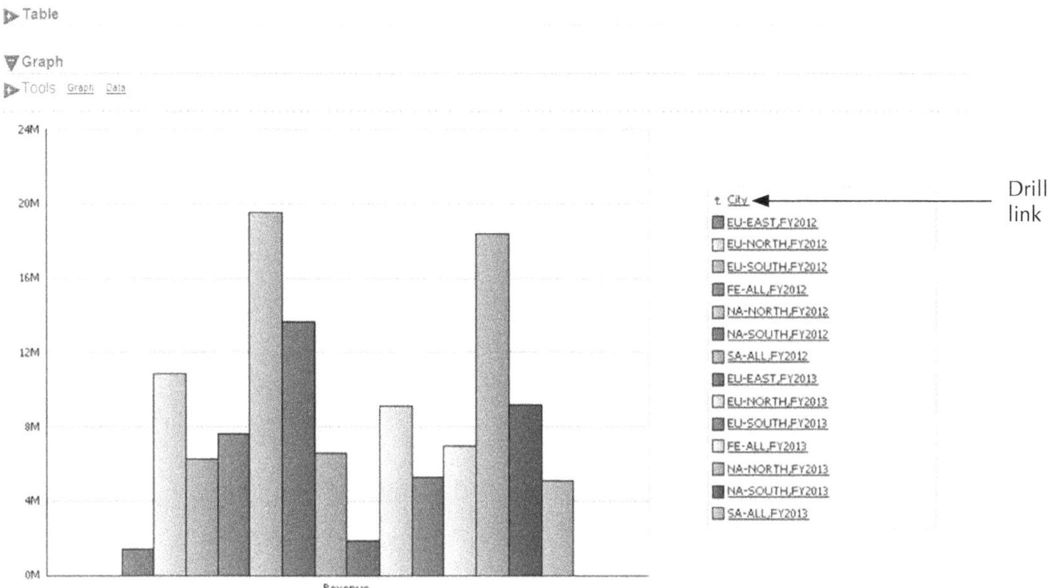


# Setting Up User Preferences in Viewer

The Preferences link opens the Preferences page. Here you have an opportunity to customize your personal Viewer environment. It is similar to the Options dialog box in Plus. Changing these options affects all worksheets, not just the current one. The page is divided into five sections.

- Query Governor
- Measure Unit
- Axis Label
- Summary Data
- Fan Trap Detection

## Query Governor

Use the Query Governor section to limit the amount of time and data retrieved when a worksheet runs. The Query Governor section is shown here.

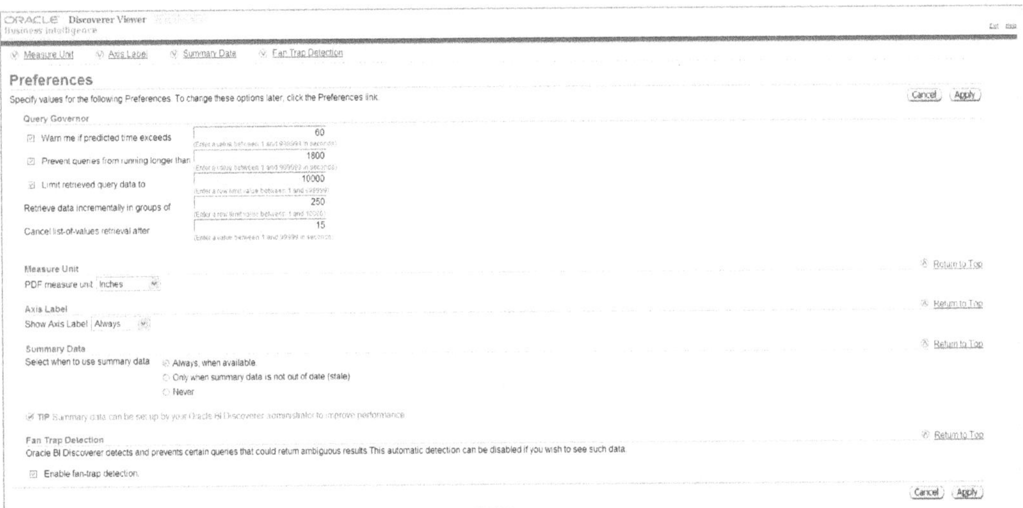

**NOTE**
*The Query Governor section options are preset by your Discoverer administrator. You cannot change these options to allow for more than the administrator has given to you. Options changed in Viewer will be reflected in Plus and vice versa.*

- **Warn me if predicted time exceeds** Check this box and enter a maximum value, in seconds, that Discoverer is allowed to use to predict how long a query will take. This value only comes into effect whenever your administrator has enabled query prediction. Most of the time you should leave this unchanged.
- **Prevent queries from running longer than** Check this box and enter a maximum value, in seconds, that Discoverer is allowed to run before canceling the query.
- **Limit retrieved query data to** Check this box and enter the maximum number of rows to retrieve for a query. If the database contains more rows than the maximum number allowed for the query, Discoverer warns you that not all rows have been retrieved. If this happens the displayed data might not be complete.
- **Retrieve data incrementally in groups of** Enter the number of rows you want to be retrieved. The smaller the number of rows to retrieve as a group, the faster the initial retrieval.
- **Cancel list of values retrieval after** Enter the maximum amount of time, in seconds, you are willing to wait for Discoverer to retrieve a list of values.

## Measure Units

Select from the drop-down list whether you want measures displayed in inches or centimeters. This only applies to PDF files.

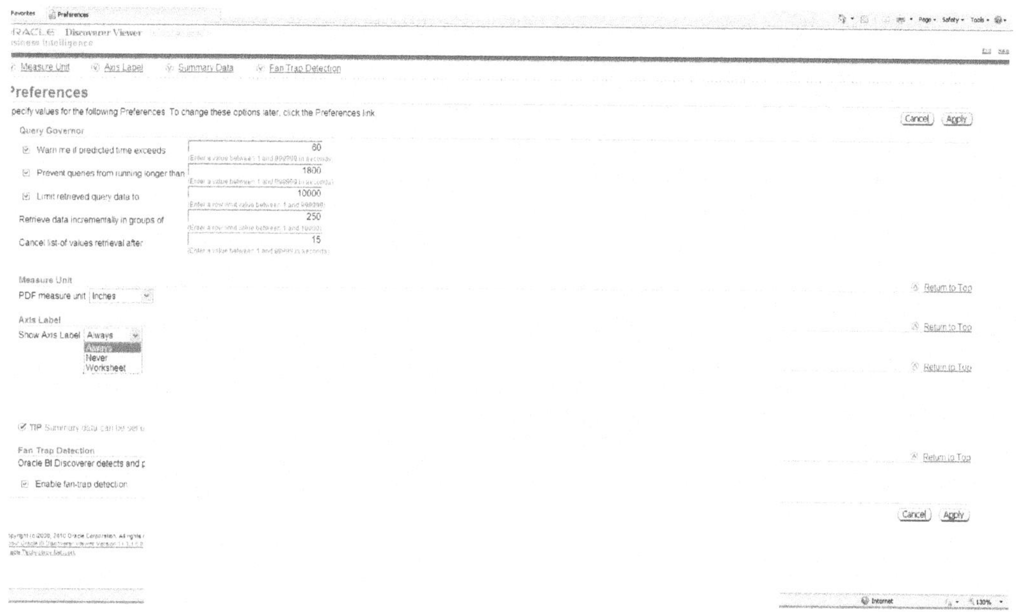


## Axis Labels

Choose when to show axis labels with the following three options:

- **Always** Axis labels are always shown in crosstab worksheets after they are opened. Any saved worksheet value is overridden.
- **Never** Axis labels are hidden in crosstab worksheets after they are opened. Any saved worksheet value is overridden.
- **Worksheet** Axis labels are shown or hidden in crosstab worksheets depending on how they were last saved.

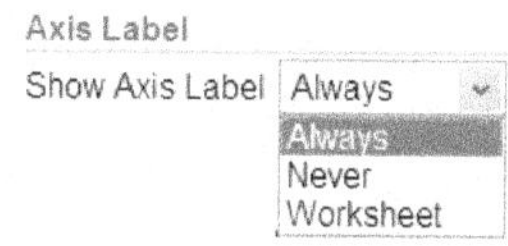


## Summary Data

Using summary data means that the work you do most often can be done faster. When you run a query, Discoverer checks summary tables set up by the Discoverer administrator to see whether saved (generally, pre-aggregated) data will satisfy your requirements. If the saved data will suffice, Discoverer loads the data quickly. If the summary tables' data does not meet your needs, Discoverer redirects the request to the rest of the database and sends the query to the database.

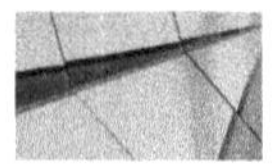

**NOTE**
*The available preferences depend on whether your database supports materialized views.*

For databases that support materialized views, the following radio button options are available:

- **Always, when available** Select this option if you don't need up-to-the-minute data for your analysis. Viewer will retrieve and display saved data from a materialized view regardless of whether the data is current.
- **Only when summary data is not out of date (stale)** Select this option if you need up-to-the-minute data. If the data in a materialized view is determined to be out of date, Discoverer will redirect your query to the full database and use the latest data for your report.
- **Never** Choose this option if you always want Discoverer Viewer to ignore the summary tables and use the latest data.

The following radio button options are available for databases that don't support materialized views (you will probably never see these options as most Oracle databases that Discoverer will work with support materialized views):

- **Always, when available** Choose this if up-to-the-minute data is not important for data analysis.
- **When summary data is more recent than n days** Choose this option when time-sensitive data is necessary for worksheets. Specify the number of days from the last data update.

# Summary

In this chapter you learned the power of Discoverer Viewer. You saw how it can be used in data analysis and how easily it slices and dices data. You saw how easy it is to format data and add special formatting such as stoplights and conditional formats.

We showed you how to rearrange columns and rows and place page items. You saw how Discoverer Viewer can be used to export and e-mail reports using a variety of common file types and how easy it is to set up a report for printing. Discoverer Viewer is also an excellent tool for viewing graphs, and graphs can be used for drilling into as well as out of hierarchical data.

Find a place for Discoverer Viewer in your organization. This powerful thin-client HTML tool will become the standard for data analysis among non–report writers.

# PART III

# Advanced Discoverer Techniques

# CHAPTER 11

# Refining Items, Drilling, and Hyper-Drilling

During the first ten chapters of this book, we taught you how to create worksheets using the Workbook Wizard, how to analyze your data, and how to convert your queries into reports.

Most queries are not very efficient when first built. You run them to make sure that they at least work. Having avoided "the query from the Twilight Zone" and decided that a query is worth keeping, you may have followed the steps in Chapter 9 and converted it into a report. Later, however, when working on a completely different problem, you may realize that a previous query satisfies most of the requirements. With a little tweaking and manipulation, you can modify or refine one query and turn it into another.

In this and the following two chapters, we will show you how to refine an existing query, how to fine-tune it, how to make it work more efficiently, and how to convert it into another query.

This chapter deals with refining the query items and drilling data. We will also show you the very powerful Plus feature called *hyper-drilling*. This allows you either to drill from one worksheet to another, going ever deeper into details, or to drill out to a URL.

# Refining Query Items

Perhaps the most frequent task you will perform in Discoverer is refining the items in a query. Refining can be as simple as adding or removing an item, but even this can have its pitfalls, as you will see in the next section. The real fun comes when you start pivoting and drilling. These techniques allow a much more sophisticated method of refining a query. It actually takes a little time to understand the full implications of what is involved, so let's begin with the simplest: adding and removing items.

## Adding and Removing Items

By far the simplest and most common ways of refining a query are to select a new item and to take an item away. Refining a query using these techniques sounds so easy, right? You take away an item or add a new item, and that's it—you have a new query. If only it really were this simple!

Unfortunately, these techniques are also one of the easiest ways to run into problems. Later in this section, we will detail some of the most common errors you may encounter.

### Adding a New Item

This is the simplest way to refine a query, but it can still be somewhat tricky. We will introduce you to a workflow plus give you an example of the most complicated way to add data: by adding an item using an intermediate folder.

There are two ways to add new items to an existing worksheet. You can use the Edit Sheet dialog box, or in Plus only, you can use the Available Items pane. As with most things with Discoverer, there is usually an easy way and, shall we say, a not-so-easy way.

First we will show you the easy way to add a new item using the Available Items pane. Then we will walk you through using the Edit Sheet dialog box, which, as you will see, is not quite as easy. If you are not yet using 11*g*, adding a new item using the Edit Sheet dialog box is the only method available. Perhaps after reading this section, you will be upgrading!

To add a new item to an existing Plus worksheet using the Available Items pane, use the following workflow:

1. Decide what item needs to be added.
2. In the Available Items pane, locate the item you want to add.

3. Use one of the following three ways to add the item:
   - Right-click the item and from the pop-up list select Add To Worksheet.
   - Drag the item from the Available Items pane to the Selected Items pane.
   - Drag the item directly from the Available Items pane to the table or crosstab. If you use this method, you can place the item exactly where you want it. This is our recommended way. Using the other methods, the item will be placed as the last item in the worksheet. You will then need to move it to the desired location.

To add a new item to an existing worksheet using the Edit Sheet dialog box, use the following workflow:

1. Decide what item needs to be added.
2. Open the Edit Sheet dialog box.
3. Examine the Discoverer open folders and see whether the item you want is in a folder you are already using. If the item you want is in one of the folders you are already using, proceed directly to step 7 of this workflow.
4. If the item you want is not in one of the folders currently in use, is it in a folder that is available? By this, we mean, is the folder containing the item you want an active folder, or is it currently deactivated? If the item you want is in an active folder, proceed to step 7 of this workflow.

**NOTE**
*Remember, a folder that is active has its name highlighted, while a folder that is inactive has its name grayed out.*

5. If the item you want is not in one of the active folders, the folder can be activated by applying a join or joins through one or more intermediate folders. If the folder you want to get to cannot be accessed this way, you will not be able to add the desired item to your current query. Unfortunately, you will have to build a new query. There are two reasons Discoverer prevents you from joining unrelated folders in queries. These are
   - To prevent you from creating meaningless queries
   - To avoid creating outer joins on two unrelated tables that could result in "the query from the Twilight Zone"

**NOTE**
*To determine whether there is an intermediate folder, look in your system's help file. If you are using NoetixViews, look in the Noetix help file and examine the Z$ items. These are joins to other folders. Refer to Appendix C for a full explanation.*

6. If the item you want is in a folder that can be accessed by joining through an intermediate folder, you will need to open the intermediate folder and then select any item from it. This should now make available the folder that contains the item you want to add.

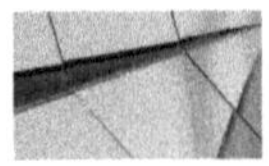

**NOTE**
*You can use multiple intermediate folders to get to the folder that contains the item you require. Repeat step 6 as many times as required, until the item you need becomes available.*

7. Open the folder containing the item you want, and add the item to your query.
8. If you used any intermediate folders to join to the folder containing the item you just added, you should remove those folder items now. Don't worry about removing these items, because Discoverer will remember exactly how to join to the folder containing the item you want.
9. Before you leave the Edit Worksheet dialog box, revise the table layout, conditions, sort order, and calculations. In the Plus Edit Worksheet, you can also revise the totals, parameters, and percentages.
10. Click OK. Discoverer now reruns the query and includes the item you want.
11. Apply any formatting you require.
12. Save the query. Remember to save it under a new name if you want to also keep a copy of the original.

## Adding an Item Using an Intermediate Folder

We will start from the following completed query and walk through all of the steps in the workflow. As you can see next, this simple query displays the total quantity ordered and the cost price for all customers.

| ▸ Cust Name | ▸ Order Qty SUM | ▸ Cost Price SUM |
|---|---|---|
| ABC WIDGET CO | 298,160 | 2621529.97 |
| ACE MANUFACTURING | 354,744 | 3430321.83 |
| BIG RIVER WIDGETS | 278,457 | 2368120.27 |
| BRIDGE THINGS | 171,041 | 1542731.00 |
| CASA DE WIDGETS | 744,294 | 6694309.10 |
| CEBU WIDGET CO | 755,633 | 6981829.49 |
| GATOR WIDGETS | 321,616 | 2754201.28 |
| HONG KONG WIDGETS | 562,448 | 4920948.71 |
| LAC WIDGETS SA | 498,452 | 4649537.16 |
| LAST RAILWAY WIDGETS | 536,368 | 4842040.18 |
| LONDON WIDGETS LTD | 535,016 | 4983079.95 |
| LOTS OF WIDGETS | 417,979 | 3698212.85 |
| MOUNTAIN WIDGETS | 510,652 | 4178928.58 |
| MUM'S WIDGET CO | 665,422 | 5960663.23 |
| OXFORD WIDGETS | 490,931 | 4461223.22 |
| PALMELA WIDGETS | 95,398 | 937186.55 |
| PATRIOT'S WIDGET CO. | 633,317 | 5316409.02 |
| REPUBLIC WIDGETS | 373,977 | 3443942.94 |

We will assume that we have been asked to change this query—to now display the totals by product line as well as by customer. Step 1 is complete, and because step 2 requires us to open the Edit Worksheet dialog box, we did just that. In steps 3 and 4, we examined the currently used and active folders and determined that the product line was not in any of those. As you can see here, the Product Line folder is inactive.

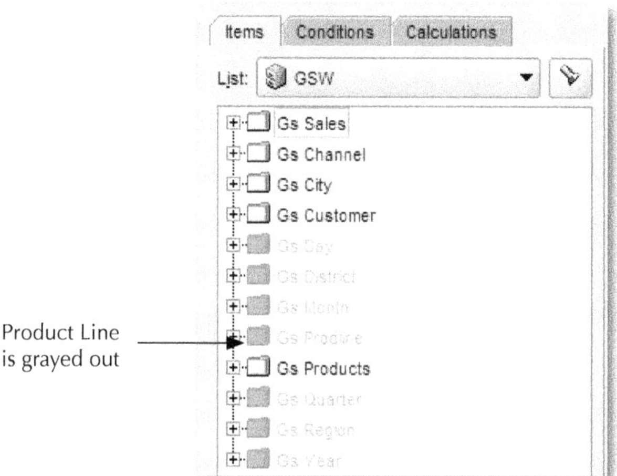


Step 5 of the workflow requires us to check whether any intermediate folder exists that can be joined to one of our in-use folders. After careful examination of our database (refer to Appendix D for a full data model of our database), we saw that there is indeed a join between the Products folder and the Product Line folder. Therefore, as required by step 6, we opened the Products folder and selected the product name. As you can see, these actions activated the Product Line folder.

Adhering to step 7 of the workflow, we now were able to open the Product Line folder and added the product line item to our query. Removing the Products folder from our list of completed items thereby completed step 8. As you can see, even though we decided not to include anything from the Products folder, that folder enabled us to select the product line.

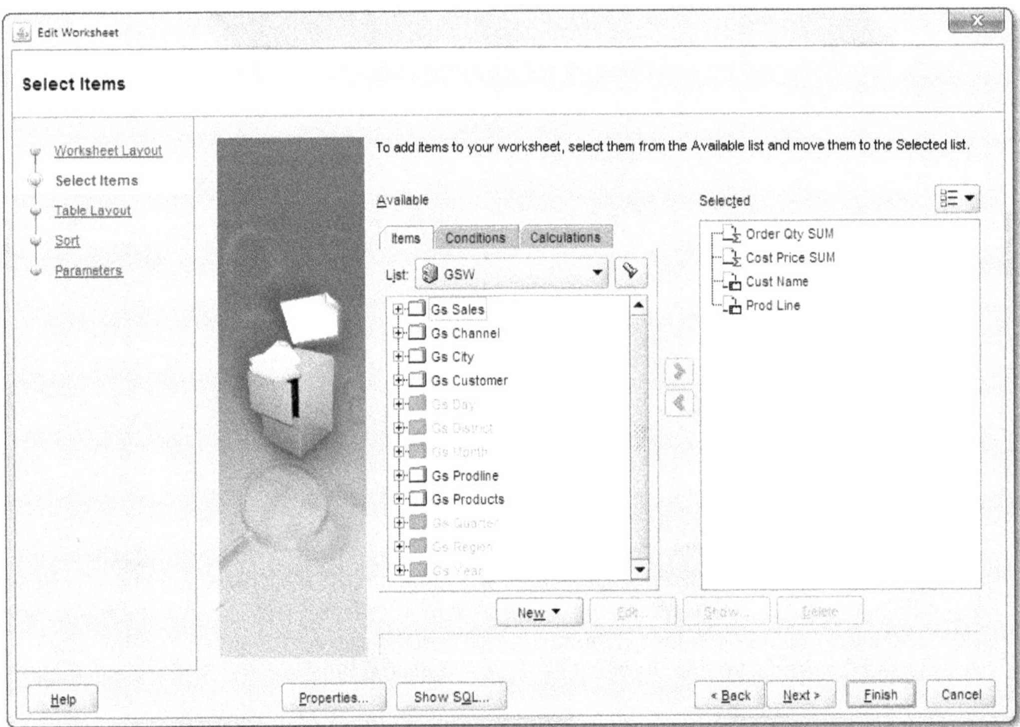


Finally, we completed the remaining steps of the workflow. We moved the product line alongside the customer name, applied a group sort on the customer, and applied a normal Low to High sort on the product line.

The final result, as just shown, has effectively demonstrated how to add an item to a query using an intermediate folder. By adhering to the workflow outlined, we completed adding the product line without any difficulty.

| Cust Name | Prod Line | Order Qty SUM | Cost Price SUM |
|---|---|---|---|
| ABC WIDGET CO | MEGA-WIDGET | 110,167 | 1060335.42 |
| | MINI-WIDGET | 38,573 | 151925.85 |
| | SUPER-WIDGET | 61,087 | 601609.56 |
| | WONDER-WIDGET | 88,333 | 807659.14 |
| ACE MANUFACTURING | MEGA-WIDGET | 86,193 | 806411.50 |
| | MINI-WIDGET | 23,939 | 95119.25 |
| | SUPER-WIDGET | 131,189 | 1439882.02 |
| | WONDER-WIDGET | 113,423 | 1088909.06 |
| BIG RIVER WIDGETS | MEGA-WIDGET | 113,525 | 1040415.18 |
| | MINI-WIDGET | 48,820 | 154401.95 |
| | SUPER-WIDGET | 47,867 | 536271.34 |
| | WONDER-WIDGET | 68,245 | 637031.80 |
| BRIDGE THINGS | MEGA-WIDGET | 49,260 | 502238.04 |
| | MINI-WIDGET | 14,754 | 58410.24 |
| | SUPER-WIDGET | 52,583 | 591311.54 |
| | WONDER-WIDGET | 54,444 | 390771.18 |
| CASA DE WIDGETS | MEGA-WIDGET | 210,221 | 1701538.28 |
| | MINI-WIDGET | 77,494 | 303773.76 |
| | SUPER-WIDGET | 249,527 | 2788824.63 |
| | WONDER-WIDGET | 207,052 | 1900172.43 |

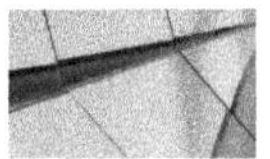

**NOTE**
*You can also add new items to a worksheet by using the drilling capabilities of Discoverer. These are explained in detail later in the section "Drilling Into and Out of Data."*

### Removing an Item from Your Query

Removing a single item from a query is straightforward. Of course, you can remove an item by launching the Edit Worksheet dialog box and removing the item from the selections, but did you know you can just highlight the item and delete it by pressing DELETE? Refer to Chapter 6 for more information on removing items from queries.

In Plus, there are two additional ways to remove an item from a query. First, you can right-click the item and from the pop-up list select Remove From Worksheet. You can also highlight the item in the Available Items pane and click the Remove From Worksheet button on the toolbar of the pane.

## Common Problems Associated with Adding or Removing Items

The most common problems users encounter when attempting to add or remove items are

- Attempting to join multiple business areas
- Attempting to combine aggregate and detail data
- Attempting to join to the same child folder from multiple parent folders
- Incorrectly joining from a child folder to a parent folder
- Missing joins
- Fan traps
- Lack of documentation

### Attempting to Join Multiple Business Areas

Unless your Discoverer manager has made it possible for you to link business areas, you will usually not be able to select items from multiple business areas at the same time.

In the following example, we already have a query that selects the order quantity and cost price by product. After editing the sheet, we tried to select from another business area.

As you can see in the following illustration, all of the folders in the other business area are deactivated:

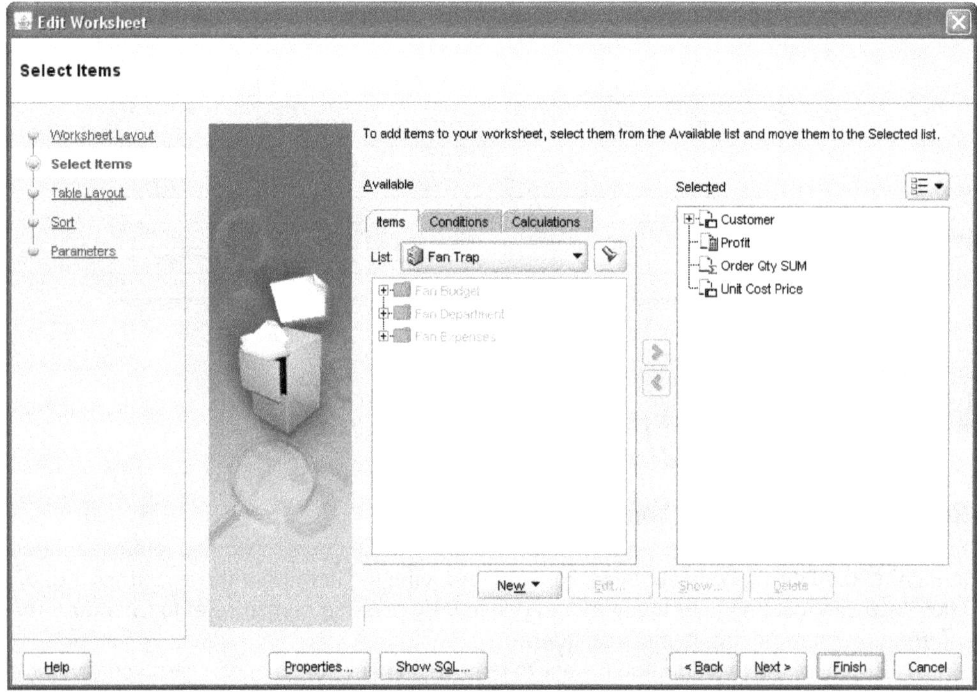


### Attempting to Combine Aggregate and Detail Data

Another common error users make when adding new items to an existing query is to fail to define the new item to be at the same level of aggregation as the existing items.

In the following example, we have an existing query that selects the total quantity ordered by sales channel for the fiscal month of February 2011. From the Available Items pane, we attempted to add the ordered quantity detail to the same query. As you can see, Discoverer gave us a warning.

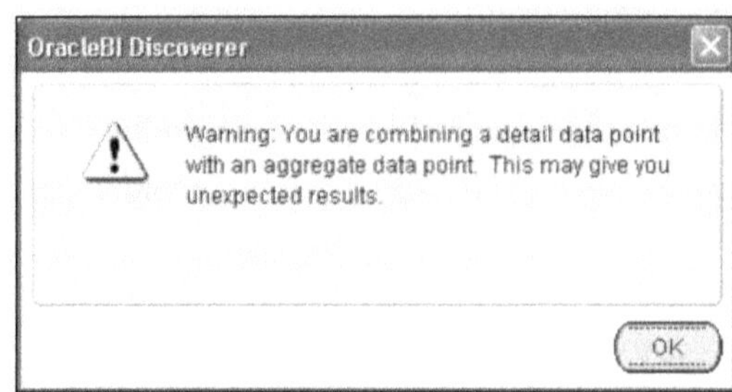

While Discoverer will not prevent you from mixing aggregate and detail data in the same query, be warned—your results may be incorrect.We ignored the warning that Discoverer gave us and ran the query anyway. This produced a very interesting result. As you can see, we placed a group sort on the channel and then subtotaled by channel. For ease of use we will show just the external channel. You might expect the subtotal for order quantity sum and order quantity total to be the same, but they are not! The correct answer is the one for the subtotal based on the order quantity sum, but if you did not know this, you could easily quote the wrong total to your manager or, worse still, to a customer or your shareholders and understate the quantity booked by almost 200,000 items!

| | ▸ Channel | ▸ Order Qty SUM | ▸ Order Qty |
|---|---|---|---|
| 1 | EXTERNAL | 3 | 1 |
| 2 | | 48 | 48 |
| 3 | | 160 | 80 |
| 4 | | 500 | 100 |
| 5 | | 320 | 160 |
| 6 | | 400 | 200 |
| 7 | | 300 | 300 |
| 8 | | 400 | 400 |
| 9 | | 1200 | 600 |
| 10 | | 2880 | 960 |
| 11 | | 2376 | 1188 |
| 12 | | 13200 | 1200 |
| 13 | | 4500 | 1500 |
| 14 | | 1600 | 1600 |
| 15 | | 1920 | 1920 |
| 16 | | 7200 | 2400 |
| 17 | | 5000 | 5000 |
| 18 | | 8100 | 8100 |
| 19 | | 8400 | 8400 |
| 20 | | 20000 | 10000 |

So what happened? The order quantity detail is shown once whereas the order quantity sum is multiplied by the detail for the number of times the item was ordered. If you look at the first row, the sum is 3 whereas the detail is 1. What this means is that there were three orders that month in the channel where the quantity was 1. Looking again in the fourth row you can see that 5 orders must have been placed where the quantity was 100.

### Attempting to Join to the Same Child Folder from Multiple Parent Folders

Pay particular attention when combining aggregate data with detail data, because this can give you problems. Data warehouses, for example, are usually built around a star schema with one or more fact tables and multiple dimensions. When multiple fact tables are employed, one of them usually contains only aggregated data, while the others contain varying amounts of detail. If you have a query that pulls data from the aggregated folder and then refine that query to also pull from the detail folder, you will have problems. Not only will Discoverer try to mix this data in the same row, but Discoverer will not be able to correctly identify which fact folder to use when joining to the remaining dimension folders.

In Discoverer terms this is a *fan trap*. As you can see in this illustration, Discoverer states that it could not add the second detail item because it has detected a fan trap. To work around this issue, please look at the "Working with Fan Traps" section later in this chapter.

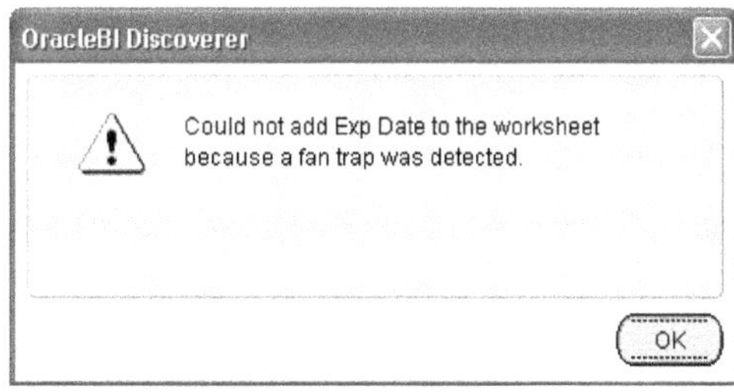
OracleBI Discoverer
Could not add Exp Date to the worksheet
because a fan trap was detected.
OK

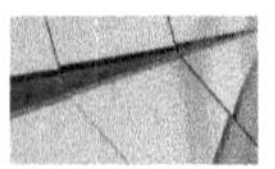

**NOTE**
*For an explanation of star schema terminology, please refer to Appendix C.*

### Incorrectly Joining from a Child Folder to a Parent Folder

Another easy-to-make mistake relates to incorrectly joining a child folder to a parent folder. The most common mistake that we have seen relates to users misunderstanding their company's use of foreign currencies and multiple currencies.

In the modern era, many companies use multiple currencies from around the world. Within the Sales Order folder, there could be amounts stored in the local, regional, and corporate currencies. A *local* currency is the currency of the transaction (USD, GBP, TWD, CHF, and so on). A *regional* currency is the currency in which a region aggregates its amounts (for example, the European region could decide to aggregate using the euro). A *corporate* currency is the currency in which the company decides to report its quarterly and annual returns.

If you are using Oracle E-Business Suite, you will probably already be aware that this application supports only the local, or *transactional*, currency and the set of books currency. The set of books currency equates to the regional currency just outlined.

However, most systems will probably have only one currency folder, containing the currency code and currency description for all currencies in use, probably using the International Organization for Standardization (ISO) set of currency codes. When users attempt to add currency codes into a query that is using multiple currencies, they need to be very careful to choose the correct link; otherwise, they could display the EURO code alongside the local amounts.

**NOTE**
*While Discoverer will prompt for which join to make, it is up to the user to make the correct choice. Making a wrong join at this stage could cause the query to produce the entirely wrong result. You will have no choice but to rebuild the query, because once you have chosen a join, there is no going back.*

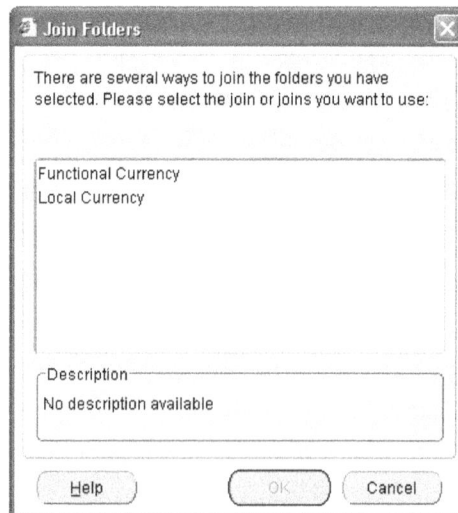

For example, using our currency code model outlined previously, suppose you have a query that reports by both regional and local currencies. Next, we want to add the currency code for the local currency. When you try to add this item, Discoverer recognizes that there is more than one way to join to this folder and opens the Join Folders dialog box.

As you can see here, Discoverer tells you that there is more than one way of joining the folders you have selected. You should select the join that you want to use and click OK.

**NOTE**

*This is a perfect example of why you need to take time to understand your data model. It is the responsibility of your Discoverer manager to display this model in terms that are meaningful to your job. Discoverer prompts you with the names of the joins. It is a poor implementation if your Discoverer manager chooses to display the primary- and foreign-key names, names that will probably be meaningless to you. It is your responsibility to know which join you need. A description of each join is displayed when selected to give you more information. If you have any doubt as to which one you should select, contact your Discoverer manager.*

A feature of 11g is the ability for Plus users to see the joins between the folders. To enable the viewing of join information in Plus, use the following workflow:

1. Launch Discoverer Plus.
2. From the menu bar, select Tools | Options. This opens the Options dialog box.
3. Click the Advanced tab. Discoverer displays the advanced options, as shown in Figure 11-1.
4. Check the Show Joins box.
5. Click OK.

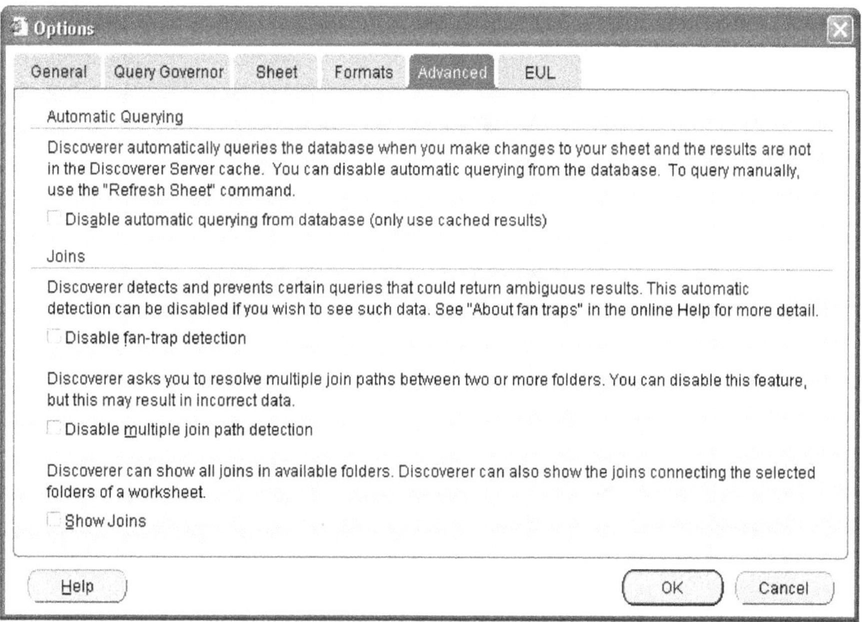


**FIGURE 11-1.** *Discoverer Plus Advanced tab of the Options dialog box*

Having enabled the viewing of join information, Discoverer Plus, shown in this illustration, shows the joins in the Available Items pane:

Sales
Channel
Currency
Currency Code
Functional Currency
Local Currency
Products
Customer

To summarize this section, when adding or removing items from a query with multiple join capabilities between the folders, you need to take extra care. You need to make sure you are fully aware of what joins are already being employed within the query.

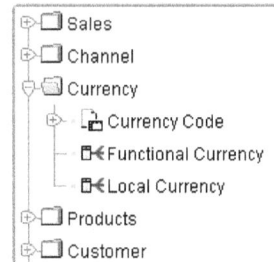

## Missing Joins

When you are attempting to add an item to your query, you may find that there is no join to the folder containing the item you want. With many databases, there is usually more than one way to join folders. First, you should see whether there is a way to open the folder you want by linking via an intermediate folder. If you cannot find a way to join to the folder you want, you need to talk to your Discoverer manager.

The two most common reasons you cannot join folders are as follows:

- The Discoverer manager did not expect this type of query to be used and has not made the join available to you.
- The Discoverer manager purposely did not make the join available to you, because it would result in incorrect aggregation or expose sensitive data.

In either of these cases, you should discuss your requirements with your Discoverer manager. They may be able to define a new join that will allow you to select the items you need.

## Working with Fan Traps

The fan trap problem has plagued administrators for a very long time, and until the launch of version 4.1 of Discoverer a few years ago, the fan trap was one of the most feared situations that could arise. Prior to that release, all Discoverer could do was detect that a fan trap had occurred and then prevent the query from running.

To protect against the fan trap occurring, Discoverer has, as the default, an option to prevent you from building a query that contains fan traps. On the Advanced tab of the Options dialog box, as shown in Figure 11-1, you can see in the center that Discoverer has an option to disable fan trap detection.

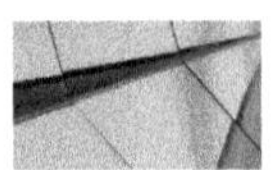

**NOTE**
*Unless you are very proficient at writing queries and know how to control fan traps, we strongly advise you not to disable this protection.*

Oracle claims that Discoverer detects fan traps, rewrites the query, and executes the query on the server. But does Discoverer really do this? We are very pleased to answer in the affirmative and will show you some example SQL later in this discussion. Discoverer rewrites a single query to use two in-line views, but actually OBIEE does this as well within the BI Server. In other words, it writes two inline queries that are sent to the database and then logically joins them, so, technically speaking, Discoverer is *not* the only product on the market any longer that does this. But what is a fan trap? Put very simply, a *fan trap* is a SQL query that generates unexpected results. The most common manifestation occurs when a master table is joined to two detail tables separately and results in incorrectly aggregated measures. To the end user, the definition is meaningless, yet the consequences can be catastrophic.

In the past, with the fan trap scenario you also needed to be careful when creating totals because Discoverer would generate incorrect values. This has now been resolved, and Discoverer will not compute a total or subtotal when a fan trap situation exists. Throughout the following section we will demonstrate this by including subtotals in all our examples.

|   | Dept Number | Department |
|---|---|---|
| 1 | 10 | SALES |
| 2 | 20 | HR |
| 3 | 30 | MIS |
| 4 | 40 | MARKETING |
| 5 | 50 | TRAINING |

We will give you an example of what we mean by a fan trap. We have created a new business area that contains three folders: a Department folder, a Budget folder, and an Expense folder. The following three illustrations show the contents of each of these folders.

This illustration shows all of the data in the Department folder. As you can see, there are just five departments. We want you to concentrate on department 10, the Sales department. We will show you how the fan trap will cause this department's amounts to be calculated incorrectly.

| Deptno | Bgt Date | Reason | Amount SUM |
|---|---|---|---|
| 10 | 19-MAR-2012 | EQUIPMENT | 5,000 |
|  | 20-MAR-2012 | TRAVEL | 40,000 |
|  |  |  | Sum: 45,000 |
| 20 | 21-MAR-2012 | EQUIPMENT | 2,000 |
|  | 21-MAR-2012 | TRAVEL | 200 |
|  |  |  | Sum: 2,200 |
| 30 | 15-APR-2012 | TRAVEL | 10,000 |
|  | 15-APR-2012 | EQUIPMENT | 25,500 |
|  |  |  | Sum: 35,500 |
| 90 | 24-FEB-2012 | TRAVEL | 25,200 |
|  | 24-FEB-2012 | EQUIPMENT | 6,340 |
|  |  |  | Sum: 31,540 |

The following illustration shows the data in the Budget folder. For each department, there is an allotted budget for the categories Equipment and Travel, along with the date the budget was set. We again draw your attention to the rows for department 10, the Sales department. As you can see, this department's budget for Equipment is 5,000, while for Travel the budget is 40,000. You can also see that subtotals have been enabled and that the totals are correct.

The next illustration shows the data in the Expense folder. For some departments, there have been some expenses recorded. As you can see, for the Sales department, 10, we have recorded three expenses so far, and inserted subtotals, so that department 10 has incurred a total amount of 1,400. Please make a note that there are no expenses for department 50, so no data is displayed.

| Deptno | Exp Date | Expenses Amt |
|---|---|---|
| 10 | 16-APR-2012 | 250 |
|  | 25-FEB-2012 | 150 |
|  |  | Sum: 400 |
| 20 | 12-APR-2012 | 1,025 |
|  |  | Sum: 1,025 |
| 40 | 28-APR-2012 | 13,000 |
|  | 26-APR-2012 | 2,750 |
|  |  | Sum: 15,750 |

Our intention is to build a query by pulling data from all three folders, with the notion of showing the total amount of budget and expenses incurred to date. For our Sales department, we know that the total budget is 45,000, and the total expenses so far are 1,400.

First, we attempted to build the query with Discoverer's fan trap detection in place. In the following illustration, you can see that we have almost completed building the query. We have already selected the detail items that we want from the Department and Expense folders and also included the total Budget Amount from the Budget folder. So far, so good, and as you can see from the next illustration, Discoverer is not only happy with our selections but has executed the query correctly and inserted subtotals.

| Deptno | Exp Date | Expenses Amt | Budget Amount |
|---|---|---|---|
| 10 | 16-APR-2012 | 250 | 45000 |
|  | 25-FEB-2012 | 150 | 45000 |
|  |  | Sum: 400 |  |
| 20 | 12-APR-2012 | 1,025 | 2200 |
|  |  | Sum: 1,025 |  |
| 40 | 28-APR-2012 | 13,000 | 80500 |
|  | 26-APR-2012 | 2,750 | 29250 |
|  |  | Sum: 15,750 |  |
| 50 | NULL | NULL | 2290 |
|  |  | Sum: NULL |  |

**NOTE**
*With the fan trap protection enabled, Discoverer will allow you to include as many detail items as you want from one of the parent folders. It will also allow you to include the total amount from the other folder.*

Before we continue, we want to draw your attention to a number of items. First, you will notice that even though there are no expenses for division 50, Discoverer has now included that item in the result. Second, take a close look at the subtotals that have been produced. You will notice that no subtotal has been generated for expenses against department 50 and that no subtotal has been produced for the budget against department 10. Can you see why?

The answer as to why no subtotal has been created for the expenses against department 50 is straightforward because, as previously mentioned, there are no expenses for that department. But why is there no budget total for department 10? This is because Discoverer has repeated the value 45,000 three times, once against each expense. If we were to attempt to add these, we would get the wrong answer.

| Deptno | Budget Amount | Exp Date | Expenses Amt |
|---|---|---|---|
| 10 | 45000 | 16-APR-2012 | 250 |
| | | 25-FEB-2012 | 150 |
| | | | Sum: 400 |
| 20 | 2200 | 12-APR-2012 | 1,025 |
| | | | Sum: 1,025 |
| 40 | 29250 | 26-APR-2012 | 2,750 |
| | 80500 | 28-APR-2012 | 13,000 |
| | | | Sum: 15,750 |
| 50 | 2290 | NULL | NULL |
| | | | Sum: NULL |

The solution is to create a group sort on the budget total and then to subtotal only on the expenses. As you can see in the following illustration, we now have the correct answer, with the budget being displayed only once for each set of expenses. There is no ambiguity and no need to total the budget.

Are you interested in the SQL that Discoverer has generated for this query? Discoverer has rewritten the SQL to use two subqueries to generate the results. In the two illustrations that follow, the first shows the SQL that Discoverer has generated, and the second shows the explain plan.

```
SELECT fx100 as E105398,fx103 as E105405,fx104 as E105404_SUM,fx101 as
E105393_SUM
 FROM ( SELECT o105397.DEPTNO AS fx102, o105401.EXP_DATE AS fx103, (
SUM(o105401.EXPENSES) ) AS fx104 FROM GSW.FAN_DEPARTMENT o105397,
GSW.FAN_EXPENSES o105401  WHERE (o105397.DEPTNO =
o105401.DEPTNO(+)) GROUP BY o105401.EXP_DATE(+), o105397.DEPTNO) ,
    ( SELECT o105397.DEPTNO AS fx100, ( SUM(o105390.AMOUNT) ) AS fx101
FROM GSW.FAN_BUDGET o105390, GSW.FAN_DEPARTMENT o105397
WHERE (o105397.DEPTNO = o105390.DEPTNO(+)) GROUP BY
o105397.DEPTNO)
 WHERE ( (fx100 = fx102))
 ORDER BY fx100 ASC , fx101 ASC ;
```

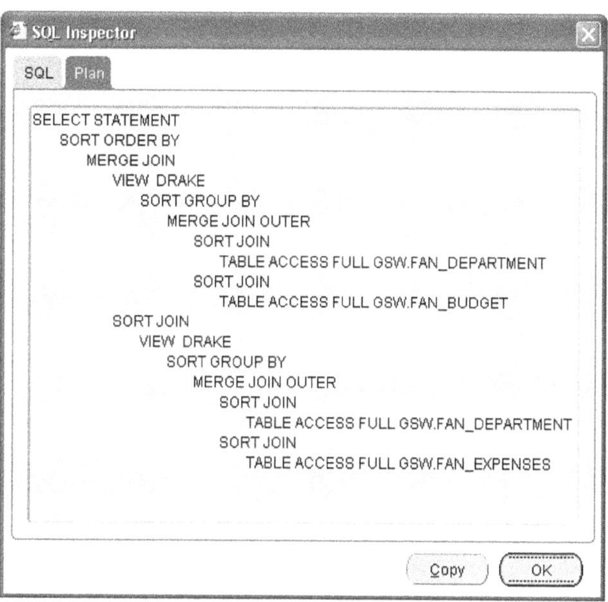

**NOTE**
*To see the SQL and Explain Plan windows, use Tools | Show SQL.*

If we now attempt to add another item from the Budget folder, for example Budget Date, we are no longer querying the total budget by expense detail. We are now attempting to query the budget detail along with the expense detail. This is the scenario that Oracle is trapping. As expected, Discoverer will not allow this but displays an error message.

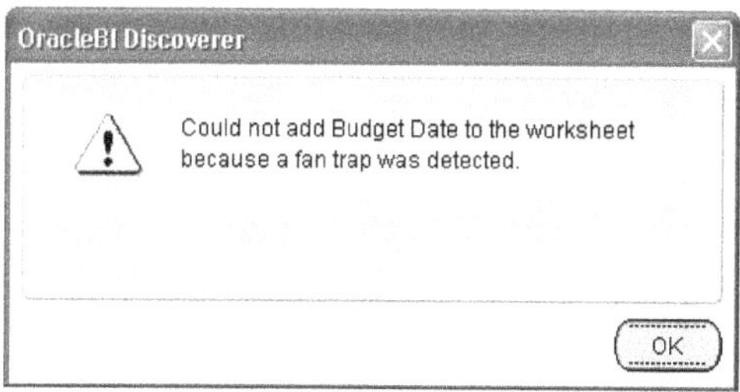


This error tells us that we are trying to create a query that pulls detail information from two parent folders at the same time. Oracle knows that this type of query usually generates incorrect results and so has inserted a trap for this.

To overcome this error and to show you what happens when the fan trap is ignored, next we disabled the fan trap protection. We were able to build and run the query, but the results were totally incorrect. Look at this illustration closely:

| Deptno | Bgt Date | Reason | Budget Amount | Exp Date | Expenses Amt |
|---|---|---|---|---|---|
| 10 | 19-MAR-2012 | EQUIPMENT | 5000 | 16-APR-2012 | 250 |
| | 19-MAR-2012 | EQUIPMENT | 5000 | 28-APR-2012 | 1,000 |
| | 19-MAR-2012 | EQUIPMENT | 5000 | 25-FEB-2012 | 150 |
| | 20-MAR-2012 | TRAVEL | 40000 | 28-APR-2012 | 1,000 |
| | 20-MAR-2012 | TRAVEL | 40000 | 25-FEB-2012 | 150 |
| | 20-MAR-2012 | TRAVEL | 40000 | 16-APR-2012 | 250 |
| | | | | | Sum: |
| 20 | 21-MAR-2012 | TRAVEL | 200 | 12-APR-2012 | 1,025 |
| | 21-MAR-2012 | EQUIPMENT | 2000 | 12-APR-2012 | 1,025 |
| | | | | | Sum: |
| 30 | 15-APR-2012 | TRAVEL | 10000 | 28-APR-2012 | 12,000 |
| | 15-APR-2012 | EQUIPMENT | 25500 | 28-APR-2012 | 12,000 |
| | | | | | Sum: |
| 40 | 24-FEB-2012 | EQUIPMENT | 4250 | 26-APR-2012 | 2,750 |
| | 24-FEB-2012 | TRAVEL | 25000 | 26-APR-2012 | 2,750 |
| | | | | | Sum: |

As you can see, we do indeed have all of the items in the query, but the answer we got for the Sales department is incorrect. If you add up the total amount budgeted for department 10, you will see that this comes to 135,000 (three times more than expected), while for expenses, the amount is 2,800 (twice more than expected). The reason that this has happened is that Discoverer has built a temporary table and made joins in the data for every occurrence of budget and expense (the master folders), by department (the detail folder). Budget is overstated threefold because there are three expense items. Expenses are doubled because there are two budget reasons. This query does not show us anything useful. We don't even get any subtotals being computed! So, we abandoned this query and re-enabled the fan trap protection.

The final example of Oracle's fan trap resolution involves displaying the total budget by department alongside the total expenses. Even with the fan trap detection enabled, Discoverer is still able to generate this query. This is because once again Discoverer rewrote the SQL and used subqueries to generate the correct results. No alert was given during this process, and the illustration that follows shows the results of running the query. As you can see, the totals for both budget and expenses are correct.

| Deptno | Budget Amount | Exp Date | Expenses Amt | Bgt Date |
|---|---|---|---|---|
| 10 | 5000 | 16-APR-2012 | 250 | 19-MAR-2012 |
| | 5000 | 28-APR-2012 | 1,000 | 19-MAR-2012 |
| | 5000 | 25-FEB-2012 | 150 | 19-MAR-2012 |
| | 40000 | 16-APR-2012 | 250 | 20-MAR-2012 |
| | 40000 | 25-FEB-2012 | 150 | 20-MAR-2012 |
| | 40000 | 28-APR-2012 | 1,000 | 20-MAR-2012 |
| | | | Sum: | |
| 40 | 2200 | 12-APR-2012 | 2,050 | 21-MAR-2012 |
| | | | Sum: 2,050 | |
| 60 | 35500 | 28-APR-2012 | 24,000 | 15-APR-2012 |
| | | | Sum: 24,000 | |
| 80 | 29250 | 26-APR-2012 | 5,500 | 24-FEB-2012 |
| | | | Sum: 5,500 | |

### Lack of Documentation

Probably the one thing that will put you at the biggest disadvantage is a lack of adequate documentation. It is essential that you, and preferably your company, keep documentation about queries. It is very common to find users building queries, saving them, using them for a while, and then totally forgetting all about them.

At some point in the future there is a change requirement. Perhaps the person who created the query is no longer with the company, or you find a batch of queries sitting in a folder on your network and you have no idea who created them. So, what do you do? What usually happens is that someone reinvents the wheel—sits down in their cubicle for several weeks and produces a complete new batch of queries.

Adequate documentation could have avoided some of this work. At least recording who did what and why, along with a specimen printout and a list of items and conditions, could have circumvented the need to draft a new batch of queries. If your company has not yet recognized the need for documenting Discoverer queries, that time will come.

When all is said and done, prevention is better than the cure. What a wonderful feeling you will have when you can sit back and relax while your co-workers document their queries, safe in the knowledge that your queries were all documented a long time ago.

# Pivoting and Drilling

Pivoting and drilling are two of the really "nice to use" features of Discoverer. In an experienced user's hands, the tools can be made to manipulate data in ways that were undreamed of only a couple of years ago.

## Pivoting Data

In Chapter 9, we showed you how to move items between the various axes. If you recall, there are three of these: the top axis, the side axis, and the page axis. Simple tables and crosstabs have both side and top axes, even if the side axis on a table is used only to display row numbers. Turning on Page Items opens the third axis, the page axis.

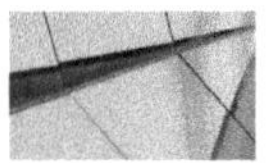

**NOTE**
*The Oracle development team refers to the top axis as the row-edge and the side axis as the column-edge. We have included this comment just in case you may hear the axes being described this way in the future.*

The term given to moving data between these axes is called *pivoting*. Using this technique, you can rearrange your data to reveal relationships that may not be apparent. To many people, pivoting is also known as *dicing*.

If you are using Plus, you can perform what is called *interactive* pivoting. This type of pivot swaps items between axes.

To interactively pivot items in Plus, use the following workflow:

1. Decide on the two items that you want to interactively pivot. For ease of explanation, we will call the first item the *base* item and the other item the *target* item.
2. Click one of the items and hold down the left mouse button.

3. Drag the base item on top of the target item.
4. Release the mouse button. You will see that Discoverer interactively pivots the two items.

## Duplicating Tables and Crosstabs as New Worksheets

There are times when you will build a query that you think is just right and you don't want to touch it for fear of messing it up. However, you can see that with a few changes it will serve another purpose. You have two choices: you can save the workbook as a new file, leaving the original workbook intact, or you can duplicate the query within the workbook. It is a good idea to keep queries with a similar purpose together as a means of data management. Discoverer has made it very easy to duplicate queries as new worksheets within the same workbook.

You can duplicate either a crosstab or a table as a table. You do this through the Duplicate as Table dialog box. The Duplicate as Table dialog box is identical to the Edit Sheet Worksheet dialog box; however, when you finish making your refinements and click OK, you will have a new worksheet in your workbook.

### Duplicating a Worksheet as a Table in Desktop

You have three methods of opening the Duplicate as Table dialog box in Desktop:

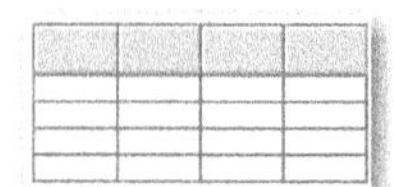

- From the menu bar by clicking Sheet | Duplicate as Table
- From the toolbar by clicking the Duplicate as Table button
- From a pop-up list, which you access by right-clicking the Sheet tab at the lower-left corner of the worksheet and clicking Duplicate As Table

### Duplicating a Worksheet as a Table in Plus

You have two methods of opening the Duplicate as Table dialog box in Plus.

- From the menu bar, select Edit | Duplicate Worksheet, and then click Duplicate As Table.
- From the toolbar, click the drop-down alongside the New Worksheet button, and from the list select Duplicate As Table.

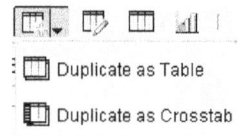

### Duplicating a Worksheet as a Crosstab in Desktop

The method for duplicating a worksheet as a crosstab is virtually identical to that for a table. These are the only differences:

- From the menu bar, select Sheet | Duplicate As Crosstab
- From the toolbar, click the Duplicate As Crosstab button shown here

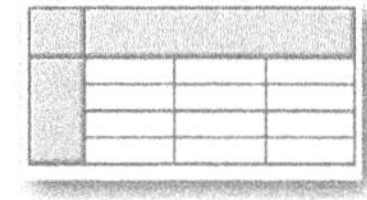

- From a pop-up list, which you access by right-clicking the Sheet tab at the lower-left corner of the worksheet and clicking Duplicate as Crosstab

### Duplicating a Worksheet as a Crosstab in Plus

The method for duplicating a worksheet as a crosstab is virtually identical to that of a table. The only differences are

- From the menu bar, select Edit | Duplicate Worksheet, and then click Duplicate as Crosstab.
- From the toolbar, click the drop-down alongside the New Worksheet button, and from the list select Duplicate As Crosstab, as shown here.

Duplicate as Table
Duplicate as Crosstab

## Renaming Worksheets

If you are going to have multiple worksheets in a workbook, it is a good idea to give them meaningful names. Discoverer gives them the default names of Sheet 1, Sheet 2, and so on. It is a simple task to rename the sheets, and it will help keep you organized within the workbook. We like meaningful names, and Discoverer will allow you to give the sheets very long names. However, just as with filenames, don't get carried away, because if you use too long a sheet name, you will not be able to see the tabs of the other sheets without using a set of navigation arrows in the lower left of the workbook.

### Renaming Worksheets in Discoverer Desktop

You can access the Rename Sheet dialog box in the following three ways:

- From the menu bar, by clicking Sheet | Rename Sheet
- From a pop-up list, which you access by right-clicking the Sheet tab at the lower-left corner of the worksheet and clicking Rename Sheet
- By double-clicking the Sheet tab at the lower-left corner of the worksheet

To rename a worksheet, use the following workflow:

1. Use one of the preceding methods to open the Rename Sheet dialog box.
2. Type in the new worksheet name.
3. Click OK.

### Renaming Worksheets in Discoverer Plus

The Rename Sheet dialog box that you have been used to working with in Desktop has been replaced with the much more comprehensive Worksheet Properties dialog box, which has three tabs. Here you can set sheet gridlines color, row numbers, inline-outline mode, and worksheet description, and you can also view the worksheet identifier and a description. Using the Aggregation tab, you can change the way that Discoverer Plus computes totals. If you find that Discoverer fails to compute a total, you can use this tab to alter the way that the computations are calculated.

To rename a worksheet in Discoverer Plus, use the following workflow:

1. Double-click the Sheet tab at the lower-left corner of the worksheet. This opens the Worksheet Properties dialog box shown here:

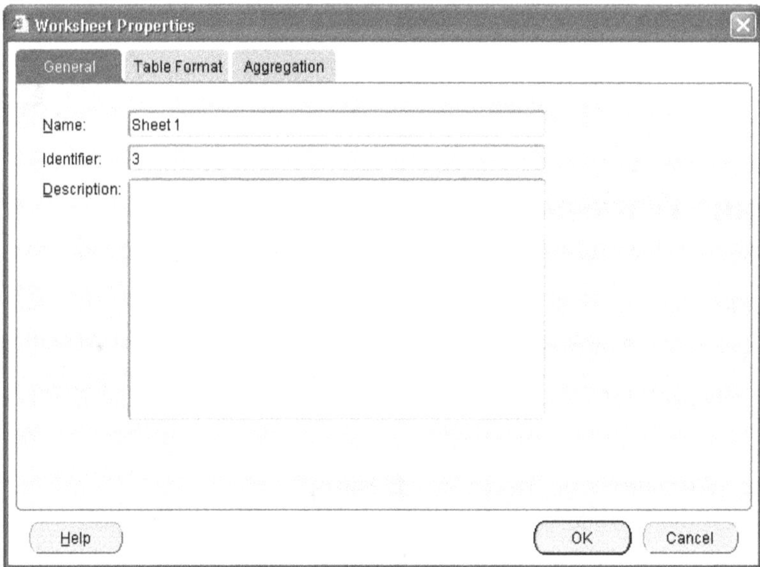


2. Click the General tab.
3. Type in the new worksheet name.
4. Click OK.

# Drilling Into and Out of Data

Drilling into and out of data is a technique that enables you to view more data about a related item. Drilling is also a shortcut for adding another item to your query. For example, suppose you have a query that shows all votes cast for each person in a presidential election and you want to see how those votes were cast in each state. Discoverer will allow you to view this data with a few clicks of the mouse, without having to rebuild the query. Drilling can be done from the Drill dialog box or directly from a drill icon located alongside the headings in your result set.

You can drill to any item in the same folder(s) even if those items are not available in the current hierarchy. This gives you yet another way of adding items to a worksheet, even from Viewer!

## Drilling in Desktop

To drill within Desktop, use the following workflow:

1. Click in the cell, row, or column containing the data you want to drill from.
2. Right-click and select Drill from the drop-down list, or select Sheet | Drill from the menu bar. This opens the Drill dialog box, as shown in Figure 11-2.
3. Make the desired selections.

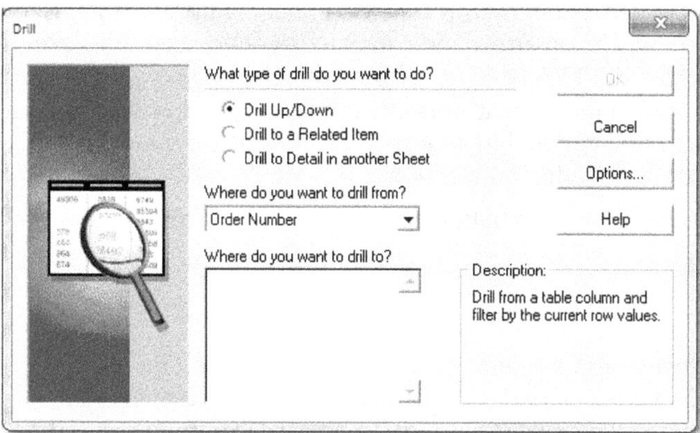


**FIGURE 11-2.** *The Drill dialog box in Desktop*

The Drill dialog box used in Desktop has the following features:

- **Drill Up/Down** Click this radio button to drill to an item in the Where do you want to drill to? selection box. If there are no items available in the selection box, the OK button will be disabled. This option allows you to drill to items that belong to a predefined hierarchy, such as Customer Name to a Region to District. An exciting aspect of Discoverer's drilling capabilities is that you can drill to any level in the hierarchy, skipping the levels you don't need. You can even do filtered drills. This ability to drill up or down a hierarchy is available within the Plus Drill dialog box and also directly from within the heading of any item that is part of a hierarchy.
- **Drill To A Related Item** Click this radio button to drill up or down to an aggregate level to data that is related but is not part of a predefined hierarchy, such as Customer Name to Order Number or City Name to Address. Discoverer will restrict the list of drillable items to only those items that exist within the folders that form the basis of the original query. This ability to drill to a related item is available within the Plus Drill dialog box and also directly from within the heading of any item in Plus.
- **Drill To Detail In Another Sheet** Click this radio button to drill to data in another worksheet. When you click OK, Discoverer opens a New Sheet dialog box that initially contains all of the items that come from the folders in the original query. Before completing the New Sheet dialog box, you should remove unwanted items and rearrange the order. This ability to drill to detail in another sheet is also available within the Plus Drill dialog box.
- **Where do you want to drill from?** The row or column that you were in when you opened the dialog box will appear as the default. To change the item to be drilled from, click the down arrow for a drop-down list of available items. Depending upon whether the item now selected is part of a predefined hierarchy, the content of some of the other boxes may change.
- **Where do you want to drill to?** This is a list of available drill items. The content of the list varies, depending upon other selections you make within the dialog box. For

example, if you check the Drill Up/Down box and select to drill from an item that is part of a predefined hierarchy, this box will contain a list of the items in the hierarchy. Beside each item will be an arrow, indicating whether you can drill up or down to that item. If you opt to drill to a related item, this box will give you a list of the remaining items in the folders used in the current worksheet. Use this to add single items to your worksheet. If you opt to drill to detail in another sheet, this box displays Show Component Rows Of Selected Values as the only option.

- **Options** Clicking this button opens the Desktop Drill Options dialog box, as shown in Figure 11-3.

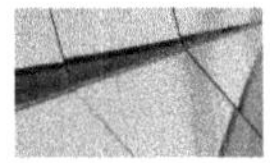

**NOTE**
*Discoverer remembers the settings you make in the Drill Options dialog box, and it uses them as the default each time you drill. Even if you don't open the Drill Options dialog box, these options will still be applied.*

The Desktop Drill Options dialog box allows you to customize the drill results. As shown in Figure 11-3, the Desktop Drill Options dialog box consists of the following areas:

- **When drilling to a new item, current item is** This area allows you to either expand the query to include the new item or replace the current item with the new item.
- **Place drill results in** Here, you decide whether you want the drill results to be displayed in the current worksheet or in a new worksheet.
- **Display results as** If you want to display the results in a new worksheet, in this area you can decide whether to display them as a table or a crosstab.

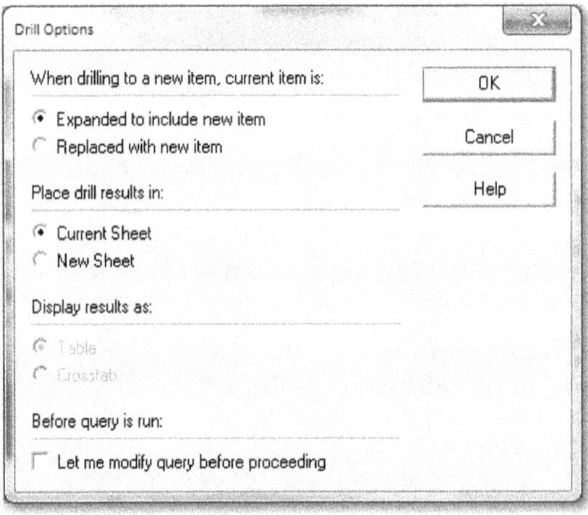


**FIGURE 11-3.** *The Desktop Drill Options dialog box*

- **Before query is run** Tick the box in this section if you want to modify the new worksheet before it runs. When you complete the drill by clicking OK in the Drill dialog box, Discoverer opens the New Sheet dialog box. This box is identical to the Edit Sheet dialog box and allows you to make any edits and modifications you want before the query runs.

## Drilling in Plus

To drill within Plus, use the following workflow:

1. Click in the cell, row, or column containing the data you want to drill from.
2. Right-click and select Drill from the drop-down list, or select Tools | Drill from the menu bar. This opens the Drill dialog box, as shown in Figure 11-4.

The Drill dialog box used in Plus has the following features:

- **Where do you want to drill from?** Use the drop-down list to select the item you want to drill from.
- **Where do you want to drill to?** This drop-down list has four options: Drill Up/Drill Down, Drill To A Related Item, Drill To Detail, and Drill To Link. The drill selection box, located immediately below the drop-down, changes depending upon the selection chosen from the list. Apart from the Drill To Link option, the other three options work the same way as the selections that you can make in the Desktop Drill dialog box described in the previous section. If drill links to other worksheets or to a URL have been enabled, when this option is selected you will be able to drill out using those links.
- **Show Advanced** Clicking this button opens the extended version of the Plus Drill dialog box, as shown in Figure 11-5.

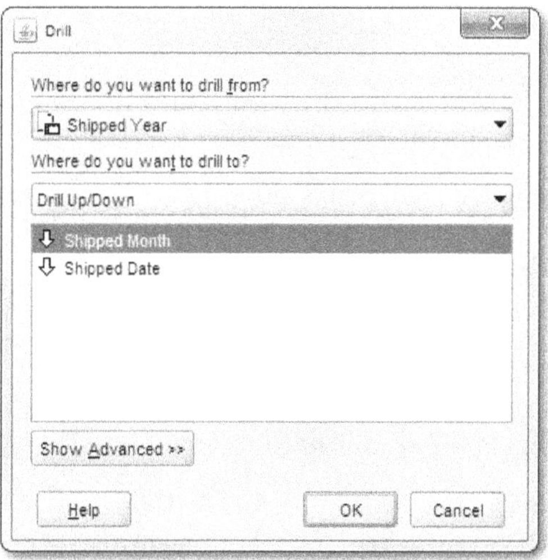


**FIGURE 11-4.** *The Drill dialog box in Plus*

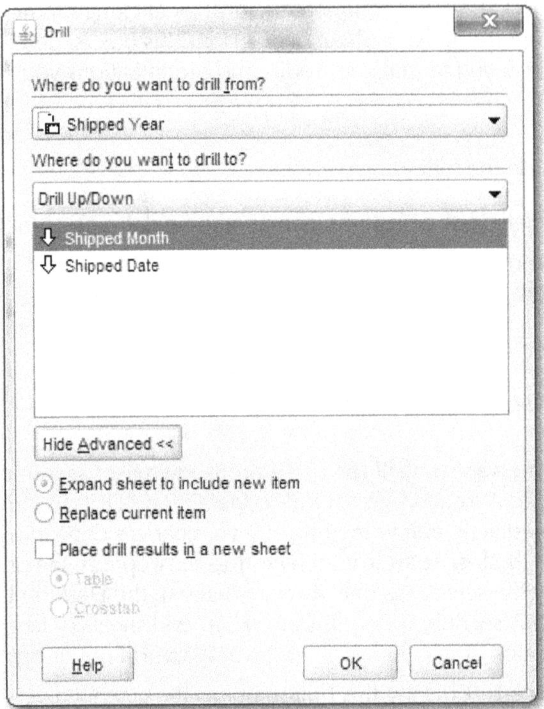


**FIGURE 11-5.** *The Plus extended Drill dialog box*

The Plus extended Drill dialog box has the same functionality as the Desktop Drill Options dialog box but is much tidier and easier to work with. This extended box has the following features:

- **Expand Sheet To Include New Item** Check this radio button if you want Discoverer to expand the sheet to include the new item. This is available only if you select Drill Up/Drill Down or Drill To A Related Item.
- **Replace Current Item** Check this radio button if you want Discoverer to replace the existing item with the item being drilled to. This is available only if you select Drill Up/Drill Down or Drill To A Related Item.
- **Place Drill Results In A New Sheet** Check this box if you want to place the drill results in a new sheet. Having checked this box, you then have to decide whether the new sheet should be a table or a crosstab. If you select Drill To Detail, this box will be checked by default. In addition, the new sheet type will default to the same worksheet you are drilling from. This option is available for all drill types except Drill To Link.

Plus has no equivalent of the Desktop Let Me Modify Query Before Proceeding button. Therefore, if you opt to see the results of the drill in a new worksheet, after clicking OK, the new worksheet will be created immediately, the query will be executed, and the results will be displayed. Further, if you chose Drill To Detail, every single item within the folders used in the current worksheet will now be included within a new worksheet. This can result in a very cumbersome and unwieldy report, especially if you elected to create a new crosstab. Unless your Discoverer administrator has paid dutiful attention when assigning the default positions of data items within the EUL, you may well find that you end up with dozens of items in the top axis of a crosstab, effectively creating an unusable worksheet. You therefore need to take great care when drilling to detail in a new worksheet.

### Drilling from Within the Heading

Drilling directly from within the heading of an item can be done whenever you see the drill icon being displayed alongside the heading. The drill icon looks like a small triangle.

**NOTE**
*In Desktop, the drill icon is displayed only whenever the item is part of a predefined drill hierarchy. In Plus, the drill icon is always available.*

Three types of drilling are available from within the heading:

- Drill using a predefined drill hierarchy
- Drill to related
- Drill by collapsing the data

**Drill Using a Predefined Drill Hierarchy** If the item is part of an existing drill hierarchy, Discoverer will enable the drill icon. Clicking this item allows you to drill to another item within the hierarchy. When drilled, the new item will be included within the current worksheet.

**Drill to Related** This type of drill, accessible from within Plus only, is available from within the heading of every item in the worksheet. When selected, Discoverer displays a pop-up list of all items that exist within the folders that form the basis of the original query. Clicking an item causes Discoverer to include that item within the current worksheet. You cannot select multiple items for inclusion. If you want to include multiple items, you need to repeat the drill for each item.

**NOTE**
*If you get into the habit of keeping the Available Items pane open, you will find that it is far easier to add items to your worksheet from this pane than by using the drill to related method.*

**Drill by Collapsing the Data** This type of drill, accessible from a Plus crosstab only, is available from within the group-sorted items in the side axis. When the pop-up list of drill options is displayed, a new option, Collapse, will be inserted into the list. If you choose this option, Discoverer will remove all of the remaining side items for the row you are in, effectively displaying a subtotal for the item you just collapsed.

Be careful using Collapse, because once the worksheet is collapsed, the only way to return it to its original state is to undo the drill by using Edit | Undo from the menu bar. If you execute multiple consecutive collapses, only the last collapse can be undone. To rectify this situation, you will have to edit the worksheet, remove all of the collapsed items, and then add them back in.

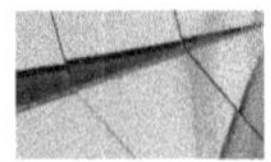

**NOTE**

*Do not save worksheets that contain collapsed items. Because Discoverer handles the collapse by creating multiple SQL statements, if you save a worksheet that has collapsed items, the next time you open that worksheet, Discoverer will be forced to execute multiple SQL queries before it can display any results. This is a common reason for extremely poor worksheet performance.*

## Drilling into Data from a Graph

Discoverer allows you to drill into data from a graph. This is a clever feature for those of us who are visual in the way that we work. Graph drilling is also available in both Plus and Viewer with 11g. You can now single-click (or double-click, depending on where you are in the graph) and drill to a greater or lesser level of detail. Graph drilling follows a drill-and-replace model of drilling. You can choose to drill from the axis labels, from the legend, or even from the series bars (in the case of bar graphs).

To drill into data from a graph, use the following workflow:

1. From the graph that you have created, double-click the item you want to drill from. This opens the Drill dialog box.
2. Determine the type of drill you want to do.
3. Click the Options button in Desktop or the Show Advanced button in Plus to define whether you want to add items in a new sheet.
4. If you are going to use a new sheet, in the New Sheet dialog box, remove any items that are not required and define any other criteria that you want to use.
5. Click OK.

For example, we have a pie graph (see the following illustrations, which show the results in Desktop and then in Plus) showing the status of all of our sales for the third quarter of 2010.

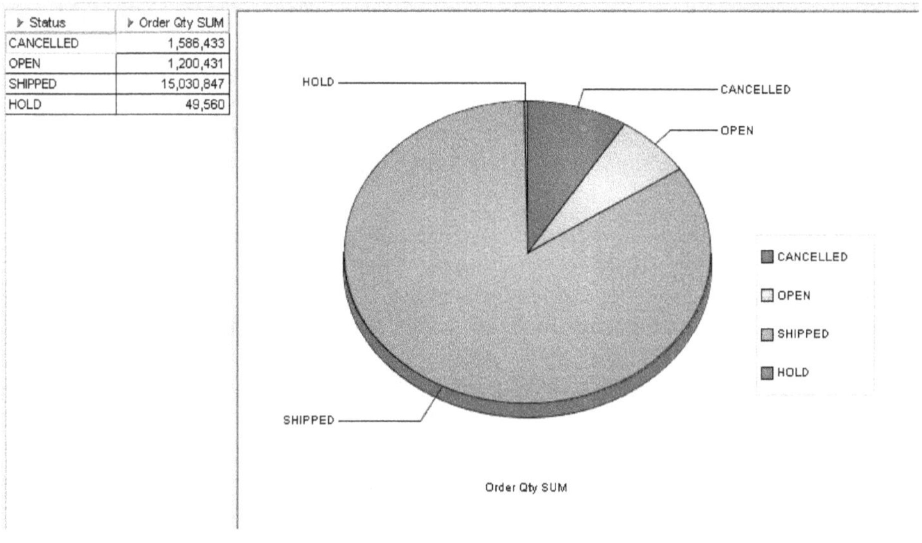

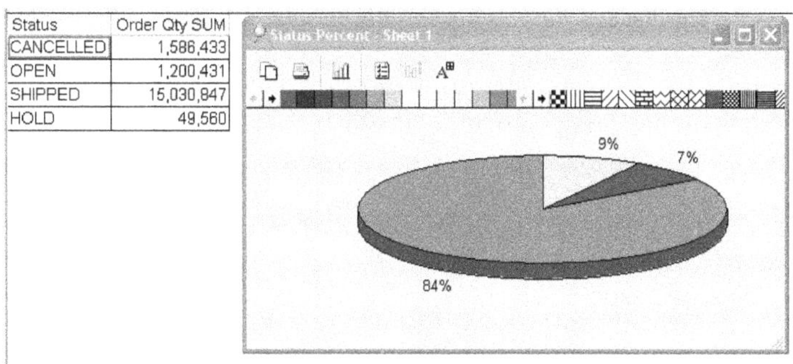


We can see instantly that the cancellations for that quarter are extremely high. When compared to the other totals, cancellations make up the third largest order quantity. Looking then at the third largest piece of the pie graph, it is evident that cancellations are making up more than 9 percent of the total. We want to know why this is so, and we will use Discoverer's drill capability to find out. The process for doing this is simple. Because you are already familiar with the Drill dialog box, we will not explain it again here. However, we will show you the end result of drilling into data from a graph.

First, we double-clicked in the graph on the Cancellations wedge in the pie. This opened the Drill dialog box. Because we wanted to see more of the detail associated with the cancellations, we opted to display the results in a new sheet. Because we believe that analysis is easier in a crosstab, this is the type of worksheet that we selected. Before we completed the drill, we edited the new worksheet and removed the items that did not appear to be of interest. The resulting crosstab is shown next.

Page Items: Status: CANCELLED

| | Order Qty SUM | Cost Price SUM | Selling Price | Margin | Markup | Profit |
|---|---|---|---|---|---|---|
| 1121 | 160 | 1699.20 | 3548.80 | 0.52 | 1.09 | 1849.60 |
| 1267 | 700 | 11158.00 | 24255.00 | 0.54 | 1.17 | 13097.00 |
| 1286 | 1,200 | 19128.00 | 41580.00 | 0.54 | 1.17 | 22452.00 |
| 1685 | 20 | 124.20 | 305.00 | 0.59 | 1.46 | 180.80 |
| 1690 | 6 | 59.28 | 127.50 | 0.54 | 1.15 | 68.22 |
| 1701 | 50 | 621.00 | 1172.50 | 0.47 | 0.89 | 551.50 |
| 1731 | 1,200 | 19128.00 | 41580.00 | 0.54 | 1.17 | 22452.00 |
| 1757 | 1,000 | 12420.00 | 23450.00 | 0.47 | 0.89 | 11030.00 |
| 1802 | 200 | 3188.00 | 6930.00 | 0.54 | 1.17 | 3742.00 |
| 1804 | 50 | 416.50 | 883.00 | 0.53 | 1.12 | 466.50 |
| 1833 | 5 | 79.70 | 173.25 | 0.54 | 1.17 | 93.55 |
| 1836 | 3,400 | 24548.00 | 45900.00 | 0.47 | 0.87 | 21352.00 |
| 1837 | 14,100 | 101802.00 | 190350.00 | 0.47 | 0.87 | 88548.00 |
| 1885 | 1 | 12.42 | 23.45 | 0.47 | 0.89 | 11.03 |

# Hyper-Drilling

*Hyper-drilling* allows a user to drill out from the current worksheet to either another worksheet or a URL. You can use the drill-to-worksheet feature to drill down from a high-level report to see a lower level of data or from a lower-level report to roll up into a higher level of aggregation. The drill-to-URL feature allows a user to drill to an Internet page. Using this feature, you could, for example, decide to drill out to a customer's web site or to one of your own company intranet pages.

The individual drill itself, available in Desktop, Plus, and Viewer, is called a *drill link*. Multiple drill links can exist at the same time, thus enabling you to drill out to several worksheets and, if you want, several URLs. You can follow only one drill path at a time and cannot simultaneously drill out in more than one direction at the same time.

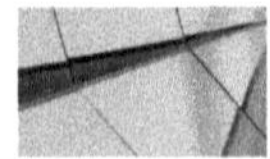

**NOTE**
*User-defined hyper-drills can be created only in Plus. Once they are created, though, you can use any of the end-user tools, Desktop, Plus, or Viewer, to execute that drill.*

A third type of hyper-drill exists, but this one gets created for you by the Discoverer manager. This type of hyper-drill allows a user to drill out to a file. Using this type of drill, you could, for example, drill out to open the customer's contract (stored as a Microsoft Word file) to view the customer's latest credit report (stored as an Excel spreadsheet), or even to send an e-mail to your customer contact via your e-mail system. This section of the book will focus on the hyper-drills that an end user can create. We will cover Discoverer manager–created hyper-drills later in the book.

As previously mentioned, these are the hyper-drills a user can create:

- Drilling out to another worksheet
- Drilling out to a URL

## Drilling Out to Another Worksheet

Effective drilling from one worksheet to another takes a little planning and forethought. We recommend that you take some time to think about what drills you intend to create. In other words, step back and try to see the big picture. You cannot create a hyper-drill if you have nowhere to drill to, so when creating a worksheet hyper-drill, you need to have created and saved the lower-level worksheet first. We know this sounds obvious, but you would be surprised how many people miss this step and jump right into creating the higher-level worksheet.

**NOTE**
*The two worksheets can be in the same workbook or in different workbooks. While the choice is yours, we recommend you think carefully before mixing worksheets with differing intents in the same workbook.*

Having created the drill-to worksheet, you can now create the drill-from worksheet. First, we will show you what the hyper-drill looks like in use. In the following example, we created two workbooks, Drill Master and Drill Detail. The Drill Master, as you can see in the next illustration, shows the selling price by Region and District.

**Drill Master - All Regions**

| | ▸ Region | ▸ District | ▸ Selling Price |
|---|---|---|---|
| 1 | EUROPE | ▸ EU-EAST | 7,623,655 |
| 2 | EUROPE | ▸ EU-NORTH | 47,977,651 |
| 3 | EUROPE | ▸ EU-SOUTH | 28,554,612 |
| 4 | FAR EAST | ▸ FE-ALL | 32,548,685 |
| 5 | NORTH AMERICA | ▸ NA-NORTH | 95,115,056 |
| 6 | NORTH AMERICA | ▸ NA-SOUTH | 40,278,515 |
| 7 | SOUTH AMERICA | ▸ SA-ALL | 22,572,670 |

If you take a closer look at the cells in the District column, you will notice that there is a small upright triangle alongside the data in each cell. This is the hyperlink button. Clicking this pops up a list of the available hyperlinks. As you can see next, in our case we have only one link, a link that allows us to Drill to Year.

**Drill Master - All Regions**

| | Region | District | Selling Price |
|---|---|---|---|
| 1 | EUROPE | EU-EAST | 7,623,655 |
| 2 | EUROPE | EU-NORTH | 47,977,651 |
| 3 | EUROPE | EU-SOUTH | 28,554,612 |
| 4 | FAR EAST | FE-ALL | 32,548,685 |
| 5 | NORTH AMERICA | NA-NORTH | 95,115,056 |
| 6 | NORTH AMERICA | Drill to year | 278,515 |
| 7 | SOUTH AMERICA | | ,572,670 |

If this link is followed in Viewer or Desktop, a second worksheet is automatically opened, displaying the selling price by year for the District that was chosen in the higher-level worksheet. In Plus you will get a warning telling you that you are about to close the current worksheet and open another one. You will be prompted "Do you wish to continue?"

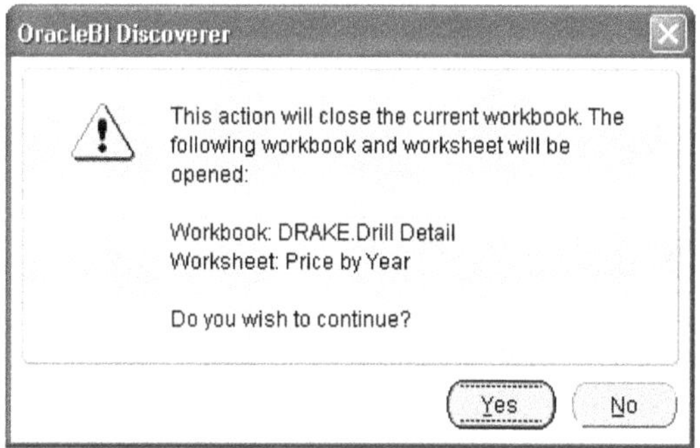

OracleBI Discoverer
This action will close the current workbook. The following workbook and worksheet will be opened:
Workbook: DRAKE.Drill Detail
Worksheet: Price by Year
Do you wish to continue?
Yes
No


If you click Yes, Discoverer will close the current worksheet and open the drilled-to worksheet. Discoverer will also pass on any parameter or cell values as necessary. Following the link through to the lower-level workbook, you can see that Discoverer displays the selling price by year for the district that we clicked in the higher-level worksheet.

**Drill Detail - Price by Year**

Page Items: Region: NORTH AMERICA

| | District | Year | Selling Price |
|---|---|---|---|
| 1 | NA-SOUTH | FY1998 | 935,035 |
| 2 | NA-SOUTH | FY1999 | 844,362 |
| 3 | NA-SOUTH | FY2000 | 2,062,873 |
| 4 | NA-SOUTH | FY2001 | 2,192,424 |
| 5 | NA-SOUTH | FY2002 | 4,391,377 |
| 6 | NA-SOUTH | FY2003 | 6,855,802 |
| 7 | NA-SOUTH | FY2004 | 13,557,250 |
| 8 | NA-SOUTH | FY2005 | 9,439,393 |
| 9 | | | 40,278,515 |

## Building a Hyperlink to Another Worksheet

To build a hyperlink to another worksheet, follow this workflow:

1. Build the lower-level worksheet and note the parameters you want to pass.
2. Create and save a higher-level worksheet.
3. Execute the higher-level worksheet so that data is displayed onscreen.
4. Locate the cell from where you want your users to be able to drill.
5. Right-click the cell and, from the pop-up menu, select Manage Links. The Manage Links dialog box, as shown in Figure 11-6, will now open.
6. The Manage Links dialog box is the place where you create, edit, delete, or reorder the links in your worksheet. It has the following areas:
   - **Item** This is the name of a worksheet item.
   - **New Link** Click this button to create a new hyperlink.

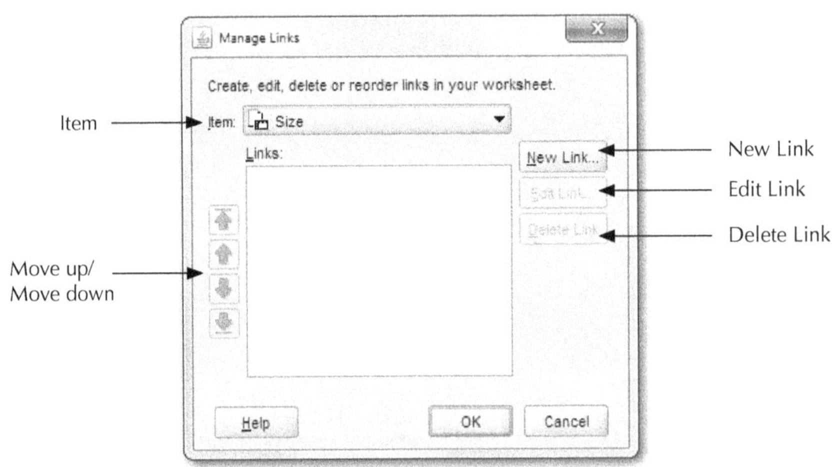


**FIGURE 11-6.** *Manage Links dialog box*

- **Edit Link** Click this button to edit an existing hyperlink.
- **Delete Link** Click this button to delete an existing hyperlink.
- **A set of Move Up/Move Down buttons** If there are multiple links from the same items, these buttons allow you to order the list of links. You can move an item up or down one place, or you can move an item to the top or to the bottom of the list.
- **OK** Click this button to save the changes that you have made and return to Discoverer Plus.

7. Click the New Link button. This opens the New Link dialog box, as shown in Figure 11-7.
8. The New Link dialog box is where you create a new hyperlink. It has the following areas:
   - **What would you like to name this link?** Type a meaningful name into this area. The name that you type here is the name that will appear in the list of hyperlinks when the user clicks in the cell.
   - **Where do you want to link to?** Your valid options are Worksheet and URL. Use the drop-down button to change the selection.
   - **Destination** This area will be displayed only when you are creating a URL link. Discoverer automatically inserts the characters *http://* and is waiting for you to type the remainder of the URL.
   - **Destination Workbook** This area will be displayed only when you are creating a worksheet link. Use the Browse button to select the workbook containing the worksheet that you want to use.
   - **Destination Worksheet** This area will be displayed only when you are creating a worksheet link. It will be accessible only after you have selected the workbook that contains the worksheet you want to use. Use the drop-down button to select the worksheet you will be using.

**FIGURE 11-7.** *The New Link dialog box for drilling to a worksheet*

- **Parameters** If the worksheet that you are drilling to has parameters, you can optionally choose what values Discoverer will pass to those parameters whenever the user drills through. You are not mandated to preassign any parameters. If you choose not to preassign the parameters, then the user who is following your link will be required to supply the parameters at run time. However, should you decide to preassign parameters, and we recommend that you do, click the Parameters button. Discoverer will display the Parameters dialog box shown next.

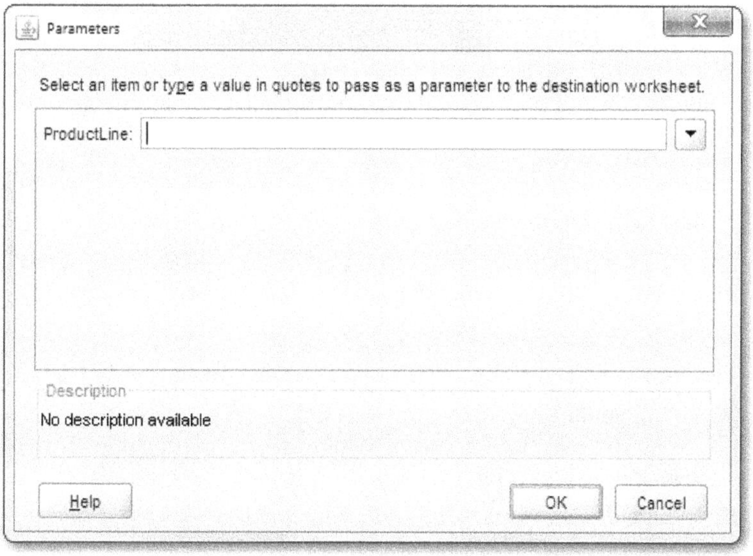

9. The Parameters dialog box enables you to preassign values to the parameters that exist in the lower-level worksheet. You assign one of the following values:
   - The parameter that was accepted as input to the current worksheet
   - The cell value from the current worksheet
10. To pick a value to pass to the next worksheet, click the drop-down button alongside the parameter. Discoverer will now display the valid values that can be passed. These will be displayed in the following order:
    - Data points
    - Cell values
    - Parameter values
11. Continue assigning values to the parameters in the lower-level worksheet. When all parameters have been assigned a value, click OK to close the New Link dialog box. Then, click OK to close the Manage Links dialog box.

**NOTE**
*The OK button will be grayed out until you have completed the New Link dialog box.*

## Drilling Out to a URL

Drilling out to a URL is very straightforward. If the worksheet that you are in contains a URL hyper-drill, you will know because Discoverer displays a different icon than for a worksheet hyper-drill. In this illustration you can see two hyper-drills, one for a worksheet and one for a URL.

### Building a Hyperlink to a URL

To create a hyperlink to a URL, follow this workflow:

1. Build the lower-level worksheet and note the parameters that you want to pass.
2. Create and save a higher-level worksheet.
3. Execute the higher-level worksheet so that data is displayed onscreen.
4. Locate the cell from where you want your users to be able to drill.
5. Right-click the cell and, from the pop-up menu, select Manage Links. The Manage Links dialog box, as shown earlier in Figure 11-6, will now open.
6. Click the New Link button. This opens the New Link dialog box, as shown in Figure 11-8.
7. The New Link dialog box is where you create a new hyperlink. It has the following areas:
   - **What would you like to name this link?** Type a meaningful name into this area. The name you type here is the name that will appear in the list of hyperlinks when the user clicks in the cell.
   - **Where do you want to link to?** Your valid options are Worksheet and URL. Use the drop-down button to change the selection to URL.

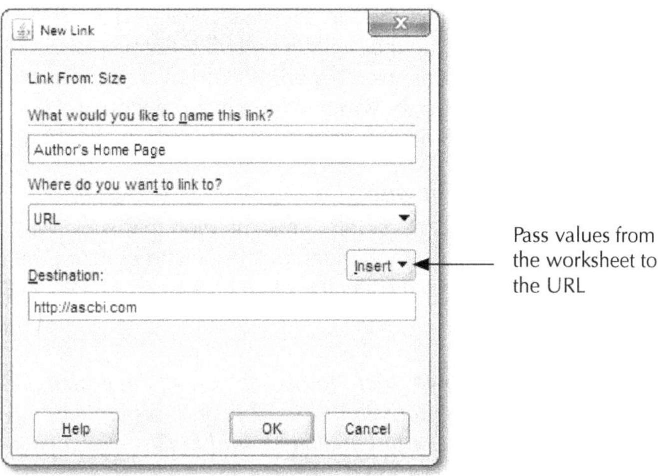


**FIGURE 11-8.** *New Link dialog box for drilling to a URL*

- **Destination** This area will be displayed only when you are creating a URL link. Discoverer automatically inserts the characters *http://* and is waiting for you to type the remainder of the URL.

8. Click OK to complete the New Link dialog box.
9. Click OK to close the Manage Links dialog box.

# Drilling Out to an Application

If you are used to working with an Internet browser, you will know that a link such as file:///C:/Book/pfile.txt will work. Unfortunately, Discoverer's end-user URL hyperlink functionality does not allow drilling to an application in this method. Do not despair, however, because your Discoverer manager can create hyper-drills to external applications. As mentioned earlier, we will not explain how to create these in this section, because this functionality will be explained later in the book.

So, how can you tell whether your Discoverer manager has created an application hyperlink for you? The answer to this depends upon whether you are using Desktop, Plus, or Viewer to execute the query.

## Drilling to a File in Desktop

If you are using Desktop, Discoverer displays the name of the file that it will call and also inserts an icon alongside the item. If you are familiar with previous versions of Desktop, you will be disappointed to know that the application icons that used to be displayed no longer appear to be used. Now only one icon is shown for all file types, the same icon that is used for hyper-drilling to a worksheet.

### Drilling to a File in Plus

In Plus, Discoverer displays the same icon as displayed in Desktop. However, Discoverer does not display the name of the file that will be called. If the worksheet is a table and you place your cursor over a cell that contains a hyperlink, Discoverer will show you the file that it will call. If the worksheet is a crosstab, you need to click the icon and then select Drill To Link from the pop-up box. Only then will Discoverer show you the name of the file that it will call.

### Drilling to a File in Viewer

In Viewer, Discoverer displays only the same icon that is displayed in Desktop and Plus. When the icon is clicked, a very small blank box opens up beneath the icon. If you click this box, Discoverer will attempt to display the file that is listed.

**NOTE**

*Neither Plus nor Viewer seem to be able to call the e-mail application. This seems to be the domain of Desktop, and this limitation is a great pity because the ability to e-mail from within Discoverer is one of Desktop's best, if little known, features.*

## Summary

In this chapter you saw how to further manipulate your queries to make them more powerful. You saw how to add and remove items from your queries and the most common problems associated with doing so. You also learned about the fan trap and how to avoid it, as well as possible solutions to this problem.

You learned how pivoting data items between axes allows you to view the same data in different ways. You also saw how sometimes when pivoting the data items there are no data points displayed at all. It happens to us all, so work with it and become more expert; then, your queries can become more meaningful.

We showed you how to duplicate tables and crosstabs. This is a simple process, and because so many queries can be created using almost the same data, you should try it. This will keep you from creating almost the same workbook over and over and help you to organize your work. Another method of organization is renaming workbooks within worksheets. You were taught how a few simple steps will save you time and possible frustration in the future.

Finally, you saw how to drill into data to "dig deeper" into a data item. Drilling is an excellent way to get a closer look at a particular piece of the data. You also learned how easy it is to drill from a graph. Using the visual approach can sometimes keep you from missing something that would not jump out at you if it were viewed only as numbers or text.

In the next chapter, you will learn the power of creating conditions, from the simple to the complex.

# CHAPTER 12

# Building Effective Conditions

After refining the query items and pivoting the data, perhaps the next most common way to refine a query is to refine the conditions. The ability to add, edit, or remove conditions is one of the things you need to master in order to become an expert in Discoverer.

In Chapter 4, we introduced you to the Workbook Wizard. One of the essential steps that you were shown was setting user-defined conditions. However, in that chapter, we advised you to create only enough conditions to avoid "the query from the Twilight Zone." Those conditions were very simple. In this chapter, we will show you how to build effective conditions and explain all of the options that are available to you.

# Adding Conditions

The most frequently used way of adding conditions is to use the Conditions dialog box, but as you will see in this section, this is not the only way.

There are, in fact, three ways to add conditions to a Discoverer query. These are as follows:

- Using Show Values from a drop-down list
- Using the Conditions area buttons on the analysis bar
- Clicking New in the Conditions dialog box

## Using Show Values to Add a Condition in Desktop

This menu item is probably one of the least known yet, at the same time, one of the best features of Discoverer Desktop. It is also one of the easiest ways to create new conditions. While this feature has not yet been added to Plus, in Plus you have the Available Items and Selected Items panes that you do not have in Desktop.

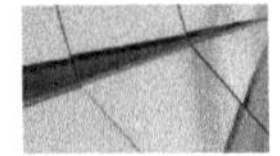

**NOTE**
*Conditions can be created, using Show Values, only for items that have a list of values. If you have a data item that does not have a list of values, you should ask your Discoverer administrator if it is possible to have such a list made available. Until a list of values exists, you will not see the Show Items menu option.*

Whenever you add conditions using this method in Desktop, Discoverer opens the Values dialog box. As shown in Figure 12-1, this dialog box consists of the following features:

- **Select values for** Discoverer displays the full list of values for the item concerned, along with a check box indicating whether the item is already being used in the query. If there is no active condition currently in use for the item concerned, Discoverer automatically checks all of the boxes. If there is a condition on the item, Discoverer checks only those items that are constrained by the current condition. Discoverer then allows you to manually check and uncheck items using the mouse.
- **Select All** Click this button if you want Discoverer to include all values for the item in your query.

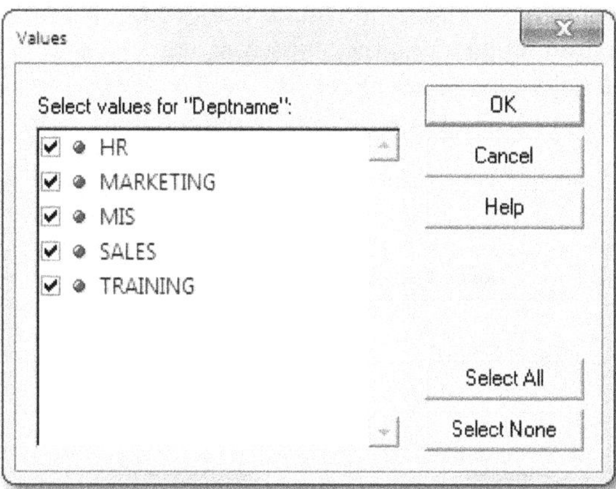


**FIGURE 12-1.** *Discoverer Desktop Values dialog box*

- **Select None** Click this button if you want Discoverer to include no values at all for the item in your query. Doing this and clicking OK causes Discoverer to return nothing. This option should be used only as a means of clearing the current selections, before manually selecting the items that you want.

To use Show Values to add a new condition to a query, use the following workflow:

1. Right-click the heading for any axis item that has a list of values.
2. From the drop-down menu, select Show Values. This opens the Values dialog box as displayed in Figure 12-1.
3. Make the desired selections.
4. Click OK. Discoverer will now create a condition based upon your selections and then rerun the query.

We'll show you how quickly you can modify a query and add new conditions using Show Values. We have started with a very simple query containing just the department name, department number, expense amount and date, and no conditions. This caused Discoverer to display a list of all expenses currently on file. There are only six of these, and you can see here that this is a very simple query:

| | Dept Number | Department | Expenses | Expense Date |
|---|---|---|---|---|
| 1 | 10 | SALES | 150.00 | 25-FEB-2012 |
| 2 | 10 | SALES | 250.00 | 16-APR-2012 |
| 3 | 10 | SALES | 1000.00 | 28-APR-2012 |
| 4 | 20 | HR | 1025.00 | 12-APR-2012 |
| 5 | 30 | MIS | 12000.00 | 28-APR-2012 |
| 6 | 40 | MARKETING | 2750.00 | 26-APR-2012 |

To demonstrate how easy it is to add a condition using Show Values, we right-clicked the heading for the department name and selected Show Values from the drop-down list. This opened the Values dialog box. Examining the contents of the box, you can see (in Figure 12-1) that all of the departments, as you would expect, are checked.

Next, we unchecked the box alongside the MIS department.

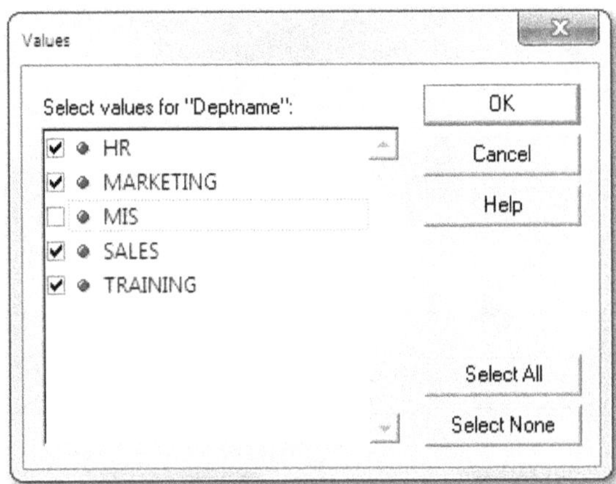


After we clicked OK, Discoverer reran the revised query, omitting the MIS department from the result. Opening the Conditions dialog box, you can see that Discoverer has indeed created a new condition for using the IN expression.

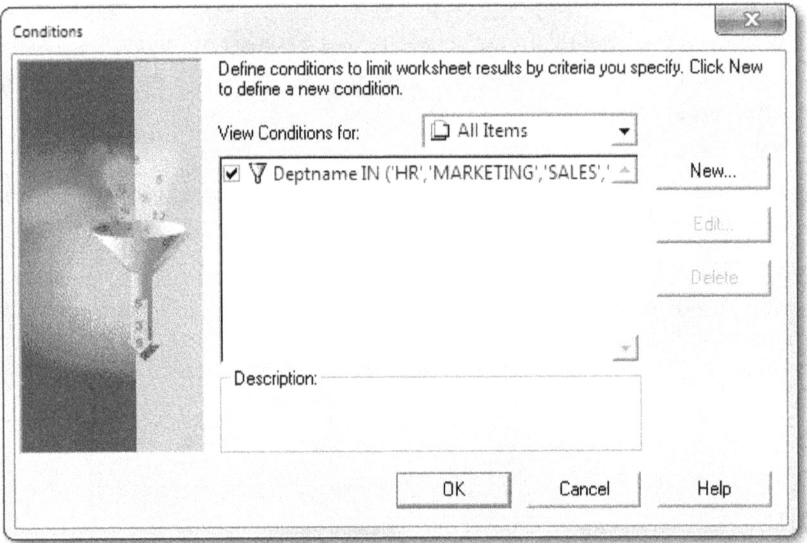


We'll now revise the query again, by once more opening the Values dialog box and changing the criteria for the department. This time we will check the MIS department but uncheck both Marketing and Training. Taking a close look at the Conditions dialog box that follows, you can see that Discoverer did not amend the original condition. Instead, Discoverer created a new condition and deactivated the original one.

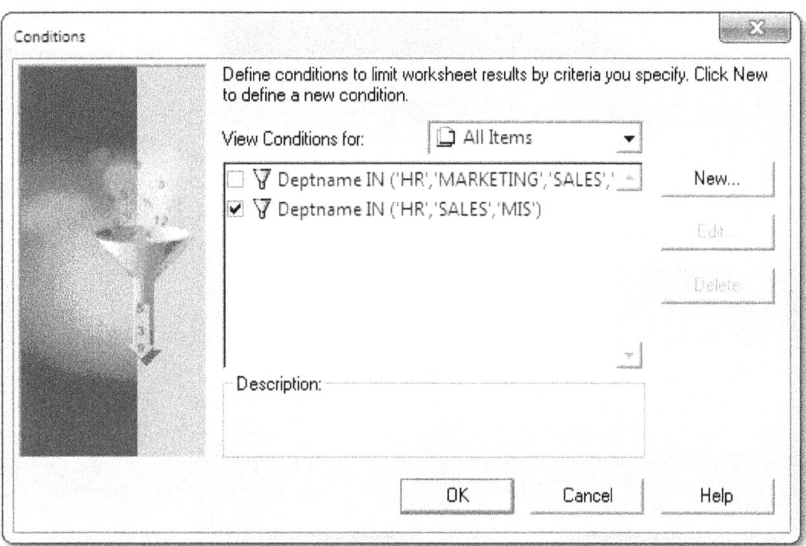


To make the situation even more complicated, we reopened the Values dialog box and re-created the situation as it was a few steps ago. That is, we checked all departments except MIS. Looking at the following illustration, you can see that Discoverer has created a third condition and deactivated the second one:

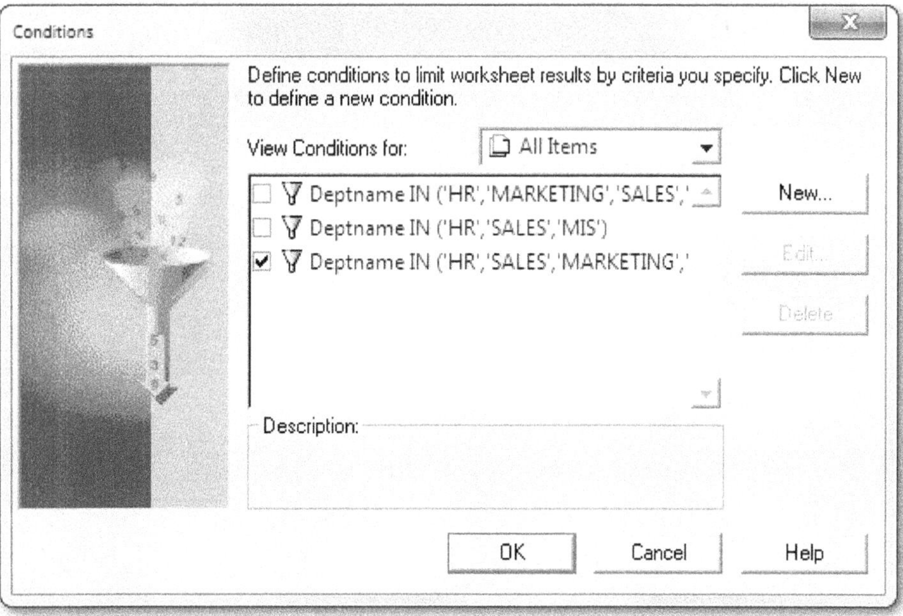

This new condition has the same constraint set as the first condition we created, yet Discoverer did not recognize this. This fault of Discoverer—to not be able to detect that a condition already exists—is the only drawback that we can see to stop us from recommending that you always create conditions using Show Values.

Be aware when using Show Values that these conditions are created when using the IN expression. When using IN, you are restricted to using 254 items. If you have more than 254 items, Discoverer will report an error. You will have to use a different construct, perhaps using a complex condition.

## Adding Conditions Using the Toolbar

The analysis bar in Discoverer Desktop and the Conditions toolbar button in both Desktop and Plus offer you another way to create conditions.

As we explained in Chapter 9, the Desktop analysis bar has four areas. The fourth area, shown in Figure 12-2, is what we call the Conditions area. Chapter 9 introduced you to the analysis bar and gave a brief description of each of the four areas.

In Plus, there is no separate analysis bar; instead, there are four buttons on the toolbar, each with its own unique set of drop-downs. Each drop-down contains the buttons that are available on the Desktop analysis bar. We think this is a great idea, as it requires fewer toolbar buttons and allows for more viewable real estate space for building and executing your query. Figure 12-3 shows the Conditions button and its drop-down of condition types.

The Conditions area of the toolbars has seven buttons; each button allows you to create conditions based on whether terms are equal (=), nonequal (<>), less than (<), less than or equal to (<=), greater than (>), or greater than or equal to (>=), plus a button to launch the Conditions dialog box. In Desktop, the first six buttons are active only when a column, row, or cell is highlighted. In Plus, these six buttons are always active. In both versions, however, the Conditions button is always active.

**NOTE**
*In Plus, if you click one of the six buttons without a column, row, or cell being highlighted, Discoverer opens the New Condition dialog box and waits for you to define the condition manually. This is another great feature and one we are sure you will love.*

### Using the Buttons to Create a New Condition in Desktop

Clicking one of the first six condition buttons opens the New Condition dialog box, which is described later in the chapter. When you enter the box as a result of clicking one of the buttons,

**FIGURE 12-2.** *Conditions area of the Desktop analysis toolbar*

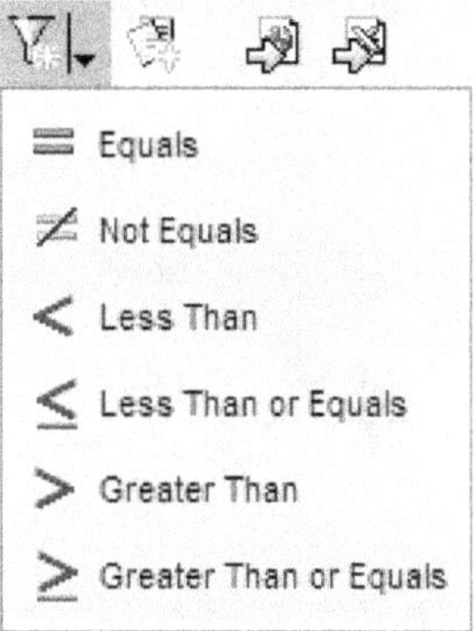


**FIGURE 12-3.** *Conditions drop-down area of the Plus toolbar*

you will find that all three of the basic components of a condition (the item, the expression, and the value) have been completed for you. All that is required to complete the condition is to click OK.

As we explained, clicking in a data cell or a column or row heading activates the main Conditions buttons on the analysis bar. We gave you a simple example of its use in Chapter 9, but to save your having to go back to that section, we will give you that workflow once again.

To create a condition using the Desktop analysis bar, use the following workflow:

1. Click either a column or row heading or any cell.
2. Click the button for the condition you want to apply. Discoverer opens the New Condition dialog box and fills in as much information as it can.
3. Amend the condition if required.
4. Click OK. Discoverer now creates the condition and executes the query.

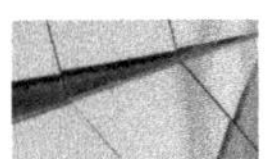

**NOTE**
*If you want to make other changes to the query, you must cancel the running of the query. To do this, click Cancel while the query is running. When prompted to return the query to its original state, click No.*

We'll give you an example. We built the following crosstab of the total quantity ordered, by product and by order status. As you can see, all of the buttons in the Conditions area of the analysis bar, except the Conditions button, are inactive.

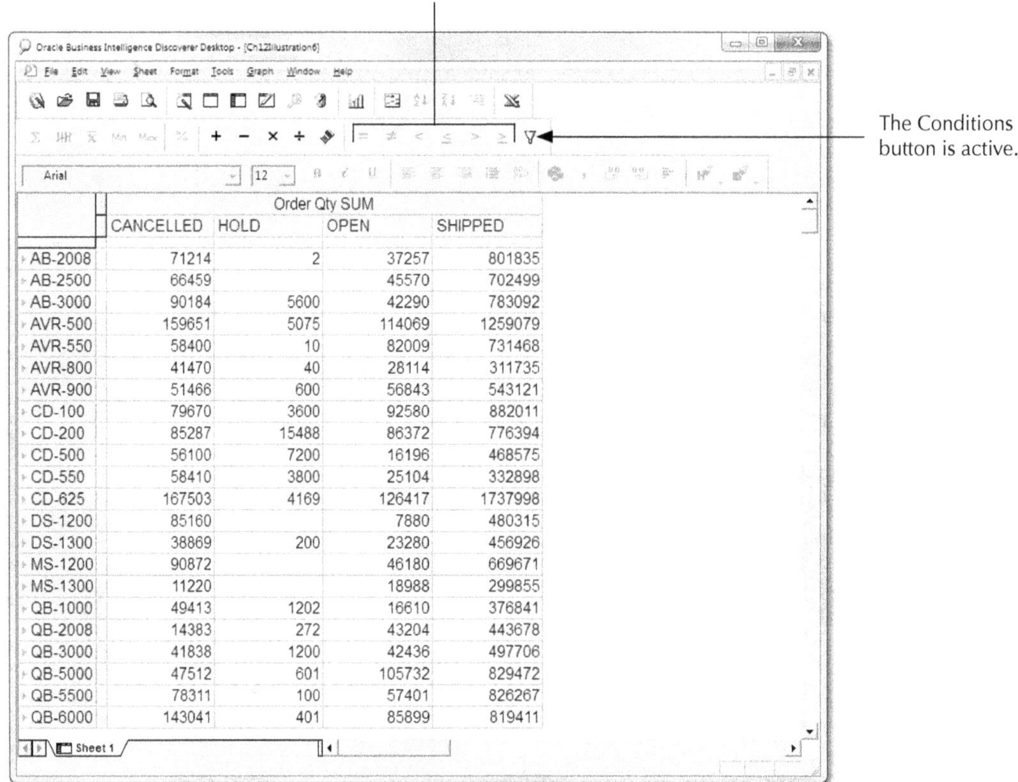
All six condition buttons are inactive.
The Conditions button is active.
Oracle Business Intelligence Discoverer Desktop - [Ch12Illustration6]
Sheet 1

| | Order Qty SUM | | | |
|---|---|---|---|---|
| | CANCELLED | HOLD | OPEN | SHIPPED |
| AB-2008 | 71214 | 2 | 37257 | 801835 |
| AB-2500 | 66459 | | 45570 | 702499 |
| AB-3000 | 90184 | 5600 | 42290 | 783092 |
| AVR-500 | 159651 | 5075 | 114069 | 1259079 |
| AVR-550 | 58400 | 10 | 82009 | 731468 |
| AVR-800 | 41470 | 40 | 28114 | 311735 |
| AVR-900 | 51466 | 600 | 56843 | 543121 |
| CD-100 | 79670 | 3600 | 92580 | 882011 |
| CD-200 | 85287 | 15488 | 86372 | 776394 |
| CD-500 | 56100 | 7200 | 16196 | 468575 |
| CD-550 | 58410 | 3800 | 25104 | 332898 |
| CD-625 | 167503 | 4169 | 126417 | 1737998 |
| DS-1200 | 85160 | | 7880 | 480315 |
| DS-1300 | 38869 | 200 | 23280 | 456926 |
| MS-1200 | 90872 | | 46180 | 669671 |
| MS-1300 | 11220 | | 18988 | 299855 |
| QB-1000 | 49413 | 1202 | 16610 | 376841 |
| QB-2008 | 14383 | 272 | 43204 | 443678 |
| QB-3000 | 41838 | 1200 | 42436 | 497706 |
| QB-5000 | 47512 | 601 | 105732 | 829472 |
| QB-5500 | 78311 | 100 | 57401 | 826267 |
| QB-6000 | 143041 | 401 | 85899 | 819411 |

Assume that we wanted to print the order quantities for what is currently open. We need to have a condition where the status is OPEN. This is a very simple condition to build. Following our workflow outlined earlier, we did the following:

1. We clicked the cell containing the status OPEN. This caused Discoverer to activate the conditions buttons.
2. We next clicked the = button. This opened the New Condition dialog box. As you can see here, Discoverer correctly populated the Item, Condition, and Value(s) boxes for us.

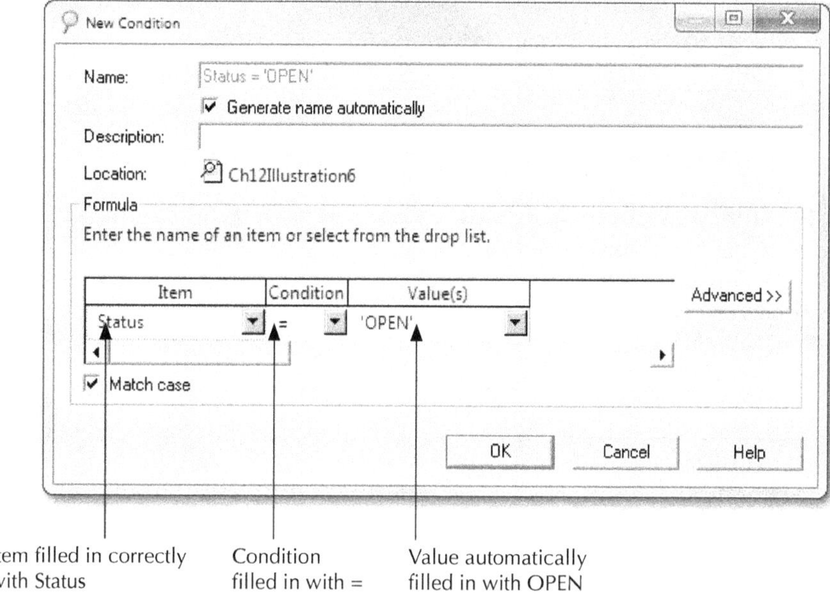


3. There is nothing to amend because Discoverer has created everything we need.
4. To complete the condition, we clicked OK. As you can see, Discoverer adjusted the query for us and created a list of only the open order quantities. We could now send this list to our planning department, which would ensure that we had enough purchase orders to satisfy the demand.

| | Order Qty SUM |
|---|---|
| | OPEN |
| AB-2008 | 37257 |
| AB-2500 | 45570 |
| AB-3000 | 42290 |
| AVR-500 | 114069 |
| AVR-550 | 82009 |
| AVR-800 | 28114 |
| AVR-900 | 56843 |
| CD-100 | 92580 |
| CD-200 | 86372 |
| CD-500 | 16196 |
| CD-550 | 25104 |
| CD-625 | 126417 |
| DS-1200 | 7880 |
| DS-1300 | 23280 |
| MS-1200 | 46180 |
| MS-1300 | 18988 |

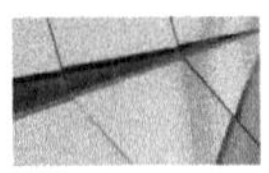

**NOTE**
*Be careful when using the Conditions area buttons. Regarding Show Values, Discoverer is not smart enough to recognize that a condition already exists. If we repeat the preceding exercise, clicking Open, followed by the = symbol, Discoverer will create another condition identical to the first.*

## Using the Toolbar Buttons to Create a New Condition in Plus

Using the toolbar buttons to create new conditions in Plus is more intuitive and requires fewer steps than in Desktop. It is fully automated with the click of a button. This does not, however, mean you cannot refine the condition later.

To create conditions with the Plus toolbar buttons, use the following workflow:

1. Click either a column or row heading or any cell.
2. Click the button for the condition you want to apply. The conditions will be applied automatically.

If you have the Available Items pane open, click the Conditions tab and look in the My Conditions area. You will see that a condition has been created and that it has a check mark to the side of the condition name. This means that the condition is in use. If the condition needs refinement, you can open it for editing.

**NOTE**
*If you have the Selected Items pane open, you will also see the condition get added to the list of selected items.*

We will use the same example we gave in the preceding section on Desktop. We built the following crosstab of total quantity ordered, by product and by order status:

| | Order Qty SUM | | | |
|---|---|---|---|---|
| | CANCELLED | HOLD | OPEN | SHIPPED |
| AB-2008 | 71214 | 2 | 37257 | 801835 |
| AB-2500 | 66459 | NULL | 45570 | 702499 |
| AB-3000 | 90184 | 5600 | 42290 | 783092 |
| AVR-500 | 159651 | 5075 | 114069 | 1259079 |
| AVR-550 | 58400 | 10 | 82009 | 731468 |
| AVR-800 | 41470 | 40 | 28114 | 311735 |
| AVR-900 | 51466 | 600 | 56843 | 543121 |
| CD-100 | 79670 | 3600 | 92580 | 882011 |
| CD-200 | 85287 | 15488 | 86372 | 776394 |
| CD-500 | 56100 | 7200 | 16196 | 468575 |
| CD-550 | 58410 | 3800 | 25104 | 332898 |
| CD-625 | 167503 | 4169 | 126417 | 1737998 |
| DS-1200 | 85160 | NULL | 7880 | 480315 |
| DS-1300 | 38869 | 200 | 23280 | 456926 |
| MS-1200 | 90872 | NULL | 46180 | 669671 |
| MS-1300 | 11220 | NULL | 18988 | 299855 |
| QB-1000 | 49413 | 1202 | 16610 | 376841 |
| QB-2008 | 14383 | 272 | 43204 | 443678 |
| QB-3000 | 41838 | 1200 | 42436 | 497706 |
| QB-5000 | 47512 | 601 | 105732 | 829472 |
| QB-5500 | 78311 | 100 | 57401 | 826267 |
| QB-6000 | 143041 | 401 | 85899 | 819411 |

Let's assume we wanted to print the order quantities for what is currently open. We need to have a condition where the status is OPEN. This is a very simple condition to build. Following our workflow outlined earlier, we did the following:

1. We clicked the cell containing the status OPEN.
2. We next clicked the drop-down arrow for the Conditions button and selected = Equals from the drop-down list. The query runs automatically and creates a list of only the open order quantities. We could now send this list to our planning department, which would ensure that we had enough purchase orders to satisfy the demand.

**NOTE**
*As with Desktop, Discoverer Plus is not smart enough to recognize that a condition already exists. If we repeat the preceding exercise, Discoverer Plus will create another condition identical to the first.*

# Using the Conditions Dialog Box to Add a Condition in Desktop and Plus

The third way to add new conditions to your query is via the Conditions dialog box. In fact, if you want to use Advanced conditions, you can create them only using the Conditions dialog box. To open this box, use one of the following three methods:

- Click the Conditions button on the analysis bar in Desktop, or click the Conditions toolbar button in Plus.
- From the menu bar, select Tools | Conditions.
- Use the Conditions tab on the Edit Sheet/Worksheet dialog box.

  In Plus only, there is a fourth way to add a new condition. From the Available Items pane, click the Conditions tab, and then from anywhere in the pane, right-click. From the pop-up you should select New Condition.

## Creating a Condition Using the Conditions Dialog Box or Conditions Tab

When creating conditions using the Desktop Conditions dialog box or the Plus Conditions tab, you should use the following workflow:

1. If you are working in Plus, click the New Condition button on the toolbar. The New Condition dialog box will open, and you should proceed to step 4.
2. If you are working in Desktop, click the Conditions button on the analysis bar. The Conditions dialog box will open. If you know the item on which you want to build the condition, from the View Conditions for drop-down list of the Conditions dialog box, select the item you want to apply the condition to. If you do not yet know the item or you want to choose an item that is not being used within the worksheet, proceed to the next step.
3. In Desktop click New.
4. Discoverer will open the New Condition dialog box, as shown in Figures 12-4 and 12-5. In Desktop, Discoverer automatically inserts the item you selected in step 2 into the Item field of the formula area. In Plus, Discoverer automatically inserts the item from the cell that you were in when you launched the New Condition dialog box.

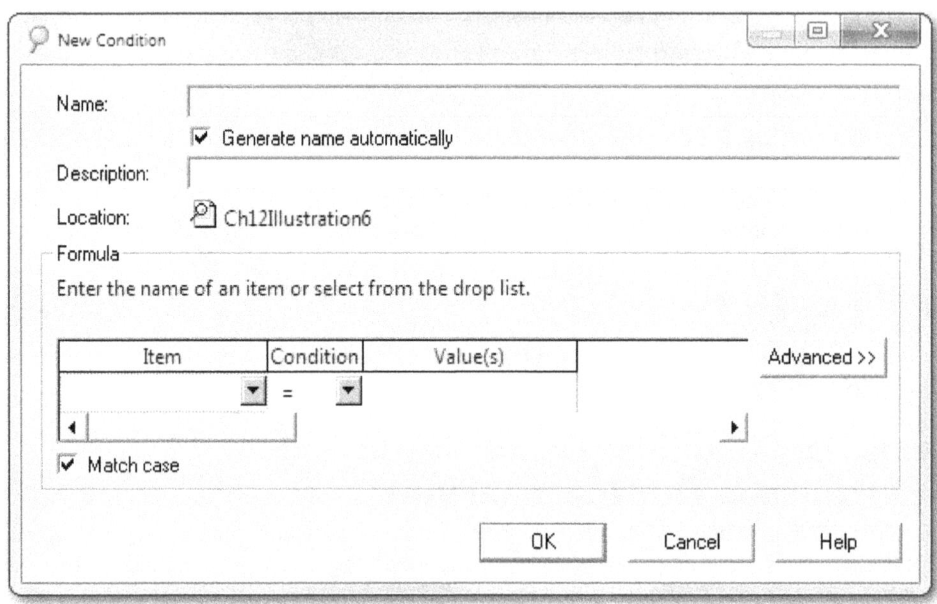


**FIGURE 12-4.** *Discoverer Desktop New Condition dialog box*

5. If this is not the item you want or if there is no item shown, select one now from the drop-down list. A detailed explanation of the choices available to you at this point is given in the "The Basic Components of a Condition" section when we deal with the basic components of a condition.
6. From the Condition drop-down list, select the expression you want to apply to the item. By default, Discoverer inserts the expression =. The available expressions are explained later in this chapter when we deal with the basic components of a condition.
7. In the Values box, type in the values you want Discoverer to constrain the item on, or from the drop-down list select one or more values. This drop-down list, in addition to a list of values, also contains options to select multiple values, create a calculation, select an item, create a new parameter, and create a new subquery. These options are explained in detail in the "The Basic Components of a Condition" section when we discuss the basic components of a condition.

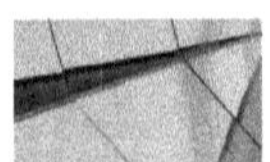

**NOTE**
*In Plus, Discoverer automatically inserts the item value from the cell that you were in when you launched the New Condition dialog.*

8. Make sure the box Match Case in Desktop, or Case-Sensitive in Plus, is checked. The reason for this is explained in the "The New Condition Dialog Box" section when we discuss the New Condition dialog box in detail.

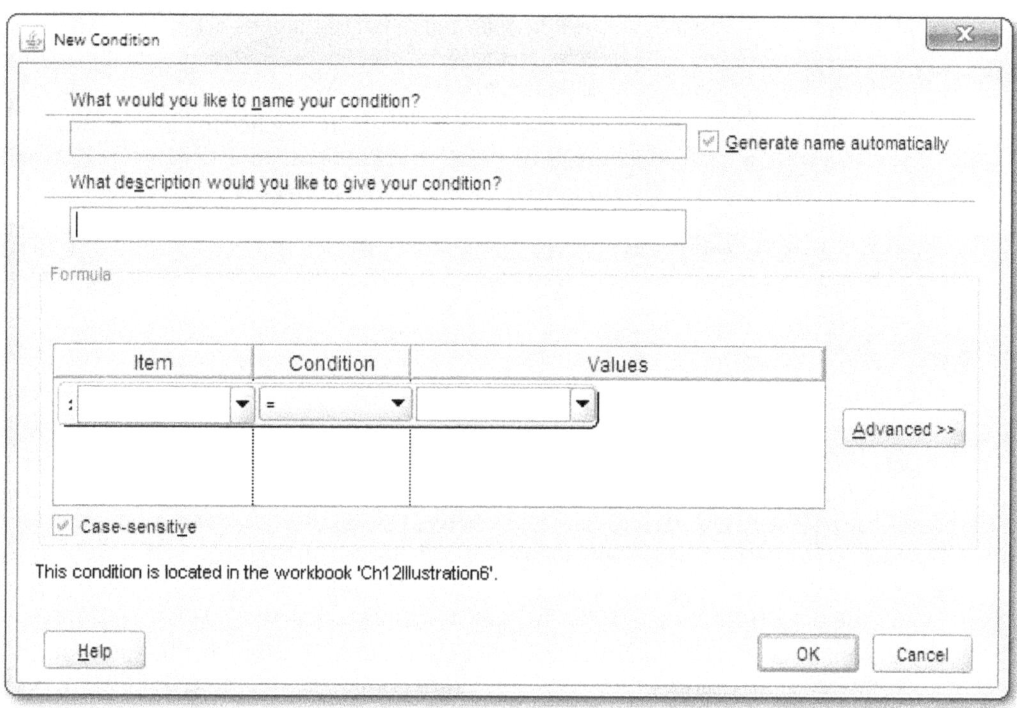


**FIGURE 12-5.** *Discoverer Plus New Condition dialog box*

9. If you want to define an advanced condition, click the Advanced button. Discoverer's advanced condition features are discussed later in this chapter.
10. If the name that Discoverer has generated for you is not to your liking, uncheck the Generate Name Automatically box and type a suitable name for the condition into the Name box.
11. Enter a description, if desired. This is optional. Remember that if others will use this worksheet, giving a description to the condition will help them decide whether they should use it. Adding a meaningful description will also help you in the future when you are asked to modify the worksheet.

**NOTE**
*We advise you to listen to the voice of experience and add meaningful descriptions whenever you can. They are an invaluable part of your documentation. No matter how good your memory is, we guarantee that you will never be able to remember why you created all conditions. In addition, you need to think of your successor and be as complete as you can with your documentation. After all, you don't want to be responsible for your organization's workbooks forever, do you?*

12. Click OK to close the New Condition dialog box.
13. If you are using Desktop, you will be returned to the Conditions dialog box, where you will see your condition highlighted in the list of conditions. To execute the condition, you need to close the Conditions dialog box by clicking OK.
14. If you are using Plus, the condition will automatically be applied to the worksheet, and you will see that the condition has been added to the list of conditions in the Conditions tab of both the Available and Selected Items panes.

### The New Condition Dialog Box

Figures 12-4 and 12-5 showed the New Condition dialog box. This box consists of the following features:

- **Name** Discoverer automatically generates a name for your condition based on the criteria that you use to build the condition. Normally, the name given by Discoverer will suffice. However, Discoverer will allow you to create your own name, but only if you uncheck the box described next.
- **Generate Name Automatically** By default, Discoverer names conditions for you, and it does this very well. Uncheck this box only if you want to name the condition yourself; then go back to the Name box and type in your own name.
- **Description** For simple queries, the name generated by Discoverer is more than adequate for identifying what will happen when a condition is selected. However, sometimes when using complex conditions, the name alone will not be sufficient. When the name generated by Discoverer does not accurately convey what will happen when the condition is selected, you should type in a description here.
- **Location** In case you have forgotten in which workbook you are working, Discoverer Desktop inserts the name of the current workbook here. Discoverer Plus also has a location, but it is not labeled. You will see the workbook name under the Case-Sensitive button.
- **Item** This is a drop-down list of available items, upon which you can base the condition. You must select something here; otherwise, Discoverer will be unable to create your condition. A full explanation of the options open to you is given in the next section. An example of an item is the ship date.
- **Condition** This is a drop-down list of expressions, from which you have to select one. A full list of all available expressions is given in the next section. An example of an expression is the = symbol, such that the condition now looks like "ship date =."
- **Value(s)** This is another drop-down list. This time, there is a list of values, from which you must select one or more in order to complete the condition. For example, we could enter the date 01-AUG-2011, thus completing our condition to be ship date = 01-AUG-2011. A full explanation of all available values is given in the next section.

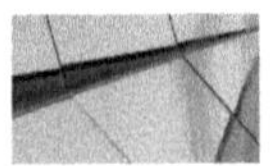

**NOTE**
*The previous three components are the three required elements of any Discoverer condition. The next section explains each of them in detail. Remember also that when you enter values that are dates or text, you must enter them inside single quotes.*

- **Advanced** Click this button if you want to access the advanced features associated with creating conditions. These features are explained in detail later in this chapter.
- **Match Case/Case-Sensitive** Uncheck this box only if you do not want Discoverer to match the case values in your query. Normally, you would not want to uncheck this, especially if you have selected from a list of values to begin with. In Desktop the box is labeled Match Case, whereas in Plus it is labeled Case-Sensitive.

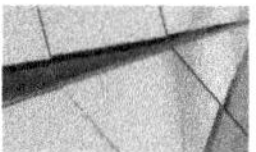

**NOTE**

*Queries will take much longer if you uncheck this box; in fact, in our experience, it is not uncommon to find query times increasing by 200 percent or more. This is because Discoverer is creating the query exactly as instructed, by ignoring match case and therefore causing the database to search for all possible combinations of the value. For example, say we were searching for the name Michael in our condition but did not check the Match Case or Case-Sensitive box. The database would scan for Michael, michae, MICHAEL, and all combinations of the uppercase and lowercase values of the seven letters in the name! You can see how long this would take and how much of an impact this would have on your own queries.*

Basically, the burden is being switched to the database. Discoverer itself does not scan for all combinations, but you will add a burden to the database. Look at the following sample code:

**The original SQL:**

```
WHERE (i100155 IN ('Central','East'))
GROUP BY i100155, i100195, i100203
```

**With Match Case unchecked:**

```
WHERE (UPPER(i100155) IN (UPPER('Central'), UPPER('East')))
GROUP BY i100155, i100195, i100203
```

## Building a Simple Condition Using the Workflow

Following the previous workflow, we will show you how to create a simple condition using the New Condition dialog box in Plus. We will follow each step exactly as specified.

We have a query that reports, for all products and statuses, the total quantity shipped and the margin. There are no conditions in this query so far, but we want to add one that shows the margin only when the product has shipped.

Step 1 of the workflow requires you to launch the New Condition dialog box. If possible, you should have placed the focus into the cell on which you want to place the condition. In this example, we want the condition to be on Status. The following illustration shows the New Condition dialog box with the item we selected already populated:

Step 5 says that if the item displayed is not the item you want to base the condition on, you should pick another item. In this case, the item that we want is Status, so we will proceed to step 6.

Step 6 of the workflow is where you set the expression. As Discoverer has already inserted the default of =, there is no need to pick an expression, so we will proceed directly to step 7.

In step 7, you have to open the drop-down list and select the value you want to constrain the status on. As we are not building a complex condition, only a simple condition, we will just select the status SHIPPED from the list of values. As you can see in the following illustration, when we opened the drop-down list, we were presented with a number of options, below which is the list of values from which we selected SHIPPED.

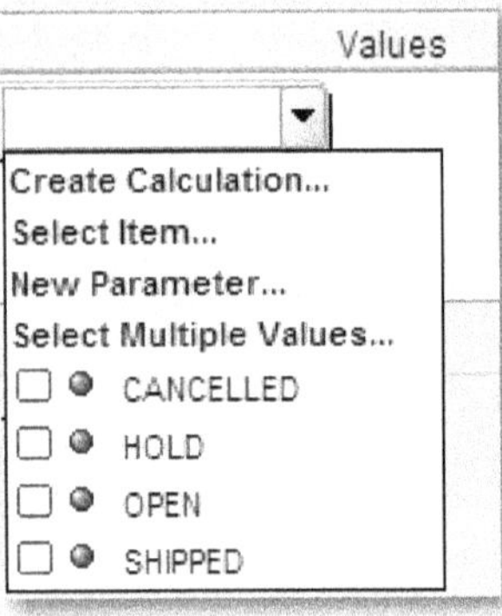

**NOTE**
*For an explanation of all the options in the drop-down list, please read the "Basic Components of a Condition" section that explains the basic components of a condition.*

Step 8 requires you to make sure Match Case in Desktop or Case-Sensitive in Plus is checked. By default, it is checked. The next three steps—for creating advanced conditions, naming the condition, and giving the condition a description—are not required. Therefore, we will proceed directly to finishing the condition. All that remains now is for us to click OK. At this point, Discoverer will rerun the query and apply the condition we have just created.

If you follow the preceding workflow, you will quickly master the art of building simple conditions. Advanced conditions are more difficult and are dealt with later in this chapter.

# The Basic Components of a Condition

As stated in the previous section, three basic components must be supplied for all Discoverer conditions. Without these components, Discoverer will be unable to build your condition. The three components are as follows:

- The item upon which the condition is based
- The expression being applied to the item
- A value (not always required)

In this section, you will take an in-depth look at these three basic components.

## Basic Component 1: The Item

When building a condition, you must specify the item you want Discoverer to use. You do this in one of two ways:

- Outside the New Condition dialog box
- Inside the New Condition dialog box

### Specifying an Item Outside the New Condition Dialog Box

How to specify the item that Discoverer must build the condition on from outside the New Condition dialog box depends on whether you are using Desktop or Plus.

In Desktop you must select the item from the drop-down list of the Conditions dialog box. After that, you should click New. Discoverer will then open the New Condition dialog box and populate the Item field with whatever item you chose.

In Plus you need to make sure that the item has the focus before you click the New Condition button. Discoverer will then open the New Condition dialog box and populate the Item field with whatever item you chose. We showed you how to do this in the preceding section.

**NOTE**

*The drop-down list of items in the Desktop Conditions dialog box contains only the items that are used within the worksheet. However, in the drop-down list of items in the New Condition dialog box, you can select from all the items contained in the folders used in the worksheet.*

### Specifying an Item Inside the New Condition Dialog Box

Specifying the item inside the New Condition dialog box gives you more flexibility. This method should be used in any of these cases:

- You are not 100 percent sure which item you want to use in your condition.
- You want to build the condition on an item that is not currently used within the worksheet.

- You want the item to be a calculation (advanced condition).
- You want the item to be a predefined or user-defined condition (advanced condition).

To build conditions based on the preceding types, use the drop-down list in the New Condition dialog box. Doing this, you will always see at the top of the list an option to create a calculation. If you have other conditions available, whether they be predefined or user-defined, you will also see an option to use them. The list will also contain all of the available items in the query, whether or not you have included them in your worksheet selections.

For example, suppose you have a folder containing ten items and you include five of them in your worksheet. Opening the drop-down list of items in the New Condition dialog box will display all ten items.

Building conditions based on other conditions or calculations will be explained in the "Building a Condition Based on Another Condition" section when we discuss advanced conditions.

## Basic Component 2: The Expression

The second basic component that you must supply, when building a condition, is the expression. Table 12-1 lists all of the available expressions.

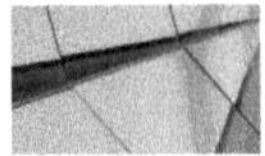

**NOTE**
*The expressions IS NULL and IS NOT NULL do not require a value. The Value field is removed when you select one of these expressions.*

Discoverer will automatically change the expression if the value you subsequently pick is incompatible with the current expression. For example, if you select = and then select two or more items from the list of values, Discoverer will change the expression to IN. This is because = takes only a single value, whereas IN can take single and multiple values.

## Basic Component 3: The Value

The third basic component of a condition is the value. As you saw in the preceding section, most, but not all, conditions take a value. If you select the expression BETWEEN, Discoverer will expect you to provide two values, a lower (or start) value and a higher (or end) value. It is up to you to ensure that the end value is indeed higher than the start value, because Discoverer will not validate your condition. So, if you build a condition where the start date is between 31-DEC-2011 and 01-JAN-2012, you will get no rows returned. If you do not spot this, for example when accepting begin and end values via parameters, your users could be fooled into thinking that there is no data.

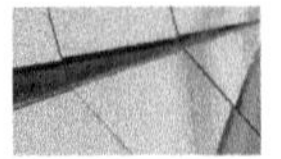

**NOTE**
*Many times date fields can have minutes and seconds and they will not match up. It is usually a good idea to use the TRUNC function to truncate the minutes/seconds and make the equation even, such as trunc(datefield1) = trunc(datefield2), or build the timestamp.*

| Symbol | Description | Examples |
|---|---|---|
| = | The item must equal the value. | Ship Qty = 15000 |
| <> | The item must not equal the value. | Ship Qty <> 15000 |
| > | The item must be greater than the value. | Ship Qty > 15000 |
| < | The item must be less than the value. | Ship Qty < 15000 |
| <= | The item must be less than or equal to the value. | Ship Qty <= 15000 |
| >= | The item must be greater than or equal to the value. | Ship Qty >= 15000 |
| LIKE | The item must match the value. You can use wildcards to find like values. The value must be enclosed in single quotes. Wildcards are valid but can be used only with text strings. | |
| | In Oracle, the % sign indicates that everything after this is ignored. For those familiar with Microsoft, the % character equates to the asterisk (*). | City Name LIKE 'D%'. This will return both *Dallas* and *Denver*. |
| | In Oracle, the _ (underscore symbol) matches a single character. For those familiar with Microsoft, the underscore equates to the question mark (?). | Product LIKE 'B_t'. This will return both *Bat* and *Bit* but not *Bet*. |
| IN | The item must be in one of the values. The values must be separated by commas and enclosed in brackets. | City IN ('Madrid', 'San Francisco', 'Tokyo'). This will find data that is in at least one of these cities. |
| IS NULL | The item must equal the NULL value. This expression returns values only when the named item is null (no value whatsoever, not even zero). | Cancel Date IS NULL. This returns only rows of data that do not have a cancel date. |
| IS NOT NULL | The item must not equal the NULL value. This expression returns values only when the named item is not null. | Ship Qty IS NOT NULL. This returns only rows of data when there is a ship quantity. |
| NOT IN | The item must not be in the set of values. The values must be separated by commas and enclosed in brackets. | City NOT IN ('Madrid', 'San Francisco', 'Tokyo'). This will find data for all cities except those listed. |
| BETWEEN | The item must be within the range of values defined. All data that is between the two values will be returned. | Ship Date BETWEEN '01-JUN-2010' and '30-JUN-2010'. This will find all shipments that took place in the month of June. Note that both the start and end dates are included. |

**TABLE 12-1.** *Available Expressions*

| Symbol | Description | Examples |
|---|---|---|
| NOT BETWEEN | The item must not fall within the range of values defined. All data that is outside of the two values will be returned. | Ship Date NOT BETWEEN '01-JUN-2012' and '30-JUN-2012'. This will find all shipments excluding those that took place in the month of June. Note that both the start and end dates are excluded. |
| NOT LIKE | The item must not match the value. You can use wildcards to omit like values. The value must be enclosed in single quotes. Wildcards are valid but can be used only with text strings. | City Name NOT LIKE 'D%'. This will exclude both *Dallas* and *Denver*. |
| != | Identical to <>. | This works the same as <>, but because some versions of SQL do not support SQL, Discoverer offers you these alternatives. |
| ^= (Desktop only) | | You should always use <> if available. |

**TABLE 12-1.** *Available Expressions* (Continued)

Having selected the item on which to build a condition and the expression, you should click in the Value field. Unless you created the condition using one of the condition buttons on the analysis bar, the Value field will be blank.

If you know the value that you want, you can type it in; otherwise, open the drop-down list. Depending on whether the data item has a list of values, the drop-down list does not always give the same options. When there is no list of values, the options are as follows:

- Create Calculation
- Select Item
- New Parameter
- Create Subquery (Desktop only)

When there is a list of values, the preceding options are supplemented by the following:

- Select Multiple Values
- The list of values (LOV)

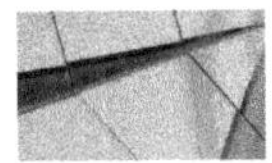

**NOTE**
*Until you have selected an item upon which to base the condition, you will not be able to see the drop-down list options for values. This is because Discoverer needs to ascertain whether a list of values is associated with the item. Even with a list of values, you can choose to ignore the LOV and select one of the other options.*

### Create Calculation

This option opens the Edit Calculation dialog. This box is identical to the New Calculation dialog box that was described in Chapter 5. Creating calculations as part of a condition is described later in this chapter, while stand-alone calculations will be dealt with when we show you how to refine calculations in Chapter 13.

### Select Item

This option opens the Items dialog box. This box lists all of the items in the folders used in the worksheet. You could reverse the contents of the Item and the Value fields, by inserting, for example, SHIPPED in the item and selecting STATUS from the list of items. You can also create conditions that use two items, such as shipped date equals ordered date, so that you can analyze all of the orders that shipped the same day that they were ordered.

### New Parameter

This option opens the New Parameter dialog box. Use this box to convert a condition into a parameter or define a new parameter for your worksheet. Defining parameters from the Workbook Wizard was covered in Chapter 5, while converting conditions into parameters will be covered in Chapter 13.

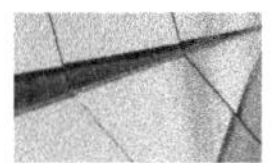

**NOTE**
*The New Parameter option cannot be used unless you have chosen an item from a folder. If you have typed a value, such as SHIPPED, into the item field, Discoverer will not allow you to create a parameter based on this.*

### Create Subquery (Available in Desktop Only)

This option opens the Create Subquery dialog box. You use this box to apply a condition on an item or value that is in another worksheet. Discoverer will let you associate a condition with an item in an existing worksheet, or it will allow you to create a new worksheet for the purpose.

The use of subqueries can be thought of as an advanced form of condition. This topic is covered in detail later in this chapter.

**NOTE**
*Oracle has not added subqueries to Plus. However, subqueries created in Desktop will work in Plus. They cannot be edited or maintained in Plus, though, because only Desktop has this ability. In many instances, the use of hyper-drilling will eliminate the need for subqueries altogether. Please refer to Chapter 10 for details on how to set up and manage hyper-drills.*

### Select Multiple Values

This option, available only if a list of values has been defined for the item, opens the Values dialog box, as shown earlier in Desktop in Figure 12-1 and in Plus in Figure 12-6. Use of the Desktop version of this dialog box was covered in the first part of this chapter when we explained creating conditions using Show Values. The difference between opening the Values dialog box using Show Values and doing so using Select Multiple Values is that Show Values checks the items that are currently in use, whereas Select Multiple Values displays all values unchecked.

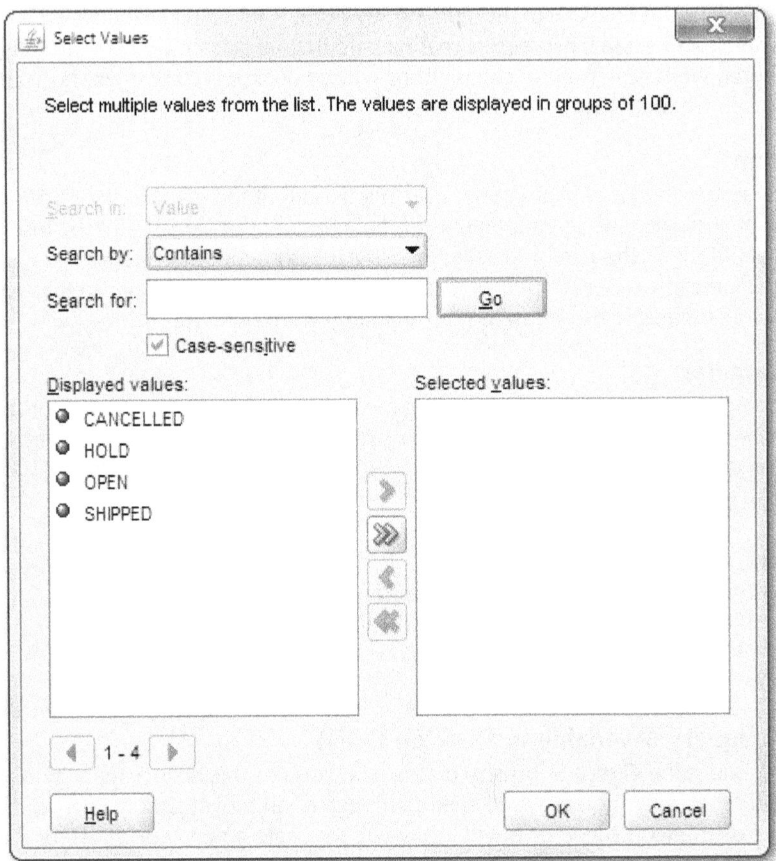


**FIGURE 12-6.** *Discoverer Plus Select Values dialog box*

In the Plus version, as shown in Figure 12-6, you select and deselect items by dragging them between the Available and Selected boxes. Alternatively, you can also use the paste buttons to move items between the boxes. If the list of items is large but you know the items that you want to select all begin with the same characters, you should use the Search By and Search For boxes in conjunction with the Go button to restrict the list to only the subset you want to work with.

The exception to this is if you have already selected items from the list of values and then clicked Select Multiple Values—the values previously selected will remain selected. For example, we have selected from the list of values the status OPEN. We then clicked Select Multiple Values and, as you can see in the following illustration, OPEN has remained selected:

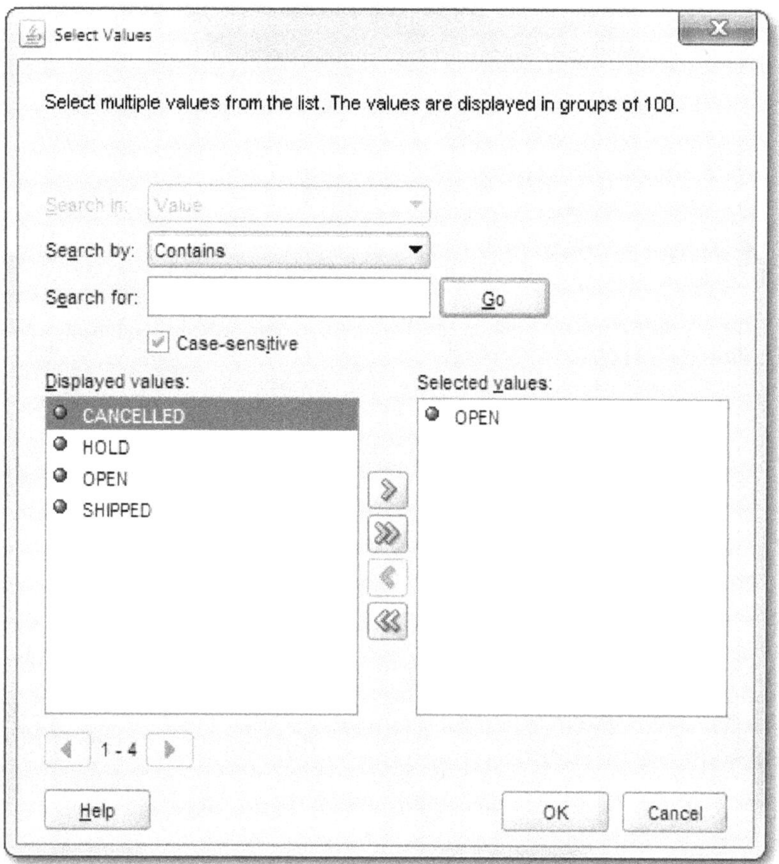


## The List of Values

When an item has a list of values, Desktop Discoverer displays all of the items, which could take a while if the list has a lot of values. In Plus, however, as you can see from this illustration, if the list contains more than 100 items, Discoverer displays the items in groups of 100 at a time. The forward and back buttons at the bottom of the screen will cause Discoverer to display the previous or next 100 rows. The number 100 is not cast in stone but is controlled by your Discoverer manager. As an organization, if you do not want to go with the default of 100, you should choose how many items should be fetched in any one set. Be careful not to set this too high; otherwise, Discoverer will time out while fetching the list of values.

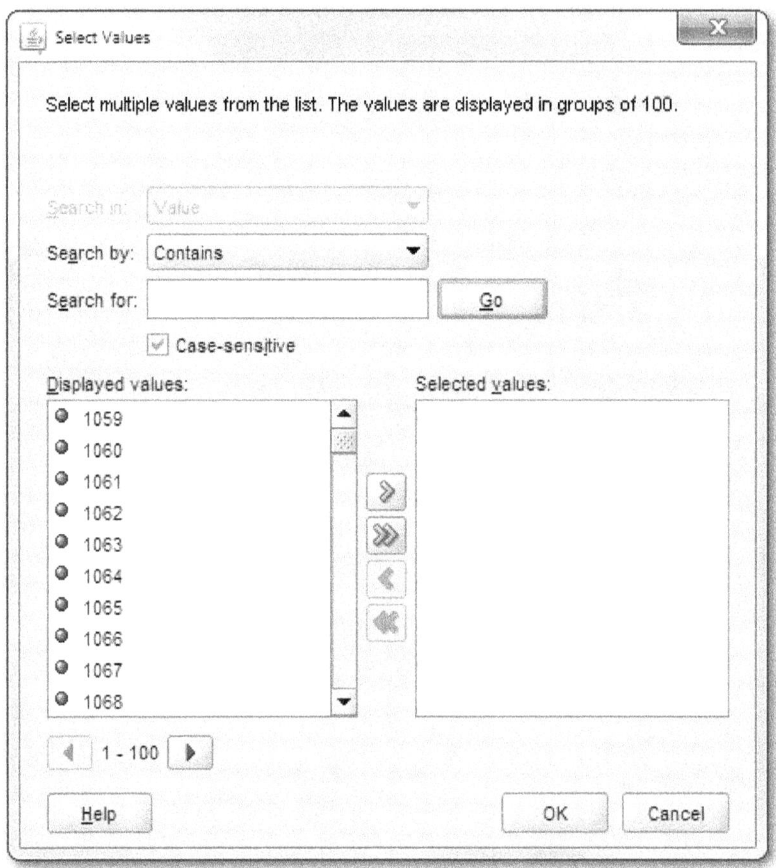


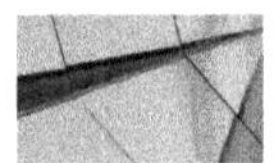

**NOTE**

*Remember, when you are using the BETWEEN expression, you must provide two values, a lower, start value and a higher, end value. Discoverer does not check the validity of the start and end values. If you enter an end value that is lower than the start value, Discoverer will accept the condition but will return no data.*

# Editing an Existing Condition

Another technique commonly used when refining queries is to edit an existing condition. In this situation, you are neither adding nor removing existing conditions, just changing an existing definition. If you find that the same query constantly needs modifying just to edit a single condition, we recommend you change that condition to a parameter. Changing conditions into parameters is dealt with in detail in Chapter 13.

To edit an existing condition, use the following workflow:

1. Open the Conditions dialog box in Desktop or select the Conditions tab from the Available Items pane in Plus.
2. From the list of conditions displayed, highlight the condition you want to edit.
3. Click the Edit button, or additionally in Plus right-click the condition and from the pop-up list select Edit. This opens the Edit Condition dialog box.
4. Change the condition as required.
5. Click OK to exit from the Edit Condition dialog box. In Desktop, click OK again to exit from the Conditions dialog box.

**NOTE**

*As stated earlier, if you realize at this point that you have made a mistake and edited the wrong condition or changed it incorrectly, you can reverse the changes by clicking Edit | Undo Conditions or pressing* CTRL-Z. *Do not do anything else; otherwise, you will not be able to undo your mistake. This is because Discoverer allows you to undo, or redo, only the last action you did.*

When you have completed editing the condition, Discoverer will execute the query and display the new results. In Desktop you can change multiple conditions and the query will execute only when you exit the Conditions dialog box. In Plus, however, there is no Conditions dialog box, and unless you uncouple the database from the query or use the Edit Worksheet dialog box, the query will execute every time you change a condition.

To uncouple Discoverer Plus from the database, from the menu bar select Tools and uncheck the Auto Refresh box. You can now change as many conditions as you want and Discoverer will requery the database only when you click the Refresh button on the toolbar.

Another way to maintain multiple conditions in Plus without executing the query every time is to launch the Edit Worksheet dialog box by using Tools | Conditions from the toolbar. As Discoverer opens the Edit Worksheet dialog box, it will navigate to the Conditions subtab on the Select Items tab. You can now change or create as many conditions as you want. When you have finished working with your conditions, click OK to close the Edit Worksheet dialog box. Discoverer will now requery the database.

# Using Advanced Conditions

Probably the most daunting aspect of creating or editing conditions is knowing how to use advanced conditions effectively. Following the workflow given earlier in this chapter, it is very easy to create simple conditions. To fully master Discoverer, you need to spend time learning how Discoverer handles complex, advanced conditions.

Using Discoverer, we have identified the following four types of advanced conditions:

- Conditions based on calculations
- Conditions based on other conditions

- Conditions using Boolean operators
- Conditions using subqueries

# Creating Conditions Based on Calculations

As you saw earlier in this chapter, when we discussed the three basic components of a condition, both the Item and Value drop-down boxes have options to create calculations. In this section we will show you how this is done.

There are two ways of creating conditions based on calculations. They are

- Using an existing calculation
- Creating a new calculation as part of the condition

There, in a nutshell, is the reason why Discoverer allows you to create two types of conditions based on calculations.

## Using an Existing Calculation

Existing calculations will appear in the list of items, even if they are not being displayed in the final output. If you base a condition on an existing calculation and then delete the calculation from the worksheet by deleting the column, the condition can still use the calculation. You can even create a new condition based on the calculation.

However, if you delete a calculation from the Calculations dialog box, it can no longer be used. Any conditions that used that calculation are also deleted. Conditions based on existing calculations are therefore vulnerable because the calculation could accidentally be deleted, unaware that it is used in a condition. Discoverer will not warn you that you are deleting a needed calculation. Unless you realize it in time and do an Undo (CTRL-Z), once the damage is done, you will have to start over!

To use an existing calculation within a condition, use the following workflow:

1. Open the New Condition dialog box.
2. In the Item field, open the drop-down list.
3. From the options provided, select the calculation.
4. Set the expression and value you require.
5. Click OK.

We'll give you an example. We built a query of shipments, showing the order number and quantity shipped, sorted by order number. We next added a profit calculation, being defined as the sum of the selling price minus the sum of the cost price. The illustration on the right shows how this looks.

| | ▸ Order Number | ▸ Shipped Qty SUM | ▸ Profit |
|---|---|---|---|
| 1 | 1059 | 10000 | 113700.00 |
| 2 | 1060 | 1200 | 10848.00 |
| 3 | 1061 | 1000 | 9040.00 |
| 4 | 1062 | 1920 | 29702.40 |
| 5 | 1063 | 1920 | 29702.40 |
| 6 | 1064 | 48 | 301.44 |
| 7 | 1065 | 50 | 338.00 |
| 8 | 1066 | 10000 | 113700.00 |
| 9 | 1067 | 1600 | 18496.00 |
| 10 | 1068 | 8400 | 97104.00 |
| 11 | 1069 | 10000 | 115600.00 |
| 12 | 1070 | 15000 | 280650.00 |
| 13 | 1071 | 200 | 3742.00 |
| 14 | 1072 | 1200 | 11196.00 |
| 15 | 1073 | 1200 | 11196.00 |
| 16 | 1074 | 1200 | 13236.00 |

Next, we opened the New Condition dialog box. From the drop-down list of items we selected the profit, as you can see here:

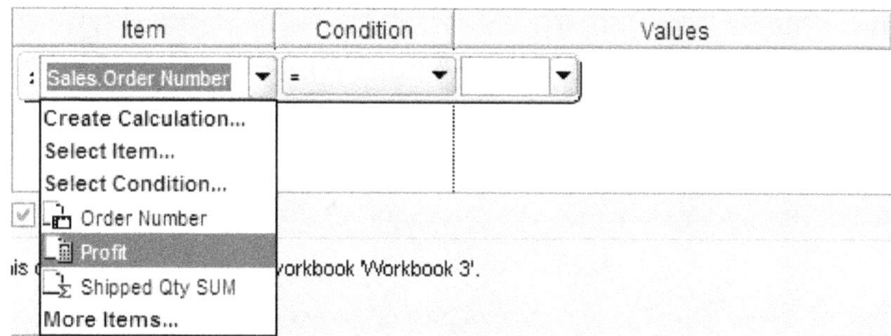


Finally, as shown here, we selected the expression > (greater than) and entered a value of 20000.

After we clicked OK, Discoverer ran the query using the condition just created, and the query was constrained to show only orders with a profit greater than 20,000.

### Creating a New Calculation as Part of the Condition

Calculations created as part of a condition will not appear in the list of items, nor will they be listed in the Calculations dialog box. They exist only as part of the condition and cannot be manipulated outside of the condition. Calculations created this way will be used only internally by the condition; they cannot be displayed as a column of the worksheet, and they cannot be used in other conditions. If you delete the condition, the calculation is also deleted.

Because these calculations are created as part of the condition, they are not vulnerable to being accidentally deleted.

To build a condition, with a calculation created as part of it, use the following workflow:

1. Open the New Condition dialog box.
2. From the options provided, select Create Calculation. This opens the Edit Calculation dialog box.
3. Create the calculation.
4. Click OK. This returns you to the New Condition dialog box.
5. Set the expression and value you require.
6. Click OK.

Using the same query of shipments we used in the example for creating conditions based on an existing calculation, we will show you how to create the same condition. This time, however, we will create the calculation from within the New Condition dialog box.

After opening the New Condition dialog box, we selected Create Calculation from the Item drop-down list. In Plus, as you can see here, Discoverer opens the New Calculation dialog box:

**NOTE**
*In Desktop the box is called the Edit Calculation dialog box.*

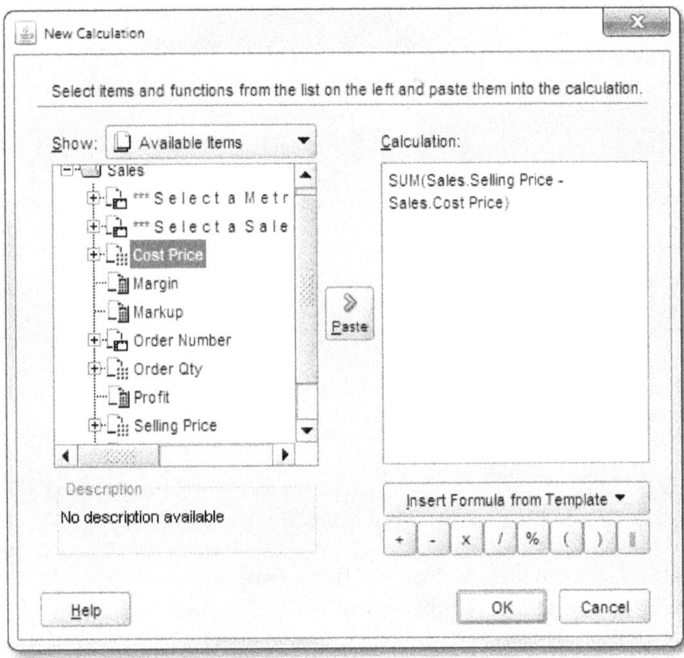


Looking at the preceding illustration, you will notice that this box looks almost identical to the standard New Calculation dialog box. However, if you look closely and you are in Desktop, you will notice that the Name field is deactivated. In Plus, as shown in the illustration, Discoverer suppresses the name altogether. This is because the calculation belongs to the condition that created it. It cannot be used in any other context and, therefore, needs no name.

As you can see in the illustration, we have also created the profit calculation. This is the sum of the selling price minus the cost price. Looking at the illustration, you will see that we used the SUM function to build the calculation.

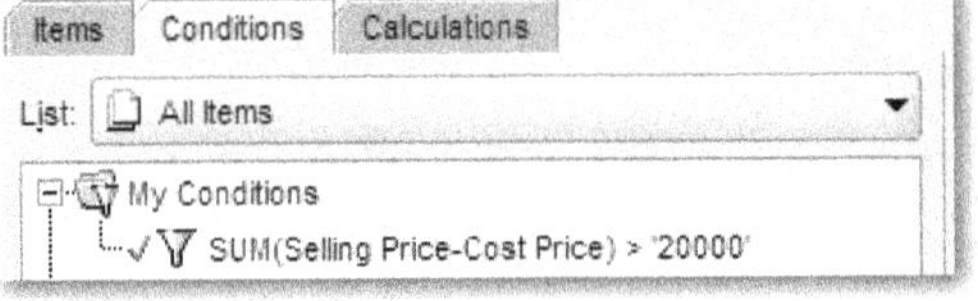


After clicking OK, we were returned to the New Condition dialog box. In here, we entered the expression > and a value of 20000. In the completed condition, the calculation displays in its entirety in the Item field, obviating the need to name the calculation.

After we clicked OK, Discoverer ran the query using the condition just created, and the query was constrained to show only orders with a profit greater than 20,000.

## Creating Conditions Based on Conditions

The second of the advanced types of conditions is to create a condition based on an existing condition. Whether these existing conditions are administrator- or user-defined is irrelevant. The important thing you need to know is that Discoverer allows you to create these conditions. Extending your skill set to include creating conditions based on other conditions will greatly enhance your expertise in Discoverer.

Perhaps the simplest way to explain why you would even bother to build a condition based on another is as follows. If you have created, or have available to you, multiple existing conditions and you are using more than one of them at the same time, Discoverer will apply an AND between each one.

For example, let's say you have two conditions in your worksheet, an administrator-defined one, which constrains the order quantity to be greater than 15,000, and a user-defined condition, which limits the status to SHIPPED. In the Conditions dialog box, you can only decide whether to use or not use these conditions. If you check both of them, Discoverer will select data only when both of the conditions are true. However, what if you want your query to return data when one or the other condition is true, such as order quantity > 15000 OR status = 'SHIPPED'? The only way to do this is to create a new condition, based on both of these conditions, combining them with the Boolean operator OR.

As you have seen in the Item drop-down list, one of the options is to use Select Condition. To build a condition based on another condition, use the following workflow:

1. Open the New Condition dialog box.
2. From the options provided, choose Select Condition. In Desktop, this opens a Conditions dialog box. Don't confuse this dialog box with the Conditions dialog box. In Plus, the dialog box is more appropriately named Select Condition. The box that has been opened here merely contains a list of the available conditions upon which you can base another condition.
3. From the list, select the condition you want to use.
4. Click OK. This returns you to the New Condition dialog box, with both the Expression and Value fields removed. At this stage, you could click OK, but all this will do is create another condition with identical functionality to the original. What you should do instead is use the advanced features of Discoverer and use Boolean logic to combine the existing condition with something else, perhaps another condition.
5. Click Advanced. This opens an extended version of the Edit Condition dialog box, in which you should create a Boolean condition (see the next section for details on how to do this).
6. When you have finished creating the Boolean condition, click OK.

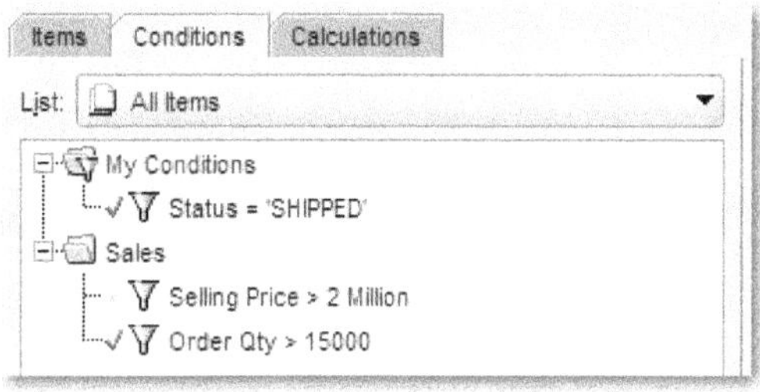

Using the example just outlined, the following illustration shows a worksheet with the two existing conditions, order quantity > 15000 and status = 'SHIPPED'. With both conditions checked, we would see only 11 rows of data. Discoverer has applied the Boolean operator AND between the two conditions.

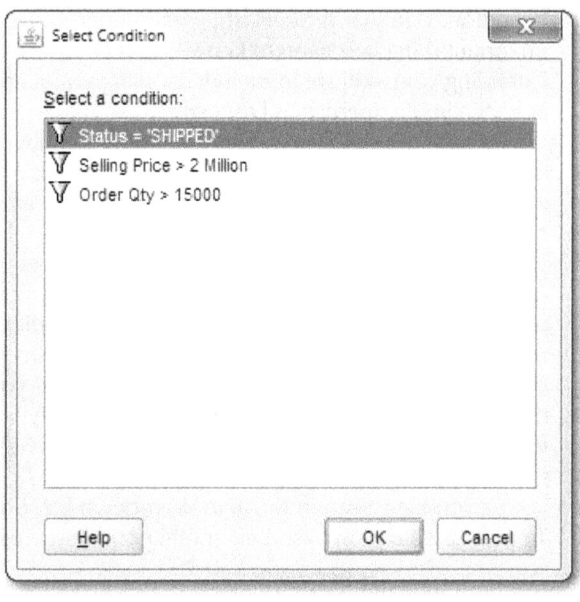


However, we don't want to see only the rows that satisfy both conditions; we want to see all orders with an order quantity > 15000 *or* a status of SHIPPED. By creating a new condition that combines both of the existing conditions, we can do just that.

Therefore, we opened the New Condition dialog box, and from the Item drop-down list we selected the option Select Condition. This opened the Select Condition dialog box shown in the following illustration. As you can see, both of our existing conditions are available to use, including another administrator-defined condition that we are not using.

We selected the first condition, Status = SHIPPED, and clicked OK. As you can see next, this inserted the condition into the New Condition dialog box and removed both the Expression and Value fields.

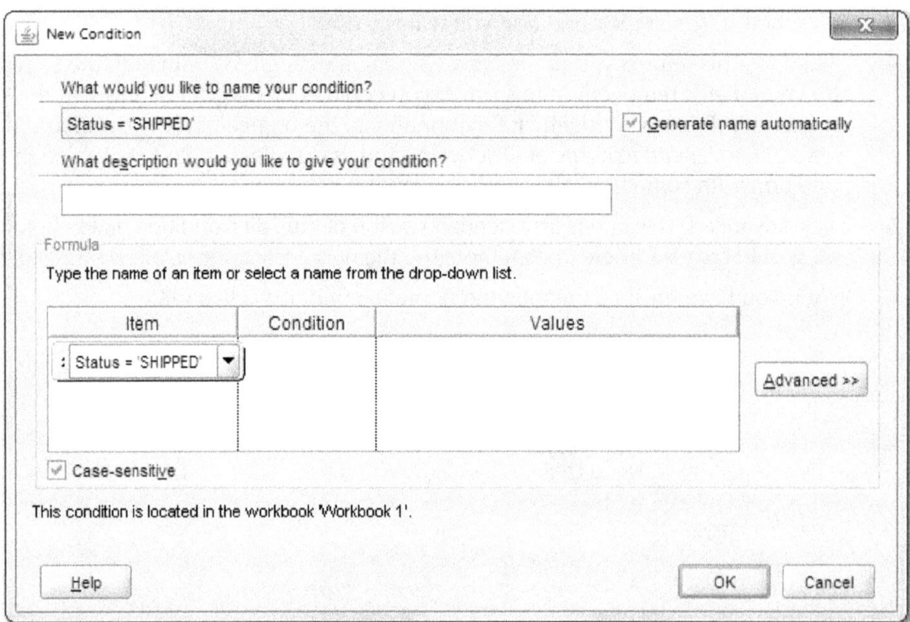

Next, we clicked Advanced. This opened the extended New Condition dialog box, as shown in the following illustration. This box, and all its functionality, will be explained in the next section when we deal with Boolean conditions.

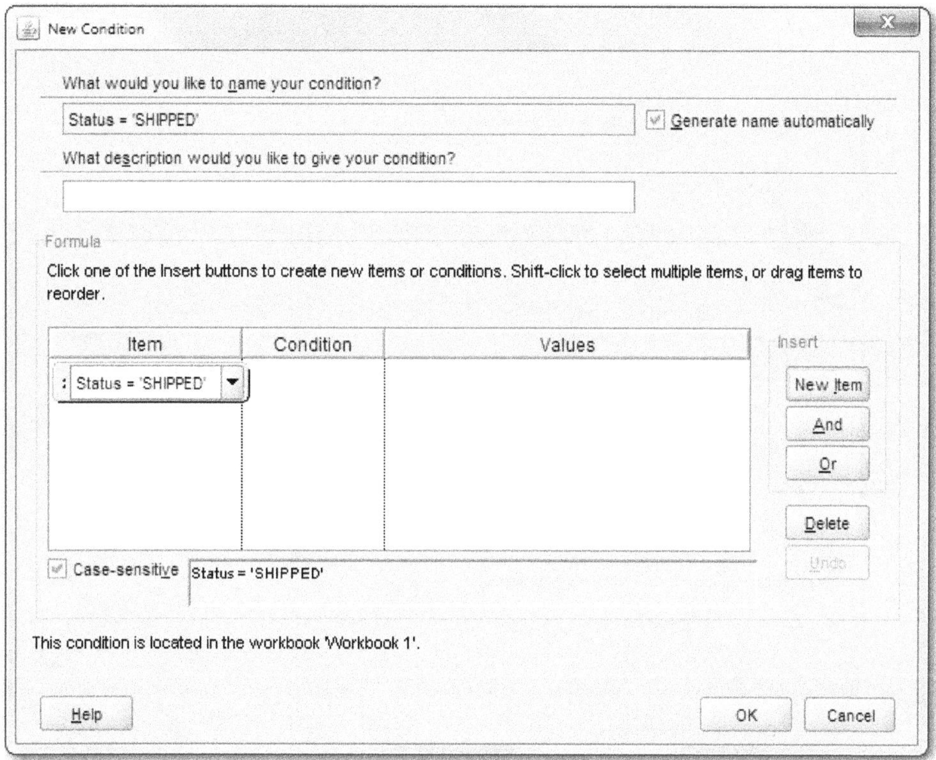


To combine the two existing conditions, we need to add the second condition to the one that is already selected. To do this, we clicked the New Item button. In Desktop the button is labeled Add; however, the functionality is the same. Discoverer has changed the display of the dialog box and inserted another set of the three basic components of a condition, as you can see in the following illustration:

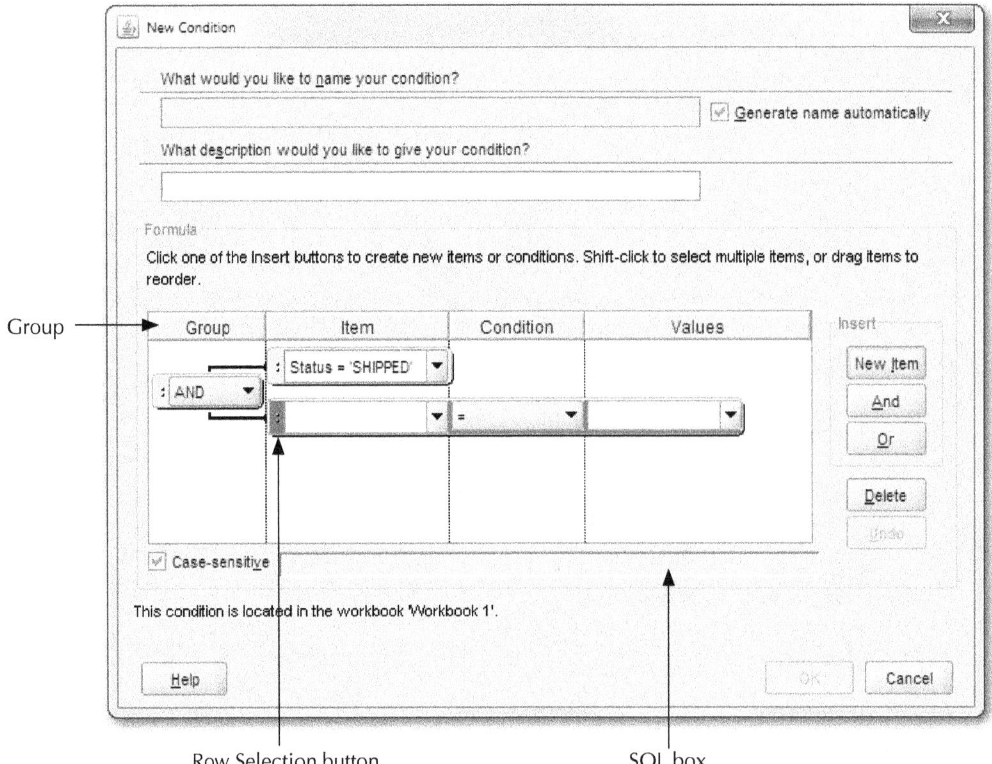

We're not quite done. To add the second condition, from the new Item drop-down list we again chose Select Condition. From the list of available conditions, we selected the second one and clicked OK. This resulted in the following illustration. As you can see, Discoverer has now combined the two conditions into one, using the Boolean operator AND.

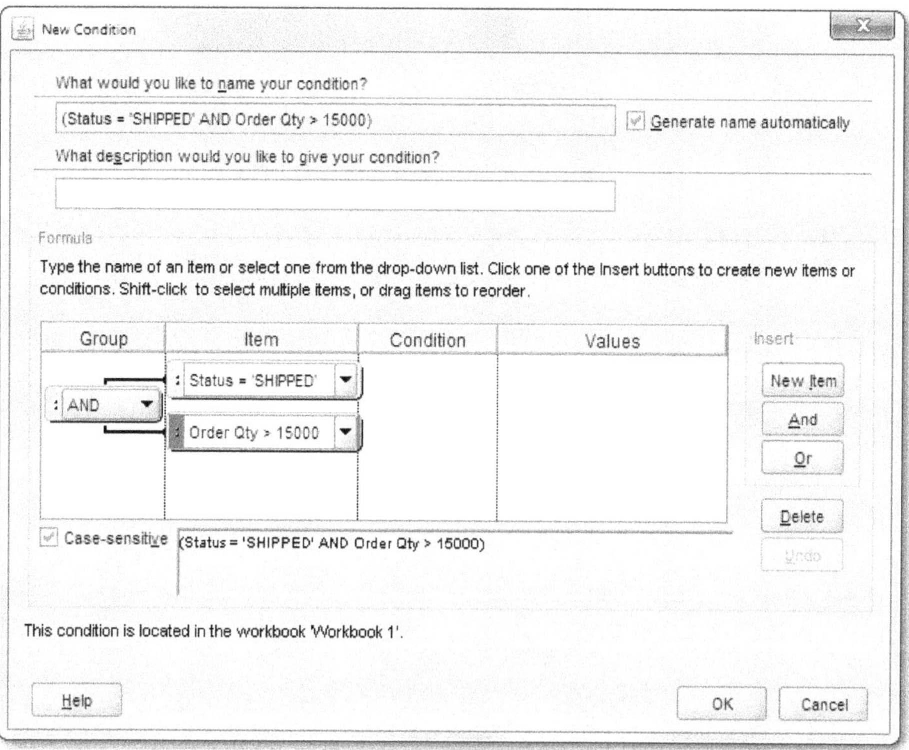

Almost there! We now have to change the Boolean operator to OR. To do this, we clicked the AND joining the two conditions, and from the drop-down list we selected OR. In Desktop you will need to click the Or button.

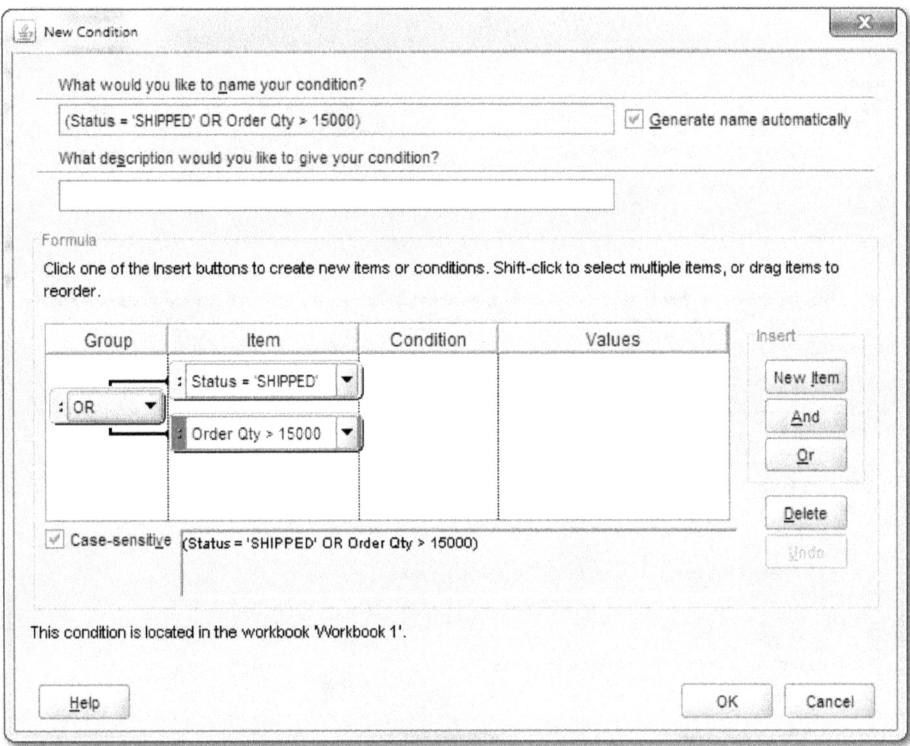


We then clicked OK to save this new condition. In Plus the new condition was added to the list of conditions on the Conditions tab, and the query was reexecuted. To complete our worksheet, we right-clicked each of the two original conditions and from the pop-up menu selected Remove From Worksheet. Our final Conditions tab looks like this:

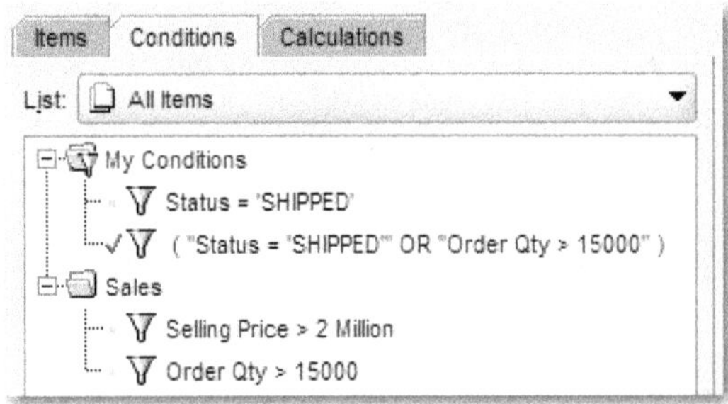


In Desktop, however, you will be returned to the Conditions dialog box without executing the query. All you need to do now is to deselect the two original conditions and then click OK.

As you can see in the next illustration, the result of running with this condition is quite different from the 11 rows that we started with:

| | Status | Order Number | Order Qty SUM |
|---|---|---|---|
| 1 | OPEN | 2822 | 16000 |
| 2 | | 3134 | 24000 |
| 3 | | 3392 | 34800 |
| 4 | | 3394 | 30000 |
| 5 | SHIPPED | 1059 | 10000 |
| 6 | | 1060 | 1200 |
| 7 | | 1061 | 1000 |
| 8 | | 1062 | 1920 |
| 9 | | 1063 | 1920 |
| 10 | | 1064 | 48 |
| 11 | | 1065 | 50 |
| 12 | | 1066 | 10000 |
| 13 | | 1067 | 1600 |
| 14 | | 1068 | 8400 |
| 15 | | 1069 | 10000 |
| 16 | | 1070 | 15000 |

Where the two conditions match exactly, we see all data values displayed. However, where only one or the other condition is true, the values that correspond to the false condition are displayed as NULL.

**NOTE**
*Don't forget to deselect the existing conditions upon which you have created the new condition. If you forget this, Discoverer will give you a result based on the combination of all three conditions.*

## Using Boolean Operators

The third of Discoverer's advanced types of conditions uses Boolean operators. We touched on this subject in the previous section, when we showed you how to combine conditions using Boolean operators. In this section, we will explore the whole gamut of Boolean operators and show you how to make effective use of them.

First, if you are not familiar with Boolean operators, we will give you a brief explanation. Boolean algebra, a system of symbolic logic dealing with operands, was devised by G. Boole (1815–1864), an English mathematician. This system includes any logical operation in which each of the operands and the result take one of the two values, true or false. These operations form the basis of logic gates in computers.

Within Discoverer there are operands and operators. An operand is anything that equates to a true or false value, such as status = shipped or quantity > 15000. An operator is a symbol that allows you to make a connection between operands, such as status = shipped AND quantity > 15000. Discoverer allows you to use the operators AND, OR, and NOT.

Now that you understand the concept of Boolean operators, it is a straightforward task to convert these into conditions. We will show you how to build both simple and complex Boolean conditions. Before you start building complex conditions, you should check that there are no existing conditions that will satisfy what you are trying to do.

## Creating Boolean Conditions

When creating Boolean conditions, use the following workflow:

1. Open the New Condition dialog box.
2. Because you know you will be creating a Boolean condition, click Advanced. This opens the extended New Condition dialog box, as shown in Figures 12-7 and 12-8.
3. Create a condition, or use the Item drop-down list to create a new calculation or select an existing condition. This step creates the first part of the Boolean condition.
4. Click Add in Desktop or New Item in Plus to create or insert another condition.

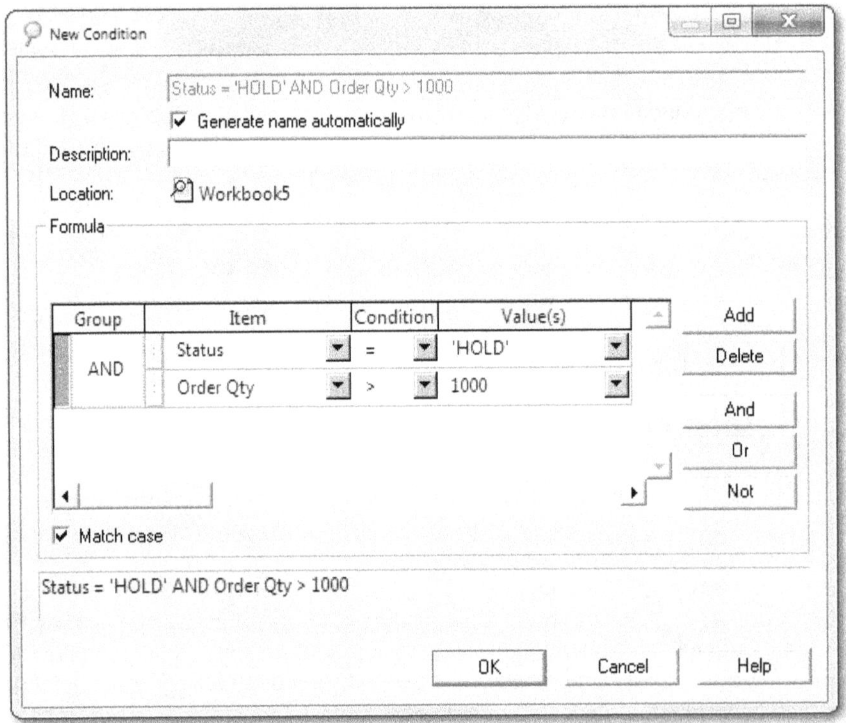


**FIGURE 12-7.** *Desktop extended New Condition dialog box*

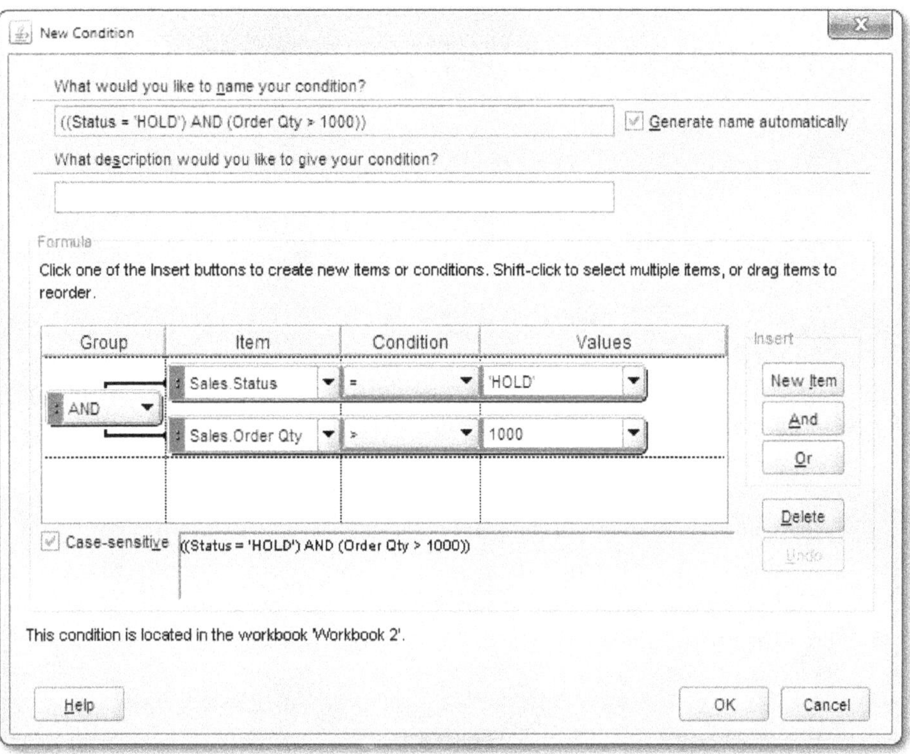


**FIGURE 12-8.** *Plus extended New Condition dialog box*

5. Set the Boolean operator you want to be applied between the conditions.
6. Repeat steps 4 and 5, adding new conditions and operators, until you have created the desired complex condition.
7. Click OK.

## The Extended New Condition Dialog Box

Whenever you are creating complex conditions, Discoverer opens the extended New Condition dialog box. This dialog box has all of the fields from the New Condition dialog box, as shown previously in Figures 12-4 and 12-5, but in addition, it has several more. As shown in Figures 12-7 and 12-8, this extended dialog box consists of the following additional features:

- **Group** This is an area containing the Boolean operators being used to join the elements of the complex condition together. Clicking one of the operators in this area highlights it. You can then click one of the Boolean operator buttons to change the join operator.
- **Row selection button** Click this button to highlight a condition that is to become part of a sublevel.

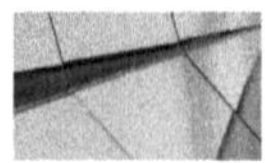

**NOTE**

*Sublevels are used to group together conditions that are to have different Boolean operators to the main conditions. This allows you to create complex conditions such as A = 1 or (A = 2 and B = 4), where conditions A = 2 and B = 4 are combined in a sublevel using the AND operator, as compared to A = 1, which is joined to the sublevel using the OR operator. In essence, this query returns all rows where A = 1 or where A = 2 and B = 4.*

- **Add or New Item** When active, click this button to add a new condition to the complex condition you are creating or editing.
- **Delete** When active, click this button to delete a highlighted condition from the complex condition.
- **Undo** This button, available in Plus only, allows you to undo a delete. If you delete a condition by mistake, clicking this button will reinstate the condition. This has already rescued us several times!
- **And** When active, click this button to change the join operator between two elements of the complex condition to the AND operator.
- **Or** When active, click this button to change the join operator between two elements of the complex condition to the OR operator.
- **Not** This button, available in Desktop only, allows you to negate the meaning of the current Boolean operator. When active, clicking this button negates the current highlighted item in the dialog box. With a join operator highlighted, Discoverer adds the word *NOT* as a prefix to the current join operator. Clicking the Not button a second time returns the join operator to its original state. With an expression highlighted, Discoverer negates that expression. For example, IN would become NOT IN, and >= (greater than or equal to) would become < (less than). To use the NOT construct in Plus, you need to click the current operator under the Group heading. From the drop-down, you can now insert the NOT operator.
- **SQL box** As you create the condition formula, a box at the bottom of the dialog box displays the SQL syntax for the condition you are entering. If you know SQL very well, you can use this box to validate that Discoverer is defining the condition as you would like it.

When you enter the extended New Condition dialog box for the first time, all of the Boolean operator buttons, apart from Not, are deactivated. This is because Add, Delete, And, and Or cannot be used until you have created at least one condition. Clicking Not would change the default condition to <>.

In both Plus and Desktop, do not click OK until you have built at least one condition. If you click OK too early, Discoverer will give you the error message shown here:

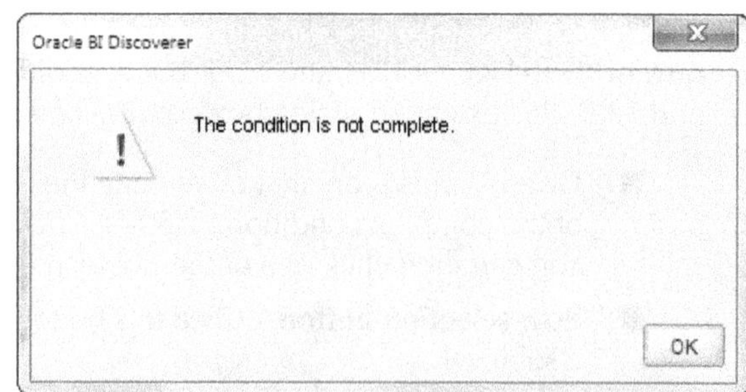
Oracle BI Discoverer
The condition is not complete.
OK

**NOTE**
*In Discoverer 10g Plus, Discoverer disabled the OK button until you had a valid construct. In 11g it is always active.*

## Building a Simple Boolean Condition

Before building a Boolean condition, you need to work out in advance what you want to know and convert that into simple Boolean algebra.

For example, let's build a condition that constrains a query to orders that are on hold and have a quantity ordered in excess of 1,000. The Boolean algebra for this is as follows:

Order Status = HOLD AND Quantity Ordered > 1000

Having ascertained that there are no existing conditions that will satisfy what we want, we opened the New Condition dialog box and clicked Advanced. This opened the extended New Condition dialog box, as shown previously in Figures 12-7 and 12-8.

Using the status to constrain the worksheet to only those orders that are on hold, we will now build the first condition. There are no illustrations for any of these steps, because by now you should know how to do this. Having created the first condition, all of the Boolean operator buttons are now activated.

Next, we clicked Add, opened another row of basic components, and built the second condition. The final complex condition appears in Figures 12-7 and 12-8.

## Building a Complex Boolean Condition

Once you know how to build simple Boolean conditions, building complex ones is straightforward. A complex Boolean condition takes three or more separate conditions and uses Boolean operators to join them. Many people have asked us if it is possible to combine different Boolean operators in the same condition. The answer is yes, and in this section, we will show you how.

First, as always, we need to think in advance what it is that we are trying to do. The complex Boolean that we are going to build uses the following logic to analyze our query of sales orders and quantities:

Order quantity > 10000 OR (order quantity between 7000 and 8000, AND the status is OPEN)

The portion in parentheses is to be considered a single condition, such that our result will display all orders that have an order quantity in excess of 15,000, along with all open orders that have a quantity between 7,000 and 8,000. Do you have a mathematical grounding? If so, you might want to think back to school and the principle of BODMAS. Here you determined the precedence of calculations as being the following: Brackets, Order and Division, Multiplication and Addition, and finally Subtraction. It is the same with conditions.

**NOTE**
*It is quite common for people to forget that parentheses always come first, which means you must calculate the answer of whatever is in the parentheses before you attempt to calculate the rest of the problem. Once you have worked out whatever is in the parentheses, usually the rest of the problem resolves easily!*

So, where do we begin? As always with complex conditions, we need to proceed directly to the extended New Condition dialog box, by clicking Advanced in the normal New Condition box. By examining our documentation of the system, we discovered that there is already an administrator-defined condition for the order quantity being in excess of 15,000. Therefore, we opened the Item drop-down list and selected Select Condition. Doing this opened the following Select Condition dialog box. As you can see in this illustration, the condition we want already exists, so all we need to do is to select it.

Clicking OK returned us to the extended New Condition dialog box, placing the condition we just selected in the first row. Next, we clicked New Item, or Add if you are following along using Desktop, to add the second part of our complex condition, the order quantity between 7,000 and 8,000. When we opened the Item drop-down list this time, we see that Discoverer has added another option to the list, Copy Condition.

Because the second part of our condition uses the same item as the first part so that we cannot possibly select the wrong item in error, we will copy the first condition and then change it. Selecting Copy Condition reopens the Conditions dialog box, from where we once again selected the administrator-defined condition. This resulted in the following:

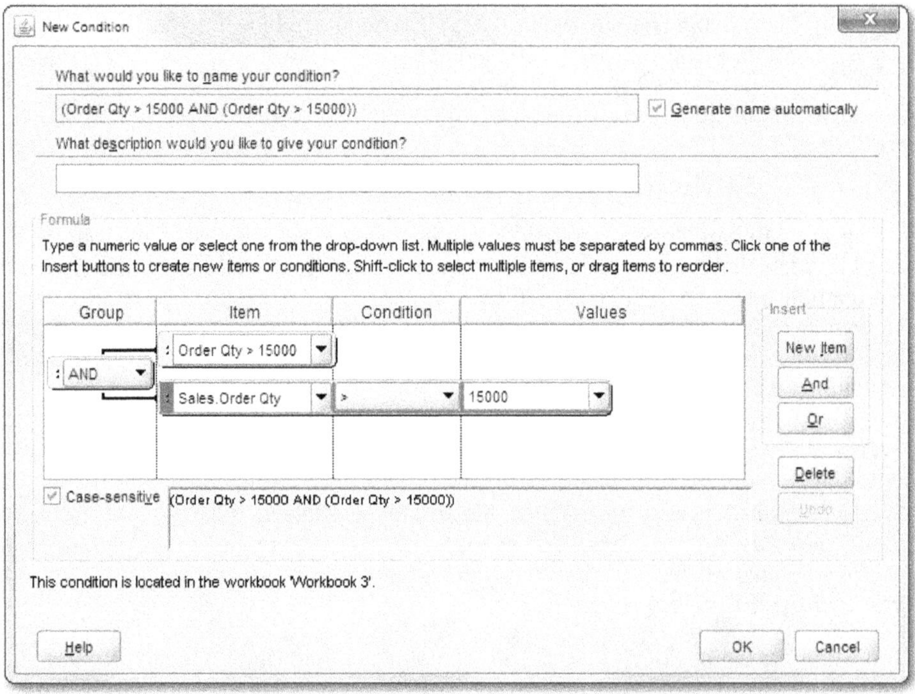

As you can see in the preceding illustration, Discoverer has added a second instance of the condition, but this time it has made it available for editing. Isn't that nice?

**NOTE**
*Remember, you cannot edit administrator-defined conditions. By copying them, you are in effect creating a new condition, a condition that you can edit. Basically, the original condition is used as a template.*

We edited this second condition and changed it so that it now selects quantities between 7,000 and 8,000, as shown here:

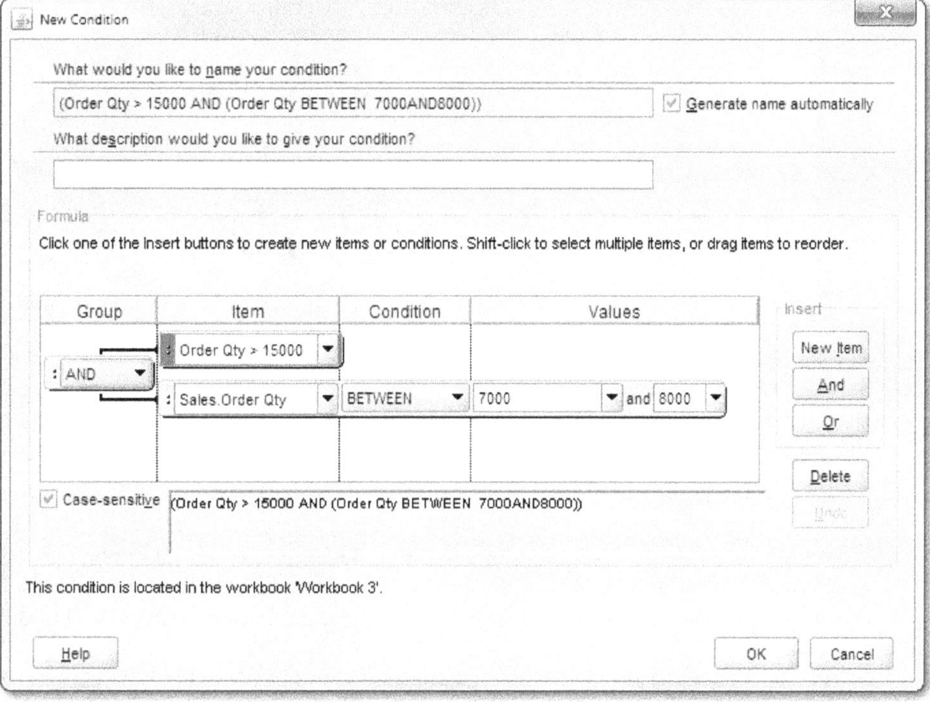

**NOTE**
*To show you the preceding illustration, we had to widen the extended New Condition dialog box. You can do this by clicking one of the sides and dragging it to the required size.*

As you can see from the preceding illustration, the two parts of this condition are out of sync with each other. It is not possible to select order quantities in excess of 15,000 while at the same time selecting order quantities between 7,000 and 8,000. Discoverer will allow you to complete this condition, but the query will return no data.

We now have to add the third component of this complex condition, the bit that constrains the status to only orders that are on hold. We clicked New Item, or Add if you are using Desktop, and then added the third condition so that our complex condition now looks as shown here:

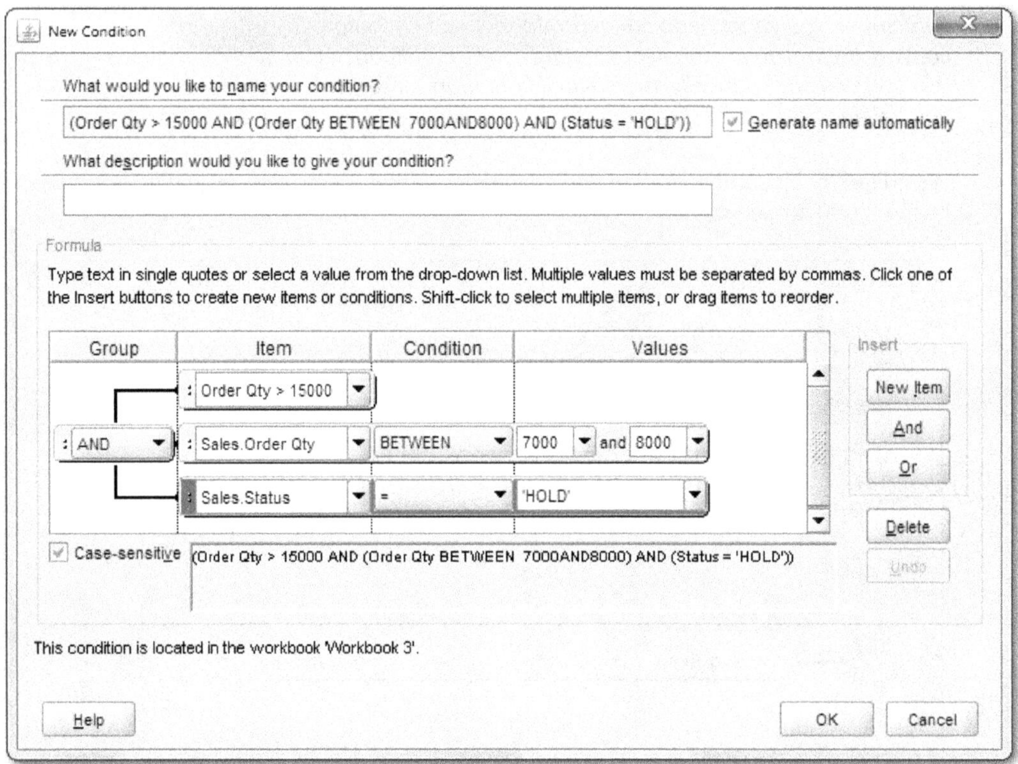


You will notice that our current complex condition has three separate components joined together using AND. We need to convert the structure of our condition such that it satisfies our original request for Order quantity > 15000 'OR' (order quantity between 7000 and 8000, 'AND' the status is open).

To accomplish this, we needed to create a sublevel within our condition based on the items that are in parentheses. Before we did that, we changed the overall Group item to be OR. To do this, we clicked the AND operator in the Group area and then clicked the OR button. This gave us the complex condition shown next. In particular, notice how Discoverer has defined the SQL syntax.

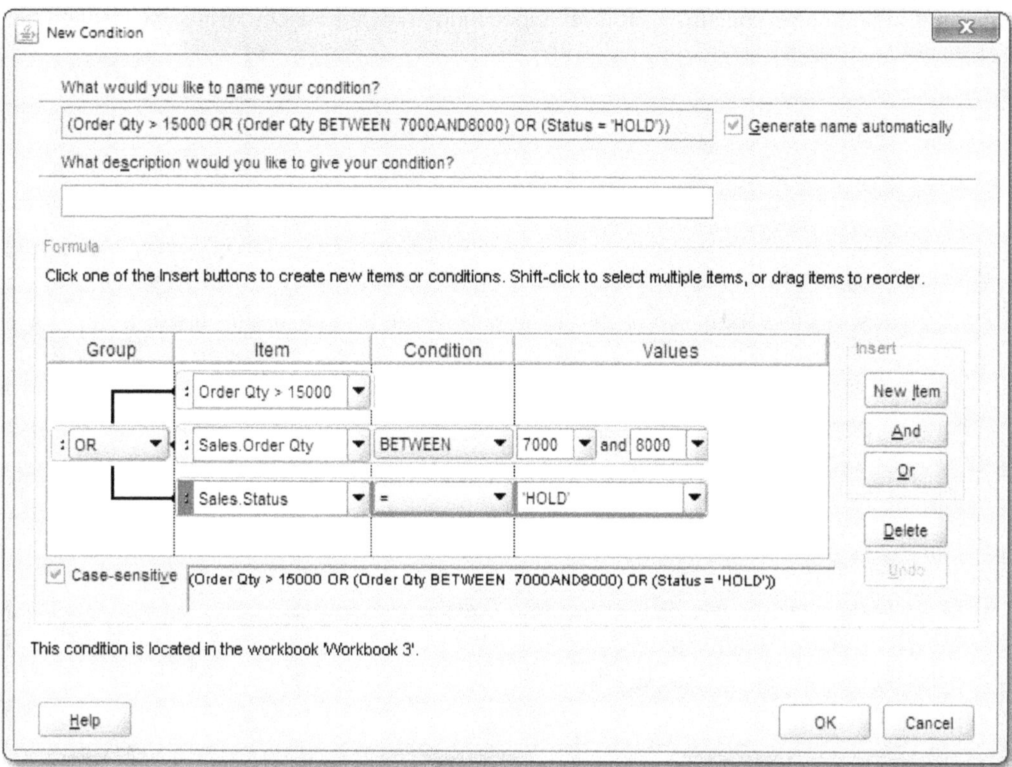


To complete our condition, we need to insert the sublevel. To create a sublevel in a complex condition, use this workflow:

1. Determine which items need to be part of the sublevel.
2. Click the row selection button to the left of the first item that needs to be part of the sublevel. This highlights the row selection button (see Figures 12-7 and 12-8).
3. Hold down CTRL and click the row selection button for the next condition that needs to be part of the sublevel.
4. Click the Boolean operator button you want to apply to the two conditions selected. Discoverer will now create a new sublevel to your condition.
5. Check that the Boolean operator linking the new sublevel to the remainder of the complex condition is correct. If not, click it and change it.
6. Repeat steps 2–5 as many times as needed, creating as many sublevels as is necessary.
7. When you have finished creating sublevels, click OK.

Using this workflow, we clicked the row selection button for the second order quantity condition (between 7,000 and 8,000), held down CTRL, clicked the row selection button for the status condition, and then finally clicked AND. You can see in the following illustration how our complex condition now contains a sublevel. Once more, notice how Discoverer has defined the SQL syntax.

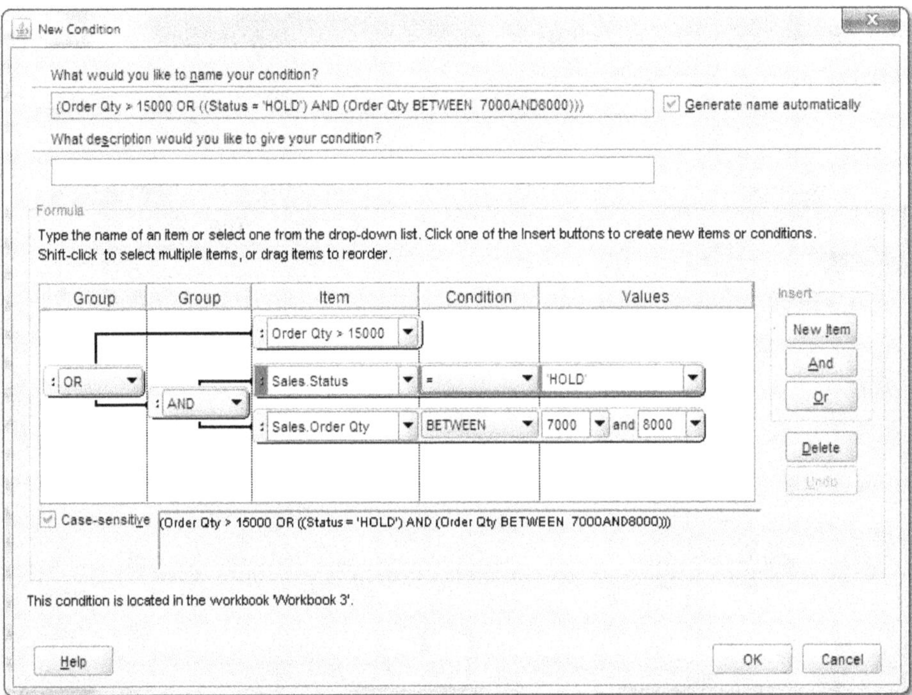


Finally, when we clicked OK to complete the condition, Discoverer ran the query again and gave us the following result. As you can see in the next illustration, we do indeed have both conditions satisfied. We have a row containing an on-hold order with a quantity between 7,000 and 8,000, while at the same time we have several other rows containing quantities in excess of 15,000.

| | ▸ Status | ▸ Order Number | ▸ Order Qty SUM |
|---|---|---|---|
| 1 | HOLD | 2818 | 8000 |
| 2 | OPEN | 2822 | 16000 |
| 3 | | 3134 | 24000 |
| 4 | | 3392 | 34800 |
| 5 | | 3394 | 30000 |
| 6 | SHIPPED | 2404 | 18000 |
| 7 | | 2414 | 15600 |
| 8 | | 2559 | 26400 |
| 9 | | 4395 | 16000 |
| 10 | | 4748 | 26400 |
| 11 | | 4810 | 15600 |
| 12 | | 4924 | 18000 |
| 13 | | 5649 | 18000 |
| 14 | | 5923 | 16000 |
| 15 | | 6831 | 15600 |
| 16 | | 7015 | 26400 |

## Using Subqueries

The final type of complex condition uses subqueries. These conditions use the results from another worksheet to determine the value or values to be used within the conditions. You can build very complex queries using this type of condition. In fact, you can even combine the results from different worksheets to be applied as values to be used within conditions of your current worksheet.

**NOTE**
*Remember, you cannot create a condition based on a subquery in Plus, but conditions created in Desktop using subqueries can be used in Plus.*

These types of queries are very easy to use and build, but they can dramatically increase the length of time it will take for your query to run. Many queries using subqueries could be rewritten as Boolean conditions. You should, therefore, use subqueries only when it is impossible to build a condition or conditions within the main query that would give you the result you are looking for.

There are two types of subquery conditions. They are

- Subqueries using single items
- Subqueries using correlated items

Whichever type of subquery condition you decide to build, you will use the Create Subquery dialog box.

## Create Subquery Dialog Box

The only way to create a condition based on a subquery is to use the Create Subquery dialog box. This box, as shown in Figure 12-9, has the following features:

- **Subquery sheet selection** In this area, you can type in or use the associated drop-down list to tell Discoverer which sheet to use.
- **Item Match** In this area, you can type in or use the associated drop-down list to tell Discoverer which item to use in the sheet being linked to.

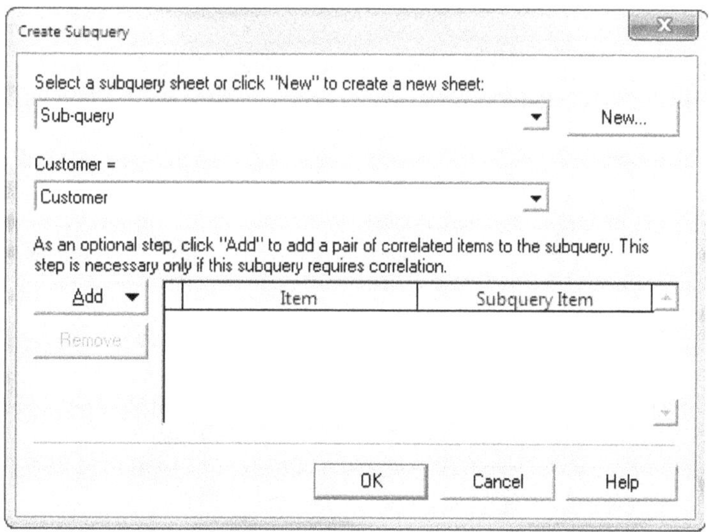


**FIGURE 12-9.** *The Create Subquery dialog box*

- **New** Click this button to create a new worksheet, in which you intend to build constraints to define the item you want your main query to link to.
- **Add** Click this button to add a pair of correlated items to the subquery.
- **Remove** Click this button to remove a pair of correlated items from the subquery.

### Building a Condition Using a Subquery

Whether you decide to build a condition using a single value from a subquery or using correlated items, the way you build the condition is the same.

To build a condition based on a subquery, use the following workflow:

1. Open the New Condition dialog box.
2. Select the item you want to use to link to the subquery, and then select an expression.
3. From the Values drop-down list, choose Create Subquery. This opens the Create Subquery dialog box shown in Figure 12-9.
4. Discoverer tries to find a link to the item you chose in step 2 within an existing worksheet in the workbook. If a link can be found, Discoverer inserts both the sheet and item names into the dialog box. If multiple sheets exist and the one you want is not the one Discoverer has defaulted to, use the drop-down list of worksheets to locate the worksheet that you want and then use the drop-down list of items to locate the item.
5. If the worksheet does not exist, use the New button to create a new worksheet. This opens the Workbook Wizard, ready for you to build the new worksheet. After you have specified the new worksheet, Discoverer will return you to the Create Subquery dialog box.
6. If you are using correlated items, Discoverer will allow you to link to an item only in the same worksheet that you based the initial subquery on.
7. Click OK. Discoverer applies the condition, creating any new worksheet that was defined in step 5.

This workflow, while not having many steps, is complex. Take your time learning this workflow. Steps 4, 5, and 6, in particular, involve much more than the mere clicking of a button.

Please take it easy when building conditions based on subqueries, because the time taken to run the query could be very long. This is especially true if you are scanning the whole database against several values in a subquery. We have found that basing the subquery on items that have small lists of values, such as sales channels, statuses, codes, or customer names, will improve the performance of these types of conditions. Using items that have large lists of values, such as sales order numbers, quantities, amounts, and dates, will take much longer.

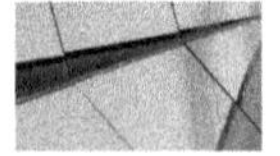

**NOTE**

*If you edit a subquery and cause the values to change, Discoverer will not recognize that the values being linked to have changed, even if you manually make Discoverer rerun the original query. This limitation prevents us from building template queries that automatically work out, using subqueries, new sets of values based on time. The only way to make Discoverer refresh a link to a subquery is to edit the subquery condition itself. For details on how to force Discoverer to use the latest subquery data, refer to the section "Editing a Subquery" later in this chapter.*

### Subqueries Without Correlated Items

These are the simplest type of subquery condition to build and understand. Whether you build the subquery first or build it from within the main worksheet makes no difference to Discoverer. However, if the subquery requires some manipulations or extremely complicated mathematical computations, we advise you to create the subquery first. Spending time refining subqueries to make them efficient in terms of indexes and items being selected will prove to be time well spent.

A good example, and the one that we will show you here, makes sheet 1 (the subquery) return a list of all customers who have had a cancellation in the current month; then, using that list, it makes the current query return a list of those customers who also have outstanding orders not yet shipped. You might want to have a heads-up and be aware that these orders could be in risk of being cancelled as well. At the very least, you should have the salesperson call the customer and make sure the outstanding orders are still required.

The preceding query could be created both ways, either building the subquery first or building the main query and then building the subquery as part of the condition. We will show you both ways.

**Example Subquery, Building Subquery First** First, we built the query that is destined to become the subquery. In this example, we selected the customer name, the fiscal cancellation month of April 2013, and the total quantity ordered. We don't need to use the status in this query because orders with a cancellation date are cancelled! When we ran this query, as you can see in this illustration, it returned a list of the 15 customers who had cancelled an order in April.

Page Items: Cancelled Month: APR-13

| | Customer | Order Qty SUM |
|---|---|---|
| 1 | ABC WIDGET CO | 50 |
| 2 | BIG RIVER WIDGETS | 1200 |
| 3 | CASA DE WIDGETS | 1300 |
| 4 | CEBU WIDGET CO | 10000 |
| 5 | HONG KONG WIDGETS | 15000 |
| 6 | MOUNTAIN WIDGETS | 200 |
| 7 | PATRIOT'S WIDGET CO. | 50 |
| 8 | RIO WIDGETS | 2600 |
| 9 | WE'VE GOT WIDGETS | 700 |
| 10 | WIDGET SUPPLY CO. | 4320 |
| 11 | WIDGETS DE MEXICO | 200 |
| 12 | WIDGETS MARKET | 2400 |
| 13 | WIDGETS OESTE | 100 |
| 14 | WIDGETS R US | 100 |
| 15 | WILD WEST WIDGETS | 1200 |

To make this example easier to follow, we have named this sheet Sub-query.

Next, we opened a new sheet in the workbook (Sheet | New Sheet from the menu bar). In this sheet, we selected the customer name (for the link), the same fiscal order month of April 2013, the status OPEN, and the total quantity ordered for all customers who currently have a balance of 2,000 or more items. The status is required this time because we need to identify which orders are not shipped. When we ran this query, as you can see here, it returned a list of 13 customers with open orders.

Page Items: Order Month: APR-13 | Status: OPEN

| | Customer | Order Qty SUM |
|---|---|---|
| 1 | ACE MANUFACTURING | 3100 |
| 2 | BIG RIVER WIDGETS | 2700 |
| 3 | CASA DE WIDGETS | 14500 |
| 4 | CEBU WIDGET CO | 15600 |
| 5 | LAST RAILWAY WIDGETS | 3900 |
| 6 | OXFORD WIDGETS | 6440 |
| 7 | THE LITTLE WIDGET | 2400 |
| 8 | THING'S | 2680 |
| 9 | WARSAW WIDGETS | 2400 |
| 10 | WE'VE GOT WIDGETS | 9420 |
| 11 | WIDGETS R US | 10000 |
| 12 | WILD WEST WIDGETS | 5000 |
| 13 | YAMATA WIDGET LTD. | 7480 |

We now need to build a new condition restricting the main sheet to only the customers from sheet 1. To do this, we will follow the workflow we gave you earlier.

First, we opened the New Condition dialog box, and then from the drop-down list of items we selected the customer name, set the expression to be =, and set the value to be Create Subquery. As you can see earlier in Figure 12-9, this opened the Create Subquery dialog box. Discoverer has already found another sheet in our query, the sheet entitled Sub-query, and has also scanned all of the items in that sheet, locating a Customer Name item. These values have automatically been inserted into the Create Subquery dialog box.

Because all required items within the Create Subquery box were complete, we clicked OK. Discoverer returned us to the New Condition dialog box, where we could see the resulting condition was Customer Name = Sub-query. Clicking OK this time caused Discoverer to rerun the query using the condition that we had just defined, returning only those customers with current orders of 2,000 or more items who placed an order in April 2013 and also had a cancellation in the same month.

As you can see here, we have six customers who match the criteria that we defined.

Page Items: Order Month: APR-13 ▾ | Status: OPEN ▾

| | Customer | Order Qty SUM |
|---|---|---|
| 1 | BIG RIVER WIDGETS | 2700 |
| 2 | CASA DE WIDGETS | 14500 |
| 3 | CEBU WIDGET CO | 15600 |
| 4 | WE'VE GOT WIDGETS | 9420 |
| 5 | WIDGETS R US | 10000 |
| 6 | WILD WEST WIDGETS | 5000 |

**Example Subquery, Building Main Query First** This time we built the main query first and then opened the New Condition dialog box. We will not show you any illustrations, because these are the same as in the preceding example. We again selected the Customer Name from the Item drop-down list, set the expression to be =, and set the value to be Create Subquery. This time when we entered the Create Subquery dialog box (see Figure 12-9), Discoverer was unable to populate any of its fields because there was no subquery within the workbook.

We therefore needed to add a new sheet. Clicking Add launched the Workbook Wizard. In there, we created a new query using the customer name and quantity ordered for April 2013. When we clicked Finish to complete this query, rather than running it, Discoverer returned us to the Create Subquery dialog box. Because the subquery was now complete, we clicked OK and completed the condition.

## Subqueries Using Correlated Items

Queries using correlated items are simply queries that link to more than one item in the subquery. For example, suppose you had a subquery that returned the average unit selling price for each product sold in the past month. Using correlated items, you could analyze the selling price of the same products by customer, returning a list of customers who had paid more than the average selling price for their goods. Obviously, last month these customers were willing to pay more than the average price for these items. Therefore, if you want to quickly increase your profits for the current month, all you need to do is have a salesperson contact these customers and see whether they are willing to buy some more. You could even offer them a discount yet still sell to them at above the average selling price!

We will show you how to create this query. We have chosen to build the subquery first, although we could just as easily have opted to build the main query first.

For the subquery, we selected the product name, the average selling price, and the average quantity shipped for January 2013. We then created a calculation to derive the average unit price, by dividing the average quantity shipped into the average selling price. This produced the list as shown here.

For the main query, we selected the customer name, average selling price, average quantity shipped, and product name for the same month. We also calculated the customer's unit price, and then we launched the New Condition dialog box. Here, we created a new condition where the customer's unit price was greater than the unit price in the subquery. We then clicked Add in the Create Subquery dialog box to add a correlated item.

Page Items: Shipped Month: JAN-13

| | Product | Selling Price AVG | Shipped Qty AVG | Unit Price |
|---|---|---|---|---|
| 1 | AB-2008 | 18630.00 | 1380 | 13.50 |
| 2 | AB-2500 | 40690.71 | 3163 | 12.87 |
| 3 | AB-3000 | 36186.63 | 1703 | 21.25 |
| 4 | AVR-500 | 59724.57 | 2216 | 26.95 |
| 5 | AVR-550 | 128551.50 | 4770 | 26.95 |
| 6 | AVR-800 | 19473.30 | 562 | 34.65 |
| 7 | AVR-900 | 135828.00 | 3777 | 35.96 |
| 8 | CD-100 | 43838.20 | 2875 | 15.25 |
| 9 | CD-200 | 14091.00 | 924 | 15.25 |
| 10 | CD-500 | 16413.20 | 740 | 22.18 |
| 11 | CD-550 | 15526.00 | 700 | 22.18 |
| 12 | CD-625 | 62542.38 | 2814 | 22.23 |
| 13 | DS-1200 | 9354.85 | 1491 | 6.27 |
| 14 | MS-1200 | 22755.00 | 4100 | 5.55 |
| 15 | MS-1300 | 11400.00 | 1900 | 6.00 |
| 16 | QB-1000 | 52653.07 | 2245 | 23.45 |
| 17 | QB-2008 | 32751.83 | 1397 | 23.45 |
| 18 | QB-3000 | 64878.33 | 2767 | 23.45 |
| 19 | QB-5000 | 44301.37 | 2509 | 17.66 |
| 20 | QB-5500 | 43237.57 | 2444 | 17.69 |
| 21 | QB-6000 | 13562.88 | 1085 | 12.50 |

In the following illustration, you can see both the New Condition and Create Subquery dialog boxes. In the New Condition dialog box, we selected Cust Unit Price from the Item drop-down box, changed the expression to >, and then selected Create Subquery from the Values drop-down list. This opened the Create Subquery dialog box, in which Discoverer detected the existence of an existing sheet but was unable to detect a Cust Unit Price field. We had to select Unit Price from the drop-down list. After clicking Add to add a correlated item, from the drop-down list we selected Product Name. Discoverer, finding a matching item in sheet 1, automatically made the correlation.

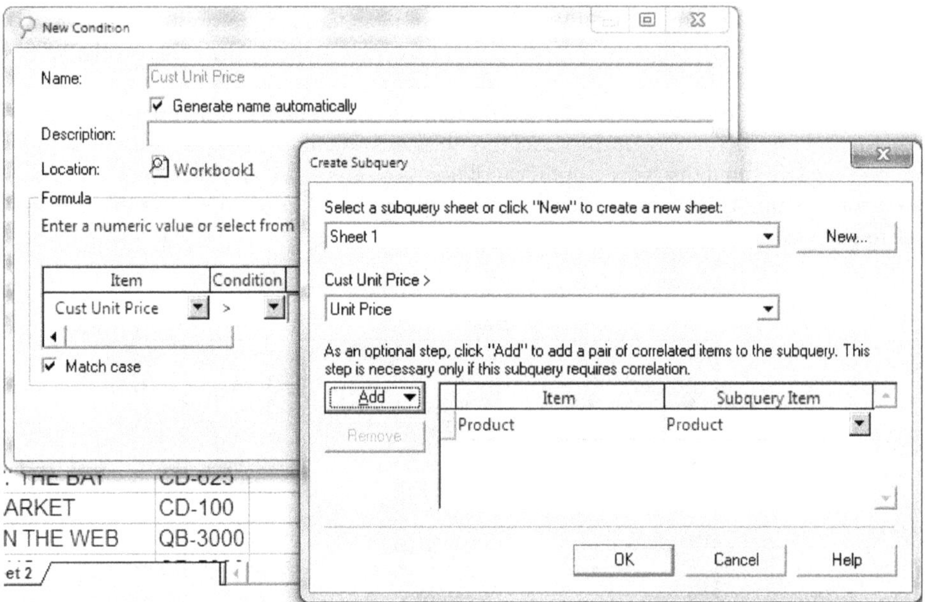


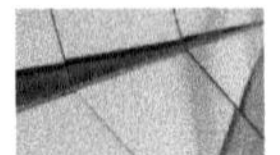

**NOTE**
*In the previous example, both the subquery and the main query use division to calculate the unit cost. To ensure that reports such as these work correctly, you should make sure you trap any divide-by-zero errors. The easiest way of doing this is to add an additional condition to both queries so that you select only the data where the average quantity shipped is greater than zero.*

## Editing a Subquery

Unfortunately, as previously mentioned, Discoverer will not detect that the data being returned in a subquery has changed. Therefore, changing a subquery will have no impact on the main query that it is referenced by. This will produce totally unexpected results when comparing the output of the worksheets.

In the preceding example, when we showed you how to build a subquery excluding correlated items, we constrained the subquery to return a list of customers who had cancellations in April 2013. Editing the subquery by adding a new condition to show only those customers who had total cancellations with a quantity in excess of 3,000 will result in a smaller list of customers. This will cause the subquery result to change, but not the main query. Even if you refresh the main sheet, it will not recognize the new list and will continue to be constrained on the original subquery.

To compound the problem, if we share this query with someone who is not very proficient in Discoverer, that person will look at the conditions for the subquery and assume that the main query result is correct, totally unaware that there is a mismatch.

The only way to correct this is to edit the subquery condition. This will cause Discoverer to recognize that the subquery has changed. To show you how this works, we added a new condition to the subquery, where the order quantity is greater than 3,000. When we ran the query in the master sheet, as expected, Discoverer did not warn us that the subquery had changed.

As we were aware of the situation, we launched the Conditions dialog box, highlighted the Customer Name IN Sub-query condition, and then clicked the Edit button. In the Edit Condition dialog box, we opened the drop-down list in the Value field. As you can see here, Discoverer added another option to the list, the option Edit Subquery:

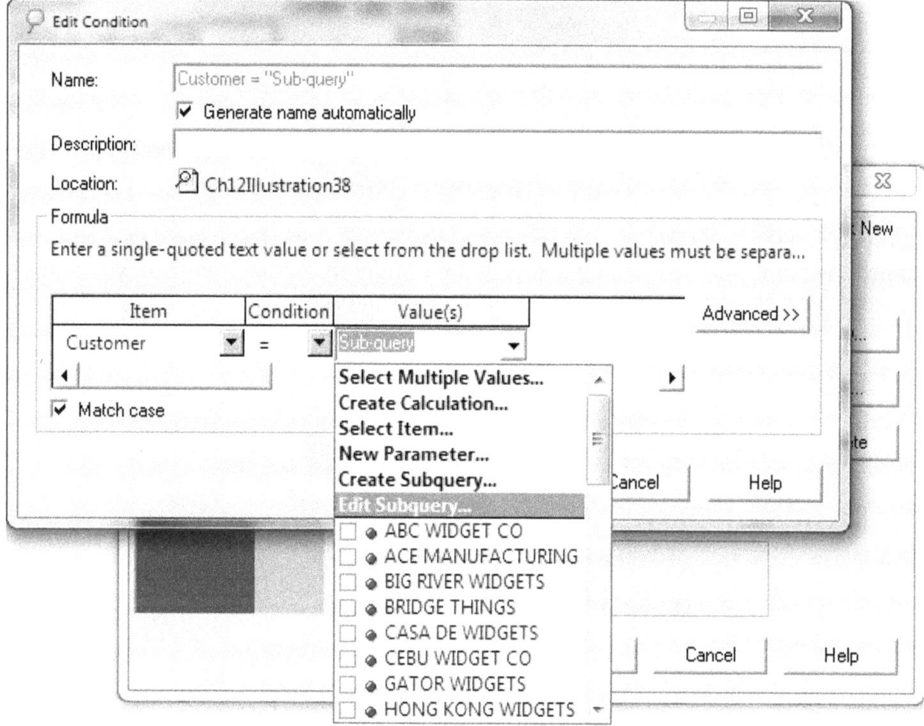


Selecting Edit Subquery caused Discoverer to at last recognize that the subquery had changed. As you can see in the next illustration, we were given the following warning that the subquery had changed. We clicked Yes, then clicked OK in the Edit Subquery box, and completed the condition. This caused Discoverer to rerun the query correctly.

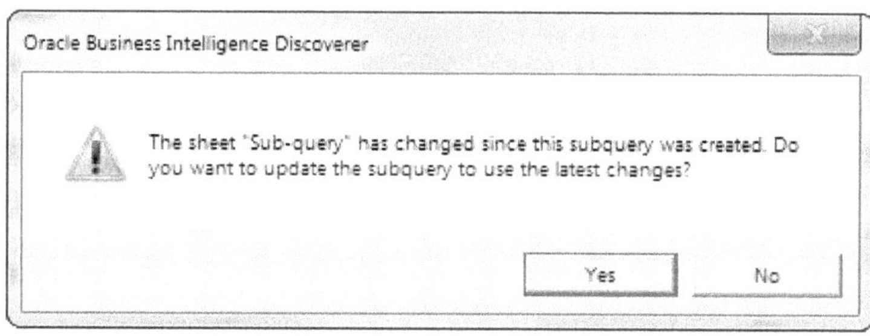

## Subqueries and Discoverer Plus

As previously mentioned, in Discoverer Plus you cannot create, maintain, or edit conditions that are based on subqueries. However, you can execute worksheets that use subqueries. Look at the following illustration:

Page Items: Order Month: APR-13 | Status: OPEN

| | Customer | Order Qty SUM |
|---|---|---|
| 1 | BIG RIVER WIDGETS | 2700 |
| 2 | CASA DE WIDGETS | 14500 |
| 3 | CEBU WIDGET CO | 15600 |
| 4 | WE'VE GOT WIDGETS | 9420 |
| 5 | WIDGETS R US | 10000 |
| 6 | WILD WEST WIDGETS | 5000 |

As you can see, we have run our report for April 2013 using Discoverer Plus and have obtained the correct answer. Looking now at the Conditions tab, shown here, you will see that Discoverer Plus correctly identifies that a subquery is in use:

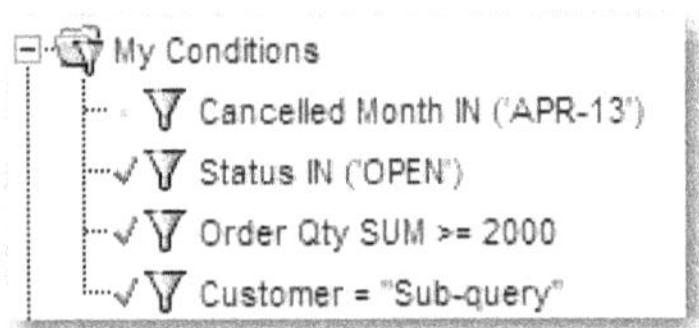


However, if we try to edit the Sub-query condition, we will get the following message:

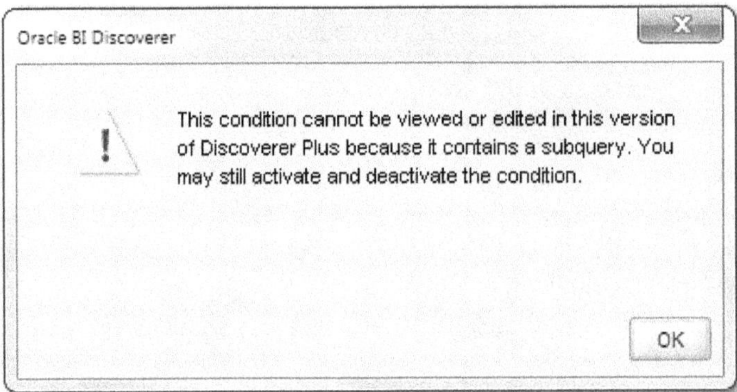

Oracle BI Discoverer
This condition cannot be viewed or edited in this version of Discoverer Plus because it contains a subquery. You may still activate and deactivate the condition.
OK


As you can see, Plus has reminded us that we cannot edit or view this condition because it contains a subquery. We can still activate and deactivate the condition, though.

# Removing Conditions

There are three very good reasons you may want to remove a condition. They are

- To return a query to its original state following analysis or printing
- Because you made a mistake and created an incorrect condition
- Because you avoided "the query from the Twilight Zone" and now want to open the query to produce some more meaningful results

There are two ways to permanently remove a condition from a query and one way to deactivate a condition yet still leave it *in situ* in case of a future requirement.

# Permanently Removing Conditions

As stated, there are two methods of permanently removing a condition from a query. They are

- To undo the last condition
- To delete the condition from the query

**NOTE**
*Deleting a condition from a workbook removes it from all worksheets in the workbook. If you have multiple worksheets in your workbook, you should be very careful not to delete a condition that is used by a worksheet other than the one you are currently working with. Discoverer will not warn you or prevent you from doing this.*

## Permanently Removing a Condition by Undoing the Last Condition

If you made a mistake and created an incorrect condition, you can return your query to its original state very easily by either pressing CTRL-Z or from the menu bar selecting Edit | Undo Conditions.

Either of these methods causes Discoverer to automatically undo the condition you just created. In fact, Discoverer actually deletes the condition.

**NOTE**
*You can use undo only immediately following the creation of a condition, although it does not matter which method you used to create the condition.*

## Deleting a Condition from a Workbook in Desktop

To delete a condition from a workbook in Desktop, you should use the following workflow:

1. Open the Conditions dialog box.
2. From the list of conditions displayed, highlight the condition you want to delete.
3. Click the Delete button.
4. Click OK.

### Deleting a Condition from a Workbook in Plus

To delete a condition from a workbook in Plus, you should use the following workflow:

1. Click the Conditions tab in the Available Items pane.
2. From the list of conditions displayed, highlight the condition you want to delete.
3. Right-click and from the drop-down select Delete.

## Deactivating a Condition

Deactivating a condition does not delete a condition from a workbook. In fact, unless you are certain that you no longer require a condition, you would be better advised to deactivate it. This recommendation has even more merit when there are multiple worksheets in the workbook.

### Deactivating a Condition in Desktop

To deactivate a condition in Desktop, use the following workflow:

1. Open the Conditions dialog box.
2. From the list of conditions displayed, uncheck the condition you want to deactivate.
3. Click OK.

### Deactivating a Condition in Plus

To deactivate a condition in Plus, use the following workflow:

1. Click the Conditions tab in the Available Items pane.
2. From the list of conditions displayed, right-click the condition you want to deactivate.
3. From the drop-down, select Remove From Worksheet.

# Removing Columns Upon Which Conditions Are Based

At first sight, this may seem a rather dangerous thing to do. However, the ability to remove a column from the display, without impacting any condition based upon that column, is another really useful feature in Discoverer. Discoverer will remember the item and will continue using it. There are two types of columns that you can remove. They are

- Columns based on data items from the database
- Columns based on calculations

## Removing a Database Item Used in Conditions

You are quite safe removing a database item from a query, even if that item is used in one or more conditions. This is because the item, being in the database, is still accessible. Discoverer will continue being able to apply conditions on that item, even if you no longer want to display the item in the final results set.

## Removing Calculations Used in Conditions

You can even remove calculated columns from the results set, and Discoverer will continue using those calculations within conditions. This is because when you remove a calculated column, Discoverer does not delete the calculation. Instead, Discoverer leaves the calculation in the workbook but marks it as being inactive. You can deactivate a calculation yet still allow Discoverer to use that calculation in a condition.

### Deactivating a Calculation Used in a Condition in Desktop

You have two ways to deactivate a calculation used in a condition in Desktop. They are as follows:

- Deactivate the calculation in the Calculations dialog box by removing the check mark alongside the calculation.
- Highlight the column heading and then press DELETE on your keyboard. This does not delete the calculation from the worksheet. The calculation is deactivated just as if you had unchecked it in the Calculations dialog box.

### Deactivating a Calculation Used in a Condition in Plus

You have two ways to deactivate a calculation used in a condition in Plus. They are as follows:

- Deactivate the calculation on the Calculations tab of the Available Items pane by right-clicking the calculation and selecting Remove From Worksheet from the drop-down list.
- Highlight the column heading, then right-click, and from the drop-down select Remove From Worksheet.
- Highlight the column heading and then press DELETE on your keyboard. This does not delete the calculation from the worksheet. The calculation is deactivated just as if you had unchecked it in the Calculations dialog box.

## Deleting Calculations Used in Conditions

Take care when deleting calculations from worksheets if those calculations are used in a condition. If you delete a calculation from a worksheet and that calculation is used in a condition, Discoverer also deletes the condition. You will not be warned that there is a condition dependent upon the calculation you are about to delete. The query will be rerun automatically, and the results you see will be minus both the calculation and the condition.

# Summary

In this chapter, we showed you how to build effective conditions and how learning this skill will allow you to unleash the power of Discoverer. You learned to add a condition using the analysis bar buttons to create a new condition. You saw how to use the Conditions dialog box to add a condition. We introduced you to a workflow to create a condition and showed you how to effectively use the New Condition dialog box.

You also saw how to put into practice the skills learned in the early part of the chapter, building skill by skill. We showed you real-world examples of building conditions using the workflow.

Next, you learned about the basic components of a condition: the item, the expression, and the value. Using these basic components, you learned to edit an existing condition. We also showed you how to take it a step further by using the Advanced button. This allows you to create conditions based on other conditions, conditions based on calculations, conditions using Boolean operators, and conditions using subqueries. We taught you how to create conditions using correlated items and how to edit a subquery.

Finally, we showed you how to remove conditions temporarily and permanently, as well as how to undo a condition. You learned how to delete a condition from a workbook and how to deactivate a condition. We also explained how you can remove items from a worksheet, while still allowing Discoverer to use those items in conditions.

In the next chapter, you will continue to learn important advanced techniques that will allow you greater and greater control of this powerful product.

# CHAPTER 13

# Refining Parameters, Calculations, Sorting, and Percentages

This, the third chapter in the advanced techniques section of the book, will deal with parameters, calculations, sorting, and percentages. As you become more expert in Discoverer, your queries will become more complex. A change in one data item could bring about the need to change a variety of query definitions. Chapter 12 took an in-depth look at conditions. By changing a condition, you may need to reevaluate one or more of the following items: parameters, conditions, sorts, and percentages.

In this chapter, you will learn to change a condition to a parameter, use dynamic parameters, activate and deactivate parameters, edit parameters, and rearrange the order of parameters. We will also show you how to define mandatory and optional parameters and to manage cascading parameters. We will show you how to refine calculations by defining the main components of a calculation and how to define the calculation in advance. You will learn how to convert an algorithm into a Discoverer script as well as how to avoid division-by-zero errors. For information about how to create calculations using analytic functions, please see Chapter 21.

We will show you housekeeping techniques to use after editing a condition by reviewing conditions based on calculations and reviewing the data items used in the edited calculation. We will explain how to use standard functions and show you how to define calculations for standard margin and markup. You will be taught how to place a final refinement on the sort order, as well as how to remove an item from the sort order. Finally, we will show you techniques for refining percentages, including how to change and how to remove them.

# Refining Parameters

After dealing with conditions, as we did in Chapter 12, the next most common way to refine a query is to refine or define parameters. The ability to convert conditions into parameters is essential if you are going to build queries on behalf of your department.

Parameters can be considered as placeholders that are used instead of hard-coded values in the definition of a condition. Unlike normal conditions, which always return the same results each time the worksheet is executed, parameters offer you the chance to enter a value before the worksheet is executed. The value entered is then fed to the condition, with the net result that the same worksheet can produce a variety of results.

Parameters are particularly useful if many people have access to the same worksheet. Discoverer will then produce a result that is of interest only to a particular person or department. As you can see, the use of parameters can save time and money, allowing you the freedom to move on to other tasks. Later, when a change is required to this query, you have only one worksheet to worry about. If, however, you had built one workbook per user, you would have many queries to refine.

Chapter 5 has detailed instructions on creating parameters and explains the difference between parameters and conditions. We also showed you how to build a parameter. However, we did not show you how to convert a condition into a parameter. In this section on refining parameters, we will show you how to convert a condition into a parameter as well as how to edit a parameter.

## Changing a Condition to a Parameter

In Chapter 4, we advised you to avoid "the query from the Twilight Zone" by applying strict conditions. Those hard-coded conditions need to be either replaced or converted into parameters to make the query more useful and flexible.

## Workflow to Convert a Condition into a Parameter

To change a condition to a parameter, use the following workflow:

1. Open the Edit Condition dialog box and make any changes to the condition that may be required.

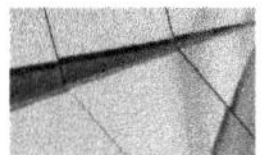

**NOTE**
*If you want your users to be able to use wildcard characters in the Parameter Wizard, you must ensure that you build the condition using the LIKE expression. Creating conditions using expressions such as = and < will return no data and need changing.*

2. From the Values drop-down list, select New Parameter. This opens the New Parameter dialog box, as shown in Figures 13-1 and 13-2. Refer to Chapter 5 if you are unsure how to use this box.
3. Enter a meaningful name if you so choose. This is not a required field, but if you do add your own name, we recommend that you use meaningful names. Later, when you are editing your conditions or placing them in the title of your worksheet, this will help you differentiate between hard-coded conditions and parameters.

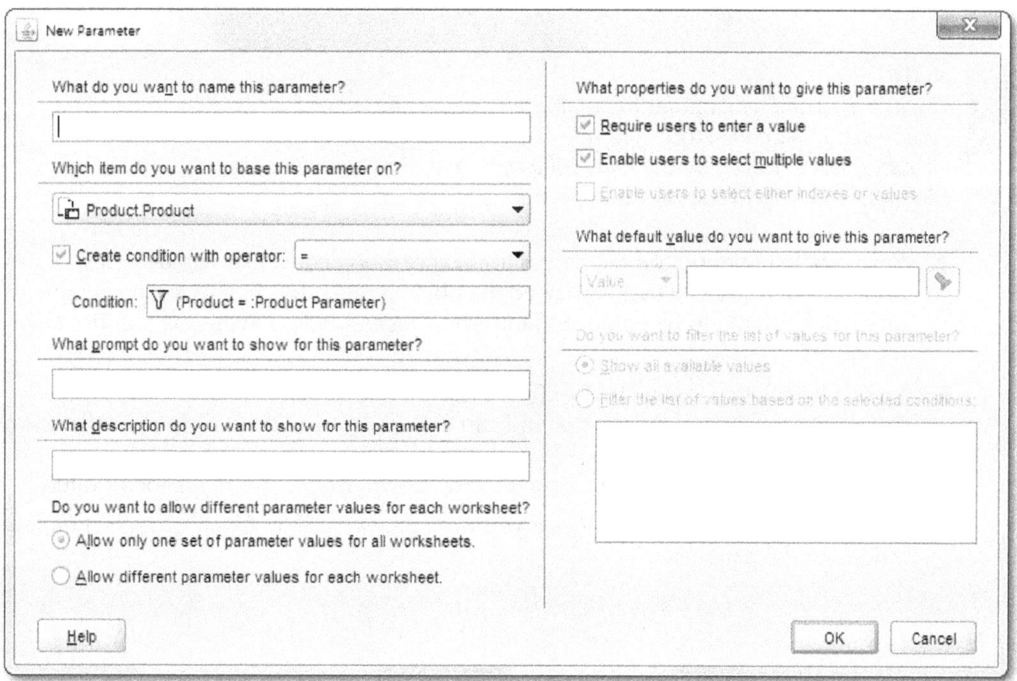


**FIGURE 13-1.** *Plus New Parameter dialog box*

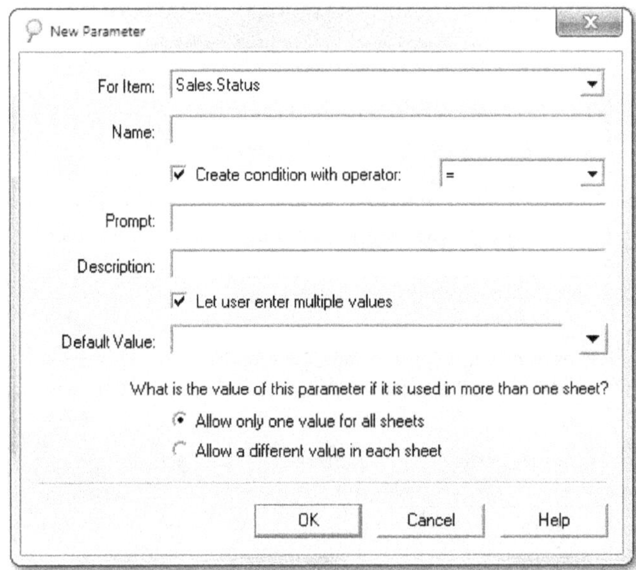


**FIGURE 13-2.** *Desktop New Parameter dialog box*

**NOTE**
*The use of meaningful names in parameters extends the power of Discoverer. In a header, footer, or title, if you type the ampersand character (&) followed by the name of a parameter or page item, you can make that object display exactly where you want it.*

4. Enter a helpful prompt for the end user. This needs to be text that will be easily understood by the end user. It may not be obvious what the choices for the parameter are. It doesn't hurt to be polite, and the words *please, bitte, s'ilvous plait,* or *por favor* go a long way.
5. Enter a description if you choose. This is not a required field. However, this is an excellent extension of the prompt and can actually contain the list of values that the end user may choose from. We like to use this field as context-sensitive help. It's where we add comments such as "Select from the drop-down list or leave blank for *all* values."
6. Check the box for multiple values if you want the end user to be able to select multiple values for the parameter.

7. Enter a default value if you choose. If a drop-down list is available, you should select the default from that list. This is not a required field.
8. Decide whether you want the values entered into this parameter to be applicable to the current worksheet only or to the whole workbook. In Desktop, the radio buttons are Allow Only One Value For All Sheets and Allow A Different Value In Each Sheet. In Plus, the radio buttons are Allow Only One Set Of Parameter Values For All Worksheets and Allow Different Parameter Values For Each Worksheet. The default is to make the parameter values available across the whole workbook.
9. In Plus only, you can choose whether the parameter is mandatory or optional by checking or unchecking the Require Users To Enter a Value box. We describe the use of mandatory and optional parameters later in this chapter.
10. Click OK and complete editing the condition. You will notice that Discoverer references the parameter by placing a colon followed by the parameter name.

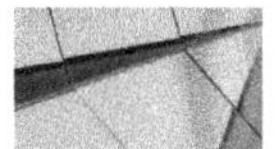

**NOTE**
*The workflow outlined here is different from the workflow given in Chapter 5. This workflow is based on an existing condition, which means the data item and operator are already selected for you. You cannot change them.*

### Converting a Condition into a Parameter Using the Workflow

In our database, we have an existing query that has multiple conditions and no parameters. Following the preceding workflow, we will show you how to change one of the conditions to a parameter. Once you have learned this skill, you will be able to convert any condition to a parameter.

Our example query displays the order number, product name, shipped quantity, shipped date, and status. The status is located on the page axis. We are editing the workbook in Discoverer Plus, and our current worksheet has two conditions.

- Order Qty > 15000 (an administrator-defined condition)
- Status = SHIPPED

Following the workflow, we opened the Edit Condition dialog box for the Status condition, and then from the Values drop-down list we selected New Parameter. This opened the New Parameter dialog box, as shown in Figure 13-1.

As you can see in the following illustration, we have completed the dialog box and given the parameter the name Status. We could have chosen not to add our own name, allowing Discoverer to create one for us, but we like to name our parameters. The rest of the fields are self-explanatory.

When we add a default of 'SHIPPED', the parameter duplicates the original condition, thereby allowing the end user to run the query as it was originally built.

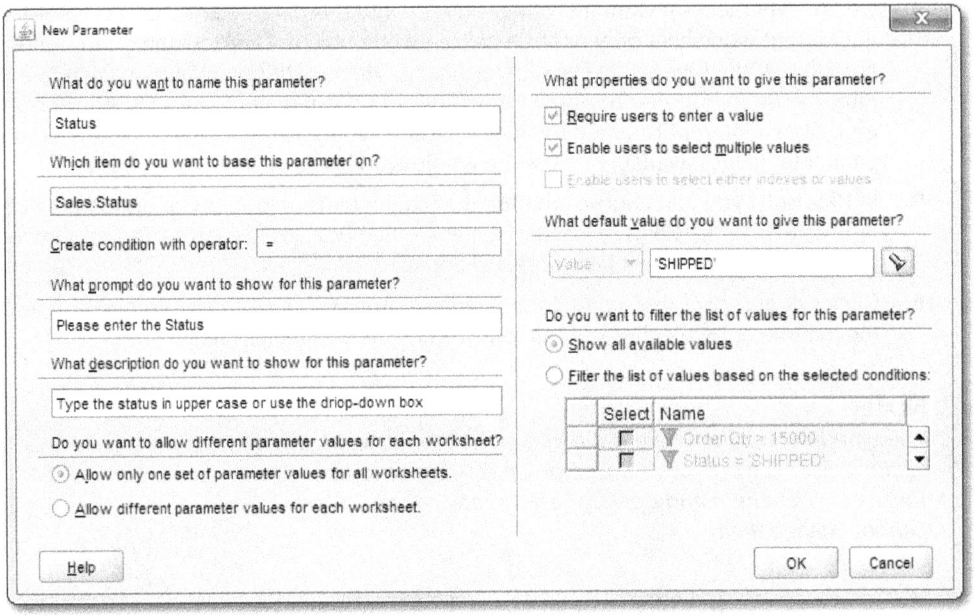

The parameter is now complete, so we click OK. This returns us to the Edit Condition dialog box shown next. As you can now see, Discoverer has changed the condition value to be the name of the parameter prefixed by a colon.

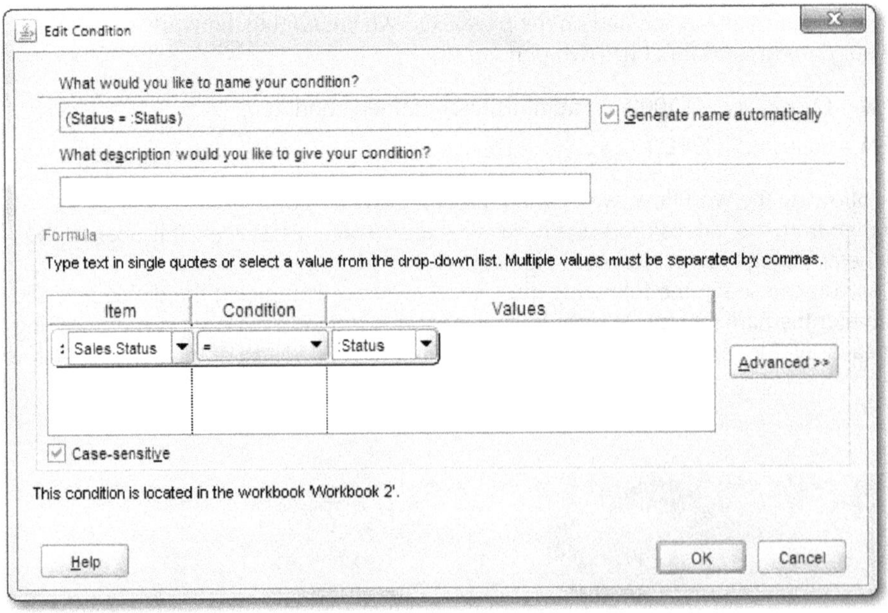

The condition is now complete, and we click OK to complete the condition. Discoverer now runs the query and, in Plus, presents us with the following Edit Parameter Values dialog box. In Desktop this is called the Parameter Wizard dialog box. As you can see, Discoverer has inserted the default and description that we specified. If the item that the parameter is based upon has a list of values, you can see that Discoverer has also added a flashlight button (this will be a drop-down arrow in Desktop) alongside the default.

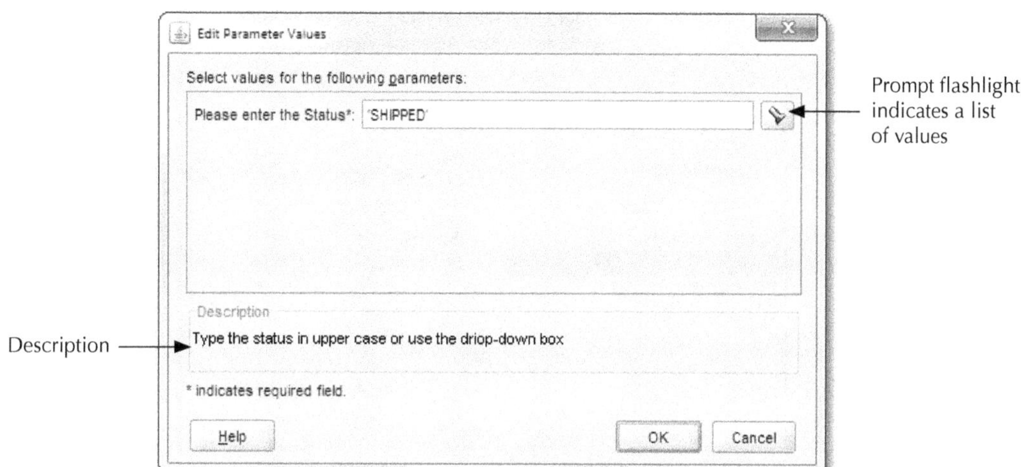


When we click the flashlight alongside the default, Discoverer opens the Select Values dialog box. As you can see, the list contains all the values for the Status item, along with buttons for adding or removing items from the selected list. If you are using Desktop and the user is allowed to select multiple values, this dialog box will have an additional item called Select Multiple Values at the bottom of the list.

In addition, and also available only in Plus, at the top of the box is a Search For area. Using this area, you can search for items within the list of values, thereby reducing the list to only those items that match your chosen search criteria. In our example we have only four values, so there is probably no need to search. However, you may easily have parameters that have hundreds of values. Your users can cut down the number of displayed values by making effective use of Discoverer's search technology. As an example, however, we keyed the value ED into the Search for box and clicked Go. As you can see in the illustration that follows, Discoverer now only displays CANCELLED and SHIPPED.

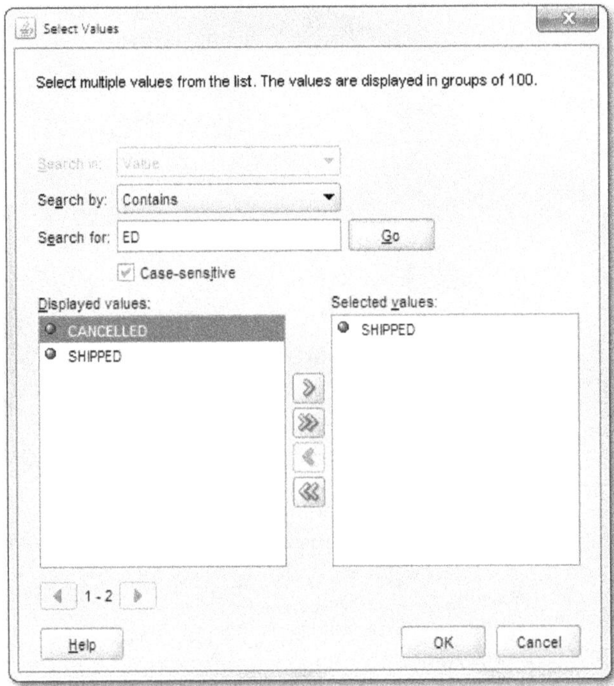


Having selected one or more values from the list provided, clicking OK in the Select Values dialog box returns the user to the Edit Parameter Values dialog box. Clicking OK in Plus, or Finish in Desktop, causes Discoverer to run the query using the parameters entered.

**NOTE**

*By carefully using the default values in parameters, you can force the query to run as it was originally built. If a user clicks OK in Plus, or Finish in Desktop, when prompted, without changing the default, the query will return the same result as if there were still a hard-coded condition.*

## Creating a Condition from a Parameter

By now, you should understand that while you are creating conditions, you can create an associated parameter. Perhaps you are not aware that you can also do the reverse. Discoverer allows you to create an associated condition while you are creating a parameter. This is probably one of the least used features of Discoverer.

To create an associated condition while creating a parameter, use the following workflow:

1. Launch the New Parameter dialog box by selecting Tools | Parameters from the toolbar or in Plus by clicking the New Parameter button.
2. In the dialog box, click New. See Figure 13-1 shown earlier.
3. Give the parameter a meaningful name.
4. When prompted "which item do you want to base this parameter on," use the drop-down and select the item.
5. Check the Create Condition With Operator box.
6. Set the operator.
7. Discoverer will create a name for the condition based on the item, operator, and parameter name. You can leave the name as defined by Discoverer, or you can insert your own name. We generally leave Discoverer to create the condition name.
8. Enter a suitable prompt.
9. In the description box, provide some context-sensitive help.
10. Complete the rest of the dialog box using your own preferences.
11. Click OK to complete the parameter.
12. Click OK to close the Edit Worksheet dialog box, if open.
13. Discoverer will automatically create the condition, associate it with the parameter, and activate it for use.
14. Execute the worksheet.

## Creating Instant Parameters

Another little known feature of Discoverer is its ability to create instant, quick-and-dirty parameters. These are parameters that are created "on the fly"—either by design or by accident—by referencing soon to be created parameters inside a condition. As you know, when working with calculations or conditions, parameters are indicated by a colon followed by the parameter name. For example, if you have a parameter called Status, you can use it in a calculation by typing **:Status**.

When creating or editing an existing condition, you can associate the condition with an existing parameter by choosing Select Parameter from the Values drop-down list. If you know the name of the parameter, you can also type it directly into the Values box. However, you need to be very careful to make sure you spell the name correctly, because if you type the name wrong, Discoverer creates another parameter.

Thus, if you have a parameter called Status and by mistake you type **:stats**, Discoverer creates another parameter. You will still be prompted only once, but you will probably be unaware that Discoverer is not using your original parameter. Your first inkling that something is wrong may come from a user who complains that there is no list of values. When you launch the Edit Sheet dialog box to try to solve the problem, you still may not be aware, especially if there are lots of parameters in the worksheet, that there are two parameters, one called Status and one called Stats. Editing the parameter that you originally created will show no issues because it will have a list of values, and you will be left scratching your head. It's at this point that you go to My Oracle Support and ask for help.

Unless you are an expert Discoverer user, do not create these instant parameters. Should you create one of these parameters and then edit it, you may be surprised to see that it is not in fact associated with a data item. Instead, you will see that the parameter is based on the item called <NONE>. You have in fact just created a dynamic parameter by mistake!

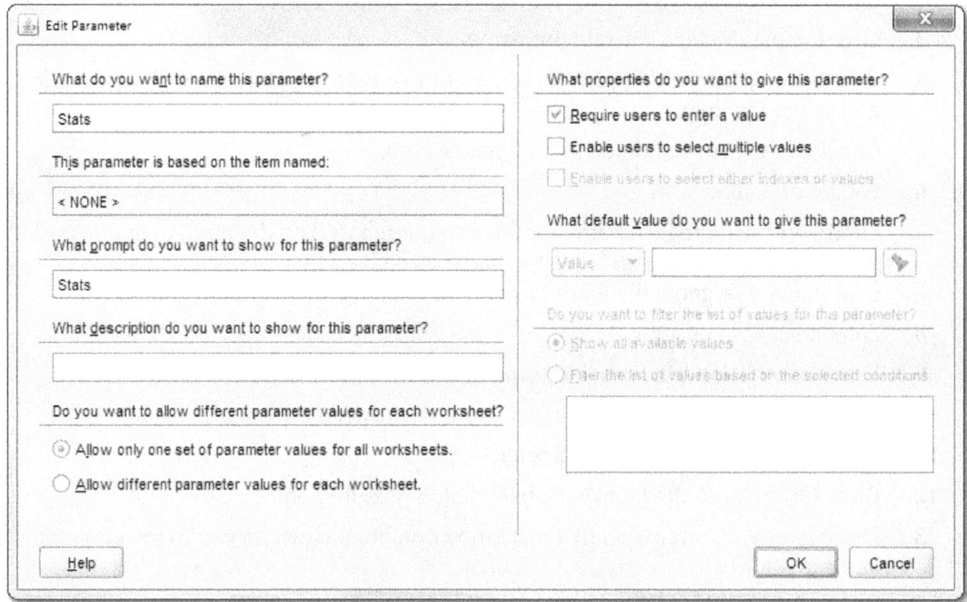


Having created a dynamic parameter by mistake, we will now show you the correct way to create and use these useful parameters.

# Dynamic Parameters

*Dynamic* parameters are not associated with any data item in the database. They are essentially free-form parameters that can later be "associated with" or "attached to" both calculations and conditions at will.

If required, these parameters can also be linked to multiple conditions in different worksheets within the same workbook. As mentioned, you can also create dynamic parameters that interact with calculations.

Here are a couple of examples of dynamic parameters:

- A Y/N parameter that controls whether one course of action is followed or another.
- A Percentage parameter that when passed to a calculation adjusts a sales amount by that percentage—useful for what-if analysis, extrapolation analysis, or simply applying discounts.

## Using Dynamic Parameters

After you have created a dynamic parameter, it will not be applied to the worksheet until you have associated or attached the parameter to a calculation or condition and you have activated that calculation or condition. For more information relating to activating or deactivating parameters, please see the next section in this chapter.

There are, therefore, two types of dynamic parameter.

- **Attached** Parameters that are linked to a calculation or condition
- **Unattached** Parameters that are not linked to a calculation or condition

**NOTE**
*You need to be aware that if the user executes a workbook that contains an unattached dynamic parameter, Discoverer will not prompt the user to enter a value for that parameter. There will be no impact to the worksheet results, and your user will be blissfully unaware that any such parameter should have been prompted.*

To create a dynamic parameter, use the following workflow:

1. Launch the New Parameter dialog box by selecting Tools | Parameters from the toolbar or in Plus by clicking the New Parameter button.
2. In the dialog box, click New.
3. Give the parameter a meaningful name.
4. When prompted "which item do you want to base this parameter on," use the drop-down and select <NONE>.
5. Enter a suitable prompt.
6. In the description box, provide some context-sensitive help.
7. Click OK.
8. Attach the parameter to a calculation or condition.

We have an existing workbook that contains a customer name, a price, and a calculation named *discount* that is taking the price and multiplying it by 0.9, effectively applying a discount of 10 percent. Now, let's say we want to apply the discount only when a switch says Y. We therefore need a dynamic parameter for this switch. After reopening the worksheet, we launched the New Parameter dialog box and entered the following values:

1. In Name, we entered **DiscParam**.
2. We changed Item to <NONE>.
3. In Prompt, we typed **Should we apply a discount?**.
4. In Description, we typed **Enter Y for Yes, any other character for No**.
5. We unchecked the option to allow users to enter multiple values.
6. In Default, we entered **N**.

**NOTE**
*Remember, you launch the New Parameter dialog box by using Tools | Parameters and then clicking the New button. In Plus, you can click the New Parameter button. This button is the third button from the right on the toolbar.*

The following illustration shows the preceding settings:

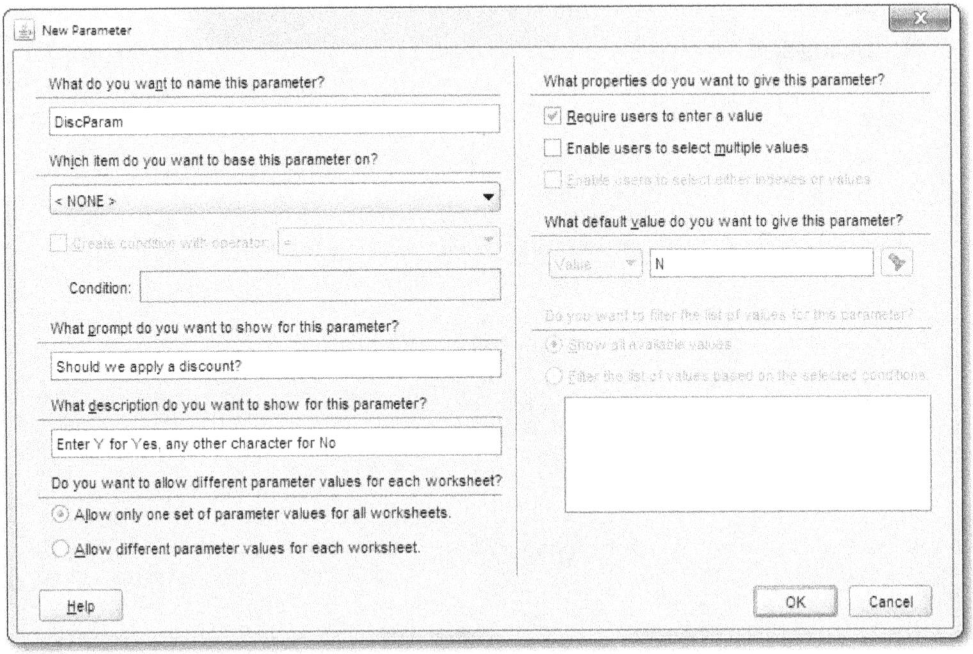

After completing the New Parameter dialog box, we clicked OK. As expected, when we ran the query, the results did not change. The parameter is not being offered, and the discount of 10 percent is still being applied. To complete this parameter and bring it into use, we have to edit the calculation for the discount.

To complete our calculation, we need to alter it such that the following logic is applied:

IF Discount Parameter = Y
THEN apply a 10% discount to the price
ELSE leave the price unchanged

The standard SQL set of functions that are available in Discoverer do not include a function called IF. However, both CASE and DECODE, which are explained in depth later in this chapter, can be used to complete the calculation. We changed our existing calculation:

```
SELLING PRICE SUM * 0.9
```

to the following:

```
DECODE(:DiscParam, 'Y', SELLING PRICE SUM * 0.9, SELLING PRICE SUM)
```

We also could have used a CASE statement like this:

```
CASE WHEN :DiscParam = 'Y' THEN SELLING PRICE SUM * 0.9 ELSE SELLING PRICE SUM END
```

Discoverer now prompts the user to enter the discount. If the user types a *Y*, the discount will be applied. If the user types any other character, including *y*, the discount will not be applied.

To make the parameter more user friendly, try altering the calculation as follows:

```
DECODE(UPPER(:DiscParam), Y', SELLING PRICE SUM * 0.9, SELLING PRICE SUM)
```

This alteration allows the user to type either an uppercase or a lowercase *Y*, thereby making the query much more user friendly.

**NOTE**

*Don't worry about the syntax for the functions used in this example at this time. We cover advanced calculations in depth later in this chapter, and Appendix B lists all of the functions along with their syntax.*

The worksheet used in the preceding example could easily be further refined. Let's say we no longer want to hard-code the discount of 10 percent but want to allow the user to key in the percentage amount from the keyboard. This is another excellent use of a dynamic parameter. To do this, we will need to create another dynamic parameter, this time prompting the user to enter the discount percentage. Having created the parameter, remember that it will not be brought into use until you attach it to a calculation or condition.

Therefore, let's say we have added a new dynamic parameter called DiscPct. All we need to do is use this in our discount calculation, and we now have an extremely powerful worksheet. Not only do we ask whether we should apply a discount, but we even ask what percentage should be applied. If you are interested, the discount calculation has been further amended as follows:

```
DECODE(UPPER(:DiscParam),'Y', Selling Price SUM *
 (1-(:DiscPct/100)),Selling Price SUM)
```

Again, here it is as a CASE statement:

```
CASE WHEN DECODE(UPPER(:DiscParam) = 'Y' THEN Selling Price SUM *
 (1-(:DiscPct/100)) ELSE Selling Price SUM END
```

After we amended the calculation and executed the worksheet, the following two parameters were prompted:

Edit Parameter Values

Select values for the following parameters:

Should we apply a discount?*: Y

Please enter the discount percentage*: 10

Description

Enter Y for Yes, any other character for No

* indicates required field.

Help OK Cancel

The use of dynamic parameters opens up a completely new set of possibilities. You no longer need to export data into a spreadsheet to perform complex what-if scenarios. A recent client of ours asked if we could help them with their payroll calculations. For years they had been extracting data to a spreadsheet and then applying calculations to generate the new pay rates. Using dynamic parameters, we were able to create a single Discoverer worksheet that prompted for the pay raise percentage for each of the different levels of employees and then applied those percentages to the current payroll data for each employee. The company is now able to try various what-if scenarios without ever having to export their sensitive payroll data from the system. Not only did we save time by simplifying the process but we helped their security by not having sensitive data stored outside of the database.

## Mandatory and Optional Parameters

In all previous releases of Discoverer, parameters were mandatory. What this meant for your users is that until they entered a value into every parameter, the OK button remained grayed out. With this release of Plus, you can now choose whether to create mandatory or optional parameters. Previously, your only other option was to prepopulate parameters with default values like %—which was never very appealing because it did not offer a great deal of control.

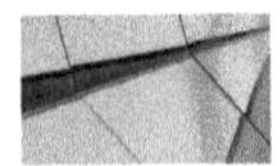

**NOTE**
*A mandatory parameter can be recognized because Discoverer places a small asterisk alongside the prompt. If there is no asterisk, the parameter is optional and the user can leave the parameter blank.*

### Optional Parameters

As previously mentioned, the Discoverer 11*g* Plus release allows you to create optional parameters. Essentially, these are parameters that do not need to have a value entered in order for the worksheet to be executed. If you omit a value (in other words, if you leave the box blank), Discoverer will assume that you want to query *all* values. Remember, Discoverer does not display an asterisk alongside optional parameters.

**NOTE**
*Even though Desktop cannot edit or create optional parameters, it will allow their use, and it does use the asterisk to signify that the parameter is mandatory.*

### Defining Mandatory and Optional Parameters

By default, all parameters are mandatory. If you want to switch a parameter from being mandatory to optional, or vice versa, you need to alter its definition. This can be done only in Plus, where you can use either the New Parameter dialog box or the Edit Parameter dialog box. The switch is a check box that can be found in the top-right corner of the dialog box. As shown in the following illustration, it is the Require Users To Enter A Value box.

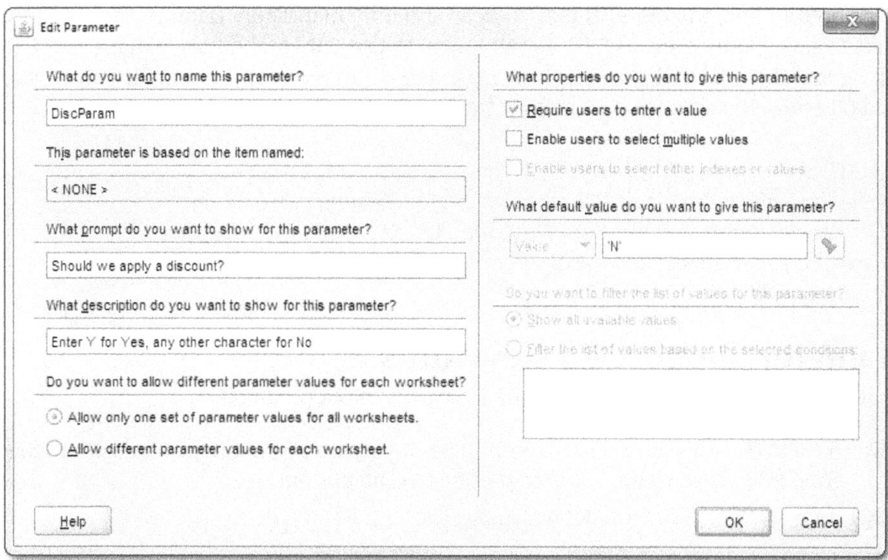


## Optional Parameters and Calculations

You cannot use optional parameters in calculations. Depending upon how you go about doing this, you will get a different error message.

If you create an optional parameter and then try to create a new calculation or amend an existing calculation using that parameter, Discoverer will give you the following error message:

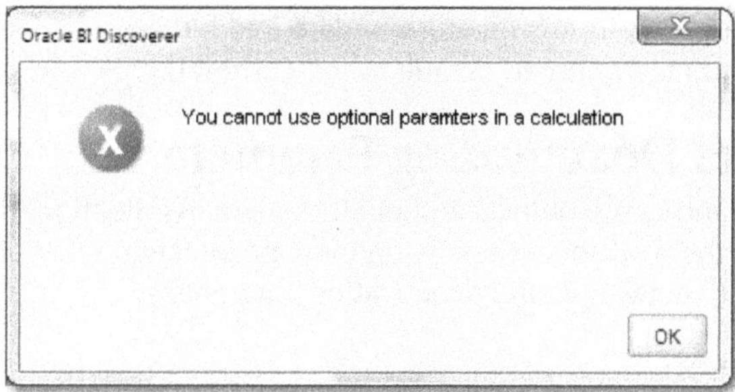


If you attach a mandatory parameter to a calculation and then try to alter the parameter to make it optional, you will get this error message:

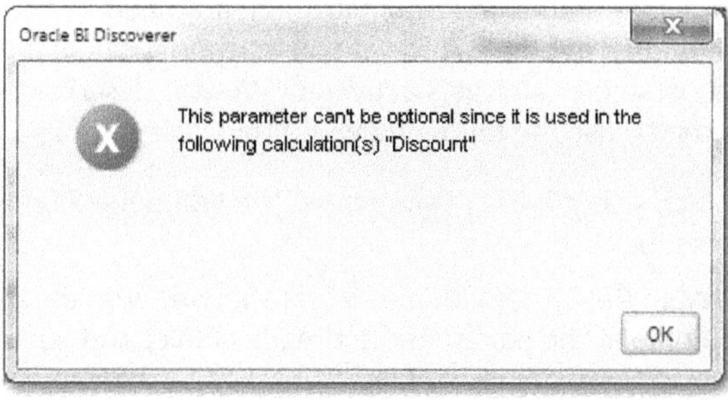

The bottom line, therefore, is that you can use only mandatory parameters in calculations. As we like to say, "Purity prevails." By allowing you to use only mandatory parameters, Oracle is ensuring that the final SQL that is submitted to the database does not contain any ambiguities that would otherwise prevent your worksheet from executing.

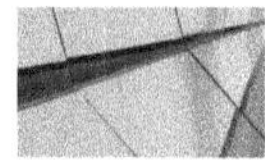

**NOTE**
*When creating a new calculation or editing an existing calculation, Discoverer suppresses the display of optional parameters. While you cannot create calculations based on optional parameters, you can create conditions.*

## Parameter Support for Keywords

Discoverer will now accept the following keywords into a parameter:

- **SYSDATE** This inserts the current date. If you are prompting for a date and the user types SYSDATE, Discoverer will interpret this as the current date.
- **NULL** This inserts the NULL value.
- **USER** This inserts the name of the user who is logged in.

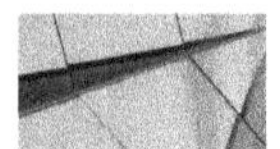

**NOTE**
*Even though we show these keywords in uppercase, they are not case sensitive.*

Of the three keywords available to you, the one that you will use most frequently is SYSDATE. As mentioned, this keyword inserts the current date into a date parameter. It is useful in parameter defaults when you want the query to default to the current date.

## Activating and Deactivating Parameters

Parameters are not stand-alone objects within Discoverer. As mentioned previously, parameters become activated in the worksheet only when they are attached to a calculation or condition. This section deals with activating and deactivating parameters.

### Activating Parameters

Before you can get Discoverer to prompt for a parameter, that parameter needs to be activated. Unlike other parts of Discoverer, such as items, conditions, calculations, totals, and percentages, which all have a right-click drop-down capability to add or remove them from the worksheet, no such functionality exists for parameters. Parameters are activated by association or by attachment to calculations or conditions. In other words, if you activate a calculation or condition that in turn uses a parameter, that parameter also gets activated. We will describe this in Plus.

To activate a parameter, use the following workflow:

1. From the toolbar, select Tools | Parameters. The Edit Sheet dialog box will now open at the Parameters tab.
2. Look at the text in the Order column. If it is showing *n/a*, the parameter is not active. If it is showing a number, the parameter is already active, and you can exit this workflow.

3. Click the Select Items tab.
4. If the parameter is associated with a condition, click the Conditions subtab and add the condition to the worksheet.
5. If the parameter is associated with a calculation, click the Calculations subtab and add the calculation to the worksheet.
6. Click OK to close the Edit Sheet dialog box.
7. Execute the worksheet.

### Deactivating Parameters

Because there is no right-click drop-down capability to add or remove parameters from a worksheet, the only way to deactivate a parameter is to deactivate the calculation or condition to which the parameter is associated. We will describe this in Plus.

To deactivate a parameter, use the following workflow:

1. From the toolbar, select Tools | Parameters. The Edit Sheet dialog box will now open at the Parameters tab.
2. Look at the text in the Order column. If it is showing *n/a*, the parameter is already inactive and you can exit this workflow. If it is showing a number, the parameter is active.
3. Click the Select Items tab.
4. If the parameter is associated with a condition, click the Conditions subtab and remove the condition from the worksheet.
5. If the parameter is associated with a calculation, click the Calculations subtab and remove the calculation from the worksheet.
6. Click OK to close the Edit Sheet dialog box.
7. Execute the worksheet.

## Cascading Parameters

*Cascading* parameters are parameters that are constrained by having a filter on a preexisting condition. That condition can be either a hard-coded condition or a condition that is associated with a previously prompted parameter. Using cascading parameters, you can ensure that lists of values are seeded so as to ensure that only the correct list is offered for selection.

We recommend that, in order to effectively use cascading parameters, you create these parameters on items that have lists of values and are contained within the same Discoverer drill hierarchy. This is simply for performance reasons and will not be enforced by Discoverer.

Oracle advises users not to create cascading parameters on non-drill-hierarchy items, though users can still go ahead and do so if they want.

But what do we mean by a drill hierarchy?

### Drill Hierarchies

According to Oracle, a Discoverer *drill hierarchy* is "a set of related items that provide a predefined path to help Discoverer users navigate worksheets." We understand that this description is a little difficult to follow at first, so we will help you by providing the following example.

In the next illustration, which is part of the entity-relationship diagram (ERD) for our database, you can see that our customer hierarchy is based on joins between the following four tables:

- Customer
- City
- District
- Region

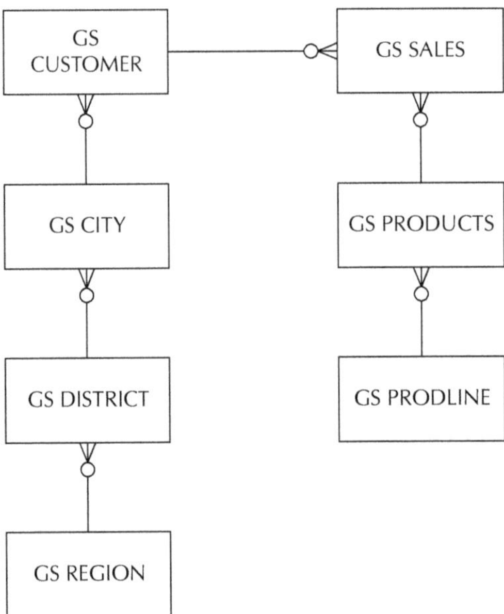


At the lowest level, you can see that the Customer table joins to our Sales table. Using this information, our users can thus create worksheets that report sales by customer. To help us even further, our Discoverer manager has created a drill path that utilizes the joins between the four tables. Using this, our users can drill from Customer down to City, thus enabling them to create worksheets that are summarized by city. There is a similar link between City and District and, finally, another one between District and Region, which is our lowest level. Our users can therefore now create reports that report sales only by region. This query will return significantly fewer rows of data than if they queried by customer.

## Creating Cascading Parameters

Taking advantage of the drill hierarchy and lists of values that exist on each item within the hierarchy, if we create a parameter that prompts for the region and then have a second parameter that prompts for the district, we can force Discoverer to display only the districts that lie within the region we chose for the first parameter. This is what is called a *cascading parameter*.

To create a cascading parameter, use the following workflow:

1. Create a worksheet that uses two or more items from the same hierarchy.
2. Create a parameterized condition on the highest-ranked item in the hierarchy.

3. Create another parameterized condition on a lower-ranked item in the hierarchy.
4. When you create the second parameter, check the radio button Filter The List Of Values Based On The Selected Conditions.
5. From the list of conditions that are now displayed, check one or more conditions that should be used as filters for this parameter.
6. Complete the condition.
7. Execute the worksheet.

We will now walk you through creating a worksheet that uses the preceding workflow to create cascading parameters. In this example, we will be using the same drill hierarchy that we outlined earlier in this section. We will create a worksheet that uses two parameters, one for Region and one for District, with the parameter for District being constrained by the values obtained from Region. Thus, if the user selects EUROPE for the Region, the District list should display only EU-EAST, EU-NORTH, and EU-SOUTH.

1. We will start a new workbook and select the following items:
   A. Order Qty from Sales
   B. District and Region from Customer/Geography
2. If we execute this worksheet without any constraints, the results that we get are as follows:

| | Region | District | Order Qty SUM |
|---|---|---|---|
| 1 | EUROPE | EU-EAST | 493291 |
| 2 | | EU-NORTH | 3203429 |
| 3 | | EU-SOUTH | 1772980 |
| 4 | FAR EAST | FE-ALL | 2025531 |
| 5 | NORTH AMERICA | NA-NORTH | 6335702 |
| 6 | | NA-SOUTH | 2576580 |
| 7 | SOUTH AMERICA | SA-ALL | 1459758 |

3. Create a parameterized condition on the region.
4. When creating the parameter, do the following:
   A. In Name, type **Region**.
   B. In Prompt, type **Please enter the Region**.
   C. Allow multiple values.
   D. Do not set a default.
   E. Complete the parameter by clicking OK.
   F. Complete the condition by clicking OK.
5. Create another parameterized condition on District.

6. When creating this parameter, do the following:

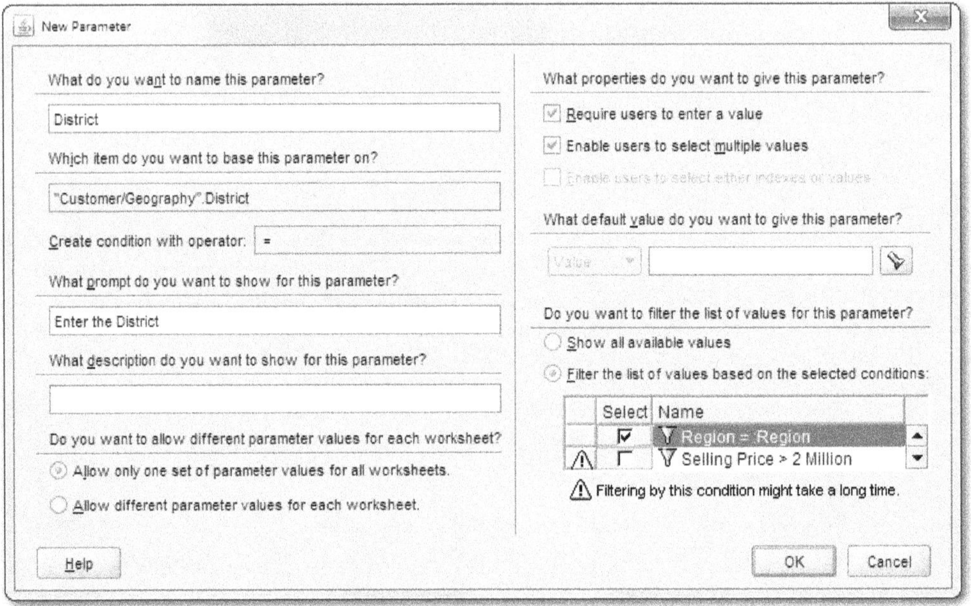


A. In Name, type **District**.
B. In Prompt, type **Enter the District**.
C. Allow multiple values.
D. Do not set a default.
E. Click the radio button Filter The List Of Values Based On The Selected Conditions.
F. Check the box alongside the Region condition.
G. Complete the parameter by clicking OK.
H. Complete the condition by clicking OK.

**NOTE**
*If Discoverer detects that you already have created a condition on another item that is in the same hierarchy as the item you are creating this parameter for, Discoverer will check that condition by default. This is a really clever feature and one that we recommend you take into account.*

7. Execute the worksheet by selecting EUROPE when prompted for the region.
8. As you can see in the following illustration, when we click the flashlight alongside the district, we can see only the districts that are within Europe:

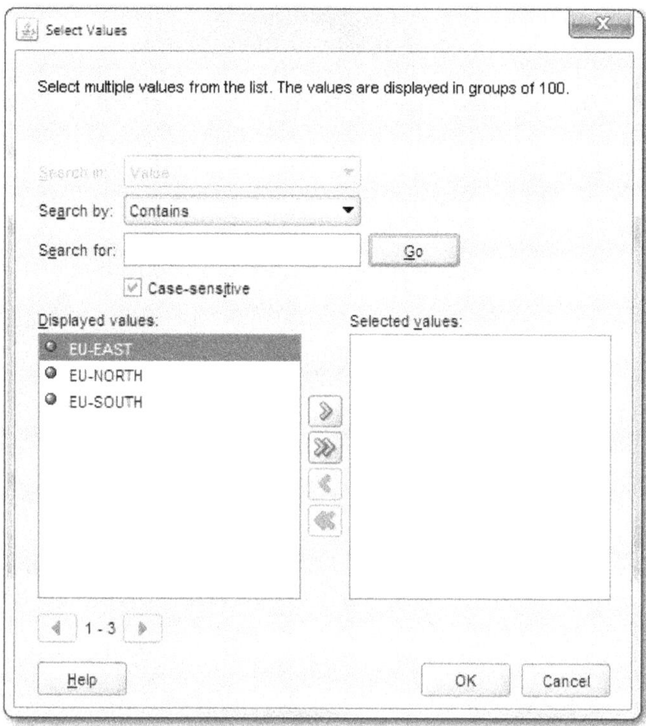


You can see from this example just how easy it is to create cascading lists of values. There is no rocket science about this. The creation of cascading parameters works so well that you will wonder how you ever managed to use Discoverer without them.

## Editing Parameters

Perhaps you want to add a bitmap to the Desktop Parameter Wizard entry screen. Maybe you want to place your newest parameter at the top of the Parameter list. Neither of these things can be done during the creation of a parameter. You will have to edit the parameter if you want to make changes like these.

If you allowed Discoverer to name the parameter, the name will contain the word *Parameter*. If you named the parameter yourself and you followed our recommendation, your name will also contain the word *Parameter*.

If you want to edit a parameter that has been based on a condition, other than renaming the parameter, you have to amend the parameter definition in the Edit Parameter dialog box, available from the menu bar using Tools | Parameters, and the condition itself in the Edit Condition dialog box. This dual process can seem somewhat irritating at first, but in our experience, you will soon learn to handle this. However, if you want to edit only the name of the parameter, changing it in the Edit Parameter dialog box also changes it in the associated condition. The authors like this dynamic interaction that Discoverer has.

### Workflow to Edit a Parameter

To edit an existing parameter, use the following workflow:

1. From the menu bar, select Tools | Parameters. In Desktop, this opens the Parameters dialog box. In Plus, this opens the Edit Sheet dialog box and places the focus on the Parameters tab.

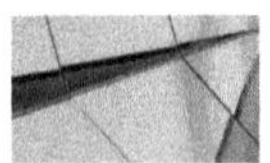

**NOTE**
*Unlike for calculations and conditions, there is no drop-down button alongside the New Parameter button.*

2. Highlight the parameter you want to edit.
3. Click the Edit button. This opens the Edit Parameter dialog box.
4. Change the parameter as required.
5. Click OK.
6. If required, adjust the ordering of the parameters.
7. If required, and in Desktop only, you can optionally add your company logo by clicking Bitmap. This opens a drop-down list. From the list, select Set Bitmap, and then browse to the bitmap you desire and click Open. This causes Discoverer to display the logo to the left of the available parameters. It will also display on the Parameter Wizard screen.

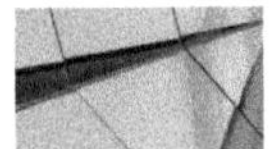

**NOTE**
*Attaching a bitmap to the dialog box is unique to Desktop. If you add a bitmap to the dialog box in Desktop, it will not display in either Plus or Viewer. However, if your organization does not use Plus or Viewer or you are a dyed-in-the-wool Desktop user, you will find this to be a really cool feature.*

8. Click OK.

### Rearranging the Order of Parameters

After adding a parameter that is based on a calculation or condition or following an edit of an existing parameter, you need to review the order in which the parameters will be presented to the end user. The section "Rearranging the Parameter Order" in Chapter 5 explains how to do this. We recommend you position the most important parameters at the top of the list. If you have cascading parameters, you must place the highest-level parameter before any dependent parameter, with each of the dependent parameters being placed in descending order of their dependency. Discoverer does not enforce the sequential placement of cascading parameters, but it's actually a good idea to do so and a habit that we heartily recommend you adopt.

In the following illustration you can see that we have created a worksheet with four parameters. When a user runs this worksheet in Desktop, the Parameter Wizard opens and displays the first three parameters. The user has to input or select the required criteria for each of these three parameters and then click Next to set the criteria for the final parameter. This restriction of three parameters to a page in Desktop was not carried through into Plus or Viewer, where Discoverer dynamically expands the list to accommodate the parameters.

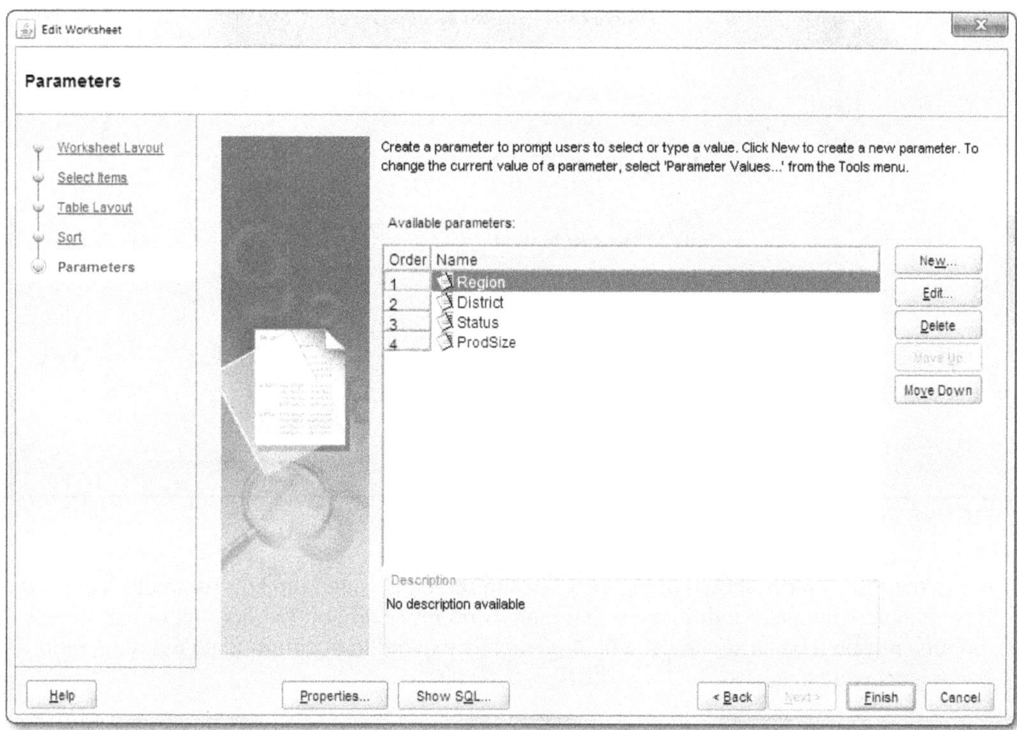

**NOTE**
*Discoverer remembers the last set of criteria that you entered into the Parameter Wizard and will insert these as the default the next time that the worksheet is run.*

When the user runs this query, Discoverer opens one of the following parameter screens. First, in Desktop, as you can see in Figure 13-3, there is a Parameter Wizard. This wizard presents parameters to the user in the order in which they appear in the Parameters dialog box. Because there are more than three parameters, the Next button is active.

**NOTE**
*As previously commented, the Desktop Parameter Wizard can show only three parameters per screen. If there are more than three parameters, Discoverer creates multiple three-parameter entry screens. Users can navigate between these screens using the Next and Back buttons. However, until all of the mandatory parameters have a value, the Finish button will be grayed out.*

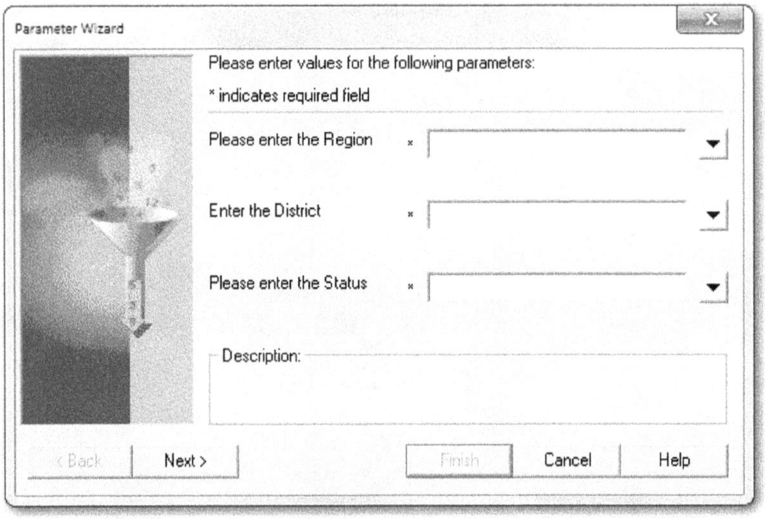

**FIGURE 13-3.** *Desktop Parameter Wizard*

In the Plus screen, shown in Figure 13-4, the screen is called the Edit Parameter Values dialog box. The nice thing about this box is that there is no restriction on the number of parameters that will be prompted because the list will dynamically expand to accommodate the number of parameters you have.

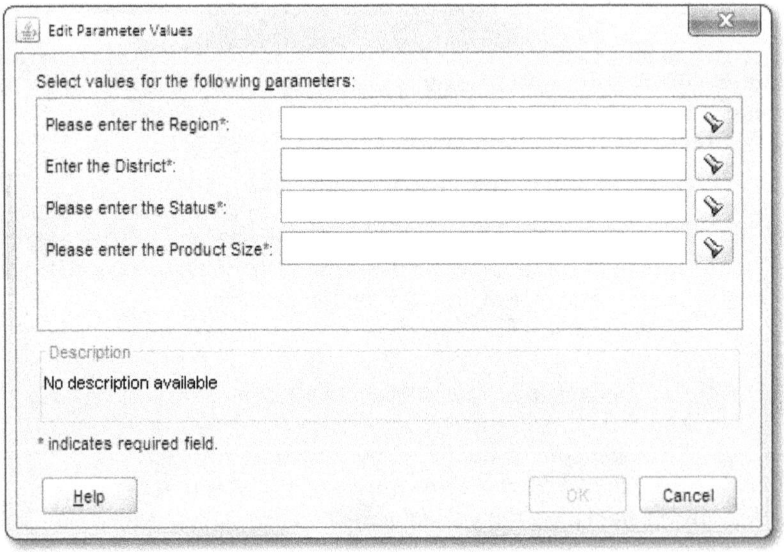

**FIGURE 13-4.** *Plus Edit Parameter Values dialog box*

**NOTE**
*Do you see the small asterisk alongside some of the parameters? This indicates that the parameter is mandatory. Optional parameters have no asterisk and can be left blank. Discoverer will not activate the Finish or OK button until you have entered something for each mandatory parameter.*

**Rearranging Cascading Parameters** When cascading parameters are in use, you need to take great care when rearranging your parameters. Do not move, or attempt to move, one of the dependent parameters above one of the parameters on which it depends. Doing this will cause Discoverer to generate the following warning:

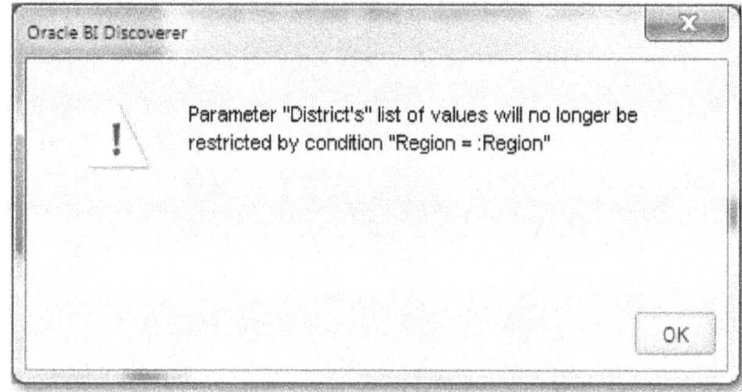

Oracle BI Discoverer
Parameter "District's" list of values will no longer be restricted by condition "Region = :Region"
OK


Unfortunately, Oracle does not provide a cancel button, so at this point you are up the creek without a paddle, or so you might think. Even though your only option at this point is to click OK, do not despair. Go ahead, click OK. When you do so, Discoverer rearranges the parameters and moves the dependent parameter above the one on which it depends. It appears as though you have lost your cascading parameter, and you may think that you have no choice but to rebuild the cascade, redefining the order of the parameters as you do.

We even tried clicking the *X* on the title bar to close the dialog box, but this did not work either. Discoverer still moves the parameter and we lost our cascade, or so we thought. Before you do anything else, click the Cancel button. This will restore the previous settings for the ordering of the parameters. The flip side of this is that if you had added or edited any parameters, these changes will also be lost, but we think this is a small price to pay for not losing the cascade.

## Using Parameters in the Title, Header, or Footer

Placing parameters on the worksheet title or in the header or footer is a good way for users to see at a glance what parameters have been chosen. You can choose to globally insert all parameters, or if you can remember the names that you gave your parameters, you can place individual parameters in the title, header, or footer.

Do you recall our recommending that you give your parameters meaningful names? Apart from the fact that it makes good sense, this ability to place individual parameters into the title, header, or footer is a good enough reason in itself.

Be careful inserting parameters into the title, header, or footer when the parameter uses a keyword such as SYSDATE or USER. Even though, as you know, these are interpreted as the current date and current user, what Discoverer displays in the title, header, and footer will be the keyword itself and not its interpreted meaning. To insert the current date, you should use &Date. Unfortunately, there is no shortcut or token that you can use for inserting the username.

### Inserting Parameters into the Title

If you cannot see the title to your worksheet, you need to make it visible.

In Desktop, you do this from the menu bar using Tools | Options followed by selecting the Table or Crosstab tab, depending upon the type of worksheet you are working with. Then you need to check the Title box and click OK.

In Plus, the title is also made visible from the menu bar, but this time you only need to select View | Title. There is no check box and no need to click OK. You can see that it is much easier to turn on the title in Plus.

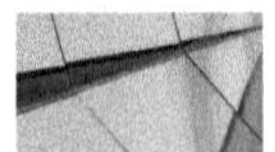

**NOTE**

*To turn the title off, just reverse the preceding logic. However, please note that this does not delete the title. It is simply not being displayed. Re-enabling the title later will restore the title to its previous state. This smart feature of Discoverer works in both Desktop and Plus, even if you close and subsequently reopen the workbook later.*

After having turned on the title, you can choose to insert all of the parameters or just selected parameters. First you need to launch the title editor. To do this, you simply double-click the title, which, by the way, kindly defaults to "Double click here to edit this title." This is a nice touch and one of the many reasons why Discoverer is a really pleasant tool to work with.

To insert parameters into the title, use this workflow:

1. If it is not already visible, display the title.
2. Launch the Edit Title dialog box by double-clicking the title.
3. To insert all parameters, click the Insert button, and from the drop-down list select Parameters. Discoverer inserts all of the parameter names and all of their associated values.
4. To insert a single parameter, type the ampersand character, **&**, followed by the name of the parameter. Be wary, though, because if you have parameters and page items in use at the same time and you have named a page item the same as a parameter, it is the page item that takes priority.

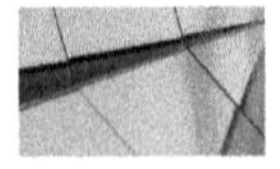

**NOTE**

*Remember, parameter names are also case-sensitive, so if you display individual parameters in the title, make sure to type the names exactly as they appear in the list of parameters.*

5. Click OK.

## Inserting Parameters into the Desktop Header or Footer

Just as with the title, you can insert parameter names and values into the header and footer. Unlike with the title, there is no activation step for editing headers and footers.

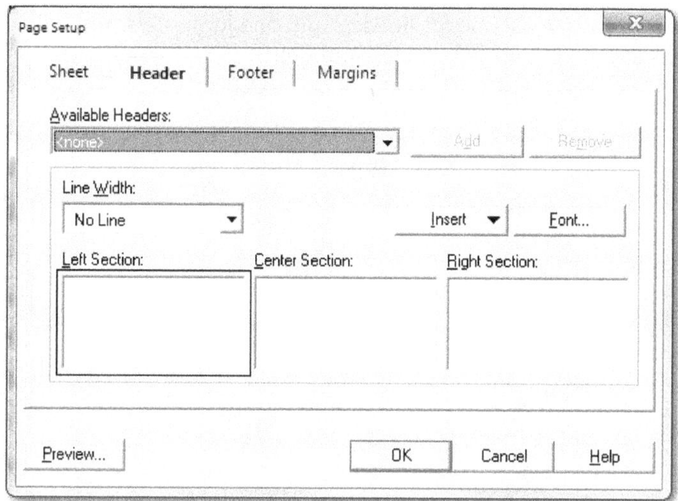


To insert parameters into the Desktop header or footer, use this workflow:

1. From the menu bar, select File | Page Setup.
2. Click either the Header or Footer tab. As shown in this illustration, you will notice that there are three sections: left, center, and right.
3. Pick the section where you want the parameters to be inserted by clicking in the appropriate area.
4. To insert all parameters, click the Insert button, and from the drop-down list select Parameters. Discoverer inserts all of the parameter names and all of their associated values.
5. To insert a single parameter, type the ampersand character, **&**, followed by the name of the parameter. Just like with the title, please remember that if you have parameters and page items in use at the same time and you have named a page item the same as a parameter, the page item will take priority.
6. Click Preview to see what the page will look like with the parameters inserted into the header and/or footer.
7. Click OK.

## Inserting Parameters into the Plus Header or Footer

Just as with Desktop, you can insert parameter names and values into the Plus header and footer. Once again, there is no activation step for editing headers and footers.

To insert parameters into the Plus header or footer, use this workflow:

1. From the menu bar, select File | Page Setup.
2. Click the Header/Footer tab. As shown in the following illustration, you will notice that this tab has two areas, one for headers and one for footers. You will also notice that each area has three sections, left, center, and right.

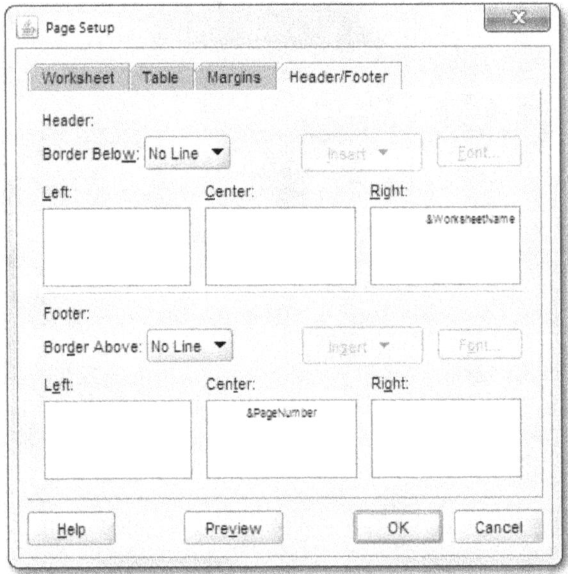


3. Pick the area and section where you want the parameters to be inserted by clicking in the appropriate section.
4. To insert all parameters, click the Insert button, and from the drop-down list select Parameters. Discoverer inserts all of the parameter names and all of their associated values.
5. To insert a single parameter, type the ampersand character, **&**, followed by the name of the parameter. Just as with Desktop, if you have parameters and page items in use at the same time and you have named a page item the same as a parameter, the page item will take priority. We've repeated this warning several times now, so you won't forget, will you?
6. Click Preview to see what the page will look like with the parameters inserted into the header and/or footer.
7. Click OK.

# Refining Calculations

After dealing with parameters, the next most common way to refine a query is to refine the calculations. The ability to manipulate data by the use of both simple and complex calculations and the ability to create new items using calculations are very useful skills to master.

# Main Components of a Calculation

Before we get too deep into the complexities of calculations, we think it is appropriate to remind you of the main components of a calculation. Whether you are creating or editing a calculation, Discoverer opens the New Calculation dialog box shown in Figure 13-5. This box allows you to give your calculation a meaningful name and to build your calculation using a combination of items from the database, functions, and operators. In Chapter 5, we introduced you to calculations using the Workbook Wizard. Appendix B contains a full list of all the functions used within Discoverer, along with many useful practical examples, and we strongly recommend that you spend some time learning how to use these functions.

# Define the Calculation in Advance

As with just about everything that we have taught you so far, once again we want to impress upon you the need to think ahead. Unless the calculation is very simple and can be obtained by adding one column to another or something equally straightforward, we recommend that you work out the calculation in advance. Yes, even in this super-modern world, this is still a use for pencil and paper.

In our experience, even the simplest of algorithms can prove difficult to translate into a script that Discoverer can understand. In this section, we will outline a few fundamentals that you should bear in mind, which may help you when dealing with calculations. They are as follows:

- How to convert an algorithm into a Discoverer script
- How to avoid division-by-zero errors
- How to choose the correct level of aggregation for a calculation

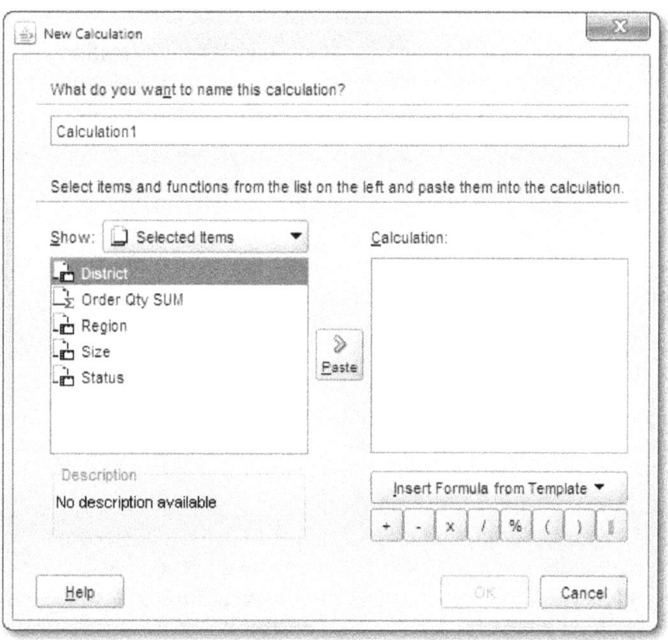


**FIGURE 13-5.** *New Calculation dialog box*

## How to Convert an Algorithm into a Discoverer Script

Converting an algorithm into a Discoverer script need not be daunting, yet many people make it so. This is because they don't remember, or don't know, that the basic language of all computers is a sequential series of zeros and ones. When working with a computer, you need to break everything down into its simplest form, and the same applies to Discoverer.

You need to remember that there is a hierarchy when dealing with Discoverer's mathematical operators. Put simply, this mathematical hierarchy is as follows:

1. Powers and square roots
2. Multiplication and division
3. Addition and subtraction

Normally, Discoverer will work out a calculation from left to right—exactly as you key it in, providing all of your operators are at the same level. If you have operators from mixed levels, Discoverer will evaluate the operators from the highest level first, again left to right, then the next level down, and so on. If you are not careful with your operators, you will end up with incorrect calculations.

For example, look at the following algorithm:

5 – 2 * 6 + 10 / 2

What do you think is the right answer, and how do you think Discoverer will evaluate this? Look at the algorithm again. A human will evaluate this expression literally from left to right and get the answer 14 in the process. This is the answer that we want Discoverer to generate.

In fact, the answer given by Discoverer is –2. Is this the answer you received? What Discoverer did was to evaluate the multiplication and division parts first, followed by the subtraction and the addition.

If we insert parentheses into the formula, grouping the multiplication and division components together, and then evaluate the mathematics contained within those parentheses first, this may help you understand what Discoverer is doing.

5 – (2 * 6) + (10 / 2), which evaluates to 5 – 12 + 5, which is –2.

If you want to force Discoverer to evaluate an expression differently than its natural hierarchy, you have to use parentheses.

For example, suppose we wanted the preceding expression to be calculated exactly as written, that is, subtract 2 from 5, multiply by 6, add 10, and finally divide by 2. Inserting parentheses as follows evaluates to 14 as required:

(((5 – 2) * 6) + 10) / 2

We hope this explanation helps you understand how Discoverer performs mathematical calculations and that you will be able to take advantage of this in your query building.

## How to Avoid Division-by-Zero Errors

As with all things computational, you cannot divide by zero in Discoverer. You must be very careful defining expressions that use division to ensure that the divisor does not evaluate to zero. A calculation that has worked for the last six months may suddenly stop working because the divisor has now evaluated to zero.

In Discoverer, if you attempt to create a calculation such as X divided by Y when Y is zero, the calculation will not work. As the report writer, it is your responsibility to look for and trap this error during the construction of the worksheet.

We think that it is folly to assume that a divisor will never be zero. Even the best-designed systems occasionally have glitches that cause erroneous data to get into the database. Perhaps an upload mechanism that was designed to add the cost price for new products did not run when it was supposed to, leaving those costs at zero! You cannot leave your users in the unenviable situation of having worksheets that will not run.

There may also be valid zero values in the database. Sales orders that have not yet shipped will genuinely have an invoiced amount of zero.

So, if you cannot guarantee that the divisor will never be zero, what can you do? There are two ways to overcome the divide-by-zero error:

- Use a condition to omit the zero values.
- Use functions to avoid divide-by-zero errors.

**Use a Condition to Omit the Zero Values** This is the simplest way to avoid divide-by-zero errors. If you are going to use this method, you must ensure that the item you are going to place the condition on is in fact the same item that Discoverer is using within the calculation.

Sounds obvious, doesn't it? At first sight, we expect that you will say something like "That's obvious," and so it is, yet many users make the mistake of pulling the wrong item into the condition. For example, using our test database, we built a query that showed the total quantity shipped and the selling price by month for the third quarter of 2012, and then we calculated the unit price by dividing the price by the quantity. As you can see next, there are no zero values. But is this the right answer?

Page Items: Quarter: 2012-Q3

| | Month | Selling Price SUM | Shipped Qty SUM | Unit Price |
|---|---|---|---|---|
| 1 | APR-12 | 7166306.78 | 354680 | 20.20 |
| 2 | MAY-12 | 6451287.97 | 290452 | 22.21 |
| 3 | JUN-12 | 8988363.91 | 492565 | 18.25 |

Without investigating further, it would be very easy to take the answer at face value and assume that the unit price is correct. In fact, as we will show you, the answer is not correct. We first noticed we had a problem when we attempted to drill into the data for May 2012 and opted to view the status for that month from the Sales Order folder. Discoverer Plus will not let us do this and reports the following divide-by-zero error:

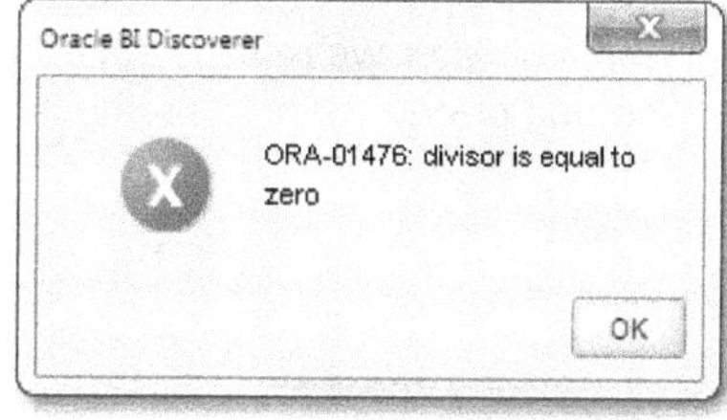
Oracle BI Discoverer
ORA-01476: divisor is equal to zero
OK

The same error is reported in Desktop, which is different functionality from what used to happen in Discoverer 10*g*. In the previous version, when we tried the same thing within Desktop, we were able to execute the query, but we did not get the expected results. If you are still using Discoverer 10*g*, you will see the characters #DIV/0! overlaid into every cell where the divide-by-zero error occurred. This could actually be quite useful because it would tell you which row was causing the problem.

From our calculation, in order to not divide by zero, the logical solution would be to make sure that Ship Qty SUM was not equal to zero. This would at least solve the divide-by-zero error. Doing just that resulted in the output you see next:

Page Items: Quarter: 2012-Q3

| | Month | Selling Price SUM | Shipped Qty SUM | Unit Price | Status |
|---|---|---|---|---|---|
| 1 | JUN-12 | 8508480.11 | 492565 | 17.27 | SHIPPED |
| 2 | MAY-12 | 6220159.97 | 290452 | 21.42 | SHIPPED |
| 3 | APR-12 | 6787942.38 | 354680 | 19.14 | SHIPPED |

So far, so good. Having avoided our divide-by-zero error, we glanced at the unit price and wondered why this was lower for all of our months than in our query before we began drilling. Leaving the condition in place, in Desktop we used Show Values on the Month heading to get back to the original selections, and we removed the status. As you can see next, the result is identical to the result we had when we first started:

Page Items: Quarter: 2012-Q3

| | Month | Selling Price SUM | Shipped Qty SUM | Unit Price |
|---|---|---|---|---|
| 1 | APR-12 | 7166306.78 | 354680 | 20.20 |
| 2 | MAY-12 | 6451287.97 | 290452 | 22.21 |
| 3 | JUN-12 | 8988363.91 | 492565 | 18.25 |

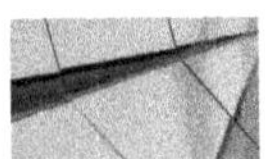

**NOTE**
*Rather than use Show Values, which does not exist in Plus, you can just as easily use Edit | Undo Drill.*

Have you spotted the error yet?

By applying the condition to be on Ship Qty SUM, as opposed to applying it on Ship Qty not being equal to zero, we have uncovered a fundamental flaw in our query. In fact, we should be excluding all items that have a ship quantity of zero because these items are causing our unit price calculation to be too high. We have been adding the selling price for items that have not shipped. After we refined the condition, the result looked as in the next illustration. Notice how the unit price is now the same as what we had when we drilled in to the data a few steps back!

Page Items: Quarter: 2012-Q3

| | Month | Selling Price SUM | Shipped Qty SUM | Unit Price |
|---|---|---|---|---|
| 1 | APR-12 | 6787942.38 | 354680 | 19.14 |
| 2 | MAY-12 | 6220159.97 | 290452 | 21.42 |
| 3 | JUN-12 | 8508480.11 | 492565 | 17.27 |

We hope the preceding example has shown you how critical it is to place the condition on the right item when trying to avoid the divide-by-zero error. At first glance, it appeared as though the condition should have been on Ship Qty SUM, whereas in fact the correct condition needed to be applied to Ship Qty.

Do not be drawn into believing that all divide-by-zero errors can be solved by placing the condition on the item, as opposed to on SUM, because they cannot. Databases that use negative values to store amounts and quantities to represent returns may require that the condition be placed on SUM. For example, suppose you have a sales database where positive values are used to represent actual shipments, and negative values are used to store customer returns. You may not have any zero values in the individual items, yet you may still end up with zero values in the result. This is caused by the total amount for the returns exactly counteracting the amount of real shipments. If you place a condition on the individual items not being zero, the total amount will still be zero.

For example, suppose you had total shipments of 8,000 items to various customers during August 2012, and then you received a single return from a major customer, also for 8,000 items. As you can see, adding the two together, you will get a total stock movement of zero. You would be wrong to place a condition on SUM because the answer is correct and this row should be included in the result. The only way to overcome this situation is to use either the CASE or DECODE function as described in the next section.

**Use Functions to Avoid Divide-by-Zero Errors** As we showed you in the preceding section, there are times when a zero value belongs in a column that will be used as a divisor. In these cases, you cannot use a condition to omit the item because the end result will be wrong. Perhaps the calculation is the reason why, the *raison d'être*, the worksheet exists in the first place. If this is the case, then you cannot use a condition to remove the items with zero. To avoid the divide-by-zero error and yet leave zero values in the divisor column, you must use some sort of SQL function.

We would like to say this:

IF Y = zero
THEN zero
ELSE compute X / Y

Oracle does not have a direct IF . . . THEN construct. Instead, Oracle provides two functions that allow you to compute IF . . . THEN scenarios. These are as follows:

- CASE
- DECODE

**Using the CASE and DECODE Functions to Overcome Divide-by-Zero Errors** What are the CASE and DECODE functions? These functions equate directly to the IF functions used in Excel and 1-2-3 spreadsheets and to the IF . . . THEN . . . ELSE constructs used in traditional programming languages.

To avoid the divide-by-zero error, we therefore need to tell the computer the following:

- **IF** the column being used as the divisor equals zero
- **THEN** place a zero in the calculated column
- **ELSE** perform the calculation

Let's take a simple case and calculate X divided by Y; say we want to trap the condition when Y equals zero using zero as the result in this case. In simple syntax, this would be written as follows:

**IF** Y = 0
**THEN** 0
**ELSE** X / Y

In Discoverer, this would be written as follows:

```
CASE WHEN Y = 0
THEN 0
ELSE X / Y
END
```

or as follows:

```
DECODE(Y, 0, 0, X / Y)
```

You will notice that the CASE function is the closest thing we have to a genuine IF . . . THEN . . .ELSE construct. However, if you can master the syntax, you will find that DECODE is an equally powerful function.

Please refer to Appendix B for a full description of the syntax of the CASE and DECODE functions, and see the section "Using Standard Functions in a Query" later in this chapter for a basic overview of how to use functions in your worksheet.

**Data Type Manipulation with CASE and DECODE** When using CASE or DECODE, you need to be aware that the data type for the function takes its format from the first result obtained within the code. In the following examples, we use RESULT1 and RESULT2 to signify the two possible results that can be returned by these functions:

```
CASE WHEN X = Y THEN RESULT1 ELSE RESULT2 END
```

or this function:

```
DECODE(X, Y, RESULT1, RESULT2)
```

Because RESULT1 is referred to first, Discoverer uses the format of that item for the overall format of the function. You therefore need to be very careful creating functions that look like this:

```
CASE WHEN X = Y THEN 'No Sales' ELSE A / B END
```

or this:

```
DECODE(X, Y, 'No Sales', A / B)
```

In fact, because Discoverer does not allow you to mix formats within a CASE statement, the first function, using CASE and 'No Sales', cannot be created. Discoverer will generate an error at this point informing you that inconsistent or invalid data types cannot be used in a CASE statement.

The latter function, DECODE, will compute, but the format of the ensuing calculation will be textual and not numeric as you would expect. Interestingly enough, although you cannot apply numeric formatting to the cells, such as adjusting the number of decimal places, you can still use totals, and they will compute correctly.

Because of the error that will be generated by a CASE statement and the wrong data type that will be generated by DECODE, we therefore recommend not mixing data types in either of these functions. If you want to be clever and use a phrase such as 'No Sales', we recommend you use the NULL result and make use of Discoverer's NULL-replacement functionality. The following examples show both functions using the NULL result:

```
CASE WHEN X = Y THEN NULL ELSE A / B END
```

or

```
DECODE(X, Y, NULL, A / B)
```

## How to Choose the Correct Level of Aggregation for a Calculation

Similar to our advice to use care when applying conditions to avoid the divide-by-zero error, you must be careful when selecting items that will be used inside calculations. Be sure to select the data item that is being used within a column, rather than the data item that is within the database. We understand that this may be a little confusing at first, so please take the time to stay with us while we explain.

For example, let's say we have a worksheet in which we have created two calculations, both of which subtract the value in one column from another. The following illustration shows the end result, with both the correct and incorrect calculations, plus a column showing the factor of incorrectness. Looking at the factor for the first row of data, you can see that the incorrect calculation is 13 times higher than the correct calculation. This is because there are 13 sales orders on the system that have a selling price of 1,172.50 and a cost price of 621.00.

| | ▸ Selling Price | ▸ Cost Price | ▸ Correct Calc | ▸ Incorrect Calc | ▸ Factor |
|---|---|---|---|---|---|
| 1 | 1172.50 | 621.00 | 551.50 | 7169.50 | 13 |
| 2 | 1161.00 | 620.92 | 540.08 | 540.08 | 1 |
| 3 | 1149.05 | 608.58 | 540.47 | 540.47 | 1 |
| 4 | 1134.00 | 606.48 | 527.52 | 1055.04 | 2 |
| 5 | 1125.60 | 596.16 | 529.44 | 4764.96 | 9 |
| 6 | 1110.00 | 790.00 | 320.00 | 11840.00 | 37 |
| 7 | 1109.00 | 531.00 | 578.00 | 15606.00 | 27 |
| 8 | 1108.80 | 510.08 | 598.72 | 1197.44 | 2 |
| 9 | 1098.00 | 447.12 | 650.88 | 1301.76 | 2 |
| 10 | 1080.00 | 577.60 | 502.40 | 9043.20 | 18 |
| 11 | 1078.00 | 459.20 | 618.80 | 6188.00 | 10 |
| 12 | 1071.00 | 503.16 | 567.84 | 567.84 | 1 |
| 13 | 1070.00 | 770.00 | 300.00 | 8700.00 | 29 |
| 14 | 1064.64 | 509.76 | 554.88 | 17201.28 | 31 |
| 15 | 1062.50 | 494.00 | 568.50 | 6822.00 | 12 |
| 16 | 1059.60 | 499.80 | 559.80 | 2799.00 | 5 |
| 17 | 1039.50 | 478.20 | 561.30 | 3367.80 | 6 |
| 18 | 1024.28 | 483.14 | 541.14 | 1082.28 | 2 |
| 19 | 1020.00 | 474.24 | 545.76 | 2183.04 | 4 |
| 20 | 1020.00 | 479.20 | 540.80 | 5408.00 | 10 |

As you can see in the following illustration, the correct calculation uses the data without any aggregation so that we are subtracting the cost price detail from the selling price detail, not the sum of these.

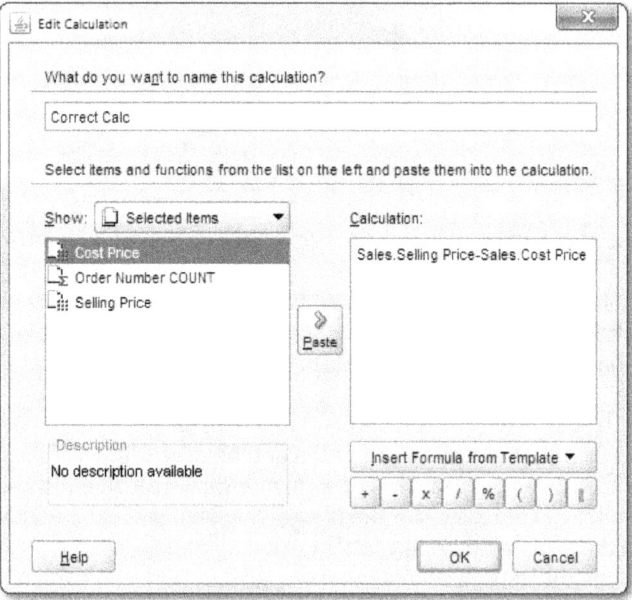


The incorrect calculation, shown next, uses the sum of aggregation. This causes Discoverer to add all instances where the selling price is the same and the cost price is the same.

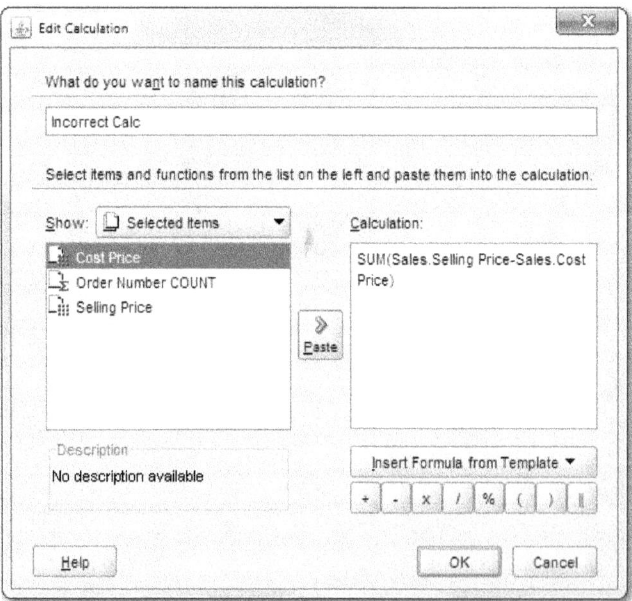

During the construction of the incorrect calculation, Discoverer recognized that there was a potential problem by giving us this warning.

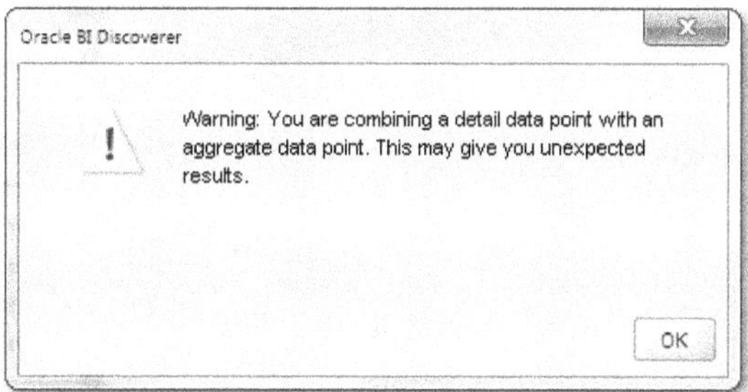


Ignore these warnings at your peril, because there is always a good reason why Discoverer issues warnings like these.

## Using COUNT in a Crosstab

Another of the less-used aggregations is COUNT. Rather than select an item in a worksheet, click the plus key alongside the item and take a look at the options. You will find that if you use COUNT on the item that is unique, such as an employee ID or a sales order number, you can generate calculations such as the headcount and number of orders. We will build a simple crosstab for you to demonstrate this.

Let's start by selecting the order status, the count of the order number, and the order date year. These three items alone make for an interesting query, as you can see here.

| | Number of Orders | | | |
|---|---|---|---|---|
| | CANCELLED | HOLD | OPEN | SHIPPED |
| FY2006 | 7 | 0 | 0 | 371 |
| FY2007 | 43 | 0 | 1 | 680 |
| FY2008 | 129 | 35 | 430 | 1087 |
| FY2009 | 109 | 0 | 0 | 1057 |
| FY2010 | 119 | 0 | 0 | 1541 |
| FY2011 | 150 | 0 | 0 | 1640 |
| FY2012 | 160 | 0 | 0 | 1897 |
| FY2013 | 151 | 6 | 255 | 1561 |

We will save this workbook and come back to it when we visit percentages later in this chapter.

As we were creating this worksheet, we had to click the plus character alongside the order number to choose COUNT. However, because there was a list of values on the order number, notice how Discoverer warned us that it was displaying only the first 1,000 order numbers:

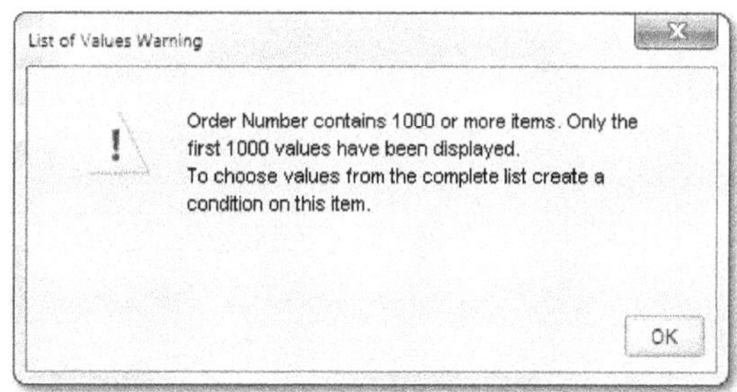

This setting is managed by the Discoverer administrator to protect the system from creating huge lists of values. By default this setting is 1,000. Many organizations consider this to be too high and set a much lower value, such as 50.

## Housekeeping After Editing a Calculation

After you have edited a calculation, you should undertake some housekeeping measures to maintain the efficiency of the worksheet. There are two steps to take after editing a calculation.

- Review any conditions based on the edited calculation.
- Review the data items used in the edited calculation.

### Review Conditions Based on Calculations

As we showed you in Chapter 12, one of the advanced condition types that Discoverer allows is to build a condition based on a calculation. If you create a condition based on a calculation and subsequently edit that calculation, you should evaluate whether the condition is still valid. Discoverer will automatically use the new calculation; however, the condition may no longer do what you wanted.

### Review the Data Items Used in the Edited Calculation

After editing a calculation in which you have changed data items, you should check to see whether the original data items are still needed in the worksheet. If they are no longer needed, delete them. If you have used additional items, you may need to add them. This will add to the integrity of the workbook as well as keep the query running efficiently.

For example, suppose you have a worksheet in which you are calculating the unit cost price for each sales order by dividing the order quantity into the cost price sum. For clarity, the worksheet will probably include both source items. If you now edit the calculation to base the unit price on the selling price, without changing the items displayed in the result, you could confuse the recipient of your report.

The following illustration perfectly demonstrates this situation. We have a query where the unit price was based on the cost price. The calculation has been changed, and the unit price is now based on the selling price. As you can see, you could easily be led into believing that the unit price is still based on the cost price. You should edit the worksheet, remove the cost price, and insert the selling price in its place.

| | Order Number | Order Qty SUM | Cost Price SUM | Unit Price |
|---|---|---|---|---|
| 1 | 1100 | 4800 | 50976.00 | 22.18 |
| 2 | 1200 | 2000 | 24840.00 | 23.45 |
| 3 | 1300 | 500 | 5310.00 | 22.18 |
| 4 | 1400 | 200 | 1242.00 | 15.25 |
| 5 | 1500 | 1000 | 8330.00 | 17.66 |
| 6 | 1600 | 500 | 7970.00 | 34.65 |
| 7 | 1700 | 20 | 248.40 | 23.45 |
| 8 | 1800 | 200 | 2124.00 | 22.18 |
| 9 | 1900 | 2400 | 17328.00 | 13.50 |
| 10 | 2000 | 2900 | 18009.00 | 15.25 |
| 11 | 2100 | 10 | 83.30 | 17.66 |
| 12 | 2200 | 960 | 15302.40 | 34.65 |
| 13 | 2300 | 2400 | 29808.00 | 23.45 |
| 14 | 2400 | 200 | 2124.00 | 22.18 |
| 15 | 2500 | 100 | 722.00 | 13.50 |
| 16 | 2600 | 2400 | 25488.00 | 22.18 |
| 17 | 2700 | 2400 | 25488.00 | 22.18 |
| 18 | 2800 | 2400 | 17328.00 | 13.50 |
| 19 | 2900 | 500 | 4165.00 | 17.66 |
| 20 | 3000 | 100 | 1242.00 | 23.45 |

If you are interested in how we managed to display only sales orders that were exactly divisible by 100, we used these two conditions:

```
ORDER NUMBER <= 3000
```

and

```
MOD(ORDER_NUMBER,100) = '0'
```

## Using Standard Functions in a Query

Perhaps the most difficult part about using calculations in Discoverer is learning how to use the functions that are available to you. When you open the New Calculation dialog box (see Figure 13-2 shown earlier) and click the Functions button in Desktop, or in Plus select Functions from the drop-down of available options, Discoverer displays the folders shown here:

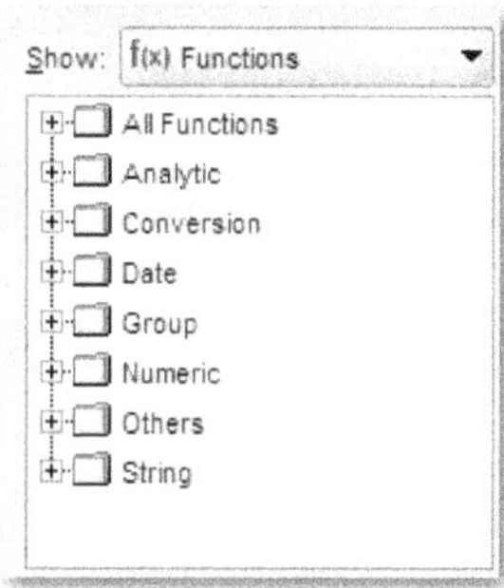


Nine folders of functions are available to you:

- **All Functions** Opening this folder displays all the functions available to you, listed in alphabetical order.
- **Analytic** This folder displays all the analytic functions available to you. These functions are all applied to the result of your query and are not calculated on a row-by-row basis. Please refer to Appendix B for more details on how to use these functions.
- **Conversion** This folder contains functions relating to converting data from one format into another. There are functions to convert strings into dates, dates into strings, and so on.
- **Database** This folder contains user-defined functions that are specific to the database you are currently using. This folder will not be in the list unless your Discoverer administrator has created some functions for you.
- **Date** This folder contains functions that manipulate dates. There are functions to generate the system date and time, functions to truncate the time, and so on.
- **Group** This folder contains functions that work on groups of data. These functions include SUM, MAX, MIN, and so on.
- **Numeric** This folder contains functions that are used in mathematical computations, such as +, –, *, /, and so on.

- **Others** This folder contains functions that cannot be categorized into one of the other folders. Examples of these include NVL, CASE, DECODE, and so on.
- **String** This folder contains functions that manipulate strings. Examples of these include UPPER, LENGTH, CONCAT, and so on.

In the remainder of this section, we will demonstrate the use of some of the more common, nonanalytic, functions available to you in Discoverer. In particular, we will show you the following:

- Advanced use of the CASE and DECODE statements
- Manipulation of dates
- Use of TO_CHAR with the number format mask

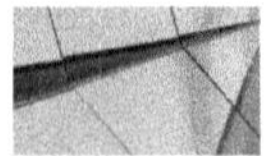

**NOTE**
*You can find a full explanation of all the functions used in Discoverer in Appendix B, along with many examples. Appendix B also contains a full listing of the format masks available to you.*

### Advanced Use of the CASE and DECODE Statements

Not a lot of people have harnessed the power of the CASE and DECODE functions, yet their usage is one of the most powerful features of Discoverer. Three of the best uses of these functions are

- Defining a list of new values
- Creating new data types
- Creating calculations based on data subsets

**Defining a New List of Values** Few people understand that you can use the CASE and DECODE functions to change a list of values as defined in your database to one that is more meaningful. For example, in many Oracle Applications tables you will notice that Oracle uses the character *Y* for Yes but uses a null value for No. To make a report more meaningful and user friendly, you might want to display the words *Yes* and *No* instead of *Y* and *null*. You can intercept the Oracle list of values and replace it with your own by using one of the following example pieces of code:

```
CASE WHEN Oracle field name = 'Y' THEN 'Yes' ELSE 'No' END
```

or

```
DECODE(Oracle field name, 'Y', 'Yes', 'No')
```

Using our example database, we will now show you how to replace one list of values with another. As you have seen in our test database, the original list of values for Status is

- CANCELLED
- HOLD
- OPEN
- SHIPPED

Let's say that our shipping department has decided that they want to use the value Pending instead of OPEN for the Status. Also, they want the remaining values to appear with the first letter capitalized and the rest in lowercase. In the following illustration, we have used a DECODE statement to give us the desired result.

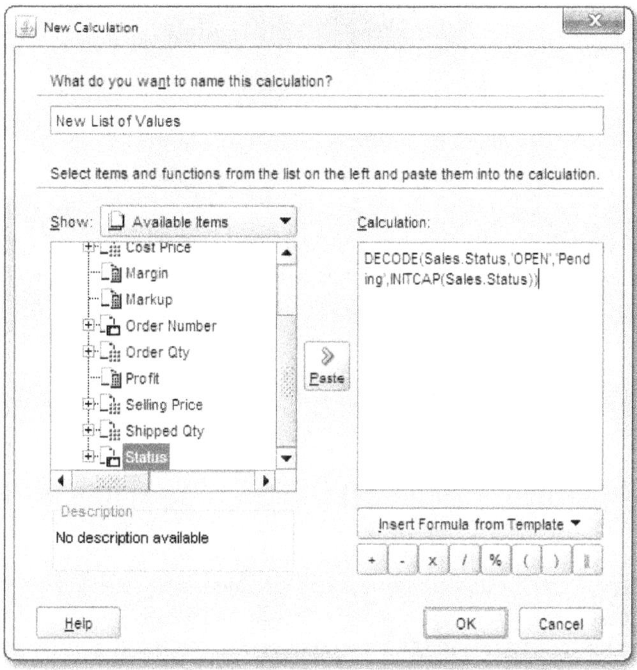


We could easily have written this using a CASE statement as follows:

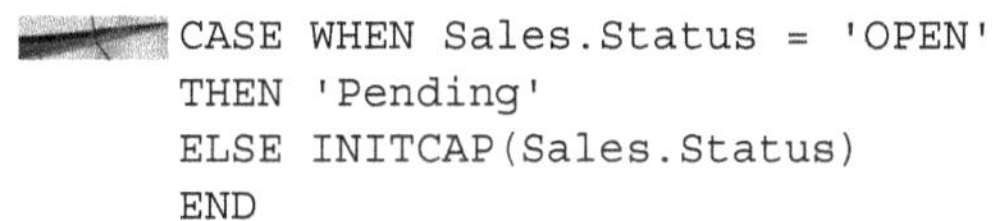

```
CASE WHEN Sales.Status = 'OPEN'
THEN 'Pending'
ELSE INITCAP(Sales.Status)
END
```

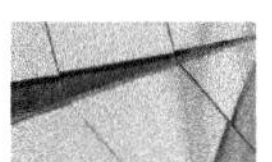

**NOTE**
*In the previous examples, INITCAP is the function that causes the first letter of the word to be capitalized with all the rest of the letters in lowercase.*

Running either of these calculations will produce the following list of values:

- Cancelled
- Hold
- Pending
- Shipped

Calculations and conditions can use either the original or amended list of values, but our report will always display the new list.

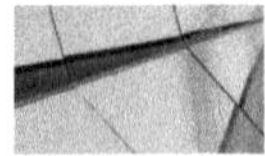

**NOTE**
*When the current data cannot be sorted into the order you desire, creating a sort using a new list of values will do the trick. This technique, common in programming circles, is a clever use of calculations. In the example just given, we created a new list of values. However, in our final report we want them sorted as Shipped, Hold, Pending, and then Cancelled. By prefixing the items using A-, B-, or 1., 2., and so on, you can reorder any list of values in any arrangement.*

**Creating New Data Types** You can use calculations to create new data types within your worksheet, but these new types will exist only within that worksheet. However, you can apply sorts and totals and even base other calculations on these data types.

Let's say we want to generate a new data type called Category and that this category has three values.

- High
- Middle
- Low

We want to analyze our sales and work out our top-ranking customers, such that customers with sales greater than nine million are in the High category, customers with sales greater than four million but less than nine million are in the Middle category, and customers with sales less than or equal to four million are in the Low category.

Here is the basic syntax:

```
IF Sales > 9000000
THEN High
ELSE IF Sales > 4000000
THEN Middle
ELSE Low
```

Using a CASE statement, this translates into the following:

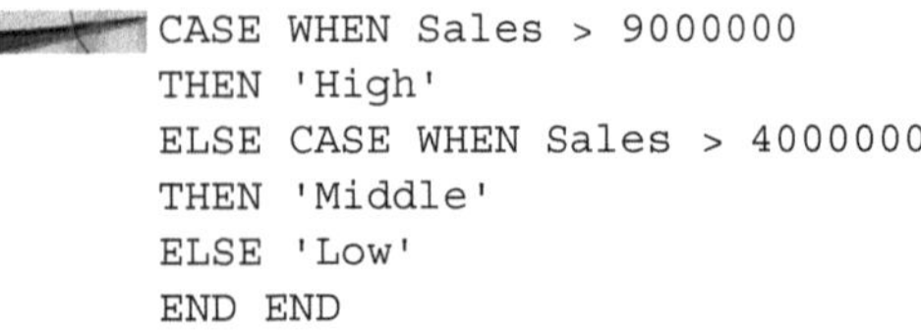

```
CASE WHEN Sales > 9000000
THEN 'High'
ELSE CASE WHEN Sales > 4000000
THEN 'Middle'
ELSE 'Low'
END END
```

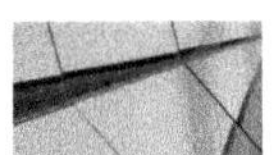

**NOTE**
*If you use multiple CASE statements in the same calculation, you must remember that each statement is completed by the END clause. Thus, in the preceding example, you can see that two END clauses are required. You can also see that the new data types are enclosed in single quotes.*

You can also use a single CASE statement with multiple WHEN clauses, like this:

```
CASE WHEN Sales > 9000000
THEN 'High'
WHEN Sales > 4000000
THEN 'Middle'
ELSE 'Low'
END
```

We like to call this a WHEN-WHEN situation.

CASE statements with multiple WHEN clauses remove data from the original set by executing the WHEN clauses in order. It is therefore vitally important to place the WHEN clauses in the right order. Starting with Sales > 9 million will allocate everything matching this condition to High and then work on what is left. If we had written our calculation starting with Sales > 4 million, allocating these to Middle, then ALL of the sales more than 4 million would be classified this way. There would be none left to allocate to High. This calculation therefore will give the wrong answer:

```
CASE WHEN Sales > 4000000
THEN Middle'
WHEN Sales > 9000000
THEN 'High'
ELSE 'Low'
END
```

We will now build this worksheet so that you can see the power of new data types. First, we started by pulling in our selling price and customer name, and we added a condition such that the status of the order is Shipped. This ensures that we produce statistics for only those customers to whom we have actually shipped widgets.

Next, we created a new calculation called Category, using the CASE statement outlined earlier. To help you, the following illustration shows the New Calculation dialog box:

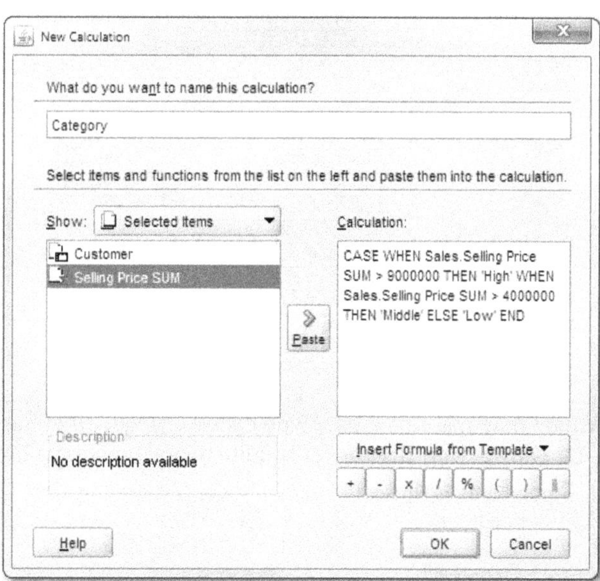

If you are comfortable with Discoverer, then you can use the WIDTH_BUCKET analytic function to create binning-type calculations on your data. Another very powerful way to perform best/worst kind of analysis on your data is to use the NTILE analytic function. You would use NTILE for rank-based bucketing and WIDTH_BUCKET for value-based bucketing.

| | Category | Customer | Selling Price SUM |
|---|---|---|---|
| 1 | High | CASA DE WIDGETS | 14095914.00 |
| 2 | | CEBU WIDGET CO | 14651508.52 |
| 3 | | MUM'S WIDGET CO. | 12502448.08 |
| 4 | | PATRIOT'S WIDGET CO. | 10985408.88 |
| 5 | | THING'S | 11277298.19 |
| 6 | | WIDGET SUPPLY CO. | 11228821.65 |
| 7 | | WIDGETS DE MEXICO | 11959138.26 |
| 8 | | WIDGETS R US | 10977463.86 |
| 9 | | WONDER WIDGETS | 12907276.06 |
| 10 | Low | BRIDGE THINGS | 3283503.23 |
| 11 | | PALMELA WIDGETS | 1943482.77 |
| 12 | | WILD WEST WIDGETS | 3369545.77 |
| 13 | Middle | ACE MANUFACTURING | 7209301.26 |
| 14 | | LOTS OF WIDGETS | 7684154.22 |
| 15 | | MOUNTAIN WIDGETS | 8521306.30 |
| 16 | | REPUBLIC WIDGETS | 7268283.69 |
| 17 | | THE LITTLE WIDGET | 7605566.23 |
| 18 | | TRICOLOR WIDGETS | 6942313.33 |
| 19 | | WE'VE GOT WIDGETS | 7488845.26 |
| 20 | | WIDGETS BY THE BAY | 7209164.99 |
| 21 | | YAMATA WIDGET LTD. | 7815671.97 |

**Manipulating New Data Types** As mentioned earlier, after you create a new data type, you can manipulate it as if it were a normal data type. You can sort by the new data type, you can use it in page items, and you can even use it in other calculations or percentages. Your only restriction is your own imagination.

Using the new data type we created earlier, in this illustration you can see that we successfully created a group sort on the category.

Next we enabled page items. Remember you do this by selecting View | Page Items from the menu bar. Finally, after enabling page items, as you can see next, we moved the category into the page axis.

Page Items: Category: High

High
Low
Middle
<All>

| | Customer | Selling Price SUM |
|---|---|---|
| 1 | CASA DE WIDGE | 14095914.00 |
| 2 | CEBU WIDGET C( | 14651508.52 |
| 3 | HONG KONG WID | 10407698.62 |
| 4 | LAC WIDGETS SA | 9580460.18 |
| 5 | LAST RAILWAY WIDGETS | 10107526.30 |
| 6 | LONDON WIDGETS LTD. | 10446212.26 |
| 7 | MUM'S WIDGET CO. | 12502448.08 |
| 8 | OXFORD WIDGETS | 9313706.72 |
| 9 | PATRIOT'S WIDGET CO. | 10985408.88 |
| 10 | THING'S | 11277298.19 |
| 11 | WARSAW WIDGETS | 9436866.33 |
| 12 | WIDGET AIR | 9423983.70 |
| 13 | WIDGET O THE MERSEY | 10706584.49 |
| 14 | WIDGET SUPPLY CO. | 11228821.65 |
| 15 | WIDGETS DE MEXICO | 11959138.26 |
| 16 | WIDGETS MARKET | 10712334.41 |
| 17 | WIDGETS ON THE WEB | 10663243.58 |
| 18 | WIDGETS R US | 10977463.86 |
| 19 | WONDER WIDGETS | 12907276.06 |

Our final worksheet now has a new data type called Category that has three values: High, Middle, and Low. You can see that Discoverer is quite happy creating a list of values on this new category.

**Creating a Calculation on the Subset of an Item** The third advanced use of the CASE and DECODE functions is a bit trickier. In our database we have two sales channels: External and Internet. Discoverer will normally see these as being a subset of the channel and will not allow us to apply a calculation to one without it being applied to the other. For example, suppose we want to see the unit price for the External channel only. Defining a calculation as we have done previously will cause Discoverer to show the unit price for both channels.

However, let's suppose we want to see the following output, in which we have displayed the unit price for the External channel and displayed *N.A.* for the Internet.

Page Items: Order Month: JUN-13

| | Channel | Order Qty SUM | Cost Price SUM | Retail Unit Price |
|---|---|---|---|---|
| 1 | EXTERNAL | 140875 | 1289804.25 | 9.16 |
| 2 | INTERNET | 414142 | 3471330.59 | N.A. |

The only way to do this is to use either CASE or DECODE. These code extracts show exactly how to do this:

```
CASE WHEN Channel = 'INTERNET' THEN NULL ELSE Cost Price Sum / Order Qty Sum
END
```

or

```
DECODE(Channel, 'INTERNET', NULL, Cost Price Sum / Order Qty Sum)
```

Here is the calculation as a DECODE:

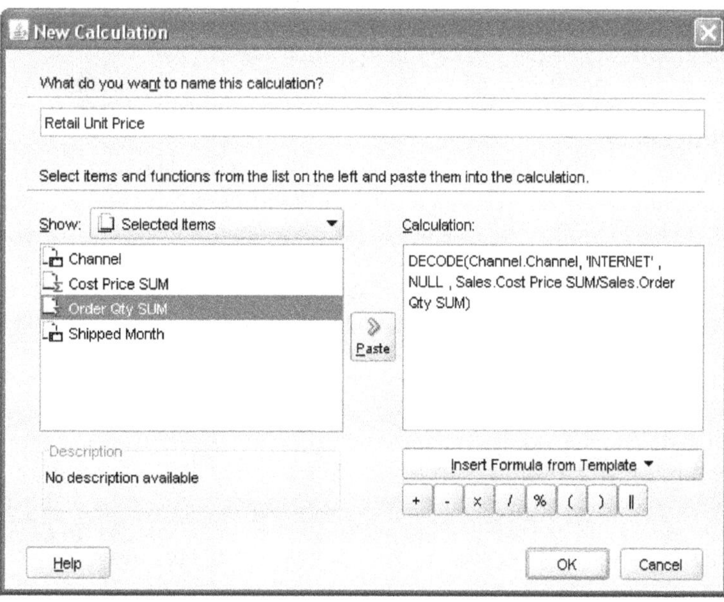

To complete the report, we made Discoverer display *N.A.* instead of the null value. This was done by right-clicking anywhere within the worksheet and from the pop-up selecting Format Table. This opened the Table Format tab of the Worksheet Properties dialog box. In the section called Sheet Content we simply selected N.A. from the drop-down.

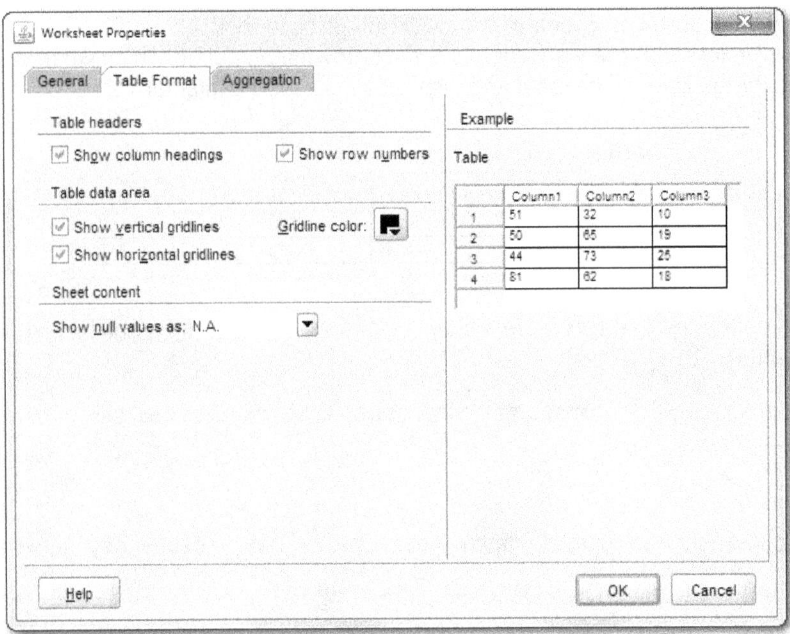


When done, we clicked OK, and the formatting was complete.

Please refer to Chapter 15 for a full explanation of how to manipulate null values.

## Manipulating Dates

Many date functions are available to you in Discoverer, and the skilled application of these coupled with other functions will greatly enhance your skill set. The ability to effectively manipulate and understand date logic is vitally important to your becoming proficient in Discoverer.

**Manipulating the Current Date** Current date manipulation lies at the heart of most date manipulations. Once you have mastered it, you can apply the same techniques to other dates, creating more and more powerful queries as you advance your knowledge.

The SYSDATE function returns the current date *and* time. We have italicized the word *and* to draw your attention to the fact that this function returns the time as well as the date. The TRUNC(SYSDATE) function returns the current date alone, with the time portion truncated. It is vitally important that you remember these two uses of the SYSDATE function.

The addition of the time to the date means you can apply both time and date formats to the SYSDATE, but you should not use it alone in calculations or conditions. To demonstrate this, look at the illustration at right. In it we have a single item, the SYSDATE, which has been formatted to show the current date and time in the 24-hour-clock format.

| | System Date |
|---|---|
| 1 | 23-APR-13 00:08:07 |

And here is the calculation:

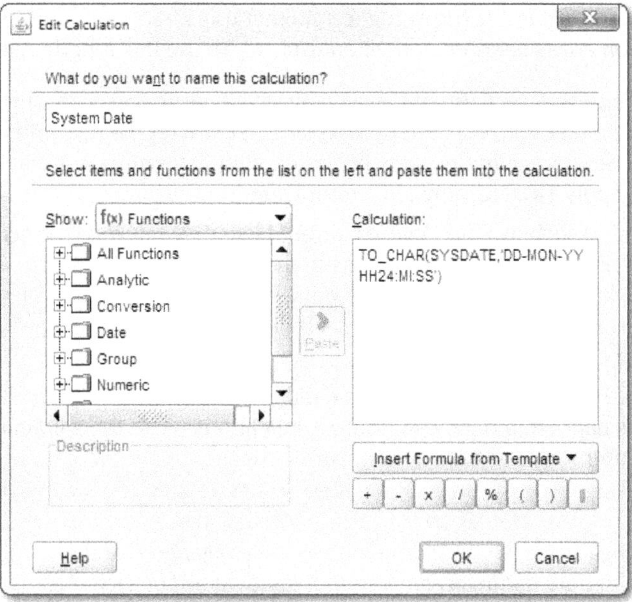


As you can see, if you attempt to find all shipments using this date, you would find only shipments that took place at precisely 8 minutes and 7 seconds past midnight on April 23, 2013! That's an unlikely scenario, we think you will agree. You might be lucky, but probably not.

To use the current date in calculations and conditions, you will apply the TRUNC function to all dates that you use. This will truncate the time portion from the date and allow you to do comparisons and computations safe in the knowledge that you are comparing apples with apples.

To find all shipments that have taken place today, you should use this construct:

```
TRUNC(SYSDATE)=TRUNC(Ship Date)
```

Most data warehouse applications will truncate transaction dates as they are being loaded into the warehouse. This will help you considerably because now your construct will become

```
TRUNC(SYSDATE)=Ship Date
```

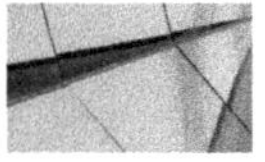

**NOTE**

*Unless you apply formatting criteria to the results of your calculation, the result of a date calculation will always be displayed in the default date format as specified by your Discoverer administrator. Most Oracle systems display the date as either DD-MON-YY or DD-MON-YYYY, meaning that December 25, 2013, will display either as 25-DEC-13 or 25-DEC-2013.*

**Common Problems Associated with Not Using TRUNC** Because the correct manipulation of the current date requires the application of the TRUNC function to all dates used when comparing one date with another, it is not surprising to find that users frequently run into problems with this. The most common errors encountered when users try to use this function are as follows:

- A condition such as Current Date = Ship Date returns no data. This is because one or both of the dates have a time portion associated with them. Some databases—data warehouses, for example—may be stored with dates already truncated, so you would need to apply TRUNC only to Current Date.
- A condition such as Ship Date < Current Date may return incorrect results by including some of the current day's shipments in the result. Suppose the current time is 4:30 p.m. and you last made a shipment at 4 p.m. This last shipment would be included in the result because the date and time combination on the shipment is prior to the current date and time combination.
- Ship Date <= Current Date returns data, but Ship Date = Current Date does not. We have seen this happen in data warehouse applications when the ship date has been truncated but the user forgot to truncate the current date.

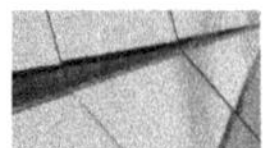

**NOTE**
*If you are using Oracle Applications, you will generally find that the transaction dates are not truncated and that the time will be stored as well. You therefore have to be very careful with your date manipulations when using Apps to ensure that your end results are correct. The following example shows you how to search for all of today's transactions when the time is stored as part of the transaction date.*

**Manipulating Other Dates** We will conclude this section with some more examples of date manipulation. Suppose you wanted to find the earliest date that an item first shipped. A combination of the DECODE or CASE, SUM, and MIN functions will give you the answer you are looking for, using one of these constructs:

```
DECODE(SUM(Qty Shipped), 0, NULL, MIN(Ship Date))
```

or

```
CASE WHEN SUM(Qty Shipped) = 0 THEN NULL ELSE MIN(Ship Date) END
```

If we take a closer look at this construct and break it down into plain English, you will be able to follow what is happening. Translating this into words, we get this: If the sum of the quantity shipped is 0, then return a null value; otherwise, return the earliest ship date on file. You may think that MIN(Ship Date) alone would return the answer you are looking for, but it will not.

The following example will explain why not. Imagine that product A has three sales orders: one has not shipped, one shipped last month, and one shipped this month. MIN(Ship Date) will return a null value because it encountered a null value in the ship date. Null values anywhere in the set of results will cause the whole result to be null; therefore, we need to eliminate them.

Last, to find yesterday's date, the function TRUNC(SYSDATE -1) can be used irrespective of the current date. Some Discoverer administrators supply a prebuilt condition for their users in tables that require a lot of reporting on data from yesterday.

**Using TO_CHAR to Manipulate Dates** There are three ways to use the TO_CHAR function in Discoverer: with dates, with numbers, and with labels. In the following section we will show you a practical use of the TO_CHAR function being applied to dates. Later in this section we will also show you how to manipulate numbers using the TO_CHAR function.

We have been asked many times how to display dates in various formats other than the format in which the database normally displays dates. For example, you may want to show and manipulate only the month component of the ship date. You might want to convert an Oracle E-Business Suite flex field into a date that you can use in other date manipulations.

First, before we show you how to use the TO_CHAR function to manipulate the month, we recommend you take a look at Appendix B, which outlines all of the date formats. There you will see other practical uses for what we are about to show you.

So, let's manipulate the ship month so that we can find all sales orders that have shipped during the current month. As you know, the SYSDATE function returns the current date.

If we use TO_CHAR(SYSDATE, 'MON'), this will convert today's date to the month. Comparing this with TO_CHAR(Ship Date, 'MON') will return all orders that have shipped in the current month. When you know how, it's simple.

**Using TO_CHAR with the Number Format Mask** In this section we will show you a practical use of the TO_CHAR function being applied to numbers.

We have frequently been asked whether there is a way to make Discoverer apply a grand total to a select number of columns in a single statement. The answer, as you will by now have realized, is no. You can define individual totals to the columns you want to total, or you can apply the total to all of the data points. There is no middle ground; however, there is a workaround using the TO_CHAR function.

Let's assume you have three columns of data: one for quantity shipped, one for the local currency amount, and one for the regional currency amount. If you are using multiple currencies, you cannot apply a total to the local currency amount. However, you also do not want to create individual totals for the remaining columns, each with its own label. What you want is a way to apply the grand total to all of the data points, except the local currency, with a single label of Grand Total.

The answer is simple. Well, it's simple if you know how! You create a new calculation, using TO_CHAR, based on the column or columns that you do not want to include in the grand total. For example, the syntax for converting the local currency amount into a string is as follows:

```
TO_CHAR(local currency amount)
```

However, on its own, the TO_CHAR function will not retain any formatting that you applied to the original number. To do this, you must add a format mask to the calculation. Let's use the same example and assume you want the local currency to be formatted with leading zeros and two decimal places. The following is the revised syntax:

```
TO_CHAR(local currency amount,'999990D99')
```

For a full description of all of the format masks available to you, refer to Appendix B.

# Calculating Standard Margin and Markup

If you are working in a manufacturing or order entry environment, these two mathematical formulae are arguably two of the most used formulas within Discoverer queries. The ability to be able to know how to create calculations for these is fundamental to becoming a master of Discoverer in this area.

There is a marked difference between margin and markup. Confusing the two may cause you to create an incorrect calculation or compute a quotation that is too low. *Margin* is defined as the percentage of the selling price represented by the gross profit. *Markup* is the amount (usually stated as a percentage of cost) that has to be added to the cost to achieve the selling price.

### Standard Margin

Using the definition just outlined, the calculation for standard margin is therefore calculated by taking the difference between the selling price and the cost price and then dividing this by the selling price.

To transform this into Discoverer format, we need to place the subtraction portion of this definition in brackets so that it now becomes (selling price – cost price) / selling price. In other words, Margin = (10 – 5) / 10, which works out to be 50 percent.

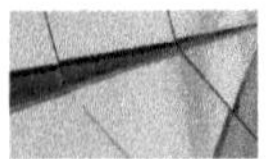

**NOTE**
*Look closely at the calculation in the following illustration. You will see that once again we have used parentheses to force Discoverer to calculate the subtraction before we perform the division.*

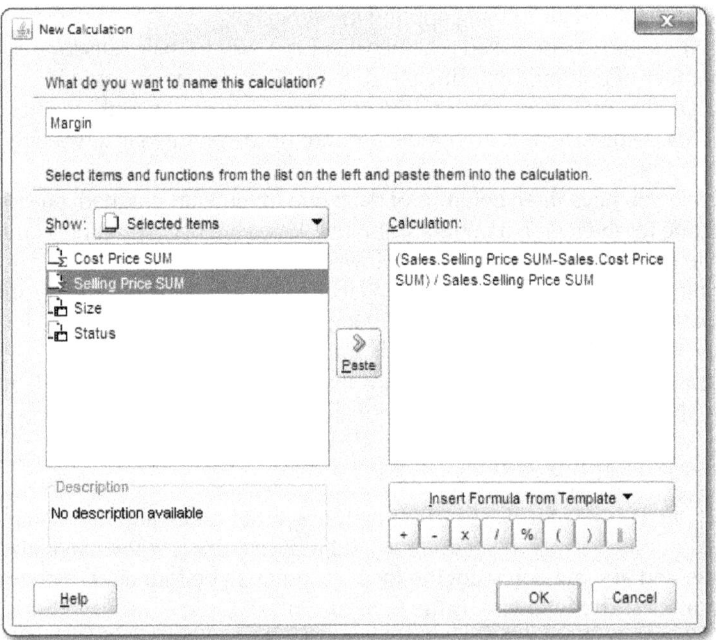


The final result of this calculation needs formatting as a percentage to two decimal places. When done, Margin looks like this:

| | Size | Status | Cost Price SUM | Selling Price SUM | Margin |
|---|---|---|---|---|---|
| 1 | MINI | CANCELLED | 849188.58 | 1202512.05 | 0.29 |
| 2 | | HOLD | 804.00 | 1190.00 | 0.32 |
| 3 | | OPEN | 384185.40 | 539596.00 | 0.29 |
| 4 | | SHIPPED | 7231369.32 | 10289549.45 | 0.30 |
| 5 | SMALL | CANCELLED | 1956923.31 | 3933474.55 | 0.50 |
| 6 | | HOLD | 69322.84 | 131146.90 | 0.47 |
| 7 | | OPEN | 1351942.50 | 2487595.15 | 0.46 |
| 8 | | SHIPPED | 18194814.19 | 36752039.75 | 0.50 |
| 9 | MEDIUN | CANCELLED | 5941241.26 | 13308146.27 | 0.55 |
| 10 | | HOLD | 358324.01 | 775642.66 | 0.54 |
| 11 | | OPEN | 6499755.77 | 14109687.50 | 0.54 |
| 12 | | SHIPPED | 54244826.48 | 121726092.77 | 0.55 |
| 13 | LARGE | CANCELLED | 5239287.26 | 10858018.30 | 0.52 |
| 14 | | HOLD | 194845.76 | 427691.46 | 0.54 |
| 15 | | OPEN | 3521376.21 | 7130347.90 | 0.51 |
| 16 | | SHIPPED | 51673187.71 | 105903161.93 | 0.51 |

The calculation, Selling Price minus Cost Price, is generally referred to as the *profit*. You could calculate the profit separately and then feed the result of that calculation into the margin as follows: profit / selling price.

## Standard Markup

Using the definition outlined earlier, the calculation for standard markup is therefore calculated by taking the difference between the selling price and the cost price and then dividing this by the cost price.

Again, in order to transform this into Discoverer format, we need to place the subtraction portion of this definition in brackets so that it now becomes: (selling price – cost price) / cost price.

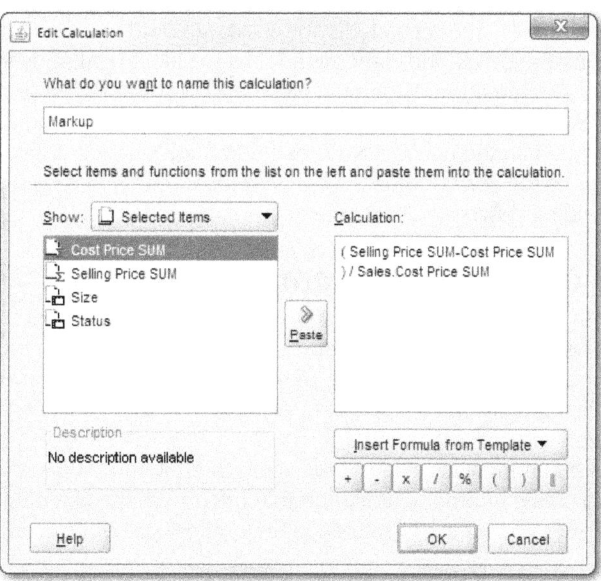


Markup = (10 – 5) / 5, which works out to be 100 percent. Once again, if you have precalculated the profit, you could use this formula: profit / cost price.

**Alternate Method to Create Margin or Markup** Assuming that you already have a calculation called Profit, there is another way of performing either the margin or markup calculation that does not involve the use of the New Calculation dialog box. This method uses the analysis toolbar.

Let's start with the following simple workbook:

| | ▸ Size | ▸ Status | ▸ Cost Price SUM | ▸ Selling Price SUM | ▸ Profit |
|---|---|---|---|---|---|
| 1 | MINI | CANCELLED | 849188.58 | 1202512.05 | 353323.47 |
| 2 | | HOLD | 804.00 | 1190.00 | 386.00 |
| 3 | | OPEN | 384185.40 | 539596.00 | 155410.60 |
| 4 | | SHIPPED | 7231369.32 | 10289549.45 | 3058180.13 |
| 5 | SMALL | CANCELLED | 1956923.31 | 3933474.55 | 1976551.24 |
| 6 | | HOLD | 69322.84 | 131146.90 | 61824.06 |
| 7 | | OPEN | 1351942.50 | 2487595.15 | 1135652.65 |
| 8 | | SHIPPED | 18194814.19 | 36752039.75 | 18557225.56 |
| 9 | MEDIUM | CANCELLED | 5941241.26 | 13308146.27 | 7366905.01 |
| 10 | | HOLD | 358324.01 | 775642.66 | 417318.65 |
| 11 | | OPEN | 6499755.77 | 14109687.50 | 7609931.73 |
| 12 | | SHIPPED | 54244826.48 | 121726092.77 | 67481266.29 |
| 13 | LARGE | CANCELLED | 5239287.26 | 10858018.30 | 5618731.04 |
| 14 | | HOLD | 194845.76 | 427691.46 | 232845.70 |
| 15 | | OPEN | 3521376.21 | 7130347.90 | 3608971.69 |
| 16 | | SHIPPED | 51673187.71 | 105903161.93 | 54229974.22 |

As you can see in the figure, we have Profit already calculated. Because Margin is Profit divided by Selling Price, we can use the quick-and-dirty method for creating a calculation. You need to click the heading for Profit and then, holding down CTRL on the keyboard, you need to next click the heading for Selling Price. With these two columns selected, you click the Divide icon in the calculation drop-down, as shown at right, to obtain the new calculation.

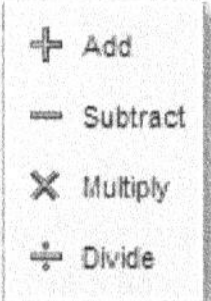


Finally, you need to rename the calculation to Margin and then format it as a percentage.

The trick to using the quick-and-dirty method, as we like to call it, is to be aware of the order of precedence for the calculation. When the calculation uses addition or multiplication, it does not matter which item you select first so that multiplying *a* by *b* can equally be represented as *a* * *b* or *b* * *a*. However, when the calculation uses subtraction or division, you have to make sure you select the items in the correct order. When you want to divide *a* by *b*, you must select *a* first and then, while holding down CTRL, click the heading for *b*.

## Ambiguous or Duplicate Item Names

When working with calculations within Discoverer, you are at liberty to name a calculation by any name you choose. You will even be allowed to name a calculation the same as an item in the database. We do this ourselves many times, perhaps when altering a formula or making data easier to read by changing from all-uppercase characters to strings that have only the first character capitalized.

The danger with naming a calculation the same as an item in the database is that occasionally you will attempt to create another calculation that references the first calculation but Discoverer will not know whether you meant to reference the original calculation or the item in the database.

When this happens, you will get the following *ambiguous or duplicate item names* error message shown here:

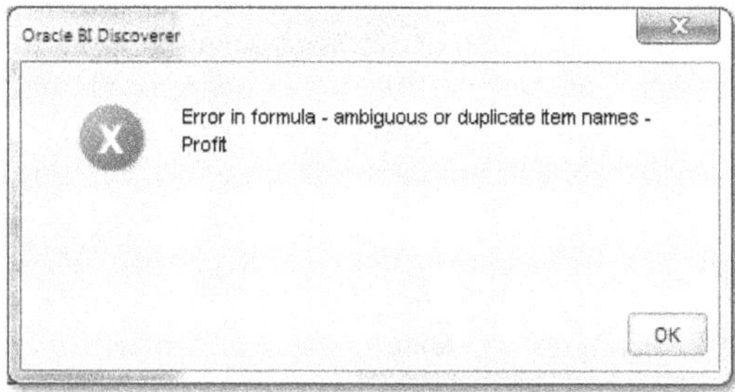


The fix in this case would be to edit the original calculation and give it a different name.

## Activating and Deactivating Calculations

Calculations are stand-alone objects within Discoverer and as such can be activated and deactivated. This section deals with activating and deactivating calculations.

### Activating Calculations

Before Discoverer can display a calculation, that calculation needs to be activated. To activate a calculation, use this workflow:

1. From the menu bar select Tools | Calculations, or in Plus click the Calculations tab.
2. Select the calculation you want to activate.
3. In Desktop, check the box alongside the calculation and click OK.
4. In Plus, right-click the calculation and from the drop-down list select Add To Worksheet.

**NOTE**
*Some calculations are used as intermediary calculations for other calculations or within conditions. Even though these calculations may be displayed as being inactive, because another calculation or condition is using that calculation, it is actually active.*

### Deactivating Calculations

Discoverer has the ability to deactivate a calculation without deleting its definition. To deactivate a calculation, use this workflow:

1. From the menu bar select Tools | Calculations, or in Plus click the Calculations tab.
2. Select the calculation you want to deactivate.
3. In Desktop, uncheck the box alongside the calculation and click OK.
4. In Plus, right-click the calculation and from the drop-down list select Remove From Worksheet.

# Refining the Sort Order

After you have refined conditions, parameters, and especially calculations, the next logical step is to refine the sort order. Perhaps the addition of a new calculation has added a new column. Maybe the calculation was created specifically for the purpose of defining a new list of values. It is also likely that an erroneous data item was removed from the worksheet when you refined your calculations.

Therefore, after you have refined calculations, you will need to revisit sorting if one of the following is true:

- You deleted a column upon which a sort had been created.
- You added a new item that needs to be part of a sort.
- You added a new list of values and a sort exists on the old list.
- The new items that have been added to the worksheet fundamentally changed the essence and meaning.

In Chapter 5, we explained in detail how to sort, add group sorts, add multiple sorts, and rearrange the order. We even showed you how to add or remove sorts using the menu bar or from a drop-down list. If you are not sure how these are done, you should read the section on sorting in Chapter 5 again.

## Sort Order Manipulation

When you have multiple sorts in your worksheet, you can choose, using Tools | Sort, the order in which those sorts are applied. By default, Discoverer has a hierarchy for sorting. This hierarchy places group sorts above standard High-to-Low or Low-to-High sorts.

It is important to remember that Discoverer has this sorting hierarchy because adding or removing sorts with a different rank will cause the sort order to change. This may not be what you intended.

In the following illustration, we have three sorts in operation. They are

- A Low-to-High group sort on Quarter
- A Low-to-High group sort on Channel
- A High-to-Low normal sort on Status

| | Order Quarter | Channel | Status | Selling Price SUM |
|---|---|---|---|---|
| 1 | 2013-Q1 | EXTERNAL | CANCELLED | 329015.26 |
| 2 | | | SHIPPED | 4563120.60 |
| 3 | | INTERNET | CANCELLED | 1981750.09 |
| 4 | | | SHIPPED | 13320887.94 |
| 5 | 2013-Q2 | EXTERNAL | CANCELLED | 126188.80 |
| 6 | | | OPEN | 64680.00 |
| 7 | | | SHIPPED | 6421429.74 |
| 8 | | INTERNET | CANCELLED | 1499149.82 |
| 9 | | | OPEN | 731214.00 |
| 10 | | | SHIPPED | 15937596.65 |
| 11 | 2013-Q3 | EXTERNAL | CANCELLED | 962248.20 |
| 12 | | | HOLD | 58625.00 |
| 13 | | | OPEN | 2467145.75 |
| 14 | | | SHIPPED | 3712079.88 |
| 15 | | INTERNET | CANCELLED | 1666755.85 |
| 16 | | | HOLD | 4379.64 |
| 17 | | | OPEN | 5401743.48 |
| 18 | | | SHIPPED | 11193598.73 |

On the Sort tab of the Edit Worksheet dialog box, the sort definitions look like this:

| | Column | Direction | Sort Type | Hidden |
|---|---|---|---|---|
| Sort by | *Order Quarter* | Low to High | Group Sort | ☐ |
| then by | *Channel* | Low to High | Group Sort | ☐ |
| then by | Status | Low to High | Normal | ☐ |

Using one of the techniques shown to you in Chapter 5, we will change the group sort on Quarter to become a standard Low-to-High sort. If you recall, you do this by right-clicking in the column that has the sort you want to change and from the drop-down list clicking Group Sort. This removes the Group Sort rule and changes the sort to become a standard sort. When we did this on Quarter, this is what happened.

| | Order Quarter | Channel | Status | Selling Price SUM |
|---|---|---|---|---|
| 1 | 2013-Q1 | EXTERNAL | CANCELLED | 329015.26 |
| 2 | 2013-Q1 | | SHIPPED | 4563120.60 |
| 3 | 2013-Q2 | | CANCELLED | 126188.80 |
| 4 | 2013-Q2 | | OPEN | 64680.00 |
| 5 | 2013-Q2 | | SHIPPED | 6421429.74 |
| 6 | 2013-Q3 | | CANCELLED | 962248.20 |
| 7 | 2013-Q3 | | HOLD | 58625.00 |
| 8 | 2013-Q3 | | OPEN | 2467145.75 |
| 9 | 2013-Q3 | | SHIPPED | 3712079.88 |
| 10 | 2013-Q1 | INTERNET | CANCELLED | 1981750.09 |
| 11 | 2013-Q1 | | SHIPPED | 13320887.94 |
| 12 | 2013-Q2 | | CANCELLED | 1499149.82 |
| 13 | 2013-Q2 | | OPEN | 731214.00 |
| 14 | 2013-Q2 | | SHIPPED | 15937596.65 |
| 15 | 2013-Q3 | | CANCELLED | 1666755.85 |
| 16 | 2013-Q3 | | HOLD | 4379.64 |
| 17 | 2013-Q3 | | OPEN | 5401743.48 |
| 18 | 2013-Q3 | | SHIPPED | 11193598.73 |

As you can see, Quarter is no longer group sorted. You can also see that Channel is no longer sorted after Quarter, but that Quarter is now being sorted after Channel. Looking at the Sort tab of the Edit Worksheet dialog box, the sort definitions now look like this:

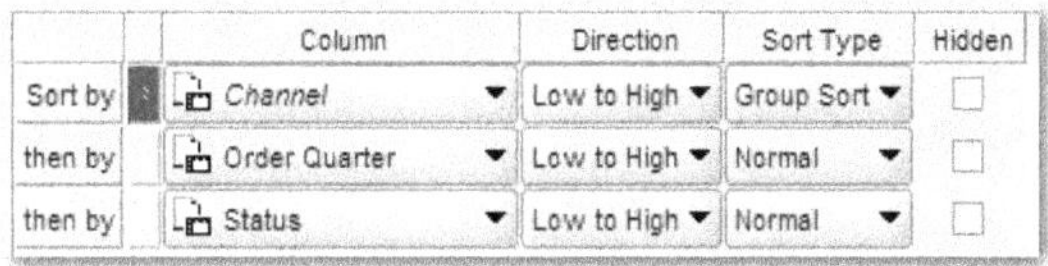

| | Column | Direction | Sort Type | Hidden |
|---|---|---|---|---|
| Sort by | *Channel* | Low to High | Group Sort | ☐ |
| then by | Order Quarter | Low to High | Normal | ☐ |
| then by | Status | Low to High | Normal | ☐ |

By comparing this illustration to the one given earlier, you can see that Discoverer has switched the sort order so that Channel now sorts before Quarter. This is because of the precedence being given to group sorts where group sorts are always applied *before* normal sorts.

As an experiment, try highlighting Quarter in the Sort tab and then clicking the Move Up button. If you do this, because you will be moving a standard sort above a group sort, Discoverer will change the sort on Quarter to once again become a group sort.

### Deleting a Sort Using the Sort Tab

In Chapter 5 you were shown how to delete a sort using a drop-down list. However, you can also delete sorts from the Sort tab of the Edit Sheet dialog box.

If you have decided that a sort is no longer needed, you can delete it, using the Sort tab, by using the following workflow:

1. From the menu bar, select Tools | Sort, or you can also click the Sort tab in the Edit Sheet dialog box. This will open the Sort dialog box.
2. Highlight the sort you want to delete.
3. Click the Delete button.
4. Click OK.

## Refining Percentages

Finally, the last component to refining a worksheet is refining percentages. Very little of the previous refinements will have had any significant impact on the percentages, which is why we have left this section until last. However, you may have changed the definition of a calculation that was used in a percentage. That change may now require you to either amend or remove the percentage definition.

In Chapter 5, we explained in great detail how to create percentages. We also gave you examples of all the different types of percentage you can create in Discoverer. In Chapter 9, we showed you many examples of percentages being used to analyze data. In this chapter, we will give you workflows for editing a percentage and for removing an unwanted percentage.

### Using COUNT and Percentages in a Crosstab

Earlier in this chapter we created a worksheet that used the count of the sales orders. We will now refine that worksheet to add a percentage and show you how the different percentage options work.

Let's start by reloading the worksheet that used the order status, the count of the order number, and the year. By clicking anywhere in the data for this worksheet and then clicking the New Percentage button, as you can see next, Discoverer automatically creates a percentage based on the order number count.

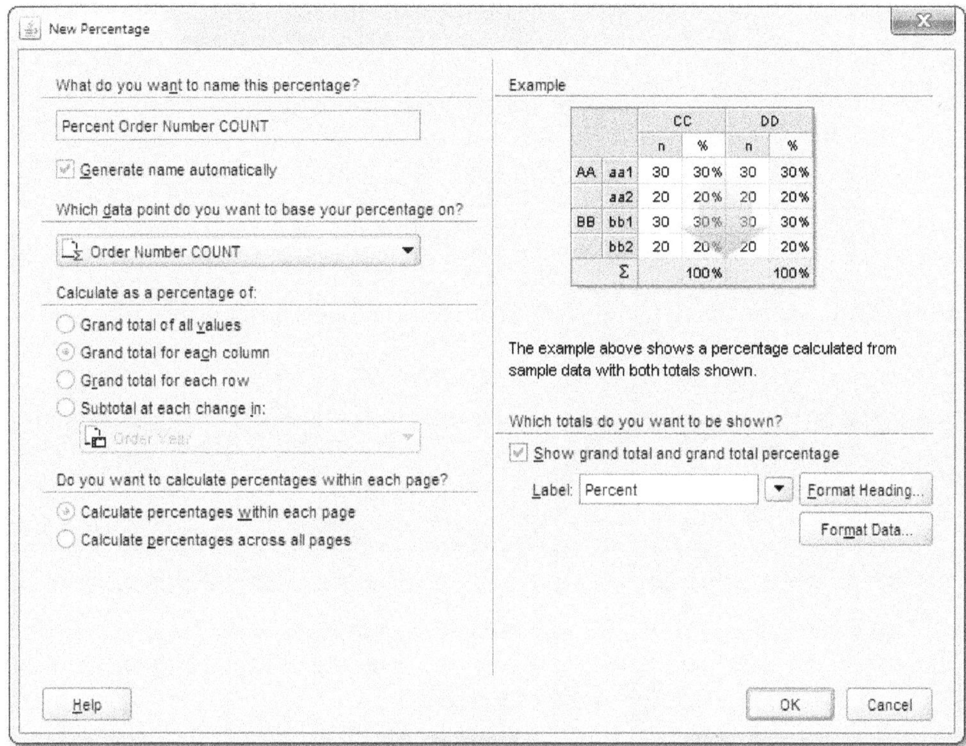


Editing the percentage shows that we have four main options for calculating the percentage.

- Grand total of all values
- Grand total for each column
- Grand total for each row
- Subtotal at each change in group sort

The next three illustrations show how this simple percentage worksheet looks when each of the first three options are selected.

The following illustration shows a percentage based on a grand total of all values:

| | Number of Orders | | | | Percent | | | |
|---|---|---|---|---|---|---|---|---|
| | CANCELLED | HOLD | OPEN | SHIPPED | CANCELLED | HOLD | OPEN | SHIPPED |
| FY2006 | 7 | 0 | 0 | 371 | 0.06% | 0 | 0 | 3.25% |
| FY2007 | 43 | 0 | 1 | 680 | 0.38% | 0 | 0.01% | 5.95% |
| FY2008 | 129 | 35 | 430 | 1087 | 1.13% | 0.31% | 3.76% | 9.51% |
| FY2009 | 109 | 0 | 0 | 1057 | 0.95% | 0 | 0 | 9.25% |
| FY2010 | 119 | 0 | 0 | 1541 | 1.04% | 0 | 0 | 13.48% |
| FY2011 | 150 | 0 | 0 | 1640 | 1.31% | 0 | 0 | 14.35% |
| FY2012 | 160 | 0 | 0 | 1897 | 1.40% | 0 | 0 | 16.60% |
| FY2013 | 151 | 6 | 255 | 1561 | 1.32% | 0.05% | 2.23% | 13.66% |
| Percent | 868 | 41 | 686 | 9834 | 7.59% | 0.36% | 6.00% | 86.04% |

The following illustration shows a percentage based on a grand total for each column:

| | Number of Orders | | | | Percent Order Number COUNT | | | |
|---|---|---|---|---|---|---|---|---|
| | ▸ CANCELLED | ▸ HOLD | ▸ OPEN | ▸ SHIPPED | ▸ CANCELLED | ▸ HOLD | ▸ OPEN | ▸ SHIPPED |
| ▸ FY2006 | 7 | 0 | 0 | 371 | 0.81% | 0 | 0 | 3.77% |
| ▸ FY2007 | 43 | 0 | 1 | 680 | 4.95% | 0 | 0.15% | 6.91% |
| ▸ FY2008 | 129 | 35 | 430 | 1087 | 14.86% | 85.37% | 62.68% | 11.05% |
| ▸ FY2009 | 109 | 0 | 0 | 1057 | 12.56% | 0 | 0 | 10.75% |
| ▸ FY2010 | 119 | 0 | 0 | 1541 | 13.71% | 0 | 0 | 15.67% |
| ▸ FY2011 | 150 | 0 | 0 | 1640 | 17.28% | 0 | 0 | 16.68% |
| ▸ FY2012 | 160 | 0 | 0 | 1897 | 18.43% | 0 | 0 | 19.29% |
| ▸ FY2013 | 151 | 6 | 255 | 1561 | 17.40% | 14.63% | 37.17% | 15.87% |
| Percent | 868 | 41 | 686 | 9834 | 100.00% | 100.00% | 100.00% | 100.00% |

The following illustration shows a percentage based on a grand total for each row:

| | Number of Orders | | | | | Percent Order Number COUNT | | | | |
|---|---|---|---|---|---|---|---|---|---|---|
| | ▸ CANCELLED | ▸ HOLD | ▸ OPEN | ▸ SHIPPED | Percent | ▸ CANCELLED | ▸ HOLD | ▸ OPEN | ▸ SHIPPED | Percent |
| ▸ FY2006 | 7 | 0 | 0 | 371 | 378 | 1.85% | 0 | 0 | 98.15% | 100.00% |
| ▸ FY2007 | 43 | 0 | 1 | 680 | 724 | 5.94% | 0 | 0.14% | 93.92% | 100.00% |
| ▸ FY2008 | 129 | 35 | 430 | 1087 | 1681 | 7.67% | 2.08% | 25.58% | 64.66% | 100.00% |
| ▸ FY2009 | 109 | 0 | 0 | 1057 | 1166 | 9.35% | 0 | 0 | 90.65% | 100.00% |
| ▸ FY2010 | 119 | 0 | 0 | 1541 | 1660 | 7.17% | 0 | 0 | 92.83% | 100.00% |
| ▸ FY2011 | 150 | 0 | 0 | 1640 | 1790 | 8.38% | 0 | 0 | 91.62% | 100.00% |
| ▸ FY2012 | 160 | 0 | 0 | 1897 | 2057 | 7.78% | 0 | 0 | 92.22% | 100.00% |
| ▸ FY2013 | 151 | 6 | 255 | 1561 | 1973 | 7.65% | 0.30% | 12.92% | 79.12% | 100.00% |

## Workflow to Change a Percentage

To change a percentage definition, use the following workflow:

1. From the menu bar, select Tools | Percentages, or in Plus click the Calculations tab in the Available Items pane. In both versions you will see a list of percentages.

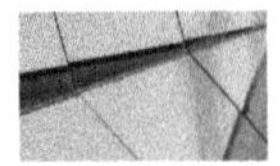

**NOTE**
*Clicking the Percentage button on the Desktop analysis bar or the Plus menu bar does not open the Percentages tool. These buttons create a percentage based on the column currently highlighted.*

2. Double-click the percentage that you want to change. Discoverer now opens the Edit Percentages dialog box.
3. Change the percentage definition (refer to Chapter 5 for an explanation of percentage definitions).
4. Click OK.

## Workflow to Delete a Percentage

To delete a percentage definition, use the following workflow:

1. From the menu bar select Tools | Percentages, or in Plus click the Calculations tab. Either one of these methods displays the list of percentages.

2. Highlight the percentage you want to remove, and then in Desktop click Delete or in Plus right-click the Percentage and from the drop-down menu select Delete.
3. In Desktop only, click OK.

## Activating and Deactivating Percentages

Percentages are stand-alone objects within Discoverer and as such can be activated and deactivated. This section deals with activating and deactivating percentages.

### Activating Percentages

Before Discoverer can display a percentage, the percentage needs to be activated. To activate a percentage, use this workflow:

1. From the menu bar select Tools | Percentages, or in Plus click the Calculations tab.
2. Select the percentage you want to activate.
3. In Desktop, check the box alongside the percentage and click OK.
4. In Plus, right-click the percentage and from the drop-down list select Add To Worksheet.

### Deactivating Percentages

Discoverer has the ability to deactivate a percentage without deleting its definition. To deactivate a percentage, use this workflow:

1. From the menu bar select Tools | Percentages, or in Plus click the Calculations tab.
2. Select the percentage you want to deactivate.
3. In Desktop, uncheck the box alongside the percentage and click OK.
4. In Plus, right-click the percentage and from the drop-down list select Remove From Worksheet.

# Summary

In this chapter you learned to change a condition to a parameter, edit parameters, and rearrange the order of parameters. We also showed you how to refine calculations by defining the main components of a calculation and defining the calculation in advance. We taught you how to convert an algorithm into a Discoverer script as well as how to avoid division-by-zero errors. We showed you how to use DECODE and CASE to overcome divide-by-zero errors, as well as how to create custom lists of values. We showed you how to review conditions based on calculations and review the data items used in the edited calculation. We showed you how to use standard functions to define calculations for standard margin and markup.

We taught you how to refine the sort order, as well as how to remove an item from the sort order. And finally, we gave you workflows for refining percentages, including how to change percentages and how to remove them.

In the following chapter, we will teach you techniques for managing queries, including sharing, security, and understanding your access to the queries of others.

# CHAPTER 14

# Managing Queries

Once a workbook has been formatted into a valuable report, you need to decide who will have access to it. Will it be distributed in print only, or will others have access to it through Discoverer? Will it be e-mailed to your manager or even become a company-wide report used by many people every day? Is it destined to find its way into your enterprise portal?

In this chapter, you will learn a little about the role of the Discoverer manager and how the position is an important part of report management. You will need to know what access you have to any given report. A good relationship with your Discoverer manager plays an important role in that access. You might be given access to a report that has been developed by another person, perhaps a library manager or superuser. Perhaps the access you are given might be limited and you will be allowed only to view the report, not to make any changes to it.

We will talk about libraries in depth and show you how they can help you organize your workbooks. You will learn how to work with libraries and see how helpful they can be in avoiding duplication of workbooks.

We will show you how to share workbooks that you have created as well as how to open workbooks that have been shared with you. You will learn the benefits of sharing workbooks as well as the involvement of superusers in the management of shared workbooks. We will teach you how to use and edit shared workbooks.

Deleting unwanted or unused workbooks from the database is another important part of report management. An equally important facet is managing the properties of a report. This chapter will teach you how to perform these functions as well as why caution should be used. We will explain how security is set up to protect sensitive company data and how that affects you.

The section "Worksheet Manipulation" will show you how to manage worksheets within your workbooks. We will show you how to reorder worksheets, how to rename worksheets, and how to delete unwanted worksheets. You will also learn how to find data within a worksheet and even how to copy or move worksheets between workbooks.

Use of the Workbook Scheduler will be covered, as well as the benefits to you of executing your workbooks at a scheduled time. You will learn how to schedule a workbook, how to view the results, and how to unschedule a workbook. You will also learn how to share the results of scheduled workbooks with other users.

We will show you the added flexibility that using a third-party scheduler provides by using the command line. We will further show you how to use the native scheduler in Windows XP to set up your own third-party scheduling.

We will also cover the Discoverer command-line utility and will introduce you to the features that give additional power to the end user. We will provide an overview to give you the syntax of all of the command-line functions, along with many examples that will show you how to use the command line.

Another topic to be covered in this chapter is the management of SQL code: importing, exporting, and using structured SQL. You will also see how to send reports to others via e-mail.

# The Discoverer Manager and the End User

Before you can begin to work with Discoverer, your Discoverer manager needs to have granted, or arranged for you to have been granted, various rights and privileges. The most important of these is the creation of a user account for the databases you will be accessing. This setup will assign you a user ID and password and will create the basic database privileges you will need. Your Discoverer administrator will convey these to you, probably in an e-mail.

**NOTE**
*If you are using Oracle E-Business Suite, your user ID, password, and responsibility will be assigned to you by the system administrator. You need to liaise with the Discoverer manager as to what rights and privileges your particular responsibility has been granted. You may well need to be granted a separate responsibility for accessing Discoverer.*

With your account now created, your Discoverer manager will now grant you access to one or more business areas as well as specify your end-user privileges. The rights that you are assigned at this stage dictate whether you have the power to grant access for other people to share your queries, whether you have the power to save and delete queries within the database, and whether you have the power to schedule queries.

## Managing Libraries

We introduced you to the concept of libraries in Chapter 2. If you are unsure as to the definitions of a Discoverer library and Discoverer manager, please go back and read those sections in Chapter 2. In this section, we expand on the concept and show you how we think libraries should be an integral part of your Discoverer environment.

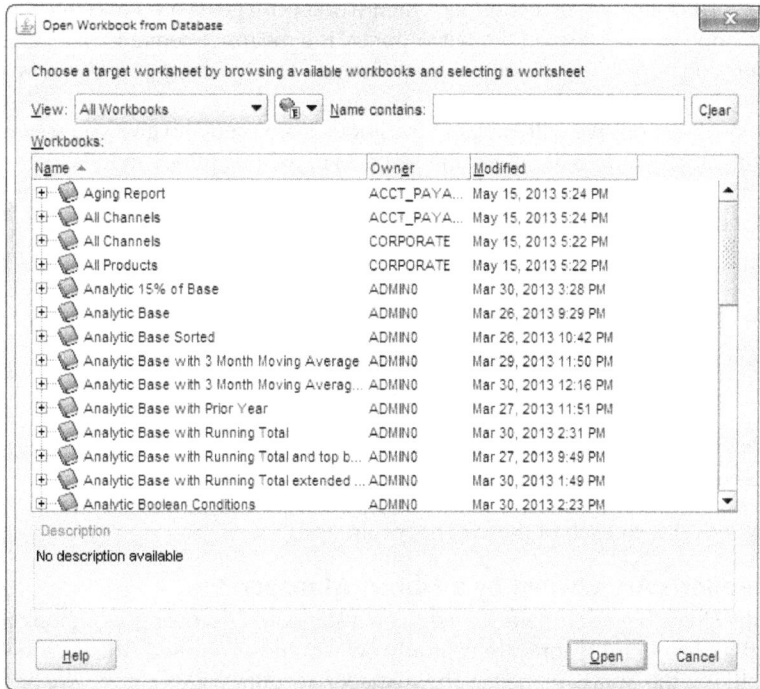

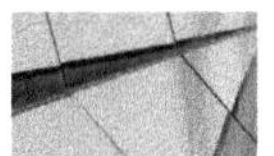

**NOTE**
*The concept of a Discoverer library is not a native Discoverer concept but one that we advocate for more efficient management of Discoverer content.*

## Expanded Library Concept

The concept of a Discoverer library is a mechanism that we invented to help our clients better manage Discoverer. Discoverer lends itself ideally to working with a library.

You can think of a library as a collection of Discoverer workbooks all based around a common theme. For example, you could have one set of workbooks dedicated to human resources, another dedicated to accounting, another dedicated to order entry, and yet another library dedicated to maintaining inventory. If you are using the Oracle E-Business Suite, in other words Oracle Applications, you can see how easy it would be to set up one library for each module of the system. Each library has a dedicated, generic user account such that you will create accounts called HR Library, OE Library, and INV Library.

Next you will create two sets of roles, or *responsibilities* if using Oracle Applications. One set will be for the library managers, with names such as HR Library Manager, OE Library Manager, and INV Library Manager. The second set is for end-user access, with names such as HR User, OE User, and INV User. Using the Discoverer Administrator tool, the Discoverer manager will assign these roles or responsibilities access to the required business areas.

Next, you assign the library manager roles to designated users. These users will be responsible for maintaining the workbooks inside their libraries. Logging into Discoverer Plus, the library manager can share workbooks with the user roles or responsibilities, such that a person with the HR Library Manager role can share the HR Workbooks with the HR User role.

All that remains is to grant the HR role or responsibility to a real HR user. The user will then automatically have access to all of the workbooks in the HR library.

The use of libraries maintains sets of corporate workbooks that adhere to corporate standards, are documented, and are guaranteed to work. End users cannot modify these workbooks, because they are not the owner. Only the library manager has the power to add or remove workbooks and worksheets. The manager also controls which workbooks get shared and which do not.

As we hope you can see, a Discoverer library is a means of centrally managing and maintaining Discoverer workbooks. The concept is not restricted to 11*g*, though, and can be used with every release of Discoverer.

In the next sections we will explain how libraries are used and give you some simple workflows for changing library reports and for gaining access to existing library reports.

Six important features of a library report make it different from a Discoverer workbook. Library documents are different from normal Discoverer workbooks in that they are

- Owned by a library manager
- Guaranteed to be accurate and perform efficiently
- Guaranteed to adhere to corporate standards
- Centrally documented
- Centrally maintained
- Secure, with access being strictly controlled

We will deal with each of these concepts in turn.

### Library Reports Are Owned by a Library Manager

Perhaps the single biggest difference between a standard Discoverer workbook and a library report is that the library reports are centrally owned and controlled. The person who has this responsibility is the library manager. The manager account will not normally be a real user account but a database account, or Apps account, which is responsible for a set of workbooks. Adopting this method of working ensures the continued existence of the library following the departure of the manager, either from the company or from that position.

**NOTE**
*By default, the Discoverer manager also has the library manager role for all libraries.*

### Library Documents Are Guaranteed to Be Accurate and Perform Efficiently

Candidate reports will have stringent user testing to confirm that they do what they are supposed to do. Before being put forward as candidates for the library, new reports will require user sign-off and documentation. The users need to confirm that the report indeed does what it sets out to do. However, not only must the report do what it is supposed to do, but it should do it effectively and efficiently without putting undue overhead on the system. In other words, where required, the report's underlying SQL will have been optimized for good performance. This may require the writing of special SQL code, as either a Custom folder or a database view.

### Library Reports Adhere to Corporate Standards

These standards dictate the layout, style, and naming conventions that will be used. There should be an agreed list of abbreviations to which all library reports will conform. Standard headers and footers should be employed, and the data should be displayed in your organization's corporate colors. A confidentiality statement will be used where necessary. The adoption of these standards ensures that reports display a corporate image. The library manager is responsible for checking that the standards are being correctly used and that your corporate look and feel is being maintained. Reports that do not conform will be rejected and sent back to the report writer.

**Library and Workbook Prefixing** Another standard you may want to consider is the use of prefixes in the naming of your libraries and workbooks. We like to use two- or three-character prefixes for all of our corporate libraries and workbooks. Using prefixes helps us keep track of which workbooks belong to which library and, if we similarly prefix our business areas and folders, which business area the workbook uses. For example, let's say we have a human resources business area. Using this standard, we would prefix the business area name with the letters *HR*, perhaps naming it HR – Human Resources. All folders within the business area will also get the same prefix; thus, for instance, our employee folder will be called HR – Employees. Following this theme, our library would be called HR – Human Resources Library, and all library reports will be prefixed similarly.

### Library Reports Are Centrally Documented

Library reports will have meaningful descriptions for the report requirements, column names, and function definitions. Any special requirements such as parameter usage will be explained in detail. There should also be a set of example screenshots from the report. Users should be able to use this documentation to understand what the report does and thus decide whether it satisfies the need that they have.

### Library Reports Are Centrally Maintained

Following a request for a change to a library report, the library manager will consult with the requesting end user or department head and that department's report writer. The end result of this consultation will be either acceptance or rejection of the request. When a change request is accepted, the library manager will release the workbook containing the report and assign it to a report writer. Following a change, the report will need user testing, sign-off, and updated documentation prior to acceptance back into the library.

### Library Reports Are Secure, with Access Being Strictly Maintained

Access to a library report will require a request from either an end user or the end user's manager. No user will be allowed to change a library report. Following the approval of a request, the library manager will work with the Discoverer manager to ensure that the user has access to the relevant business area. When this confirmation has been received, the library manager will share the report with the user's role or responsibility. Finally, the user will be informed that their request has been accepted and that the report is now available to them.

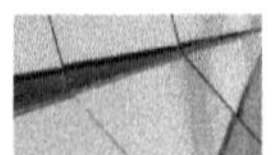

**NOTE**

*Some reports need to get assigned to a subset of the user base. In this case, we recommend that rather than sharing the report with the user directly, you create another role or responsibility for this purpose. Then, if another user needs to have access to the same report, the library manager only needs to ensure that the user gets granted the role or responsibility.*

### Creating New Library Reports

If you are working in an organization that is using libraries and you need to get a new report created and added to the library, use this workflow:

1. Raise a new report request, including a justification and specification for the new report, and send this request to the library manager.
2. The library manager checks existing library reports to see whether such a report already exists.
3. If no report currently exists, a report writer is assigned the task.
4. After the report has been built, user acceptance testing must be completed.
5. The library documentation is produced by the report writer.
6. The report writer shares the new report with the library manager and requests that the report be included in the library.
7. Upon receipt of a request for a report to be included in the library, the manager
   - Checks that corporate standards have been met.
   - Checks that naming standards have been met.
   - Checks that the user requirements have been met.
   - Checks that the documentation is complete.
   - Accepts the new report into the library by using Save As.
   - Makes the report available to the end users using Discoverer's share functionality. The report will normally be shared with a role or responsibility, not with a named user.
8. The report writer deletes the report from their account.

### Gaining Access to a Library Report

Before a user can log in and run a report contained within a Discoverer library, the following steps need to have been completed:

1. The user or the user's manager will need to request that access to Discoverer be made available. This request should specify to which database the user needs to have access and to which business areas access should be granted. The request should also contain the user's contact information, the user's position, and whether the user needs to have full Discoverer access (report writer) or just the ability to run prewritten reports (report viewer).
2. The library manager will take the request and coordinate it with the DBA, Apps administrator, and Discoverer manager. After the DBA or Apps administrator has created the user account and granted the appropriate roles or responsibilities, the Discoverer manager will complete their tasks by granting access to the required business areas or roles and possibly arranging for the user to attend a training course.
3. After the Discoverer manager has completed their tasks, the request will be passed back to the library manager for completion. The library manager will ensure that all relevant reports to which the user needs to have access have been shared with that user's role or responsibility. Departmental training will also now be arranged.
4. Finally, when all of the preceding steps have been completed, the user will receive notification from the library manager that the account has been set up and has been activated.

## Sharing Workbooks with Other Users

Sharing workbooks allows you to grant other people rights to run your workbooks. These other users will be allowed to view, analyze, and print the results from your workbook, but they will not be allowed to save any changes to your query. Users who execute shared workbooks will see that the Save option on the menu bar is disabled. However, users will be allowed to save the workbook under their own name, leaving the original intact.

Apart from the convenience of having the ability to share your workbooks with other users, there are a number of other benefits to sharing workbooks. Sharing gives users without the right to create workbooks the ability to run them and perform analysis on the data.

Another key benefit of sharing workbooks is the all-important matter of saving resources. There is nothing more frustrating to a manager than finding that two of that manager's staff used time and effort creating virtually the same report. Communication among the Discoverer users in a department will keep staff members from *reinventing the wheel*. Even when the reporting needs of two separate users are different, the same workbook may satisfy both needs as the foundation to build upon.

If you are using scheduling in your organization, you will be pleased to know that users using Plus can now share the results of scheduled workbooks with other users, thus disseminating information across your organization.

**NOTE**

*A great feature of sharing in Plus is the ability to share not only with an individual user but also with a role or responsibility. This is one of the ways that setting up libraries in Discoverer has been facilitated.*

## Superuser Involvement with Shared Workbooks

One of the real pluses of having a superuser is the ability to appoint them as your departmental workbook guru or report writer. Having a single person in this position can be extremely advantageous. Involvement with shared workbooks could then be the responsibility of the superuser in the following three ways:

- **For development of shared workbooks** Given that your superuser has increased knowledge of the database, they could be tasked with workbook development. These workbooks, once written, could then be shared with other members of your department or even shared company-wide.
- **For support of shared workbooks** If you have a superuser who has taken on the responsibility for creating your department's workbooks, the same person should be tasked with supporting those workbooks by essentially creating your first Discoverer library. They would become the first line of support for your department's users.
- **For maintaining documentation** When shared workbooks are used, it is vitally important that documentation is provided about those workbooks. It is natural that the person who creates the workbooks also creates and maintains that documentation. When using libraries, this documentation becomes part of the central documentation.

## How to Share a Workbook

To share a workbook, you need to have been granted the appropriate rights and privileges. If you do not have the correct privileges, both at the database and end-user layer levels, you will not be able to share a workbook. The privileges are set by the Discoverer administrator, and you will need to submit a request to have these set up for you.

You can share workbooks in one of two ways.

- You can allow one or more users, roles, or responsibilities to share one of your workbooks or the workbooks you are managing.
- You can allow one or more workbooks to be shared by one user, role, or responsibility.

### Sharing a Workbook Using Desktop

To share a workbook in Discoverer Desktop, use the following workflow:

1. From the menu bar select File | Manage Workbooks | Sharing. This opens the Share Workbooks dialog box, as shown in Figure 14-1. As you can see, the Share Workbooks dialog box has two tabs: one for Workbook > User and one for User > Workbook.
2. Select the tab Workbook > User.
3. The Workbook drop-down list displays all of the queries you have created. From the Workbook drop-down list, select the workbook you want to share.
4. The user list displays all of the users who have access to the same database as yourself, although they may not have access to the business area that the workbook is using. From the list of available users, click the user you want to share the workbook with.

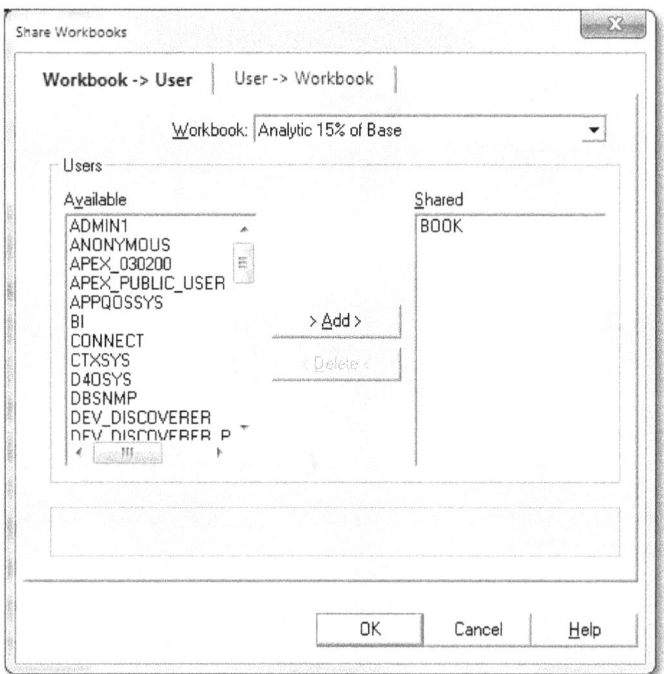


**FIGURE 14-1.** *Desktop Share Workbooks dialog box*

**NOTE**
*To highlight more than one user, hold down* CTRL *while clicking the usernames. This allows you to share the workbook with multiple users at the same time.*

5. Click Add. This moves the users to the Shared box.
6. Click OK. This closes the Share Workbooks dialog box and completes the sharing of the workbook with the users concerned.

## Sharing a Workbook Using Plus

To share a workbook in Discoverer Plus, use this workflow:

1. From the menu bar, select Tools | Manage Workbooks. This opens the Manage Workbooks dialog box shown in Figure 14-2. Until you select a workbook to share, the Share button is grayed out.
2. Expand the list of workbooks that you own.
3. Click one of your workbooks. You will notice that the Share button has now been activated.

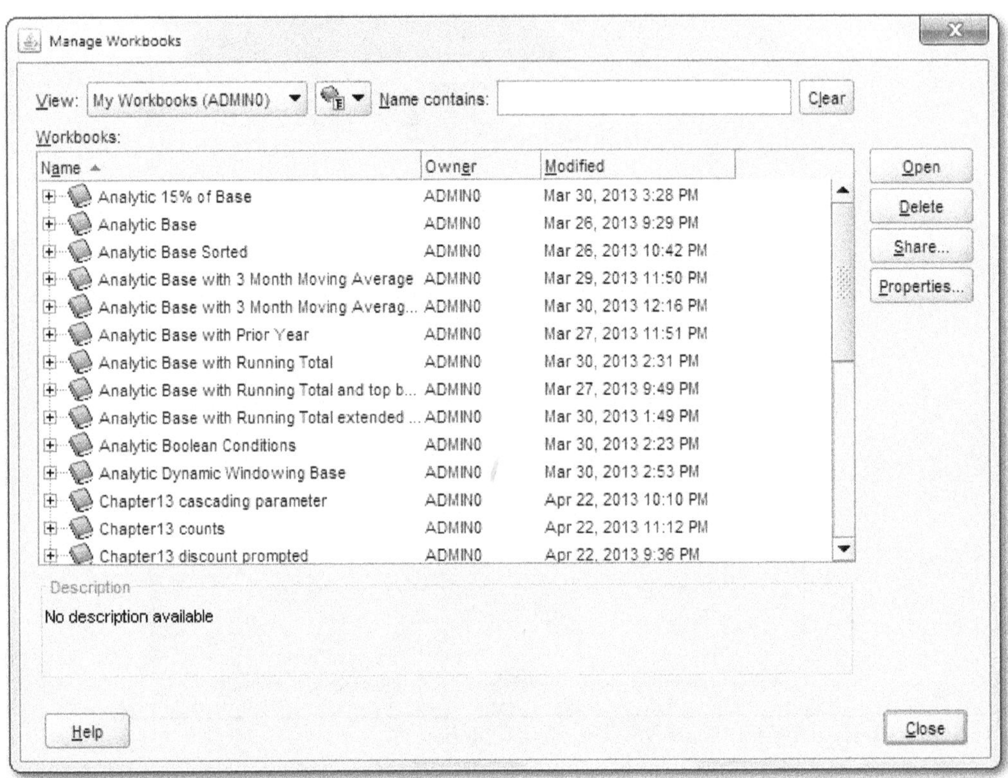


**FIGURE 14-2.** *Plus Manage Workbooks dialog box*

4. Click Share. This opens the Share Workbooks dialog box shown in Figure 14-3.
5. As you can see in Figure 14-3, the Plus Share Workbooks dialog box, like the Desktop equivalent, also has two tabs: one for Workbook > User and one for User > Workbook.
6. Unlike when using the Desktop dialog box, you now have the ability to share with a database role or, if using E-Business Suite, an Apps responsibility.
7. Using the Workbook > User tab, you can share one workbook with one or more users, database roles, or Apps responsibilities. The workbook was already selected in step 4. From the Available pane, select the user, role, or responsibility you want to share the workbook with and move it to the Shared pane.

**NOTE**
*Users and roles are identified by different icons, as are scheduled workbooks.*

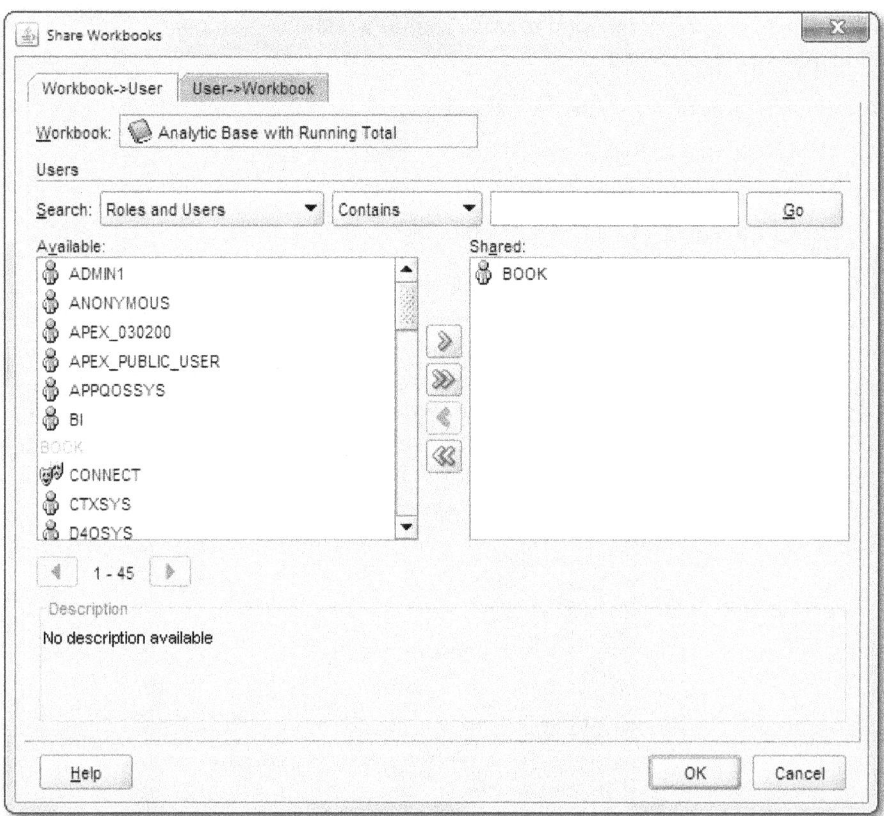


**FIGURE 14-3.** *Plus Share Workbooks dialog box*

8. Using the User > Workbook tab, you can share multiple workbooks with one user, database role, or Apps responsibility. Use the Select User button to choose one user, role, or responsibility and then from the Available pane select one or more workbooks you want to share, moving them to the Shared pane.

**NOTE**
*When working with E-Business Suite, you should always share with an Apps responsibility rather than an individual user. Similarly, if you are a library manager and you are sharing a library report, make sure you share it with a database role or Apps responsibility and not with an individual user.*

9. After you have made your selections, click OK to close the Share Workbooks dialog box.
10. Click Close to close the Manage Workbooks dialog box.

# Using a Shared Workbook

If you have been granted permission to use a shared workbook, you need to know a number of things, including the following:

- How to recognize a shared workbook
- How to open a shared workbook
- How to manage missing items
- How to edit and save a shared workbook

### How to Recognize a Shared Workbook

When you log in to Discoverer to open an existing workbook, Discoverer prefixes shared workbooks with the name of the owner or library. In the following illustration, you can see that this user has many workbooks available from the database. The first two in the list are the user's own workbooks, and the last ones have been shared by library owners. In Desktop, shared workbooks always appear at the bottom of the list of available workbooks. In Plus, workbooks can be viewed either alphabetically or by owner. The following is the Desktop dialog box:

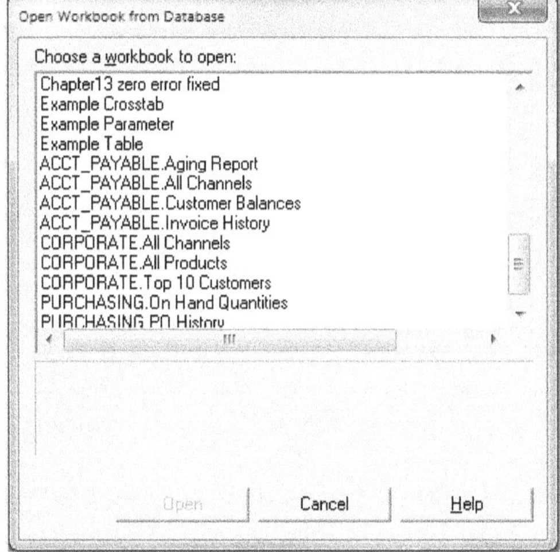


# How to Open a Shared Workbook

To open and execute a shared workbook, use the following workflow:

1. From the menu bar, select File | Open.
2. Locate and click a workbook that has been shared with you.
3. Click Open. In Plus, Discoverer automatically opens and executes the workbook. In Desktop, Discoverer prompts you with the Workbook in Other Database Account dialog box.

In the Desktop box shown here, you can see that you have three options:

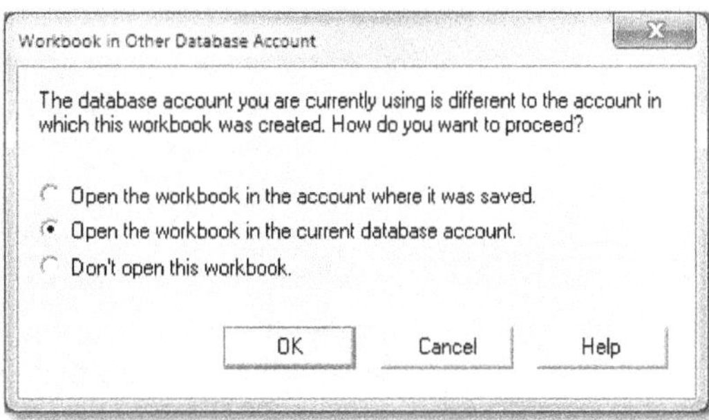


- **Open The Workbook In The Account Where It Was Saved** Clicking this button and then clicking OK closes your current database connection. You will then be prompted to type in the password for the owner of the workbook. If you enter the correct password, Discoverer will launch the workbook and ask whether you want to run the sheet.
- **Open The Workbook In The Current Database Account** Clicking this button (the default) and then clicking OK launches the workbook. Discoverer validates whether you have access to the required business area and then asks whether you want to run the sheet. If you do not have rights to the business area used by the workbook, you will be unable to open the workbook. See the following sections, "How to Manage Missing Items in Desktop" and "How to Manage Missing Items in Plus."
- **Don't Open This Workbook** This option does just as it says and returns you to the workbook selection list, from which you should select another workbook.

### How to Manage Missing Items in Desktop

When working in Desktop, every time you open a workbook that has been shared with you by another user or from a library, Discoverer validates that you have the rights to the business area used by the workbook. If this validation fails, you will see the following Missing Item or Condition dialog box. Unless you successfully manage these missing items, you will not be able to run the workbook that has been shared with you.

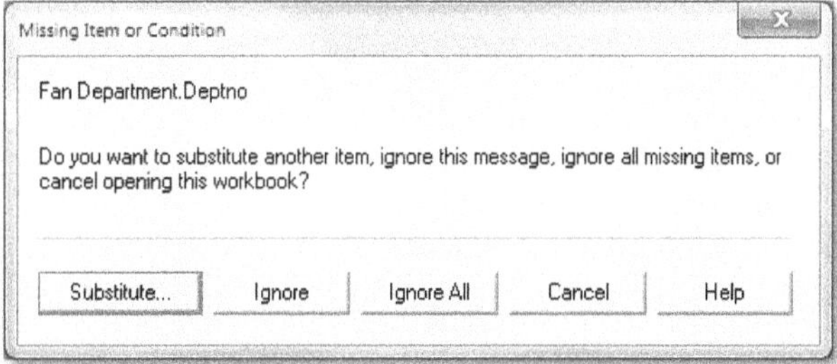


As you can see in the preceding illustration, this dialog box has a number of buttons. The first item that Discoverer is unable to find will be displayed in the box. You will be informed of the name of the folder and the name of the item. At this point, you have the following options:

- **Substitute** Clicking this button opens the following Substitute Item dialog box. In this box, Discoverer will once again display the item that you do not have access to, along with all of the business areas and folders that you do have access to. You should select another item that will be substituted for the missing item. For example, many companies have business areas that are broken down by region or department. If you have been granted access to a workbook that was created using the European region and you have access only to the Middle East region, you should open the Middle East business area, locate the matching folder and item, and then substitute it. When done, click OK.

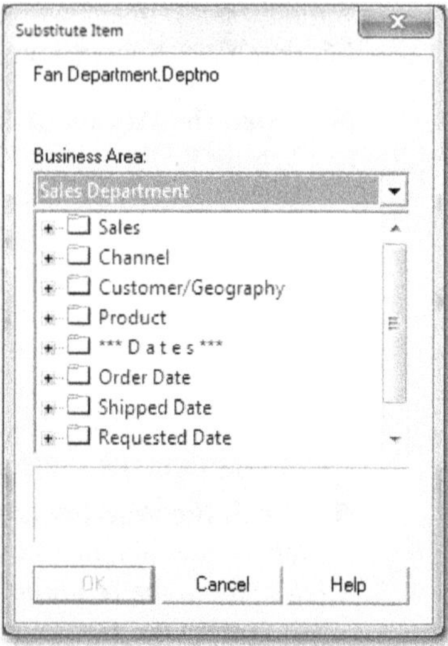


- **Ignore** Clicking this button ignores the current item and displays the next item that Discoverer could not validate.
- **Ignore All** Clicking this button causes Discoverer to ignore all invalid items.
- **Cancel** Clicking this button cancels the opening of the workbook.
- **Help** Clicking this button opens the Discoverer help system.

When you have completed substituting items, Discoverer either runs the query or displays the following "Item dependency" error message. This message means you did not successfully substitute a new item for every item that was missing.

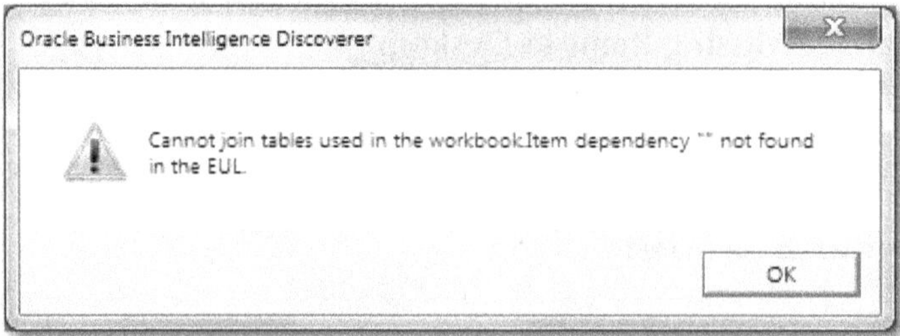


Clicking OK in the error box causes Discoverer to display the "failed" workbook error message. You will not be able to continue opening this workbook.

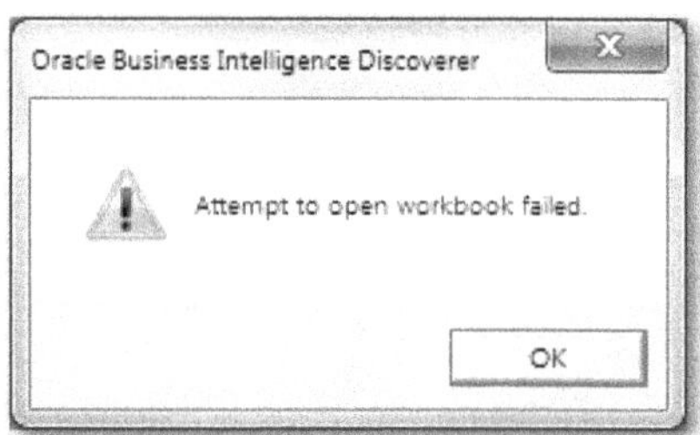


At this stage, you now have two options available to you. The first option is to speak with the person who owns the workbook. The owner, or library manager, may be able to share another workbook with you that uses a business area to which you do have access. The second option is to speak with your Discoverer manager, who may be able to grant you access to the business area that this workbook tried to open.

## How to Manage Missing Items in Plus

When working in Plus, every time you open a workbook that has been shared with you, Discoverer validates that you have the rights to the business area used by the workbook. If this validation fails, you will see a message like this one:

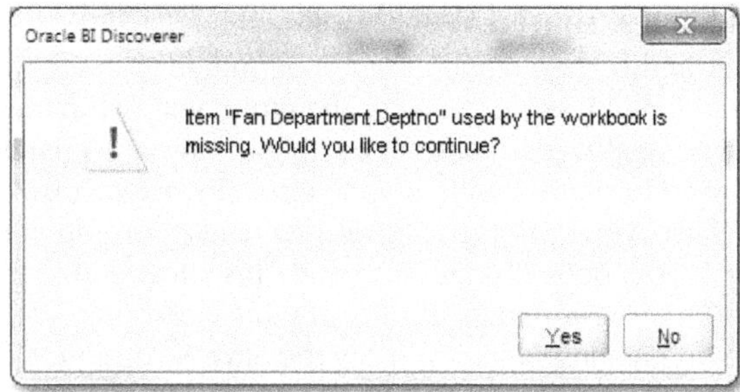


As you can see in the illustration, Plus warns you that you do not have access to an item that is used in the workbook and asks you if you want to continue. If you click No, Discoverer abandons the attempt to open that workbook. However, if you click Yes, unlike with Desktop, Plus does not offer you any chance to substitute for the missing item.

Instead, Plus now informs you about the next missing item, repeating the process for all of the missing items. Eventually, Plus will have no more items to check and will do one of the following three things:

- Open the workbook with all of the items missing
- Tell you that the workbook failed because of the dreaded "Item dependency not found in the EUL" message

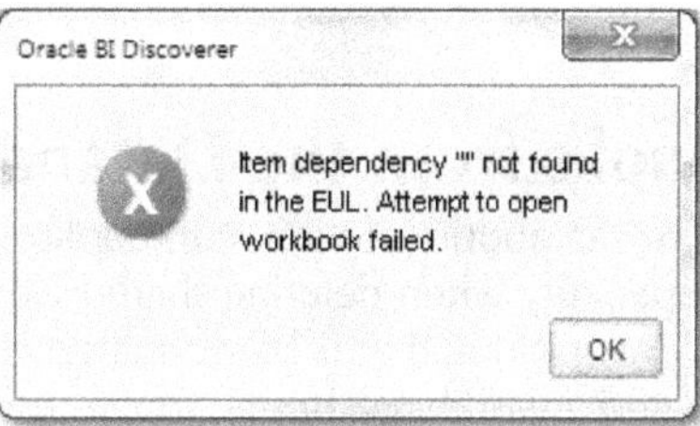


- Tell you that the workbook failed because it has no items

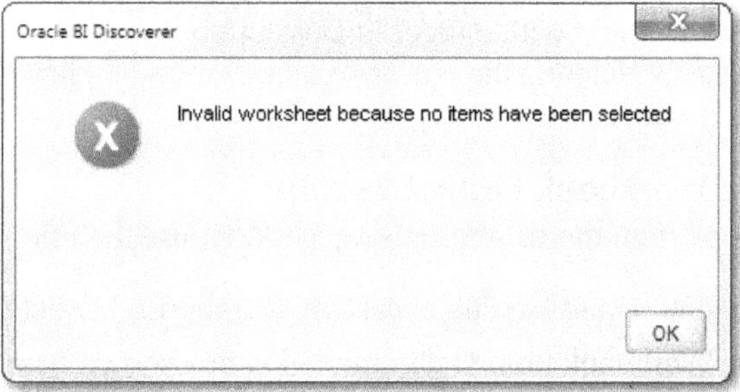


If the opening of the workbook fails, as with Desktop, you now have two options. Option 1 is to speak with the owner of the workbook and see whether there is another workbook they can share with you. Option 2 is to speak with the Discoverer manager and see whether there is a way for you to be granted access to the business area that the workbook is using.

### How to Edit and Save a Shared Workbook

As mentioned earlier in this chapter, you are not permitted to make permanent changes to workbooks that are owned by someone else. Therefore, you will notice that some of the menu items are deactivated. Notably, you will not be able to save any changes to the original workbook, nor will you be allowed to share it with anyone else. However, you will be allowed to schedule it. In older versions of Discoverer prior to 10*g*, you were also forbidden from turning page items on or off, but just as with 10*g*, both 11*g* Desktop and Plus allow you to do so.

If you do want to make permanent changes to this workbook, you will have to save the workbook to your own database account using the Save As option. However, if you have spotted an error in the workbook—perhaps an incorrect calculation or a missing condition, for example—the correct approach would be to report this to the owner.

**NOTE**
*Do not try sharing a workbook that has been shared with you. You are not the owner, and you do not have the required sharing privileges. Discoverer will therefore not allow you to share that workbook with anyone else.*

# Workbook Manipulation

Managing the workbooks within your environment is an important aspect of Discoverer management. In this section we will show you how to delete unwanted workbooks from your database account, how to add a description to your workbooks, and how to manage the workbook identifiers.

## Deleting Workbooks from the Database

The most important thing to say about deleting workbooks from the database is that caution should always be used, especially when deleting shared workbooks. Discoverer will not warn you if you are about to delete a workbook that is being shared with someone else.

Let's say you have created a workbook but no longer use it. Because you are conscientious and care about not wasting space on the database, your inclination is to delete it. However, before you do so, please check whether you have shared that workbook with someone else. That person may be using your workbook on a regular basis, and deleting it could be devastating. The situation is even more fraught with danger in Desktop, because Desktop does not even ask you to confirm whether you are deleting the correct workbook. If you click the Delete button, that will be the end of the workbook!

### How to Delete a Workbook Using Desktop

To delete a workbook from the database using Desktop, use the following workflow:

1. From the menu bar, select File | Manage Workbooks | Delete.
2. The Delete Workbook from Database dialog box shown next will open. Notice that the Delete button is grayed out.

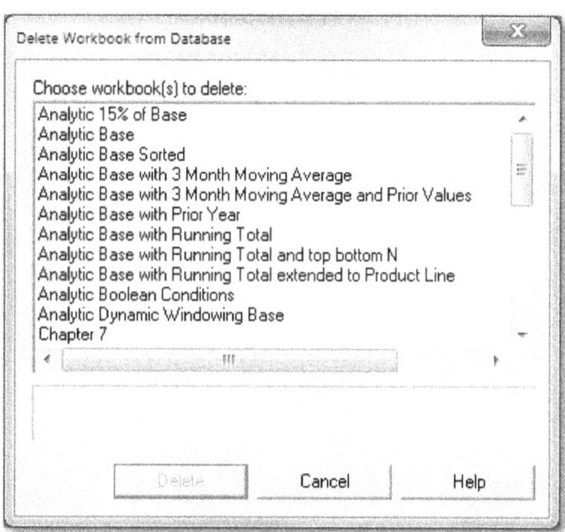


3. Select the workbook you want to delete. The Delete button is now activated.
4. Click Delete.

**NOTE**
*Be sure you really want to delete a workbook from the database before you click the Delete button, because Discoverer will delete it without any further prompting. There is no Undo option! However, in Desktop, after deleting an open workbook, it is still open, so you have the option of resaving it. You will be prompted for the name when you try to save it.*

### How to Delete a Workbook Using Plus

To delete a workbook from the database using Plus, use the following workflow:

1. From the menu bar, select Tools | Manage Workbooks. This opens the Manage Workbooks dialog box shown in Figure 14-2. Unless you have a workbook highlighted, you will notice that the Delete button is currently grayed out.
2. Expand the list of workbooks that you own.
3. Select the workbook you want to delete. The Delete button is now activated.
4. Click Delete.
5. Discoverer will now ask you to confirm that you want to delete this workbook.
6. If you click Yes, the workbook and all associated sharing will be deleted. If you click No, the workbook will be retained.

## Managing Workbook Descriptions and Identifiers

For those of us who affectionately remember the DOS days with naming conventions that limited us to eight-character filenames with three-character extensions, long filenames are a real blessing. We have, however, gotten over our giddiness now and tend to be fairly utilitarian in the naming of our files. Discoverer gives you the added option of adding a description to your files that will help you keep track of queries and the purpose they serve. You can also control the identifier by which the workbook will be known to the system. Both of these are handled using what are known as the *workbook properties*.

To manage workbook properties, use the following workflow:

1. Open the workbook you want to manage.
2. From the menu bar, in Desktop select File | Manage Workbooks | Properties, or in Plus select File | Workbook Properties. This opens the Workbook Properties dialog box shown in this illustration:

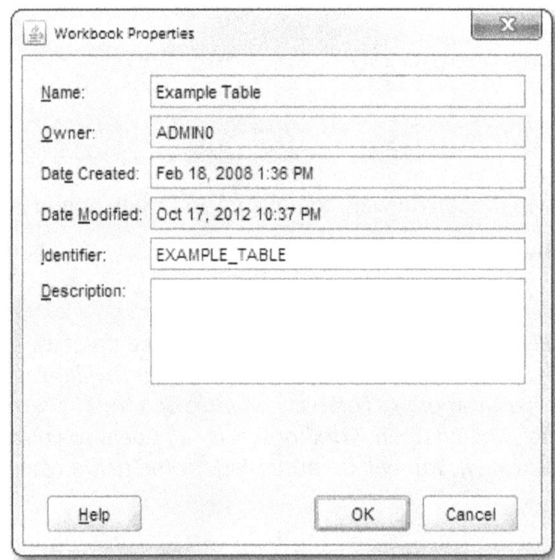


3. Enter a meaningful description of the workbook in the Description field.

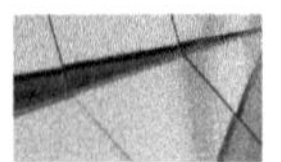

**NOTE**
*Spaces are permitted in the description.*

4. If desired, enter a meaningful identifier for the workbook. Spaces are not permitted in the workbook identifier. If you are a library manager, it is recommended that you enter the library prefix as a prefix to the workbook identifier to help associate it with the library you are managing. Identifiers should be used very carefully, as they are used by Discoverer to uniquely identify every object in the EUL. This is also known internally as the developer key of an object. Discoverer by default will give every object—workbooks, worksheets, parameters, and so on—a unique identifier value.
5. Click OK.

**NOTE**

*In Plus, using Tools | Manage Workbooks, selecting a workbook and clicking Properties allows you to view the properties for the chosen workbook. Even though you may own the workbook, you cannot edit its properties this way. You need to open the workbook and then use File | Workbook Properties.*

# Worksheet Manipulation

Managing the worksheets within a workbook is an important aspect of workbook management. In this section we will show you how to reorder your worksheets, how to rename worksheets, and how to delete unwanted worksheets. Then we will also show you how to add a description to your worksheets. After that, we show you how to copy and move worksheets between workbooks. Finally, we will show you how to find data in your worksheet results.

## Reordering Worksheets

As you go about building workbooks, you will undoubtedly have workbooks that have multiple worksheets. The order in which you present those worksheets to your users may or may not have any importance. We have noticed that when worksheets have differing levels of data, users usually like to see the higher-level, or summarized, worksheets before they see the lower-level, detailed worksheets. This means you need to know how to rearrange the order of your worksheets. Because this is handled differently in Desktop and Plus, we will show you each separately.

### Reordering Worksheets in Desktop

To rearrange the order of the worksheet in Desktop, use the following workflow:

1. Open the workbook that contains the worksheets you want to reorder.
2. Click the tab name of the worksheet you want to move.
3. Drag and drop the worksheet into its new position. Discoverer will reorder the worksheets.

**NOTE**

*Older versions of Discoverer may require you to hold* CTRL *while you drag the worksheet to its new position.*

### Reordering Worksheets in Plus

To rearrange the order of the worksheets in Plus, use the following workflow:

1. Open the workbook that contains the worksheets you want to reorder.
2. Right-click the tab name of any worksheet, and from the pop-up menu select Move Worksheet.

3. As shown in this illustration, Discoverer now opens the Move Worksheets dialog box.
4. In the Move Worksheets dialog box, drag and drop worksheets or use the Promote and Demote buttons to rearrange the order of the worksheets in the workbook.
5. When you have rearranged the order of your worksheets, click OK. Discoverer now rearranges the worksheets.

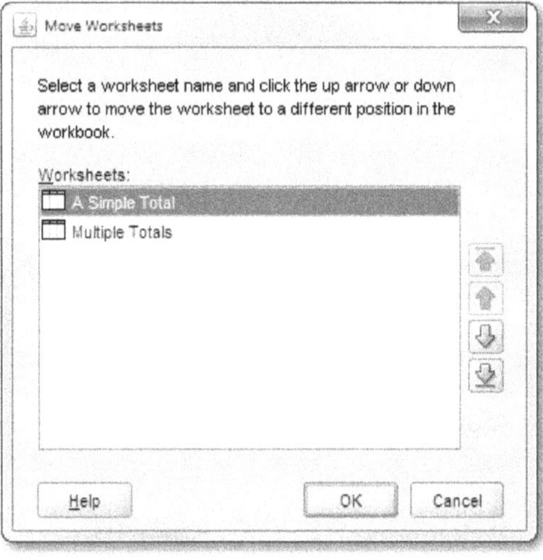

**NOTE**
*The Move Worksheets dialog box can also be launched from the menu bar by selecting Edit | Move Worksheet.*

## Renaming Worksheets

Throughout this handbook we have stressed the need to use meaningful names whenever you can. This naming standard applies to worksheets, too. Giving worksheets meaningful names will greatly help your users, allowing them to choose which worksheet to run by simply looking at its name.

To rename a worksheet, use the following workflow:

1. Open the workbook that contains the worksheets you want to rename.
2. Double-click the worksheet name. In Desktop this opens the Rename Worksheet dialog box, whereas in Plus this opens the Worksheet Properties dialog box.
3. Give the worksheet a suitable, meaningful name.
4. Click OK.

**NOTE**
*In Plus, the Worksheet Properties dialog box can also be launched by right-clicking the worksheet name and from the pop-up list selecting Worksheet Properties. It can also be launched from the menu bar in Plus by selecting either Edit | Rename Worksheet or Edit | Worksheet Properties or in Desktop by selecting Sheet | Rename Sheet.*

## Deleting Worksheets

As time goes by, you will find that some worksheets either are no longer needed or have been superseded by another worksheet, either in the same workbook or in another workbook. Rather than clog up your system with these unwanted worksheets, you should delete them. Thus, another essential aspect of worksheet manipulation is the removal of unwanted worksheets. Because this is handled differently in Desktop and Plus, we will show you each separately.

### Deleting a Worksheet in Desktop

To remove an unwanted worksheet in Desktop, use the following workflow:

1. Open the workbook that contains the worksheet you want to delete.
2. Right-click the worksheet you want to delete, and from the pop-up menu select Delete Sheet.
3. When prompted with "Are you want to delete the sheet?" click Yes or No.

**NOTE**
*You can also delete a worksheet from the menu bar by selecting Sheet | Delete Sheet.*

### Deleting a Worksheet in Plus

To remove an unwanted worksheet in Plus, use the following workflow:

1. Open the workbook that contains the worksheet you want to delete.
2. Click the worksheet name you want to delete, and wait for the name to become highlighted. The worksheet has now become the focus.
3. Right-click the worksheet name, and from the pop-up list select Delete Worksheet.
4. When prompted with "Are you sure you want to delete the worksheet?" click Yes or No.

**NOTE**
*In Plus only, with the worksheet name highlighted, you can also press DELETE or select Edit | Delete Sheet from the menu bar. Either of these methods causes Discoverer to pop up the same prompt referred to in step 4 of the preceding workflow.*

## Adding a Description to a Worksheet

Another excellent way to help your users determine what a worksheet does is to provide a meaningful description. Unfortunately, you can add worksheet descriptions only in Plus. By the way, the requirement to expose a worksheet identifier is one of the reasons Oracle introduced the Worksheet Properties dialog box. The other reason is the need to cleanly separate workbook- and worksheet-level properties.

To add a description to a worksheet in Plus, use the following workflow:

1. Open the workbook that contains the worksheet for which you want to enter a description.
2. Double-click the tab for the worksheet name. This launches the Worksheet Properties dialog box.
3. Enter a suitable, meaningful description for the worksheet.
4. Click OK.

**NOTE**
*In Plus, the Worksheet Properties dialog box can also be launched by right-clicking the tab for the worksheet name and from the pop-up list selecting Worksheet Properties. It can also be launched from the menu bar by selecting either Edit | Rename Worksheet or Edit | Worksheet Properties. Either method allows you to change the description.*

## Copying and Moving Worksheets Between Workbooks

Another little-known feature of Discoverer is its ability to copy and move worksheets between workbooks. You can do this only in Desktop. The reason this will not work in Plus is that you can open and work with only one workbook at a time in Plus, whereas Desktop can open and manipulate several workbooks at the same time.

To copy or move worksheets between workbooks, use the following workflow:

1. Launch Desktop.
2. Open the two workbooks you want to manipulate.
3. From the menu bar, select Window | Tile Horizontally. Discoverer places the workbooks one above the other, with the first opened workbook at the top and the last opened workbook at the bottom.
4. To initiate the copy process, press and hold down CTRL on your keyboard. To initiate the move process, press and hold down SHIFT on your keyboard.

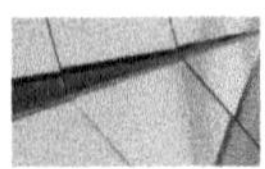

**NOTE**
*You cannot move a worksheet if it is the only worksheet in the workbook.*

5. While holding down either CTRL or SHIFT, click the name tab of the worksheet you want to copy or move and hold the mouse button down. You can now release CTRL or SHIFT.

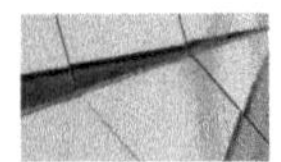

**NOTE**
*Make sure you keep holding the left mouse button down after you release CTRL or SHIFT.*

6. Drag the worksheet out of its current workbook and into the receiving workbook but do not release the mouse button until you have placed the worksheet alongside or on top of one of the worksheet names in the receiving workbook. Release the mouse button only when you see a small arrow appear above the worksheet name.

**NOTE**
*Be very careful to make sure you place the worksheet correctly before you release the mouse button. If you release the mouse button before you have placed the worksheet in position, Discoverer creates a new workbook and places the worksheet in that workbook.*

7. Discoverer now copies or moves the worksheet into the receiving workbook.

**NOTE**
*You can place the new worksheet alongside an existing worksheet only when you are copying. If you are moving a worksheet, you must drag it on top of one of the existing worksheets in the receiving workbook. Discoverer will reorder the worksheets automatically.*

8. You may want to check the names of conditions, parameters, and calculations. If the second worksheet has an identically named condition, parameter, or calculation, Discoverer does not share these objects. Instead, Discoverer creates a second object and appends a 1 to its name.

## Finding Data in Your Worksheet Results

When you execute a worksheet that has many pages of results, sometimes you would like to quickly find out whether a particular value or item was returned in the set of results. Fortunately, Discoverer provides such a mechanism.

To search for a value or item in a set of results, use the following workflow:

1. Open and execute the worksheet.
2. On the keyboard, press CTRL-F. This launches the Find dialog box shown in the following illustration:

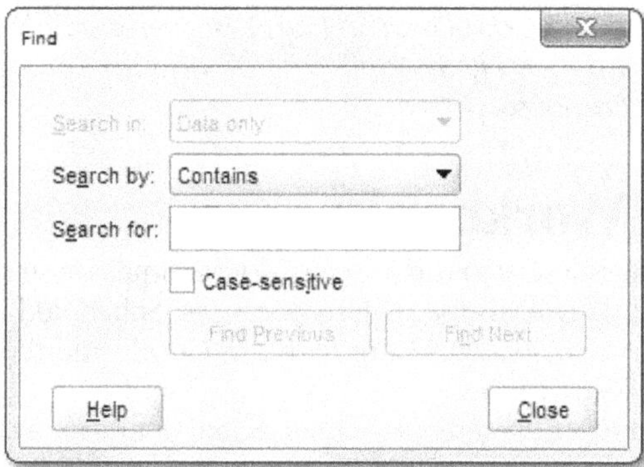


3. In the Find dialog box, enter the value or name of the item you want to search for. In Desktop this is labeled Search Text. In Plus, this is labeled Search For.
4. You need to tell Discoverer how to perform the search. In Desktop this is labeled Find Text That. In Plus this is labeled Search By. By default this is set to Contains. Your valid options are
   - Exactly matches
   - Contains (this is the default and the one you most often use)
   - Begins with (in Plus this option is called Starts with)

- Ends with
- Is NULL

5. You now need to tell Discoverer whether to take the case of the value or item into account during the search. In Desktop, the button is Match Case. In Plus, this button is Case-Sensitive. By default this is unchecked and is the setting you will use the most.
6. After you have made your selections, click Find Next. Because Plus has an additional button called Find Previous, you can click this instead if you want.
7. Discoverer will now search for the value or item that you entered, using the search criteria that you set. If the value or item that you are searching for is found in the worksheet, Discoverer locates the first instance of that value or item in the direction you are searching, and places the cursor on it. The Find dialog box will remain open and on top of the open worksheet. If the value or item that you are searching for cannot be found within the worksheet, a suitable message will be displayed.
8. To find further occurrences of the value or item, click Find Next or, in Plus only, click Find Previous.
9. When you have finished searching the worksheet, click Close.

**NOTE**
*In Desktop, when Discoverer cannot find any more items matching the value or item you selected, a box saying "Cannot find the specified value in the sheet" will be displayed. In Plus, Discoverer simply returns you to the first or last found item, depending on whether you clicked Find Next or Find Previous.*

# Scheduling Workbooks

Scheduling workbooks is a way to run a report at a set time. These reports will probably not be the ones you use on a daily basis for analysis purposes. Scheduled reports are the ones that you want, for example, to run daily, weekly, or monthly. Good candidates for scheduled reports might be monthly profits or weekly sales.

Another reason to schedule a report is time. Some queries are complex and take a long time to run. A query of this type may take so long to run, in fact, that the time it takes exceeds the time that your Discoverer manager has allotted for you to run queries. Scheduling a workbook of this nature allows the query to run in the background during *off-peak* hours, when you are not under the same exacting time constraints. If you are using Desktop, another advantage to scheduling is that the scheduled workbook runs on the server. You don't even need to leave your computer on.

The Scheduling Wizard in Discoverer is intuitive and easy to use; however, it does have some limitations. At the end of this section, we have included a discussion addressing some third-party scheduling applications and their use.

## The Benefit of Scheduling Workbooks

Scheduling workbooks has a number of benefits. The five main benefits of scheduling workbooks are as follows:

- The user does not need to be logged in to Discoverer while the queries run.

- If you have limited bandwidth or frequently see network congestion at peak times, scheduling workbooks to run off-peak will help.
- The user can run key reports prior to the start of the working day at off-peak hours.
- The user can run queries that normally exceed the time they are allowed by the Discoverer manager.
- The user can schedule special reports to run as weekly or monthly reports. Such reports will run automatically without user intervention.

## How to Schedule a Workbook

To schedule a workbook, you need to have been granted the appropriate rights and privileges. If you do not have the correct privileges, both at the database and EUL levels, you will not be able to schedule a workbook. These privileges are controlled by the Discoverer manager, and should you find that your scheduling options are grayed out, you will need to submit a request to have these set up for you.

### Using the Desktop Schedule Workbook Wizard

To schedule a workbook in Discoverer Desktop using the Schedule Workbook Wizard, use the following workflow:

1. If the workbook you want to schedule is the one currently open on your screen, from the menu bar select File | Schedule. This automatically opens the first part of the Schedule Workbook Wizard, as shown in Figure 14-4. Proceed to step 7 of this workflow.

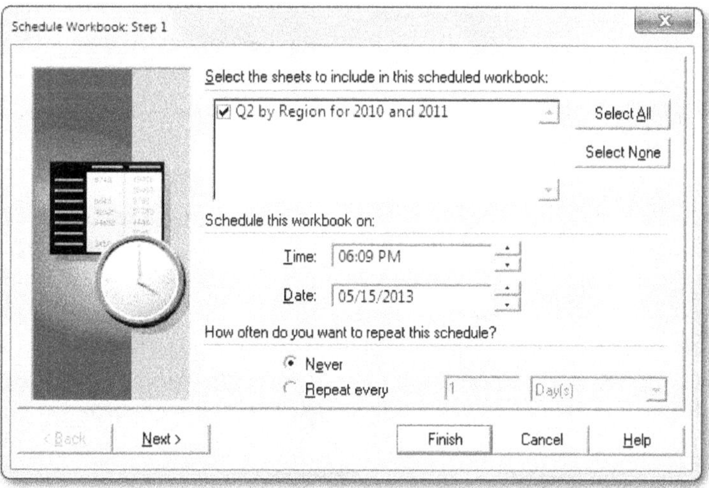


**FIGURE 14-4.** *Desktop Schedule Workbook Wizard, step 1*

2. To schedule any other workbook, from the menu bar select File | Manage Workbooks | Scheduling Manager. This opens the Scheduling Manager dialog box.

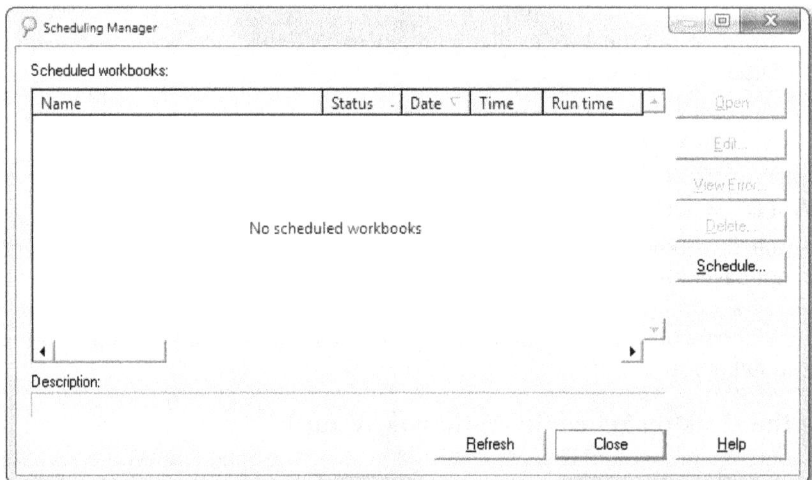


3. Click Schedule. This opens the Schedule Workbook dialog box. This box, as you can see, has two selection buttons: one for My Computer and the other for Database.

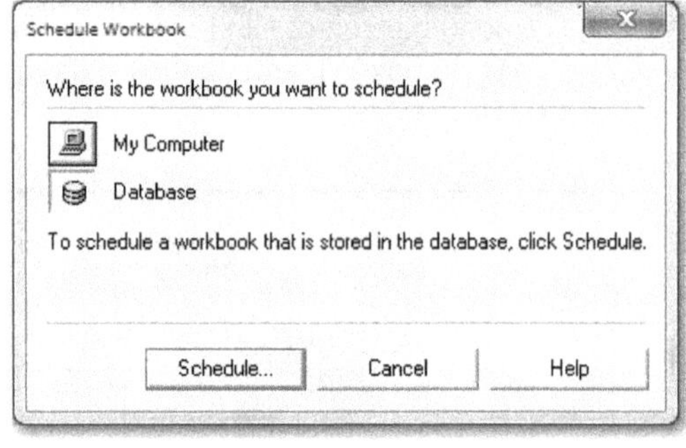


4. Select the location where the Discoverer workbook has been saved.
5. Click Schedule. This opens either the Open dialog box, if scheduling a workbook that was saved to the file system, or the Schedule Workbook from Database dialog box.
6. From within either the Open or Schedule Workbook from Database dialog box, locate the workbook you want to schedule, and then click Open or Schedule, respectively. Discoverer opens the first part of the Schedule Workbook Wizard, as shown in Figure 14-4.
7. Define which sheet or sheets are to be scheduled by clicking in the check box to the left of the worksheet names. Click Select All to include all of this workbook's worksheets. Click Select None to deselect all of the worksheets. Once all worksheets have been deselected, you should check the individual sheets that you want.

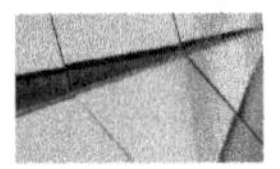

**NOTE**
*All worksheets in the workbook will be listed by their name. This is another reason we recommend giving your worksheets meaningful names, because Sheet1, Sheet2, and so on, might not be obvious.*

8. Set the date and time you want the workbook to run.
9. Define a repeat schedule, if required. Under the prompt "How often do you want to repeat this schedule?" there are two radio buttons: Never and Repeat Every. This is your opportunity to set this schedule up to run periodically, daily, weekly, or however often you choose. To do this, click Repeat Every, type in a number, and then select a time period from the drop-down list illustrated next. The default is Never, which will run the scheduled workbook only once.

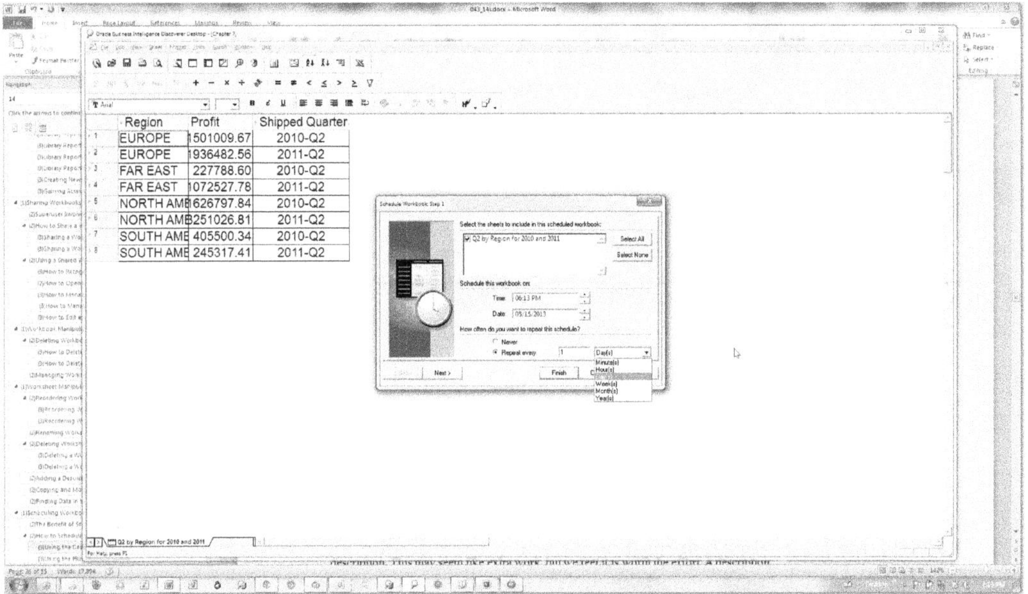


10. Having completed step 1 of the Schedule Workbook Wizard, click Next. Discoverer opens step 2 of the wizard, as shown in Figure 14-5.
11. Enter a name for the workbook you are scheduling. This is an optional step, as Discoverer will automatically give your workbook the same name as the original; however, we recommend you give it a name that is meaningful to you.

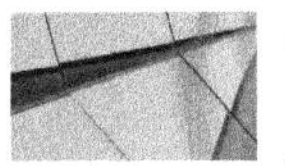

**NOTE**
*This functionality is different from Discoverer 10g, which would not allow you to save a scheduled workbook using the same name as the original.*

12. Enter a description for the workbook you are scheduling. This is another optional step; however, again, we recommend you take some time to give your scheduled workbook a description. This may seem like extra work, but we think it is worth the effort. A description might include why you have scheduled the worksheet and what is to be done with it after it has run. The description you enter will be displayed at the bottom of the Desktop Scheduling Manager dialog box shown later in Figure 14-8.

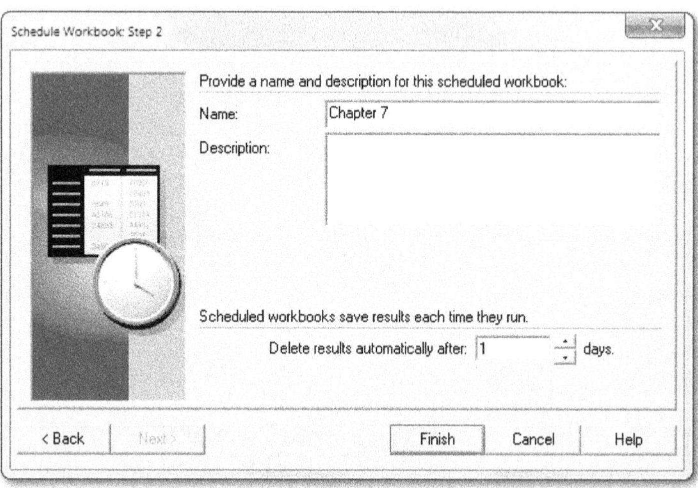


**FIGURE 14-5.** *Desktop Schedule Workbook Wizard, step 2*

**NOTE**
*Discoverer will automatically give your scheduled workbook a description, based on the original workbook name, the name you have given the scheduled workbook, and the date upon which the workbook is to run.*

13. Define the delete criteria. Discoverer automatically deletes the results after 30 days.
14. Having completed step 2 of the wizard, click Finish.
15. If there are any parameters in the worksheets within the workbook, Discoverer will now prompt you for those parameters. This illustration shows the sheet prompt. Enter the parameters that you want.
16. Click Finish.

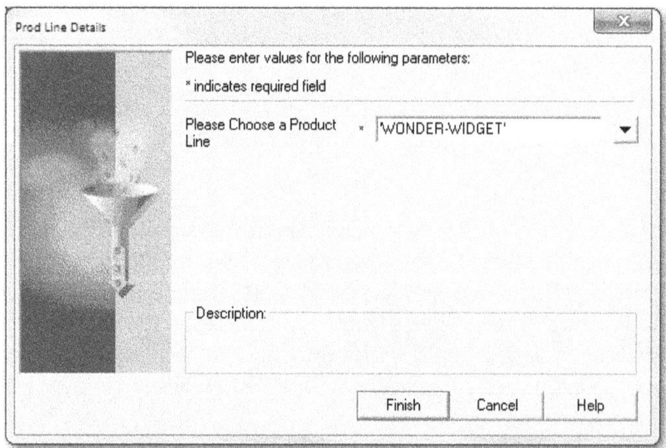

The worksheets you have just scheduled will be run on the date and time you specified.

### Using the Plus Schedule Wizard

To schedule a workbook in Discoverer Plus using the Schedule Wizard, use the following workflow:

1. If the workbook you want to schedule is the one in active memory, from the menu bar select File | Schedule. This automatically opens the first part of the Schedule Wizard, as shown in Figure 14-6. Proceed to step 5 of this workflow.
2. To schedule any other workbook, from the menu bar select Tools | Manage Schedules.
3. Click Schedule.
4. From the list of workbooks, locate the workbook you want to schedule and click Select.
5. Enter a unique name for the workbook you are scheduling. This is a mandatory step, as Discoverer requires that all workbooks have a unique name. If you do not enter a unique name, Discoverer displays the Scheduling Error box. In the box, you must either type a

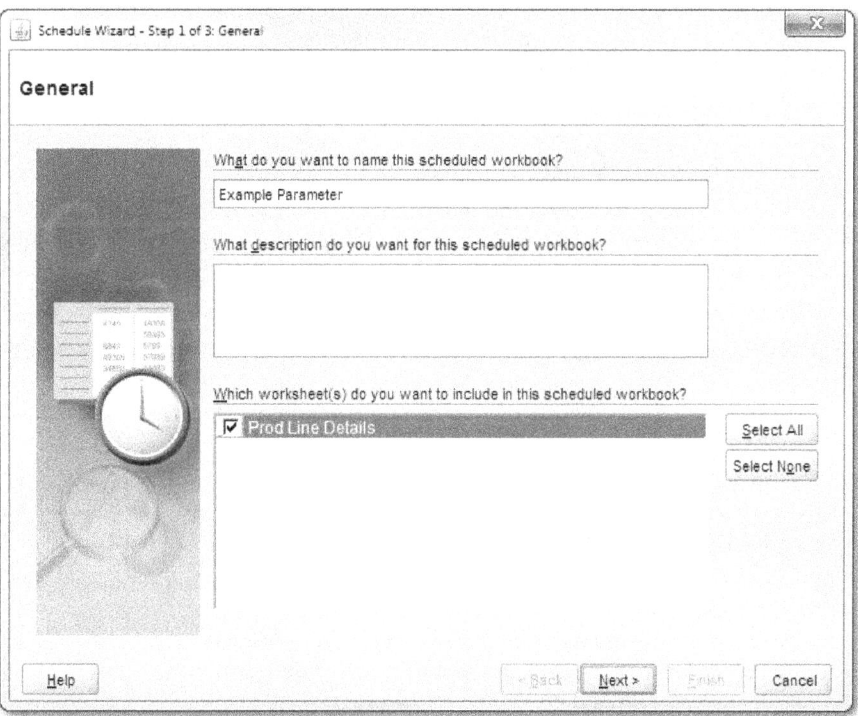


**FIGURE 14-6.** *Plus Schedule Wizard, step 1*

unique name or elect to have Discoverer keep the name but delete the existing workbook and its results. After you have made your choice, click OK.

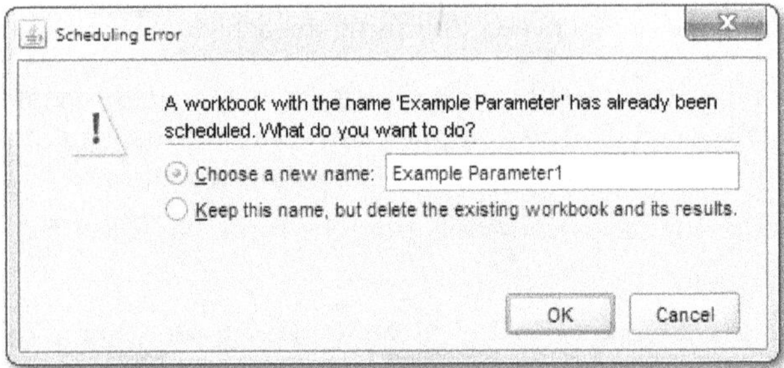


6. Enter a description for the workbook you are scheduling. This is another optional step; however, again, we recommend you take some time to give your scheduled workbook a description. The description you enter will be displayed at the bottom of the Plus Scheduling Manager dialog box shown later in Figure 14-9.
7. Define which sheet or sheets are to be scheduled by clicking in the check box to the left of the worksheet names. Click Select All to include all of this workbook's worksheets. Click Select None to deselect all of the worksheets. Once all worksheets have been deselected, you should check the individual sheets that you want.
8. Having completed step 1 of the Schedule Workbook Wizard, click Next. If everything has been defined correctly, proceed to step 10. If you did not enter a unique name in step 5, Discoverer displays the Scheduling Error box just shown.
9. In the Scheduling Error box, you must either type a unique name for the workbook or elect to have Discoverer keep the name but delete the existing workbook and its results. After you have made your choice, click OK.
10. Discoverer now opens step 2 of the wizard, as shown in either Figure 14-7 or Figure 14-8.
11. If there are any parameters in the worksheets within the workbook, Discoverer will now prompt you for those parameters, as shown in Figure 14-7. Enter the parameters you want and then click Next. Discoverer will now open the final step of the wizard, as shown in Figure 14-8.
12. Set the date and time you want the workbook to run. You can either choose Immediately or use the Calendar pop-up to select a date for when you want the workbook to be scheduled. You need to also set the time.

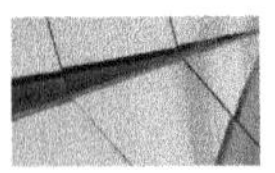

**NOTE**
*If you choose not to schedule immediately, Discoverer automatically adds one day to the current date and sets the time to be one minute past midnight. Change this if need be.*

13. Define a run time for the schedule. Under the prompt "When do you want to schedule this schedule?" there are two radio buttons: Immediately and Time. This is your opportunity to decide when the schedule should be. Complete this area as follows:
    - **Immediately** Check this if you want the schedule to start straightaway.

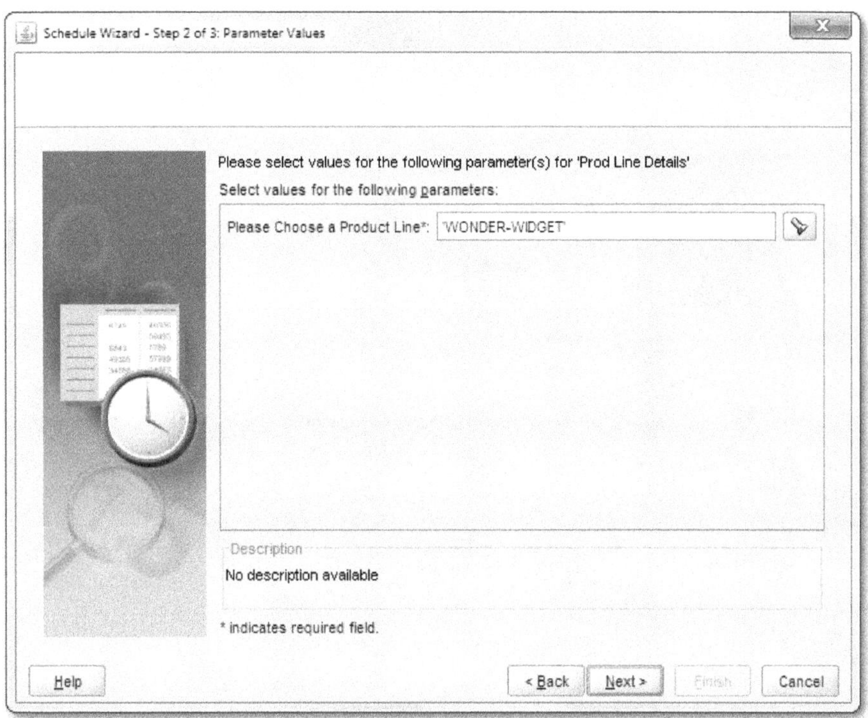


**FIGURE 14-7.** *The Plus Schedule Wizard, step 2 with parameter*

- **Time** This is the default. If it's checked, you need to determine the day, month, year, and time for when the schedule should start. You can use the Calendar pop-up to help you choose. If you highlight one of the time components, for example the month, you can then use the Up and Down buttons alongside to move one component at a time.

14. Define a repeat schedule, if required. Under the prompt "When do you want to repeat this schedule?" there are two radio buttons: Never and Repeat Every. This is your opportunity to set this schedule up to run periodically, daily, weekly, or however often you choose. Complete this area as follows:
    - **Never** This is the default. Leave this checked if you want the report scheduled once.
    - **Repeat Every** Check this if you want to set up a repeating schedule. You should type in a number and then select a time period from the drop-down list.
15. Under the prompt "Do you want to keep all versions of results?" there are two radio buttons: Yes and No. Complete this area as follows:
    - **Yes, Keep All The Results** This is the default. Leave this checked if you want Discoverer to keep all of the results.
    - **No, Just Keep The Latest Set Of Results** Check this if you want only the latest results.

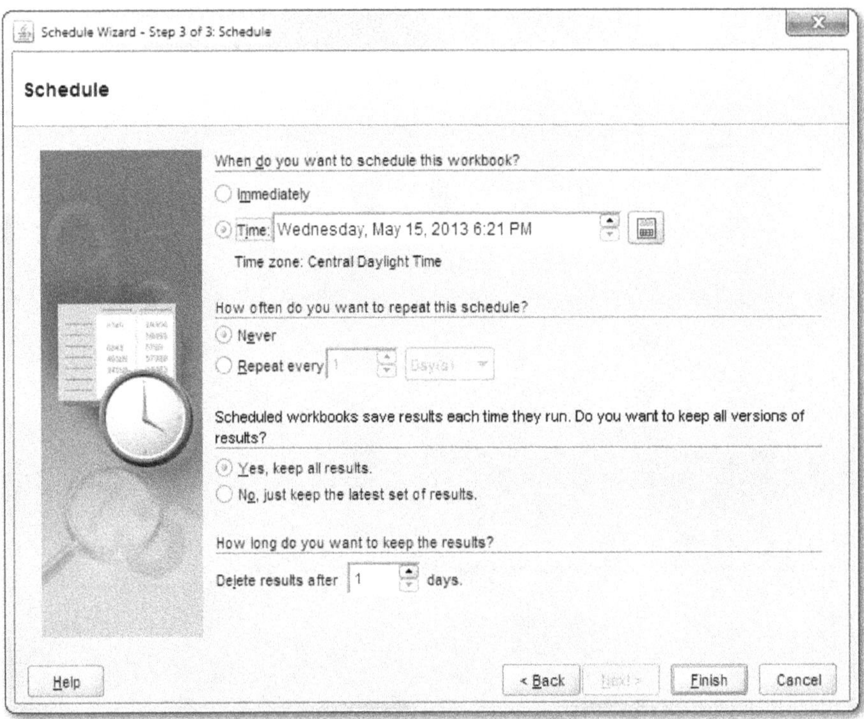


**FIGURE 14-8.** *The Plus Schedule Wizard, final part parameter*

16. Under the prompt "How long do you want to keep the results?" is a single box with up and down buttons. This is where you define the delete criteria.
17. Having completed the final step of the wizard, click Finish.

The worksheets you have just scheduled will be run on the date and time you specified. The schedule time is based on the database time when scheduling from Desktop and Plus. Thus, if the database is in California and the user is in Denver, this may cause some confusion.

## The Scheduling Manager Dialog Box

The Desktop Scheduling Manager dialog box, as shown in Figure 14-9, and the Plus Scheduling Manager dialog box, as shown in Figure 14-10, have the following features:

- **Scheduled workbooks** In this area, Discoverer displays details about all of your scheduled workbooks. This includes those scheduled to run, those that are running, and those that have already run. The Status column will tell you whether the workbook is Scheduled (Pending in Plus), running, expired, or completed (Report ready), or if it has encountered an error. It is also possible for you to see a status that your Discoverer manager has unscheduled your workbook.

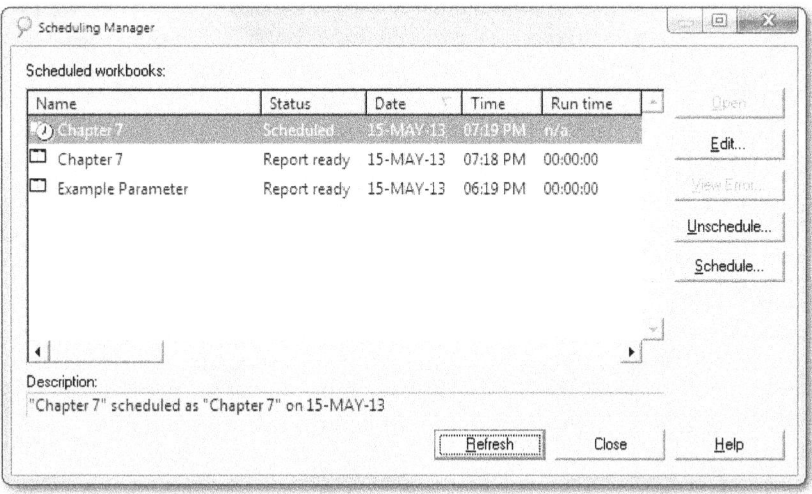


**FIGURE 14-9.** *The Desktop Scheduling Manager dialog box*

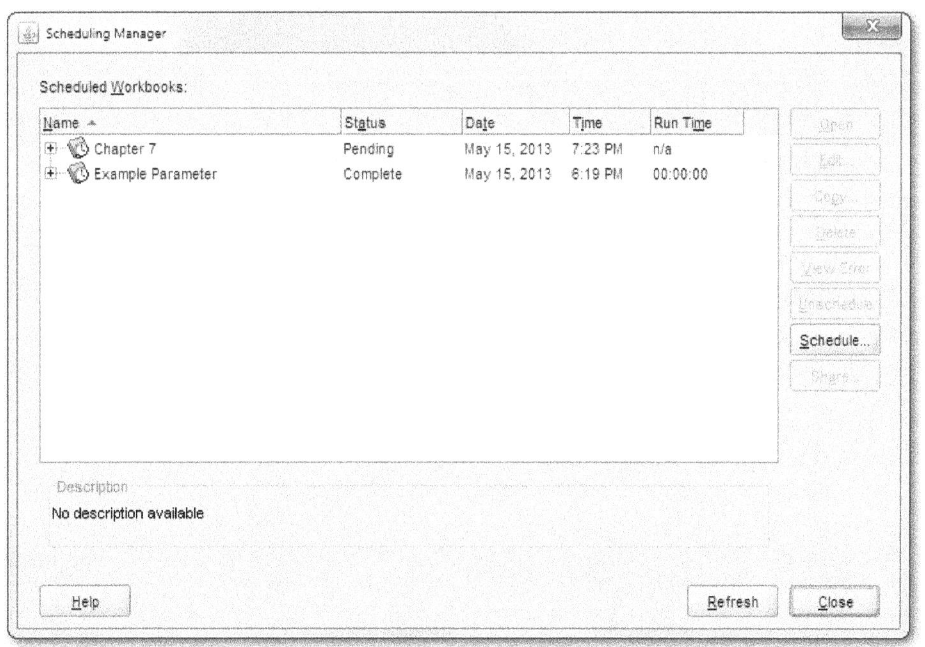


**FIGURE 14-10.** *The Plus Scheduling Manager dialog box*

In addition to the Status column, there are columns for the date and time that the workbook is scheduled to run and how long the workbook took to run. To the left of the workbook name are icons indicating the status of the workbook. The Clock icon indicates that the workbook is scheduled to run or is running. The icon without a clock indicates that the workbook has run and that the report is ready for viewing. In Plus, you must click the small plus sign alongside a workbook that has a status of Complete in order to see the actual results. These results will have the status Report ready.

- **Open** If your workbook has the status Report ready, this means the workbook has run and that the results are ready to be viewed. Highlight the report you want to view and then click this button or double-click the report name to view the results. In Desktop, you may get prompted whether you want to see the results or leave the sheet empty.
- **Edit** Click this button to edit a report's schedule. Discoverer reopens the Schedule Workbook Wizard. When this opens, you will see two tabs, one called General and one called Schedule. On the General tab you will find the name and description of the workbook. On the Schedule tab is where you alter the timings.
- **View Error** If your scheduled workbook is showing an error status, click this button to view the details. Viewing errors might be frustrating, because they generally describe database conditions, and these error messages can be difficult to understand. If you encounter errors with your scheduled queries, see your Discoverer manager.
- **Delete** Click this button to delete the output from a completed scheduled workbook. If the workbook was scheduled not to repeat, this also causes the scheduled workbook itself to be deleted.

**NOTE**
*The original workbook is still intact because Discoverer uses a copy of the workbook within the scheduler. It is important for you to remember this when you change the original. It has changed, but the scheduled one has not. If you want the scheduled workbook to reflect the changes to the original, you will need to delete and reschedule the workbook.*

- **Schedule** Click this button to schedule a new workbook.
- **Unschedule** Click this button to unschedule a currently scheduled workbook.

**NOTE**
*In Desktop, Discoverer toggles between Delete and Unschedule depending upon the status of the report. In Plus, Discoverer has two different buttons, one for Delete and one for Unschedule.*

- **Refresh** Click this button to refresh the status of all scheduled workbooks. Discoverer will not automatically refresh the statuses while you are in the dialog box. Therefore, if the status is Running Query and you are waiting for the query to complete, keep clicking Refresh until the status changes to Report ready.

- **Close** Click this button to exit from the Scheduling Manager dialog box.
- **Description** This area displays the description you typed in when you first scheduled the workbook.
- **Share** This button, available only in Plus, allows you to share a scheduled workbook with other users, roles, or responsibilities.

## How to Share the Results of a Scheduled Workbook

The ability to share the results of scheduled workbooks is one of the most requested features in previous versions of Discoverer.

To share the results of a scheduled workbook with other users, use this workflow:

1. From the menu bar, select Tools | Manage Schedules. This opens the dialog box shown in Figure 14-10.
2. Select the scheduled workbook you want to share.
3. Click the Share button. This opens the Plus Share Workbooks dialog box shown earlier in Figure 14-3.

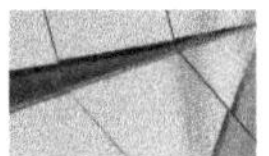

**NOTE**
*The ability to share scheduled workbooks is available only in Plus.*

## Viewing Results

There are several ways to view the results of a scheduled workbook.

- In Desktop, from the menu bar use File | Open | Scheduling Manager or File | Manage Workbooks | Scheduling Manager.
- In Plus, from the menu bar use File | Open to launch the Open Workbook from Database dialog box. In this box, click the View drop-down list and from the list select Scheduled Workbooks.
- Also in Plus, again from the menu bar, select Tools | Manage Schedules.

### Viewing Results from the Open File Dialog Box

In both Desktop and Plus, to view the results of a scheduled workbook from the Open File dialog box, use the following workflow:

1. From the Desktop menu bar, select File | Open | Scheduling Manager and then click the Open button. From the Plus menu bar, select File | Open and from the View drop-down select Scheduled Workbooks. These launch the Open File dialog boxes shown in Figures 14-11 and 14-12.
2. Continue with step 3 of the workflow in the following section.

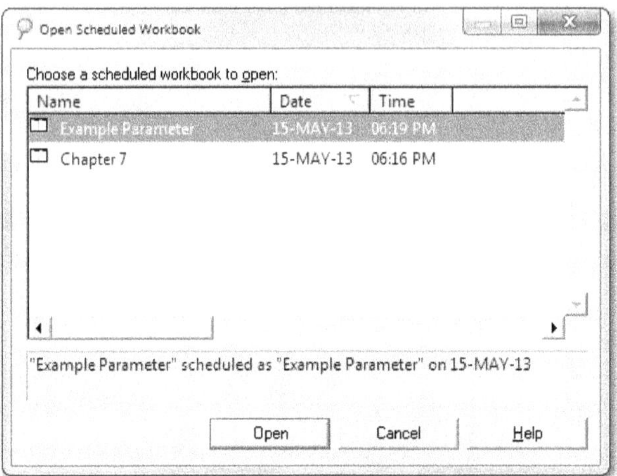


**FIGURE 14-11.** *The Desktop Open Scheduled Workbook dialog box*

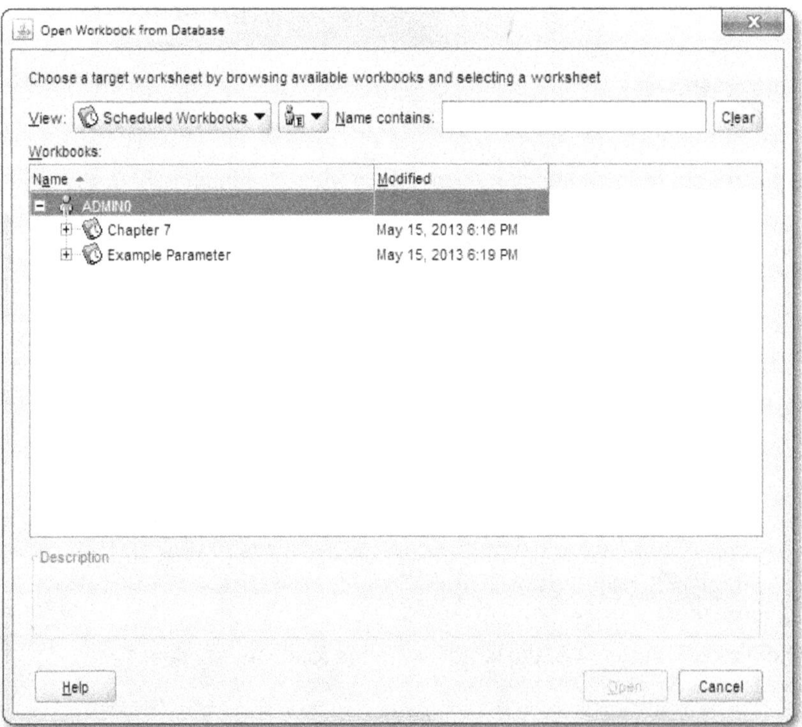


**FIGURE 14-12.** *The Plus Open Workbook from Database dialog box*

## Viewing Results from the Scheduling Manager Dialog Box

Both Desktop and Plus have the ability to view the results of scheduled workbooks using the Scheduling Manager. To view the results of a scheduled workbook from the Scheduling Manager dialog box, use the following workflow:

1. From the menu bar in Desktop, select File | Manage Workbooks | Scheduling Manager, whereas for Plus, select Tools | Manage Schedules. Either of these methods will open the Scheduling Manager dialog boxes, as were shown in Figures 14-9 and 14-10.
2. In Desktop highlight the worksheet result you want to view. In Plus, as shown here, you need to first click the workbook name and then highlight the worksheet result that you want to view:

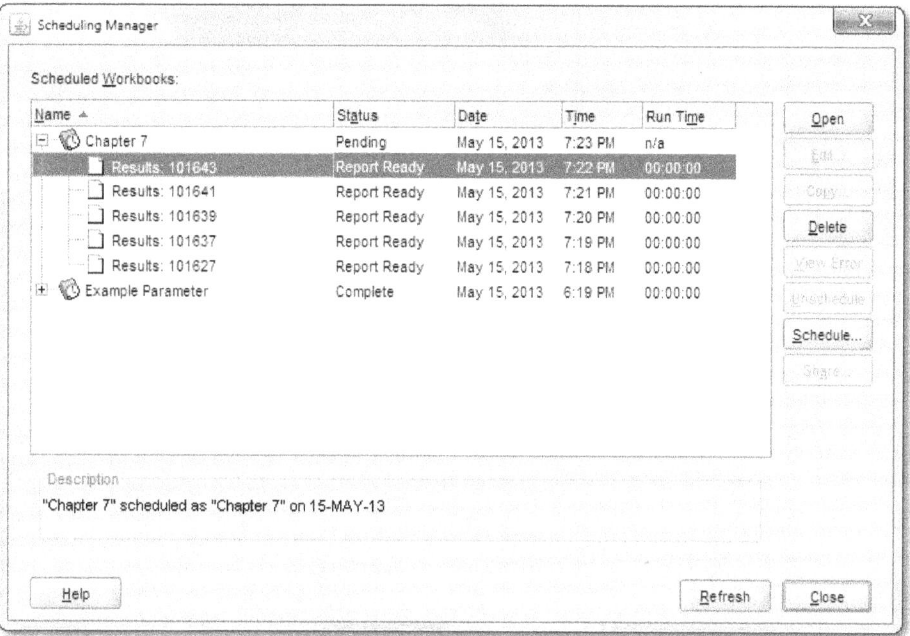

**NOTE**

*In Desktop the results are sorted by the order in which the results were generated so that the most recent set of results will be at the bottom of the list. However, Plus has a rather nice feature that sorts the results with the most recent first.*

3. Click the Open button, or double-click the results you want to view. You may be asked to confirm whether you want to view the results or leave the worksheet empty.
4. If you were asked whether you wanted to view the results, clicking Yes causes Discoverer to open the workbook and display the results. Clicking No still opens the workbook but leaves the display empty.

5. If you selected No and you later decide that you want to refresh the data in the sheet, clicking the Refresh button causes Discoverer to ask whether you now want to re-query for the latest data or to continue viewing the results. Clicking Yes causes Discoverer to re-query the database and display the results using the latest data. Clicking No in Desktop now displays the results from the scheduled workbook. In Plus, clicking No continues to leave the worksheet empty.

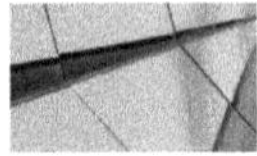

**NOTE**
*Discoverer will always keep the results of a scheduled workbook until you either refresh the data from the database or delete the output. Careful management of the results of scheduled queries will allow you to retain important results virtually indefinitely. We do not recommend that you keep results forever; however, retaining them for a couple of months should satisfy your need for the output. This is especially true if you want to manipulate the results in the future.*

## Unscheduling a Scheduled Workbook

Because the method used to unschedule a workbook is different in Desktop and Plus, we will show both methods separately.

### Unscheduling a Workbook in Desktop

To unschedule a scheduled workbook in Desktop, use the following workflow:

1. Open the Desktop Scheduling Manager dialog box, as shown in Figure 14-9.
2. Highlight the scheduled workbook.
3. Click Unschedule. This opens the following Confirm Unschedule dialog box:

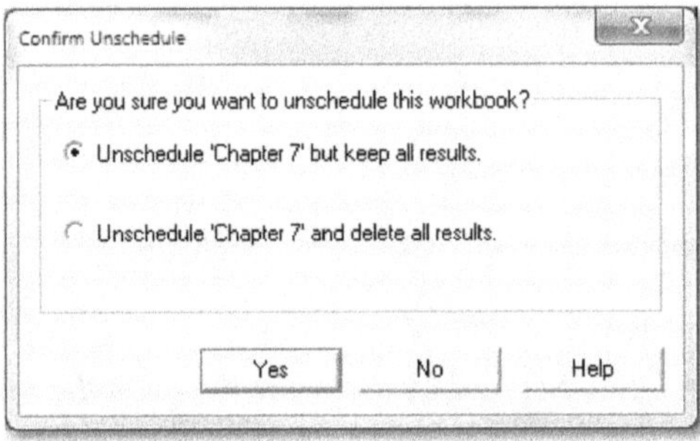


4. As you can see in the dialog box, you can choose to unschedule and keep the results, or you can unschedule and delete all of the results.
5. Click Yes to unschedule or No to leave the schedule unchanged.
6. Close the Desktop Scheduling Manager dialog box.

**NOTE**
*In Desktop, clicking the Delete button with a set of results highlighted allows you to delete those results. As mentioned earlier, the Delete button is not available in Desktop when the workbook itself is highlighted. You must use Unschedule to remove the workbook.*

### Unscheduling a Workbook in Plus

To unschedule a scheduled workbook in Plus, use this workflow:

1. Open the Plus Scheduling Manager dialog box, as shown earlier in Figure 14-10.
2. Click the workbook you want to unschedule.
3. Click the Unschedule button. This opens the Confirm Unschedule dialog box:

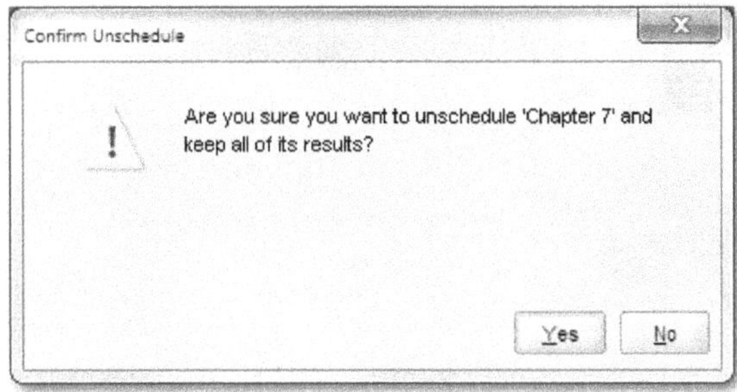


4. As you can see in the dialog box, your only choice is to unschedule the workbook while keeping all of the results.
5. Click Yes to unschedule or No to leave the schedule unchanged.
6. Close the Plus Scheduling Manager dialog box.

**NOTE**
*In Plus, clicking the Delete button with the workbook selected gives you the chance to delete the workbook and all of the results. Clicking the Delete button with a set of results highlighted allows you to delete just those results.*

## Editing a Scheduled Workbook

Editing a schedule workbook allows you to adjust the settings that will be applied to the next run. To edit a scheduled workbook that has not yet run, use the following workflow:

1. Open the Desktop or Plus Scheduling Manager dialog box, as shown earlier in Figures 14-9 and 14-10.
2. Click the workbook you want to edit.
3. Click the Edit button. This opens the Schedule Workbook dialog box. As you can see in Figure 14-13 and Figure 14-14, the Desktop box has two tabs, Schedule and General, whereas the Plus box has a single tab with a workflow on the left side. The workflow changes depending upon whether the scheduled workbook uses parameters. The three possible workflow steps of the Plus Edit Scheduled Workbook dialog box are shown in Figures 14-15, 14-16, and 14-17.

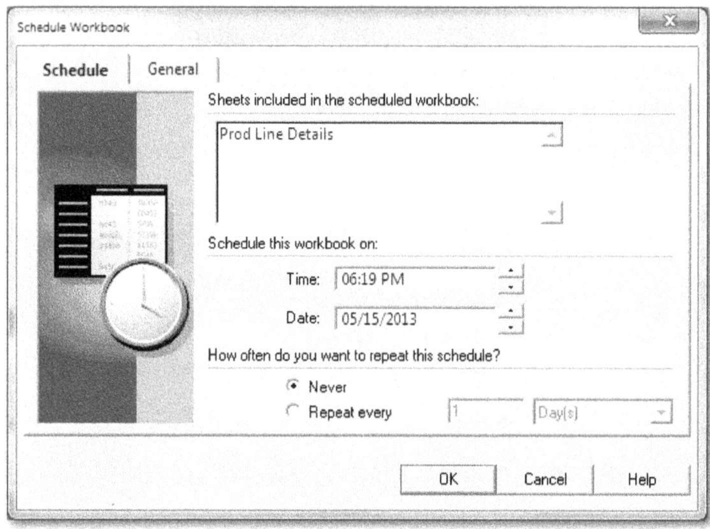


**FIGURE 14-13.** *Desktop Schedule Workbook, Schedule tab*

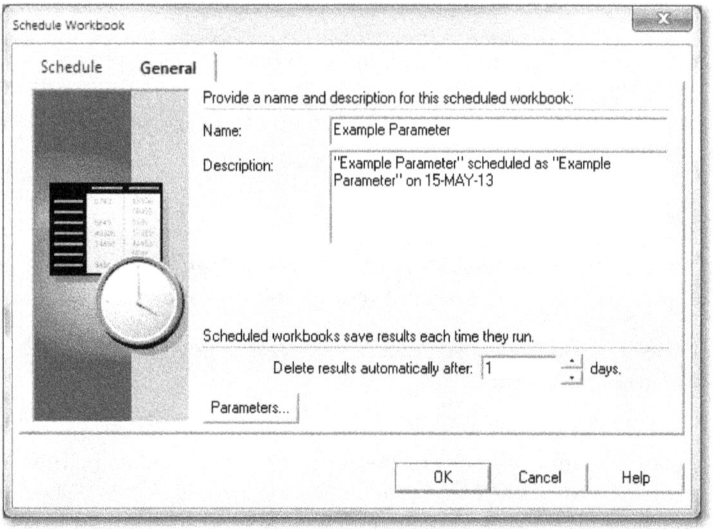


**FIGURE 14-14.** *Desktop Schedule Workbook, General tab*

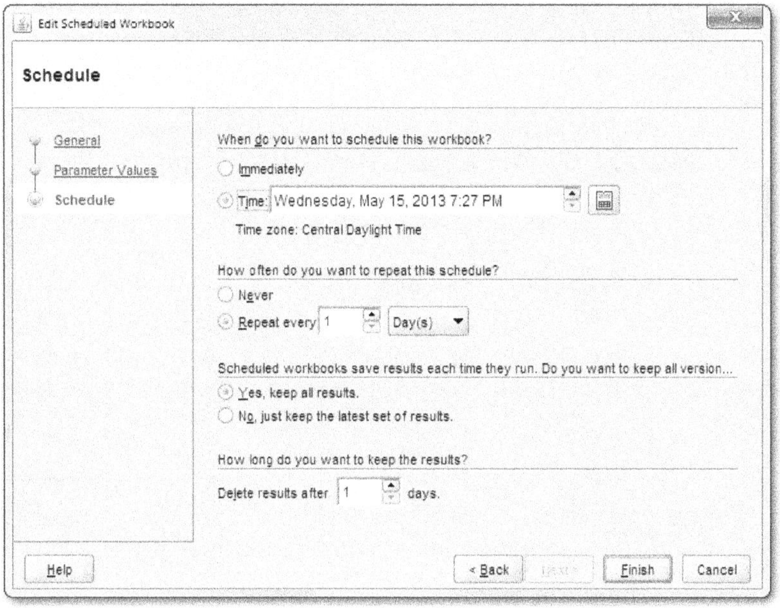

**FIGURE 14-15.** *Plus Edit Schedule Workbook, Schedule workflow step*

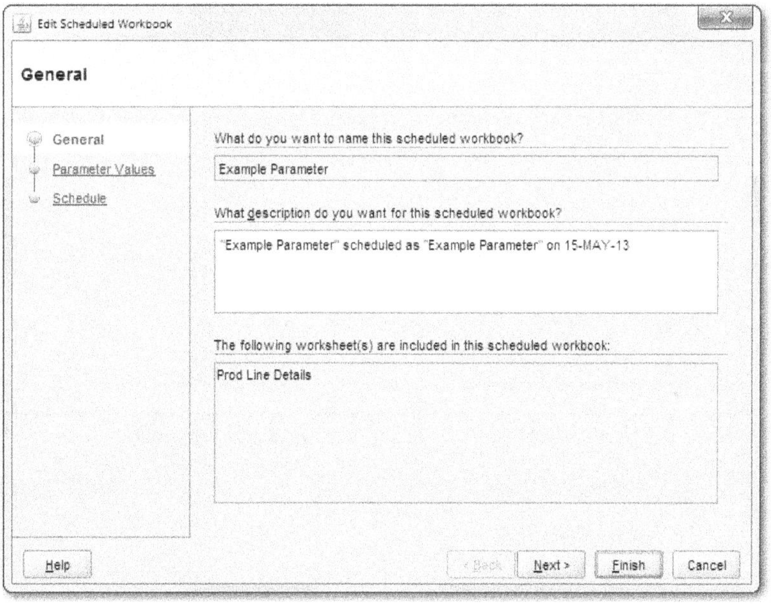

**FIGURE 14-16.** *Plus Edit Schedule Workbook, General workflow step*

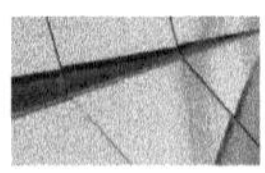

**NOTE**

*The preceding dialog boxes are almost the same as the Schedule Workbook Wizard that we showed you earlier in this chapter. It differs in that the Desktop dialog box has tabs instead of the Back and Next buttons you saw earlier and the Plus dialog box used a workflow.*
*As you can see in Figure 14-14, when the worksheet uses parameters in Desktop, there is an additional button on the General tab. In Plus there is an additional workflow step called Parameter Values, shown in Figure 14-17.*

4. From the forms, make any edits you require.
5. If you need to edit the parameters for the workbook, in Desktop click the Parameters button, and in Plus click the Parameter Values workflow link. Follow the instructions given earlier in this chapter for setting parameters in a scheduled workbook.

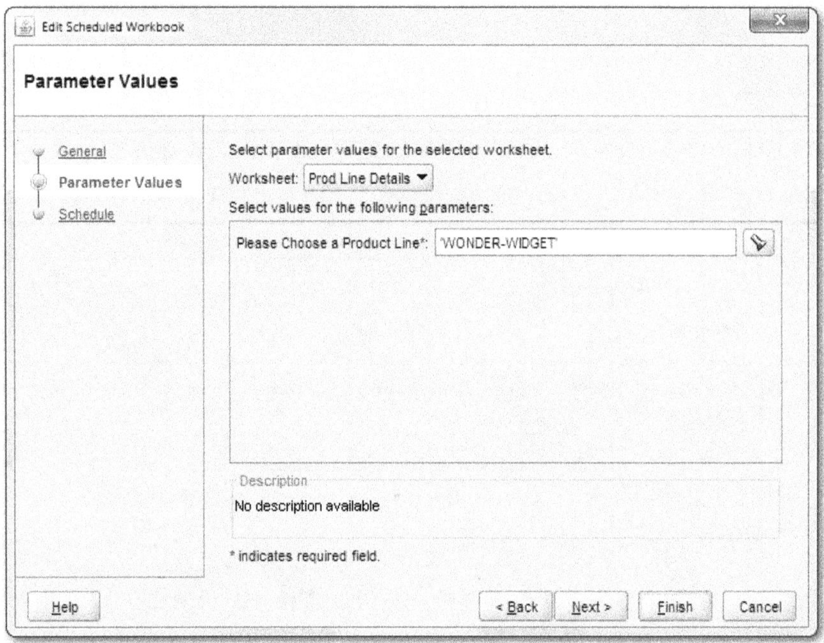


**FIGURE 14-17.** *Plus Edit Schedule Workbook, Parameter Values workflow step*

6. When you have finished editing, in Desktop click OK, or in Plus click Finish.
7. If you have made changes to the schedule, in Plus you will be prompted that Discoverer needs to delete the old results. If you are sure that this is what you want to do, click Yes; otherwise, click No. Discoverer Plus does not delete the old results.

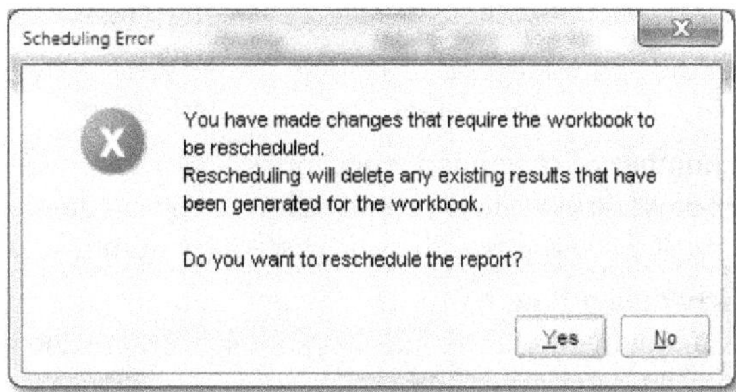


# Security

For a user to be able to schedule a workbook, the Discoverer manager must grant scheduling privileges to that user. The following illustration, from the Discoverer Administrator tool, shows the security privileges that are controlled by the Discoverer manager:

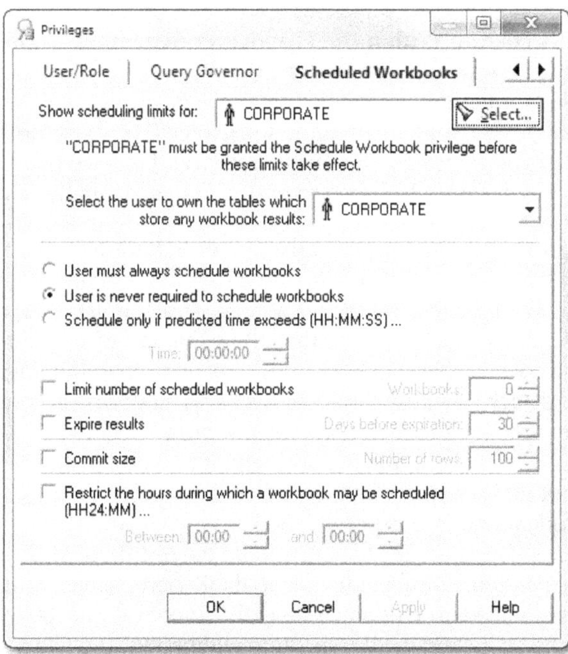

Among the privileges that are controlled are the following:

- **Owner of the results** The Discoverer manager dictates who owns the results of scheduled workbooks that you create. Normally, this is yourself; however, you may agree to transfer your viewing rights to a colleague. When your Discoverer manager deems that the database privileges required to schedule workbooks are beyond the level they want you to possess, they can grant these privileges to another database user. This will enable you to still schedule and view reports as if the results were owned by you. This is different from allowing another user to read the scheduled report.
- **Maximum number of scheduled workbooks** Your Discoverer administrator can restrict the number of workbooks that you are allowed to schedule. If you think you should have more, you must discuss this with your Discoverer administrator.
- **Limits on scheduling time** Your Discoverer administrator can limit the times between which you are allowed to schedule workbooks. Perhaps the peak hours will be off-limits, maybe during system backup, and so on.

### Limitations of the Discoverer Scheduler

There are two major limitations of the Discoverer scheduler. They are as follows:

- There is no export feature within the Discoverer scheduler.
- There is no e-mail feature within the Discoverer scheduler.

**There Is No Export Feature Within the Discoverer Scheduler** Using the previous weekly sales report scenario, you would love for the Discoverer scheduler to automatically export the results in a specified format into a specific folder. Then, your e-mail system could scan the folder, pick up the contents, and e-mail them to the sales force. The sales force would not even need to have access to Discoverer; instead, the sales force would receive the reports via e-mail. Alas, Discoverer cannot do this. You will need to either do this manually or use a third-party scheduler.

**There Is No E-mail Feature Within the Discoverer Scheduler** For those of you who are used to scheduling jobs overnight and e-mailing the results to company managers, customers, vendors, and so on, you will be disappointed in the Discoverer scheduler. We know that there are many companies who have old legacy systems that allow this sort of scheduling, and we have heard complaints that Discoverer does not allow this directly from within the scheduler.

All is not lost, though, because there are two ways of getting around this problem. The first is to use a third-party scheduler to export the results into a specified folder and then use an agent on the e-mail application to pick up the file and send it to a designated recipient. Lotus Notes, for example, can be set up very easily to do just this.

The second workaround is to export the SQL from your worksheet into an Oracle Reports format and then get Oracle's Report Queue Manager to do the rest. To do this, you would export the file as an RDF file and then manually submit the file to the Reports server, from which the report can be run and the results e-mailed. In Plus and Viewer the Reports format is Reports XML, and the export file contains both the query and the layout. From within Plus, use File | Export to launch the Export dialog box. In the second step of this box, use the drop-down alongside the format and from the list pick Oracle Reports (*.xml). From within Viewer, click the Export link. On the Choose export type page, use the drop-down to pick Oracle Reports XML (*.xml) from the list.

**NOTE**
*There is no option to export to Oracle Reports from within Desktop.*

# Third-Party Scheduling

As you now know, the Discoverer scheduler cannot output your data to a file, nor can the results be made available to other users. However, using the command-line interface, you can use third-party schedulers to run queries and create output automatically, without the intervention of the human hand.

The use of third-party schedulers can be advantageous because they offer more flexibility and allow users to open reports in formats such as HTML without the need to have Discoverer installed. There are many scheduling products on the market, including the following:

- **Winat.exe** The Windows NT native scheduler
- **Task Scheduler** The Windows 7 native scheduler
- **Norton Program Scheduler** The Norton Utilities scheduler
- **JIT Scheduler** A freeware utility available from the Web
- **AT Scheduler** The Windows XP native scheduler
- **Febooti Automation Workshop** Point and click software for automation of complex and recurring processes that would otherwise require programming code.

## Third-Party Scheduling Using Windows 7

We have had many requests from clients asking about third-party scheduling and how to make it work. In the following sections, we will show you how to use the Windows 7 scheduler to set up some third-party Discoverer scheduling. We will cover

- Using the Task Scheduler dialog box
- Scheduling a new task in Windows 7
- Setting advanced properties
- Modifying a scheduled task
- Removing a scheduled task
- Pausing and restarting scheduled tasks

### Using the Task Scheduler

Windows 7 has an extremely powerful, built-in scheduling tool that can be used to launch Discoverer and run workbooks via the command line. How to set up the command line to execute Discoverer workbooks and worksheets is explained later in this chapter.

To open Task Scheduler, use the following workflow:

1. Click the Windows Start button.
2. Navigate to Control Panel | Administrative Tools | Task Scheduler.

### Scheduling a New Task in Windows 7

To schedule a new task, use the following workflow:

1. Follow the steps from the previous page to open the Task Scheduler, shown here:

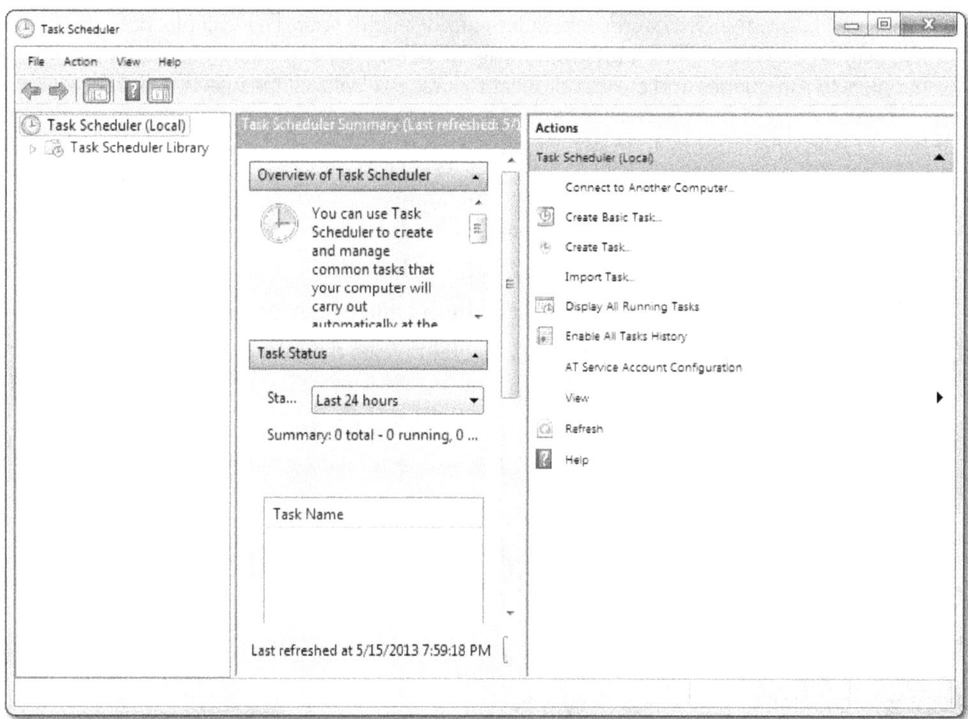

**NOTE**
*Confirm that the system date and time on your computer are accurate. Task Scheduler relies on this information to run the tasks. To verify or change this information, double-click the time indicator on the Windows taskbar.*

2. Click Create Basic Task to open the first screen of the Create Basic Task Wizard, as shown here:

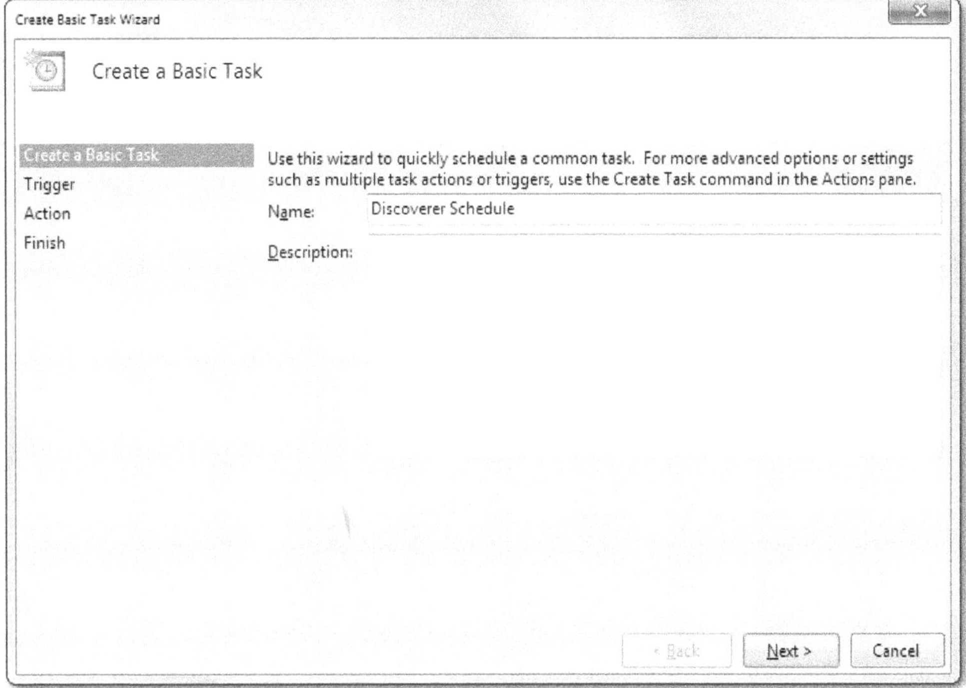

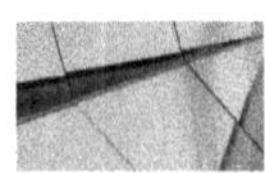

**NOTE**
*As you can see, the Create Basic Task Wizard is a workflow template with links on the left side to the appropriate tasks. You can use these links to jump directly to the step you want. Alternatively, a set of Next and Previous buttons allows you to move from one logical workflow step to the next.*

3. On the first step you need to supply a name and an optional description for the task.
4. When done, click Next to display the second step, the Task Trigger step.

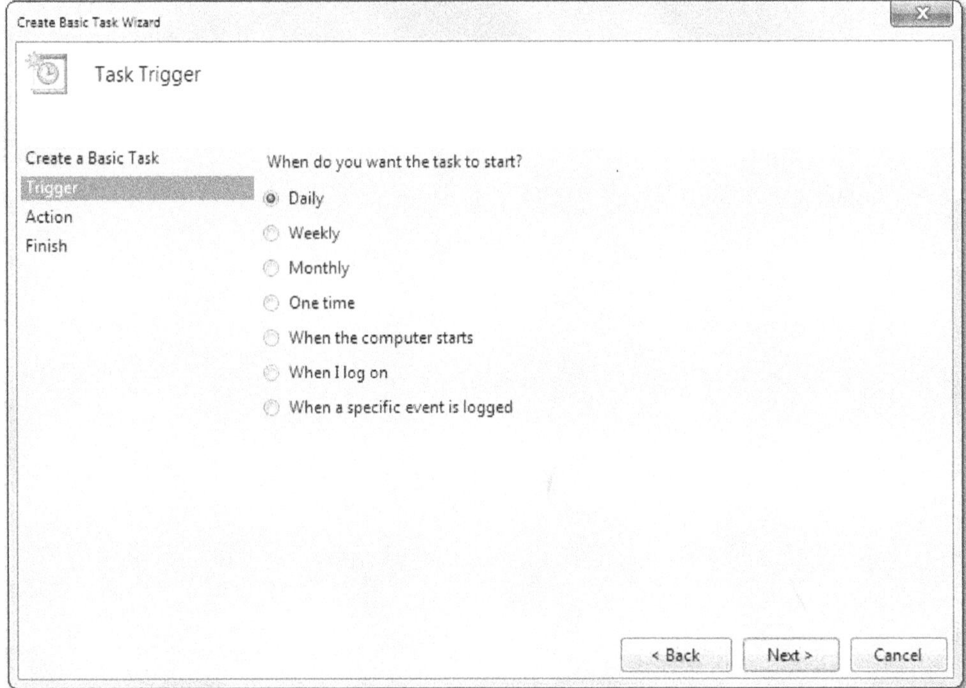


5. Complete the Task Trigger step as follows:
   A. Select the frequency for the task. You do this by checking one of the following seven radio buttons:
      - Daily
      - Weekly
      - Monthly

- One Time
- When The Computer Starts
- When I Log On
- When A Specific Event Is Logged

**B.** When you're done, click Next. The next screen you see depends upon which radio button you selected.

**6.** If you choose Daily, the following screen will be displayed:

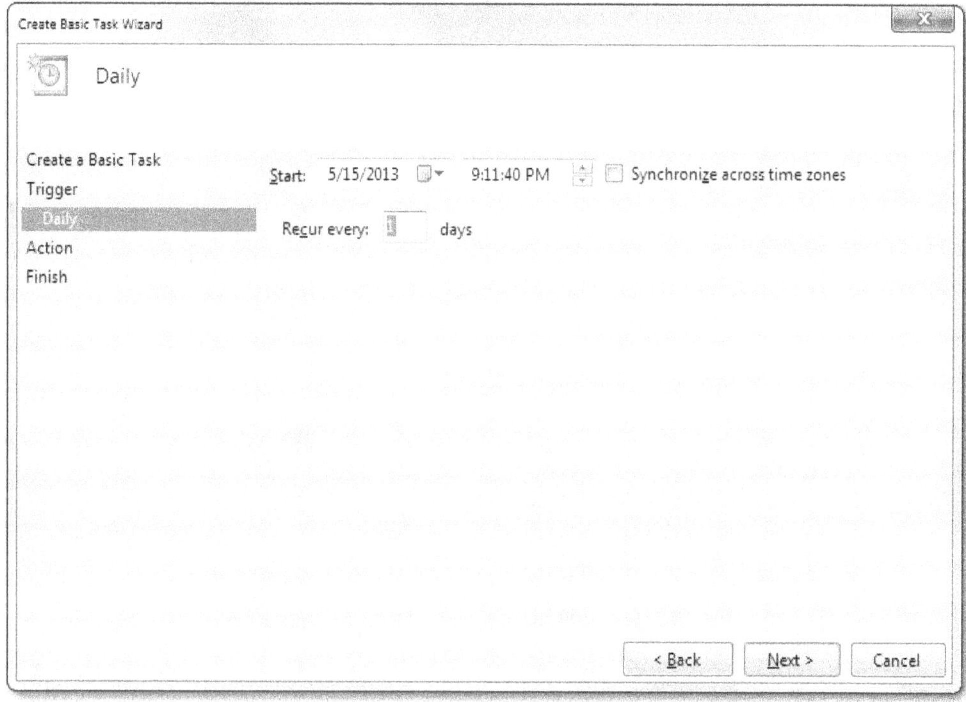


Complete the Daily screen as follows:

**A.** Specify a start date and time.

**B.** Specify how many days the schedule should recur.

**C.** Click Next and then proceed to step 11.

7. If you choose Weekly, the following screen will be displayed:

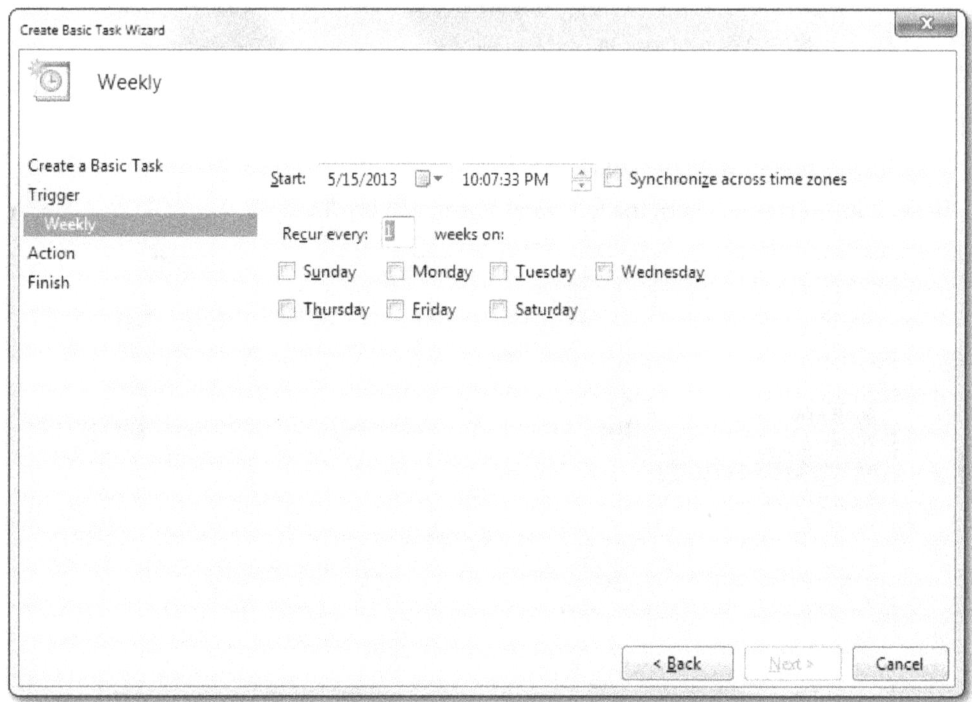


Complete the Weekly screen as follows:

A. Specify a start date and time.

B. Specify how many weeks the schedule should recur.

C. Specify which days of the week the schedule should run.

D. Click Next and then proceed to step 11.

8. If you choose Monthly, the following screen will be displayed:

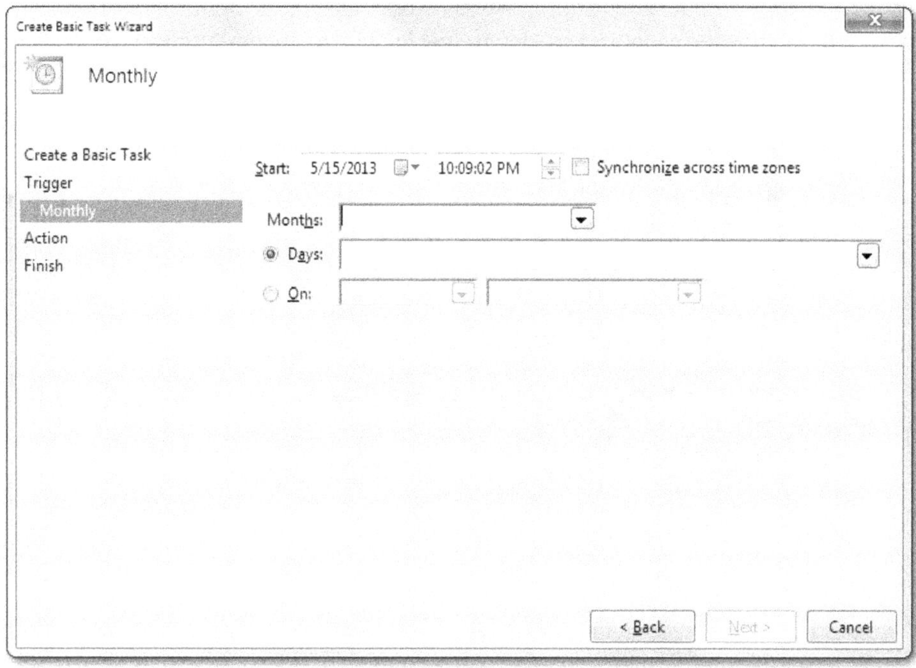

Complete the Monthly screen as follows:

**A.** Specify a start date and time.

**B.** Using the Months drop-down, specify which months you want. You can choose between the following:

- All months
- A single month
- Multiple months

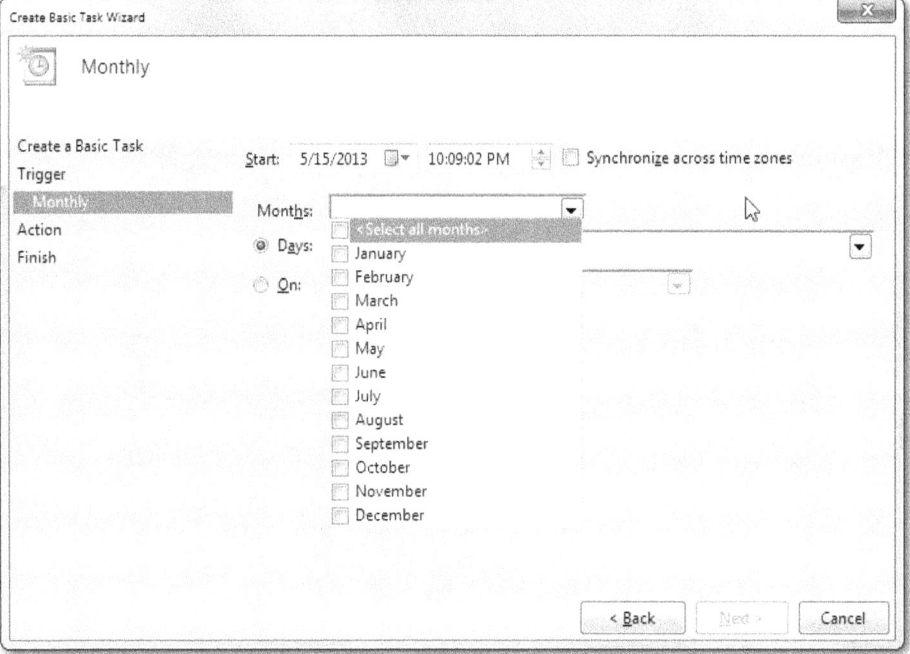

C. Use the Days radio button if you want to run the schedule on specific dates. Having selected the Days radio button, you use the drop-down alongside to pick which days of the month to run the schedule.

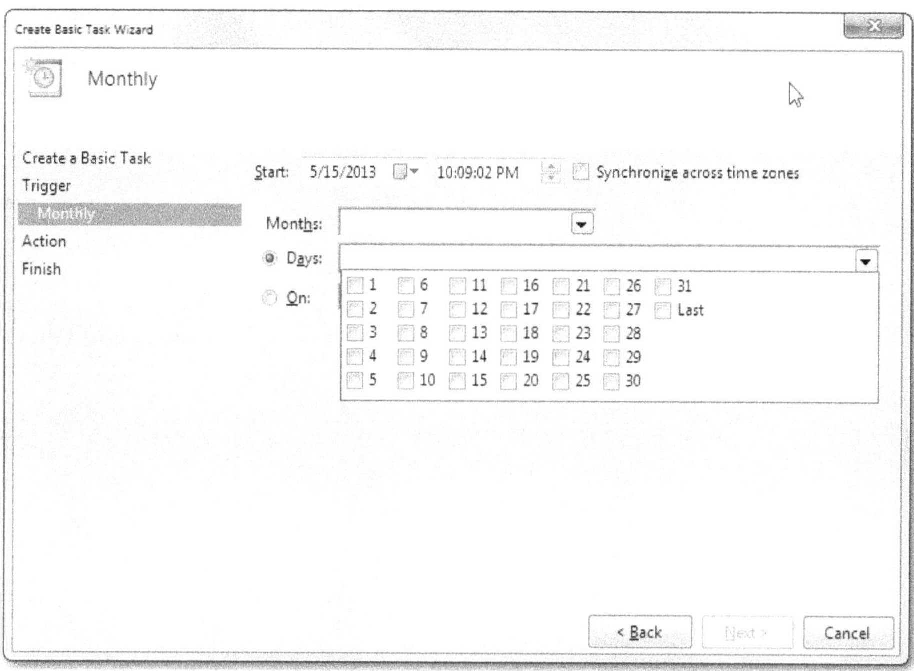

**D.** Use the On radio button if you want to run the schedule on specific times of the month. Using the first drop-down, choose between the following:

- First
- Second
- Third
- Fourth
- Last

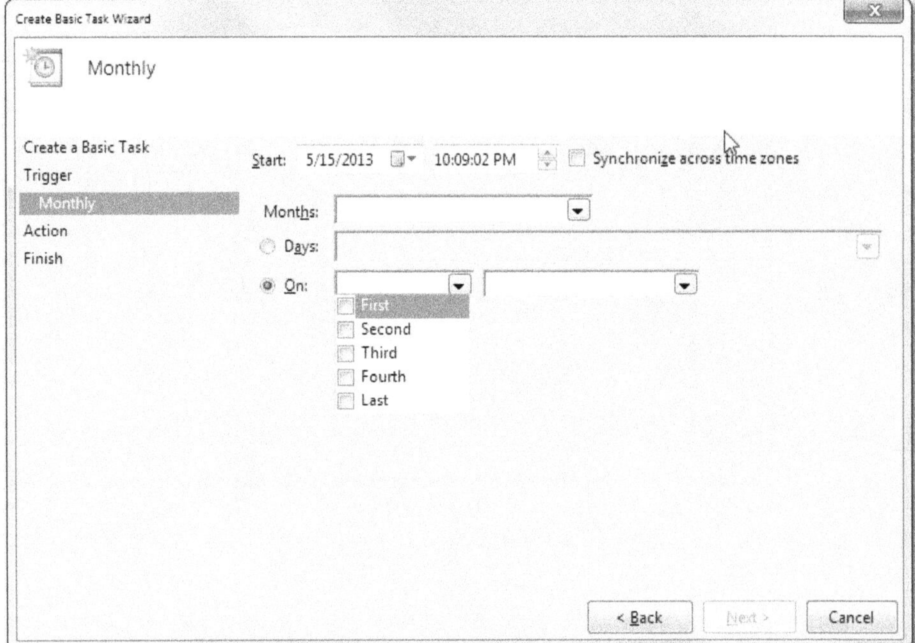

**E.** Using the second drop-down, choose which days of the week the previous choice applies to.

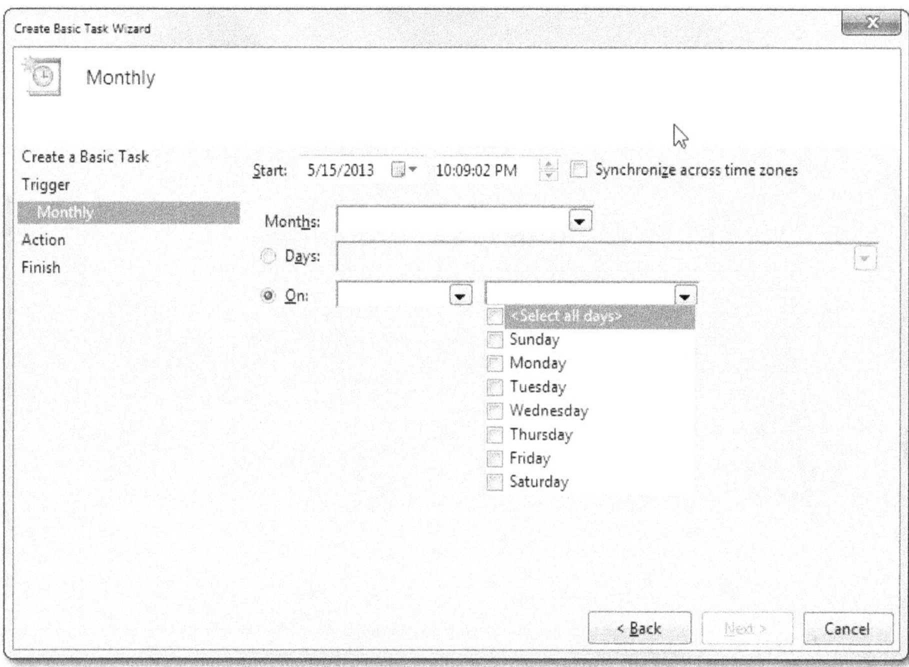


**F.** Click Next and then proceed to step 11.

9. If you choose One Time, the following screen will be displayed:

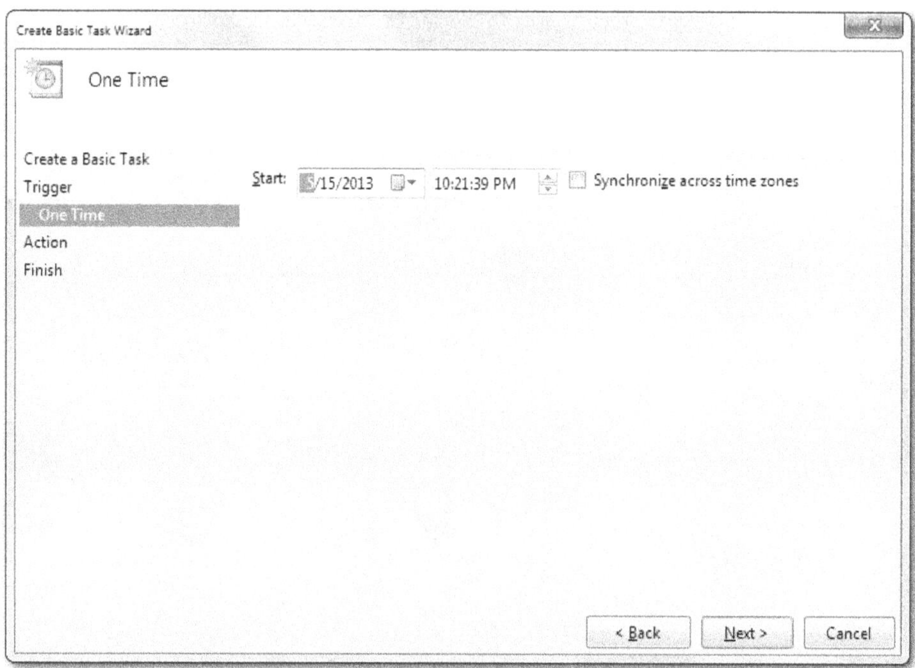


Complete the One Time screen as follows:

A. Specify a start date and time.

B. Click Next and then proceed to step 11.

**10.** If you choose When A Specific Event Is Logged, you will be taken to this screen. We do not describe this screen in conjunction with using Discoverer because it does not appear to have any use with regard to scheduling a Discoverer report. When done, click Next, and proceed with the next step.

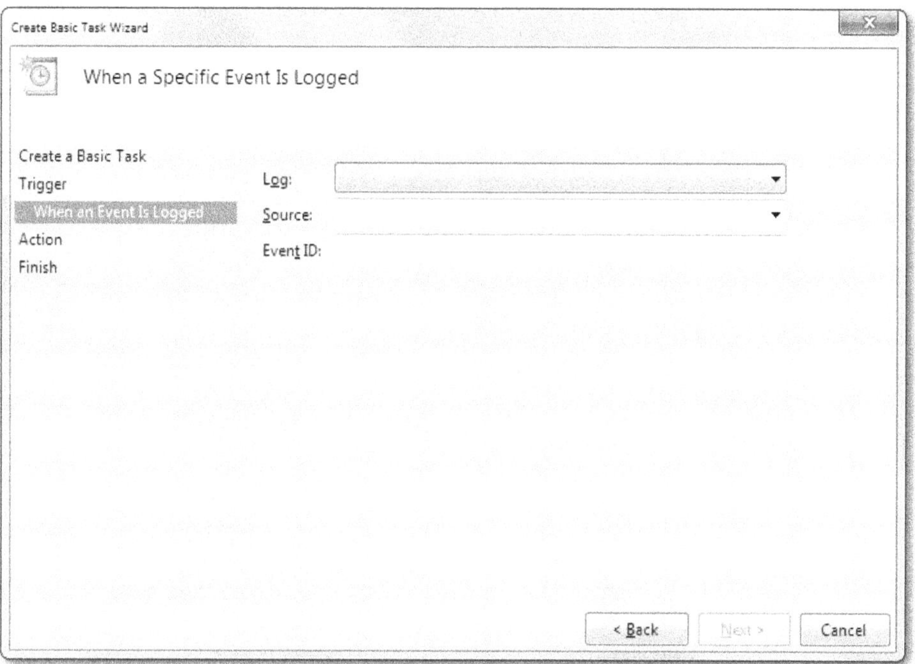

11. If you choose When The Computer Starts or When I Log On or click Next on any of the previous screens, you will be taken to this Action screen:

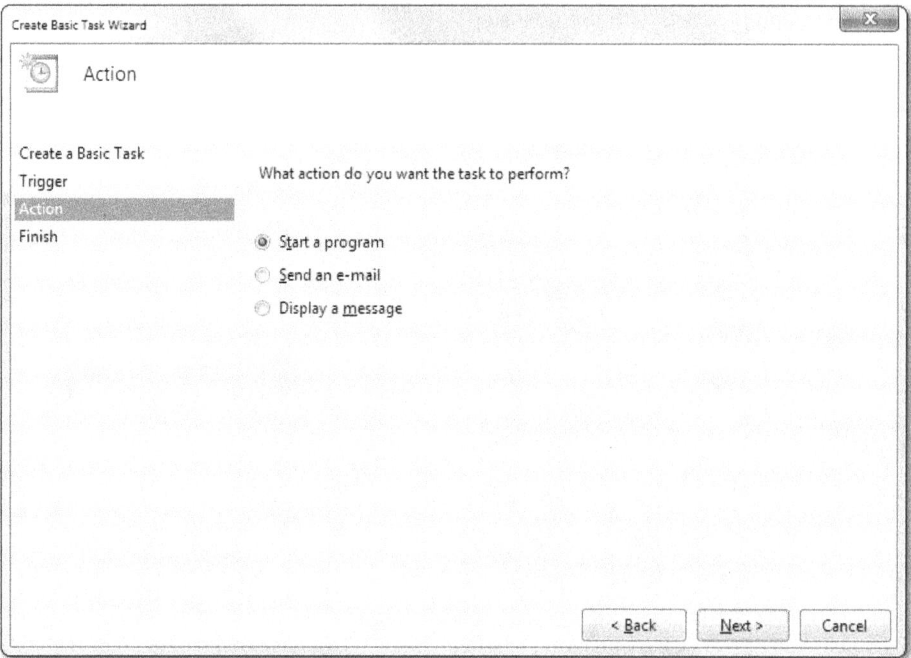


12. Complete the Action screen as follows:

    A. Select one of the following actions:

        - Start A Program
        - Send An E-mail
        - Display A Message

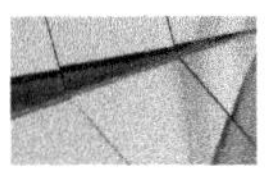

**NOTE**
*For the purposes of scheduling a Discoverer report, you would check Start A Program.*

**B.** Click Next.

**13.** The following Start a Program screen will be displayed:

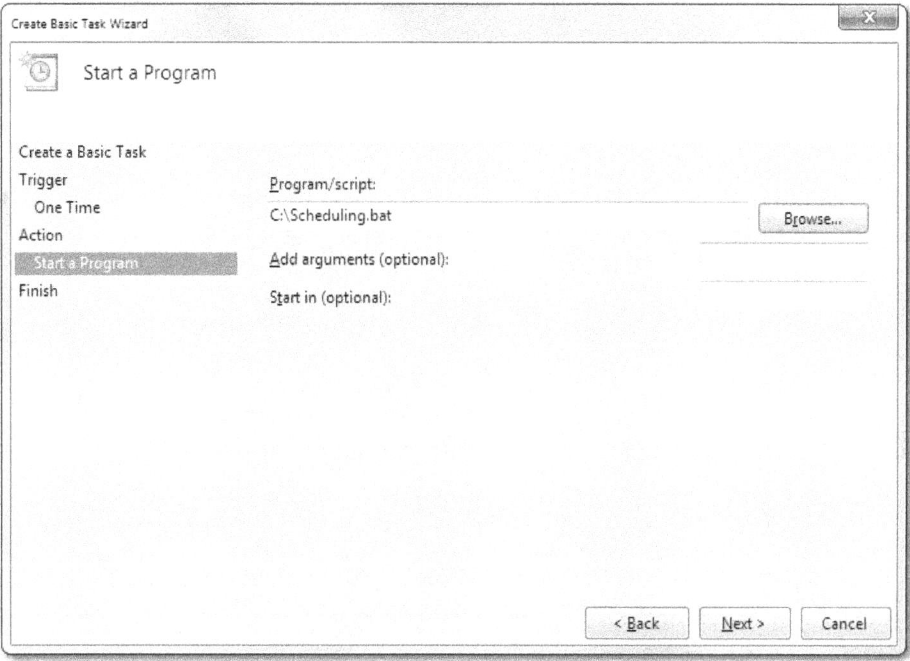

Complete this screen as follows:

A. Click the Browse button and then navigate to the script you want to run.
B. Highlight the file you want to schedule and then click Open.
C. Click Next.

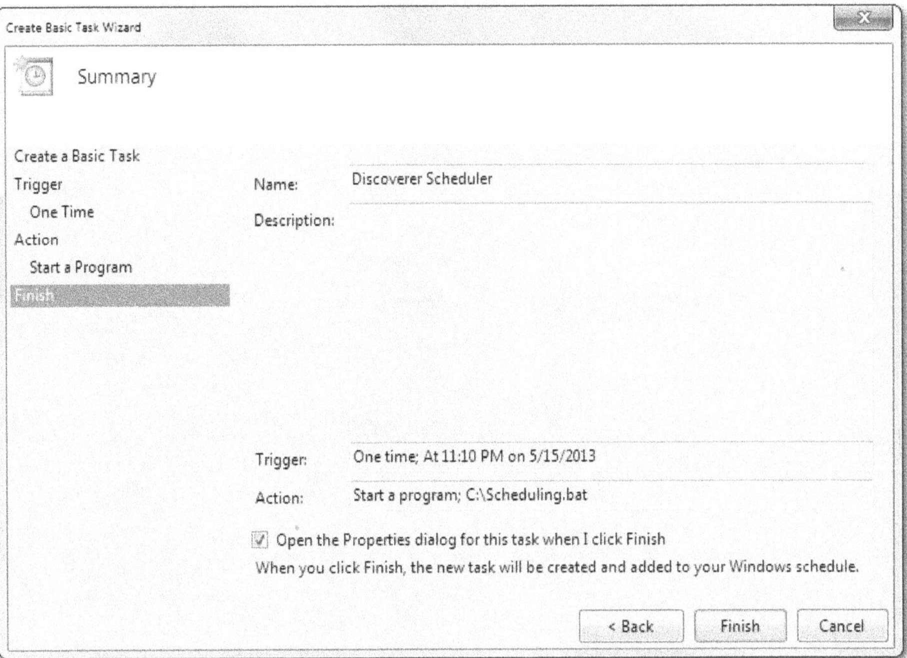


D. Look over the schedule.
E. If any part of the schedule is not right, use the workflow links on the left or the Back button to go back and modify it.
F. If you are happy with the schedule, click Finish.
G. The Discoverer job is enabled.
H. Back in the Task Scheduler main screen, you can see that the job is enabled.

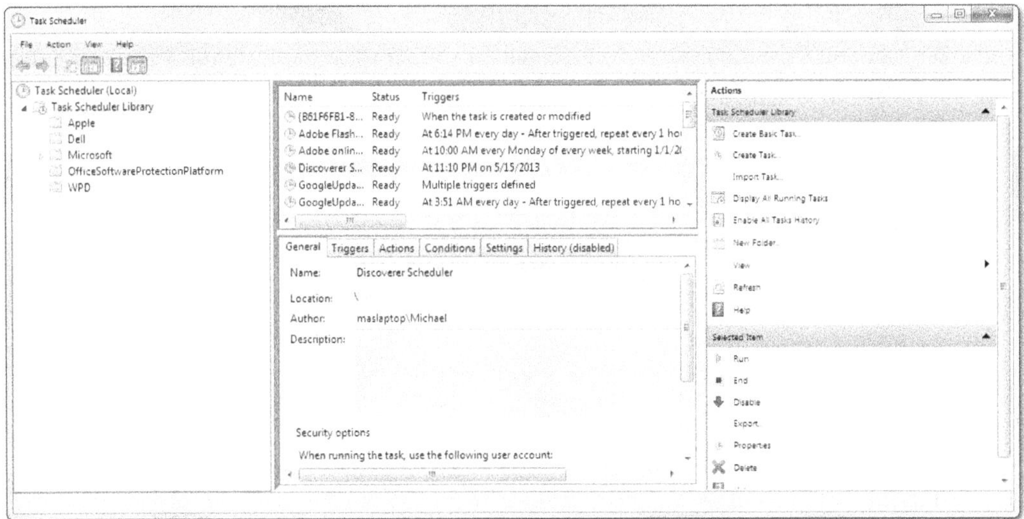


**Modifying a Scheduled Task** To modify a scheduled task, use the following workflow:

1. Open the Task Scheduler.
2. Right-click the task you want to modify, and then click Properties. A multitabbed window will open with tabs equating to the major screens you completed when creating the schedule.

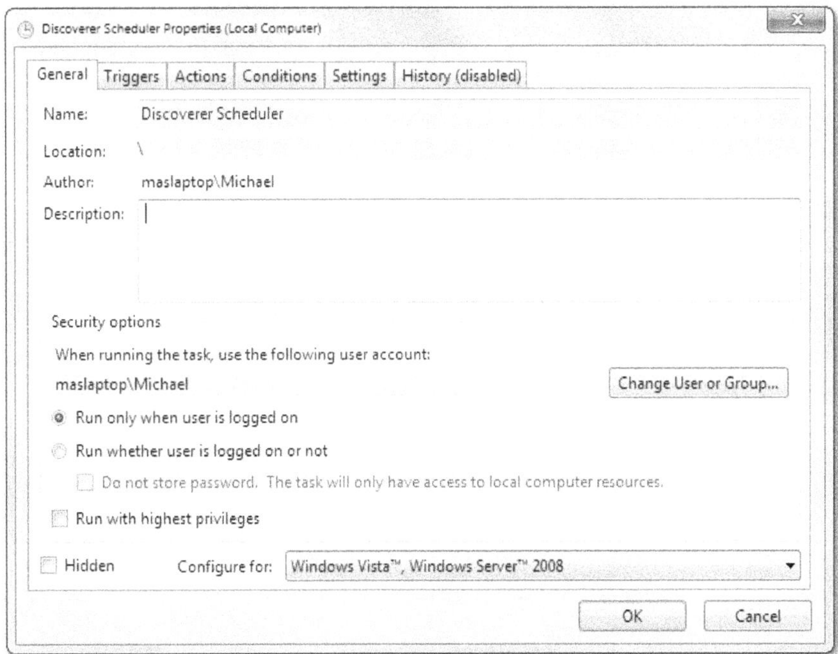

3. Do one or more of the following:

- **General** On this tab you can change the account and determine whether to run the task only when the user is logged on or run it regardless of whether the user is logged on.
- **Triggers** On this tab you can use the Edit button to change the frequency for the task and when the task will run.
- **Actions** On this tab you can pick a different job to run.
- **Conditions** On this tab you can define the criteria that must be true for the task to run. For example, you could decide to run only when the computer is idle or to run when the power is connected or only when a certain network connection is available.
- **Settings** On this tab you specify additional settings that affect the behavior of the task. For example, you can decide to allow the task to run on demand, you can specify what to do if the task fails, or you can specify when the task should be deleted following its last run.
- **History** On this tab you can view the history of the task, providing it has been set up to run more than once. If the task was a one-off task, the History tab will be disabled.

**Removing a Scheduled Task** To remove a scheduled task, use the following workflow:

1. Open the Task Scheduler.
2. Right-click the task you want to remove and then click Delete.

**NOTE**
*Removing a scheduled task removes the task only from the schedule. The program file that the task runs is not itself removed.*

**Stopping a Scheduled Task** To stop a schedule task that is running, use the following workflow:

1. Open Task Scheduler.
2. Right-click the task you want to stop and then click End.

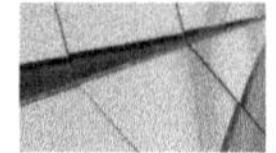

**NOTE**
*If a scheduled task is started and then stopped, End does not stop all the other programs that the scheduled task might have started. You may experience a delay of several minutes before the actual task shuts down.*

To restart a stopped task, right-click the task, and then click Run.

We hope that this section has shown you how easy it is to use the Windows 7 native scheduler to set up jobs to be run. In the next section, we will deal with running Discoverer from the command line.

# Running Discoverer Desktop from the Command Line

Perhaps one of the less-known capabilities of Discoverer Desktop is the ability to specify many of its functions directly from the command line. Using this command-line interface, you can, without opening Discoverer itself, run queries, automate printing, and export the results. You can also use third-party schedulers to control the running of queries outside of normal hours.

## Running Discoverer from the Command Line

To run Discoverer from the command line, use the following workflow:

1. From the Windows Start button, type **Run** into the Search box and then click the Run program. This opens the Run dialog box, as shown here:

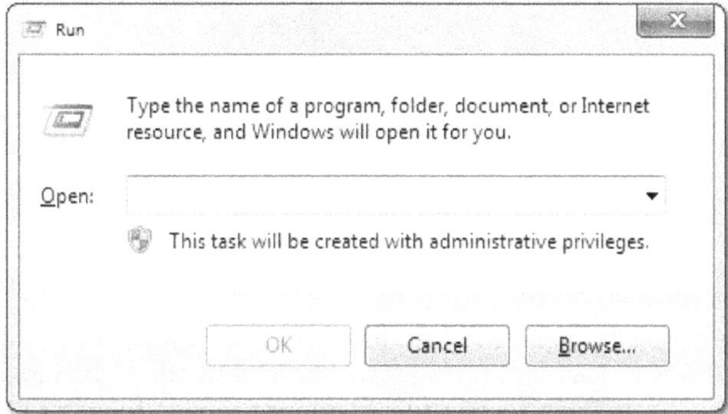


2. Click Browse. This opens the following Browse dialog box:

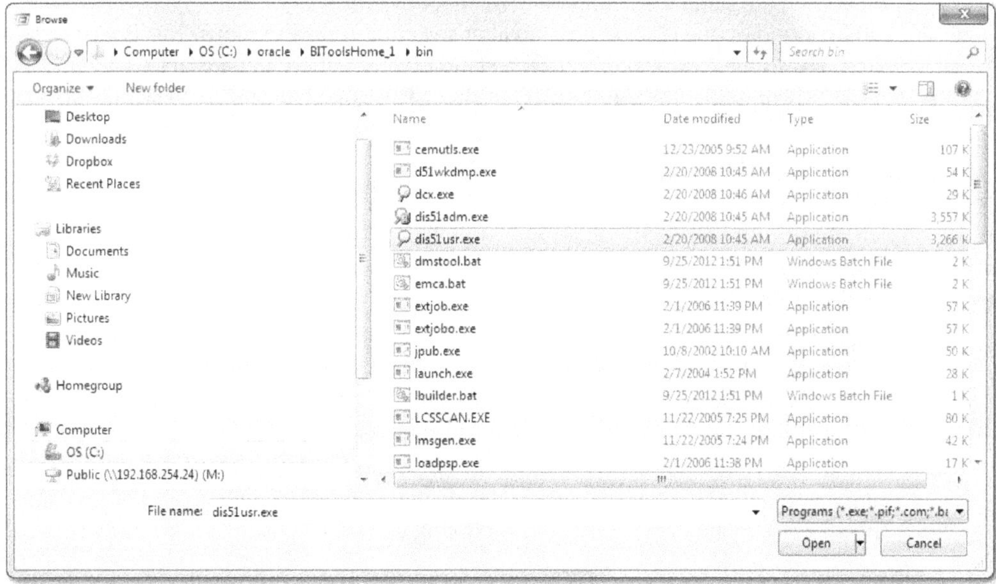

3. Locate the Discoverer end-user run-time program, dis51usr.exe, and then click Open. As shown here, Windows now inserts the path and location of Discoverer into the Run dialog box.
4. Add the options that you require to pass to Discoverer, which will be explained in the following section.
5. Click OK. Windows now performs the command-line instructions, opening and running Discoverer.

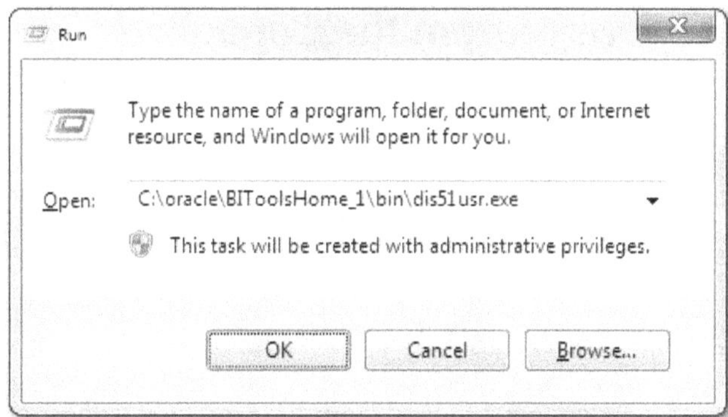


## Optional Command-Line Parameters

To increase the efficiency of the command-line interface, Discoverer will accept various parameters when launched this way. Each option begins with the forward slash character (/) and is preceded and followed by a space. The command-line options are as follows:

- **/apps_fndnam<foundation-name>** When working in Apps mode, this causes Discoverer to override the standard setting for the FNDNAM (foundation name) parameter, which can be found on the Connection tab after selecting Tools | Options. This is passed as a parameter to the /connect option. The standard foundation name is apps.
- **/apps_gwyuid<gwy-userid> / <gwy-password>** When working in Apps mode, this causes Discoverer to override the standard setting for the GWYUID (gateway user ID) parameters, which can be found on the Connection tab after selecting Tools | Options. This is passed as a parameter to the /connect option. The standard gateway user ID is applsyspub, and the standard gateway password is pub.
- **/apps_user** When you have an Apps-mode EUL, this switch tells Discoverer to log in as an Apps user.
- **/apps_responsibility** When this modifier is coupled with the previous/apps_user command, you can supply an Apps responsibility as part of the login information. Standard practice dictates that you should enter the responsibility name inside double quotes, especially if there are spaces in the name.
- **/batch** This causes Discoverer to run in batch mode. This mode does not wait for user interaction and will process one workbook after another, even if an earlier one fails. This mode is mandatory if you are scheduling workbooks using a third-party scheduler.

When using this command, you must also include either an /export or one of the two print, /pt or /p, commands; otherwise, you will get an error.

- **/cmdfile<filename>** This causes Discoverer to open the text file named in the command and execute it. Inside the text file, you should place all of the parameters you need to run one job. To run multiple jobs one after the other, use DOS batch files.
- **/connect userid/password@database** This is a means for you to pass your login information to Discoverer. If the information that you specify is correct, in that you have provided a valid user ID, password, and database connect string, Discoverer will bypass the login screen and log you in. For example, if your user ID is Michael, your password is happy, and the database you want to connect to is odbc:polite, the following command-line option will log you in automatically:

```
/connect Michael/happy@odbc:polite
```

**NOTE**

*If the information you specify is incorrect, Discoverer will display the standard Desktop login screen populated with the information that you have entered and will wait for you to manually complete logging in.*

- **/eul<eul-name>** This allows you to specify the EUL against which you will be running. You must have access privileges to the EUL that you name. In the real world, this parameter is rarely used; if it is omitted, Discoverer will connect you to the default EUL.
- **/export <format><export-file-name>** This exports the results of executing a worksheet to the file named, in the format specified. If you do not specify a worksheet on the command line, Discoverer exports the results from the active worksheet. If you nominate /sheet ALL on the command line, Discoverer exports all of the worksheets in the workbook and names the output files as <file><sheet-name>.<ext>, identically to the behavior of the Export Data command.
- **/open <my-workbook>** This opens a Discoverer workbook (DIS) from the file system in My Computer. You need to specify the full path and location of the workbook and to combine this with a valid /connect parameter.
- **/opendb<db-workbook>** This opens the named workbook from the database.
- **/p<workbook-name>** This opens a workbook, executes it, and prints a file located in My Computer to the default printer.
- **/pt<file><printer><driver><port>** This opens, runs, and prints a file located in My Computer to a specified printer, with specified printer driver and port.
- **/parameter <parameter-name><parameter-value>** This option is a means for you to pass a value to a parameter in a worksheet. If you do not pass a parameter value, Discoverer will use the default value. If you are running in /batch mode, Discoverer will run the worksheet using the defaults; otherwise, it will prompt you when Discoverer opens.
- **/savedb<file>** This copies a workbook from the file system in My Computer and saves it to the database. Again, you need to specify the full path and location of the workbook, and you must have supplied a valid /connect parameter.

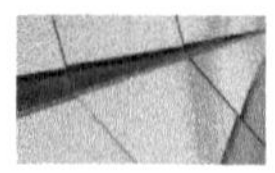

**NOTE**
*To copy and save multiple workbooks, use multiple /savedb parameters in the same command line.*

- **/sheet ALL** This forces Discoverer to open and run all of the worksheets in the workbook.
- **/sheet <sheet-name>** This forces Discoverer to open and run the worksheet specified by the worksheet name.
- **/sheet <sheet-number>** This forces Discoverer to open and run the worksheet specified by the worksheet number.
- **/?** This option displays the command-line help dialog box.

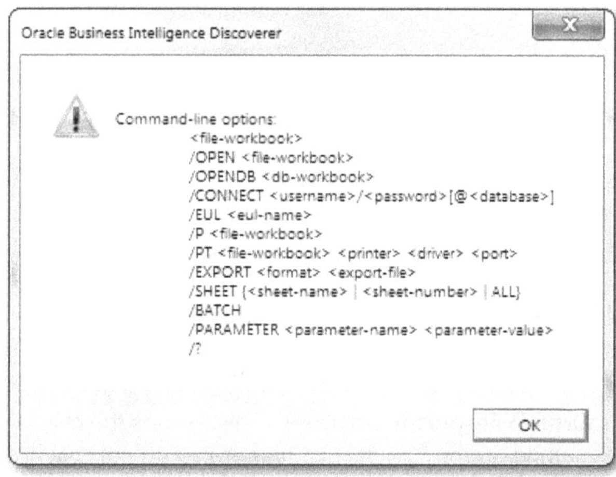


## Command-Line Examples

The following is a list of command-line examples. Most of the commands can be mixed together, and Discoverer allows you to place them in any order.

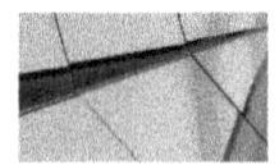

**NOTE**
*If you make a mistake with any of the command-line options, Discoverer abandons the command and just launches the login screen. The username and database will be populated, but the password will be blank, even if you provided a valid password.*

**c:\oracle\BIToolsHome_1\bin\dis51usr.exe /connect bob/apple@report** This example logs the user Bob, using the password apple, into the report database. The login screen is bypassed, and Discoverer launches with the screen that asks whether the user should open an existing report or create a new one.

**c:\oracle\BIToolsHome_1\bin\dis51usr.exe /connect darlene/motbo@prod /apps_user / apps_responsibility "HR User" /eul prod1** This example logs the Apps user Darlene, using the password motbo, into the prod database using the responsibility HR User. The user will be connected to the EUL called prod1.

**NOTE**

*The preceding Apps login can also be entered asc:\oracle\BIToolsHome_1\bin\dis51usr.exe /connect "darlene:HR User/motbo@prod" /apps_user /eul prod1.*

**c:\oracle\BIToolsHome_1\bin\dis51usr.exe /connect sean/nashville@prod /apps_user / apps_responsibility "Inv User" /apps_fndnam apps /apps_gwyuidapplsyspub/pub** This example logs the Apps user Sean, using the password nashville, into the prod database using the Inv User responsibility. Because the /eul parameter is omitted, the user will be connected to the default EUL. However, as you can see, we have provided the foundation name, the gateway user ID, and the gateway user password.

**c:\oracle\BIToolsHome_1\bin\dis51usr.exe /connect john@odbc:polite /opendb workbook5 /sheet 1** This example connects john to an Oracle Lite database named polite, using ODBC connectivity. It opens the file workbook5 from the database and runs sheet 1. As this user has no password, the password component has been omitted.

**NOTE**

*The preceding is an example of poor workbook and worksheet naming. Compare this with the following example command line.*

**c:\oracle\BIToolsHome_1\bin \dis51usr.exe /connect michael/hidehi@disco11g /opendb "Product History" /sheet "Prod Summary"/parameter product_param AB-2000** This example logs in Michael using the password hidehi into the database called disco11g. It opens a worksheet called Prod Summary in the workbook called Product History and passes the value AB-2000 to the parameter called product_param. This time, Discoverer runs the query without prompting us for input. The parameter name you specify must match exactly with the name you gave the parameter when you created the worksheet. If you recall, we recommended giving your workbooks, worksheets, and parameters meaningful names. This is one of the reasons why.

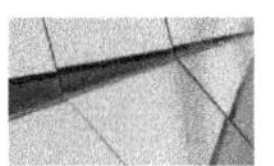

**NOTE**

*Workbook and worksheet names are case sensitive, and if they contain spaces, you must enclose the name in double quotes as in the preceding example.*

**c:\oracle\BIToolsHome_1\bin \dis51usr.exe /connect michael/hidehi@disco11g /opendb "Product History" /sheet "Prod Summary" /parameter product_param AB-2000 /batch / export HTML prodlist** This example, building on the preceding one, runs the query in batch mode and exports the result in HTML format to the file called prodlist.

**NOTE**

*Discoverer recognizes the following format options in the command line: XLS for an Excel spreadsheet, WKS for a Lotus spreadsheet, TEXT for a text file, CSV for a comma-separated file, HTML for a file in HTML format, SYLK for a symbolic link file, FIXED for a PRN file, DIF for a data interchange file, SQL for an export of the SQL used in your worksheet, and RDF for an Oracle Report format file.*

**c:\oracle\BIToolsHome_1\bin\dis51usr.exe /connect byron/doodlebug@home /open c:\myqueries\small_fry /sheet detail /parameter child_prompt MADISON /export SQL c:\export\ myexport.sql /batch** This example logs in Byron using the password doodlebug into the database called home. It then opens the workbook called small_fry from the file system and executes the worksheet called detail, passing the value MADISON to the parameter called child_prompt. Running in batch mode, this command exports the SQL for the worksheet into the file called myexport.sql located on the file system at c:\export.

**c:\oracle\BIToolsHome_1\bin \dis51usr.exe /connect bob/apple@report /opendb "bob's report" /sheet ALL** This example opens the file "bob's report" from the database and runs all sheets. Notice how we have enclosed the filename in double quotes. This is because the filename contains spaces.

**c:\oracle\BIToolsHome_1\bin \dis51usr.exe /connect byron/doodlebug@home /open c:\myqueries\small_fry /sheet detail /parameter child_prompt 'RYAN', 'MADISON' , 'ASHLEY'** This example shows you how to pass multiple values to a parameter and open a file from your hard disk. In this case, because we have not specified batch mode, the query will run online with the output being visible onscreen. When passing multiple values to a parameter, separate each value from the next with a comma, with no spaces. We have seen reports that Discoverer wants the parameters to be enclosed in double quotes, but we have not needed to do this with our system.

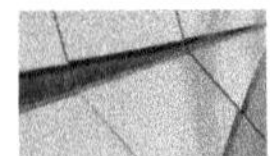

**NOTE**

*When exporting results, you can export either one sheet or all sheets. If you want to export more than one sheet but not all of them, you will have to create batch files for each sheet that you want to export.*

### Known Command-Line Problems

There are a number of known problems with the command line, three of which are

- Giving a parameter the name *prompt*
- Passing a parameter value to an unattached parameter
- Defining the parameter prompt to be the same as the parameter name

**Giving a Parameter the Name Prompt** While you may think of this as being obvious, Discoverer itself does not have a problem with this construct. However, running this from the command line, with older versions of Discoverer, results in either a Dr. Watson error or an illegal operation error. While this has been fixed in this release, we have left this warning here in case you are using an older version. We therefore recommend you do not give any of your parameters the name *prompt*.

**Passing a Parameter Value to an Unattached Parameter** The illegal operation error message will also be caused when you have not associated a parameter with any particular item and you pass a value to that parameter in the command line.

**Defining the Parameter Prompt to Be the Same as the Parameter Name** During the normal course of worksheet development you can define a parameter prompt as being the same as the parameter name itself. However, under the following special combination of events you will also generate an illegal operation error message when you execute the workbook using the command line:

- You have defined the parameter prompt to be the same as the parameter name itself.
- You have not associated the parameter with any particular item.
- You have used the parameter inside a calculation.

**NOTE**
*We think you will agree that this is an interesting phenomenon. To remedy this, change the prompt for the parameter to anything other than the name of the parameter.*

# SQL Management

As we stated earlier in the book, when Discoverer runs a query, it converts it into SQL. This SQL is then submitted to the database. Discoverer allows you to view the SQL, view the explain plan, and export or import the SQL.

## Viewing SQL

If you want to see what the SQL being used in your worksheet looks like, from the menu bar in Desktop select View | SQL Inspector, or in Plus select Tools | Show SQL. Discoverer now opens a two-tabbed dialog box in which you can see the SQL code. Here is the Plus dialog box with the SQL tab selected.

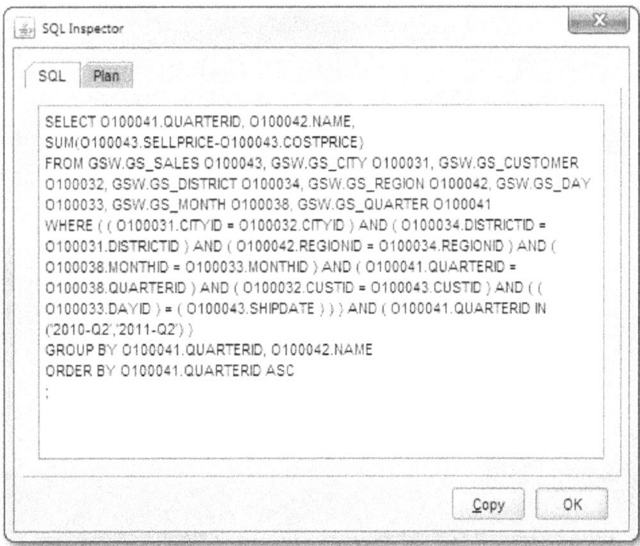

SQL Inspector
SQL
Plan
SELECT O100041.QUARTERID, O100042.NAME,
SUM(O100043.SELLPRICE-O100043.COSTPRICE)
FROM GSW.GS_SALES O100043, GSW.GS_CITY O100031, GSW.GS_CUSTOMER
O100032, GSW.GS_DISTRICT O100034, GSW.GS_REGION O100042, GSW.GS_DAY
O100033, GSW.GS_MONTH O100038, GSW.GS_QUARTER O100041
WHERE ( ( O100031.CITYID = O100032.CITYID ) AND ( O100034.DISTRICTID =
O100031.DISTRICTID ) AND ( O100042.REGIONID = O100034.REGIONID ) AND (
O100038.MONTHID = O100033.MONTHID ) AND ( O100041.QUARTERID =
O100038.QUARTERID ) AND ( O100032.CUSTID = O100043.CUSTID ) AND ( (
O100033.DAYID ) = ( O100043.SHIPDATE ) ) ) AND ( O100041.QUARTERID IN
('2010-Q2','2011-Q2') )
GROUP BY O100041.QUARTERID, O100042.NAME
ORDER BY O100041.QUARTERID ASC
;
Copy
OK


As you can see in the dialog box, there are two tabs. The first tab, called SQL, allows you to view the SQL used in your worksheet. The second tab, called Plan, allows you to look at the explain plan, as described next.

Both tabs have a Copy button and an OK button. In Desktop only, there is an additional Export button, which is active only while you are on the SQL tab.

## Viewing the Explain Plan

To most end users, the content being displayed on the Plan tab will be meaningless gobbledygook. If you are one of the 99 percent of end users to whom SQL is a big mystery and something that just happens, we recommend you take just a quick peek to see what excites the geeks in your company and then forget all about it.

For example, if you are one of the 1 percent of end users with a masochistic tendency to know everything that Discoverer can do, here is a brief description of what you see when you look at the Plan tab. The explain plan, as it is called by SQL tuning experts, is a mechanism that forces Oracle to explain how it plans to execute the SQL that you can see in the SQL tab. It is simply an aid to performance tuning and is something that your DBA may look at should you have a worksheet that is performing badly.

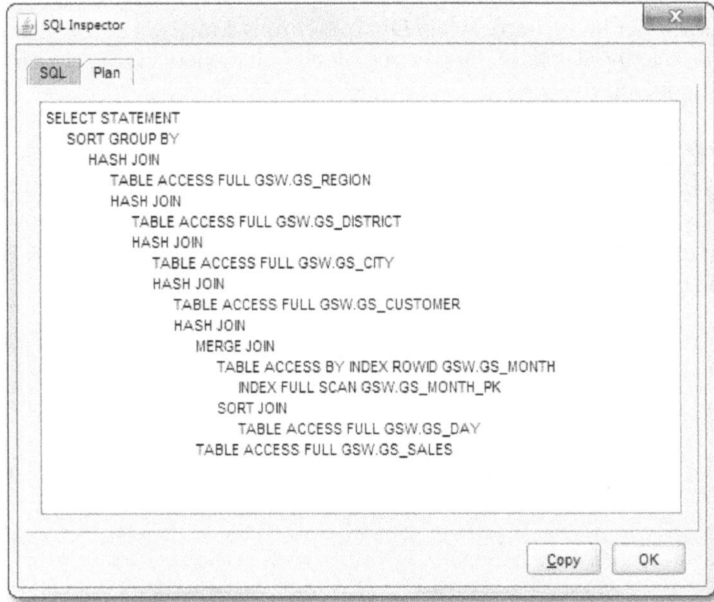


There, now you can go and bamboozle your friends with another piece of useless trivia!

## Exporting SQL

Only Desktop allows exporting of the SQL code. To export the SQL code from your worksheet, use the following workflow:

1. From the Desktop menu bar, select View | SQL Inspector. This opens the SQL Inspector dialog box.
2. Click Export. This opens the Save As dialog box.
3. Select the location to which the code should be saved.

4. Give the export file a name.
5. Click Save.
6. Close the SQL Inspector dialog box.

**NOTE**
*You can also use the Desktop command line to export SQL. Please refer to the section "Running Discoverer Desktop from the Command Line" earlier in this chapter for more details.*

## Importing SQL

Once again, only Desktop allows you to import SQL. To import SQL code into a worksheet, use the following workflow:

1. From the menu bar, select File | Import SQL. This launches the Open dialog box.
2. Locate the SQL file you want to import.
3. Click Open. Discoverer imports the code into a new worksheet.
4. If the code has parameters, Discoverer opens the Parameter Wizard dialog box. Enter the parameters. When you have entered all of the parameters, click Finish.

**NOTE**
*Discoverer deactivates the Finish button until you have entered all of the parameters. When Discoverer imports code with parameters, it gives each prompt the same name as the name of the parameter. You will need to edit each parameter and give it a correct and meaningful prompt.*

## Structured SQL

If you are unfamiliar with SQL, looking at the code in the SQL Inspector dialog box might be daunting. No matter how complex and involved the SQL code appears, there are in fact only four basic components of a SQL query.

- **Select** This command begins all SQL queries. Following it is a list of all the items that are to be displayed in the final result of the query. Each item is usually prefixed by the name of the table or folder in which the item resides. Multiple items are separated from each other by a comma. There is no comma after the last item.
- **From** This command follows the last selected item and starts on a new line. Following this command is a list of all the tables and folders used in the query. Each folder or table is normally prefixed by the name of the owner of the object. Multiple entries are separated from each other by a comma. There is no comma following the last table or folder.
- **Where** This command follows the last table or folder and again starts on a new line. In this section of the query, you will see the joins, conditions, and parameters. However, as Discoverer usually protects you from knowing the joins between folders, you will probably see only conditions and parameters here. If there are multiple statements, each will be separated from the next by the word *AND*.

- **Group By** If used, this statement follows the last join, condition, or parameter. This construct allows aggregations to group by the items listed.

This illustration shows the example of SQL code that was exported from our database earlier in this section. As you can see, each of the four basic components starts on a new line.

Q2_by_Region_for_2010_and_2011.sql - Notepad

File Edit Format View Help

```
SELECT O100041.QUARTERID, O100042.NAME, SUM(O100043.SELLPRICE-O100043.COSTPRICE)
FROM GSW.GS_SALES O100043, GSW.GS_CITY O100031, GSW.GS_CUSTOMER O100032, GSW.GS_DISTRICT
O100034, GSW.GS_REGION O100042, GSW.GS_DAY O100033, GSW.GS_MONTH O100038, GSW.GS_QUARTER
O100041
WHERE ( ( O100031.CITYID = O100032.CITYID ) AND ( O100034.DISTRICTID = O100031.DISTRICTID ) AND
( O100042.REGIONID = O100034.REGIONID ) AND ( O100038.MONTHID = O100033.MONTHID ) AND (
O100041.QUARTERID = O100038.QUARTERID ) AND ( O100032.CUSTID = O100043.CUSTID ) AND ( (
O100033.DAYID ) = ( O100043.SHIPDATE ) ) ) AND ( O100041.QUARTERID IN ('2010-Q2','2011-Q2') )
GROUP BY O100041.QUARTERID, O100042.NAME
ORDER BY O100041.QUARTERID ASC
;
```

While not pretending to even begin teaching you all about SQL, we hope this small section on the basic components of a SQL query will be of some help when you view the SQL.

# E-mailing Worksheets and Reports

An excellent way to share the results of worksheets and reports is by e-mail. This feature can be used only if your e-mail system supports this kind of linking, and it can be used only from within Desktop and Viewer. In Desktop, if you do not see the Send option on the File menu, your e-mail application does not support this feature. For e-mailing in Viewer, see Chapter 10.

Discoverer can send a workbook in a variety of formats, including the following:

- Discoverer Workbook (*.dis)
- Excel Workbook (*.xls)
- HTML (*.htm)
- Text file (tab delimited) (*.txt)
- CSV (comma delimited) (*.csv)
- Formatted text (space delimited) (*.prn)
- Oracle Report Definition File (*.rdf)
- Data Interchange Format (DIF) (*.dif)
- Symbolic Link (SYLK) (*.slk)
- Lotus 1-2-3 (*.wks)

Available in Plus and Viewer are the following additional formats:

- **IQY** Web query for Microsoft Excel 2000 and newer.
- **XML** Oracle Reports.
- **PDF** Native PDF export. This does not rely on the Reports DLLs.

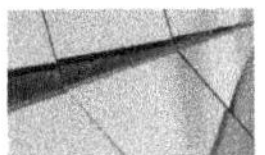

**NOTE**
*Depending upon what software has been installed on your system, you may also see options to send workbooks in the PDF and RDF formats. If you are using OLAP, you will see a slightly different set of export formats.*

You can send these files as attachments to an e-mail. Or, message text can be sent directly in the body of the e-mail. This would be the recommended method only if the e-mail system you or the recipient uses does not support attachments. The following three formats can be sent as message text:

- Text file (tab delimited)
- CSV (comma delimited)
- Formatted text (space delimited)

## To Send a Discoverer Workbook via E-mail

To send a Discoverer workbook or results via e-mail using Desktop, use the following workflow:

1. From the menu bar, click File | Send.
2. This opens the Prepare Mail dialog box, as shown here:

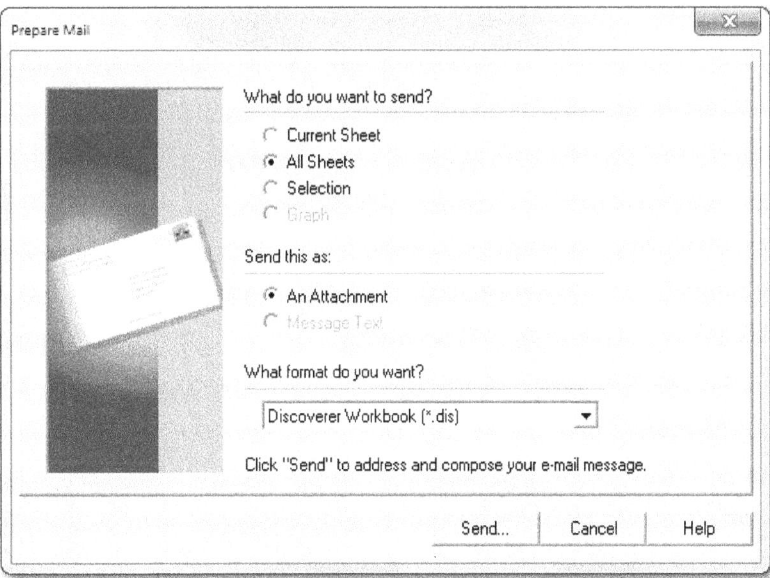


3. Tell Discoverer what you want to send. Will you send the current sheet, all sheets, a selection, or a graph? Graph will be inactive if there is no graph in the workbook you want to send.

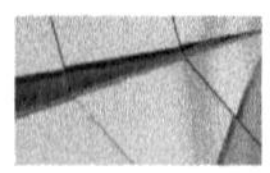

**NOTE**
*To send a selection, you need to highlight the rows and columns you want to send before you launch the dialog box.*

4. Choose whether you will send it as an attachment or as message text.
5. Select the file type, the format, in which you will send the workbook or the results. If you select the type HTM and you are sending the results from only one worksheet, Discoverer inserts the HTML code directly into the e-mail as message text, irrespective of whether you chose to send it as an attachment.

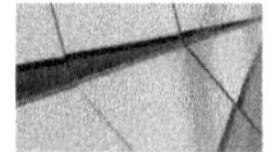

**NOTE**
*The drop-down menu is not available for graphs, because graphs are always sent as a Windows Metafile (WMF). This format is the recognized format for sending a graph. Do not worry if you have not exported a document in the format in which you want to send the attachment. Discoverer will create this for you when it sends the e-mail.*

6. Click Send. Your e-mail application system will open. Depending on the selections that you made in the Prepare Mail dialog box, the worksheet or workbook will appear either as an attachment or in the message body.

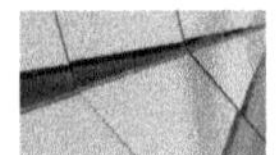

**NOTE**
*If you are e-mailing all sheets or a sheet that you have not yet run, Discoverer will prompt you to run those sheets before you e-mail the results.*

7. Using your normal e-mail system, address the message and send the e-mail.

### Known Problem with E-mailing from Within Discoverer

Some e-mail systems are unable to decipher graph documents. If you see an error message when attempting to send a graph, this means that your e-mail application is unable to handle files sent as WMFs.

## Summary

In this chapter, we showed you the importance of the system administrator and their relationship with the end user. You learned the security issues of giving access rights, sharing rights, and scheduling privileges, all of which are established by the Discoverer manager. We explained in depth how to use and manage libraries.

You learned the benefits of sharing queries with other users and the importance of superuser involvement with shared workbooks. We taught you how to share a workbook and gave you a workflow for sharing a workbook with another user. You learned how to use a shared workbook and how to recognize a shared workbook. We showed you how to open, edit, and save a shared workbook.

In this chapter, we taught you about manipulating workbooks, including how to delete workbooks from the database and the caution that should be used. We taught you how to add a description to the workbook properties.

In the section "Worksheet Manipulation," we showed you how to manage worksheets within your workbooks. We showed you how to reorder worksheets, how to rename worksheets, and how to delete unwanted worksheets. You also learned how to find data within a worksheet and even how to copy or move worksheets between workbooks.

You were next taught the power of scheduling workbooks and the benefit of scheduling workbooks, and you got to try a workflow showing you how to schedule a workbook. We taught you how to view the results of a scheduled workbook and how to unschedule a scheduled workbook. You learned how to edit a scheduled workbook and saw the security issues surrounding a scheduled workbook. You were introduced to the benefits of third-party scheduling, how to use the XP native scheduler, and how to use the Discoverer command-line utility for scheduling. We taught you how to run Discoverer from the command line and gave you many command-line examples that will help you set these up for yourself. We also outlined a few of the known command-line problems.

In this chapter, we taught you how to manage SQL code. We taught you about exporting, importing, and structuring SQL. And finally, we showed you how to e-mail workbooks and reports and how to send a Discoverer workbook via e-mail. We also covered one of the known problems with e-mailing from within Discoverer.

In the next chapter, you will learn about some of your options in setting up user preferences. You will learn to customize some of Discoverer's features and establish defaults for some common formatting issues. We will also give you a more in-depth look at the Discoverer administrator.

# CHAPTER 15

# Setting Up User Preferences, the Toolbar, and Working with the Discoverer Administrator

You can set up a variety of user preferences within Discoverer. Most of these are done using the Options dialog box. In this chapter, we will show you the various settings available to you for customizing Discoverer to suit your particular needs. Because Discoverer Desktop and Plus have enough differences, we will show you the Options dialog box in both versions.

In this chapter, we will also give you a quick-reference guide to the Discoverer Desktop and Plus toolbars. We will describe each button's functionality and its location on the toolbar.

You will also learn more about your Discoverer administrator and that role in your successful use of Discoverer. We will teach you about the various tasks a Discoverer administrator needs to perform as well as what they can do for you.

# Customizing User Preferences

Discoverer allows you to customize many of the day-to-day features you will be using. These features include setting file locations, setting how queries run by default, tailoring how your reports are set up, and many more. This customization is done using the Options dialog box. You have already been introduced to this dialog box in relation to creating reports and formatting queries, as well as in setting up how your queries run. We want to be sure nothing is missed and so will take you through each section of the Options dialog boxes for both Desktop and Plus.

The Options dialog box is accessed through the Tools menu on the menu bar. To open the Options dialog box, select Tools | Options.

**NOTE**

*You can also access the Options dialog box from a button in the Workbook Wizard. This button is active in all steps of the Workbook Wizard except step 1. Before the button can be activated, you need to have chosen a table or crosstab layout. In Desktop, if you click Options in the Workbook Wizard, only the Query Governor, Table/Crosstab Format, and Default Format tabs are available. In Plus, if you click Properties in the Workbook Wizard, only the General, Table/Crosstab Format, and Aggregation tabs are available.*

# Desktop Options

The Desktop Options dialog box consists of seven tabs; however, only five of them can be seen at the same time. There are left and right arrows in the upper-right corner that give you access to the additional tabs. The seven tabs are as follows:

- General
- Query Governor
- Sheet Format (Table or Crosstab)
- Default Formats
- Cache Settings
- Advanced
- EUL

Our tutorial on the Options dialog box will begin with the General tab.

## General

The General tab in Desktop, as shown in Figure 15-1, is divided into three areas.

The first area, Viewers, concerns how you want to view multimedia files. If the Discoverer workbook contains video, images, or sound items, click these boxes to have Discoverer's built-in viewers open and play these files.

The second area, Workbooks, is for setting up preferences for how and when your workbooks run. As you can see in Figure 15-1, there are three radio buttons to choose from, a check box, and an input box. The radio buttons are as follows:

- **Run Query Automatically** When you open a workbook, Discoverer will automatically run the active worksheet if you select this option. Discoverer will not run any of the other worksheets until you click the corresponding worksheet tab.
- **Don't Run Query (Leave Sheet Empty)** When you open a workbook, Discoverer will not run any of the worksheets if you select this option. You will, however, be in the active worksheet with no data displayed.
- **Ask For Confirmation** When you open a workbook, Discoverer will ask for confirmation that you want to run the active worksheet. Clicking Yes will run the worksheet, and clicking No will not.

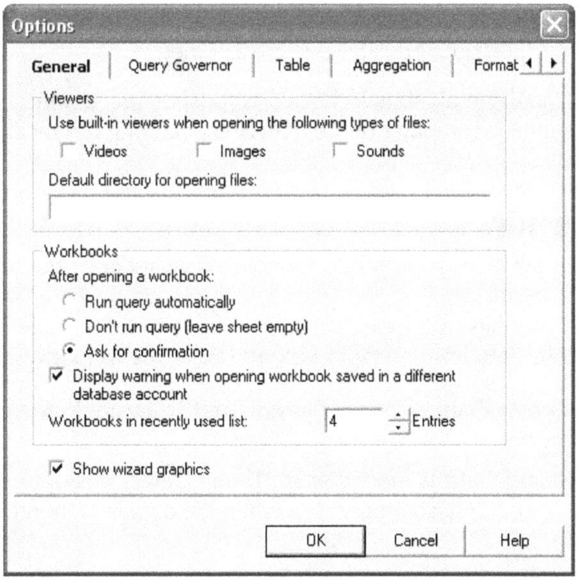

**FIGURE 15-1.** *The Desktop Options dialog box General tab*

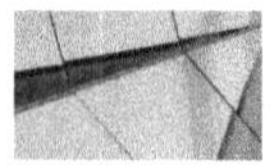

**NOTE**
*Because Discoverer has sticky features, it remembers the last worksheet that was opened in the workbook. This worksheet is called the active worksheet. We think the best option to choose is Ask For Confirmation. If you are anything like us, you don't remember which worksheet you last had open. By selecting this option, you have the chance to choose whether Discoverer runs the active worksheet. If you are not sure what the active worksheet does, click No when prompted, and then open the Edit Sheet dialog box and check it out. With the other options, you could be waiting for a query to run when it is not even the one you need.*

**NOTE**
*In Plus, users have the option of selecting which workbook they want to open, so this makes life a bit simpler.*

The remaining options in the Workbook area are as follows:

- **Display Warning When Opening Workbook Saved In A Different Database Account** Check this box to display a warning if you are about to open a workbook that has been saved in a different database account. This is checked by default, and we think it is a good idea to leave it that way.
- **Workbooks In Recently Used List** This is a selection box to the right, near the bottom of this area. In this box, enter how many files you want to see in the recently used file list. The default is four, but you can select up to nine.

The last area in the General tab is a check box for showing graphics in the Workbook Wizard. If you have a slow-running computer or are querying over long distances, we recommend you deselect this option.

## Query Governor

The Query Governor tab gives you options for how you want large queries to run. Figure 15-2 shows the Query Governor tab.

The Query Governor has two areas, Summary Data and Query Governor.

The Summary Data area has two radio buttons. These are as follows:

- **Always, When Available** Select this option if you want to force Discoverer to always use summary data.
- **When Summary Data Is More Recent Than** Select this option if you want to force Discoverer to use only summary data when the data is more recent than the number of days specified.

Later in this chapter, we will teach you about summary data and how it can be set up by your Discoverer administrator.

The second area of the Query Governor tab allows you to customize the following five query options:

- **Warn Me If Predicted Query Time Exceeds** This option allows you to ask Discoverer for a warning if the query will take more than a designated time to run. Select from 1 minute

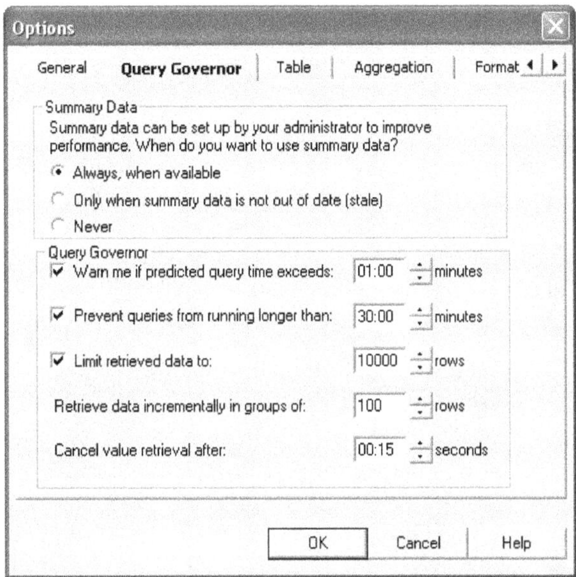


**FIGURE 15-2.** *The Options dialog box Query Governor*

to 99 hours and 59 minutes. Your Discoverer administrator can set a maximum default time. If this has happened, you can only set lower time limits.

This option is relevant only if your company's Discoverer administrator has not disabled Discoverer's query predictor. Discoverer's query predictor is a clever feature that predicts approximately how long a query will take to run. To do this, Discoverer needs certain database settings to have been made by the DBA. When these options are set correctly, Discoverer will maintain a log of past queries and compare your query with those results. If your query uses items that have been queried before, Discoverer will be able to give you an approximation of how long it will take this time. Unfortunately, the settings that Discoverer's query predictor needs are incompatible with Oracle Applications prior to 11*i*. If your Discoverer administrator has not disabled the query predictor, your queries will take much longer to run. Discoverer also utilizes the Oracle database's cost-based optimizer along with its own gathered query statistics to come up with the query prediction values.

- **Prevent Queries From Running Longer Than** This option allows you to create a time limit for your queries. Worksheets that reach this deadline are terminated. The Discoverer administrator can set a default time period. If this has happened, you can set only a lower time limit.
- **Limit Retrieved Data To** Here you can designate the maximum number of rows of data you want a query to retrieve. If your Discoverer administrator has set a maximum value, you cannot set a limit that is higher.
- **Retrieve Data Incrementally In Groups Of** Here you can select the number of rows of data you want Discoverer to retrieve at one time. The default is 100 rows. As each group of data is retrieved, Discoverer displays what has been retrieved so far. Assuming the data is good, you can continue by retrieving the next group.

- **Cancel Value Retrieval After** This setting is used by Discoverer when displaying lists of values. To display a list of values, Discoverer queries the databases to find a unique list. These queries can take a long time. If the search for a list of values exceeds the time allotted, Discoverer will abandon the search.

## Table/Crosstab

The third tab in the Options dialog box is the Table or Crosstab tab. Depending upon the worksheet format you have chosen, this tab will be labeled either Table or Crosstab. On this tab, you can determine how the worksheet will be seen on the screen and how it will look when printed. Most of the options for Table and Crosstab are the same. When there is a difference, we will bring this to your attention. Figure 15-3 shows the Table tab, while Figure 15-4 shows the Crosstab tab.

The options for the Table and Crosstab tabs are as follows:

- **Title** Here you can turn on or turn off the title display of your worksheets. When this is checked, the worksheet title will be displayed.
- **Default Title** Click this button to open the Edit Title dialog box. We covered the functionality of this box in Chapter 6, so we will not do so again here. When you create a title using the Default Title button, the title you create will become the default for all future workbooks. It will not, however, apply to any of the titles in the current workbook.
- **Page Items When Printing** This option allows you to turn on or turn off the printing of page items. When checked, the page items will be printed.
- **Horizontal Gridlines** This option allows you to turn on or turn off the horizontal gridlines. When checked, the horizontal gridlines will be displayed.
- **Vertical Gridlines** This option allows you to turn on or turn off the vertical gridlines. When checked, the vertical gridlines will be displayed.

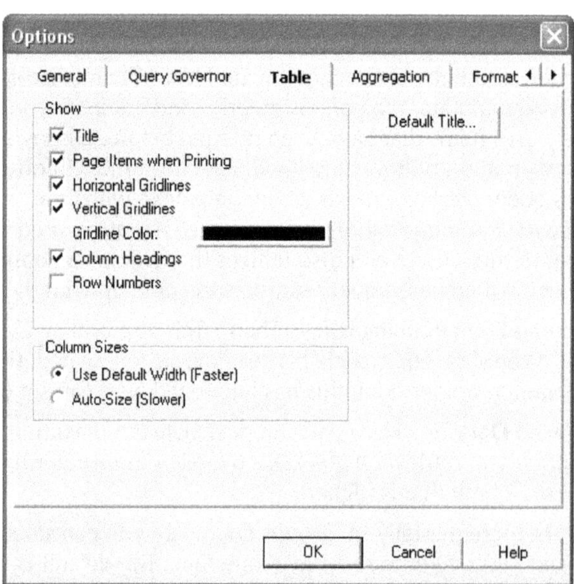


**FIGURE 15-3.** *The Options dialog box Table tab*

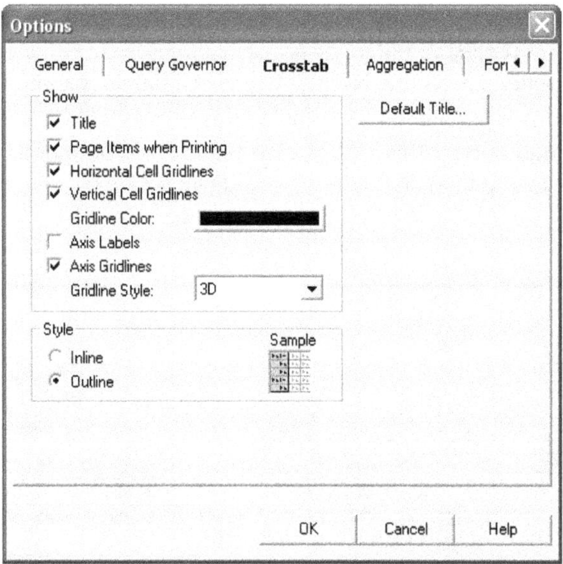


**FIGURE 15-4.** *The Options dialog box Crosstab tab*

- **Gridline Color** This button allows you to change the color of the gridlines in your worksheet. Click the button to open the color box and then select the color you desire.
- **Column Headings (Table only)** This option allows you to turn on or turn off the column headings. When it's checked, the column headings will be displayed.
- **Row Numbers (Table only)** This option allows you to turn on or turn off the row numbers. When it's checked, the row numbers will be displayed.
- **Column Sizes (Table only)** This area has two radio buttons. You can choose between Use Default Width (Faster) and Auto-Size (Slower). We have tried both settings and have seen no appreciable difference in speed. However, if you are concerned about performance, you should use the default width as recommended by Oracle.

**NOTE**
*This is likely to be an issue when working over the Web for very large data sets. When using Auto-Size, Discoverer will attempt to size the column according to the width of the widest cell for that column, as opposed to the default option, where the width is set according to the heading width.*

- **Axis Labels (Crosstab only)** This option allows you to turn on or turn off the side axis labels. When checked, the axis labels will be displayed.

**NOTE**
*There is no option for turning off the column labels in a crosstab. These are always displayed.*

- **Axis Gridlines (Crosstab only)** This option allows you to turn on or turn off the axis gridlines. When checked, the axis gridlines will be displayed.
- **Gridline Style (Crosstab only)** This box contains two choices, 3D and Normal. 3D is the default setting. Selecting Normal will give a flat appearance to the axis gridlines. We don't see any performance issues either way. This is simply a user preference issue.
- **Style (Crosstab only)** This area gives you two radio buttons to choose from. The first, Inline, will lay out the Y axis labels (the side axis) side by side, as shown in Figure 15-5. This is the default for a crosstab style.

Global Widges Profits - By Region 2

| | | 2010-Q2 | | |
|---|---|---|---|---|
| | | JAN-10 | FEB-10 | MAR-10 |
| | | Profit | Profit | Profit |
| EUROPE | ACE MANUFACTURING | 8,122 | 15,072 | 30,989 |
| | CASA DE WIDGETS | 131,897 | 34,303 | 17,819 |
| | LAC WIDGETS SA | 69,360 | 42,449 | 504,055 |
| | LONDON WIDGETS LTD. | 34,140 | | |
| | MUM'S WIDGET CO. | 27,462 | 25,161 | 50,648 |
| | OXFORD WIDGETS | | 12,979 | 89,664 |
| | TRICOLOR WIDGETS | 38,675 | 21,018 | 56,229 |
| | WARSAW WIDGETS | 162,978 | 22,199 | 10,852 |
| | WIDGET O THE MERSEY | 2,987 | 10,494 | 58,864 |
| | WIDGETS ON THE WEB | 222,248 | 15,729 | 71,354 |
| FAR EAST | ABC WIDGET CO | 1,359 | 31,722 | |
| | CEBU WIDGET CO | 49,749 | 35,051 | 25,383 |
| | HONG KONG WIDGETS | 24,345 | 3,432 | 29,905 |
| | YAMATA WIDGET LTD. | | 3,110 | 52,807 |
| NORTH AMERICA | BIG RIVER WIDGETS | 40,472 | 25,500 | 69,942 |
| | BRIDGE THINGS | | 24,762 | 2,036 |
| | GATOR WIDGETS | 1,119 | 18,944 | 46,308 |
| | LAST RAILWAY WIDGETS | 57,322 | | |
| | LOTS OF WIDGETS | 22,887 | 35,632 | 57,545 |
| | MOUNTAIN WIDGETS | 97,854 | 20,615 | 54,768 |
| | PATRIOT'S WIDGET CO. | 3,882 | 5,719 | 9,804 |
| | THE LITTLE WIDGET | 28,799 | 35,126 | 32,712 |
| | WE'VE GOT WIDGETS | 1,164 | 9,568 | 45,152 |
| | WIDGET AIR | | 9,330 | 24,491 |
| | WIDGET SUPPLY CO. | 89,818 | | |
| | WIDGETS BY THE BAY | 11,735 | 15,559 | 108,742 |
| | WIDGETS DE MEXICO | 73,372 | 52,251 | 87,228 |
| | WIDGETS MARKET | | 33,110 | 115,785 |
| | WIDGETS R US | 77,688 | 205 | 11,355 |
| | WIDGETS SA | 2,265 | | |
| | WIDGETS Y GADGETS | 73,901 | 130 | 41,853 |
| | WILD WEST WIDGETS | 2,824 | 5,008 | |
| | WONDER WIDGETS | 38,860 | 6,533 | 46,136 |
| SOUTH AMERICA | REPUBLIC WIDGETS | 127,572 | 136,297 | 13,908 |
| | RIO WIDGETS | 22,538 | | |
| | THING'S | 5,369 | 42,864 | 56,953 |

**FIGURE 15-5.** *An inline crosstab*

The second radio button is for an outline-style crosstab. This style of crosstab places the first side axis item above the second side axis item, and so on. It also creates a subtotal on the data items for the topmost side axis item. Figure 15-6 shows the same table shown in Figure 15-5, but this time as an outline crosstab. Notice how each item is indented from the previous one.

**Global Widges Profits - By Region 2**

| | 2010-Q2 | | |
|---|---|---|---|
| | JAN-10 | FEB-10 | MAR-10 |
| | Profit | Profit | Profit |
| EUROPE | 697,869 | 199,404 | 890,474 |
| ACE MANUFACTURING | 8,122 | 15,072 | 30,989 |
| CASA DE WIDGETS | 131,897 | 34,303 | 17,819 |
| LAC WIDGETS SA | 69,360 | 42,449 | 504,055 |
| LONDON WIDGETS LTD. | 34,140 | | |
| MUM'S WIDGET CO. | 27,462 | 25,161 | 50,648 |
| OXFORD WIDGETS | | 12,979 | 89,664 |
| TRICOLOR WIDGETS | 38,675 | 21,018 | 56,229 |
| WARSAW WIDGETS | 162,978 | 22,199 | 10,852 |
| WIDGET O THE MERSEY | 2,987 | 10,494 | 58,864 |
| WIDGETS ON THE WEB | 222,248 | 15,729 | 71,354 |
| FAR EAST | 75,452 | 73,314 | 108,095 |
| ABC WIDGET CO | 1,359 | 31,722 | |
| CEBU WIDGET CO | 49,749 | 35,051 | 25,383 |
| HONG KONG WIDGETS | 24,345 | 3,432 | 29,905 |
| YAMATA WIDGET LTD. | | 3,110 | 52,807 |
| NORTH AMERICA | 623,962 | 297,991 | 753,858 |
| BIG RIVER WIDGETS | 40,472 | 25,500 | 69,942 |
| BRIDGE THINGS | | 24,762 | 2,036 |
| GATOR WIDGETS | 1,119 | 18,944 | 46,308 |
| LAST RAILWAY WIDGETS | 57,322 | | |
| LOTS OF WIDGETS | 22,887 | 35,632 | 57,545 |
| MOUNTAIN WIDGETS | 97,854 | 20,615 | 54,768 |
| PATRIOT'S WIDGET CO. | 3,882 | 5,719 | 9,804 |
| THE LITTLE WIDGET | 26,799 | 35,126 | 32,712 |
| WE'VE GOT WIDGETS | 1,164 | 9,568 | 45,152 |
| WIDGET AIR | | 9,330 | 24,491 |
| WIDGET SUPPLY CO. | 89,818 | | |
| WIDGETS BY THE BAY | 11,735 | 15,559 | 108,742 |
| WIDGETS DE MEXICO | 73,372 | 52,251 | 87,228 |
| WIDGETS MARKET | | 33,110 | 115,785 |
| WIDGETS R US | 77,688 | 205 | 11,355 |
| WIDGETS SA | 2,265 | | |
| WIDGETS Y GADGETS | 73,901 | 130 | 41,853 |
| WILD WEST WIDGETS | 2,824 | 5,008 | |
| WONDER WIDGETS | 38,860 | 6,533 | 46,136 |
| SOUTH AMERICA | 155,479 | 179,161 | 70,861 |
| REPUBLIC WIDGETS | 127,572 | 136,297 | 13,908 |
| RIO WIDGETS | 22,538 | | |
| THING'S | 5,369 | 42,864 | 56,953 |

**FIGURE 15-6.** *An outline crosstab*

## Formats

The fourth tab in the Options dialog box is the Formats tab. This tab allows you to view the currently defined formats for five of the most common worksheet options and for determining what Discoverer will display when null values are returned in your query. Figure 15-7 shows the Formats tab.

If you want to amend the current default format of one of the five options described next, select the format you want to amend and click Change. This opens the relevant Edit dialog box. These were described in detail in Chapter 6.

To reset an option to Discoverer's default, select the format you want to change and click the Reset button.

The five default options you can set are as follows:

- **Data** Setting this controls how your data will look onscreen. You can set font, alignment, and background color. The Discoverer default is Arial 10 point, in a regular typeface, left justified, using black text on a white background.
- **Headings** Setting this controls how your column headings will look onscreen. You can set font, alignment, and background color. The Discoverer default is Arial 10 point, in a regular typeface, center justified, using black text on a light gray background.

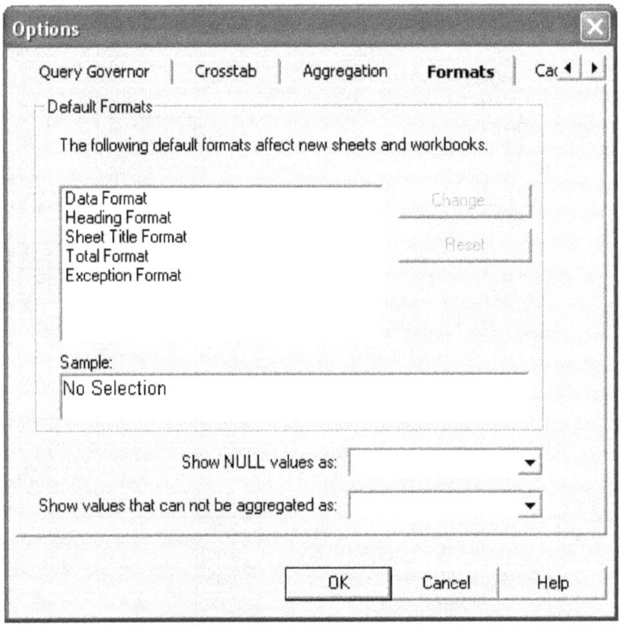

**FIGURE 15-7.** *The Desktop Options dialog box Formats tab*

- **Sheet Titles** Setting this controls how your sheet titles will look onscreen. You can set font and background color. The Discoverer default is Arial 10 point, in a bold typeface, center justified, on a white background.
- **Totals** Setting this controls how your totals will look onscreen. You can set font and background color. The Discoverer default is the same as for the data option (Arial 10 point, in a regular typeface, left justified, on a white background).
- **Exceptions** Setting this controls how your exceptions will look onscreen. You can set font and background color. The Discoverer default is Arial 10 point, in a regular typeface, left justified, on a red background.

The last option on the Formats tab, as shown in Figure 15-7, is for formatting null values. In the field entitled Show NULL values as, you can either select from the drop-down list or type in your default. Normally, a null value displays as nothing, but you can change this to any text value, number, or date that you want to see.

## Cache Settings

The Cache tab is where you set the options for memory and disk caching. On the tab shown in the illustration that follows, Discoverer allows you to set various caching options. You should not change any of these settings without the approval of your Discoverer administrator.

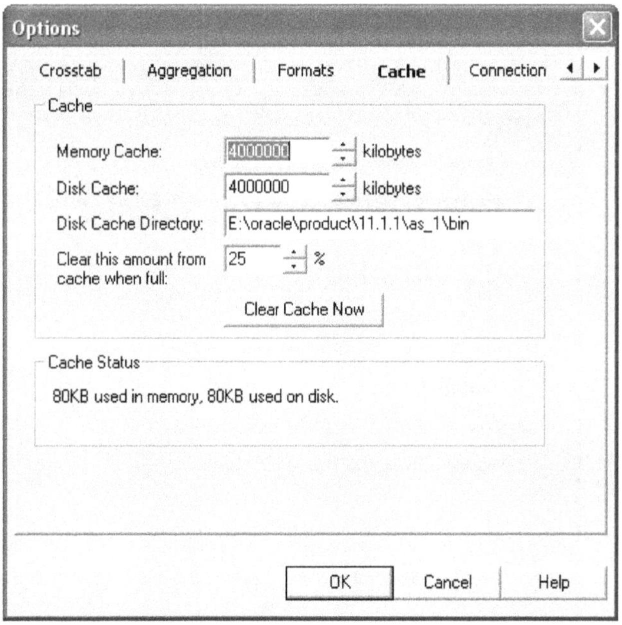

If you encounter errors such as "Cannot create virtual memory swap file" or "No data can be retrieved because the disk is full," your settings may need changing. However, as stated, do not attempt to make these changes without consulting your Discoverer administrator.

The default settings that you see have been well thought out by Oracle and rarely need changing. These are not settings you should tinker with, and you should never lower the settings from their defaults.

## Connection

The Connection tab is where you set the connection options. You choose whether to connect to standard or Oracle Applications EULs. There are three choices.

- Connect To Standard EULs
- Connect To Applications EULs
- Connect To Both Standard And Applications EULs

If you choose to connect to an Oracle Applications EUL, you will need to give the application's gateway user ID and password as well as the foundation name. The typical values for these are

- **Gateway user ID/password:** applsyspub/pub
- **Foundation name:** apps

You should not change any of these settings without the approval of your Discoverer administrator.

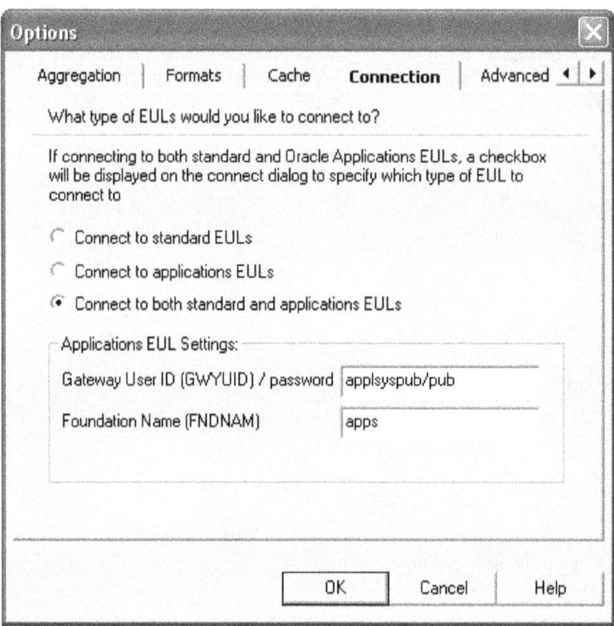

## Advanced

On the Advanced tab, as shown in Figure 15-8, Discoverer allows you to turn on or turn off automatic querying and the trapping of join errors.

The options for the Advanced tab are as follows:

- **Disable Automatic Querying** Check this box if you want to prevent Discoverer from automatically requerying the database after you have made changes to the worksheet. With this box checked, you will need to manually refresh the worksheet. We do not recommend that you check this box without approval from your Discoverer administrator.
- **Disable Fan-Trap Detection** Check this box if you want to prevent Discoverer from detecting fan traps. Fan traps were covered in detail in Chapter 10. Unless you are using Discoverer version Desktop 4.1 or newer, we do not recommend you check this box. In any case, you should not check this without approval from your Discoverer administrator.
- **Disable Multiple Join Path Detection** Check this box if you want to prevent Discoverer from detecting multiple join paths. This topic was also discussed in detail in Chapter 10. Do not check this box without approval from your Discoverer administrator.

## EUL

On the EUL tab, as shown in Figure 15-9, Discoverer allows you to change the End User Layer you are using. This feature is primarily used by the Discoverer administrator, who needs access to both development and production Discoverer End User Layers. Unless you are a very experienced

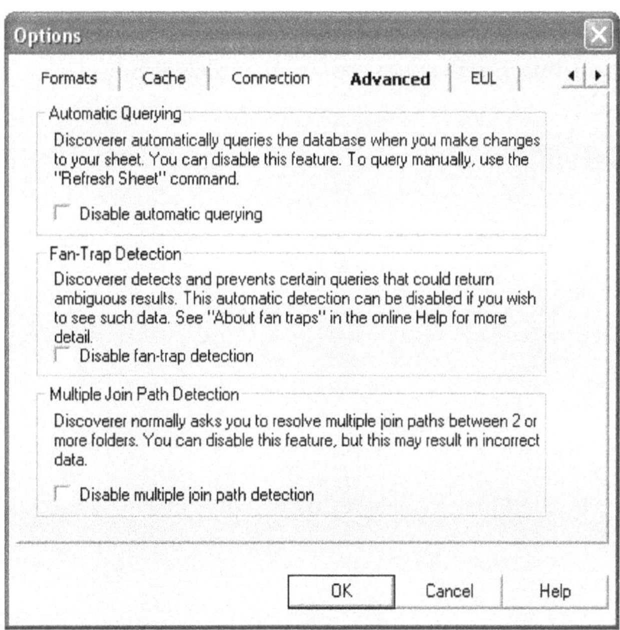


**FIGURE 15-8.** *The Desktop Options dialog box Advanced tab*

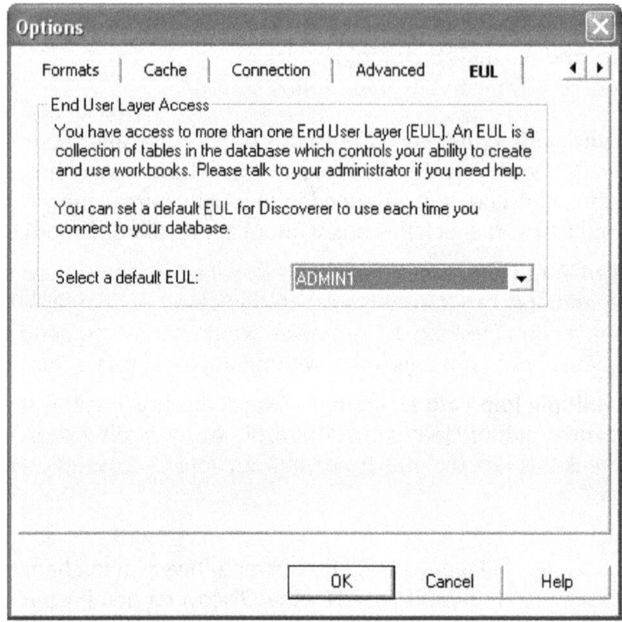


**FIGURE 15-9.** *The Desktop Options dialog box EUL tab*

user, you should not attempt to change the default setting. If you are unsure about what EUL should be the default, check with your Discoverer administrator.

# Plus Options

The Plus Options dialog box has six tabs. The six tabs are as follows:

- General
- Query Governor
- Sheet Format
- Formats
- Advanced
- EUL

Our tutorial on the Plus Options dialog box will begin with the General tab.

## General

The General tab is for setting up preferences for how and when your workbooks run. Figure 15-10 shows the General tab in Plus.

As you can see in Figure 15-10, there are three radio buttons to choose from. They are as follows:

- **Run Query Automatically** When you open a workbook, Discoverer will automatically run the active worksheet if you select this option. Discoverer will not run any of the other worksheets until you click the corresponding worksheet tab.
- **Don't Run Query (Leave Sheet Empty)** When you open a workbook, Discoverer will not run any of the worksheets if you select this option. You will, however, be in the active worksheet with no data displayed.
- **Ask For Confirmation** When you open a workbook, Discoverer will ask for confirmation that you want to run the active worksheet. Clicking Yes will run the worksheet; clicking No will not.

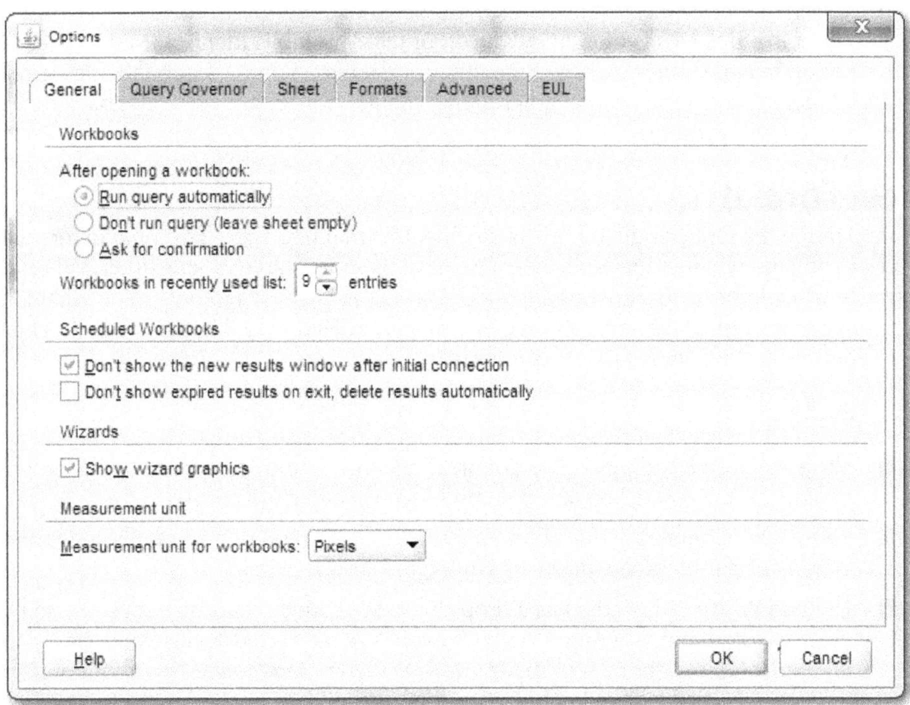


**FIGURE 15-10.** *The Plus Options dialog box General tab*

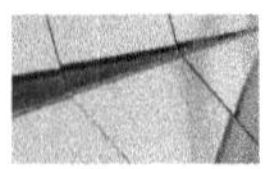

**NOTE**
*Because Discoverer has sticky features, it remembers the last worksheet that was opened in the workbook. This worksheet is called the active worksheet. We think the best option to choose is Ask For Confirmation. If you are anything like us, you don't remember which worksheet you last had open. By selecting this option, you have the chance to choose whether Discoverer runs the active worksheet. If you are not sure what the active worksheet does, click No when prompted and then open the Edit Sheet dialog box and check it out. With the other options, you could be waiting for a query to run when it is not even the one you need. You can now use the slightly improved Workbook navigator in Plus to select the worksheet you want to open.*

The last area in the General tab is a check box for showing graphics in the Workbook Wizard. Graphics use a tremendous amount of system resources and can seriously decrease performance. If you have a slow-running computer or are querying over long distances, we recommend you deselect this option.

## Query Governor

The second of the Plus tabs is the Query Governor tab. This tab is identical to the Query Governor tab in Desktop in appearance and functionality. For details on the Desktop tab, please refer to the Desktop "Query Governor" section earlier in this chapter. You should also refer back to Figure 15-2 to see the Query Governor tab.

## Sheet Format

The third tab in the Options dialog box is the Sheet Format tab. There are some differences in this tab, depending on whether the worksheet you have open is a table or a crosstab. When there is a difference, we will bring this to your attention. This tab is also used to determine what Discoverer will display when null values are returned in your query. Figure 15-11 shows the Sheet tab.

The options for the Sheet tab are as follows:

### Table Headers

- **Show Column Headings** This option allows you to turn on or turn off the column headings. When checked, the column headings will be displayed.
- **Show Row Numbers** This option allows you to turn on or turn off the row numbers. When checked, the row numbers will be displayed.
- **Column Width** This area has a drop-down list. You can choose between Use Default Width (Faster) and Use Auto Width (Slower). We have tried both settings and have seen no appreciable difference in speed. However, if you are concerned about performance, you should use the default width as recommended by Oracle. Use Default Width (Faster) will size the columns by the column heading width, while Use Auto Width (Slower) will format the size by either the widest column heading or the widest data item in the column.

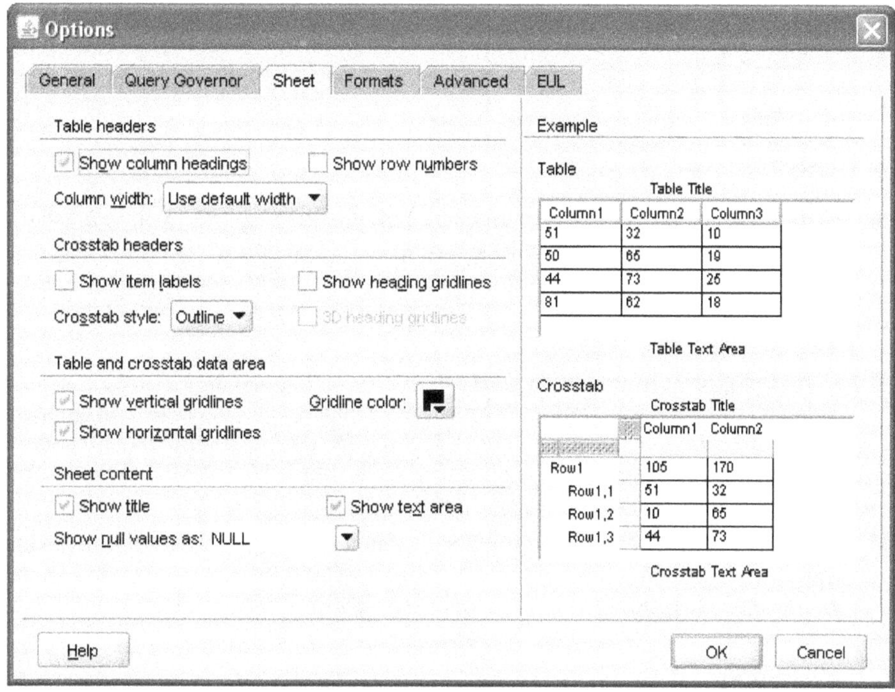


**FIGURE 15-11.** *The Plus Options dialog box Sheet tab*

## Crosstab Headers

- **Show Item Labels** This option allows you to turn on or turn off the item labels. When checked, the item labels will be displayed.
- **Show Heading Gridlines** This option allows you to turn on or turn off the heading gridlines. When checked, the heading gridlines will be displayed.
- **Crosstab Style** This area has a drop-down list. You can choose between outline or inline crosstab styles. Figure 15-5 showed an inline crosstab where the first child record is on the same row as the parent record. Figure 15-6 showed the same crosstab as an outline crosstab where the first child record is one row lower than the parent record.
- **3D Heading Gridlines** Use this check box to display the crosstab heading gridlines in 3D. This check box is enabled only when the Show Heading Gridlines check box has been selected.

## Table and Crosstab Detail Area

- **Show Vertical Gridlines** Here you can turn on or turn off the vertical gridlines. When checked, the vertical gridlines will be displayed.

- **Show Horizontal Gridlines** Here you can turn on or turn off the horizontal gridlines. When checked, the horizontal gridlines will be displayed.
- **Gridline Color** Here you can choose to use a color other than black for your gridline colors. Click the button to open a palette of colors or create a custom color for your gridlines.

### Sheet Content Area

- **Show Title** Here you can turn on or turn off the title display of your worksheets. When checked, the worksheet title will be displayed. When you uncheck this box, the Title check box will be unchecked by default when you create new worksheets. If you elect to not show titles by default, you can turn on titles for a specific worksheet by using View | Title from the menu bar.
- **Show Text Area** Here you can turn on or turn off the text area display of your worksheets. When checked, the worksheet text area will be displayed. When you uncheck this box, the Text area check box will be unchecked by default when you create new worksheets. If you elect to not show the text area by default, you can turn it on for a specific worksheet by using View | Text Area from the menu bar.
- **Show Null Values As** This option allows you to either select from the drop-down list or type in your default. Normally, a null value displays as nothing, but you can change this to any text value, number, or date that you want to see. The drop-down list contains these values:
  - **Blank** Nothing will be displayed.
  - **NULL** The word *NULL* will be displayed.
  - **–** The dash character will be displayed.
  - **0** A zero will be displayed. Please note that this is the zero character, not the number that is being displayed instead of the NULL value. The underlying value is still NULL, so you may need to watch for this when creating calculations.
  - **N.A.** The characters *N.A.* will be displayed.

## Formats

The fourth tab in the Options dialog box is the Formats tab. This tab allows you to view the currently defined formats for seven of the most common worksheet options. Figure 15-12 shows the Formats tab.

If you want to amend the current format of one of the seven options described next, click the Change button. To reset the option to Discoverer's default, click the Reset button.

The seven default options you can set are as follows:

- **Data Format** Setting this controls how your data will look onscreen. You can set font, alignment, and background color.
- **Heading Format** Setting this controls how your column headings will look onscreen.
- **Total Format** Setting this controls how your totals will look onscreen.

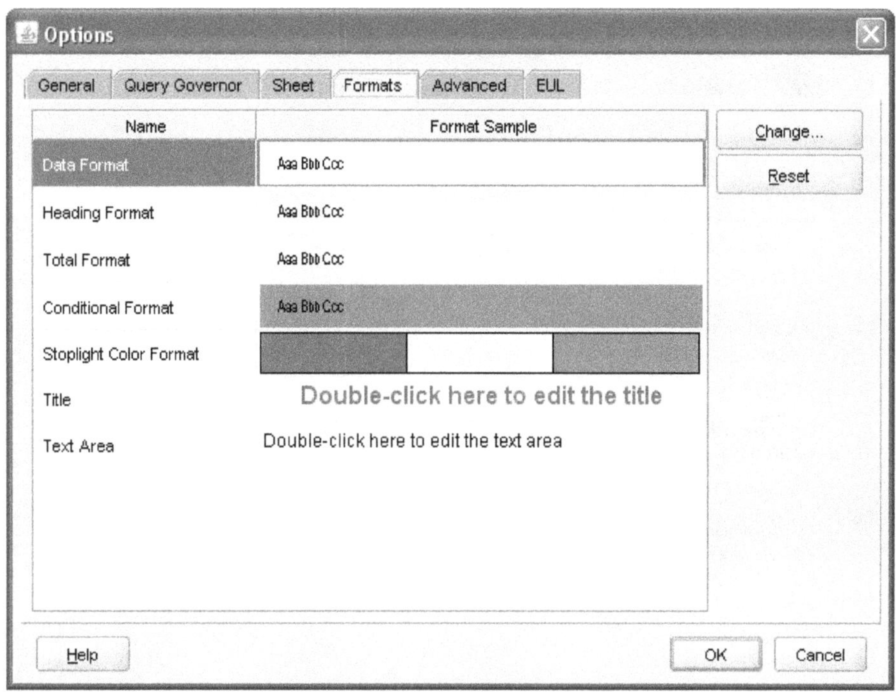


**FIGURE 15-12.** *The Plus Options dialog box Formats tab*

- **Conditional Format** Setting this controls how your conditional formats will look onscreen.
- **Stoplight Color Format** Setting this controls how your stoplight formats will look onscreen.
- **Title** Setting this controls how your title will look onscreen.
- **Text Area** Setting this controls how your text area will look onscreen.

# Advanced

The fifth tab in the Options dialog box is the Advanced tab, as shown in Figure 15-13. Discoverer allows you to turn on or turn off automatic querying and the trapping of join errors.

The options for the Advanced tab are as follows:

- **Disable Automatic Querying** Check this box if you want to prevent Discoverer from automatically requerying the database after you have made changes to the worksheet. With this box checked, you will need to manually refresh the worksheet. We do not recommend that you check this box without approval from your Discoverer administrator.

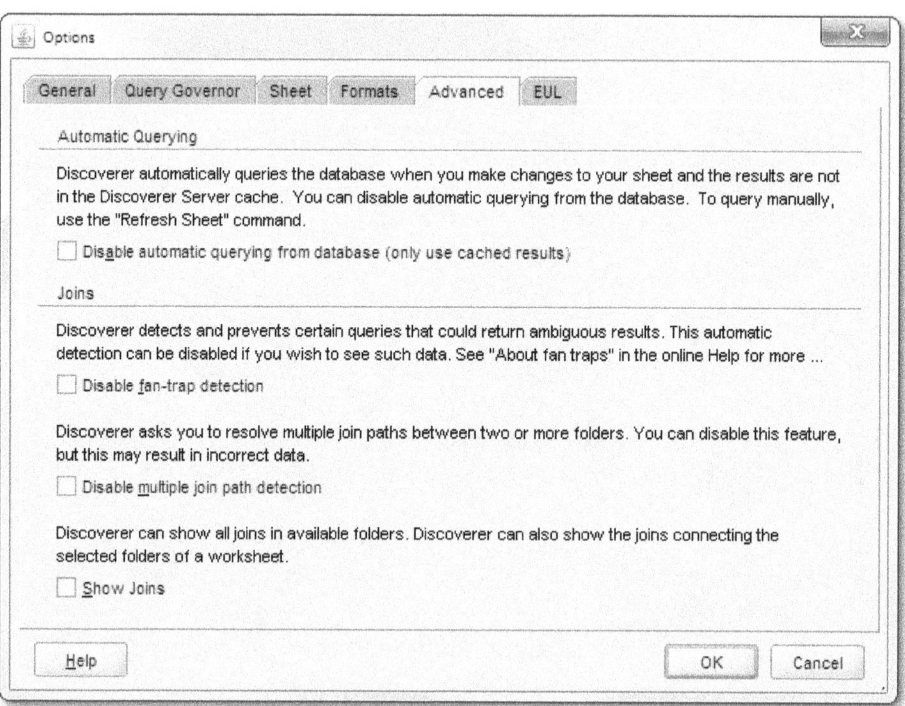


**FIGURE 15-13.** *The Plus Options dialog box Advanced tab*

- **Disable Fan-Trap Detection** Check this box if you want to prevent Discoverer from detecting fan traps. Fan traps were covered in detail in Chapter 10. We do recommend you disable your fan-trap detection without approval from your Discoverer administrator.
- **Disable Multiple Join Path Detection** Check this box if you want to prevent Discoverer from detecting multiple join paths. This topic was also discussed in detail in Chapter 10. Do not check this box without approval from your Discoverer administrator
- **Show Joins** Check this box if you want to have Discoverer show you the joins that are in use between the various folders. This can be very useful for troubleshooting troublesome reports. We like this option and usually have it enabled.

## EUL

The sixth tab in the Options dialog box is the EUL tab. This tab in Plus is identical to the EUL tab in Desktop in both appearance and functionality. For details on this tab, please refer to the Desktop "EUL" section of this chapter. Also, refer back to Figure 15-9 to see the EUL tab.

# The Toolbar

For the sake of not wanting to miss anything, we are adding this section on the toolbar. We are the types who, when we get new software, point at all of the buttons on the toolbar to see what they are for. If you are used to working in a Windows environment, you may have done the same. If not, you might not be in the habit of "checking out" the toolbar.

Many of the buttons on the toolbar have been covered in the preceding chapters. However, we will show them all here as a reference guide.

# The Discoverer Desktop Toolbar

The Discoverer Desktop toolbar buttons are grouped in a logical manner and in a very similar order to other Windows programs. The toolbar has been divided into five sections, so we will show them to you by these sections.

## Workbook Section of the Desktop Toolbar

The first section of the toolbar is used for managing workbooks: opening, saving, and printing. The following illustration shows the first section of the toolbar:

The workbook section of the Desktop toolbar has the following five buttons:

- **New Workbook** Opens the Workbook Wizard.
- **Open Workbook** Opens the Open Workbook dialog box.
- **Save** Saves the workbook. If the workbook has not already been saved, the Save Workbook dialog box will open.
- **Print** Prints the current worksheet.
- **Print Preview** Displays how the current worksheet will print. When the Print Preview dialog opens, it has the following seven buttons:
    - **Print** This prints the worksheet.
    - **Next Page** If the worksheet has more than one page, this button allows you to see the next page. If there are no more pages or there is only one page, the button is grayed out. You must navigate one page at a time.
    - **Prev Page** If the worksheet has more than one page and you are not currently previewing the first page, this button allows you to see the previous page. If you are already previewing the first page, the button is grayed out. You must navigate one page at a time.
    - **Two Page** If the worksheet has more than one page, this button will allow you to view two pages side by side. If there is only one page, the button is grayed out. If you are viewing two pages at a time, the button gets renamed to One Page. Clicking One Page returns you to previewing one page at a time.

- **Zoom In** Click this button to zoom in to see the page in a bigger font. Discoverer allows you to zoom in twice. If you have already zoomed in twice, this button will be grayed out.
- **Zoom Out** Click this button to zoom out to see the page in a smaller font. Discoverer allows you to zoom out several times. If you have already zoomed out back to the original size or if you have never zoomed in, this button will be grayed out.
- **Close** Click this button or press the ESC key to exit the Print Preview dialog.

### Worksheet Section of the Desktop Toolbar

The second section of the toolbar is used for managing worksheets: creating new worksheets, editing, copying, drilling, and refreshing. The following illustration shows the worksheet section of the toolbar:

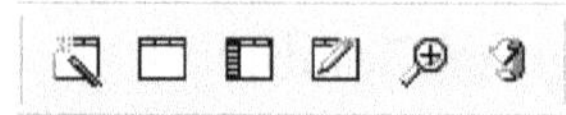

The worksheet section of the Desktop toolbar has the following six buttons:

- **New Sheet** Opens the New Sheet Wizard
- **Duplicate as Table** Opens the Duplicate as Table dialog box
- **Duplicate as Crosstab** Opens the Duplicate as Crosstab dialog box
- **Edit Sheet** Opens the Edit Sheet dialog box
- **Drill** Drills to the data for the column selected
- **Refresh** Refreshes the data in the worksheet

### Graph Section of the Desktop Toolbar

The third section of the toolbar has only one button and is used for managing graphs. The first time you click this button, the Graph Wizard will open. Once a graph has been created, the button will open the graph.

### Sorting Section of the Desktop Toolbar

The fourth section of the toolbar is used for formatting exceptions and sorting. The fourth section of the toolbar is shown here:

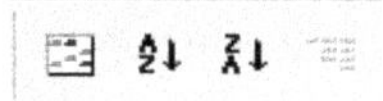

The sorting section of the Desktop toolbar has the following four buttons:

- **Format Exceptions** Opens the Exceptions dialog box
- **Sort Low to High** Sorts the data in the column selected in ascending order

- **Sort High to Low** Sorts the data in the column selected in descending order
- **Group Sort** Group sorts the data in the column selected

### Excel Section of the Desktop Toolbar

The fifth section of the toolbar is used for exporting the data in the worksheet into an Excel worksheet. If there is more than one worksheet in a workbook, Discoverer will export the first sheet by the same name as the workbook. After the first worksheet has been exported, you will be prompted to name the additional worksheets to be exported.

## The Discoverer Plus Toolbar

The Discoverer Plus toolbar buttons are grouped into five sections, much the same as the Desktop toolbar. There are a few differences in the Plus toolbar because of differences in the functionality of the two products. Just as we did when we explained the Desktop toolbar, we will show the Plus toolbar to you by sections.

### Workbook Section of the Plus Toolbar

The first section of the toolbar is used for managing workbooks: opening, saving, printing, and print preview. The illustration, as shown here, displays the first section of the toolbar.

The workbook section of the Plus toolbar has the following five buttons:

- **New Workbook** Opens the Workbook Wizard.
- **Open Workbook** Opens the Open Workbook dialog box.
- **Save** Saves the workbook. If the workbook has not already been saved, the Save Workbook dialog box will open.
- **Print** Prints the workbook.
- **Print Preview** Shows a print preview of the workbook.

### Worksheet Section of the Plus Toolbar

The second section of the toolbar has five buttons. These buttons are used for managing worksheets: creating new worksheets, editing, and copying. Unlike in Desktop, you cannot drill from the toolbar in Plus, and the Refresh button has been moved into its own section. Oracle has also added an extra button to this section. This extra button opens the Table Layout dialog box. The worksheet section of the toolbar is shown here:

The worksheet section of the Plus toolbar has the following buttons:

- **Add Worksheet** Opens the New Sheet Wizard. It also has a drop-down with two additional options, as shown here:

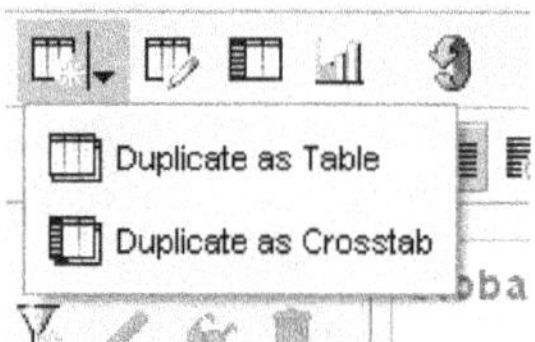


  - **Duplicate As Table** Opens the Duplicate as Table dialog box.
  - **Duplicate As Crosstab** Opens the Duplicate as Crosstab dialog box.
- **Edit Worksheet** Opens the Edit Sheet dialog box.
- **Edit Table/Crosstab** Opens the Table/Crosstab Layout dialog box.

### Refresh Data Section of the Plus Toolbar

The third section of the toolbar has only one button, which is used to refresh the data in the query.

### Sort Section of the Plus Toolbar

The fourth section of the toolbar is used for sorting. The following illustration shows the sort section of the toolbar:

The sort section of the Plus toolbar has the following three buttons:

- **Sort Low to High** Sorts the column in ascending order
- **Sort High to Low** Sorts the column in descending order
- **Group Sort** Places a group sort on the column

### Tools Section of the Plus Toolbar

The fifth section of the toolbar is used for opening five of the various tool dialog boxes. The buttons also have drop-down lists of common functions and can be used to create simple operations. The following illustration shows the tools section of the toolbar:

The tools section of the Plus toolbar has the following five buttons:

- **Totals** Opens the Totals dialog box
- **Percentages** Opens the Percentages dialog box
- **Calculations** Opens the Calculations dialog box
- **Conditions** Opens the Conditions dialog box
- **Parameters** Opens the Parameters dialog box

### Export Section of the Plus Toolbar

Plus has two export buttons in the sixth section of the toolbar. Using these buttons, you can export the data in the worksheet into an Excel worksheet or as an HTML page. The sixth section of the toolbar is shown here:

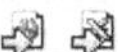

- **Export to HTML** We like the HTML option for distributing a worksheet's results. It is basically a snapshot of the worksheet that keeps all of the formatting.
- **Export to Excel** This option should be chosen when the data needs to be manipulated in some way. Most of the formatting is exported, but you may need to do some column resizing.

**NOTE**

*More export formats are available using the File | Export feature of the menu bar.*

### The Plus Graph Toolbar

The graph toolbar is available when the graph is activated. As you can see, you can do all of your manipulation of the graph from the toolbar. We think it is a great tool and allows you to make changes on the fly without any cumbersome dialog boxes. The buttons of the graph toolbar are covered in Chapter 7.

# The Discoverer Administrator

We cannot tell you everything that the Discoverer administrator does, but in this section we will try to give you a brief glimpse behind the scenes. We hope this will give you a better understanding and insight into the job that this person does. Later in this section, we will outline just what the Discoverer administrator can do for you. Here, you will find a list of all of the things that your Discoverer administrator can change on your behalf.

## The Discoverer Administrator's Role

As far as Discoverer is concerned, the most important person you will come into contact with is your Discoverer administrator. Without this person, there will be no Discoverer. The role of the Discoverer administrator is a very specialized role indeed. Each company has at least one, and all of the users are thankful that they are there. The Discoverer administrator understands how to design business areas that support your company's way of doing things. At least one of the Discoverer administrators is also a database guru. This is the person who knows everything about your company's databases—where they are located, how they are stored, and how the data is all linked together. It is not required that every Discoverer administrator be a database guru or even a DBA. The only prerequisite is that they understand the portion of data (tables, views, and joins) for which they are responsible. In addition, users who understand the data can share some of the responsibilities of administering the Discoverer End User Layer. For example, a user who understands the business terms used by the rest of the user community could be responsible for defining descriptions for folders and items.

Being able to design business areas and being a database guru are just two of the roles. The third role of the Discoverer administrator is somewhat more abstract than the other two, both of which are primarily technical. This third role requires good interpersonal skills and a really good sense of business acumen, something not usually associated with "techies." The Discoverer administrator knows the decision makers within your company. They are able to talk with users at their level and in their language, omitting the jargon and techno-babble that is the domain of programmers. We feel strongly that this third role of the Discoverer administrator is the most important and cannot be overemphasized. Having built a good rapport with the business management, the Discoverer administrator is in a perfect position to identify what data is needed within your business areas.

## You Can Help Your Discoverer Administrator Identify the Data Needed

Before your company makes Discoverer available to you, the user, it is your Discoverer administrator's responsibility to identify the data that is needed. They do this by talking with you and your fellow co-workers.

If you are lucky enough to be selected as a key user during the analysis phase, you can help your Discoverer administrator by having answers to some of the following questions:

- What reports do you create today, and who do you send them to?
- What is wrong with the data that you have today, and how would you like to see it made better in the future?
- Do you know where the data is kept today? Is it kept in a database, or do you perhaps use spreadsheets?
- Do you have an EDI system and need Discoverer to take a feed from that?
- Are you able to define any corporate algorithms or calculations that you want to see standardized?

Do not keep quiet at this point. If you do not understand something at this stage, be sure to ask. Waiting until you have access to Discoverer is far too late.

Once the data has been identified, your Discoverer administrator will design the business areas that you will eventually see inside Discoverer. These are designed on paper first and are refined many times before the admin edition is even touched! It is a very complex and expensive process to unbundle badly created business areas, even with a product as good as Discoverer. Time spent analyzing and designing will repay itself over and over again.

Once the business areas have been created and you have a working system, the fun really starts. No Discoverer system can ever be considered finished. It is your responsibility to ensure that the system delivers what you need. You must keep in touch with your Discoverer administrator and be aware what they can do for you.

## What Can the Discoverer Administrator Do for You?

Perhaps the most interesting part of the interaction between yourself and your Discoverer administrator is knowing what they can do for you. Using this knowledge, you should be better able to make requests of your Discoverer administrator. They can then take your request, act on it, and make modifications on your behalf. These modifications will make your life easier and enable you to write more cost-effective queries.

The following is a list of all the items that your Discoverer administrator has control over. Use this list to see what your Discoverer administrator can do for you.

- **Adding new users** The Discoverer administrator is responsible for adding new users to the system. Whether they do it or whether the DBA is assigned the task is irrelevant. Any request for access should initially be directed to the Discoverer administrator. If you are able to specify exactly what type of access is required, this will make the job that much easier.
- **Granting access to business areas** If you find that you do not have access to a business area that you need, you should raise a request to your Discoverer administrator to have that access granted. Perhaps you have changed your job, or maybe your responsibilities have been extended.
- **Granting privileges within the user edition** If you feel that your privileges are not sufficient, you should discuss this with your Discoverer administrator. On the Privileges tab of the Discoverer Admin Edition, your Discoverer administrator grants access to the Discoverer 11g End User Edition. Having granted you access to run the End User Edition, your Discoverer administrator also determines whether you can create or edit a query, whether you can drill, whether you can share or schedule workbooks, and whether you can save workbooks to the database. The Discoverer administrator Privileges tab is shown here:

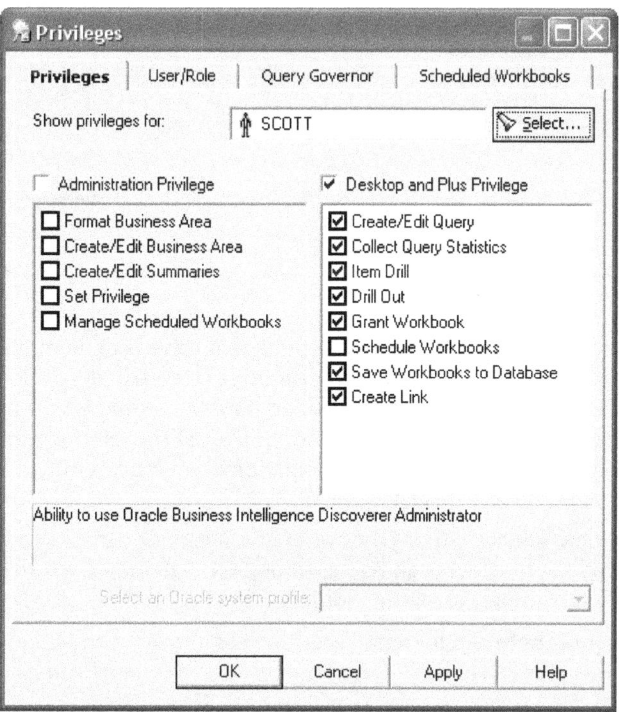

- **Adding meaningful descriptions to business areas, folders, and data items** A very simple, yet very useful, means of helping you understand your data better is to add descriptions to the data objects. This adds no overhead to the processing of the system, yet it is incredible to us how many business areas and folders are not given meaningful descriptions. In the following illustration, you can see that a description has been created for the main business area of our tutorial database. Similar descriptions can be created for each folder, making it a lot easier for you to understand what the folder contains.

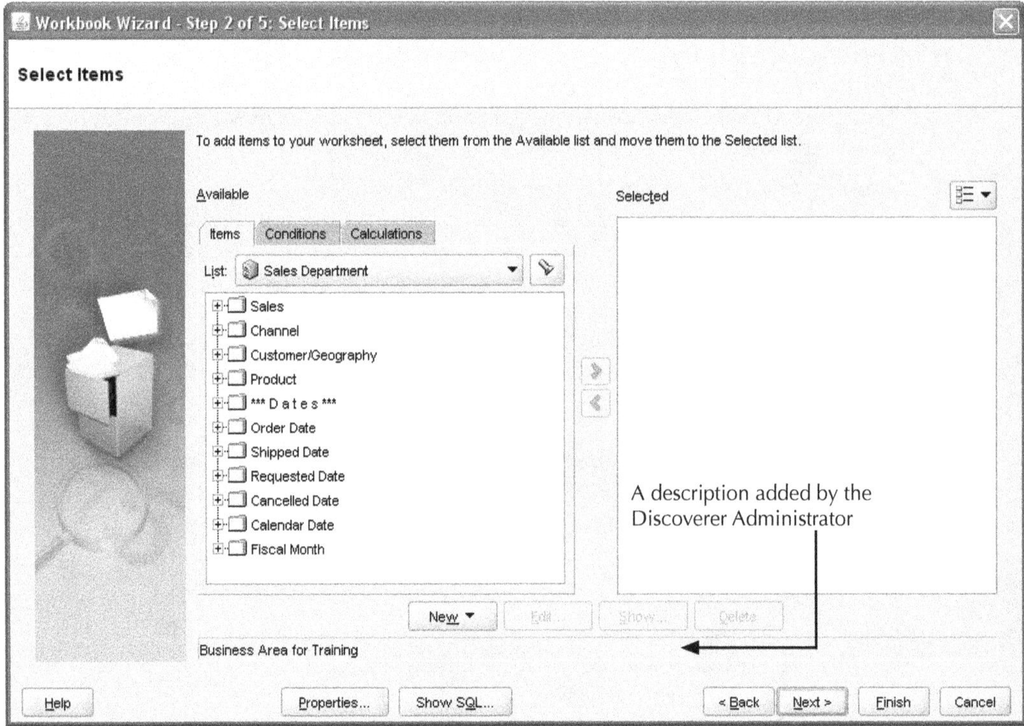


- **Adding new items to folders** If you think that there is an item missing from a folder, you should talk to your Discoverer administrator. They are able to add new items to folders. Adding items to a data warehouse folder, however, could be a lengthy process. If the item already exists in your warehouse and your Discoverer administrator has determined that it does not contain sensitive information, then it takes only a few minutes for the administrator to make this item available.
- **Creating new folders** Your Discoverer administrator can create new folders within Discoverer. These folders can be based on SQL statements, extracts from the database, or even items contained in existing folders.
- **Creating joins between folders** There will be times when Discoverer deactivates folders. This is because there is no join between the items you have chosen and the

deactivated folder containing the item you want. It may be possible for your Discoverer administrator to create a join for you, thus enabling you to choose the item you want.

- **Creating lists of values** Many users do not know that the lists of values you see inside Discoverer have actually been created by the administrator. It is a misconception that these lists are created by the database—they are not. If you see a data item in a folder and you think that there should be a list of values, contact your administrator and request that one be created.
- **Creating alternative sorts** Another way that your administrator can help you is by creating alternative sorts. An example of an alternative sort is sorting the months of the year into the order in which they occur. Month names are text values, and a text list would place January after February. Your Discoverer administrator can create a custom sort, placing the months in the order in which they occur. You can even have the months sorted by fiscal year.
- **Creating new items based on calculations** If you have standardized calculations within your company, it makes sense to include these as items in Discoverer. Your administrator can create these custom calculations and add them as items to folders. You can then select these new items, saving you the step of creating the calculation in the query.
- **Creating new conditions** Another simple task for your Discoverer administrator is the creation of conditions. Perhaps you have a large list of part numbers, of which only a certain range of numbers are available for shipment to customers. The remainder could be components or for internal use only. Your Discoverer administrator can create a condition based on the part number, constraining the list to only those that are shippable. You would then be able to select this condition just as you would any item.
- **Creating drill hierarchies** One of the least-used features of Discoverer is the use of hierarchical drilling. This type of drill uses a predefined hierarchy of items, within which you can drill up or down by a click of the mouse. Typical hierarchies used are dates and geographic data, such as ZIP Code drilling up to State, State drilling up to Country, and so on. If you can define a drill of this type, your Discoverer administrator can build a hierarchy for you.
- **Modifying an item's type** A little-used function available to your Discoverer administrator is the ability to change an item's data type. If you always need to be able to manipulate a date—for example, as a string—you can ask your administrator to change the item's type.
- **Creating summary data** When reporting from transaction systems, you do not want to be querying from the detail tables if you can help it. This will cause long delays while querying and can seriously reduce the performance of your OLTP system. Your Discoverer administrator can create summary folders that contain preaggregated data. If these have been created for you, your Discoverer administrator will advise you of the correct setting to make in the summary data section of the Query Governor tab of the Options dialog box. By default, summary administration is transparent to users and probably does not require any action.
- **Rearranging the order of folders in a business area** When you select items from folders, in a business area it is nice to see the folders arranged in an order that makes sense to you. For example, in an HR system, you always want to add the employee name and

identification number from the Employee Info folder first, then you want to add salary information from the Salary folder, and, last of all, you want to add training information from the Training folder. The Discoverer manager can make this easier by putting the folders in that order in the business area.

- **Rearranging the order of items in a folder** When you are querying from a folder, you may notice that you are always scrolling down the list of items to get the one you want. You can ask your Discoverer administrator to change the ordering of the items within the folder. This has no impact on the system, yet it can be a tremendous timesaver.
- **Changing refresh cycles** Many Discoverer systems are based on either a snapshot of the OLTP system or data warehouses. Both of these types of databases use a refresh mechanism to update. If you believe that the refresh schedule is insufficient, you can ask your Discoverer administrator to change it. Perhaps you would like an extra collection during the lunch period. It is possible that your Discoverer administrator will be able to accommodate you, if your justification is strong. Always remember that it doesn't hurt to ask; your Discoverer administrator can only say no!
- **Allowing scheduling of workbooks** Not all users are granted permission to schedule workbooks. Not all users need to schedule workbooks. If you believe that you should be given permission to schedule, you should bring that to the attention of your Discoverer administrator. You may be asked to provide justification. The screen that your Discoverer administrator uses to control scheduling is shown here:

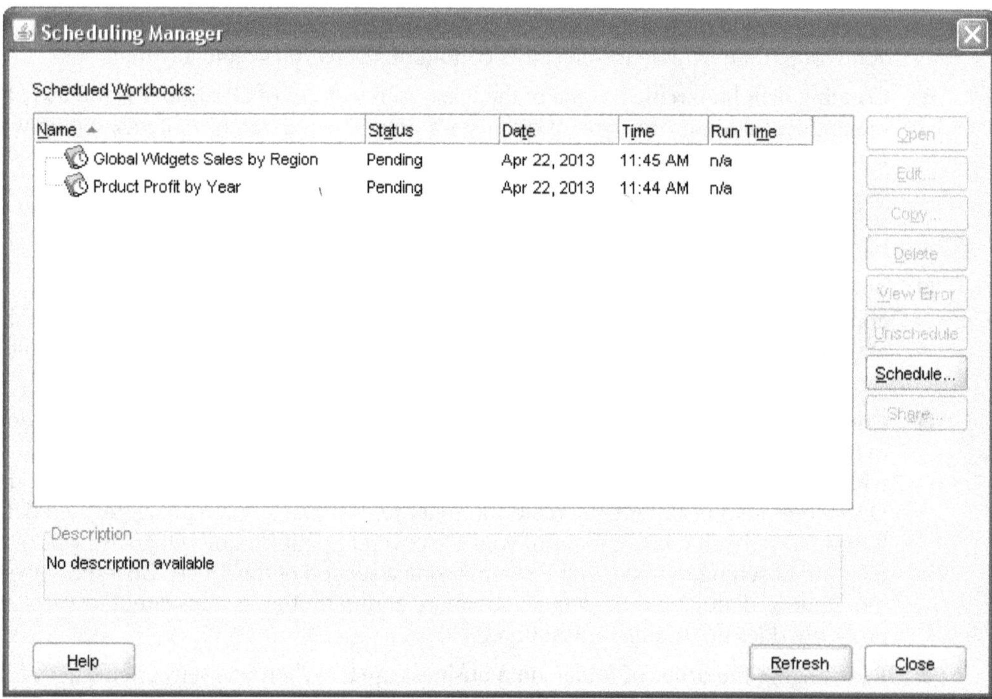

- **Creating new functions** Discoverer already has a vast array of functions at your disposal. Refer to Appendix A for an alphabetical list of all the functions. However, sometimes you need a new function. Your Discoverer administrator has the ability to create new functions and make these available within the system. If you are familiar with SQL, you will notice that not all SQL functions are available in Discoverer. If there is a SQL function that you want to use, your Discoverer administrator might be able to add it.
- **Being another source of help** Your Discoverer administrator is an expert in Discoverer, and you should treat that person as a resource. If you are stuck with a tricky calculation or cannot define the right conditions, pick up the telephone.

# Discoverer Desktop Directory Structures

Two important directories must be set in order for Discoverer Desktop to work correctly. Your Discoverer administrator is responsible for determining the location of these directories. The two vital directories are as follows:

- **Discoverer's default directory for opening files** On the General tab of the Discoverer Desktop Options dialog box is a placeholder for entering the default directory for opening files. If this directory is located on a shared drive—such as on a network, on a terminal server, or on a shared PC—your Discoverer administrator will help you determine the correct entry for this placeholder. They are also responsible for ensuring that you have the correct read and write access to this directory. If the directory is to be located on your local PC, you should use a folder such as c:\temp.
- **Discoverer's cache directory** On the Cache tab of the Discoverer Desktop Options dialog box is a placeholder for entering the default directory for disk caching. Unless advised by your Discoverer administrator, you should not change this directory.

**NOTE**
*If you have many users sharing drives, particularly when using terminal servers, you may want to consider not sharing the same cache drive between all users. The reasoning behind this is that no one can determine exactly when Discoverer will need the disk cache. If two users swap to disk at the same time, it is possible that the caching may get impacted, with the resulting crash of the system.*

## Terminal Server Directories

This section is applicable only if your company uses terminal servers for accessing Discoverer. When using these shared machines, your network administrator will not take kindly to your saving files all over their server. Your Discoverer administrator, therefore, will work with the network administrator to create directories into which you can save workbooks.

If you have been advised to use a certain directory for your files, please use it. It is not just out of courtesy that we say this, although this is certainly a consideration. The biggest concern we have is that your saved workbooks may get deleted if they are stored outside of the agreed area. Having spent a great deal of time making a query work, we are sure that the last thing you want right now is to start all over again!

## Summary

In this chapter, you learned how to use the Options dialog box in both versions of Discoverer. We showed you the various settings you can select to create defaults to customize Discoverer to meet your needs. Included in these options, you learned how to create default formats for some of the most common data types. You saw how to format tables and crosstabs to present your data better. We taught you which of these settings to use care in setting and when to contact your Discoverer administrator for assistance.

You were given a quick-reference guide to the Discoverer Desktop and Plus toolbars, with all of the functions. And finally, you learned about your Discoverer administrator. You learned about the privileges you can be granted and how the Discoverer administrator provides you with them. You also learned how you can help the Discoverer administrator to determine the kinds of data and business areas you will need to create your queries and reports. We showed you how a directory structure is set up in Discoverer and why it is important to save your workbooks to the correct directory folders.

# PART IV

# Using the Discoverer Administration Edition

# CHAPTER 16

# Getting Started in the Administration Edition

Welcome to the first of the chapters dedicated to the Discoverer Administrator tool. If you have never used the Discoverer Administrator tool, you are going to be surprised at how easy it is. In this chapter, we will teach you about the main features of the tool. We will then devote the rest of the chapter to showing you how to install the End User Layer and then build the business area that has been used throughout the end-user sections of this book. We will show you how to pull in objects from the database and then show you how to check the items that are used within the folders, making use of item separators to break up the items into logical groups or sets. In this chapter, you will also learn how to hook up Discoverer to an E-Business Suite database using Applications mode.

# Key Definitions

Before we get into using the tool, we will briefly describe some of the key definitions as used in Discoverer administration. You should read this section in conjunction with Chapter 3, where we explained the key definitions of the following:

- Workbooks and worksheets
- Queries
- Reports
- Libraries

## End User Layer

Commonly referred to as the EUL, the End User Layer is a metadata repository that stores all the object definitions used by Discoverer. Using the EUL, you hide the complexity of the underlying system from the users, allowing them to interact with the database using familiar business language and terms. A well-designed End User Layer means that users do not need to know the underlying structure of the database.

The End User Layer also protects and preserves the integrity of the database. This integrity is preserved because using Discoverer, neither the Discoverer manager nor any Discoverer end user can change the underlying database. The only thing the Discoverer manager can change is the End User Layer, with access to the underlying database being read-only.

But what does the End User Layer look like? The End User Layer is a series of approximately 50 tables and views that all begin with the characters *EUL5*. For example, the table that stores the users is called EUL5_EUL_USERS, while the table that stores the workbooks is called EUL5_WORKBOOKS.

The main way to maintain the End User Layer is to use the Discoverer Administrator tool when logged in as an administrator. You can also use the EUL Command Line utility for Java to manage the Discoverer EUL. While not as powerful as the Discoverer Administrator tool, this utility will allow you to perform many of the standard maintenance tasks such as authorizing users to access the EUL, exporting/importing EUL objects, and others. We do not cover the Command Line utility for Java in this book. If you want to learn more about it, we recommend you take a look at the Oracle Business Intelligence Discoverer EUL Command Line for Java user guide, which you can find on OTN.

As the administrator, you are responsible for maintaining the EUL and the conceptual view of the database. This conceptual view helps the end user navigate through the data more easily when performing queries. The EUL contains enhanced definitions of folders and their items, as well as the relationships between the folders, and other constructs that help users explore their data.

## Business Areas

A *business area* is a set of common, related information with a single business purpose in mind. One business area, for example, might be created for Accounting, while another might be created for Purchasing, with yet another created for Human Resources. End-user access is maintained by the Discoverer administrator. Business areas are organized into:

- **Folders** These are a collection of related items. Each folder can be thought of as being like a table in a database. There are three types of folders.
  - **Simple** A simple folder maps directly to a database object such as a table or a view.
  - **Custom** A custom folder is a single SQL statement that you type directly into Discoverer.
  - **Complex** A complex folder groups items from other folders.
- **Joins** These map the links between folders. Each join can be thought of as being like a join between tables in a database. Joins can be either predefined or user-defined. If the folders are based on database objects and if foreign-key/primary-key constraints exist between the objects, you can import the predefined joins for use within Discoverer. If no predefined constraints exist, you can manually create them. Joins can be either one-to-many or one-to-one. Discoverer also supports the concept of outer joins, although performance can deteriorate if they are used.
- **Items** These are components of a folder or worksheet. Each item can be thought of as being like a column in a database table. Folder items can be either predefined or user-defined. Predefined folder items are loaded from the database as part of the folder definition. User-defined folder items are manually created by the Discoverer administrator, as either a calculation or a condition. To the report writer, both of these are regarded as predefined and therefore reusable. Predefined worksheet items are loaded from the EUL. A user-defined worksheet item is manually created by the report writer and can be either a calculation, condition, or parameter. Items can be made to appear on various axes.

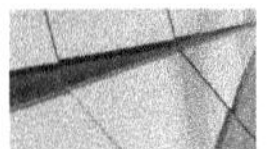

**NOTE**
*Discoverer Admin has no concept of a predefined parameter, so parameters must be created by the report writer directly within the workbook. As such, these parameters are not reusable and must be defined on a workbook-by-workbook basis.*

## Axes

You can think of an *axis* as being a placeholder into which an end user can position data within a worksheet. As part of the setup and maintenance of business areas, the Discoverer administrator gets to choose the default location for every item. During the creation of a report, the report writer chooses the axes where the data should be displayed, overriding the default assigned by the Discoverer administrator if need be. During the execution of a report, a report viewer can further customize the output to see the data displayed on yet a different axis. Every item must have a default axis, and every item used within a worksheet must be displayed on an axis. Discoverer uses four axes.

- **Page axis** This axis is used to break up a report into multiple pages. If you place, for example, a customer name in the page, Discoverer will display that customer's details only on the current page of the report. Discoverer will dynamically create a list of values (LOV) for every item that is placed on the page axis.

- **Top axis** This axis can be thought of as the column headings in a report. Moving an item to the top axis causes Discoverer to place the item's name in the column heading with each data value displayed in a different row.
- **Side axis** In a table worksheet, this is where Discoverer places the row numbers. In a crosstab, this is where the row headings are displayed. A user can drag an item from the top or page axis and place it on the side axis to create a crosstab or a pivot table. Such a worksheet must have at least one item on the side axis; otherwise, it cannot be constructed. Moving an item to the side axis causes Discoverer to place the item's name in the row heading with each data value displayed in a different column.

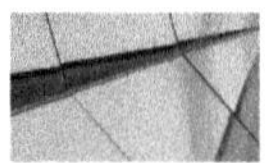

**NOTE**
*In reality, a top axis and a side axis don't really make a lot of sense in the case of a table, but we hope you understand what we are getting at.*

- **Data points** This axis is used to hold items that can be used for aggregation, such as totals and averages. A crosstab worksheet must have at least one data point; otherwise, it cannot be constructed.

Figure 16-1 shows the relationship between the various axes. It also shows the location of the title and text areas.

## Item Classes

*Item classes* are lists of values—drop-down lists that aid users when they are selecting items for a query. Lists of values are predefined and are created by the Discoverer manager. Not all items get a list of values to begin with, and if users see an item that does not have a list of values that they believe should have one, the user should contact the Discoverer administrator. We will discuss these in depth in Chapter 17.

## Hierarchies

A *hierarchy*, in Discoverer terms, is a default drill path between related items in a folder. Hierarchies can be used in Discoverer even when there is no relationship between the items in the database. Users can then roll up to see aggregated data or drill down to see detail data.

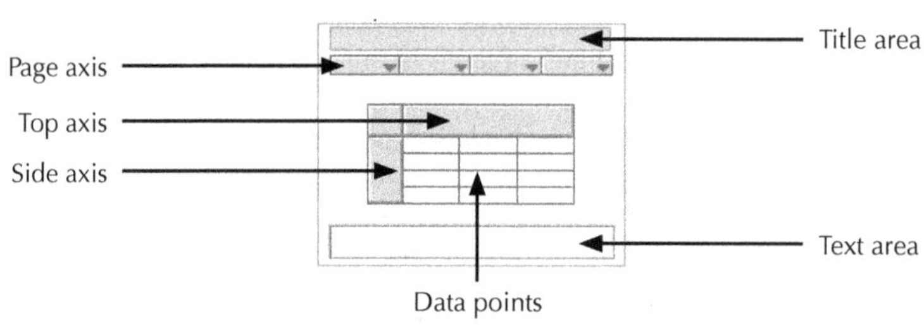


**FIGURE 16-1.** *Axes used in Discoverer*

Hierarchies are created by the Discoverer administrator and as such are predefined. Using a hierarchy, for example, a user could roll up from all the months in a year to just the year itself or drill down from one particular month to see all of the daily transactions for that month. In Discoverer, there are two types of hierarchy.

- **Item hierarchies** These map the relationship between items such as City, State, and Country, thus allowing end users to drill between those items.
- **Date hierarchies** These map the relationship between key time elements of a date such as Day, Month, Quarter, and Year. Date hierarchies work best when the fiscal year that you are using corresponds to the calendar year, such that Q1 runs from January to March, Q2 runs from April to June, and so on. While you can use a modified date hierarchy to create fiscal time hierarchies, we like to use item hierarchies to create hierarchies based on fiscal years that do not correspond to calendar years, such as when using a 4-4-5 notation, where quarters are determined by the number of weeks in the period.

The use of hierarchies is explained in detail in Chapter 17.

## Summaries

*Summaries* are preaggregated tables of results against which Discoverer can query. In database terms these are materialized views (MVs), and if they exist, the Oracle database optimizer will rewrite a user's query to go after an MV if it can be determined that it will satisfy the requirements. Discoverer can work with a preexisting MV, or it can even build it for itself, provided that the Discoverer administrator has been granted the required database privileges by the DBA. Within the Discoverer Administrator tool there is a Summary Wizard that allows the Discoverer administrator to analyze user queries to determine whether a summary table, MV, will help. Using this wizard, Discoverer can even create the materialized view and set up the automated refreshes for it. Discoverer has the ability to preaggregate data that is being used by user queries into prebuilt tables. Essentially, you are creating materialized views. You use these summary folders to improve query response time for your end users. The response time is improved because the query will use preaggregated and prejoined data rather than accessing the underlying database tables at run time. Summary management is discussed in detail in Chapter 21.

## Properties

Most of the components of the End User Layer have properties. These are placeholders for you to define additional characteristics about the component you are working with. Properties exist for business areas, folders, and items. We will discuss properties in detail in Chapter 17, with further comments in Chapter 18.

# Sticky Features

The Discoverer Administrator tool has a memory. From time to time, Discoverer will make a note in the system registry of "last used" options. The next time you are given a choice for one of these options, Discoverer will remember what you last did and default to that setting. We call this Discoverer's sticky feature.

# The Steps to a Successful Discoverer Implementation

There are six steps that you must follow if you are to implement Discoverer successfully.

1. Understand and anticipate user requirements.
2. Create the End User Layer.
3. Create a business area.
4. Refine the business area.
5. Grant access to the business area.
6. Deploy.

## Understand and Anticipate User Requirements

The Discoverer administrator should understand and anticipate user requirements, have knowledge of the application database, and be able to set up the relational structure in the EUL to best display the application data.

Of these tasks, perhaps the most difficult is to understand and anticipate user requirements. You need to be able to work with your users to analyze their data requests. At the very least, you will probably need to conduct interviews with your users to determine what it is that they are asking for. You need to be able to understand your business using the terminology of the end users, essentially being able to use user-speak when talking with your users and geek-speak when talking with others in your IT department.

Be wary, though, because users will usually demand everything and insist that it is delivered at breakneck speed. You will need to be a good mediator, setting reasonable expectations. Perhaps the best approach is to deliver the data in bite-size chunks as opposed to trying to deliver everything all at the same time.

During the discussion phase you should encourage your users to show you how they use the information that they currently have and what they have to do to make good reports out of it. Perhaps they cannot get any reports at the moment, which is why they approached you in the first place!

## Create the End User Layer

You must have an End User Layer before you can create a business area. We will walk you through the steps of creating your first End User Layer later in this chapter.

## Create a Business Area

You must create at least one business area. In a real-world implementation, you will consider using several business areas, each with its own particular business purpose. You will point these business areas at particular tables and views of the data within the database, thus ensuring that each business area covers one succinct business purpose. While you can create business areas that cover multiple business purposes, this is not good practice, because it makes life difficult when you come to manage the user access to those areas.

Later in this chapter, we will walk you through the steps in creating your first business area, the business area that is used in the end-user sections of this book.

## Refine the Business Area

After you have created a business area, the business of maintaining that business area begins. This is where you refine the business area to add new folders, new calculated items, conditions, and lists of values. This is covered in Chapters 17 and 18, when we discuss editing the business area and how to interact with the users.

## Granting Access to the Business Areas

As you go about determining the user requirements, you should also have a pretty good idea of what type of access the users will need. The lowest level of control that you have within Discoverer relates to a business area. User access is therefore managed at the business area level. You cannot restrict access to a particular folder. This is one of the reasons why we recommend restricting business areas to one particular business purpose. The granting of access to a business area is discussed in Chapter 18.

## Deploy

If your organization is like most organizations, you will be considering a 70:30 split between report viewers and report writers. The report writers will need to be able to create workbooks and therefore will need to have access to Discoverer Plus, while your report viewers will want only to run workbooks that have been created for them by someone else. These users need to have access to Discoverer Viewer.

In Chapter 18 we will show how you to interact with the users and how to grant access to the business area.

# Source to Destination

Before we begin, we need to think a little about what we are going to do. We are going to take a set of relational data definitions from a source database and load them into our End User Layer as a business area. That business area will then be worked on to produce the final result that we will present to our users. The final result, our destination schema, will be a new set of data definitions that our users can understand.

## Source Database

Our source database, as shown in Figure 16-2, has 12 tables. As you can see in the figure, our 12 database tables are all based around a single Sales table. From the Sales table there are joins to the Day, Channel, Customer, and Products folders.

### Source Hierarchies

If you take a close look at the database schema in Figure 16-2, you may be able to spot some of the hierarchies that we will eventually be using in our business area. At first glance you should be able to spot three: Day, Customer, and Products.

The Date table joins to a hierarchy of interrelated tables containing Month, Quarter, and Year data. The Customer table joins to a hierarchy of tables containing City, District, and Region data. The Product table joins to a Product Line table, thus in effect producing a small product hierarchy. Because the Channel table links to no other tables, it is not part of any hierarchy and will thus end up becoming a single folder inside our business area.

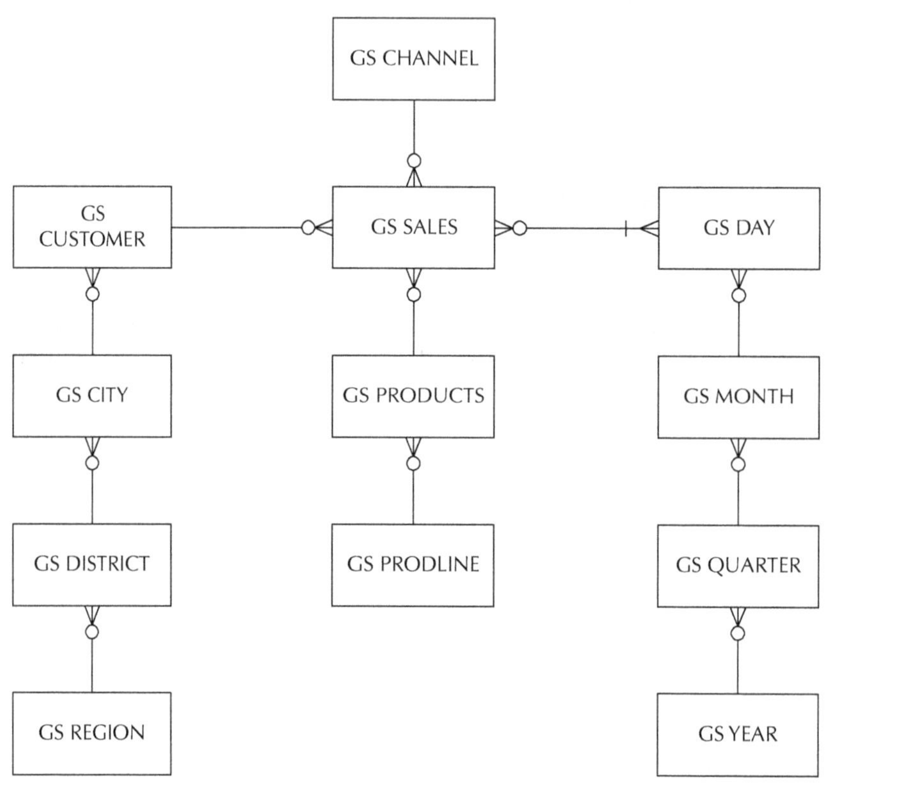


**FIGURE 16-2.** *Source database*

## Destination Schema

In Figure 16-3 we show you the design for our final business area. The hierarchy based around the Customer table has become a single complex folder called Geography. The hierarchy based around the Product table has become a single complex folder called Products. The hierarchy that is based around the Date table has become four complex folders, one each for our Order Date, Cancel Date, Request Date, and Ship Date. Do not worry about how you create these complex folders and hierarchies at this stage. This will all be explained in Chapter 18.

As mentioned earlier, because the Channel table is not part of any hierarchy, it will become its own folder in the final business area. Oh, yes, we must not forget the Sales table, which is at the heart of the source database. This will become the key folder in our new business area, in which our users will find the metrics.

Take a close look at the destination schema in Figure 16-3. If you are familiar with data warehousing, you should recognize this as being a star schema. Wherever possible, you should always try to design relational business areas using star schemas. These types of schema make for excellent performance within Discoverer and, as an added bonus, are the easiest for end users to understand. They are what we like to call *less join intensive*. By this we mean that users do not have to open numerous tables in order to find the joins they need.

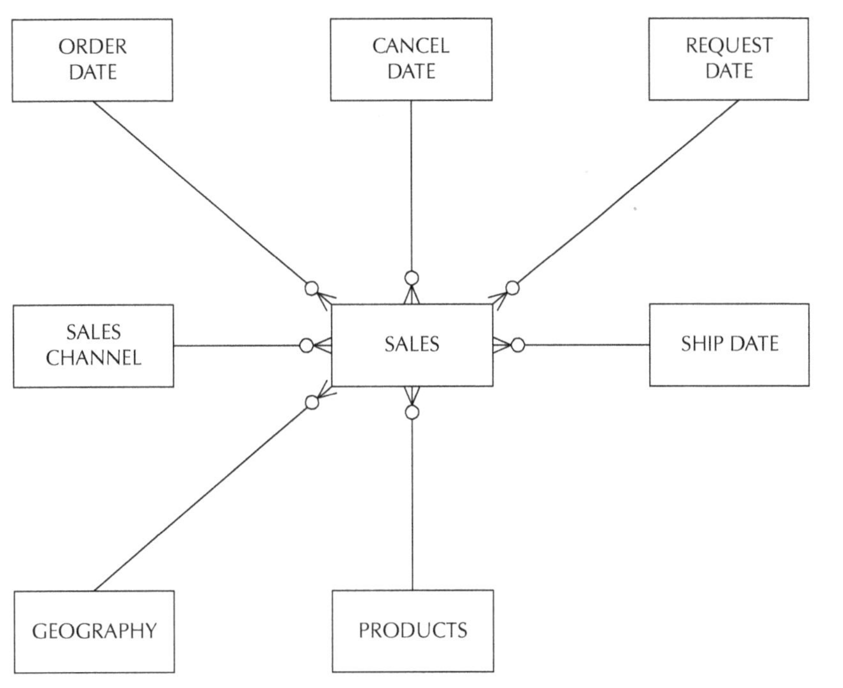


**FIGURE 16-3.** *Destination schema*

Take a look at Figure 16-2 again. Let's say you build the End User Layer exactly as per this diagram, with 12 folders joined using the primary- and foreign-key constraints defined within the database. If a user wants to build a worksheet that uses something from the Sales folder along with Region and Year, can you see that there are numerous ways to do this? You could start in the Sales folder, but then where would you go next? The only folders available to you at this time are Channel, Customer, Products, and Day. You cannot see the Region or Year folder because you need to make joins between several other folders to get where you want to be. This type of worksheet is join intensive and something you need to avoid.

Unfortunately, many companies do exactly this, and as consultants we spend a great deal of time explaining why this is not a good idea. As we have stated, what starts right stays right. A good conceptual model minimizes the number of joins a user needs to make to find the data they need. Take another look at Figure 16-3. Can you see that if the user starts by pulling something, anything, from the Sales folder, that all of the other folders are instantly available? This is a good design and one that you should strive to follow. We have also mentioned that a good design hides the complexity of the database from the end user. This is what we mean. Behind the scenes the user does not need to know that we have overlaid the database with six complex folders to create the business area.

All you need to do is tell your users that they should select something from the fact or metric folder first and then select one or more items from the dimension folders. You will find that your users have a greater chance of understanding your model and thus making use of the business area that you have built for them.

For example, let's say a user wants to build a query that selects the total quantity shipped by channel by product. You can easily explain that the two BY clauses, by channel and by product, are both dimensions. If you now teach the user that all of the metrics, such as total quantity shipped, can be found in the Sales folder and that they should begin their selections in there, the user will find this easy. Imagine how much easier it becomes when the Sales folder is right at the top of the list of folders. If you place all of the other dimension folders beneath the main metric folder, it now becomes very easy for the user to understand the model and make the necessary selections for the query.

# Creating the End User Layer

Before you can begin creating business areas, you need to have an End User Layer. Let's assume you do not have an End User Layer. Where do you begin? Well, first you need to create a new database user for the End User Layer.

## New User Privileges

Whether you have the ability to do this yourself or you need to ask your DBA to do it for you, to create and maintain an End User Layer in an Oracle database you need certain database privileges. We have broken these privileges into three kinds.

- Standard database privileges
- Summary management privileges
- Other privileges

### Standard Database Privileges

The standard database privileges that you must have in order to create an End User Layer in an Oracle database are as follows:

| | |
|---|---|
| CONNECT | CREATE TABLE |
| RESOURCE | CREATE VIEW |
| CREATE SESSION | CREATE SEQUENCE |
| CREATE PROCEDURE | CREATE ROLE (see the following note) |

In addition to these privileges, the database user must also have the following:

- A default tablespace, which must not be a temporary tablespace
- A quota set in the default tablespace (Oracle recommends a minimum of 3MB)

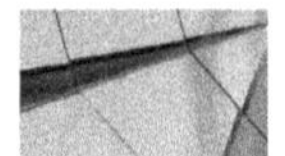

**NOTE**

*If you create the database user using Discoverer Administrator, Discoverer will automatically grant the CREATE ROLE privilege. If you are going to be using a predefined user as the EUL owner, you ensure that this user also has the CREATE ROLE privilege. Database roles that are created outside Discoverer will enable the administrator (within Discoverer) to define security configurations using those roles. The DBA will then be able to associate security access to the underlying tables through the roles you have created. It is vitally important to understand that security is not compromised by allowing a Discoverer EUL owner the privilege to create roles.*

### Summary Management Privileges

If you are creating the EUL in an Oracle Enterprise Edition database, to use Discoverer's manual summary management and automated summary management (ASM) functionality you will also need the following privileges:

| | |
|---|---|
| ANALYZE ANY | CREATE ANY MATERIALIZED VIEW |
| ALTER ANY MATERIALIZED VIEW | DROP ANY MATERIALIZED VIEW |
| GLOBAL QUERY REWRITE | SELECT ON SYS.V_$PARAMETER |
| EXECUTE ON SYS.DBMS_JOB | UNLIMITED TABLESPACE (optional) |

The ALTER, CREATE, and DROP ANY MATERIALIZED VIEW, or SNAPSHOT, privileges are required if you want to use the summary management capabilities of Discoverer. Having the less powerful ALTER, CREATE, or DROP MATERIALIZED VIEW, or SNAPSHOT, without the word ANY, is not sufficient. This is because Discoverer will create the materialized view directly in the database schema that owns the objects upon which the materialized view is based. When this has been done, the database optimizer will be able to rewrite queries correctly.

This is another reason why the EUL owner needs to have the unqualified UNLIMITED TABLESPACE privilege as opposed to the lesser privilege that would grant unlimited space against a named tablespace.

In addition to the previous database privileges, the following must be true if you want to use summary management:

- The database must support PL/SQL.
- The DBMS_JOB package must be installed. For help about determining whether the package has been installed, see Appendix A.

### Other Privileges

The following are the other privileges that may be needed:

EXECUTE ANY PROCEDURE (recommended)

SELECT ANY TABLE (optional)

CREATE USER

DBA

**NOTE**
*Your DBA may consider the SELECT ANY TABLE privilege to be too powerful and may not want to let you have it. If this is the case, then you will need to assign SELECT rights over the individual objects you need.*

Another privilege that you may have access to is CREATE USER. If you do have this privilege, the Discoverer Administrator tool will make use of it, as you will see later in this chapter. Some organizations also grant the DBA privilege to the EUL owner. This is not really necessary and can be very dangerous in the wrong hands. However, if your Discoverer administrator is also your DBA, you won't have to worry.

For more information relating to privileges, particularly for the privileges needed for scheduling, please see Chapter 18 and Appendix A.

For more help on this subject, please look at the following section in the Discoverer Administration manual:

http://docs.oracle.com/cd/E23943_01/bi.1111/b32519/maintain_eul.htm#i1004636

For demonstrating how to create an End User Layer in this book, we are using a user called BOOK, which was created using the standard privileges mentioned earlier.

## Software Installation

Having created your new user account, you need to install the Discoverer Administrator software on your PC into a new Oracle home. The default home that the software wants to use is called BIToolsHome_1. We recommend you leave this as the default if you can. Because the installation is easy, we will not cover it in any detail here. Please see Appendix A for an explanation about how to install both the Administrator and Desktop tools at the same time.

## Create the EUL

Having installed the Discoverer Administrator software, you will create your first EUL. Assuming you installed it into the default Oracle home, from the Windows Start button, select Start | Programs | Oracle Business Intelligence Tools - BIToolsHome_1 | Oracle Discoverer Administrator. This launches the login screen shown here:

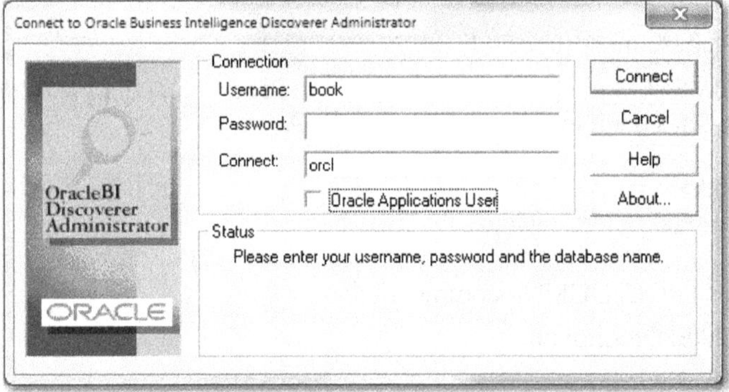


You should enter your username, password, and database. In our case, we will connect using the BOOK user we created earlier.

Assuming you enter a valid username, password, and database, Discoverer checks whether any End User Layer exists for the user you entered. If the EUL does exist, Discoverer opens it. However, in our case, the EUL does not exist and so we were given the message shown here:

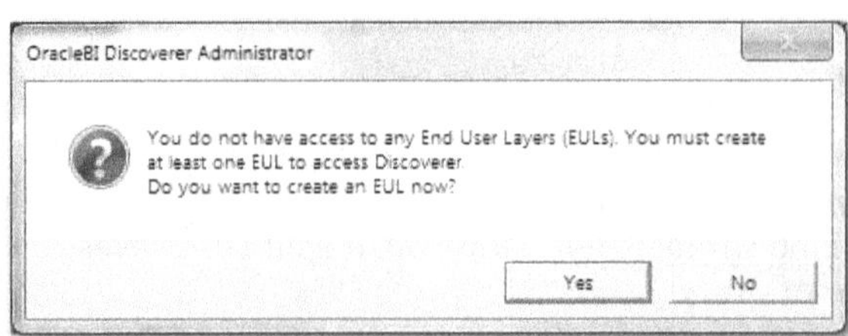

As you can see, the only options you have are to click Yes to create the EUL or No to not create the EUL. When we clicked Yes, Discoverer opened the EUL Manager dialog box.

Discoverer prompts "What do you want to do?" Once again, you really have only one option. You should click the Create An EUL button; Discoverer will then take you to step 1 of the Create EUL Wizard.

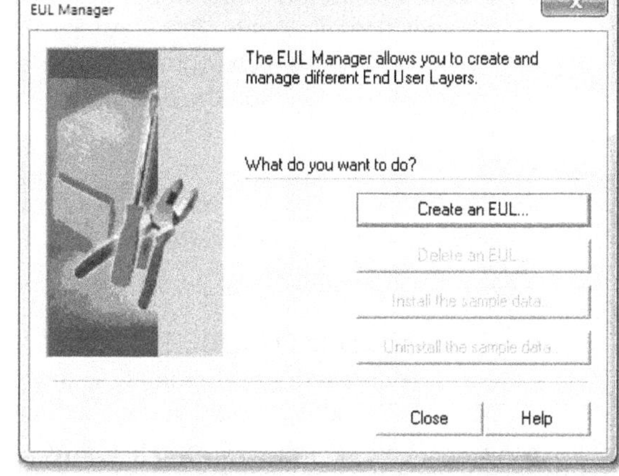


## Create EUL Wizard

The Create EUL Wizard has three steps.

1. Select the owner and type of EUL (if you are installing a standard EUL, this is the only wizard screen you will see).
2. Select the schema containing the FND tables (Apps mode only for E-Business Suite).
3. Select the tablespaces to be used in the installation (available only if creating a new user).

**Create EUL Wizard: Step 1** The first step, to select the owner and type of EUL, has the following areas, as illustrated here:

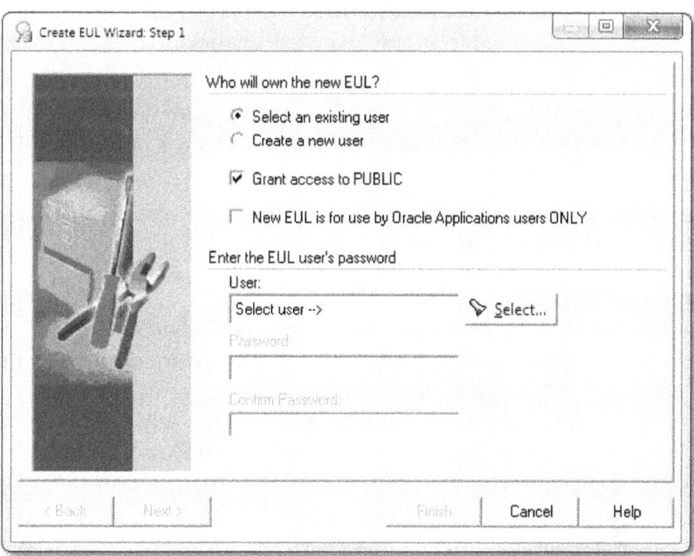


- **Who will own the new EUL?** In response to this question, you have two choices. The first choice is to select an existing user, while the second is to create a new user. The option to create a new user will be available only if you have been granted the CREATE

USER database privilege. In our case, the user has already been created for us, so we clicked the radio button Select An Existing User. If you do have the CREATE USER privilege, you will be required to enter a name and password for the new user. You will be required to provide the default tablespaces for the user later.

**NOTE**
*You can have only one Discoverer EUL in a user's schema. This is because all of the EUL tables and views, from version 9.0.2 onward, begin with the characters EUL5.*

- **Grant Access To PUBLIC** This box is checked by default. In most cases you will leave this box checked, as this will allow any user of the system to have access to the EUL that you have created. Should you want to create a private EUL, you should uncheck this box.
- **New EUL Is For Use By Oracle E-Business Suite Users ONLY** Check this box only if you are creating an Apps-mode EUL. In our case we are not creating an Apps-mode EUL, so will leave this box unchecked.

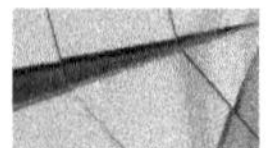

**NOTE**
*If you check this box, the Next button on the bottom of the screen will become active.*

- **Select** Click this button to display a list of users against whom you can create the EUL. If you pick a user other than the user who you logged in as or you are creating a new user, you will be required to supply that user's password. For this example, we chose the existing BOOK user.
- **Finish** If you are creating a standard EUL and you are creating it in an existing user's schema, having made all of your selections on screen 1 of the wizard, your only option will be to click Finish.
- **Next** If you are creating an Apps-mode EUL or are creating a new user for the EUL, your only option will be to click Next.

### Create EUL Wizard: Step 2

The screen that displays at this point varies, depending upon whether you are creating an Apps-mode EUL and whether you are creating a new user. If you are not creating an Apps-mode EUL but are creating a new user, in this step of the wizard, as you can see in the illustration that follows, you will be required to tell Discoverer which default and temporary tablespaces should be used for the new standard EUL owner. To tell Discoverer which tablespace to use, you need to click it to highlight it. Having specified which tablespaces Discoverer should use, your only option is to click Finish.

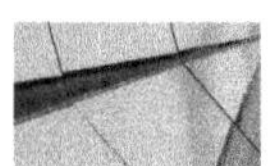

**NOTE**
*Even if there is only one temporary tablespace available, the Finish button will not activate until you highlight both the default and temporary tablespaces. If you are new to Discoverer and the Finish button is grayed out, you now know why.*

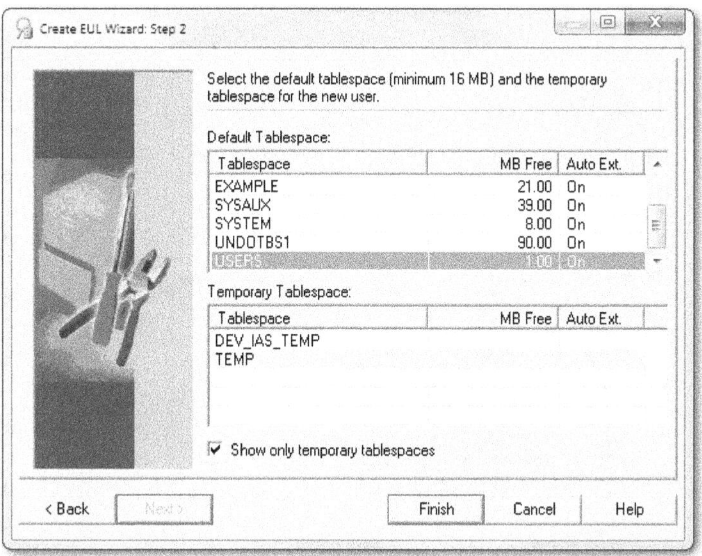


If you are creating an Apps-mode EUL, in this step of the wizard, as shown in the following illustration, you will be required to tell Discoverer the username and password of the database schema that contains the Apps foundation tables. In most cases, this will be the APPS user. Having provided this information, your only option is to click Next.

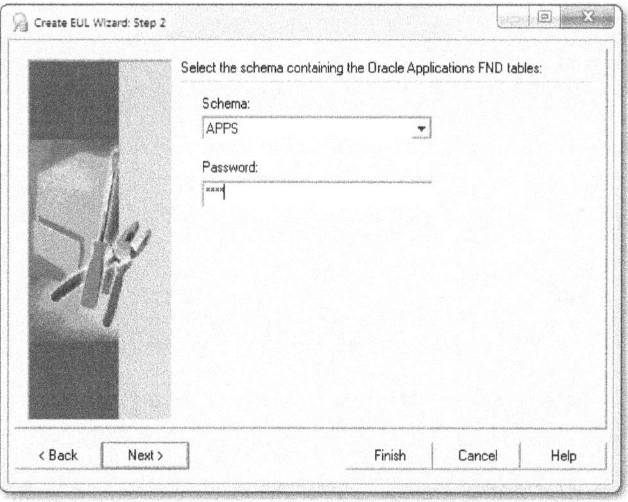


### Create EUL Wizard: Step 3

You will see a third step to the Create EUL Wizard only if you are creating an Apps-mode EUL and a new user at the same time. In this step, you will be required to tell Discoverer which default and temporary tablespaces should be used for the new Apps-mode owner. Even if there is only one temporary tablespace available, the Finish button will not activate until you highlight both the default and temporary tablespaces.

### Creating the EUL for Real

Once you have clicked Finish in the Create EUL Wizard, Discoverer will create the End User Layer. As the install progresses, you will see a series of three identically sized message screens. The install goes through three stages.

- Creating tables and views
- Populating tables with default data
- Granting access on EUL tables

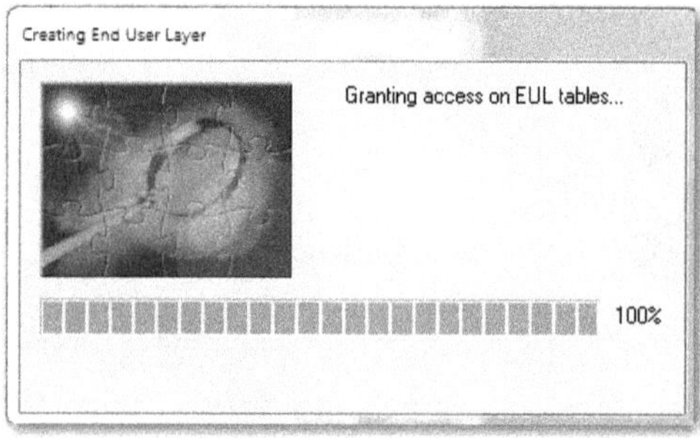


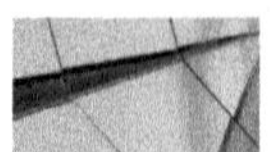

**NOTE**
*As a bit of fun, watch the jigsaw gradually fill in as the status moves toward 100 percent.*

When the installation has completed, you will be given the message saying that the EUL has been successfully created.

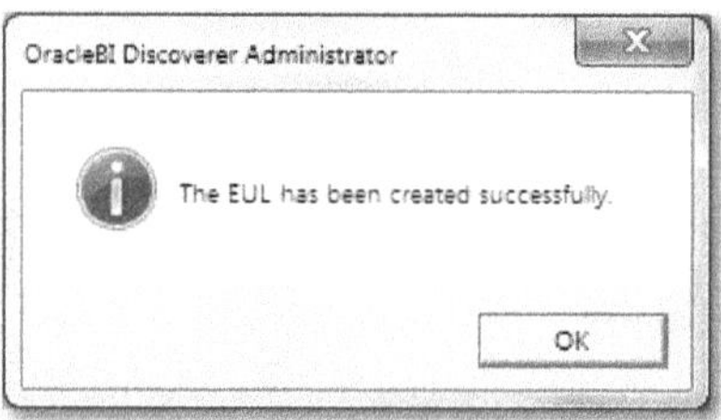


As you can see here, your only option is to click OK. At that point, Discoverer might present you with the following screen:

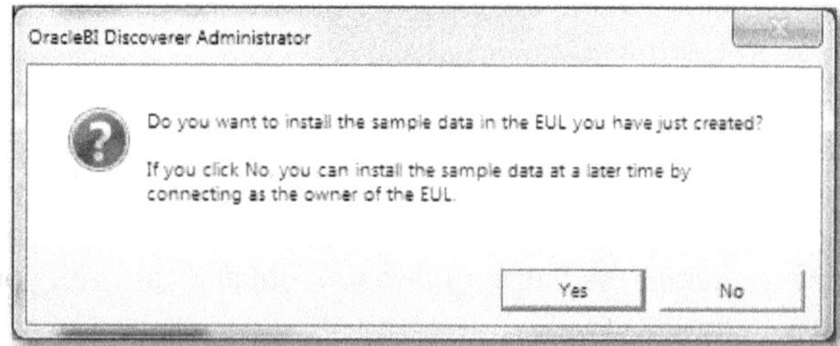

This screen will appear only if Discoverer detects that a database user called VIDEO5 exists in the database or that the user does not exist but you have the CREATE USER privilege. This is the schema used by Oracle's Video Store tutorial. If you want to have this tutorial installed, click Yes. If you have the CREATE USER privilege and the VIDEO5 user does not exist, during the install of Oracle's sample data, Discoverer will create the user and give it the default password VIDEO5. We don't need this for our EUL, so we clicked No.

Finally, to complete the installation of the End User Layer, close the EUL Manager dialog box by clicking Close.

If you installed the EUL into a new user account, you will now be prompted to connect as that user. When prompted "Do you want to connect as the owner of the EUL which you just created?" click Yes.

If you are creating an Apps-mode EUL, you have not yet finished and need to follow the steps in the next section. However, if you are creating a standard EUL, well done, you are finished. Please move on to the section "Creating Your First Business Area."

## Completing the Apps-Mode EUL

The remainder of this section is required only if you are creating an Apps-mode EUL.

After the EUL has been created, Discoverer will display the box shown later in Figure 16-4. As you have not yet completed setting up Discoverer to operate in Apps mode, you should click Cancel and then follow the instructions.

To complete setting up an Apps-mode EUL, use the following workflow:

1. From the toolbar, select Tools | Options, and then, as shown in the following illustration, click the Connection tab.

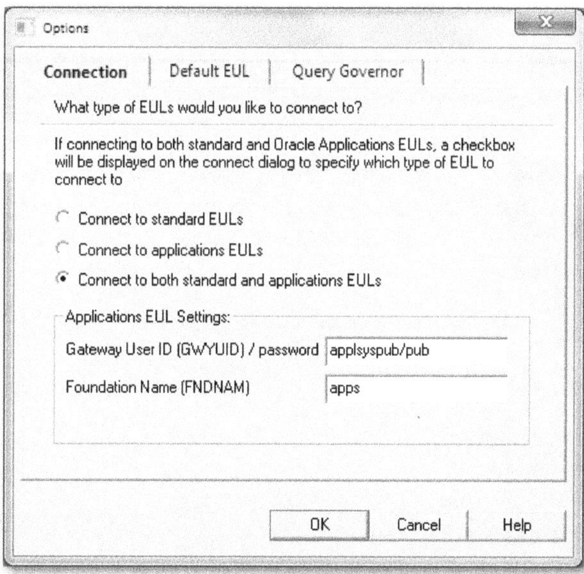


2. As you can see, the Connection tab has three radio buttons and an area called Applications EUL Settings. The three radio buttons are

   ■ **Connect To Standard EULs** Check this if your organization will only ever be using Discoverer in standard mode.

- **Connect To Applications EULs** Check this if your organization will only ever be using Discoverer in Apps mode.
- **Connect To Both Standard And Applications EULs** Check this if your organization will be using Discoverer in both Apps and standard modes. If you are wondering how this can be, let us explain. Some organizations use Discoverer in Apps mode against their Oracle Apps database but use it in standard mode against another database, such as a data warehouse. Because there is only one Administrator tool, the same tool needs to be able to administer Discoverer in both modes, which is the reason for the third option on the screen.

3. Having enabled Discoverer in Apps mode and specified whether you will only be administering Apps EULs or a combination of standard and Apps EULs, you are now required to provide the following information in the Applications EUL Settings area:
   - **Gateway user ID (GWYUID)/password** Enter **applysyspub/pub** as one string. This is the default, but it could be different, so please check with your E-Business Suite DBA.
   - **Foundation name (FNDNAM)** Enter **apps** or whichever user your organization is using for the ownership of the Apps foundation tables.
4. When you have completed this screen, click OK.
5. From the menu bar, select File | Connect. The Discoverer Administrator login screen will be displayed, and you should reconnect as the owner of the EUL. There is now an additional check box called Oracle Applications User. Do not check this box at this time.
6. When prompted with the standard load screen shown in Figure 16-4, click Cancel.

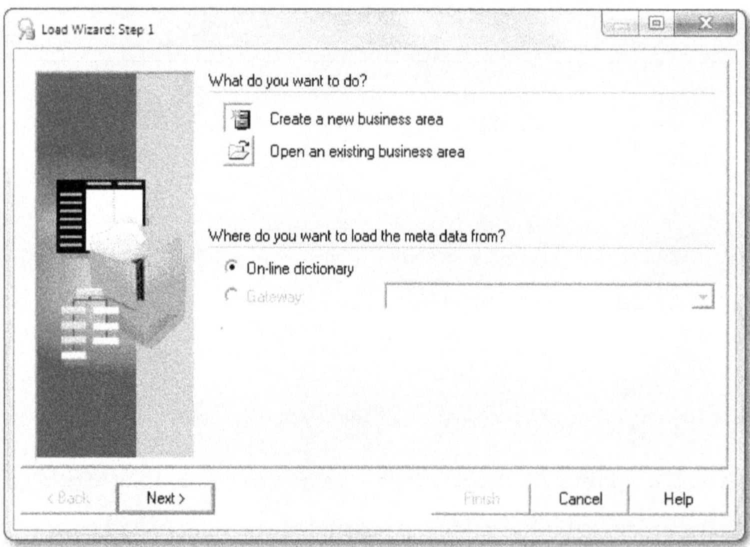


**FIGURE 16-4.** *Load Wizard, part 1: create a new business area*

7. From the menu bar, select Tools | Privileges and grant the SYSADMIN user the following privileges by checking the boxes alongside each privilege:
   - Administration Privilege, plus all subprivileges
   - Desktop and Plus Privileges, plus all subprivileges

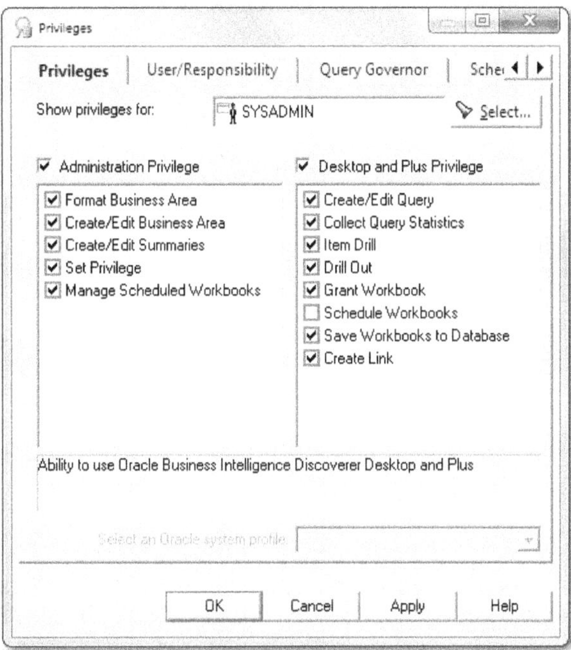


8. When you have completed assigning privileges to the SYSADMIN user, click OK.
9. From the menu bar, select File | Connect. The Discoverer Administrator login screen will be displayed once more, but this time you should reconnect as the SYSADMIN user. You will, of course, need to know the SYSADMIN password, and you must make sure that you check the Oracle Applications User box.

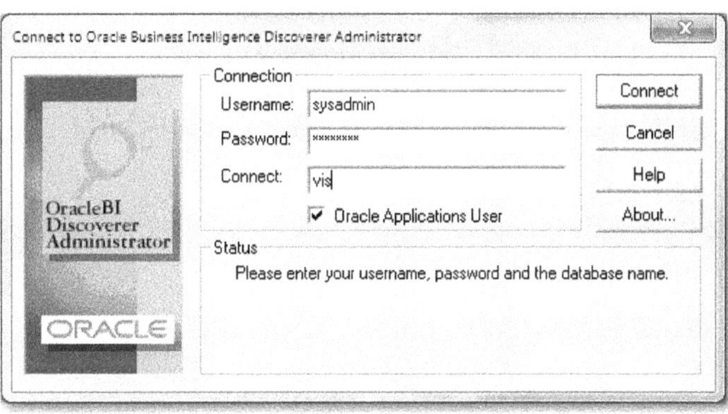

10. Discoverer will now authenticate the SYSADMIN user against the Oracle Applications E-Business Suite. If the credentials are correct, you will be presented with the following Choose a Responsibility dialog box:

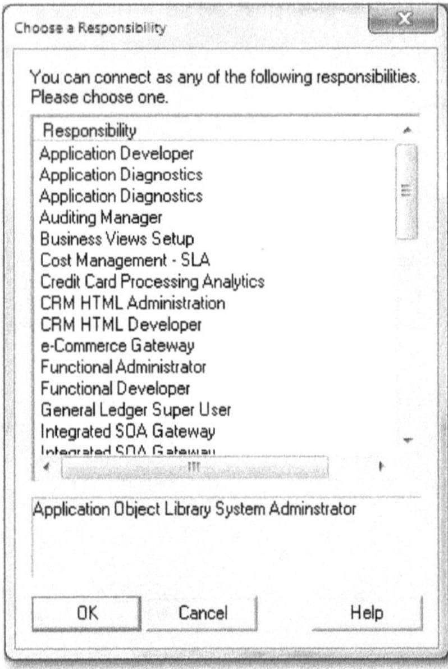


11. Select the System Administrator responsibility and click OK.
12. From here on, you should log in to the Administrator tool only as the Apps SYSADMIN user.

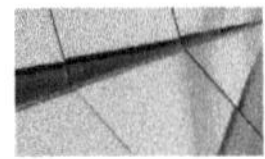

**NOTE**
*Do not attempt to administer an Apps-mode EUL as the EUL owner. This account is used to store the EUL tables and views, but it is not an Apps account. You will run into serious trouble if you start administering the EUL with it, so please do not try.*

# Creating Your First Business Area

Once you have created your empty End User Layer, Discoverer displays the first screen of the Load Wizard. You will use this wizard to create business areas. The Load Wizard has the following five steps:

1. Create or open a business area.
2. Select the schema.
3. Select the objects to use.
4. Define the import options.
5. Name the business area and provide final preferences.

## Load Wizard Step 1: Create or Open a Business Area

On the first screen of the Load Wizard, shown in Figures 16-4 and 16-5, you are asked whether you want to create a new business area or open an existing business area.

**NOTE**
*Having created your EUL, from now on, each time you log in to Discoverer Administrator, this is the screen you will see.*

There are two buttons on the first screen of the Load Wizard. As you can see in Figures 16-4 and 16-5, the screen changes depending upon which button you click. As we do not have any existing business areas, we will show you how to create one.

### Creating a New Business Area

Having decided that you want to create a new business area, take a look at Figure 16-4. On that screen, you will see that there are two ways to create a business area.

- **On-line Dictionary** Use this radio button to select objects from the database data dictionary. This is the most common way of bringing objects into a business area.
- **Gateway** Use this radio button to select objects from a *gateway*. A *gateway* is a link between another application and Discoverer. For example, if you are using Warehouse Builder, you might create a gateway between the warehouse metadata repository and Discoverer.

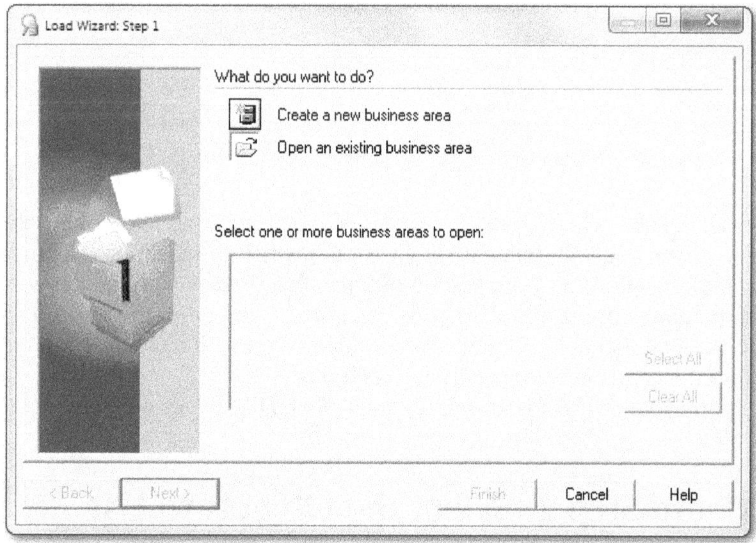


**FIGURE 16-5.** *Load Wizard, part 1: open an existing business area*

As we do not have a gateway installed, we clicked the On-line Dictionary radio button and then clicked Next. Discoverer will now open the second screen of the Load Wizard.

## Load Wizard Step 2: Select the Schema

In the second step of the Load Wizard, you need to pick the user who owns the database objects that you want to use within the business area. If there is a database link in use, you should select it first. In most cases, there will not be a database link and you will be selecting objects directly from the database in which the End User Layer has been created.

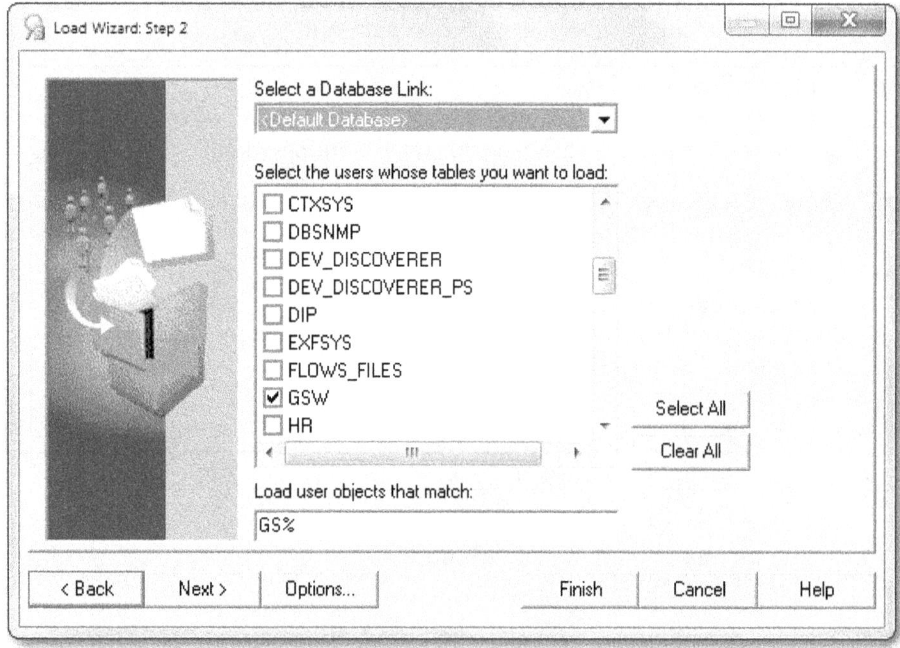


In our case, the user who we will be using is called GSW, short for Global Sales Widgets. At the bottom of the screen you will notice a Load User Objects That Match box. If you are aware of the name of the table or view you want to load or know that there is a prefix that you can use, enter the name of the object or the prefix into this box immediately prior to the wildcard character. In our case, because all the tables that we want to load begin with the letters *GS*, we entered these characters into the Load User Objects That Match box.

Having made your selections for step 2, click Next. Discoverer will now open the third screen of the Load Wizard.

## Load Wizard Step 3: Select the Objects to Use

As you can see in the next illustration, the third screen of the Load Wizard has an Available items box and a Selected items box. In the Available items box, Discoverer presents you with a list of the objects that are available for selection into your End User Layer. In the Selected items box, Discoverer lists the objects that you have already selected for inclusion in your End User Layer.

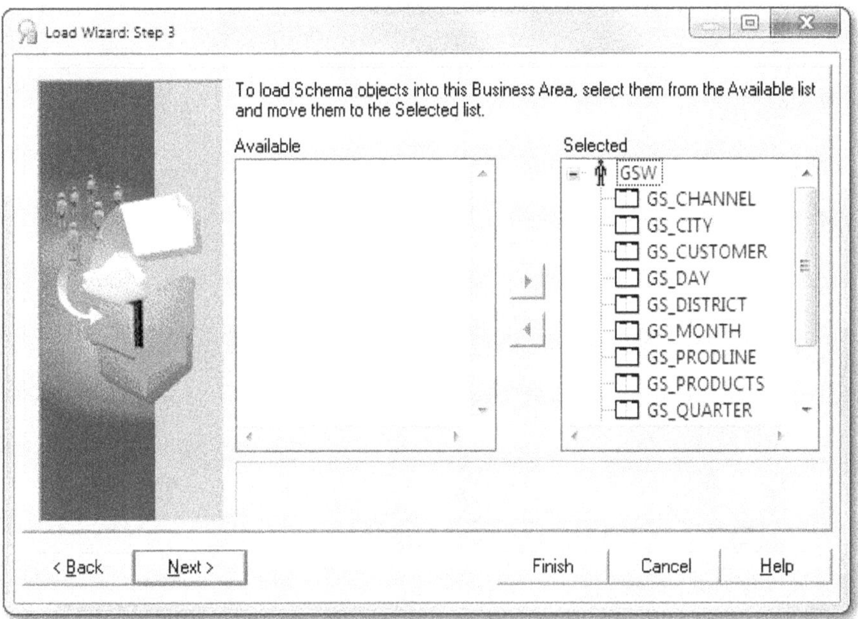

**NOTE**
*Discoverer does not remember what items you have previously selected for your End User Layer. So, if your EUL already contains a table called Sales and you reopen the wizard, the wizard will not place Sales in the Selected items list. You have to remember that you have already done this.*

On the third screen of the Load Wizard, Discoverer lists the objects owned by the user you selected in step 1, constrained by the match criteria you entered in step 2. As you can see in the preceding illustration, the GSW user owns a number of objects that all begin with the characters *GS*.

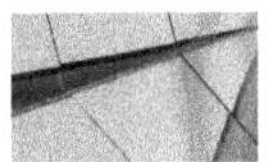

**NOTE**
*Discoverer initially displays an empty screen with just the usernames you selected. If you click the plus character alongside the username, Discoverer will now display the objects owned by that user.*

If you look back at Figure 16-2, you can see that we want all of the objects that begin with *GS*. Therefore, drag and drop or push each object from the Available items list to the Selected items list, and then click Next. Discoverer will now open the fourth screen of the Load Wizard.

## Load Wizard Step 4: Define the Import Options

The fourth screen of the Load Wizard has the following areas:

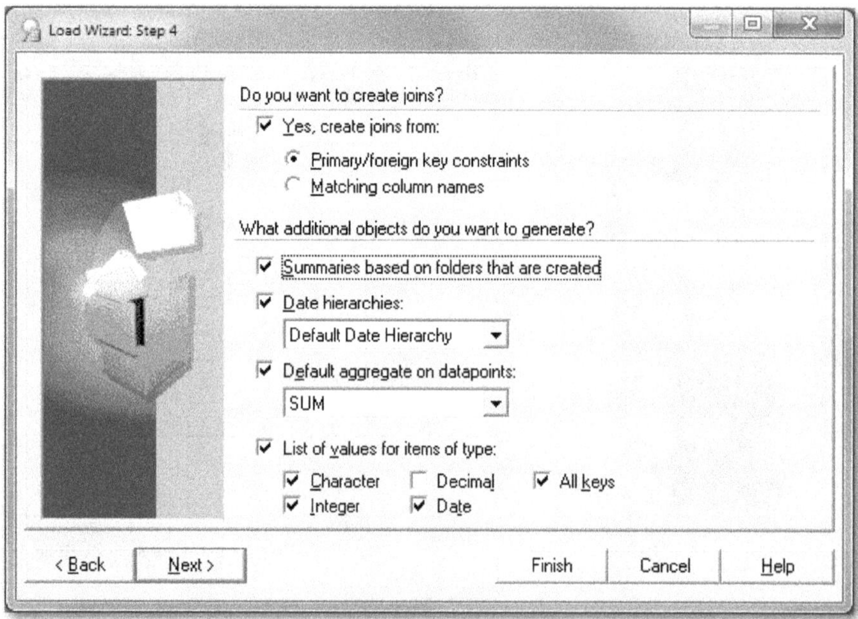


- **Do you want to create joins?** Check the Yes box if you want Discoverer to automatically create joins for you. You have the option to create joins from primary-key/foreign-key constraints or matching by column names. If we are aware that primary-key/foreign-key constraints exist in the database, we will generally allow Discoverer to go ahead and create the joins for us. By default this box will be checked with the option set to primary-key/foreign-key constraints. However, be wary of allowing Discoverer to create joins based on matching column names, because in that case you are relying on whoever created the database to have designed it with this in mind.

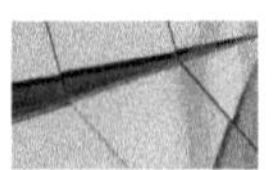

**NOTE**

*When using Discoverer against Oracle E-Business Suite, take note that Oracle does not generally use primary-key/foreign-key constraints, so all that you will have to go on is the column names. Make sure the joins really do exist before allowing Discoverer to create them. For example, you do not want to be joining every occurrence of SEGMENT1 or ATTRIBUTE1.*

- **Summaries Based On Folders That Are Created** Check this box if you want Discoverer to create summaries, materialized views, based on the folders that are being created. You will rarely use this feature. We recommend that you not check this box at this time. You can always create summaries later, and unless you really know what you are doing, you could easily overpower your system with materialized views. By default this option will be unchecked.
- **Date Hierarchies** Check this box if you want Discoverer to create date hierarchies for every date that is being imported into the business area. Having checked the box, you next need to tell Discoverer which hierarchy type it should use to create the new hierarchies. Again, we do not recommend that you check this box at this time. As not all dates will warrant a hierarchy, it is better to create hierarchies later, when you have had a chance to look at the data. By default this option will be checked.
- **Default Aggregate On Datapoints** Check this box if you want Discoverer to assign a default aggregate to each of the data points being imported into the End User Layer. We like this feature and recommend you keep this box checked. Having checked the box, you now need to tell Discoverer what default aggregate it should use. Discoverer checks this box by default, with SUM being the chosen option. SUM is the one that you will most often use.
- **List Of Values For Items Of Type** Check this box if you want Discoverer to automatically create lists of values for the imported objects. If you check the box, you also need to tell Discoverer which objects should have lists of values associated with them. Discoverer does not enable the creation of automatic lists of values by default, so if you want to take advantage of this option, you need to manually check the box. You can associate lists of values with the following types:
    - Character
    - Integer
    - Decimal
    - Date
    - All keys

If you do elect to allow Discoverer to create lists of values, it will select Character, Integer, All Keys, and Integer by default. Carefully make sure you have checked only the data types you intend; otherwise, you could find your system being clogged up with lots of unwanted lists of values.

**NOTE**
*We recommend not letting Discoverer create its own item classes (lists of values) because you cannot control the name of the item class and cannot prevent Discoverer from creating duplicate item classes should the same item exist in multiple folders.*

When we create EULs for our customers, we typically only check the Default Aggregate On Datapoints box with everything else being unchecked. In the case of this tutorial, because our database was defined with primary keys and constraints, we will allow Discoverer to create joins from primary-key/foreign-key constraints, as shown here:

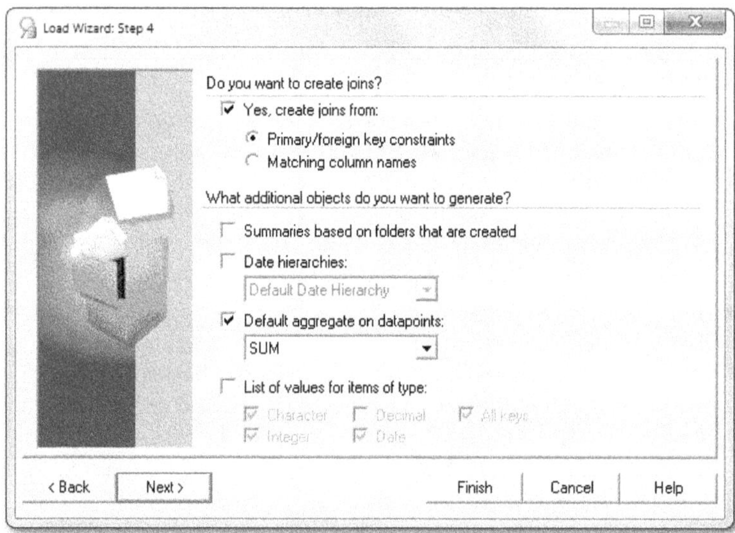


Having made your choices for step 4, click Next. Discoverer will now open the fifth and final screen of the Load Wizard.

## Load Wizard Step 5: Name the Business Area and Provide Final Preferences

The fifth screen of the Load Wizard, shown next, is a screen for inputting the name of the business area plus setting a number of preferences:

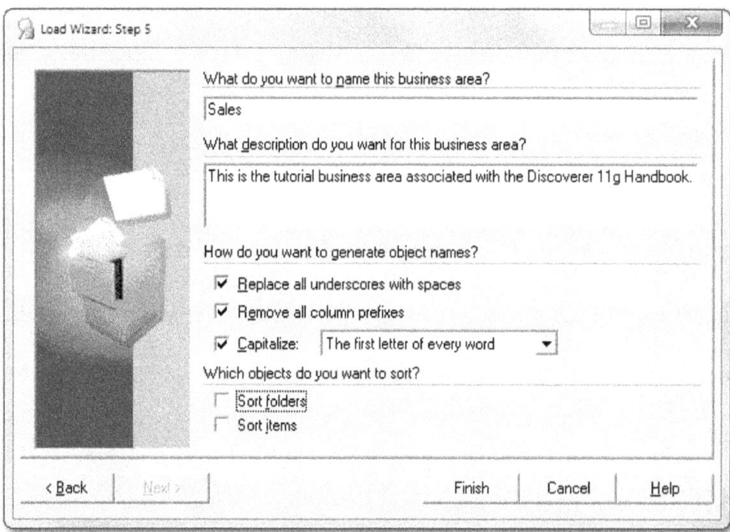

It has the following areas:

- **What do you want to name this business area?** Give the business area a meaningful name that fits in with your corporate naming standards. In our case, we will call it Sales, which is the sales area associated with our fictitious company Global Software Widgets.
- **What description do you want to give this business area?** Provide a meaningful description of the business area to help your users understand what it is used for. In our case, we entered "This is the tutorial business area associated with the Discoverer 11*g* Handbook."
- **Replace All Underscores With Spaces** This setting is based on user preference and will be part of your corporate standards. In our case, we always replace underscores with spaces, such that the name order_qty will become order qty. This option is checked by default.
- **Remove All Column Prefixes** This setting is based on user preference, but if it is checked, Discoverer will remove any prefixes that it finds in the column names. This option is checked by default.
- **Capitalize** This setting is also down to user preference and will be part of your corporate standards. In our case, we always capitalize the first letter of every word, but you can use the associated drop-down list to capitalize only the initial letter if you so want. If we do this with order_qty, it will become Order Qty when used in conjunction with replacing underscores with spaces. This option is checked by default.
- **Sort Folders** This preference allows you to alphabetically sort all of the folders. We do not recommend doing this, as you will be placing folders exactly where you want them in a later step. This is not checked by default.
- **Sort Items** This preference allows you to alphabetically sort all of the items within the folders. We do not recommend doing this, as one of the important steps to good business area design calls for the placement of items in the order that we choose. Be careful because this option will be checked by default.

At this stage you are ready to create your business area. If you are unsure as to any of the settings that you have made, use the Back button to go back and check. You can use the Back and Next buttons to navigate through all of the wizard steps.

When you have made all of your choices, come back to the fifth screen of the wizard and click Finish. Discoverer will now create the business area, loading the data objects that you have selected and setting the preferences and options you input to the wizard. Once again, Discoverer will create a jigsaw, gradually filling in more and more pieces as the business area is created.

Congratulations, you have now created your first business area.

# Key Business Area Objects

There are three very important objects that must have unique names within Discoverer.

- Business area
- Folders
- Joins

Discoverer cannot have duplicate business area, folder, or join names anywhere within the End User Layer. These objects must have unique names. Part of your job as the Discoverer manager is to make sure these are unique. If you do not ensure uniqueness using names that are under your control, then Discoverer will do it for you. However, Discoverer does this by appending a number to the end of the name. If you are not proactive and do not take control of the names, this can have disastrous consequences for exporting and importing objects between End User Layers when Discoverer will not be able to import objects using the name that they were originally assigned.

In addition to names, Discoverer uses unique object identifiers. These unique identifiers are initially assigned by Discoverer but can be changed by you. We recommend you always make sure you have both meaningful names and identifiers for the three objects just listed.

We will explain why.

When Discoverer saves a workbook, it saves both the object names and the object identifiers for the business area, folders, and joins used within each worksheet. When that workbook is subsequently opened either in the same End User Layer or in a new End User Layer, Discoverer first looks for the objects by name. If it cannot find the objects by name, it will look for the objects by their identifiers. If it finds either the name or the identifier, the workbook will open. If neither the name nor the identifier can be found, workbook validation will fail and the workbook will not open.

If you have been sloppy and allowed Discoverer to name folders as FOLDER_1 and so on, then during an export of objects from one End User Layer to another, Discoverer may already have a folder called FOLDER_1 in the new EUL and will thus rename the second one to something like FOLDER_11. Any workbook using that folder will fail validation when it looks for the name and will then try to find the folder using the identifier. If you have also not taken care to assign meaningful identifiers, it is possible that an existing folder had the same identifier as the one you were trying to import and that the identifier also got renamed. At this point, the workbook will fail to open.

Thus, it is essential that after you have created a new business area or added new critical objects to a business area, you make checks on the business area.

# Checking a Business Area

Having created a new business area or added new critical objects to a business area, such as folders or joins, you need to check the business area. We check it by doing the following:

- Check the business area name, description, and identifier.
- Check the folder names, descriptions, and identifiers.
- Check the order of the folders.
- Check the names of the items.
- Check the order of the items.
- Check or create lists of values.
- Check the names and identifiers for the joins.

## Check the Business Area Name, Description, and Identifier

As previously explained, the business area's name and identifier must be unique and meaningful. You should already have assigned the new business area a meaningful name and description during the creation stage. However, this is the first time you have had a chance to look at the identifier.

To check the identifier for a business area, use the following workflow:

1. Right-click the business area name.
2. From the pop-up menu, select Properties.
3. Make sure the name, description, and identifier meet your standards.
4. If not, change the name, description, and identifier.
5. When done, click OK.

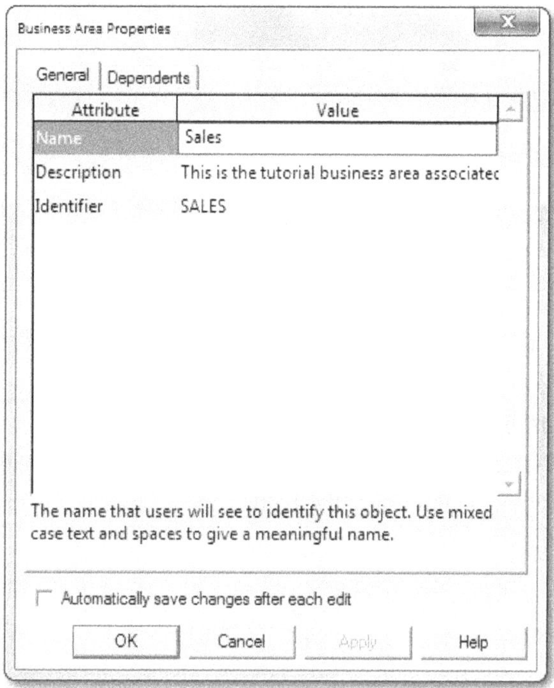

**NOTE**

*Folder names can use a combination of upper- and lowercase characters and the space character. Identifiers are all in uppercase and can have no spaces.*

## Check the Folder Names, Descriptions, and Identifiers

Many times, especially when importing objects from the database, you will find that the name of the table is not user friendly. We therefore need to rename all non-user-friendly folder names. In our case, the folder names are okay, so we will not rename them. However, two other things should be checked at this point. These are the folder descriptions and identifiers.

To change the name, description, or identifier of a folder, use the following workflow:

1. Right-click the folder you want to check.

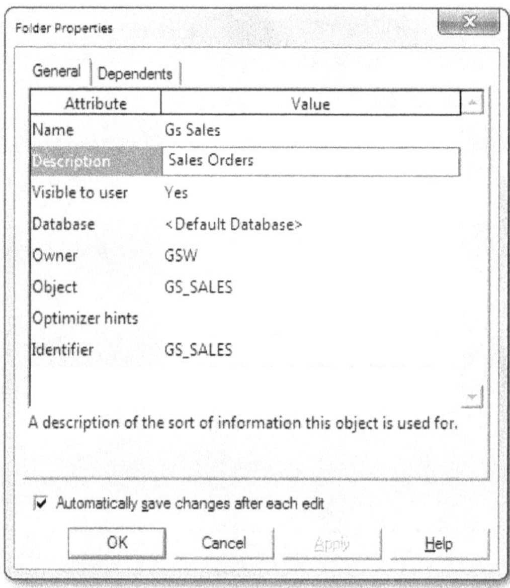


2. From the pop-up menu, select Properties.
3. Make sure the name, description, and identifier meet your standards.
4. If not, change the name, description, and identifier.
5. When done, click OK.

If you do decide to change the name of an identifier, you will be presented with the following warning:

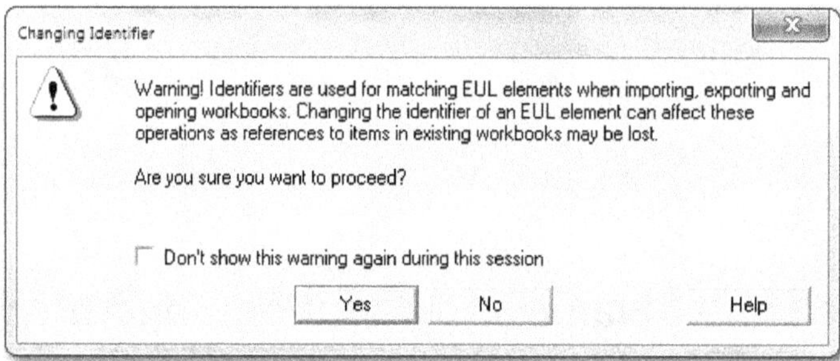


Discoverer is warning you that changing an identifier after workbooks have been created can cause those workbooks not to open. Be careful therefore when renaming identifiers to do so only during the object creation stage and not after the users have started creating workbooks against the business area.

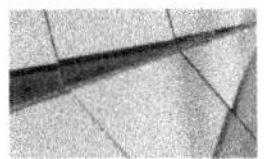

**NOTE**
*Click the Dependents tab to view all items that reference this folder. Discoverer will list all the other folders, items, summaries, and workbooks that reference the folder you are working on.*

## Check the Order of the Folders

As mentioned earlier, it is important that you place folders in the most logical order in which they will be used by users. In particular, you should place folders in this order:

1. Place fact or metric folders first.
2. Place nondate dimension folders next, in alphabetic order.
3. Place date dimension folders next, in either alphabetical or business use order.

In our case, because the Sales folder contains the metrics for our business area, we will move this "fact" folder to the top of the list of folders. Because all of the other folders, apart from the Channel folder, will be used to create hierarchies, we will make sure that the Channel folder sits second in the list beneath the Sales folder.

To move the location of a folder, use the following workflow:

1. Click the folder you want to move and hold the mouse button down.
2. Move the mouse cursor to the location where you want this folder to be.
3. Wait until Discoverer highlights the destination folder.
4. Release the mouse button.The folder will now move to the chosen position.

This illustration shows our business area with the Sales folder at the top of the list and the Channel folder next. The position of the remaining folders does not matter because they will all be used to define hierarchies.

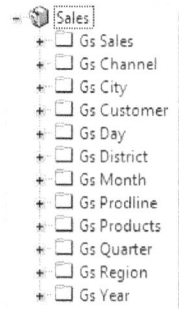

Sales
Gs Sales
Gs Channel
Gs City
Gs Customer
Gs Day
Gs District
Gs Month
Gs Prodline
Gs Products
Gs Quarter
Gs Region
Gs Year

### Grouping Folders

The business area we are building is a relatively simple business area that will have less than ten folders in the final iteration. However, some business areas can have as many as twenty or even thirty folders. If you have more than thirty folders, we recommend you consider breaking the business area up into two or even three smaller areas.

However, sometimes your business will dictate that you have a lot of folders. In this case, you may want to consider grouping your folders into logical sets. One way to group folders is to group them using a theme, where aggregate folders are listed first followed by detail folders. Another way to group folders is to group them by type, with all of the metric folders first followed by all of the dimension folders. A third grouping method consists of grouping the folders by subject area, with all of the folders relating to sales in one group and all of the folders relating to invoices in another group. Of course, you might say that these should be in their own business area, and from the purist perspective so would we. However, we cannot dictate the business area design of all companies, and where this style would not work for your company, for another company this may be exactly what they need.

Whichever method you choose for grouping folders, we believe you ought to use separator folders to split the folders into separate groups.

### Separator Folders

A *separator* folder is really an empty folder that is being used to group sets of folders together. Users cannot select anything from these folders, but that is exactly what we want.

To create a separator folder, use the following workflow:

1. Right-click the name of the business area into which you want to insert a separator folder.
2. From the pop-up menu, select New Folder. Discoverer now adds a new folder, called NewFolder1, to the bottom of the list of folders. The identifier for this new folder will also be NEWFOLDER1, all in uppercase.
3. Using the Folder Properties dialog box, give the folder a new name and a new identifier. Use something like *****D a t e s***** for the name and **DATES_SEPARATOR** for the identifier. We like to use asterisks on both sides of the words, with each word having a space between each letter and with three spaces between words. As you can see, this makes the name of the separator visually stand out.

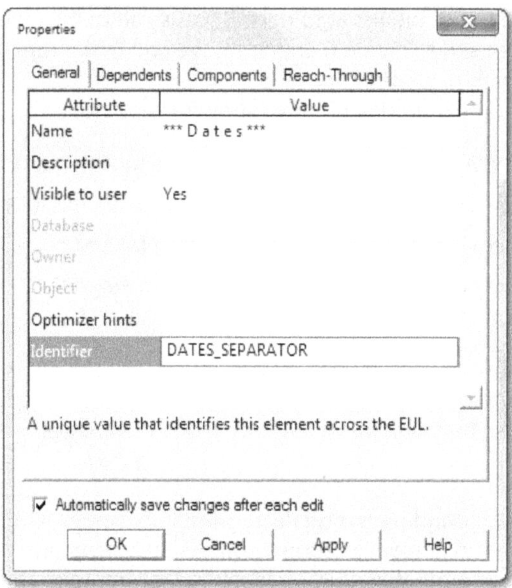


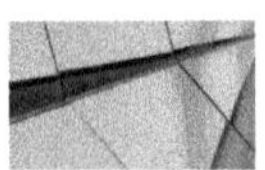

**NOTE**

*As mentioned previously, changing an identifier will prompt Discoverer to ask you to confirm that you understand that any workbooks that use this folder might no longer open. We also mentioned that the object creation stage is the time to do this. Because we are in that stage, not only should you click Yes but we recommend you also check the Don't Show This Warning Again box. Doing so will prevent the warning message from coming up again during the session. The first time you do this you will be prompted twice.*

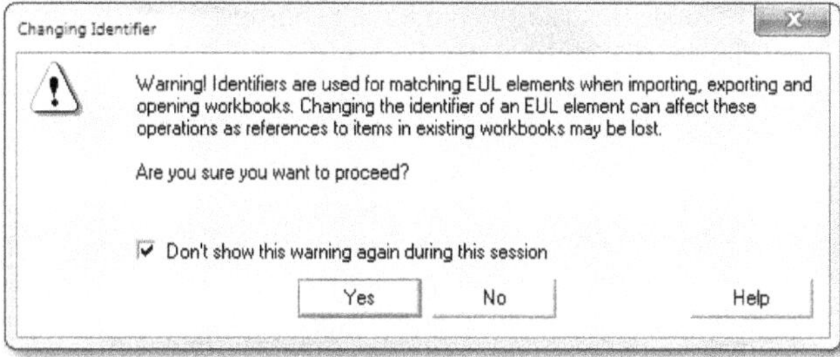


4. Move the separator folder to its new position.

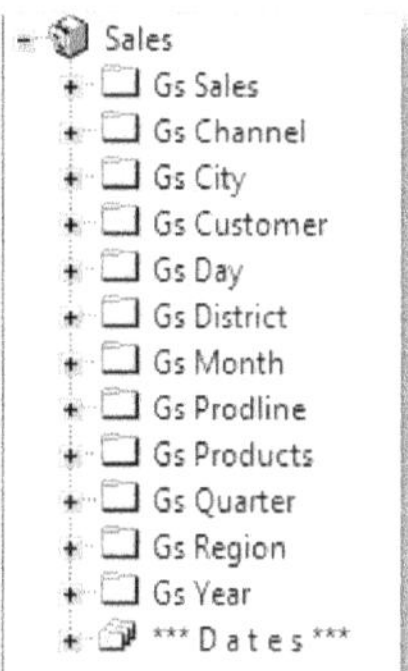


This illustration shows the use of separator folders in our own business area. As you can see, we have placed our separator at the end of the list. This is because it is a placeholder for other folders that we will add later. Notice how the separator name stands out.

## Check the Names of the Items

Even though we told Discoverer to replace underscores with spaces and to remove prefixes from our item names, we need to check the names to ensure that they have meaningful names. Many times, especially when importing objects from the database, you will find that the name of the item is not user-friendly.

If you look here at the names of the items in our Sales folder, you will notice that many of these are cryptic with no spacing and the occasional use of a not-so-obvious abbreviation. These need to be changed.

To rename an item, use this workflow:

1. Right-click the item you want to rename.
2. From the pop-up menu, select Properties.
3. Click in the Name field.
4. Enter a more business-friendly name.
5. Optionally, provide a description.
6. Click OK.

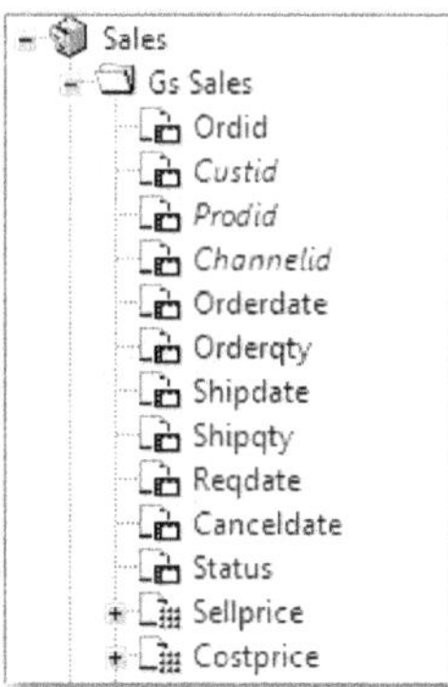

As you can see in the next illustration, we have renamed all of the items that are used as joins (except the three identifier items) in the Sales folder.

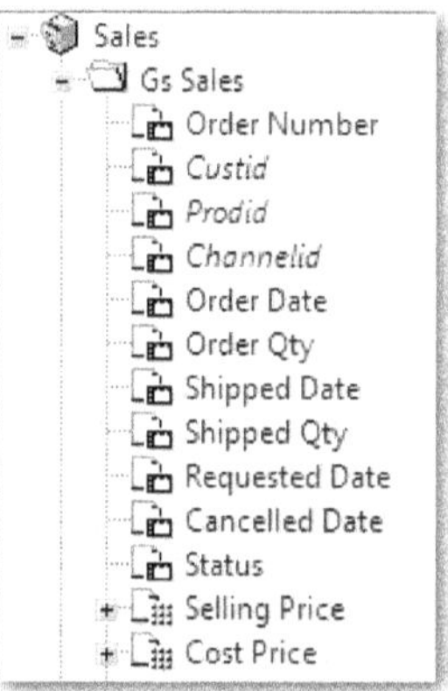


If you have downloaded the database and are following along with us as we create this business area, you need to rename the item names for all of the other folders in the database. The following table lists the items, folder by folder, indicating which need to be renamed and which should be left as they are:

| **Folder** | **Original Name** | **New Name** | **Comment** |
|---|---|---|---|
| GS Channel | Name | Channel | Ignore Channelid |
| GS City | Name | City | Ignore Cityid and Districtid |
| | Countrycode | Country Code | |
| GS Customer | Name | Customer | Ignore Custid and Cityid |
| | Contactname | Contact Name | |
| | Creditlimit | Credit Limit | |
| | Postcode | Post Code | |
| GS Day | Dayid | Calendar Date | Ignore Monthid |
| GS District | Name | District | Ignore Districtid and Regionid |
| GS Month | Monthid | Fiscal Month | Ignore Sequenceno and Quarterid |
| | Enddate | Month End Date | |
| GS Prodline | Name | Prod Line | Ignore Lineid |
| GS Products | Name | Product | Ignore Prodid and Lineid |
| | Prodsize | Size | |
| | Cost | Unit Cost Price | |
| | Sell | Unit Selling Price | |

| Folder | Original Name | New Name | Comment |
|---|---|---|---|
| GS Quarter | Quarterid | Fiscal Quarter | Ignore Yearid |
| | Enddate | Quarter End Date | |
| GS Region | Name | Region | Ignore Regionid |
| GS Year | Yearid | Fiscal Year | |
| | Enddate | Year End Date | |

# Check the Order of the Items

After you have renamed all of the items within the folders, it is now time to check the order of the items. We need to open each folder and look at the ordering of the items, rearranging the order to make selections for users easier.

We moved metrics to the top, followed by descriptor items, dates, and finally nonessential identifiers. After we moved the items into their correct positions, we used item separators to break up the items into logical sets or groups.

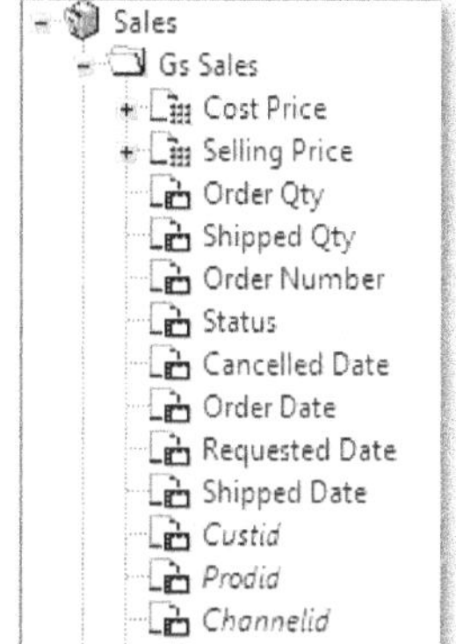


To change the position of an item, use this workflow:

1. Click the item you want to move and hold the mouse button down.
2. Move the mouse cursor to the location where you want this item to be.
3. Wait until Discoverer highlights the destination item.
4. Release the mouse button. The item will now move to the new position.

We have split up the items into the following four logical groups:

- **Metrics** Cost Price, Selling Price, Order Qty, and Ship Qty
- **Descriptor items** Order Number and Status
- **Dates** Cancelled Date, Order Date, Requested Date, and Shipped Date
- **Identifiers** Channelid, Custid, and Prodid

## Using Item Separators

Item separators are used to break up and group sets of items. They help users understand about the different data sets that are in our folders. We can also use the Description field of these items to provide more generic help about how to use the folder.

To insert an item separator, use this workflow:

1. Right-click the name of the folder into which you want to insert an item separator.
2. From the pop-up menu, select New Item. Discoverer opens the New Calculation dialog box.
3. Give the item a separator name such as *** **Metrics** ***.

4. In Calculation, use NULL.
5. Click OK to complete the calculation.
6. Move the item to its correct position.

Take a close look at this illustration to see how we have inserted item separators into the Sales folder to logically break up our folder into two groups:

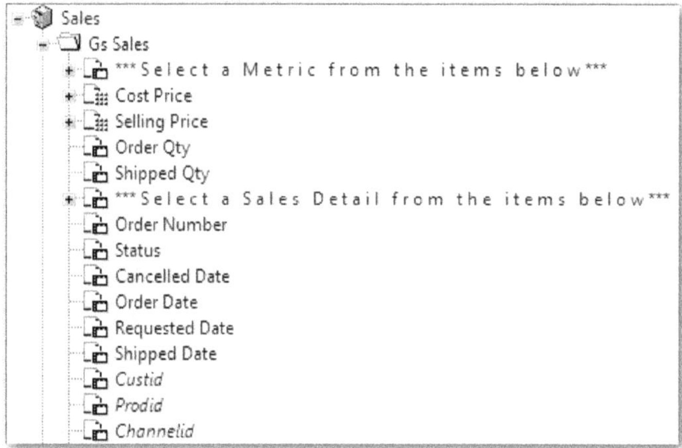


## The Remaining Folders

Because the rest of the folders, with the exception of the Channel folder, will be used to create hierarchies and complex folders, there is no need to alter the order of the items in these folders. Even the Channel folder does not need reordering, because it contains only two items, the channel ID and the channel name. In our final business area, the channel ID will be hidden from the end user, leaving just the channel name, and as only one item will then be visible to the user, there is no need to reorder.

We hope this discussion gives you a good idea when items should be reordered and when they should not be. Here are a few simple rules that should help you decide:

- Reorder when the folder will be visible to the user and more than one item in the folder will be visible to the user.
- When reordering, place items in the following order:
  - Metrics
  - Descriptor items
  - Dates
  - Identifiers
- Do not reorder folders that will be used as the basis for complex folders, but don't forget to reorder the items in the actual complex folders. We will handle this in the next chapter.

## Check Default Positions

Having worked out the positions for all the items in our folders, we need to look at the default positions that have been assigned to those items. In particular, we need to pay close attention to items that could have mathematical possibilities.

By default, when Discoverer imports data items, they are assigned the following default positions:

| **Data Type** | **Default Axis** |
|---|---|
| Dates | Top axis |
| Integers | Top axis |
| Numbers with decimal places | Data point |
| Strings | Top axis |

As you can see in the table, most of the default positions are fine, except for integers. By default, Discoverer assigns integers to the top axis. This is because most integers in a database are items such as identifiers, order numbers, line numbers, and units of measure that do not need to be summed. However, integers such as order quantity and ship quantity do need to be summed and therefore need to have their default format changed.

To change an item's position, use this workflow:

1. Right-click the item whose position you want to change.
2. From the pop-up menu, select Properties.
3. Click in the field called Default Position, and from the drop-down menu, select the new position.
4. Your options are Data Point, Page, Side, Top, Top, or Side.
5. When done, click OK.

**NOTE**
*To change the default position of multiple items at the same time, hold down* CTRL *while clicking each item with the mouse. When you right-click any of the highlighted items, all will be selected at the same time.*

Whenever we change an item's default position like this, we will change it to become a data point, thus allowing us to manage aggregations on the items.

In our business area, two items in the Sales folder need to have their default position changed. These are Order Qty and Ship Qty. This illustration shows the metrics area of the Sales folder as it stands following the change of these two default positions:

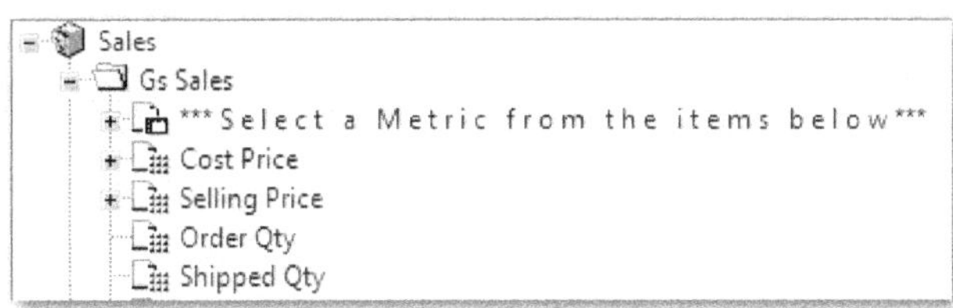

Note how the icon alongside both Order Qty and Ship Qty has changed to look like a small calculator.

## Check Item Aggregation

Having reassigned the default position for our items, we need to look at the default aggregation properties of these items. This is because when you change an item's position to become a data point, Discoverer sets the aggregation property to Detail.

However, if you recall, when we first imported the data definitions from the database, we told Discoverer to set the default position to SUM. Unfortunately, while Discoverer Administrator has many "sticky" features, this is not one of them. When you change an item's default position to data point, Discoverer *always* sets the new aggregation to Detail. Therefore, after you have changed an item's default position, you now have to also check the default aggregation.

**NOTE**
*The same situation applies when you bring in a new data point item from the database. Discoverer assigns the default aggregation of these items to Detail also.*

To change an item's default aggregation, use this workflow:

1. Right-click the item whose property you want to change.
2. From the pop-up menu, select Properties.
3. Click in the Default Aggregate field, and from the drop-down menu select the new aggregate.
4. Your options are AVG, COUNT, Detail, MAX, MIN, and SUM.
5. When done, click OK.

**NOTE**
*To change the default aggregate of multiple items at the same time, hold down* CTRL *while clicking each item with the mouse. When you right-click any of the highlighted items, all will be selected at the same time.*

In our business area, there are two items in the Sales folder that need to have their default aggregation changed. These are Order Qty and Ship Qty. The illustration here shows the Properties dialog box as it looks after we selected SUM from the drop-down menu:

**NOTE**
*In the preceding dialog box, note how the name of the database column is blank. This is because we changed the default aggregate for more than one item at the same time.*

## Check Default Formats

When Discoverer imports data items from the database, it automatically assigns the default format of the data items as follows:

- **Dates** DD-MON-RRRR, or to whatever is the default NLS date format
- **Integers** As defined within the database, as in 9999999999
- **Numbers with decimal places** As defined within the database, as in 999999D99
- **Strings** As defined in the database

So, if the item formats have been defaulted to the way in which they were defined within the database, why do we need to check them? We check the format for a number of reasons, among which are these:

- To allow for leading zeros in numbers that have decimals
- To increase the number of decimal places to allow for better mathematical accuracy
- To increase the number of places before the decimal to allow for summations
- To insert comma separators
- To truncate dates
- And many other reasons

To change an item's default format, use this workflow:

1. Right-click the item whose format you want to change.
2. From the pop-up menu, select Properties.
3. Click in the Format field.
4. Change the format.
5. When done, click OK.

In our business area, we need to change the format of two data items. We will change the following:

- Cost Price and Selling Price, from 999999D99 to 999999990D99, thus increasing the number of places to the left and inserting a leading zero. This will allow users to compute summations on the total cost or revenue without worrying that the computation will fail.

## Summary

In this chapter we introduced you to the Discoverer Administrator tool. You learned the key components of the tool as well as your responsibilities as an administrator. We showed you how to build an End User Layer and a business area based on the Global Sales Widgets database. We described to you the importance of understanding and anticipating end-user requirements and the six steps to a successful Discoverer implementation.

We also showed you all of the steps required to make Discoverer work in Apps mode.

You learned how to refine the business area by arranging the folders and items in a meaningful way. You also learned how to change an item's properties in order to improve performance. We taught you how to create folders that hide the complexities of the database from the users and hierarchies to improve drilling capabilities.

Using Discoverer Admin is truly an art and not just a science. In the next few chapters, we will show you how to create an environment for reporting that is truly exceptional.

# CHAPTER 17

# Editing the Business Area

In this chapter we will expand on what you learned in Chapter 16 and show you how to continue with the remaining business area checks. We will show you how to manage lists of values and joins. Later we will show you how to add new folders, followed by managing hierarchies. Finally, we will show you some of the more advanced mechanisms for item management, culminating in an explanation of how to manage descriptive lists of values.

# Remaining Business Area Checks

The last three checks you need to make on a new business are

- Reviewing folder names
- Managing lists of values
- Managing joins

## Review Folder Names

Before we continue with the next set of business area checks, we need to make sure we have finished everything from the previous chapter. In that chapter, we advised you to rename all of your folders; however, we only provided you with a workflow and did not ask you to rename the folders. As a recap, here is the workflow once again to change the name, description, or identifier of a folder:

1. Right-click the folder you want to check.
2. From the pop-up menu, select Properties.
3. Make sure the name, description, and identifier meet your standards.
4. If not, change the name, description, and identifier.
5. When done, click OK.

The following table lists the folders, in the order that they appear in the business area, indicating the new names that will be used:

| Folder | New Name |
|---|---|
| GS Sales | Sales |
| GS Channel | Channel |
| GS City | City |
| GS Customer | Customer |
| GS Day | Calendar Date |
| GS District | District |
| GS Month | Fiscal Month |
| GS Prodline | Prodline |
| GS Products | Products |

| Folder | New Name |
|---|---|
| GS Quarter | Fiscal Quarter |
| GS Region | Region |
| GS Year | Fiscal Year |

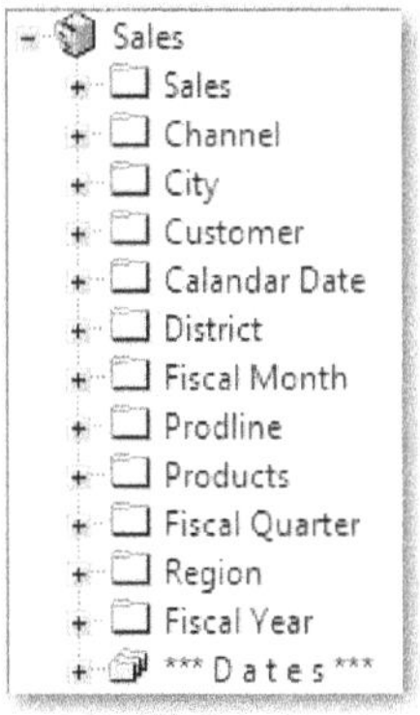

When done, your business area should look like the illustration shown here.

Sales
Sales
Channel
City
Customer
Calandar Date
District
Fiscal Month
Prodline
Products
Fiscal Quarter
Region
Fiscal Year
*** D a t e s ***

## Managing Lists of Values

The next stage to successful business area management is to create lists of values. Whether you allowed Discoverer to create its own lists of values during the import stage determines whether you will have to create your own list of values or check existing lists of values. As we advised you not to allow Discoverer to automatically create lists of values, we will start by showing you how to create them.

### Defining Lists of Values

If you followed our advice and did not allow Discoverer to create its own lists of values during the import stage, you get to have some fun and create them now. Just as when riding the Tour de France, you have come over that monstrous climb in the middle of the stage to find that you have a long downhill section before the next climb, so creating lists of values following all that checking comes like a breath of fresh air. This is a chance to catch your breath before the next climb.

In the language of Discoverer, a list of values is an item class. According to the Discoverer Administration 11*g* help guide, *item classes* are "groups of items that share some similar properties. An item class enables you to define item properties once and then assign the item class to other items that share similar properties."

Now that you have set up the business area with the items you want, it is time to create the lists of values that your users will need when creating their worksheets. Before we show you the steps required to create a list of values, we will discuss how they will be used.

### Lists of Values Usage

You do not need to place a list of values on every item in a folder. We have rarely seen an occasion when users need to query lists of identifiers. They usually don't need to see lists of values on dates either. If you recall from our discussions with the Plus tool, Discoverer Plus will display a calendar pop-up whenever a user is offered a parameter that is a date. You, as the administrator, do not need to do anything to enable this behavior, so why go to the trouble of creating a list of values on the date?

Another reason for not allowing Discoverer to automatically create its own lists of values is that during the automatic creation stage Discoverer does not check to see whether an existing item class already exists. For example, let's say you create a new business area and import two objects, one for the Purchase Order header and one for the Purchase Order detail. Both objects may well contain identical items. At the very least you will probably have the PO Number in both. If you allowed Discoverer to automatically create its own lists of values, it would have created two, one for the PO Number in the Header folder and one for the PO Number in the Detail folder. This may not sound like too big of a deal, but imagine that you have created a large business area that has 10 folders, each of which contains a product number. Discoverer will create 10 item classes, which is not a very efficient way of working.

**NOTE**
*We deliberately used the word object in the preceding paragraph because you can import data definitions based on tables, views, or materialized views.*

Continuing with the usage of lists of values, we will give you another very good reason not to automatically allow Discoverer to create its own lists of values. Let's say you have a table that contains ten million rows, not an uncommon scenario. Let's say the table contains a column called Gender that has two values, Male and Female. If you allow Discoverer to create a list of values based on the Gender column in this table, every time a user clicks the list of values, SQL will execute a select distinct gender clause from that table. In essence you are forcing the database to look for two values out of a ten million row table. Later in this chapter we will show you how to overcome this by using a custom folder to generate this list of values.

## Creating a List of Values

Now that we have explained why you should not allow Discoverer to automatically create its own list of values, we will walk you through creating manual lists of values.

To create a manual list of values, use the following workflow:

1. Determine the item for which you want a list of values.
2. Navigate to and right-click the item, and from the pop-up menu select New Item Class.
3. Discoverer launches the Item Class Wizard and starts at step 2.

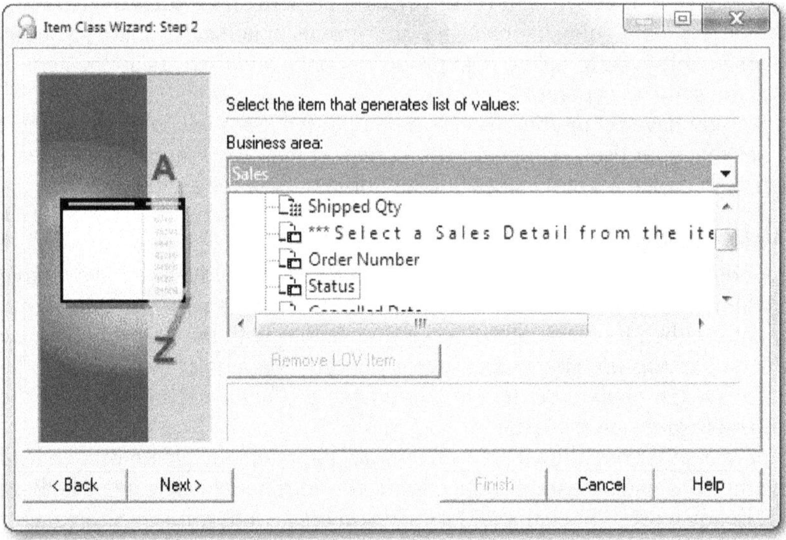

**NOTE**

*If you want to create a list of values using an alternative sort or for use in a drill to detail, you can find these switches on step 1 of the wizard. To get to step 1 of the wizard, click the Back button. For this exercise, we will create a standard list of values.*

4. The item you right-clicked in step 1 of this workflow will be selected automatically. Although you can change it if you want, we don't recommend you alter the settings once you have started. Having confirmed that the item checked is the one that you want to use for generating this new list of values, click Next.

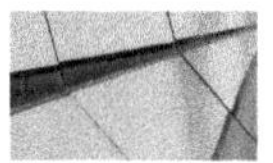

**NOTE**

*If you have opted to create a list of values using an alternative sort, Discoverer inserts an additional step into the wizard at this point. Because we will discuss alternative sorts later in the chapter, you should not see this screen at this time.*

5. You are in step 3 of the wizard or step 4 if you are creating an alternative sort. In this step, as you can see next, you can optionally associate the new list of values with other items in the business area. Unless you are an experienced Discoverer administrator, we don't recommend you do this, because you can easily make a mistake and assign the list of values to the wrong item.

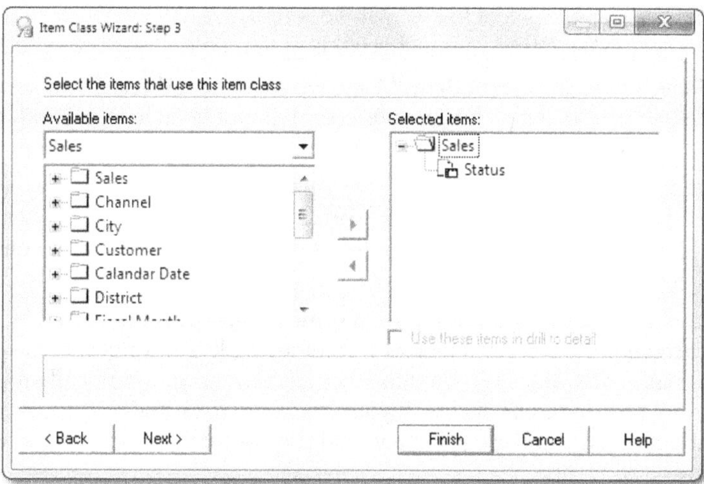


6. Click Next.

7. Step 4 of the wizard (step 5 if you created an alternative sort) is where you assign advanced options. As you can see in the following illustration, you can assign five options:

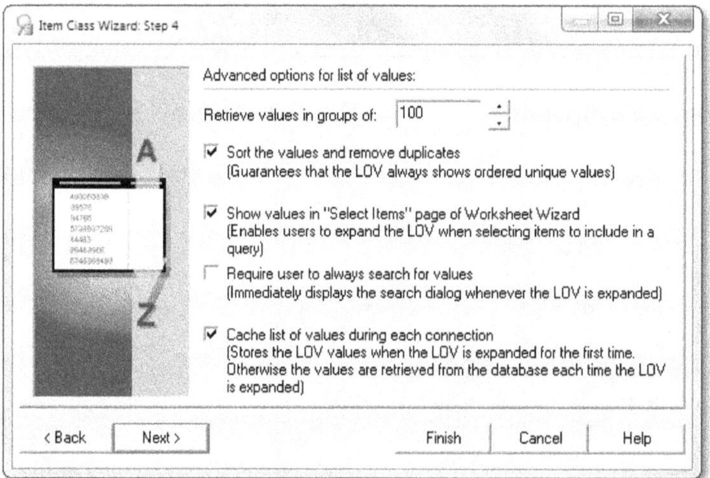


- **Retrieve Values In Groups Of** This defaults to 100, and unless you have a real need to alter this value, you should leave this setting as is.
- **Sort The Values And Remove Duplicates** This is checked by default because this option guarantees that the list will be sorted and will not contain duplicates. We do not recommend that you uncheck this option unless you have good reason.
- **Show Values In "Select Items" Page Of Worksheet Wizard** This is checked by default. If you uncheck this, your users will not be able to expand the list of values when creating worksheets. We do not recommend you uncheck this option.
- **Require User To Always Search For Values** This is unchecked by default. If you check this, Discoverer will launch the Search dialog box whenever a user clicks the list of values. Should you have a large list of values, you may want to consider turning on this option.
- **Cache List Of Values During Each Connection** This is checked by default because caching is the most efficient way of retrieving lists of values. If you do not want to cache the values but want to force Discoverer to dynamically re-create the list every time the users access it, you should uncheck this box. If you are worried about security and are using a virtual private database, you might want to consider unchecking this.

8. After you have assigned your advanced options, click Next.
9. Step 5 of the wizard (step 6 if you created an alternative sort) is where you assign a meaningful name and optional description. We recommend you name these ChannelLOV, ProductLOV, and so on. While not mandatory, we recommend you use the description box if you have changed any of the default options. It is acceptable to have spaces and mixed case in the names; however, since the end user will not see these names, we don't add spaces. It is really a holdover from the days when few applications

allowed spaces, and we have become accustomed to omitting spaces when they are not needed. This step is shown here.

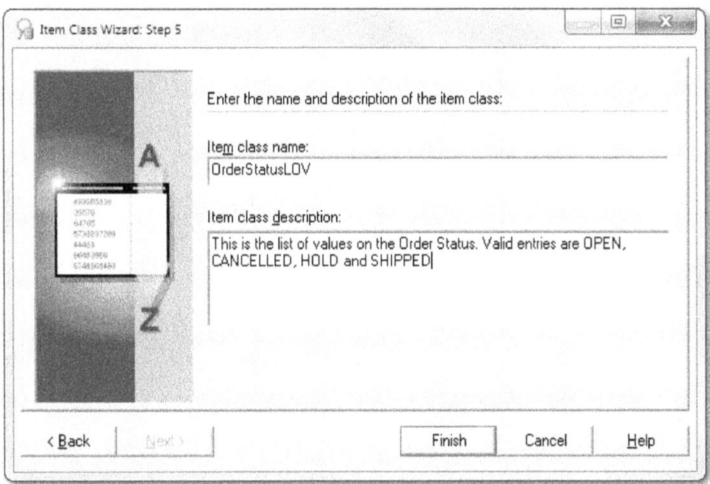


10. When done, click Finish. Discoverer creates the list of values, which you should test by clicking the plus icon alongside the item.

**NOTE**

*If Discoverer gives you a warning saying that this could take a long time, ignore it. As the administrator, you need to test that your list of values works and is efficient! If the retrieval times out, you can increase the limit by selecting Tools | Options from the menu bar and going to the Query Governor tab and increasing the default value.*

When you click Finish, you may encounter a "no privileges on tablespace" error. If this happens, this means your user does not have all of the necessary privileges to be a Discoverer administrator. To correct this particular problem, you need to ask your DBA to issue the following grant:

GRANT UNLIMITED TABLESPACE TO user

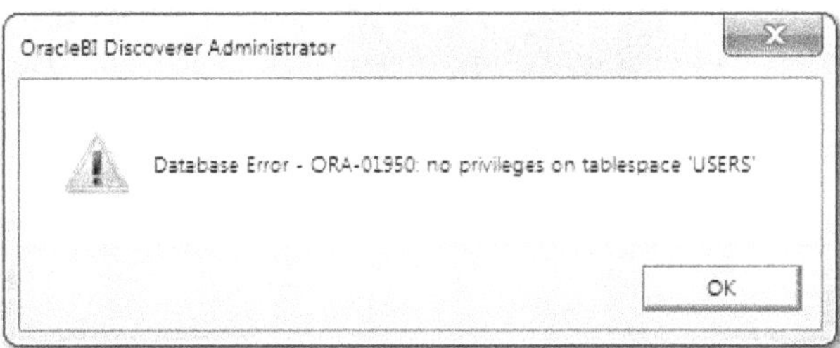


## Removing a List of Values

From time to time it will become necessary for you to remove a list of values from the system. This is easy to do.

To remove a list of values, use the following workflow:

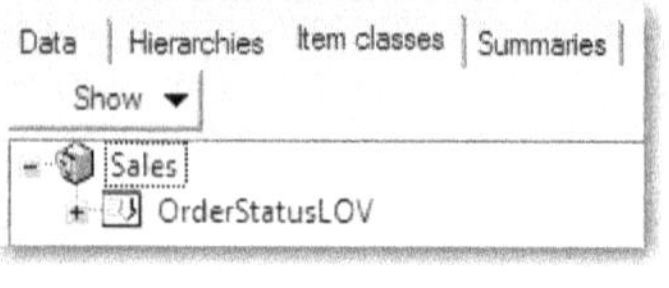


1. Click the Item Classes tab in the main Administrator window, as shown here.
2. Locate and right-click the list of values you want to remove, and from the pop-up menu select Delete Item Class, as shown here.

3. The Confirm Delete dialog box will open.

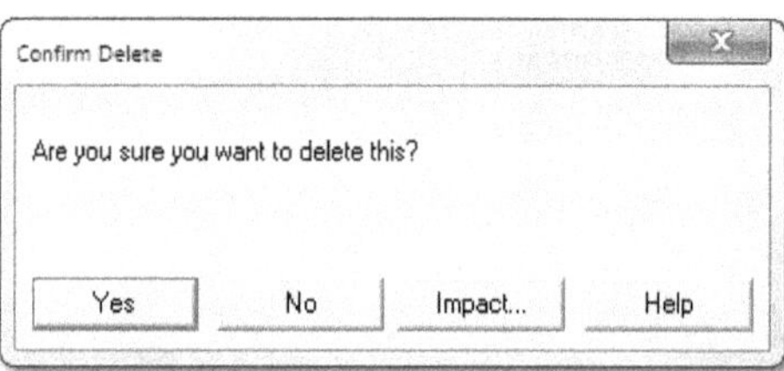


4. When prompted "Are you sure you want to delete this," you have four options.
   - **Yes** Click this to delete the item class.
   - **No** Click this to cancel.
   - **Impact** Click this to see what impact deleting this item class will have. If Discoverer displays only one item in the Impact dialog box, you are probably safe in deleting the item class. If Discoverer displays more than one impacted item, you might want to reconsider.

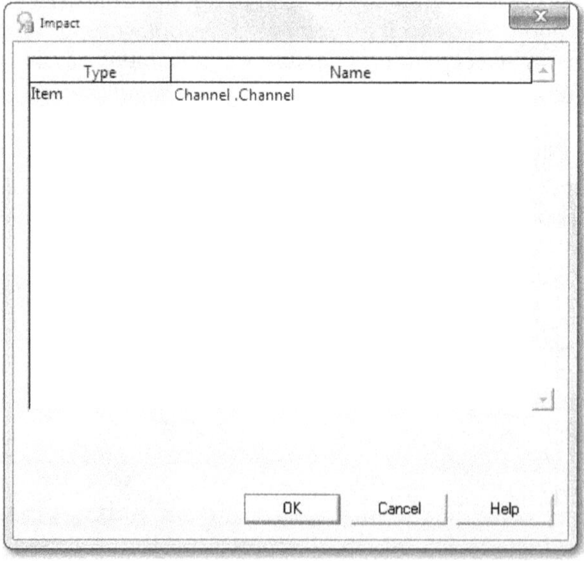


   - **Help** Click this to open context-sensitive help in a browser window.
5. If you click Yes, the item class will be deleted.

## Checking Lists of Values

If we had allowed Discoverer to automatically create its own lists of values or if you need to undertake a cursory examination of an existing list, you will need to examine the item class settings.

To check a list of values, follow this workflow:

1. Click the Item Classes tab in the main Administrator window.
2. Locate and right-click the list of values you want to check, and from the pop-up menu select either Edit Item Class or Properties.
3. If you selected Edit Item Class, as you can see next, Discoverer opens the Edit Item Class dialog box.

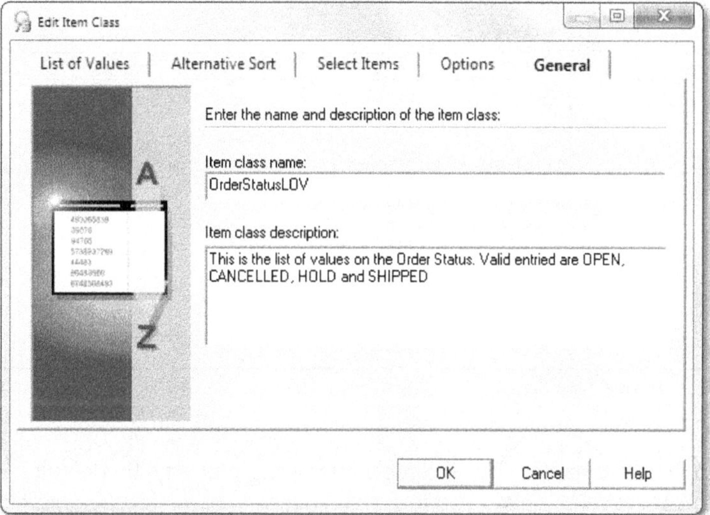


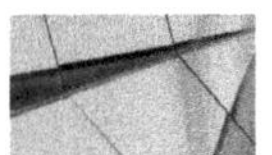

**NOTE**

*The Edit Item Class dialog box is a multitabbed box that corresponds to the steps in the Item Class Wizard. After making any required changes, click OK.*

4. If you selected Properties, as you can see in Figure 17-1, Discoverer opens the Item Class Properties dialog box.

The Item Class Properties dialog box is a form that allows you to view or change the properties of a list of values. If you take a close look at this box, you will notice that there are a couple of additional properties that cannot be set anywhere else. These are explained in the following section.

### Additional Item Class Properties

In the preceding section we showed you how to examine the properties of an item class by launching the Item Class Properties dialog box, shown in Figure 17-1. In this box there are two additional properties that cannot be set anywhere else.

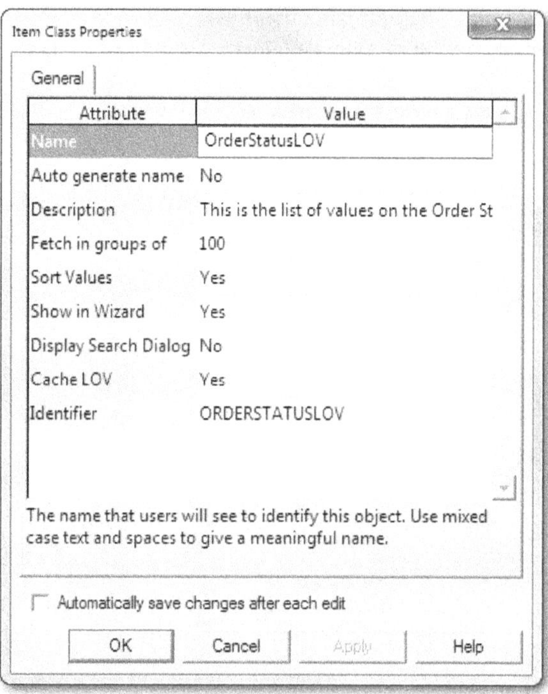


**FIGURE 17-1.** *Item Class Properties dialog box*

- **Auto generate name** This is a most interesting property. By default it is set to No, which means Discoverer allows you to assign your own name for the item class. If you change this to Yes, Discoverer replaces your name with an autogenerated name consisting of the folder name and the item name upon which the item class is based. Unless you switch this property to No, you will not be allowed to edit the name again. Furthermore, although we cannot show this to you in a black-and-white illustration, Discoverer colors the name of the item class on the Item Classes tab. If you redisplay the Item Class Properties dialog box, you will notice that the name is now grayed out. This indicates that the item class name is noneditable.
- **Identifier** Discoverer assigns unique identifiers to item classes. By default, this is the uppercased value of the item class name. There is no need to change this name unless your corporate standards dictate.

**NOTE**
*Even though setting the "Auto generate name" property to Yes causes Discoverer to rename the item class, this has no impact on the Identifier. The Identifier can be changed only manually.*

### Required Lists of Values

In our tutorial business area, we need to create 14 lists of values. The following table shows the lists of values we will create:

| Folder Name | Item Name | List of Value Name |
|---|---|---|
| Sales | Status | StatusLOV |
| Channel | Channel | ChannelLOV |
| City | City | CityLOV |
| Customer | Customer | CustomerLOV |
| District | District | DistrictLOV |
| Month | Fiscal Month | MonthLOV |
| Products | Product | ProductLOV |
| | Size | ProdSizeLOV |
| Prod Line | Prod Line | ProdLineLOV |
| Quarter | Fiscal Quarter | QuarterLOV |
| Region | Region | RegionLOV |
| Year | Fiscal Year | YearLOV |

Having created the lists of values, click the Item Classes tab. You should see the lists displayed, as shown here.

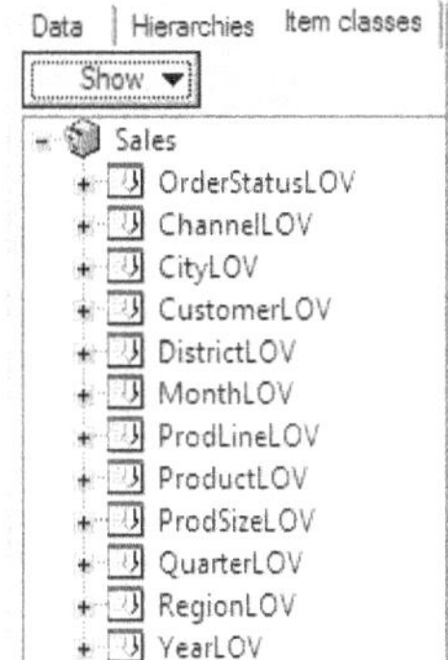


### Issues with Lists of Values

These are the most common issues that occur with lists of values:

- Lists of values take too long to generate and time out.
- Lists of values show the data in the wrong sort sequence.

If users report that the list of values is timing out or it is not producing the full list, you have the following three possible solutions.

**Increase the Time Out Limit** If the user is using Desktop or Plus, tell them to do the following:

1. Launch Discoverer Desktop.
2. From the Tools menu, select Options | Query Governor.
3. Change the option "Cancel value retrieval after" to a higher value.
4. Click OK.

If the issue is occurring in Plus, do the following:

1. Launch Discoverer Plus.
2. From the Tools menu, select Options | Query Governor.
3. Change the option "Cancel list-of-values retrieval after" to a higher value.
4. Click Apply.

If the issue is occurring in Viewer, do the following:

1. Launch Discoverer Viewer.
2. Click the Preferences link.
3. Change the option "Cancel list-of-values retrieval after" to a higher value.
4. Click Apply.

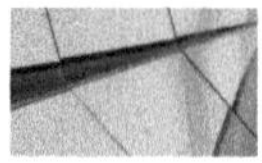

**NOTE**
*Between Plus and Viewer there is only one set of preferences, so if a user changes the retrieval value in one, it is automatically reflected in the other the next time the user connects.*

If the issue is occurring in the Administrator edition, do the following:

1. Launch Discoverer Administrator.
2. From the Tools menu, select Options | Query Governor.
3. Change the option "Cancel value retrieval after" to a higher value.
4. Click OK.

**Force the Use of the Search Dialog Box** Launch the Item Class Properties dialog box and set the property called Display Search Dialog to Yes. This will force the Discoverer end user to be prompted for the item that they want rather than displaying a large list of values.

**Use Another Data Item to Create the List of Values** If neither of the preceding two options rectifies the situation, you should try creating the list of values on an alternate item, perhaps from another table. You might also want to consider using a custom folder for this purpose.

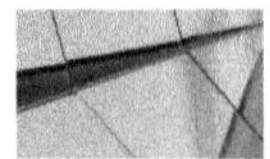

**NOTE**
*Another option for improving retrieval times is to optimize the database table by adding an index.*

When checking lists of values, you need to be aware that Discoverer creates them based on the following underlying data types:

- DATE
- NUMBER
- VARCHAR or VARCHAR2

Sorts based on dates and numbers will always be in the correct order. Sorts based on VARCHAR or VARCHAR2 data types, strings to us, can create problems because they will sort alphabetically. Sometimes this is not the order we want them to sort in. The following section on alternative sorts addresses this issue.

## Using Alternative Sorts

Sometimes, when you look at a list of values, you will see that it is not in the order that you would like. To overcome this, you can use what is called an *alternative sort*. To use an alternative sort, you must have another unique item available in the folder that contains the item on which you created the list of values.

This alternative item must be one of the following:

- Another unique and available item, such as month end date
- An artificially created sequence number

Among the most common data elements that sort in the wrong order are days of the week and months of the year. For both of these, you will need to create an alternative sort if you want your users to see the list displayed in the right order.

For example, look at the following table:

| Natural Order | Logical Order |
|---|---|
| April | January |
| August | February |
| December | March |
| February | April |
| January | May |
| July | June |
| June | July |
| March | August |
| May | September |
| November | October |
| October | November |
| September | December |

**Creating an Alternative Sort** Let's look at the Month data in the sample database. Open the Month folder and click the plus character alongside the Fiscal Month data item. This opens the current list of values, which, as you can see here, is displayed in alphabetical order.

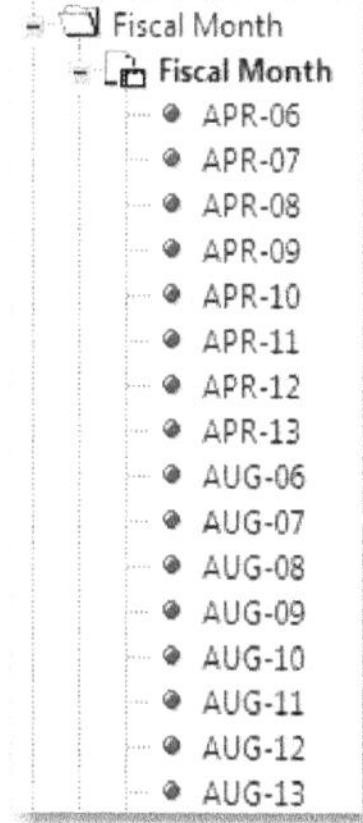


To add an alternative sort, use the following workflow:

1. Click the Item Classes tab.
2. Expand the list of item classes.
3. Locate the list of values that needs the alternative sort. In our case, we are looking for the MonthLOV.
4. Right-click the item class, and from the pop-up menu select Edit Item Class.
5. In the Edit Item Class dialog box, click the Alternative Sort tab.
6. Select the item that will be used to generate the new alternative sort. In our case, we can use the Month End Date because for any one month there is only one month ending date.

As mentioned previously, because dates always sort correctly, this is an excellent item on which to sort.

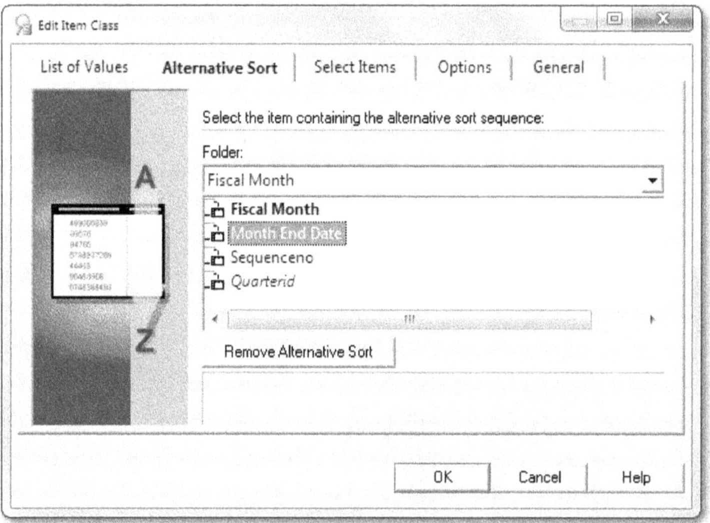


7. Click OK.
8. Recheck the list of values. As you can see in this illustration, the months are sorted correctly.

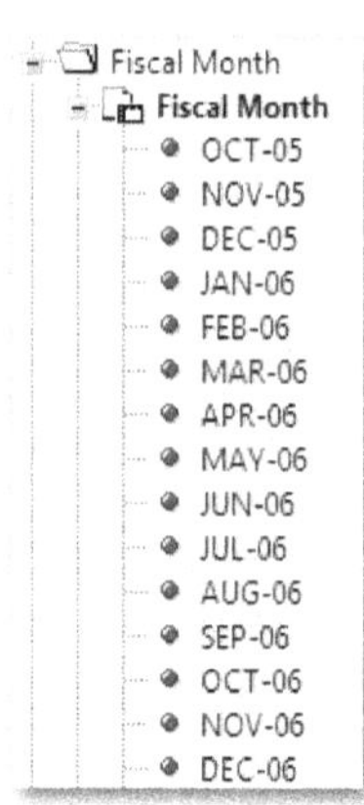

**NOTE**

*Days of the week are trickier because there is no obvious alternative item that you can use to sort by. However, if we think outside the box, we can create an artificial sort using a sequence number as the alternate item. We will show you how to do this when we discuss custom folders later in this chapter.*

**Removing an Alternative Sort** If you make a mistake by setting an alternative sort for an item that does not need this type of sort, you can remove the alternative sort. This is a new feature. If you have used previous versions of Discoverer, you will know how hard it was to remove an alternative sort until now.

To remove an alternative sort, use the following workflow:

1. Right-click the item class that has the alternative sort you want to remove, and from the pop-up menu select Edit Item Class.
2. Click the Alternative Sort tab.
3. Click the Remove Alternative Sort button.
4. Click OK.

# Managing Joins

The next thing you need to do in working with a newly created business area is to create the joins that you need between your folders or check the joins that already exist. As we hope you recall from the creation of our business area, we asked Discoverer to automatically create joins for us based on the primary- and foreign-key constraints in the database. Looking at Figure 17-2 of the data model that we used for the tutorial database, you see that there are 12 tables, interlinked by a series of one-to-many relationships.

## Defining Joins

In Discoverer, a join relates two folders using one or more matching items, whereas in the database a join relates two tables using one or more matching columns. Just like in the database, where the DBA has to know which table is the parent and which is the child, Discoverer needs to know which folder is the master and which is the detail. What we are looking for are one-to-many (1:N) or one-to-one (1:1) relationships. A many-to-many (N:N) relationship cannot be handled by Discoverer, so these relationships need to be resolved in some other way.

When you create a join between two folders, Discoverer gives end users the rights to pull items out of both folders into the same worksheet. The user does not need to know how the join was created or which folder is the master. This complexity is hidden from the end user by the End

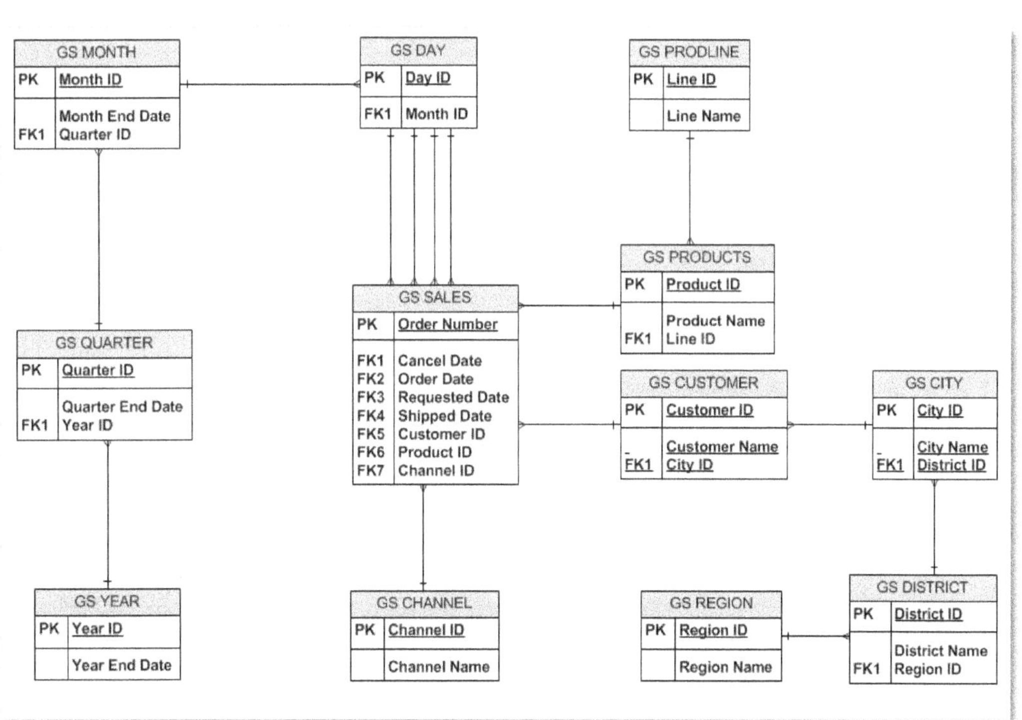


**FIGURE 17-2.** *Tutorial database schema*

User Layer's metadata. Our job, as Discoverer administrators, is to make life as easy as possible for our end users. We should be looking for ways to make it easier for the end users to build the queries they need. One of the best ways we can do this is to create joins between folders. Users do not have this power, so if we do not create joins, our end users will have a difficult time.

If you look back at Figure 17-2, which outlines the GSW data model, you will see that there are 12 tables, interlinked by a series of one-to-many relationships.

## Data Types

Discoverer has a rule that the data items on both ends of a join must be of the same data type and size; otherwise, it cannot create the join. The prime responsibility therefore rests with the data designer and the DDL creator to ensure that the items are the same. However, as the Discoverer administrator, if you find that the data items do not match, what can you do?

The real question is, what should you do? Our first piece of advice is to take a deep breath and not panic. These things happen from time to time, and ideally this data mismatch is just an oversight. Go back to the data designer and the DDL creator to see whether they are aware of this situation and ask whether this was intentional. Tact will dictate that you should not use the words *bug* or *bad design* when discussing a data model with your data designer. You do need to find out whether a data model revision is planned. If the answer is no and the data model cannot be changed, the question is—what can you do?

Correcting this situation in Discoverer is not the most effective way and will almost certainly cause performance issues. However, by using a function to convert the data type and size of one of the items to match the data type and size of the other item, you can at least create the join. Should you do this? Ideally, no—but sometimes you will have no choice. Workarounds are one of our greatest weapons!

But which item should you change? Speaking logically, you need to change the one that has the least impact. In most master-detail relationships you will typically be joining from the primary key of a master folder to an item in the detail folder that may or may not be associated with an index. You do not need primary-key/foreign-key constraints enabled in the database to make this work.

Applying a function to change the data type of an item in the primary key of the master folder could have serious consequences for performance. Doing this will probably negate searches on the primary key and cause the Oracle database to do a full table scan, something you want to avoid if you can. We therefore need to look at the other end of the relationship, at the properties of the detail item. We will cover this later in this section when we discuss creating a complex join.

## Creating a Simple Join

Let's focus on one pair of tables, the GS_Prodline and GS_Products folders. Looking at the data model, we can see that the primary key of the GS_Prodline table is the column called Line ID. When we look inside the GS_Products table, we can see that there is also a column called Line ID. There is a 1:N join between these tables, and the parent table is the GS_Prodline.

Looking inside Discoverer, we have folders that correspond to these two tables. The Discoverer folder corresponding to the GS_Prodline table is called Prodline, while the folder corresponding to the GS_Products table is called Products. We therefore need to create a join from the ProdLine folder to the Products folder.

To create a join, use the following workflow:

1. Determine the two folders that need to be joined.
2. Determine the names of the items that need to be joined.

3. Determine which folder is the master and which folder is the detail.
4. Navigate to and open the folder that contains the master item.
5. Navigate to and right-click the master item, and from the pop-up menu select New Join.
6. Discoverer opens the Join Wizard. Looking at the first screen of the Join Wizard, you can see that it has the following seven areas:

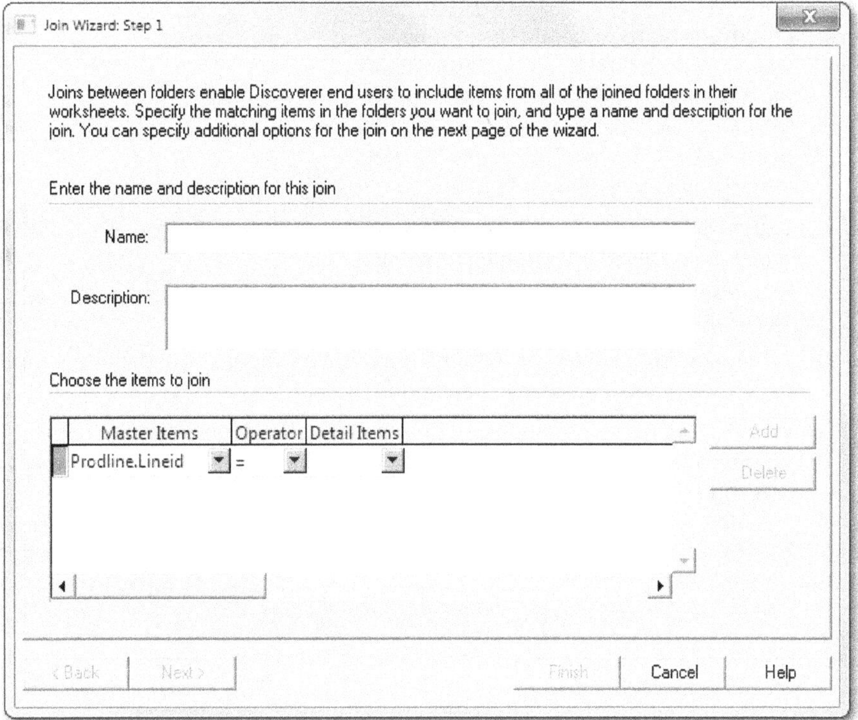


- **Name** Join names are critical to the successful operation of Discoverer workbooks. Every join must have a unique name, not only in the business area but across the entire EUL. Discoverer will autogenerate a name if you leave this blank.
- **Description** This is a placeholder for you to type a description about the join.
- **Choose the items to join** This area comprises three components: a master item, an operator, and a detail item. These components are the heart of the join and tell Discoverer exactly how the join is put together.
- **Add** Use this button to add additional join items, in effect creating a composite join between multiple items. For example, in Apps you might have both a category code and a category item code joining the two tables together.
- **Delete** Use this button to delete the secondary components that are in use in a composite join.

- **Next** Use this button to navigate to the second screen of the Join Wizard. It will be active only when the three join items, the master item, the operator, and the detail item, have been entered.
- **Finish** Use this button to complete the join. It is active only in step 2.

7. Discoverer starts to create the join by inserting, under the heading Master Items, the folder and item names of the item we selected. Click the drop-down icon under the heading Detail Items. This opens the New Join dialog box, as shown here.

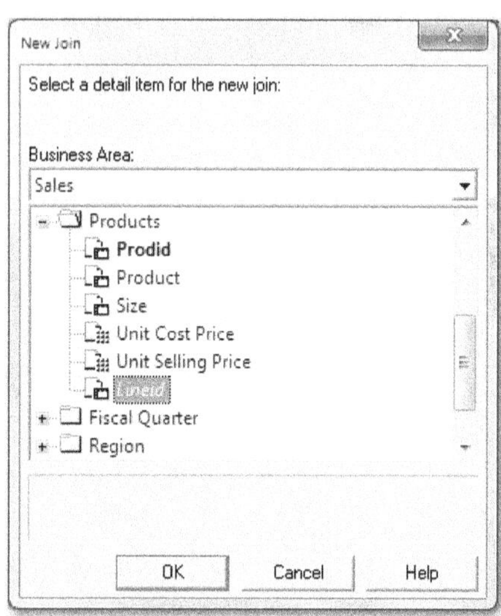


8. In the New Join dialog box you need to select the business area, folder, and detail item required to complete the join and then click OK.
9. When control is passed back to the wizard, you should notice that the folder and item name of the detail item have been filled in.
10. While a join name is mandatory, Discoverer will autogenerate the name for you based on the names of the folders. Therefore, you should notice that the Next key is now active. You should also note that the Finish button is still grayed out.

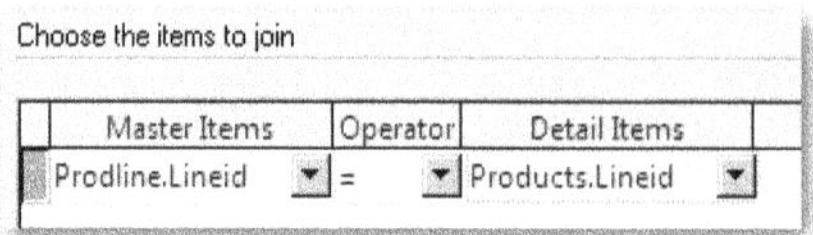

**NOTE**

*In version 9.0.4, and continued with 10.1.2, Oracle added a number of SQL optimizations to the SQL generation capabilities of Discoverer. One of these is join trimming, which means that in a query that joins two or more tables, if the query can be answered and still satisfy all constraints by not including a table at all in the SQL, then Discoverer will drop that table from the SQL that it sends to the database. The Next screen when defining a join is for that purpose: to force the Discoverer administrator to make a choice and not simply rely on the defaults. It is therefore good practice to pay more attention to this second screen than ever before.*

11. Click Next to proceed to the second screen of the wizard.
12. In step 2 of the Join Wizard, you need to provide information about the join details and set any optional configurations you need. These are the two main areas of this screen:

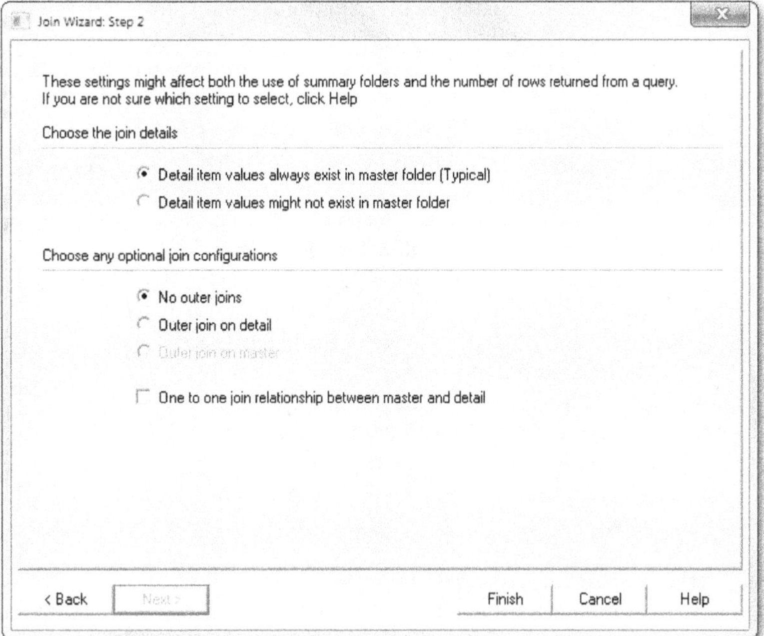


- **Choose the join details** In this area you must tell Discoverer whether the detail items always exist in the master folder or whether these are optional. You must check one of the two radio buttons. Typically, you will nearly always encounter the situation where the detail items do exist in the master folder. This is the default.
- **Choose any optional configurations** In this area you must tell Discoverer about the join itself, whether there is an outer join, whether the outer join is on the detail or the master, or whether the join is a one-to-one. Normally, the configuration is such that the join is not an outer join. This is the default.

**NOTE**
*The option Outer Join On Master is grayed out. This option is available only when you check the button Detail Item Values Might Not Exist In Master Folder in the join detail section. Unless you really need to and you know what you are doing, take care adjusting these settings. Making incorrect join settings will result in worksheets that at best run slow or at worst give incorrect results.*

13. Click Finish.
14. Discoverer completes the join and closes the wizard.

## Creating Complex Joins

A complex join occurs in two situations.

- When one of the data types is wrong
- When multiple items are used to join the folders

What follows is a fictitious example of a multi-item join. This is a join between a Product folder and a materialized view that has been created against Sales. After speaking with the data modeler, it was determined that the items shown in the following table make up this join:

| Master Folder | Master Item | Detail Folder | Detail Item | Join Type | Join Order |
|---|---|---|---|---|---|
| Product | Org ID | Sales MV | Org ID | Complex | First |
| Product | Prod ID | Sales MV | Prod ID | Complex | Second |

As mentioned earlier, the only stipulation that Discoverer has is that the data types of all the items in the join must match. However, in our situation we have a further complication. As defined in the database, the data type of Prod ID in the Product table is NUMBER(4), whereas in the Sales materialized views it is defined as VARCHAR2(4). The lengths are the same, but the data types are not. When we tried building this join, Discoverer responded with the error message shown here.

Clicking OK returned us to the Join Wizard, and we cannot continue with the join. One of the data types must be changed.

**Changing Data Types for a Join** Whenever you have a situation where the data types are not the same and you need to create a join, you need to change the data type for one of the join items.

To change the data type, use the following workflow:

1. Click the heading for the folder that contains the data type you want to change, in this case the Sales MV.
2. From the pop-up menu, select New Item.
3. Discoverer displays the following New Item dialog box:

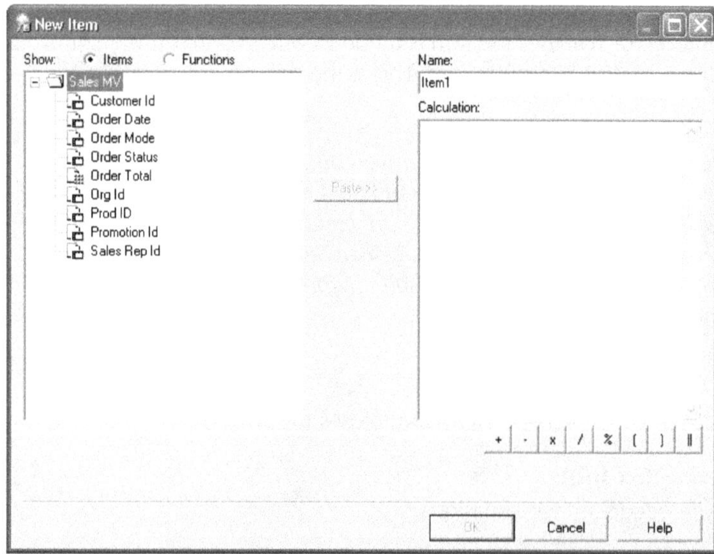


4. Enter a meaningful, unique name for the item. In our case we will name it New Prod ID.

5. Expand the list of items in the Show box and locate the item you want to change.
6. Paste or push the item into the Calculation box and use a converter function to make the change. Your calculation should look like this:

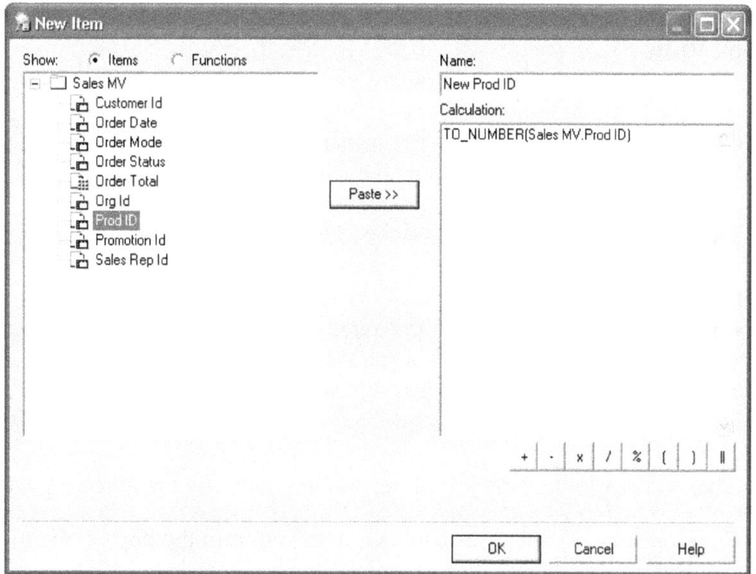


7. Click OK to close the Edit Calculation dialog box.
8. Because the new item was created using the TO_NUMBER function, it will have been created with a default position of Data Point. Using the Properties dialog box, change the default position to Side.

Now you can use this new item in the join.

**Creating a Multi-item Join** Now that we have added a new item with the data type we need for the complex join, we can create the join. We are referring to the new item in the Sales MV folder.

| Master Folder | Master Item | Detail Folder | Detail Item | Join Type | Join Order |
|---|---|---|---|---|---|
| Product | Org ID | Sales MV | Org ID | Complex | First |
| Product | Prod ID | Sales MV | New Prod ID | Complex | Second |

To create the complex multi-item join, use the following workflow:

1. Use the workflow that was outlined earlier in this section and create a simple join on the Org ID between the Product and Sales MV folders. Do not click Next after you have added this first element, but click Add.
2. Add a second join item between the Prod ID in the Product folder and our new item. Call this second item New Prod ID in the Sales MV folder.
3. The screen should look like the screen shown here.
4. Click Next, and then click Finish.

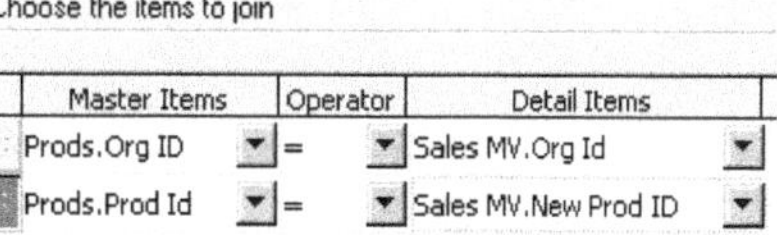

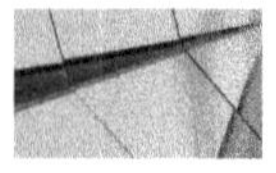

**NOTE**
*Do not forget that when you bring tables into Discoverer, each table equates to a folder, and the columns in the table equate to items within the folder.*

## Checking Joins

From time to time it may become necessary for you to check a join. Let's expand the Channel folder so that we can see all of the items.

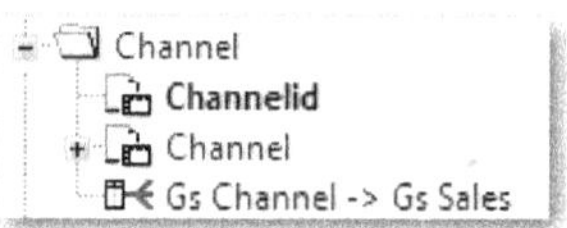


As you can see in this illustration, this folder has only two items, a channel and a channel ID. The channel ID is in bold, while below it is another item with a "crow's-foot" icon. These are the join items.

The channel ID is in bold because it is the primary key in the primary-key/foreign-key relationship.

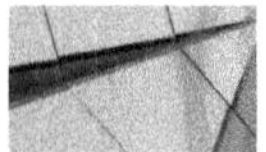

**NOTE**
*The corresponding foreign key in the Sales order will be italicized. Discoverer bolds all primary keys and italicizes all foreign keys. It also names the join using the folder names as they were when the join was created.*

Let's take a closer look at the join. To examine a join, use the following workflow:

1. Right-click the join you want to examine, and from the pop-up menu select Edit Join.
2. Discoverer displays the following Edit Join dialog box:

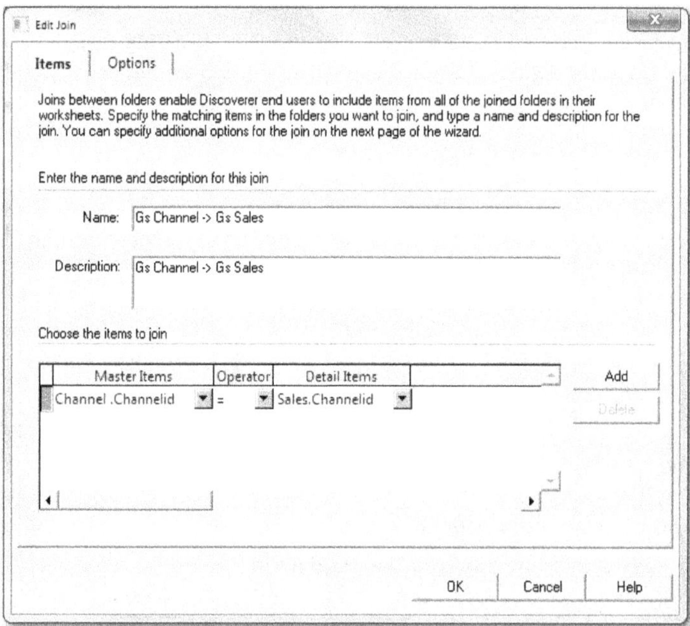


As you can see in the illustration, the Edit Join dialog box has two tabs: one called Items and one called Options.

**The Items Tab** The Items tab has the following five areas:

- **Name** Join names are critical to the successful operation of Discoverer workbooks. Every join must have a unique identifier, not only in the business area but across the entire EUL. Even though join names can be duplicated within the business area, we recommend giving joins unique names to match the identifiers. You will find this to be extremely helpful if you need to debug the system later.
- **Description** This is a placeholder for you to type a description about the join.
- **Choose the items to join** This area comprises three components: a master item, an operator, and a detail item. These components are the heart of the join and tell Discoverer exactly how the join is put together.
- **Add** Use this button to add additional join items, in effect creating a composite join between multiple items. For example, in Apps you might have both a Category Code item and a Category Item Code item joining two tables together.
- **Delete** Use this button to delete the secondary components that are in use in a composite join.

**The Options Tab** The Options tab, illustrated here, has two main areas.

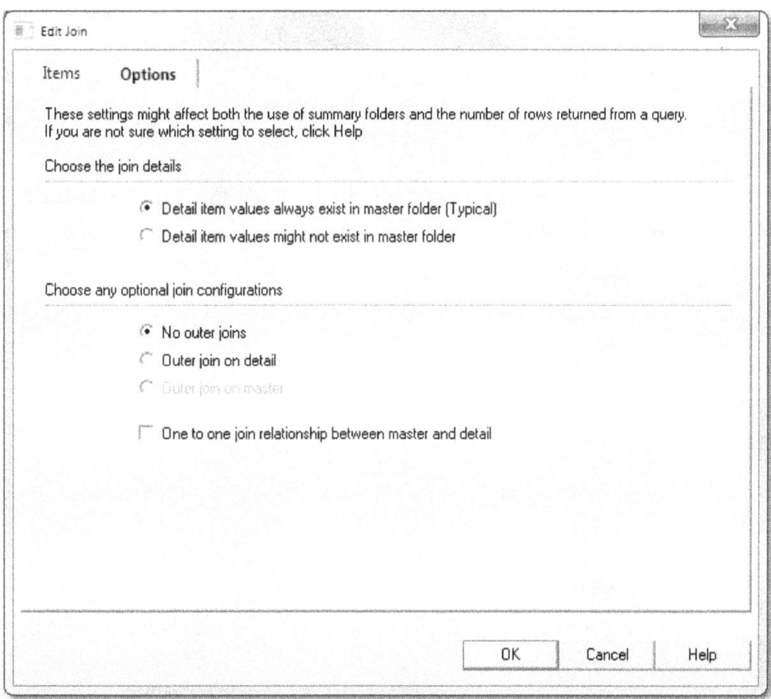


- **Choose the join details** In this area you must tell Discoverer whether the detail items always exist in the master folder or whether they are optional. You must check one of the two radio buttons. Typically, you will nearly always encounter the situation where the detail items do exist in the master folder.

- **Choose any optional configurations** In this area you must tell Discoverer about the join itself, whether there is an outer join, whether the outer join is on the detail or the master, or whether the join is a one-to-one relationship. Normally, the configuration is such that the join is not an outer join.

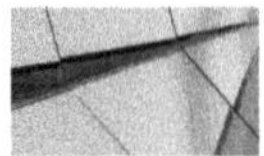

NOTE
*You will notice that the option Outer Join On Master is grayed out. This option is available only when you check Detail Item Values Might Not Exist In Master Folder in the join detail section. Do not adjust any of these settings unless you really need to and you know what you are doing. Making incorrect join settings will result in worksheets that at best run slow or at worst give incorrect results.*

Now that you know how to look at the join settings, you need to check that Discoverer has correctly created all of the joins that you were expecting. If all of your joins are in place, well done; you have successfully completed checking your new business area. We will discuss joins in more detail in the next section when we discuss maintaining business areas.

# Enhancing Business Areas

After you have created a new business area and made all of the necessary checks to ensure that the items you imported and their associated properties are correct, you can begin your enhancements. Unfortunately, many inexperienced Discoverer administrators think that they have finished at this point. You would be amazed at some of the horror stories that we could tell about poorly designed business areas.

We will outline the enhancements that need to be made to complete your business area. We have identified five major areas of work still needed.

- Folder enhancements
- Hierarchy enhancements
- Item enhancements
- User access
- Testing

For the remainder of this chapter we will discuss the first three of these major work areas in some detail.

## Folder Enhancements

The folder enhancements that we will discuss primarily concern adding new folders. There are three types of new folders.

- **New** This type of folder is the sort we will use when we want to create a new, complex folder. A complex folder is one that consists of items from existing folders. You will use these folders often.

- **Custom** This type of folder allows you to key the SQL yourself directly into Discoverer. We use these folders for manually adding lists of values or alternative sorts.
- **From Database** This type of folder is associated with an object from the database. These objects could be a table, a view, or a materialized view.

### Creating New Folders

To create a new folder, follow this workflow:

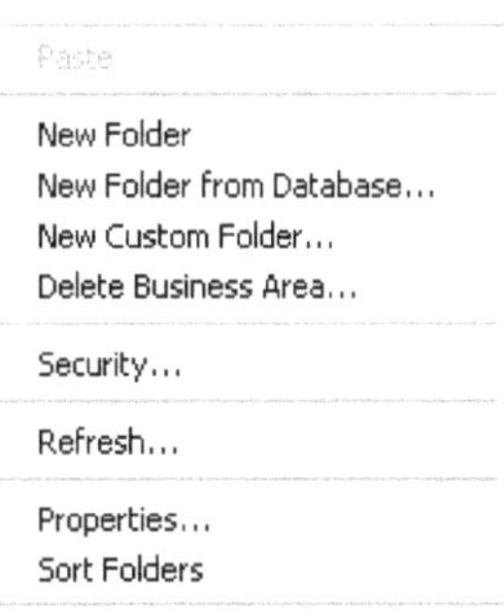


1. Click the business area heading such that the business area name is highlighted.
2. Right-click the business area name; Discoverer will pop up a context menu.
3. From the context pop-up menu, shown here, click the type of folder you want to create.

**NOTE**
*An alternate method for step 2 is to select Insert | Folder from the menu bar.*

### Adding Complex Folders

Complex folders are folders that combine data from one or more other folders in the End User Layer. They enable your users to see data from multiple folders at the same time, somewhat similar to the way a view works in the database. You use complex folders to simplify what the user sees when logging in. Rather than seeing numerous interlinking folders, the user will see one folder. If your company has strict rules for creating database views, you may want to consider complex folders because you do not need the CREATE VIEW privilege to create a complex folder. You can also use complex folders to create subsets of the data for different parts of your organization, leaving the original folders intact.

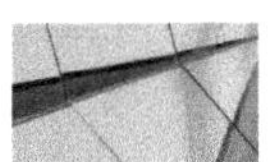

**NOTE**
*To combine data from multiple folders, just as with a database view, there must be joins in place between the folders.*

**Choosing New Complex Folders** How do you choose when to use a complex folder? Take a look back at Figure 17-2, which gives you an entity-relationship diagram for the database we are using in this book. While this may look like a star schema, it is actually a snowflake schema.

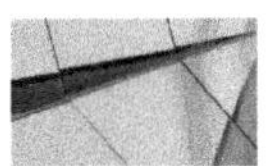

**NOTE**
*You will find information concerning star and snowflake schemas in Appendix C.*

Look at the joins that radiate out from the GS Sales folder. You can see that there are four, one each to GS Channel, GS Customer, GS Day, and GS Product, respectively. Beyond the GS Customer, GS Day, and GS Product folders, there are more folders. Beyond Products, there are Product Lines, while beyond Customer there is a complete geographic hierarchy linking to Cities, District, and Region. Looking beyond the Day folder, you can see a time hierarchy linking to Month, Quarter, and Year. We will use complex folders based around each of these hierarchies so that our end users will see one Geographic folder containing all of the items from Customer, City, District, and Region; and one Products folder containing all of the items from Products and Product Lines.

You might ask, "What about the time hierarchy? Shouldn't we create a complex folder on this too?" The answer is yes, we will do this, but we will not build one complex folder but four, one folder for each of the dates that we have in our Sales folder: Cancel Date, Order Date, Requested Date, and Ship Date. Why four complex folders; wouldn't one suffice? The answer is no. If we want our users to build queries such as "Show me how many of the sales orders ordered in Q3 did not ship until Q4," they cannot do this if we have one date folder. However, if we have a separate Order Date folder, containing our month, quarter, and year data along with the calendar dates, and we have another, similarly defined Ship Date folder, our users can build such a query.

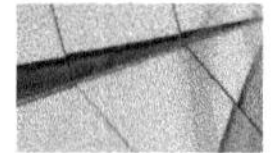

**NOTE**
*GSW, our fictitious retailing company, uses a fiscal time calendar running from October to September. Our Q1 is therefore October to December, while Q2 is January to March of the following fiscal year. We thus cannot use the standard Discoverer date hierarchy.*

We need to create six complex folders. The data model in Figure 17-3 shows the business area model after we have added the new folders. If you think that this looks like a star schema,

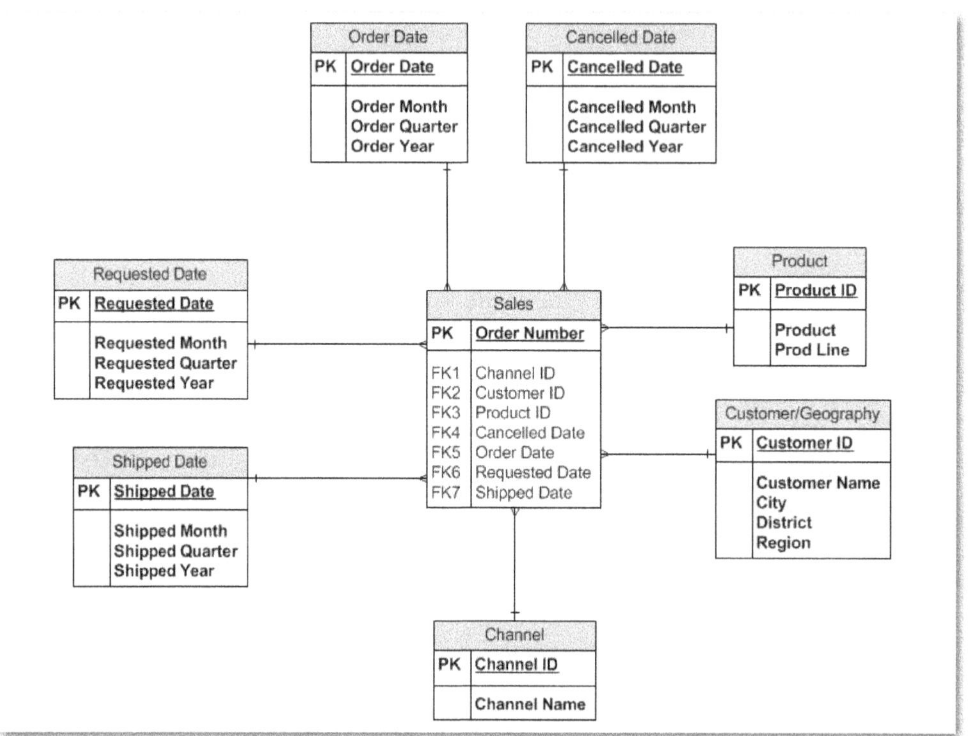


**FIGURE 17-3.** *Data model shown as a star schema*

you would be right. Discoverer works well with star schemas, and this is what you should be trying to do with your models. If you cannot create a star schema in the database, you should try to use complex folders to do this for you in the tool. Users understand star schema data models better than any other kind of data model.

**Fiscal Date Complex Folders** As mentioned previously, and as shown in Figure 17-3, in our Sales folder there are four dates, one each for

- Cancelled Date
- Order Date
- Requested Date
- Shipped Date

We will create one new folder for each date and populate it from the existing Calendar Date, Fiscal Month, Fiscal Quarter, and Fiscal Year simple folders. We will describe the process in detail only for the new Cancelled Date folder. Having shown how to do this for Cancelled Date, we will then show you how to create the other three folders by copying and pasting what you have just done.

**NOTE**
*As shown in the following illustration, it is much easier to do the next tasks if you split the screen into two windows using Window | Split Window from the menu bar.*

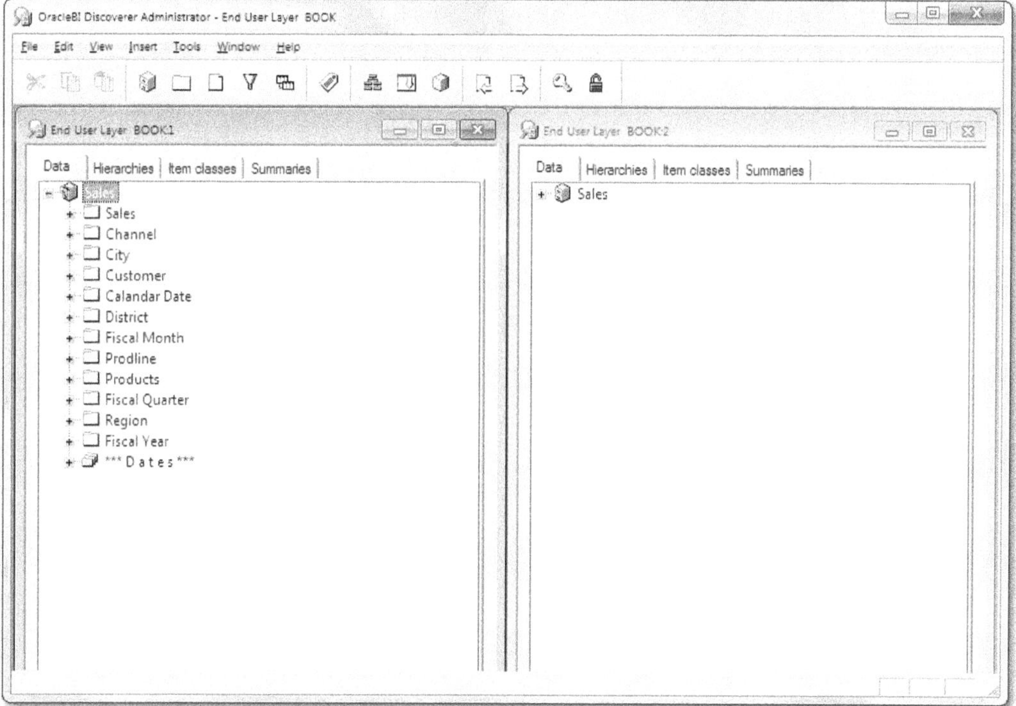

To create the Cancelled Date complex folder, use the following workflow:

1. In the right-hand window, right-click the business area name, and from the pop-up menu select New Folder.
2. As you can see next, Discoverer creates a new empty folder named NewFolder1, expands the list of existing folders, and places the new folder at the bottom of the list.

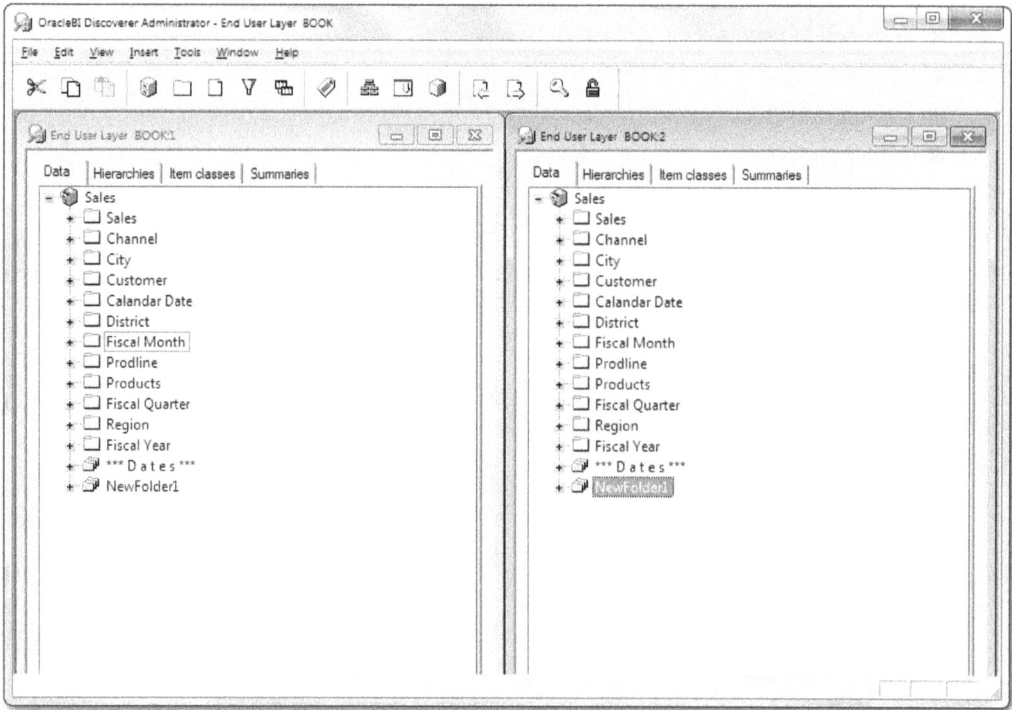


3. Right-click the new folder, and from the pop-up menu select Properties. The Folder Properties dialog box will open. Using the General tab, rename the folder to **Cancelled Date** and change Identifier to **CANCELLED_DATE_FOLDER**.

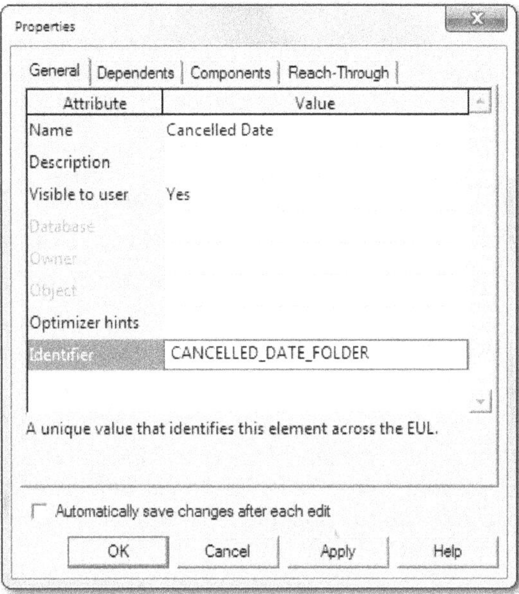


4. Click OK when warned that changing identifiers can be risky.

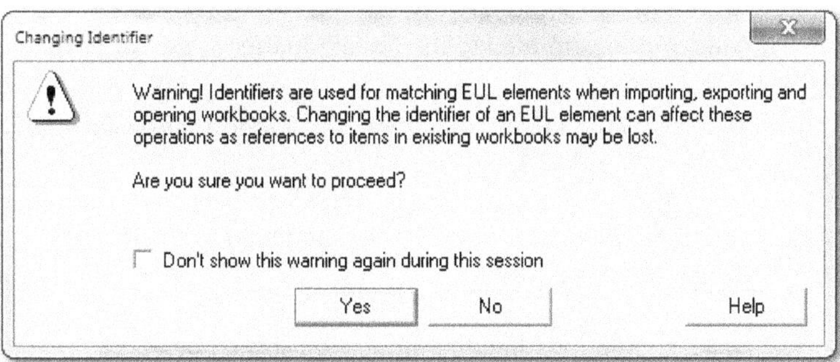


5. If there is already a folder in the EUL by the name you are trying to use, Discoverer will give this warning telling you that the name must be unique:

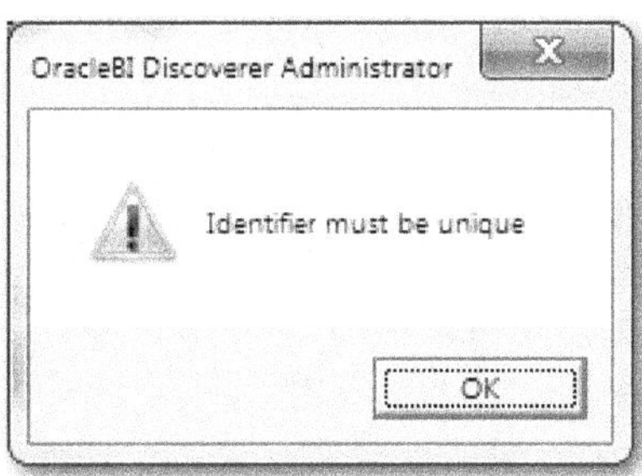

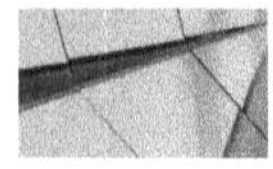

**NOTE**
*It is perfectly safe to change the identifier when creating a new folder. Waiting until later, however, when users may well have workbooks based on the folder, increases the risk that workbooks will no longer open and is not recommended.*

6. In the left-hand window, expand the Calendar Date folder.
7. Click the Calendar Date item and drag it across the window separator into the new folder.
8. In the left-hand window, minimize the Calendar Date folder and expand the Fiscal Month folder.
9. Click the Fiscal Month item and drag it across the window separator into the new folder.

**NOTE**
*To drag multiple items at the same time, click one of the items to highlight that item, and hold down* CTRL *while you click the other items. With all items highlighted, you can drag the set across the window separator into the new folder.*

10. In the left-hand window, minimize the Fiscal Month folder and expand the Fiscal Quarter folder.
11. Click the Fiscal Quarter item and drag it across the window separator into the new folder.
12. In the left-hand window, minimize the Fiscal Quarter folder and expand the Fiscal Year folder.
13. Click the Fiscal Year item and drag it across the window separator into the new folder.

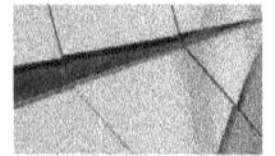

**NOTE**
*Existing lists of values are maintained and remain attached to the items as they are dragged into the new folder.*

14. Your new folder should look like the illustration shown here.

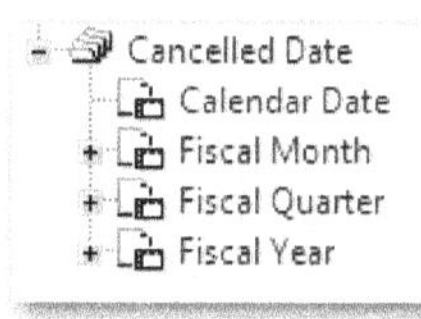

**NOTE**
*As you become more comfortable with highlighting and dragging items between folders, you may well find it easier to highlight the items in all of the simple folders first and then drag them over at the same time.*

After creating our base complex folder, we need to make it ready for use. If the items in the new folder do not have meaningful names, they should be renamed. To help our users, we will rename the item called Calendar Item to Cancelled Date and then rename each of the other items to remove the word *Fiscal* and replace it with the word *Cancelled*.

Having created a new folder, we need to join it to the Sales folder. The new folder we created is for the Cancelled Date, so it makes sense to create a join from here to the Cancelled Date item in the Sales folder, as shown here.

To finish the remaining date folders, we need to create three more complex folders, one each for Order Date, Requested Date, and Shipped Date. This process is much easier than creating the Cancelled Date folder because we can take advantage of what we have just done by copying the new Cancelled Date folder and pasting a replica of its definition into the business area three times.

**Replicating a Folder** To replicate a complex folder, use the following workflow:

1. Click the name for the folder you want to copy so that the name is highlighted.
2. Right-click the folder, and from the pop-up menu select Copy.
3. Right-click the heading for the business area, and from the pop-up menu select Paste.
4. Give the new folder a meaningful name and identifier.

**Completing the Date Folders** To complete our complex data folders, use the following workflow:

1. Use the workflow in the previous section to copy the Cancelled Date folder three times.
2. After you have made these three copies, rename the new folders to **Order Date**, **Requested Date**, and **Shipped Date**, respectively.
3. Make sure you assign a unique identifier to each new folder.
4. Rename all of the items in these folders to remove the *Cancelled* prefix and replace it with the prefixes **Order**, **Requested**, and **Shipped**, respectively.
5. Add one join from each new folder to the Sales folder. As you do this, make sure you join on the correct items, with the Order Date folder joining to the Order Date item, the Requested Date joining to the Requested Date item, and the Shipped Date joining to the Shipped Date item.
6. Hide the four original Calendar Date, Fiscal Month, Fiscal Quarter, and Fiscal Year folders. You do this by changing the folder property called Visible to user from Yes to No. If you use CTRL, you can select all four folders at the same time, making it much easier to effect the change.
7. Expanding the Sales folder, it now looks like the illustrations shown here.

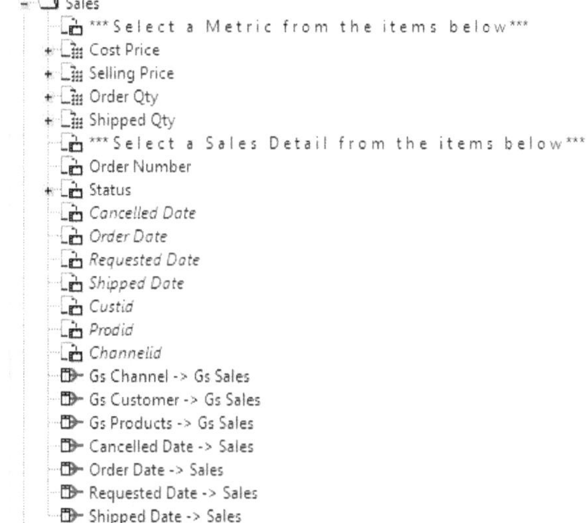

As you can see in the illustration, there are now seven joins into the Sales folder.

**Creating a New Complex Geographic Folder** We will create one new folder for the geographic rollup, containing all of the customer data, along with the city, district, and region data.

In our Sales fact folder there is a Customer ID, which has an N:1 join to the customer folder. The customer folder, in turn, has an N:1 join to the City folder, which in turn joins to the District folder, which joins to the Region folder.

To create the Geographic rollup, use the following workflow:

1. Create a new complex folder.
2. Name the new folder **Customer/Geography**.
3. Name the identifier **CUSTOMER_GEOGRAPHY_FOLDER**.
4. Drag Cust ID from our Customer folder into the new folder.
5. Drag all of these Customer items: Customer, Contact Name, Credit Limit, Address, State, and Post Code.
6. Drag the City and Country Code from the City folder.
7. Drag District from the District folder.
8. Drag Region from the Region folder.
9. Create a new join from the new folder to the Sales folder, joining on the Cust ID.
10. Add new item separators and rearrange the order of the items, as shown in Figure 17-4.
11. Hide Cust ID in both Sales and the new folders. You do this by changing the item's Visible to user property from Yes to No.
12. Hide the four original Customer, City, District, and Region folders. Remember you do this by changing the folder's Visible to user property from Yes to No.

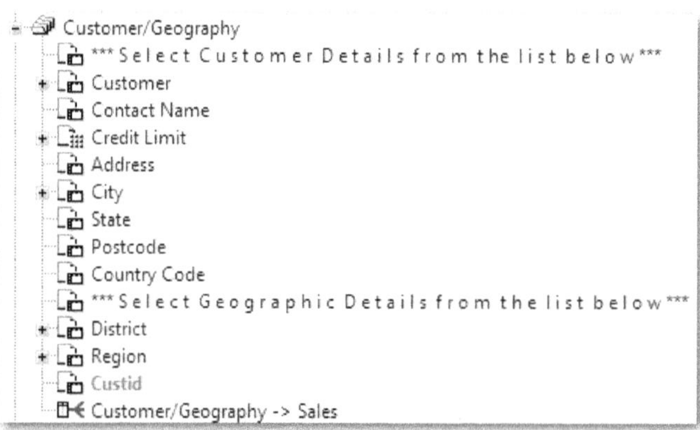


**FIGURE 17-4.** *Completed Customer/Geography complex folder*

**Creating a New Complex Products Folder** We will create one new folder for the product rollup, containing all of the product and product line data. In our Sales folder there is a Product ID, which has an N:1 join to the Products folder. The Products folder, in turn, has an N:1 join to the Prodline folder.

To create the Product rollup, use the following workflow:

1. Create a new complex folder.
2. Name the new folder **Product**.
3. Name the identifier **PRODUCT_FOLDER**.
4. Drag Prod ID from the Products folder into the new folder.
5. Drag all of these product items: Product, Size, Unit Cost Price, and Unit Selling Price.
6. Drag Prod Line from the Prod Line folder.
7. Create a new join from the new folder to the Sales folder, joining on the Product ID.
8. Hide the Product ID in both the Sales and Product folders.
9. Hide the two original Products and Prod Line folders.

**Notes About Complex Folders** Whenever you use complex folders, note these points:

- Lists of values are copied, and the item classes are shared with the original items.
- Joins are not copied; they must be created manually.
- Complex folders make great candidates for creating hierarchies.
- Hierarchies make great candidates for cascading parameters. A prerequisite of being able to create cascading parameters is that the items must belong to a hierarchy.

## Adding Custom Folders

A custom folder is based on SQL that you type directly into Discoverer. While there are many reasons for using custom folders, we will discuss three here:

- To create a new list of values
- To create an alternative sort sequence for a data set that does not have a natural sort
- To pull data from a database link

We will discuss each of these in turn, but first we will show you how easy it is to create a custom folder.

To create a custom folder, use the following workflow:

1. Click the business area heading such that the business area name is highlighted.
2. Right-click the business area name; Discoverer will pop up a context menu.

3. From the context pop-up menu, select New Custom Folder. Discoverer opens the following Custom Folder dialog box:

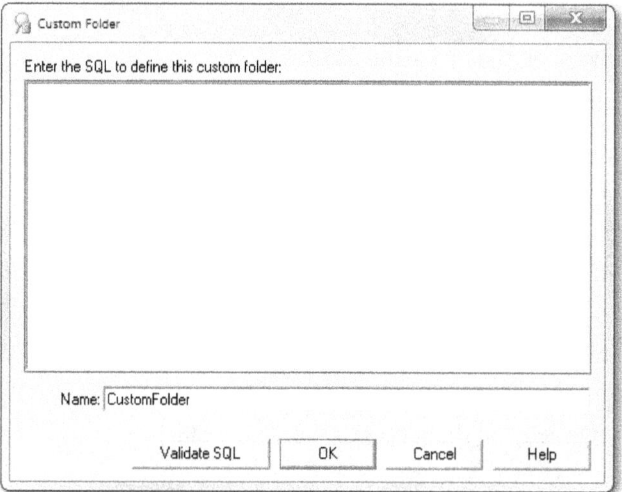


4. Type or paste the SQL code into the box.
5. Give the folder a unique name.
6. Click the Validate SQL button to check whether the SQL is okay for Discoverer to use.
7. If the SQL is invalid, you will see the following message:

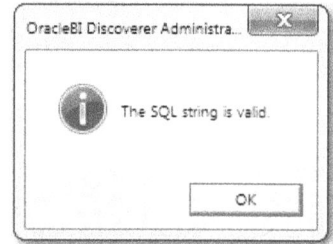

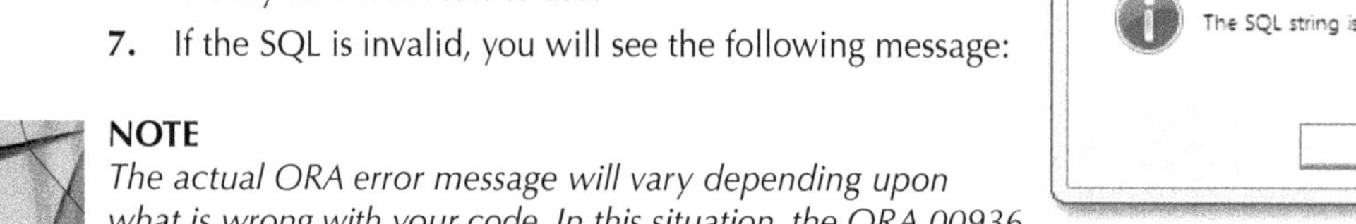

**NOTE**
*The actual ORA error message will vary depending upon what is wrong with your code. In this situation, the ORA 00936 means that we have forgotten to include a required element. We actually forgot to select anything from our SQL!*

8. Please note that not all SQL that is valid in SQL Plus is valid in Discoverer. We will explain this in the next section. You may have to keep plugging away until Discoverer says it is valid.
9. If the SQL is valid, you will see the following message:

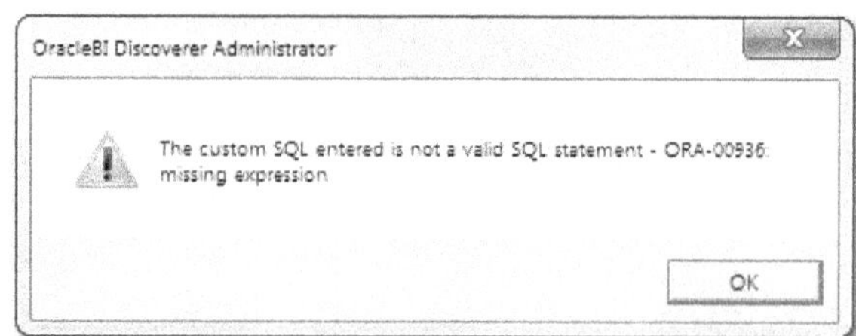


10. Whether you have entered valid or invalid SQL, so long as you enter a unique name for the folder, Discoverer will allow you to click OK and save the folder.

**NOTE**
*Discoverer will allow you to create a custom folder with invalid SQL. This is done for development purposes, allowing you to save what you have done so far and come back to it later when you have figured out what the problem is. This also allows you to create some SQL and then ask a colleague to take a look at it to see whether they can figure out why it is not working. We think this ability to save invalid code is a great feature, one of many that Oracle has incorporated into Discoverer over the years.*

If you have a custom folder that has invalid code, perhaps you should save what you have done so far and return to it later. When the code is invalid and you click OK, Discoverer displays the following message:

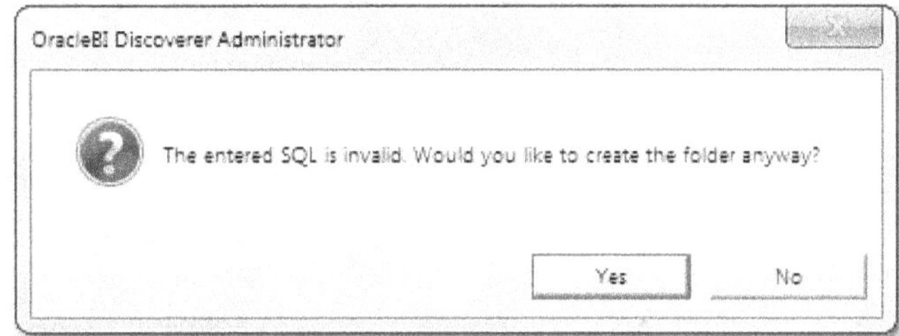
OracleBI Discoverer Administrator
The entered SQL is invalid. Would you like to create the folder anyway?
Yes
No

If you click Yes, Discoverer will save the folder. Don't worry, your users will not be able to select from this folder while it is in an invalid state.

If you have a custom folder that is currently valid and you add some code that makes it invalid, you will see this message:

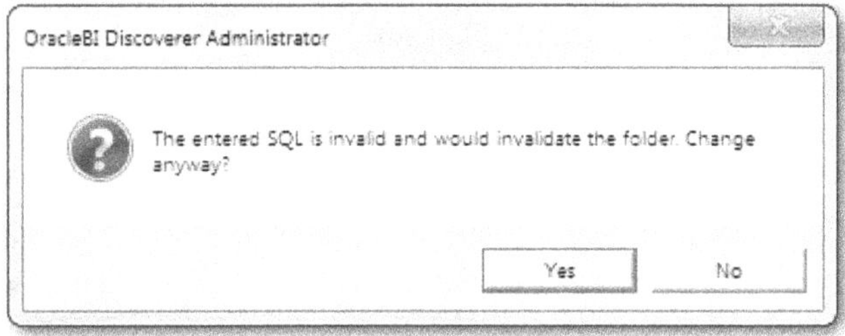
OracleBI Discoverer Administrator
The entered SQL is invalid and would invalidate the folder. Change anyway?
Yes
No

**Getting the SQL Valid in a Custom Folder** One of the most common complaints we hear from inexperienced administrators is that Discoverer says their SQL is invalid. As mentioned in the preceding section, not all SQL that is valid in SQL Plus will compile in Discoverer. You have to remember that Discoverer needs to have a unique name for every item in the SELECT statement.

Look at the following code, which is the E-Business Suite code to join sales order headers with sales order lines. The code is valid in SQL Plus but not valid in Discoverer. Because Discoverer strips off table prefixes from custom code, it will not be able to differentiate between the two HEADER_ID columns.

```
SELECT
SOH.HEADER_ID,
SOL.HEADER_ID
FROM
ONT.OE_ORDER_HEADERS_ALLSOH,
ONT.OE_ORDER_LINES_ALL SOL
WHERE
SOL.HEADER_ID = SOH.HEADER_ID
```

Changing the code to add unique column aliases as follows overcomes the problem and will make your folder valid:

```
SELECT
SOH.HEADER_IDSOH_HEADER_ID,
SOL.HEADER_IDSOL_LINE_ID
FROM
ONT.OE_ORDER_HEADERS_ALLSOH,
ONT.OE_ORDER_LINES_ALL SOL
WHERE
SOL.HEADER_ID = SOH.HEADER_ID
```

**Using a Custom Folder to Create a New List of Values** We mentioned earlier in this chapter that you should not be creating lists of values from tables that have millions of rows of data. This is because of the performance hit on the database by Discoverer executing a SELECT DISTINCT from a million-row table. To overcome this, the solution is to use a custom folder.

To use a custom folder to create a list of values, use the following workflow:

1. Determine what the list of values should be. You can do this either by selecting from a separate dimension folder or by using DUAL.
2. Create a custom folder using the SQL you have developed.
3. Create a new list of values based on the item in the custom folder.
4. Attach the list of values to the original item by right-clicking the item and, from the pop-up menu, selecting Properties.
5. In the Item Properties box,look for the property Item Class. When you click in it, you will be presented with a list of the valid item classes that Discoverer thinks could be suitable.
6. Select the new item class from the list presented.

**NOTE**
*Discoverer does some filtering on the item classes to not show you the lists of values that are not suitable. For example, if the column you are working on is defined as being a Number, Discoverer will offer you only numeric lists of values. It won't offer you anything based on a VARCHAR or DATE, because it knows these would not work!*

7. Click OK.

From here on, every time a user clicks the plus icon alongside the item in the original folder, Discoverer will execute the code contained in the custom folder to generate the list of values. The following two examples show this to good effect.

We will explore custom folders in depth in Chapter 21 when we discuss more advanced Discoverer administration techniques.

### Custom Folder Based on a Dimension Table

Staying within E-Business Suite for our examples, let's say you need to get a list of values based on the currency contained in PO Lines but you have millions of purchase orders and it takes too long to get the list by querying PO Lines. The following code will give you a list of just the active currency codes contained in the system:

```
SELECT CURRENCY_CODE
FROM APPS.FND_CURRENCIES_ACTIVE_V
```

If you place this code in a custom folder, you will see a single item called CURRENCY_CODE. Creating a list of values on this item will produce the list in seconds.

### Custom Folder Using DUAL

Let's say you have a system that has ten million rows and you have a column called Active that has only two values, a Y to indicate Yes and an N to indicate No. The following code will give you a list containing just two values, Y and N:

```
SELECT 'Y' ACTIVE_STATUS FROM DUAL
UNION
SELECT 'N' ACTIVE_STATUS FROM DUAL
```

Placing this code within a custom folder will cause Discoverer to generate a new folder containing a single item called ACTIVE_STATUS. Creating a list of values on this item will produce the list in a fraction of a second.

**Using a Custom Folder to Create an Alternative Sort Sequence** Earlier in this chapter we mentioned that we would show you how to use a custom folder to generate the days of the week list of values. The following code will give you a new folder containing two items, one called DOY and one called SEQUENCE:

```
SELECT 'SUNDAY' DOY, 1 SEQUENCE FROM DUAL
UNION
SELECT 'MONDAY' DOY, 2 SEQUENCE FROM DUAL
UNION
SELECT 'TUESDAY' DOY, 3 SEQUENCE FROM DUAL
UNION
SELECT 'WEDNESDAY' DOY, 4 SEQUENCE FROM DUAL
UNION
SELECT 'THURSDAY' DOY, 5 SEQUENCE FROM DUAL
UNION
SELECT 'FRIDAY' DOY, 6 SEQUENCE FROM DUAL
UNION
SELECT 'SATURDAY' DOY, 7 SEQUENCE FROM DUAL
```

If you create a new list of values based on DOY, using SEQUENCE as the alternative sort item, the list will be generated in the order you want.

**Using a Custom Folder to Pull Data from a Database Link** Sometimes when working with data, you may find that the piece of data you need is located in another database. Once again, using E-Business Suite as our base system, let's say you have a data warehouse that has pulled in the SALESREP ID but somehow not the SALESREP NAME and your users want to see the name. You might have asked your data warehousing team if they can correct the code, but they have said they can but not for another six months. Rather than telling your users that the request will have to wait, you can use the following code inside a Discoverer custom folder to pull both the SALESREP_ID and SALESREP_NAME:

```
SELECT DISTINCT
JRS.SALESREP_IDSALESREP_ID,
JRR.RESOURCE_NAMESALESREP_NAME
FROM
JTF.JTF_RS_SALESREPS@DW_TO_PRODRSA,
JTF.JTF_RS_RESOURCE_EXTNS_TL@DW_TO_PRODJRR
WHERE
JRS.RESOURCE_ID = JRR.RESOURCE_ID
AND JTS.ORG_ID IS NOT NULL
```

### Adding New Folders from the Database

You can add new folders from the database easily. In fact, this is what we did to create the business area in the first place.

To create a new folder from the database, use the following workflow:

1. Click the business area heading so the business area name is highlighted.
2. Right-click the business area name; Discoverer will open a pop-up menu.
3. From the context pop-up menu, select New Folder From Database.

Discoverer reopens the Load Wizard that we used at the beginning of Chapter 16.

## Managing Folder Properties

Like all other objects in Discoverer, folders have properties. These properties are managed from the Folder Properties dialog box.

To display the Folder Properties dialog box, use the following workflow:

1. Right-click the folder whose properties you want to maintain, and from the pop-up menu select Properties.
2. Discoverer displays the Folder Properties dialog box, as shown in Figures 17-5 and 17-6.
3. Having changed any property, click OK to commit the change.

As you can see in Figures 17-5 and 17-6, there are four tabs to the Folder Properties dialog box:

- **General** On this tab, shown in Figure 17-5 for a complex folder and in Figure 17-6 for a folder based on a database object, you will find the following general properties:
  - **Name** This is the name of the folder and must be unique in the EUL.
  - **Description** This is an optional property and one that is greatly underused. When an end user clicks a folder that has a description, Desktop or Plus displays the text that is contained in it. You should therefore make good use of this property.

- ■ **Visible to user** This is a Yes/No property. When set to No, the folder will not be visible to the end user. Be careful making folders invisible after the fact because this can upset users and even prevent existing workbooks from opening.
- ■ **Database** If the folder is based on a database object, Discoverer displays the name of the database where the object is located.
- ■ **Owner** If the folder is based on a database object, Discoverer displays the name of the owner of the object here.
- ■ **Object** If the folder is based on a database object, Discoverer displays the name of the object here.
- ■ **Optimizer hints** If you are used to working with optimizer hints and you find that end-user performance is bad, you might want to try adding optimizer hints here. In our experience, if you find that hints are necessary, you may well need to create a database view instead and base the folder on that view.
- ■ **Identifier** This is the unique identifier for the folder in the EUL.

■ **Dependents** On this tab Discoverer will display a list of all the secondary objects that are dependent upon this folder. Examples of secondary objects are

- ■ Item classes (lists of values)
- ■ Joins
- ■ Workbooks

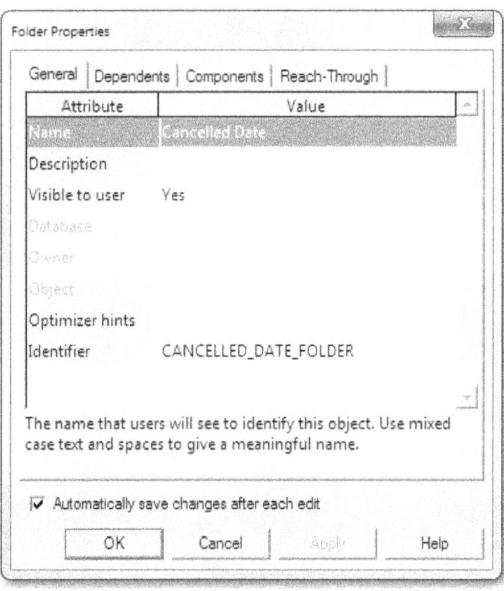


**FIGURE 17-5.** *Folder Properties dialog box for a complex folder*

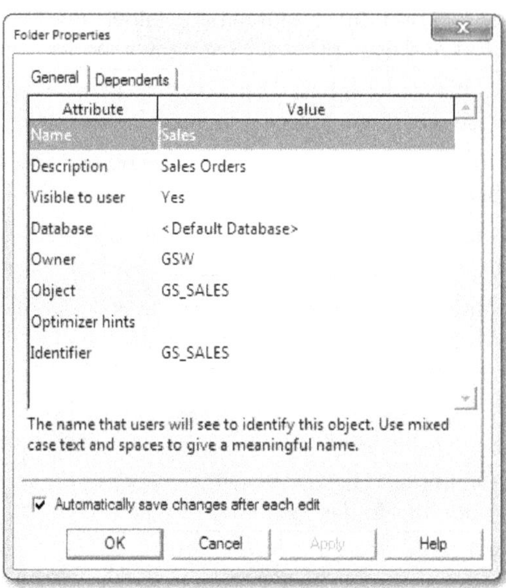


**FIGURE 17-6.** *Folder Properties dialog box for a folder based on a database object*

The following illustration shows the Dependents tab for our Sales folder. We recommend you always check for workbook dependencies whenever you are about to make a major change to a folder, such as to remove a join or disable reach-through to a base folder.

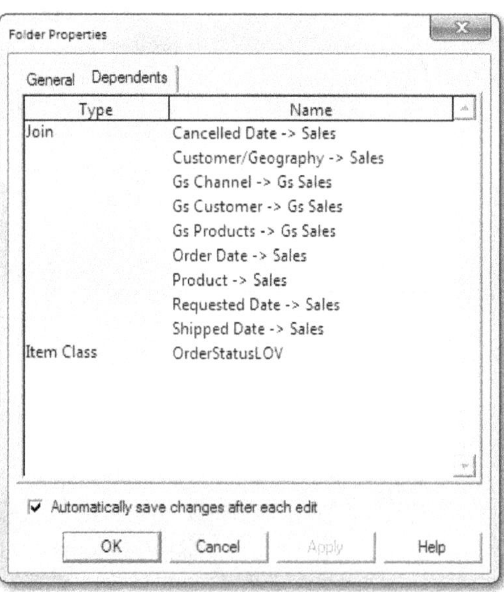

**NOTE**

*If you do not check for dependent workbooks and you proceed with your change, the workbooks will no longer open and it will be your fault. We can almost guarantee that when the user complains that a workbook no longer opens, you will not connect the two events and will be left scratching your head.*

- **Components** On this tab, which is displayed only for a complex folder, Discoverer displays a list of the objects that are being used to create the complex folder. These objects include
  - Folders
  - Items
  - Joins

Here, you can see the Components tab for our Cancel Date folder:

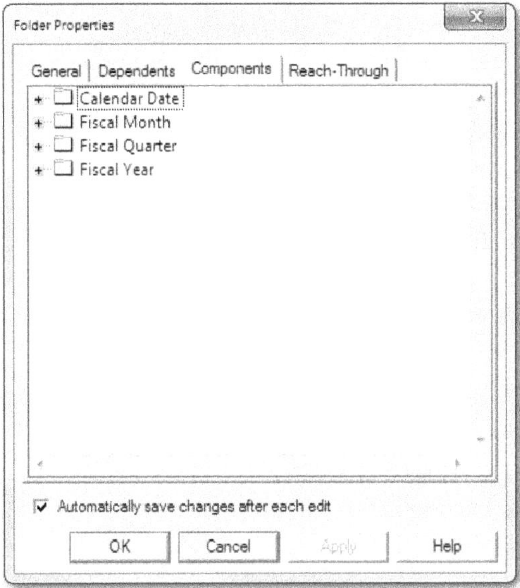


- **Reach-Through** On this tab, which is also displayed only for a complex folder, Discoverer allows you to define the objects that can be reached through this folder. We will describe reach-through in detail in the next section.

**Using Reach-Through from a Complex Folder** One of the really clever features of Discoverer is *reach-through*. This feature allows Desktop and Plus users to add items to their worksheets from the base folders that were used to create the complex folders. A base folder can be any of the following:

- A simple folder based on a database object
- A custom folder based on SQL
- Another complex folder

If reach-through is enabled, when a user selects from one of the complex folders, all of the enabled reach-through folders from which the complex folder was created become available for selection.

You may say that you could already achieve this by adding joins from the complex folder back to its base folders. This is true, except it is not very elegant or very efficient. For a start, you have all those extra joins to maintain, and it can also affect performance. The best way is to enable reach-through.

To enable reach-through from a complex folder back to one or more of its constituent base folders, use the following workflow:

1. Right-click the complex folder you want reach-through to enable, and from the pop-up menu select Properties. Discoverer displays the Folder Properties dialog box.
2. Click the Reach-Through tab.
3. Click the check box against the base folders you want to allow the users to reach.
4. Click OK to complete the reach-through.

This illustration shows the Reach-Through tab for our Cancelled Date folder with reach-through enabled back to the original Fiscal Month and Fiscal Quarter folders.

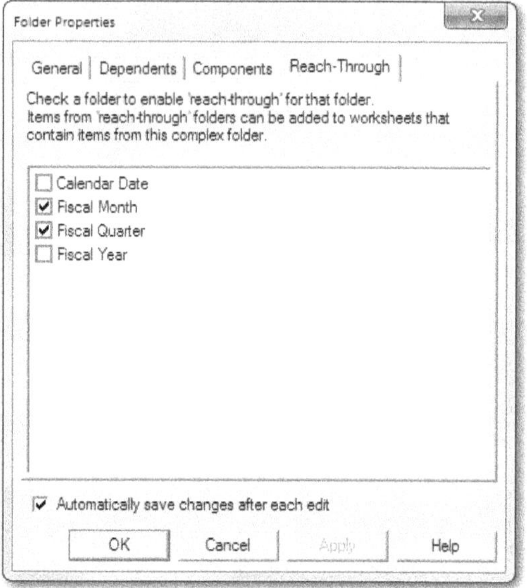


**Canceling Reach-Through** While canceling reach-through is a simple task, you need to be careful. If you cancel reach-through to a folder that has been used in a user's workbook, the user will no longer be able to open that workbook.

To cancel reach-through, use the following workflow:

1. Right-click the complex folder that is currently reach-through enabled, and from the pop-up menu select Properties. Discoverer displays the Folder Properties dialog box.
2. Click the Reach-Through tab.
3. Uncheck the box against the base folder that you no longer want to allow users to reach.
4. Discoverer understands that disabling reach-through can have disastrous consequences for your users and displays the Remove Reach-Through dialog box.

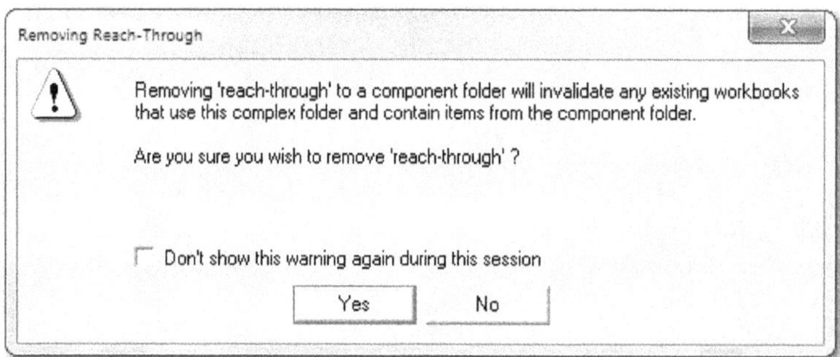


5. Discoverer prompts you with "Are you sure you want to remove 'reach-through'?" Clicking Yes confirms your understanding of the consequences, while clicking No

abandons the reach-through removal. If you continue with the removal and there was a workbook using the reach-through-enabled folder, the user will get this message in Desktop:

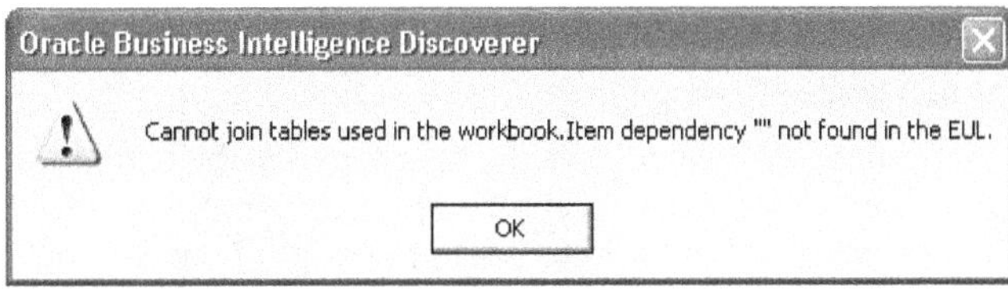


The user will get a similar message in Plus.

To rectify this situation, all you have to do is reenable the reach-through, if you can remember what you did. Perhaps it is better to check dependencies first!

Even if you clicked Yes in the previous step, it is still not too late to abandon the removal. Clicking Cancel will abort what you have started.

If you are sure that you want to remove the reach-through, click OK.

**Reach-Through Restrictions** As an administrator, you need to be aware of several points when working with the reach-through capability of Discoverer.

- The Discoverer Administrator tool will not allow you to enable reach-through if there is a join in existence between the base folder and the complex folder. Discoverer will generate the following error message:

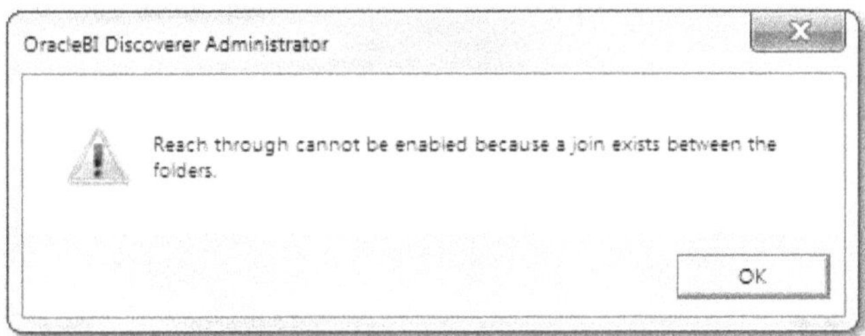


- The Discoverer Administrator tool will not allow you to create a join between a base folder and its associated complex folder if reach-through has been enabled. Discoverer will generate the following error message:

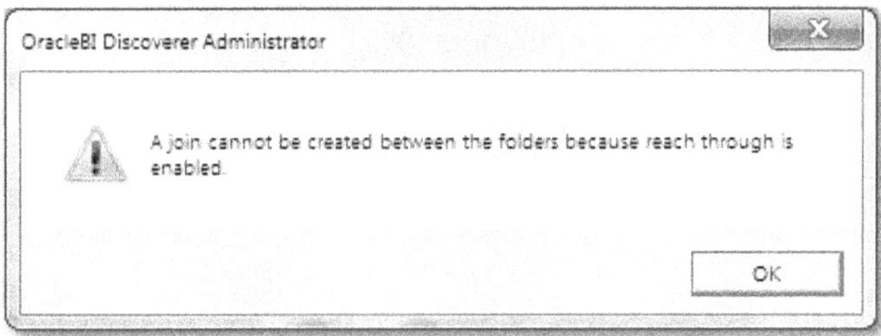

- When you have a reach-through-enabled folder and you are using Discoverer's automatic summary management (ASM) feature to create summary folders, Discoverer will not generate summary folder information on the folders that are reach-through enabled.
- Items that are in folders that are joined to the reach-through-enabled folder are not available for selection by the end user. The reach-through works only to the folder that is reach-through enabled using the implied join.
- There must be at least one item from the base folder in the complex folder for reach-through to work. In other words, if you edit a complex folder and remove all the items from a reach-through-enabled base folder, the implied join between the two folders will be removed. Any user workbook that was using the implied join to get data from the base folder will fail.
- If you remove a join between a complex folder and a base table in order to enable reach-through and a user's workbook was using that join, the workbook will no longer open and the user will see the dreaded "Cannot join tables used in the workbook. Item dependency" error message. Therefore, before removing any join, please check the impact.

### Hiding a Folder

After you have created complex folders, it is common practice to hide the non-reach-through-enabled base folders upon which the complex folder has been created.

To hide a folder, use this workflow:

1. Right-click the folder you want to hide.
2. From the pop-up menu select Properties.
3. Change Visible to user from Yes to No.
4. Click OK.

## Hierarchy Enhancements

A hierarchy allows a user to drill through the data. Typically, we use 1:N relationships to define hierarchies in a business area so that users can roll up data or drill down. In a database, there are two types of drill.

- **Rolling up** This reduces a query by allowing a user to include data from a higher level of the hierarchy, essentially summarizing the data. For example, you could roll up from a month to a quarter to see the whole quarter's revenue.
- **Drilling down** This expands a query by allowing a user to include data from a lower level, essentially bringing in more detail items to the query. For example, you could drill down from a quarter to a month to see the revenue for all of the months in the quarter.

In both types, Discoverer may requery the database. As well as the two database hierarchy types, there are two kinds of Discoverer hierarchy.

- **Item hierarchies** According to Oracle, these are hierarchies on anything that is not a date; however, we will show you how to use these for dates too.
- **Date hierarchies** These work only on dates. When you opt to allow Discoverer to create a date hierarchy, you need to be aware of what Discoverer will do and how this can impact performance. We will cover this later in the chapter.

## Date Hierarchy or Item Hierarchy?

We are frequently asked where we stand with regard to using date hierarchies. To be truthfully honest, we rarely use date hierarchies and never use them for anything other than the simplest of folders. Let us explain.

As a concept, Oracle's implementation of date hierarchies in Discoverer is clever, really clever. What happens is that Discoverer creates a hierarchy of date format masks, inserting new items into the folder, one for each time element. At run time, Discoverer applies those format masks, using the TO_CHAR function, to evaluate each element of the hierarchy. The problem here is that these functions have to be evaluated against every row of the data in order to determine whether a filter that is being applied against one of those elements is true or false.

During the early summer of 2005, and several times since, we had cause to visit a client of ours who was having trouble with performance. They complained that a worksheet running against a single table was taking longer than ten minutes to run. The first thing we noticed is that they had defined a date hierarchy on every date in the transaction folder. There were ten dates in that folder, and every one of them was using five different time elements. This made us step back and think. Our curiosity aroused, we wondered how many rows of data there were in that table. When we looked at the database, we were amazed to find that the table in question had more than two million rows. To make things worse, the users had constructed workbooks that used all of the time elements for all of the dates. In effect, fifty TO_CHAR functions were being performed on every row of the data, and of course the users were filtering on nonindexed items.

The first thing we did was to drop all of the date hierarchies. We then created a new materialized view that had all of the time elements prebuilt and pre-indexed. Next we created individual date folders, as you have seen us do in our tutorial, for each of the important dates. Finally, we created new item hierarchies, one per date folder, to replace the old date hierarchies. The time filter was applied against an index in this folder, joining back to an index in the main folder. When we ran a workbook against this setup, it ran in less than one minute.

You may think this is an extreme case. Believe us, it is not. There are organizations with billions of rows of data in single tables. If you attempt to create a date hierarchy on them, you will be asking for trouble. Our recommendation is to use a materialized view for your date elements using an item hierarchy that simply links the elements together. No functions, no TO_ CHAR, no hassle.

**Date Hierarchies and Indexes** We recommend that you not create date hierarchies on dates that are indexed. This is an area of great concern to us and one that we have seen affect performance so many times.

According to Oracle, "If you apply a date hierarchy to a date item from an indexed table, a query that includes one of these date items will not use the indexes (which can reduce performance)." We will qualify this statement by saying that this *will* affect performance, big time. The index will not be used, and Oracle will undertake full table scans every time.

We will show you how to create both types of Discoverer hierarchy. In both cases we will use Cancel Date for the hierarchy.

## Creating an Item Hierarchy

To create an item hierarchy, use the following workflow:

1. Click the Hierarchies tab.
2. Right-click the business area in which you want to create the hierarchy, and from the pop-up list select New Hierarchy. This opens the Hierarchy Wizard, as shown in Figure 17-7.

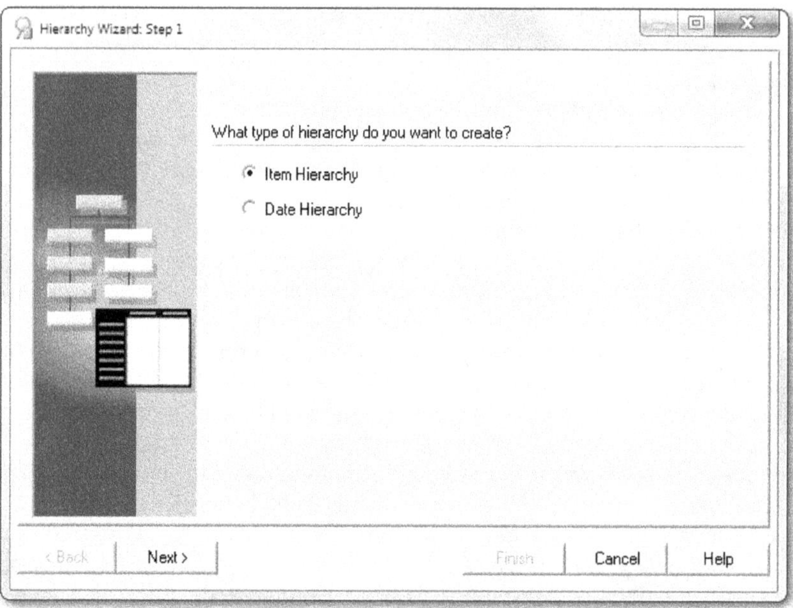


**FIGURE 17-7.** *Hierarchy Wizard, step 1*

3. Check Item Hierarchy.
4. Click Next. This opens the second screen of the Hierarchy Wizard.

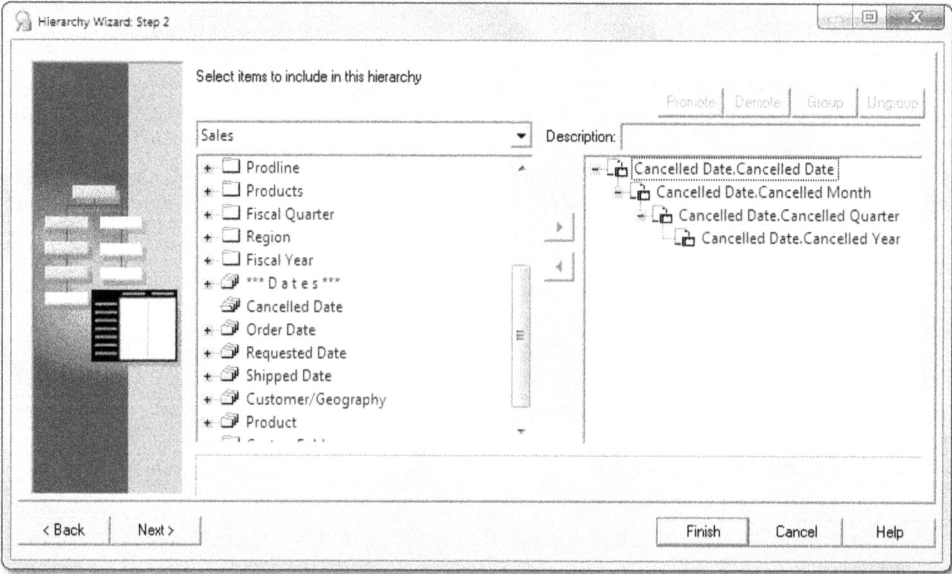

5. Locate and open the folder containing the items that will be in the hierarchy. As you can see in the preceding image, we have selected Cancelled Date, Cancelled Month, Cancelled Quarter, and Cancelled Year.
6. Select the lowest-level drill item and move or paste it in the right side.
7. Select the next items, in order, until you have selected all the items you need.
8. When all items are selected, click Next. This opens the third and last screen of the Hierarchy Wizard.

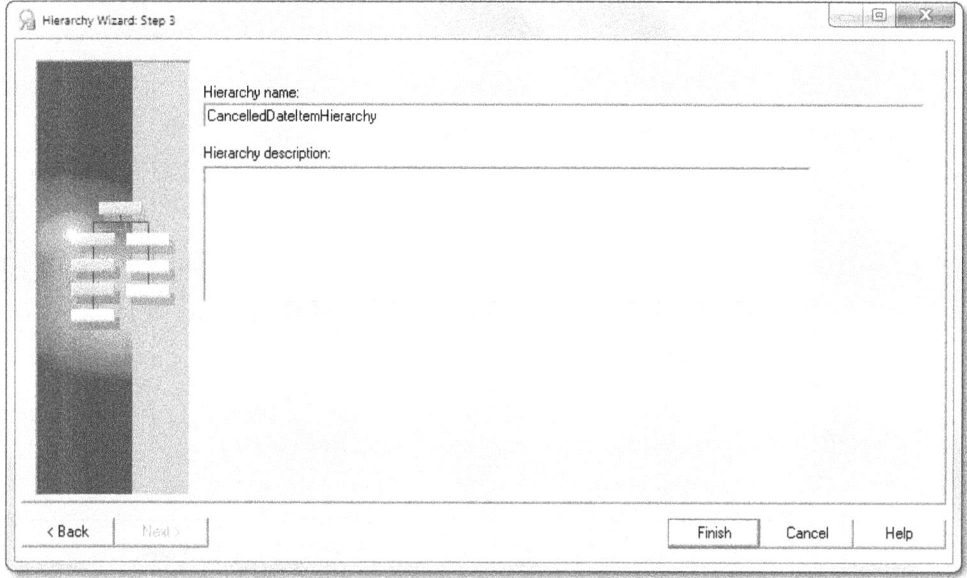


9. Give a meaningful name and optional description to the hierarchy.
10. Click Finish.

## Creating a Date Hierarchy

To create a date hierarchy, use the following workflow:

1. Click the Hierarchies tab.
2. Right-click the business area in which you want to create the hierarchy, and from the pop-up list select New Hierarchy. This opens the Hierarchy Wizard, as was shown in Figure 17-7.
3. Check Date Hierarchy.

4. Click Next. This opens the second screen of the Hierarchy Wizard.

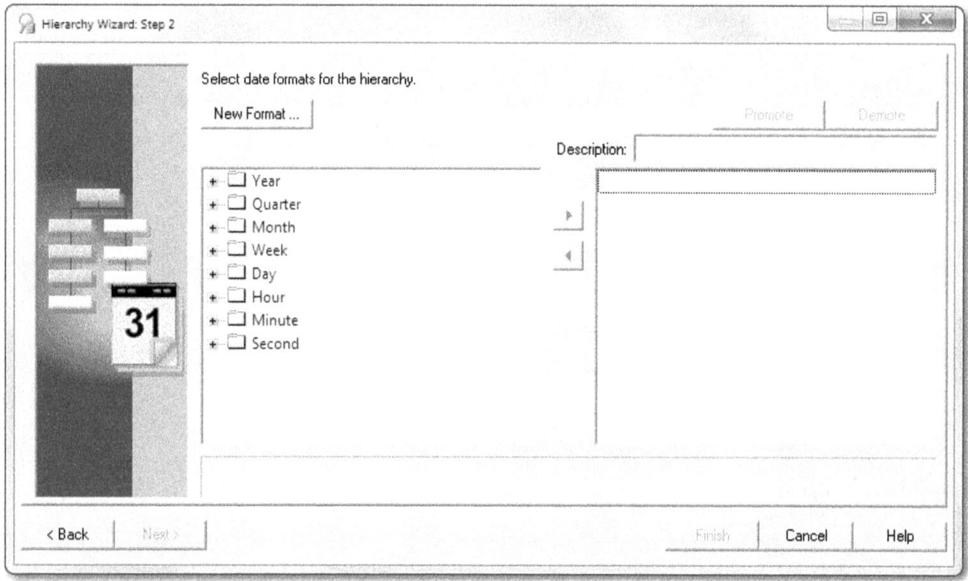


5. Select the hierarchy items that you want to include by expanding the group elements and pasting the required time element into the right side.
6. If the time element you need is not among the available elements in a group, click the New Format button. This opens the New Date Format dialog box. Select the group you want to define a new element for, and in the New Format box type the format mask for the new time element. When done, click OK. The new element will be available in the chosen group.

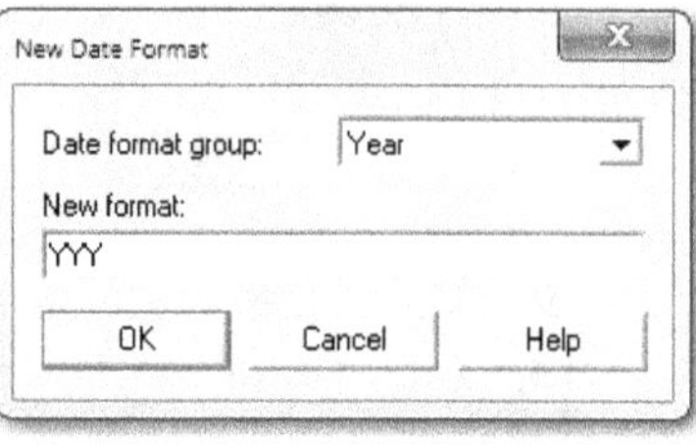


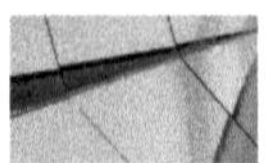

**NOTE**
*In the preceding box, we have defined a new element called YYY in the Year group. For a list of all the valid date format masks, please refer to Appendix B.*

7. Select the time elements, in descending order of group, until you have selected all of the elements that you need.
8. In the following example, you can see that we have chosen YYYY from the Year group, "Q"Q from the Quarter group, Mon-RR from the Month group, and DD-Mon-YYYY from the Date group.

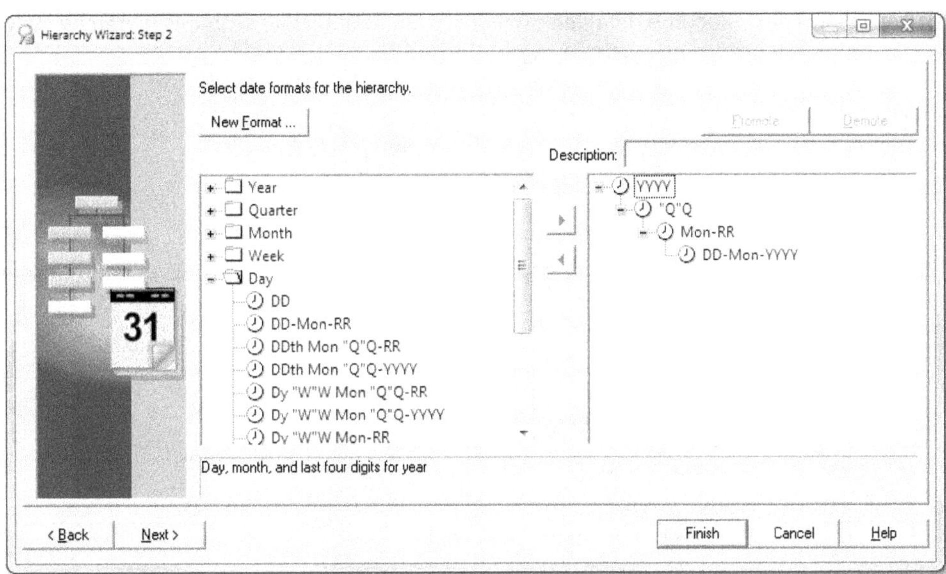

**NOTE**
*The Promote, Demote, and Description boxes in the Hierarchy Wizard will be grayed out until you click one of the elements you have chosen. Then you can provide a description for the element and manipulate the hierarchy by demoting and promoting elements.*

9. When all elements have been selected, click Next. This opens the third screen of the Hierarchy Wizard.

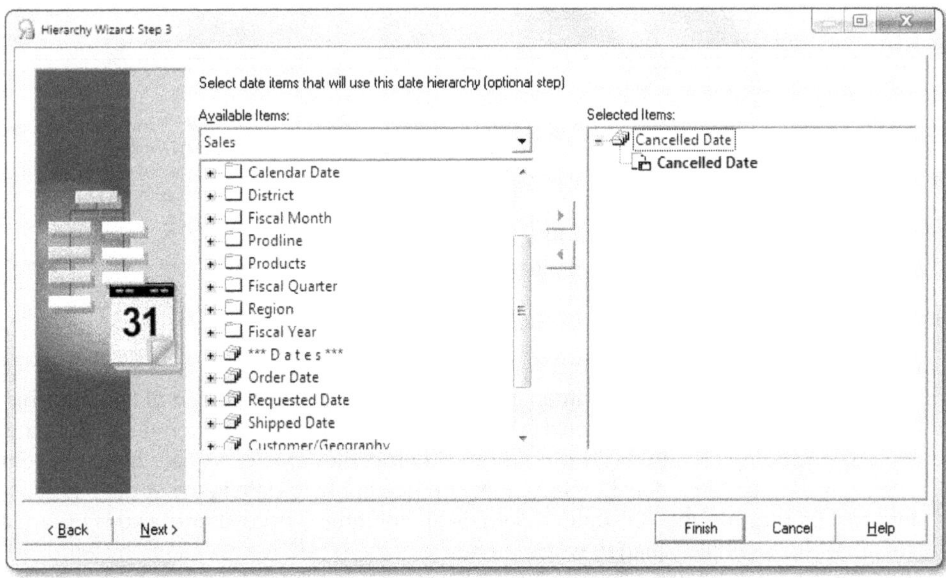

10. Optionally, select the date item that you want to associate with this hierarchy. As you can see in the preceding example, we have used Cancelled Date.

**NOTE**
*You do not need to select any date item in this step. If you leave the Selected box empty, you will be creating a new template. For more information on date templates, see the next section.*

11. When you have finished with step 3, click Next. This opens the fourth and last screen of the Hierarchy Wizard.

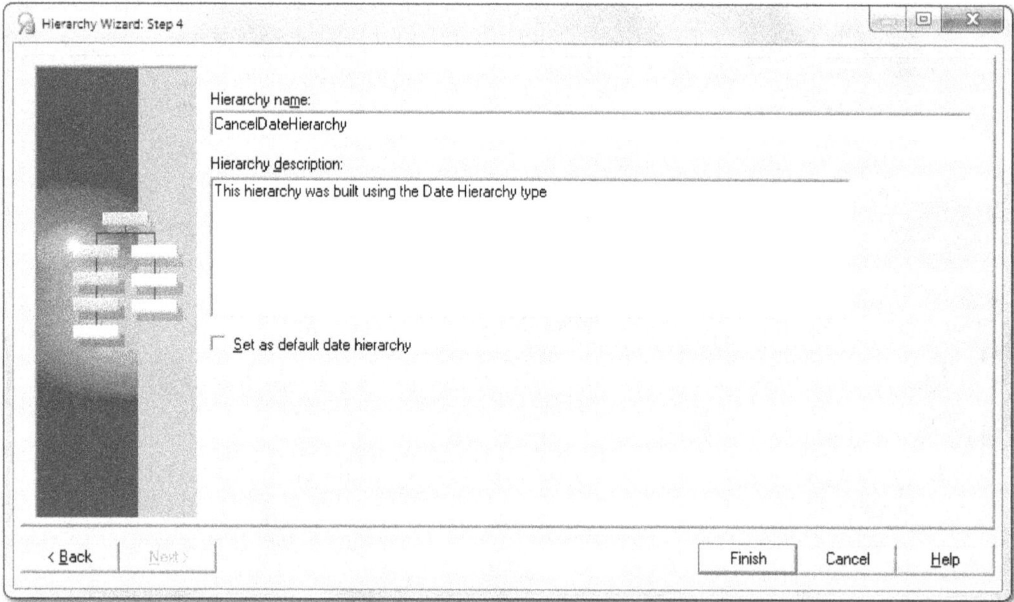


12. Give a meaningful name and optional description to the hierarchy.
13. Click Finish.
14. Discoverer creates and adds one new item per time element to the folder, as you can see in the illustration shown here.

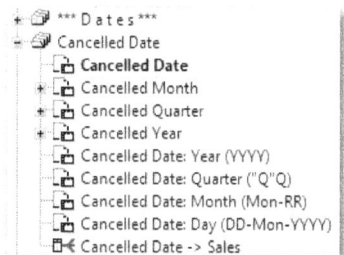

*** Dates ***
Cancelled Date
Cancelled Date
Cancelled Month
Cancelled Quarter
Cancelled Year
Cancelled Date: Year (YYYY)
Cancelled Date: Quarter ("Q"Q)
Cancelled Date: Month (Mon-RR)
Cancelled Date: Day (DD-Mon-YYYY)
Cancelled Date -> Sales

## Date Hierarchy Templates

In the preceding section we commented that if you left the third screen of the Date Hierarchy Wizard empty, you would in effect be creating a new date hierarchy template. But what is a date hierarchy template? Put in its simplest form, according to Oracle, "A date hierarchy template enables you to define a date hierarchy that you can apply to date items. A date item uses information that specifies the date, month, year, and time. Discoverer uses this information to calculate, for example, quarter, week, and days of the week. A date hierarchy template automatically creates items based on a date item, for example to represent the year or month."

It is far more efficient to reuse a date hierarchy than to have to redefine the hierarchy every time you want to create a new one. This is where the template comes in. By saving a set of date hierarchy elements as a date hierarchy template, you can reuse this any number of times.

### Creating and Selecting Your Hierarchies

How many hierarchies do you need in your business area? The number will vary depending upon how many rollups or drills you need. However, in our case, we need to create one item hierarchy for each of the six new complex folders we have created:

- Cancelled Date
- Order Date
- Requested Date
- Shipped Date
- Geography
- Product

We have already shown you how to create the Cancelled Date hierarchy using both item and date hierarchies. Because we are using a custom fiscal calendar that has been prebuilt and pre-indexed, we will use item hierarchies for all of our dates. Simply following the instructions given earlier for creating an item hierarchy, we created the three other time hierarchies on the Order Date, Requested Date, and Shipped Date folders.

Turning to the Geographic and Product hierarchies, these are simple to build. They are both item hierarchies.

### Geographic Hierarchy

Our geographic hierarchy is based on the Geography folder. At the lowest level, this folder joins on the Customer ID to our Sales folder. The customer is the lowest-level item in the hierarchy. Looking at the available items, we can see that Customer Name is available to use in the Geography folder. In turn, we need to pick something from the other base folders that make up our complex Geography folder. If you recall, we have four 1:N folders making up the complex folder:

- Customer
- City
- District
- Region

It makes sense, therefore, that because the tables these folders are based on have a primary-key/foreign-key relationship, we select one City item, one District item, and one Region item. In our final hierarchy, we chose the following:

- Customer
- City
- District
- Region

Any sort of drilling on these items will perform very fast.

### Product Hierarchy

We will turn our attention to the product hierarchy that will be based on the Product complex folder. At the lowest level, this folder joins on the Product ID to our Sales folder. The product is therefore the lowest-level item in this hierarchy. Looking at the available items, we can see that both Product Name and Product Size are available to us in the Product folder. However, the join between the base Products folder and the Sales folder is on the Product ID, which in turn is linked to Product Name. Therefore, Product Name becomes the lowest element in our hierarchy. We need to pick something from the other base folder that forms part of our complex Product folder. If you recall, we have two 1:N folders making up this complex folder.

- Products
- Product Line

It makes sense that because the tables that these base folders are based on have a primary-key/foreign-key relationship, we should select Product Line. In our final hierarchy, we have the following:

- Product Name
- Product Line

## Item Management

Why do we create new items? We create new items in the End User Layer to enable our users to

- Make better sense of the data
- Avoid mistakes
- Have guaranteed working algorithms

For these reasons, we will always look to create new algorithms in the business area whenever possible. If you look back to the early part of this chapter where we created a new item to convert a string into a number for use in a complex join, you already know how to add a new item to a folder. We therefore will not dwell on this point, other than to say you will be using the New Item dialog box.

In this section we will not belabor how to create new items but concentrate instead on the following:

- Types of items
- Useful algorithms
- Sorting items
- Assigning indexes to an item

## Types of Items

Discoverer understands three types of items.

- **Columns** These items are based on columns from objects in the underlying database.
- **Components** These items are based on the components of a custom folder.
- **Calculations** These items are based on calculated items that you, the administrator, create on behalf of your users.

## Useful Algorithms

A number of useful, standard algorithms can be created in Discoverer. We will describe three of them.

- **Profit** Calculated as the selling price minus the cost price
- **Standard margin** Calculated as profit divided by the sum of the selling price
- **Standard markup** Calculated as profit divided by the sum of the cost price

When creating calculated items using division, you must make sure you allow for and ensure that you do not introduce divide-by-zero errors. This subject was covered in depth in Chapter 13, where we described the techniques you must use to avoid these errors.

## Adding Items to a Complex Folder

If you are creating new items in a complex folder, Discoverer lists all of the folders that were used to create the complex folder. Discoverer also displays all of the items in the original base folders, irrespective of whether they are being used in the complex folder. This is very useful to know, especially if you are adding calculated items to the complex folder.

This allows you to build new items on any item from the base folders, not just on the items in the complex folder.

## Sorting Items

Should you want to sort the items in a folder, Discoverer provides a means to do so. To sort the items in a folder, use the following workflow:

1. Right-click the folder you want to sort.
2. From the pop-up menu, select Sort Items.
3. Discoverer displays the following Alphabetical Sort dialog box:

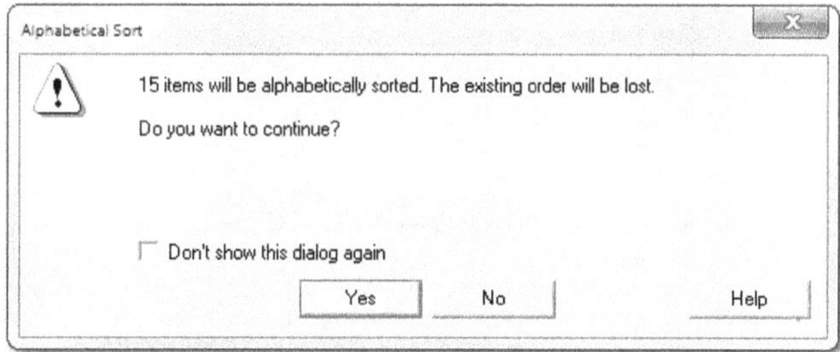


4. As you can see in the preceding illustration, Discoverer tells you how many items are to be sorted and prompts "Do you want to continue?" Click Yes to sort or No to cancel.

## Descriptive Lists of Values: Assigning Indexes to an Item

Another new feature of Discoverer is the ability to add an indexed item to another item to improve parameter selection performance in the end-user tools. So long as both items exist in the same folder and neither is hidden, you can tell Discoverer to search an index rather than the original item.

Let's explore this some more by using the following example. Suppose you have a base table that has a Product Name and a Product ID, with the Product ID being indexed and the Product Name not indexed. Most users will know a product by its name, not by its ID value, and so will want to create parameters based on the name. However, because the name is not indexed, the query could take a long time. To overcome this poor performance, Oracle has introduced the concept of *descriptive* lists of values. The list of values, on the parameter selection screen, is shown along with its associated ID. However, when the query is executed, Discoverer uses the ID.

To set up a descriptive list of values, use the following workflow:

1. Expand a folder that contains both the item and the indexed item.
2. Right-click the item, and from the pop-up menu select Properties.
3. Navigate to the property Indexed item. It is located toward the bottom of the list.

**NOTE**
*For this to work, the item must have a list of values associated with it before the Indexed item property is available. If you do not have a list of values associated with the item, the property will be grayed out.*

4. Click the Indexed item property, and from the pop-up list select the indexed item you want to use.

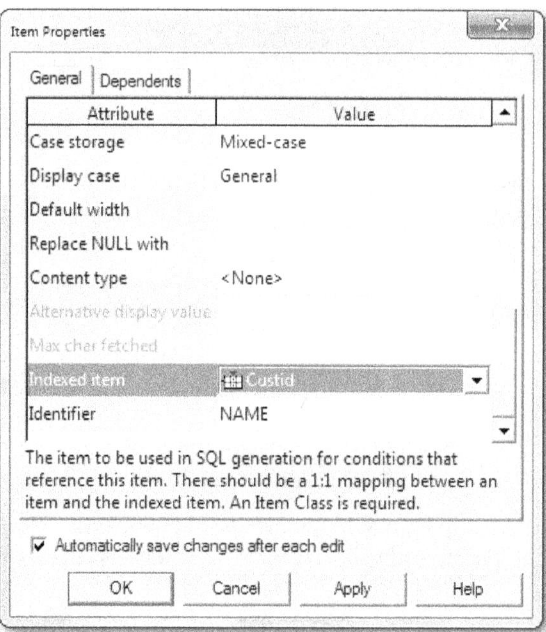

5. As you can see in the preceding illustration, Discoverer inserts a marker alongside any indexed item that it finds in the folder.
6. Select the indexed item that matches one-to-one with the original item and click OK.
7. If there is no index in the database on the item you are trying to create the descriptive list of values, Discoverer prompts that you need to create one.

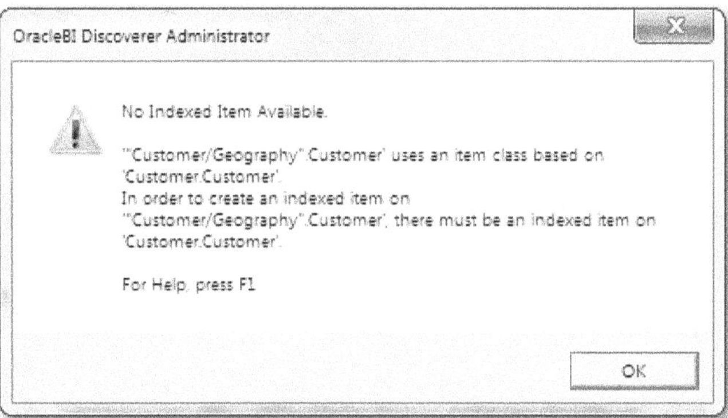

OracleBI Discoverer Administrator
No Indexed Item Available.
"Customer/Geography".Customer' uses an item class based on 'Customer.Customer'.
In order to create an indexed item on "Customer/Geography".Customer', there must be an indexed item on 'Customer.Customer'.
For Help, press F1
OK


8. If there is no list of values on the indexed item, as you can see next, Discoverer prompts "Setting an indexed item requires a new LOV to be created" and offers you OK or Cancel.

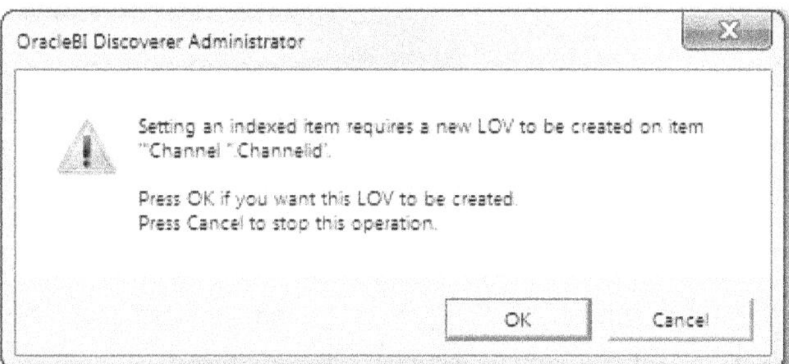

OracleBI Discoverer Administrator
Setting an indexed item requires a new LOV to be created on item "Channel".Channelid'.
Press OK if you want this LOV to be created.
Press Cancel to stop this operation.
OK
Cancel


9. Click OK to complete the attachment of the index.
10. If you look at the list of values on the item class, you will see that Discoverer has created a new list of values for itself, shown here.

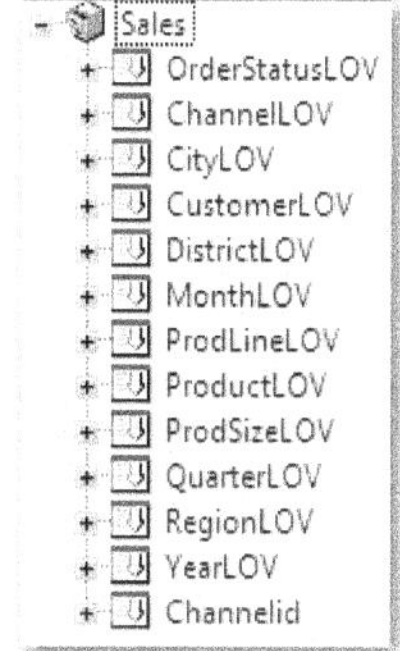


In Discoverer Plus, whenever the user creates a parameter on the customer name, they will be given the opportunity to search by name or by the index. Searching by the index will greatly improve performance.

### Using Descriptive Lists of Values in Plus

Having set up the descriptive lists of values, perhaps you might be interested in seeing how an end user can take advantage of this in Discoverer Plus. For this example, we created a descriptive list of values on the Channel using the Channel ID as the indexed item.

We created a new workbook using the Channel and then started to create a new condition using a parameter. As you can see in the illustration that follows, Discoverer now allows the user to check the box Enable Users To Select Either Indexes Or Values.

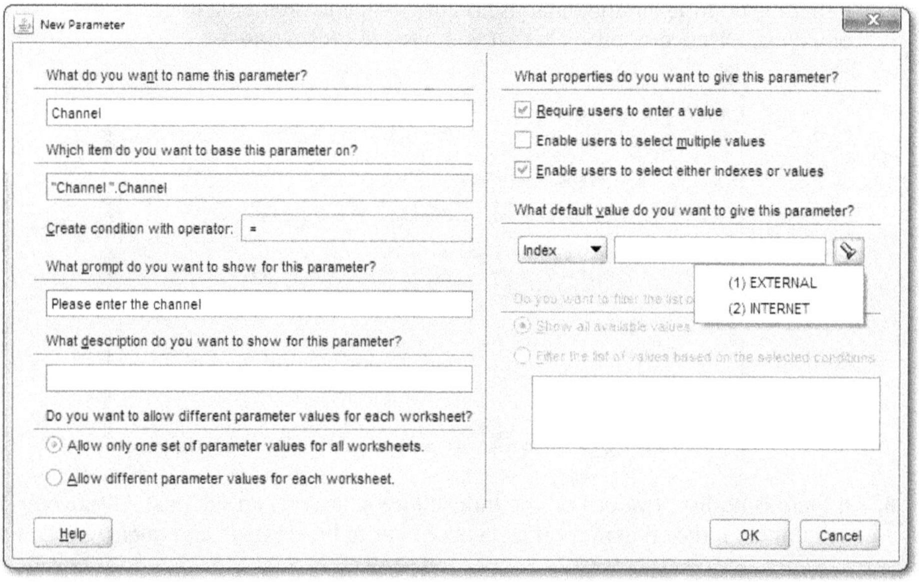

With the indexes or values box checked, the boxes immediately below are enabled. The first, as you can see in the preceding image, is a drop-down that allows the user to specify that an index or a value should be used as the default. As you can see, we have opted to use the index as the default, and when we click the drop-down, we get a list of the two channels available to us along with their IDs. If we select (2) INTERNET from the drop-down, Discoverer will put 2 into the default.

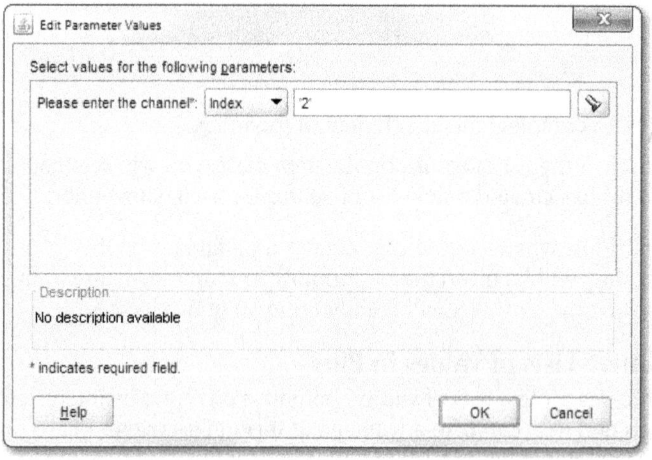

When this parameter is presented to a user in a working query, Discoverer displays the revised Edit Parameter Values dialog box.

In the dialog box, you can see that Discoverer is allowing the user to choose whether they want to input the index value or the actual value. Many users actually know the index values or codes that are being used on the system and may prefer to type in the code value when selecting parameters. This is particularly true for users in HR situations where they prefer to type a user's employee number rather than the name. The preceding explanation shows you how to enable this.

Turning our attention now to Discoverer Desktop, if we save the report that was created in Plus and open it in Desktop, you will see that the functionality for the user to be prompted whether to use the index values or codes exists here too. You can even edit a parameter that uses indexed items in Desktop. However, the workbook and original parameter must have been created inside Plus first. You cannot create new indexed parameters in Desktop; you can edit only existing parameters.

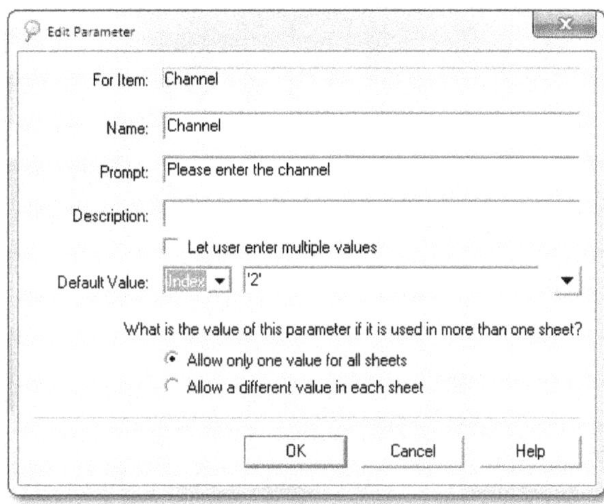


# Summary

In this chapter, you learned how to continue with the remaining business area checks. You learned the value of a well-designed business area as it affects the end user. We demonstrated how to manage lists of values and joins. We showed you how to add new folders, followed by managing hierarchies. Finally we showed you some of the more advanced mechanisms for item management, culminating in an explanation of how to manage descriptive lists of values.

# CHAPTER 18

# Interacting with the End User

This chapter, another in the series of chapters dedicated to the Discoverer administrator, is packed with useful workflows that will help you interact with your end users. The intention of this chapter is to complement one of the sections in Chapter 15. If you look back at the "What Can the Discoverer Administrator Do for You?" section, you will see it contains a list of approximately 20 topics. This chapter will take each of those topics in turn and describe or provide you with a workflow that will tackle the topic.

Several of the workflows that are needed to answer questions posed by the users have already been given in previous chapters. We will not repeat those workflows here but simply direct you to the relevant chapter. However, in this chapter you will find some concepts being introduced or explained for the first time. Among the new topics that you will find in this chapter are managing access, managing privileges, creating predefined conditions, and managing scheduling.

In many of the workflows used within this chapter, you will be asked to click Cancel when the first screen of the Load Wizard appears. To understand what we are suggesting, please take a look at Figure 18-1.

# Adding New Users

If you receive a request for a new user, you need either to ask your DBA to create an account or, if using Oracle Applications, to direct the user to the applications system administrator. For a standard EUL, the DBA will also need to know which privileges and roles should be granted. For an Apps-mode EUL, the system administrator will need to know which responsibilities should be granted.

Special database privileges are required for scheduling. These privileges are dealt with later in this chapter.

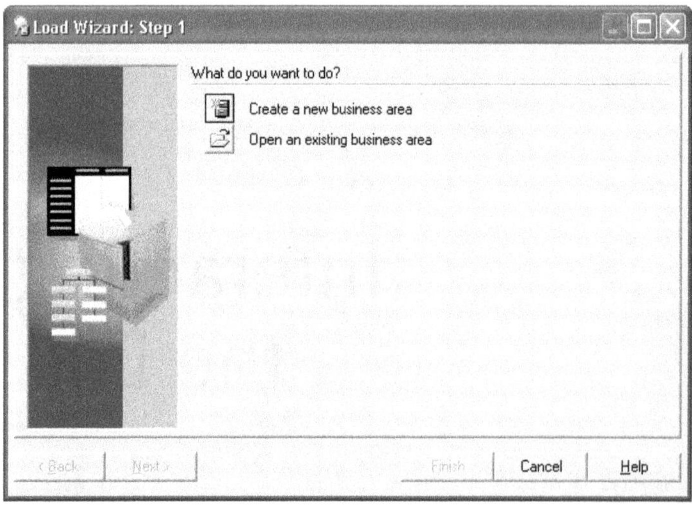


**FIGURE 18-1.** *Load Wizard, step 1*

In some cases, the user you will be creating will have all or partial access to some of the features of the Discoverer Administrator tool. You need to work with the user to determine how much administration is required. If the user is to be a second administrator, you will need to ask your DBA to create a user who has the identical database privileges that you have.

Having created the user accounts, you need to assign the Discoverer privileges and grant access to the required business area. These topics are dealt with later in this chapter.

# Granting Access to Business Areas

Having received a request from a user for access to a business area, before you log in to the Administrator tool to do the work, there are some other tasks you need to do first.

Presumably, the user already has an account. If not, you need to address this issue first. So, let's assume the user has an account but does not have access to the business area they are requesting. It is not your responsibility as the Discoverer administrator to decide who gets access to what. Your job is only to ensure that you obtain the necessary approval or rejection and that the access is maintained on an ongoing basis.

There are two types of access for you to consider. They are

- Open
- Restricted

## Open Access

Some business areas are considered open. By this we mean that anyone can have access without the need for higher-level approval. The only consideration should be, does the person need to have this access to do their job? If the answer is yes—and usually the manager can confirm this—the access should be granted.

## Restricted Access and Insider Trading

However, many organizations have what are called *restricted*, or secure, business areas. These business areas need higher-level approval. All you need to do is submit the request to the person responsible. An example of a "restricted" business area is one that contains revenue information. If you are in an organization that releases periodic results to your shareholders, access to the revenue business area should be restricted to only those people who are allowed to see the results prior to publication. Using this data, an unauthorized user could use that information to buy or sell stock in your company or influence others to do so. This practice, called *insider trading*, is prohibited by law. It is therefore essential that those sensitive business areas are protected.

**NOTE**
*If you grant access to secure data to a role or responsibility, you are in effect delegating the access for that secure data to whomever is responsible for managing those roles or responsibilities. Unless you have created special roles or responsibilities for this purpose, we strongly recommend you grant secure access to user accounts only.*

## Workflow to Grant Access

Assuming the user has been approved for access to a business area, to grant access to that business area, use the following workflow:

1. Launch the Discoverer Administrator tool.
2. When the Load Wizard displays, as shown in Figure 18-1, click Cancel.
3. From the menu bar, select Tools | Security. Discoverer opens the Security dialog box.
4. The Security dialog box has two tabs.
   - **Users -> Business Area** This tab allows you to grant a single user or role to have access to one or more business areas.

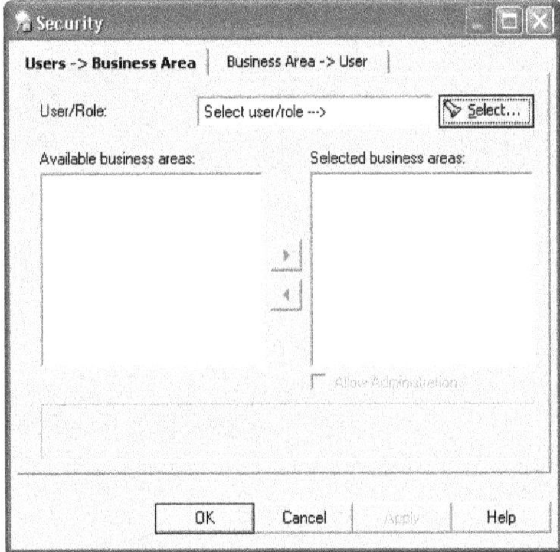


   - **Business Area -> User** This tab allows you to grant access to a single business area for one or more users or roles.

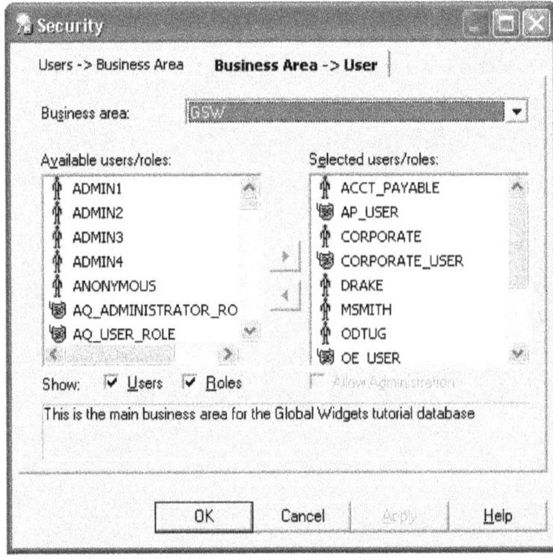

5. On the Users -> Business Area tab, you first need to select the user you want to work with. Having selected the user or role, as shown next, Discoverer shows you the access currently assigned to that user or role:

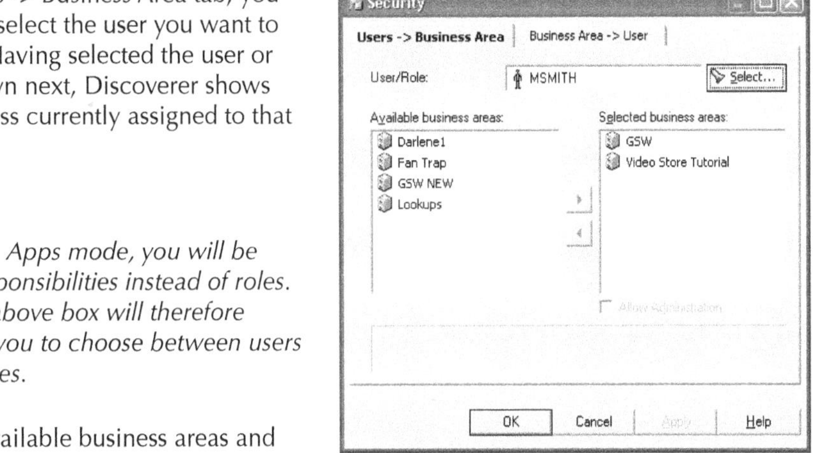

**NOTE**
*When working in Apps mode, you will be working with responsibilities instead of roles. The label in the above box will therefore change to allow you to choose between users and responsibilities.*

6. Using the Available business areas and Selected business areas boxes, adjust the access for the user, role, or responsibility and then click OK.
7. On the Business Area -> User tab, use the drop-down alongside the Business area box to select the area you want to work with.
8. Using the Available users/roles and Selected users/roles boxes, adjust the access for the business area and then click OK.
9. Inform the user that the access has been adjusted.

# Granting User Edition Privileges

If a user comes to you and suggests that their Discoverer privileges are insufficient, you should discuss this with the user. Having determined what additional privileges the user needs, you should use the Privileges tab of Discoverer Administrator.

To grant additional user edition privileges, use the following workflow:

1. Launch the Discoverer Administrator tool.
2. When the Load Wizard displays, as shown in Figure 18-1, click Cancel.
3. From the menu bar, select Tools | Privileges. Discoverer opens the Privileges dialog box.

As you can see in Figure 18-2, the Privileges dialog box has four tabs.

- **Privileges** This tab allows you to assign multiple privileges to a single user or role.
- **User/Role** This tab allows you to assign multiple users, roles, or responsibilities to a single privilege.
- **Query Governor** This tab allows you to assign query governor privileges to a single user, role, or responsibility.
- **Scheduled Workbooks** This tab allows you to maintain the scheduling privileges for a single user. Scheduling is dealt with later in this chapter.

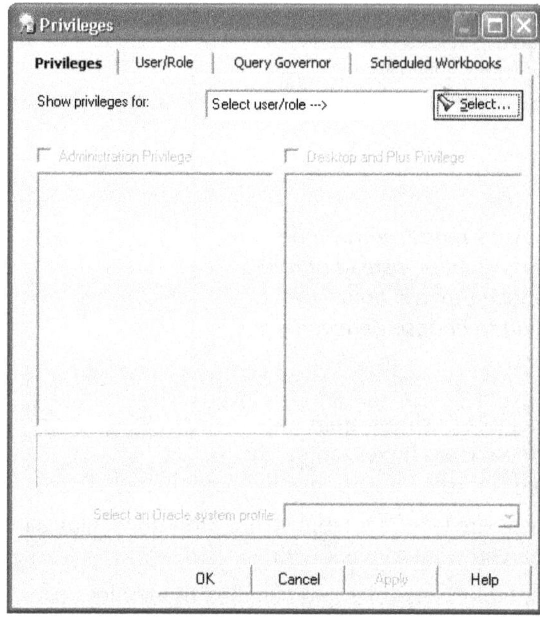


**FIGURE 18-2.** *Privileges dialog box*

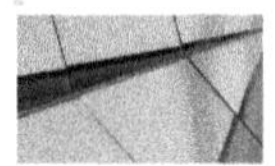

**NOTE**
*In Apps mode, the User/Role tab is labeled User/Responsibility.*

We will deal with the Privileges, User/Role, and Query Governor tabs separately in the following sections.

## Working with the Privileges Tab

To work with the Privileges tab, use the following workflow:

1. Launch the Privileges dialog box, shown in Figure 18-2, and click the Privileges tab.
2. Click the Select button. Discoverer opens the Select User/Role or Select User/Responsibility search box.
3. Type or search for the user, role, or responsibility for whom you want to assign privileges.

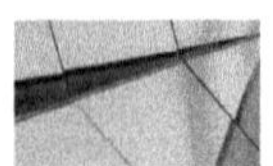

**NOTE**
*If you have used previous versions of Discoverer, you may notice that this box has changed. Whereas in older versions this was a drop-down, it has now become a field that you have to search for first. This has been done to improve performance. Oracle tell us that it had cases where the user population ran into tens of thousands, and populating a drop-down with 10,000 or more values takes time—sometimes a lot of time. Hence, Oracle has provided this new search-then-assign workflow.*

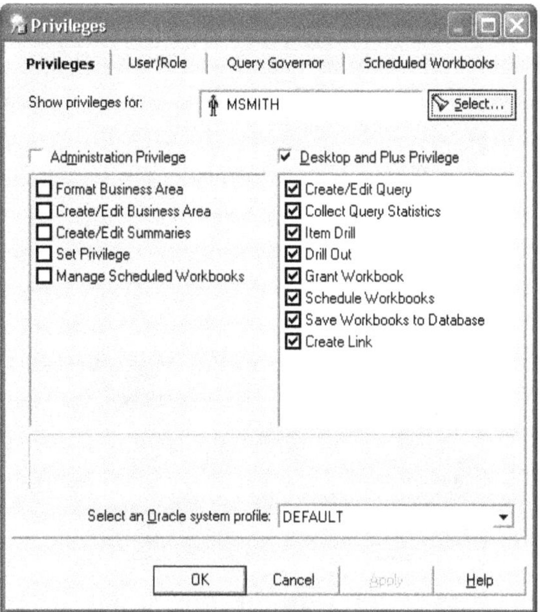


**FIGURE 18-3.** *Privileges tab*

4. Click OK to close the Select User/Role or Select User/Responsibility search box.
5. As shown in Figure 18-3, Discoverer displays the current privileges for the user, role, or responsibility.

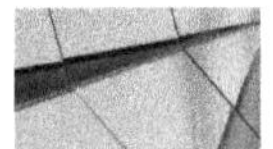

**NOTE**
*For an explanation of what each privilege allows, please read the section "Discoverer Privileges Explained."*

6. Grant the privileges needed by checking the appropriate privilege boxes.
7. Having worked with the privileges, use one of the following options:
   - **Apply** Click this to apply the privileges you have set and stay within the tab.
   - **OK** Click this to apply the privileges you have set and exit the tab.
   - **Cancel** Click this to exit the tab without applying privileges.

## Working with the User/Role or User/Responsibility Tab

To work with the User/Role or User/Responsibility tab, use the following workflow:

1. Launch the Privileges dialog box, shown earlier in Figure 18-2, and click the User/Role or User/Responsibility tab.

2. Note the different areas of this tab, as shown here and described after these steps:

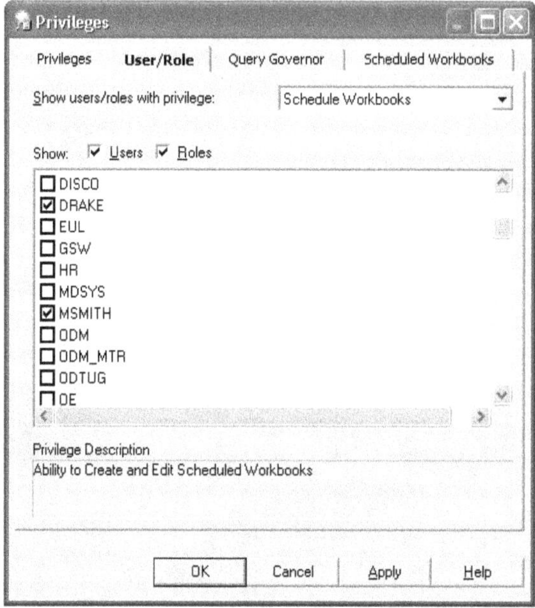


3. Having worked with the privileges, use one of the following options:
   - **Apply** Click this to apply the privileges you have set and stay within the tab.
   - **OK** Click this to apply the privileges you have set and exit the tab.
   - **Cancel** Click this to exit the tab without applying privileges.

These are the options available to you on the User/Role or User/Responsibility tab:

- **Show users/roles with this privilege** Use the drop-down to select the privilege you want to administer.
- **A Show area** This contains two check boxes.
  - **Users** Check this box to show only users who have the privilege.
  - **Roles** Check this box to show only roles who have the privilege.
- **A list of users** Use the check boxes alongside the user or role to grant or remove the privileges.

**NOTE**
*In Apps mode, the word User is replaced by the word Responsibility.*

## Working with the Query Governor Tab

To work with the Query Governor tab, use the following workflow:

1. Launch the Privileges dialog box, shown in Figure 18-2, and click the Query Governor tab.

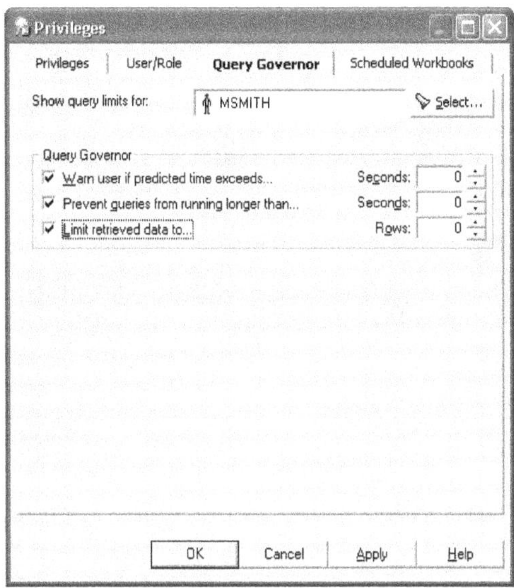


2. As you can see in the preceding illustration, this tab has the areas described next.

**NOTE**
*Using the Discoverer Viewer Preferences tab or the Query Governor tab from Tools | Options in both Desktop and Plus, users can apply their own query governor settings. However, users can apply only settings that are lower than or equal to the settings that the administrator has set.*

3. Having made the query governor settings for the user, use one of the following options:
   - **Apply** Click this to apply the settings you have set and stay within the tab.
   - **OK** Click this to apply the settings you have set and exit the tab.
   - **Cancel** Click this to exit the tab without applying the settings.

These are the options available to you on the Query Governor tab:

- **Show query limits for** Use the Select button to pick the user you want to administer.
- **A Query Governor area** This contains three check boxes.
  - **Warn User If Predicted Time Exceeds** Check this box and then use the Seconds box to set a query limit for the user. When set, with the query predictor enabled, Discoverer will estimate how long a query will take and warn the user if the predicted time exceeds this limit.

- **Prevent Queries From Running Longer Than** Check this box and then use the Seconds box to set a maximum query limit for the user. When set, with the query predictor enabled, Discoverer will estimate how long a query will take and prevent the user from running any query that is predicted to exceed this time limit.
- **Limit Retrieved Data To** Check this box and then use the Rows box to set a maximum query limit for the user. When set, Discoverer prevents the user from pulling more than the number of rows defined here.

# Discoverer Privileges Explained

In this section, we will give a detailed explanation of both the administration and user privileges that are under your control.

## Administration Privileges Explained

The Privileges tab of the Privileges dialog box, shown in Figure 18-3, shows all the administration privileges you can grant. Table 18-1 gives a detailed explanation of each of these privileges.

| Privilege | Description |
|---|---|
| Administration Privilege | Checking this allows a user or role to log in to the Discoverer Administrator tool. Until this box is checked, you will not be able to assign the individual administrator privileges. |
| Format Business Area | Grant this privilege if you want to allow the administrator to edit formatting information in an existing business area to which they have access. Such formatting information includes folders, summary folders, joins, and items. Granting this privilege allows the user or role to specify names, descriptions, default format masks, and placement. |
| Create/Edit Business Areas | Grant this privilege if you want to allow the administrator to create and modify business areas, folders, summary folders, joins, calculations, conditions, hierarchies, and item classes. |
| Create/Edit Summaries | Grant this privilege if you want to allow the administrator to create summary folders using the Discoverer Administrator tool. The use of this privilege also requires database privileges for materialized views. |
| Set Privilege | Grant this privilege if you want to allow the administrator to maintain and modify user privileges using this dialog box. You cannot grant this privilege to a role. |
| Manage Scheduled Workbooks | Grant this privilege if you want to allow the administrator to monitor and maintain the schedule for scheduled workbooks. |

**TABLE 18-1.** *Administration Privileges*

### User Privileges Explained

The Privileges tab of the Privileges dialog box, shown in Figure 18-3, also shows all the user privileges you can grant. Table 18-2 gives a detailed explanation of each of these privileges.

| Privilege | Description |
|---|---|
| Desktop and Plus Privilege | Checking this allows a user or role to log in to Discoverer Desktop and Discoverer Plus. Until this box is checked, you will not be able to assign the individual privileges.<br>A user who has been authorized to use Discoverer will always be able to log in to Viewer—you cannot revoke this privilege. |
| Create/Edit Query | Grant this privilege if you want to allow the user or role to create new worksheets and workbooks. Without this privilege, the user will be able to run only existing workbooks. You should therefore unset this if the user needs only to run Viewer and does not need to make changes. |
| Collect Query Statistics | Grant this privilege if you want Discoverer to maintain statistics about how the user's queries perform. |
| Item Drill | Grant this privilege if you want to allow the user or role to be able to drill to detail within a worksheet. If you want to grant this privilege, you must also grant the Drill Out privilege. |
| Drill Out | Grant this privilege if you want to allow a user or role to be able to launch another application to see related information. Before a user can use this privilege, the administrator must create the drill using the Item Class Wizard or edit the item properties and set Content Type to <FILE>. |
| Grant Workbook | Grant this privilege if you want to allow a user or role to be able to share their workbooks with other users so that they can run and view them. |
| Schedule Workbooks | Grant this privilege if you want to allow a user to schedule a workbook to run at a later time and at regular intervals (i.e., daily, weekly, monthly). You cannot grant this privilege to a role, and the user must have certain database privileges; otherwise, this will not work. |
| Save Workbooks to Database | Grant this privilege if you want to allow a user or role to save their workbooks to the database. By default, Discoverer Desktop workbooks are saved on the user's hard drive. If the user is using Plus and you have not checked this box, the user will be unable to save. |
| Change Password | This privilege is not used in this release. |
| Create Link | This privilege allows you to control who is allowed to create their own drill links. A drill link is a way to access another worksheet or URL from a particular worksheet cell value. |

**TABLE 18-2.** *User Privileges*

# Adding Meaningful Descriptions to Business Areas, Folders, and Data Items

A very simple, yet very useful, means of helping users understand the data better is to add descriptions to the data objects. This adds no overhead to the processing of the system, yet many administrators do not assign meaningful descriptions. Of particular help to end users is the addition of meaningful descriptions to the following EUL objects:

- Business areas
- Folders
- Items

## Adding a Meaningful Description to a Business Area

To assign a meaningful description to a business area, use the following workflow:

1. Launch the Discoverer Administrator tool.
2. When the Load Wizard displays, as shown earlier in Figure 18-1, click Open An Existing Business Area.
3. Open the business area that needs a description.
4. Right-click the business area, and from the pop-up menu select Properties. Discoverer opens the Business Area Properties dialog box, shown here.
5. Enter a meaningful description for the business area.
6. Click OK.

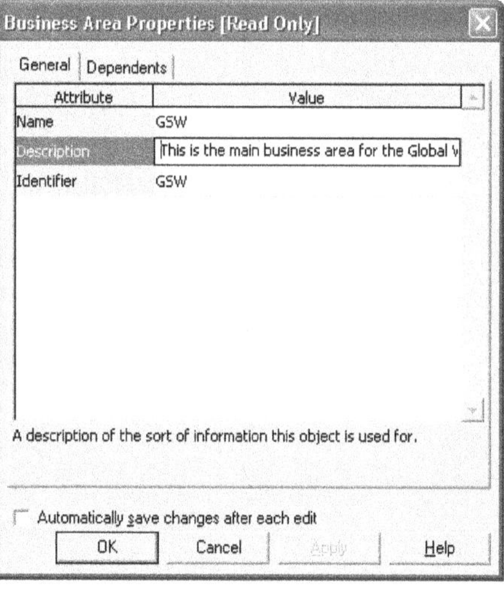


## Adding a Meaningful Description to a Folder

To assign a meaningful description to a folder, use the following workflow:

1. Launch the Discoverer Administrator tool.
2. When the Load Wizard displays, as shown in Figure 18-1, click Open An Existing Business Area.
3. Open the business area that contains the folder.
4. Expand the business area and locate the folder.

5. Right-click the folder, and from the pop-up menu select Properties. Discoverer opens the folder Properties dialog box, shown here.
6. Enter a meaningful description for the folder. Take a close look at the identifier. It looks like we should change this as well!
7. Click OK.

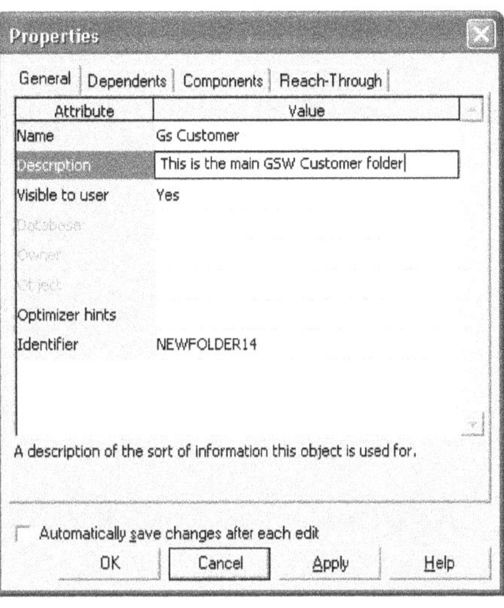


## Adding a Meaningful Description to an Item

To assign a meaningful description to an item, use the following workflow:

1. Launch the Discoverer Administrator tool.
2. When the Load Wizard displays, as shown earlier in Figure 18-1, click Open An Existing Business Area.
3. Open the business area that contains the folder.
4. Expand the business area and locate the folder that contains the item.
5. Expand the folder and locate the item.
6. Right-click the item, and from the pop-up menu select Properties. Discoverer opens the Item Properties dialog box.

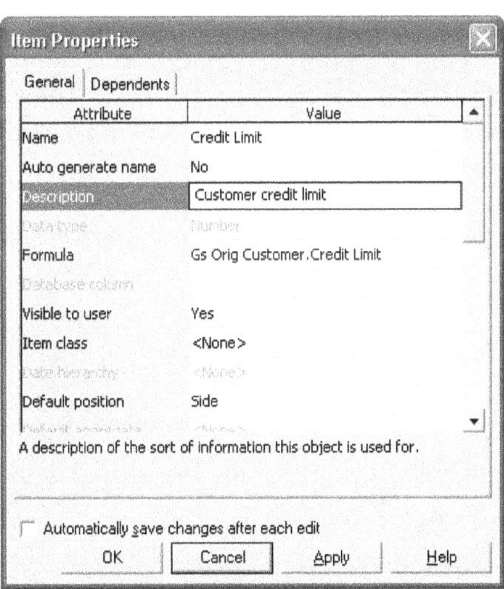


7. Enter a meaningful description for the item.
8. Click OK.

# Adding New Items to Folders

If you are approached by an end user who believes an item is missing from a folder, you need to sit down with the user and talk about it. You will probably also need to take a look at the user's worksheet to see whether you can pull the item in from another folder.

Having determined that the item is currently not available within any of the folders that the user currently has access to, you first need to determine whether the item exists within the EUL.

If it does exist but is not accessible to the user's worksheet, you should look to create a join to the folder that contains the item. To do this, please look at the section "Managing Joins" in Chapter 17.

At this stage, you have determined that the item does not exist within the EUL, so you need to add it. There are still some decisions that need to be taken, and these differ depending upon what type of folder you are working with.

# Adding New Items to Simple Folders

As you know, a simple folder is one that is based on an underlying database object, where that object is a table, a view, or a materialized view. You need to examine these objects to determine whether the required item already exists within the object. If it does, all you need to do is refresh the folder. If the item does not exist, you will need to add it. However, adding a new item to a table can be difficult, especially if you are working in an Oracle Applications or data warehousing environment. If the item that is required can be evaluated using items that already exist, you might want to consider adding a calculated item to the folder. To do this, please look ahead to the section "Creating New Items Based on Calculations."

If the item cannot be evaluated using items that already exist but the underlying object is a view or materialized view, you have a much better chance of getting the object changed. Assuming you have been able to get the object changed, to make the new item available within the EUL, you need to refresh the object. If the object is a table and you are forbidden from altering it, we recommend you consider creating a view and then switching the folder to point at the view instead of the table. We will show you both of these two workflows.

## Refreshing a Folder

To refresh a folder in order to bring in a new item, use the following workflow:

1. Launch the Discoverer Administrator tool.
2. When the Load Wizard displays, as shown earlier in Figure 18-1, click Open An Existing Business Area.
3. Open the business area that contains the folder you want to refresh.
4. Locate the folder, right-click it, and from the pop-up menu select Refresh.
5. Discoverer will open the Refresh Wizard.
6. In step 1 of the Refresh Wizard, shown next, you need to tell Discoverer from where it should refresh the folder.

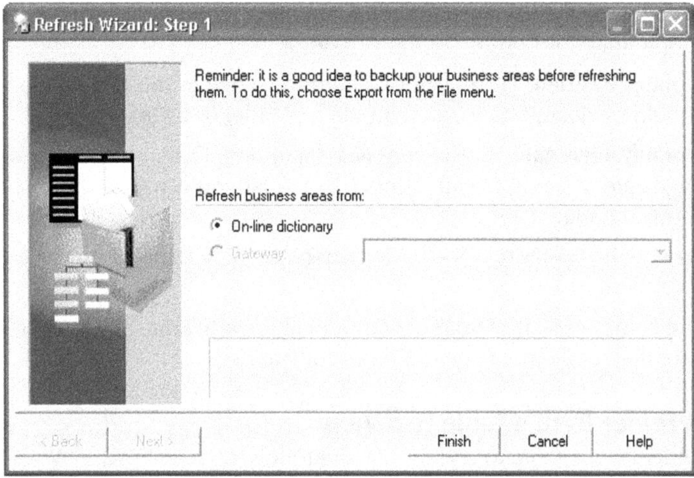


7. Having determined where the folder will be refreshed from, click Finish.
8. Discoverer will now analyze the folder by comparing the contents of the folder with the contents of the database object.
9. When the analysis is complete, Discoverer will either tell you that no changes were found or display a dialog box of the changes. If any changes were uncovered, Discoverer will display the Refresh Business Area dialog box.

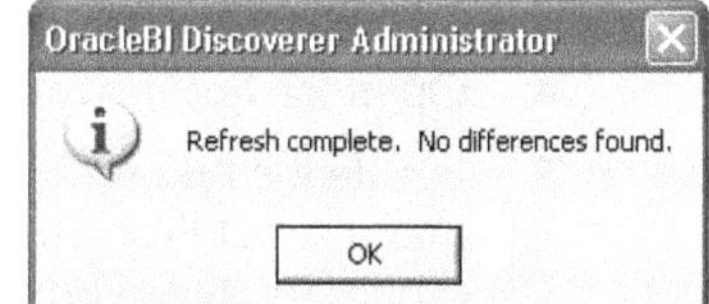


10. Use the check boxes alongside the changed items to signify whether you accept or reject the change.
11. Having made all of your selections, click OK.
12. Discoverer will make the necessary changes to your folder.

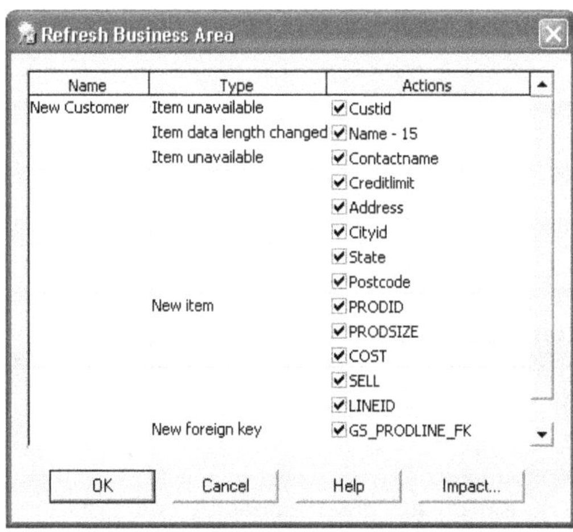

13. Before opening the folder to the user, you need to check the properties of the new item to make sure that it is correct. At the very least, you need to check the following:
    - **Default Position** You need to determine whether this is a data point or whether it should by default be located on the top, side, or page axis.
    - **Default Aggregate** If the item is a data point, Discoverer will assign the default aggregate as being Detail. If this is not what you want—and it probably is not—you should change it.
14. Determine the position in the folder where the new item should be and move it to its final position.
15. Having completed all of your checks and made any adjustments, you should now inform the user that the item has been successfully added.

### Switching a Folder from a Table to a View

To switch a folder from a table to a view, use the following workflow:

1. Create a new view in the database containing all of the original items.
2. Launch the Discoverer Administrator tool.
3. When the Load Wizard displays, as shown earlier in Figure 18-1, click Open An Existing Business Area.
4. Open the business area that contains the folder you want to refresh.
5. Locate the folder, right-click it, and from the pop-up menu select Properties. Discoverer will open the folder Properties dialog box.
6. In the Object property, click the object you want to change. Discoverer will open the Choose table or view dialog box, shown here.

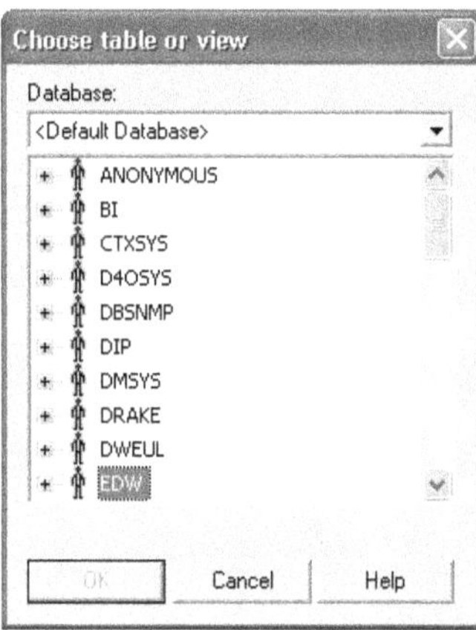


7. Having chosen the new object, click OK. Discoverer does not validate that the new object contains all of the items, so you need to be very careful not to pick the wrong object.
8. Follow all of the steps in the preceding section to refresh the folder. Discoverer should locate the new item but should not detect any other changes.
9. If any additional changes are found, you should revisit the view and then restart this workflow.

### Renaming a New Item and Using Headings

New items will come through from the database using the name of the column as it exists in the source table or view. Therefore, having added a new item from the database, you should check the name to make sure it complies with your organization's naming standard. If the name does not comply, you should change it.

As you know, when a user creates a worksheet, by default Discoverer takes the name of the item and uses that as the column heading. However, there are times, especially when the name is long, that you will want to use a different heading. Fortunately, Discoverer has a mechanism for doing just this.

To force Discoverer to use a different heading than the item's name, use the following workflow:

1. Right-click the item, and from the pop-up menu select Properties. Discoverer will open the Item Properties dialog box.
2. Scroll down to the Heading property.
3. Change the value for the heading.
4. Click OK.

**NOTE**
*By default, the item's heading is linked to the item's name; thus, if you change the name, the heading will also change. However, if you edit the heading, the link is broken, and the two properties must now be managed separately.*

## Adding New Items to Complex Folders

As you know, a complex folder is one that is based on one or more joined base folders. A base folder can be a simple, complex, or custom folder. Adding a new item to a complex folder is a simple task.

To add a new item to a complex folder, use the following workflow:

1. Determine which base folder contains the item that needs to be added to the complex folder.
2. Launch the Discoverer Administrator tool.
3. When the Load Wizard displays, as shown earlier in Figure 18-1, click Open An Existing Business Area.
4. Open the business area that contains the complex folder to which you want to add the new item.
5. Open a second window by using Window | New Window on the menu bar.
6. Expand the base folder that contains the item that needs to be added to the complex folder.
7. Click the item and drag it into the complex folder.
8. Before opening the folder to the user, you need to check the properties of the item to make sure it is correct. At the very least, you need to check the following:
   - **Default Position** You need to determine whether this is a data point or whether it should by default be located on the top, side, or page axis.
   - **Default Aggregate** If the item is a data point, Discoverer will assign the default aggregate as being Detail. If this is not what you want—and it probably is not—you should change it.
9. Determine the position in the folder where the item should be and move it to its final position.
10. Having completed all of your checks and made any adjustments, you should now inform the user that the item has been successfully added.

## Adding New Items to Custom Folders

As you know, a custom folder is a SQL script you have created. This script is stored in the EUL and can be edited using the Custom Folder Properties dialog box.

To add a new item to a custom folder, use the following workflow:

1. Launch the Discoverer Administrator tool.
2. When the Load Wizard displays, as shown earlier in Figure 18-1, click Open An Existing Business Area.
3. Open the business area that contains the custom folder to which you want to add the new item.
4. Right-click the custom folder, and from the pop-up box select Properties. Discoverer opens the Custom Folder Properties dialog box.

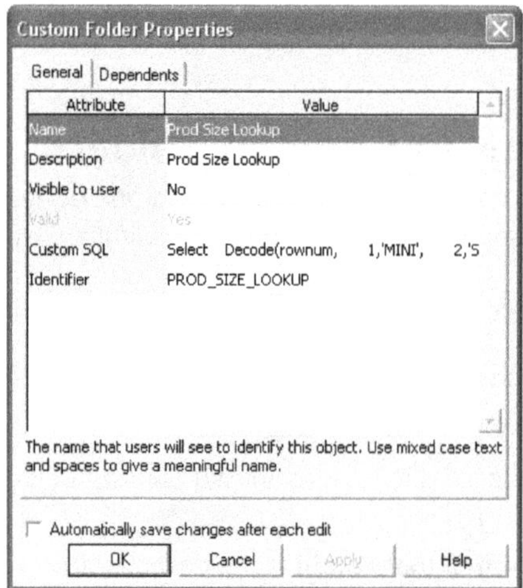


5. Click the Custom SQL property. Discoverer opens the following Edit Custom Folder dialog box.
6. Change the SQL.
7. Use the Validate SQL button to confirm that the SQL is valid.
8. When you have valid SQL, click OK.
9. Click OK to close the Custom Folder Properties dialog box.
10. Before opening up the folder to the user, you need to check the properties of the item to make sure that it is correct. At the very least, you need to check the following:

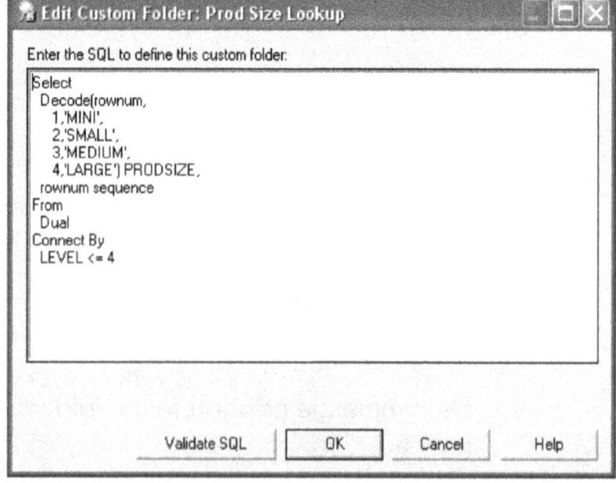

- **Default Position** You need to determine whether this is a data point or whether it should by default be located on the top, side, or page axis.
- **Default Aggregate** If the item is a data point, Discoverer will assign the default aggregate as being Detail. If this is not what you want—and it probably is not—you should change it.

11. Determine the position in the folder where the item should be and move it to its final position.
12. Having completed all of your checks and made any adjustments, you should now inform the user that the item has been successfully added.

# Creating New Folders

Your Discoverer administrator can create new folders within Discoverer. These folders can be based on SQL statements, extracts from the database, or even items contained in existing folders. If, as the administrator, you want to create a new folder, please look at the section "Creating New Folders" in Chapter 15.

# Creating Joins Between Folders

In both Desktop and Plus, Discoverer will gray out a folder if there is no join to it from any other folder that has been used as the basis for a worksheet. Sometimes this is just an oversight and there really should be a join. Perhaps you have just added a new folder to the EUL and you now need to join to the other folders. In either case, you need to manually add this join.

To create joins, please look at the section "Managing Joins" in Chapter 17.

# Creating Lists of Values

Most business areas are created with either none or the minimum number of lists of values. As time goes by and more and more users begin to use the system, the demand for additional lists of values will increase. As users cannot add lists of values, they will come to you, the administrator, and ask you to do this for them.

Adding a list of values to an existing data item is a very simple process. Please look at the section "Managing Lists of Values" in Chapter 17.

# Creating Alternative Sorts

If a user comes to you and says that the list of values is not sorting in the right order, you need to add what is called an *alternative sort*. An example of an alternative sort is sorting the months of the year into the order in which they occur. Because month names are text values, a text sort would place *January* after *February*.

Adding an alternative sort to an existing list of values is a very simple process if you have an item that can be used for the alternative sort.

Please look at the section "Using Alternative Sorts" in Chapter 17.

# Creating New Items Based on Calculations

If you have standardized calculations within your company, it makes sense to include these as items in Discoverer. You can create these custom calculations on behalf of your users and then add them as items to folders. Users can then select these new items, saving themselves the step of creating the calculation in the query.

To create a new item based on a calculation, use the following workflow:

1. Determine which folder needs to have the calculated item.
2. Launch the Discoverer Administrator tool.
3. When the Load Wizard displays, as shown earlier in Figure 18-1, click Open An Existing Business Area.
4. Open the business area that contains the folder to which you want to add the new item.
5. Locate and right-click the folder, and from the pop-up box click New Item.
6. Discoverer opens a New Item box. You use this box in the same way that an end user would create calculations. You should therefore continue this workflow by looking at the section "Workbook Wizard Step 6: Creating User-Defined Calculations" in Chapter 5.
7. After you have created the new item, you need to determine the position in the folder where the item should be and move it to its final position.
8. You should also make sure to check the format and aggregation properties.
9. Having completed all of your checks and made any adjustments, you should now inform the user that the item has been successfully added.

# Creating New Conditions

Another simple task for you, as the Discoverer administrator, is the creation of predefined conditions. We can best show you how to do this by using an actual example. Let's say we want to allow users to create reports that use only sales orders that are past due. But what is the formula for past due, and how do you ensure that users comply with this definition?

First, here is our formula: an order is past due when it is still open and the order date is more than two weeks in the past. If we allow users to create their own conditions, they could easily get this wrong. To avoid this, we will create the condition for them.

Before we show you how to create an administrator-defined condition, we need to tell you about mandatory and optional conditions. In Chapter 4 we showed you how an end user could create conditions, and we also discussed the use of predefined conditions. When, as an administrator, you create a condition, you have the ability to specify whether this condition is mandatory or optional. If you create a mandatory condition, it will always be applied, and the user will have no choice whether to use that condition. If you create an optional condition, the user will get a choice and will be allowed to decide when to use it.

To create our administrator-defined condition, use the following workflow:

1. Launch the Discoverer Administrator tool.
2. When the Load Wizard displays, as shown earlier in Figure 18-1, click Open An Existing Business Area.
3. Open the GSW business area.

4. Expand the GS Sales folder.
5. To begin the condition, we need to locate the first item for the condition. In our case this is the status. Right-click the status and from the pop-up box select New Condition. Discoverer opens the New Condition dialog box with the item Status selected.

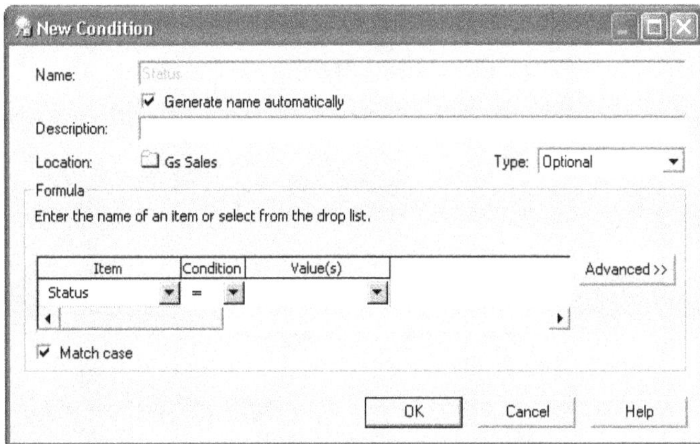


6. Use the drop-down button under Value(s) and select OPEN.
7. Take a close look at the dialog box. You will notice that there is an area of the screen called Type. This area is where you specify whether the condition is mandatory or optional. In our case, we will leave it set to the default of Optional.
8. We need to extend this condition to also include the fact that the order date must be more than seven days in the past. To do this, click Advanced. Discoverer opens an extended dialog box.

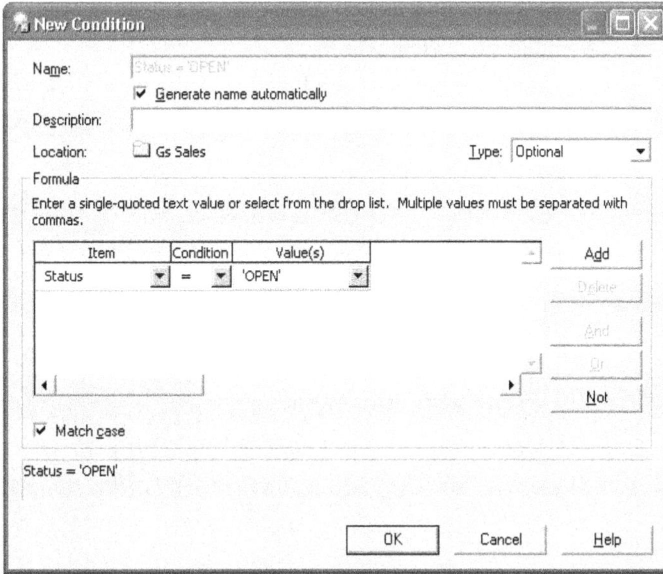

9. Just as with end user conditions, the extended dialog box allows you to add extra components to the condition. Click the Add button and then under the Item drop-down select Create Calculation.
10. In the New Calculation dialog box, enter this algorithm: **TRUNC(SYSDATE) - 14**.
11. Upon return to the extended New Condition dialog box, complete the condition by setting the condition itself to greater than; then select Order Date in the Value(s) box.
12. Name this condition **Past Due Orders** by unchecking the Generate Name Automatically box and typing the name. The final condition looks like this:

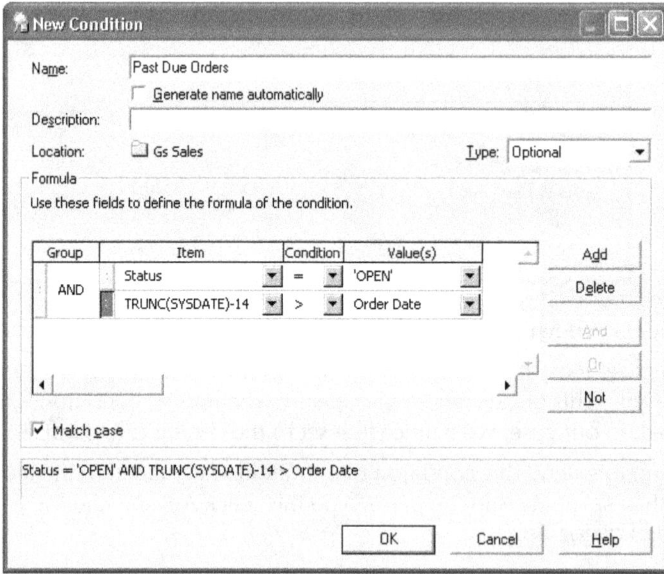


13. Complete the condition by clicking OK.
14. At the bottom of the list of items for the folder, as shown in the following illustration, you will see a new item called Order Date (Optional):

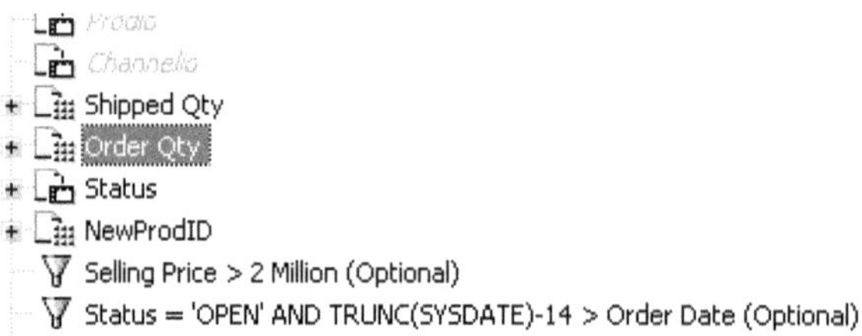


When an end user opens the folder for item selection, that user will now see this new condition and can select it into their worksheet just like any other item. Users are not permitted to edit predefined conditions, so if any changes are required, they will have to be done by the administrator.

# Deleting Predefined Conditions

Deletion of predefined conditions must be done by the administrator. However, you must be very careful because deleting a predefined condition that has already been used by a user in a workbook will cause that workbook to return incorrect results. Before you delete a predefined condition, you need to check the impact of the deletion.

To correctly delete a predefined condition, use the following workflow:

1. Locate the predefined condition you want to delete.
2. Right-click the condition and from the pop-up menu select Delete Condition. Discoverer will display the Confirm Delete dialog box, shown here.
3. In the Confirm Delete dialog box, click Impact. Discoverer will display the Impact dialog box. As you can see, Discoverer will let you know whether there are any workbooks that use the condition. You should not delete the condition if it is in use.

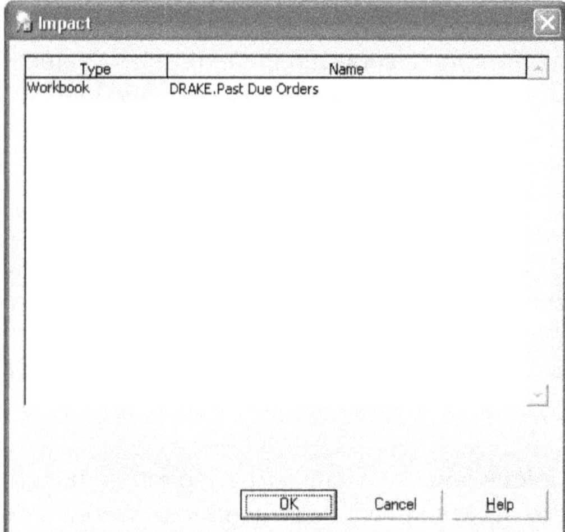


4. Click OK to close the Impact dialog box and return to the Confirm Delete dialog box.
5. If there will be no impact, click Yes; otherwise, click No.

If you did not check the impact or if you ignored the impact and you deleted a predefined condition, the next time the user tries to open a workbook that uses the condition, they will see this warning:

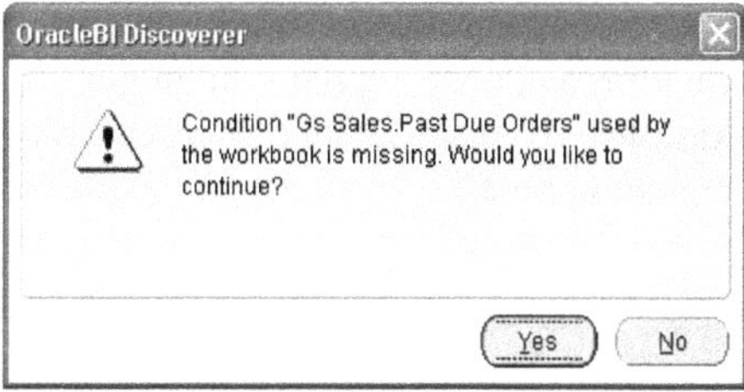

OracleBI Discoverer
Condition "Gs Sales.Past Due Orders" used by the workbook is missing. Would you like to continue?
Yes
No


The workbook will continue to open, but the results will be wrong.

# Creating Drill Hierarchies

As we have mentioned, one of the least-used features of Discoverer is hierarchical drilling. In this type of drill a user navigates up or down a predefined hierarchy of items. Over the years, we have received many requests for drill hierarchies from users who do not understand the relationships that must exist between the component items in a hierarchy. Unless you fully understand the intricacies of a hierarchy, you can easily create Discoverer hierarchies that result in erroneous drills.

When a user comes to you and asks you to create a hierarchy, you need to take your time and not rush into creating it. First, you need to determine whether there are one-to-many relationships between all of the items in the proposed hierarchy. There can be no ifs or buts, no maybes, and no exceptions. There has to be a one-to-many relationship between every item, period! Do not allow someone in a position of authority to browbeat you into creating a hierarchy when the relationships are wrong. Equally, do not be tempted to insert an additional item into an existing hierarchy when that item is not unique within the entity that it comes from.

Let's look at one of our hierarchies: the geographic hierarchy. As we have explained several times in this book, there are one-to-many relationships between Region and District, District and City, and City and Customer. Conversely, there are many-to-one relationships going the other way. This sounds obvious, we hear you say, but it is these relationships that lie at the heart of the hierarchy. For every many-to-one relationship there must be a value for the entity that is on one end of the relationship. This cannot be an optional item, and the join cannot be an outer join. In our case, our joins are mandatory, and thus the unique items within each table—Customer Name, City Name, District Name, and Region Name—are the perfect candidates for a hierarchy.

**NOTE**
*You must pick a unique item from within every one of the entities for the hierarchy to work. There is no point trying to create a hierarchy from Customer to City using Contact Name because there is no guarantee that there are not two people with the same name, albeit in different companies.*

Having found the unique items that can be used to form a hierarchy, the next step, if you have not already done so, is to make sure that these items exist within a single Discoverer folder. Sometimes the best way to do this is to use a predefined object in the database. Views and materialized views are perfect candidates for hierarchy generation. However, many times you will have to use a complex folder. In Chapter 16 we showed you in detail how to create both complex folders and hierarchies.

If you are using Oracle Applications, you are probably aware that the table called GL_ PERIODS is the one that contains your organization's fiscal time calendar. Time and time again, we have seen organizations make the base GL_PERIODS table available to end users. This is wrong and will cause your queries to perform badly. You need to create a materialized view of GL_PERIODS and prebuild all of the hierarchical information against each date. Allowing users to dynamically manipulate GL_PERIODS is asking for disaster. We have a client who was doing just this. They had daily reports that were taking longer than seven hours to complete. Following our recommendation, they created a hierarchical materialized view. The same reports now run in five minutes.

# Modifying an Item's Type

A little-used function is the ability to change an item's data type. If one of your users comes to you and says that they always have to change the data type of a certain item, you should create another item whose data type and format has been set the way the user needs it. Let's say the user has said that they want to be able to display the order date as a string and that it is to be formatted differently. Rather than the system showing 01-JAN-2012, the user wants to print January 1, 2012. Now we know what you may be saying. You are saying that the user could do this without your help. While this is true, the art to being a good administrator is to make the user's life a little easier. Why make the user do this when you could do it for the user?

To add a new item for the order date with a different item type, use the following workflow:

1. Open the GSW business area and expand the list of folders.
2. Locate and right-click the heading for the Sales folder. From the pop-up menu, select New Item.
3. Complete the New Item dialog box as follows and then click OK:
   - **Name** Enter **New Order Date**.
   - **Calculation** Enter **TO_CHAR(GsSales.OrderDate,'Month D, YYYY')**.
4. Move the new item to its correct location within the folder.

NOTE
*Please refer to Appendix B for a listing of all the available format masks that can be used with dates.*

# Creating Summary Data

Performance is the reason we use summary tables. Please look at Chapter 22 for full details on managing summary tables. In this chapter, we give you workflows for managing Discoverer's automated summary management feature and show you how to manually manage summary tables.

# Rearranging the Order of Folders in a Business Area

In Chapter 16 we recommend that you order the folders in a business area in a way that makes sense to your users. With all the best will in the world, we can still have folders in the wrong order. If a user comes to you with a request to change the order of the folders within a business area, it is an easy task to change it. However, before you jump in and start changing things, you might want to step back and think about what the user is asking for.

Perhaps the user is unaware that the organization has a standard for the way that folders are presented. Perhaps the user is relatively new to the company and is not yet fully on board with the reasons a business area has been set up the way it is being presented. You may need to arrange for the user to get some training.

Notwithstanding all of these points, it could be that the user's idea really is a good one and that the order does need changing. We have already given you a workflow for rearranging the order of the folders in a business area. You will find this in Chapter 16.

# Rearranging the Order of Items in a Folder

In Chapter 16 we recommend that you order the items in a folder in a way that makes sense to your users. We also recommend that you set up a corporate standard for this ordering, making use of item separators to group items into logical sets. Even with all our planning and standards, we can still have items in the wrong order. If the user's idea really is a good one and the order does need changing, you should take a look at the workflow that we have already provided in Chapter 16.

# Changing Refresh Cycles

Many Discoverer systems are based either on a snapshot of the OLTP system or on data warehouses. Both of these types of databases use a refresh mechanism to update. If a user comes to you with the belief that the refresh schedule is insufficient, you are in the perfect position to do something about it.

Perhaps the users would like to see an extra data warehouse collection during the lunch period. Perhaps the users need to have materialized views refreshed more frequently. Perhaps the business needs to have an additional copy of the OLTP database to coincide with the start of the business day in another part of the world.

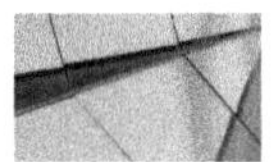

**NOTE**
*Some organizations keep a backup copy of the database and apply the database logs from the production environment to bring the copy up to date.*

Some Discoverer managers will have more power than others, and some of you will be directly responsible for one or more of the refreshes that we have outlined. However, before you set off making wholesale changes, remember that these refreshes could have a bigger impact than just the user or business unit that requested them. You may need to liaise with other IT departments, perhaps the data warehouse production team. Even if you don't have responsibility over these areas, you will surely have input and be required to provide feedback from the end-user community.

# Allowing Scheduling of Workbooks

Not all organizations make use of scheduling. Assuming your organization is using scheduling, not all users are automatically granted permission to schedule workbooks. In fact, not all users need to schedule workbooks. If a user asks for permission to schedule, you will need to either validate the request with the user's manager or discuss this in more depth with the user.

## Scheduling Privileges

For a user to be able to schedule workbooks, that user needs to have the following database privileges:

- CREATE PROCEDURE
- CREATE TABLE
- CREATE VIEW

- EXECUTE ANY PROCEDURE
- UNLIMITED TABLESPACE
- EXECUTE ON SYS.DBMS_JOB
- SELECT ON SYS.V_$PARAMETER

We have been asked many times, especially by DBAs, just why these privileges are required. You can find the answer to this, and much more, in Appendix A.

**NOTE**
*Scheduled workbooks can be shared, so these privileges can be provided to only a few users. These users can then share scheduled workbooks with other users. Of course, with shared scheduled workbooks, the data that a user sees is the data that the owner of the scheduled workbook would have seen. Your users therefore need to be very careful not to share secure data!*

## Enabling Scheduling

Having determined that the user's request is valid, to allow the user to schedule, use the following workflow:

1. Make sure the user has the necessary database privileges outlined in the preceding section.
2. Launch the Discoverer Administrator tool.
3. When the Load Wizard displays, as shown earlier in Figure 18-1, click Cancel.
4. From the menu bar, select Tools | Privileges. Discoverer opens the Privileges dialog box.
5. As you saw in Figure 18-2, the Privileges dialog box has four tabs. They are
   - **Privileges** This tab allows you to assign multiple privileges to a single user or role. The Privileges tab was dealt with earlier in this chapter; however, we need to use it again now.
   - **User/Role** This tab allows you to assign multiple users or roles to a single privilege. The User/Role tab was dealt with earlier in this chapter.
   - **Query Governor** This tab allows you to assign query governor privileges to a single use or role. The Query Governor tab was dealt with earlier in this chapter.
   - **Scheduled Workbooks** This tab allows you to maintain the scheduling privileges for a single user. This tab will be used in this section.
6. Click the Privileges tab.
7. Click the Select button. Discoverer opens the Select User/Role search box.
8. Type or search for the user for whom you want to manage scheduling.
9. Click OK to close the Select User/Role search box.

10. Check the box Schedule Workbooks. The Schedule Workbooks privilege can be assigned only to a user. It cannot be assigned to a role or an Apps responsibility. If you attempt to do so, you will receive this error message:

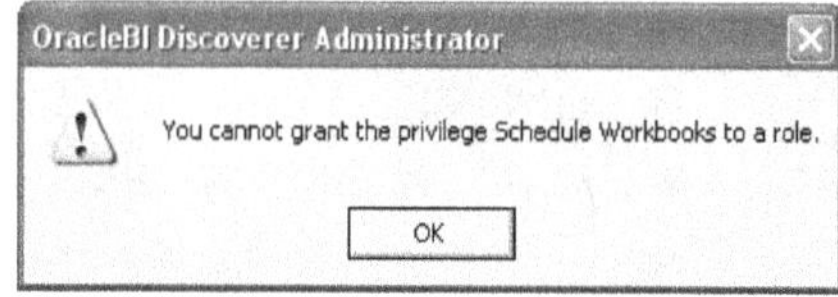


11. Click Apply. The user now has the power to schedule. However, you have not finished yet, because you need to make sure the user has the correct scheduling powers.
12. Click the Scheduled Workbooks tab. As you can see here, this is a rather busy screen. However, it is a very important screen and one you need to master.

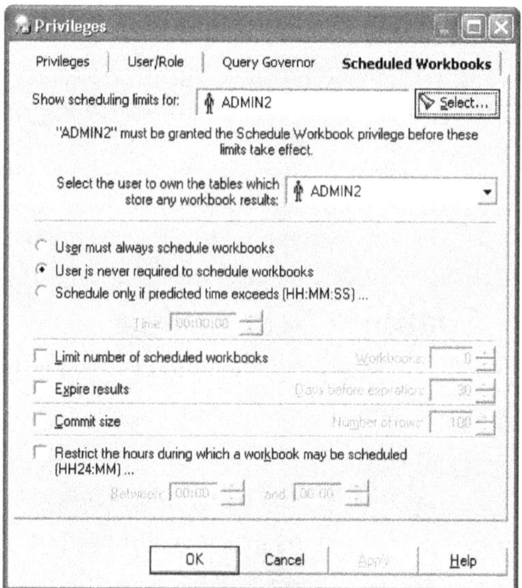


13. If you want another user to own the tables that store the workbook results, use the drop-down alongside and select another user. A discussion on this topic follows at the end of this section.
14. In the middle of the screen are the following three radio buttons:
    - **User Must Always Schedule Workbooks** Check this radio button if you want this user to be forced to always schedule their workbooks. The user will not be able to run workbooks in Plus or Viewer, unless the workbook has been scheduled.
    - **User Is Never Required To Schedule Workbooks** Use this radio button if you do not want to force the user to have to schedule. The user will then be able to choose. This is the default option and the one you will use most often.
    - **Schedule Only If Predicted Time Exceeds** Use this radio button if you want to force the user to have to schedule if the predicted time for the query exceeds the limits set here. After checking the box, you need to define the time limit.
15. At the bottom of the screen are the following check boxes:
    - **Limit Number Of Scheduled Workbooks** Check this box if you want to limit the number of scheduled workbooks that the user can have at any moment in time. After checking the box, you need to define the maximum number the user can use.

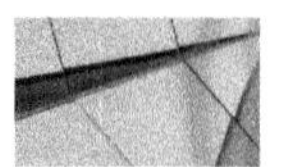

**NOTE**
*This option allows you to prevent users from submitting so many scheduled workbooks that no other jobs in the DBMS_JOB queue can run.*

- **Expire Results** Check this box if you want to limit the length of time that the user's results will be retained within the database. After checking the box, you need to define the time limit. This is typically set to 30 days but can be set lower or higher depending upon user and organizational needs. Following expiry, the results are deleted the next time the user exits the EUL.
- **Commit Size** Contrary to popular belief, this box does not restrict the number of rows of data that can be saved in a scheduled workbook. This check box is to set the commit frequency. For example, if this is set to 100, then Discoverer will issue a commit every time 100 rows of data have been retrieved. After checking the box, you need to define the commit size. According to Oracle, little gain will be achieved by setting this higher than 1000.
- **Restrict The Hours During Which A Workbook May Be Scheduled** Check this box if you want to restrict the hours during which the user can schedule. This will be of particular importance to organizations that have users all across the globe. By restricting the hours that a user can schedule, you can, for example, prevent a user in the United States from being able to schedule during the European hours of operation. After checking the box, you need to define the start and end times. You can go across midnight; thus, if you set the start time to 23:00 and the end time to 03:00, the user will be able to schedule only between 11 p.m. and 3 a.m.

16. Having set all of the scheduling privileges, click Apply or OK to make the changes take effect.

### User Selection

If you have used previous versions of Discoverer, you may notice that the Privileges dialog box has changed. Whereas in older versions the user selection used to be a drop-down, it has now become a field that you have to search for first. As commented elsewhere, this has been done to improve performance.

Oracle tell us that there were cases where the user population ran into tens of thousands, and populating a drop-down box, as you will appreciate, with 10,000 or more values takes time, sometimes a lot of time. Hence, Oracle has provided this new search-then-assign workflow that you will see used throughout the Privileges dialog box.

## Storing Workbook Results

When a scheduled workbook is run, Discoverer stores the results in database tables. Discoverer's default behavior is to store the scheduled workbooks in the EUL owner's schema. Before an end user can schedule a workbook, you must decide which database user is to own those tables. The results can be stored in one of two places.

- The schema of the user who is running the scheduled workbook
- A scheduled workbook results schema

### Storing the Results in the Owner's Schema

The main advantage to storing the results of scheduled workbooks directly in the owner's schema is that a database limit can be specified on the maximum amount of data that the user can store in the database. The DBA can control the maximum amount of space that the user can fill with their results. If that user should fill their allotted space, this will affect only that user.

**NOTE**
*The previous option should not be taken if you are using Discoverer in Apps mode.*

### Storing the Results in a Scheduled Workbook Results Schema

The advantage of storing the results in a separate schema is that individual users do not need to have the special database privileges that are needed to run scheduled workbooks. Some organizations think that it is easier to manage the data when it is stored in a central repository than when there are multiple user schemas to manage.

Of course, the disadvantage of storing the results in a central repository is that one user could run a scheduled workbook that fills the available storage space, thus preventing other scheduled workbooks from running. The storage space quota is thus shared and could easily be used by a single user.

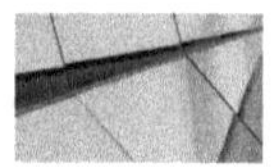

**NOTE**
*If you are working in Apps mode, you need to use the APPS schema for this purpose.*

## Setting Up a Scheduled Workbook Results User

To set up workbook scheduling using a centralized repository schema, you must log in to the database as a SYSDBA and run the batchusr.sql script found at $ORACLE_HOME/ discoverer/util.

**NOTE**
*If you are using Discoverer in Apps mode, you must use the batchusr_ app.sql script.*

This script creates a new user who is granted the appropriate privileges. In addition, the user will be granted the SELECT ANY TABLE database privilege. If you do not want the user to have this powerful privilege, you will need to manually revoke it later. You will also need to make sure the user has appropriate SELECT privileges to all the objects that will be needed. In our opinion, this is one of the times when you should use the SELECT ANY TABLE privilege.

In addition to creating the user, the Discoverer manager must also use the Scheduling Privileges screen to set up all users who will schedule under this new user account.

If the scheduled workbook user is to be a user's real schema, then it is sufficient to grant the appropriate privileges. You do not have to run the batchusr.sql script in this case.

## Managing Scheduled Workbooks

As the Discoverer manager, you have the ability to monitor the jobs that users have scheduled. This is done from the menu bar by selecting Tools | Manage Scheduled Workbooks. You can use the Manage Scheduled Workbooks dialog box to:

- Edit the user's scheduled workbook
- Delete a scheduled workbook from the processing queue
- View the status of a scheduled workbook
- Read an error message that a scheduled workbook has incurred

**NOTE**
*You must have the Manage Scheduled Workbooks administration privilege to access the Manage Scheduled Workbooks dialog box.*

To manage scheduled workbooks, use the following workflow:

1. Launch the Discoverer Administrator tool.
2. When the Load Wizard displays, as shown earlier in Figure 18-1, click Cancel.
3. From the menu bar, select Tools | Manage Scheduled Workbooks. Discoverer opens the Manage Scheduled Workbooks dialog box.
4. You need to either check the box called Select All Users or use the Select button to choose one user.

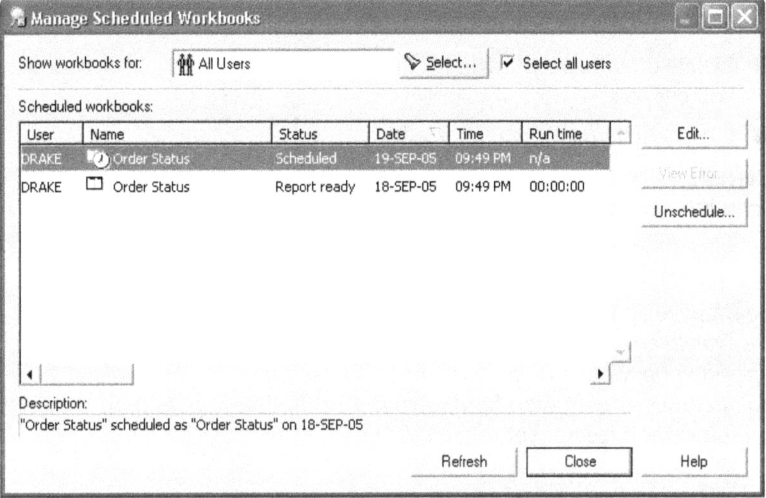


5. As you can see in the preceding image, Discoverer displays the scheduled workbooks for the users.
6. When you have completed your management, click Close.

These are the components of the screen just shown:

- **Show workbooks for** This displays the users you are managing.
- **Select** Click this button to locate a single user.
- **Select All Users** Check this box to display the schedules for all users.
- **Scheduled workbooks** This area displays the actual scheduled workbooks, along with their names, statuses, and when to run. At the end of this section, you will find a list of the possible statuses.
- **Edit** Click this button to edit the scheduled workbook.

- **View Error** If the results show that there was an error, click this button to get more information about the error.
- **Unschedule** Click this button to unschedule a workbook that has not yet run. You will see this screen and two additional options. Select your option and click Yes to cause Discoverer to take the requested action; otherwise, click No.
  - Unschedule but keep all results
  - Unschedule and delete all results

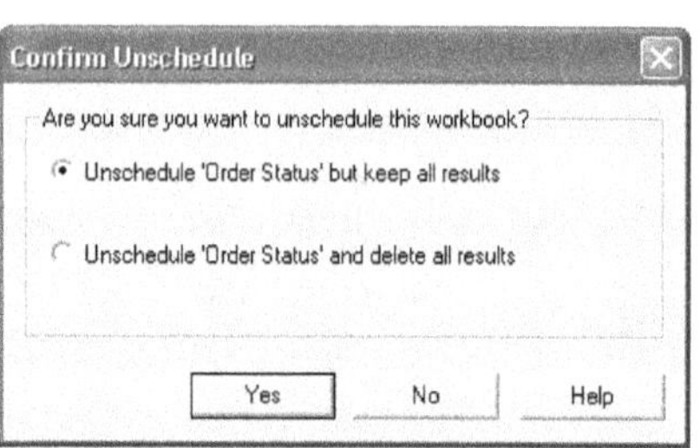


- **Delete** Click this button to delete a workbook that has already been run. You will see this screen and two options. Select your option and click Yes to cause Discoverer to take the requested action; otherwise, click No.
  - Delete only the results run for the date you clicked
  - Unschedule and delete all results

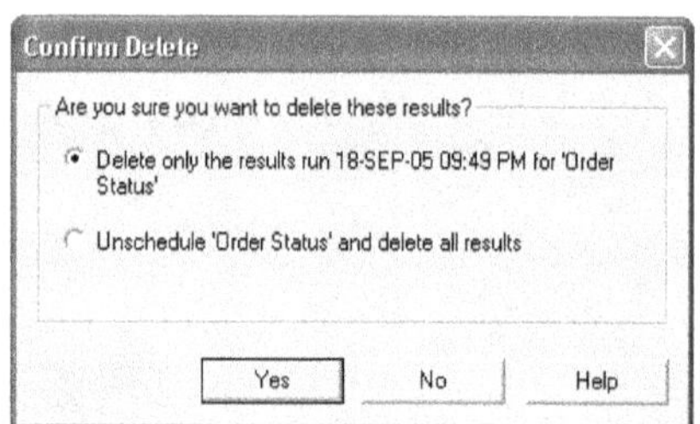


- **Refresh** Click this button to refresh the list of scheduled workbooks.

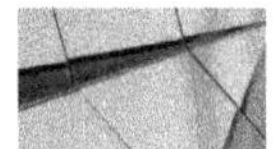

**NOTE**
*On the Manage Scheduled Workbooks screen you will not see the buttons Delete and Unschedule at the same time because they use the same position on the screen and are mutually exclusive. Delete applies only to already executed workbooks, while Unschedule applies only to schedules that have not yet executed.*

## List of Scheduled Statuses

The following are the possible statuses that you could see when managing scheduled workbooks:

| Status | Description |
|---|---|
| Could not schedule | The workbook could not be submitted to the processing job queue. |
| Error while running query | Running the query produced an error. You will need to click the View Error button for more details. |
| EUL has changed, reschedule report | A change occurred in the EUL that has affected the workbook; for example, a folder was deleted. |
| Number of rows limit exceeded | The "Limit retrieved data" threshold set on the Scheduled Workbooks tab has been exceeded. |

| Status | Description |
|---|---|
| Report deleted by Administrator | This workbook has been set for deletion by the administrator. |
| Report expired | The workbook has expired and will be deleted the next time the user exits from the EUL. |
| Report ready | The workbook ran successfully, and the report is ready. As the administrator, you cannot see the results; only the user can do this using Plus or Viewer. |
| Running query | The workbook is running, and the result set is being built. |
| Scheduled | The workbook is scheduled to run at a future time. |

# Creation of New Functions

Discoverer already has a vast array of functions at your disposal, and you should refer to Appendix B for an alphabetical list of all the available functions. However, sometimes you need a new function.

For the purposes of this exercise, we have created the following simple function:

```
CREATE OR REPLACE function f_eul_month
  (day date)
return varchar2 is month varchar2(6) := 'JAN-10';
begin
   select monthid into month
  from gsw.gs_day
where day = dayid;
  return (month);
  exception
when no_data_found then
return (month);
end f_eul_month;
/
```

If you execute this function in SQL Plus using

```
selectf_eul_month('29-AUG-2011') from dual
```

the database will reply with SEP-04. The function takes a date as an argument and returns the fiscal month.

To make a new function available in Discoverer, use the following workflow:

1. Use SQL Plus to create the function in the database.
2. Launch the Discoverer Administrator tool.
3. When the Load Wizard displays, as shown earlier in Figure 18-1, click Cancel.

4. From the menu bar, select Tools | Register PL/SQL Functions. Discoverer opens the following PL/SQL Functions dialog box:

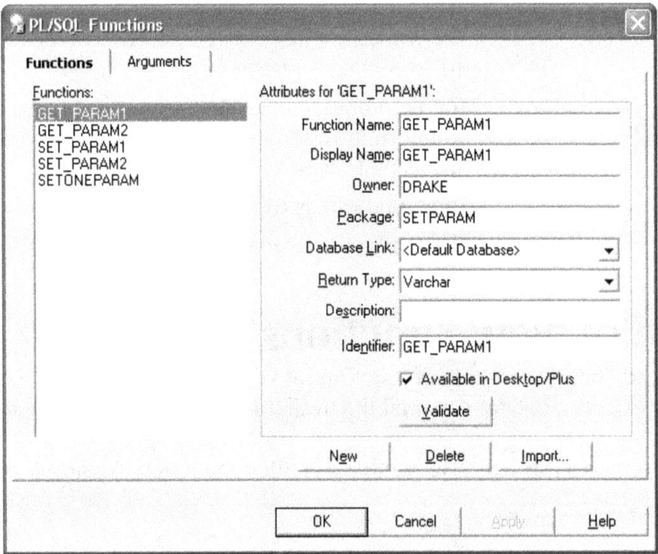


5. Click Import. Discoverer displays the second screen of the Import PL/SQL Functions Wizard.

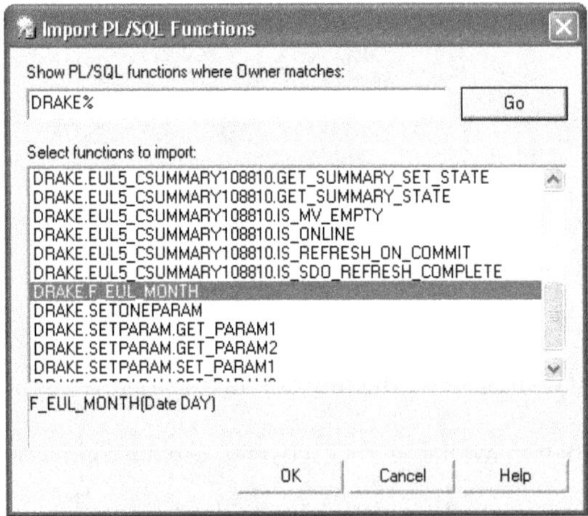


6. On the preceding screen, you need to select the user you want to work with and then locate the function you want to import.

7. Having located the function, click OK. As shown next, Discoverer imports all the features about the function and displays them on the main screen.

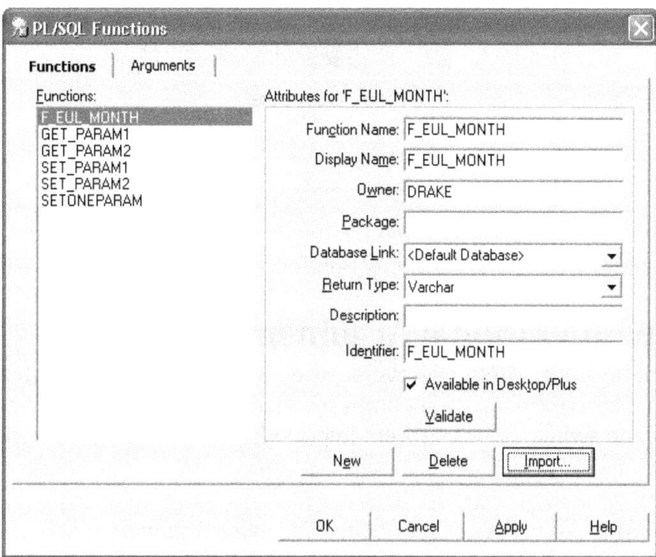


8. Click the Arguments tab to look at the arguments that Discoverer needs to supply to the function. As you can see at the bottom of the screen, there is a Usage area that has two radio buttons: Optional and Required. Discoverer has correctly recognized that our function has a single, mandatory (Required) date argument.

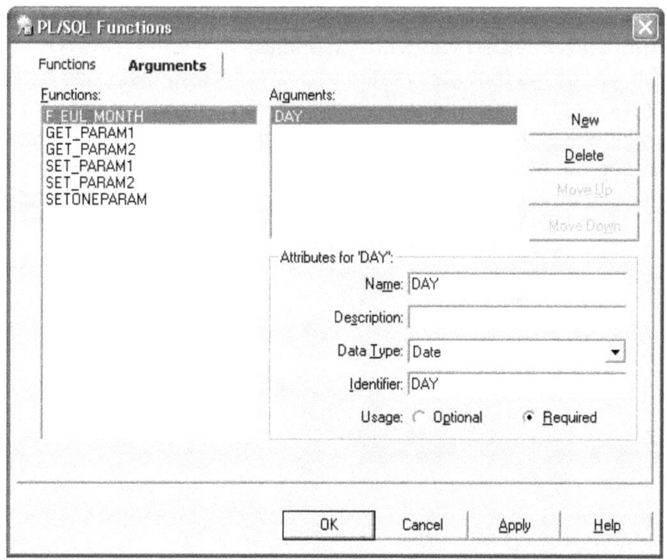

9. Return to the Functions tab and click Validate. This causes Discoverer to validate that the function is okay to work within the EUL.
10. If you have done everything correctly, you will see this box:

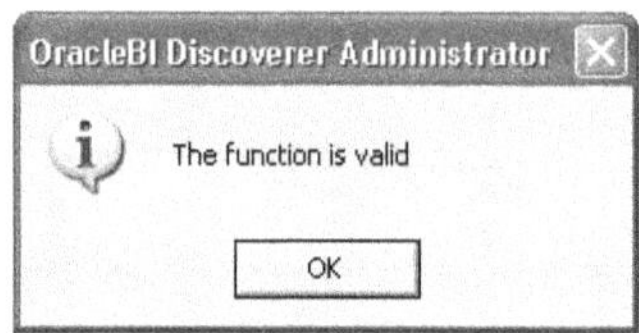
OracleBI Discoverer Administrator
The function is valid
OK

11. Close the box informing you that the function is valid and then click OK to complete the importation of the function. The function is now available for use within Discoverer.

## Working with Optional Arguments

There appears to be a bug within Discoverer when importing PL/SQL functions with optional arguments in that Discoverer can sometimes see them as being required. You will need to check these manually and switch those that were imported with the wrong usage definition.

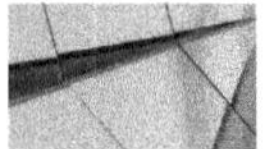

**NOTE**
*You should therefore make a point of checking every argument when you are importing new functions.*

## Summary

In this chapter, you have learned how to interact with your end users. The intention of this chapter is to be complementary to the "What Can the Discoverer Administrator Do for You?"section of Chapter 15. That section contains a list of approximately 20 topics. This chapter took each of those topics in turn and provided you with a workflow that will tackle the topic.

Several of the workflows that are needed to answer questions posed by the users have already been given in previous chapters. These were not repeated here, but we simply directed you to the relevant chapter. However, in this chapter we did introduce or explain to you some concepts for the first time. Among the new topics that you found in this chapter were managing access, managing privileges, creating predefined conditions, and managing scheduling.

# CHAPTER 19

# Configuring Discoverer

This chapter is intended for a different audience than the rest of this book. This discussion is aimed at technical team members who are responsible for managing and configuring the Oracle Discoverer installation and, in particular, for administrators who need to control the WebLogic environment. In this chapter we will describe the Discoverer installation types and list all of the components of a Discoverer installation. Next we discuss the various ways to start the WebLogic Server, WebLogic Node Manager, and Discoverer Service. Following this will be a discussion of Oracle Process Manager and Notification (OPMN) server. After discussing OPMN, we will discuss Fusion Middleware Control and show you how to log in. Next we will discuss Oracle HTTP Server (OHS) and introduce you to the key Apache directives and key OHS modules. We will then show you how to manually manage OHS followed by the much easier method of using Fusion Middleware Control. Next we will discuss configuring Web Cache and show you how to configure Web Cache to load balance multiple Discoverer servers. At the end of the chapter we will introduce you to the topic of single sign-on (SSO) and show you how to enable it for both Discoverer 10*g* and 11*g*, concluding with a description of how to configure Oracle Access Manager to control SSO for Discoverer 11*g*.

If you are looking for advanced administration to manage the Discoverer settings and Discoverer preferences, please refer to Chapter 20, which is where we show you how to use Oracle Fusion Middleware, also referred to as Oracle Enterprise Manager (OEM), to configure Discoverer for a corporate look and feel.

The 11*g* Release 2 Business Intelligence Application Server provides three primary Discoverer components.

- Plus
- Viewer
- Portlet Provider

As the application server administrator, it is your responsibility to guarantee that these three components are available, performing correctly, and configured appropriately to your organization's business intelligence needs. To be able to accomplish this goal, you must be familiar with Discoverer and the components it depends on.

This chapter contains many references to file locations. Here's an example:

```
$MIDDLEWARE_HOME/wlserver_10.3/server/bin
```

Please be aware that the $ sign is a Unix/Linux environment variable reference. In Windows this is replaced with a % sign before and after the name. The / (forward slash) character is also unique to Unix/Linux because Windows will use a \ (backslash) character. The previous example from Unix/Linux will convert to the following in Windows:

```
%MIDDLEWARE_HOME%\wlserver_10.3\server\bin
```

Throughout the chapter we will primarily be using the Unix/Linux method.

## Architecture

As shown in Figure 19-1, Discoverer has the following three-tier architecture:

- The Discoverer client tier of Discoverer Plus and Discoverer Viewer
- The Discoverer middle tier, otherwise known as the middleware tier, with the following three components:
  - One or more Discoverer servers
  - A Discoverer preference server
  - A WebLogic application server
- The database tier, which includes the data that Discoverer will be reporting on and the metadata (the EUL or catalog) that controls how the data is made available to the users.

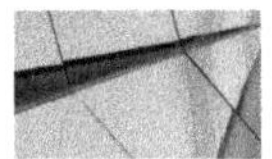

**NOTE**
*We discuss Discoverer's three-tier architecture in detail later in this section.*

Technically speaking, the Discoverer and preference servers are C++ components. If you are looking for these executables in your Discoverer Bin folder, dis51ws is the Discoverer server, and

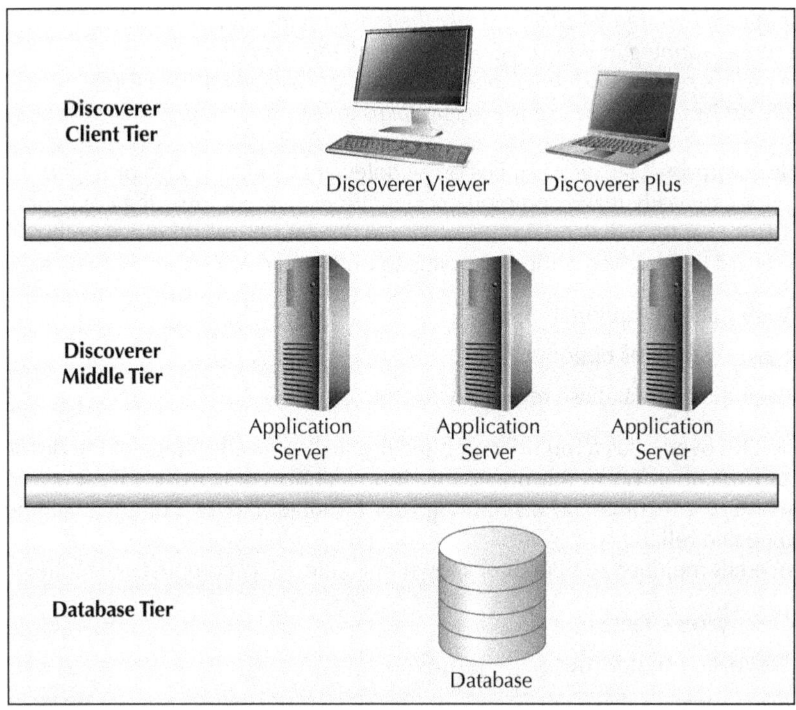


**FIGURE 19-1.** *Discoverer's multitier architecture*

dis51pr is the preference server. These executables reside within the *application server* as binaries and are not Java components that run within the WebLogic application server. A connection servlet exists in the application.

The application server includes many different components that all work together to deliver a rich business intelligence environment to the user. When an end user makes a web request to Discoverer, the first component that user will reach is Oracle Web Cache, which is a caching reverse proxy server, designed to accelerate mid-tier performance. If enabled for use and if Web Cache does not have the content that the user needs in its cache, Web Cache intelligently makes an additional request to the Oracle HTTP Server. OHS is responsible for routing all HTTP requests to the appropriate component. In the case of Discoverer 11*g*, all requests are routed to WebLogic, which is the heart of the system. In Discoverer 10*g* the requests are routed to OC4J.

It is WebLogic that runs Discoverer Viewer, Discoverer Plus, Discoverer Portlet Provider, and OLAP. To maintain high availability, in the sense of components on the server as opposed to running multiple load-balanced servers, every Discoverer 11*g* install includes Oracle Process Management and Notification. OPMN is essentially a heartbeat process that includes death detection and restarts any of the OPMN-managed components (such as Web Cache, Oracle HTTP Server, Discoverer preference server, and the Discoverer session server). This does not include death detection for the Java components that run within the WebLogic application server, such as the JVM that runs the Discoverer-managed server. Death detection and restarts for the JVMs are handled by the WebLogic Node Manager.

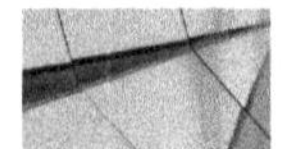

**NOTE**
*Technically speaking, Discoverer Plus is a Java applet that runs on the client machine, not in WebLogic. Only the initial connection is made via a servlet running in WebLogic. After that, all the hard work is done in the dis5ws session and the applet. The heart of Discoverer therefore is really dis5ws. This is where the magic takes place.*

Oracle Enterprise Manager 11*g* Fusion Middleware Control is also provided so that the administrator can easily make common configurations without touching configuration files or the database. This chapter will acquaint you with the configuration and usage of these components.

With regard to Discoverer, the key points to understand are

- Web Cache is optional.
- Single sign-on is optional.
- Even the 11*g* database repository is optional.

Oracle Discoverer has a multitier architecture that takes advantage of the distributed nature of the web environment. While it is possible to install all tiers of the Discoverer architecture on the same machine, we recommend distributing your installation over multiple machines to maximize performance and reliability.

Discoverer's multitier architecture, shown in Figure 19-1, comprises the following three tiers:

- Discoverer client tier
- Discoverer middle tier
- Discoverer database tier

We describe each of these in the following sections.

## Discoverer Client Tier

In its simplest form, the Discoverer client tier is the web browser that is used to connect to Discoverer Plus and Discoverer Viewer. However, the client tier also includes the Discoverer Portlet Provider and the Discoverer Web Services application programming interface (API). The client-tier Portlet Provider enables Discoverer workbooks to be published on various portals, while the client-tier Web Services enables third-party applications to return Discoverer content.

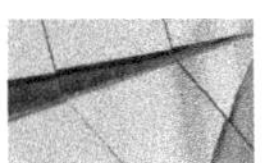

**NOTE**
*To successfully deploy Discoverer Plus and Viewer to your end users, you must provide them with the appropriate URL.*

### Client Tier: Discoverer Plus Requirements

For Discoverer Plus, the only client machine requirement is that it runs a supported Java-enabled web browser (for example, Microsoft Internet Explorer or Mozilla Firefox), with a Java Virtual Machine (JVM).

The first time that a client machine is used to connect to Discoverer Plus, the Discoverer Plus applet is downloaded from the Discoverer middle tier and cached on the client machine. This applet provides the Discoverer Plus user interface and functionality for creating workbooks and analyzing data. When the user subsequently logs on, the Discoverer Plus applet runs from the local cache and does not need to be downloaded again.

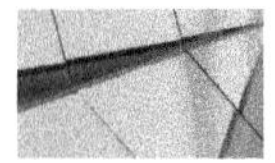

**NOTE**
*If you upgrade the JVM, you may need to clear your local Java cache to avoid clashes. Once cleared, the next time the user connects to Discoverer Plus, the applet will be downloaded again.*

### Client Tier: Discoverer Viewer Requirements

For Discoverer Viewer, the only client machine requirement is that the client machine can run HTML using a suitable web browser. This requirement is much simpler than for Discoverer Plus and requires a much smaller footprint on the computer.

## Discoverer Middle Tier

The Discoverer middle tier comprises the following two elements:

- Discoverer Java Enterprise edition (EE) applications
- Discoverer Common Object Request Broker Architecture (CORBA) components

The middle tier also contains the Discoverer Plus applet that is downloaded to the client tier whenever a user requests to use Discoverer Plus for the first time or when the system detects that the Java cache does not contain the applet.

**NOTE**
*All of the machines running the Discoverer middle tier must be on the same subnet.*

## Middle Tier: Discoverer Java EE Applications

The Discoverer Java EE applications are comprised of a series of four servlets.

A *servlet* is a module of Java code that runs on a server machine to answer requests from a client machine. The use of servlets minimizes the client-side processing. Discoverer's servlets are deployed into the WebLogic-managed server where a servlet engine runs the actual servlets.

The four middle-tier servlets are

- **Discoverer servlet** This servlet manages the connections and login for Discoverer Plus and Discoverer Viewer.
- **Discoverer Plus servlet** This servlet handles traffic between the Discoverer Plus Relational applet and the Discoverer Session process started for that session.
- **Discoverer Portlet Provider servlet** This servlet provides a user interface for publishing Discoverer worksheets and links to Discoverer workbooks on a portal page.
- **Discoverer Web Services servlet** This servlet provides an API to obtain Discoverer connections, workbooks, and worksheets; to execute worksheet queries; and to return worksheet content through Simple Object Access Protocol (SOAP; see the following note).

**NOTE**
*SOAP is a protocol for exchanging structured information in the implementation of web services. It uses XML for its message format but uses other protocols, such as Hypertext Transfer Protocol (HTTP) or Simple Mail Transfer Protocol (SMTP) for message negotiation and transmission.*

## Middle Tier: Discoverer CORBA Components

The Discoverer CORBA components are responsible for activating Discoverer when an end user starts a Discoverer session. This happens whenever a user connects to Discoverer Plus or Discoverer Viewer.

The Discoverer CORBA components are used by all four of the Discoverer client-tier components: Discoverer Plus, Discoverer Viewer, Discoverer Portlet Provider, and Discoverer Web Services.

There are two CORBA components. They are

- **Discoverer Sessions component** This component, sometimes referred to as the CORBA server, performs operations such as connecting to the database and opening a workbook. The session component also provides the link between the Discoverer servlet or applet and the database. There is one Discoverer session component per active user login session.
- **Discoverer Preferences Server component** This component provides a single location for preference settings for all Oracle Discoverer Plus and Viewer users. The Discoverer middle tier relies on stored preference settings to specify the default Discoverer behavior and to hold previously defined user preferences. For a complete listing of the user preferences managed by this component, please refer to Chapter 20.

**NOTE**

*In a multimachine environment where different Discoverer session components are running on different machines, there is always a single preference server. For more information regarding designating a single preference server, please refer to: http://docs.oracle.com/cd/E28280_01/bi.1111/b40107/multimachineinstall.htm#i1011966.*

## Discoverer Database Tier

The Discoverer database tier comprises the following five elements:

- **An End User Layer** Used for non-OLAP environments. The EUL is metadata that exposes data stored in relational tables. It is designed to overcome the need for an end user to know the underlying database.
- **One or more Discoverer workbooks** Used to store the metadata about queries that will be submitted to the database. Discoverer workbooks can be likened to a Microsoft Excel workbook. Each Discoverer workbook contains one or more Discoverer worksheets which can be likened to a Microsoft Excel worksheet. Each Discoverer worksheet contains the SQL code needed to query the database along with the formatting rules needed to present the results in a meaningful way to the user.
- **An active catalog** Used for OLAP only. The catalog is a set of relational views exposing the metadata stored within the analytic workspaces. Once exposed, the data can be accessed by SQL.
- **One or more analytic workspaces** Used for OLAP only. These are multidimensional schemas stored in a relational manner.
- **Business intelligence data** Contains the data the user wants to report against. Before users can use Discoverer to analyze relational data, you must first have installed and configured a EUL. Similarly, before users can use Discoverer to analyze multidimensional data, you must first have installed an active catalog. We show you how to create a EUL earlier in the book. In Chapter 20 we show you how to install the catalog.

# Discoverer Installation Types

Discoverer 11*g* can be installed in a stand-alone manner the same as 10*g*. However, the installation guide does not make this very clear, and many people are convinced that stand-alone mode is no longer available. We really had to read between the lines of the installation guide before it became obvious that we could in fact still do this.

The following notes are provided courtesy of Oracle Support from the following document: 1225255.1.

Discoverer 10*g* has a separate media install to perform a Discoverer middle-tier installation, without any dependency or requirement for an infrastructure metadata repository database or Oracle Internet Directory (OID)/single sign-on.

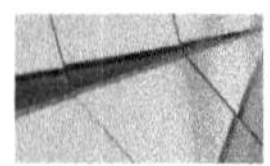

**NOTE**

*There is no separate media for 11*g *(10*g *had separate media). For 11*g*, you use the same media and download links to the documentation as referenced by our support note later in the section.*

The metadata repository basically equates to the old 10*g* infrastructure. It stores the same information it did in 10*g*, namely, the tables for the portal definitions, for scheduling, and for storing public and private connection information.

Discoverer 11*g* uses a single install media to perform each installation type, and it is built in a *modular* style for flexibility. By single install media we mean that there is only one set of installation materials. While these may cover multiple installation discs each installation type can be done from the same media. There is therefore no need to download multiple media. You will of course be required to purchase the relevant licenses before using the software.

The following are all the available components. In the list, the components that are not available in a stand-alone install appear in italics.

- Discoverer Plus Relational and Discoverer Plus OLAP
- Discoverer Viewer
- *Discoverer Portlet Provider* (see following note)
- *Discoverer Web Services* (see following note)
- Oracle HTTP Server
- WebLogic Server
- OPMN
- Oracle Fusion Middleware Control
- Oracle Web Cache
- *Oracle Single Sign-On*
- *Discoverer Connections Management page*
- *Private and Public Discoverer connections*
- SSL functionality in Discoverer
- *Oracle Identity Management*

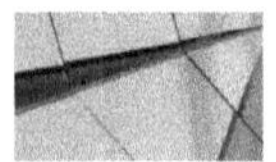

**NOTE**

*Discoverer Portlet Provider and Discoverer Web Services are both installed during a stand-alone install but are not operational.*

Following a stand-alone install, users start Discoverer by using the direct login page. Public and private connections and single sign-on are not available.

Following a full install, users can still start Discoverer by using the direct login page if they want, and many choose to do it this way. However, public connections and private connections, as well as authentication via single sign-on, are all now available.

After performing a stand-alone installation, if there is a requirement to associate Discoverer with an Oracle Internet Directory and the database schemas, then you must rerun the Discoverer

Configuration tool (config.sh) to configure Discoverer by associating it with an Oracle Internet Directory and the database schemas. For this new instance, you can point to the same ORACLE_HOME as that of the stand-alone instance. You can, optionally, discard the first stand-alone instance.

**NOTE**
*No manual process exists for associating an existing stand-alone installation with an Oracle Internet Directory and the database schemas.*

For more information regarding installing Discoverer in stand-alone mode, please log in to My Oracle Support and look at document 1225255.1: How To Install Discoverer 11g "Standalone" Without A Metadata Repository Requirement.

As mentioned earlier, the metadata repository basically equates to the old 10g infrastructure. However, it is possible to extend the system by configuring Discoverer to use a powerful set of identity management and security features. These features include Oracle SSO, OID, and the Delegated Administration Service (DAS). We will briefly discuss these components and the configuration needed to use them with Discoverer.

Discoverer 11g also supports the Oracle Access Manager SSO solution. In fact, this is the recommended solution. We will comment further on this later in the chapter.

# Starting the Discoverer Components

To launch Discoverer so that users can connect, it is important to start all of the components in the correct order.

The correct order for starting Discoverer is shown in the following workflow:

1. Start the TNS listener; we will assume you know how to do this or you have a DBA to do this step for you.
2. Start the 11g database; we will assume you know how to do this or you have a DBA to do this step for you.
3. Start the WebLogic administration server; see the section "Starting the WebLogic Server."
4. Start WebLogic Node Manager; see the section "Starting the WebLogic Node Manager."
5. Start the WLS_DISCO server; see the section "Starting the Discoverer Server." One of the ways to do this is from a browser by launching the WebLogic console; see the section "Starting the Discoverer Server."

**NOTE**
*You can start the WLS_DISCO server in multiple ways, with the WebLogic console being just one of them. As with all middleware products that employ a managed server, you can actually use the command line, the WebLogic Scripting Tool (WLST), or the WebLogic console (as mentioned). You can even convert the WebLogic administration server and managed server to run as Windows services. We don't cover all of these alternatives in this book but mention them so that you know what can be done.*

6. Start the Discoverer service; see the section "Starting the Discoverer Service."
7. Test that Discoverer is working; see the section "Testing That Discoverer Is Working."
8. If necessary to save memory, you can also stop both Web Cache and OHS.

# Starting WebLogic Server and Node Manager

There are various ways to start WebLogic Server and Node Manager, but we found that attempting to start these using the Windows Start menu on our Windows 7 64-bit machine would not always work.

Following discussions with the Oracle WebLogic team, we determined that the most reliable way to start both WebLogic Server and Node Manager is to use the command line.

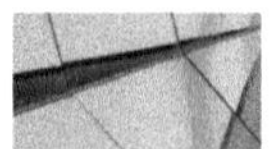

**NOTE**
*We do not recommend running a production environment using Windows 7. The best you could get away with is as a demo or, as we did, for writing a book! Oracle does not support running the server on a Windows client operating system, so if you do this, you may well not get any support. The point we are trying to make is that if you have trouble with the menu scripts, you should use the command line.*

## Starting WebLogic Server

There is more than one way to start WebLogic Server. The two that we will discuss are

- Starting WebLogic Server from the Windows Start menu
- Starting WebLogic Server from the command line

### Starting WebLogic Server from the Windows Start Menu

We found that starting WebLogic Server from the Windows Start menu is straightforward but occasionally troublesome, especially on a Windows 7 64-bit machine. If you are using Windows and find that you have difficulty starting the server from the Start menu, please look at the section "Starting WebLogic Server from the Command Line."

To start WebLogic Server from the Windows Start menu, use the following workflow:

1. From the Windows Start menu All Programs link, navigate to and click the Oracle WebLogic folder.
2. Click the User Projects folder.
3. Click the Classic Domain folder.
4. Click Start Admin Server For WebLogic Server Domain. Windows will open a command window and launch the server.
5. If prompted for your login credentials, enter them as follows:
   A. **Username** This is typically **WebLogic**.
   B. **Password** This is the password you provided when WebLogic was installed.

**NOTE**
*If you want to avoid having to always provide your username and password, please see the section "Automating Your WebLogic Server Login Credentials."*

6. When you have successfully entered your credentials, the WebLogic server start utility will run.
7. When you see the server started in RUNNING mode, your WebLogic server is up and running.
8. Leave the command line window open; this is very important.

**NOTE**
*One reason most customers would run this as a service on Windows is so that it runs in the background without the problems you will encounter if you accidentally kill the DOS shell on a production machine. The WLS documentation contains those steps, and they are universal to any WLS install or managed server.*

### Starting the WebLogic Server from the Command Line

If you are using Linux or Unix, the command line is the way you will always start the server. If you are using Windows and you have any trouble with starting the server from the Start menu, please use this method.

To start WebLogic Server from the command line, use the following workflow:

1. Open a command-line window. In Windows you do this from the Start menu by typing **cmd** in the "Search programs and files" box and then clicking cmd.exe when it appears at the top of the list.
2. Navigate to the WebLogic bin folder in the Middleware directory.
3. Thus, if your Middleware home is located here:

   ```
   /oracle/Middleware
   ```

   the full path to the bin folder will therefore be as follows:

   ```
   $MIDDLEWARE_HOME/user_projects/domains/ClassicDomain/bin
   ```

4. From the bin folder, locate and run the program called startweblogic.

   In Windows this is a CMD file, whereas for Linux or Unix this will have the extension SH.

**NOTE**
*startWebLogic.cmd or startWebLogic.sh is a script file and can be viewed in any suitable text editor. If you have the time to study it, you will see how the WebLogic server is started.*

5. If prompted for your login credentials, enter them as follows:
   - **A. Username** This is typically **WebLogic**.
   - **B. Password** This is the password you provided when WebLogic was installed.

**NOTE**
*If you want to avoid having to always provide your username and password, please see the section "Automating Your WebLogic Server Login Credentials."*

6. When you have successfully entered your credentials, the WebLogic start utility will run.
7. When you see the server started in RUNNING mode, your WebLogic server is up and running.
8. Leave the command line window open; this is very important.

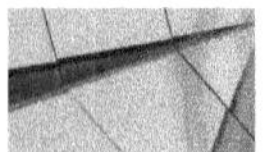

**NOTE**
*Closing the command-line window stops WebLogic. If you do this by mistake, just redo the steps in this section.*

## Automating Your WebLogic Server Login Credentials

If you are like us, you will quickly get fed up with having to remember your WebLogic login ID and password every time you start the program. This can be automated.

To automate the passing of your credentials, use the following workflow:

1. Either in an Explorer window or from the command line, navigate to the AdminServer folder under your Middleware directory.

   Thus, if your Middleware home is located here:

   ```
   oracle/Middleware
   ```

   the full path to your administration server will therefore be as follows:

   ```
   $MIDDLEWARE_HOME/user_projects/domains/ClassicDomain/servers/AdminServer
   ```
2. Check whether you have a folder called *security* under AdminServer.
3. If you do not have a folder called *security*, create it now.
4. In the security folder, create a text file called *boot.properties*. If you are doing this in Linux or Unix, do not forget to set your access permissions and ownership.
5. Edit boot.properties and in clear text enter the following two lines:

   username=<Your **WebLogic** username> usually WebLogic
   password=<Your **WebLogic** password>
6. Save and exit from boot.properties.
7. Start or restart your WebLogic server using the steps in the previous section.
8. You should no longer be prompted for your credentials.

**NOTE**
*During the startup sequence, the WebLogic server will encrypt the boot.properties file. If you need to change the login username or password again, you simply need to repeat the steps in this section and enter the credentials again in clear text.*

## Starting WebLogic Node Manager

Just as with WebLogic Server, there is more than one way to start WebLogic Node Manager. The two that we will discuss are

- Starting WebLogic Node Manager from the command line
- Starting WebLogic Node Manager from the Windows Start menu

### Starting WebLogic Node Manager from the Command Line

Starting Node Manager from the command line in the background is the only way to start it when using Linux or Unix.

Starting Node Manager this way from Windows is risky because the window needs to be kept open throughout the session. If the window is closed, the JVM session will be killed, and therefore Node Manager will stop working. We do not recommend running a production environment from a Windows server using the command line. Our recommendation is to transform the procedure into a Windows-managed service. This topic is really outside the scope of the book and will not be covered.

**NOTE**
*In a Windows install, WebLogicNodeManager is automatically created as a service. The default name is similar to Oracle WebLogic NodeManager (oracle/middleware/wlserver_10.3). It is the administration server and the managed server (WLS_DISCO) that we recommend could be transformed into Windows services.*

To start Node Manager from the command line, use the following workflow:

1. Open a command window and navigate to the Node Manager server bin folder under the Middleware directory.

   Thus, if your Middleware home is located here:

   ```
   oracle/Middleware
   ```

   the full path to your Node Manager will therefore be as follows:

   ```
   $MIDDLEWARE_HOME/wlserver_10.3/server/bin
   ```

2. From the bin folder, locate and run startnodemanager.

   In Windows this is a CMD file, whereas for Linux or Unix this has the extension SH.

**NOTE**
*The startnodemanager.cmd or startnodemanager.sh file is a script file and can be viewed in any suitable text editor. If you have the time to study it, you will see how Node Manager is started.*

3. There are no login credentials for starting Node Manager.

4. When you see a message saying "Secure socket listener started on Port 5556," your Node Manager is up and running.
5. Leave the command-line window open; this is very important.

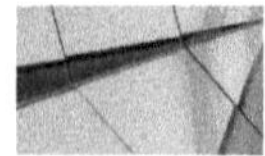

**NOTE**
*As mentioned, if you are using Windows, you should be using a Windows server. This is true if you start the command line in a shell (for example, in Windows). In Unix/Linux, you would start in the background on the command line.*

### Starting WebLogic Node Manager from the Windows Start Menu

We found that starting WebLogic Node Manager from the Windows Start menu to be very much hit-and-miss, especially on a Windows 7 64-bit machine. If you are using Windows and find you have difficulty starting Node Manager from the Start menu, please look at the section "Starting WebLogic Node Manager from the Command Line."

To start WebLogic Node Manager from the Windows Start menu, use the following workflow:

1. From the Windows Start menu All Programs link, navigate to and click the Oracle WebLogic folder.
2. Click the User Projects folder.
3. Click the WebLogic Server 11gR1 folder.
4. Click the Tools folder.
5. Click Node Manager. Windows will open a command window and launch Node Manager.
6. There are no login credentials for starting Node Manager.
7. When you see a message saying "Secure socket listener started on Port 5556," your Node Manager is up and running.
8. Leave the command-line window open; this is very important.

## Starting the Discoverer Managed Server

The Discoverer managed server is started from the Oracle WebLogic Server Administration Console. The console itself is a web service and as such is accessed via a web browser. If you installed the WebLogic server onto a Windows machine, you can launch the Oracle WebLogic Server Administration Console on that machine directly from the Windows Start menu. For all other installs or if you are not located at the machine where WebLogic is installed, you launch a web browser and type the URL for the Administration Console into the address window. We will discuss the Administration Console more in depth later in this chapter. For now, we will just use it to start the Discoverer managed server.

**NOTE**
*As mentioned, starting from the Windows Start menu is only one of the ways to start the managed server. Please look here for more information: http://docs.oracle.com/cd/E28280_01/bi.1111/b40107/maint.htm#CHDBDAIE.*

To launch the Administration Console from the Windows Start menu, use the following workflow:

1. From the Windows Start menu All Programs link, navigate to and click the Oracle WebLogic folder.
2. Click the User Projects folder.
3. Click the Classic Domain folder.
4. Click Admin Server Console. Windows will open your default web browser and launch the console login screen shown in Figure 19-2.

To launch the Administration Console from a web browser, use the following workflow:

1. Launch a web browser.
2. Type the following into the address window:

   **http://myserver:7001/console**

The browser will open the console login screen shown in Figure 19-2.

Having successfully launched the Administration Console login screen, to complete the start of the Discoverer server, continue with this workflow:

1. Enter your login credentials as follows:
   A. **Username** This is typically **WebLogic**.
   B. **Password** This is the password you provided when WebLogic was installed.
2. Windows will open the WebLogic Server Administration Console shown in Figure 19-3.

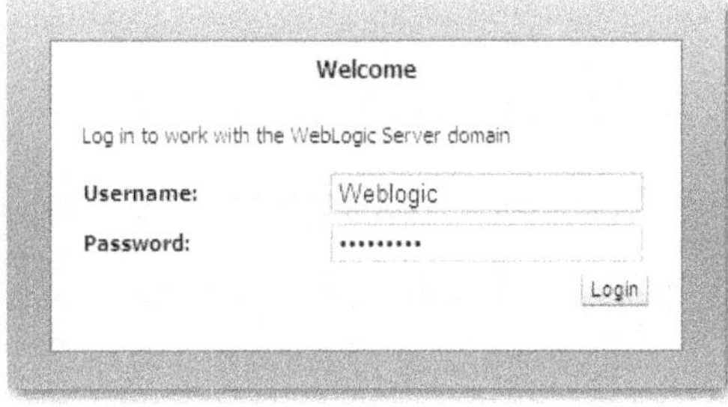


**FIGURE 19-2.** *The WebLogic console login screen*

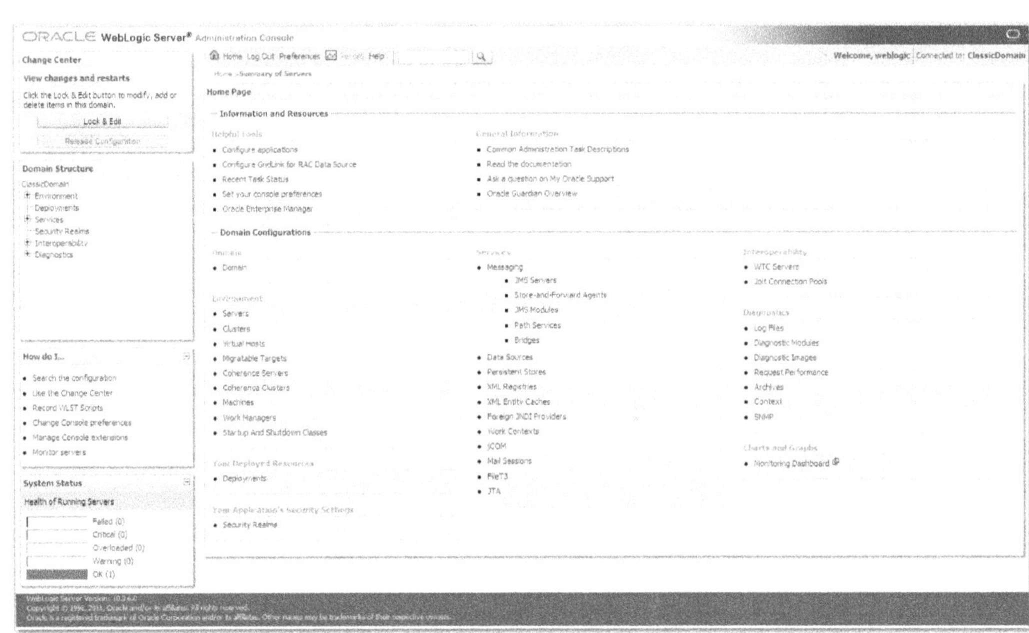


FIGURE 19-3. *The WebLogic Server Administration Console*

3. Under Environment, click Servers. As shown here, the Summary of Servers screen will open:

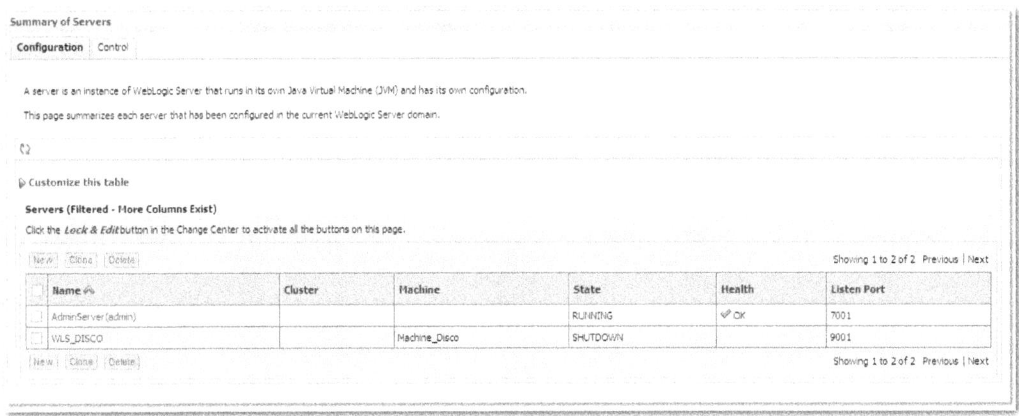

4. On the Summary of Servers screen, you will see two tabs: the default, named Configuration, and the second, named Control.
5. When you first come to this screen, you will be on the Configuration tab. You should see a server called AdminServer in a state of RUNNING, with the health being OK and the listen port listed. The listen port will typically be 7001 and is the one you used to launch the browser.
6. You should also see a second server, this time entitled WLS_DISCO. This server will be in a SHUTDOWN state, with no health and with its listen port listed. As you can see, in our situation the listen port for WLS_DISCO is 9001.

**NOTE**
*The check boxes alongside the servers are grayed out on the Configuration tab. They become active only on the Control tab.*

7. Click the Control tab; the screen changes as shown here:

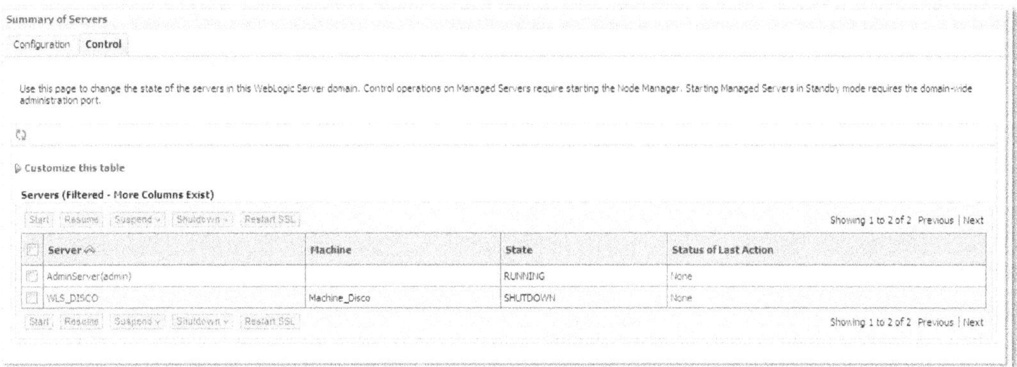


8. Click in the check box alongside the Discoverer server (remember in our case this is called WLS_DISCO). Notice how the buttons above the server listing have now become active.

9. Click the Start button.

10. When prompted by the Server Life Cycle Assistant, click the Yes button.

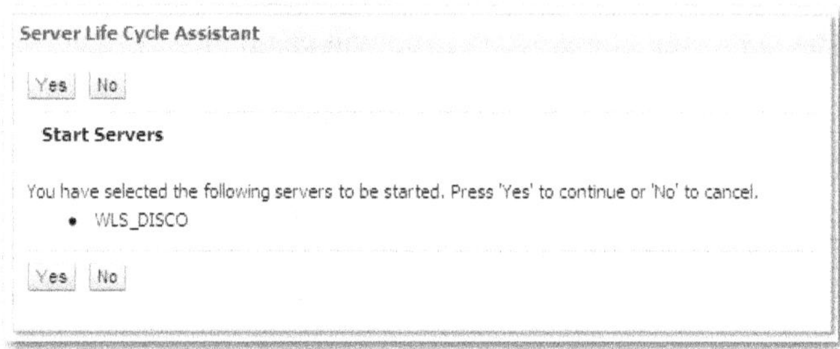

Server Life Cycle Assistant
Yes
No
Start Servers
You have selected the following servers to be started. Press 'Yes' to continue or 'No' to cancel.
WLS_DISCO
Yes
No


11. The state will change to STARTING, and the status of the last action will change to TASK IN PROGRESS.
12. Click the Refresh button to monitor the progress of the task.
13. When the task is done, the state will change to RUNNING, and the status of the last action will change to TASK COMPLETED.

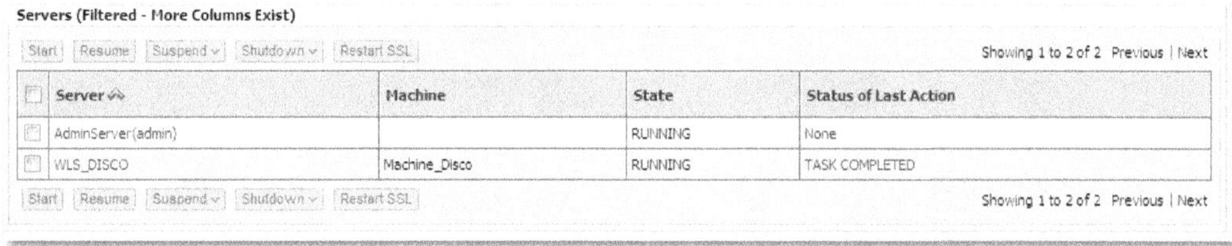

**NOTE**
*The check mark is automatically removed when the task completes, and the buttons above the list of servers revert to being grayed out.*

14. Click the Refresh button to stop monitoring.
15. If you click the Configuration tab again, you will see that the state says RUNNING and that the health is OK.

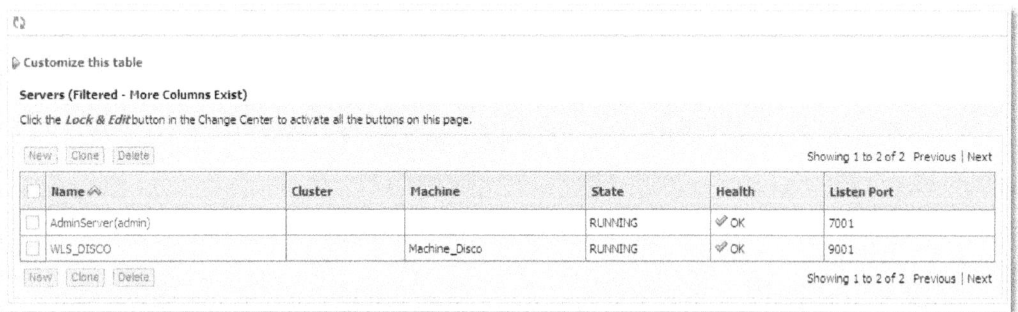

Customize this table
Servers (Filtered - More Columns Exist)
Click the Lock & Edit button in the Change Center to activate all the buttons on this page.
New
Clone
Delete
Showing 1 to 2 of 2 Previous | Next
Name
Cluster
Machine
State
Health
Listen Port
AdminServer(admin)
RUNNING
OK
7001
WLS_DISCO
Machine_Disco
RUNNING
OK
9001

16. Close the web browser.
17. You can also close the Node Manager command-line window. This is optional.

## Starting the Discoverer OPMN Managed Components

The Discoverer OPMN managed components are comprised of Web Cache, OHS, the Discoverer preference server, and the Discoverer session server.

As is nearly always the case these days, there is more than one way of starting the components. If you are using Windows, you can start it from the Start menu, from the Services box, or from the command line. If you are using Linux or Unix, you can do this only from the command line. Before you attempt to start the Discoverer services, you must have started the WebLogic server and have the database that is housing the repository up and running.

### Starting the Discoverer OPMN Components from the Windows Start Menu

To start the Discoverer OPMN components from the Windows Start menu, use the following workflow:

1. From the Windows Start menu All Programs link, navigate to and click the Oracle Classic Instance folder; it is usually called asinst1, as shown here:

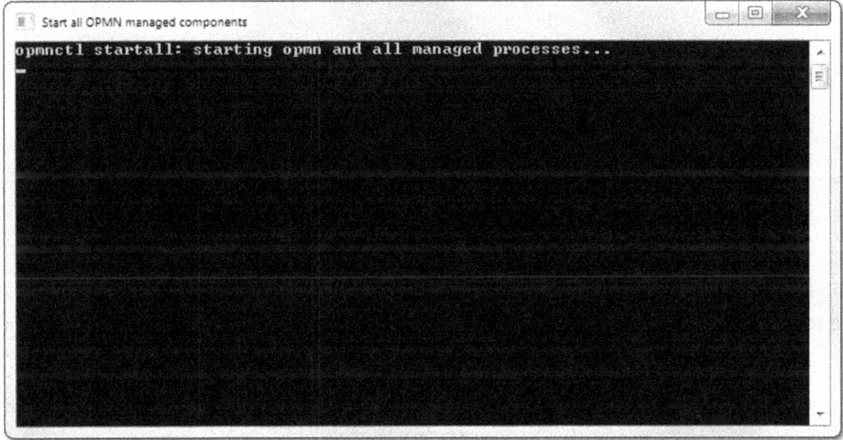


2. Click the Start all OPMN managed components link.
3. A Windows command prompt will open, and the service will begin to start.
4. While the service is starting, the window will remain open, and you should not close it.
5. When the service has started, the window will close automatically.

### Starting the Discoverer OPMN Components from the Windows Services Box

To start the OPMN components from the Windows Services box, use the following workflow:

1. From the Windows Start button, select Control Panel.
2. Click Administrative Tools.
3. Double-click Services.

4. Navigate to the service called Oracle Process Manager (asinst_1).
5. Right-click the service and from the pop-up select Start.

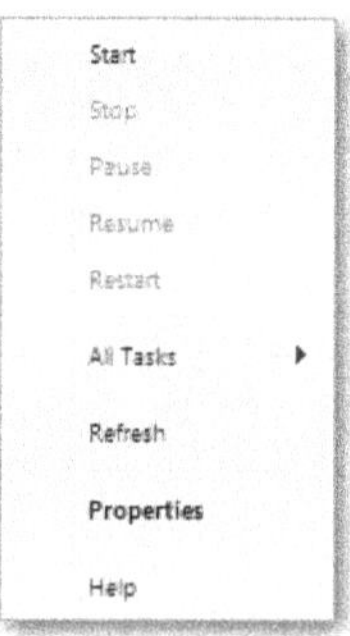


6. Windows will display a message saying that it is starting the service.
7. When the task has finished, the status of the service will change to Started.

Offline Files The Offline ... Started Automatic Local System
Oracle ORCL VSS Writer Service Manual Local System
Oracle Process Manager (asinst_1) Started Manual Local System
Oracle WebLogic NodeManager (C_ora... Manual Local System
OracleDBConsoleorcl Manual Local System
OracleJobSchedulerORCL Disabled Local System
OracleMTSRecoveryService Started Automatic Local System
OracleOraDb11g_home1ClrAgent Manual Local System
OracleOraDb11g_home1TNSListener Started Automatic Local System
OracleServiceORCL Started Manual Local System


8. Close the Services window.

### Starting the Discoverer OPMN Components from the Command Line

To start the Discoverer OPMN components from the command line, use the following workflow:

1. Open a command window and navigate to the Discoverer bin folder under the Middleware directory.

   Thus, if your Middleware home is located here:

   ```
   c:\oracle\Middleware\
   ```

   the full path to your Discoverer Service will therefore be as follows:

   ```
   c:\oracle\Middleware\asinst_1\bin
   ```

2. From the bin folder locate and run opmnctl startall.

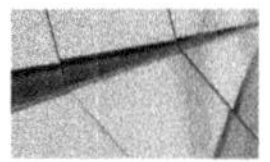

**NOTE**
*opmnctl.cmd or opmnctl (with no extension on Unix/Linux) is a script file and can be viewed in any suitable text editor. If you have the time to study it, you will see how the OPMN control is scripted. For more information about the use of OPMN, please refer to the "Oracle Process Management and Notification (OPMN)" section later in this chapter.*

3. There are no login credentials for starting the Discoverer service.
4. While the service is starting, you will see the following message: "opmnctl startall: starting opmn and all managed processes…."
5. For now, leave the command-line window open.
6. When the service has started, the command prompt will return.
7. To confirm that everything has started correctly, type the following: **opmnctl status**.
8. You should see that all of the services have started and are alive.

```
C:\oracle\Middleware\asinst_1\bin>opmnctl status

Processes in Instance: asinst_1
---------------------------------+--------------------+---------+---------
ias-component                    | process-type       |     pid | status
---------------------------------+--------------------+---------+---------
emagent_asinst_1                 | EMAGENT            |    8908 | Alive
Discoverer_asinst_1              | PreferenceServer   |    4052 | Alive
Discoverer_asinst_1              | ServicesStatus     |    6768 | Alive
webcache1                        | WebCache-admin     |    1812 | Alive
webcache1                        | WebCache           |    6888 | Alive
ohs1                             | OHS                |    8720 | Alive
```

9. Close the command-line window.

## Confirming That Discoverer Has Started

Before you inform the users that Discoverer is up and running, it is a good idea to test it for yourself. You can do this by launching Discoverer Plus and then Discoverer Viewer. If they both launch OK, then you can safely inform the users that Discoverer is up and running.

There are a number of ways to start the end-user tools. By this we mean you can use a number of ports. You can use one of the following:

- The Discoverer listen port, usually 8090, or 8890 if using HTTPS
- The WLS_DISCO listen port, usually 9001
- The Discoverer Oracle HTTP Server listen port, usually 8888

To test Discoverer, use the following workflow:

1. Launch a web browser.
2. Type the following URL:

   **http://servername:port/discoverer/plus**

   You can use any of the ports listed earlier.
3. Make sure you can log in.
4. Close Discoverer Plus.
5. Type the following URL:

   **http://servername:port/discoverer/viewer**

   Once again, you can use any of the ports listed earlier.
6. Make sure you can log in.

# Oracle Process Management and Notification (OPMN)

This component of the Oracle application server is used to start, stop, and monitor many of the components in the server, including Discoverer. It will ping Discoverer and all other components on a configurable interval. If it determines that a component has crashed or is no longer responding, it will notify MOD_OC4J (in 10*g*) or the Discoverer servlet in WebLogic (for 11*g*) to stop routing requests to that component and then attempt to restart the component. When the component is running again, the component will notify either MOD_ OC4J or the Discoverer servlet that it is able to accept requests again.

## OPMN Basic Commands

The Oracle Process Manager and Notification server uses the opmnctl utility to manage all Oracle Application Server 11*g* server processes. The powerful startall and stopall commands will manage all server components. Unless a tier consists of a stand-alone component such as the Web Cache, opmnctl should be used rather than the separate component control program. These are the basic OPMN commands:

- **Opmnctl start** Use this command to start OPMN.
- **Opmnctl shutdown** Use this command to shut down OPMN and all of its managed processes.
- **Opmnctl startall** Use this command to start OPMN and all of the managed processes.
- **Opmnctl stopall** Use this command to stop OPMN and all of the managed processes.
- **Opmnctl status** Use this command to list the status for each OPMN component. Adding the additional switch -l after the command causes the system to display an extended status showing the uid, memory used, uptime (in hours, minutes, and seconds), and ports used. The following is sample output from the standard command, omitting the –l switch:

```
Processes in Instance: asinst_1
---------------------+-----------------+-------+------------------
ias-component        | process-type    |  pid  | status
---------------------+-----------------+-------+------------------
emagent_asinst_1     | EMAGENT         |  6280 | Alive
Discoverer_asinst_1  | PreferenceServer|  2804 | Alive
Discoverer_asinst_1  | ServicesStatus  |  8548 | Alive
Web Cache1           | Web Cache-admin |  8252 | Alive
Web Cache1           | Web Cache       |  10808| Alive
ohs1                 | OHS             |  3044 | Alive
```

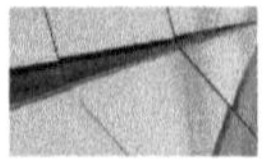

**NOTE**

*If you are still using 10g, from time to time you may see a Log Loader process. This is usually down. The Log Loader is a feature that compiles log messages from various log files into a single repository. There is no Log Loader process in 11g.*

- **Opmnctl startproc ias-component=Discoverer_asinst_1** Use the startproc command to start an individual process. If no process attribute is supplied to this command, all opmn-managed processes except components with id-matching=true will be started. The previous command will start the Discoverer component. It starts both of the processes, PreferenceServer and ServicesStatus.
- **Opmnctl stopproc ias-component=Discoverer_asinst_1** Use the stopproc command to stop an individual process. This command will stop both of the components associated with the Discoverer instance.
- **Opmnctl restartproc ias-component=Discoverer_asinst_1** Use restartproc to stop and then restart a process. This command will stop and then restart the components associated with the Discoverer instance. This works only when a process is alive. If no processes are alive at the time you issue a restartproc command, you will receive a message telling you that no processes are alive.
- **Opmnctl stopproc process-type=PreferenceServer** This command starts just the Discoverer preference server.
- **Opmnctl help** Use this command to display a brief description of all the commands available for use with opmnctl.
- **Opmnctl usage** Use this command to display a detailed description of all the commands available for use with opmnctl. Adding an optional switch of the command name displays just the description for that command. For example, typing **opmnctl usage start** displays a full description of the usage for the start command.

OPMN is primarily configured using opmn.xml. If you explore this file, you will recognize many key parameters. In the following section, we will list several of the key parameters. However, please note that there are many more parameters than those in the following text. The goal of this discussion is to identify OPMN as a key Discoverer component that deserves exploration whenever problems occur.

You should also explore $ORACLE_INSTANCE/diagnostics/logs/OPMN/opmn as a first priority when troubleshooting Discoverer.

## OPMN.XML Example

The opmn.xml file, found in $ORACLE_INSTANCE/config/OPMN/opmn, is used to tell OPMN the processes it manages. The file is much simplified in 11*g* from the 10*g* version and is not as long or complicated as it used to be. This is because several of the 10*g* components have been deprecated. However, the file is still broken up into sections beginning with the command ias-component id=. In a typical opmn.xml file, you will a section for each ias-component listed when you typed **status –l**. You will find one ID for each of the following component types:

- OHS, with a single component, called ohs1 in our case
- Web Cache, with two components
  - Web Cache
  - WebCache-admin
- Discoverer, with three components
  - ServicesStatus

  - PreferenceServer
  - SessionServer
- EMAGENT, with a single component typically also called EMAGENT

The IDs associated with the previous types set the respective environment variables. If you look back to the section "OPMN Basic Commands," you will notice that the example output in that section contains entries that equate to the ias components listed previously.

The section of our opmn.xml that manages Discoverer is shown here:

```
<ias-component id="Discoverer_asinst_1" type="Discoverer">
<environment>
<variable id="PREFERENCE_PORT" value="16002"/>
<variable id="PREFERENCE_HOST" value="localhost"/>
<variable id="DISCO_DIR" value="$ORACLE_HOME"/>
<variable id="DC_LOG_LOG_DIR"
value="ORACLE_INSTANCE/diagnostics/logs/$COMPONENT_TYPE/$COMPONENT_NAME/"/>
<variable id="LD_LIBRARY_PATH"
value="$ORACLE_HOME/discoverer/lib$:$ORACLE_HOME/lib$:/usr/lib"
append="true"/>
<variable id="DC10_REG" value="$ORACLE_INSTANCE/config/
PreferenceServer/$COMPONENT_NAME/"/>
<variable id="FND_TOP" value="$ORACLE_INSTANCE/config/$COMPONENT_
TYPE/$COMPONENT_NAME/"/>
<variable id="FND_SECURE" value="$ORACLE_INSTANCE/config/$COMPONENT_
TYPE/$COMPONENT_NAME/"/>
<variable id="TNS_ADMIN" value="$ORACLE_INSTANCE/config/"/>
</environment>
<process-type id="ServicesStatus" module-id="Disco_ServicesStatus"
status="enabled">
<process-set id="ServicesStatus" numprocs="1"/>
</process-type>
<process-type id="PreferenceServer" module-id="Disco_PreferenceServer"
working-dir="$DC_LOG_DIR " status="enabled">
<process-set id="PreferenceServer" numprocs="1"/>
</process-type>
<process-type id="SessionServer" module-id="Disco_SessionServer" working-
dir="$DC_LOG_DIR" status="enabled">
<start retry="0" timeout="180"/>
<port id="ses" range="0"/>
<process-set id="SessionServer" parallel-requests="true" restart-on-
death="false" maxprocs="50" minprocs="0"/>
</process-type>
</ias-component>
```

In the previous extract, you will notice various switches and settings:

- **range="0"** This identifies the ports used by the Discoverer session servers. You must have enough ports to handle the number of processes. If set, ports should have a low value and a high value like 3801-3950.

- **minprocs="0"** This identifies the number of session processes that are started when Discoverer is started. You may choose either 0 or 1.
- **maxprocs="50"** This is the maximum number of Discoverer sessions. Set this as high as your server's resources will permit.
- **restart-on-death="false"** If a process dies, this tells OPMN whether it should restart it. For the session server, this must remain at false.
- **parallel-requests="true"** This tells OPMN whether it should process requests in parallel or serially.
- **"TNS_ADMIN" value="$ORACLE_INSTANCE/config/"** This tells you where the TNSNAMES.ORA file is located. In Discoverer 10*g*, this file used to be in the network/admin folder. This folder still exists but is not where Discoverer will look for the file.

# Oracle Fusion Middleware Control

Oracle Fusion Middleware is a collection of standards-based software products, ranging from Java EE and developer tools to integration services, identity management, business intelligence, and collaboration tools. Oracle Fusion Middleware offers complete support for development, deployment, and management.

To manage and control middleware, you use Oracle Fusion Middleware Control, otherwise known as Oracle Enterprise Manager (OEM). We recommend you familiarize yourself with all the facets of Fusion Middleware Control because you will need to use it frequently.

## Oracle Fusion Middleware Components

Oracle Fusion Middleware provides a large number of components. When discussing Discoverer, the components we are interested in are as follows:

- Oracle WebLogic Server
- Oracle HTTP Server (explained in detail later in this chapter)
- Oracle Web Cache (explained in detail later in this chapter)
- Oracle Internet Directory
- Oracle Portal
- Oracle Business Intelligence (includes Discoverer; discussed in detail in Chapter 20)

In this section, we will describe how to log into Fusion Middleware Control. Later in the chapter we will discuss managing Oracle HTTP Server and Oracle Web Cache. First, however, you need to be able to connect to Oracle Fusion Middleware Control.

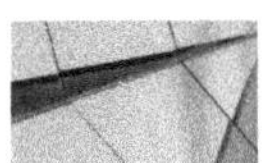

**NOTE**
*Please refer to Chapter 20 for information about using Oracle Fusion Middleware Control to manage Discoverer.*

## Connecting to Fusion Middleware Control

To connect and log in to Oracle Fusion Middleware Control, use the following workflow:

1. From a browser, enter http://fully_qualified_domain_name:7001/em. The Fusion Middleware Control login page will be displayed.

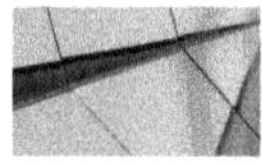

**NOTE**
*The port depends upon your installation and may not be 7001. It may be anywhere in the range 7001–9000.*

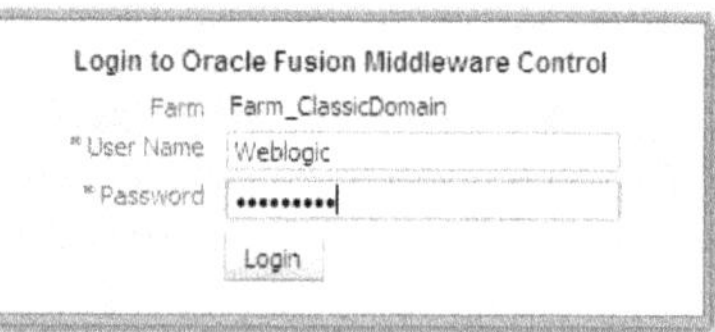


2. In User name, enter **Weblogic**, as shown here.
3. In Password, enter the WebLogic password.

**NOTE**
*The WebLogic password is the password you provided during the install of the server. You should not lose this password. Equally, you should not lightly give it away.*

4. The Fusion Middleware Control home page shown in Figure 19-4 will be displayed. On this page you will see all of the clusters and instances in your farm.
5. From the Fusion Middleware Control home page, select the component you want to administer.

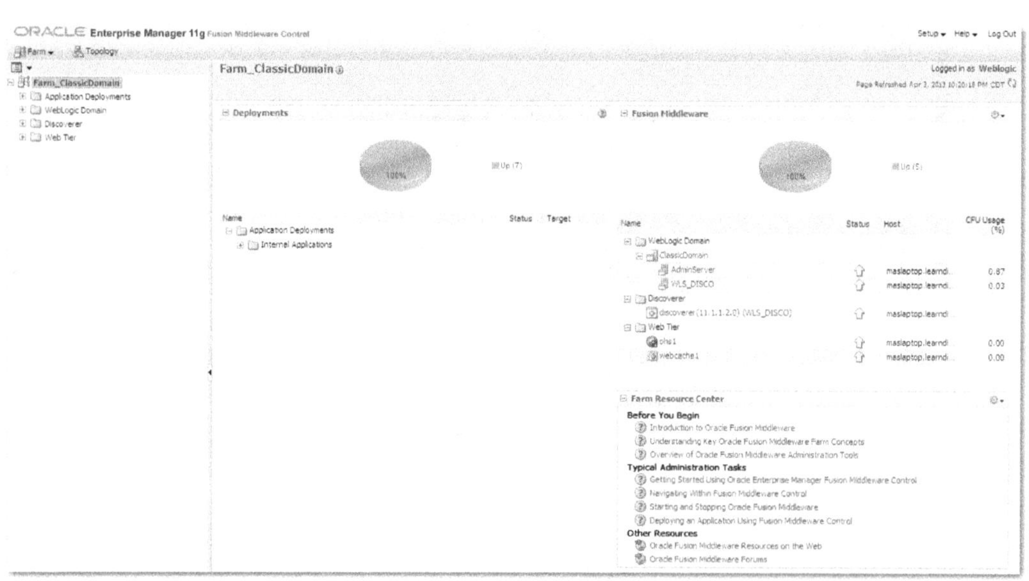


**FIGURE 19-4.** *Fusion Middleware Control home page*

# Oracle HTTP Server

Oracle HTTP Server (OHS from here onward) is based on Apache 2.2.10 infrastructure with some additional Oracle-supplied modules underneath the covers. Apache has been the most popular web server on the Internet for quite some time. According to the September 2012 Netcraft Web Server Survey (http://news.netcraft.com/archives/2012/09/10/september-2012-web-server-survey.html), even though the percentage share has dropped in recent years, almost 60 percent of all web sites on the Internet are using Apache, making it more widely used than all other web servers combined.

OHS has the following components to handle client requests:

- **HTTP listener** This handles incoming requests and routes them to the appropriate processing utility.
- **Modules** Otherwise known as *mods*, modules come in two forms. There are the standard Apache modules and several modules specific to Oracle Fusion Middleware. The latter are how Oracle extends the basic functionality of OHS to support integration between OHS and other middleware components.
- **Perl interpreter** A persistent Perl runtime environment is included within OHS via the use of the mod_perl module.

**NOTE**
*Perl is a powerful scripting language that is often used to provide dynamic content. The Perl version used by Oracle Fusion Middleware is 5.10.*

## Key Apache Directives

OHS receives all requests from Oracle Web Cache (if used) and then routes the request to the WebLogic server. Apache has many sophisticated features and configuration options that you can explore. These configurations either can be found in $ORACLE_INSTANCE/config/OHSComponent/ohs-comp-name/httpd.conf or are files referenced in the httpd.conf file using the include directive. In our system, the ORACLE_INSTANCE is

```
c:\oracle\Middleware\asinst_1
```

The OHS Component is simply called OHS, and the ohs-comp-name is ohs1. Therefore, the path to our httpd.conf file is

```
c:\oracle\Middleware\asinst_1\config\OHS\ohs1
```

Here are some of the key Apache directives:

- **Timeout** This is the maximum number of seconds allowed for a command to complete. The default value is 300.
- **KeepAlive** Setting this to On allows Apache to keep the connection open for that client when the client requests it. Because the connection has to be set up only once, this can improve performance. The trade-off is that the server process cannot be used to service other requests until the client disconnects, the connection times out (as controlled by the

KeepAliveTimeout directive), or the MaxKeepAliveRequests value has been reached. The default value for KeepAlive is On.

- **MaxKeepAliveRequests** This is the maximum number of requests to allow during a persistent connection. Setting this to 0 allows an unlimited amount, which is not recommended. If you have long client sessions, you might want to increase this value. See the preceding item, KeepAlive, for additional comments. The default value is 100. To obtain maximum performance, we recommend you leave this set to a high value.
- **KeepAliveTimeout** This is the number of seconds that the system will wait for the next request from the same client on the same connection. Once again, please see the previous item, KeepAlive, for additional comments. The default value in 11*g* is 5. In 10*g* it was 15.
- **MaxRequestsPerChild** This is the number of requests that each child process is allowed to process before the child dies. The child will then exit, thus avoiding the problems that can occur after prolonged use when Apache memory leaks happen. On most operating systems this is not really an issue; however, Solaris is renowned for leaks in its libraries. For Solaris we therefore recommend setting this to a number such as 10000. If you set this to 0, which is usually the default, your setting will be unlimited. According to Oracle, if you use Windows, you should set this to 0 because in Windows there is only one server process.
- **ThreadsPerChild** This setting specifies the number of requests that each child process is allowed to handle before the child process dies. Requests in excess of this number will be required to wait in the TCP/IP queue. Allowing such requests to wait in the TCP/IP queue often results in the best response time and throughput. While setting this value high will allow more requests to be active at the same time, you need to be aware that this could seriously affect performance as the requests end up being handled more slowly. According to information from Oracle on some in-house testing that it has done, "A setting of 20 ThreadsPerChild per CPU produces good response time and throughput results. For example, if you have four CPUs, set ThreadsPerChild to 80. If, with this setting, CPU utilization does not exceed 85%, you can increase ThreadsPerChild, but ensure that the available threads are in use." Thus, as you can see, altering this setting can help with performance tuning. The default for this in 11*g* is 25, whereas in 10*g* it was 50. According to Oracle, the ThreadsPerChild setting in Windows works like the MaxClients setting in Unix.
- **MinSpareServers** The MinSpareServers and MaxSpareServers (see the next item) settings allow the HTTP server to dynamically adapt to the system load as it sees fit. It will maintain enough processes to handle the load, keeping a few in reserve just in case. The server does this by periodically checking how many clients are waiting for a request. If that number is less than MinSpareServers, it will create a new spare, whereas if there are more than the MaxSpareServers, some of them will be killed off. Unless you really need to alter these settings, we recommend you leave these set with their default. The default for MinSpareServers is 5.
- **MaxSpareServers** See the preceding item for a description of this setting, the default for which will be either 10 or 20. On our system it was 10.
- **MaxClients** This sets a limit on the total number of clients that can connect simultaneously. If this limit is ever reached, then subsequent clients will be locked out and will be unable

to connect. Thus, please do not set this too low! Oracle has designed this to be used as a brake to stop a runaway server from taking the system down with it. The default for this setting is 150 and has been set by Oracle following exhaustive tests. According to information obtained from the 10*g* Application Server Performance Guide, "Tests on a 2-processor, 168 MHz Sun UltraSPARC on a 100 Mbps network showed that saturation of the network occurs when MaxClients is set to 150. Even on 4- and 6-processor, 336 MHz systems, there was no significant performance improvement seen by increasing the MaxClients setting from 150 to 256, based on static page and servlet tests with up to 1000 users." You should therefore understand that increasing MaxClients when system resources are saturated will not improve performance. In fact, when the system is overloaded, we recommend you reduce the number of MaxClients to force requests to stay in the network queue. It might be better to have requests time out and get the system to retry rather than having long response times. According to Oracle, the MaxClients setting in Unix works like the ThreadsPerChild setting in Windows.

- **Listen** This allows you to bind Apache to specific IP addresses and/or ports. Usually the default is set to an HTTP listener port during the installation of the application server. The default is usually 8888 but can be higher.
- **Port** This is the port to which the stand-alone server listens. If you encounter issues, please disable any firewall, security, and other services. The default port is 80.

Here is an example include directive:

```
include"C:\oracle\Middleware\asinst_1/config/OHS/ohs1/mod_wl_ohs.conf"
```

**NOTE**

*The previous directive includes a combination of forward and backslash characters. This is not a mistake nor is it mistyped. In a Windows httpd.conf all of the include directives adopt this approach.*

We included the previous example because mod_wls_ohs.conf is the module in the Oracle HTTP Server that allows requests to be proxied from OHS to the Oracle WebLogic Server. This include directive must therefore not be removed because it is vitally important.

You will probably notice that if you look at your system, every line in mod_wl_ohs.conf is commented out and therefore not really doing anything. This is the file used in most custom installations and in some Oracle Fusion Middleware products, but for the portal, forms, reports, and Discoverer installation, the WebLogic proxy is in here:

```
$ORACLE_INSTANCE/config/OHS/ohs1/moduleconf/module_disco.conf
```

For further information regarding OHS, please take a look at the E10144-01 Oracle Fusion Middleware Administrator's Guide for Oracle HTTP Server. In particular, you will find the "Getting Started" section particularly useful. You can find this at http://docs.oracle.com/cd/E12839_01/web.1111/e10144/getstart.htm.

Please also review the httpd.conf file and www.apache.org for a discussion of these directives. Unless you really have cause to do otherwise, we recommend you leave all of Apache's configurations set to the defaults. Apache scales really well and, in most cases, will be the least of your problems. Any initial changes that you make will relate to enabling the Secure Sockets Layer

(SSL) and single sign-on (SSO) or disabling Web Cache. It is important to know that any change to OHS's httpd.conf file requires a restart. Instead of going into detail about OHS's standard directives, which is a complete topic by itself, we will discuss the procedure you must follow to make changes to OHS's configuration. You can make changes to OHS via Enterprise Manager or directly updating configuration files. The preferred method is to use Enterprise Manager because you are far less likely to make mistakes.

## Key Oracle HTTP Server Modules

The Oracle HTTP Server has more than 50 modules, among which the following are considered key to Discoverer:

- **mod_wl_ohs** This module replaces the mod_oc4j module found in 10*g* that was used to route requests from OHS to OC4J. The new module routes requests from OHS to WebLogic. This module is enabled by default. It provides the same functionality as the Oracle WebLogic Server Plug-in for Apache HTTP Server (mod_weblogic) except for some minor differences, as follows:
    - Uses Oracle's security layer (NZ) to provide SSL support for the module. A new directive, WlSSlWallet, has been added to OHS through the mod_wl_ohs module that allows the use of Oracle Wallets.
    - Supports two-way SSL between OHS and Oracle WebLogic Server.
    - Supports IPv6 for communication with Oracle WebLogic Server.

  For more information on the mod_wl_ohs module, please refer to this page: http://docs.oracle.com/cd/E12839_01/web.1111/e10144/under_mods.htm#BABGCGHJ.

  For more information on the Oracle WebLogic Server Plug-in for Apache HTTP Server (mod_weblogic) module, please refer to this page: http://docs.oracle.com/cd/E12839_01/apirefs.1111/e14395/toc.htm.
- **mod_osso** This module redirects requests for protected content to SSO for authentication and authorization. In other words, this module enables SSO for OHS. When used, this module examines incoming requests and determines whether the requested resource is protected. If the resource is protected, mod_osso retrieves the OHS cookie. By default, this module is disabled. The mod_osso module is enabled on the Server Configuration properties page of OEM.

  For more information about using Fusion Middleware Control to specify server properties, please refer to this page: http://docs.oracle.com/cd/E12839_01/web.1111/e10144/getstart.htm#BEHEIJED.
- **mod_ossl** This module provides the facilities to support HTTPS (SSL) requests. It enables strong cryptography for OHS. The module is a plug-in to OHS that enables the server to use SSL. Oracle states that this module is similar to the standard mod_ssl module except it is based on Oracle's implementation of SSL rather than OpenSSL.

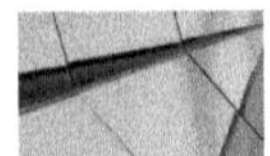

**NOTE**
*For those readers who are technically savvy with SSL, mod_ossl supports SSL 3 and TLS 1 and is based on Certicom and RSA cryptography technologies.*

To configure HTTP Server using Oracle Enterprise Manager, please see the "Using Middleware Control to Manage OHS" section.

## Manual Oracle HTTP Server Configuration

To perform manual OHS configuration, use the following workflow:

1. Locate the httpd.conf file, which you will find in $ORACLE_INSTANCE/config/OHS/ohs1.
2. Take a backup of this file.
3. Make any changes you want to make.
4. Save the file.
5. Restart the OHS component by executing the following command:

   ```
   $ORACLE_INSTANCE/opmn/bin/opmnctl restartproc ias-component=ohs1
   ```

6. You can see your component names and check whether they are up or down by executing the following command, which gives you a tabular view of the component names:

   ```
   $ORACLE_INSTANCE/opmn/bin/opmnctl status
   ```

**NOTE**
*You do not need to stop and restart* all *the components. You can merely restart OHS so it picks up the configuration changes.*

## Using Fusion Middleware Control to Manage OHS

In a previous section we showed you how to manually configure Oracle HTTP Server. In this section, we will show you how to use Oracle Fusion Middleware Control to manage and control OHS. Ideally, you will find that this is much easier.

To get to the OHS home page, use the following workflow:

1. From the Middleware Control home page shown in Figure 19-4, navigate to the ClassicDomain area at the top-left side of the page where you will see a listing of the component headings.
2. Click the Web Tier link. As shown in Figure 19-5, the listing will expand to show the components available in this area.

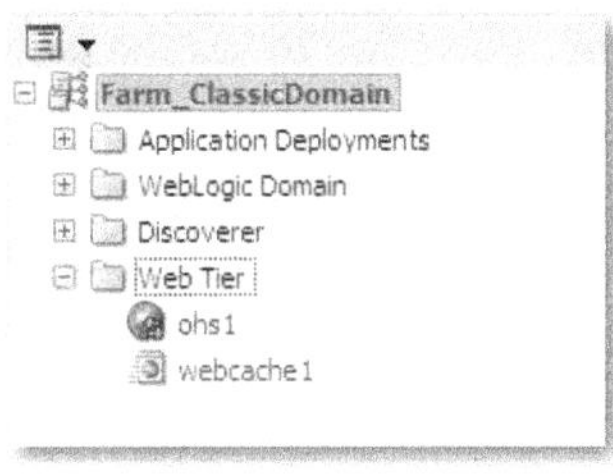


**FIGURE 19-5.** *Fusion Middleware Control Web Tier listing*

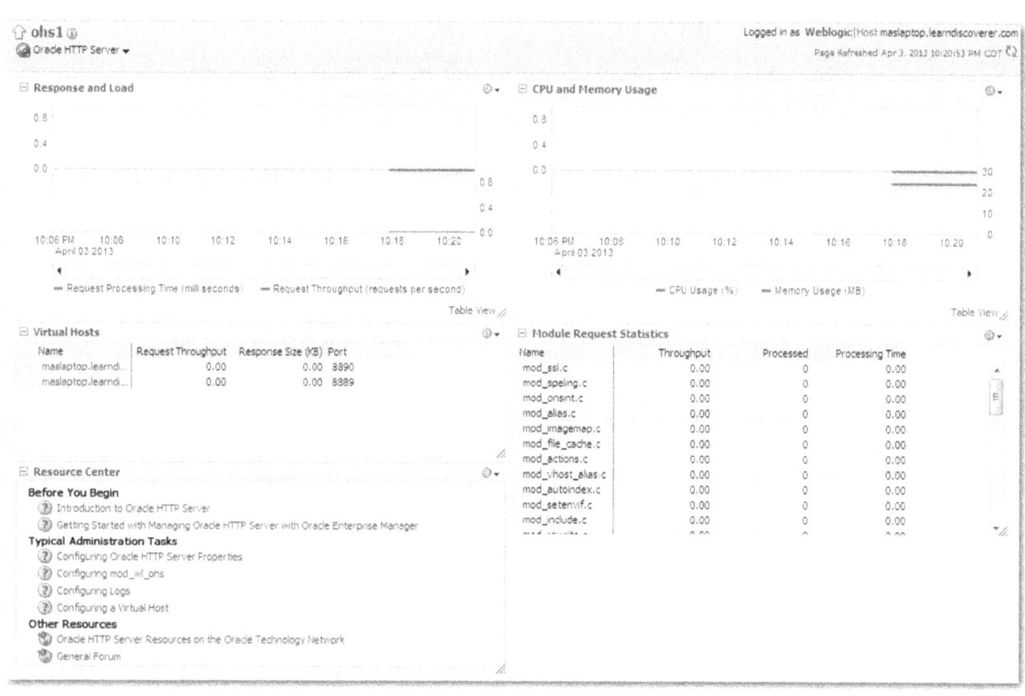


**FIGURE 19-6.** *Fusion Middleware Control HTTP Server home page*

3. Click the link called ohs1. The Oracle HTTP Server home page shown in Figure 19-6 will open.
4. On the HTTP Server home page, you will see the following areas:
   - **An Oracle HTTP Server drop-down link (very top of the screen)** We will discuss this in more detail shortly.
   - **A Response and Load area** This displays a graph showing the load on the server.
   - **A CPU and Memory Usage area** This displays a graph showing how much CPU and memory is being consumed.
   - **A Virtual Hosts area** This lists the virtual hosts that exist in this server. Clicking the name of a virtual host allows you to see the performance details of that host.
   - **A Module Request Statistics area** This lists all of the modules that are being managed along with their throughput, number of times processed, and processing time.
   - **A Resource Center area** This area has a set of links that link to various Oracle documents for helping with administering the HTTP server.

   Before we move away from this page and look in detail at how to configure OHS, we will point out some of the features of this page.

First, the layout of this page is configurable, as are all pages in Fusion Middleware Control. You can therefore move the areas of the page around by clicking the View Actions Menu button, which is located at the top right of every area. Using this, you can, for example, move the Virtual Hosts area above the Response and Load area.

Second, we encourage you to make great use of the Resource Center area because it contains links to a vast library of online help. For example, clicking Introduction to Oracle HTTP Server opens the Oracle Enterprise Manager online help, as shown in Figure 19-7, in a separate window.

5. Clicking the drop-down link alongside Oracle HTTP Server at the top of any of the OHS pages opens the drop-down list at right.

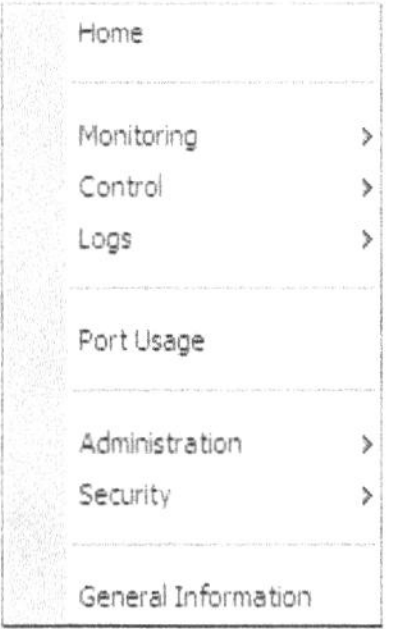


6. As you can see, the list provides access to the following:

   - **Home** Selecting this returns you to the Oracle HTTP Server home page.
   - **Monitoring** Selecting this opens a submenu that offers you a single option called Performance Summary. Selecting this option opens the Performance Summary page where you can monitor such things as CPU usage, memory usage, and request processing. We do not discuss this page further in the book.

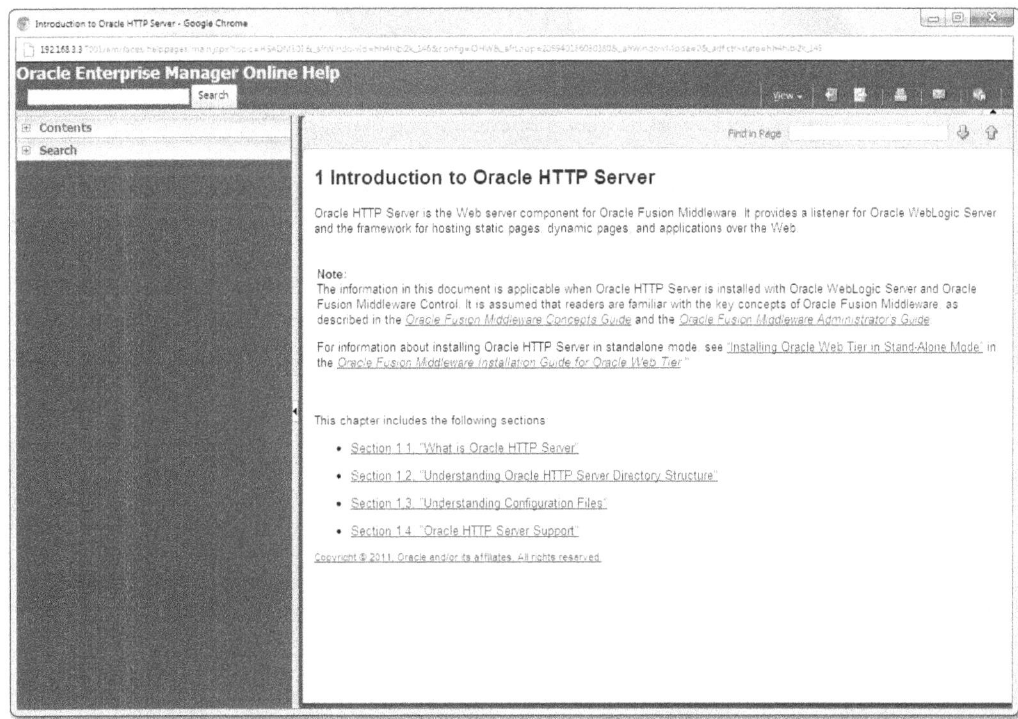


**FIGURE 19-7.** *Oracle Enterprise Manager online help*

For more information about monitoring the server performance, please refer to the following page: http://docs.oracle.com/cd/E16764_01/web.1111/e10144/man_server.htm#BACJGEJI.

- **Control** Selecting this opens a submenu that offers you the following three choices:
   i. **Start Up** Selecting this runs the startup process for Oracle HTTP Server. If the server is already running, you will receive a message telling you that the operation failed because the component is already alive. If the server is currently down, the startup process will run. When the process completes, you will be informed that the process was successful. Your only option now is to click the Close button.

   ii. **Shut Down** Selecting this runs the shutdown process for Oracle HTTP Server. When asked to confirm that you want to shut it down, your choices are Shutdown and Cancel. Clicking Shutdown starts the shutdown process. If the server is already down, you will receive a message telling you that the operation failed because the component is already down. When the process completes, you will be informed that the process was successful. Your only option now is to click the Close button.

   iii. **Restart** Selecting this runs the shutdown process, if the server is up, followed by the startup process. If the server is already down, only the startup process is executed. When the process completes, you will be informed that the process was successful. Your only option now is to click the Close button.

   For more information about starting, stopping, and restarting Oracle HTTP Server, please refer to http://docs.oracle.com/cd/E16764_01/web.1111/e10144/getstart.htm#BEHFGCAE.

- **Logs** Selecting this opens a submenu that offers you a single option called View Log Messages. Selecting this option opens the Log Messages page where you can view or examine all of the HTTP Server logs. We do not discuss this page further in the book.

- **Port Usage** Selecting this opens the following Port Usage page. As you can see from this page, you can determine which ports are being used as the HTTP listener and the HTTPS listener.

Port Usage

| Port in Use | IP Address | Component | Protocol |
|---|---|---|---|
| 8889 | ALL | ohs1 | https |
| 8890 | ALL | ohs1 | https |
| 8888 | ALL | ohs1 | http |

For more information about port usage, please refer to http://docs.oracle.com/cd/E16764_01/web.1111/e10144/man_network.htm#i1005601.

- **Administration** Selecting this opens a submenu that has nine options. We will discuss the Administration drop-down options in the next section.

- **Security** Selecting this opens a submenu that offers you the following two choices:
   i. **Audit Policy** Selecting this opens the Audit Policy page. You use this page to view and set the audit policies for this Oracle HTTP Server instance. Any changes

made to audit policies will require a restart of Oracle HTTP Server. We do not discuss audit policies further in this book.

ii. **Wallets** Selecting this opens the Wallets page. A *wallet* is a keystore that stores X.509 certificates and private keys in industry-standard, PKCS #12 format. On this page, you can create wallets, manage wallets, and even create self-signed wallets that use self-signed certificates. We do not discuss wallets further in this book

- **General Information** Selecting this opens a pop-up that displays the following information:
  i. **Target Name** Example: /Farm_ClassicDomain/asinst_1/ohs1
  ii. **Version** Example: 11.1.1.6.0
  iii. **Oracle Home** Example: c:\oralce\middleware\as1
  iv. **Oracle Instance** Example: c:\oracle\middleware\asinst_1
  v. **Host** Example: maslaptop.learndiscoverer.com

### HTTP Server Administration Drop-Down Options

In the previous section, we explained most of the options available to you from the drop-down button alongside Oracle HTTP Server. The one option we did not explain was Administration. In this section, we will walk you through the administrative options available to you.

Selecting Administration from the drop-down opens a submenu that offers you the following nine choices:

- **Virtual Hosts** Selecting this opens the Virtual Hosts page where you can create virtual hosts to maintain more than one server on one computer, as differentiated by their apparent hostname, enabling Oracle HTTP Server to serve different web sites simultaneously. You can select a virtual host row from the table and, using the Configure menu, specify mod_wl_ohs, mod_perl, SSL, MIME, and log configuration for the selected row. We do not discuss virtual hosts further in this book. For more information about managing virtual hosts, please refer to http://docs.oracle.com/cd/E16764_01/web.1111/e10144/man_network.htm#CIHBHHIE.
- **Performance Directives** Selecting this opens the Performance Directives page where you can tune performance-related directives for Oracle HTTP Server. After you have made any change to these directives, you need to click one of the Reset To Default, Apply, or Revert buttons on the top of the page. If you clicked Apply or Reset To Default after already applying a different setting, you will be required to restart the server. The directives you can tune are
  - **Maximum Requests per Child Server Process** The default is No Limit, but you can set the limit if you want.
  - **Request Timeout (seconds)** The default is 300.
  - **Maximum Connection Queue Length** There is no default for this.
  - **Multiple Requests per Connection** The default is Allow with Connection Timeout of 5 seconds, but you can change this to any number of seconds you want. You can also choose Not Allowed.
  - **Threads per Child Server Process** The default for this is 150.

For more information about performance directives, please refer to http://docs.oracle.com/cd/E16764_01/web.1111/e10144/man_server.htm#BGBIIDFH.

- **Log Configuration** Selecting this opens the Log Configuration page. Oracle HTTP Server records server error information in error logs. Specify the error log settings, including whether to generate log messages in Oracle Diagnostic Logging (ODL) text, ODL XML, or Apache format. ODL is a standard format and mechanism for correlating the diagnostics messages from components across Oracle Fusion Middleware. If you made any changes to the configuration of the logs, you should click the Apply button. You will then need to restart the server. For more information about log configuration, please refer to http://docs.oracle.com/cd/E16764_01/web.1111/e10144/man_logs.htm#BACFFJJI.
- **Server Configuration** Selecting this opens the Server Configuration page. You use this page to configure basic OHS settings, such as document root directory, the user and group under which the server runs, installed modules, and aliases. On this page is where you can enable or disable the mod_perl, mod_fcgi, and mod_osso modules. If you made any changes to the configuration of the server, you should click the Apply button. You will then need to restart the server. For more information about configuring the server, please refer to http://docs.oracle.com/cd/E16764_01/web.1111/e10144/getstart.htm#BEHCBCDE.
- **MIME Configuration** Selecting this opens the MIME Configuration page. You use this page to manage the Multipurpose Internet Mail Extension (MIME) languages and types. This is where you associate file extensions with language codes so that, for example, the extension .fr is associated with France and the extension .zh_CN is associated with China. To apply a MIME type as the default for unknown types, select a row and click Set As Default. The page also includes areas to configure MIME encodings and MIME languages. If you made any changes to the MIME configuration, you should click the Apply button. You will then need to restart the server. For more information about MIME configuration, please refer to http://docs.oracle.com/cd/E16764_01/web.1111/e10144/getstart.htm#BEHEHJFC.
- **Ports Configuration** Selecting this opens the Ports Configuration page. The ports used by Oracle HTTP Server can be set during and after installation. In addition, you can change the port numbers, as needed. If you change the port or make other changes that affect the URL, such as changing the hostname and enabling or disabling SSL, you will need to re-register partner applications with the SSO server using the new URL. We do not describe this process in the book or discuss port configurations further. For more information about configuring ports, please refer to http://docs.oracle.com/cd/E16764_01/web.1111/e10144/man_network.htm#BHCICADE.
- **mod_perl Configuration** Assuming you have enabled the mod_perl module using Server Configuration, selecting this opens the mod_perl Configuration page. For more information about enabling and configuring the mod_perl module, please refer to http://docs.oracle.com/cd/E16764_01/web.1111/e10144/getstart.htm#BEHEJCFG.
- **mod_wl_ohs Configuration** Selecting this opens the mod_wl_ohs Configuration page. The mod_wl_ohs module allows requests to be proxied from Oracle HTTP Server to Oracle WebLogic Server. In here you specify parameters common for all URLs directed to the mod_wl_ohs handler and use the MatchExpression and Location sections to specify any overrides. If you made any changes to the configuration, you should click the Apply

button. You will then need to restart the server. For more information about mod_wl_ohs configuration, please refer to http://docs.oracle.com/cd/E16764_01/web.1111/e10144/getstart.htm#BEHGIDCB.

- **Advanced Configuration** Selecting this option opens the Advanced Server Configuration page. On this page you can view or edit an Oracle HTTP Server configuration file. Earlier in the book we described how to manually edit the httpd.conf file. On the page, there is a drop-down alongside Select File. One of the options on the list, in fact the first one, is httpd.conf. Having selected the file you want to view or edit, click the Go button. The contents of the file will be displayed. If you make any changes to a configuration file, you should click the Apply button. You will then need to restart the server. For more information about modifying an Oracle HTTP Server configuration file, please refer to http://docs.oracle.com/cd/E16764_01/web.1111/e10144/getstart.htm#BEHDGFEB.

**NOTE**
*There is a great deal of information in the preceding section, and we appreciate that some of these settings do not directly affect Discoverer. However, we have provided this information as a direct response to requests that we have received from system administrators who wanted to know just what settings can and cannot affect Discoverer.*

# Oracle Web Cache

The number-one question that most people ask us is, will Web Cache help Discoverer? The answer is, it depends. You see, Web Cache provides web content compression, load balancing, and, of course, caching. Web Cache caches static and dynamically generated files in memory. You can configure the caching rules and expiration schedules for Web Cache content.

For example, a data warehouse that is refreshed every Saturday can have Discoverer Viewer pages expire on Saturday also.

However, because Discoverer Plus is a web applet, Web Cache will not provide any performance benefit through caching. The Oracle Java Client caches the applet on the client machine. On the other hand, Web Cache can provide significant benefits for both Discoverer Viewer and Discoverer Portlets. Therefore, in the following discussion, we will show you how to administer Web Cache and how to configure Discoverer Viewer to use Web Cache.

**NOTE**
*Discoverer 10*g *could also use JInitiator. This has been deprecated in 11*g *and now only the Oracle Java Client (previously Sun) can be used.*

Oracle Web Cache is administered in the following two places:

- In Oracle Fusion Middleware Control (discussed next)
- In the Web Cache Administration tool (discussed in the section "Configuring Viewer with Web Cache" later in this chapter)

## Using Fusion Middleware Control to Manage Web Cache

In this section, we will show you how to use Middleware Control to manage and control Web Cache.

To get to the Web Cache home page, use the following workflow:

1. From the Middleware Control home page shown earlier in Figure 19-4, navigate to the ClassicDomain area at the top-left side of the page where you will see a listing of the component headings.
2. Click the link Web Tier. As was shown in Figure 19-4, the listing will expand to show the components available in this area.
3. Click the link Web Cache1. The Web Cache home page shown in Figure 19-8 will open.
4. On the Web Cache home page you will see the following areas:
   - **A Web Cache drop-down link (very top of the screen)** We will discuss this in more detail shortly.

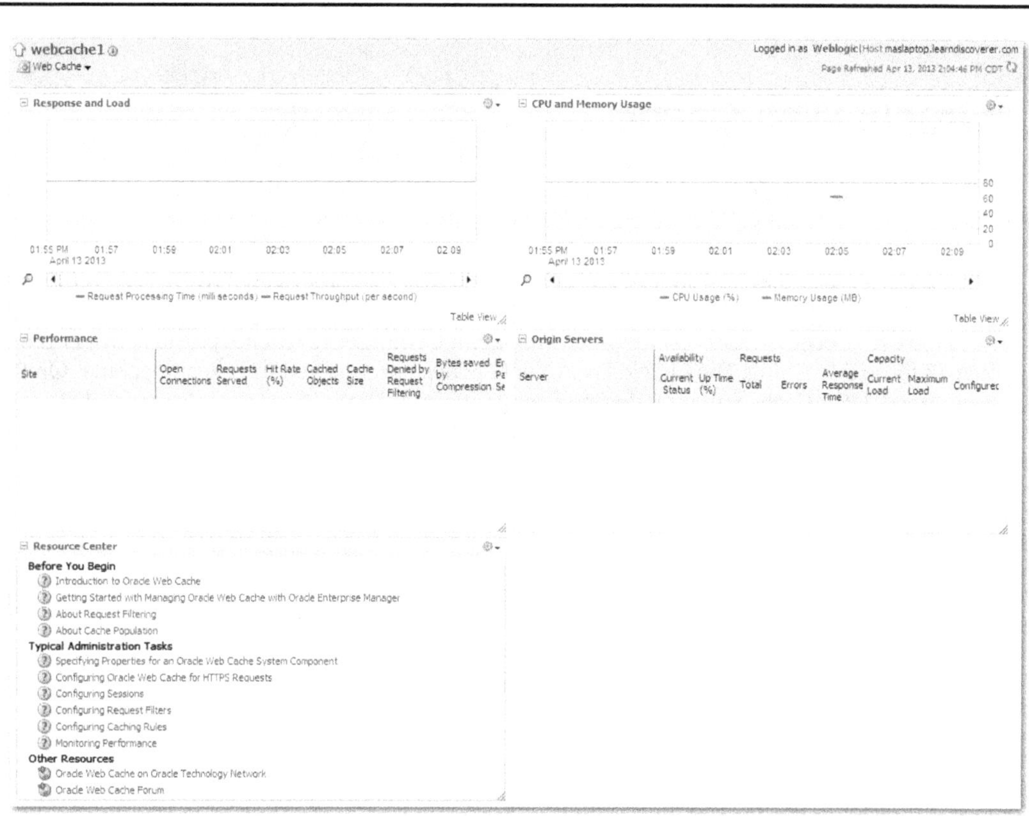


**FIGURE 19-8.** *Fusion Middleware Control Web Cache home page*

- **A Response and Load area** This displays a graph showing the load on the server.
- **A Performance area** Among the statistics being displayed are the number of open connections, the number of requests served, and the number of objects stored in the cache.
- **An Origin Servers area** Among the statistics being displayed are the name of the origin server, the current status, and the load on the server.
- **A Resource Center** This area has a set of links to various Oracle documents for helping with administering Web Cache.

Before we move away from this page and look in detail at how to configure Web Cache, we will point out some of the features of this page.

First, the layout of this page is configurable, as are all pages in Fusion Middleware Control. You can therefore move the areas of the page around by clicking the View Actions Menu button, which is located at the top right of every area. Using this you can, for example, move the Performance area above the Response and Load area.

Second, as previously mentioned, we strongly encourage you to make great use of the Resource Center area because it contains links to a vast library of online help.

5. Clicking the drop-down link alongside Web Cache at the top of any of the Web Cache page opens the drop-down list at right.

6. As you can see, the list provides access to the following:
   - **Home** Selecting this returns you to the Web Cache server home page.
   - **Monitoring** Selecting this opens a submenu that offers you the following two choices:
     i. **Performance Summary** Taking this option opens the Performance Summary page where you can monitor such things as CPU usage, memory usage, and request processing. We do not discuss this page further in the book. For more information about monitoring the server performance, please refer to http://docs.oracle.com/cd/E14571_01/web.1111/e10143/diagnostic.htm#CHDFIFBC.

     ii. **Popular Request** Selecting this option enables you to view the most popular requests for determining whether the caching rules are caching the correct objects. For more information about monitoring popular requests, please refer to http://docs.oracle.com/cd/E14571_01/web.1111/e10143/diagnostic.htm#CHDDIIGG.
   - **Control** Selecting this opens a submenu that offers you the following three choices:
     i. **Start Up** Selecting this runs the startup process for Web Cache. If Web Cache is already running, you will receive a message telling you that the operation failed because the component is already alive. If Web Cache is currently down, the startup process will run. When the process completes, you will be informed that the process was successful. Your only option now is to click the Close button.

     ii. **Shut Down** Selecting this runs the shutdown process for Web Cache. When asked to confirm that you want to shut it down, your choices are Shutdown and Cancel. Clicking Shutdown starts the shutdown process. If the server is already down, you will receive a message telling you that the operation failed because the component is already down. When the process completes, you will be informed that the process was successful. Your only option now is to click the Close button.

iii. **Restart** Selecting this runs the shutdown process, if Web Cache is up, followed by the startup process. If Web Cache is already down, only the startup process is executed. When the process completes, you will be informed that the process was successful. Your only option now is to click the Close button.

For more information about starting and stopping Web Cache, please refer to http://docs.oracle.com/cd/E14571_01/web.1111/e10143/getstarted.htm#BEHJGAGB.

- **Logs** Selecting this opens a submenu that offers you a single option called View Log Messages. Selecting this option opens the Log Messages page where you can view or examine all of the Web Cache logs. We do not discuss this page further in the book.
- **Port Usage** Selecting this opens the following Port Usage page. As you can see from this page, you can determine which ports are being used as the Web Cache HTTP and HTTPS listeners as well as the admin port.

Port Usage

| Port in Use | IP Address | Component | Protocol | Port Type |
|---|---|---|---|---|
| 8091 | maslaptop.learndisco... | webcache1 | http | admin |
| 8092 | maslaptop.learndisco... | webcache1 | http | stat |
| 8093 | maslaptop.learndisco... | webcache1 | http | invalidation |
| 8094 | maslaptop.learndisco... | webcache1 | https | listen |
| 8090 | maslaptop.learndisco... | webcache1 | http | listen |

For more information about port usage, please refer to http://docs.oracle.com/cd/E14571_01/web.1111/e10143/getstarted.htm#CHDCBGAD.

- **Administration** Selecting this opens a submenu with 13 options. We will discuss the Administration drop-down options in the next section.
- **Security** Selecting this opens a submenu that offers you the following three choices:

i. **Audit Policy** Selecting this opens the Audit Policy page. You use this page to view and set the audit policies for this Web Cache instance. Any changes made to audit policies will require a restart of Oracle HTTP Server. We do not discuss audit policies further in this book, but you can find more information here: http://docs.oracle.com/cd/E14571_01/core.1111/e10043/audpolicy.htm#JISEC2904.

ii. **SSL Configuration** Selecting this opens the SSL Configuration page. On this page you specify and manage which SSL wallet to use for Oracle Web Cache connections to origin servers. We do not discuss SSL configuration further in this book, but you can find more information here: http://docs.oracle.com/cd/E14571_01/web.1111/e10143/security.htm#CDDDBGGA.

iii. **Wallets** Selecting this opens the Wallets page. A *wallet* is a keystore that stores X.509 certificates and private keys in industry-standard, PKCS #12 format. On this page you can create wallets, manage wallets, and even create self-signed wallets that use self-signed certificates. We do not discuss wallets further in this book, but you can find more information here: http://docs.oracle.com/cd/E14571_01/web.1111/e10143/security.htm#CDDCEFFD.

- **General Information** Selecting this opens a pop-up that displays the following information:
  - **i. Target Name** Example: /Farm_ClassicDomain/asinst_1/Web Cache1
  - **ii. Version** Example: 11.1.1.6.0
  - **iii. Oracle Home** Example: c:\oralce\middleware\as1
  - **iv. Oracle Instance** Example: c:\oracle\middleware\asinst_1
  - **v. Host** Example: maslaptop.learndiscoverer.com

## Web Cache Administration

In the previous section we explained most of the options available to you from the drop-down button alongside Web Cache. The one option we did not explain was Administration. In this section, we will walk you through the administrative options available to you. High-level documentation about the Administration options is available here: http://docs.oracle.com/cd/E14571_01/web.1111/e10143/getstarted.htm#CHDEAEEH.

Selecting Administration from the drop-down opens a submenu with the following 13 choices:

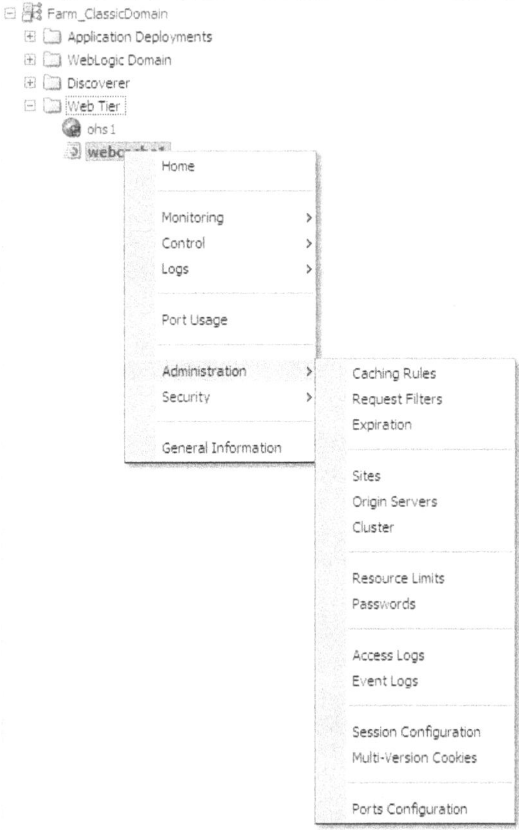

- **Caching Rules** Selecting this opens the Caching Rules page where you can create the caching rules for Web Cache. Caching rules determine which objects to cache. When you establish a caching rule, objects matching the rule are not cached until there is a client request for them. When a client first requests an object, Oracle Web Cache sends the request to the origin server. This request is a cache miss. Because this URL has an associated caching rule, Oracle Web Cache caches the object for subsequent requests. When Oracle Web Cache receives a second request for the same object, Oracle Web Cache serves the object from its cache to the client. This request is a cache hit. When you stop Oracle Web Cache, the cache clears all objects. In addition, Oracle Web Cache clears and resets statistics. We do not discuss caching rules further in this book, but you can find more information here: http://docs.oracle.com/cd/E14571_01/web.1111/e10143/caching.htm#CEGIBDEB.
- **Request Filters** Selecting this opens the Requests Filters page where you can enable filters to protect you against common HTTP request attacks. Common attacks include planting malicious code that when executed by a user attempts to steal the user's identity of private information, trying to execute arbitrary code, or bombarding sites with high volumes of bogus requests. In addition, request filtering controls which clients and requests are allowed access to a web site or certain parts of a web site. To defend against web site attacks, you can enable a series of filters that each request must pass through before being processed. Each filter is composed of customizable rules that can identify the requests to either allow or deny access. We do not discuss request filters further in this book, but you can find more information here: http://docs.oracle.com/cd/E14571_01/web.1111/e10143/requestfilter.htm#BABFDDJB.
- **Expiration** Selecting this opens the Expiration Policies page where you can create expiration policies that specify when to expire objects in the cache and how you want Oracle Web Cache to process objects after they have expired. When an object expires, Web Cache removes it either immediately or as permitted by the origin server capacity up to a maximum time limit. To apply an expiration policy for an object, associate the appropriate expiration policy when creating a caching rule for the object. We do not discuss expiration policies further in this book, but you can find more information here: http://docs.oracle.com/cd/E14571_01/web.1111/e10143/caching.htm#CEGCFDAD.
- **Sites** Selecting this opens the Site Definitions page where you can configure Oracle Web Cache with information about the named web sites. For Oracle Web Cache to act as a virtual server for one or more web sites, you must configure Oracle Web Cache with information about the named web sites. We do not discuss site definitions further in this book, but you can find more information here: http://docs.oracle.com/cd/E14571_01/web.1111/e10143/getstarted.htm#CHDHIIFI.
- **Origin Servers** Selecting this opens the Origin Servers page where you can configure the application web server or proxy server to which Oracle Web Cache sends cache misses. We do not discuss origin servers further in this book, but you can find more information here: http://docs.oracle.com/cd/E14571_01/web.1111/e10143/getstarted.htm#CHDCBFEC.
- **Cluster** Selecting this opens the Cache Cluster page. To increase the availability and scalability of your web site, you can configure multiple instances of Oracle Web Cache to run as members of a cache cluster. To configure a cache cluster, you configure two or

more Oracle Web Cache instances as cache cluster members and then specify properties for the cluster. A cache cluster uses one configuration that is synchronized from the current cache (the cache to which your client browser is connected) to all cluster members. The configuration contains settings that are the same for all cluster members as well as cache-specific settings for each cluster member. We do not discuss clustering further in this book, but you can find more information here: http://docs.oracle.com/cd/E14571_01/web.1111/e10143/highav.htm#i1006978.

- **Resource Limits** Selecting this opens the Resource Limits page where you can specify caching and network thresholds to ensure Oracle Web Cache runs efficiently. We do not discuss resource limits filters further in this book.
- **Passwords** Selecting this opens the Passwords page where you can change or set the passwords for the Web Cache invalidation and administration accounts. The *invalidator* account is an administrator authorized to send invalidation requests. This account sends HTTP POST requests to invalidate objects in the cache. The *administrator* account is the Oracle Web Cache administrator authorized to log in to Oracle Web Cache Manager and make configuration changes through that interface. This administrator is also authorized to send statistic monitoring requests to the Oracle Web Cache statistics monitoring port. The default password for these accounts is the password you supplied on the Web Cache Administrator page of the Oracle Universal Installer. Before you begin configuration, change the passwords for these accounts to a secure password. You must perform this configuration in Fusion Middleware Control. Because you will need to enable the administration password before you can use the Web Cache Administration tool, we discuss setting the administration password in the next section. You can find more information here: http://docs.oracle.com/cd/E14571_01/web.1111/e10143/security.htm#CDDBGGDA.
- **Access Logs** Selecting this opens the Access Log Configuration page. Oracle Web Cache records information about the received HTTP and HTTPS requests in access logs. Each web site defined in Oracle Web Cache can have its own access log. By default, the access log has a filename of access_log and is stored in the following directories:

  ```
  (UNIX) ORACLE_INSTANCE/diagnostics/logs/WebCache/<webcache_name>
  (Windows) ORACLE_INSTANCE\diagnostics\logs\WebCache\<webcache_name>
  ```

  We do not discuss access logs further in this book, but you can find more information here: http://docs.oracle.com/cd/E14571_01/web.1111/e10143/log.htm#CEGBBACA.
- **Event Logs** Selecting this opens the Event Log Configuration page. Oracle Web Cache records event and error information in event logs. An event log entry can help you determine what objects have been inserted in the cache and alert you to any cache-related issues. Configure settings for each cache and general settings for all the logs. If you have a high-volume site, specify a daily or hourly policy in the Rollover Policy section. We do not discuss event logs further in this book, but you can find more information here: http://docs.oracle.com/cd/E14571_01/web.1111/e10143/log.htm#i1011050.
- **Session Configuration** Selecting this opens the Session Configuration page. A session is associated with a caching policy. You can direct Web Cache to use a single origin server for all requests for a given user session, called *session binding*, or personalize content using session-encoded URLs in HREFs. The page is also used to configure session

policies and session binding in the Session Policy Configuration and Session Binding Configuration sections. You complete configuration for session-encoded URLs when you create a caching rule where you can create virtual hosts to maintain. We do not discuss session configuration further in this book, but you can find more information here: http://docs.oracle.com/cd/E14571_01/web.1111/e10143/getstarted.htm#CHDECBEJ.

- **Multi-Version Cookies** Selecting this opens the Multi-Version Cookies page. The content of a response might depend upon a cookie value. You use this page to create cookie definitions for these responses and then associate caching rules with them, enabling Web Cache to cache multiple versions of the same object. We do not discuss multiversion cookies further in this book, but you can find more information here: http://docs.oracle.com/cd/E14571_01/web.1111/e10143/caching.htm#CEGJJCBH.
- **Ports Configuration** Selecting this opens the Ports Configuration page. The ports used by Oracle Web Cache can be set during and after installation. In addition, you can change the port numbers as needed. If you change the port or make other changes that affect the URL, such as changing the port type, IP address, port number, or enabling or disabling SSL, you will need to restart the server. We do not describe this process in the book or discuss port configurations further. For more information about configuring ports, please refer to http://docs.oracle.com/cd/E14571_01/web.1111/e10143/getstarted.htm#CHDCBGAD.

**NOTE**
*There is a great deal of information in the preceding section, and we appreciate that some of these settings do not directly affect Discoverer. However, we have provided this information as a direct response to requests that we have received from system administrators who wanted to know just what settings can and cannot affect Discoverer.*

## Maintaining the Web Cache Passwords

One of the tools you will use for administering Web Cache is the Web Cache Administration tool. Before you can use this tool, you need to ensure that you have set a Web Cache administration password.

To set the Web Cache administration password, do the following:

1. From the Web Cache drop-down, select Web Cache | Administration | Passwords.

Passwords

Apply Revert

You can change passwords for Web Cache invalidation and administration accounts. These accounts are used for sending invalidation, statistics monitoring requests, and administrative requests to Web Cache. If you change the password for the administrator account, then Web Cache configuration pages in Enterprise Manager will not be available. You must restart Web Cache. To restart, from the Web Cache menu, select Control > Restart. In a cache cluster, set the administrator password individually for each cache member. It is not possible to synchronize an administrator password change through the Cluster page.

Invalidation User Password

Specify the password for the invalidator user. This user is permitted to send cache invalidation requests.

User invalidator
New Password
Confirm Password

Administration User Password

Specify the password for the administrator user. This user is authorized to view statistics monitoring requests, as well as to log into Web Cache Manager and submit configuration and administrative requests.

User administrator
New Password •••••••••
Confirm Password •••••••••

2. Complete the Administration User Password section as follows:
   A. **New Password** Enter a password that complies with the following rules:
      - Must be between five and characters long
      - Must contain at least one number
      - Only alphanumeric characters and the underscore permitted
      - Must begin with a character
      - Cannot be an Oracle reserved word
   B. **Confirm Password** Reenter the password.
   C. **Apply** Click this to set the password.
3. When done, you will need to stop and restart Web Cache.

**NOTE**
*The Web Cache admin port can be determined from the Ports Usage page. To access this page, click the drop-down alongside Web Cache and from the list select Port Usage. The port type is admin.*

## Configuring Viewer with Web Cache

To configure Discoverer Viewer to use Web Cache, use the following workflow:

1. Launch OEM Application Server Control for the Discoverer mid-tier.
2. Click the Discoverer link.
3. Click the Discoverer Viewer link.
4. Click the Configure link.

5. Check the box Use Web Cache. By default it will be checked.
6. Click Apply. You may have to wait a couple of minutes for this to take effect.
7. Stop and restart the Discoverer server.

**NOTE**
*If SSO has been enabled, disable it. Please see the following section for more information.*

8. Click the Discoverer Viewer link on the top of the screen.
9. Click the Customization button.
10. In the Layout area of the page is the box Action Links. Oracle recommends you deselect as many of the Actions check boxes as possible. Now that you are using Web Cache, their usefulness may be limited. For example, deselecting the Rerun Query box is a good idea because if a user tries to rerun a query, all that will happen is that the page will reload from the cache. However, if you are using Discoverer with a combination of secure and insecure web pages, you cannot use Web Cache.
11. If you changed any of the action links, click the Apply button and then stop and restart the Discoverer server.
12. Launch Web Cache Administration from a browser by entering the following:

    ```
    http://myserver:WebCacheadminport/WebCacheadmin
    ```

**NOTE**
*The Web Cache admin port can be determined from the Ports Usage page. To access this page, click the drop-down alongside Web Cache and from the list select Port Usage. The port type is admin.*

13. Log in using the username **administrator** and the password you set during the install. If you have not yet set a password, please refer to the previous section "Maintaining the Web Cache Passwords."
14. Select Expiration Policy Definitions, located in the section Rules for Caching.

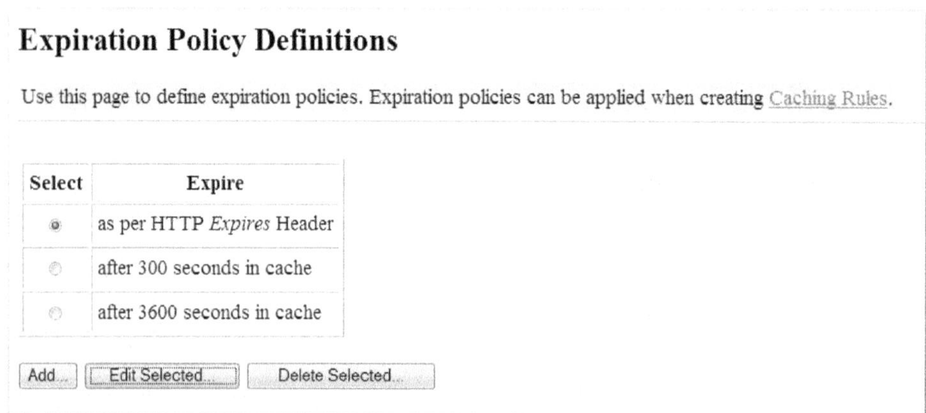

15. Check an existing policy or click Add to create your own expiration policy. After you have added your own policy, click Submit.

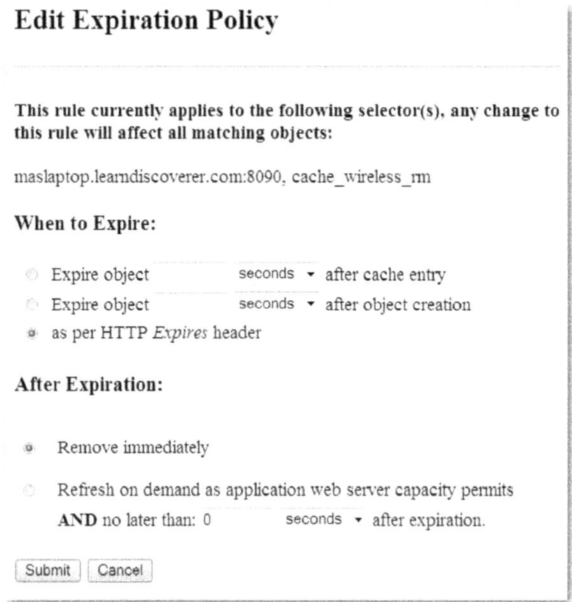

Edit Expiration Policy
This rule currently applies to the following selector(s), any change to this rule will affect all matching objects:
maslaptop.learndiscoverer.com:8090, cache_wireless_rm
When to Expire:
Expire object seconds after cache entry
Expire object seconds after object creation
as per HTTP Expires header
After Expiration:
Remove immediately
Refresh on demand as application web server capacity permits
AND no later than: 0 seconds after expiration.
Submit
Cancel


16. Select Caching, Personalization, and Compressions Rules. It is also located in the Rules for Caching section. Part of this page is shown here:

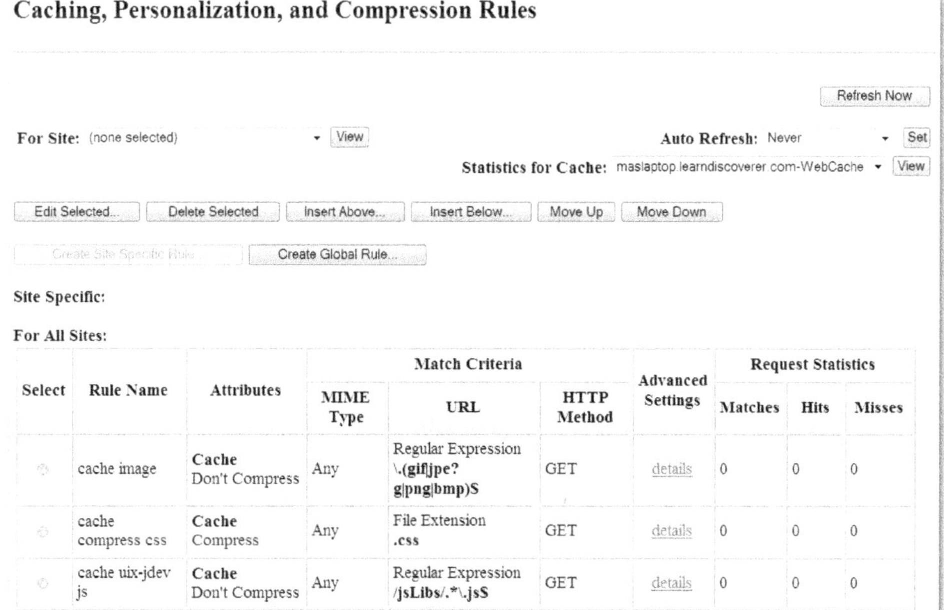


| Select | Rule Name | Attributes | Match Criteria | | | Advanced Settings | Request Statistics | | |
|---|---|---|---|---|---|---|---|---|---|
| | | | MIME Type | URL | HTTP Method | | Matches | Hits | Misses |
| | cache image | **Cache** Don't Compress | Any | Regular Expression **\.(gif\|jpe?g\|png\|bmp)$** | GET | details | 0 | 0 | 0 |
| | cache compress css | **Cache** Compress | Any | File Extension **.css** | GET | details | 0 | 0 | 0 |
| | cache uix-jdev js | **Cache** Don't Compress | Any | Regular Expression **/jsLibs/.*\.js$** | GET | details | 0 | 0 | 0 |

17. Complete the Caching, Personalization, and Compression Rules page as follows:
    - In the table called For All Sites, select any radio button, and then click the Insert Above button.

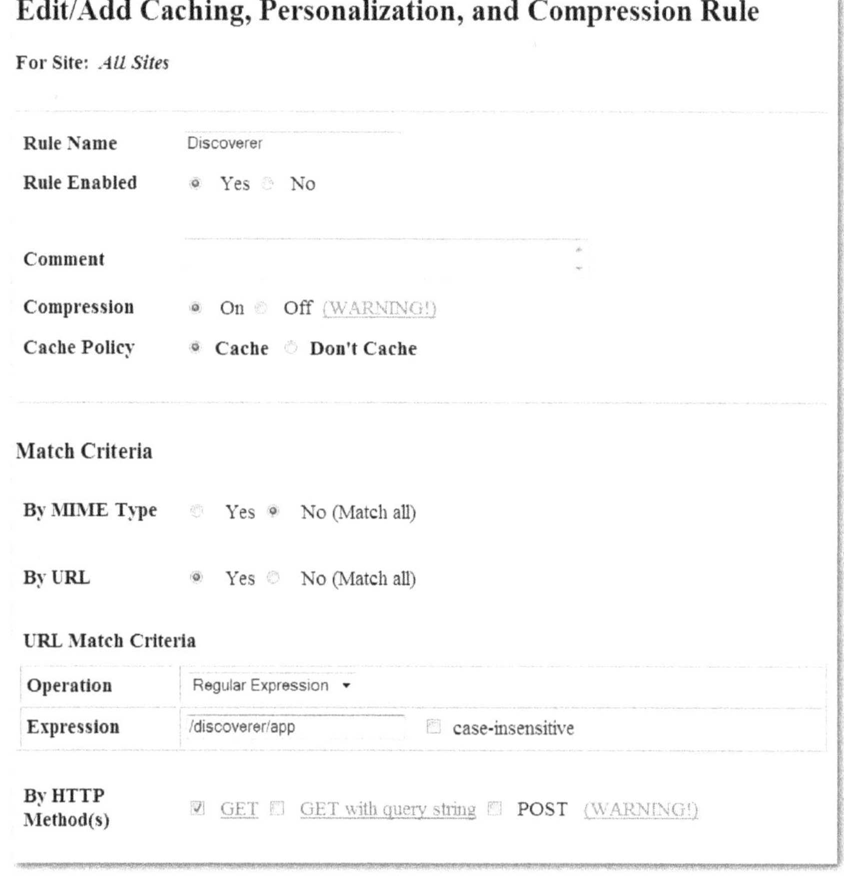


    - In the Rule Name field, enter **Discoverer**.
    - In the Compression field, check **On**.
    - In the Cache Policy field, check **Cache**.
    - In the URL Expression field, enter **/Discoverer/app**.
    - Select the expiration policy you just created.
    - Click Submit. You may need to scroll down to see this button.
18. Click Apply Changes.
19. Web Cache will display the following Cache Operation page:

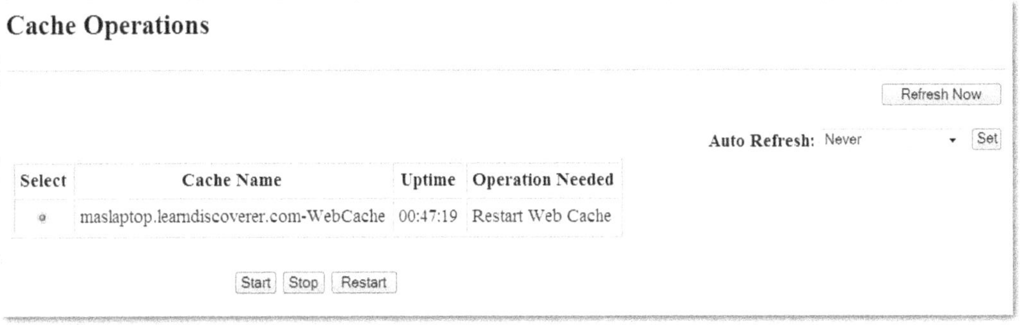

**Cache Operations**

Refresh Now

**Auto Refresh:** Never Set

| Select | Cache Name | Uptime | Operation Needed |
|---|---|---|---|
|  | maslaptop.learndiscoverer.com-WebCache | 00:47:19 | Restart Web Cache |

Start Stop Restart

**20.** Click Restart. At this point, Web Cache will maintain all Discoverer Viewer content for the amount of time you specified after the data enters the cache. If you have many users running the same report, you will see significant performance improvement with Web Cache enabled.

### Web Cache and Single Sign-On

It is vitally important that you not attempt to use Web Cache with sensitive data. This is because Web Cache has no mechanism to protect its content. When a request is made to Web Cache for a page that is cacheable (as defined by the caching rules) but has not yet been cached, then Web Cache makes a request on behalf of the user to the Oracle HTTP Server (Apache). OHS has the mod_osso add-on module, whose job it is to guarantee that a user must be authorized to view a page.

The first time such a request is received, the Single Sign-On connection screen will appear, and the user will need to provide their SSO username and password. But, because the page is cacheable, Web Cache will keep a copy of it in memory. Then, any subsequent request from any user will deliver the page to the user without authentication. This is why Oracle explains that you must cache only Discoverer Viewer content delivered through a Discoverer public connection. The long and the short of this is that you should not cache pages in Web Cache unless it is okay for everyone to see them.

## Configuring Discoverer for High Availability

Two fundamental advantages exist to having multiple Discoverer middle tiers. One is high availability; the other is load balancing. In our experience, most organizations that we have come across that have a need for high availability use one of the standard hardware load balancers.

If your organization does not have a hardware load balancer, you can configure Oracle Web Cache to perform the load balancing for you. The fundamental challenge to load-balancing Discoverer is that each user must stay connected to the same Discoverer server for their entire session. Fortunately, Oracle Web Cache has a feature called *session binding* that will guarantee this. If you are going to use a hardware load balancer, this is known as *sticky-bit* configuration.

### Load-Balancing Multiple Discoverer Servers Using Web Cache

Before you can begin to configure Web Cache for high availability, you must have created an Oracle farm using Fusion Middleware Control. Using Fusion Middleware Control, you need to add two or more BI Discoverer instances to the farm and ensure that Oracle Web Cache is running in at least one of the instances.

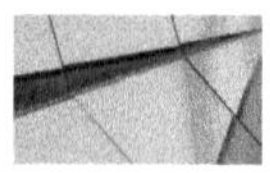

**NOTE**
*Before starting with the configuration, we strongly recommend you confirm that you can start Discoverer directly from the machine you selected for the preference server. Having confirmed that the server will start, make sure that it runs correctly. You will be surprised at the number of organizations that try to load-balance using a nonworking server.*

Having confirmed that Discoverer works correctly on the chosen machine, you are ready to configure the load balancing.

Configuring Oracle Web Cache for load balancing involves the following tasks:

- Choose which machine you want to specify as the proxy machine and start Oracle Web Cache on that machine. We will assume you have done this.
- Define the Oracle BI Discoverer middle-tier machines to use to provide load balancing (using the Origin Servers page in Oracle Web Cache).
- Define the load-balancing relationship between Oracle Web Cache and the Oracle BI Discoverer installations (using the Sites page in Oracle Web Cache).
- Enable the Default Session Binding option (using the Session Configuration page in Oracle Web Cache).
- Restart Oracle Web Cache (using the Cache Operations page in Oracle Web Cache).

To load-balance multiple Discoverer servers using Oracle Web Cache, use the following workflow:

1. Install each Discoverer mid-tier.
2. Use the portlist.ini file from the first mid-tier during the installation of the second and subsequent mid-tiers. This will guarantee that the port numbers are the same for all installations.
3. Configure the tnsnames.ora files to be the same on all of the Discoverer servers. You might find it easier to copy the file from one of the middle-tier machines and save it onto all of the others, making sure they all contain the same database names and aliases.

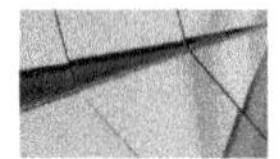

**NOTE**
*Remember to keep a note that you now have multiple tnsnames files. Should you bring on a new database server and change the hostname or port of an existing database, you will need to do this in each of the Discoverer instances.*

4. Determine which Discoverer server will be used as the centralized preference server and note the hostname. You can do this from a command prompt by typing **hostname** and pressing ENTER.
5. On the server that is now the preference server, locate and open the file $ORACLE_INTANCE/config/opmn/conf/opmn.xml and find an entry like this one:

```
<variable id = "PREFERENCE_PORT" value = "16002">
```

Take note of the number after value="#####". This is your preference server's listening port. In the example just listed, and illustrated next, this is 16002:

```
- <ias-component id="Discoverer_asinst_1" type="Discoverer">
  - <environment>
      <variable id="PREFERENCE_PORT" value="16002"/>
      <variable id="PREFERENCE_HOST" value="localhost"/>
      <variable id="DISCO_DIR" value="$ORACLE_HOME"/>
      <variable id="DC_LOG_DIR" value="$ORACLE_INSTANCE/diagnostics/logs/$COMPONENT_TYPE/$COMPONENT_NAME/"/>
      <variable id="LD_LIBRARY_PATH" value="$ORACLE_HOME/discoverer/lib$:$ORACLE_HOME/lib$:/usr/lib" append="true"/>
      <variable id="DC10_REG" value="$ORACLE_INSTANCE/config/PreferenceServer/$COMPONENT_NAME/"/>
      <variable id="FND_TOP" value="$ORACLE_INSTANCE/config/$COMPONENT_TYPE/$COMPONENT_NAME/"/>
      <variable id="FND_SECURE" value="$ORACLE_INSTANCE/config/$COMPONENT_TYPE/$COMPONENT_NAME/"/>
      <variable id="TNS_ADMIN" value="$ORACLE_INSTANCE/config/"/>
    </environment>
```

6. Close the opmn.xml file on the preference server.
7. Open and edit the opmn.xml file on each of the other machines and enter the hostname and port values you obtained in steps 4 and 5 into PREFERENCE_HOST and PREFERENCE_PORT, respectively.
8. Locate the PreferenceServer process type, and change its status to disabled. You are looking for this line:

```
<process-type id = "PreferenceServer" module-id="Disco_PreferenceServer"
working-dir="$DC_LOG_DIR status="enabled">
```

9. After you have changed enabled to disabled, all in lowercase, save opmn.xml.
10. Stop the Discoverer service on that machine and then restart it.
11. Launch Fusion Middleware Control on each Discoverer server. Here's an example:

```
http://ascserver.learndiscoverer.com:7001/em
```

12. From the home page, expand the web tier under the domain for your farm. In our case, this is called Farm_ClassicDomain.
13. Right-click Web Cache1 and from the pop-up select Administration; then select Origin Servers.
14. The following Origin Servers page will be displayed:

**Origin Servers** Apply Revert

Configure Web Cache with the application Web servers for internal sites and proxy servers for external sites outside a firewall to which it sends cache misses. These settings are required for load balancing, failover, and site-to-server mappings.

Create... | Edit... Delete...

| Host | Port | Protocol | Routing Enabled | Capacity | Proxy Server |
|---|---|---|---|---|---|
| maslaptop.learndiscoverer.com | 8888 | HTTP | ✓ | 100 | |
| maslaptop.learndiscoverer.com | 8890 | HTTPS | ✓ | 100 | |

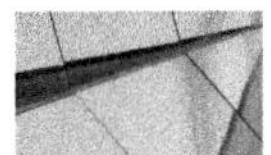

**NOTE**

*In our previous example, we have only one Discoverer server, and it is shown with its HTTP and HTTPS ports. When configuring for high availability, you will have two or more servers, one of which will be the server used for Web Cache.*

15. Assuming you have multiple servers, determine which server you will be using for Web Cache, highlight it, and then click the Edit button.

Edit Origin Server

OK Cancel

Specify the settings for the origin server. In order for Web Cache to forward requests to origin server, you must map a site to the origin server on the Sites page.

* Host maslaptop.learndiscoverer.coi

* Port 8888

Capacity 100

Protocol HTTP

Routing Enabled

Failover

If another cluster member repeatedly fails to respond, Web Cache will assume that the cache server process for that member has failed. Then it will periodically ping the cache server until it receives a successful response.

Failover Threshold 5

Ping URL /

Ping Frequency (seconds) 10

Proxy Server

Select proxy server for external sites protected by firewall. If the proxy server does not require a username and password leave those fields blank.

Proxy Server

Username

Password

16. Make a note or set the following properties:

    A. **Host** Do not enter protocol information such as http or https. Simply enter something like maslaptop.learndiscoverer.com.

    B. **Port** Enter the Oracle Web Cache listening port, usually 8888 for HTTP or 8890 for HTTPS.

    C. **Capacity** The recommended value is 100.

    D. **Protocol** From the drop-down list, decide whether you will be using HTTP or HTTPS.

    E. **Routing Enabled** Check this box if you want routing to be enabled. It will be enabled by default.

    F. **Failover Threshold** The recommended value is 5.

    G. **Ping URL** The recommended value is /.

    H. **Ping Frequency (seconds)** The recommended value is 10.

    I. **Proxy Server settings** If enabled or if required, click the Proxy Web server box and then enter the username and password of the proxy server administrator.

17. Right-click Web Cache1 again and from the Administration pop-up select Sites.

18. Edit an existing or create a new site.

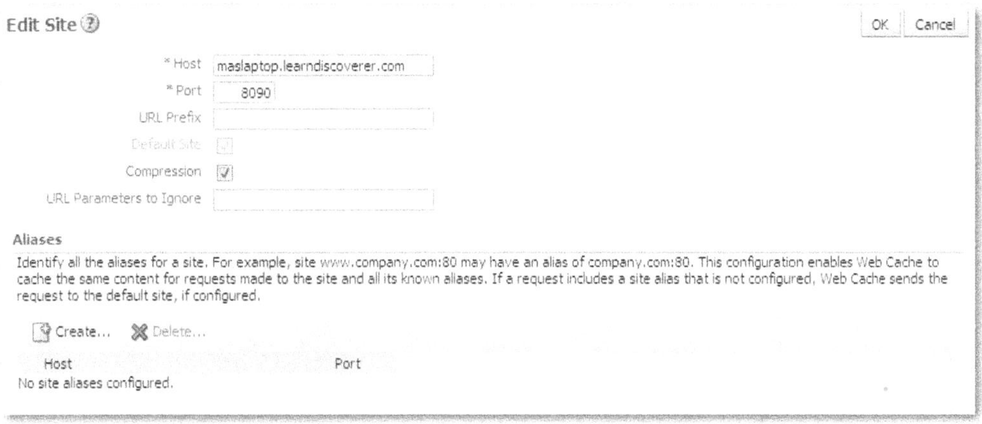
Edit Site
OK
Cancel
* Host maslaptop.learndiscoverer.com
* Port 8090
URL Prefix
Default Site
Compression
URL Parameters to Ignore
Aliases
Identify all the aliases for a site. For example, site www.company.com:80 may have an alias of company.com:80. This configuration enables Web Cache to cache the same content for requests made to the site and all its known aliases. If a request includes a site alias that is not configured, Web Cache sends the request to the default site, if configured.
Create...
Delete...
Host
Port
No site aliases configured.

19. Set the following properties:

   A. **Host** Do not enter protocol information such as http or https. Simply enter something like maslaptop.learndiscoverer.com. You use the same host that you noted in step 16.

   B. **Port** Enter the HTTP or HTTPS listening port. Right-click Web Cache1 and select Port Usage to determine your listening port.

**Port Usage**

| Port in Use | IP Address | Component | Protocol | Port Type |
|---|---|---|---|---|
| 8091 | maslaptop.learndisco... | webcache1 | http | admin |
| 8092 | maslaptop.learndisco... | webcache1 | http | stat |
| 8093 | maslaptop.learndisco... | webcache1 | http | invalidation |
| 8094 | maslaptop.learndisco... | webcache1 | https | listen |
| 8090 | maslaptop.learndisco... | webcache1 | http | listen |

   C. **URL Prefix** To distinguish sites that share the same hostname, enter the path prefix of the URLs. Ensure the prefix starts with /. Do not include the filename or embedded URL parameters in the prefix.

   D. **Default Site** Click this option to make this site the default site Oracle Web Cache uses to forward requests without host information.

   E. **Compression** Click to instruct Oracle Web Cache to serve cacheable and noncacheable content compressed to browsers. Not selecting this option means you are instructing Oracle Web Cache to not serve compressed content for this site.

   F. **Aliases** Specify all the possible aliases for the site to ensure requests are directed to the correct site. An alias specifies the host and port that browsers use to connect to the site.

   G. **OK** When done with aliases, click the OK button.

20. Repeat steps 18 and 19 as many times as needed to create the sites you need.
21. When done creating sites, click the Apply button.
22. On the Sites page, use the Move Up and Move Down buttons to order the site definitions.

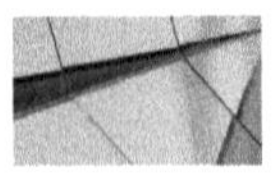

**NOTE**
*Oracle Web Cache resolves incoming requests to a site definition and then to the first matching site-to-origin server mapping. Make sure there is a space character between the existing text and the new text. Enter the hostname and port you obtained in steps 4 and 5. See http://docs.oracle.com/cd/E23943_01/web.1111/e10143/getstarted.htm#CHDJCHID for more information regarding how Oracle Web Cache uses the order of site definitions and site-to-server mappings to match requests.*

23. When done ordering the sites, click the Apply button.
24. Next you need to define a site-to-server mapping. You do this from the Sites page by working in the lower section entitled Site-to-Server Mapping.

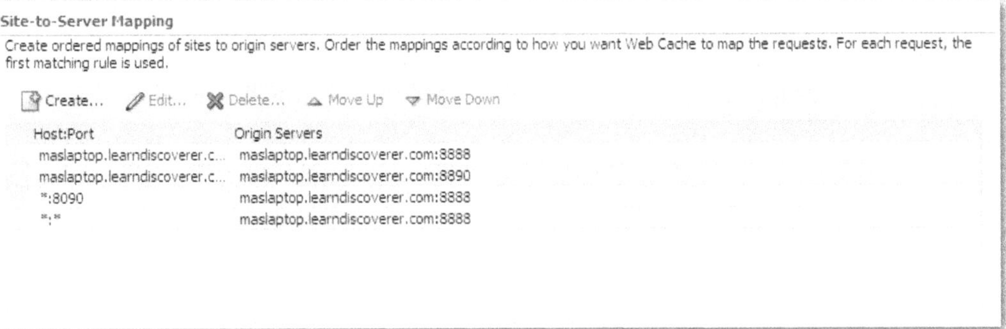


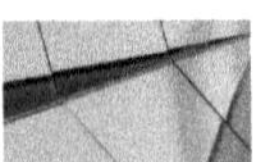

**NOTE**
*If Oracle HTTP Server was installed, the installation process creates a default site-to-server mapping based on the hostname and listening port of Oracle HTTP Server. You can see this in the previous illustration.*

25. Looking at our mappings, you can see that we have two entries for maslaptop.learndiscoverer.com; they both came from the HTTP Server install. One of these, port 8888, is our HTTP port, while the other, 8890, is our HTTPS port. Editing one of these entries, for example the one for 8888, opens the following box:

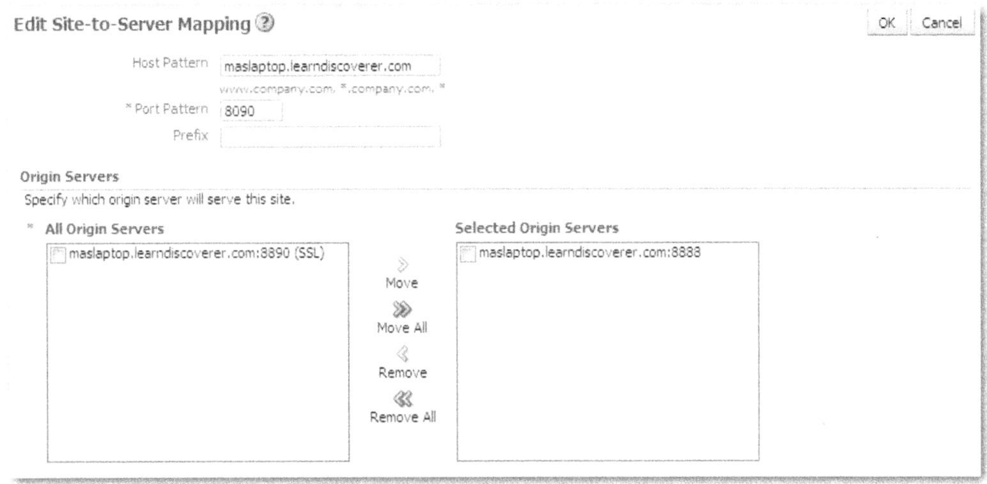


26. You should be able to see that port 8890 is being redirected to port 8090. If we edit the entry for 8888, we will see a similar redirect; however, this time the SSL port of 8890 is being redirected to 8094, which in our case is not yet configured as a site. Because 8888 is being redirected to 8090, this means that we can launch Discoverer Plus, Viewer, or Portal using either port 8090 or port 8888.

27. If you have created multiple origin server sites, you need to edit or create one site-to-server mapping and then map all of the origin servers to one selected origin server (either your HTTP or HTTPS port for the preferred server).

28. Set the following properties:

    A. **Host Pattern** Do not enter protocol information such as http or https. Simply enter something like maslaptop.learndiscoverer.com. You use the same host that you noted in step 16. This time, however, you can use the * character to indicate a wildcard; for example, we could enter *.learndiscoverer.com. Doing this will map all machines on the domain.

    B. **Port Pattern** Enter the HTTP or HTTPS listening port for the web site from which Web Cache is listening. Right-click Web Cache1 and select Port Usage to determine your listening port. Again, you can use the * character as a wildcard.

    C. **Prefix** To distinguish sites that share the same hostname, enter the path prefix of the URLs. Ensure the prefix starts with /. Do not include the filename or embedded URL parameters in the prefix.

D. **All Origin Servers** Select one or more origin servers. If you select more than one origin server, the servers must be of the same type and use the same protocol on their listening port. You cannot mix HTTP and HTTPS servers.

E. **Selected Origin Servers** This list contains the origin servers you have selected.

F. **OK** Click this to complete the page and return to the Sites page.

29. Repeat steps 27 and 28 as many times as necessary.
30. When done creating mappings, click the Apply button.
31. In the Mappings area of the Sites page, use the Move Up and Move Down buttons to order the mapping definitions.
32. When done, click the Apply button.
33. Next you need to define the resource limits. You do this from the Administration pop-up by selecting Resource Limits. The resource limits are very much similar to the Java Options settings in the Discoverer 10*g* server.

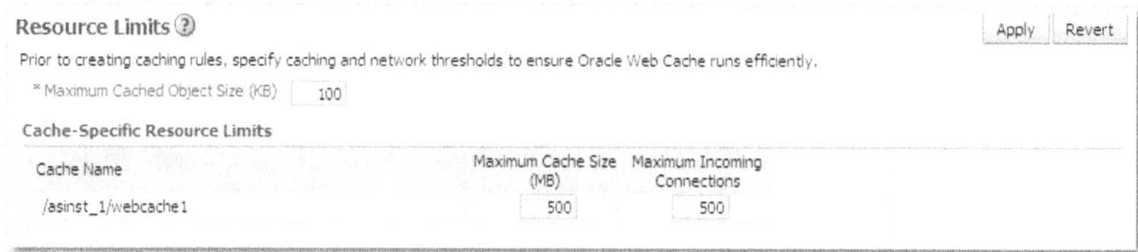


34. Set the resource limits as follows:

A. **Maximum Cached Object Size** Enter the maximum size in kilobytes (KB) as the maximum size of the objects to be stored in the cache. In our system, this defaulted to 100 KB. For more on this setting please refer to http://docs.oracle.com/cd/E23943_01/web.1111/e10143/getstarted.htm#i1041667.

B. **Maximum Cache Size** Enter the maximum size in megabytes (MB) for the total memory to be made available to Oracle Web Cache. In our system, this defaulted to 500MB. For more on this setting, please refer to http://docs.oracle.com/cd/E23943_01/web.1111/e10143/getstarted.htm#i1041388.

C. **Maximum Incoming Connections** Enter the maximum number of connections allowed to Oracle Web Cache. In our system, this defaulted to 500. For more on this setting, please refer to http://docs.oracle.com/cd/E23943_01/web.1111/e10143/getstarted.htm#i1041521.

35. When done, click the Apply button.
36. Next, you will need to define the network timeouts. To do this, you need to launch the Web Cache Administration tool. Before you can do this, you need to ensure that you have set a Web Cache administration password.

**NOTE**
*If you have not set the Web Cache administration password, please refer to the section "Maintaining the Web Cache Passwords" earlier in this chapter.*

**37.** Launch Web Cache Administration from a browser by entering the following:

```
http://myserver:WebCacheadminport/WebCacheadmin
```

In our system, this is as follows:

```
http://ascserver.learndiscoverer.com:8091/webcacheadmin
```

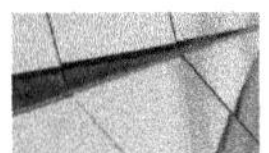

**NOTE**
*The Web Cache admin port can be determined from the Ports Usage page. To access this page, click the drop-down alongside Web Cache and from the list select Port Usage. The port type is admin.*

**38.** When prompted, enter your administrator username and password. Typically, the username is administrator. The Web Cache Admin home page will open.

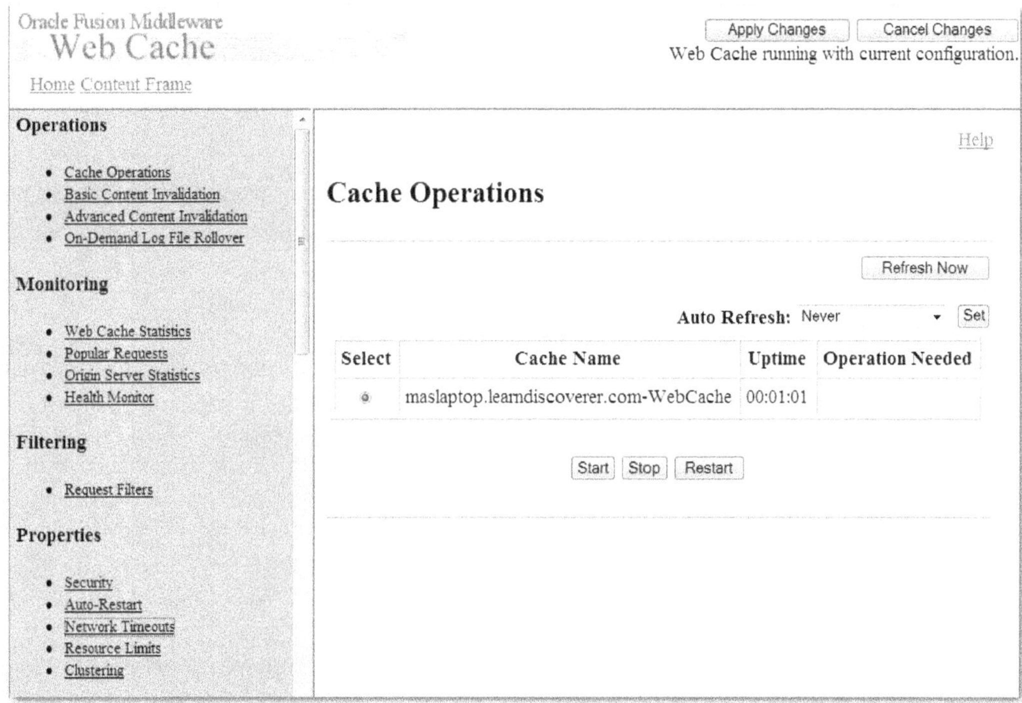

**39.** From the side navigator frame, in the Properties section click Network Timeouts to open the Network Timeouts page.

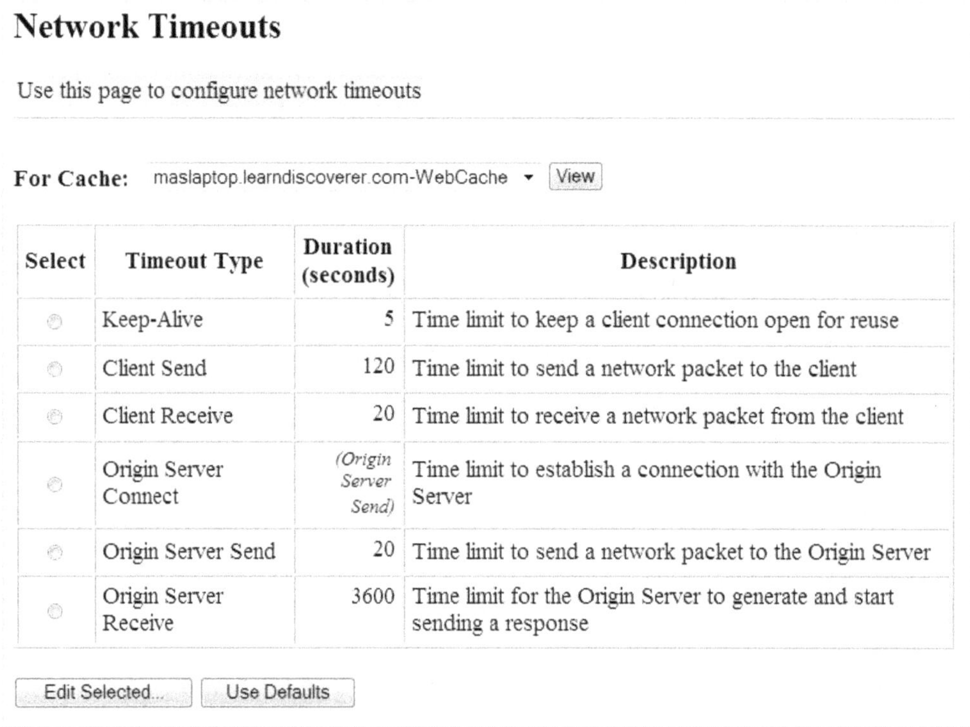

Network Timeouts
Use this page to configure network timeouts
For Cache: maslaptop.learndiscoverer.com-WebCache
View
Select
Timeout Type
Duration (seconds)
Description
Keep-Alive
5
Time limit to keep a client connection open for reuse
Client Send
120
Time limit to send a network packet to the client
Client Receive
20
Time limit to receive a network packet from the client
Origin Server Connect
(Origin Server Send)
Time limit to establish a connection with the Origin Server
Origin Server Send
20
Time limit to send a network packet to the Origin Server
Origin Server Receive
3600
Time limit for the Origin Server to generate and start sending a response
Edit Selected...
Use Defaults


**40.** Edit the properties on the Network Timeouts page as follows:

**A. For cache** Select the Web Cache instance you want to administer.

**B. Keep-Alive Timeout** The keep-alive timeout is the time limit for the client to process a request from Oracle Web Cache. After Oracle Web Cache sends a response to a client, the connection is left open for this number of seconds, which is typically enough time for the client to process the response from Oracle Web Cache. If the network between the client and Oracle Web Cache is slow, consider increasing the keep-alive timeout. The default is five seconds. If you set the value to 0, the connection to the client is *not* kept open.

**C. Client Send** This specifies the allowed time for Oracle Web Cache to finish a send operation to the client. The typical default is 120 seconds.

**D. Client Receive** This specifies the allowed time for Oracle Web Cache to wait for a receive operation to complete from the client. The typical default is 20 seconds.

E. **Origin Server Connect** This specifies the time allowed for Oracle Web Cache to complete connection establishment to an origin server. If an origin server has multiple IP addresses (for example, IPv4 and IPv6) that will be retried, the timeout refers to connecting to one origin server IP address. If the origin server cannot generate a response within that time, Oracle Web Cache drops the connection and sends a network error page to the client. If your application requires a shorter period, adjust the timeout. The typical default is the same as Origin Server Send.

F. **Origin Server Send** This specifies the time allowed for the Oracle Web Cache to finish a send operation to the origin server. The typical default is 20 seconds.

G. **Origin Server Receive** This specifies the time allowed for the origin server to generate and start sending a response to Oracle Web Cache. The typical default is 3600 seconds (10 minutes).

H. **Use for all caches in the cluster** If this option is available, you have multiple Web Cache instances in the cluster. Checking this will apply the duration to all clusters. To apply to only the current cluster, make sure this box is deselected.

I. **Edit Selected** To use this button, click the radio button alongside the timeout you want to edit and then click this button. An edit dialog box will display. The box shown here is the box for the Keep-Alive setting. You either enter your own timeout, in seconds, or click the Use default box. When done, you click either the Submit or Cancel button.

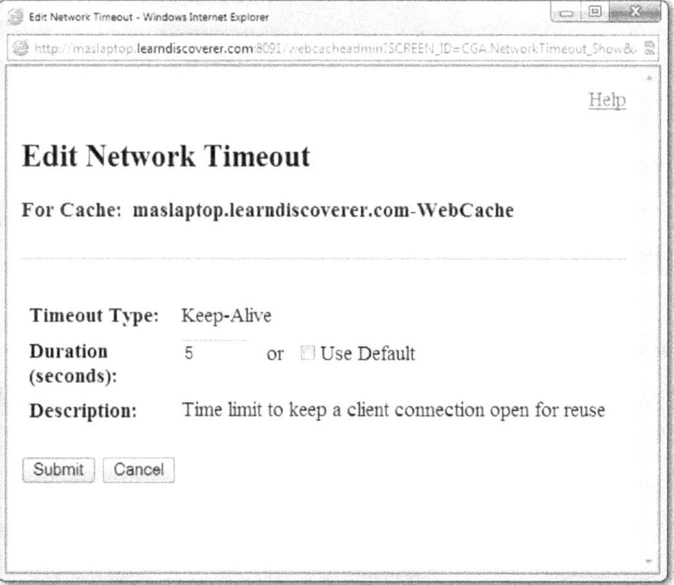


J. **Use Defaults** To revert to the system defaults, click this button.

K. When done, if you made changes to any of the settings, click either the Apply Changes or Cancel Changes button. You can find these buttons at the top right of the page. If you did not make any changes, you can close the Web Cache Admin session.

**41.** Optionally, you can choose to configure error pages. For situations in which there is a network communication error, site busy error, or ESI <esi:include> error, applications serve error pages. Rather than burden the origin server with this task, you can configure these pages to be served from Oracle Web Cache. To configure Oracle Web Cache to serve error pages for a site, do the following:

**A.** Create error pages and place them in the following locations:

```
UNIX: ORACLE_INSTANCE/instance_name/config/WebCache/WebCache_name/files
Windows: ORACLE_INSTANCE\instance_name\config\WebCache\WebCache_name\files
```

The defaults settings are as follows:

- For network errors, the default setting is set to network_error.html. This error page is served when there is a network problem while connecting, sending, or receiving a response from an origin server for a cache-miss request.
- For site busy errors, the default setting is set to busy_error.html. This page is served when origin server capacity is reached.
- For ESI default fragments, the default setting is set to esi_fragment_error.txt. This page is served when Oracle Web Cache cannot fetch the source specified in an <esi:include> tag and the alt attribute, onerror attribute, or try|attempt|except block are either not present or fail.

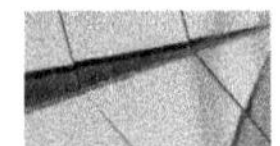

**NOTE**
*For a production environment, Oracle recommends you modify the defaults or create entirely new error pages to be consistent with other error pages for your site.*

**B.** From Oracle Web Cache Manager, from the side navigator frame, in the Origin Servers, Sites, and Load Balancing section, click Error Pages to open the Error Pages page.

## Error Pages

Use this page to configure the error pages that Web Cache will serve to Web browsers when different errors occur.

**Note:** For a production environment, Oracle Corporation advises that you modify the defaults or create entirely new error pages to be consistent with other error pages for the site.

| Select | Site Name | Network Error | Site Busy Error | ESI Default Fragment |
|---|---|---|---|---|
| | maslaptop.learndiscoverer.com:8090 | *(default page)* | *(default page)* | *(default page)* |
| | ***Default Pages*** | /network_error.html | /busy_error.html | /esi_fragment_error.txt |

Edit Selected...

C. Select either Default Pages or a site name in the table and then click the Edit button.

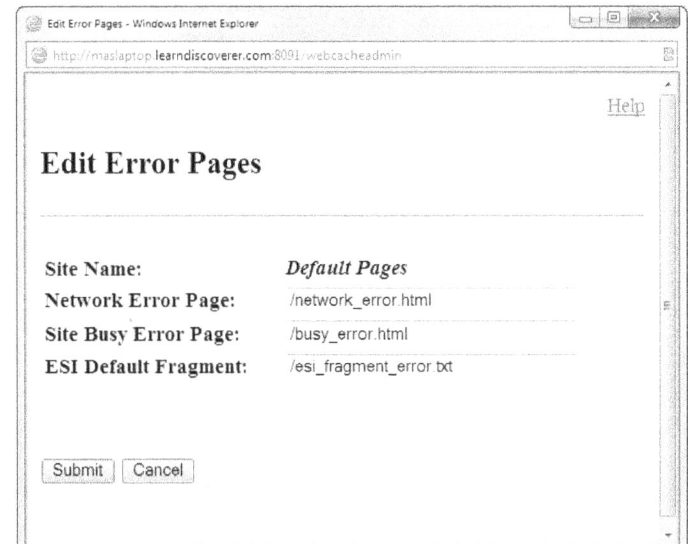


D. Complete the Edit Error Pages page as follows:

  i. **Network Error Page** Enter the filename of the error page delivered for network communication problems between Oracle Web Cache and the web site. The Oracle default entry is /network_error.html.

  ii. **Site Busy Error Page** Enter the filename of the error page delivered when a web site is saturated with requests. The Oracle default entry is /busy_error.html.

  iii. **ESI Default Fragment** Enter the filename of the page delivered when Oracle Web Cache cannot retrieve an HTML fragment for an <esi:include> tag. If you are not using <esi:include> tags for partial page caching or you want to use only ESI language elements for exceptions, do not enter a value. The Oracle default entry is /esi_fragment_error.txt.

  iv. When done with the dialog box, click either the Submit or Cancel button.

  v. When done, if you made changes to any of the settings, click either the Apply Changes or Cancel Changes button. These buttons can be found at the top right of the page. If you did not make any changes, you can close the Web Cache Admin session.

42. From the Cache Operations page, click Restart to stop and restart Web Cache.

# Single Sign-On (SSO)

SSO provides a great deal of flexibility and allows for easier integration with Discoverer and Oracle Portal. You must decide whether using SSO with Discoverer is cost-effective. Deciding on whether your organization is interested in investing in an Identity Management server is another discussion. If you already have implemented Oracle Identity Manager and Oracle Single Sign-On for other Oracle products, such as Oracle Portal, then this discussion is for you.

**NOTE**
*For Discoverer 11g Oracle recommends using Oracle Access Manager for enabling SSO. We discuss this topic later in the section.*

SSO is a component of Oracle Fusion Middleware that enables users to access multiple web applications (for example, Discoverer Plus, Discoverer Viewer, and Oracle Portal) using a single username and password that is entered only once.

When you install Oracle, the Oracle Single Sign-On service is installed automatically. However, it is not enabled for Discoverer by default. In this section we will show you how to do so. Discoverer connections work in both SSO mode and non-SSO mode. If you are using Discoverer in SSO mode and a user launches Discoverer without yet having authenticated to the SSO server, the user will be challenged to provide an SSO username and password.

After the user provides their name and password, SSO checks with OID to see whether this is a valid user. If so, SSO places a temporary cookie in the user's browser indicating the user has been authenticated. Then, the user is redirected to Oracle HTTP Server (OHS) that the original request was made to. Upon returning, SSO identifies that Discoverer is still protected, but this time because the cookie exists, the SSO component, mod_osso, allows the user to access Discoverer.

Once authenticated, providing the user stays within the same browser session, the user can switch to other SSO-enabled applications without being prompted for the username and password over and over again.

Here are two more advantages of using single sign-on:

- Users can have their own set of connections that will follow them wherever they log in. This can be a great help if your company frequently clears out browser cookies because clearing cookies will cause some connection information to be lost.
- If you are using a virtual private database (VPD) for data security, you can pass user contexts using SSO.

**NOTE**
*When enabled for Discoverer, SSO is enabled for both Discoverer Plus and Discoverer Viewer. You cannot enable it for only one of them.*

## Configuring Single Sign-On

If you are using 10*g*, you will need to configure SSO.

To configure SSO for 10*g*, use the following workflow:

1. Launch a web browser and enter the URL to manage SSO. Here's an example:
   `http://infraserver.learndiscoverer.com:7777/orasso`
2. Log in using **orcladmin** and the ias_admin password you provided during installation.
3. You have the following three choices:
   - **Edit SSO Server Configuration** Set the SSO session duration. This is how long a user may stay logged into SSO. Also, verify the IP addresses for requests made in the SSO server. This security check compares the IP address of the browser to the IP address provided in the HTTP request. Do not check this if you are using Oracle Portal.

- **Administer Partner Applications** A partner application is any application that delegates authentication to SSO. The implication here is that the web application does not have its own login mechanism and will solely depend upon using SSO to protect its content. If you configure SSO using mod_osso configuration, you have configured a partner application.
- **Administer External Applications** An external application is one where SSO maintains the additional username and password for the other application, and then upon navigation to the other application, SSO submits the username and password. It is very simple to set up an external application. All you need to provide is the URL to submit the username and password to and the field names for the username and password. You can easily find this information by exploring the HTML source of the application's login page.

# Enabling Discoverer with SSO

As explained earlier, it is actually the mod_osso module in OHS that is configured to protect an application like Discoverer. The steps to enable SSO for Discoverer 10*g* and Discoverer 11*g* are different, so we will explain them separately. Oracle recommends you use Oracle Access Manager with Discoverer 11*g* rather than the older method. We will show you both.

## Enabling Discoverer 10*g* with SSO

To enable SSO for Discoverer10*g*, use the following workflow:

1. Navigate to the mod_osso.conf file located here:

   ```
   $ORACLE_HOME/Apache/Apache/conf
   ```

2. Make a backup copy of mod_osso.conf.
3. Edit mod_osso.conf and locate these lines:

   ```
   #
   # Insert Protected Resources:
   #
   ```

4. Insert the following lines:

   ```
   <Location /Discoverer/plus*>
    require valid-user
    AuthType Basic
   </Location>
   <Location /Discoverer/viewer>
    Header unset Pragma
    OssoSendCacheHeaders off
    require valid-user
    AuthType Basic
   </Location>
   ```

   You will notice that the Discoverer Viewer parameters are different from Discover Plus. This is because of a Microsoft Internet Explorer problem that occurs when exporting data from Viewer.

**NOTE**
*In the changes just outlined, an asterisk (*) must follow the word* plus*, as in /discoverer/plus*.*

5. Save mod_osso.conf.
6. In a command shell, navigate to this folder:

```
$ORACLE_HOME/dcm/bin
```

7. Run this command: **dcmctl updateconfig**.

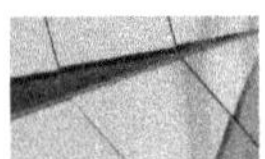

**NOTE**
*This step can take several minutes, so please be patient while it runs and make sure you do nothing else at this time. Well, maybe get a coffee!*

8. When the dcm step has finished, start a browser and launch the Discoverer OEM.
9. Connect to the Discoverer mid-tier.
10. Restart Oracle HTTP Server.
11. After SSO has been enabled, you should test it using the ias_admin username.
12. When you are happy that SSO is working, you can use any SSO login to create SSO users using OIDDAS.

## Enabling Discoverer 11*g* with SSO: Older Method

To enable SSO for Discoverer 11*g*, use the following workflow:

1. Navigate to the mod_osso.conf file located here:

```
$ORACLE_HOME/config/OHS/ohs1/moduleconf
```

**NOTE**
*If no mod_osso.conf exists in the moduleconf folder, there is an example located here:*

```
$ORACLE_HOME/config/OHS/ohs1/backup/disabled
```

2. Make a backup copy of mod_osso.conf.
3. Edit mod_osso.conf and locate these lines:

```
<IfModule osso_module>
    OssoIpCheck off
    OssoIdleTimeout off
```

4. Insert the following lines after the OssoIdleTimeout line:

```
<Location /Discoverer/plus>
 require valid-user
 AuthType Osso
</Location>
<Location /Discoverer/viewer>
 require valid-user
 AuthType Osso
</Location>
</Location>
```

```
<Location /discoverer/app>
require valid-user
AuthType Osso
</Location>
```

5. Save the mod_osso.conf file
6. Using OEM, stop and restart the OHS component.

**NOTE**
*Rather than manually editing the mod_osso.conf file from the command line, you may find it easier to edit it directly from within OEM. You do this selecting mod_osso.conf from the list of files on the Advanced Server Configuration screen of the Oracle HTTP Server. You can find more information about this in the section "HTTP Server Administration Drop-Down Options."*

## Enabling Discoverer 11*g* Using Oracle Access Manager

Oracle Access Manager (OAM) is a component in Oracle Fusion Middleware that provides an SSO solution to access multiple web applications using a single username and password.

OAM is now the recommended enterprise-wide SSO solution. This section describes how to use OAM with Discoverer 11*g*. You may find the following document describing Oracle Access Manager to be very useful:

http://docs.oracle.com/cd/E28280_01/bi.1111/b40107/security2.htm#BIDCG848

To enable SSO for Discoverer 11*g* using OAM, use the following workflow:

1. Install OAM as described in the chapter called "Installing Oracle Identity Management in the Oracle Fusion Middleware Installation Guide for Oracle Identity Management" here: http://docs.oracle.com/cd/E28280_01/install.1111/e12002/instps2.htm#BGBCHIJI.
2. Using the following document, configure OAM and ensure that the Oracle Access Manager server is running after the deployment: http://docs.oracle.com/cd/E28280_01/doc.1111/e36891/oam.htm#INDGW1230.
3. Register the OSSO agent (mod_osso) with OAM 11*g* using the steps in this document: http://docs.oracle.com/cd/E23943_01/doc.1111/e15478/agents.htm#AIAAG234.
4. Create a new folder called osso in this location:

   ```
   $ORACLE_HOME/config/OHS/ohs1
   ```

5. Locate the osso.conf file that was created during the registration process in step 3 and copy it into the folder you created in the previous step.
6. Locate the mod_osso.conf file here:

   ```
   ORACLE_HOME/config/OHS/ohs1/backup/disabled
   ```

7. Copy the file into this location:

   ```
   $ORACLE_HOME/config/OHS/ohs1/moduleconf
   ```

8. Edit the mod_osso.conf file and delete all current content.

9. Insert the following lines:

```
LoadModule osso_module "${ORACLE_HOME}/ohs/modules/mod_osso.so"
<IfModule osso_module>
  OssoIpCheck off
  OssoIdleTimeout off
OssoHttpOnly off
OssoSecureCookies off
OssoConfigFile MW_Home1/asinst_1/config/OHS/ohs1/osso/osso.conf
<Location /discoverer/plus>
  require valid-user
  AuthType Osso
</Location>
<Location /discoverer/viewer>
  require valid-user
  AuthType Osso
</Location>
<Location /discoverer/app>
  require valid-user
  AuthType Osso
</Location>
</IfModule>
```

10. Save mod_osso.conf.
11. Restart Oracle HTTP Server.
12. Restart Oracle Access Manager.
13. Make sure both of the Discoverer URLs can be accessed through the OAM authentication screen.

# Summary

We have traveled through the architecture of the Oracle Application Server 11*g* WebLogic environment. We started by describing the Discoverer installation types and listed the components of a Discoverer installation. Next, we discussed the various ways to start the WebLogic server, WebLogic Node Manager, and Discoverer Service. Following this was a discussion of OPMN. After discussing OPMN, we discussed Oracle Fusion Middleware Control and showed you how to log in. Oracle HTTP Server (OHS) came next, and after introducing you to the key Apache directives and key OHS modules, we then showed you how to configure OHS. Next, we discussed managing Web Cache, showed you how to use it with Discoverer Viewer, and showed you how to configure Web Cache to load-balance multiple Discoverer servers. Finally, we introduced you to the topic of single sign-on and showed you how to enable it for both Discoverer 10*g* and 11*g*, concluding with a description of how to configure Oracle Access Manager to control SSO for Discoverer 11*g*.

The only way to really become familiar with configuring middleware is to explore and test the various options. Don't worry, though, because you can always roll back—that is, if you are in the habit of taking backups!

# CHAPTER 20

# Advanced Discoverer Administration

In the previous chapter we focused on WebLogic and how to administer Oracle HTTP Server and Oracle Web Cache. This chapter is intended for technical team members who are responsible for managing and configuring the Oracle Discoverer installation and, in particular, for administrators who need to control the Discoverer environment. We will show you how to use Oracle Fusion Middleware Control to manage the Discoverer settings as well as the Discoverer preferences that can be set for the middle tier. Carefully applying the Discoverer preferences will allow you to configure Discoverer for a corporate look and feel. The Discoverer Plus timeout is controlled from the middle-tier preferences. However, these do not apply to Discoverer Viewer, so we will show you how to use the WebLogic Administration Console to change the timeout values for Discoverer Viewer. Following this, we will discuss how you can optimize Discoverer for optimal performance. Next, we will explain how to use EUL parameters in a browser and give you some practical examples of their use. The chapter will conclude with a brief discussion of migrating Discoverer to OBIEE using the Discoverer Metadata Migration Assistant (DOMA).

# Oracle Fusion Middleware Control

Oracle Fusion Middleware is a collection of standards-based software products, from Java EE and developer tools, to integration services, identity management, business intelligence, and collaboration. Oracle Fusion Middleware offers complete support for development, deployment, and management.

To manage and control Oracle Fusion Middleware, you use Oracle Fusion Middleware Control, otherwise known as Oracle Enterprise Manager (OEM). We recommend you familiarize yourself with all the facets of Fusion Middleware Control because you will need it frequently.

## Oracle Fusion Middleware Components

Oracle Fusion Middleware provides a large number of components. When discussing Discoverer, the components we are interested in are as follows:

- **Oracle WebLogic Server**
- **Oracle HTTP Server** Explained in detail in Chapter19
- **Oracle Web Cache** Explained in detail in Chapter19
- **Oracle Internet Directory**
- **Oracle Portal**
- **Oracle Discoverer** Explained in detail in this chapter

In this section we will describe how to log in to Fusion Middleware Control. Later in the chapter we will discuss managing using Middleware Control to manage Discoverer.

**NOTE**
*Please refer to Chapter 19 for information about using Fusion Middleware Control to manage Oracle HTTP Server and Oracle Web Cache.*

## Connecting to Fusion Middleware Control

Even though we covered this in Chapter 19, because this chapter is aimed at a different administrator, we will also show you how to connect and log in to Oracle Middleware Control in this chapter.

To connect and log in to Oracle Middleware Control, use the following workflow:

1. From a browser, enter **http://fully_qualified_domain_name:7001/em**. The Fusion Middleware Control login page will be displayed.

**NOTE**
*The port depends upon your installation and may not be 7001. It could be anywhere in the range 7001–9000.*

2. In Username, enter the username you used when you installed the system. Most of the time it will be **Weblogic**.
3. In Password, enter the WebLogic password.

**NOTE**
*The WebLogic password is the password you provided during the install of the server. You should not lose this password. Equally, you should not lightly give it away.*

4. The Fusion Middleware Control and farm home page shown in Figure 20-1 will be displayed. On this page you will see all of the clusters and instances in your farm.
5. From the Middleware Control home page, select the component you want to administer.

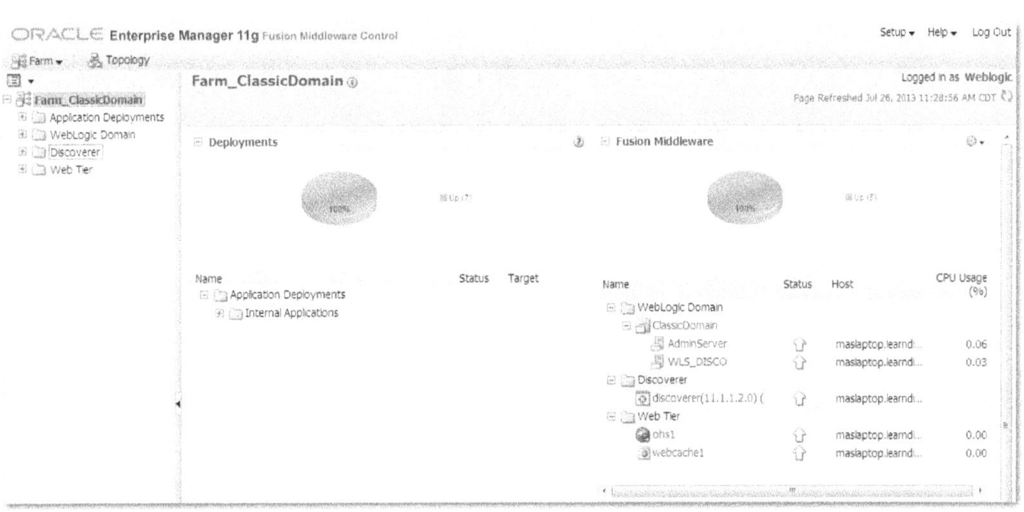


**FIGURE 20-1.** *Middleware Control home page*

# Using Fusion Middleware Control to Manage Discoverer

In Chapter 19 we showed you how to configure Oracle HTTP Server (OHS) and Oracle Web Cache. In this section we will show you how to use Middleware Control to manage and control Discoverer.

To get to the Discoverer home page, use the following workflow:

1. From the Middleware Control home page shown in Figure 20-1, navigate to the Farm_ClassicDomain area at the top-left side of the page where you will see a listing of the component headings.

2. Expand the Discoverer link. The listing will expand to show the components available in this area.
3. Click the discoverer link. The Discoverer home page shown in Figure 20-2 will open.
4. On the Discoverer home page you will see the following areas:
   - **The Discoverer status** A green arrow indicates that Discoverer is up and running.
   - **A Discoverer drop-down link (very top of the screen)** We will discuss this in more detail later in the chapter.

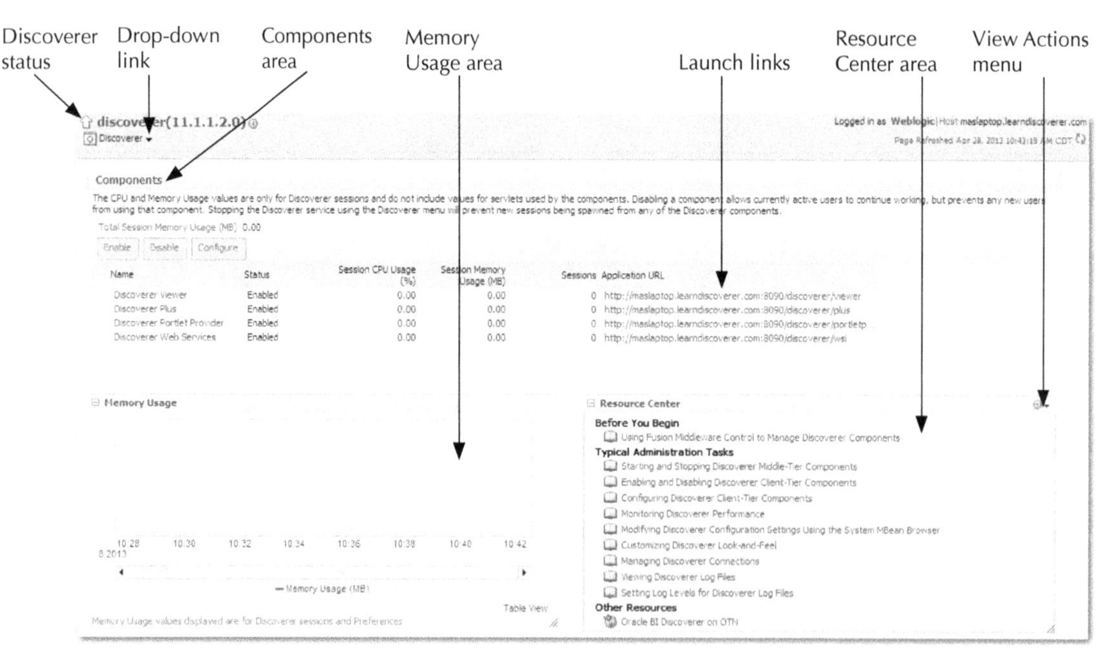


**FIGURE 20-2.** *Middleware Control Discoverer home page*

- **A Components area** This displays the four main components with page and launch links to the following:
  - i. **Discoverer Viewer** Clicking the left link opens the Discoverer Viewer home page shown in Figure 20-3. The right link launches the Discoverer Viewer login page.
  - ii. **Discoverer Plus** Clicking the left link opens the Discoverer Plus home page shown later in the chapter in Figure 20-6. The right link launches the Discoverer Plus login page.
  - iii. **Discoverer Portlet Provider** Clicking the left link opens the Discoverer Portlet Provider home page shown later in the chapter in Figure 20-7. The right link displays the Portlet Provider test page shown here:

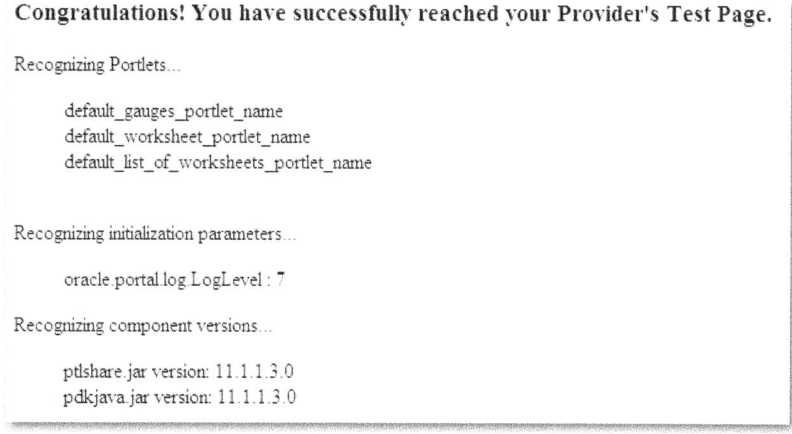


  - iv. **Discoverer Web Services** Clicking the left link opens the Discoverer Web Services home page shown later in the chapter in Figure 20-10. The right link is the link that launches the Web Services page. The first time you click this link, you will be informed that a username and password are required for this task. To log in, you should use WebLogic for the username and the same password you used to log in to Fusion Middleware Control; then click the Log In button.

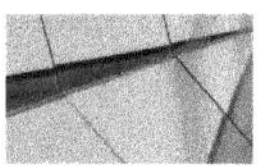

**NOTE**

*You will be required to log in only once per browser session. Subsequent clicks on the right Web Services link while in the same session will directly open the Web Services page.*

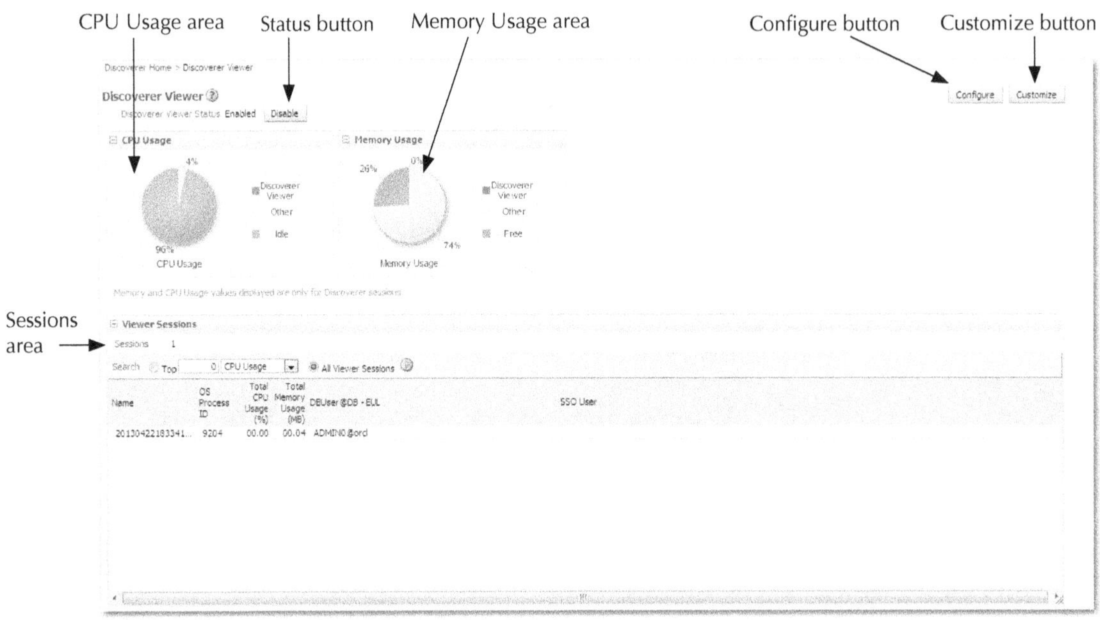


**FIGURE 20-3.** *Discoverer Viewer home page*

After you have logged in or if you click the right link again while in the same session, the following Web Services page will open.

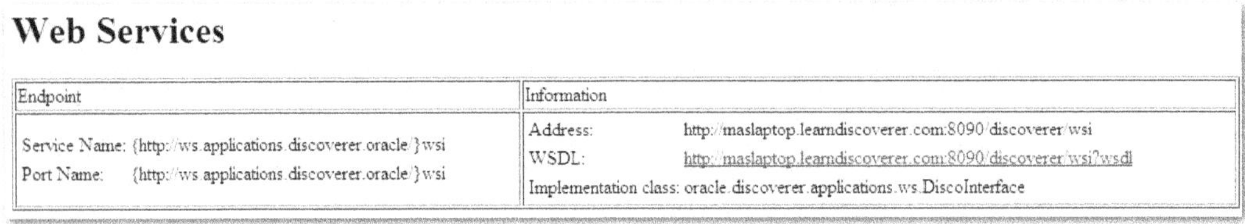


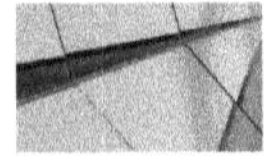

**NOTE**
*For each component you will see the status, the CPU usage, the memory usage, and a URL. If you click the link for one of the components, the system will try to launch that component. This is a great way to test whether the components are in use.*

- **A Memory Usage area** This displays a graph showing how much memory is being consumed.
- **A Resource Center** This area has a set of links going to various Oracle documents for helping with administering Discoverer.

Before we move away from this page and look in detail at how to configure Discoverer, we will point out some of the features of this page.

First, as we have mentioned previously in the book, the layout of all the pages in Fusion Middleware Control is configurable. You should therefore be able to move the areas of the page around by clicking the View Actions menu button located at the top right of every area. However, on the Discoverer home page, only the Resource Center area has this button. Because only the Resource Center area has this capability, clicking the link to move the page up or down does not in fact do anything. The button is obviously there in case there are other moveable areas above or below.

Second, we encourage you to make great use of the Resource Center because it contains links to a vast library of online help. For example, clicking the link Using Fusion Middleware Control to Manage Discoverer Components takes you to the Managing and Configuring section (Chapter 4) of the Middleware Configuration Guide for Oracle Business Intelligence Discoverer. You will find this guide online at http://docs.oracle.com/cd/E14571_01/bi.1111/b40107/maint.htm.

In the following sections, we will cover each of the four Discoverer components in detail.

## Components Area: Discoverer Viewer Link

Clicking the Discoverer Viewer link in the Components area opens the Discoverer Viewer home page shown in Figure 20-3. Some of the greatest enhancements, starting with the Discoverer 10*g* Release 2 edition and continuing with 11*g*, relate to the configuration of Discoverer Viewer. If you take time and care when setting up these configurations, you can configure Discoverer Viewer so that it looks and feels like part of your corporate web site.

On the Discoverer Viewer home page you will see the following areas:

- **Page breadcrumbs** These appear horizontally across the top of the web page, below the header. The breadcrumbs provide links back to each previous page the user navigated through to get to the current page.
- **Viewer status** This button is labeled Disable when Viewer is currently enabled and labeled Enable when Viewer is currently disabled. You might want to disable Discoverer Viewer for the following reasons:
  - To prevent new users from connecting to Discoverer Viewer
  - To restrict access to Discoverer Viewer

  When you disable Viewer, the following happens:
  - All existing Discoverer Viewer sessions continue to run until users end their sessions.
  - A message is displayed informing the Discoverer end user that Viewer is disabled.
  - Requests for new user sessions are not accepted. Users whose sessions time out because of inactivity cannot continue to use Viewer. The timeout for Viewer is determined by using the servlet.
  - When a user attempts to access the Discoverer Viewer URL, Discoverer displays an error message explaining that the service is unavailable.

- **Configure** Clicking this button launches the Discoverer Viewer Configuration page shown in Figure 20-4. This page is described in detail in the "Configuring Discoverer Viewer" section.
- **Customize** Clicking this button launches the Discoverer Viewer Customization page shown in Figure 20-5. This page is described in detail in the "Customizing Discoverer Viewer" section.
- **CPU Usage** This area displays a graph showing the amount of CPU currently being consumed for all Discoverer Viewer sessions.
- **Memory Usage** This area displays a graph showing the amount of memory currently being consumed for all Discoverer Viewer sessions.
- **Viewer Sessions** This area allows you to view the various Discoverer sessions that are currently in use. The Viewer Sessions area is explained as follows:
  - **Sessions** This displays the total number of current Viewer sessions.
  - **Top** Select this radio button to specify that you want to see information about the top *N* Viewer sessions. Having selected this button, you use the left box to enter a value for the number of sessions you want to view and then use the drop-down box alongside to specify whether you want to see information about CPU usage or memory usage.

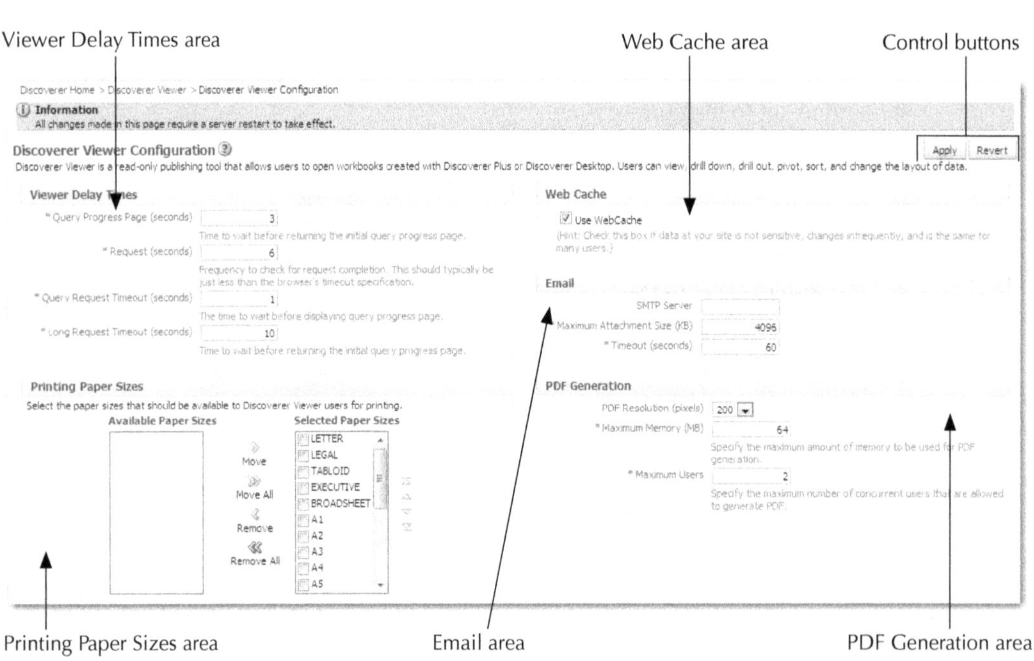


**FIGURE 20-4.** *Discoverer Viewer Configuration page*

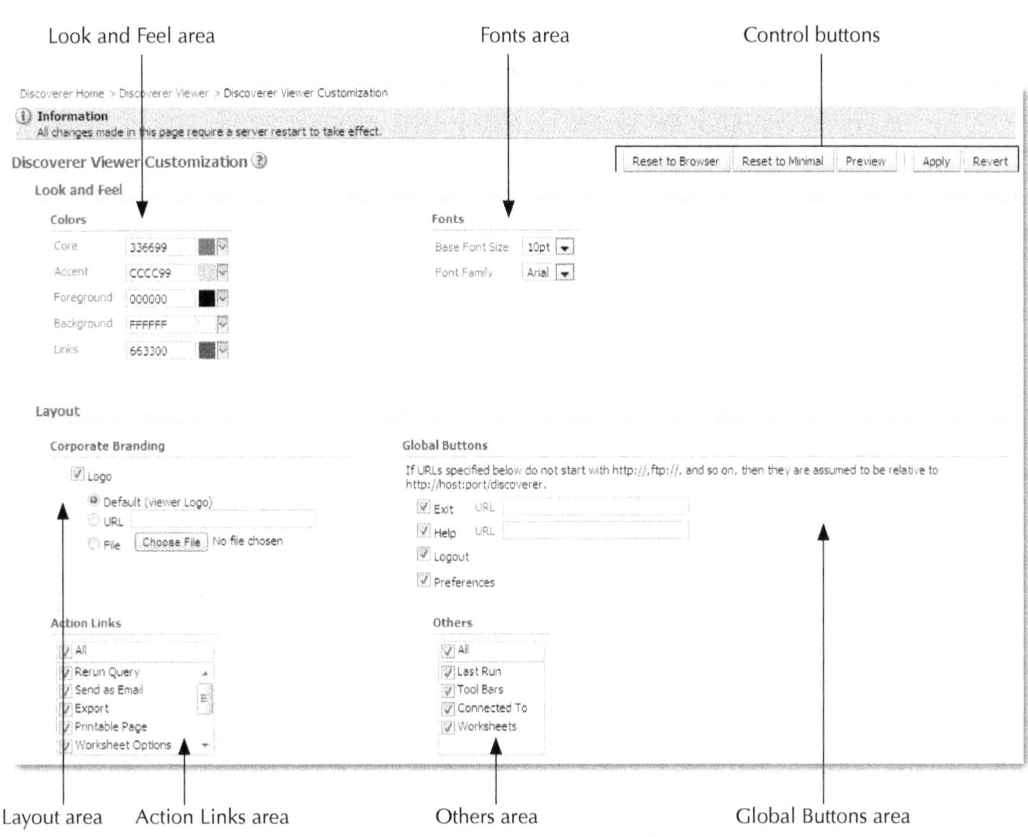


**FIGURE 20-5.** *Discoverer Viewer Customization page*

- **All Viewer Sessions** Select this radio button to tell Discoverer that you want to see information about all of the current Viewer sessions. The drop-down box for CPU usage and memory usage is still available.
- **Go** Click this button to view the session details.
- **Name** This is the session ID of the Discoverer Viewer session.
- **OS Process ID** This is the operating system process ID.
- **Total CPU Usage %** This is the total percentage of CPU that is currently being used by the session.
- **Total Memory Usage** This is the total amount of memory that is currently being used by the session.

**NOTE**
*The CPU and memory usage statistics shown here do not include the CPU and memory being consumed by the servlets. To see the amount of resources being used by the servlets, you need to view the usage statistics of the individual servlet. You do this by navigating to the Discoverer page from the home page.*

- **DBUser@DB** This displays the database user, database name, and EUL for the session.
- **SSO User** If SSO is enabled, this displays the name of the SSO that is using the session.

## Configuring Discoverer Viewer

The Discoverer Viewer Configuration page is shown in Figure 20-4. On the Discoverer Viewer Configuration page you will see the following areas:

- **Page breadcrumbs** These appear horizontally across the top of the web page, below the header. The breadcrumbs provide links back to each previous page the user navigated through to get to the current page
- **Viewer Delay Times area** This area has four settings that enable you to specify how long to wait before Discoverer Viewer displays a query progress page or the frequency for checking for export completion. All of the settings are in seconds. The four settings you can control are
    - **Query Progress Page** This is the number of seconds to wait before returning the initial query progress page. The default is 3 seconds. Oracle recommends setting this to a high value of around 60 seconds if you have enabled Web Cache.
    - **Request** This is the frequency to check for request completion. This should typically be just less than the browser's timeout specification. The default is 6 seconds. Internet Explorer's default timeout is 60 seconds, so please do not set the delay to be higher than this. Should you do this, we will leave you to guess what will happen! We recommend lowering the default from 6 seconds to 1 second. Otherwise, a page that would normally take 4 to 9 seconds will always take 10 seconds.
    - **Query Request Timeout** This is the number of seconds to wait before displaying the query progress page. The default is 1 second.
    - **Long Request Timeout** This is the number of seconds to wait before returning the initial query progress page. The default is 10 seconds.
- **Web Cache** This area contains a single check box: Use Web Cache. If you want to allow Web Cache to cache your Discoverer Viewer pages, you need to check this box. How to set up Web Cache was discussed at length in Chapter 19. Although Oracle Web Cache is installed with Oracle Business Intelligence, it is disabled for use with Discoverer Viewer by default. To make use of Oracle Web Cache with Discoverer, you must enable it. For example, you might want to cache Discoverer Viewer pages or use a Discoverer middle-tier machine to provide load balancing.

**NOTE**
*Although Fusion Middleware Control might display the status of Oracle Web Cache as Enabled in the Components table, this does not mean it is enabled for use with Discoverer Viewer. You must also ensure that this Use Web Cache check box is checked on the Discoverer Viewer Configuration page.*

- **Printing Paper Sizes** Prior to Discoverer 10*g*, one of the weakest areas of Discoverer Viewer was its printing features. Starting with 10*g* and continuing into 11*g*, you can preselect a variety of different paper sizes that Discoverer end users are allowed to use. Using the two boxes in this area, you can enable or restrict the paper sizes that users can pick for printing. By default, you will generally find that all of the available paper sizes have already been enabled for use. If you see a page size that you know will not be needed, you should move it back into the available box using the remove buttons.
- **Email** This is where you set the SMTP server, the timeout, and the maximum attachment size. During the install of the Discoverer mid-tier, you would have been asked for the SMTP server to use for your e-mail application. Whatever SMTP server you entered at that time will be displayed here. However, as you know, the completion of the SMTP server screen of the installer is optional, and you can install the mid-tier without setting your e-mail server. If you did not have an e-mail server or could not remember the name of your e-mail server when you installed the mid-tier, here is where you enter it.

**NOTE**
*Later in this section we will show you how you can set up Discoverer's e-mail so that it always sends from the same e-mail address.*

- **PDF Generation** You can set the resolution of the Portable Document Format (PDF) documents, the maximum memory used to generate the PDFs, and the maximum number of concurrent users allowed to create PDFs. The defaults for these are a resolution of 200 pixels (your options are 100 to 600), a maximum memory of 64MB, and a maximum number of two users. The latter two options are free-form, and you can set these to any reasonable value that will support your configuration.

After you have made your changes, click the Apply button. You will then need to restart the server. The next time a user logs into Viewer, the system will pick up and use these new settings.

## Customizing Discoverer Viewer

The Discoverer Viewer Customization page is shown in Figure 20-5. On the Discoverer Viewer Customization page you will see the following areas:

- **Page breadcrumbs** These appear horizontally across the top of the web page, below the header. The breadcrumbs provide links back to each previous page the user navigated through to get to the current page.
- **Look and Feel** As you can see in Figure 20-5, this area has two components: Colors and Fonts. Each will be described in detail now.

- **Colors** You can either type hex codes or use palette buttons to set the colors; for example, #000000 is white, meaning 00 for red, 00 for green, and 00 for blue. There are five colors you can set.
    - **Core** This is used to define the following colors:
        - The actions and worksheet headings
        - The arrow icons
        - The column headings
        - The connected-to text
        - The crosstab or table heading
        - The header panel
        - The last-run date
        - The text color of the header cells for the Connections table on the Connections page
        - The tools headings
        - The worksheet name
    - **Accent** This is used to define the following colors:
        - The background color of the Connections table on the Connections page
        - The background color of the Workbook Explorer
        - The text background for the actions and worksheets
    - **Foreground** This is used to define the following colors:
        - The Connections table
        - The final breadcrumb text (the text that displays the current location within Viewer)
        - The text used in drop-down lists, such as lists of values
        - The Workbook Explorer
    - **Background** This is used to define the main background color used in all Discoverer Viewer pages.
    - **Links** This is used to define colors for all link text used in Viewer.
- **Fonts** This is used to define the base font size and font family that Viewer will use.

- **Base Font Size** You use this field to specify the font size for most of the text displayed within the Viewer user interface. It does *not* control the following:
    - The actions heading
    - The Exit, Help, and Preferences links in the header
    - The Go button
    - The text used for crosstab tools and layout controls
    - The worksheet name

- **Font Family** Use this field to specify the font family that is to be used for text displayed within Viewer. You can choose one of the following:
  - Arial (this is the default)
  - Courier
  - Times New Roman

As you make changes to the look and feel, use the Preview button to see what your settings will look like. Unlike 10*g*, Discoverer 11*g* does not maintain an example screen to the right of your selections. You need to use the Preview button. When clicked, as shown in Figure 20-6, Discoverer shows you how the changes will look. To exit the Preview page, click the OK button.

When you have selected the set of colors and fonts you want to use, click the Apply button. Unlike 10*g*, where no restart was required, in 11*g* you need to restart the server in order for the changes to take effect.

**NOTE**

*If you click the Reset To Minimal button, then Viewer pages will be assembled faster. This is because Discoverer will have to perform the minimum amount of rendering to put a worksheet screen together.*

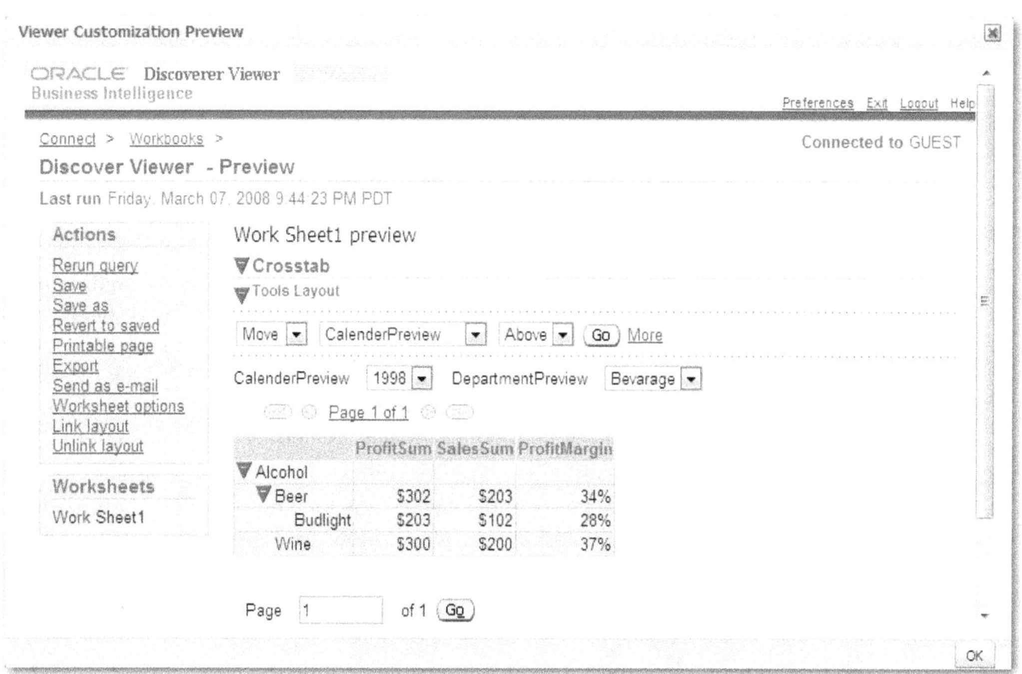


**FIGURE 20-6.** *Preview page for Viewer configuration*

- **Layout** As you can see in Figure 20-5, this area has the following four components. Corporate Branding, Global Buttons, Action Links, and Others. Each component will now be described in detail.
  - **Corporate Branding** In this area, you can tell Discoverer that it should use your corporate logo rather than use the generic logo that is normally displayed. This area has the following radio features:
    - **Logo** Use this check box to indicate whether Viewer should display a logo. If it's unchecked, the remaining features will be disabled.
    - **Default** Check this button if you want to use the standard Discoverer Viewer logo.
    - **URL** Check this button if you want to use a URL address for the logo. You must then complete the box alongside by providing a valid URL.
    - **File** Check this button if you want to use a logo contained within a file. Use the Choose File button to locate the file.

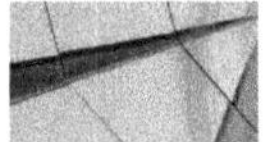

**NOTE**
*The logo you set here is applied only to the Discoverer Viewer pages. It is not applied to the Discoverer Plus pages.*

  - **Global Buttons** Both the top right and very bottom of the Viewer screen have placeholders for the following five buttons. You can choose whether to individually hide or display these buttons. In addition, Oracle has provided a way for you to customize the behavior of the Exit, Logout, and Help buttons by allowing you to enter your own URLs for these three buttons.
    - **Exit** Use this check box to display or hide the Exit link that normally displays at the top right and immediately below all Discoverer Viewer worksheets. If you select this check box, you can optionally define a target URL. If you decide not to define a target URL and a user clicks the Exit link, Discoverer Viewer will display a standard exit page.
    - **Help** Use this check box to display or hide the Help link that normally displays at the top right and immediately below all Discoverer Viewer worksheets. If you select this check box, you can optionally define a target URL for your own help. If you decide not to define a target URL and a user clicks the Help link, Discoverer Viewer will display the appropriate help page for the page that they are currently in. This feature is useful if your company has created its own help system as it bypasses the standard Oracle help and replaces it with your homegrown system.
    - **Logout** Use this check box to display or hide the Logout link that normally displays at the top right and immediately below all Discoverer Viewer worksheets. In 10*g*, if you select this check box, you can optionally define a target URL. If you are using 11*g* or decide not to define a target URL and a user clicks the Logout link, Discoverer Viewer will log the user out of Discoverer.
    - **Preferences** Use this check box to display or hide the Preferences link that normally displays at the top right and immediately below all Discoverer Viewer worksheets. The Preferences page enables end users to specify their own values for

several of the Discoverer Viewer settings (for example, the query governor). If this box is not checked, your users will not be able to set their own preferences.

- **Return To Portal** Use this check box to display or hide the Return to Portal link that normally displays at the top right of Discoverer Viewer worksheets that have been reached from a Discoverer Portlet page.

**NOTE**
*If you have not installed Portal, you will not see the Return To Portal button. If you have enabled SSO, your users will see a Logout button instead of an Exit button.*

- **Action Links** On the left side of the main Viewer screen your users will be presented with a box of actions. This box is a placeholder for the following eight options. You can choose whether to individually hide or display these buttons.
  - **Rerun Query** If this is enabled, your users will see a Rerun Query link. When a user clicks this link, the user will be able to rerun the query to obtain the latest information from the database.
  - **Send As Email** If this is enabled, your users will see a Send as Email link. When a user clicks this link, Discoverer will allow the user to send the results via e-mail, provided of course that you have specified your SMTP e-mail settings.
  - **Export** If this is enabled, your users will see an Export link. When a user clicks this link, Discoverer will allow the user to export the data from the report in a number of different formats.
  - **Printable Page** If this is enabled, your users will see a Printable Page link. When a user clicks this link, Discoverer will display a page called Printable Page Options, where users can set up their own preferences for things such as whether the headers and footers should print and whether to show the title on the first page or all pages. Users will also get the chance to use Page Setup to determine the page size, margins, and scaling.
  - **Worksheet Options** If this is enabled, your users will see a Worksheet Options link. When a user clicks this link, Discoverer will display a page that allows the user to decide whether the title, graph, table, or crosstab should be displayed.
  - **Save/Save As** If this is enabled, your users will see Save and Save As links. Turning this feature off does still not prevent a user from saving. You will need to remove the user's Save to Database privilege in the Administrator edition to completely prevent a user from saving within Viewer.
  - **Revert to Saved** If this is enabled, Viewer will display a Revert to Saved link. When a user clicks this link, Discoverer will rerun the query from the database, restoring any formatting or layout changes to the way that they are set within the saved workbook.
  - **Link/Unlink Layout** If this is enabled, and in OLAP only, your users will see a Link or Unlink Layoutlink. When a user clicks this link, Discoverer will allow the user to link or unlink the screen layout from the query.

**NOTE**
*You will be asked to hide several of these buttons if you choose to enable Oracle Web Cache.*

- **Others** You can hide or display the toolbars, the connections the user is connected to, the date the query was last run, and the available worksheets by using these buttons:
  - **Last Run** If this is enabled, your users will see when the query was last run. This information will be displayed at the top-left corner of each worksheet.
  - **Tool Bars** If this is enabled, your users will see the Layout, Format, and Sort tools links on the screen, which will allow them to modify and analyze the data. By default these are enabled.
  - **Connected To** If this is enabled, your users will see a label at the top-right corner of each worksheet informing them of their connection information.
  - **Worksheets** If this is enabled, your users will see the list of available worksheet links on the left side of each worksheet.

Just as you did with the Look and Feel section, as you make changes to the Layout section, use the Preview button to see what your settings will look like. Unlike 10*g*, Discoverer 11*g* does not maintain an example screen to the right of your selections, so you will need to make good use of the Preview button. When clicked, as shown in Figure 20-6, Discoverer shows you how the changes will look. To exit the Preview page, click the OK button.

## Customizing Viewer Manually

We are frequently asked whether it is possible to customize Discoverer Viewer further. The answer to this is yes. To customize Discoverer Viewer even further than is allowed using Fusion Middleware Control, you need to edit the Discoverer UIX files. You will appreciate that we cannot give you all of the customizations possible. This would require a complete book to itself! However, just to show you what is possible, we will explain how to manually suppress the display of the export types and how to force users to send Discoverer reports from a prespecified e-mail account.

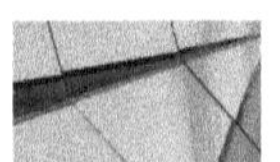

**NOTE**
*Before you jump in and start editing your UIX files, please see the section "Warning Concerning Editing UIX Files" and make sure you understand all of the warnings.*

**Manually Suppressing the Display of Export Types in Viewer** It is possible to construct a Viewer export page with only certain export formats available.

To begin with, it is important to know which export format corresponds to which resource key. If you are used to working and exporting from within Viewer, you will know that not all formats are supported for both relational and OLAP worksheets. Some, like HTML, CSV, and PDF, are supported only on relational connections, while others such as Excel and pivot tables are supported on only relational connections; still other export formats work for both relational and OLAP worksheets. Table 20-1 lists all the export types and indicates which can be used in relational worksheets, OLAP worksheets, or both.

| ID | Resource Key | Extension | Supported Connection |
|---|---|---|---|
| 0 | export.type.csv | *.csv | Relational/OLAP |
| 1 | export.type.excel | *.xls | Relational |
| 2 | export.type.excel.pivot | *.xls | Relational |
| 3 | export.type.html | *.htm | Relational |
| 5 | export.type.reports | *.xml | Relational |
| 6 | export.type.txt | *.xml | Relational/OLAP |
| 7 | export.type.pdf | *.pdf | Relational/OLAP |
| 8 | export.type.dif | *.dif | Relational |
| 9 | export.type.slk | *.slk | Relational |
| 10 | export.type.wks | *.wks | Relational |
| 11 | export.type.prn | *.prn | Relational |
| 12 | export.type.gif | *.gif | Relational/OLAP |
| 13 | export.type.png | *.png | Relational/OLAP |
| 14 | export.type.iqy | *.iqy | Relationalnon-SSO |
| 16 | export.type.html.excel | *.zip | Relational/OLAP |
| 17 | export.type.excel | *.zip | OLAP |

**TABLE 20-1.** *Valid Export Types When Editing ExportTypes.uix*

To hide the display of the export types, use the following workflow:

1. Locate this file:

   $MIDDLEWARE_HOME/user_projects/domains/ClassicDomain/servers/WLS_DISCO/tmp/_WL_user/discoverer_11.1.1.2.0/<tmpfolder>/war/ExportTypes.uix

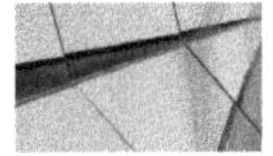

**NOTE**
*In our system, the name of the tmp folder is 51oeh7. You may have a different name for <tmpfolder> on your system and so may need to do a search for* ExportTypes.uix.

2. Make a safe backup of ExportTypes.uix.
3. Locate these lines:

```
<choice name="${uix.data.constants.EXPORT_TYPE_PARAM}"
selectedValue="${uix.eventResult.selectedExportTypeValue}">
```

4. Delete the following content lines:

```
<contents childData="${uix.eventResult.exportTypeList}">
<option value="${uix.current.exportTypeValue}"
text="${uix.data.nls[uix.current.resourceKey]}" />
</contents>
```

5. Examine the following lines. Each line you add represents the export type you want to make available to your users. Add these lines in the same location where you deleted the previous set of lines:

```
<contents>
<option value="1" text="${uix.data.nls['export.type.excel']}"/>
<option value="2" text="${uix.data.nls['export.type.excel.pivot']}"/>
<option value="7" text="${uix.data.nls['export.type.pdf']}"/>
</contents>
```

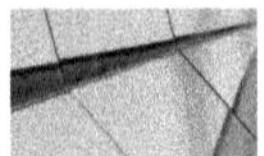

**NOTE**
*As you can see, we have enabled only Excel, Excel pivot tables, and PDFs. For a full listing of the available options and ID values, please look at Table 20-1.*

6. Save the file.
7. Take a backup of the modified file and place it somewhere safe.
8. Stop and restart the WLS_DISCO server in the WebLogic Server Administration Console.

When you let Discoverer construct the export formats drop-down list, it knows which formats to include for relational and which ones to include for OLAP. However, when you explicitly specify the export formats to show in the drop-down, the same options will be displayed, irrespective of the worksheet type, whether relational or OLAP. Therefore, if you are working with a relational worksheet and you specify that it be exported using one of the OLAP formats, you will get an error message.

Now, you could argue that Discoverer could handle this better by looking to see what export types you have made available and use some smart logic to display only those that actually can be used, as opposed to generating an error. However, if you think about it, Discoverer is handling matters by throwing out an error instead of doing something weird like churning out odd results. Second, as we have mentioned, the whole notion of editing UIX files is not encouraged or supported by Oracle because you are basically hacking the product to do something it was not built to do in the first place. The fact that UIX technologies are so clever and make so many things possible is a definite advantage; you just need to be careful.

There is one more place in Discoverer Viewer where you can select the export type. Do you remember where? Yes, that's right, on the e-mail export type selection page! When you specify that a worksheet should be e-mailed, you first have to select the format in which the worksheet should be e-mailed. So, if you have modified the available export formats for a standard export, you probably should customize the export formats available on this page too. To do that, you need to follow the same steps as earlier, but this time the UIX file that needs to be modified is EmailExportTypes.uix. You will find it in the same folder where you found the ExportTypes.uix file. The changes are the same, so we will not repeat them here.

**Forcing Viewer to Use a Predefined E-mail Account** If you want to force users to send Discoverer reports from a prespecified e-mail account, use the following workflow:

1. Locate this file:

   $MIDDLEWARE_HOME/user_projects/domains/ClassicDomain/servers/WLS_DISCO/tmp/_WL_user/discoverer_11.1.1.2.0/<tmpfolder>/war/Email.uix

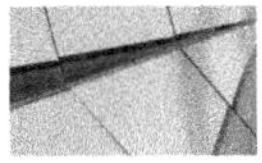

**NOTE**
*Once again, in our system the name of the tmpfolder is 51oeh7. You may have a different name for <tmpfile> on your system and so may need to do a search for* Email.uix.

2. Make a safe backup of Email.uix.
3. Find the following line and add the information in bold:

```
<contents>
<messageTextInput required="yes" name="sender"disabled="true"
tip="john.doe@company.com" columns="40"
prompt="${uix.data.nls['email.text.sender']}" text="Discoverer@company.com"/>
```

4. Find the following line and add the line in bold below it:

```
<formValue name="event" value="sendEmail" />
<formValue name="sender" value=Discoverer@company.com />
```

**NOTE**
*Make sure the domain name you provide is the same domain you are using for the SMTP server; otherwise, your Discoverer Viewer users will not be able to send e-mail.*

5. Take a backup of the modified file and place it somewhere safe.
6. Stop and restart the WLS_DISCO server in the WebLogic Server Administration Console.

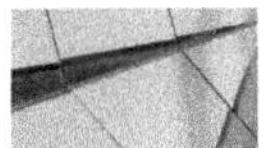

**NOTE**
*Once again, we cannot overstress the need for you to read the "Warning Concerning Editing UIX Files" section. Please make sure you understand all of the warnings and make all the recommended backups before you start.*

**Warning Concerning Editing UIX Files** Before you jump into editing the UIX files and make wholesale changes to your underlying configurations, we need to give you the following words of warning:

- *Never* make any changes without first backing up the UIX file you intend to work on. You need to go slowly and carefully, making backups as you go and trying your modifications on a test system first.
- Any changes you make to a UIX file will not be supported by Oracle, and if you run into any problems with changes you make to a UIX file, you will be on your own, which is why you need a backup.
- If you need future support, you will need to be able to prove that the issue you are encountering is not because of any changes you have made. You will basically need to have a clean instance to prove that the issue is still there.
- Any upgrades or patches that you subsequently apply may overwrite any custom changes that you have made to the UIX files. It will be your responsibility to keep copies of any changes you have made, and it will be your responsibility to make sure these changes are still valid after any upgrade or patch.

- Oracle does not guarantee that it will continue using UIX in future releases. Therefore, any effort you spend in gaining UIX expertise for the purpose of customizing Discoverer could be useless in the future. We issued the same warning in our 10*g* handbook but were delighted to see that Discoverer 11*g* has continued the use of UIX technology.

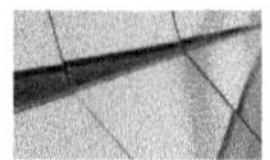

**NOTE**
*We cannot be held responsible if you tamper with your UIX files and mess up your system. You have been warned! That said, there are many examples for editing UIX files on Oracle's Support site. So long as you are careful and heed the warnings mentioned, you should be fine.*

## Components Area: Discoverer Plus Link

Clicking the Discoverer Plus link in the Components area opens the Discoverer Plus home page shown in Figure 20-7.

On the Discoverer Plus home page you will see the following areas:

- **Page breadcrumbs** These appear horizontally across the top of the web page, below the headers. The breadcrumbs provide links back to each previous page the user navigated through to get to the current page.

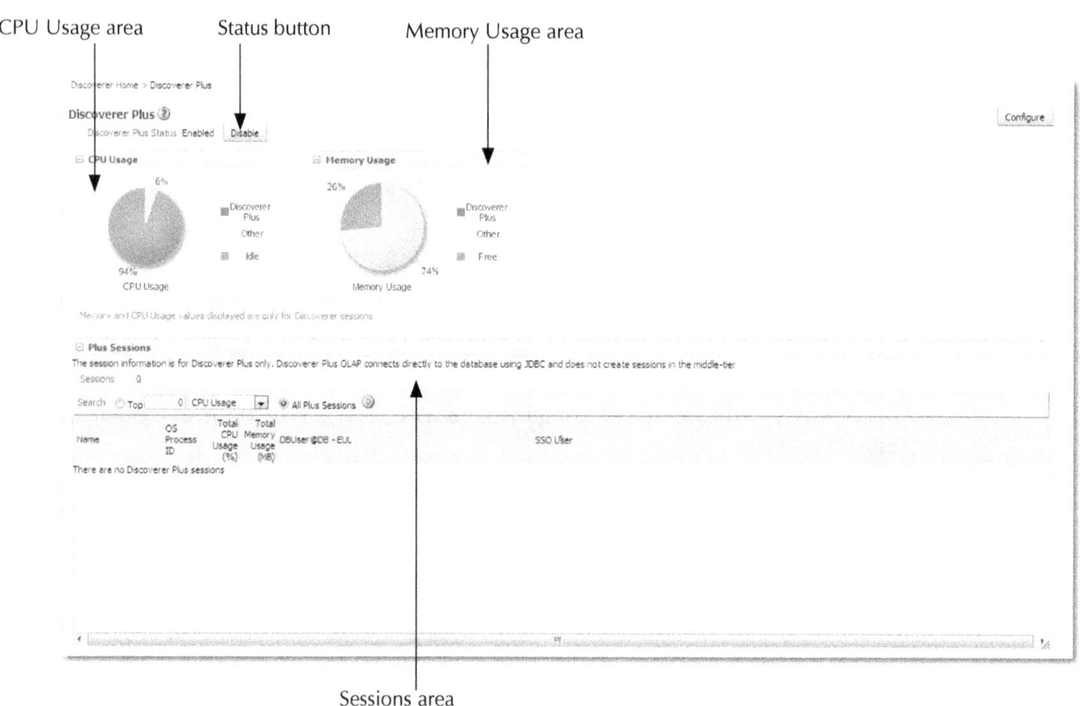


**FIGURE 20-7.** *Discoverer Plus home page*

- **Plus status** This button is labeled Disable when Plus is currently enabled and labeled as Enable when Plus is currently disabled. You might want to disable Discoverer Plus for the following reasons:
  - To prevent new users from connecting to Discoverer Plus
  - To restrict access to Discoverer Plus

  When you disable Plus, the following happens:
  - If Discoverer Java EE applications are not running, nothing happens.
  - All existing Discoverer Plus sessions continue to run until users end their sessions.
  - A message is displayed informing the Discoverer end user that Plus is disabled.
  - Requests for new user sessions are not accepted. Users whose sessions time out because of inactivity cannot continue to use Plus. The timeout for Plus is determined by using the server settings.
  - When a user attempts to access the Discoverer Plus URL, Discoverer displays an error message explaining that the service is unavailable.
- **Configure** Clicking this button launches the Discoverer Plus Configuration page shown in Figure 20-8. This page is described in detail in the section "Configuring Discoverer Plus."
- **CPU Usage** This area displays a graph showing the amount of CPU currently being consumed for all Discoverer Plus sessions.

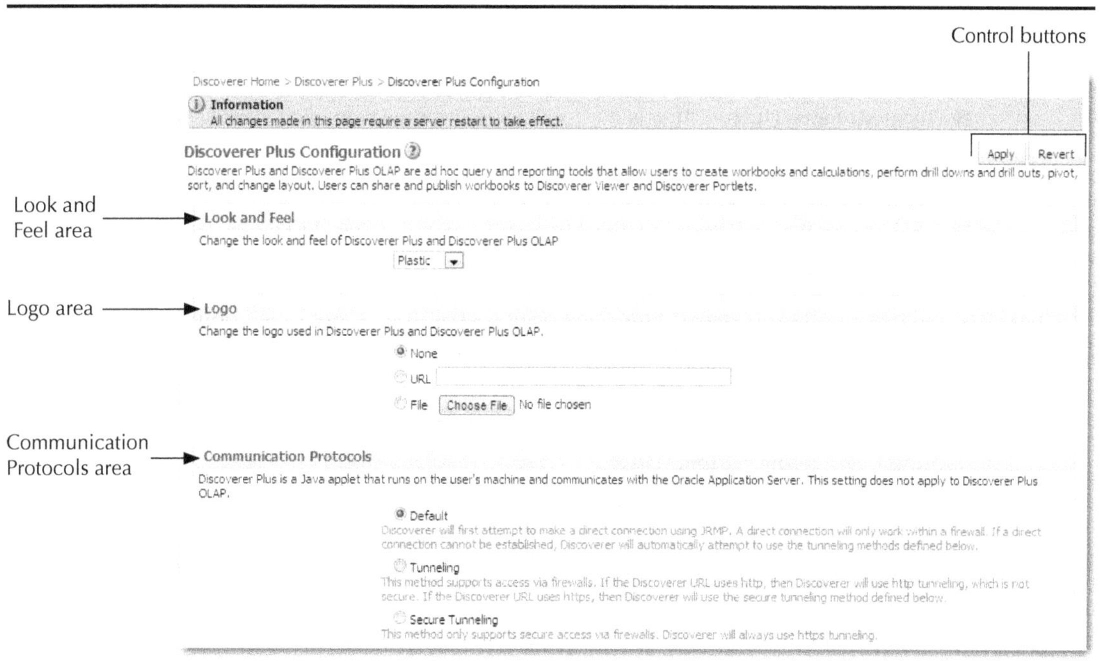


**FIGURE 20-8.** *Discoverer Plus configuration page*

- **Memory Usage** This area displays a graph showing the amount of memory currently being consumed for all Discoverer Plus sessions.
- **Plus Sessions** This area allows you to view the various Discoverer sessions that are currently in use.

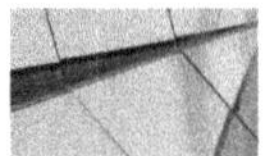

**NOTE**
*This session information is for Discoverer Plus relational only. Because Discoverer Plus OLAP connects directly to the database using JDBC, you will not see any OLAP sessions in this area.*

The Plus Sessions area contains the following:

- **Sessions** This displays the total number of current Plus sessions.
- **Top** Select this radio button to specify that you want to see information about the top *N* Plus sessions. Having selected this button, you use the left box to enter a value for the number of sessions you want to view and then use the drop-down box alongside to specify whether you want to see information about CPU usage or memory usage.
- **All Viewer Sessions** Select this radio button to tell Discoverer that you want to see information about all the current Plus sessions. The drop-down box for CPU usage and memory usage is still available.
- **Go** Click this button to view the session details.
- **Name** This is the session ID of the Discoverer Plus session.
- **OS Process ID** This is the operating system process ID.
- **Total CPU Usage %** This is the total percentage of CPU that is currently being used by the session.
- **Total Memory Usage** This is the total amount of memory that is currently being used by the session.
- **DBUser@DB** This displays the database user, database name, and EUL for the session.
- **SSO User** If SSO is enabled, this displays the name of the SSO that is using the session.

## Configuring Discoverer Plus

Clicking Configure on the Discoverer Plus page displays the Discoverer Plus Configuration page shown in Figure 20-8. This page has the following areas:

- **Page breadcrumbs** These appear horizontally across the top of the web page, below the headers. The breadcrumbs provide links back to each previous page the user navigated through to get to the current page.
- **Look And Feel** This feature allows you to change the general appearance of the Discoverer Plus applet. The choice you make here applies to both the standard and OLAP versions of Discoverer Plus. You can pick from one of four types: Browser, Oracle, Plastic, and System. However, if you intend to use Oracle JInitiator, please note that the Plastic look and feel will default to the browser. The main differences between the types are as follows:
  - **System** This type uses the same light gray colors for the background of the Plus screens and the background for the menus as the color used in the Plastic type.

Whenever the focus is placed in a cell, the bottom gridline of the cell becomes a series of dots in the same color as the main gridline color. Tabs that have the focus get a small orange bar on the outer edge of the tab name. Slider bars are in blue.

- **Plastic** This type uses a very light gray color for both the background of the Plus screens and the background of the menus. Nonfocused tabs get a more medium gray background for the tab names. Whenever the focus is placed in a cell, the gridlines for that cell become orange. When a tab receives the focus, the background for the tab changes to the same light gray color as the remainder of the backgrounds. Slider bars are in blue. This is the default.
- **Browser** This type picks up the colors from your Windows theme.
- **Oracle** This type uses dark gray for the background of the Plus screens and a medium gray for the background of the menus and the nonfocused tab names. Whenever the focus is placed in a cell, the outline of the cell becomes dark gray. When a tab receives the focus, the background for the tab changes to the same medium gray as the background for the menus. Slider bars are in the medium gray.

After you have completed changing the look and feel of Discoverer Plus using Fusion Middleware Control, click the Apply button. You will then need to restart the server. The next time a user logs into Plus,the system will pick up this new look and feel.

**NOTE**
*You can also use a custom look and feel. To use a custom look and feel, please see the section "Defining a Custom Look and Feel for Discoverer Plus."*

- **Logo** This area allows you to manage your corporate logo for both the standard and OLAP versions of Discoverer Plus. This area has the following radio buttons:
  - **None** Check this button if you are not using a logo.
  - **URL** Check this button if you want to use a URL address for the logo. You must then complete the box alongside by providing a valid URL.
  - **File** Check this button if you want to use a logo contained within a file. Use the Choose File button to locate the file.

**NOTE**
*The logo that you set here is applied only to the Discoverer Plus and Plus for OLAP screens. It is not applied to the Viewer screens.*

- **Communication Protocols** This area allows you to control how the Discoverer applet that runs on the user's machine communicates with the Oracle application server. This setting does not apply to Discoverer Plus OLAP. You have the following three protocols to choose from:
  - **Default** If you check this button, Discoverer will first make an attempt to communicate using Java Remote Method Protocol (JRMP). A direct connection will work only within a firewall. If a direct connection cannot be established, Discoverer will attempt to connect first via HTTP (Tunneling) and then via Secure Tunneling (HTTPS).

- **Tunneling** If you are using a firewall, checking this button will cause Discoverer to initially attempt to communicate with the server using HTTP. If this fails, Discoverer will then try to use the Secure Tunneling protocol of HTTPS. You should use tunneling if a firewall exists between your users and Discoverer and you mainly use HTTP. It will allow much faster connectivity.
- **Secure Tunneling** If you are using a firewall, checking this button will cause Discoverer to always use HTTPS for all connections. You should use Secure Tunneling only if a firewall exists and you use only HTTPS. Your connections will be fast.

After you have made your changes, click the Apply button. You will then need to restart the server. The next time a user logs into Plus, the system will pick up the new logo or use the appropriate communications protocol.

## Defining a Custom Look and Feel for Discoverer Plus

You can deploy Discoverer with your own look and feel (LAF) by defining a custom LAF. To define a custom LAF, use the following workflow:

1. Copy the JAR file containing the LAF class into the following folder:

   <ORACLE_HOME>/discoverer/lib
2. Start the MBean browser and navigate to the PlusConfig node. Refer to the section "Configuring Discoverer Using the System MBean Browser" later in this chapter.

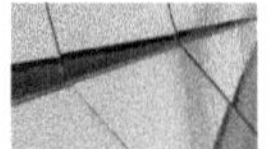

**NOTE**
*The PlusConfig node is found in the Application Defined MBeans area. You should navigate to Application Defined MBeans | com.oracle | Server: WLS_DISCO | Application: Discoverer | Xml.PlusConfig.*

Application Defined MBeans
EMDomain
com.oracle
Domain: ClassicDomain
Server: AdminServer
Server: WLS_DISCO
Application: discoverer
DiscovererCatalogExportFileDownloadStream
DiscovererCatalogImportFileUploadStream
DiscovererCatalogManager
DiscovererConnection
DiscovererLogoFileUploadStream
DiscovererPreviewLogoFileCopy
DiscovererPreviewLogoFileUploadStream
Xml.CustomizationPreviewStyleSheet
Xml.CustomizationStyleSheet
Xml.PlusConfig
PlusConfig
Xml.PlusPreviewConfig
Xml.PortletConfig
Xml.PortletPreviewConfig
Xml.ServerConfig
Xml.ServerPreviewConfig
Xml.ViewerConfig
Xml.ViewerPreviewConfig
Xml.WebServicesConfig
Xml.WebServicesPreviewConfig
Xml

**3.** After clicking the Xml.PlusConfig link, the PlusConfig node shown here will display on the right:

Application Defined MBeans: Xml.PlusConfig:PlusConfig

Apply | Revert

Show MBean Information

Attributes | Operations | Notifications

| | Name | Description | Access | Value |
|---|---|---|---|---|
| 1 | ConfigMBean | If true, it indicates that this MBean is a Config MBean. | R | true |
| 2 | D4O | D4O configuration parameters. | R | javax.management.openmbean.CompositeDataSupport(compositeT... |
| 3 | EnablePlusStatus | This attributes determines whether to enable Discoverer Plus. | RW | true |
| 4 | EnablePlusValue | Discoverer Plus Status Description. | RW | Plus was stopped by your Administrator. |
| 5 | eventProvider | If true, it indicates that this MBean is an event provider as defined by JSR-77. | R | true |
| 6 | eventTypes | All the event's types emitted by this MBean. | R | jmx.attribute.change |
| 7 | HelpSet | Help Set. | RW | help |
| 8 | Jvm | JVM configuration parameters. | R | [Ljavax.management.openmbean.CompositeData;@3dbc3300 |
| 9 | LAF | Look and feel. | RW | plastic |
| 10 | LafClass | LAF Class. | RW | |
| 11 | LafJar | LAF jar. | RW | |
| 12 | LogLevel | Logging level. | RW | Unavailable |
| 13 | LogoFile | Logo file name. | RW | |
| 14 | LogoRendered | This attributes determines whether the logo is rendered. | RW | true |
| 15 | LogoSource | This attributes determines whether the logo source is file,url or default. | RW | default |
| 16 | LogoURL | Logo URL. | RW | |
| 17 | objectName | The MBean's unique JMX name | R | com.oracle:name=PlusConfig,type=Xml.PlusConfig,Application=disc... |
| 18 | Plugin | Java Plug-in. | RW | sun |
| 19 | ReadOnly | If true, it indicates that this MBean is a read only MBean. | R | false |
| 20 | RestartNeeded | Indicates whether a restart is needed. | R | false |
| 21 | SystemMBean | If true, it indicates that this MBean is a System MBean. | R | false |
| 22 | Transport | List of communication protocols. | R | [Ljavax.management.openmbean.CompositeData;@eb864aa |
| 23 | TransportProtocols | List of communication protocols. | RW | jrmp,http |

**4.** Change the value of the LAF attribute to Custom.

**5.** In the Value field of the LafJar attribute, enter the name of the JAR file containing the custom LAF.

**6.** In the Value field of the LafClass attribute, enter the fully qualified Java class name for the LAF, such as **javax.swing.plaf.metal.MetalLookAndFeel**.

**7.** Click Apply.

# Components Area: Discoverer Portlet Provider Link

Clicking the Discoverer Portlet Provider link in the Components area opens the Discoverer Portlet Provider home page shown in Figure 20-9.

On the Discoverer Portlet Provider page you will see the following areas:

- **Page breadcrumbs** These appear horizontally across the top of the web page, below the headers. The breadcrumbs provide links back to each previous page the user navigated through to get to the current page.
- **Portlet Provider status** This button is labeled Disable when the Portlet Provider is currently enabled and labeled as Enable when the Portlet Provider is currently disabled. You might want to disable the Discoverer Portlet Provider for the following reasons:
    - To prevent new users from connecting to the Discoverer Portlet Provider
    - To restrict access to the Discoverer Portlet Provider

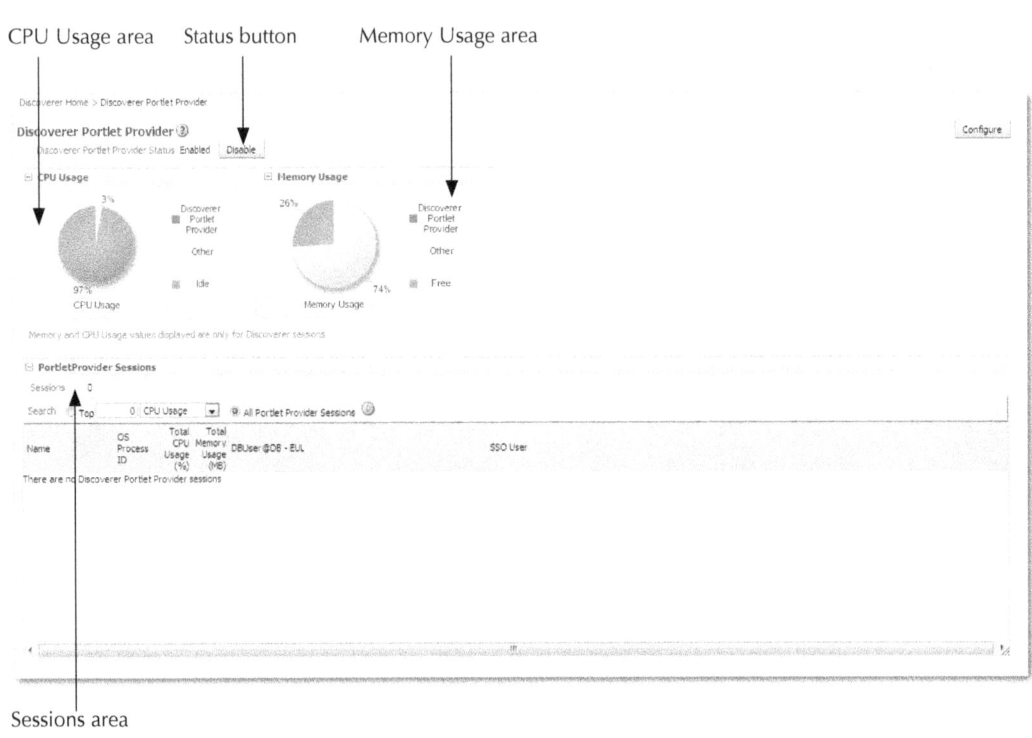


**FIGURE 20-9.** *Portlet Provider home page*

When you disable the Portlet Provider, the following happens:

- If Discoverer Java EE applications are not running, nothing happens.
- New Discoverer Portlets cannot be added to Portal pages.
- A user cannot use the Edit Defaults option or the Customize option for existing portlets.
- If a user is editing defaults or customizing a portlet when the component is disabled, they can finish the task.
- Scheduled refreshes that are in progress can continue until they are complete. However, scheduled refreshes that have not yet started do not run until you enable the Portlet Provider component.
- If a user attempts to add a new portlet, edit defaults, or customize an existing portlet, Discoverer displays a message explaining that the service is not available.
- Discoverer continues to display data in existing Discoverer portlets using the last-cached data.

- **Configure** Clicking this button launches the Discoverer Portlet Provider page shown in Figure 20-10. This page is described in detail in the "Configuring Discoverer Portlet Provider" section.

Session area

Control buttons

Discoverer Home > Discoverer Portlet Provider > Discoverer Portlet Provider Configuration

Information
All changes made in this page require a server restart to take effect.

Discoverer Portlet Provider Configuration

Apply Revert

The Discoverer Portlet Provider generates portlets for use on Oracle Portal and Oracle WebCenter. Discoverer portlets can be created when setting up a Portal page.

Discoverer Session

Discoverer Portlet Provider uses Discoverer Sessions to update cached data for Discoverer Portlets. These sessions can be pooled for reuse by different Discoverer portlets, saving CPU and Memory

* Maximum Sessions 20

A small number of maximum sessions in the pool saves memory but causes requests to be queued for a short time if all sessions are in use.

* Maximum Session Inactivity (minutes) 17

The maximum number of minutes a session is allowed to be inactive in the pool before being removed.

* Maximum Session Age (hours) 35

The maximum number of hours a session is allowed to be in the pool even if it is active.

* Maximum Wait Time (minutes) 1

The maximum number of minutes to wait for a session to become available before cancelling a portlet refresh.

Portlet Generic Parameters

Discoverer Worksheet Portlet uses generic portlet parameters in order to support Portal Page parameters. Specify the number of generic parameters that you want Discoverer Worksheet Portlet to expose.

* Maximum Generic Parameters 10

Typically the maximum number of generic parameters should be equal to the maximum number of query parameters that may be present in any Discoverer worksheet that is published as a portlet.

Generic Parameters area

**FIGURE 20-10.** *Discoverer Portlet Provider Configuration page*

- **CPU Usage** This area displays a graph showing the amount of CPU currently being consumed for all Discoverer Portlet Provider sessions.
- **Memory Usage** This area displays a graph showing the amount of memory currently being consumed for all Discoverer Portlet Provider sessions.
- **Portlet Provider Sessions** This area allows you to view the various Discoverer sessions that are currently in use. The Portlet Provider Sessions area is explained as follows:
  - **Sessions** This displays the total number of current Portlet Provider sessions.
  - **Top** Select this radio button to specify that you want to see information about the top *N* Portlet Provider sessions. Having selected this button, you use the left box to enter a value for the number of sessions you want to view and then use the drop-down box alongside to specify whether you want to see information about CPU usage or memory usage.
  - **All Viewer Sessions** Select this radio button to tell Discoverer that you want to see information about all of the current Portlet Provider sessions. The drop-down box for CPU usage or memory usage is still available.
  - **Go** Click this button to view the session details.
  - **Name** This is the session ID of the Discoverer Portlet Provider session.

- **OS Process ID** This is the operating system process ID.
- **Total CPU Usage %** This is the total percentage of CPU that is currently being used by the session.
- **Total Memory Usage** This is the total amount of memory that is currently being used by the session.
- **DBUser@DB** This displays the database user, database name, and EUL for the session.
- **SSO User** If SSO is enabled, this displays the name of the SSO that is using the session.

## Configuring Discoverer Portlet Provider

Clicking Configure on the Discoverer Plus page displays the Discoverer Portlet Provider Configuration Page shown in Figure 20-10. This page has the following areas:

- **Page breadcrumbs** These appear horizontally across the top of the web page, below the headers. The breadcrumbs provide links back to each previous page the user navigated through to get to the current page.
- **Discoverer Session** Discoverer Portlet Provider uses Discoverer sessions to update cached data. These sessions can be pooled for reuse by different Discoverer portlets, saving CPU and memory. The session controls you have are
    - **Maximum Sessions** The default is 20. A small number of maximum sessions in the pool saves memory but causes requests to be queued for a short time if all sessions are in use. If you find that user sessions are not becoming active very quickly and you believe you need more, you should increase this value. We recommend increasing it only in increments of 10.
    - **Maximum Session Inactivity** This is the maximum number of minutes a session is allowed to be inactive in the pool before being removed. The default is 17 minutes. To improve the performance of Discoverer Portlet Provider, you should reduce the value of maximum session inactivity. We recommend taking it down to 10 but only if you have noticed a deterioration in performance.
    - **Maximum Session Age** This is the maximum number of hours a session is allowed to be in the pool even if it is active. The default is 35 hours. To improve the performance of Discoverer Portlet Provider, you should reduce the value of maximum session age. We recommend taking it down in increments of five but only if you have noticed a deterioration in performance. You probably do not want to reduce this to less than two hours. If you find that performance is still poor, you should look at your resources and consider increasing CPU and memory or even load balancing across multiple servers.
    - **Maximum wait time** This setting determines how long Portal will wait, in minutes, for a session to become available before cancelling a portlet refresh. The default is one minute. To improve the performance of Discoverer Portlet Provider, you should increase the value of maximum wait time. We recommend taking it up in increments of five minutes but only if you have noticed deterioration in performance.
- **Portal Generic Parameters** If you so choose, you can pass parameters that Portal maintains to Discoverer portlets. The Portal Generic Parameters setting sets the maximum number of generic parameters that may be mapped. The default value of 10 should be sufficient unless workbooks have been developed with more than 10 user-defined parameters to which Portal needs to provide values.

After you have made your changes, click the Apply button. You will then need to restart the server. The next time a user logs into Portal, the system will pick up and use these new settings.

## Components Area: Discoverer Web Services Link

Clicking the Discoverer Web Services link in the Components area opens the Discoverer Web Services home page shown in Figure 20-11.

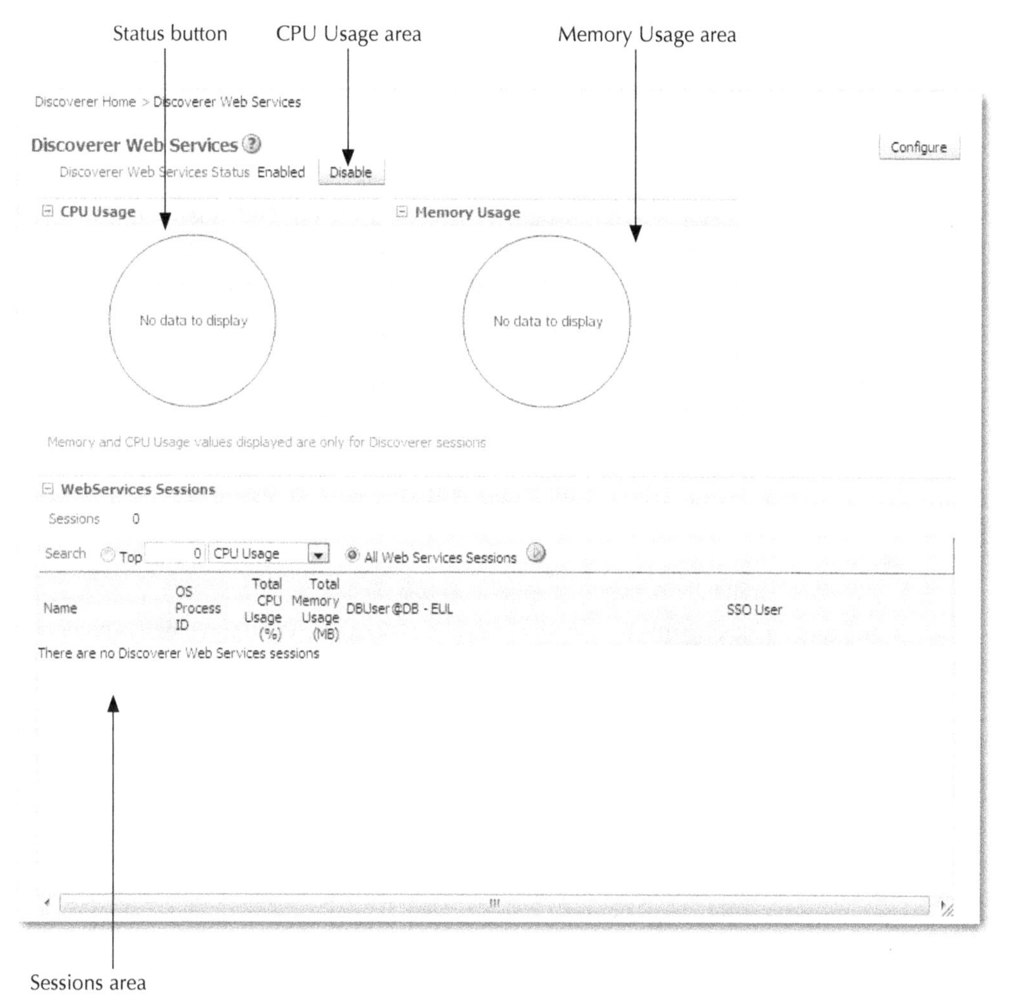


**FIGURE 20-11.** *Web Services home page*

Oracle Discoverer Web Services are part of an application programming interface (API) that enables a client to do the following:

- Obtain Discoverer connections, workbooks, and worksheets
- Execute worksheet queries
- Obtain worksheet content using the SOAP protocol (version 1.1 with JAX-WS/document wrapped format). The SOAP endpoint URL for Discoverer Web Services is as follows: http(s)://<host>:<port>/discoverer/wsi.

On the Discoverer Web Services page you will see the following areas:

- **Page breadcrumbs** These appear horizontally across the top of the web page, below the headers. The breadcrumbs provide links back to each previous page the user navigated through to get to the current page.
- **Web Services status** This button is labeled Disable when Web Services are currently enabled and labeled as Enable when Web Services are currently disabled. You might want to disable the Discoverer Web Services for the following reasons:
  - To prevent new users from connecting to the Discoverer Web Services
  - To restrict access to the Discoverer Web Services

  When you disable Web Services, the following happens:
  - If Discoverer Java EE applications are not running, nothing happens.
  - All existing Web Services sessions continue to run until users end their sessions.
  - A message is displayed informing the end user that Discoverer Web Services are disabled.
  - Requests for new user sessions are not accepted. Users whose sessions time out because of inactivity cannot continue to use Web Services.
- **Configure** Clicking this button launches the Discoverer Web Services Configuration page shown in Figure 20-12. This page is described in detail in the section "Configuring Discoverer Web Services."
- **CPU Usage** This area displays a graph showing the amount of CPU currently being consumed for all Discoverer Web Services sessions.

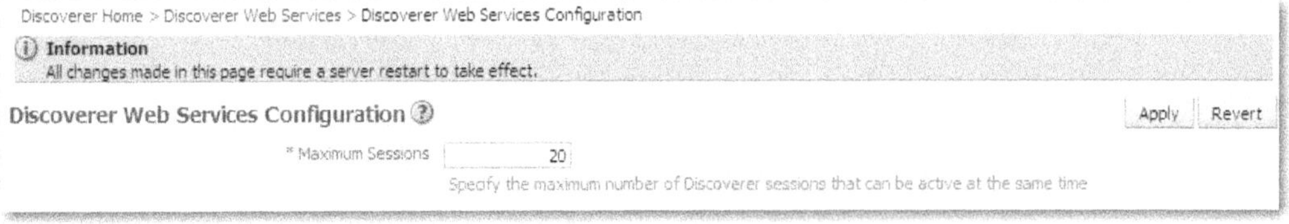

Discoverer Home > Discoverer Web Services > Discoverer Web Services Configuration
Information
All changes made in this page require a server restart to take effect.
Discoverer Web Services Configuration
Apply Revert
* Maximum Sessions 20
Specify the maximum number of Discoverer sessions that can be active at the same time

**FIGURE 20-12.** *Discoverer Web Services Configuration page*

- **Memory Usage** This area displays a graph showing the amount of memory currently being consumed for all Discoverer Web Services sessions.
- **Web Services Sessions** This area allows you to view the various Discoverer sessions that are currently in use. The Web Services Sessions area is explained as follows:
  - **Sessions** This displays the total number of current Web Services sessions.
  - **Top** Select this radio button to specify that you want to see information about the top *N* Web Services sessions. Having selected this button, you use the left box to enter a value for the number of sessions that you want to view and then use the drop-down box alongside to specify whether you want to see information about CPU usage or memory usage.
  - **All Web Services Sessions** Select this radio button to tell Discoverer that you want to see information about all of the current Web Services sessions. The drop-down box for CPU usage or memory usage is still available.
  - **Go** Click this button to view the session details.
  - **Name** This is the session ID of the Discoverer Web Services session.
  - **OS Process ID** This is the operating system process ID.
  - **Total CPU Usage %** This is the total percentage of CPU that is currently being used by the session.
  - **Total Memory Usage** This is the total amount of memory that is currently being used by the session.
  - **DBUser@DB** This displays the database user, database name, and EUL for the session.
  - **SSO User** If SSO is enabled, this displays the name of the SSO that is using the session.

## Configuring Discoverer Web Services

Clicking Configure on the Discoverer Plus page displays the Discoverer Web Services Configuration page shown in Figure 20-12. This page has the following areas:

- **Page breadcrumbs** These appear horizontally across the top of the web page, below the headers. The breadcrumbs provide links back to each previous page the user navigated through to get to the current page
- **Web Services Configuration** This area has the following single configurable element:
  - **Maximum Sessions** This is the maximum number of Web Services sessions that can be active at the same time. The default is 20. A small number of maximum sessions in the pool saves memory but causes requests to be queued for a short time if all sessions are in use. If you find that user sessions are not becoming active very quickly and you believe you need more, you should increase this value. We recommend increasing it only in increments of 10.

After you have made your changes, click the Apply button. You will then need to restart the server. The next time a user begins using an API that has a link back to the Discoverer Web Services, this maximum session setting will be used.

## Discoverer Drop-Down Menu

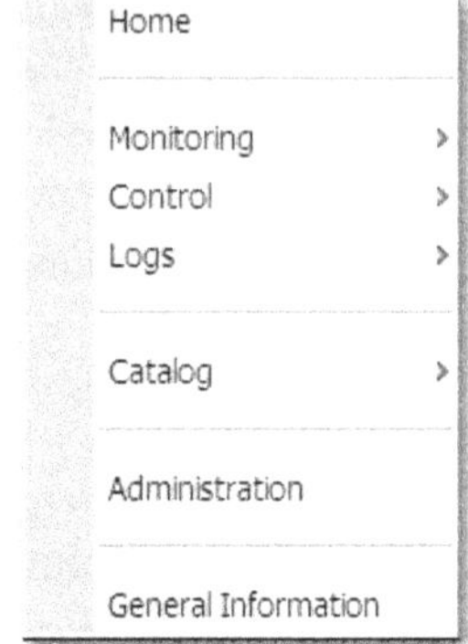


Clicking the drop-down link alongside the word *Discoverer* at the top of any of the Discoverer pages opens the drop-down list at right

As you can see, the list provides access to the following:

- **Home** Selecting this returns you to the Discoverer home page shown in Figure 20-2.
- **Monitoring** Selecting this opens a submenu that offers you the following two choices:
  - **Performance Summary** Selecting this option opens the Performance Summary page. The Performance Summary page contains charts for selected performance metrics.

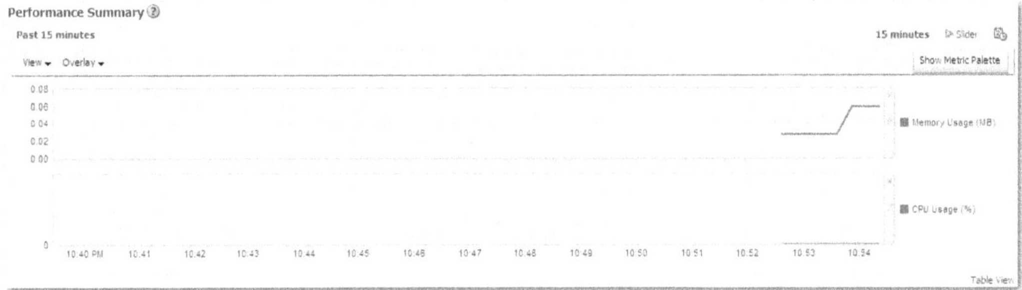


To add or remove metrics in the Performance Summary page, click the Show Metric Palette button. Then, in the Metric palette, select or deselect the metric to add or remove. For example, in the Metric palette, if you click the Response folder and select the UpDown Status check box, a new chart is displayed in the Performance Summary page showing the value of the UpDown Status Response metric. For more information about monitoring the server performance, please refer to http://docs.oracle.com/cd/E21764_01/bi.1111/b40107/maint.htm#BIDCG876.

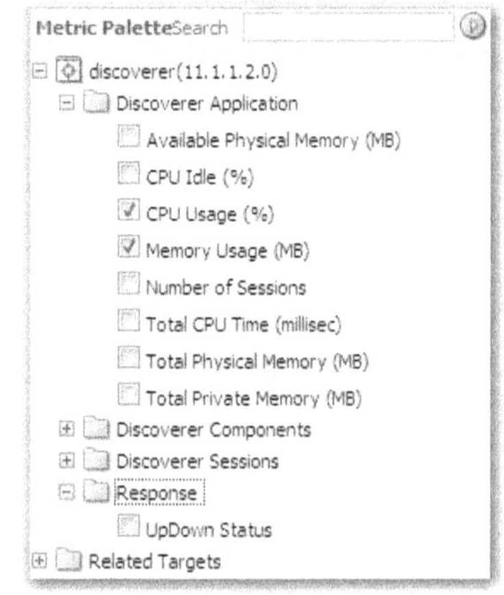


  - **Discoverer Sessions** Selecting this option opens the Discoverer Sessions page. The Discoverer Sessions page shows session information for Discoverer Plus, Discoverer Viewer, Discoverer Portlet Provider, and Discoverer Web Services. It does not show session information for Discoverer Plus OLAP because this connects directly to the database using JDBC and does not create sessions in the middle tier.

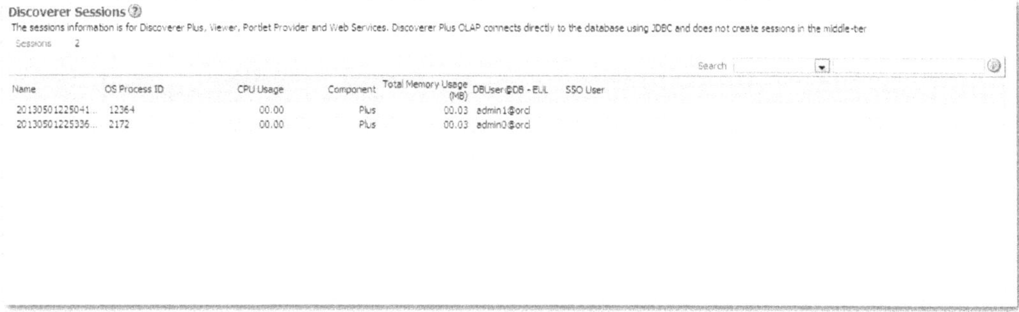

Discoverer Sessions
The sessions information is for Discoverer Plus, Viewer, Portlet Provider and Web Services. Discoverer Plus OLAP connects directly to the database using JDBC and does not create sessions in the middle-tier
Sessions 2
Search
Name
OS Process ID
CPU Usage
Component
Total Memory Usage (MB)
DBUser@DB - EUL
SSO User
20130501225041... 12364 00.00 Plus 00.03 admin1@orcl
20130501225336... 2172 00.00 Plus 00.03 admin0@orcl


At the top of the screen is a Search area. The drop-down in this area allows you to home in on just one of the following elements:

- **Name** This is the session ID of the Discoverer session.
- **OS Process ID** This is the operating system process ID.
- **Total CPU Usage %** This is the total percentage of CPU that is currently being used by the session.
- **Component** This is the Discoverer component that is responsible for the session.
- **Total Memory Usage** This is the total amount of memory that is currently being used by the session.
- **DBUser@DB** This displays the database user, database name, and EUL for the session.
- **SSO User** If SSO is enabled, this displays the name of the SSO that is using the session.

- **Control** Selecting this opens a submenu that offers you the following three choices:
  - **Start Up** Selecting this runs the startup process for Discoverer. If Discoverer is already running, you will receive a message telling you that the operation failed because the application is already running. If Discoverer is currently down, the startup process will run. When the process completes, you will be informed that the process was successful. Your only option now is to click the Close button.
  - **Shut Down** Selecting this runs the shutdown process for Discoverer. When asked to confirm that you want to shut it down, your choices are Shutdown and Cancel. Clicking Shutdown starts the shutdown process. If the server is already down, you will receive a message telling you that the operation failed because the application is already down. When the process completes, you will be informed that the process was successful. Your only option now is to click the Close button.
- **Logs** Selecting this opens a submenu that offers you the following two choices:
  - **View Log Messages** Selecting this option opens the Log Messages page where you can view or examine all of the Discoverer logs. We do not discuss this page further in the book; however, you can find more information here: http://docs.oracle.com/cd/E21764_01/bi.1111/b40107/logging_diagnostics.htm#i1028628.

- **Log Configuration** Selecting this option opens the Log Configuration page shown here:

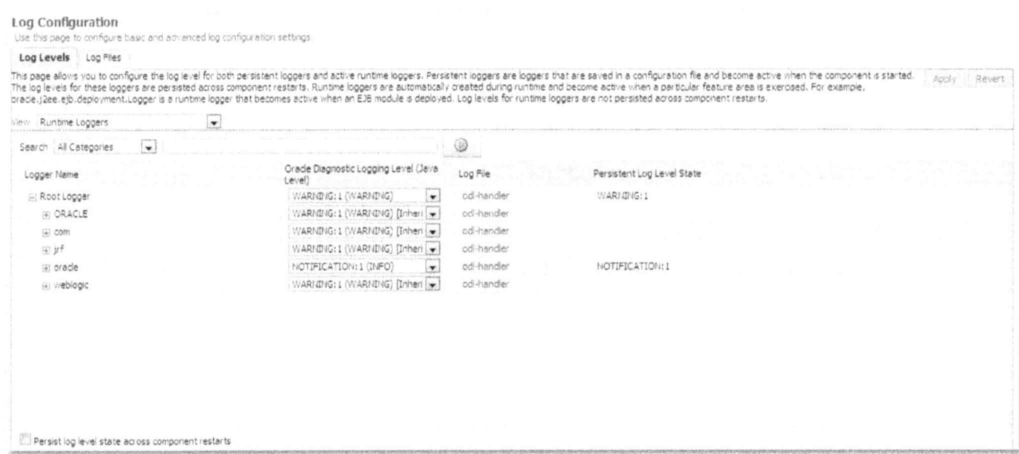


For Discoverer we are really interested in five loggers that Fusion Middleware provides just for Discoverer. They are

- **ORACLE.DISCOVERER.SERVER** For the Discoverer session server
- **ORACLE.DISCOVERER.VIEWER** For Discoverer Viewer
- **ORACLE.DISCOVERER.WEB_SERVICES** For Discoverer Web Services
- **ORACLE.DISCOVERER.PORTLET_PROVIDER** For Discoverer Portlet Provider
- **ORACLE.DISCOVERER.MODEL** For logging messages pertaining to common internal components that are used by the Viewer, Plus, and Web Services components

To see details about these five loggers, expand the ORACLE link directly underneath the Root Logger heading. You will now see the following:

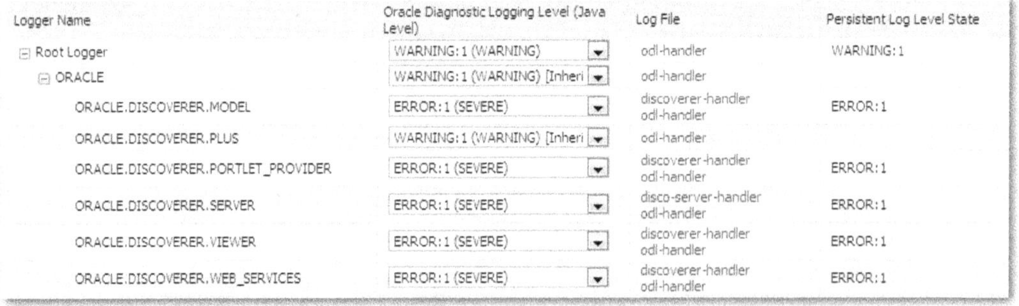


For each of these loggers, you can configure the Oracle Diagnostic Logging (ODL) level. You set the log level for individual Discoverer components when you want to monitor Discoverer component session activity at a specific level of detail. When you are done, click Apply.

When managing logging, you can choose one of five message types. They are

- **INCIDENT_ERROR** A serious problem that may be caused by a bug in the product and that should be reported to Oracle Support. Examples are errors from which you cannot recover or serious problems.
- **ERROR** A serious problem that requires immediate attention from the administrator and is not caused by a bug in the product. An example is if Oracle Fusion Middleware cannot process a log file but you can correct the problem by fixing the permissions on the document.
- **WARNING** A potential problem that should be reviewed by the administrator. Examples are invalid parameter values or a specified file does not exist.
- **NOTIFICATION** A major life-cycle event such as the activation or deactivation of a primary subcomponent or feature. There are two levels of notification, described in the next list.
- **TRACE** Trace or debug information for events that are meaningful to administrators or Oracle Support. There are three levels of trace, described in the next list.

Each of these have a level number associated with them, and some have more than one level. There are three levels: 1, 16, and 32.

The combination of trace and level number determines the performance impact, as follows:

- **Level 1** For Incident Error, Error, Warning, and Notification, a level of 1 has no performance impact.
- **Level 1** For Trace, a level of 1 has a small performance impact. You can enable this level occasionally on a production environment to debug problems. This returns trace or debug information for events that are meaningful to administrators, such as public API entry or exit points.
- **Level 16** For Notification, a level of 16 means there is a minimal impact on performance.
- **Level 16** For Trace, a level of 16 means there is a high impact on performance. This level should not be enabled on a production environment, except on special situations to debug problems. This returns detailed trace or debug information that can help Oracle Support diagnose problems with a particular subsystem.
- **Level 32** This exists for Trace only. This level should not be enabled in a production environment. It is intended to be used to debug the product on a test or development environment. This returns very detailed trace or debug information that can help Oracle Support diagnose problems with a particular subsystem.

The default setting for most logs is Notification level 1. This is the setting that has the least impact to the system. The remaining options log activity in greater and greater detail starting with Error and going up to Trace. You should enable Trace logging only when you already have serious issues and you are trying to find out what is going wrong. We recommend that under normal situations you use either Notification or Warning, both at level 1.

You can find more information on logging at http://docs.oracle.com/cd/E21764_01/bi.1111/b40107/logging_diagnostics.htm#i1028628.

- **Catalog** The Discoverer Catalog is where you manage OLAP. Discoverer Plus OLAP is installed automatically when you install Discoverer Plus. Discoverer Plus OLAP depends on the Discoverer Catalog to store the objects that users need for analyzing data. The Discoverer Catalog, however, is not installed automatically. Instead, you use Fusion Middleware Control to install and manage the Discoverer Catalog. Discoverer OLAP does not use an End User Layer but rather uses a catalog for storing workbooks, worksheets, and all of the Discoverer OLAP metadata.

**NOTE**
*You need the Discoverer Catalog only if you intend to use Discoverer Plus OLAP.*

Selecting Catalog opens a submenu that offers you the following three choices:

- **Install** As shown next, you will use this link to install the Discoverer Catalog. You must provide a hostname (fully qualified domain name), DBA username (we use SYSTEM), and password in order to install the catalog. In our experience, you will probably also need to provide the port and database SID. You will find the catalog under the D4OSYS schema.

Install Catalog
Step 1 Step 2
Step 1
Cancel Step 1 of 2 Continue
Install Catalog
Enter the database connection information.
When you install the Discoverer Catalog, a D4OSYS user is automatically created and populated with the schema objects required for workbooks, worksheets and other objects in Discoverer Plus OLAP. A database can contain only one Discoverer Catalog.
* Host
Port
SID
* DBA User Name
* DBA Password

After you have completed this page, click Continue.
On the second screen, you enter the D40SYS password (twice) and select a tablespace. When done, click Finish.

Install Catalog
Step 1 Step 2
Step 2
Cancel Back Step 2 of 2 Finish
Install Catalog: D4OSYS Details
The Discoverer Catalog will be installed in the D4OSYS Schema. Enter the D4OSYS password and specify the tablespace to be used.
* D4OSYS Password
* Confirm Password
Tablespace

You will be asked to confirm that you are sure you want to install the Discoverer Catalog. If you are sure, click Yes; otherwise, click No.

**NOTE**
*Don't be afraid when the system initially reports that the install failed. It displays this message until the operation has completed, and then it changes to Completed Successfully.*

- **Uninstall** As shown here, you will use this link to uninstall the Discoverer Catalog. In addition to the required parameters you used when installing the catalog, you will also need to provide the D4OSYS password.

Uninstall Catalog
Cancel OK
When you uninstall the Discoverer Catalog, the D4OSYS user is removed from the database. As a result, all workbooks, worksheets and other objects that were created by Discoverer Plus OLAP are also removed. If you want to save these objects, then export the Discoverer Catalog before uninstalling it.
* Host
Port
SID
* DBA User Name
* DBA Password
* D4OSYS Password

After you have provided the uninstall credentials, click OK. You will be prompted whether you really want to uninstall the Discoverer Catalog. Click Yes to remove the catalog, or click No to leave it in place.

- **Manage** As shown next, you will use this link to manage the Discoverer Catalog.

Manage: Discoverer for OLAP Login
Enter connection information for the Catalog schema. D4OSYS is the schema in which the Catalog is installed.
* Host
Port
SID
* D4OSYS Password
Login

You must provide the host name, port, SID, and password for the D4OSYS schema. After you click the Login button, Discoverer validates your credentials and, if successful, displays the following Manage Catalog page:

Discoverer Home > Manage Catalog
Manage Catalog
Export Import Authorize Users
Database maslaptop.learndiscoverer.com:1521:orcl
Tablespace USERS
Discoverer Catalog Version 3.2.3.2.13

On the Manage Catalog page there are the following three links:

- **Export Catalog** When you click this link, Discoverer automatically generates an export file called d4o_export.xml. If you are using Windows XP, you may well see the following download box being displayed. Back in OEM, you will also see a message saying that the catalog has been successfully exported.
- **Import Catalog** When you click this link, you will be asked to provide the name of a file that contains the information you want to import. You can use this mechanism to import workbooks, worksheets, or other objects into the catalog.

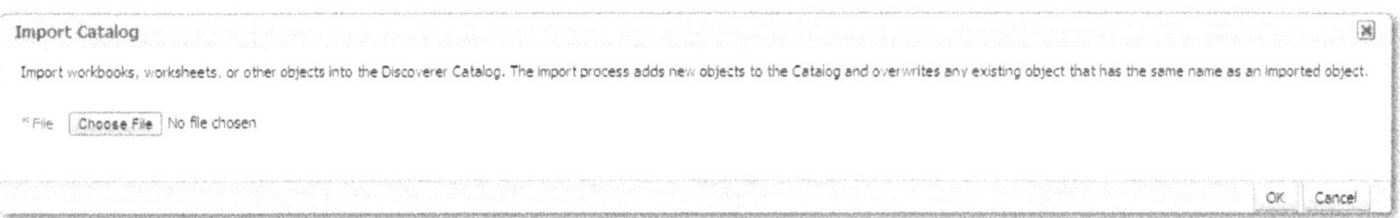

Import Catalog
Import workbooks, worksheets, or other objects into the Discoverer Catalog. The import process adds new objects to the Catalog and overwrites any existing object that has the same name as an imported object.
* File
Choose File
No file chosen
OK
Cancel


- **Authorize Users and Roles** When you click this link, Discoverer displays the following Authorize Users page. Use this page to grant or revoke users and roles access to the catalog.

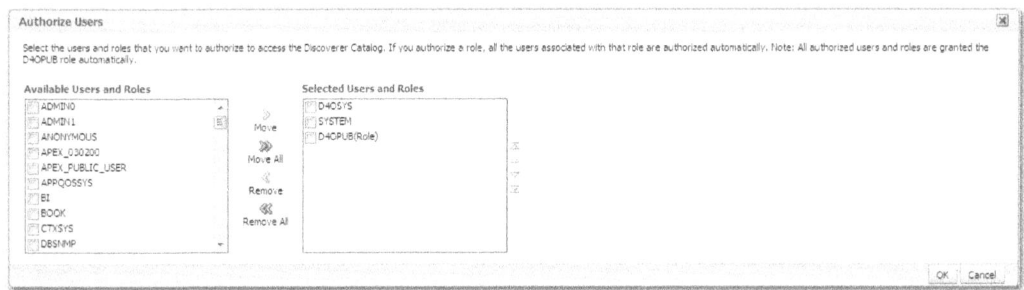


For more information about catalogs, please use http://docs.oracle.com/cd/E21764_01/bi.1111/b40107/disco_catalog_config.htm#BIDCG196.

- **Administration** Selecting this opens the Discoverer Administration page shown here:

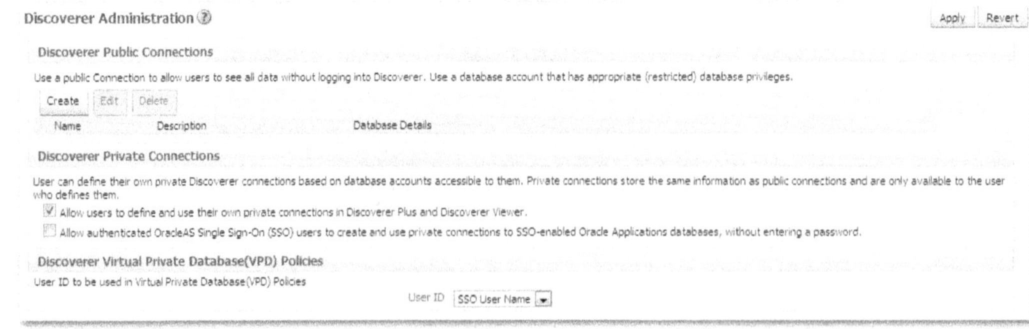

Discoverer Administration
Apply
Revert
Discoverer Public Connections
Use a public Connection to allow users to see all data without logging into Discoverer. Use a database account that has appropriate (restricted) database privileges.
Create
Edit
Delete
Name
Description
Database Details
Discoverer Private Connections
User can define their own private Discoverer connections based on database accounts accessible to them. Private connections store the same information as public connections and are only available to the user who defines them.
Allow users to define and use their own private connections in Discoverer Plus and Discoverer Viewer.
Allow authenticated OracleAS Single Sign-On (SSO) users to create and use private connections to SSO-enabled Oracle Applications databases, without entering a password.
Discoverer Virtual Private Database(VPD) Policies
User ID to be used in Virtual Private Database(VPD) Policies
User ID
SSO User Name

The Discoverer Administration page has the following three areas:

- **Discoverer Public Connections** In this area you can create, edit, and delete Discoverer public connections. These are connections that are available to all users. Only the application server administrator can create public connections.
  - **Create** Click this button to open the Create Public Connection page. As you can see, you need to provide the following:

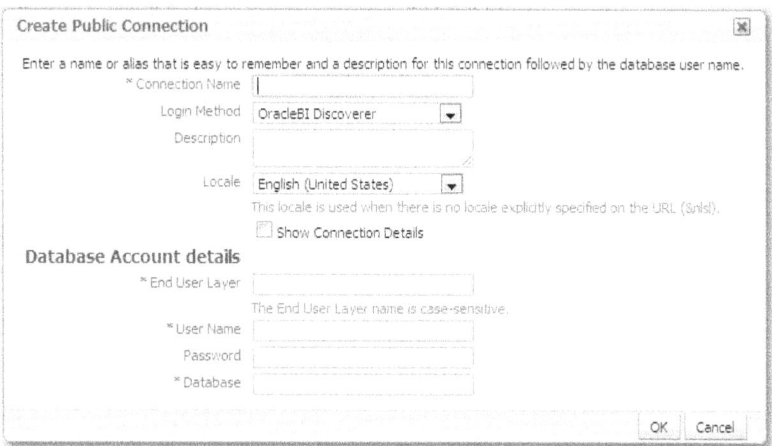


- **Connection Name** This is a free-format name.
- **Login Method** Use this drop-down to select from one of the following:
  - **Oracle BI Discoverer** For a connection to a standard EUL
  - **Oracle Applications** For a connection to E-Business Suite
  - **Oracle BI Discoverer for OLAP** For an OLAP connection
- **Description** This is optional.
- **Locale** Pick the language the connection is for. It will default to the language being used by the administrator.
- **Show Connection Details** Check this box if you want the user to be able to see the EUL and username being used for the connection. By default it is not checked.
- **End User Layer** Enter the EUL where the workbooks are stored. This is not available for an OLAP connection.
- **User Name** Enter the name of a Discoverer user who owns workbooks. This is the user who will be logged in automatically when the user clicks the connection.
- **Password** Enter the password of the Discoverer user who owns workbooks.
- **Database** Enter the database connection where the workbooks are stored.
- **Responsibility** This is available only for an Oracle Applications connection. It is a required field.

- **Security Group** This is available only for an Oracle Applications connection. It is not mandatory.

- **Edit** Click this button to open the Edit Public Connection page. As you can see, you have the ability to edit all of the information provided when the connection was first created.

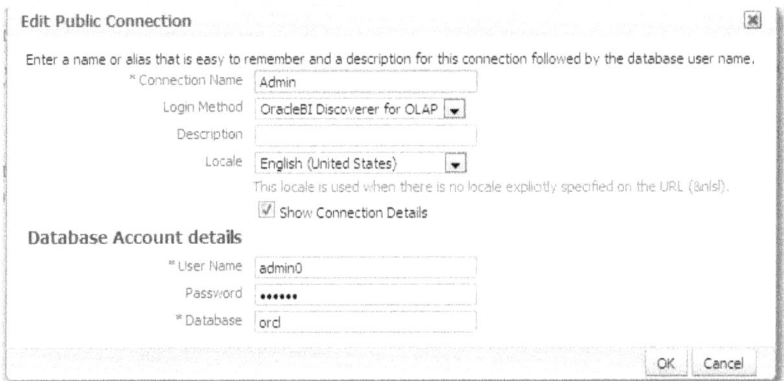


- **Delete** Click this button to delete a public connection. You will be asked to confirm if you are sure you want to delete the connection. If you are sure click Yes; otherwise, click No.

- **Discoverer Private Connections** Private connections are created by the end user and, unless you are using SSO, are stored as cookies on the end user's computer. If you are using SSO, the connections are stored within the database. This allows the user to keep their connections as they move from one computer to another. It is also quite annoying for users to lose their Discoverer connections when they clear their cookies, but this is what will happen unless you enable SSO. From the Discoverer configuration page you may create public connections and allow or disallow users to create their own private connections. The Discoverer Private Connections page has the following two check boxes:

  - Allow users to define and use their own private connections in Discoverer Plus and Discoverer Viewer. This is checked by default.
  - Allow authenticated Oracle AS single sign-on (SSO) users to create and use private connections to SSO-enabled Oracle Applications databases, without entering a password.

  Without SSO, as mentioned, a user's private connection is stored as a cookie. Because non-SSO URLs are unprotected, anyone who has access to the computer has access to the cookie, thus exposing the Discoverer URL to just about anyone. In this situation, even though the user provided a password when creating the connection, the password will always be prompted, thus affording Plus and Viewer the same protection as Desktop.

- **Discoverer Virtual Private Database (VPD)** Policies use this drop-down to inform Discoverer whether the SSO username or global user ID (GUID) is to be used when a VPD policy is encountered. For more information about using a VPD policy, please refer to http://docs.oracle.com/cd/E21764_01/bi.1111/b40107/security2.htm#BIDCG371.

- **General Information** Selecting this opens a pop-up that displays the following information:
    i. **Target name** Example: /Farm_ClassicDomain/asinst_1/ohs1
    ii. **Version** Example: 11.1.1.6.0
    iii. **Oracle home** Example: c:\oralce\middleware\as1
    iv. **Oracle instance** Example: c:\oracle\middleware\asinst_1
    v. **Host** Example: maslaptop.learndiscoverer.com

**Connection Tip for Bypassing the Connection Screen** If you want to bypass the Discoverer connection screen, use the following workflow:

1. Create a public connection using Fusion Middleware Control.
2. Enter the URL to launch Discoverer. Here's an example:
   **http://maslaptop.learndiscoverer.com:8890/discoverer/viewer**
3. Expand the details for the public connection and note the connection key.
4. Add the connection key to the URL as a parameter. For example, if the connection key you noted in step 3 was cn=cf_a105, you will enter the following:
   **http://maslaptop.learndiscoverer.com:8890/discoverer/viewer?cn=cf_a105**

# Configuring Discoverer Using the System MBean Browser

The System MBean Browser is part of Fusion Middleware Control and is used to update configuration settings for the middle-tier components. You can use the System MBean Browser to enter or modify Discoverer configuration settings that are not available in the Fusion Middleware Control Discoverer pages.

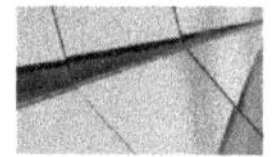

**NOTE**
*You should not use the System MBean Browser unless you are an advanced middle-tier administrator.*

To modify Discoverer configuration settings by using the System MBean Browser, use the following workflow:

1. Start Enterprise Manager Fusion Middleware Control and navigate to the farm home page. For more information, see the "Connecting to Fusion Middleware Control" section earlier in this chapter about starting Fusion Middleware Control. You can get more information here: http://docs.oracle.com/cd/E17904_01/bi.1111/b40107/maint.htm#CHDCADJC.

2. Expand Application Deployments.
3. Expand Internal Applications.

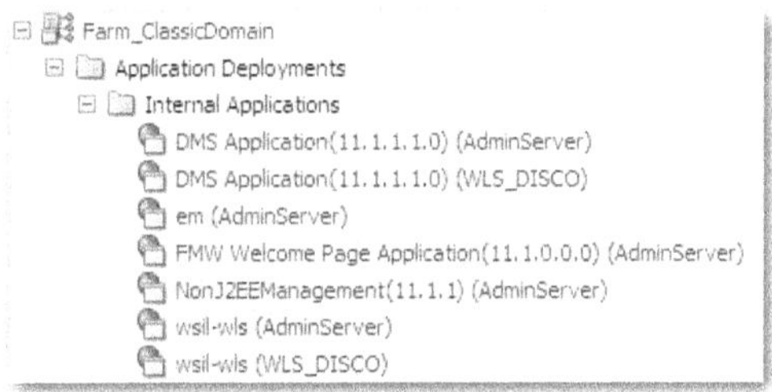


4. Right-click WLS_DISCO and from the drop-down select System MBean Browser.

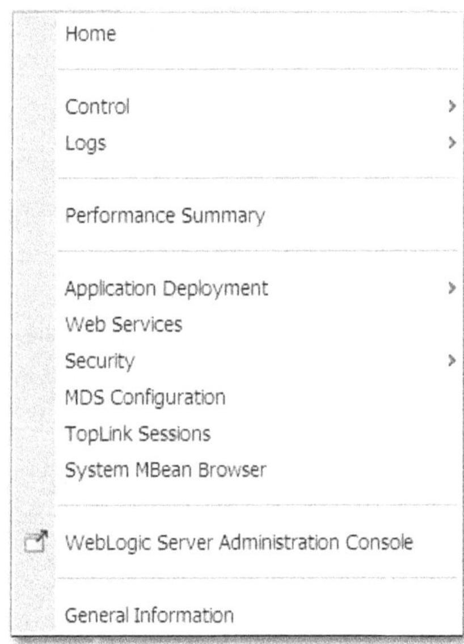


5. Fusion Middleware Control displays the System MBean Browser page.

**NOTE**
*You need to be careful when working with the System MBean Browser. Many times you will be required to lock the domain, make your changes, and then unlock the domain. Please also note that MBeans can be accessed with a JMX browser and even WLST scripting.*

6. Click the plus (+) symbol to the left of the appropriate node in the navigation tree, and drill down to the specific MBean to modify.

7. The navigation tree expands to display links for viewing or updating settings. Each node in the navigation tree represents settings in a configuration file.
8. Click a node in the navigation tree and select the Attributes tab, to display the details for a group of attributes. For example, click the Plus Viewer node and the Attributes tab to display attributes for Discoverer Plus configuration settings. Part of this node is shown here:

| | Name | Description | Access | Value |
|---|---|---|---|---|
| 1 | AuthenticationTokenTimeout | How long, in seconds, the web-cache authentication token remains valid for. 86400 = 1 day in seconds | RW | 86400 |
| 2 | Charting | Attribute exposed for management | W | |
| 3 | ConfigMBean | If true, it indicates that this MBean is a Config MBean. | R | true |
| 4 | ConnectedToLabelRendered | Attribute which determines whether the label to display connection should be rendered | R | true |
| 5 | DefaultLocale | The default locale to use if the browser does not specify a supported locale. | RW | en |
| 6 | DisableBrowserCaching | Attribute exposed for management | W | |
| 7 | EmailMaxAttachment | Maximum email attachment size in MB | RW | 4096 |
| 8 | EmailSmtpServer | SMTP server for email | RW | |
| 9 | EmailTimeout | Email time-out | RW | 60000 |
| 10 | EnableAppsSSOConnection | Attribute exposed for management | W | |
| 11 | EnableDataSelection | Attribute exposed for management | W | |
| 12 | EnableViewerStatus | This attributes determines whether to enable Discoverer Viewer. | RW | true |
| 13 | EnableViewerValue | Discoverer Viewer status description | RW | Viewer was stopped by your Administrator. |
| 14 | eventProvider | If true, it indicates that this MBean is an event provider as defined by JSR-77. | R | true |
| 15 | eventTypes | All the event's types emitted by this MBean. | R | jmx.attribute.change |
| 16 | IsCurrentPageItemsExportForOLAF | Attribute exposed for management | W | |
| 17 | LAF | Look and Feel | RW | dc_blaf |
| 18 | LastRunLabelRendered | Attribute which determines whether the label to display last Run time should be rendered | RW | true |
| 19 | LogLevel | Log level for viewer | RW | SEVERE |
| 20 | LogoFile | Logo image file | RW | |
| 21 | LogoRendered | Attribute to determine whether the logo should be rendered | RW | true |
| 22 | LogoSource | Source of the logo | RW | default |
| 23 | LogoURL | URL for the logo image | RW | |
| 24 | LongRequestRefreshPeriod | Request refresh period | RW | 6000 |
| 25 | LongRequestTimeout | Period, in milliseconds, between first long request progress page an subsequent long request progress pages | RW | 10000 |
| 26 | NumberOfLOVsToBeDisplayed | The Number of LOVs to be displayed in the parameter search dialog box. Defaults to 25. | RW | 25 |
| 27 | objectName | The MBean's unique JMX name | R | com.oracle:name=ViewerConfig,type=Xml.ViewerConfig,Applicati... |
| 28 | PageNavigation | Attribute exposed for management | W | |
| 29 | PassNullParameterAsNull | This variable decides whether a parameter value should be passed as NULL always to another worksheet when we drill from one sheet to another ( when the value is actually NULL) | RW | false |
| 30 | PrintingMaxMemory | Maximum memory in MB that can be used while printing | RW | 64 |
| 31 | PrintingMaxUsers | Maximum users allowed for printing | RW | 2 |

9. Update values of the attributes to modify by entering the new value in the Value field.
10. Click Apply.

# Discoverer User Preferences

Discoverer has a sophisticated component called *preferences*. During installation, Discoverer uses factory-supplied default values (stored in defaults.txt) to create user preferences for all Discoverer users (stored in pref.txt). All of the preferences in pref.txt are compiled into a file called .reg_key.dc.

When a new user starts a Discoverer session for the first time, the settings in the pref.txt file take effect as that user's default settings.

After installation, the user preferences can be changed in the following three ways:

- Discoverer end users can change their own user preferences using options within Discoverer Plus or Discoverer Viewer. For example, a Discoverer Viewer end user might click Preferences and change their personal preferences. When an individual user changes a preference, this change is stored in the .reg_key.dc file on the Discoverer middle tier. Unless a user changes a preference value, the value of that preference is as specified in the pref.txt file.
- You can set individual preferences for a specific user using the dis51pr command-line utility. Changes made via this method are also compiled into the .reg_key.dc file. Changing user preferences using the command line is described later in this chapter.
- You can change the global defaults for all of your Discoverer users by editing the pref.txt file. For the changes to take effect, you must "apply" the preferences. Once again, these are compiled into the .reg_key.dc file.

Both the pref.txt and .reg_key.dc files are usually located in the same folder, as follows:

$ORACLE_HOME/<instance_name>/config/PreferenceServer/Discoverer_<instance>

On Unix implementations, .reg_key.dc is a hidden Unix file (in other words, the filename is prefixed with a .). Type the command **ls -al** to list hidden files.

In our case, because our $ORACLE_HOME is c:\oracle\Middleware and our instance is called asinst_1, the folder is located here:

C:\oracle|middleware\asinst_1\config\PreferenceServer\Discoverer_asinst_1

In the .reg_key.dc file, you will get all the defaults as set by pref.txt along with any individual preferences that have been made by users either in Plus or in Viewer. The system first reads the default settings and then overrides these with individual user settings.

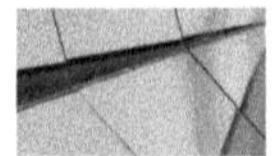

**NOTE**

*Even though .reg_key.dc looks like a file that could be edited manually using a standard text editor, do not be tempted to do so. This file is intended for system use only, and editing it manually could cause Discoverer to no longer work correctly. Please also note that its name begins with a period.*

If you lose or delete the .reg_key.dc file, you will lose all preferences that were set by your Discoverer end users or preferences set using the Discoverer preferences command-line utility. Default preferences stored in pref.txt are applied.

The factory-supplied default values for pref.txt are contained in the defaults.txt file. If you make a mistake when editing the pref.txt file (or lose or corrupt the file), refer to defaults.txt to restore the content of pref.txt to the original values. The defaults.txt file is located in the same folder as the pref.txt file.

## Discoverer Preference Server

Discoverer has what is called a *preference server* that manages the user preferences. This server has its own process, called dis51pr. It even has its own port. But why do preferences need to be a separate process? The primary reason is for Discoverer load balancing. Let's say you have two or more Discoverer servers and that one of your users has set their background color to be light green. Unless you have a preference server, the next time the user logs on, if that user is directed to another Discoverer server, they would lose the light green background.

Therefore, in a multiple-host Discoverer environment, you will start the preferences server on one host. The preferences will then be stored in the hidden .reg_key.dc file on this single mid-tier.

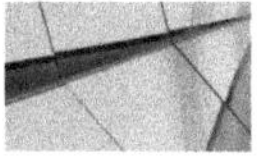

**NOTE**
*Using a single preference server is a potential high-availability issue, because this server now becomes a single point of failure, at least for your user preferences. Discoverer will continue to work using default preferences, so this is not a high-availability issue in the sense of a catastrophic single point of failure.*

## Changing Preferences by a User

An end user can set their own preferences from within Discoverer Plus using Tools | Options or from within Discoverer Viewer by clicking the Preferences link on the main Viewer page.

When a user adjusts their preferences, Discoverer contacts the preference server and requests that it handle the change. Any changes that the user has made in that session are written to the .reg_key.dc file. If a user has never set that preference before, a new entry is written. If the user has previously entered a different preference for the same setting, the setting will be updated.

## Changing Global User Preferences Using pref.txt

To change Discoverer's global user preferences, use the following workflow:

1. Open and edit pref.txt located here:

   $ORACLE_HOME/<instance_name>/config/PreferenceServer/Discoverer_<instance>
2. In Unix or Linux, run applypreferences.sh or enter **dis51pr -apply -file pref.txt**; while in Windows, run applypreferences.bat. The applypreferences file for Discoverer 11*g* can be found in the following folder:

   $ORACLE_HOME/<instance_name>/Discoverer/Discoverer_<instance>/util
3. Restart the Discoverer mid-tier server.

**NOTE**
*In Discoverer 10g the applypreferences executable is located in the same folder as pref.txt.*

## Changing User Preferences Using the Command Line

To change Discoverer's preferences via the command line, use the following workflow:

1. Navigate to the bin folder for the application server instance, which in our case is as follows:

   $ORACLE_HOME/as_1/bin – where $ORACLE_HOME = c:\oracle\Middleware
2. Execute **dis51pr -user username@eulname -setpref** ***areanameprefname*** ***pref setting***.

For example, to set the default EUL for user msmith on the bookdbdatabase to Marketing, use the following:

**dis51pr -user msmith@bookdb -setpref "Database""DefaultEUL"\\"Marketing\\"**

This command sets the new preferences and creates a new version of reg_key.dc. It uses the following syntax:

```
dis51pr -user <user> -setpref <"preference category"><"preference
name"><"preference value">
```

The syntax is explained as follows:

- <user> is the name of the user for which you want to set the preference value, followed by the @ symbol, followed by the name of the database (for example, msmith@bookdb).
- <"preference category"> is the category of the preference you want to change (for example, Database).
- <"preference name"> is the name of the preference you want to change (for example, DefaultEUL).
- <"preference value"> is the value you want the preference to have.

Here are some examples:

- If you want to set the default EUL to Sales for the user msmith, use the following at a command prompt:

  ```
  dis51pr -user msmith@bookdb -setpref "Database" "DefaultEUL" \\"Sales\\"
  ```

- If you want to set the maximum amount of heap memory allowed for the data cache to 768000 for a user msmith, use the following at a command prompt:

  ```
  dis51pr -user msmith@bookdb -setpref "Application""MaxVirtualHeapMem"
  768000
  ```

The following rules apply to setting preferences via the command line:

- To display online help for the Discoverer preferences command-line utility, type the name of the script followed by -help (for example, **dis51pr -help**).
- Preference names and values are case-sensitive.
- When specifying a string as a preference value, prefix the string with \\" and end the string with \\". For example, if the preference value is Sales, enter \\"**Sales**\\".

## Listing of User Preferences

Table 20-2 lists the preferences that can be set inside the pref.txt file. The pref.txt file is broken into the following four areas:

- Session Manager
- Application

- Database
- Generic Properties

The areas are shown in square brackets in the table.

**NOTE**
*Unlike Discoverer 10g in which all of the preferences were visible inside pref.txt, in Discoverer 11g only the most commonly used preferences are made available upon install. If you find that a preference you need to set is not in your pref.txt, you will need to add it in the appropriate area. We have indicated in the table which preferences are not available out of the box by displaying their name in italics. Also, most preference names have no spaces between the words. We have included a note for those preferences that do have spaces in their name.*

| Preference | Default Setting | Description |
|---|---|---|
| [Session Manager] | | |
| Timeout | 1800 | Discoverer Plus, the web applet, will warn the user, and if the user does not respond, it will close the session after the number of seconds indicated. Upon installation, the default is 1,800 seconds (30 minutes). The minimum allowed is 180.<br>Take care raising the timeout limit, as this will cause Discoverer to hold sessions open for longer.<br>**Note:** For SSO-based connections, Discoverer Plus does not consider the Global User Inactivity Timeout (GUIT) setting defined in the SSO server. To get the same SSO timeout behavior for Discoverer Plus, you can set the Timeout value in pref.txt to the same value as the GUIT setting.<br>To set the timeout for Discoverer Viewer, you need to set the viewerSessionTimeOut variable in the Discoverer deployment plan of the WebLogic Server Administration Console. For instructions on how to do this, please refer to the section "Setting the Timeout Value for Discoverer" later in this chapter. |
| [Application] | | |
| RowsPerHTML | 25 | This setting controls the number of rows per page that should be used to display the results on a report. The range is 1–999, with the default being 25. Be careful, because if you set this number too high, it will have an adverse effect on performance. |

**TABLE 20-2.** *Discoverer User Preferences* (continued)

| Preference | Default Setting | Description |
|---|---|---|
| EuroCountries | "de,de_AT,de_DE,de_LI,de_LIECHTENSTEIN,de_LU,de_LUXEMBOURG,el,el_GR,en_IE,es_ES,fi,fi_FI,fr, fr_BE,fr_FR,fr_LU,fr_LUXEMBOURG,it,it_IT,nl,nl_BE,nl_NL,pt,pt_PT,sv_FI" | This setting controls the list of countries that use the euro as their unit of currency. You will probably never have a need to change this setting unless a new country is admitted to the Euro zone or a country opts out of the euro.<br>The list is a comma-delimited list of Java locales. |
| PrintHeadersOnce | 0 | This setting controls whether headers will print only once or for each printed page. It has two valid settings.<br>0: Print the header only once.<br>1: Repeat the heading on each printed page.<br>The default is 0.<br>**Note:** Setting this value to 1 will reduce the number of pages that Discoverer Plus generates (for example, in a crosstab worksheet where headers are repeated often). |
| PrintPercentageOfTitle | 60 | If the title does not fit on a printed page, use this setting to automatically show a percentage of the title. The range is 20–60, and the default is 60. When used, the remaining part of the title will be truncated. |
| GraphAxesAutoScaledFromZero | 1 | This setting controls whether Discoverer will scale graphs starting from zero. It has two valid settings.<br>0: Scale graphs automatically. Discoverer will choose the minimum scale value based on the data being graphed.<br>1: The minimum scale value is set to 0.<br>The default is 1. |
| CacheFlushPercentage | 25 | This setting determines the percentage of cache that Discoverer will flush when the cache fills up. The range is 0–100, with the default being 25. |
| MaxVirtualDiskMem | 1024000000 | This setting specifies the maximum amount of virtual memory, in bytes, to use for the data cache. You need to make sure that this is greater than MaxVirtualHeapMem. The setting alongside equates to 1GB.<br>The minimum is 0.<br>The maximum is 4GB.<br>The default is 1GB, specified as 1024000000. |
| MaxVirtualHeapMem | 5120000 | This specifies the maximum amount of heap memory, in bytes, to make available for the data cache. The setting alongside equates to 5MB.<br>The minimum is 0.<br>The maximum is 4GB.<br>The default is 5MB, specified as 5120000. |

**TABLE 20-2.** *Discoverer User Preferences* (continued)

| Preference | Default Setting | Description |
|---|---|---|
| QueryBehavior | 0 | This setting controls what Discoverer will do when a workbook is opened. It has three valid settings.<br>0: Automatically run the query when the workbook is opened.<br>1: The query will not run automatically, and the user needs to click the refresh button to run the query.<br>2: Discoverer will prompt the user every time the user opens this workbook to see whether they want to run the query.<br>The default is 0.<br>This can be overridden by a user setting their own value using Tools \| Properties \| General by checking one of the following radio buttons:<br>■ Run Query Automatically<br>■ Don't Run Query (Leave Sheet Empty)<br>■ Ask For Confirmation |
| ShowDialogBitmaps | 1 | This setting controls whether Discoverer shows images inside the wizard dialogs. It has two valid settings.<br>0: Do not show images. Setting this to 0 will maximize the amount of real estate available to a user when inside the wizard. This can be very useful when you have folders with lots of items or business areas with lots of folders.<br>1: Show the images.<br>The default is 1.<br>This can be overridden by a user setting their own value using Tools \| Properties \| General and then checking/unchecking the check box called Show Wizard Graphics. |
| SaveLastUsedParamValue | 0 | When a workbook that has parameters is saved, this setting determines what the default will be the next time a user enters a parameter value. It has two valid settings.<br>0: Use the default value that was set by the report writer when the workbook was created.<br>1: Save the value that the user just entered and use that as the next default. The value will be stored with the workbook.<br>The default is 0. |
| NotifyNewRunsOnConnect | 0 | This setting controls whether a user will be alerted to scheduled jobs when logging in. It has two valid settings.<br>0: The user will not be alerted to scheduled jobs that have finished when the user logs in.<br>1: The user will receive a message notifying the user that their scheduled jobs are completed. It causes Discoverer to launch the New Schedule Runs dialog box on login.<br>The default is 0.<br>This can be overridden by a user setting their own value using Tools \| Properties \| General and then checking/unchecking the check box Don't Show The New Results Window After Initial Connection. |

**TABLE 20-2.** *Discoverer User Preferences* (continued)

| Preference | Default Setting | Description |
|---|---|---|
| ShowExpiredRunsAtExit | 1 | This setting controls whether the user will be notified about expired and deleted jobs when logging out. It has two valid settings.<br>0: The user will not be notified about expired and deleted scheduled workbook results when logging out. The results will be deleted.<br>1: The user will be notified about expired and deleted scheduled workbook results when logging out.<br>The default is 1.<br>This can be overridden by a user setting their own value using Tools \| Properties \| General and then checking/unchecking the check box Don't Show Expired Results On Exit, Delete Results Automatically. |
| GraphShowRollupAggregates | 1 | This setting controls whether graphs that are associated with an outline crosstab show rollup values. It has two valid settings.<br>0: Do not show the rollup values.<br>1: Show the rollup values.<br>The default is 1. |
| ExportGroupSortedItemsAsBlank | 1 | This setting controls how group-sorted items or items displayed in the left axis of a crosstab are exported when users export to a CSV or TXT file. It has two valid settings.<br>0: Export all group-sorted values causing the value of the group-sorted items to repeat for each row.<br>1: Export the first group-sorted value and then send the remainder of the values as empty cells, aka NULL values.<br>The default is 1. |
| AxisLabelBehavior | 1 | This setting controls how axis labels are managed. It has three valid settings.<br>1: Always show the axis labels.<br>2: Never show axis labels.<br>3: Let the user control whether axis labels are displayed.<br>The default is 1. |
| Data Format | "<fontFormat fontName="Dialog" pitch="11" bold="false" italic="false" underline="false" strikethrough="false" foreground="0,0,0" background="255,255,255" halign="right" valign="top" wordWrap="true"></ fontFormat>" | This is where you may provide HTML to control how the data in the worksheet cells are displayed.<br>End users can override this setting by using Tools \| Options \| Formats from the toolbar and setting their own default data format.<br>**Note:** The name of this preference has spaces between the words. |
| Heading Format | "<fontFormat fontName="Dialog" pitch="11"bold="false" italic="false" underline="false" strikethrough="false" foreground="0,0,0" background="247,247,231" halign="left" valign="top" wordWrap="true"></ fontFormat>" | This is where you provide HTML to control how the headings appear in the worksheet.<br>End users can override this setting by using Tools \| Options \| Formats from the toolbar and setting their own default heading format.<br>**Note:** The name of this preference has spaces between the words. |

**TABLE 20-2.** *Discoverer User Preferences* (continued)

| Preference | Default Setting | Description |
|---|---|---|
| Totals Format | "<fontFormat fontName="Dialog"pitch="11" bold="false" italic="false" underline="false" strikethrough="false" foreground="0,0,0" background="247,247,231" halign="right" valign="top" wordWrap="true"></ fontFormat>" | This is where you provide HTML to control how totals appear in the worksheet.<br>End users can override this setting by using Tools \| Options \| Formats from the toolbar and setting their own default totals format.<br>**Note:** The name of this preference has spaces between the words. |
| NullValue | "NULL" | This specifies what Discoverer should display when a value is null.<br>This can be overridden by a user setting their own global value using Tools \| Properties \| Sheet or in an individual worksheet. |
| NonAggregableValue | "" | This specifies what Discoverer should display when a value cannot be aggregated.<br>A cell is classified as "non-aggregable" if the aggregation function being applied does not make sense for the values being aggregated. |
| ExcelExportWithMacros | 1 | This setting controls whether Discoverer will export macros when exporting to Excel. If this is disabled by changing the value to 0, no formats or macros will be exported. It has two valid settings.<br>0: Do not export macros to Excel.<br>1: Export macros to Excel. This causes Discoverer to also export the formats to Excel.<br>The default is 1.<br>**Note:** Macros must be enabled for pivot table exports to work correctly. |
| CellPadding | "1" | This setting determines how many pixels will be padded around cells. The range is 0–5.<br>For example, 0 = no pixels, 1 = one pixel, 2 = two pixels, and so on.<br>**Note:** Setting this value to 0 will reduce the size of printed reports by removing extra spaces.<br>**Tip:** For more information about reducing the size of a printed report, see the PrintHeadersOnce preference.<br>The default is 1. |
| ShowGraphToolBar | true | This setting controls whether the graph toolbar is displayed. It has two valid settings.<br>false: Do not show the graph toolbar.<br>true: Show the graph toolbar.<br>The default is true. |
| ShowFormatToolBar | true | This setting controls whether the format toolbar is displayed. It has two valid settings.<br>false: Do not show the format toolbar.<br>true: Show the format toolbar.<br>The default is true. |

**TABLE 20-2.** *Discoverer User Preferences* (continued)

| Preference | Default Setting | Description |
|---|---|---|
| StandardToolBar | true | This setting controls whether the standard toolbar is displayed. It has two valid settings.<br>false: Do not show the standard toolbar.<br>true: Show the standard toolbar.<br>The default is true. |
| ShowJoins | false | This is a really cool setting and a much-awaited feature. The default is false, meaning the joins will be hidden from Discoverer Plus users. Sometimes more sophisticated users become frustrated, because they do not know which folders are related. Changing this to true will allow the join icons to appear in Plus as they do in the Administrator tool. It has two valid settings.<br>false: Do not show the joins to the user.<br>true: Show the joins to the user.<br>The default is false.<br>This can be overridden by a user setting their own value using Tools \| Properties \| Advanced and checking/unchecking the check box Show Joins. |
| ShowDrillIcon | false | This setting controls whether to show the drill icons in worksheets. It has two valid settings.<br>false: Do not show the drill icon.<br>true: Show the drill icon.<br>The default is false. |
| ColumnWidth | 100 | This setting controls the default column width.<br>The setting must be greater than 1.<br>The default is 100. |
| DefaultExportPath | "" | This setting controls the default export path for Discoverer Plus.<br>If set to "", Discoverer saves exported files in the client browser machine's home directory (that is, the profile directory in Windows). For example, on a Windows XP client, this path might be c:\Documents and Settings\<Windows username>, whereas for Windows 7 this would be c:\Users\\<Windows username>.<br>The default is to allow Discoverer to export files in the client browser machine's home directory. |
| RowsPerPage | 25 | This setting controls the number of rows per scrollable page that are available within Discoverer Viewer. Each page down will move down the RowsPerPage.<br>The default is 25. |
| ColsPerPage | 128 | This setting controls the number of columns per scrollable page in Discoverer Viewer.<br>The default is a very large 128. |

**TABLE 20-2.** *Discoverer User Preferences* (continued)

| Preference | Default Setting | Description |
|---|---|---|
| ScatterGraphDataModel | 0 | This setting controls how to display a scatter graph.<br>It has three valid settings.<br>0: Use the Discoverer Plus style.<br>1: Use the Discoverer Desktop style.<br>2: Use the Microsoft Excel style.<br>The default is 0. |
| Cell Gridcolor | 0 | This setting controls the default cell color. The value entered must be entered as a hex value using the RRGGBB format, where RR is the value for red, GG is for green, and BB is for blue.<br>The default is 0 for black.<br>**Note:** The name of this preference has spaces between the words. |
| Show Text Area | 1 | This setting controls the default display of the text area at the bottom of the Plus screen. It has two valid settings.<br>0: Do not show the text area.<br>1: Show the text area.<br>The default is 0.<br>This can be overridden by a user in each worksheet.<br>**Note:** The name of this preference has spaces between the words. |
| Show Title | 1 | This setting controls the default display of the title. It has two valid settings.<br>0: Do not show the title.<br>1: Show the title.<br>The default is 1.<br>This can be overridden by a user in each worksheet.<br>**Note:** The name of this preference has spaces between the words. |
| Cell XGridline | 1 | This setting controls the default display of the horizontal and vertical gridlines. It has two valid settings.<br>0: Do not show the gridlines.<br>1: Show the gridlines.<br>The default is 1.<br>**Note:** The name of this preference has spaces between the words. |
| Cell YGridline | 1 | This setting controls the default display of the horizontal and vertical gridlines. It has two valid settings.<br>0: Do not show the gridlines.<br>1: Show the gridlines.<br>The default is 1.<br>**Note:** The name of this preference has spaces between the words. |

**TABLE 20-2.** *Discoverer User Preferences* (continued)

| Preference | Default Setting | Description |
|---|---|---|
| Default Title | "" | This setting controls what will be displayed as the default title. You can set this to anything you like. The default is null.<br>This can be overridden by a user setting their own value using Tools \| Properties \| Formats, selecting Title, and then clicking the Change button.<br>**Note:** The name of this preference has spaces between the words. |
| Default Text Area | "" | This setting controls what will be displayed as the default in the text area. You can set this to anything you like.<br>The default is null.<br>This can be overridden by a user setting their own value using Tools \| Properties \| Formats, selecting Text Area,and then clicking the Change button.<br>**Note:** The name of this preference has spaces between the words. |
| Measurement Units | 0 | This setting controls the default for the unit of measure. It has three valid settings.<br>0: Use pixels.<br>1: Use inches.<br>2: Use centimeters.<br>The default is 0.<br>This can be overridden by a user setting their own value using Tools \| Properties \| General and selecting a different value from the drop-down Measurement unit for workbooks.<br>**Note:** The name of this preference has spaces between the words. |
| DisableClassicExports | 0 | This setting controls whether the classic export formats of DIF, SLK, and WKS will be displayed. It has two valid settings.<br>0: Do not enable these export formats.<br>1: Allow users to export in these formats.<br>The default is 0. |
| AggregationBehavior | 0 | This setting controls whether Discoverer linearly aggregates values that otherwise cannot be computed. It has two valid settings.<br>0: Disallow linear aggregation.<br>1: Allow Discoverer to linearly aggregate values that it could not have done otherwise (except for analytics and repeated values, the latter of which has its own setting; see the next setting). This has no effect if EDA is enabled.<br>The default is 0. |
| AllowAggregationOverRepeatedValues | 0 | This setting controls whether Discoverer is allowed to aggregate repeated values. It has two valid settings.<br>0: Do not allow aggregation over repeated values.<br>1: Allow aggregation over repeated values.<br>The default is 0. |

**TABLE 20-2.** *Discoverer User Preferences* (continued)

| Preference | Default Setting | Description |
|---|---|---|
| AdjustPlusFontSize | false | This setting controls whether Discoverer is allowed to adjust the font size to handle a Java bug. It has two valid settings.<br>false: Do not adjust the font size.<br>true: Adjust the font size. Setting this to true allows Discoverer Plus to visually display results in the same font as Discoverer Viewer. You need to change this only if you notice that the font sizes are different.<br>The default is false. |
| MRUEnabled | 1 | This setting controls whether Discoverer will keep a list of the most recently used (MRU) workbooks. It has two valid settings.<br>0: Do not keep the most recently used workbooks.<br>1: Keep a list of the most recently used workbooks. The actual number of workbooks that will be kept in the list is under user control and can be set from within the Tools \| Options menu of the Plus screen.<br>The default is 0.<br>This can be overridden by a user setting their own value using Tools \| Properties \| General and selecting a value from 0 through 9 from the box Workbooks In Recently Used List. A setting of 0 indicates that Discoverer should not keep a list of the most recently used workbooks. A nonzero value indicates how many workbooks should be remembered. |
| genericHeaderScroll | false | This setting controls whether Discoverer Plus Relational enables end users to scroll in large headers.<br>If crosstabs have large row headers, end users might have difficulty viewing the data unless they can scroll in the header.<br>It has two valid settings.<br>false: Do not enable scrolling in headers.<br>true: Enable scrolling in headers.<br>The default is false. |
| EnableWebQueryRun | 0 | This setting controls whether Discoverer response messages are displayed in Microsoft Excel when a query is run in Microsoft Excel. It has two valid settings.<br>0: Enable web query run.<br>1: Disable web query run.<br>The default is 0.<br>See also ExportToWebQuery and WebQueryBaseURL |

**TABLE 20-2.** *Discoverer User Preferences* (continued)

| Preference | Default Setting | Description |
|---|---|---|
| ExportToWebQuery | 1 | This setting controls whether Discoverer Plus and Discoverer Viewer end users can export worksheets to Web Query (*.IQY) format.<br>You typically add this preference and set the value to 0 to disable exporting to Web Query format.<br>If this preference is not present or applied, the default value is 1.<br>If export to Web Query is enabled, when Discoverer end users export a worksheet, they will see this format in the list of export types available.<br>It has two valid settings.<br>0: Disable export to web query.<br>1: Enable export to web query.<br>The default is 0.<br>See also EnableWebQueryRun and WebQueryBaseURL |
| WebQueryBaseURL | <Discoverer Viewer URL> | This setting controls the base Discoverer URL (for example, "http://machine-name:port#/discoverer/viewer"). If not present or applied, Discoverer uses the default Discoverer Viewer URL.<br>See also EnableWebQueryRun and ExportToWebQuery. |
| [Database] | | |
| DisableFanTrapDetection | 0 | This setting controls Discoverer's fan trap protection. It has two valid settings.<br>0: Enable fan trap detection.<br>1: Disable fan trap detection.<br>The default is 0. |
| DisableFanTrapResolution | 0 | This setting controls whether Discoverer is allowed to resolve fan traps. When enabled, Discoverer will prevent certain queries from running if the end result could be ambiguous. In particular, this is meant to trap and prevent summary data from being pulled from a folder that is designated as the master folder in a relationship. You can overcome this by changing the properties of the join in the Discoverer Administration tool to be 1:1.<br>It has two valid settings.<br>0: This turns on Discoverer's fan trap resolution.<br>1: This turns off Discoverer's fan trap resolution.<br>The default is 0.<br>Discoverer uses a patented mechanism for resolving fan traps. For more information on this, you should take a look at Chapter 10. We do not recommend turning off Discoverer's fan trap resolution mechanism unless you have good reason to do so.<br>This can be overridden by a user setting their own value using Tools \| Properties \| Advanced and then checking/unchecking the check box Disable Fan-Trap Protection. |

**TABLE 20-2.** *Discoverer User Preferences* (continued)

| Preference | Default Setting | Description |
|---|---|---|
| DisableMultiJoinDetection | 0 | When multiple joins between folders are detected, this setting controls whether Discoverer prompts a user as to which join should be used. It has two valid settings.<br>0: Ask the user which join to use.<br>1: Discoverer will select the first join it finds, even if it is incorrect. Changing this setting to 1 can have adverse effects on your reports, so take care doing so and do so only if you have good reason.<br>The default is 0.<br>This can be overridden by a user setting their own value using Tools \| Properties \| Advanced and then checking/unchecking the check box Disable Multiple Join Path Detection. |
| DisableAutoQuery | 0 | This setting controls whether Discoverer should automatically run a query when the user makes a change to a sheet and the data is not in the Discoverer cache. It has two valid settings.<br>0: Turns off automatic querying. The user will need to use the Refresh Sheet command to see the data.<br>1: Turns on automatic querying. Discoverer will automatically rerun a query following a change if it detects that the data is not in the cache.<br>The default is 0.<br>This can be overridden by a user setting their own value using Tools \| Properties \| Advanced and then checking/unchecking the check box Disable Automatic Querying From Database. |
| DisableAutoOuterJoinsOnFilters | 0 | This setting controls how Discoverer uses outer joins when conditions or filters exist. It has two valid settings.<br>0: When a query has a filter, a setting of 0 will not disable outer joins and allow outer joins to be used.<br>1: Disable outer joins on filters.<br>The default is 0. |
| EnhancedAggregationStrategy | 1 | This feature dictates how the database executes the GROUP BY clause. It has five valid settings.<br>0: Use ordinary GROUP BY, which is the slowest.<br>1: Use the Grouping Sets command on the GROUP BY clause.<br>2: Optimize grouping sets by possibly submitting multiple queries to the database.<br>3: Use cube and rollup commands as well.<br>4: Let Discoverer decide the fastest way to execute the query. |

**TABLE 20-2.** *Discoverer User Preferences* (continued)

| Preference | Default Setting | Description |
|---|---|---|
| *Continued* | 1 | Whichever version of the application server you are using will determine what the current default level of this switch is. In 11*g* and 10*g*, it is defaulted to 1, whereas in 9*i*, it was defaulted to 4. If you are using 10*g* or 11*g*, we recommend leaving this set to 1; however, if you are reading this and are still using 9*i*, we would first try switching it from 4 to 1. If performance is still poor, you can then try switching it to 0.<br>We have to say that performance in 11*g* Plus is better than in 10*g* Plus, which in turn is better than in 9*i* Plus, and so you should have fewer issues. Nevertheless, we have seen complex crosstabs run for a long time in 11*g* initially, only for them to run in just a few seconds when we set this switch to 0.<br>In some rare cases (for example, a complex query where a CUBE aggregation strategy is chosen), an Enhanced AggregationStrategy setting of 4 can lead to Discoverer becoming unresponsive while it generates a large number of aggregation combinations. Accordingly, we endorse Oracle's recommendation to set this to 1. |
| ItemClassDelay | 15 | This setting controls the maximum number of seconds that Discoverer is allowed to use when determining a list of values. If the LOV takes longer than this setting, it will time out and not display the list.<br>The default is 15.<br>This can be overridden by a user setting their own value using Tools \| Properties \| Query Governor and then changing the value in the box Cancel List-Of-Values Retrieval After. |
| PredictionThresholdSeconds | 60 | This setting controls the number of seconds after which Discoverer will warn the user that the query might take a while.<br>The default is 60.<br>The minimum value that you can set is 1.<br>This can be overridden by a user setting their own value using Tools \| Properties \| Query Governor, checking/unchecking the check box Warn Me If Predicted Query Time, and setting the number of minutes and seconds the query is allowed to run before a warning is issued. |
| PredictionThresholdSecondsEnabled | 1 | This setting controls whether the query predictor threshold is enabled. It has two valid settings.<br>0: Do not enable the query prediction threshold.<br>1: Enable the query prediction threshold. If your database does not have a cost-based optimizer (in other words, it is a non-Oracle database or older than Oracle 8), then you must set this to 0.<br>The default is 1. |

**TABLE 20-2.** *Discoverer User Preferences* (continued)

| Preference | Default Setting | Description |
|---|---|---|
| QueryTimeLimit | 1800 | This setting controls the maximum number of seconds that a query is allowed to run. If the query exceeds this limit, then it will time out, discarding all work.<br>The default is 1,800 seconds, or 30 minutes.<br>The minimum value that you can set is 1.<br>This can be overridden by a user setting their own value using Tools \| Properties \| Query Governor, checking/unchecking the check box Prevent Queries Running Longer Than, and setting the number of minutes and seconds the query is allowed to run. |
| QueryTimeLimitEnabled | 1 | This setting controls whether the query time limit is enabled. It has two valid settings.<br>0: The query time limit is disabled.<br>1: The query time limit is enabled.<br>The default is 1. |
| RowFetchLimit | 10000 | If enabled, this setting defines the maximum number of rows a query is allowed to fetch. This setting is designed to protect the database from bad queries and Cartesian products.<br>The default is 10000.<br>The minimum value you can set is 1.<br>This can be overridden by a user setting their own value using Tools \| Properties. |
| RowFetchLimitEnabled | 1 | This setting controls whether the row fetch limit is enabled. It has two valid settings.<br>0: The row fetch limit is disabled.<br>1: The row fetch limit is enabled.<br>The default is 1.<br>This can be overridden by a user setting their own value using Tools \| Properties \| Query Governor, checking/unchecking the check box Limit Retrieved Data To, and setting the number of rows to be retrieved. |
| MaxRowsPerFetch | 250 | This setting determines the maximum number of database rows to be delivered with each fetch.<br>The default is 250.<br>The minimum value you can set is 1.<br>The maximum value you can set is 10000.<br>**Notes**:<br>■ If the MaxRowsPerFetch value is greater than the RowsPerFetch value, use the RowsPerFetch value.<br>■ If the MaxRowsPerFetch value is less than or equal to the RowsPerFetch value, use the MaxRowsPerFetch value.<br>■ If the RowsPerFetch value is not set, use the MaxRowsPerFetch value.<br>This can be overridden by a user setting their own value using Tools \| Properties \| Query Governor and then setting the value in the box Retrieve Data Incrementally In Groups Of.<br>See also RowsPerFetch. |

**TABLE 20-2.** *Discoverer User Preferences* (continued)

| Preference | Default Setting | Description |
|---|---|---|
| RowsPerFetch | 250 | This setting determines how many rows are delivered per fetch.<br>The default is 250.<br>The minimum value you can set is 1.<br>The maximum value you can set is 10000.<br>**Notes**:<br>■ If the RowsPerFetch value is less than or equal to the MaxRowsPerFetch value, use the RowsPerFetch value.<br>■ If the RowsPerFetch value is greater than the MaxRowsPerFetch value, use the MaxRowsPerFetch value.<br>■ If the RowsPerFetch value is not set, use the MaxRowsPerFetch value.<br>See also MaxRowsPerFetch. |
| SummaryThreshold | 60 | If enabled, this setting controls how summary folders are used.<br>0 means do not use summaries.<br>Any other value determines how many days old a summary can be and still be used. |
| SummaryThresholdEnabled | 1 | This setting controls whether the summary threshold is used. It has two valid settings.<br>0: The summary threshold is disabled.<br>1: The summary threshold is enabled.<br>The default is 1.<br>This can be overridden by a user setting their own value using Tools \| Properties \| Query Governor and then checking one of the three radio buttons.<br>■ Always, When Available<br>■ Only When Summary Data Is Out Of Date<br>■ Never |
| MaterializedViewRedirectionBehavior | 0 | This setting controls how Discoverer uses materialized views. It has three valid settings.<br>0: This setting means always use materialized views.<br>1: This setting means use the materialized view only if the source data has not changed (not stale).<br>2: This setting means never use materialized views.<br>The default is 0. |
| DefaultEUL | "VIDEO5" | This identifies the default End User Layer. When installing a new EUL, Discoverer sets this to VIDEO5, the EUL for the Oracle sample data.<br>You should change this setting for your own system to specify the EUL to which you want all users to connect.<br>This can be overridden by a user entering their own preferred EUL on the Discoverer Plus Tools \| Options \| EUL tab. |

**TABLE 20-2.** *Discoverer User Preferences* (continued)

| Preference | Default Setting | Description |
|---|---|---|
| DisableAlternateSortOptimisation | 0 | This setting controls whether Discoverer will write optimized alternate queries for sorts. It has two valid settings.<br>0: Do not disable alternate sort optimization.<br>1: Disable alternate sort optimization. You should set this only if you are using unregistered external summaries and you want Discoverer's alternate sort queries to be redirected to those summaries.<br>The default is 0. |
| SQLFlatten | 1 | This setting controls whether Discoverer will avoid inline views by flattening the SQL. It has two valid settings.<br>0: Discoverer will not flatten the SQL, thus not avoiding inline views.<br>1: Discoverer will avoid inline views (subqueries in the FROM clause) by flattening the SQL.<br>The default is 1. |
| SQLItemTrim | 1 | This setting controls whether Discoverer includes nonrequired items in the query. It has two valid settings.<br>0: Discoverer might include extra items in a query. This could make for faster drilling but could cause additional CPU and memory usage.<br>1: Discoverer will not include items the user does not want.<br>The default is 1. |
| SQLJoinTrim | 1 | This setting controls whether Discoverer includes joins to items that are not used in the query. It has two valid settings.<br>0: Discoverer might include extra joins in the query.<br>1: Discoverer will not join items the user does not need.<br>The default is 1. |
| AppsGWYUID | "APPLSYSPUB/PUB" | This is the default setting if you are querying an E-Business Suite database and you want to connect using an E-Business Suite user and responsibility. Unless you are using different settings, there will be no need to change this setting. |
| AppsFNDNAM | "APPS" | This is the foundation name, or main user, of the Oracle E-Business Suite application. This is used for connecting Discoverer in Apps mode. Unless you are using a different foundation username, there will be no need to change this setting. |

**TABLE 20-2.** *Discoverer User Preferences* (continued)

| Preference | Default Setting | Description |
|---|---|---|
| BusinessAreaFastFetchLevel | 1 | This setting controls how much caching occurs when loading business areas. In general terms, the lower the value, the fewer folders and items are fetched into the Navigator dialog immediately. It has five valid settings.<br>0: No fast fetch is performed.<br>1: Discoverer will cache only the business area when it opens it. This makes for a faster opening of the business area. If you are not constantly changing business areas and trust that they are valid, you can safely use this setting.<br>2: Discoverer will cache the business area and all items within the business area that are used by the users.<br>3: Discoverer will cache the business area and all items within the business area that are used by the Administrator tool.<br>4: Discoverer will cache the business area and all items within the business area.<br>The default is 1.<br>This setting is an internal setting only, and the end user has no visibility of it and has no way of setting it as an individual preference. |
| ObjectsAlwaysAccessible | 1 | This setting controls whether objects are to be assumed always accessible to the users. It has two valid settings.<br>0: This setting causes Discoverer to check that the objects exist and that the user has access to the objects every time the user opens the items in a folder.<br>1: If every user can access every folder, set this to 1. The security checks will then be deferred until query execution time, thus causing the business areas to load much faster.<br>The default is 1.<br>By default, in any of the user editions, whenever folders and items are displayed in the Navigator, Discoverer validates that the tables/views that they refer to exist and that the user has access to them. If you want, you can switch this validation off by setting this registry setting to be any number greater than 0. This will speed up the display of folders and items in the Navigator. However, if the database objects do not exist or the user does not have access to them when this setting is greater than 0, the user will see an error when they execute the query.<br>This setting is an internal setting only, and the end user has no visibility of it and has no way of setting it as an individual preference. |

**TABLE 20-2.** *Discoverer User Preferences* (continued)

| Preference | Default Setting | Description |
|---|---|---|
| SummaryObjectsUseCachedAccessibility | 0 | This setting controls whether summary data should be accessed using Discoverer's results cache. It has two valid settings.<br>0: Use summary data from Discoverer's results cache.<br>1: Do not use the cache.<br>The default is 0.<br>This setting is an internal setting only, and the end user has no visibility of it and has no way of setting it as an individual preference. |
| AvoidServerWildcardBug | 0 | The database has a wildcard bug that Discoverer can avoid by setting this to 1. |
| RdbFastSQLOff | 0 | If you are using RDB, set this to 1. |
| QPPEnable | 1 | This setting controls query prediction. It has two valid settings.<br>0: Query prediction is disabled.<br>1: Query prediction is enabled. In fact, any nonzero value enables query prediction.<br>The default is 0.<br>This setting is an internal setting only. An end user has no visibility of it and has no way of setting it as an individual preference. |
| QPPCreateNewStats | 1 | This setting determines whether Discoverer will record new statistics in the EUL for query performance and prediction. A value greater than 0 enables the capturing of new statistics, while a setting of 0 turns it off. The statistics are stored in a table called EUL5_QPP_STATS. It has two valid settings.<br>0: Do not capture statistics.<br>1: Enable the capture of statistics. Any nonzero setting will work.<br>The default is 1.<br>This setting is an internal setting only. An end user has no visibility of it and has no way of setting it as an individual preference. |
| QPPLoadStatsByObjectUseKey | 1 | This setting controls whether Discoverer will load statistics for same objects first before others. It has two valid settings.<br>0: Do not load same objects first.<br>1: Load same objects first.<br>The default is 1. |
| QPPUseCpuTime | 1 | This setting controls whether the CPU time should be included within the prediction estimates. It has two valid settings.<br>0: Do not include the CPU time when predicting.<br>1: Include the CPU time when predicting.<br>The default is 1. |
| QPPMaxObjectUseKey | 30 | This setting determines how many statistics to cache in memory.<br>The default is 30. |

**TABLE 20-2.** *Discoverer User Preferences* (continued)

| Preference | Default Setting | Description |
|---|---|---|
| QPPCBOEnforced | 2 | This setting determines whether the use of the cost-based optimizer is enforced. It has three valid settings.<br>0: The use of the cost-based optimizer is not enforced.<br>1: The use of the cost-based optimizer is enforced.<br>2: The use of the cost-based optimizer will be enforced only for an Oracle 8.1.6 or newer database.<br>The default is 2.<br>Setting QPPCBOEnforced to be 1 forces Discoverer to use the cost-based optimizer, but setting it to 0 does not turn if off. To stop Discoverer using CBO altogether, you need to turn off query prediction, which is done by setting QPPEnable to 0. |
| QPPObtainCostMethod | 1 | If the cost-based optimizer is enabled, this setting controls how the costs are estimated. It has two valid settings.<br>0: Use the explain plan for the estimates.<br>1: Use dynamic views for the estimates.<br>The default is 1.<br>Because of a bug in the Oracle 11*g* database (4024370) as recorded in a posting on MetaLink on January 15, 2005, we need to use a workaround for Discoverer that will force Discoverer to use an explain plan instead of dynamic views. Therefore, when using an 11*g* database, you must set this setting to 0. |
| QPPMinCost | 0 | The setting controls how many statistics to record. A setting of 0 means record all statistics, no matter how low the cost. The default is 0. |
| QPPMaxStats | 500 | This setting controls how many previous statistics to load.<br>The default is 500. |
| QPPMinActCpuTime | 0 | To use CPU time or not to use CPU time, that is the question. A value of 0 is yes; anything greater is no. |
| QPPMinActElapsedTime | 0 | A setting of 0 will record all statistics. Any number greater than 0 means record statistics only if the actual elapsed time is greater than the setting. |
| QPPMinEstElapsedTime | 0 | This setting controls whether you will record statistics only if the actual elapsed time is less than this setting.<br>The default is 0. |
| UseOptimizerHints | 0 | This setting controls whether optimizer hints can be added to the SQL. It has two valid settings.<br>0: Do not add optimizer hints.<br>Any other value: Add optimizer hints to SQL.<br>The default is 0. |

**TABLE 20-2.** *Discoverer User Preferences* (continued)

| Preference | Default Setting | Description |
|---|---|---|
| QuerySQLFastFetchLevel | 1 | This setting controls how much SQL precaching occurs. Set this to 4; it is the fastest. It has five valid settings.<br>0: No fast fetch<br>1: Fast fetch (slow)<br>2: Fast fetch (medium)<br>3: Fast fetch (fast)<br>4: Fast fetch (super-fast) |
| SQLTrace | 0 | This setting controls whether a SQL trace is maintained of every query sent to the database. It has two valid settings.<br>0: SQL tracing is turned off.<br>1: SQL tracing is turned on. Discoverer copies SQL statements to a trace file for analysis.<br>The default is 0. |
| SQLType | 2 | This specifies the SQL style displayed in the SQL Inspector dialog in Discoverer Plus. It has three valid settings.<br>0: Flattened.<br>2: Default SQL with no flattening.<br>3: Flattened SQL without object aliases.<br>The default is 0. |
| Axis Label | 0 | This setting controls whether axis labels are displayed in a crosstab. It has two valid settings.<br>0: Do not display crosstab axis labels.<br>1: Show the crosstab axis labels.<br>The default is 0.<br>**Note:** The name of this preference has spaces between the words. |
| Axis Style | 2 | This setting controls the axis style for a crosstab worksheet. It has two valid settings.<br>1: Display crosstabs using the inline method.<br>2: Display crosstabs using the outline method.<br>The default is 2.<br>**Note:** The name of this preference has spaces between the words. |
| Column Headings | 1 | This setting controls whether column headings will be displayed. It has two valid settings.<br>0: Do not display column headings.<br>1: Display column headings.<br>The default is 1.<br>**Note:** The name of this preference has spaces between the words. |
| Row Headings | 0 | This setting controls whether row numbers will be displayed in a table. It has two valid settings.<br>0: Do not display row number for tables.<br>1: Display the row numbers.<br>The default is 0.<br>**Note:** The name of this preference has spaces between the words. |

**TABLE 20-2.** *Discoverer User Preferences* (continued)

| Preference | Default Setting | Description |
|---|---|---|
| QPPEnableEstimateWithNo Stats | 0 – if set | This preference controls how query prediction works during the first execution of a new workbook. When a query is run, statistics are collected and are then used the next time the query time is predicted. However, the first time a query is run, there will be no historical statistics available. In this case, Discoverer will try to get its information from the database using the explain plan. However, if the tables have not recently been analyzed, even the database may not be able to give the correct information the first time. This preference has two valid settings.<br>0: Query estimation is not based on statistics. Discoverer returns a predicted time of one second and does not waste time trying to predict the query run time. The users will not see any warning, and the query will run immediately.<br>1: Query estimation is based on the database explain plan.<br>In Discoverer 3.1.*x*, the following prediction message appeared even if the Discoverer workbook was being run for the first time: "This query will take approximately X seconds."<br>In Discoverer 4.1.*x*, the workbook must be run at least once to collect statistics for query prediction, and after the workbook is saved, closed, and reopened, the query prediction message appeared.<br>Many Oracle customers found this change in behavior inconvenient and wanted to have control over it. This preference was introduced in 4.1.46 for the first time, went away in 9.0.2, returned in 9.0.4, and has been retained in 10.1.2. You will not find this preference within the existing pref.txt file, so if you want to use it, you will need to add it in the [Database] section, setting the preference to 0. You also need to ensure that QPPEnable is set to 1; otherwise, query prediction will not be enabled. |
| DefaultPreserveDisplayPropertyForRefresh | 0 | When refreshing, this setting specifies whether an updated item description is discarded and replaced with the original description or whether the updated description is retained. It has two valid settings.<br>0: Use updated description.<br>1: Use original description.<br>The default is 0. |
| [Generic Properties] | | |
| GenericFormatToolBar | true | This specifies whether to display the Formatting toolbar by default in Discoverer Plus. It has two valid settings.<br>true: Display toolbar.<br>false: Do not display toolbar. |

**TABLE 20-2.** *Discoverer User Preferences* (continued)

| Preference | Default Setting | Description |
|---|---|---|
| GenericGraphToolBar | true | This specifies whether to display the Graph toolbar by default in Discoverer Plus. It has two valid settings.<br>true: Display toolbar.<br>false: Do not display toolbar. |
| GenericDefaultCacheCapacity | 80 | This specifies the default capacity of the cache to hold the rows above when you scroll down a worksheet in Discoverer Plus.<br>The minimum is 1. |
| GenericMaxCacheCapacity | 500 | This specifies the maximum capacity of the cache to hold the rows above when you scroll down a worksheet in Discoverer Plus.<br>The minimum is 1. |
| GenericStandardFetchSpan | 80 | This specifies the number of rows to be fetched from a worksheet at a time in Discoverer Plus.<br>The minimum is 1. |
| EUL Object Navigator | 1 | This setting controls the Available Items pane in Discoverer Plus. It has two valid settings.<br>0: This hides the Available Items pane for new users or for users who have never set their own preferences.<br>1: This enables the Available Items pane for new users and for users who have never set their own preferences.<br>The default is 1.<br>If the user changes their own settings, this will override whatever is set inside pref.txt.<br>**Note:** The name of this preference has spaces between the words. |
| Selected Object Navigator | 1 | This setting controls the Selected Items pane in Discoverer Plus. It has two valid settings.<br>0: This hides the Selected Items pane for new users or for users who have never set their own preferences.<br>1: This enables the Selected Items pane for new users and for users who have never set their own preferences.<br>The default is 1.<br>If the user changes their own settings, this will override whatever is set inside pref.txt.<br>**Note:** The name of this preference has spaces between the words. |

**TABLE 20-2.** *Discoverer User Preferences*

## Setting the Timeout Value for Discoverer

You specify a Discoverer timeout if you want Discoverer sessions to shut down automatically after a specified time period if no user interaction has occurred during that time. Before Discoverer shuts down, a warning message is displayed in Discoverer Plus. For example, if a Discoverer session is not used for ten minutes, the Discoverer session shuts down. The Discoverer end user must reconnect to use Discoverer again.

Discoverer timeout values are specified as follows:

- **Discoverer Plus** The Timeout value in the pref.txt file specifies the timeout value for Discoverer Plus. This was covered in the previous section.
- **Discoverer Viewer** The session-timeout value in the web.xml file specifies the timeout value for Discoverer Viewer. The value is called viewerSessionTimeOut and is found in the Discoverer deployment plan.

Use the following workflow to change the timeout value for Discoverer Viewer:

1. Locate the Discoverer deployment plan.
2. Change the timeout in the Discoverer deployment plan.
3. Redeploy the Discoverer application.

These steps are described in the following sections.

## Locating the Discoverer Deployment Plan

The Discoverer deployment plan is an XML file that you will need to manually edit in order to change the timeout value for Discoverer Viewer.

To view the location of the Discoverer deployment plan using WebLogic Server Administration Console, use the following workflow:

1. Log in to Oracle WebLogic Server Administration Console.
2. In the Domain Structure area, shown here, click Deployments.
3. The Summary of Deployments page will open. The main area on this page, as shown here, is called Deployments.

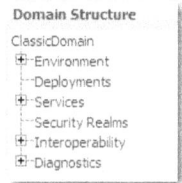

Domain Structure
ClassicDomain
Environment
Deployments
Services
Security Realms
Interoperability
Diagnostics

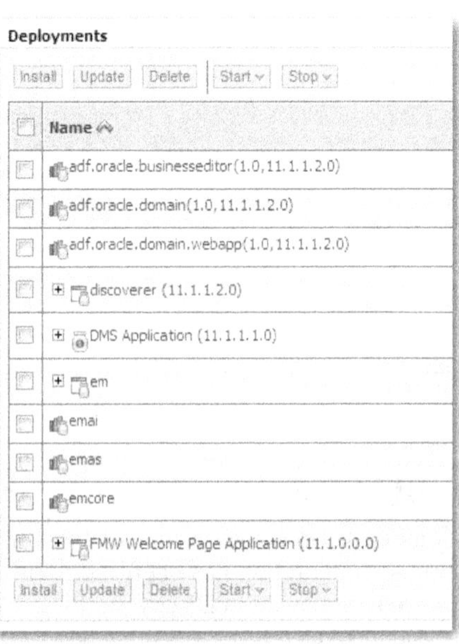

4. Click the deployment for Discoverer 11.1.1.2.0. The Settings page will open, a part of which is shown below:

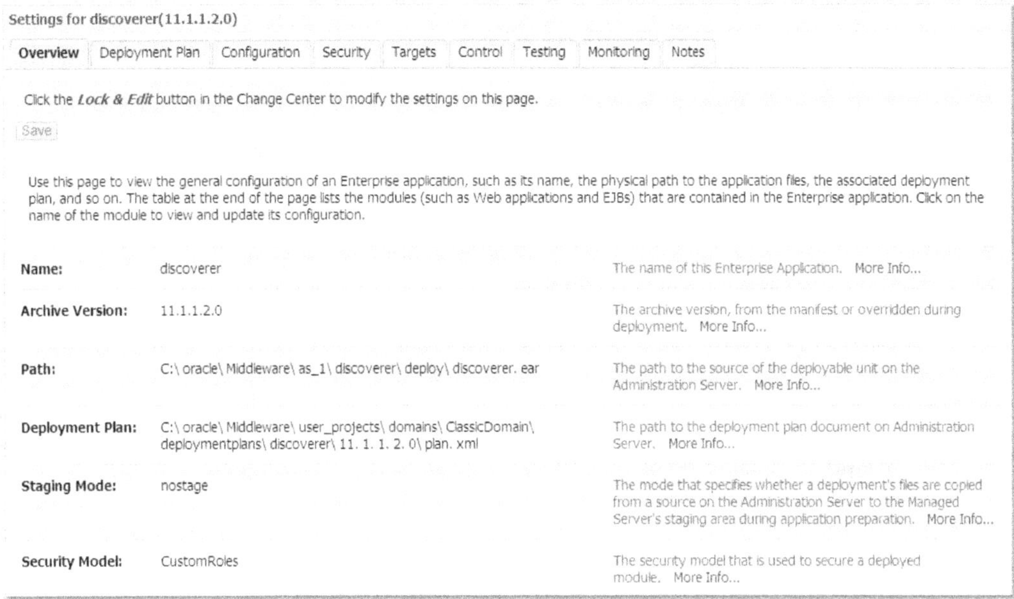

Settings for discoverer(11.1.1.2.0)
Overview
Deployment Plan
Configuration
Security
Targets
Control
Testing
Monitoring
Notes
Click the Lock & Edit button in the Change Center to modify the settings on this page.
Save
Use this page to view the general configuration of an Enterprise application, such as its name, the physical path to the application files, the associated deployment plan, and so on. The table at the end of the page lists the modules (such as Web applications and EJBs) that are contained in the Enterprise application. Click on the name of the module to view and update its configuration.
Name:
discoverer
The name of this Enterprise Application. More Info...
Archive Version:
11.1.1.2.0
The archive version, from the manifest or overridden during deployment. More Info...
Path:
C:\oracle\Middleware\as_1\discoverer\deploy\discoverer.ear
The path to the source of the deployable unit on the Administration Server. More Info...
Deployment Plan:
C:\oracle\Middleware\user_projects\domains\ClassicDomain\deploymentplans\discoverer\11.1.1.2.0\plan.xml
The path to the deployment plan document on Administration Server. More Info...
Staging Mode:
nostage
The mode that specifies whether a deployment's files are copied from a source on the Administration Server to the Managed Server's staging area during application preparation. More Info...
Security Model:
CustomRoles
The security model that is used to secure a deployed module. More Info...


5. On the Settings page, make sure you are on the Overview tab. Locate the setting called Deployment Plan and note the name of the file and the path to its location. In our case, the file is named plan.xml, and it is located here:

   C:\oracle\Middleware\user_projects\domains\ClassicDomain\deploymentplans\discoverer\11.1.1.2.0

## Changing the Viewer Timeout in the Discoverer Deployment Plan

Having identified the name of the file and its location, you need to modify the deployment plan and set a new timeout value.

To edit the deployment plan and set a new timeout value, use the following workflow:

1. Using an XML editor, open the deployment plan from the location you obtained in the previous section.
2. Navigate to the variable-definition section shown here:

```
...
<variable-definition>
<variable>
<name>discoWsrpPrefStoreSharedPath</name>
<value>portletData</value>
</variable>
<variable>
```

```
<name>discoPlusFilesDirectroy</name>
<value>C:\oracle\Middleware\as_1/discoverer</value>
</variable>
<variable>
<name>viewerSessionTimeOut</name>
<value>30</value>
</variable>
</variable-definition>
...
```

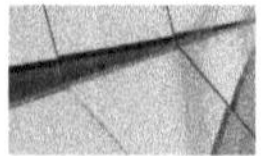

**NOTE**
*The viewer SessionTimeOut variable is defined in both the variable-definition and variable-assignment sections of the deployment plan. You should modify only the viewer SessionTimeOut variable, which is defined in the variable-definition section. The value is defined in minutes. It is highlighted in bold in the code snippets.*

3. Change the value of the viewerSessionTimeOut variable to a valid integer value. For example, change the value to 20 (twenty minutes), as shown here:

```
...
<variable-definition>
<variable>
<name>discoWsrpPrefStoreSharedPath</name>
<value>portletData</value>
</variable>
<variable>
<name>discoPlusFilesDirectroy</name>
<value>C:\oracle\Middleware\as_1/discoverer</value>
</variable>
<variable>
<name>viewerSessionTimeOut</name>
<value>20</value>
</variable>
</variable-definition>
...
```

4. Save your changes and close the XML file.

## Redeploying the Discoverer Application

When you update an application, you can specify that WebLogic Server redeploy the original archive file or exploded directory, or you can specify that WebLogic Server deploy a new archive file in place of the original one. You can also change the deployment plan that is associated with the application. Update an application if you have made changes to the application and you want to make the changes available to WebLogic Server clients, if you have made changes to the deployment plan, or if you want to redeploy an entirely new archive file in a new location.

Having changed the deployment plan, you need to update the Discoverer application. To do this, you will redeploy the Discoverer application.

To redeploy the Discoverer application, use the following workflow:

1. If you have not already done so, in the Change Center of the Administration Console, click the Lock & Edit button. It is located at the top-left of the Administration Console.

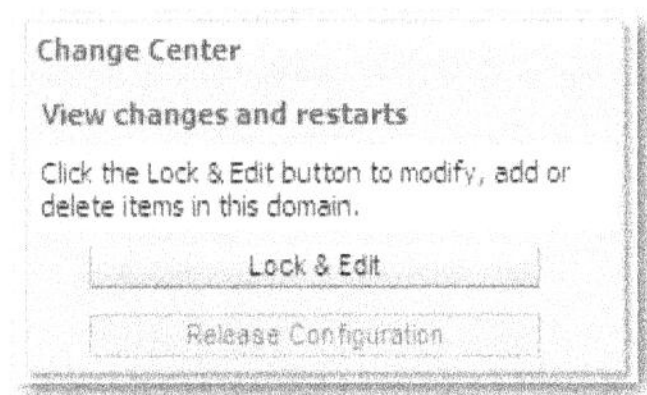


2. In the Domain Structure area, located immediately below the Change Center, select Deployments. A table in the right pane displays all the deployed enterprise applications and application modules.
3. The Summary of Deployments page will open. The main area on this page is called Deployments.
4. Select the check box next to the name of the enterprise application you want to update. In our case, this is Discoverer 11.1.1.2.0.
5. Click the Update button. The following Update Application Assistant window will open:

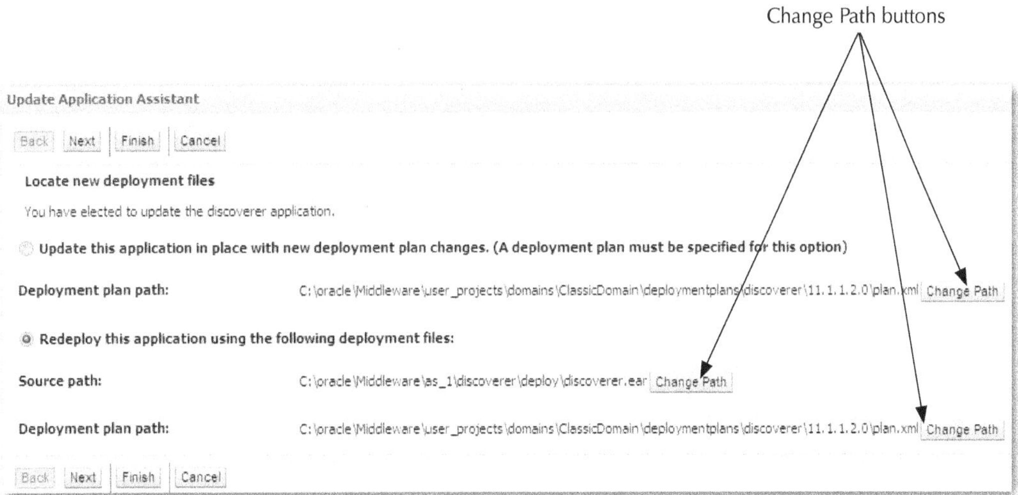


6. In the Locate New Deployment Files area of the Update Application Assistant, use the Change Path buttons if you want to change the source file of the application or change the associated deployment plan.

7. In our case, because we edited the existing deployment plan, there is no need to change the path, so all we need to do is click the Next button, located in the Control Buttons area. The Update Application Assistant page will change with the following Review your choices area, replacing the Locate New deployment Files area:

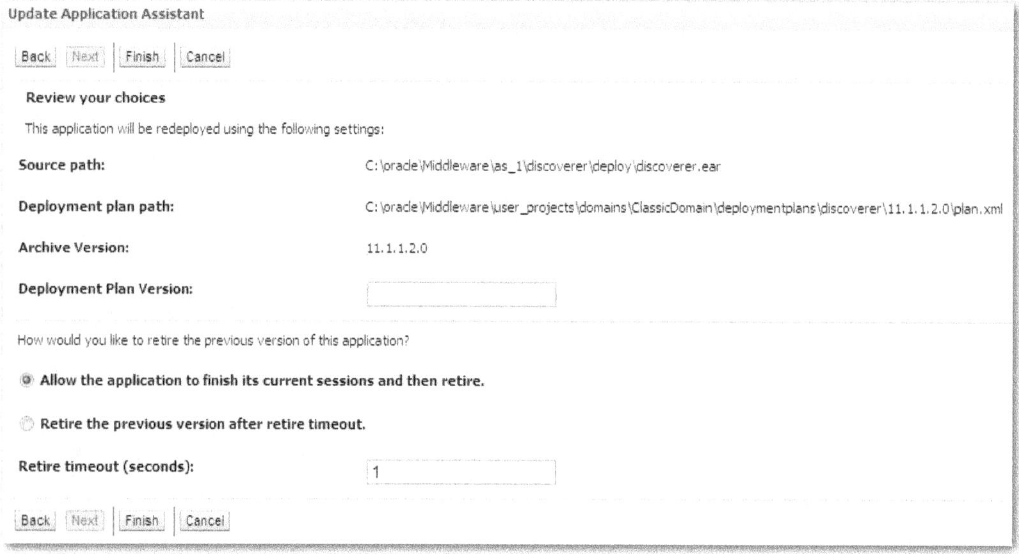


Source path:

8. In the Review your choices area, decide whether to allow the application to finish its current session or retire the previous version after retire timeout and then click the Finish button.
9. When the task has completed, you need to go back to the Change Center of the Administration Console and click Activate Changes.

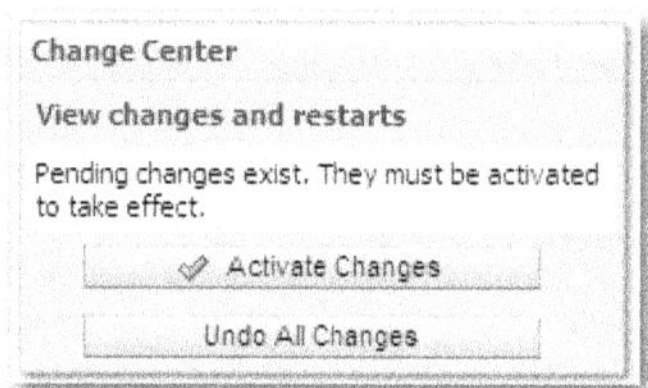

Change Center
View changes and restarts
Pending changes exist. They must be activated to take effect.
Activate Changes
Undo All Changes


10. Look at the Messages area to determine whether a restart is required. In our case, as you can see here, no restart is needed.

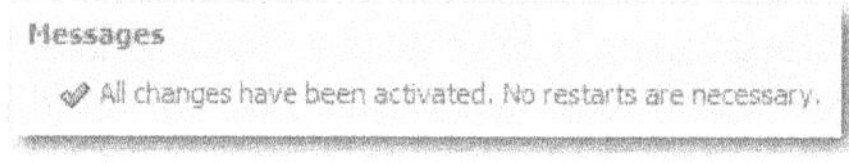

All changes have been activated. No restarts are necessary.

**NOTE**
*Not all changes take effect immediately—some will require a restart, so it is important to look in the Messages area to make sure.*

11. When users next start Discoverer Viewer, Discoverer imposes the specified timeout value.

**NOTE**
*If single sign-on is enabled, Discoverer Viewer also considers the Global User Inactivity Timeout (GUIT) value defined in the SSO server. In this case, the smallest value among the session-timeout and GUIT values takes the precedence over the other.*

# Optimizing Discoverer for Optimal Performance

The performance of a Discoverer system refers to the time Discoverer takes to complete a specific task. Performance time might be the time taken to do the following:

- Return the results of a query (that is, display a worksheet)
- Perform a pivot or drill
- Add a new user to the system

In this section of the chapter, we will look at the following facets of optimizing Discoverer for optimal performance:

- Scaling Discoverer
- Using worksheets and page items appropriately
- Setting preferences
- Using summary folders
- Increasing the size of the array used to fetch rows from the database
- Basing lists of values on tables with distinct values
- Using Web Cache with Discoverer Viewer
- Load balancing

## Scaling Discoverer for Optimal Performance

You have probably heard of the term *scalability* often, but what does it mean? The scalability of a Discoverer system refers to its ability to handle increasing numbers of users or tasks without compromising performance.

To take advantage of the inherently scalable architecture in Discoverer, you can install Discoverer on multiple machines and share the workload between those machines. We discussed this a little in Chapter 19 when we showed you how to you can use Web Cache for load balancing. However, there is a lot more to managing Discoverer in a multi-machine or multi-instance environment. For more information on this subject, please visit http://docs.oracle.com/cd/E17904_01/bi.1111/b40107/multimachineinstall.htm#CHDFECGB.

The main factors that determine Discoverer's scalability are

- The number of server CPUs
- The distribution of processing across CPUs
- The total server memory (both RAM and virtual memory)
- The specific tasks requested by each user (individual workload)
- The number of Discoverer middle-tier machines

Other than having multiple machines to handle the load, as you can see, the main factors that determine Discoverer's scalability are the number of CPUs and the amount of memory. In the following section, we outline our algorithm for sizing a Discoverer application server.

## Sizing the Application Server

In our many years in this business, we have been asked many times how much memory and how many CPUs a server should have in order to give the best performance for Discoverer.

We have included two scenarios, both of which are for 100 users. The first is when all 100 users will be using Discoverer Plus; the second is when there is a split of 40 Plus users and 60 Viewer users. These numbers can be used for making recommendations as to the kind of hardware you need to be using when it comes to buying a Discoverer server. Please also remember that we strongly recommend placing Discoverer on its own server.

We have five base rules, which are

- **Base CPU rule** Every 4GB RAM needs one CPU, but please make sure you buy hardware that can be expanded if you can.
- **Base memory rule** A typical Linux operating system will need at least 500MB to load, and you will need to allow in the region of at least 1.5GB for a Windows load. On top of this you need to allocate 1GB for the middle tier and Fusion Middleware Control components. Thus, you will need between 1.5GB and 2.5GB just to get the machine up and running. This is called the *base memory*. We recommend you start with 2.5GB in all cases.
- **End-user memory rule** The user rules are split into the requirements for a Plus user and a Viewer user as follows:
  - **Discoverer Plus** A single Plus user needs to have 85MB available.
  - **Discoverer Viewer** A single Viewer user needs to have 15MB available.
- **Total memory rule** The total memory required is calculated as follows:
  - Base memory +
  - Maximum number of Plus users × 85MB +
  - Maximum number of Viewer users × 15MB
- **Memory percentage rule** Total memory must never exceed 85 percent of the available memory during day-to-day usage.

Let's look at our two scenarios in turn.

**Scenario 1: Requirements for 100 Plus Users** For these 100 Plus users, you will need to have 8.5GB available (100 × 85MB) on the server, to which you must add the 4GB for the base memory (see earlier), making an intermediate total of 12.5GB. As this must be no more than 85 percent of the available memory, this scenario needs 14.7GB. Because of this, you should start with 16GB, although we would recommend a machine that is capable of being extended to 24GB.

Because every 4GB RAM needs one CPU, you will need to get either a 4CPU machine, a double dual-core machine, or a quad-core, or perhaps even start with an eight-core.

We have to say that having only Discoverer Plus users is very uncommon and therefore recommend you consider using the Discoverer Viewer tool for those users who only need to run prebuilt reports.

In the following scenario, also based on 100 users, we will use a split of Plus and Viewer users.

**Scenario 2: Requirements for 40 Plus and 60 Viewer Users** For the 40 Plus users, you will need to have 3.4GB available (40 × 85MB).

For the 60 Viewer users, you will need to have 900MB available (60 × 15MB).

Adding the two together, along with the base memory (4.0GB), means you will need an intermediate total of 8.3GB. As this must be no more than 85 percent of the available memory, this scenario needs 9.75GB. Because of this, you should start with 12GB, although we recommend having a machine that is capable of being extended to 16GB. Because every 4GB RAM needs one CPU, this scenario starts out with a three-CPU machine, if limiting to 12GB, or a four-CPU allocation if you adopt our expansion recommendation and allocate 16GB.

## Using Worksheets and Page Items Appropriately

The time that Discoverer takes to query and display data depends on the worksheet layout, that is, table or crosstab, and whether the worksheet layout uses page items.

Here are some examples:

- When populating a tabular worksheet that does not contain page items, Discoverer uses an incremental fetch (for example, retrieves rows 250 at a time) and therefore does not have to load the entire results set, which might be much larger. The data for tabular layouts that do not contain page items is therefore displayed faster because Discoverer does not have to create an index of cached items as it would do if the page items were displayed.
- When populating a tabular worksheet that contains page items or a crosstab worksheet, Discoverer takes longer to display the data, regardless of the number of rows fetched at a time. The data takes longer to display because Discoverer spends additional time creating an index by page item or by items in the left axis of a crosstab on the cached results set.

To enhance performance, encourage Discoverer Plus users to follow these guidelines when designing Discoverer workbooks:

- Try to use tabular reports rather than crosstab reports.
- Minimize the number of page items in reports.
- Avoid wide crosstab reports.
- Avoid creating reports that will return tens of thousands of rows of data.
- Whenever possible, provide parameters to reduce the amount of data being returned.
- Minimize the number of worksheets in workbooks. We recommend a maximum of six worksheets per workbook.
- Remove extraneous worksheets from workbooks. This is especially true if end users frequently use the Discoverer export option.

**NOTE**
*When end users export data in Discoverer Plus or Discoverer Viewer, they can export either the current worksheet or all the worksheets. In other words, they cannot selectively choose the worksheets to be exported. Removing extraneous worksheets will reduce the amount of time taken to export whenever the user chooses to export all worksheets.*

The following worksheet scenarios all increase the overhead in index creation and therefore have a negative impact on Discoverer performance:

- Wide crosstabs
- Crosstabs with multiple items in the left axis
- Reports that have page axis items
- Page axis items with a large number of values

All of these override Discoverer's natural tendency to pull data incrementally. The use of page items and crosstabs will force Discoverer to pull all of the data before it can display any results.

## Setting Preferences for Optimal Performance

Earlier in this chapter we outlined all the middle-tier preferences that you can set. In this section we will draw your attention to those specific preferences that can help you maximize your Discoverer performance. These are the preferences that are most likely to help improve performance.

The preferences that can help you maximize your Discoverer performance are

- **ObjectsAlwaysAccessible** This controls how quickly the list of available business areas and folders are presented to the user. Before displaying the list, Discoverer makes a database security check to confirm that the user has access to *all* of the tables referenced in *all* the folders. Although the security check makes sure that the user cannot create workbooks that they cannot run, the security check can also increase the time taken to display the list, particularly if the user has access to a great number of business areas and folders.

  This preference setting controls whether the security check is made when the user starts a new report. A setting of 1 disables the check and assumes that the user has security clearance to all of the business areas and folders to which they have access, passing the security check to the run time, still therefore respecting database security. At run time, if a user does not have access to a table referenced by a folder, the worksheet will return no data. A setting of 0 executes the security check whenever a user starts a new report.

  We recommend always setting ObjectsAlwaysAccessible to 1.
- **SQLItemTrim** Item trimming refers to the mechanism whereby Discoverer can remove references to irrelevant or unused columns and expressions in the query SQL, thus improving performance.

  A setting of 1 enables item trimming, whereas 0 disables it.

  We recommend always setting SQLItemTrim to 1.
- **SQLJoinTrim** Join trimming refers to the mechanism whereby Discoverer detects and eliminates joins, whenever possible, from queries without affecting the result set. This can greatly improve query performance.

  A setting of 1 enables item trimming, whereas 0 disables it.

  We recommend always setting SQLJoinTrim to 1.
- **SQLFlatten** SQL flattening refers to the mechanism whereby Discoverer minimizes the use of inline views in the query SQL, which makes it easier for the database to efficiently parse the SQL and select an optimal execution path.

  A setting of 1 enables item trimming, whereas 0 disables it.

We recommend always setting SQLFlatten to 1.

- **QPPEnable** This setting controls the query predictor. When databases are not analyzed frequently or primary-key and foreign-key constraints are not enabled, the query predictor can
  - Take a long time to run
  - Produce exaggeratedly high or low predictions

  We strongly recommend always setting this to 0 unless you really need to use query prediction and you are sure the prediction results are accurate.

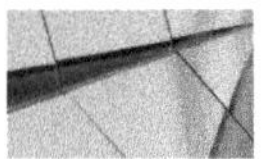

**NOTE**
*E-Business Suite does not have primary-key and foreign-key constraints, and most organizations using EBS turn off query prediction.*

- **MaxRowsPerFetch** This controls how many rows of data should be brought into the results for each fetch from the database. If it is likely or intended that Discoverer should fetch large numbers of rows, in the order of thousands, from the database, you can improve performance by increasing the size of the array that Discoverer uses to fetch the rows.

  If you anticipate Discoverer will be retrieving thousands of rows, we recommend increasing this setting at first to 500 but even as high as 1000 to increase the size of the array.

  Discoverer end users can override this default value as follows:
  - **Discoverer Plus** By choosing Tools | Options | Query Governor and then using the Retrieve data incrementally in groups of field.
  - **Discoverer Viewer** By selecting the Preferences link to display the Preferences page and then using the Retrieve data incrementally in groups of field.

**NOTE**
*In the case of table worksheets, there is a trade-off between perceived performance and actual performance. Tables display the data immediately after the first array is retrieved. If MaxRowsPerFetch is set to 100, a Discoverer end user will see the first 100 rows more quickly than if MaxRowsPerFetch is set to 1000.*

- **Cache Settings** Data retrieved from the database is stored in a middle-tier Discoverer cache for each user session. This cache supports Discoverer's rotation, drilling, and local calculation capabilities.

  You can control the performance of the cache using the following settings:
  - **CacheFlushPercentage** This defaults to 25 percent.
  - **MaxVirtualDiskMem** This defaults to 1GB.
  - **MaxVirtualHeapMem** This defaults to 512MB.

  The default settings for the cache are typically sufficiently large enough to enable Discoverer to take advantage of the available memory. If the system has more resources available, you can increase one or more of the default memory values being used. However, we recommend not increasing the resources system-wide but rather doing this on a user-by-user basis. You will find that only some users need this increased caching, so it is likely to be beneficial only for users whose queries return large result sets. It can be decidedly detrimental to the system to increase these system-wide, especially if you have users who do not understand how to avoid queries from the Twilight Zone.

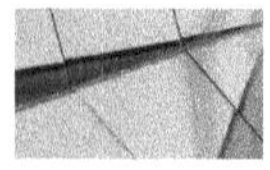

**NOTE**
*The default values are the requirements for each user, but you can change the values for specific users using the Discoverer preferences command-line utility dis51pr. For more information about setting preferences for individual users, please refer to the section "Changing User Preferences Using the Command Line" in this chapter.*

## Using Summary Folders for Optimal Performance

When used correctly, Discoverer summary folders significantly improve query response times. For example, queries that use summary folders might take only seconds to run, whereas queries that return the same result set but do not use summary folders might take several hours. Summary folder management is the key to good performance with Discoverer implementations.

Summary folders can be based on database materialized views or Discoverer summary tables, with the following differences in behavior:

- If a Discoverer query includes a summary folder that is based on a materialized view, the database automatically rewrites the query to use the materialized view.
- If a Discoverer query includes a summary folder that is based on a summary table, Discoverer automatically rewrites the query to use the summary table (providing the summary table has been registered with the EUL).

You can use the SQL Inspector dialog to view the path taken by the query and to find out whether the database has rewritten the query.

### Discoverer Summary Tables

Discoverer summary tables are database tables created by the Discoverer administrator that contain summarized data. These summary tables contain preaggregated and prejoined data and can significantly improve query performance in both Discoverer Plus and Discoverer Viewer.

Discoverer will automatically recognize when a summary table is available and rewrite the query to use the summary table. For more information on this aspect of summary tables, please see http://docs.oracle.com/cd/E23943_01/bi.1111/b32519/add_sum_info.htm#i1008906.

For example, when a query is run for the first time in Discoverer Plus, it retrieves data from the detail tables. This may require a multiple table join and aggregation over thousands or millions of rows, which could take some time to complete. If Discoverer has created a suitable summary table, the same query retrieves data from the summary table and will return results in a few seconds. Both queries will produce the same results.

**NOTE**
*If you are using a data warehouse, you can achieve the same result because the tables in the data warehouse will also contain summarized data.*

For more information about Discoverer and rewriting queries to summary tables with Oracle Standard edition databases, see "Example illustrating the advantages of rewriting a query to use a summary table" here: http://docs.oracle.com/cd/E23943_01/bi.1111/b32519/add_sum_info.htm#i1009057.

### Materialized Views

Materialized views are database objects that contain the results of a query created by an Oracle Enterprise edition database. The query results contain preaggregated and prejoined data and can improve query performance in Discoverer Plus and Discoverer Viewer.

Oracle Enterprise edition databases automatically recognize when a materialized view can be used to satisfy a query request. The database rewrites the query to use the materialized view. Queries are then directed to the materialized view and not to the underlying detail tables or views.

Materialized views have the following characteristics:

- Materialized views consume storage space.
- Unlike ordinary views, materialized views contain data resulting from a query against one or more detail tables.
- Materialized views must be refreshed when data changes.

The Oracle database maintains data in materialized views by refreshing the materialized views after changes are made to the detail tables.

You can configure the following for Discoverer:

- **Refresh Type** This determines how the refresh is performed and has the following two settings:
  - **Incremental** That is, fast refresh, where only the changes made to the detail tables are refreshed
  - **Full** That is, complete, where the database executes the defining subquery of the materialized view
- **Refresh** This determines when the refresh will be performed and has the following two settings:
  - **On demand** When this is used, the refresh is manually maintained by the Discoverer manager.
  - **On commit** When this is used, the materialized view is updated whenever a database transaction commits its changes to the detail tables. This method keeps the materialized view synchronized with the database but can create a significant overhead on the system if a large number of commits are being performed.

Materialized views are transparent to Discoverer users.

## Basing Lists of Values on Tables with Distinct Values

By default, a Discoverer list of values (LOV) is populated using a SELECT DISTINCT statement in the query on the underlying data table. To populate the LOV, all of the rows must be scanned before the list of distinct values can be displayed. However, this default query is inefficient if the LOV is populated from a column that has a large number of rows but relatively few distinct values.

To improve performance, avoid creating LOVs on items based on columns in tables that have a large number of rows. Instead, consider the following options:

- Create LOVs for items based on columns in small "dimension" tables (containing only distinct allowable values) attached to the fact table. If such tables do not exist, create and populate them using SQL*Plus.
- If the list of allowable values is small or changes relatively infrequently, define the LOV within Discoverer Administrator by creating a custom folder based on SQL statements that select the allowable values from SYS.DUAL.

For example, if your database has 4 regions, one for each of the points of the compass, to create an LOV containing  all regions, you might do the following:

Create a custom folder to list all regions based on the following SQL statement:

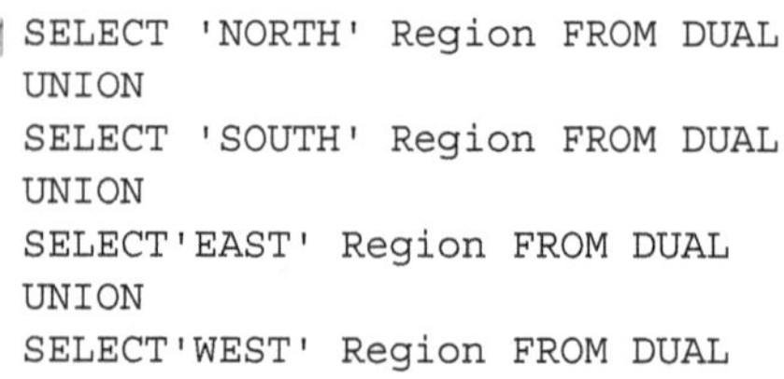

```
SELECT 'NORTH' Region FROM DUAL
UNION
SELECT 'SOUTH' Region FROM DUAL
UNION
SELECT'EAST' Region FROM DUAL
UNION
SELECT'WEST' Region FROM DUAL
```

You would then edit the item class for the Region item so that it uses the previous custom folder for its list of values.

### LOV Business Area

When we build Discoverer systems for customers, one of the first business areas that we create is a special LOV business area, typically called Lookups.

We have such a business area in use in the EUL that we used for this book. It is called Lookups and is shown here:

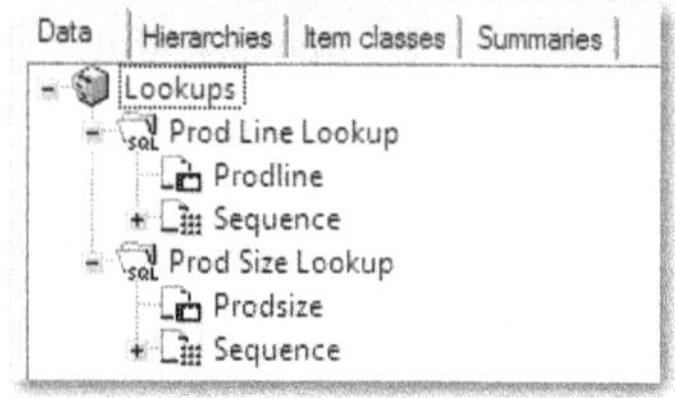


As you can see, we have only two folders, both of which are custom folders containing SQL code to generate the LOVs that we want.

Another way that we use a Lookups business area is with a data warehouse. Typically, a data warehouse will refresh once per day, sometimes more often such as evening and lunchtime. Data warehouse tables can contain millions of rows of data, so we create a special table that contains the results of LOV queries against our data warehouse. As part of the data warehouse load, the last job populates our Lookup Values database.

Here's an example:

```
INSERT INTO ASC_LOOKUP_VALUES
   SELECT DISTINCT
'ITEM_CATEGORY_NAME' LOOKUP_TYPE,
      CATEGORY_NAME LOOKUP_CODE,
      CATEGORY_NAME MEANING,
TRUNC(SYSDATE)
   FROM ASC_ITEMS
```

All we have to do now is to create a custom Discoverer folder using this table in our Lookups business area and create an LOV. Here is the custom SQL that was used for the LOV based on the previous table:

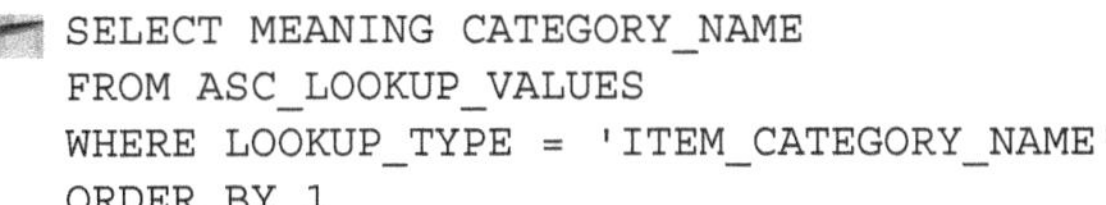

```
SELECT MEANING CATEGORY_NAME
FROM ASC_LOOKUP_VALUES
WHERE LOOKUP_TYPE = 'ITEM_CATEGORY_NAME'
ORDER BY 1
```

## Using Web Cache with Discoverer Viewer

If your workbooks remain relatively stable, Oracle Web Cache can greatly improve Discoverer Viewer performance. Please refer to the section "Configuring Viewer with Web Cache" in Chapter 19.

## Load Balancing

The scalable architecture of Oracle enables you to install the Discoverer services tier on multiple machines.

You can balance the load between the different machines using the following:

- **Oracle Web Cache** We discuss this in some detail in Chapter 19. This would be a software load balancer.
- **Standard commercial HTTP/IP router load balancers** These would be hardware load balancers.

If you are in a heavy usage environment, we recommend you look to invest into a hardware load balancer. We have seen, and even configured, Oracle Web Cache several times, and it works very well in a small to medium-sized environment.

For more information regarding using Discoverer in a multi-machine or multi-instance environment, please look here: http://docs.oracle.com/cd/E17904_01/bi.1111/b40107/multimachineinstall.htm#CHDFECGB.

## Performance Troubleshooting

Complaints about the system running slow can be very hard to troubleshoot. Although this section of the book cannot explore all the facets of troubleshooting a poorly performing Discoverer installation, we can give you some high-level tips and tricks that will get you started.

If you have looked through all of the preceding performance optimizing suggestions, our troubleshooting tips are as follows:

- If in use, ensure that summaries are refreshed when necessary in Discoverer Administrator.
- Attempt to run the same code in a SQL tool such as SQL*Plus or SQL Developer.
- Increase the amount of virtual memory available for the Discoverer data cache (using the MaxVirtualDiskMem preference in pref.txt).
- If Discoverer's workbook dialogs are slow to update (for example, the Open Workbook from Database dialog), ensure that Discoverer end users delete their old workbooks and worksheets when they are no longer required.

- If Discoverer's user dialogs are slow to update (for example, the Share Workbook dialog in Discoverer Plus Relational), ensure that the Discoverer manager removes old database accounts and roles when they are no longer required.
- Minimize the amount of Discoverer log information being recorded, and do not enable Trace logging unless you have issues and are trying to resolve them. Once the issue is resolved, you should reset your logging back to either Notification or Warning. For more information about how to change the amount of log information recorded, see http://docs.oracle.com/cd/E17904_01/bi.1111/b40107/logging_diagnostics.htm#i102727.
- If the Discoverer server is underperforming, you might want to increase the amount of memory available or the amount of swap space on the Discoverer middle-tier machine.
- If you encounter workbooks that take a long time to save to the database, do the following:
  - Increase MaxVirtualDiskMem for all users to 2GB.
  - Increase MaxVirtualHeapMem for all users to 100MB.

**NOTE**
*While not exactly a performance solution, should you find that users are not being permitted to connect, you may want to increase the number of MaxProcs from 50 to 100. You should also ensure that you have enough CPU and memory available. The MaxProcs setting is stored in the OPMN.XML file, which was discussed in Chapter 19.*

# Starting Discoverer Using URL Parameters

Discoverer end users usually start Discoverer by manually choosing a Discoverer connection (or connecting directly), opening a worksheet, and then optionally specifying workbook parameter values. To speed up this process, you can create a URL with parameters to start Discoverer with specific settings.

For example, you might want to provide a URL to Discoverer end users that automatically logs into Discoverer and opens a particular worksheet. For examples of Discoverer URL parameters, see the section "URL Parameter Examples" later in this chapter.

Having created a URL that meets your requirements, you can do the following:

- Give the URL to end users to enter in their web browser address box.
- Add the URL as a link on a web site so that end users can start Discoverer by selecting a single hot link.

## URL Parameter Syntax

URL parameters must conform to the following syntax: http://<host.domain>:<port>/<Discoverer application name>? arg1=value1...&argN=valueN.

The syntax is explained as follows:

- <host.domain> is the server name and domain on which Oracle HTTP Server is installed (for example, maslaptop.learndiscoverer.com).
- <port>is the port number on which Oracle HTTP Server is installed (for example, 8090).

**NOTE**
*To start Discoverer Plus OLAP, you must also specify the SID after the port number.*

- <Discoverer application name> is one of the following:
  - discoverer/plus
  - discoverer/viewer
- ?, which is optional, tells Discoverer that what follows are parameters.
- arg1=value1 is the first parameter and again is optional. Subsequent parameters are prefixed with the &character.

The following rules apply to providing URL parameters:

- URL parameters are not case-sensitive. For example, 'Locale=' and 'locale=' are the same.
- URL parameter values are case-sensitive. For example, 'workbooksource=Database' is different from 'workbooksource=DataBase'.
- The order of the URL parameters is not important.
- When you specify login details, either you can specify a username, database, and EUL, or you can specify the connection ID of a Discoverer connection. If you specify a username, database, and EUL (for example, http://maslaptop.learndiscoverer.com:8090/discoverer/viewer?us=video5&db=db1&eul=VIDEO5), the end user is prompted to specify a database password before they can start Discoverer.
- If you specify login details using the ID of a Discoverer connection, you specify the EUL when you create the connection.
- If the following mandatory parameters are not specified on the URL, end users are prompted for them:
  - User Name
  - Responsibility (for an Oracle E-Business Suite login)
  - Security Group (for an Oracle E-Business Suite login)
- Where names contain spaces, concatenate the words with a plus (+). For example, if a workbook is called April Analysis 2014, the URL parameter is as follows: &wb=April+Analysis+2014.
- To include other special characters in a URL, you must replace those characters with the equivalent ASCII (or in some cases Unicode) codes. This process is known as *URL encoding*. For example, to replace a vertical bar (|),you replace it with ~7c. Any characters not in the following lists must be URL encoded:
  - Capital letters (that is, A B C D E F G H I J K L M N O P Q R S T U V W X Y Z)
  - Lowercase letters (that is, a b c d e f g h i j k l m n o p q r s t u v w x y z)
  - Numerals (that is, 0 1 2 3 4 5 6 7 8 9)
  - Certain special characters (for example, _ ! ~ ( ) * ' )

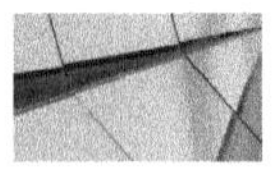

**NOTE**
*For a listing of the ASCII codes, please see the "ASCII Character Set" section in Appendix B.*

- Discoverer uses a proprietary encoding mechanism that is similar to HTTP URL encoding, except that Discoverer uses a tilde character (~) instead of a percent character (%). For more information about URL encoding, refer to any standard HTML guide.
- The maximum number of characters you can put in a URL depends on which web browser you are using, as follows:
  - Internet Explorer 4 and newer: 2,048 characters
  - Mozilla Firefox: No known limit

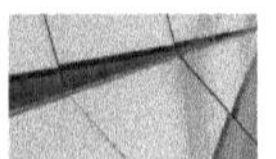

**NOTE**
*Apache Web Server, on which the Oracle HTTP Server is based, has a limit of 8,192 characters.*

## Specifying Login Information Using URL Parameters

You can specify login information in a URL in either of the following two ways:

- By specifying login details individually using the following URL parameters:
  - us=<database username> to specify a database username
  - either database=<database name> (for Discoverer Plus) or db=<database name> (for Discoverer Viewer) to specify a database name
  - eul=<EUL name> to specify a Discoverer End User Layer

**NOTE**
*For security reasons, you cannot specify a database password using a URL parameter.*

For examples of specifying login details using URL parameters, please see the section "URL Parameter Examples" later in this chapter.

- By specifying the connection ID of a Discoverer connection
  - **Public connections** If you use a public connection, the end users are not prompted for a database password.
  - **Private connections** If you use a private connection, the end users are always prompted at least once for a database password. You can also add the reuseConnection URL parameter to reuse login details in the same browser session so that end users do not have to enter a database password repeatedly for the same private Discoverer connection.

For information about how to specify login information using a connection ID, see the section "Specifying Login Information for Discoverer Connections" later in this chapter.

**NOTE**
*If you do not specify login information, Discoverer will prompt the end user for login details.*

When you specify connection information in URL parameters, please note the following restrictions:

- If Discoverer end users are not allowed to create private connections in Discoverer Plus or Discoverer Viewer, you can use URL parameters containing only public connection information. In other words, you *must* include the connection ID in a URL parameter string for a public connection because end users can start Discoverer only using public connections.
- If a Discoverer URL parameter string does not work, it might be because you are trying to use a private connection when private connections are not allowed. In other words, the Allow Users To Define And Use Their Own Private Connections In Discoverer Plus And Discoverer Viewer check box is cleared on the Discoverer Administration page in Fusion Middleware Control.

Discoverer end users should navigate to the required Discoverer worksheet and store the URL as a bookmark in their browser.

## Specifying Login Information for Discoverer Connections

You can use the login details stored in an existing Discoverer connection to start Discoverer.

To specify login information using a connection, use the following workflow:

1. If you do not have a Discoverer connection, create a Discoverer connection using the login details that access the worksheet you want to open.
2. Find out the connection ID of the Discoverer connection (please see the section "Locating the Connection ID of a Connection" later in this chapter).

   For example, a connection ID might be cf_a102.
3. Create a URL using the cn= URL parameter, as follows: http://<host.domain>:<port>/discoverer/viewer?cn=<connection ID value>.

For example, if the connection ID is cf_a102and the host and port are the same as before, create a URL parameter as follows: http://maslaptop.learndiscoverer.com:8090/discoverer/viewer?cn=cf_a102.

Discoverer end users can now use this URL to start Discoverer. If you use a public connection, end users are not prompted for a database password. If you use a private connection, end users are prompted for a database password.

## Locating the Connection ID of a Connection

You find out the connection ID, oftentimes referred to as a *connection key*, of a connection so that you can start Discoverer without specifying connection details. For example, you might want to start Discoverer without prompting the end user for connections.

**NOTE**
*If you use a public connection, end users are not prompted for a database password. If you use a private connection, end users are prompted for a database password. You can also use the reuseConnection URL parameter to reuse login details in the same browser session so that end users do not have to enter a database password repeatedly for the same connection.*

You can find out the connection ID of a connection in either Discoverer Viewer or Discoverer Plus by using the following workflow:

1. Start a web browser.
2. Start Discoverer Viewer or Discoverer Plus to display the connections page containing the connection you want to use.
3. The following example shows the Connect to Oracle BI Discover page. Both Viewer and Plus use the same log in page.

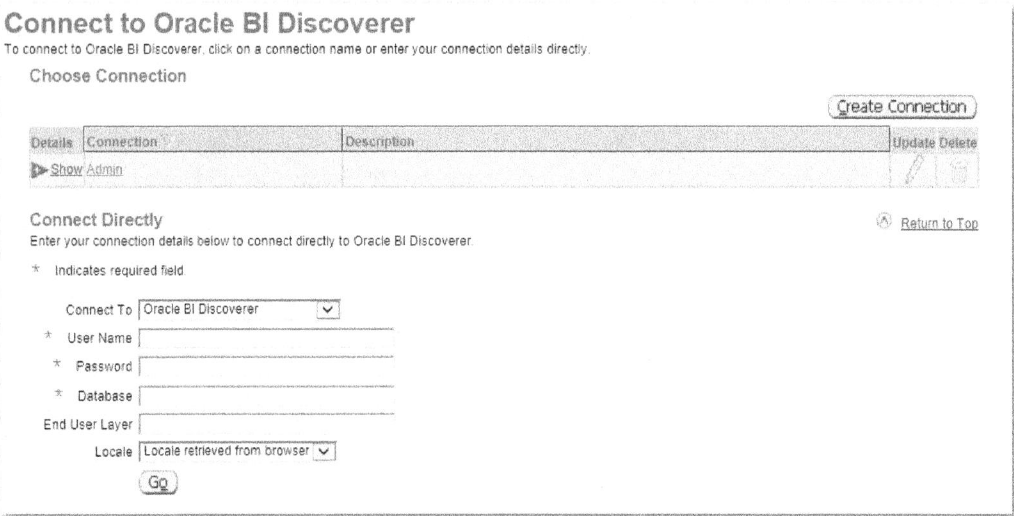


4. In the Details column, select the Show link next to the connection to expand the connection details.

**TIP**
*If the Show links are not available in your browser, use Microsoft Internet Explorer to display the connection page.*

5. Note the value of the connection key.
6. You can now use the value of the connection key with the cn= URL parameter.

## Finding Out the Unique ID of a Workbook

You find out the unique workbook ID of a workbook so that you can specify a workbook on a Discoverer URL using its unique workbook ID.

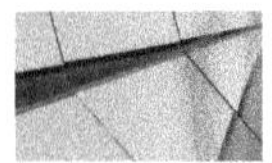

**NOTE**
*You identify a workbook using its workbook ID in preference to using its workbook name to avoid encoding problems and problems caused by large workbook names.*

To find out the unique ID of a workbook in Discoverer Plus, follow this workflow:

1. Start a web browser.
2. Run Discoverer Plus and display the Workbook Wizard.
3. Click Browse to display the Open Workbook from Database dialog.
4. Right-click the workbook and select the Properties option to display the Workbook Properties page.
5. To find out the unique ID of a workbook, note the value in the Identifier field.

**NOTE**
*Alternatively, if you have a workbook open in Discoverer Plus, choose File | Workbook Properties to display the Workbook Properties dialog and note the value in the Identifier field.*

You can use a workbook ID value to specify a workbook as follows:

- In a Discoverer Plus URL using opendbid=<workbook ID>
- In a Discoverer Viewer URL using wbk=<workbook ID>

## Finding Out the Unique ID of a Worksheet

You find out the unique worksheet ID of a worksheet so that you can specify a worksheet on a Discoverer URL using its unique worksheet ID.

**NOTE**
*You identify a worksheet using its worksheet ID in preference to using its worksheet name to avoid encoding problems and problems caused by large worksheet names.*

To find out the unique ID of a worksheet in Discoverer Plus, follow this workflow:

1. Start a web browser.
2. Run Discoverer Plus and open the worksheet.
3. Choose Edit | Worksheet Properties to display the Worksheet Properties dialog.
4. Display the General tab and look at the value in the Identifier field.

You can use a worksheet ID value to specify a worksheet as follows:

- In a Discoverer Plus URL using sheetid=<worksheet ID>
- In a Discoverer Viewer URL using wsk=<worksheet ID>

## URL Parameter Examples

This section contains examples of using URL parameters with Discoverer.

### Starting Discoverer Viewer

To start Discoverer Viewer, connect automatically as msmith, and open a worksheet called January Analysis in a workbook called Monthly Analysis, you might use the following URL: http://<host.domain>:<port>/discoverer/viewer?cn=cf_a102&wbk=MONTHLY_ANALYSIS&wsk=179.

The following rules apply to starting Discoverer Viewer using URL parameters:

- http://<host.domain>:<port>/discoverer/viewer? is the Discoverer Viewer URL.
- cn=<value> specifies the connection ID of a Discoverer connection.

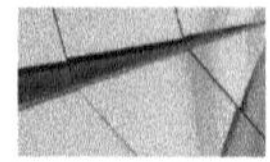

**NOTE**
*For more information about finding out connection IDs, see the section "Locating the Connection ID of a Connection" earlier in this chapter.*

- wbk=<value> specifies the workbook ID of a Discoverer workbook.
- wsk=<value> specifies the worksheet ID of a Discoverer worksheet.

In the previous example, MONTHLY_ANALYSIS is the workbook ID of the Monthly Analysis workbook, and 179 is the worksheet ID of the January Analysis worksheet.

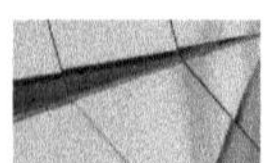

**NOTE**
*For more information about finding out workbook IDs and worksheet IDs, see the sections "Finding Out the Unique ID of a Workbook" and "Finding Out the Unique ID of a Worksheet" earlier in this chapter.*

### Starting Discoverer Viewer with a Worksheet Parameter

To start Discoverer Viewer, connect automatically as msmith to the Sales EUL, open a worksheet called January Analysis in a workbook called Monthly Analysis, and enter the worksheet parameter value East; you might use the following URL: http://<host.domain>:<port>/discoverer/viewer?cn=cf_a102&wbk=MONTHLY_ANALYSIS&wsk=179&qp_regionparam=East.

The following rules apply to starting Discoverer Viewer using URL parameters and worksheet parameters:

- http://<host.domain>:<port>/discoverer/viewer? is the Discoverer Viewer URL.
- cn=<value> specifies the connection ID of a Discoverer connection.

**NOTE**
*For more information about finding out connection IDs, see the section "Locating the Connection ID of a Connection" earlier in this chapter.*

- wbk=<value> specifies the workbook ID of a Discoverer workbook.
- wsk=<value> specifies the worksheet ID of a Discoverer worksheet.
- qp_regionparam=<value> specifies a value for a parameter called region param.

In the previous example, MONTHLY_ANALYSIS is the workbook ID of the Monthly Analysis workbook, and 179 is the worksheet ID of the January Analysis worksheet.

**NOTE**
*For more information about finding out workbook IDs and worksheet IDs, see the sections "Finding Out the Unique ID of a Workbook" and "Finding Out the Unique ID of a Worksheet" earlier in this chapter.*

### Starting Discoverer Plus

To start Discoverer Plus, connect automatically as msmith to the Sales EUL, and open a worksheet called January Analysis in a workbook called Monthly Analysis, you might use the following URL: http://<host.domain>:<port>/discoverer/plus?cn=cf_a102&opendbid=MONTHLY_ANALYSIS&sheetid=179.

The following rules apply to starting Discoverer Plus using URL parameters:

- http://<host.domain>:<port>/discoverer/plus? is the Discoverer Plus URL.
- cn=<value> specifies the connection ID of a Discoverer connection.

**NOTE**
*For more information about finding out connection IDs, see the section "Locating the Connection ID of a Connection" earlier in this chapter.*

- opendbid=<value> specifies the workbook ID of a Discoverer workbook.
- sheetid=<value> specifies the worksheet ID of a Discoverer worksheet.

In this example, MONTHLY_ANALYSIS is the workbook ID of the Monthly Analysis workbook, and 179 is the worksheet ID of the January Analysis worksheet.

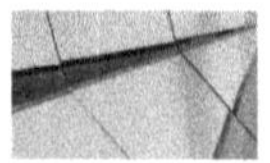

**NOTE**

*For more information about finding out workbook IDs and worksheet IDs, see the sections "Finding Out the Unique ID of a Workbook" and "Finding Out the Unique ID of a Worksheet" earlier in this chapter.*

### Starting Discoverer Viewer and Prompt for a Password

In this example, you want end users to be prompted to specify a password before they can access Discoverer. You therefore specify a username, database, and EUL on the URL.

To start Discoverer Viewer, connect as msmith to the EUL called book on database orcl, and open a worksheet called January Analysis in a workbook called Monthly Analysis, you might use the following URL: http://<host.domain>:<port>/discoverer/viewer?us=msmith&db=orcl&eul=book&wbk=MONTHLY_ANALYSIS&wsk=179.

The following rules apply to starting Discoverer Plus using URL parameters:

- http://<host.domain>:<port>/discoverer/viewer? is the Discoverer Viewer URL.
- us=<value> specifies the database username.
- db=<value> specifies the database.
- eul=<value> specifies the End User Layer.
- wbk=<value> specifies the workbook ID of a Discoverer workbook.
- wsk=<value> specifies the worksheet ID of a Discoverer worksheet.

In this example, MONTHLY_ANALYSIS is the workbook ID of the Monthly Analysis workbook, and 179 is the worksheet ID of the January Analysis worksheet.

**NOTE**

*For more information about finding out workbook IDs and worksheet IDs, see the sections "Finding Out the Unique ID of a Workbook" and "Finding Out the Unique ID of a Worksheet" earlier in this chapter.*

### Starting Discoverer Plus in Apps Mode and Prompt for a Password

In this example, you want end users to connect to an Apps-mode EUL and be prompted to specify a password before they can access Discoverer. You therefore specify a username, database, and EUL on the URL.

To start Discoverer Plus, connect automatically as msmith to the Apps-mode EUL called eul_us on database orcl, and open a worksheet called January Analysis in a workbook called Monthly Analysis, you might use the following URL: http://<host.domain>:<port>/discoverer/plus?us=msmith&lm=applications&database=orcl&eul=eul_us&responsibility=SalesUser&opendbid=MONTHLY_ANALYSIS&sheetid=179.

The following rules apply to starting Discoverer Plus in Apps mode using URL parameters:

- http://<host.domain>:<port>/discoverer/plus? is the Discoverer Plus URL.
- us=<value> specifies the E-Business Suite username.
- database=<value> specifies the database.

- eul=<value> specifies the Apps-mode End User Layer.
- lm=applications specifies to connect using Apps mode.
- responsibility=<value> specifies the responsibility.
- opendbid=<value> specifies the workbook ID of a Discoverer workbook.
- sheetid=<value> specifies the worksheet ID of a Discoverer worksheet.

In this example, MONTHLY_ANALYSIS is the workbook ID of the Monthly Analysis workbook, and 179 is the worksheet ID of the January Analysis worksheet.

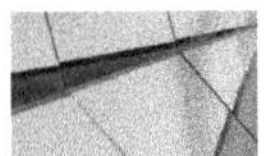

**NOTE**
*For more information about finding out workbook IDs and worksheet IDs, see the sections "Finding Out the Unique ID of a Workbook" and "Finding Out the Unique ID of a Worksheet" earlier in this chapter.*

## List of URL Parameters

When entering URL Parameters, you can use three types of parameters.

The three types of URL parameters that you can use are

- URL parameters common to both Discoverer Plus and Viewer
- URL parameter specific to Discoverer Plus
- URL parameters specific to Discoverer Viewer

We will look at all three types in the following sections.

### URL Parameters Common to Both Discoverer Plus and Viewer

There are 14 URL parameters that are common to both Discoverer Plus and Discoverer Viewer.

Table 20-3 lists the 14 URL parameters common to both Discoverer Plus and Discoverer Viewer.

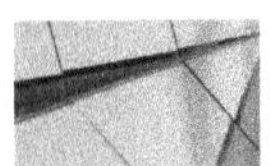

**NOTE**
*All of the parameters listed in Table 20-3 are available for use with OLAP unless specifically excluded.*

### URL Parameters Specific to Discoverer Plus

There are 20 URL parameters that are specific to Discoverer Plus.

Table 20-4 lists the 20 URL parameters specific to only Discoverer Plus.

**NOTE**
*In Table 20-4, a parameter is not available for use with OLAP unless specifically stated.*

| Parameter and Values | Description | Example |
|---|---|---|
| cn=<connection ID> | Specifies the private or public connection containing the login details with which to start Discoverer.<br>See also "Locating the Connection ID of a Connection." | cn=cf_a102<br>**Note:** If Discoverer end users are not allowed to create private connections, the specified connection must be a public connection.<br>**Note:** This parameter is not available when using OLAP. |
| cs=[APPS_SECURE]<dbc file name> | Specifies whether to connect in secure mode. <dbc filename> refers to the E-Business Suite DBC file that contains the E-Business Suite connection information. | cs=[APPS_SECURE]purchase_orders<br>**Note:** This parameter is not available when using OLAP. |
| eul=<EUL name> | Specifies the name of the EUL to which to connect. You must specify this parameter only if you want to override the default EUL.<br>**Note:** EUL names are case-sensitive. | eul=myEUL<br>**Note:** This parameter is not available when using OLAP. |
| nls_date_format=<date format> | Specifies the default date format for the session. | nls_date_format='MM/DD/YY' |
| nls_date_language=<date language> | Specifies the language for day and month names displayed in Discoverer. | nls_date_language=Spanish |
| nls_lang=<language> | Specifies the language and territory that Discoverer uses.<br>**Note:** Use Oracle naming conventions to specify language and territory. | nls_lang=spanish_spain |
| nls_numeric_characters=<separator characters> | Specifies the default characters to use as the decimal and group separator.<br>**Note:** You must specify the decimal separator first, followed by the group separator. | nls_numeric_characters='.,' |
| nls_sort=<sort name or binary> | Specifies the session collating sequence for ORDER BY queries and string comparisons, as follows:<br>■ Use <sort name> to specify an alphabetical sort sequence.<br>■ Use binary to specify a binary sort. | nls_sort=binary |
| nls_sort=<sort type> | Specifies a character sort sequence. For more information about the nls_sort command, see Oracle Database Globalization Support Guide. | nls_sort=XSpanish |

**TABLE 20-3.** *URL Parameters Common to Both Discoverer Plus and Viewer* (continued)

| Parameter and Values | Description | Example |
|---|---|---|
| reuseConnection=<true or false> | Specifies whether end users must always enter a password when using URL links containing the same login details in a browser session.<br>**Note:** Use this preference with private Discoverer connections. End users are not prompted for a database password when using public Discoverer connections.<br>Discoverer checks whether the end user has specified a database password in a browser session and, if so, whether to prompt the user again for a database password.<br>For example, a web page might contain URL links to five Discoverer worksheets. If an end user selects the first worksheet and enters a database password, you might want them not to have to enter the password again if they return to the web page and select from the other four worksheet links.<br>Use false if you always want end users to enter a password.<br>Use true if you want end users to enter a password only the first time they use a private connection in a browser session. | reuseConnection=true<br>**Note:** This parameter is not available when using OLAP. |
| sg=<security group> | Specifies the Oracle E-Business Suite security group you want to connect with.<br>**Note:** If you do not specify a username, responsibility, or security group, the Discoverer end user is prompted to enter the missing login information. | sg=securityGroup<br>**Note:** This parameter is not available when using OLAP. |
| us=<database username> | Specifies a database username with which to connect to Discoverer.<br>**Tip:** You can also use this parameter to specify a database username as a single parameter.<br>**Note:** If you do not specify a username, the Discoverer end user is prompted for a username. | us=video5 |

**TABLE 20-3.** *URL Parameters Common to Both Discoverer Plus and Viewer* (continued)

| Parameter and Values | Description | Example |
|---|---|---|
| wbkowner=<workbook owner name> | Specifies the name of the owner of the workbook to open in Discoverer.<br>**Note:** This parameter is used when workbooks are saved with the same name under different schemas. | wbkowner=guest<br>**Note:** This parameter is not available when using OLAP. |
| lm=<applications, OLAP or discoverer> | Specifies the login method, as follows:<br>■ applications connects as an Oracle E-Business Suite user.<br>■ discoverer (default) connects as a database user.<br>■ OLAP specifies that you are not deploying OLAP Discoverer in a single sign-on environment.<br>**Note:** According to the Oracle documentation, this parameter is specific to Discoverer Viewer only. However, upon testing we noticed that it also works with Discoverer Plus; therefore, we have moved it into the set of common parameters. | lm=applications<br>**Tip:** If omitted, discoverer is assumed.<br>**Note:** This parameter is available when using OLAP, but only the OLAP setting is permitted. In non-OLAP environments, you must use applications or discoverer. |

**TABLE 20-3.** *URL Parameters Common to Both Discoverer Plus and Viewer*

| Parameter and Values | Description | Example |
|---|---|---|
| _plus_popup=<true or false> | Specifies whether to launch Discoverer Plus in a new browser window or in the Discoverer Connections page, as follows:<br>■ true (default) launches Discoverer Plus in a new browser window.<br>■ false launches Discoverer Plus in the current browser window.<br>This URL parameter can be used with framedisplaystyle (for more information, see framedisplaystyle=). | _plus_popup=true<br>**Note:** If omitted, Discoverer is launched in the current browser window. |
| autoconnect=<yes or no> | Specifies whether to automatically connect when all parameters are present. The default is yes.<br>■ yes (default) automatically connects when all parameters are present.<br>■ no does not automatically connect, even when all parameters are present. | autoconnect=yes<br>**Note:** This parameter is available only when using OLAP. |

**TABLE 20-4.** *URL Parameters Specific to Discoverer Plus* (continued)

| Parameter and Values | Description | Example |
|---|---|---|
| brandimage=<logo_file_name> | Specifies that you display a logo in the top-right corner of the Discoverer Plus OLAP screen.<br>You can reference this file in the following two ways:<br>■ Using a path that is relative to the location of the d4o.jar file on the server<br>■ Using an absolute path | brandimage=http://server.com:7777/discoverer/common/mylogo.gif<br>**Note:** This parameter is available only when using OLAP. |
| database=<database name or alias> | Specifies which database to connect to when Discoverer starts.<br>**Tip:** You can also use the connection ID URL parameter cn=<value> to specify the database and username as a single parameter. | database=mydb |
| framedisplaystyle=<separate or embedded> | Specifies how to launch the Discoverer main window.<br>■ separate launches Discoverer's main window as a separate frame from the browser (that is, from the Discoverer Connections page). The browser window contains a Discoverer image and must remain open while Discoverer is being used.<br>■ embedded causes Discoverer's main window to launch within the current browser window.<br>When using _pop_up with framedisplaystyle= in a non-OLAP environment, the four possible combinations are<br>■ _plus_popup=true and framedisplaystyle=embedded launches Discoverer Plus in a new pop-up browser window that contains the Plus applet embedded in it.<br>■ _plus_popup=true and framedisplaystyle=separate opens a new pop-up browser window *and* launches Discoverer Plus in a new applet window. | framedisplaystyle=separate<br>**Note:** This parameter is available in all of the Discoverer environments including OLAP. |

**TABLE 20-4.** *URL Parameters Specific to Discoverer Plus* (continued)

| Parameter and Values | Description | Example |
|---|---|---|
| (*Continued*) | This combination launches three windows: the original browser window (that is, Discoverer Connections page), the new browser window containing the Discoverer image, and the JFrame window containing the Discoverer Plus applet.<br>■ _plus_popup=false and framedisplaystyle=embedded launch Discoverer Plus in the current browser window.<br>■ _plus_popup=false and framedisplaystyle=separate launch Plus in a JFrame window. The current browser window contains the Discoverer image. | framedisplaystyle=separate<br>**Note:** This parameter is available in all of the Discoverer environments including OLAP. |
| helpset=<br><path>/<locale>/<HS file> | Specifies a help set location that is different from the default Discoverer Plus help set, where<br>■ path = Directory that contains the help set<br>■ locale = Two-character locale<br>■ helpset_file_name = Name of the help set file, such as myhelp.hs<br>**Note:** The help must be in subdirectories named by the standard two-character locale.<br>**Tip:** As an alternative to using the HelpSet URL parameter to customize the help, edit the plusug.hs file and its related files. | helpset=Plus_files/My_custom_help<br>(where the Plus_files/My_custom_help directory contains the language folders, such as /en, /es, /fr).<br>**Note:** This parameter is available in all of the Discoverer environments including OLAP. |
| locale=<language[_country]<br>[_variant]> | Specifies the language (and optionally the country and variant) that is used by Discoverer Plus OLAP. This parameter overrides the browser's language setting on the end user's client machine.<br>**Tip:** Use ISO codes to specify the language, country, and variant. | locale=es_ES<br>In this example, the language is Spanish, and the country is Spain.<br>**Note:** This parameter is available only when using OLAP. |
| loglevel=<type> | Specifies the level of log messages to display for end users.<br>The values for type are<br>■ none = No messages (default)<br>■ error = Error messages<br>■ warning = Warning messages<br>■ informational = Informational messages<br>■ trace = Trace messages | loglevel=error<br>**Note:** This parameter is available only when using OLAP. |

**TABLE 20-4.** *URL Parameters Specific to Discoverer Plus* (continued)

| Parameter and Values | Description | Example |
|---|---|---|
| lookandfeelname=<system or oracle or browser or plastic or custom> | Specifies a look and feel. For example, a user might want to run Discoverer Plus using the Windows look and feel.<br>This setting overrides the LAF specified in Oracle Fusion Middleware Control.<br>Your options are<br>■ system<br>■ plastic<br>■ browser<br>■ oracle<br>■ custom<br>■ metal (OLAP only)<br>■ motif (OLAP only)<br>If you specify the lookandfeelname value as custom, Discoverer uses the LAF class and JAR specified in the configuration.xml file. For more information regarding setting a custom LAF, see the "Defining a Custom Look and Feel for Discoverer Plus" section in this chapter. | lookandfeelname=plastic<br>**Note:** This parameter is available in all of the Discoverer environments including OLAP. |
| opendb=<workbook name> | Specifies the name of a workbook to open (Discoverer assumes that the workbook is stored in the database, not as a scheduled workbook). If you use the opendb parameter more than once in the URL, Discoverer uses the last one.<br>**Tip:** This URL parameter is included for backward compatibility. Oracle recommends that you use the following opendbid to specify workbooks.<br>**Note:** opendb=Video+Sales+Workbook is the equivalent of workbookname=Video+Sales+Workbook&workbooksource=Database.<br>See also workbookname and workbooksource. | opendb=Video+Sales+Workbook<br>**Note:** You must also specify a workbook source (that is, workbooksource=Database or Scheduled). Here's an example: workbooksource=Scheduled&opendb=Video+Sales+Workbook. |
| opendbid=<unique ID> | Specifies the unique ID of the workbook you want to open.<br>Discoverer assumes the workbook is stored in the database, not as a scheduled workbook.<br>For more information about how to find the unique ID of a workbook, see the "Finding Out the Unique ID of a Workbook" section in this chapter. | opendbid=JanuarySales<br>**Note:** You must also specify a workbook source (that is, workbooksource=Database or Scheduled).<br>Here's an example: workbook source=Scheduled&opendbid=JanuarySales. |

**TABLE 20-4.** *URL Parameters Specific to Discoverer Plus* (continued)

| Parameter and Values | Description | Example |
|---|---|---|
| param_<parameter_ name>=<parameter_value> | Specifies values for parameters. **Note:** If the workbook does not contain a parameter of that name, Discoverer ignores the parameter. | param_regionparam=East |
| responsibility= <responsibility name> | Specifies the Oracle E-Business Suite responsibility for Oracle Applications end users. **Note:** If you do not specify a username, responsibility, or security group, the user is prompted to enter the missing login information. | responsibility=Manager (Discoverer bypasses the Responsibility dialog and assigns the end user an Oracle E-Business Suite responsibility of Manager.) |
| sheet=<worksheetname> | Specifies the name of the worksheet to open by default. **Note:** If you use the sheet parameter more than once in the URL, Discoverer opens the last one. **Tip:** In a non-OLAP environment, this URL parameter is included for backward compatibility. Oracle recommends you use the following sheet ID to specify worksheets in a non-OLAP environment. | sheet=Sales+Detail+Sheet **Note:** This parameter is available in all of the Discoverer environments including OLAP. |
| sheetid=<unique ID> | Specifies the unique identifier of the worksheet to open. For more information about how to find the unique ID of a worksheet, see the section "Finding Out the Unique ID of a Worksheet" in this chapter. **Note:** You must also specify a workbook using opendbid. | sheetid=7 |
| username=<database username> | Specifies a database username with which to connect to Discoverer. **Tip:** You can also use this parameter to specify a database username as a single parameter. **Note:** If you do not specify a username, the Discoverer end user is prompted for a username. | username=video5 **Note:** This parameter is available in all of the Discoverer environments including OLAP. |
| windowheight= <number of pixels> | Specifies the height in pixels of the Discoverer application frame. If you do not use this parameter, Discoverer uses a default value. | windowheight=600 **Note:** This parameter is available in all of the Discoverer environments including OLAP. |
| windowwidth= <number of pixels> | Specifies the width in pixels of the Discoverer application frame. If you do not use this parameter, Discoverer uses a default value. | windowwidth=800 **Note:** This parameter is available in all of the Discoverer environments including OLAP. |

**TABLE 20-4.** *URL Parameters Specific to Discoverer Plus* (continued)

| Parameter and Values | Description | Example |
|---|---|---|
| workbookname=<workbookname> | Specifies the name of the Discoverer workbook to open.<br>**Tip:** Unless you are using OLAP, use this URL parameter with workbooksource.<br>For example, workbookname=Video+Sales+Workbook&workbook source=Database is the equivalent of opendb=Video+Sales+Workbook.<br>**Tip:** In a non-OLAP environment, this URL parameter is included for backward compatibility. Oracle recommends that you use the opendbid to specify worksheets in a non-OLAP environment. | workbookname=Video+Sales+Workbook<br>**Note:** This parameter is available in all of the Discoverer environments including OLAP. |
| workbooksource=<Database or Scheduled> | Specifies the location of the workbook to open:<br>■ Database specifies that the workbook is saved in the database.<br>■ Scheduled specifies that the workbook is a scheduled workbook that is updated periodically.<br>**Tip:** Use this URL parameter with opendbid or workbookname. | workbooksource=Database |

**TABLE 20-4.** *URL Parameters Specific to Discoverer Plus*

## URL Parameters Specific to Discoverer Viewer

There are 13 URL parameters specific to Discoverer Viewer.

Table 20-5 lists the 13 URL parameters specific to only Discoverer Viewer.

**NOTE**

*In Table 20-5, all the parameters are available for use with OLAP unless specifically excluded.*

| Parameter and Values | Description | Example |
|---|---|---|
| anlsdf=<date format> | Specifies the date format for the session for Oracle Applications end users (synonym of nls_date_format). | anlsdf='MM/DD/YY' |
| anlsdl=<date language> | Specifies the language to use for the spelling of day and month names and date abbreviations (AM, PM, AD, BC) for Oracle Applications end users (synonym of nls_date_language). | anlsdl=fr |

**TABLE 20-5.** *URL Parameters Specific to Discoverer Viewer* (continued)

| Parameter and Values | Description | Example |
|---|---|---|
| anlsl=<language> | Specifies the session language for Oracle Applications end users (synonym of nls_lang). | anlsl=en-gb |
| anlss=<sortname or binary> | Specifies the session collating sequence for ORDER BY queries and string comparisons for Oracle Applications end users (synonym of nls_sort).<br>Values are<br>■ the name of an alphabetical sort sequence<br>■ binary, specifying a binary sort | anlss=binary |
| db=<database name><br>db=<host:port:database> | Specifies the database to connect to when Discoverer starts. When just a name is specified, the database name must equate to an entry in your LDAP or TNSNAMES.ORA file.<br>In an OLAP environment, you fully qualify the database by quoting the host, port, and database directly. | db=video<br>db=http://<host.domain>:<port>/discoverer/plus?db=host1:1521:ora925 |
| pi_<page item name>=<page item value> | Specifies the name of a page item and the value to select. | pi_Region=West |
| qp_<parameter name>=<parameter value> | Specifies values for parameters.<br>**Note:** If the workbook does not contain a parameter of that name, Discoverer ignores the parameter. | qp_City=Denver |
| rs=<responsibility> | Specifies the Oracle E-Business Suite responsibility for Oracle Applications end users.<br>**Note:** If you do not specify a username, responsibility, or security group, the user is prompted to enter the missing login information. | rs=Manager<br>(Discoverer bypasses the Responsibility dialog and assigns the end user an Oracle E-Business Suite responsibility of Manager.)<br>**Note:** This URL parameter is not available when using OLAP. |
| wb=<workbook name> | Specifies the name of the Discoverer workbook to open.<br>**Tip:** This URL parameter is included for backward compatibility. Oracle recommends that you use wbk to specify workbooks.<br>**Note:** Use + to indicate spaces in workbook names. | wb=My+Workbook<br>**Note:** This URL parameter is not available when using OLAP. Please see the parameter called worksheetName at the end of this table. |

**TABLE 20-5.** *URL Parameters Specific to Discoverer Viewer* (continued)

| Parameter and Values | Description | Example |
|---|---|---|
| wbk=<unique ID> | Specifies the unique ID of the workbook to open.<br>Discoverer assumes that the workbook is stored in the database, not as a scheduled workbook.<br>For more information about how to find the unique ID of a workbook, see the "Finding Out the Unique ID of a Workbook" section in this chapter. | wbk=JanuarySales<br>**Note:** This URL parameter is not available when using OLAP. Please see the parameter called worksheetName at the end of this table. |
| ws=<worksheetname> | Specifies the name of the worksheet to open by default.<br>**Tip:** This URL parameter is included for backward compatibility. Oracle recommends that you use wsk to specify worksheets.<br>**Note:** Use + to indicate spaces in worksheet names. | ws=Sales+Detail+Sheet<br>**Note:** This URL parameter is not available when using OLAP. Please see the parameter called worksheetName at the end of this table. |
| wsk=<unique ID> | Specifies the unique identifier of the worksheet to open.<br>For more information about how to find the unique ID of a worksheet, see the "Finding Out the Unique ID of a Worksheet" section in this chapter.<br>**Note:** You must also specify a workbook using wbk. | wsk=7<br>**Note:** This URL parameter is not available when using OLAP. Please see the parameter called worksheetName at the end of this table. |
| worksheetName=workbook_path/worksheet_name | Specifies the folder location, OLAP workbook name, and name of the OLAP worksheet to open.<br>You must prefix folder names, workbook names, and worksheet names with a slash (/) or the URL-encoded value for slash:%2F). For example, to specify a worksheet called Export 1 in Workbook A, which is stored in the Users/msmith/ folder in the Discoverer Catalog, specify &worksheetName=Users/msmith/Workbook+A/Export+1.<br>**Note:** Do not prefix the root folder name with a slash. For example, specify &worksheetName=Users, not&worksheetName=/Users. | worksheetName=Users/msmith/Workbook+A/Export+1<br>**Note:** This URL parameter is available only when using an OLAP worksheet in Discoverer Viewer. |

**TABLE 20-5.** *URL Parameters Specific to Discoverer Viewer*

# Migrating Discoverer to OBIEE

Prior to February 2013 there really was no way to migrate Discoverer content to OBIEE. But that's when Oracle released the Discoverer Metadata Migration Assistant (DOMA). We have not had time to test DOMA because it was released too late for full testing for the book; however, we have been given permission by Oracle to quote from the migration document.

There is a very comprehensive migration user guide available from Oracle at http://www.oracle.com/technetwork/developer-tools/discoverer/disco-metadata-migration-user-guide-1908439.pdf.

The document provides a single source of information about translating the metadata from an Oracle BI Discoverer system to that which can be used by Oracle BI Enterprise Edition (OBIEE).

OBIEE is an innovative and comprehensive BI platform that delivers the full range of BI capabilities on a next-generation architecture designed for true enterprise deployment. It enables organizations to define a single, logical view of all enterprise data, whether in a single data warehouse or across multiple operational and analytic sources. Business users benefit from new levels of self-sufficiency to access, interact with, and utilize this information to increase effectiveness.

## Similarities with Discoverer

If you are used to working with Discoverer, you will be used to terms such as EUL, workbook, the Discoverer Administration tool, Discoverer Plus, Discoverer Portlet, and so on. There are equivalents to much of the Discoverer terminology within OBIEE, and in the following sections, in which we outline the major elements of OBIEE, we will point out as many as we can. This way, you can begin to understand that even though OBIEE is very much different from Discoverer, at least in terms of being able to understand what it does there is some overlap. We hope this brief introduction will help you decide whether you should migrate.

### Oracle BI Administration Tool

The metadata that is used by Oracle BI Server is created using the Oracle BI Administration tool. This is comparable to Discoverer Administrator. The OBIEE metadata is contained within a file known as an .rpdfile. This is the equivalent of a Discoverer EUL. Discoverer business areas are roughly equivalent to a presentation layer catalog, which in turn is made available as subject areas within Oracle BI Answers.

There is a key difference between the metadata models of the two products whereby OBIEE metadata consists of three layers. A physical layer contains the mappings to the objects that hold the data, such as a database, Microsoft Excel spreadsheet, XML file, and so on. This layer also contains information about how the mappings relate to each other in the form of primary/foreign keys. The logical or business model layer contains mappings of how objects in the physical layer relate to each other. Key differences with Discoverer are the creation of dimensions and facts leading to the ability to define level-based measures. The presentation layer contains the view of the metadata that the end users see. It is possible to view a diagrammatic representation of both the physical model (in other words, database model) and logical business model layers. The benefit of this is a clear and quick understanding of how the metadata objects are related.

The Oracle BI Administration tool provides support for multiuser BI metadata administration (including a check-in/out model) and multilanguage metadata. The OBIEE metadata can span multiple heterogeneous data sources, share common dimensions between multiple subject areas, and therefore provide a common and consistent reporting framework across all business functions.

### Oracle BI Interactive Dashboards

Oracle BI Interactive Dashboards provide a fully interactive collection of analytic content with a rich variety of visualizations in a pure thin client. Guided navigations and alerts drive the user to greater insight to take the right actions at the right time for their business. This is comparable to using the Discoverer Portlet provider in conjunction with Oracle Portal. Users familiar with the BI Interactive Dashboards will know how easy they are to use offering greater presentation and visualization capabilities.

### Oracle BI Answers

Oracle BI Answers is a pure thin-client adhoc query and analysis tool with a simple point-and-click interface for building queries. Users interact with a business-friendly view of their data. This is comparable to Discoverer Plus and Viewer. In Answers 10*g*, a query is known as a *request*, whereas in Answers 11*g* this is now known as an *analysis*. Both of these are equivalent to a Discoverer worksheet. Answers requests and analyses are stored in a catalog either in a user's personal area or in a shared area. There is full support in the catalog for organizing requests in folders and subfolders.

### Oracle BI Delivers

Oracle BI Delivers enables proactive notification, monitoring and alerting, and report distribution to multiple channels such as e-mail, dashboard alerts, and mobile devices. It includes a web-based interface for the creation of alerts (known as iBots in OBIEE 10*g* and Agents in OBIEE 11*g*) and the ability to execute other iBots, agents, scripts, or Java programs to build up analytic workflows. There is no comparable alerting and distribution functionality in Discoverer other than the ability to schedule worksheets and share the results with other users of the system.

### Oracle BI Publisher

Oracle BI Publisher enables pixel-perfect reports to be generated using Answers as the source. Microsoft Word or Adobe Acrobat can be used to lay out reports and create templates. BI Publisher is an excellent tool and excels at high-volume picture-perfect output. There is no equivalent functionality within Discoverer for the direct distribution of Discoverer content like this. Discoverer was designed primarily as an analysis tool and not as a report distribution tool.

Following on from the previous, many people, including ourselves, have found various ways to deliver Discoverer content using Discoverer Desktop with a combination of third-party scheduling and e-mailing tools in addition to Microsoft's native APIs and Adobe's Acrobat. We have had to do this out of necessity because Oracle never added such functionality to Discoverer. If you intend on staying with Discoverer for any length of time and want to publish Discoverer content, you should either use Discoverer 10*g* interfaced with BI Publisher 10*g* or follow our approach and use third-party tools.

**NOTE**

*BI Publisher also integrated with Discoverer as a source in OBIEE 10*g*, but this was removed in OBIEE 11*g*.*

## Discoverer to OBIEE Migration Assistant

This section provides a high-level overview of the instructions for using the Discoverer to OBIEE Migration Assistant. This is a command-line utility that is intended to greatly accelerate the translation of Discoverer metadata from the EUL into OBIEE.

### Suitability of the Migration Assistant

There are several types of system that Discoverer can be used to report against:

- **Data warehouse** In other words, this is a star or snowflake schema. This is the optimum type of metadata to use with DOMA and because of the nature of the OBIEE business model layer generates metadata that in the majority of cases needs few manual changes before being able to create queries. Discoverer too works best with this type of system.
- **Custom-built OLTP schema** This type of metadata will probably need manual changes after being run through DOMA, because the Discoverer metadata can contain joins that do not directly translate to the OBIEE business model layer, in other words, multiple join paths between folders and circular joins. DOMA can cope with these scenarios by the optional creation of additional objects in the OBIEE metadata logical layer as alias dimension or fact tables.
- **Discoverer reporting on Oracle Applications** For example, these are Oracle E-Business Suite or custom-built systems. Oracle recommends customers evaluate the Oracle BI applications in these scenarios because they offer the fastest time to value using prebuilt data warehouse star schemas, ETL routines, and OBIEE metadata and dashboards built to best practices.

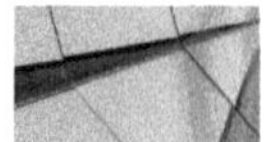

**NOTE**

*DOMA is a free toolkit. According to the DOMA release notes, it is being made available via the Oracle Technology Network on an as-is basis without any provision of support or plan for any additional enhancements. Oracle says that while care has been taken with the production of the toolkit, there are no warranties of any sort made on the outcomes it produces.*

This disclaimer is a concern to us because it clearly states that you will be on your own should things go wrong during the migration/upgrade process. This is not something to be taken lightly and is something you need to be aware of before starting. You also should not jump straight in and run DOMA on a production instance without testing it several times first.

Once the metadata has been migrated and you are operating within OBIEE, you will be fully supported just as if the content had been built natively within OBIEE. Oracle will of course point out the differences between your expected behaviors, those you were used to inside Discoverer, and OBIEE's intended behavior. Please read ahead to the following sections in this chapter in which we first describe known issues with DOMA and then point out the mapping differences between the tools. The mapping section will give you an idea of the difference between your expected behavior and OBIEE's intended behavior.

We know that many organizations have used Discoverer for a long time and have upwards of 20,000 workbooks and dozens of business areas. Migrating production environments such as these would be a monumental task. Because of the effort involved in migrating large numbers of workbooks and with the knowledge that there are some known issues, covered in a moment, if you are intent on moving to OBIEE, you may want to consider another option. This would be to take stock of your thousands of workbooks, weed out any duplication, and start fresh. As OBIEE offers capabilities, limiting yourself to importing into OBIEE only what Discoverer can do may not be your best approach.

We're not saying you have to reinvent the wheel, and we know some of you will not want to do so. However, we are realistic and understand that Discoverer may not retain its current market share for many more years. Larger organizations that have the budget to tackle a task such as starting fresh, while not reinventing the wheel in terms of current reporting, can certainly invent some new wheels to harness the improved functionality that OBIEE has to offer.

Finally, we know there are organizations still purchasing and using Discoverer in new installations and that there are smaller organizations and many "mom and pop" companies that simply cannot afford to upgrade at this time. For you this book will prove invaluable, and Oracle has stated that there will be no forced migration away from Discoverer. We recommend you stay just where you are. In time, when and if OBIEE becomes more within your budget, then would be the time to consider your migration options.

# Known Issues Migrating Discoverer to OBIEE

This section lists some of the known issues with DOMA and outlines the possible workarounds.

## CalcDecode for Character Data Types

Operations involving columns of data type VARCHAR are permitted in Discoverer with numeric values. OBIEE is stricter and requires the numbers to be surrounded by single quotes.

In such cases, Answers will display an error such as the following: "SQL ERROR:Data type doesn't match, Char is Expected but Number."

The workaround to this problem is to edit the column with the problem and add single quotes around the numbers.

## RPD May Not Return Answers Results

The Migration Assistant can take a Discoverer export in the form of an EEX file and generate an RPD. This RPD may fail to return results to Answers even if it does return results via a right-click of a physical table in the OBIEE admin tool.

To detour this problem, use the OBIEE admin tool to go to the database properties and reset its features to Default. After you have done this, verify the consistency and save.

## Worksheets with Autogenerated Names

Any worksheet items with names defined as AUTO_GENERATED_NAME cannot be migrated. Examples of this kind of worksheet are found in the Video Store tutorial sample workbooks. If Generate Column Name Automatically is selected in Discoverer, then the XML for the worksheet will not contain a real column name because Discoverer dynamically generates these. Consequently, a report cannot be built because there is no way to identify what RPD column to use.

## Dependence on Versions of Discoverer and OBIEE

The minimum version of Discover required is 10.1.2.1; the Discoverer environment must be upgraded to this level or greater before the Migration Assistant can deal with any exported EEX files. This is not an issue for Discoverer 11*g* because the version is already higher.

The only supported version of OBIEE is 10.1.3.4.1, and the required components from this are included with the DOMA bundle. The RPD and Answers reports generated must then be upgraded using the upgrade tools available with the specific version of OBIEE 11*g* that you have deployed.

## Privilege Metadata

Unfortunately, no privilege metadata is migrated from Discoverer because OBIEE has its own specific privilege and security features, and there is no simple mapping between the tools. This set of privileges includes Product, Workbook, Worksheet, and Query Governor. Once the metadata has been migrated, you will need to manage privileges and security within OBIEE.

### Title Metadata

The following title metadata is not taken across from Discoverer to Answers reports:

- Workbook name
- Worksheet name
- Conditions
- Data points
- Axis items
- Page items
- Parameters

To us, it looks as though the only title metadata that you can be assured will be migrated are titles that you have manually keyed. For the most part, we do not see this as a big problem because you will be getting new requests created in BI Answers anyway, and generating new titles should be straightforward.

### Text Formatting

The following formatting is not taken across from Discoverer to Answers reports:

- Uppercase
- Lowercase
- Capitalized

### Workbook Metadata

The following workbook metadata will not be migrated:

- Options
- Filter drills
- N-pass filters
- PL/SQL functions

### Catalog Object Schema Validation Failed

In some cases, following the upgrade of the migrated catalog to the most current version of OBIEE, you may get the following error when running a report: "Catalog object schema validation failed."

This may be because of an invalid font family. In this case, you need to specify a font family that is installed on the machine running the presentation server, such as Arial or Times New Roman.

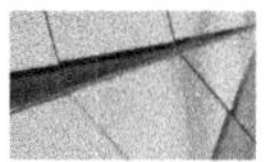

**NOTE**
*When the font family has a multipart name, enclose it with quotes.*

## OBIEE Mappings from Discoverer Administrator

This section describes the mappings used by DOMA for the metadata properties in Discoverer Administrator. It also describes any assumptions that DOMA makes when creating the three layers that make up the OBIEE metadata model.

- **End User Layer** This maps to an OBIEE *metadata repository file* (RPD).
- **Business areas** These map to a presentation catalog also known as a *subject area* in BI Answers.
- **Simple folders** These in Discoverer are mapped directly against database tables or views. They correspondingly migrate to the following tables in OBIEE:
  - Physical tables in the physical layer.
  - Logical tables in the business model layer.
  - Presentation tables in the presentation layer. The tables migrate to the presentation layer only if they are set to be visible to users in Discoverer.

**NOTE**
*Please refer to the DOMA Migration User Guide on OTN for detailed information explaining how the properties of a Discoverer simple folder are migrated.*

- **Complex folders** These are used to combine items from multiple simple folders. The analogy often used to describe complex folders is that of a database view. From a Discoverer administration perspective, they are useful for combining items into logical groups to simplify the end user's view of the metadata. From an end user's perspective, this can make life easier because they need to go to only a single folder to get all the items they need for a report rather than multiple folders.

  Complex folders appear in the presentation layer with the following mapping:
  - The item references of the complex folder will be picked from the respective base folders in the logical layer.
  - For creating the Discoverer *admin calculations* within a complex folder, a logical table corresponding to the complex folder will be created in the logical layer. Those calculations involving items from more than one base table will be created in the complex folder. The logical folder will then be moved to the presentation layer. However, if the *admin calculations* are based on a single base folder, they will be migrated to the corresponding logical folder and not the complex folder.

**NOTE**
*Complex folders based on items from another complex folder cannot be migrated automatically. Please refer to the DOMA Migration User Guide on OTN for detailed information explaining how the properties of a Discoverer complex folder are migrated.*

Custom folders enable fantastic flexibility in folder creation, such as SQL statements using set operators (e.g., UNION, INTERSECT, MINUS). On entering a SQL statement in the UI for creating a custom folder, a folder is created containing items that are referenced in the SQL statement.

In OBIEE, the custom folders are migrated to the physical layer with a table type of *select*. This is also known as an *opaque view*.

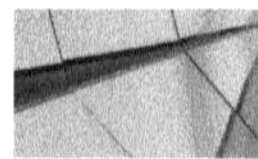

**NOTE**
*Please refer to the DOMA Migration User Guide on OTN for detailed information explaining how the properties of a Discoverer custom folder are migrated.*

- **Items** These are the basic building block for Discoverer queries. They are mapped to columns in database tables or views or created directly from calculations in Discoverer Administrator. These calculations can be based upon PL/SQL functions. Discoverer items migrate to the following columns in OBIEE:
  - Physical columns in the physical layer.
  - Logical columns in the business model layer.
  - Presentation columns in the presentation layer of OBIEE. Only items that are not hidden from end users will appear in the presentation layer.

  In Discoverer, when building a query, end users are able to either use the default aggregation for an item or select from a list of available aggregation functions. In OBIEE metadata, it is possible to specify the default aggregation for a particular column in the logical layer; however, this aggregation cannot be changed (in a similar manner to Discoverer) during the creation of the Answers worksheet. The user needs to create another column and define the required aggregation.

  To offer end users a similar experience for selecting aggregations, the Migration Assistant has an option to create a separate column in the logical layer for each default aggregation that is supported in Discoverer. This configuration option is CreateAggregatedCols. If this is set to TRUE while migrating, all aggregations supported by Discoverer will be generated. If this is set to FALSE, then a column with its aggregation function set to the Discoverer default aggregation will be created.

  Discoverer calculated items based on Oracle PL/SQL functions or Oracle analytic functions will be migrated to OBIEE metadata that uses the EVALUATE and EVALUATE_AGGR functions. These calculations will be created as a logical column with its formula being set in the setting Physical Mapping of the Logical Table Source.

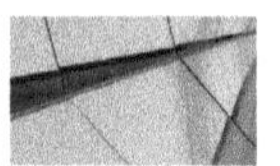

**NOTE**
*Please refer to the DOMA Migration User Guide on OTN for detailed information explaining how the properties of an item are migrated.*

- **Joins** In Discoverer these are metadata-defining relationships between the folders that are used for building queries. Usually joins are defined using the corresponding key columns of the underlying database objects but not always. Because of the differences in the metadata models between Discoverer and OBIEE, there are some differences in the types of joins that can be migrated automatically.

It is in this area of metadata that the differences between Discoverer and OBIEE metadata become apparent. The main difference is that the logical business model layer needs to be based around one or more star schema models (this is a common data model for data warehouse design).

A variation on the star schema model is known as a *snowflake* model (commonly represents the hierarchy levels of a dimension as separate tables). In these cases, the Migration Assistant collapses the snowflake dimensions to their lowest level of dimension above the fact table.

The physical metadata layer does not need to be modeled around a star schema, so this layer is created using the join information from the Discoverer metadata.

**NOTE**
*Please refer to the DOMA Migration User Guide on OTN for detailed information explaining how the properties of a Discoverer join are migrated.*

- **Multiple join paths** Discoverer folders having multiple join paths to another folder will be supported by creating object aliases that are based on the same underlying physical object but have the required alternative join paths. In the case of multiple joins to the same folder, the detail folder will be aliased.
- **Conditions** Discoverer allows the creation of conditions in the metadata. Conditions can be both mandatory and optional. Mandatory conditions are not visible to the end user and have the effect of limiting the data that can be queried. Optional conditions can be defined for end user convenience; in other words, the user (who may not be familiar with SQL syntax) can optionally use predefined conditions, perhaps containing complicated logic in their reports by dragging them into their report from a list of available conditions.
  - **Mandatory conditions** DOMA translates mandatory conditions depending on whether it is a simple, custom, or complex folder. For simple and custom folders, mandatory conditions are migrated as *content filters* in the WHERE clause section of the logical table source. For complex folders, all users migrated from the Discoverer metadata will be of the OBIEE group Everyone, so mandatory conditions on complex folders will be applied to this user group as a security filter.
  - **Optional conditions** Optional conditions that can be defined in Discoverer metadata will not be migrated to the OBIEE metadata in the initial release DOMA.

**NOTE**
*It is expected that optional conditions will be persisted as saved filters in the Web Catalog when workbook migration is available. Please refer to the DOMA Migration User Guide on OTN for detailed information explaining how the properties of a condition are migrated.*

- **Aggregate calculated items** Discoverer's aggregate calculations, also known as *admin calcs*, are calculated items that contain an aggregate function (for example, SUM). They are represented by a different icon to other items in a folder.

  For example, the formula for margin percentage could be as follows:

  ```
  SUM (Video Analysis Information.Profit)*100 / SUM (Video Analysis
  Information.Sales)
  ```

Formulas like this will be migrated using a variation of the EVALUATE function available in OBIEE.

- **Item hierarchies** Discoverer item hierarchies provide end users with a drill path through related data. A simple example is drilling through a geography hierarchy using data aggregated at a country level through region and city. These item hierarchies are migrated to OBIEE dimensions. The levels in the Discoverer item hierarchy are migrated to the associated dimension levels.

Discoverer has the ability to allow the creation of multiple hierarchy drill paths. This migrates to entries in the preferred drill path property of the OBIEE dimension-level property.

All hierarchies based on a folder will be migrated to a single dimension created on the folder. Item hierarchies based on complex folders will not be migrated since a dimension in OBIEE must be associated with a dimension table. Hierarchies spanning tables will be migrated by setting the preferred drill path appropriately.

- **Discoverer date hierarchies** There is no equivalent in OBIEE to Discoverer date hierarchy templates, so these will not be migrated. However, the resulting date hierarchies themselves will be migrated. If you have paid close attention to our earlier chapters, you will know that we do not recommend the use of date hierarchies. Therefore, if you have followed our advice, this issue will be a moot point.
- **Item classes** There is no equivalent metadata object in OBIEE, so item classes will not get migrated. When creating filters in Oracle BI Answers, lists of values are generated at runtime.
- **Summary folders** Discoverer summary folders are not migrated to OBIEE.

As we stated at the beginning of this section on DOMA, the Migration Assistant was released too late for us to fully evaluate. From what we have been able to glean from the user guide, this version of DOMA is a big step forward when compared to previous versions. The ability to migrate workbooks has long been waited for, and it is hoped that many of the organizations that have been waiting for this migration utility will now be able to move forward.

We were a little disappointed that some of the really cool Discoverer functionality does not have a migration path, but we hope that in the not too distant future Oracle will improve DOMA so we will be able to fully migrate all of Discoverer's features.

# Summary

This chapter was intended for technical team members who are responsible for managing and configuring the Oracle Discoverer installation and in particular for administrators who need to control the Discoverer environment. We showed you how to use Oracle Fusion Middleware Control to manage the Discoverer settings as well as the Discoverer preferences that can be set for the middle tier. Careful application of Discoverer's preferences will allow you to configure Discoverer for a corporate look and feel. The Discoverer Plus timeout is controlled from the middle-tier preferences. However, these preferences do not apply to Discoverer Viewer, so we next showed you how to use the Web Logic Administration Console to change the timeout values for Discoverer Viewer. Following this, we discussed how you can optimize Discoverer for optimal performance. Following this, we explained in some detail how to use EUL parameters in a browser and gave you examples of their use. The chapter concluded with a brief discussion about migrating Discoverer to OBIEE using the Discoverer Metadata Migration Assistant.

# CHAPTER 21

# Analytic Functions

In this chapter we will introduce you to Oracle's analytic functions and show you how to use these powerful objects. We will discuss some essential concepts and show you how to use a template to help you create the functions. After this, we will show you some practical examples of using analytic functions. Following the practical examples, we will explain how you can use Boolean logic to sequence conditions in such a way as to force Discoverer to apply a condition based on an analytic function first. Next, we will discuss the two types of windowing options: explicit and dynamic. Finally, we will talk a little about the power of analytics.

# What Are Analytic Functions?

Analytic functions are functions that run against the data in a query *after* the query has computed its normal results. Whereas standard functions such as margin and profit execute on a row-by-row basis as the query runs, analytic functions run against the results. These functions support basic business intelligence calculations such as moving averages, rankings, and running totals. Prior to Oracle's introduction of analytic functions in its 8*i* database, queries that required the use of this analytical horsepower were extremely difficult to build. In Discoverer, they were almost impossible. We understand that although these functions are not part of the ANSI standard set of functions, there have been discussions within the community to have some, if not all, of them included within the standard set.

As you read this chapter, please take note that Appendix B lists all of the functions available to you as you are using Discoverer.

# Business Questions

Analytic functions lend themselves perfectly to answering business questions about your data. The following are some of the typical sales questions that can be answered using analytics:

- What is my best-performing product in terms of sales?
- What are my top *n*/bottom *n* selling products?
- How do my sales from this year compare with last year?
- What is the three-month moving average of sales?
- What products sell more than 15 percent of total sales for their product line?
- Of my top ten products, how many open orders do I have?

We will show you how to use analytic functions to create reports that answer all of these questions.

# Essential Concepts

Before we get into explaining how they are used, we will explain the four basic concepts of analytical design. If you understand these concepts, you will have a much better chance of understanding how to use analytic functions.

The four basic concepts of analytical design are

- Processing order
- Partitions

- Windows
- Current row

## Discoverer Processing Order

To build a Discoverer worksheet that uses analytical functions, you need to build some worksheets in the following order:

1. Build the base query.
2. Add page items and group sorts.
3. Define the analytic function.
4. Create the remaining sorts.

## Partitions

Do not confuse the term *partitions* with database partitions. In analytic terms and as it relates to Discoverer, a partition is simply the set of page items and group sorts you are using. Thus, you would define the PARTITION BY clause of the analytic function to use the page items and group sorts.

## Windows

For each row within the partition you have defined, you can define a sliding window of data. This window determines the number of rows that will be used by the calculation. You might think that the rows would simply be the number of rows within the partition, and in most cases you would be right. However, Discoverer allows you to take a subset of the rows such that you can tell Discoverer to give you a running total, using the first row of the partition as the start point and the current row as the end point, adding up everything between those two rows.

Using windowed analytic functions such as SUM, AVG, Standard Deviation, and Variance allows you to compute cumulative, moving, and centered averages.

## Current Row

Every analytic function is executed in relation to the current row of the partition. The current row is used as the reference point to determine the start and end of the current window.

**NOTE**
*When we refer to the current row of a partition, we are referring to a row of the results, not the base rows of data as they are pulled from the database.*

# Using Analytic Functions

Prior to Discoverer 10*g*, even though the use of analytic functions was supported, you had to manually type the function into a calculation. Since 10*g*, at least in Discoverer Plus, Oracle has inserted a new button at the bottom of the New Calculation dialog box called Insert Formula From Template.

Clicking the Insert Formula From Template button lists the most commonly used analytic functions, as shown in Figure 21-1.

**NOTE**

*Many more analytic functions are available to you than just those in Figure 21-1, and Appendix B lists all of the functions that are available for use within Discoverer. We strongly recommend you get to know and use as many of the functions as you can. Doing so will set you on your way to becoming a master of Discoverer report development.*

In the following sections, we will walk you through the following six practical applications of analytic functions:

- Creating a ranking report
- Creating a running total report
- Creating a top *n*/bottom *n* report
- Creating a report to compare this year to last year
- Creating a three-month rolling-average report
- Creating previous- and next-value reports

After the examples we will discuss the concept of partitions and windows.

f(x) Rank
f(x) Percent Rank
f(x) Difference
f(x) Percent Difference
f(x) Preceding Value
f(x) Following Value
f(x) Running Total
f(x) Percent Running Contribution
f(x) Moving Total
f(x) Group Total
f(x) Percent Contribution
f(x) Band by Value
f(x) Band by Rank

**FIGURE 21-1.** *List of analytic templates*

Figure 21-2 shows the results of the base query we will use for our analytic function examples. You should notice that this is a crosstab with Product Size and Product Name on the side axis and Profit and Revenue as the data points. We have not applied any conditions, so this query scans our complete database.

| Product Size | Product Name | Profit | Revenue |
|---|---|---|---|
| LARGE | AVR-800 | $5,778,221.91 | $10,899,193.80 |
| | AVR-900 | $10,693,809.69 | $20,193,326.45 |
| | CD-500 | $6,490,671.82 | $12,297,448.18 |
| | CD-550 | $5,121,106.13 | $9,522,374.03 |
| | CD-625 | $19,945,287.32 | $39,064,837.72 |
| | QB-1000 | $4,523,599.57 | $9,437,697.71 |
| | QB-2008 | $5,284,350.01 | $10,866,016.00 |
| | QB-3000 | $5,853,476.20 | $12,038,325.70 |
| MEDIUM | AVR-500 | $20,288,355.43 | $35,776,325.41 |
| | AVR-550 | $12,324,147.95 | $21,681,080.78 |
| | CD-100 | $11,440,746.92 | $20,015,291.65 |
| | CD-200 | $10,383,271.72 | $18,181,973.60 |
| | QB-5000 | $9,570,416.13 | $18,195,109.02 |
| | QB-5500 | $9,039,564.02 | $17,172,184.28 |
| | QB-6000 | $9,828,919.51 | $18,897,604.46 |
| SMALL | AB-2008 | $5,842,488.74 | $12,685,075.60 |
| | AB-2500 | $5,907,659.67 | $11,517,752.95 |
| | AB-3000 | $9,981,105.10 | $19,101,427.80 |
| MINI | DS-1200 | $739,513.00 | $2,760,838.40 |
| | DS-1300 | $973,487.40 | $3,028,431.00 |
| | MS-1200 | $1,241,306.60 | $4,307,810.10 |
| | MS-1300 | $612,993.20 | $1,935,768.00 |

**FIGURE 21-2.** *Base query used for analytic examples*

## Creating a Ranking Report

Starting from our base query, as shown in Figure 21-2, we launched the New Calculation dialog box, shown here:

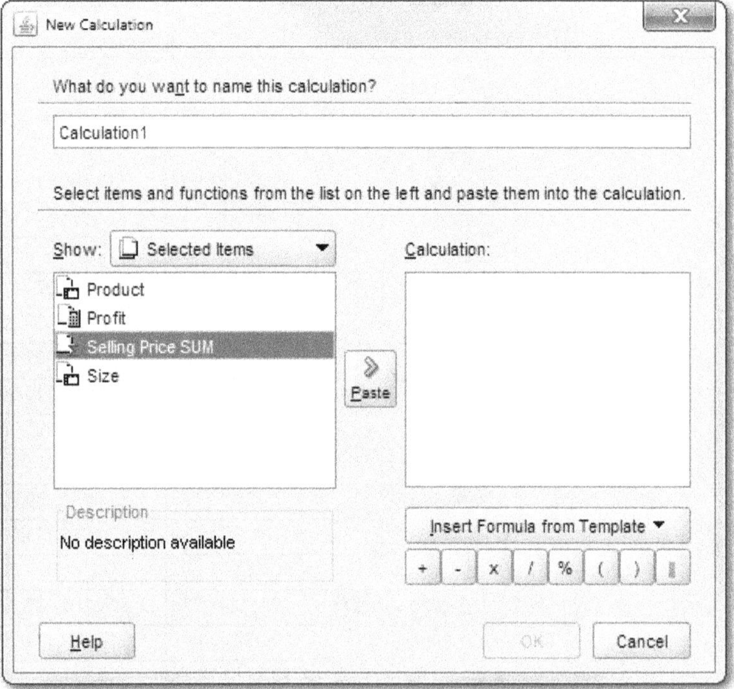


In the box, we clicked the Insert Formula From Template button. The list of available templates, as shown in Figure 21-1, is displayed, from which we selected Rank. This caused Discoverer to open the Rank dialog box shown in Figure 21-3.

In the Rank dialog box, you will notice the following four areas:

- **Rank based on** Use this area to define the item on which the ranking should be based. Discoverer will always try to populate this area for you. By default, it will use the first data point it finds. If this is not the one you want to rank by, change it. You can also change whether the highest value or the lowest value should be used to start the ranking.
- **Then rank based on** If needed, use this area to define a second item on which the ranking should be based.
- **Restart ranking at each change in** This is the partition area. Discoverer will automatically populate this area using the page items and group sorts you are using. As you can see in Figure 21-2, we have a group sort based on the product size. Discoverer has automatically brought this into the formula. Discoverer will restart the ranking according to the items you place here, inserting these items into the PARTITION BY clause of the SQL.

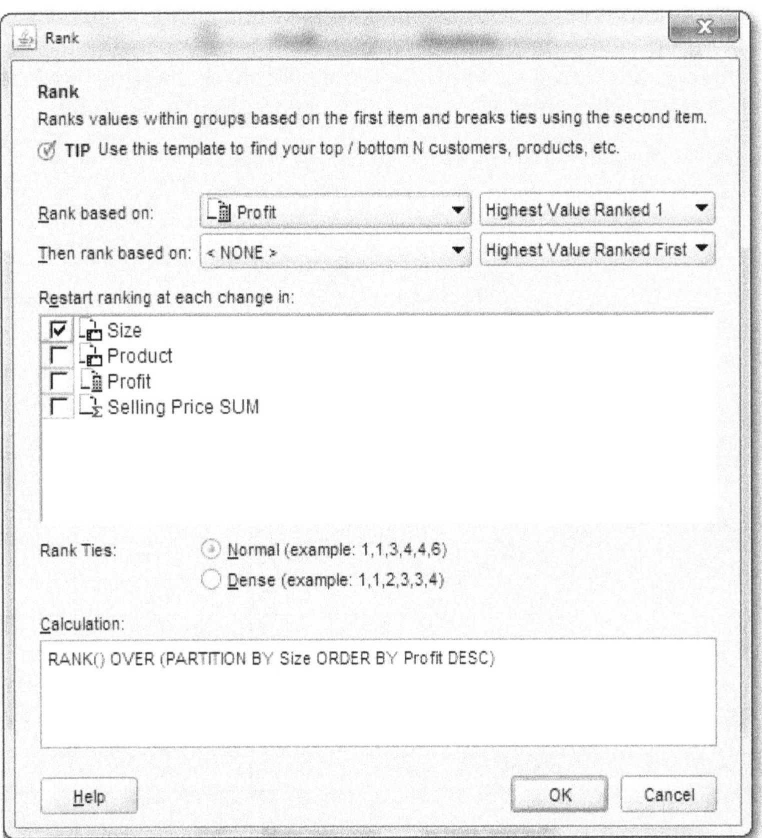


**FIGURE 21-3.** *Rank dialog box*

- **Rank Ties** This area tells Discoverer whether to use normal ranking or dense ranking. A normal ranking, as you can see in the example given in Figure 21-3, will omit a number when there is a tie for the preceding number, whereas in the dense ranking all possible values are used. So, if two values tie for first place, in a normal rank you will see 1, 1, 3, where the third value is given a rank of 3 and the 2 is omitted. In a dense rank, you will see 1, 1, 2, with the third value being given a rank of 2 and no numbers omitted. When football teams are being ranked as to their position in a league, if the first two have the same number of points, they are both ranked equal first. The third team will then be ranked third. This is an example of normal ranking. However, consider if the two top salespeople in your company have the same Sales YTD value. They will both be ranked equal first. The salesperson with the next highest Sales YTD value will be ranked second. No ranking is omitted, so this is an example of dense ranking.
- **Calculation** Discoverer uses this area to display the SQL code that will be generated when you click OK. You cannot manually change this code here. To change the code, you need to use the template.

Once you have completed the template, clicking OK causes Discoverer to create the function. Discoverer places a copy of the SQL code into the New Calculation dialog box. Assuming you have defined the function correctly, all that remains now is for you to give the function a name and click OK. After completing the function, you should check the format for both the heading and the data. We typically center all of our rank functions. Here is the result:

| Product Size | Product Name | Profit | Revenue | Rank |
|---|---|---|---|---|
| LARGE | AVR-800 | $5,778,221.91 | $10,899,193.80 | 5 |
| | AVR-900 | $10,693,809.69 | $20,193,326.45 | 2 |
| | CD-500 | $6,490,671.82 | $12,297,448.18 | 3 |
| | CD-550 | $5,121,106.13 | $9,522,374.03 | 7 |
| | CD-625 | $19,945,287.32 | $39,064,837.72 | 1 |
| | QB-1000 | $4,523,599.57 | $9,437,697.71 | 8 |
| | QB-2008 | $5,284,350.01 | $10,866,016.00 | 6 |
| | QB-3000 | $5,853,476.20 | $12,038,325.70 | 4 |
| MEDIUM | AVR-500 | $20,288,355.43 | $35,776,325.41 | 1 |
| | AVR-550 | $12,324,147.95 | $21,681,080.78 | 2 |
| | CD-100 | $11,440,746.92 | $20,015,291.65 | 3 |
| | CD-200 | $10,383,271.72 | $18,181,973.60 | 4 |
| | QB-5000 | $9,570,416.13 | $18,195,109.02 | 6 |
| | QB-5500 | $9,039,564.02 | $17,172,184.28 | 7 |
| | QB-6000 | $9,828,919.51 | $18,897,604.46 | 5 |
| SMALL | AB-2008 | $5,842,488.74 | $12,685,075.60 | 3 |
| | AB-2500 | $5,907,659.67 | $11,517,752.95 | 2 |
| | AB-3000 | $9,981,105.10 | $19,101,427.80 | 1 |
| MINI | DS-1200 | $739,513.00 | $2,760,838.40 | 3 |
| | DS-1300 | $973,487.40 | $3,028,431.00 | 2 |
| | MS-1200 | $1,241,306.60 | $4,307,810.10 | 1 |
| | MS-1300 | $612,993.20 | $1,935,768.00 | 4 |

To complete the query, we need to add a sort on the profit, which is the item being used to generate the rank. As you can see, even though the Rank function is working, our display is still sorting based on the items in the side axis.

In prior versions of Discoverer, mainly because of Java constraints, when there was more than one item on the left axis, we would not have been able to add a sort to one of the data points. In this situation, you would have no choice but to change the report to a table, losing the very elegant layout of the crosstab.

Ideally we want to be able to sort by the profit within the product size, also causing the product name to sort alongside in the left axis, and this is what we will show you next.

From the menu bar, select Tools | Sort. The following Sort Crosstab dialog box will open:

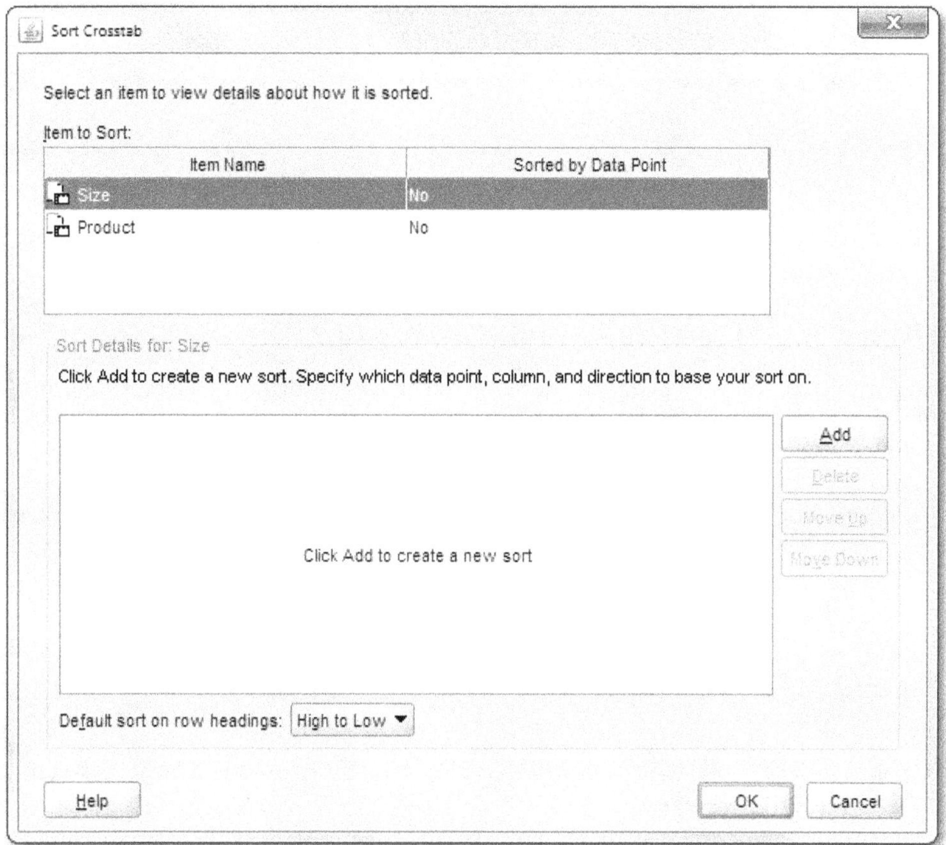


As you can see, there are no sorts on the data points. However, you can see that from the side axis the size is being sorted first followed by product. With the highlight on Size, click the Add button. Discoverer initially inserts the first named data point, which in this case, as you can see, is Profit.

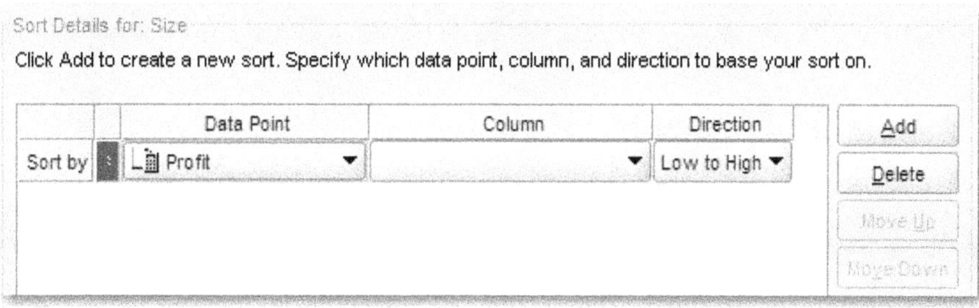

If you wanted to sort on a different data point, all you would need to do is click the drop-down alongside Profit. Discoverer will list all the data points.

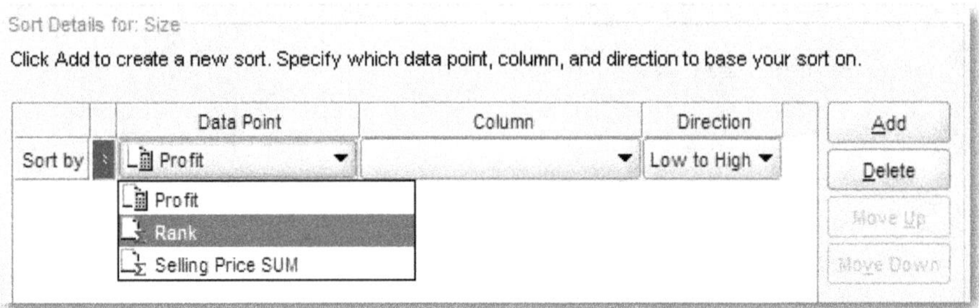


If you recall we created the rank based on the highest to lowest profit. However, left to its own devices, Discoverer will default the sort to being Low to High. Therefore, we need to make sure we change the direction for the sort to be High to Low to match the ranking. Notice how the Sorted by Data Point option alongside Size now changes to Yes.

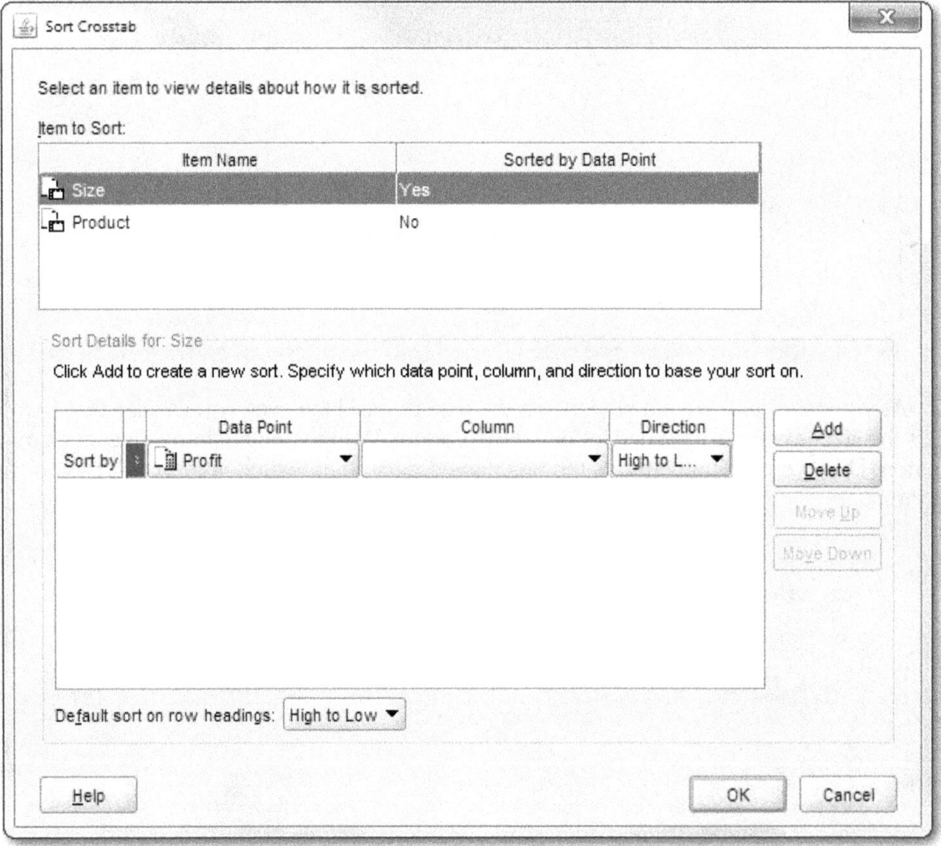

When you're done, click the OK button. The sort will now be applied, and what might appear to be our final answer is displayed here:

| Product Size | Product Name | Profit | Revenue | Rank |
|---|---|---|---|---|
| MEDIUM | AVR-500 | $20,288,355.43 | $35,776,325.41 | 1 |
| | AVR-550 | $12,324,147.95 | $21,681,080.78 | 2 |
| | CD-100 | $11,440,746.92 | $20,015,291.65 | 3 |
| | CD-200 | $10,383,271.72 | $18,181,973.60 | 4 |
| | QB-5000 | $9,570,416.13 | $18,195,109.02 | 6 |
| | QB-5500 | $9,039,564.02 | $17,172,184.28 | 7 |
| | QB-6000 | $9,828,919.51 | $18,897,604.46 | 5 |
| LARGE | AVR-800 | $5,778,221.91 | $10,899,193.80 | 5 |
| | AVR-900 | $10,693,809.69 | $20,193,326.45 | 2 |
| | CD-500 | $6,490,671.82 | $12,297,448.18 | 3 |
| | CD-550 | $5,121,106.13 | $9,522,374.03 | 7 |
| | CD-625 | $19,945,287.32 | $39,064,837.72 | 1 |
| | QB-1000 | $4,523,599.57 | $9,437,697.71 | 8 |
| | QB-2008 | $5,284,350.01 | $10,866,016.00 | 6 |
| | QB-3000 | $5,853,476.20 | $12,038,325.70 | 4 |
| SMALL | AB-2008 | $5,842,488.74 | $12,685,075.60 | 3 |
| | AB-2500 | $5,907,659.67 | $11,517,752.95 | 2 |
| | AB-3000 | $9,981,105.10 | $19,101,427.80 | 1 |
| MINI | DS-1200 | $739,513.00 | $2,760,838.40 | 3 |
| | DS-1300 | $973,487.40 | $3,028,431.00 | 2 |
| | MS-1200 | $1,241,306.60 | $4,307,810.10 | 1 |
| | MS-1300 | $612,993.20 | $1,935,768.00 | 4 |

However, if you look very closely, you will see that while some of the items have been partially sorted, everything is not as we would like. The trick is to repeat the previous steps of adding a data point sort for the profit on the other side axis item, Product Name.

With a second data point sort in place, the end result looks like this:

| Product Size | Product Name | Profit | Revenue | Rank |
|---|---|---|---|---|
| MEDIUM | AVR-500 | $20,288,355.43 | $35,776,325.41 | 1 |
| | AVR-550 | $12,324,147.95 | $21,681,080.78 | 2 |
| | CD-100 | $11,440,746.92 | $20,015,291.65 | 3 |
| | CD-200 | $10,383,271.72 | $18,181,973.60 | 4 |
| | QB-6000 | $9,828,919.51 | $18,897,604.46 | 5 |
| | QB-5000 | $9,570,416.13 | $18,195,109.02 | 6 |
| | QB-5500 | $9,039,564.02 | $17,172,184.28 | 7 |
| LARGE | CD-625 | $19,945,287.32 | $39,064,837.72 | 1 |
| | AVR-900 | $10,693,809.69 | $20,193,326.45 | 2 |
| | CD-500 | $6,490,671.82 | $12,297,448.18 | 3 |
| | QB-3000 | $5,853,476.20 | $12,038,325.70 | 4 |
| | AVR-800 | $5,778,221.91 | $10,899,193.80 | 5 |
| | QB-2008 | $5,284,350.01 | $10,866,016.00 | 6 |
| | CD-550 | $5,121,106.13 | $9,522,374.03 | 7 |
| | QB-1000 | $4,523,599.57 | $9,437,697.71 | 8 |
| SMALL | AB-3000 | $9,981,105.10 | $19,101,427.80 | 1 |
| | AB-2500 | $5,907,659.67 | $11,517,752.95 | 2 |
| | AB-2008 | $5,842,488.74 | $12,685,075.60 | 3 |
| MINI | MS-1200 | $1,241,306.60 | $4,307,810.10 | 1 |
| | DS-1300 | $973,487.40 | $3,028,431.00 | 2 |
| | DS-1200 | $739,513.00 | $2,760,838.40 | 3 |
| | MS-1300 | $612,993.20 | $1,935,768.00 | 4 |

If you look very closely at the final result and compare it to our base query shown in Figure 21-2, notice how the sort order for the side axis items has changed from Large, Medium, Small, and Mini to Medium, Large, Small, and Mini. Can you see what happened?

With the rank being based on the profit, when we added the data point sort for the size, we not only sorted the profit within the size but also sorted the size so that the size with the highest profit is listed first. Thus, Medium is sorted in first place because it contains the item with the highest profit ($20,288,355.43) of any item, namely, AVR-500.

Large comes in second place because its highest ranked item, CD-625, with a profit of $19,945,287.32, which is higher than the highest-ranked items in either Small or Mini. We encourage you to study these results closely until you understand what just happened.

You therefore need to be careful using Rank within a crosstab when there is more than one item on the side axis.

**SQL Used in Rank** Here is the SQL that Discoverer generated for the Rank function:

```
RANK() OVER(PARTITION BY Product.Size ORDER BY Sales.Profit DESC)
```

**NOTE**
*Creating conditions on Rank calculations can be very useful. For example, in our example report where we simply list all of our products ranked from highest to lowest profit, if we had created a condition such that Ranking = 1, we would see the top profit-making product for each of our sizes. Altering this to, say, Ranking <= 5 will display our top-five selling products by size. As you get used to working with the Rank function, you will find that it is an extremely versatile and useful function. We use it all the time in our reports.*

## Creating a Running Total Report

Having altered our base query to rank and sort based on the profit, we found it a very simple task to add a running total to the query. Once again we launched the New Calculation dialog box and then clicked Insert Formula From Template. The list of available templates, as shown in Figure 21-1, is displayed, from which we selected Running Total. This caused Discoverer to open the Running Total dialog box, as shown in Figure 21-4.

In the Running Total dialog box, you will notice the following four areas:

- **Running total on** Use this area to define the item upon which you want the running total. Discoverer will automatically choose the first named data point.

**FIGURE 21-4.** *Running Total dialog box*

- **Order rows by** Use this area to define the items you want to order the query by. This will typically be the same item that is being used for the running total calculation. In our case, we want to order on the profit from highest to lowest. This makes the running total synchronized with the ranking and the sorting we did earlier.
- **Restart running total at each change in** Once again, this is the partition area. Discoverer will automatically populate this area using the page items and group sorts you are using. If you are using a crosstab, it will automatically populate with the outer most item in the page axis. If you look back at Figure 21-2, because our outermost item is the product size, Discoverer has automatically brought this into the formula. Discoverer will restart the running total according to the items you place here, inserting these items into the PARTITION BY clause of the SQL.
- **Calculation** Discoverer uses this area to display the SQL code that will be generated when you click OK. You cannot manually change this code here. To change the code, you need to use the template.

Having completed the template, click OK for Discoverer to create the function. Discoverer places a copy of the SQL code into the New Calculation dialog box. Assuming you have defined the function correctly, all that remains now is for you to give the function a name and click OK. After completing the function, you should adjust the format to make sure it is displayed in the same way as the column upon which it is based. Here is the result:

| Product Size | Product Name | Profit | Revenue | Rank | Running Total |
|---|---|---|---|---|---|
| MEDIUM | AVR-500 | $20,288,355.43 | $35,776,325.41 | 1 | $20,288,355.43 |
| | AVR-550 | $12,324,147.95 | $21,681,080.78 | 2 | $32,612,503.38 |
| | CD-100 | $11,440,746.92 | $20,015,291.65 | 3 | $44,053,250.30 |
| | CD-200 | $10,383,271.72 | $18,181,973.60 | 4 | $54,436,522.02 |
| | QB-6000 | $9,828,919.51 | $18,897,604.46 | 5 | $64,265,441.53 |
| | QB-5000 | $9,570,416.13 | $18,195,109.02 | 6 | $73,835,857.66 |
| | QB-5500 | $9,039,564.02 | $17,172,184.28 | 7 | $82,875,421.68 |
| LARGE | CD-625 | $19,945,287.32 | $39,064,837.72 | 1 | $19,945,287.32 |
| | AVR-900 | $10,693,809.69 | $20,193,326.45 | 2 | $30,639,097.01 |
| | CD-500 | $6,490,671.82 | $12,297,448.18 | 3 | $37,129,768.83 |
| | QB-3000 | $5,853,476.20 | $12,038,325.70 | 4 | $42,983,245.03 |
| | AVR-800 | $5,778,221.91 | $10,899,193.80 | 5 | $48,761,466.94 |
| | QB-2008 | $5,284,350.01 | $10,866,016.00 | 6 | $54,045,816.95 |
| | CD-550 | $5,121,106.13 | $9,522,374.03 | 7 | $59,166,923.08 |
| | QB-1000 | $4,523,599.57 | $9,437,697.71 | 8 | $63,690,522.65 |
| SMALL | AB-3000 | $9,981,105.10 | $19,101,427.80 | 1 | $9,981,105.10 |
| | AB-2500 | $5,907,659.67 | $11,517,752.95 | 2 | $15,888,764.77 |
| | AB-2008 | $5,842,488.74 | $12,685,075.60 | 3 | $21,731,253.51 |
| MINI | MS-1200 | $1,241,306.60 | $4,307,810.10 | 1 | $1,241,306.60 |
| | DS-1300 | $973,487.40 | $3,028,431.00 | 2 | $2,214,794.00 |
| | DS-1200 | $739,513.00 | $2,760,838.40 | 3 | $2,954,307.00 |
| | MS-1300 | $612,993.20 | $1,935,768.00 | 4 | $3,567,300.20 |

**SQL Used in Running Total** Here is the SQL that Discoverer generated:

```
SUM(Sales.Profit) OVER(PARTITION BY Product.Size ORDER BY Sales.Profit SUM DESC
ROWS UNBOUNDED PRECEDING)
```

Do you see how this SQL has been put together and how it differs from the SQL that was generated for the Rank function?

You should notice that the name of the function being used is not RUNNING TOTAL but SUM. This is because a running total is a specialized type of SUM. You should also notice that we are using some windowing commands for the first time. Unless stated otherwise, the base row for all analytical functions is the current row.

We could easily have written the SQL to explicitly reference the current row, as follows:

```
SUM(Profit SUM) OVER(PARTITION BY Product Size ORDER BY Profit SUM DESC RANGE
BETWEEN
UNBOUNDED PRECEDING AND CURRENT ROW)
```

The end results of running these two sets of SQL are identical. This is because an implied CURRENT ROW is being used in the first example, whereas an explicit CURRENT ROW command is being used in the latter case. We will talk more about these commands later in the chapter.

# Creating a Top *n*/Bottom *n* Report

We will continue from where we left off with the Running Total report and extend it to build a report that shows the top *n* and bottom *n* values.

To create a top *n*/bottom *n* report, use the following workflow:

1. Create a calculation for a standard ranking.
2. Create a second standard ranking calculation, this time with the order reversed. This second ranking will be used within a condition but will not be displayed on the screen.
3. Add a dynamic parameter to prompt the user for the *n* value that will be passed to the condition in step 4.
4. Create a Boolean condition that filters both ranking calculations to display only the *n* values received in step 3.

To refresh your memory, here is the SQL that was used in the first ranking:

```
RANK() OVER(PARTITION BY Product.Size ORDER BY Sales.Profit DESC)
```

We will now add a second calculation using this calculation:

```
RANK() OVER(PARTITION BY Product.Size ORDER BY Sales.Profit ASC)
```

The result looks like this:

| Product Size | Product Name | Profit | Revenue | Rank | Running Total | Second Rank |
|---|---|---|---|---|---|---|
| MEDIUM | AVR-500 | $20,288,355.43 | $35,776,325.41 | 1 | $20,288,355.43 | 7 |
| | AVR-550 | $12,324,147.95 | $21,681,080.78 | 2 | $32,612,503.38 | 6 |
| | CD-100 | $11,440,746.92 | $20,015,291.65 | 3 | $44,053,250.30 | 5 |
| | CD-200 | $10,383,271.72 | $18,181,973.60 | 4 | $54,436,522.02 | 4 |
| | QB-6000 | $9,828,919.51 | $18,897,604.46 | 5 | $64,265,441.53 | 3 |
| | QB-5000 | $9,570,416.13 | $18,195,109.02 | 6 | $73,835,857.66 | 2 |
| | QB-5500 | $9,039,564.02 | $17,172,184.28 | 7 | $82,875,421.68 | 1 |
| LARGE | CD-625 | $19,945,287.32 | $39,064,837.72 | 1 | $19,945,287.32 | 8 |
| | AVR-900 | $10,693,809.69 | $20,193,326.45 | 2 | $30,639,097.01 | 7 |
| | CD-500 | $6,490,671.82 | $12,297,448.18 | 3 | $37,129,768.83 | 6 |
| | QB-3000 | $5,853,476.20 | $12,038,325.70 | 4 | $42,983,245.03 | 5 |
| | AVR-800 | $5,778,221.91 | $10,899,193.80 | 5 | $48,761,466.94 | 4 |
| | QB-2008 | $5,284,350.01 | $10,866,016.00 | 6 | $54,045,816.95 | 3 |
| | CD-550 | $5,121,106.13 | $9,522,374.03 | 7 | $59,166,923.08 | 2 |
| | QB-1000 | $4,523,599.57 | $9,437,697.71 | 8 | $63,690,522.65 | 1 |
| SMALL | AB-3000 | $9,981,105.10 | $19,101,427.80 | 1 | $9,981,105.10 | 3 |
| | AB-2500 | $5,907,659.67 | $11,517,752.95 | 2 | $15,888,764.77 | 2 |
| | AB-2008 | $5,842,488.74 | $12,685,075.60 | 3 | $21,731,253.51 | 1 |
| MINI | MS-1200 | $1,241,306.60 | $4,307,810.10 | 1 | $1,241,306.60 | 4 |
| | DS-1300 | $973,487.40 | $3,028,431.00 | 2 | $2,214,794.00 | 3 |
| | DS-1200 | $739,513.00 | $2,760,838.40 | 3 | $2,954,307.00 | 2 |
| | MS-1300 | $612,993.20 | $1,935,768.00 | 4 | $3,567,300.20 | 1 |

As you can see, all the second calculation does is display the profit ranked from lowest to highest. However, we do not need to show it, so remove the second rank from the screen.

Next we will add the dynamic parameter. You do this by launching the New Parameter dialog box. You get to this from the menu bar using Tools | Parameters and then clicking the New button.

Complete the New Parameter dialog box by giving it a name such as **Top/Bottom** and selecting <NONE> when prompted with "Which item do you want to base this item on?" Then enter a suitable prompt such as **What value should be used for the top / bottom n?** and uncheck the box Enable Users To Select Multiple Values; finally, click the OK button. The completed box is shown here:

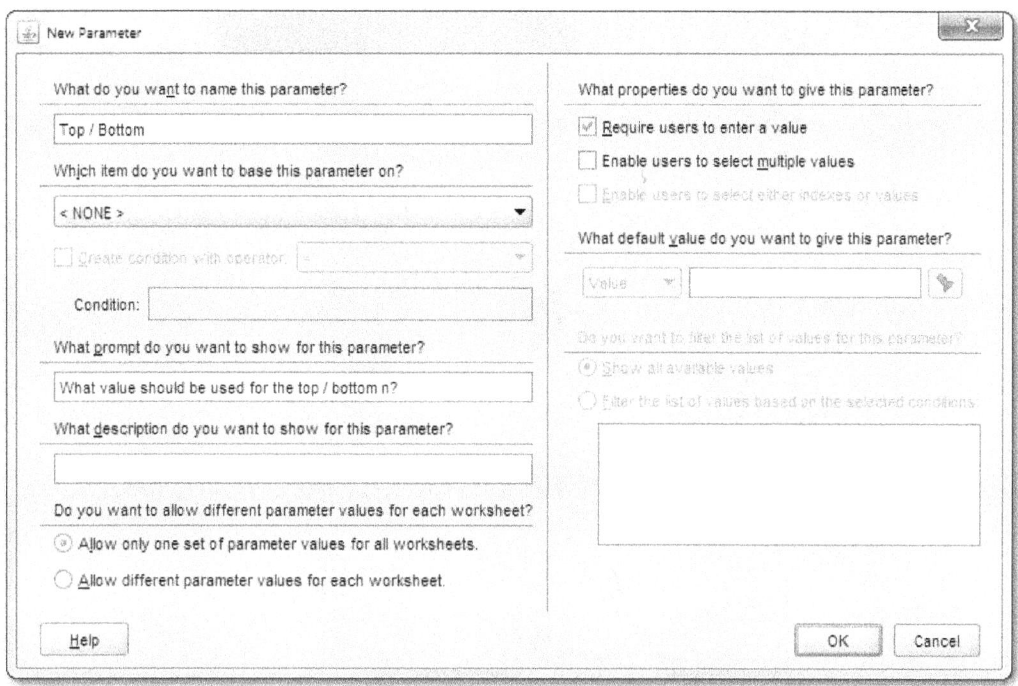


As you know, dynamic parameters will be prompted only if you associate the value from the parameter with either a condition or a calculation. In our case, we have not yet done this, so after you click the OK box to close the New Parameter dialog box, you should see that there is a small *n/a* alongside the parameter. This is correct at this stage in the report, so just click the Finish button to complete the parameter.

To use the new parameter we just created, we need to associate it with either a condition or a calculation. We will associate with the following Boolean condition:

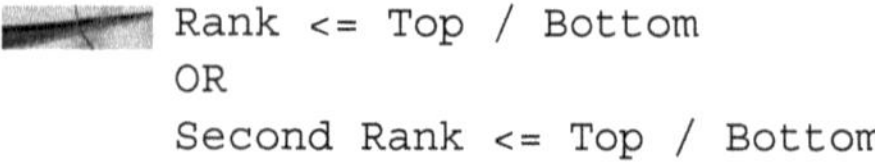

```
Rank <= Top / Bottom
OR
Second Rank <= Top / Bottom
```

To do this, launch the New Condition dialog box and create the Boolean. It should look like this:

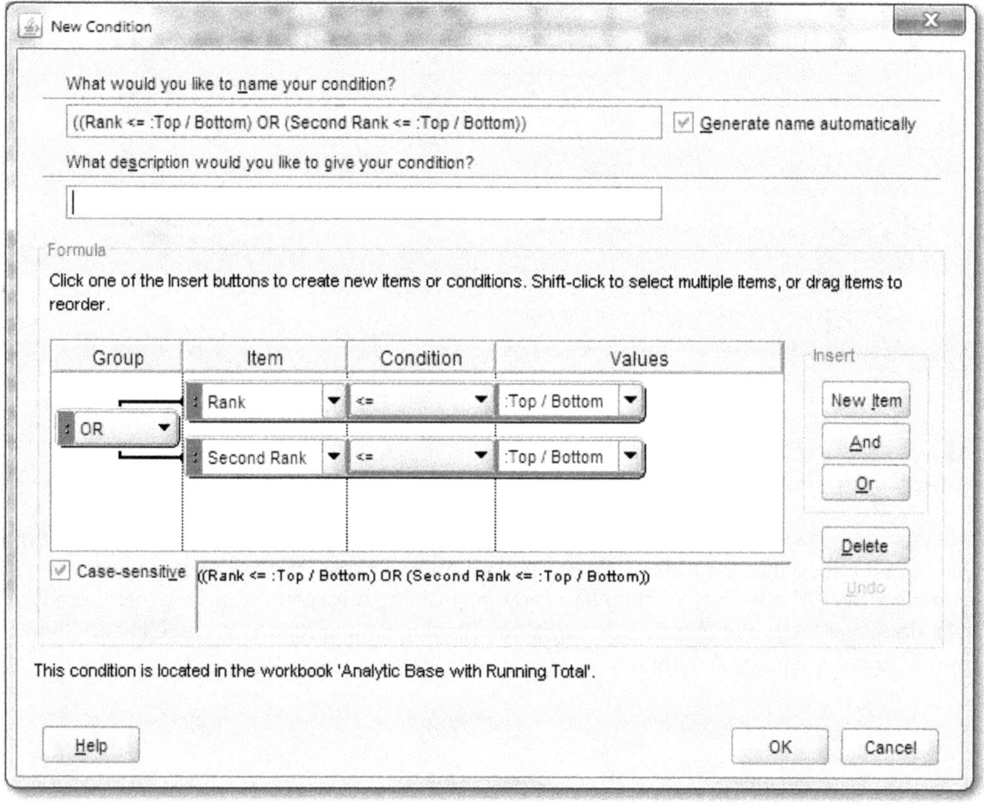

When you complete the condition by clicking the OK button, you will be prompted to provide a value for *n*.

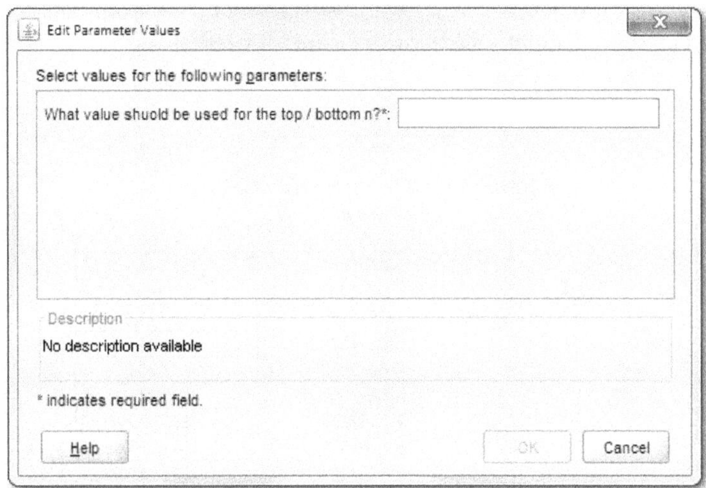


When we entered the value 2 into the parameter, we got the following result:

| Product Size | Product Name | Profit | Revenue | Rank | Running Total |
|---|---|---|---|---|---|
| MEDIUM | AVR-500 | $20,288,355.43 | $35,776,325.41 | 1 | $20,288,355.43 |
| | AVR-550 | $12,324,147.95 | $21,681,080.78 | 2 | $32,612,503.38 |
| | QB-5000 | $9,570,416.13 | $18,195,109.02 | 6 | $73,835,857.66 |
| | QB-5500 | $9,039,564.02 | $17,172,184.28 | 7 | $82,875,421.68 |
| LARGE | CD-625 | $19,945,287.32 | $39,064,837.72 | 1 | $19,945,287.32 |
| | AVR-900 | $10,693,809.69 | $20,193,326.45 | 2 | $30,639,097.01 |
| | CD-550 | $5,121,106.13 | $9,522,374.03 | 7 | $59,166,923.08 |
| | QB-1000 | $4,523,599.57 | $9,437,697.71 | 8 | $63,690,522.65 |
| SMALL | AB-3000 | $9,981,105.10 | $19,101,427.80 | 1 | $9,981,105.10 |
| | AB-2500 | $5,907,659.67 | $11,517,752.95 | 2 | $15,888,764.77 |
| | AB-2008 | $5,842,488.74 | $12,685,075.60 | 3 | $21,731,253.51 |
| MINI | MS-1200 | $1,241,306.60 | $4,307,810.10 | 1 | $1,241,306.60 |
| | DS-1300 | $973,487.40 | $3,028,431.00 | 2 | $2,214,794.00 |
| | DS-1200 | $739,513.00 | $2,760,838.40 | 3 | $2,954,307.00 |
| | MS-1300 | $612,993.20 | $1,935,768.00 | 4 | $3,567,300.20 |

Let's take a moment to study the results of the top *n*/bottom *n* query after we provided the value 2 for *n*. Look closely at the results for the Medium and Large sizes. For Medium we see only the products that are ranked 1, 2, 6, and 7, while for Large we see only the products that are ranked 1, 2, 7, and 8. This is what we wanted to see.

Look even closer at the running total. The running total continues to use all the values even though we are displaying only the top two and bottom two. One of the great features of analytic functions is that they are independent of each other. While both of the ranking calculations are filtering and displaying only the top two and bottom two, the running total is evaluating over *all* of the data. It was able to do this because it was not bound to the results of the rest of the query; the UNBOUNDED option took care of this.

## Creating a Report to Compare This Year to Last Year

Starting again from our base query shown in Figure 21-2, we will alter it to turn on the page items and populate it using the shipped year. Removing the profit gives us the start point shown here, which as you can see is currently showing the values for 2013:

Page Items: Shipped Year: FY2013

| Product Size | Product Name | Revenue |
|---|---|---|
| LARGE | AVR-800 | $2,427,232.50 |
| | AVR-900 | $4,153,183.65 |
| | CD-500 | $1,816,985.60 |
| | CD-550 | $1,368,084.58 |
| | CD-625 | $6,141,043.14 |
| | QB-1000 | $2,094,554.00 |
| | QB-2008 | $1,627,218.95 |
| | QB-3000 | $2,434,110.00 |
| MEDIUM | AVR-500 | $6,747,848.80 |
| | AVR-550 | $4,620,469.70 |
| | CD-100 | $3,005,058.25 |
| | CD-200 | $2,367,684.50 |
| | QB-5000 | $2,103,094.08 |
| | QB-5500 | $2,707,737.16 |
| | QB-6000 | $2,939,030.18 |
| SMALL | AB-2008 | $2,270,389.50 |
| | AB-2500 | $1,898,334.75 |
| | AB-3000 | $2,654,805.00 |
| MINI | DS-1200 | $682,860.95 |
| | DS-1300 | $736,485.05 |
| | MS-1200 | $739,548.60 |
| | MS-1300 | $342,180.00 |

We will now add a new calculation to pull the value for the product from the previous year. This is a much more adventurous calculation than you have seen before.

```
SUM(Selling Price SUM)
OVER(PARTITION BY Product.Size,Product.Name
ORDER BY TO_DATE(TO_NUMBER (
SUBSTR(Shipped Date."Shipped Year", 3, 4),'YYYY')
RANGE BETWEEN INTERVAL '1' YEAR PRECEDING
AND INTERVAL '1' YEAR PRECEDING)
```

We need to point out a couple of very important things about this construct.

- Whenever you use RANGE INTERVAL using YEAR, the item in the ORDER BY clause *must* return a date, which is why we're using the TO_DATE function.
- To correctly evaluate the value for the year, it *must* be a number, which is the reason for the additional TO_NUMBER and SUBSTR functions. We needed to use SUBSTR because all our year values are preceded by the characters *FY* so that 2013 is actually FY2013 and 2012 is FY2012. By pulling out the last four characters, starting at position 3, and then converting this to a number, the problem is solved. The numeric year must also appear in the page items.

**NOTE**

*If we had created a new calculation called Year that did the conversion from a string to a number already, we could call that calculation in our main calculation. The code will be much simpler to understand if you do this, but either will work. However, because we need a numeric year in our page items anyway, you may as well use the calculated year in the Prior Year calculation, as shown next:*

```
SUM(Selling Price SUM)
OVER(PARTITION BY Product.Size,Product.Name
ORDER BY TO_DATE("Year",'YYYY')
RANGE BETWEEN INTERVAL '1' YEAR PRECEDING
AND INTERVAL '1' YEAR PRECEDING )
```

Reading the previous calculation, you can see that all we are doing is pulling the total of the selling price for the prior year for the same size and product.

Here is our result showing 2013:

Page Items: Year: 2013

| Product Size | Product Name | Revenue | Prior Year |
|---|---|---|---|
| LARGE | AVR-800 | $2,427,232.50 | $1,787,212.35 |
| | AVR-900 | $4,153,183.65 | $3,746,046.15 |
| | CD-500 | $1,816,985.60 | $3,053,077.00 |
| | CD-550 | $1,368,084.58 | $1,744,900.60 |
| | CD-625 | $6,141,043.14 | $8,155,985.24 |
| | QB-1000 | $2,094,554.00 | $1,904,140.00 |
| | QB-2008 | $1,627,218.95 | $2,831,095.05 |
| | QB-3000 | $2,434,110.00 | $2,470,996.85 |
| MEDIUM | AVR-500 | $6,747,848.80 | $8,039,670.10 |
| | AVR-550 | $4,620,469.70 | $5,445,517.00 |
| | CD-100 | $3,005,058.25 | $2,860,366.25 |
| | CD-200 | $2,367,684.50 | $2,820,975.50 |
| | QB-5000 | $2,103,094.08 | $2,773,714.92 |
| | QB-5500 | $2,707,737.16 | $2,761,723.78 |
| | QB-6000 | $2,939,030.18 | $2,899,365.82 |
| SMALL | AB-2008 | $2,270,389.50 | $2,826,927.00 |
| | AB-2500 | $1,898,334.75 | $2,191,495.50 |
| | AB-3000 | $2,654,805.00 | $4,461,501.25 |
| MINI | DS-1200 | $682,860.95 | $457,146.80 |
| | DS-1300 | $736,485.05 | $812,627.20 |
| | MS-1200 | $739,548.60 | $1,278,836.55 |
| | MS-1300 | $342,180.00 | $668,754.00 |

Let's take a moment to look at this result, which displays the revenue for the year selected in the page items and displays that alongside the revenue from the prior year. We are currently displaying data for 2013. Notice how the year is just a number? This complies with the rule that the year must be numeric. Now look at the top two products for the Large size. The prior year is displaying $1,787,212.35 and $3,746,046.15.

Switching the page item to now show data for 2012, we can confirm that the correct values have indeed been pulled forward.

Page Items: Year: 2012

| Product Size | Product Name | Revenue | Prior Year |
|---|---|---|---|
| LARGE | AVR-800 | $1,787,212.35 | $1,624,357.35 |
| | AVR-900 | $3,746,046.15 | $4,009,594.05 |
| | CD-500 | $3,053,077.00 | $2,198,171.08 |
| | CD-550 | $1,744,900.60 | $1,160,967.74 |
| | CD-625 | $8,155,985.24 | $6,636,344.72 |
| | QB-1000 | $1,904,140.00 | $1,892,837.10 |
| | QB-2008 | $2,831,095.05 | $1,597,414.00 |
| | QB-3000 | $2,470,996.85 | $2,009,172.55 |
| MEDIUM | AVR-500 | $8,039,670.10 | $5,495,994.35 |
| | AVR-550 | $5,445,517.00 | $3,428,767.65 |
| | CD-100 | $2,860,366.25 | $2,709,604.75 |
| | CD-200 | $2,820,975.50 | $2,418,970.25 |
| | QB-5000 | $2,773,714.92 | $3,029,802.58 |
| | QB-5500 | $2,761,723.78 | $2,773,661.94 |
| | QB-6000 | $2,899,365.82 | $2,118,211.04 |
| SMALL | AB-2008 | $2,826,927.00 | $1,762,587.00 |
| | AB-2500 | $2,191,495.50 | $1,935,207.75 |
| | AB-3000 | $4,461,501.25 | $3,368,295.00 |
| MINI | DS-1200 | $457,146.80 | $610,905.80 |
| | DS-1300 | $812,627.20 | $456,466.15 |
| | MS-1200 | $1,278,836.55 | $675,978.90 |
| | MS-1300 | $668,754.00 | $435,432.00 |

Our system contains data only from 2006, so if we switch our page item to that year, we should not get any values for the prior year. The report bears this out. It still displays the data for 2006 but displays nothing for the prior year.

Page Items: Year: 2006

| Product Size | Product Name | Revenue | Prior Year |
|---|---|---|---|
| LARGE | AVR-800 | $183,855.00 | |
| | AVR-900 | $463,845.00 | |
| | CD-500 | $404,789.00 | |
| | CD-550 | $282,436.00 | |
| | CD-625 | $883,494.00 | |
| | QB-1000 | $384,367.12 | |
| | QB-2008 | $136,045.25 | |
| | QB-3000 | $246,745.00 | |
| MEDIUM | AVR-500 | $962,681.92 | |
| | AVR-550 | $429,632.48 | |
| | CD-100 | $2,072,866.95 | |
| | CD-200 | $575,467.20 | |
| | QB-5000 | $859,585.90 | |
| | QB-5500 | $950,124.66 | |
| | QB-6000 | $1,158,084.34 | |
| SMALL | AB-2008 | $452,350.50 | |
| | AB-2500 | $351,023.05 | |
| | AB-3000 | $442,571.85 | |

## Creating a Three-Month Rolling-Average Report

Starting again from our base query shown in Figure 21-2, we will alter it to remove both the product size and the product name from the side axis and include the shipped month instead. To aid in the display of the report, we added a condition to include only fiscal year 2011. We also removed the revenue because we want to see only the profit. The resulting output is shown at right.

| Shipped Month | Profit |
|---|---|
| OCT-10 | $2,051,379.99 |
| NOV-10 | $1,638,293.30 |
| DEC-10 | $1,950,427.14 |
| JAN-11 | $1,780,187.86 |
| FEB-11 | $2,203,660.95 |
| MAR-11 | $2,521,505.75 |
| APR-11 | $2,093,339.12 |
| MAY-11 | $2,401,178.03 |
| JUN-11 | $2,185,432.07 |
| JUL-11 | $3,077,467.18 |
| AUG-11 | $1,958,783.38 |
| SEP-11 | $3,625,419.85 |

Let's add a three-month rolling average for the profit.

Once again we launched the New Calculation dialog box and then clicked Insert Formula From Template. The list of available templates, as was shown in Figure 21-1, is displayed, from which we selected Moving Total. This caused Discoverer to open the Moving Total dialog box shown in Figure 21-5.

Moving Total

**Moving Total**

Calculates a total on all of the item values in the group from a value N rows before the current value to the current value.

Total on: Profit

Total type: f(x) Sum

Start on: 1 Rows Before Current Value

Order rows by: Shipped Month Lowest to Highest

Then order rows by: < NONE > Lowest to Highest

Restart moving total at each change in:

Shipped Month

Profit

Calculation:

SUM(Profit) OVER ( ORDER BY Shipped Month ASC ROWS BETWEEN 1 PRECEDING AND CURRENT ROW)

Help OK Cancel

**FIGURE 21-5.** *Moving Total dialog box*

In the Moving Total dialog box, you will notice the following seven areas:

- **Total on** Use this area to define the item upon which you want the running total. Discoverer will automatically choose the first named data point. In our case, we have only one, Profit.
- **Total type** Use this area to define the type of total to use. The default is SUM, and we will leave it set to SUM for the time being; however, if you click the drop-down, you get the options shown here:

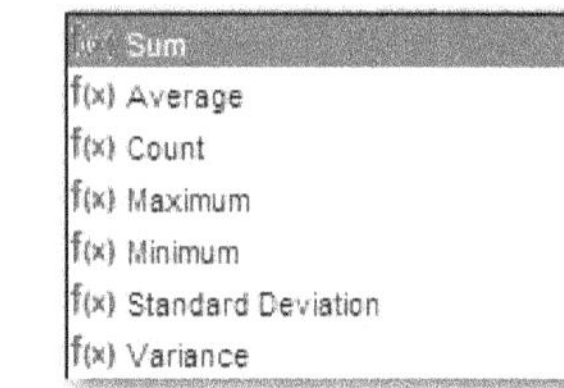


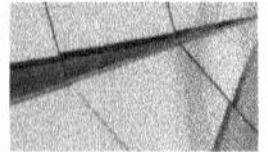

**NOTE**

*We know that we said we would be creating a three-month rolling average yet we chose Sum in the selection rather than Average. This is because we want to check our values first to make sure that the right months are being included. We can tell you in advance that our answer will initially be wrong, and we will explain why and give you the solution later in the section.*

- **Start on** Use this area to define how many rows to include in the moving total. The default is 1 Rows Before Current Value. You can change the quantity to any number you want. In our case, because we want a three-month moving average, we will change this to 2. If we had typed 3, we would have a four-month moving average. This is because the current month is always included. The only option in the template is to select rows prior to the current row. You can use following rows, but you will need to do this manually. We will show you this later in the chapter when we discuss editing a moving total.
- **Order rows by** Use this area to define the initial item you want to order the query by. This will default to the leftmost item in the worksheet. In our case, we want to order on the shipped month from lowest to highest. This makes the moving total synchronized with the display.
- **Then order rows by** Use this area to define a second item for ordering the query. This is rarely used, and most reports you create will have a single sort. You can leave this blank by setting the option to <NONE>.
- **Restart moving total at each change in** Once again, this is the partition area. Discoverer will automatically populate this area using the page items and group sorts you are using. If you are using a crosstab and you have more than one item in the side axis, Discoverer will automatically populate this with the outermost item. If you look back at Figure 21-5, because we have only one item in the side axis, Discoverer has omitted a PARTITION BY clause, showing you that this is optional in a moving total.
- **Calculation** Discoverer uses this area to display the SQL code that will be generated when you click OK. As with other templates, you cannot manually change this code here. To change the code, you need to use the template.

Having completed the template, click OK for Discoverer to create the function. Discoverer places a copy of the SQL code into the New Calculation dialog box. Assuming you have defined the function correctly, all that remains is for you to give the function a name and click OK. After completing the function, as always, you should adjust the format to make sure it is displayed in the same way as the column upon which it is based. Here is the result:

| Shipped Month | Profit | 3 Month Moving Total |
|---|---|---|
| OCT-10 | $2,051,379.99 | 6,090,851.32 |
| NOV-10 | $1,638,293.30 | 6,560,977.08 |
| DEC-10 | $1,950,427.14 | 6,002,549.64 |
| JAN-11 | $1,780,187.86 | 5,934,275.95 |
| FEB-11 | $2,203,660.95 | 6,112,871.47 |
| MAR-11 | $2,521,505.75 | 7,784,405.00 |
| APR-11 | $2,093,339.12 | 2,093,339.12 |
| MAY-11 | $2,401,178.03 | 7,108,115.85 |
| JUN-11 | $2,185,432.07 | 7,043,087.11 |
| JUL-11 | $3,077,467.18 | 7,061,315.99 |
| AUG-11 | $1,958,783.38 | 4,052,122.50 |
| SEP-11 | $3,625,419.85 | 7,315,093.14 |

**SQL Used in Moving Total** Here is the SQL that Discoverer generated:

```
SUM(Sales.Profit) OVER ( ORDER BY Shipped Date.Shipped Month ASC ROWS BETWEEN
2 PRECEDING AND CURRENT ROW
```

Let's take a closer look at the output. Does it look right to you? Focus on the total for the third month in the list, DEC-10. The calculated answer is 6,002,549.64. This is *not* the total of OCT-10, NOV-10, and DEC-10. It is in fact the total of APR-10, AUG-10, and DEC-10. The reason is that the display is being generated using an alternate sort, whereas the calculation is using the month in alphabetic order. We need to change this.

As you should understand by now, sorting strings can be hit-or-miss. For example, we understand that January comes before February, which in turn comes before March. However, a string sort will place them in this order: February, January, and then March. Similarly, if we look at days of the week, we understand that Tuesday comes before Wednesday, which in turn comes before Friday. In a string sort, the computer will place them in this order: Friday followed by Tuesday followed by Wednesday.

We therefore need to find another way to sort. Dates and numbers are excellent candidates for sorting. If we were to sort the months based on the date of the first of the month, they will sort correctly. Using the fiscal period defined as MON-YY, and therefore JAN-11 and so on, we can use the following to define the first date of the month:

```
TO_DATE(Shipped Date.ShippedMonth,'MON-YY')
```

Using the previous in a new calculation called Start Date, here is our intermediate result:

| Shipped Month | Start Date | Profit | 3 Month Moving Total |
|---|---|---|---|
| OCT-10 | 01-OCT-10 | $2,051,379.99 | 6,090,851.32 |
| NOV-10 | 01-NOV-10 | $1,638,293.30 | 6,560,977.08 |
| DEC-10 | 01-DEC-10 | $1,950,427.14 | 6,002,549.64 |
| JAN-11 | 01-JAN-11 | $1,780,187.86 | 5,934,275.95 |
| FEB-11 | 01-FEB-11 | $2,203,660.95 | 6,112,871.47 |
| MAR-11 | 01-MAR-11 | $2,521,505.75 | 7,784,405.00 |
| APR-11 | 01-APR-11 | $2,093,339.12 | 2,093,339.12 |
| MAY-11 | 01-MAY-11 | $2,401,178.03 | 7,108,115.85 |
| JUN-11 | 01-JUN-11 | $2,185,432.07 | 7,043,087.11 |
| JUL-11 | 01-JUL-11 | $3,077,467.18 | 7,061,315.99 |
| AUG-11 | 01-AUG-11 | $1,958,783.38 | 4,052,122.50 |
| SEP-11 | 01-SEP-11 | $3,625,419.85 | 7,315,093.14 |

Next, we will edit our three-month moving total to use the new calculation within the ORDER BY clause. Here is the SQL:

```
SUM(Sales.Profit) OVER(ORDER BY  Start Date ASC  ROWS BETWEEN 2 PRECEDING AND
CURRENT ROW )
```

Now our output looks like this:

| Shipped Month | Start Date | Profit | 3 Month Moving Total |
|---|---|---|---|
| OCT-10 | 01-OCT-10 | $2,051,379.99 | 2,051,379.99 |
| NOV-10 | 01-NOV-10 | $1,638,293.30 | 3,689,673.29 |
| DEC-10 | 01-DEC-10 | $1,950,427.14 | 5,640,100.43 |
| JAN-11 | 01-JAN-11 | $1,780,187.86 | 5,368,908.30 |
| FEB-11 | 01-FEB-11 | $2,203,660.95 | 5,934,275.95 |
| MAR-11 | 01-MAR-11 | $2,521,505.75 | 6,505,354.56 |
| APR-11 | 01-APR-11 | $2,093,339.12 | 6,818,505.82 |
| MAY-11 | 01-MAY-11 | $2,401,178.03 | 7,016,022.90 |
| JUN-11 | 01-JUN-11 | $2,185,432.07 | 6,679,949.22 |
| JUL-11 | 01-JUL-11 | $3,077,467.18 | 7,664,077.28 |
| AUG-11 | 01-AUG-11 | $1,958,783.38 | 7,221,682.63 |
| SEP-11 | 01-SEP-11 | $3,625,419.85 | 8,661,670.41 |

This is much better. However, we are not quite finished. Now that we can see that we are using the correct three values in our total, we need to do two things. First, we do not need to see the start date on the screen, so we will remove it (we will not delete it). Second, we can change our calculation to use AVG instead of SUM, thus truly computing the three-month moving average.

Here is the final answer:

| Shipped Month | Profit | 3 Month Moving Avg |
|---|---|---|
| OCT-10 | $2,051,379.99 | 2,072,359.56 |
| NOV-10 | $1,638,293.30 | 1,927,670.80 |
| DEC-10 | $1,950,427.14 | 1,978,091.98 |
| JAN-11 | $1,780,187.86 | 2,347,695.70 |
| FEB-11 | $2,203,660.95 | 2,353,772.00 |
| MAR-11 | $2,521,505.75 | 2,186,992.36 |
| APR-11 | $2,093,339.12 | 2,093,339.12 |
| MAY-11 | $2,401,178.03 | 2,030,283.77 |
| JUN-11 | $2,185,432.07 | 2,369,371.95 |
| JUL-11 | $3,077,467.18 | 2,594,801.67 |
| AUG-11 | $1,958,783.38 | 2,037,623.82 |
| SEP-11 | $3,625,419.85 | 2,511,543.46 |

**NOTE**

*Discoverer computes moving averages only for the actual values on the screen. Therefore, even though we wanted a three-month moving average, for the first month, the answer is the same value, while for the second month the answer is the total of January plus February divided by 2. For all other months, we have two previous values to work with, and so the answer is correct.*

## Creating Previous- and Next-Value Reports

Continuing from where we left off in the previous report where we showed you how to create a three-month moving average, we will extend that report to bring in the profit from both of the preceding months. This will allow us at a glance to visually confirm the results and also to see all three months side by side. For ease of use, we have duplicated our worksheet as the following table:

| Shipped Month | Profit | 3 Month Moving Avg |
|---|---|---|
| OCT-10 | $2,051,379.99 | 2,051,379.99 |
| NOV-10 | $1,638,293.30 | 1,844,836.65 |
| DEC-10 | $1,950,427.14 | 1,880,033.48 |
| JAN-11 | $1,780,187.86 | 1,789,636.10 |
| FEB-11 | $2,203,660.95 | 1,978,091.98 |
| MAR-11 | $2,521,505.75 | 2,168,451.52 |
| APR-11 | $2,093,339.12 | 2,272,835.27 |
| MAY-11 | $2,401,178.03 | 2,338,674.30 |
| JUN-11 | $2,185,432.07 | 2,226,649.74 |
| JUL-11 | $3,077,467.18 | 2,554,692.43 |
| AUG-11 | $1,958,783.38 | 2,407,227.54 |
| SEP-11 | $3,625,419.85 | 2,887,223.47 |

Once again we launched the New Calculation dialog box and then clicked Insert Formula From Template. The list of available templates, as was shown in Figure 21-1, is displayed, from

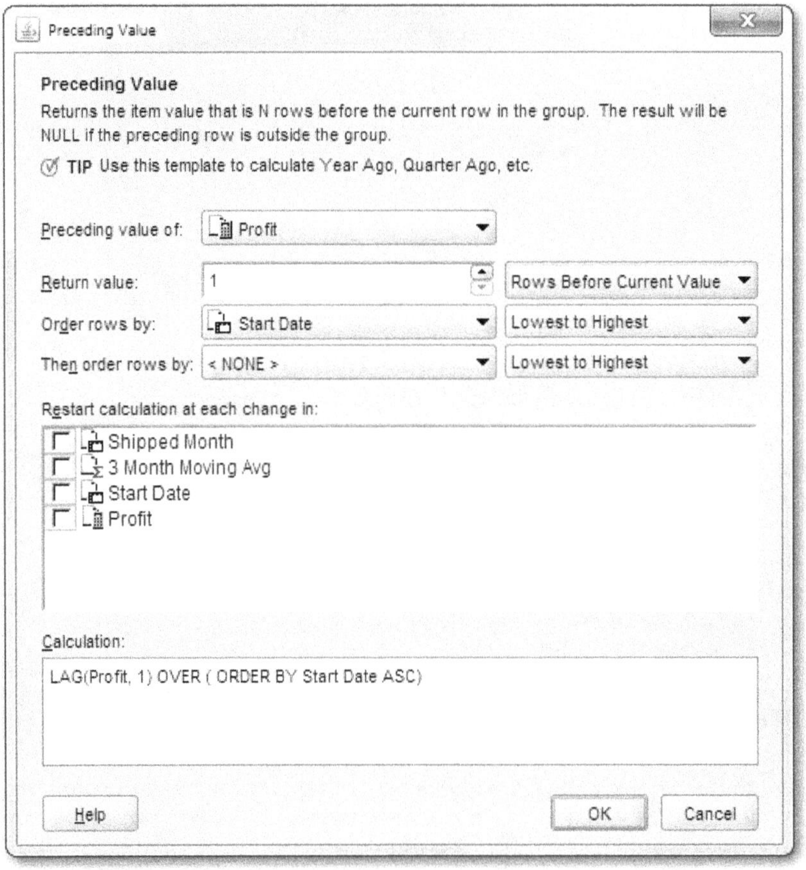

**FIGURE 21-6.** *Preceding Value dialog box*

which we selected Preceding Value. This caused Discoverer to open the Preceding Value dialog box shown in Figure 21-6.

Use this dialog box to create a preceding value calculation. A preceding value calculation returns the value that is a specified number of rows or a specified time period before each value. For example, you might want to know what the previous month's sales are for each value.

A similar template and dialog box exists for calculating following values.

In the Preceding Value dialog box, you will notice the following six areas:

- **Preceding value of** Use this area to choose the item for which you want to return the preceding value. Discoverer will automatically choose the first named data point. In our case, we will use the profit, but we easily could have chosen the three-month moving average.

- **Return value** Use this drop-down to specify the number of rows or the number of time periods over which you want to compare the values. The adjacent drop-down is used to define the type of interval to use. The default is Rows Before Current Value; however, if you click the drop-down, you get the options shown at right.

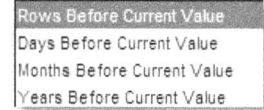

Rows Before Current Value
Days Before Current Value
Months Before Current Value
Years Before Current Value

**NOTE**
*If you have time-based data, use one of the time-based groups Days/Months/Years Before Current Value. If you are not using time-based data, you should choose the row-based group Rows Before Current Row. Using time-based or row-based intervals is also known as windowing.*

- **Order rows by** Use this area to define the initial item you want to order the query by. This will default to the leftmost item in the worksheet. In our case, we want to order not on the shipped month but on the calculation we created for the start date. If we use the shipped month and the current row was AUG-11, the prior value would be APR-11. Using the start date will cause the calculation to use JUL-11 as the prior value, thus calculating correctly. This makes the preceding value synchronized with the display.
- **Then order rows by** Use this area to define a second item for ordering the query. This is rarely used, and most reports you create will have a single sort. You can leave this blank by setting the option to <NONE>.
- **Restart calculation at each change in** Once again, this is the partition area. Discoverer will automatically populate this area using the page items and group sorts you are using. If you are using a crosstab and you have more than one item in the side axis, Discoverer will automatically populate this with the outermost item. If you look back at Figure 21-6, because we have only one item in the side axis, Discoverer has omitted a PARTITION BY clause, showing you that this is optional in a moving total. Omitting a PARTITION BY clause effectively tells Discoverer to treat the whole worksheet as a single group.
- **Calculation** Discoverer uses this area to display the SQL code that will be generated when you click OK. As with other templates, you cannot manually change this code here. To change the code, you need to use the template.

Having completed the template, click OK for Discoverer to create the function. Discoverer places a copy of the SQL code into the New Calculation dialog box. Assuming you have defined the function correctly, all that remains now is for you to give the function a name and click OK.

After completing the function, as always, you should adjust the format to make sure that it is displayed in the same way as the column upon which it is based. Here is the result:

| Prior Month | Shipped Month | Profit | 3 Month Moving Avg |
|---|---|---|---|
| NULL | OCT-10 | $2,051,379.99 | 2,051,379.99 |
| $2,051,379.99 | NOV-10 | $1,638,293.30 | 1,844,836.65 |
| $1,638,293.30 | DEC-10 | $1,950,427.14 | 1,880,033.48 |
| $1,950,427.14 | JAN-11 | $1,780,187.86 | 1,789,636.10 |
| $1,780,187.86 | FEB-11 | $2,203,660.95 | 1,978,091.98 |
| $2,203,660.95 | MAR-11 | $2,521,505.75 | 2,168,451.52 |
| $2,521,505.75 | APR-11 | $2,093,339.12 | 2,272,835.27 |
| $2,093,339.12 | MAY-11 | $2,401,178.03 | 2,338,674.30 |
| $2,401,178.03 | JUN-11 | $2,185,432.07 | 2,226,649.74 |
| $2,185,432.07 | JUL-11 | $3,077,467.18 | 2,554,692.43 |
| $3,077,467.18 | AUG-11 | $1,958,783.38 | 2,407,227.54 |
| $1,958,783.38 | SEP-11 | $3,625,419.85 | 2,887,223.47 |

**SQL Used in Preceding Value** Here is the SQL that Discoverer generated:

```
LAG(Sales.Profit, 1) OVER ( ORDER BY Start Date ASC)
```

We will repeat the previous and add a second Preceding Value calculation to get the profit from two months earlier. Here is the SQL that Discoverer generated:

```
LAG(Sales.Profit, 2) OVER ( ORDER BY Start Date ASC)
```

Let's take a closer look at the final result:

| 2 Months Prior | Prior Month | Shipped Month | Profit | 3 Month Moving Avg |
|---|---|---|---|---|
| NULL | NULL | OCT-10 | $2,051,379.99 | 2,051,379.99 |
| NULL | $2,051,379.99 | NOV-10 | $1,638,293.30 | 1,844,836.65 |
| $2,051,379.99 | $1,638,293.30 | DEC-10 | $1,950,427.14 | 1,880,033.48 |
| $1,638,293.30 | $1,950,427.14 | JAN-11 | $1,780,187.86 | 1,789,636.10 |
| $1,950,427.14 | $1,780,187.86 | FEB-11 | $2,203,660.95 | 1,978,091.98 |
| $1,780,187.86 | $2,203,660.95 | MAR-11 | $2,521,505.75 | 2,168,451.52 |
| $2,203,660.95 | $2,521,505.75 | APR-11 | $2,093,339.12 | 2,272,835.27 |
| $2,521,505.75 | $2,093,339.12 | MAY-11 | $2,401,178.03 | 2,338,674.30 |
| $2,093,339.12 | $2,401,178.03 | JUN-11 | $2,185,432.07 | 2,226,649.74 |
| $2,401,178.03 | $2,185,432.07 | JUL-11 | $3,077,467.18 | 2,554,692.43 |
| $2,185,432.07 | $3,077,467.18 | AUG-11 | $1,958,783.38 | 2,407,227.54 |
| $3,077,467.18 | $1,958,783.38 | SEP-11 | $3,625,419.85 | 2,887,223.47 |

# Editing Analytical Functions

Unfortunately, all of the templates that we have shown you in the previous section are available only at the creation stage. If you want to edit an existing analytic function, you have to do this manually, altering the SQL yourself.

At first, this can seem daunting, especially if you are not very good at SQL or have not had much exposure to it. When we wrote the 10g book, we commented that we hoped that in a future release of Discoverer Oracle would be able to bring back the template for editing purposes, not

Page Items: Prod Line: MEGA-WIDGET

| Product Size | Product Name | Profit | Revenue | Rank | Running Total |
|---|---|---|---|---|---|
| LARGE | CD-625 | $19,945,287.32 | $39,064,837.72 | 1 | $19,945,287.32 |
| | CD-500 | $6,490,671.82 | $12,297,448.18 | 3 | $37,129,768.83 |
| | CD-550 | $5,121,106.13 | $9,522,374.03 | 7 | $59,166,923.08 |
| MEDIUM | CD-100 | $11,440,746.92 | $20,015,291.65 | 3 | $44,053,250.30 |
| | CD-200 | $10,383,271.72 | $18,181,973.60 | 4 | $54,436,522.02 |
| SMALL | AB-2500 | $5,907,659.67 | $11,517,752.95 | 2 | $15,888,764.77 |

**FIGURE 21-7.** *Query modified to include the product line*

just for creation purposes. This did not materialize for 11*g*, so you have no choice but to manually edit the SQL.

We will now show you how to edit both the Rank and Running Total examples. We have added another component to our query by inserting the product line as a page item. This gave us the initial result shown in Figure 21-7.

As you can see in Figure 21-7, the inclusion of an additional page item has upset both of our calculations. This is because both calculations use a partition, and as mentioned previously, the partition consists of both page items and group sorts or side axis items.

## Editing the Rank

If we edit the Rank function and change the SQL as follows, the function will be correct:

```
RANK() OVER(PARTITION BY Product.Prod Line,Product.Size  ORDER BY  Sales.
Profit DESC )
```

The intermediate result is as follows:

Page Items: Prod Line: MEGA-WIDGET

| Product Size | Product Name | Profit | Revenue | Rank | Running Total |
|---|---|---|---|---|---|
| LARGE | CD-625 | $19,945,287.32 | $39,064,837.72 | 1 | $19,945,287.32 |
| | CD-500 | $6,490,671.82 | $12,297,448.18 | 2 | $37,129,768.83 |
| | CD-550 | $5,121,106.13 | $9,522,374.03 | 3 | $59,166,923.08 |
| MEDIUM | CD-100 | $11,440,746.92 | $20,015,291.65 | 1 | $44,053,250.30 |
| | CD-200 | $10,383,271.72 | $18,181,973.60 | 2 | $54,436,522.02 |
| SMALL | AB-2500 | $5,907,659.67 | $11,517,752.95 | 1 | $15,888,764.77 |

## Editing the Running Total

If we next edit the Running Total function and change the SQL using one of the following extracts, this function will also be correct:

```
SUM(Profit SUM) OVER(PARTITION BY Product.Prod Line, Product.Size ORDER BY
Profit SUM DESC ROWS UNBOUNDED PRECEDING)
```

```
SUM(Profit SUM) OVER(PARTITION BY Product.Prod Line, Product.Size ORDER BY
Profit SUM DESC RANGE BETWEEN UNBOUNDED PRECEDING AND CURRENT ROW)
```

The final result is shown here:

Page Items: Prod Line: MEGA-WIDGET

| Product Size | Product Name | Profit | Revenue | Rank | Running Total |
|---|---|---|---|---|---|
| LARGE | CD-625 | $19,945,287.32 | $39,064,837.72 | 1 | $19,945,287.32 |
| | CD-500 | $6,490,671.82 | $12,297,448.18 | 2 | $26,435,959.14 |
| | CD-550 | $5,121,106.13 | $9,522,374.03 | 3 | $31,557,065.27 |
| MEDIUM | CD-100 | $11,440,746.92 | $20,015,291.65 | 1 | $11,440,746.92 |
| | CD-200 | $10,383,271.72 | $18,181,973.60 | 2 | $21,824,018.64 |
| SMALL | AB-2500 | $5,907,659.67 | $11,517,752.95 | 1 | $5,907,659.67 |

# Sequencing of Conditions

Discoverer enables almost unlimited analytic capabilities with its power and flexibility. In this section, we will discuss the sequencing of conditions and let you see just how powerful and flexible Discoverer really is.

We opened up this whole chapter stating that analytic functions are functions that run against the data in a query *after* the query has computed its normal results. In this section, we will show you how you can manipulate the query to force Discoverer to apply an analytic function *prior* to computing the normal results.

To begin, like we did for our analytic examples earlier, we will start with a base query. This time, we will start with a report that returns our top ten products by size.

| | Size | Product | Status | Profit | Revenue | Ranking | Running Total |
|---|---|---|---|---|---|---|---|
| 1 | MINI | MS-1200 | OPEN | $73,888.00 | $256,299.00 | 1 | $73,888.00 |
| 2 | | MS-1300 | OPEN | $36,077.20 | $113,928.00 | 2 | $109,965.20 |
| 3 | | DS-1300 | OPEN | $33,625.40 | $127,211.00 | 3 | $143,590.60 |
| 4 | | DS-1200 | OPEN | $11,820.00 | $42,158.00 | 4 | $155,410.60 |
| 5 | SMALL | AB-3000 | OPEN | $471,810.30 | $957,072.50 | 1 | $471,810.30 |
| 6 | | AB-2500 | OPEN | $420,592.14 | $909,102.90 | 2 | $892,402.44 |
| 7 | | AB-2008 | OPEN | $243,250.21 | $621,419.75 | 3 | $1,135,652.65 |
| 8 | MEDIUM | CD-200 | OPEN | $1,358,854.56 | $2,478,090.60 | 1 | $1,358,854.56 |
| 9 | | CD-100 | OPEN | $1,334,348.00 | $2,409,781.00 | 2 | $2,693,202.56 |
| 10 | | AVR-500 | OPEN | $1,216,449.81 | $2,244,720.48 | 3 | $3,909,652.37 |
| 11 | | QB-5000 | OPEN | $1,200,122.48 | $2,300,261.20 | 4 | $5,109,774.85 |
| 12 | | AVR-550 | OPEN | $977,023.09 | $1,768,858.26 | 5 | $6,086,797.94 |
| 13 | | QB-6000 | OPEN | $934,528.53 | $1,786,738.98 | 6 | $7,021,326.47 |
| 14 | | QB-5500 | OPEN | $588,605.26 | $1,121,236.98 | 7 | $7,609,931.73 |
| 15 | LARGE | CD-625 | OPEN | $913,282.44 | $1,930,311.58 | 1 | $913,282.44 |
| 16 | | AVR-900 | OPEN | $815,716.51 | $1,654,509.75 | 2 | $1,728,998.95 |
| 17 | | QB-2008 | OPEN | $429,647.76 | $819,909.00 | 3 | $2,158,646.71 |
| 18 | | QB-3000 | OPEN | $407,859.64 | $747,025.00 | 4 | $2,566,506.35 |
| 19 | | CD-550 | OPEN | $359,815.88 | $641,731.80 | 5 | $2,926,322.23 |
| 20 | | AVR-800 | OPEN | $331,900.14 | $635,722.50 | 6 | $3,258,222.37 |
| 21 | | CD-500 | OPEN | $182,835.92 | $363,726.40 | 7 | $3,441,058.29 |
| 22 | | QB-1000 | OPEN | $167,913.40 | $337,411.87 | 8 | $3,608,971.69 |

We currently have the following two separate conditions:

- Condition 1, based on an analytic function

  ```
  Ranking <= 10
  ```

- Condition 2, based on a standard item

  ```
  Status = 'OPEN'
  ```

When there are two or more separate conditions, where one of them is based on an analytic function, there is an implied AND clause between the conditions, with the nonanalytic being applied first. It is important that you remember this.

Discoverer achieves this result by creating a subquery. The subquery finds all the data where status = OPEN and then applies an outer query to apply the ranking on this.

If you want to achieve the opposite result, where the analytic conditions are applied first followed by the nonanalytic, you have to create a Boolean condition, like this:

```
Ranking <= 10 AND Status = 'OPEN'
```

We understand that this goes against all standard logic. However, within Oracle the designers of Discoverer knew that there would be times when you would want to apply analytic conditions first. The trick is in creating the Boolean.

Let's look at the results of our query after creating the Boolean:

| | Size | Product | Status | Profit | Revenue | Ranking | Running Total |
|---|---|---|---|---|---|---|---|
| 1 | MINI | MS-1200 | OPEN | $73,888.00 | $256,299.00 | 8 | $3,464,073.60 |
| 2 | | MS-1300 | OPEN | $36,077.20 | $113,928.00 | 9 | $3,500,150.80 |
| 3 | | DS-1300 | OPEN | $33,625.40 | $127,211.00 | 10 | $3,533,776.20 |
| 4 | SMALL | AB-3000 | OPEN | $471,810.30 | $957,072.50 | 7 | $21,005,587.10 |
| 5 | | AB-2500 | OPEN | $420,592.14 | $909,102.90 | 8 | $21,426,179.24 |
| 6 | | AB-2008 | OPEN | $243,250.21 | $621,419.75 | 9 | $21,669,429.45 |
| 7 | MEDIUM | CD-200 | OPEN | $1,358,854.56 | $2,478,090.60 | 9 | $71,022,307.65 |
| 8 | | CD-100 | OPEN | $1,334,348.00 | $2,409,781.00 | 10 | $72,356,655.65 |
| 9 | LARGE | CD-625 | OPEN | $913,282.44 | $1,930,311.58 | 10 | $56,750,831.94 |

What happened this time is that Discoverer was instructed to rank all of our products' sizes with the highest profit-making products ranked first. Then and only after this analytic has been applied, the condition limiting the report to only OPEN orders was applied. What we are now seeing is a report that does the following:

"Of my top ten profit-making products, show me total of the OPEN orders."

Like previously, Discoverer creates a report using a subquery. This time, the analytic condition is being applied within the subquery, with the standard condition being applied on the outer query.

# Windowing Options

In many of the SQL examples we gave you earlier in the chapter, you can see that we have used some windowing code to define exactly the range of rows the function should use.

When working with analytic windows, you can either explicitly or dynamically tell Discoverer which rows should be used within the window.

## Explicit Windows

An *explicit* window uses fixed points to define the start and end rows. As previously mentioned, unless you state otherwise, Discoverer uses the current row as the end point. When using ranges for windows, you can use one of the following three fixed windows:

- **CURRENT ROW** Explicitly use the current row as one of the end points.
- **UNBOUNDED PRECEDING** Explicitly use the first row of the window as one of the end points.
- **UNBOUNDED FOLLOWING** Explicitly use the last row of the window as the end point.

### Explicit Example

Using both UNBOUNDED PRECEDING and UNBOUNDED FOLLOWING at the same time effectively includes the whole window. You can take advantage of this to use the SUM function over the whole range.

Here is our original code for the running total:

```
SUM(Sales.Profit) OVER(PARTITION BY Product.Size ORDER BY Sales.Profit SUM DESC
ROWS BETWEEN UNBOUNDED PRECEDING AND CURRENT ROW)
```

Try altering the Running Total calculation as follows:

```
SUM(Sales.Profit) OVER(PARTITION BY Product.Size ORDER BY Sales.Profit SUM DESC
ROWS BETWEEN UNBOUNDED PRECEDING AND UNBOUNDED FOLLOWING)
```

Without looking at the illustration that follows, can you work out what this does?

The revised calculation that we have given is no longer a running total but a grand total for the whole window. In the following illustration, we have altered and renamed the calculation:

| Product Size | Product Name | Profit | Revenue | Rank | Total Profit |
|---|---|---|---|---|---|
| MEDIUM | AVR-500 | $20,288,355.43 | $35,776,325.41 | 1 | $82,875,421.68 |
| | AVR-550 | $12,324,147.95 | $21,681,080.78 | 2 | $82,875,421.68 |
| | CD-100 | $11,440,746.92 | $20,015,291.65 | 3 | $82,875,421.68 |
| | CD-200 | $10,383,271.72 | $18,181,973.60 | 4 | $82,875,421.68 |
| | QB-6000 | $9,828,919.51 | $18,897,604.46 | 5 | $82,875,421.68 |
| | QB-5000 | $9,570,416.13 | $18,195,109.02 | 6 | $82,875,421.68 |
| | QB-5500 | $9,039,564.02 | $17,172,184.28 | 7 | $82,875,421.68 |
| LARGE | CD-625 | $19,945,287.32 | $39,064,837.72 | 1 | $63,690,522.65 |
| | AVR-900 | $10,693,809.69 | $20,193,326.45 | 2 | $63,690,522.65 |
| | CD-500 | $6,490,671.82 | $12,297,448.18 | 3 | $63,690,522.65 |
| | QB-3000 | $5,853,476.20 | $12,038,325.70 | 4 | $63,690,522.65 |
| | AVR-800 | $5,778,221.91 | $10,899,193.80 | 5 | $63,690,522.65 |
| | QB-2008 | $5,284,350.01 | $10,866,016.00 | 6 | $63,690,522.65 |
| | CD-550 | $5,121,106.13 | $9,522,374.03 | 7 | $63,690,522.65 |
| | QB-1000 | $4,523,599.57 | $9,437,697.71 | 8 | $63,690,522.65 |
| SMALL | AB-3000 | $9,981,105.10 | $19,101,427.80 | 1 | $21,731,253.51 |
| | AB-2500 | $5,907,659.67 | $11,517,752.95 | 2 | $21,731,253.51 |
| | AB-2008 | $5,842,488.74 | $12,685,075.60 | 3 | $21,731,253.51 |
| MINI | MS-1200 | $1,241,306.60 | $4,307,810.10 | 1 | $3,567,300.20 |
| | DS-1300 | $973,487.40 | $3,028,431.00 | 2 | $3,567,300.20 |
| | DS-1200 | $739,513.00 | $2,760,838.40 | 3 | $3,567,300.20 |
| | MS-1300 | $612,993.20 | $1,935,768.00 | 4 | $3,567,300.20 |

Using this calculation, you could now create other calculations that use the grand total. For example, one such calculation could divide the profit by the grand total to give you the percentage.

## Dynamic Windows

A *dynamic* window, as its name implies, uses variable pointers, or offsets, to define the window. You can take advantage of this feature to use the AVG or SUM function over that range, effectively doing a running total over a moving range. For this next example, we will use the following new query:

| | Channel | Shipped Year | Shipped Quarter | Revenue |
|---|---|---|---|---|
| 1 | EXTERNAL | FY2010 | 2010-Q1 | $4,311,979.81 |
| 2 | | | 2010-Q2 | $4,079,771.71 |
| 3 | | | 2010-Q3 | $5,326,220.26 |
| 4 | | | 2010-Q4 | $3,266,822.35 |
| 5 | | FY2011 | 2011-Q1 | $5,163,880.45 |
| 6 | | | 2011-Q2 | $4,557,318.76 |
| 7 | | | 2011-Q3 | $5,783,076.11 |
| 8 | | | 2011-Q4 | $5,123,302.83 |
| 9 | | FY2012 | 2012-Q1 | $5,849,953.20 |
| 10 | | | 2012-Q2 | $5,101,413.12 |
| 11 | | | 2012-Q3 | $6,259,831.52 |
| 12 | | | 2012-Q4 | $5,884,725.96 |
| 13 | INTERNET | FY2010 | 2010-Q1 | $4,236,903.73 |
| 14 | | | 2010-Q2 | $3,101,358.53 |
| 15 | | | 2010-Q3 | $4,421,266.66 |
| 16 | | | 2010-Q4 | $2,997,775.18 |
| 17 | | FY2011 | 2011-Q1 | $5,545,834.34 |
| 18 | | | 2011-Q2 | $7,691,568.05 |
| 19 | | | 2011-Q3 | $7,072,006.39 |
| 20 | | | 2011-Q4 | $11,411,756.82 |
| 21 | | FY2012 | 2012-Q1 | $10,128,045.09 |
| 22 | | | 2012-Q2 | $7,263,241.29 |
| 23 | | | 2012-Q3 | $13,884,504.39 |
| 24 | | | 2012-Q4 | $11,620,360.34 |

By adding the following new calculation, we can generate a moving average.

```
AVG(Selling Price SUM) OVER(PARTITION BY Channel.Channel ORDER BY Shipped
Date."Quarter End Date" ROWS 2 PRECEDING)
```

It is worth mentioning that we did not include the year or the quarter in PARTITION BY. We partitioned only by the channel so that the moving average would cross all quarters and years. As you can see in this illustration, we have generated a true three-month moving average:

| | Channel | Shipped Year | Shipped Quarter | Revenue | Moving Avg |
|---|---|---|---|---|---|
| 1 | EXTERNAL | FY2010 | 2010-Q1 | $4,311,979.81 | $4,311,979.81 |
| 2 | | | 2010-Q2 | $4,079,771.71 | $4,195,875.76 |
| 3 | | | 2010-Q3 | $5,326,220.26 | $4,572,657.26 |
| 4 | | | 2010-Q4 | $3,266,822.35 | $4,224,271.44 |
| 5 | | FY2011 | 2011-Q1 | $5,163,880.45 | $4,585,641.02 |
| 6 | | | 2011-Q2 | $4,557,318.76 | $4,329,340.52 |
| 7 | | | 2011-Q3 | $5,783,076.11 | $5,168,091.77 |
| 8 | | | 2011-Q4 | $5,123,302.83 | $5,154,565.90 |
| 9 | | FY2012 | 2012-Q1 | $5,849,953.20 | $5,585,444.05 |
| 10 | | | 2012-Q2 | $5,101,413.12 | $5,358,223.05 |
| 11 | | | 2012-Q3 | $6,259,831.52 | $5,737,065.95 |
| 12 | | | 2012-Q4 | $5,884,725.96 | $5,748,656.87 |
| 13 | INTERNET | FY2010 | 2010-Q1 | $4,236,903.73 | $4,236,903.73 |
| 14 | | | 2010-Q2 | $3,101,358.53 | $3,669,131.13 |
| 15 | | | 2010-Q3 | $4,421,266.66 | $3,919,842.97 |
| 16 | | | 2010-Q4 | $2,997,775.18 | $3,506,800.12 |
| 17 | | FY2011 | 2011-Q1 | $5,545,834.34 | $4,321,625.39 |
| 18 | | | 2011-Q2 | $7,691,568.05 | $5,411,725.86 |
| 19 | | | 2011-Q3 | $7,072,006.39 | $6,769,802.93 |
| 20 | | | 2011-Q4 | $11,411,756.82 | $8,725,110.42 |
| 21 | | FY2012 | 2012-Q1 | $10,128,045.09 | $9,537,269.43 |
| 22 | | | 2012-Q2 | $7,263,241.29 | $9,601,014.40 |
| 23 | | | 2012-Q3 | $13,884,504.39 | $10,425,263.59 |
| 24 | | | 2012-Q4 | $11,620,360.34 | $10,922,702.01 |

To change the moving average, you simply alter the value for the number of rows in the PRECEDING command; for example, with the query reporting by quarter, if you change the number of rows to be 3 PRECEDING, you are effectively creating a yearly moving average.

An interesting possibility arises when moving analytic functions to the page items. If you move the moving-average calculation out from the body of the table and into page items, you get a list of all the moving-average amounts in low-to-high order. Using the list of values that Discoverer automatically creates on a page item allows you to take in the highest or lowest moving average at a glance.

# The Power of Analytics

As we hope you have learned from the preceding discussions, the use of analytic functions opens up another dimension in Discoverer reporting. As a bit of fun and as an example of the power of analytics, we will give you one final example.

Take a look at the following example:

Products that generate at least 15% of revenue per product line

Page Items: Year: FY2013 Region: NORTH AMERICA

| | Prod Line | Total Sales per Line | Product | Revenue |
|---|---|---|---|---|
| 1 | MINI-WIDGET | $1,119,708.65 | MS-1200 | $344,993.55 |
| 2 | | | DS-1200 | $317,151.00 |
| 3 | | | DS-1300 | $290,824.10 |
| 4 | SUPER-WIDGET | $9,984,957.50 | AVR-500 | $3,087,338.10 |
| 5 | | | AVR-550 | $2,241,162.00 |
| 6 | | | AVR-900 | $1,963,996.65 |
| 7 | | | AB-3000 | $1,653,653.75 |
| 8 | MEGA-WIDGET | $8,448,853.95 | CD-625 | $2,818,967.10 |
| 9 | | | CD-100 | $1,692,460.25 |
| 10 | WONDER-WIDGET | $8,009,220.28 | QB-5500 | $1,468,746.88 |
| 11 | | | QB-1000 | $1,292,329.50 |
| 12 | | | AB-2008 | $1,289,533.50 |
| 13 | | | QB-6000 | $1,202,822.60 |

What this does is show only those products that have generated more than 15 percent of the total revenue for the product line. It uses one calculation and one condition.

The calculation shows the total revenue for a line using this analytic function:

```
SUM(Selling Price SUM) OVER(PARTITION BY Shipped Date."Shipped
Year","Customer/Geography".Region,Product.ProdLine  ORDER BY  Selling Price
SUM DESC  ROWS BETWEEN UNBOUNDED PRECEDING AND UNBOUNDED FOLLOWING )
```

This generates the same grand total for all rows. However, in order to show the result only once, we added a GROUP SORT to this item.

Next we created a new condition such that we include only those products that have generated revenue greater than 15 percent of the analytic calculation, and that's it. Discoverer handled the rest!

Even though we are displaying only those products that have revenue exceeding 15 percent, the grand total of sales for each line is being calculated on *all* the products.

This section on analytic functions is not intended to be a manual that teaches you how to use analytics but to give you a flavor of the power of them. Please use Appendix B as a reference to the analytics, using it as a cross-reference for the syntax of all the analytic functions.

# Summary

In this chapter, we introduced you to Oracle's analytic functions. We discussed the essential concepts and showed you how to use a template to help you create these powerful functions. After we showed you some practical examples of using analytic functions, we explained how you can use Boolean logic to sequence conditions in such a way as to force Discoverer to apply a condition based on an analytic function first. After this, we discussed the two types of windowing options: explicit and dynamic. Finally, we talked a little about the power of analytics.

# PART V

# Appendixes

# APPENDIX A

# Michael's Gold Mine of Answers to FAQs

In this appendix I have included more than 75 tips and tricks that I have picked up over the past 18 years of working with Oracle. This is not an exhaustive list by any means, and I have tried to include tricks on all aspects of Discoverer. These tricks are not in any particular order and should make for interesting bedtime reading. Quite a number of these tricks involve SQL code that will be available for download from the Oracle Press and Armstrong-Smith Consulting web sites.

**QUESTION:** *I have access to two EULs, an 11*g *and a 9.0.2. Recently I set my default EUL to the wrong one. After this, every time I try to launch Desktop I get a message saying "You must upgrade your EUL tables to use this software release. Please contact your Discoverer manager." I am the Discoverer manager—please help.*

**ANSWER:** When you are in Desktop and are presented with a list of EULs that you can connect to, make sure you pick one of the EULs that will work with 11*g*. A EUL created with 10*g* will work in 11*g*. If you pick an older EUL, you will not be warned, but you will also no longer be able to connect to Discoverer without editing your registry.

If you do this, you will be told that you need to reconnect in order to use this new EUL. However, when you do so, you will get a message saying "You must upgrade your EUL tables to use this software release. Please contact your Discoverer manager." You can no longer connect to Discoverer Desktop, and to add insult to injury, you will probably get a memory issue warning when you try to exit from Desktop.

The only way to fix this is to edit this registry setting on your machine:

```
[HKEY_CURRENT_USER]/Software/Oracle/Discoverer 11/Database/UEUL_username_database
```

Here, *username* is your name, and *database* is the database that you connect to. You need to change this setting to the correct one.

**QUESTION:** *Our DBA says that we cannot use scheduling because he is afraid that we won't have enough disk space. Can you help with our case?*

**ANSWER:** This question first came up several years ago, and I am surprised that even in 2013 the issue has not gone away. When I first commented on this in 2006, I found that a really fast (15,000 RPM) 150GB SCSI drive would set you back about $1,200 retail. Today you can get a 300GB SCSI drive for about $300, or put another way, you can purchase 1GB for around $1. On average, a scheduled workbook will consume around 2MB of disk space, but for argument's sake let's say they take 5MB of disk space. Some are larger, but if well built, most will be smaller. As a worst-case scenario, if you enable 500 users and allow them to create three 5MB scheduled workbooks per day with a 30-day retention period, you will consume 450GB. Let me be more reasonable. Let's assume you have 10 libraries and that you allow each library to have 20 scheduled reports daily that will be retained for 28 days. The amount of required disk space is about 28GB (10 libraries * 5MB * 20 workbooks * 28 days).

The reason for scheduling in the first place is to avoid making users waste time by waiting for long-running workbooks (in excess of 10 minutes) to run online. By allowing the same workbooks to be scheduled, you will save 200 minutes per library per day. But of course, library documents will be used by multiple users every day. If we conservatively say that each of the 20 library workbooks will be used by 5 users per day, then the amount of time wasted by these 10 users would be 1,000 minutes a day, equivalent to 83.33 hours per week per library, or about the cost of one full-time employee per year. If you have ten libraries, this equates to lost productivity of ten full-time employees. In effect, not enabling scheduling will cost you one person per library per year in lost productivity. Bear in mind that over time, the cost of disk space will go down while the cost of employees will go up. In 2006 the cost per SCSI GB was $8, whereas in 2013 this has fallen to just $1.

If I compare employee cost to the cost of disk space, about $1 per GB (and remember that we need only 28GB for those same reports), you can see why I suggest that disk space should *never* be an issue. Somehow this equation needs to be brought to the attention of senior management so that the issue over disk space is eliminated from all future discussions. The same disk space issue will prevent you from harnessing all of Discoverer's power by not enabling materialized view management. One of the biggest incentives to using ad hoc tools is performance gain. Users should never complain that the tool is too slow. If this happens, you are taking the risk that Discoverer will not be embraced by the user community.

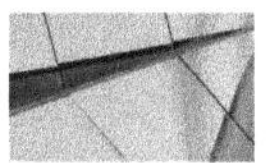

**NOTE**
*In the previous answer, the price of $1,200 was the price in January 2006. The price of $300 was the price in May 2013.*

**QUESTION:** *We recently installed Discoverer Desktop on a machine with Windows 7. The user is using Internet Explorer and Discoverer Plus and can export to Excel fine because Discoverer writes the file. However, on her older operating system, usually after Discoverer exports, it launches Excel for her to see the output. Discoverer is not doing this. I have checked her file associations, and they are correct. Do you know what we are doing wrong?*

**ANSWER:** Microsoft, as always, does not quite tell you everything it has changed. The big one this time is that there is a registry switch that by default prevents Internet Explorer from transferring applications between zones. To Microsoft, running something from a web server (Discoverer) and then running something on your PC (Excel) means running applications in two different zones. With that switch set, your PC cannot switch zones when running Internet Explorer and so cannot open Excel from within Discoverer Plus or Viewer.

To allow Discoverer Plus to call a local copy of Excel, you need to set the switch so that it allows zone switching, like the old XP. The switch should be set to 0. To reset this switch, use the following workflow:

1. From the Windows Start button, select Run to open the Run dialog box.
2. Type **regedit** and click OK.

3. Navigate to this folder:

```
[HKEY_LOCAL_MACHINE]/SOFTWARE/Microsoft/Internet Explorer/MAIN/
FeatureControl/FEATURE_ZONE_ELEVATION.
```

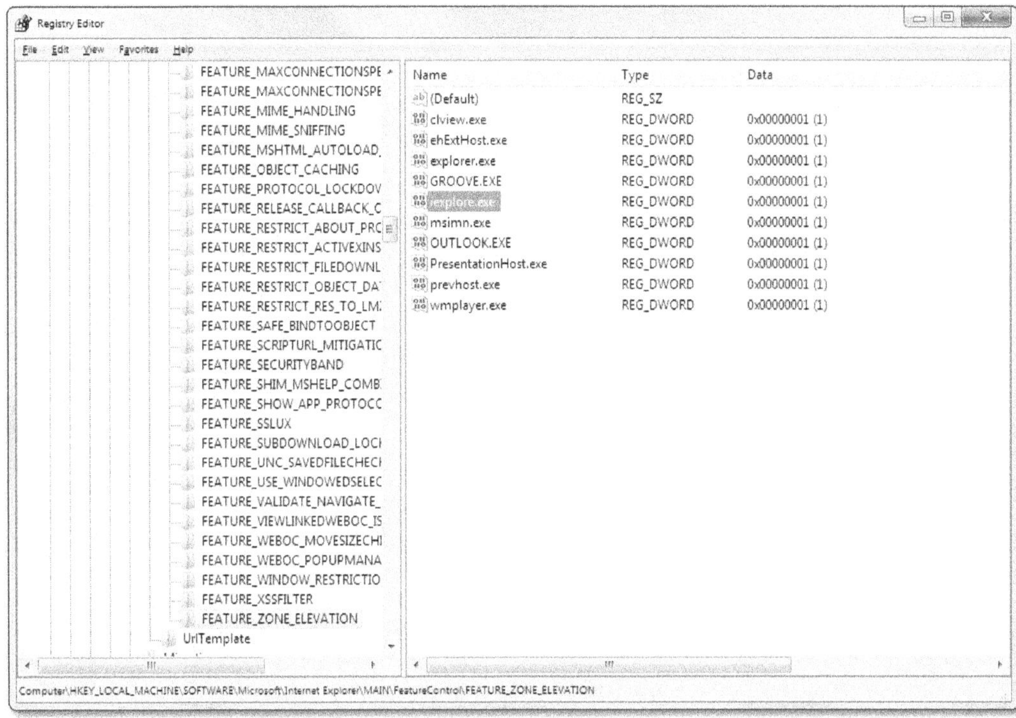


4. Click the item called iexplore. It is probably set to 1 but should be set to 0.
5. Right-click iexplore and from the pop-up select Modify.
6. In the Edit DWORD Value dialog box, change the value from 1 to 0.

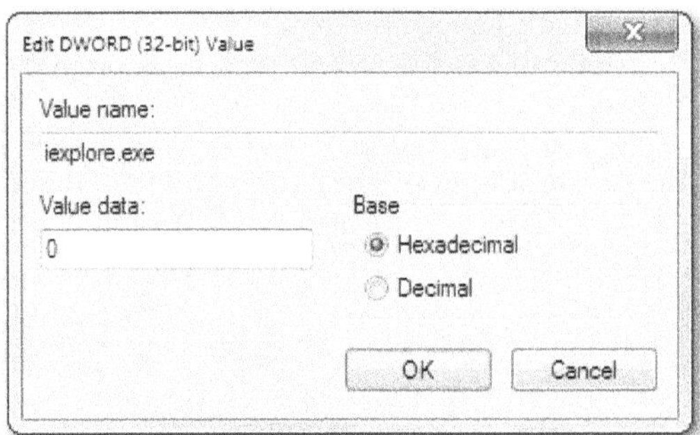


7. Click OK to close the Edit DWORD Value dialog box.
8. Close the registry Editor.

9. In XP, also do the following:
   A. Open Windows Explorer.
   B. From the toolbar, select Tools | Folder Options.

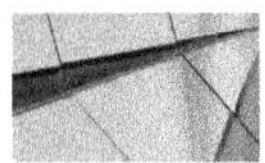

**NOTE**
*If you cannot see the menu bar, click the Organize button. From the drop-down, expand Layout and click Menu Bar. It will now be visible.*

   C. Click the File Types tab.
   D. Select the Extension XLS (or HTML) and then click Advanced.
   E. At the bottom of the screen, shown here, are three settings that use check boxes. If either of the following two are checked, uncheck them:
      - Confirm Open After Download
      - Browse In Same Window
   F. Select OK.
   G. Click Apply.
   H. Reboot the PC.

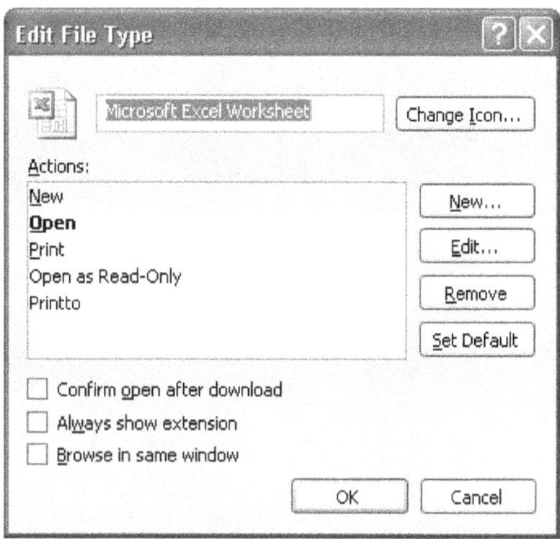

**NOTE**
*A change in Sun Java in 1.6.0_23 and newer does not allow the automatic opening of exported files. If this is the case, you should log in to Oracle Support and look at document 1319218.1.*

**QUESTION:** *I am using page items in my report, but I don't want all page items to display in my title. Is there a way for me to display just one page item in the title?*

**ANSWER:** Yes, a little known feature of Discoverer is the ability to display single page items and parameters in the title, header, or footer. You need to know the exact name of the page item or parameter that you want to display and then type an ampersand (&) followed by the name.

For example, let's say you have a page item called Cust Name. You type **&Cust Name** in the title. Discoverer will display just that page item. When you use this construct, the title will dynamically change to reflect what is being displayed onscreen. As your users switch from one page item to another, they will see the title change.

Similarly, if you have a parameter called From that is being used to store the start date, you can use &From in your title, header, or footer.

**QUESTION:** *We have many business areas in our EUL, and for one of them, when I try to open the lists of values, I get the following message: "The folder for this item class is inaccessible or invalid." The DBA checked in the database and did not find any invalid objects. Do you have any idea what I should look for?*

**ANSWER:** This usually means the object upon which the item class is based has somehow become inaccessible to the user. You may want to check that your user has been granted SELECT on the necessary underlying database objects. Another possible cause is that the item class is using a COUNT function. An item class needs to be able to return the same set of values every time; in other words, the item code that produces the list of values must be deterministic. Functions can be used to generate lists of values but only if they are deterministic. In this case, COUNT returns different values and so is considered to be nondeterministic. When you stop to think about it, it makes sense. To establish a stable list of values, each value in the calculated column must contain a known and consistent value. If the values might differ every time the row is examined, then the list will be invalid.

Another possible cause of this issue arises when you are accessing the data via a database link and one of the following situations occurs:

- The database link has become invalid; perhaps the password has changed.
- The object on the other end of the link has been deleted or renamed.
- The user account being used for the database link no longer has the appropriate select privileges.

**QUESTION:** *We are using E-Business Suite with Discoverer and have written our own views for our reports. Several of these make recursive joins to the GL_PERIODS table, and our performance is poor. One of our reports takes more than seven hours. Can you help?*

**ANSWER:** GL_PERIODS, as you know, is the E-Business Suite table that contains your organization's calendar. However, because you can have recursive joins between the elements of this table, report performance can be seriously impacted.

You should create a materialized view of your GL_PERIODS date hierarchy. After you have created the materialized view, you should place a unique index on the calendar date, with nonunique indexes on the months, quarters, and years. After you do this, inside your view you can now join your transaction date to the date in the materialized view and read off the hierarchy.

Most DBAs are rightly concerned about adding materialized views to E-Business Suite. In this case, because GL_PERIODS is updated only once a year, you have a perfect candidate for a materialized view. You just need to make sure you refresh the materialized view after you add the dates for the next year.

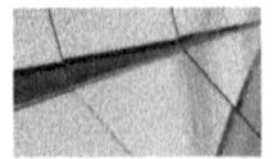

**NOTE**

*During a follow-up conversation with this client, they reported that the seven-hour report is now being produced in five minutes. They were busy similarly converting all of their long-running reports.*

The following is a sample script from an older E-Business Suite version that you can use as the beginning of a materialized view. This script builds a view of GL PERIODS using recursive joins to get the Month, Quarter, and Year information. It pulls the calendar data, starting from October 1, 1998, and runs against a fictitious calendar called GSW CALENDAR. To make this work in your organization, you will need to change the name of the calendar and the start date. You may also need to add data for the calendar dates.

```
CREATE OR REPLACE VIEW V_FISCAL_TIME
AS SELECT DISTINCT
GL_MTH.PERIOD_NAME          MTH,
GL_MTH.PERIOD_SET_NAME      SET_NAME,
```

```
GL_MTH.START_DATE          MTH_START_DATE,
GL_MTH.END_DATE            MTH_END_DATE,
GL_MTH.PERIOD_NUM          MTH_NUMBER,
GL_MTH.LAST_UPDATE_DATE    MTH_LAST_UPDATE_DATE,
(GL_MTH.END_DATE -
   GL_MTH.START_DATE) +1   MTH_TIMESPAN,
GL_QTR.PERIOD_NAME         QUARTER,
GL_QTR.START_DATE          QTR_START_DATE,
GL_QTR.END_DATE            QTR_END_DATE,
GL_QTR.QUARTER_NUM         QTR_NUMBER,
GL_QTR.LAST_UPDATE_DATE    QTR_LAST_UPDATE_DATE,
(GL_QTR.END_DATE - GL_QTR.START_DATE) + 1    QTR_TIMESPAN,
GL_YR.PERIOD_NAME          YR,
GL_YR.START_DATE           YR_START_DATE,
GL_YR.END_DATE             YR_END_DATE,
(GL_YR.END_DATE - GL_YR.START_DATE) + 1    YR_TIMESPAN,
GL_YR.LAST_UPDATE_DATE     YR_LAST_UPDATE_DATE,
GL_YR.PERIOD_YEAR          PERIOD_YEAR,
GL_QTR.ENTERED_PERIOD_NAME ACTUAL_QTR
FROM
APPS.GL_PERIODS GL_MTH,
APPS.GL_PERIODS GL_QTR,
APPS.GL_PERIODS GL_YR
WHERE
GL_MTH.PERIOD_SET_NAME = 'GSW CALENDAR'
AND GL_MTH.PERIOD_TYPE = 'Month'
AND GL_MTH.START_DATE >= '01-JAN-2010'
AND GL_QTR.QUARTER_NUM = GL_MTH.QUARTER_NUM
AND GL_QTR.PERIOD_YEAR = GL_MTH.PERIOD_YEAR
AND GL_QTR.PERIOD_TYPE = 'Quarter'
AND GL_YR.PERIOD_YEAR  = GL_MTH.PERIOD_YEAR
AND GL_YR.PERIOD_TYPE  = 'Year';
```

If you are using bill of materials (BOM), you might want to consider using another table. This is the BOM_CALENDAR_DATES table. Here is a simple script:

```
CREATE OR REPLACE VIEW V_DISCO_DAYS
AS SELECT ALL
TRUNC(BCD.CALENDAR_DATE)                    CALENDAR_DATE,
TRUNC(F_DIS_WEEK(TRUNC(BCD.CALENDAR_DATE))) WEEK_END_DATE,
SUBSTR(F_DIS_MONTH(TRUNC(BCD.CALENDAR_DATE)),1,15) MTH,
BCD.LAST_UPDATE_DATE  LAST_UPDATE_DATE
FROM
APPS.BOM_CALENDAR_DATES BCD
WHERE 1=1
AND BCD.CALENDAR_CODE = 'ABC'
AND BCD.EXCEPTION_SET_ID = -1
AND BCD.CALENDAR_DATE >= '01-APR-2011'
AND BCD.CALENDAR_DATE <= '31-MAR-2012';
```

The preceding script uses a number of constructs, which need explaining.

- **F_DIS_WEEK** This function returns the week end date for the date given. You need to create this function yourself to match your organization's requirements. If the week end date can be calculated using a combination of the TO_DATE and TO_CHAR functions, you should change the code accordingly. Some organizations end their week on a Friday, some on a Saturday, and some on a Sunday; hence, it is impossible to give you a definitive answer.
- **F_DIS_MONTH** This function returns the month name for the date given. Once again, you need to create this function yourself to meet your organization's requirements. Some organizations use constructs such as MON-YY; others use MON-YYYY, and so on. If the month can be calculated using the TO_CHAR function, you should change the code accordingly. You need to make sure the month you assign here corresponds to the month you will find in GL_PERIODS. If you do this, you will be able to combine these two scripts into one materialized view.
- **CALENDAR_CODE** Oracle E-Business Suite has the capability to use multiple calendars, especially if you are using multiple organizations. To avoid pulling multiple copies of the same calendar date, you need to choose one calendar as the base calendar for use within the reporting system.
- **DATE RANGE** This is optional but is demonstrated here for an organization whose fiscal year runs from April through March.

**QUESTION:** *Do you know of a way to generate my own table of dates that I can use inside Discoverer?*

**ANSWER:** Let me share with you some code that I have used several times at different client sites. Bear with me because the following is quite lengthy. However, if you can see it through, you will have a great date creation utility.

The utility uses two tables (a table of required dates and a master table of production dates) and a procedure to populate the data.

The two tables are

- **REQUIRED_DATES_TBL** This contains one row per required date.
- **PRODUCTION_DATES_TBL** This contains all of the additional information you might want to know about a given date, such as the month, quarter, year, and so on.

Here's the script for the REQUIRED_DATES table:

```
CREATE TABLE REQUIRED_DATES_TBL(
REQUIRED_DATE  DATE)
NOLOGGING
NOCOMPRESS
NOCACHE
NOPARALLEL
NOMONITORING;
```

Here's the script for the PRODUCTION_DATES table:

```
CREATE TABLE PRODUCTION_DATES_TBL (
CAL_DATE          DATE,
CAL_MTH           VARCHAR2(8 BYTE),
CAL_QTR           VARCHAR2(7 BYTE),
CAL_YEAR          NUMBER,
MTH_START_DATE    DATE,
MTH_END_DATE      DATE,
MTH_NUMBER        NUMBER,
QTR_START_DATE    DATE,
QTR_END_DATE      DATE,
QTR_NUMBER        NUMBER,
YEAR_START_DATE   DATE,
YEAR_END_DATE     DATE)
NOLOGGING
NOCOMPRESS
NOCACHE
NOPARALLEL
NOMONITORING;
```

Next you need to create the procedure that inserts a set of dates into the REQUIRED_DATES_TBL table and then create code that uses those dates to generate the PRODUCTION_DATES_TBL table.

Here is the code for the procedure:

```
CREATE OR REPLACE PROCEDURE XX_DATE_LOADER
(V_START_DATE IN DATE, V_END_DATE IN DATE) IS
V_DATE DATE :=TO_DATE('01-JAN-2012');
BEGIN  -- loop through and update
V_DATE := V_START_DATE;
EXECUTE IMMEDIATE 'TRUNCATE TABLE REQUIRED_DATES_TBL REUSE STORAGE';
WHILE V_DATE <= V_END_DATE LOOP
INSERT INTO REQUIRED_DATES_TBL VALUES (V_DATE);
V_DATE := V_DATE + 1;
END LOOP;


INSERT INTO PRODUCTION_DATES_TBL
SELECT DISTINCT
TRUNC(REQ.REQUIRED_DATE)                              CAL_DATE,
TO_CHAR(REQ.REQUIRED_DATE, 'MON-YYYY')                CAL_MTH,
TO_CHAR(REQ.REQUIRED_DATE,'YYYY') || '-' ||
   'Q' || TO_CHAR(REQ.REQUIRED_DATE, 'Q')             CAL_QTR,
TO_NUMBER(TO_CHAR(REQ.REQUIRED_DATE,'YYYY'))          CAL_YEAR,
TRUNC(REQ.REQUIRED_DATE,'MM')                         MTH_START_DATE,
ADD_MONTHS(TRUNC(REQ.REQUIRED_DATE,'MM'),1)-1         MTH_END_DATE,
TO_NUMBER(TO_CHAR(REQ.REQUIRED_DATE,'MM'))            MTH_NUMBER,
TRUNC(REQ.REQUIRED_DATE,'Q')                          QTR_START_DATE,
ADD_MONTHS(TRUNC(REQ.REQUIRED_DATE,'Q'),3)-1          QTR_END_DATE,
TO_NUMBER(TO_CHAR(REQ.REQUIRED_DATE,'Q'))             QTR_NUMBER,
TRUNC(REQ.REQUIRED_DATE,'Y')                          YEAR_START_DATE,
```

```
ADD_MONTHS(TRUNC(REQ.REQUIRED_DATE,'Y'),12)-1     YEAR_END_DATE
FROM
REQUIRED_DATES_TBL REQ;
COMMIT;
END;
```

All that remains to be done now is run the procedure with a set of required dates.

```
EXEC XX_DATE_LOADER('01-JAN-2012','31-DEC-2012');
```

**QUESTION:** *I seem to remember you mentioning that I could use a custom folder for generating lists of values. We are using E-Business Suite, and I need to get a listing of the customer master from the system. Do you have the code that I could use?*

**ANSWER:** Here is the script you asked for:

```
SELECT
CUST.PARTY_ID,
CUST_ACCT.ACCOUNT_NUMBER              CUSTOMER_NBR,
CUST.PARTY_NAME                       CUSTOMER_NAME,
CUST.STATUS                           PARTY_STATUS,
CUST_ACCT.STATUS                      ACCOUNT_STATUS,
CUST.ADDRESS1,
CUST.ADDRESS2,
CUST.ADDRESS3,
CUST.ADDRESS4,
DECODE (CUST.CITY, NULL, NULL, CUST.CITY || ', ')
  || DECODE (CUST.STATE,
  NULL, CUST.PROVINCE || ', ',
  CUST.STATE || ', ')
  || DECODE (CUST.POSTAL_CODE, NULL, NULL, CUST.POSTAL_CODE || ', ')
  || DECODE (CUST.COUNTRY, NULL, NULL, CUST.COUNTRY) ADDRESS5,
CUST.CITY,
CUST.POSTAL_CODE,
CUST.STATE,
CNTRY.DESCRIPTION                     COUNTRY,
CUST.CREATION_DATE,
CUST.LAST_UPDATE_DATE,
TRUNC(SYSDATE)                        DATE_LOADED
FROM
AR.HZ_PARTIES                CUST,
APPLSYS.FND_LOOKUP_VALUES CNTRY,
AR.HZ_CUST_ACCOUNTS          CUST_ACCT
WHERE 1=1
AND CUST_ACCT.CUST_ACCOUNT_ID + 0   = CUST_ACCT.CUST_ACCOUNT_ID
AND CNTRY.LOOKUP_TYPE(+)  = 'SG_COUNTRY_CODE'
AND CNTRY.LOOKUP_CODE(+)  = CUST.COUNTRY
AND CUST_ACCT.PARTY_ID = CUST.PARTY_ID;
```

If you use this script in a custom folder, you will be able to create a list of values on the customer name. As a bonus, I have also included the code that generates the party ID, customer number, customer address, party status, and customer account status. You can then create lists of values on the customer number, status, and type using the same custom folder.

**QUESTION:** *We are using lots of tablespaces. Our DBA says that it is a pain to keep checking the tablespace on the system. Do you have a script that will help us look at just the tablespaces that we need to look at?*

**ANSWER:** I've seen a lot of scripts that tell you about all the tablespaces in a database, but very few show only the ones that are going to give you problems. A colleague of mine has been using the following script for a few years now, and it has really saved him from dialing in at nights and on the weekends. He uses it as a cursor for a procedure and has it build an e-mail and/or page notification that is sent to him and others.

This script is useful because it drills down to what is going to give you a problem. My colleague does not have a lot of time to wade through pages of a report to find out which tablespace is running out of space. The following script is short and sweet and allows him to get on with his day. This script has been tested on 8, 8*i*, 9*i*, 10*g*, and 11*g* databases, but there is one proviso: you need to make sure you are using SYS, SYSTEM, or another user who has access to read the data dictionary.

```
SELECT
TSP.TABLESPACE_NAME T_NAME,
TSP.TOTAL_SPACE  TOT_SPACE,
FREE.TOTAL_FREE,
ROUND(FREE.TOTAL_FREE /TSP.TOTAL_SPACE*100)  PCT_FREE,
ROUND((TSP.TOTAL_SPACE - FREE.TOTAL_FREE),2) TOT_USED,
ROUND((TSP.TOTAL_SPACE - FREE.TOTAL_FREE)/TSP.TOTAL_SPACE*100) PCT_USED,
NEXTEXT.MAX_NEXT_EXTENT
FROM
(SELECT
TABLESPACE_NAME,
SUM(BYTES)/1024/1024 TOTAL_SPACE
FROM DBA_DATA_FILES
GROUP BY TABLESPACE_NAME) TSP,
(SELECT
TABLESPACE_NAME,
ROUND(SUM(BYTES)/1024/1024,2) TOTAL_FREE,
ROUND(MAX(BYTES)/1024/1024,2) MAX_FREE
FROM DBA_FREE_SPACE
GROUP BY TABLESPACE_NAME) FREE,
(SELECT
TABLESPACE_NAME,
ROUND(MAX(NEXT_EXTENT)/1024/1024,2) MAX_NEXT_EXTENT
FROM DBA_SEGMENTS
GROUP BY TABLESPACE_NAME) NEXTEXT
WHERE 1=1
AND TSP.TABLESPACE_NAME = FREE.TABLESPACE_NAME (+)
AND TSP.TABLESPACE_NAME = NEXTEXT.TABLESPACE_NAME (+)
AND ((ROUND(FREE.TOTAL_FREE/TSP.TOTAL_SPACE*100)) < 10
OR NEXTEXT.MAX_NEXT_EXTENT > FREE.MAX_FREE);
```

The following illustration shows a screenshot from SQL*Plus.

| T_NAME | TOT_SPACE | TOTAL_FREE | PCT_FREE | TOT_USED | PCT_USED | MAX_NEXT_EXTENT |
|---|---|---|---|---|---|---|
| SYSAUX | 660 | 35.94 | 5 | 624.06 | 95 | 1 |
| USERS | 33.75 | 1.63 | 5 | 32.12 | 95 | 1 |
| SYSTEM | 710 | 6.88 | 1 | 703.12 | 99 | 1 |

**QUESTION:** *The following error messages are displayed whenever we try to submit a scheduled workbook:*

**Database Error - ORA-04068: existing state of packages has been discarded ORA-04063: package body "<SCHEMA>.EUL5_BATCH_USER" has errors ORA-06508: PL/SQL: could not find program unit being called ORA-06512: at line 2.**

*Do you have any ideas?*

**ANSWER:** It sounds like the EUL5_BATCH_USER package body is invalid because the V_ $PARAMETER cannot be accessed.

To fix this situation, use the following workflow:

1. Using SQL Plus, connect to the database where the EUL is located and log in as the SYS or SYSTEM user.
2. Execute the following script:

```
GRANT SELECT ON SYS.V_$PARAMETER TO <eul_owner>;
```

**NOTE**
*You need to replace <eul_owner> with the name of the user who owns the EUL in your environment.*

3. You now need to recompile the EUL5_BATCH_USER package by logging in to SQL Plus as the EUL owner and execute the following:

```
ALTER PACKAGE EUL5_BATCH_USER COMPILE PACKAGE;
```

4. Finally, you need to confirm that there are no issues by executing this SQL:

```
SELECT OBJECT_NAME, OBJECT_TYPE, STATUS FROM
USER_OBJECTS
WHERE STATUS LIKE 'INVALID';
```

**QUESTION:** *We have disabled the Save option in Oracle Enterprise Manager, yet Discoverer Viewer is still prompting the user to save the changes. It gives these messages:*

**Do you want to save your changes before closing this worksheet?**
**You have not saved the changes you made to this worksheet. This worksheet must be closed to continue. Click *Yes* to save changes and continue, *No* to continue without saving changes, or *Cancel* to return to this worksheet. If you choose *Yes* and you do not own the workbook, you will be prompted to save it under a new name.**

*Can you help?*

**ANSWER:** Customization to remove the Save link will only remove the Save and Save As links from the Viewer layout, but this does not stop the user from having the privilege to save. I am guessing you probably created a public EUL. Creating a public EUL grants the Save workbooks to Database privilege to the public role, which in turn is granted to all users.

Your users will therefore be getting this warning message to save the workbook whenever some changes have been made to the formatting or the layout.

To disable this warning, use the following workflow:

1. Connect to the Discoverer Administrator.
2. Navigate to Tools | Privileges.
3. Click Select, provide the username that you want to administer, and click Go.
4. In the Desktop and Privileges section, uncheck the option Save Workbooks To Database.
5. Click Apply.

**NOTE**
*This will remove the privilege to only that particular user. To remove this privilege from all users, select the public role and revoke the privilege.*

**QUESTION:** *How can I completely remove the Discoverer applet and Java Runtime Environment (JRE) from a user's PC?*

**ANSWER:** The first time that a user accesses the Discoverer Plus URL, the Discoverer applet will be downloaded. This applet includes a Sun JRE and a signed VeriSign Class 3 certificate. These items are required for any subsequent access to Discoverer Plus.

If these need to be removed, use the following workflow:

1. From the Windows Start button, select Settings | Control Panel.
2. Double-click Add/Remove Programs (XP) or Programs and Features (Windows 7).
3. In XP do the following:
   - **A.** Click the item Java 2 Runtime Environment SE, v1.4.2_04.
   - **B.** Click the Remove button.
4. In Windows 7 do the following:
   - **A.** Right-click the item that begins with Java(TM).
   - **B.** From the pop-up select Deinstall.

**NOTE**
*The default JRE that ships with Discoverer 10*g *is version 1.4.2_04. The version on the client machine may be higher if the application server administrator has changed the Discoverer server-side configuration. You may need to remove more than one. With Discoverer 11*g *the server Java was installed independently from Discoverer. It will probably be Java 6 with an update of 27 or greater.*

5. Windows may alert the user to restart the computer to completely remove the Sun JRE.
6. The Discoverer security certificate is in the browser and can be removed only by opening Internet Explorer and editing the Internet Options settings. If you have not already done so, launch Internet Explorer.
7. From the toolbar, select Tools | Internet Options.
8. Click the Content tab.
9. Click the Publishers button.
10. Click the Trusted Root Certification Authorities tab.
11. Scroll through the list of certificates and remove any certificates issued to VeriSign Trust Network and issued by VeriSign Trust Network that display a "friendly name" of VeriSign Class 3 Primary CA.
12. Click Close to exit the Certificates dialog box.
13. Click OK to save and exit from the Internet Options settings.
14. When all actions are completed, reboot the PC. The Discoverer applet components will be completely removed from the client PC.

**QUESTION:** *Why does a user need to have the CREATE PROCEDURE, CREATE TABLE, and CREATE VIEW database privileges in order to schedule?*

**ANSWER:** For a user to be able to schedule workbooks, they need to have all of the following database privileges:

- CREATE PROCEDURE
- CREATE TABLE
- CREATE VIEW
- EXECUTE ANY PROCEDURE
- UNLIMITED TABLESPACE
- EXECUTE ON SYS.DBMS_JOB
- SELECT ON SYS.V_$PARAMETER

For all of this to work, the user needs to be able to create a procedure that will execute the job at the allotted time. The CREATE TABLE and CREATE VIEW privileges are needed for the storage of the results. Every time the query is executed, Discoverer creates a table to store those results.

In standard Discoverer, when you create and run a worksheet, the results are created dynamically. This means the data is available only within the session that is running the worksheet. More important, the data is *not* available to any other worksheet whether within that session or not.

However, if you use a scheduled workbook, then the results from the worksheet are held in a temporary table until you remove the results or you delete the scheduled workbook.

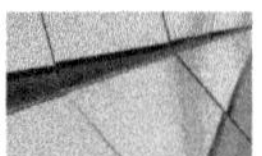

**NOTE**
*This temporary table is stored within the schema of the user who owns the workbook, not within the standard EUL schema.*

A typical table has a name in the form of EUL5_ B *YYMMDDHHMISS QN RN*, such as EUL5_B130918214946Q1R3, which can be broken into six separate pieces as follows:

- EUL5_ is a constant.
- B means Batch and is a constant.
- YYMMDD is the date that the scheduled worksheet was created; for example, 130918 means September 18, 2013.
- HHMISS is the time when the scheduled worksheet was created, given in the 24-hour clock format; for example, 214946 means 9:49:46 p.m.
- QN is the letter *Q* followed by a number, such as Q1, which signifies the query number. I believe Oracle has some plans to allow multiple queries, but for now this is always Q1.
- RN means this is the letter *R* followed by a number, such as R1, R2, and so on. This is the run number.

Using the preceding logic, therefore, this is a valid example: EUL5_B151129151025Q1R1. This is result set 1 for query 1, which was set up at 3:15:25 p.m. on November 29, 2015.

Something else that adds interest here is that the column names within the table do not match the column names in your original query. The scheduled results' column names use generic names such as BRVC1, BRVC2, BRD1, BRD2, BRN1, and BRN2. These are codes and can be interpreted as follows:

- BRCV1 and BRCV2 mean Batch Result Var Chars 1 and 2.
- BRD1 and BRD2 mean Batch Result Dates 1 and 2.
- BRN1 and BRN2 mean Batch Result Numbers 1 and 2.

So, why do you need the CREATE VIEW privilege? This is used at run time to populate the latest table of results. For every scheduled workbook that you create, Discoverer will create one view. When the appointed time arrives for the execution of the query, Discoverer executes a CREATE TABLE script like this:

```
CREATE TABLE xyz AS SELECT * FROM VIEW;
```

A typical view has a name like EUL5_B150918214946Q1V3, which, as you can see, looks almost identical to the format for the table name. This is deliberate and corresponds to the date and time when the schedule was first set up.

By the way, did you realize that what you are seeing is basically the forerunner to today's materialized views? In a materialized view, Oracle is able to combine a view definition with a table to store the results. Discoverer has been able to do this for years, albeit the view and the table are stored as separate objects.

**QUESTION:** *Could you please explain the tables that are used by scheduling?*

**ANSWER:** Apart from the tables and views created by the user at the time of scheduling, Discoverer uses a set of predefined tables to manage scheduling. They are as follows:

- **EUL5_BATCH_REPORTS** This table contains one row per scheduled worksheet and contains all of the base information that the user assigned when the schedule was set up. Of particular importance are the following columns:

- **BR_ID** Is the unique ID assigned to this scheduled worksheet.
- **BR_EU_ID** Is the user ID of the owner of the schedule. This links to the EU_ID in the EUL5_EUL_USERS tables, where the EU_USERNAME column will tell you the actual user.
- **BR_NEXT_RUN_DATE** Contains the date and time of the next run.
- **BR_EXPIRY** Contains the number of days to keep the results.
- **BR_NUM_FREQ_UNITS** Contains the number of units to be used between refreshes as qualified by BR_RFU_ID.
- **BR_RFU_ID** Contains a code indicating the time frequency for the units expressed in the preceding column. The valid values for this are as follows:
  - **2000** The time frequency is minutes.
  - **2001** The time frequency is hours.
  - **2002** The time frequency is days.
  - **2003** The time frequency is weeks.
  - **2004** The time frequency is months.
  - **2005** The time frequency is years.
- **BR_AUTO_REFRESH** This is code indicating whether the scheduled report should run once or refresh automatically. The valid values for this are as follows:
  - **0** The schedule should execute just once.
  - **1** The schedule should automatically refresh.

- **EUL5_BR_RUNS** This table contains one row for each execution of the schedule. Of particular importance are the following columns:
  - **BRR_ID** This is the unique ID assigned to this run.
  - **BRR_BR_ID** This is the ID of the scheduled worksheet being run. This corresponds to the BR_ID in the EUL5_BATCH_REPORTS table.
  - **BRR_RUN_NUMBER** This is a sequential number corresponding to the number of times the worksheet has been scheduled to run.
  - **BRR_STATE** This is a code to indicate the status of the run. I am not aware of all the possible states but the ones you are most likely to see are
    - **1** The worksheet is scheduled to run.
    - **9** The worksheet has been executed successfully.
  - **BRR_RUN_DATE** This is the date and time when the schedule was run. It will be null if BRR_STATE is 1.
- **EUL5_BATCH_SHEETS** This table contains one row per scheduled worksheet and contains a cross-reference to the actual worksheet. Of particular importance are the following columns:
  - **BS_ID** This is the unique ID assigned to this run.
  - **BS_BR_ID** This is the ID of the scheduled worksheet being run. It corresponds to the BR_ID value in the EUL5_BATCH_REPORTS table.

- **BS_SHEET_NAME** This is the name of the sheet to be executed.
- **BS_SHEET_ID** This is the ID of the worksheet being scheduled. It is usually encrypted.

- **EUL5_BATCH_QUERIES** This table contains one row per scheduled worksheet and contains the actual SQL that is to be executed. Of particular importance are the following columns:
  - **BQ_ID** This is the unique ID assigned to this query.
  - **BQ_BS_ID** This is the ID of the sheet being run. It corresponds to the BS_ID value in the EUL5_BATCH_SHEETS table.
  - **BQ_RESULT_SQL_1–4** These four columns contain the SQL that will be run to produce the results. Most of the time, the SQL can be contained in the first column. If there is more SQL than will fit in the first column, Discoverer will concatenate the columns into one string before executing the code.
- **EUL5_EUL_USERS** This table stores information about EUL users. Of particular importance are the following columns:
  - **EU_ID** This is the unique ID assigned to the user.
  - **EU_NAME** This is the name of the user or role as stored within the database.

The following script will show you all the scheduled worksheets within your EUL, including those that have already run. You need to make sure you are logged in to SQL as the EUL owner.

```
SELECT
A.EU_USERNAME"User Name",
B.BR_EU_ID"User ID",
B.BR_WORKBOOK_NAME "Workbook",
B.BR_ID"Workbook ID",
R.BRR_RUN_NUMBER"Run Number",
R.BRR_RUN_DATE"Run Date"
FROM
EUL5_BATCH_REPORTS B,
EUL5_BR_RUNS R,
EUL5_EUL_USERS A
WHERE 1=1
AND A.EU_ID  = B.BR_EU_ID
AND R.BRR_BR_ID = B.BR_ID
ORDER BY
B.BR_ID, R.BRR_RUN_NUMBER;
```

Here is what the output looks like:

| | | | | | |
|---|---|---|---|---|---|
| ADMIN0 | 100002 | Analytic Base with Running Total | 101001 | 1 | 5/14/2013 6:44:19 PM |
| ADMIN0 | 100002 | Analytic Base with Running Total | 101001 | 2 | 5/14/2013 6:45:21 PM |
| ADMIN0 | 100002 | Analytic Base with Running Total | 101001 | 3 | |

The following script will show you the scheduled worksheets within your EUL that have not yet run. You need to make sure you are logged into SQL as the EUL owner.

```
SELECT
A.EU_USERNAME"User Name",
B.BR_NAME"Workbook Name",
B.BR_CREATED_DATE"Created Date",
B.BR_NEXT_RUN_DATE "Next Scheduled Run Time",
'Every ' || B.BR_NUM_FREQ_UNITS || ' ' ||
DECODE(B.BR_RFU_ID,
 2000,'Minutes',
 2001,'Hours',
 2002,'Days',
 2003,'Weeks',
 2004,'Months','Years') "Often"
FROM
EUL5_BATCH_REPORTS B,
EUL5_EUL_USERS  A
WHERE B.BR_EU_ID=A.EU_ID;
```

Here is what the output looks like:

| User Name | Workbook Name | Created Date | Next Scheduled Run Time | Often |
|---|---|---|---|---|
| ADMIN0 | Analytic Base with Running Total | 5/14/2013 6:43:18 PM | 5/14/2013 6:47:17 PM | Every 1 Minutes |

**QUESTION:** *I need a Discoverer workbook that shows the top 15 airlines in terms of passenger count. More specifically, the top 15 should each be listed in the report with their respective percentage share (highest to lowest), with any count that is less than 15 being totaled on the last line. Can you help?*

**ANSWER:** To give you the result you want, you will need to use some rather clever calculations. Let me give you an example based on Airline and SUM.

1. Create a table worksheet that has Airline Name and Passenger SUM.
2. Rename Passenger SUM to Passengers and sort the rows high to low based on Passengers.
3. Create an analytic ranking calculation that looks like this:

   ```
   RANK() OVER(ORDER BY Passenger SUM DESC)
   ```

4. Create another analytic calculation called Grand Total that looks like this:

   ```
   SUM(Passenger SUM) OVER(ORDER BY Passenger SUM DESC RANGE
   BETWEEN UNBOUNDED PRECEDING AND UNBOUNDED FOLLOWING )/15
   ```

5. Create a calculation called Remainder that looks like this:

   ```
   Grand Total - Passenger SUM
   ```

6. Create a total on Passengers using SUM, and give this total the label Totals.
7. Create a total on Grand Total using Cell SUM; assign no label to this total.
8. Create a total on Remainder using Cell SUM; also assign no label to this total.
9. Format the data in both Grand Total and Remainder so that the background color is the same as the foreground color. This effectively hides the intermediate values, leaving just a single row at the bottom containing the total count for thc 15 airlines, a total for all airlines, and a total for the difference between all airlines and the 15 selected in the ranking.

The output is shown here:

| Rank | Airline | Passengers | Grand Total | Remainder |
|---|---|---|---|---|
| 1 | CD-625 | 1,750,997 | | |
| 2 | AVR-500 | 1,258,289 | | |
| 3 | CD-100 | 881,911 | | |
| 4 | QB-5000 | 829,052 | | |
| 5 | QB-5500 | 826,217 | | |
| 6 | QB-6000 | 819,342 | | |
| 7 | AB-2000 | 798,849 | | |
| 8 | AB-3000 | 783,452 | | |
| 9 | CD-200 | 775,574 | | |
| 10 | AVR-550 | 729,518 | | |
| 11 | AB-2500 | 702,475 | | |
| 12 | MS-1200 | 668,871 | | |
| 13 | AVR-900 | 542,121 | | |
| 14 | QB-3000 | 497,296 | | |
| 15 | DS-1200 | 480,295 | | |
| | | Totals: 12,344,259 | 15,034,172 | 2,689,913 |

**QUESTION:** *Can you give me a script that allows me to query the database tables and views and find out which business areas use them within my EUL?*

**ANSWER:** Here is the script you requested:

```
SELECT DISTINCT
BA.BA_NAME"BA Name",
OBJ.SOBJ_EXT_TABLE"Table Name",
OBJ.OBJ_EXT_OWNER"Owner"
FROM
EUL5_BAS BA,
EUL5_BA_OBJ_LINKS BOL,
EUL5_OBJS OBJ
WHERE 1=1
AND BA.BA_ID = BOL.BOL_BA_ID
AND OBJ.OBJ_ID  = BOL.BOL_OBJ_ID
AND OBJ.OBJ_EXT_OWNER IS NOT NULL
ORDER BY 1,2;
```

The output is shown here:

| BA Name | Table Name | Owner |
|---|---|---|
| Fan Trap | FAN_BUDGET | GSW |
| Fan Trap | FAN_DEPARTMENT | GSW |
| Fan Trap | FAN_EXPENSES | GSW |
| Sales Department | GS_CHANNEL | GSW |
| Sales Department | GS_CITY | GSW |
| Sales Department | GS_CUSTOMER | GSW |
| Sales Department | GS_DAY | GSW |
| Sales Department | GS_DISTRICT | GSW |
| Sales Department | GS_MONTH | GSW |
| Sales Department | GS_PRODLINE | GSW |
| Sales Department | GS_PRODUCTS | GSW |
| Sales Department | GS_QUARTER | GSW |
| Sales Department | GS_REGION | GSW |
| Sales Department | GS_SALES | GSW |
| Sales Department | GS_YEAR | GSW |

**QUESTION:** *What we want to do is know how long a person has been sick by subtracting the end date from the start date. However, if the sickness lasts from Friday until Monday, then only one day should count. In other words, we want an algorithm that works out the number of nonworking days between any two dates, excluding Saturday and Sunday. Do you have a nice workaround for this?*

**ANSWER:** This can be done, but you have to use four calculations. I will assume you have two dates: a start date and an end date. The following example will show you how to do it. Of course, you can always combine calculations into one algorithm, but for clarity I will break them out here so that you can see exactly what is going on. The algorithms can be tricky, but if you copy them into Discoverer exactly as they are shown here, they will work.

- **Calc 1: Base Diff** This counts the base number of days between the start and end dates, assuming of course that the end date is later than or equal to the start date. I add 1 because if the end date equals the start date, we still have to allow for one day's sickness.

  ```
  TRUNC(End Date) - TRUNC(Start Date) + 1
  ```

  In our example, where the end date is Monday and the start date is Friday, the base diff will be 4.

- **Calc 2: Weeks** This counts the number of whole weeks between the start and end dates. Therefore, if the Base Diff is 4, the number of whole weeks will be 0.

  ```
  TRUNC( ABS( ( Base Diff ) / 7), 0)
  ```

- **Calc 3: Variance** This works out how many odd days there are between the base number of days and the total number of weeks. Therefore, if the Base Diff is 4, the variance will be 4.

  ```
  TRUNC(Base Diff - ( Weeks * 7 ), 0)
  ```

- **Calc 4: Actual Diff** This works out how many working days there are between the start date and the end date, assuming that Saturday and Sunday are not to be counted. Basically this works out the day of the week for the end date and calculates the exact number of days the person has been sick.

  ```
  Base Diff - ( 2 * Weeks ) - DECODE(DECODE(SIGN(TO_NUMBER(TO_CHAR(End
  Date, 'D')) - Variance),1,'N','Y'),'Y',2,0)
  ```

Let's look at this last algorithm in a bit more detail. It starts with the base difference and then subtracts two times the number of whole weeks. Once again, in the example provided, where the start date is a Friday and the end date is a Monday, the number of whole weeks is zero, and so nothing is subtracted, with the number of days remaining at 4.

Next, the algorithm subtracts an additional two days if the day of the week is greater than the variance. Let's see how this works. The following is the heart of the algorithm:

```
DECODE(DECODE(SIGN(TO_NUMBER(TO_CHAR(End Date, 'D')) Variance), 1, 'N', 'Y')
,'Y',2,0)
```

TO_CHAR(End Date, 'D') returns the Day of the Week integer in a string. This needs converting to a number before we can use the SIGN function, which is the TO_NUMBER function. In our example, Monday will return 2.

Consider the inner DECODE statement, shown here:

```
DECODE(SIGN(TO_NUMBER(TO_CHAR(End Date, 'D')) - Variance),1,'N','Y')
```

This is explained as follows:

IF the Day of the Week minus the Variance is positive
THEN return the value 'N' (nothing to add)
ELSE return the value 'Y'

In our example, where the variance is 4 and the day of the week is 1, because the day of the week minus the variance is negative, the algorithm will return a 'Y'.

The outer decode simply says this:

IF the value returned by the inner decode is 'Y'
THEN subtract an additional 2 days
ELSE subtract 0 additional days

In our example, because the inner DECODE returned a 'Y', we now subtract two additional days from the base difference, making the overall answer 2.

In the final worksheet, the only calculation that you would have visible to the user would be the final one for Actual Diff.

**QUESTION:** *We need an algorithm that calculates the difference between two dates, with the result being displayed as days, hours, minutes, and seconds. Do you have an algorithm that can do this?*

**ANSWER:** This can be done, but once again you need to use several calculations. In this case, there are four. Let's assume you have two dates: a higher date and a lower date. The following example will show you how to do it. Of course, you can always combine calculations into one algorithm, but for clarity I will break them out here so that you can see exactly what is going on. The algorithms can be tricky, but if you copy them into Discoverer exactly as they are shown here, they will work.

- **Calc 1: Base Diff** This calculates the base number of days between the higher and lower dates, assuming of course that the higher date is later than or equal to the lower date. This time, unlike the answer given to the previous question, we do not use the TRUNC command.

Higher Date – Lower Date

- **Calc 2: New Mins** The following calculates the number of odd minutes between the times given:

```
TRUNC(Base Diff * 1440) - ( TRUNC(Base Diff) * 1440 ) - (
TRUNC(MOD(Base Diff, TRUNC(Base Diff)) * 24) * 60 )
```

- **Calc 3: New Secs** The following calculates the number of odd seconds between the times given:

```
TRUNC(Base Diff * 86400) - ( TRUNC(Diff) * 86400 ) - ( TRUNC(MOD(Base
Diff, TRUNC(Base Diff)) * 24) * 3600 ) - ( New Mins * 60 )
```

- **Calc 4: New Time** The following calculates the final display:

```
TRUNC(Base Diff) || ' Days, ' || TRUNC(MOD(Base Diff, TRUNC(Base Diff)) *
24) || ' Hours, '|| New Mins || ' Minutes, ' || New Secs || ' Seconds'
```

Using the preceding calculations, if Higher Time is 17:05:20 on Monday, September 26, and Lower Time is midnight on September 20, the individual calculations come out as follows:

- **Calc 1: Base Diff** 5.7120 rounded to four decimal places
- **Calc 2: New Mins** 5
- **Calc 3: New Secs** 20
- **Calc 4: New Time** 5 days, 17 hours, 5 minutes, 20 seconds

Once again, you would make only the final calculation visible to the user.

**QUESTION:** *Do you have a script that will show us the business areas and folders as well as the items that are used in each folder?*

**ANSWER:** The following script will give you what you want:

```
SELECT DISTINCT
BA.BA_NAME"BA Name",
OBJ.OBJ_NAME"Folder Name",
EXP.EXP_SEQUENCE"Item Order",
EXP.IT_HEADING"Item Heading",
```

```
DECODE(EXP.EXP_DATA_TYPE,
   1, 'VARCHAR2',
 2, 'NUMBER',
 4, 'DATE',
  EXP.EXP_DATA_TYPE) "Data Type",
DECODE(EXP.IT_HIDDEN,
   '0', 'No', 'Yes')  "Item Hidden",
OBJ.OBJ_ID"Folder ID",
BA.BA_ID"BA ID"
FROM
EUL5_BA_OBJ_LINKS BOL,
EUL5_BAS BA,
EUL5_OBJS  OBJ,
EUL5_EXPRESSIONS  EXP
WHERE 1=1
AND BOL.BOL_BA_ID  = BA.BA_ID
AND BOL.BOL_OBJ_ID = OBJ.OBJ_ID
AND EXP.IT_OBJ_ID  = OBJ.OBJ_ID
AND EXP.EXP_TYPE  IN ('CI','CO')
ORDER BY BA_NAME, OBJ_NAME, EXP_SEQUENCE;
```

Here is what the output looks like:

| BA Name | Folder Name | Item Order | Item Heading | Data Type | Item Hidden | Folder ID | BA ID |
|---|---|---|---|---|---|---|---|
| Sales Department | Calendar Date | 1 | Calendar Date | DATE | No | 100033 | 100024 |
| Sales Department | Calendar Date | 2 | Monthid | VARCHAR2 | No | 100033 | 100024 |
| Sales Department | Cancelled Date | 1 | Cancelled Date | DATE | No | 100045 | 100024 |
| Sales Department | Cancelled Date | 2 | Cancelled Month | VARCHAR2 | No | 100045 | 100024 |
| Sales Department | Cancelled Date | 3 | Cancelled Quarter | VARCHAR2 | No | 100045 | 100024 |
| Sales Department | Cancelled Date | 4 | Cancelled Year | VARCHAR2 | No | 100045 | 100024 |
| Sales Department | Channel | 1 | Channelid | NUMBER | No | 100030 | 100024 |
| Sales Department | Channel | 2 | Channel | VARCHAR2 | No | 100030 | 100024 |
| Sales Department | City | 1 | Cityid | NUMBER | No | 100031 | 100024 |

**QUESTION:** *Do you have a script that shows who has access to each business area? The output should indicate whether a user is an administrator.*

**ANSWER:** Here is the script you asked for:

```
SELECT
BA.BA_NAME"Business Area",
DECODE(PRIVS.AP_PRIV_LEVEL,1,
  'Yes','No')"Administrator",
USR.EU_USERNAME "User Name"
FROM
EUL5_EUL_USERS USR,
EUL5_ACCESS_PRIVS PRIVS,
```

```
EUL5_BAS BA
WHERE 1=1
AND USR.EU_ID = PRIVS.AP_EU_ID
AND BA.BA_ID  = PRIVS.GBA_BA_ID;
```

The output is shown here:

| Business Area | User Name | Administrator |
|---|---|---|
| Fan Trap | ADMIN0 | Yes |
| Fan Trap | ADMIN1 | Yes |
| Lookups | ADMIN0 | Yes |
| Lookups | ADMIN1 | Yes |
| Sales Department | ADMIN0 | Yes |
| Sales Department | ADMIN1 | Yes |
| Sales Department | BOOK | No |

**QUESTION:** *Can you provide me with a script to show me who has workbooks that they have saved to the database?*

**ANSWER:** As you know, the tables used by Discoverer 10*g* and Discoverer 11*g* are all prefixed with EUL5. The users are stored in a table called EUL_USERS, and the workbooks themselves are stored in a table called EUL5_DOCUMENTS, so in this version the tables are called EUL5_EUL_USERS and EUL5_ DOCUMENTS. The following SQL query, when logged in as the EUL owner, will tell you which workbooks are owned by which users:

```
SELECT
EU_USERNAME  "Doc Owner",
DOC_NAME  "Doc Name"
FROM
EUL5_EUL_USERS  USRS,
EUL5_DOCUMENTS  DOCS
WHERE USRS.EU_ID = DOCS.DOC_EU_ID
ORDER BY
"Doc Owner", "Doc Name";
```

Here is what the output looks like:

| Doc Owner | Doc Name |
|---|---|
| ADMIN0 | Analytic 15% of Base |
| ADMIN0 | Analytic Base |
| ADMIN0 | Analytic Base Sorted |
| ADMIN0 | Analytic Base with 3 Month Moving Average |
| ADMIN0 | Analytic Base with 3 Month Moving Average and Prior Values |
| ADMIN0 | Analytic Base with Prior Year |
| ADMIN0 | Analytic Base with Running Total |
| ADMIN0 | Analytic Base with Running Total |
| ADMIN0 | Analytic Base with Running Total and top bottom N |

By the way, to see who has shared what with whom, use this script in SQL when connected as the owner of the EUL:

```
SELECT
AP_CREATED_BY "Doc Owner",
DOC_NAME  "Doc Name",
EU_USERNAME  "Shared With"
FROM
EUL5_EUL_USERS  USRS,
EUL5_DOCUMENTS  DOCS,
```

```
EUL5_ACCESS_PRIVS PRIVS
WHERE 1=1
AND PRIVS.GD_DOC_ID = DOCS.DOC_ID
AND USRS.EU_ID = PRIVS.AP_EU_ID
ORDER BY
"Doc Owner", "Doc Name", "Shared With";
```

Here is what the output looks like:

| Doc Owner | Doc Name | Shared With |
|---|---|---|
| ADMIN0 | Analytic Base with Running Total | BOOK |
| ADMIN0 | Analytic Boolean Conditions | BOOK |

**QUESTION:** *We are using Discoverer in Apps mode against E-Business Suite and have too many workbooks assigned to too many responsibilities. We want to clean up the workbooks and the responsibility assignments. Can you provide us with a script that shows all of the workbooks and all of the responsibility assignments? Also, just how does the Discoverer metadata link to E-Business Suite?*

**ANSWER:** Here is a script that may well be of some use. To use it, you will need to find out the name of the schema owner for your particular EUL. You then insert that name into this script at the five locations identified by EUL_OWNER. Finally, I recommend you log in to the E-Business Suite database as the APPS user in order to run this script. If you look carefully in this script, you will see exactly how the Discoverer metadata links to E-Business Suite.

```
SELECT
USER_NAME || ':' || DOCS.DOC_NAME "Doc Name",
RESP.RESPONSIBILITY_NAME"Resp Name"
FROM
EUL_OWNER.EUL5_EUL_USERS  USRS,
EUL_OWNER.EUL5_ACCESS_PRIVS PRIVS,
EUL_OWNER.EUL5_DOCUMENTS  DOCS,
EUL_OWNER.EUL5_EUL_USERS  OWN_USR,
APPS.FND_RESPONSIBILITY_VL  RESP,
APPS.FND_USER  CRTD_BY
WHERE 1=1
AND PRIVS.AP_TYPE = 'GD'
AND PRIVS.AP_EU_ID = USRS.EU_ID
AND PRIVS.GD_DOC_ID = DOCS.DOC_ID
AND OWN_USR.EU_ID = DOCS.DOC_EU_ID
AND RESP.RESPONSIBILITY_ID =
  SUBSTR(USRS.EU_USERNAME,2,INSTR(USRS.EU_USERNAME,'#',2)-2)
AND CRTD_BY.USER_ID = SUBSTR(DOCS.DOC_CREATED_BY,2)
AND OWN_USR.EU_USERNAME NOT IN ('EUL_OWNER','PUBLIC')
ORDER BY 1,2;
```

**QUESTION:** *I am trying to create a parameter where the users can pass one of the following values:*

- *All (i.e., all values)*
- *003 (i.e., a specific value)*
- *003, 001 (i.e., multiple values)*

*So, my condition looks like this:*

```
DOMAIN IN DECODE(:p_domain,'All',Domain,:p_domain)
```

*I have checked the Let User Enter Multiple Values check box for the domain parameter. With the preceding setup, the query works correctly when I provide All and single values. However, when I execute the report with multiple parameters (in other words, '003','001' ), I get records related to only the first parameter, which in this case is '003'. How can I get this to work?*

**ANSWER:** You need to create a complex condition like this:

```
DOMAIN = DECODE(UPPER(:p_domain), 'ALL', Domain)
OR
DOMAIN IN :p_domain
```

By the way, you might be interested to know that in the first part of this condition, when we refer to DOMAIN = DECODE, this works equally well with DOMAIN IN DECODE. This is because Discoverer silently changes to the appropriate operator, depending on how many values are present when generating the SQL query. You should check out the SQL inspector to see this in action.

**QUESTION:** *When we choose a connection or enter the connection details at the Discoverer Plus login page, the screen flickers and then the connections page is displayed again. After this, the applet starts but in a different window. Is there a way to make Plus start in the same window?*

**ANSWER:** By default, Discoverer Plus is designed to launch in a separate window from the connection screen. However, to answer your question, yes, you can make Discoverer Plus use the same connection. To do this, you append the following to the end of the URL:

```
?_plus_popup=false&framedisplaystyle=embedded
```

If your standard URL is as follows:

```
http://server.my.com:8890/discoverer/plus
```

you change this to the following:

```
http://server.my.com:8890/discoverer/plus?_plus_popup=false&framedisplaystyle=
embedded
```

This time you will see the Discoverer connections page, applet loading, and Plus interface all appear in the same window. You will also see loading messages and an hourglass display as the session starts, loads, and renders. Please refer to Chapter 20 for more information about providing URL parameters in a browser.

**QUESTION:** *I cannot see an option to add the total number of pages to the footer section of my Discoverer Plus worksheet. Has this been removed?*

**ANSWER:** Yes, this feature was removed when Discoverer 10*g* was introduced and has continued through into Discoverer 11*g*. According to Oracle, the token that used to generate this code (&Pages) has been phased out and is no longer supported within Discoverer. This is because it is computationally intensive to determine the number of pages and doing so would lead to unacceptable performance degradation.

If you still want to do this, you need to use Desktop to add the &Pages token. You must also print from within Desktop. If you set this up in Desktop and then try to print from within Plus, Discoverer will print the page numbers incorrectly. For example, if the print command was submitted when viewing page 4 of 12, all of the printed pages would show "Page 4 of 12." If your printing started on page 1, all the printed pages would show "Page 1 of 12."

While this can be quite amusing at first and could be the subject of an interesting topic of conversation, we do not recommend printing from within Discoverer Plus whenever Discoverer Desktop has been used to add the total number of pages.

**QUESTION:** *From time to time I noticed that newer versions of Java are being installed on my client machines. Sometimes there is more than one version of Java on the machine. I would like to know if there is a way to get Discoverer to tell me which version of Java it is actually using.*

**ANSWER:** Yes, this can be done. All you need to do is launch Discoverer Plus on a client machine. Then, from the menu bar you select Help | About Discoverer.

Here is an example of what the output looks like:

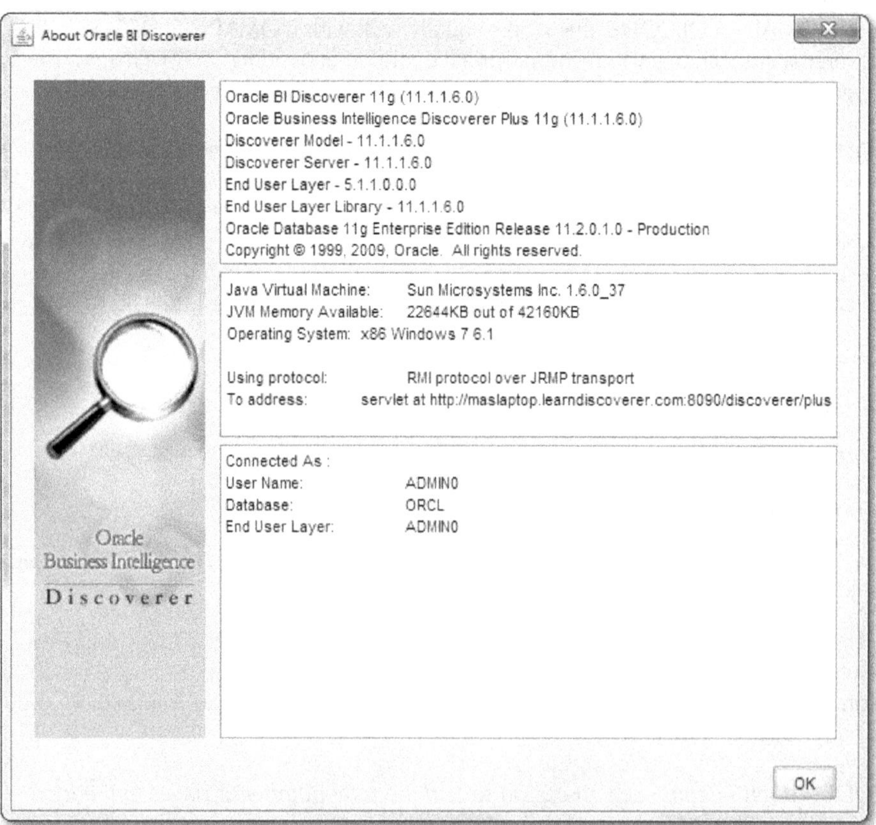

As you can see, not only does this tell you which version of Java is being used, in this case Sun Microsystems 1.6.0_37, but you also get to know a lot more information, included in which is the following:

- The version of Discoverer, in this case 11.1.1.6.0
- The EUL version, 5.1.1.0.0.0
- The database version, Oracle Enterprise 11g 11.2.0.1.0
- The operating system, x86 Windows 7.6.1
- The protocol being used, RMI protocol over JRMP transport
- Username, ADMIN0
- EUL, ADMIN0

**QUESTION:** *I cannot control the paper size inside Discoverer Plus. Do you know of a way to do this?*

**ANSWER:** On older versions of Discoverer this has not been possible. However, starting with Discoverer 10g and continued into Discoverer 11g, there is now a drop-down on the Page Setup screen for managing the page size. The older versions simply displayed the page size but did not allow you to change it.

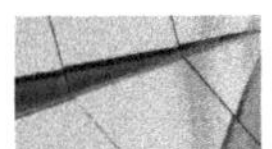

**NOTE**

*There is one proviso: you must have already saved the workbook before you can alter the page size. This is because Discoverer will store your page size preference. As a bonus, if you open the same worksheet in Viewer, Discoverer will remember the paper size that you set in Plus. This works the other way, too, in that if you set up a page size in Viewer and resave the workbook, the same setting will be available the next time you open Plus.*

To help you know whether you have saved a worksheet in Viewer, Discoverer will display an asterisk alongside the sheet name in the Worksheets area.

**QUESTION:** *One of our users created a crosstab worksheet. When she exported it to Excel, the headings were wrong and the side axis items moved up one row. Do you know why?*

**ANSWER:** You must be using Discoverer 10g because there was a bug in that release, but there was also workaround. The workaround was to turn on your Axis labels, simple as that. Without these being enabled, Discoverer exported nothing in those cells, which caused Excel to push everything up.

We are delighted to be able to tell you that this issue does not affect Discoverer 11g as the bug has been fixed.

Incidentally, in Discoverer 10g, you probably were aware that your column widths were not retained when you exported to Excel. In fact, they all got set to the width of the heading. Unfortunately, there was no workaround for this one. Our only recommendation was to keep your headings to an absolute minimum and if necessary use a set of standard abbreviations such as Avg for Average, Std for Standard, Dlvd for Delivered, and so on. Unfortunately, this issue continues to impact Discoverer 11g as the widths of column headings still do not get exported correctly to Excel. Our advice to keep heading names to the minimum therefore still applies.

**QUESTION:** *Do you know if I can pick up the "session variable" in Discoverer (Apps mode) that tells me the responsibility I am logged on as? The variable USER simply returns APPS, which is what I would expect. However, Discoverer must know the values because if I write a query, I can see that it is storing the value in the EUL5_EUL_USERS table, such as #10152#183. We are using Discoverer against E-Business Suite 11.5.9 on a 10g database.*

**ANSWER:** I use the following code in a custom folder created in Discoverer Administrator to get the responsibility plus other user information:

```
SELECT
APPS.FND_GLOBAL.RESP_ID,
APPS.FND_GLOBAL.RESP_NAME,
APPS.FND_GLOBAL.USER_ID,
APPS.FND_GLOBAL.USER_NAME,
APPS.FND_GLOBAL.EMPLOYEE_ID,
APPS.FND_GLOBAL.PER_SECURITY_PROFILE_ID,
APPS.FND_GLOBAL.ORG_ID
FROM DUAL;
```

| | Responsibility ID | Responsibility Name | User ID | User Name | Employee ID | Per Security Profile ID | Org ID |
|---|---|---|---|---|---|---|---|
| 1 | 20420 | System Administrator | 0 | SYSADMIN | -1 | 62 | 94 |

**QUESTION:** *We are using Discoverer Plus and are using a 10g database. However, we are noticing severe performance issues when running the query predictor in that the prediction takes up most of the time. When we used a 9i database, everything was fine. Do you know what we are doing wrong?*

**ANSWER:** Because of an old bug in the Oracle 10g database (4024370), if you need to use the query predictor, you need to use a workaround for Discoverer that will force Discoverer to use an explain plan instead of dynamic views. When I made these settings to the registry and the mid-tier of the production system for a client of mine, then Discoverer ran as fast as it ever did.

First I will discuss the registry entries. Two entries need to be set for every developer machine. Both of these entries need to be created in this folder:

```
HKEY_USERS\Software\ORACLE\Discoverer 11\Database
```

- **DWORD** Create an entry called QPPObtainCostMethod with a setting of 0.
- **DWORD** Create an entry called QPPEnable with a setting of 0.

Turning our attention to the application server, to make these settings on the server, use the following workflow:

1. Edit PREF.TXT in the middle tier.
2. Edit the same settings just outlined; you will find them in the [Database] section.
3. Save the PREF.TXT file.
4. Apply the preferences using applypreferences.sh on Unix or applypreferences.bat on Windows.
5. Restart the Discoverer middle tier.

By the way, if you want to turn off the query predictor, this is also controlled in two places. In the registry, it is called QPPEnable and can be found here:

```
HKEY_USERS\Software\ORACLE\Discoverer 11\Database
```

In the application server, use the preceding workflow to edit the PREF.TXT file, locate the entry for QPPEnable, and change it to 0. Don't forget to stop the middle tier before you apply the preferences.

Setting QPPEnable to 0 turns off query prediction, while setting it to 1 enables query prediction.

**QUESTION:** *I have a table that contains some columns of type NUMBER. I have created a business area that contains this table, but the columns that are NUMBER(8) in Discoverer appear with the icon of the varchar type. Then, in the Discoverer Desktop Edition, I cannot, for example, create a table report with a percentage. Do you know if I need a patch?*

**ANSWER:** It sounds like you have not defined the items to be data points. Only those items that are data points can be treated as numbers and thus be used in calculations and percentages. Items that are not defined as data points will be treated as characters and can have a list of values assigned to them. By the way, you cannot assign a list of values to an item that is defined as a data point.

To check your current settings, please follow this workflow:

1. Log in to Discoverer Administrator as the EUL owner.
2. Open the business area and folder that has the problem.
3. Locate an item that has a problem.
4. Right-click the item.
5. From the pop-up box select Properties—the Item Properties dialog box will be displayed.
6. In the Item Properties dialog box, make sure the General tab is the active tab and now look for the property called Default Position. In Default Position the valid options are
   - Data Point
   - Page
   - Side
   - Top
   - Top or Side
7. If your item is not defined as Data Point, click the current setting and from the drop-down list provided select Data Point.
8. Click Apply and, if you have more items that need to be fixed, go back to step 3; otherwise, continue with step 9.
9. When you have finished redefining the settings for all of the items you wanted to fix, click OK.
10. Exit the Administrator edition and launch one of the end-user editions to verify that all is now working as you desire.

**QUESTION:** *I have been trying to create some materialized views in the database so that I can use external summary management. However, I am having trouble specifying the refresh interval. How can I refresh a materialized view at an interval of two hours on the exact even hours through the SQL prompt?*

**ANSWER:** I am surmising but guess that you specified the materialized view using something like this:

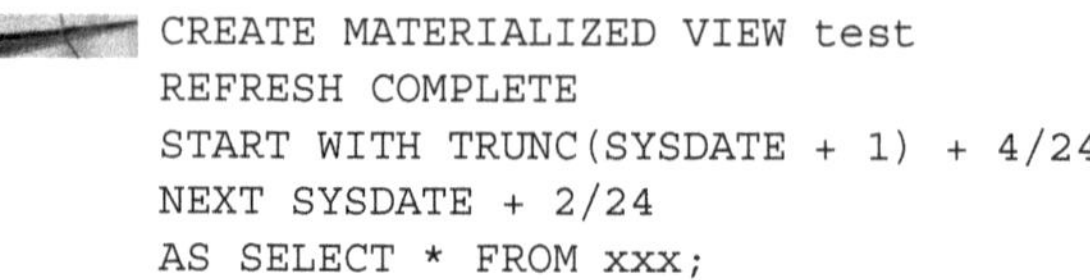

```
CREATE MATERIALIZED VIEW test
REFRESH COMPLETE
START WITH TRUNC(SYSDATE + 1) + 4/24
NEXT SYSDATE + 2/24
AS SELECT * FROM xxx;
```

This will correctly do the first refresh at 4 a.m. tomorrow morning, but it will set up the following refresh to take place two hours after the previous refresh has completed. So, if the previous refresh completes at 4:10 a.m., the next refresh will start at 6:10 a.m. and not at 6 a.m. as you might think.

What you need to do is to provide a parameter to the TRUNC command. Look at this modified script:

```
CREATE MATERIALIZED VIEW test
REFRESH COMPLETE
START WITH TRUNC(SYSDATE + 1) + 4/24
NEXT TRUNC(SYSDATE,'HH') + 2/24
AS SELECT * FROM xxx;
```

This code will set up the materialized view to do its first refresh at 4 a.m. tomorrow and then refresh every two hours on the hour, no matter when the last refresh completed (provided of course that it took less than one hour to run).

**NOTE**
*If you have a materialized view that is scheduled to refresh every two hours and it takes longer than one hour to complete each refresh, perhaps it needs to be tuned.*

Now look at this code:

```
CREATE MATERIALIZED VIEW test
REFRESH COMPLETE
START WITH TRUNC(SYSDATE + 1) + 11/24
NEXT NEXT_DAY(TRUNC(SYSDATE), 'MONDAY') + 15/24
AS SELECT * FROM xxx;
```

This code creates a materialized view called test and runs it for the first time tomorrow at 11 a.m. The following refreshes will then be each Monday at 3 p.m.

**QUESTION:** *I have just installed a new EUL, but the option to install Oracle's sample data is grayed out. Do you know how I can install this?*

**ANSWER:** The option is grayed out because you do not have a user called VIDEO5 in the database, and the account you used to connect to Discoverer Administrator does not have the privilege to create a database user either.

To get the sample to install, use the following workflow:

1. Create a new user called VIDEO5, granting these privileges.
   - CONNECT
   - RESOURCE
   - ALTER ANY MATERIALIZED VIEW
   - ANALYZE ANY
   - CREATE ANY MATERIALIZED VIEW
   - CREATE PROCEDURE
   - CREATE TABLE
   - CREATE VIEW
   - DROP ANY MATERIALIZED VIEW
   - EXECUTE ANY PROCEDURE
   - GLOBAL QUERY REWRITE
   - SELECT ANY TABLE
   - UNLIMITED TABLESPACE
2. Launch the Administrator edition and connect as the owner of the EUL.
3. Navigate to Tools | EUL Manager.
4. The Install The Sample Data Option will now be active and you should click it.
5. Give the password for the VIDEO5 user.
6. The sample database, along with its data, business area, and workbooks, will now be created. Access will be granted to PUBLIC.

**QUESTION:** *Can you tell me how to add five minutes to SYSDATE? I want to set up a job, and I want the job to fire off every five minutes until I stop it.*

**ANSWER:** The answer you want is SYSDATE + (1/288) or SYSDATE + 0.0034722.

Adding something to SYSDATE, or any other date for that matter, is a simple case of working out the decimal that needs to be added.

- **Example 1** Add one hour (1/24 of a day).

  ```
  SYSDATE + (1/24) or SYSDATE + 0.0416666
  ```
- **Example 2** Subtract 30 minutes (1/48 of a day).

  ```
  SYSDATE - (1/48) or SYSDATE - 0.0208333
  ```
- **Example 3** Add 1.5 days.

  ```
  SYSDATE + 1.5
  ```

Therefore, to add five minutes, you have to work out that there are 288 five-minute periods in a 24-hour period, so the answer is

```
SYSDATE + (1/288) or SYSDATE + 0.0034722
```

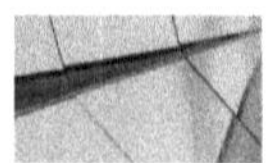

**NOTE**
*Do not forget the parentheses if you are mixing + or – with * or /.*

**QUESTION:** *What does it mean when an attribute in a folder is in bold letters or when it is italicized?*

**ANSWER:** This formatting is applied inside the Administrator edition to help you identify which items have been used in joins. The bold text signifies that the item is being used as the master item in a join; in other words, you have defined a 1:N join going from this item. Items that are formatted in italics are items that are being used as the detail item in a join; in other words, there is a join to this item from an item in another folder.

**QUESTION:** *I have heard talk of there being primary and secondary elements within Discoverer. Can you tell me what these are and how this affects my EUL?*

**ANSWER:** The primary elements in a EUL are as follows:

- Business areas
- Folders
- Items

The secondary elements are as follows:

- Joins
- Complex folder items
- Item hierarchies
- Item hierarchy nodes
- Date hierarchy templates
- Date hierarchy items
- Item classes—lists of values

Primary elements must be uniquely named within the EUL. These names are assigned by the administrator, and you should take great care naming them. In fact, we recommend you use meaningful names and identifiers for all primary elements.

Secondary elements must be uniquely named within the folder or business area, but the names can be assigned by Discoverer using the value of the Auto-Generate name property of the secondary elements.

**QUESTION:** *What does the Auto-Generate name property do?*

**ANSWER:** The Auto-Generate name property enables the names of secondary elements to be automatically updated whenever a primary element name is changed. The Auto-Generate name property is applied to secondary elements using Discoverer Administrator (its value can be set to Yes or No). When the value of the Auto-Generate name property is set to Yes for a secondary element, Discoverer generates its name using the names of its primary elements (in other words, the folder and item names used in the secondary element).

**NOTE**
*The Auto-Generate name property value is set to No by default.*

**QUESTION:** *Is there a way to set up Discoverer such that when I import new objects from the database, the secondary elements are automatically named for me?*

**ANSWER:** Yes, you do this by setting the AutogenNameOnCreate registry setting to 1. By default, this setting is not present, so you will need to create it. The AutogenNameOnCreate registry setting is a DWORD and should be located here:

```
HKEY_CURRENT_USER\Software\Oracle\Discoverer 11\Database
```

If the AutogenNameOnCreate registry setting is present in the registry and its value is set to 1, Discoverer will do the following:

- If you install the sample data, Discoverer will set the Auto-Generate name property for all secondary elements to Yes.
- When you create new secondary elements, Discoverer will set the Auto-Generate name property to Yes.
- When an item has its Auto-Generate name property value set to Yes, it will display in the EUL in a different color from the other items; for example, it will display in blue if you are using the Windows default color scheme.

If you export EUL objects and then import the EUL objects using the /auto_gen_name command modifier in the EUL Command Line for Java (or the Discoverer command-line interface), Discoverer will set the Auto-Generate name property to Yes for all the secondary elements contained in the EUL objects that you exported and imported.

**QUESTION:** *I have deleted a folder from the business area but not the EUL. Now that it's not appearing, is there any way to remove it from the EUL?*

**ANSWER:** Oracle calls these orphaned folders, and yes, you will be pleased to know that Discoverer has a mechanism to delete them.

To delete an orphaned folder, use the following workflow:

1. Launch the Discoverer Administrator edition.
2. From the toolbar, select Tools | Manage Folders.
3. In the Manage Folders dialog box, click the Orphaned Folders tab, shown here.
4. Locate the folder you do not want and click Delete.

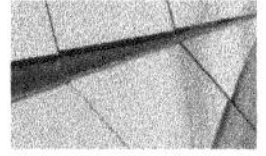

**NOTE**
*Versions of Discoverer prior to 10g do not have this feature; you will need to reassign the folder to a business area before you can delete it.*

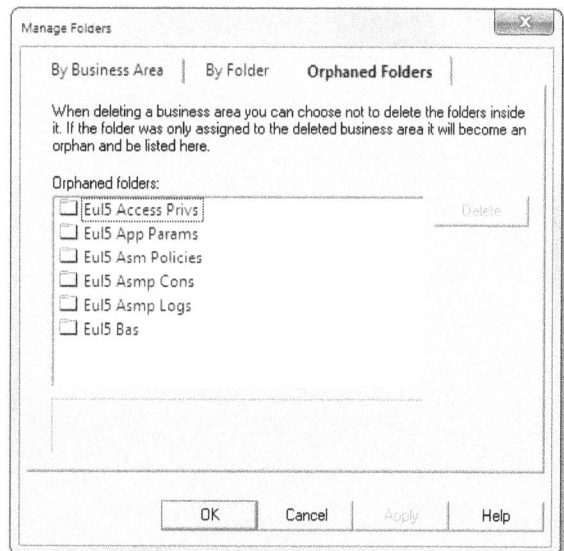

**QUESTION:** *I have the following condition in Discoverer: WHERE NAME IN :pNAME. The parameter :pNAME can accept multiple values like john, joe. How can I convert the multiple values to uppercase? Adding the function UPPER( :pNAME) to the condition will return only JOHN. I have also used my own function to convert the string and return an uppercase string to Discoverer, but Discoverer still uses only the first value. Is there a way to do this?*

**ANSWER:** You can do what you want by substituting another character for the comma and then using the REPLACE command to convert that character back into a comma. You need to do this because the UPPER function converts a single string into its uppercase values. If you include a comma inside a parameter, such as "john, joe", Discoverer will treat this as two strings. You will notice that the parameter itself gets transformed into 'john', 'joe'. Applying UPPER to this parameter will return just 'JOHN'.

However, if you key in multiple values using some character other than a comma as the delimiter, then it will work. Try using / so that the user keys in **john / joe**. The answer will be JOHN / JOE.

Now you just use the REPLACE command, and *voilà*, the comma gets reinstated.

REPLACE( UPPER(":pNAME"), '/',, ') will now return JOHN, JOE.

**QUESTION:** *I have a folder that is based on a view. I changed the folder to remove a column, yet when I launch Discoverer Administrator and use File | Refresh, Discoverer says that there are no changes. Do you have any idea why?*

**ANSWER:** You probably forgot to drop the column name from the list of aliases as well. If you edit a view definition that uses aliases, you must remember to remove the column from both places. If you edit the view and only drop a column without altering the alias list, the view will compile incorrectly. However, if you don't realize this and you go to the Discoverer Administrator and select File | Refresh, Discoverer will say nothing has changed. This is not an error because nothing really has changed yet—not until you alter the view correctly.

Let me explain with the following example:

```
CREATE OR REPLACE VIEW TEST_VIEW
(PRODUCT, DESCRIPTION, REASON)
AS
SELECT
TABLE1.PRODUCT_CODE,
TABLE2.PRODUCT_DESCRIPTION,
TABLE2.PRODUCT_RSN_CD
FROM
TABLE1,
TABLE2
WHERETABLE1.ID = TABLE2.ID
```

Let's say we want to drop the REASON and edit the view like this:

```
CREATE OR REPLACE VIEW TEST_VIEW
(PRODUCT, DESCRIPTION, REASON)
AS
SELECT
TABLE1.PRODUCT_CODE,
TABLE2.PRODUCT_DESCRIPTION
FROM
```

```
TABLE1,
TABLE2
WHERETABLE1.ID = TABLE2.ID
```

The view will not compile and will be invalid. However, if you don't spot this and try to refresh, Discoverer will think that there are no changes. Here is the correct alteration:

```
CREATE OR REPLACE VIEW TEST_VIEW
(PRODUCT, DESCRIPTION)
AS
SELECT
TABLE1.PRODUCT_CODE,
TABLE2.PRODUCT_DESCRIPTION
FROM
TABLE1,
TABLE2
WHERETABLE1.ID = TABLE2.ID
```

**QUESTION:** *I want to trim a field that has this character in common :'|' For example, 17x75|WIDGET, 17.00 X .175 should display as just 17x75. Can you please help me or direct me to the right place?*

**ANSWER:** RTRIM will not do the job for you. It only eliminates spaces to the right of your field. You will need to use a combination of the INSTR and SUBSTR functions.

- **INSTR** Finds the position of the character you are seeking (for example, INSTR('17x 75|WIDGET','|') will return position 6).
- **SUBSTR** Outputs part of a string. It takes two additional parameters, a start point and a length. It then returns a new string starting at the position you have nominated of the length you stated, such as SUBSTR('STRING', starting Position, Length).

As an example, the following:

```
SELECT SUBSTR('17x75|TIRE', 1, INSTR('17x75|TIRE','|')-1) FROM DUAL;
```

will output '17x75' as required.

**QUESTION:** *I am using Desktop and my company has introduced a new database for me to connect to. Our DBA told me to update my TNS Names file, but I don't know where it is located. Can you help?*

**ANSWER:** The TNS Names file is actually called tnsnames.ora. The version of Discoverer that you are using controls where the file is located.

- In Discoverer 10*g*, it is located here: `$ORACLE_HOME/network/ admin`.
- In Discoverer 11*g*, it is located here: `$ORACLE_HOME/asinst_1/config`.

If you used an out-of-the-box installation of Discoverer Administrator or Desktop, your Oracle home will probably be `c:\ oracle\BIToolsHome_1`, in which case tnsnames will be located here:

```
c:\ oracle\BIToolsHome_1\network\admin
```

A typical TNS Names entry looks like this:

```
VIS =
   (DESCRIPTION =
(ADDRESS = (PROTOCOL = TCP) (HOST = 192.168.2.116) (PORT = 1521))
(CONNECT_DATA =
 (SID   = VIS)
  ))
```

Here, there are three important sections that you need to fill in:

- **HOST =** You type in the IP address or the server name for the connection you want to make. If you are using a server name, you may also need to have an entry in your HOSTS file linking the server with its IP address.
- **PORT =** You type in the number of the port for the database you will be connecting to. The default port for all Oracle databases is 1521, but many DBAs will change this.
- **SID =** You type in the database identifier provided by your DBA.

I usually copy and paste a good TNS entry inside my tnsnames.ora file, replacing the relevant entries with the items specified here. You also need to make sure you assign a unique name to the entry. In the example shown, I have named this VIS. Inside Discoverer Desktop, I will use this name in the Connect box.

**QUESTION:** *I will be traveling around the country for my job and need to connect to various client systems in order to run Discoverer Plus. Someone told me that I should update my HOSTS file. Can you tell me where I can find this file and what I must do to edit it?*

**ANSWER:** Every Discoverer server that is running Plus or Viewer, no matter whether this is Linux, Unix, or Windows, needs to have a fully qualified domain name (FQDN). This FQDN is then associated with a unique IP address. On the server, this is set inside the HOSTS file.

In Linux and Unix you will find this file here: /etc.

In Windows you will find this file here: c:\windows\system32\drivers\etc.

For your laptop to connect to a client's Discoverer server, either the client needs to let you connect to their domain or you need to update your local HOSTS file. If the client has a DNS server and allows you to connect to their domain, you should have no issues.

However, in some situations where you cannot connect to the client's domain, you will need to manually add a new entry to your HOSTS file. In Windows, as mentioned, you will find this in c:\windows\system32\drivers\etc. The good news is that this file can be edited with a standard text editor such as Notepad.

When you edit this file for the first time, it will have a single entry that looks like this:

```
127.0.0.1   localhost
```

Do not change this entry. To add a new entry to this file, you need to find out from the client the name of the server that they want you to use and the IP address the server is using. Having obtained this information, you add the new entry to your HOSTS file using this syntax:

```
"IP address" "FQDN" "short name"
```

For example, if the client says that the server you should connect to is oraias.learndiscoverer.com and that it is using IP address 192.168.2.102, you should add the following entry and then save and close the file.

```
192.168.2.102 oraias.learndiscoverer.com oraias
```

When you save and close the HOSTS file, any changes that you made will take effect immediately. There is no need to reboot your laptop.

**QUESTION:** *We have an Oracle Apps EUL, and I have created a report that links the supplier header and sites with the invoices table. What I want is a list of the vendors that have never had a transaction. It sounded simple at the time, but I do not know how to create this report. Do you have any ideas?*

**ANSWER:** Presumably, what you have done is to join the vendor folder to your vendor sites and subsequently to your invoice folder. When you do this, you will get data for vendors that have transactions. If the vendor has no transactions, then the vendor record will not be available to your report.

There are two ways to overcome this within Discoverer. You can use either a subquery or a custom folder.

To use a subquery, use the following workflow:

1. Launch Discoverer Desktop—you cannot create subqueries using Plus.
2. Create a workbook that selects all vendors that have an invoice.
3. Create a new worksheet in the same workbook and make this just a listing of vendors.
4. Create a condition such that the vendor is not in the first worksheet.

**NOTE**
*You cannot create a subquery in Plus. However, if you create the report in Desktop, you will be able to run it in both Plus and Viewer.*

To use a custom folder, use the following workflow:

1. Launch the Discoverer Administrator edition.
2. Open the business area and folder you want to work in.
3. Right-click the business area, and from the pop-up menu select New Custom Folder.
4. Type in some SQL that would bring up a list of vendors that do not have a transaction, such as follows:

   ```
   SELECT VENDOR_NAME
   FROM APPS. VENDORS
   WHERE PAY_GROUP_LOOKUP_CODE = 'SUPPLIER' AND VENDOR_NAME NOT IN
   (SELECT VENDOR_NAME
   FROM APPS. VENDORS VEND, PO.PO_HEADERS_ALL TRX DISTINCT
   WHERE VEND.VENDOR_ID = TRX. VENDOR_ID);
   ```
5. Give the folder a suitable name.
6. Click the Validate SQL button and keep refining the SQL until it is valid.
7. Close the Administrator edition.
8. Open Plus and create a workbook against this new folder.

If you are comfortable with a custom folder, I recommend this approach because you have control over the SQL, performance will be better, and your users can create this report in Plus.

**QUESTION:** *We have a lot of SQL views that we would like to convert to run as custom folders in Discoverer. Do you know of a method for converting SQL to custom folders?*

**ANSWER:** Here are the basic rules for converting SQL code into code that is suitable for use within Discoverer:

- There should be no hard-coded filters or constraints unless absolutely necessary, such as when constraining for a certain set of books.
- There should be no optional parameters.
- There should be no hard-coded formatting.
- There should be no embedded formatting.
- All columns should use aliases.
- You should replace all parameters that are based on ID columns with meaningful descriptor columns that Discoverer users can build parameters against.
- You should remove all Order By clauses.
- You should remove all subqueries, if at all possible.
- You should check the new code in SQL using a tool such as TOAD before you import it into Discoverer. This will allow you to work on the explain plan to optimize the code. Don't forget that when you test the code, you need to add additional WHERE clauses equivalent to what a Discoverer user would do. Here's an example:

```
AND RAC.CUST_NAME = 'SMITH'
```

**QUESTION:** *We are using Oracle E-Business Suite and would like to know if you have a script that returns the party information.*

**ANSWER:** You should find the following script to be of use:

```
CREATE OR REPLACE VIEW DISCO_PARTIES_V
AS
SELECT
PRT.PARTY_NUMBER  ACCOUNT,
PRT.PARTY_NAME    ACCT_NAME,
PRT.PARTY_TYPE    PARTY_TYPE,
PRT.STATUS        STATUS,
PRT.CATEGORY_CODE CATEGORY_CODE,
LOC.ADDRESS1      ADDRESS1,
LOC.ADDRESS2      ADDRESS2,
LOC.ADDRESS3      ADDRESS3,
LOC.ADDRESS4      ADDRESS4,
LOC.CITY          CITY,
LOC.POSTAL_CODE   POSTAL_CODE,
LOC.STATE         STATE,
LOC.COUNTRY       COUNTRY
FROM
APPS.HZ_PARTIES      PRT,
APPS.HZ_LOCATIONS    LOC,
APPS.HZ_PARTY_SITES  STE
```

```
WHERE 1=1
AND PRT.PARTY_TYPE   = 'ORGANIZATION'
AND STE.PARTY_ID     =  PRT.PARTY_ID        -- Party to Party Sites
AND STE.LOCATION_ID =  LOC.LOCATION_ID      -- Party Sites to Locations
```

**QUESTION:** *We are using Oracle E-Business Suite and would like to know if you have a script that returns the customer site information.*

**ANSWER**: You should find the following script to be of use:

```
CREATE OR REPLACE VIEW DISCO_CUST_SITES_V
AS
SELECT
PARTY.PARTY_NAME                                  CUSTOMER_NAME,
TO_NUMBER(CUST_ACCT.ACCOUNT_NUMBER)               CUSTOMER_NBR,
PARTY_SITE.PARTY_SITE_NUMBER                      SITE_NBR,
CUST_ACCT.CUSTOMER_CLASS_CODE,
CASE WHEN INSTR(SITE.LOCATION,'-') = 0
   THEN SITE.LOCATION
   ELSE SUBSTR(SITE.LOCATION,1,INSTR(SITE.LOCATION,'-')-1)
END                                               SITE_LOCATION,
ACCT_SITE.CUST_ACCT_SITE_ID,
SITE.SITE_USE_ID,
CUST_ACCT.CUST_ACCOUNT_ID,
LOC.LOCATION_ID,
PARTY.PARTY_ID,
SITE.SITE_USE_CODE                                SITE_TYPE,
ACCT_SITE.STATUS                                  SITE_STATUS,
LOC.ADDRESS1,
LOC.ADDRESS2,
LOC.ADDRESS3,
LOC.ADDRESS4,
DECODE (LOC.CITY, NULL, NULL, LOC.CITY || ', ')
  || DECODE (LOC.STATE,
  NULL, LOC.PROVINCE || ', ',
  LOC.STATE || ', ')
  || DECODE (LOC.POSTAL_CODE, NULL, NULL, LOC.POSTAL_CODE || ', ')
  || DECODE (LOC.COUNTRY, NULL, NULL, LOC.COUNTRY) ADDRESS5,
LOC.CITY,
LOC.POSTAL_CODE,
LOC.STATE,
CNTRY.DESCRIPTION                                 COUNTRY,
PARTY_PHONE.RAW_PHONE_NUMBER                      CUSTOMER_PHONE,
SITE_PHONE.RAW_PHONE_NUMBER                       SITE_PHONE,
TRUNC(SYSDATE)                                    DATE_LOADED
FROM
AR.HZ_CUST_ACCT_SITES_ALL ACCT_SITE,
AR.HZ_PARTY_SITES         PARTY_SITE,
AR.HZ_LOCATIONS           LOC,
AR.HZ_CUST_SITE_USES_ALL  SITE,
AR.HZ_PARTIES             PARTY,
AR.HZ_CUST_ACCOUNTS       CUST_ACCT,
```

```
AR.HZ_CONTACT_POINTS       SITE_PHONE,
AR.HZ_CONTACT_POINTS       PARTY_PHONE,
APPLSYS.FND_LOOKUP_VALUES CNTRY
WHERE 1=1
AND SITE.CUST_ACCT_SITE_ID = ACCT_SITE.CUST_ACCT_SITE_ID
AND ACCT_SITE.PARTY_SITE_ID = PARTY_SITE.PARTY_SITE_ID
AND PARTY_SITE.LOCATION_ID = LOC.LOCATION_ID
AND PARTY_PHONE.CONTACT_POINT_TYPE(+)  = 'PHONE'
AND PARTY_PHONE.OWNER_TABLE_NAME(+)  = 'HZ_PARTIES'
AND PARTY_PHONE.PRIMARY_FLAG(+)  = 'Y'
AND PARTY_PHONE.OWNER_TABLE_ID(+)  = PARTY.PARTY_ID
AND SITE_PHONE.CONTACT_POINT_TYPE(+)  = 'PHONE'
AND SITE_PHONE.OWNER_TABLE_NAME(+)  = 'HZ_PARTY_SITES'
AND SITE_PHONE.PRIMARY_FLAG(+)  = 'Y'
AND SITE_PHONE.OWNER_TABLE_ID(+)  = SITE.SITE_USE_ID
AND ACCT_SITE.CUST_ACCOUNT_ID = CUST_ACCT.CUST_ACCOUNT_ID
AND CUST_ACCT.PARTY_ID = PARTY.PARTY_ID
AND SITE.ORG_ID = ACCT_SITE.ORG_ID
AND CUST_ACCT.CUST_ACCOUNT_ID + 0  = CUST_ACCT.CUST_ACCOUNT_ID
AND CNTRY.LOOKUP_TYPE = 'SG_COUNTRY_CODE'
AND CNTRY.LOOKUP_CODE = LOC.COUNTRY;
```

**QUESTION:** *We have both the 11g and 4i versions of Discoverer. When I save a workbook to the database in 4i, I am unable to see the workbook in 11g. Am I doing something wrong?*

**ANSWER:** You are not doing anything wrong. The problem is that the 4*i* workbooks are stored in a table called EUL4_DOCUMENTS, whereas the 11*g* workbooks are stored in a table called EUL5_DOCUMENTS. The 11*g* version of Discoverer does not have access to the EUL4 tables, and conversely the 4*i* version does not have access to the EUL5 tables used by 11*g*.

The reason for the difference is that the two End User Layers are different. They have different data structures and operate using different algorithms.

If you want to know which version of the EUL you are connected to, when you are logged in to Discoverer, use Help |About from the menu bar. The 11*g* screen looks like this.

| Doc Owner | Doc Name |
|---|---|
| ADMIN0 | Analytic 15% of Base |
| ADMIN0 | Analytic Base |
| ADMIN0 | Analytic Base Sorted |
| ADMIN0 | Analytic Base with 3 Month Moving Average |
| ADMIN0 | Analytic Base with 3 Month Moving Average and Prior Values |
| ADMIN0 | Analytic Base with Prior Year |
| ADMIN0 | Analytic Base with Running Total |
| ADMIN0 | Analytic Base with Running Total |
| ADMIN0 | Analytic Base with Running Total and top bottom N |

**QUESTION:** *Our working week always ends on a Friday. Can you tell me the code to use inside a Discoverer calculation that will return the date for Friday?*

**ANSWER:** When the end of the week is a Friday, use this code to get the date:

```
TRUNC(SYSDATE, 'ww')+6
```

Here are some more algorithms you may find useful:

- **Yesterday** TRUNC(SYSDATE)-1
- **Beginning of the current month** TRUNC (SYSDATE, 'mm')
- **Beginning of the previous month** ADD_MONTHS(TRUNC (SYSDATE, 'mm'),–1)
- **Monday of the current week** TRUNC (SYSDATE, 'ww')+2
- **Beginning of the current quarter** TRUNC (SYSDATE, 'Q')
- **Beginning of the previous quarter** TRUNC(TRUNC(SYSDATE,'Q')-1,'Q')
- **Beginning of second month in previous quarter** ADD_MONTHS(TRUNC(TRUNC(SYSDATE,'Q')-1,'Q'),1
- **End of the current month** LAST_DAY(TRUNC(SYSDATE, 'mm'))
- **Beginning of last week** TRUNC (SYSDATE, 'ww')–5
- **Beginning of quarter 1** TO_DATE('1/1/'|| TO_CHAR (SYSDATE, 'yy'), 'mm/dd/rr')
- **End of last year's quarter 1** TO_DATE ('3/31/'||TO_CHAR(SYSDATE -365, 'yy'), 'mm/dd/rr')

Extending this example, why not create a function that allows a user to key a token, returning one of the preceding values. For instance, look at this function:

```
CREATE OR REPLACE FUNCTION
DISCO_DATE(P_DATE IN VARCHAR2) RETURN DATE IS
THE_RESULTS DATE;
BAD_DATE_SUBMITTED EXCEPTION;
PRAGMA EXCEPTION_INIT(BAD_DATE_SUBMITTED, -20001);
BEGIN
IF UPPER(P_DATE) = 'YESTERDAY' THENTHE_RESULTS := TRUNC(SYSDATE)-1;
ELSIF UPPER(P_DATE) = 'BOM' THENTHE_RESULTS := TRUNC(SYSDATE, 'mm');
ELSIF UPPER(P_DATE) = 'BOW' THENTHE_RESULTS := TRUNC(SYSDATE, 'ww')+2;
ELSIF UPPER(P_DATE) = 'BOQ' THENTHE_RESULTS := TRUNC(SYSDATE, 'Q');
END IF;
RETURN THE_RESULTS;
EXCEPTION
WHEN OTHERS THEN
   RAISE_APPLICATION_ERROR(-20001,'Use dd/mm/yy, dd-mm-yy or dd-mon-yy
   or yesterday, '|| 'bow, bom, boq', FALSE);
END;
```

If you execute this function as follows:

```
SELECT DISCO_DATE('BOM') FROM DUAL
```

the function will return the date corresponding to the beginning of the current month.

The next step would be to import this function into Discoverer and make it available to your end users inside a condition.

**QUESTION:** *We are using Oracle E-Business Suite and want to know if you have a script that would let us interrogate the flexfields in use for a table?*

**ANSWER:** Oracle E-Business Suite stores information about flexfields in a table called FND_DESCR_FLEX_COLUMN_USAGES. The table is owned by the APPLYSYS user.

You should find the following script to be of use:

```
SELECT
APP.APPLICATION_ID,
APP.APPLICATION_NAME,
USAGES.LAST_UPDATE_DATE,
USAGES.DESCRIPTIVE_FLEXFIELD_NAME,
USAGES.APPLICATION_COLUMN_NAME,
USAGES.END_USER_COLUMN_NAME,
USAGES.COLUMN_SEQ_NUM,
USAGES.ENABLED_FLAG,
USAGES.REQUIRED_FLAG,
USAGES.DISPLAY_SIZE,
USAGES.FLEX_VALUE_SET_ID,
USAGES.DEFAULT_TYPE,
USAGES.DEFAULT_VALUE,
FLEXSETS.VALIDATION_TYPE,
FLEXSETS.UPPERCASE_ONLY_FLAG
FROM
APPLSYS.FND_DESCR_FLEX_COLUMN_USAGES USAGES,
APPLSYS.FND_FLEX_VALUE_SETS FLEXSETS,
APPLSYS.FND_APPLICATION_TL APP
WHERE 1=1
AND FLEXSETS.FLEX_VALUE_SET_ID(+) = USAGES.FLEX_VALUE_SET_ID
AND USAGES.APPLICATION_ID = APP.APPLICATION_ID
AND USAGES.DESCRIPTIVE_FLEXFIELD_NAME NOT LIKE '$%'
AND USAGES.APPLICATION_COLUMN_NAME LIKE 'ATTRIBUTE%'
AND USAGES.DESCRIPTIVE_FLEXFIELD_NAME = 'MTL_SYSTEM_ITEMS'
ORDER BY DESCRIPTIVE_FLEXFIELD_NAME, APPLICATION_COLUMN_NAME;
```

Let's look closer at this script. First, take a look at the WHERE clause and, in particular, these lines of code:

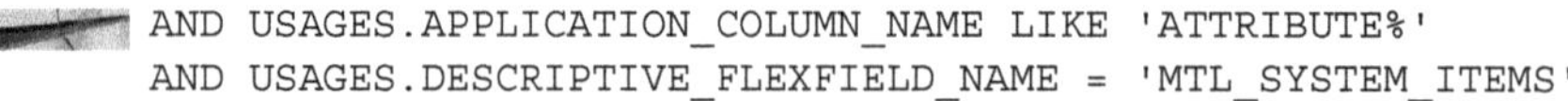

```
AND USAGES.APPLICATION_COLUMN_NAME LIKE 'ATTRIBUTE%'
AND USAGES.DESCRIPTIVE_FLEXFIELD_NAME = 'MTL_SYSTEM_ITEMS'
```

Filtering the APPLICATION_COLUMN_NAME to be like ATTRIBUTE% tells the system to return information only about the ATTRIBUTE fields.

Filtering the DESCRIPTIVE_FLEXFIELD_NAME to MTL_SYSTEM_ITEMS tells the system to return information about the Item Master.

I will explain some of the columns for you:

- **APPLICATION_ID** This is the ID of the E-Business Suite application.
- **APPLICATION_NAME** This is the name of the application.
- **DESCRIPTIVE_FLEXFIELD_NAME** This is the name of the table being controlled
- **APPLICATION_COLUMN_NAME** This is the name of the ATTRIBUTE column. Most Oracle E-Business Suite tables have 15 flexfield attributes, named from ATTRIBUTE1 to ATTRIBUTE15.
- **END_USER_COLUMN_NAME** This is the name by which the end user knows the flexfield. This will be displayed onscreen.

- **ENABLED_FLAG** This is a YN value that indicates whether the flexfield is in use.
- **REQUIRED_FLAG** This is a YN field that indicates whether the flexfield is mandatory.
- **DISPLAY_SIZE** This is the maximum length, in bytes, of the flexfield.
- **UPPERCASE_ONLY_FLAG** This is a YN flag that indicates whether the flexfield content should be stored in uppercase.

To find a listing of all the tables that have flexfields, you can run the following script:

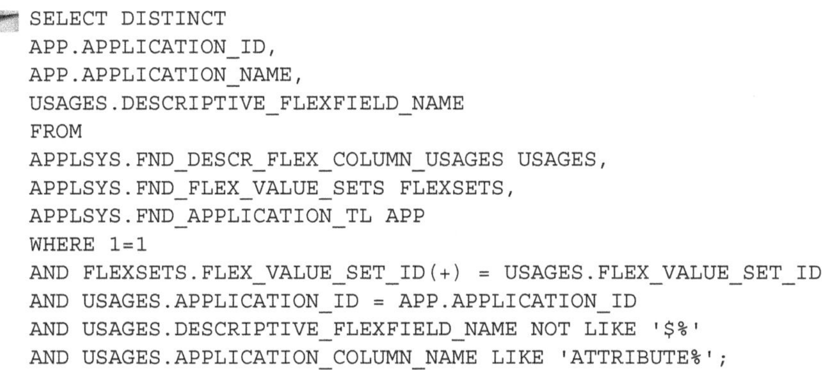

```
SELECT DISTINCT
APP.APPLICATION_ID,
APP.APPLICATION_NAME,
USAGES.DESCRIPTIVE_FLEXFIELD_NAME
FROM
APPLSYS.FND_DESCR_FLEX_COLUMN_USAGES USAGES,
APPLSYS.FND_FLEX_VALUE_SETS FLEXSETS,
APPLSYS.FND_APPLICATION_TL APP
WHERE 1=1
AND FLEXSETS.FLEX_VALUE_SET_ID(+) = USAGES.FLEX_VALUE_SET_ID
AND USAGES.APPLICATION_ID = APP.APPLICATION_ID
AND USAGES.DESCRIPTIVE_FLEXFIELD_NAME NOT LIKE '$%'
AND USAGES.APPLICATION_COLUMN_NAME LIKE 'ATTRIBUTE%';
```

**QUESTION:** *Oracle tells me that Discoverer is not certified for use on a Citrix terminal server. We have no choice but to use a terminal server because that is our organization's policy. Do you have any recommendations for optimizing Discoverer against a terminal server?*

**ANSWER:** Traditional terminal server environments place a single copy of Discoverer Desktop on the server and then allow Citrix to manage the multi-user access. First, you need to make sure you purchase the relevant number of licenses for the number of users who will be accessing Discoverer. Desktop is licensed on a named user basis, not on a concurrent user basis, which means you must own one license for every user who will be using Discoverer.

So, with licensing taken care of, there are (aren't there always) some things to think about when setting up Citrix to work with Discoverer. These are the main ones:

- You need to determine whether you will be using anonymous connections or local connections. I recommend using an anonymous connection for standard users and a local connection for both administrators and users who need to have secure connections to areas such as finance and HR.
- You need to think about whether users will be able to access their local drives and printers from within Citrix or whether you are going to set up and maintain these centrally.
- I recommend the creation of a large, centrally located, shared folder either on the terminal server or on a dedicated server nearby for users to store workbooks and results of workbooks. You should have a predefined storage hierarchy such as a folder for each department or region in your company and make users save into only the designated areas. If you don't do this, you will find that your terminal servers get clogged with user queries and output and you will have no idea who did it.
- You need to discourage users from exporting within Discoverer directly to their desktops. Discoverer does not handle this sort of long-distance exporting very well. I recommend

users save to a file on the central server first and then use Windows Explorer to copy the file to their local drive. Don't forget to tell users to delete the file on the central server to avoid wasting space; otherwise, well, you can guess what will happen next!

- I recommend purging stored workbooks and output after a period of time. You need to determine what period of time is suitable for you, but somewhere in the range of 12 to 18 months should be considered a maximum.
- You need to make sure that when users exit their session, no matter how they do it, their session is disconnected. This will prevent rogue sessions from staying open, consuming memory and terminal server sessions.
- You need to make sure that user sessions are automatically disconnected after a reasonable period of inactivity. Most user sessions can safely be disconnected after 30 minutes, but you may need to increase this timeout to 120 minutes for some power users.

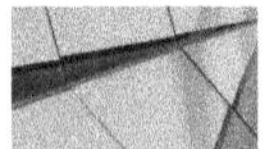

**NOTE**
*Even though Discoverer may be running a query, if a user has done nothing on the terminal server screen for a while, Citrix thinks nothing is going on and will terminate the session. This is why you need to allow power users more time than ad hoc users. Training a user to occasionally visit the terminal server screen and move the mouse is sufficient to make Citrix think that there is some ongoing activity.*

- You need to make sure you clean up your user profiles and temporary files on a weekly basis. You will find that the TEMP folder gets clogged with old sessions and profiles. These should be deleted. Citrix will not let you delete an active session. You will also find hundreds of files ending in .TMP in the Discoverer home folder. These should be removed too.
- Discoverer does not scale well on a Citrix server, and unless you have plenty of processing power and memory available to the users, you will quickly find yourself out of resources. I have seen Citrix handle 16 Discoverer sessions with ease yet max out on CPU with 17 sessions.

**QUESTION:** *Can I upgrade from 4*i *to 11*g *directly, or must I go though some other version first?*

**ANSWER:** I am pleased to tell you that you can upgrade from 4*i* to 11*g* without upgrading via any intermediate release. The upgrade is very straightforward and should be painless. You basically install and launch the 11*g* Administrator edition and connect as the owner of the 4*i* EUL. When you do this, Discoverer will display the following:

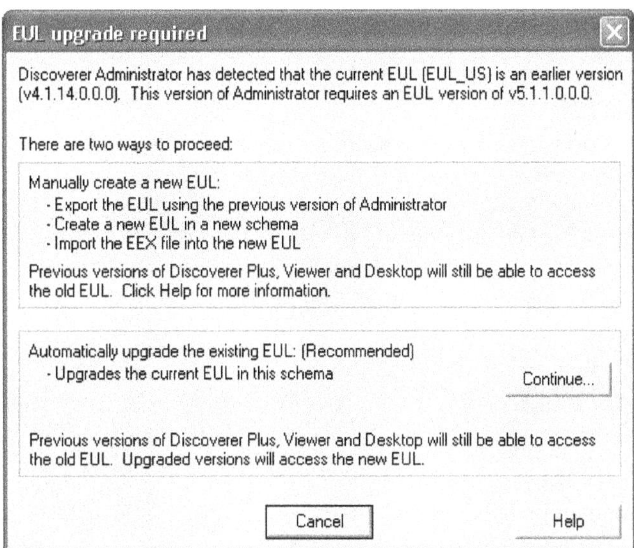

EUL upgrade required
Discoverer Administrator has detected that the current EUL (EUL_US) is an earlier version (v4.1.14.0.0.0). This version of Administrator requires an EUL version of v5.1.1.0.0.0.
There are two ways to proceed:
Manually create a new EUL:
- Export the EUL using the previous version of Administrator
- Create a new EUL in a new schema
- Import the EEX file into the new EUL
Previous versions of Discoverer Plus, Viewer and Desktop will still be able to access the old EUL. Click Help for more information.
Automatically upgrade the existing EUL: (Recommended)
- Upgrades the current EUL in this schema
Continue...
Previous versions of Discoverer Plus, Viewer and Desktop will still be able to access the old EUL. Upgraded versions will access the new EUL.
Cancel
Help


As you can see in this illustration, Discoverer has recognized that there is a 4.1 version of the EUL. The message tells you that you have two ways to continue:

- Manually create a new EUL and then export/import the old one
- Automatically upgrade the existing EUL by clicking Continue

Because the upgrade is easy, we recommend you take the automatic route. When you click Continue, Discoverer displays the following:

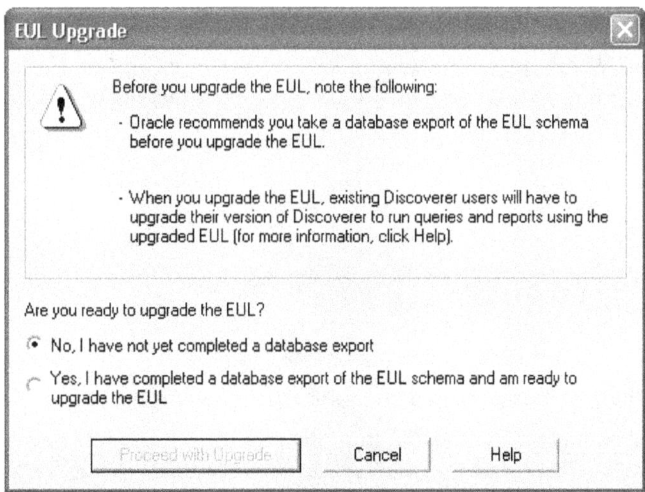

EUL Upgrade
Before you upgrade the EUL, note the following:
- Oracle recommends you take a database export of the EUL schema before you upgrade the EUL.
- When you upgrade the EUL, existing Discoverer users will have to upgrade their version of Discoverer to run queries and reports using the upgraded EUL (for more information, click Help).
Are you ready to upgrade the EUL?
No, I have not yet completed a database export
Yes, I have completed a database export of the EUL schema and am ready to upgrade the EUL
Proceed with Upgrade
Cancel
Help


On this screen you are being advised that you should take a database export of your original EUL schema before starting the upgrade. As you can see, the button called Proceed With Upgrade is grayed out and will continue to be grayed out until you check the radio button confirming that you have completed a database export of your original EUL schema.

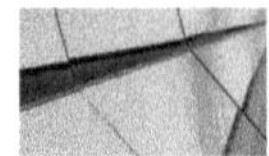

**NOTE**

*Discoverer has no way of knowing whether you have taken a database export. Even though most of the time this upgrade is 100 percent effective, because you are working with a database, any failure to create the upgrade, such as being out of tablespace, will require you to restore the schema to its original state. If you click the Confirm radio button without having taken an export, you proceed at your own risk!*

Having taken the required export, check the Confirm button and then click Proceed With Upgrade.

As the upgrade continues, you will see all of your existing objects being upgraded. Toward the end of the upgrade you will see the message shown here, saying that your workbook dependencies are being transferred.

Not long after this screen has been displayed, the EUL upgrade will finish, and you will be informed that you need to use 11*g* in order to use the new EUL.

At this point you have successfully upgraded your 4.1 EUL to 11*g*. You will now need to install the Discoverer 11*g* end-user versions, Desktop, Plus, and Viewer, before your users can connect.

**NOTE**

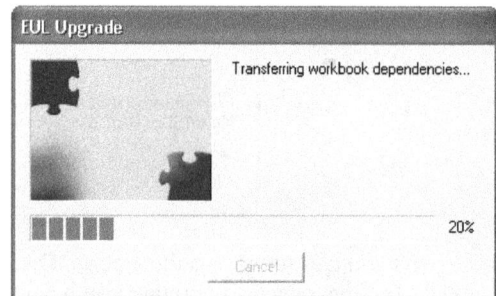

*The upgrade from version 4 to version 11g is nondestructive. This means your original EUL will be unaffected by the upgrade and your users will be able to connect to both versions at the same time. After you have tested your upgrade, you should remove the old version 4 by running the script eul4del.sql in SQL*Plus when connected as the owner of the End User Layer.*

**QUESTION:** *Two of our folders have data items that have a data type of LONG. We would like our users to be able to query these inside Discoverer reports. Do you know if there is a way to do this?*

**ANSWER:** Yes, this can be done. To make the data in a LONG variable available inside Discoverer, use the following workflow:

1. Launch the Discoverer Administrator tool.
2. Navigate to the business area and folder that contains the item.
3. Right-click the LONG item and from the pop-up menu select Properties.
4. Set Default Width to something like 50.
5. Set Max Char Fetched to the length that you want to see, such as 512.
6. Set Word Wrap to Yes.
7. Close the Item Properties dialog box.

This will allow your users to query the LONG item inside Discoverer. With these settings, Discoverer will wrap the first 512 bytes of the LONG item into a field that is 50 characters wide.

**NOTE**
*Your users must never try to include a LONG item in the same query as the SUM of anything. A SUM causes SQL to add a GROUP BY clause, and you cannot use GROUP BY with a LONG item. Therefore, you must ensure that all data items are brought in using Detail.*

**QUESTION:** *This might seem crazy, but we need to change the name of a business area. Can I change the name even when workbooks and worksheets exist that use the business area? I don't want to mess the system up.*

**ANSWER:** You just change the name of the business area using the properties in the Discoverer Administrator edition. Any workbooks that reference items in folders in the business area will continue to reference these items without any trouble.

**QUESTION:** *When I create a parameter, I want to be able to give the users some form of context-sensitive help that will let them know how to fill in the parameter correctly. Is there a way to do this in Discoverer?*

**ANSWER:** When you are creating the parameter, you should use the Description box as the placeholder for your context-sensitive help. This is a free-form box, and you can type anything you like. Here are some tips that might help:

- In Plus, if you uncheck the Require Users To Enter A Value box, you should tell users that if they leave the parameter blank, they will see all values. This parameter cannot be created in Desktop. However, your Desktop users will be able to run a query that uses an optional parameter.
- In both Desktop and Plus, there is a drop-down button to the right of the Default box. If this button is active, not grayed out, this means that a list of values exists for the parameter. You should let your users know that a list of values exists and advise them to select from the drop-down.
- If you are aware that the value you are expecting from the user must be in any special form of casing, use the Description box to tell the users. For example, if the values in your status are all in uppercase, you should tell the users this.

**NOTE**
*If uppercase input is required, you might be better advised to alter the condition that is associated with the parameter to automatically uppercase the value returned from the keyboard. Supposing that the parameter name is Status, the use of UPPER(:Status) will do this.*

**QUESTION:** *I have seen the term UIX referred to many times in conjunction with Discoverer Plus. Can you tell me what this stands for?*

**ANSWER:** User Interface XML (UIX) is a set of Oracle technologies that constitute a framework for building web applications. The main focus of this UIX is the user interface layer of an application. There is also some added functionality that manages events and manages the state of the application flow.

In both 10*g* and 11*g*the Oracle Discoverer Portlets and Discoverer Viewer pages are rendered using UIX rather than XSL, as was the case in prior versions. Therefore, if you want to make changes to the look and feel or layout, over and above what is possible with the Application Server Control, you now have the ability to change the appropriate UIX files—that is, if you feel confident about making such changes.

For more information concerning UIX, please take a look at the Oracle 11*g* XML Developer's Kits Guide, which you can find on OTN. The Oracle XML Developer Kit itself is a component of the application server.

The UIX files are all located here:

```
$MIDDLEWARE_HOME/user_projects/domains/ClassicDomain/servers/WLS_DISCO/tmp/_
WL_user/discoverer_11.1.1.2.0/<tmpfolder>/war
```

**NOTE**

*Before you start modifying these files, I cannot overly stress the importance of backing up the original files to a safe location before you start. The motto "better safe than sorry" has added significance here because you could easily stop your user interface from working if you make changes to a UIX file that you should not have changed.*

**QUESTION:** *I have created a crosstab, and I created a calculation to take one of my data items and split it into two so that both values appear side by side, rather than use a grand total at the right. When I try to do this, I get an ORA-00979, not a GROUP BY expression. Can you help?*

**ANSWER:** This is caused when you create a calculation wrong and you do not aggregate at the right level. Let me explain using my own database. I have created the following query:

| | | | Order Qty SUM | | |
|---|---|---|---|---|---|
| | | Channel | EXTERNAL | INTERNET | Sum |
| Status | Size | | | | |
| CANCELLED | MINI | | 91,762 | 134,359 | 226,121 |
| | SMALL | | 71,151 | 156,706 | 227,857 |
| | MEDIUM | | 279,912 | 371,960 | 651,872 |
| | LARGE | | 221,513 | 259,070 | 480,583 |
| HOLD | MINI | | NULL | 200 | 200 |
| | SMALL | | 5,500 | 102 | 5,602 |
| | MEDIUM | | 20,132 | 5,143 | 25,275 |
| | LARGE | | 6,543 | 11,940 | 18,483 |
| OPEN | MINI | | 35,788 | 60,540 | 96,328 |
| | SMALL | | 56,655 | 68,462 | 125,117 |
| | MEDIUM | | 245,635 | 378,427 | 624,062 |
| | LARGE | | 211,594 | 143,330 | 354,924 |
| SHIPPED | MINI | | 806,964 | 1,099,803 | 1,906,767 |
| | SMALL | | 887,777 | 1,399,649 | 2,287,426 |
| | MEDIUM | | 2,898,499 | 3,225,603 | 6,124,102 |
| | LARGE | | 2,123,507 | 2,589,045 | 4,712,552 |

As you can see, we have a grand total on the right. However, I think what you are asking for is to be able to see the data displayed like this:

| Status | Size | Order Qty SUM | External | Internet |
|---|---|---|---|---|
| CANCELLED | MINI | 226,121 | 91,762 | 134,359 |
| | SMALL | 227,857 | 71,151 | 156,706 |
| | MEDIUM | 651,872 | 279,912 | 371,960 |
| | LARGE | 480,583 | 221,513 | 259,070 |
| HOLD | MINI | 200 | 0 | 200 |
| | SMALL | 5,602 | 5,500 | 102 |
| | MEDIUM | 25,275 | 20,132 | 5,143 |
| | LARGE | 18,483 | 6,543 | 11,940 |
| OPEN | MINI | 96,328 | 35,788 | 60,540 |
| | SMALL | 125,117 | 56,655 | 68,462 |
| | MEDIUM | 624,062 | 245,635 | 378,427 |
| | LARGE | 354,924 | 211,594 | 143,330 |
| SHIPPED | MINI | 1,906,767 | 806,964 | 1,099,803 |
| | SMALL | 2,287,426 | 887,777 | 1,399,649 |
| | MEDIUM | 6,124,102 | 2,898,499 | 3,225,603 |
| | LARGE | 4,712,552 | 2,123,507 | 2,589,045 |

This illustration shows a significant saving in real estate from the original. However, it is not so easy to create as you might think, not until you know the trick, anyway!

The trick is in the calculations used to define the two new items, External and Internet. I used the following CASE statement, with an outer SUM:

```
SUM(CASE WHEN Channel = 'EXTERNAL'
THEN "Order Qty" ELSE 0 END)
AND
SUM(CASE WHEN Channel = 'INTERNET'
THEN "Order Qty" ELSE 0 END)
```

The GROUP BY error that you are seeing is caused when you create the calculations like this:

```
CASE WHEN Channel = 'EXTERNAL'
THEN "Order Qty SUM" ELSE 0 END)
```

Do you see the difference? Look carefully, and you will see that the aggregation is being done outside of the CASE statement, rather than being an integral part of it. You might think that using a CASE of the Order Qty SUM would be correct, and it would be if it were not for the implied group sort that is being done on the status.

By the way, if I convert this to a table and rename the Order Qty heading to Total, I can create a tabular worksheet that has a row-wise total. Try doing this with standard totals and you will fail miserably because you can create totals only on columns in a table!

| | Status | Size | | Total | External | Internet |
|---|---|---|---|---|---|---|
| 1 | CANCELLED | MINI | | 226,121 | 91,762 | 134,359 |
| 2 | | SMALL | | 227,857 | 71,151 | 156,706 |
| 3 | | MEDIUM | | 651,872 | 279,912 | 371,960 |
| 4 | | LARGE | | 480,583 | 221,513 | 259,070 |
| 5 | HOLD | MINI | | 200 | 0 | 200 |
| 6 | | SMALL | | 5,602 | 5,500 | 102 |
| 7 | | MEDIUM | | 25,275 | 20,132 | 5,143 |
| 8 | | LARGE | | 18,483 | 6,543 | 11,940 |
| 9 | OPEN | MINI | | 96,328 | 35,788 | 60,540 |
| 10 | | SMALL | | 125,117 | 56,655 | 68,462 |
| 11 | | MEDIUM | | 624,062 | 245,635 | 378,427 |
| 12 | | LARGE | | 354,924 | 211,594 | 143,330 |
| 13 | SHIPPED | MINI | | 1,906,767 | 806,964 | 1,099,803 |
| 14 | | SMALL | | 2,287,426 | 887,777 | 1,399,649 |
| 15 | | MEDIUM | | 6,124,102 | 2,898,499 | 3,225,603 |
| 16 | | LARGE | | 4,712,552 | 2,123,507 | 2,589,045 |
| 17 | Sum | | | 17,867,271 | 7,962,932 | 9,904,339 |

**QUESTION:** *Is there any way to filter the records for the last date of the month using Discoverer?*

**ANSWER:** You should create a calculated item using the function LAST_DAY() and then create a condition on this item. Assuming that the dates have already been truncated, the condition should look like this:

```
DATE_ITEM = LAST_DAY(date_item)
```

Otherwise, you will need to use this:

```
TRUNC(date_item) = LAST_DAY(TRUNC(date_item))
```

This will return only rows where the date is the last day of the month.

**QUESTION:** *Can you tell me how I can check which users have been granted the ability to share workbooks?*

**ANSWER:** First let's look at the privileges. You can interrogate the list of valid privileges by running the following query when logged in as the owner of the EUL:

```
SELECT APP_ID,
DECODE (PARAMS.APP_NAME_MN,
2300, ' Desktop / Plus Privilege',
2301, ' Create / Edit Query',
2302, ' Item Drill',
2303, ' Drill Out',
2304, ' Grant Workbook (sharing)',
2305, ' Collect Query Statistics',
2306, ' Administration',
2307, ' Set Privilege',
2308, ' Create / Edit Business Area',
```

```
2309, ' Format Business Area',
2310, ' Create / Edit Summaries',
2311, ' Query Statistics Minimum Cost',
2312, ' Schedule Workbooks',
2313, ' User is never required to schedule workbooks',
2314, ' Save Workbooks to Database',
2315, ' Manage Scheduled Workbooks',
2318, ' Change Password',
2324, ' Create Link',
NULL, NULL,
'Unknown Privilege'
) Description
FROM EUL5_APP_PARAMS PARAMS <Add a new line
of text:> WHERE APP_TYPE = 'PRI';
```

| APP_ID | DESCRIPTION |
|---|---|
| 1000 | Desktop / Plus Privilege |
| 1001 | Create / Edit Query |
| 1002 | Item Drill |
| 1003 | Drill Out |
| 1004 | Grant Workbook (sharing) |
| 1005 | Collect Query Statistics |
| 1006 | Administration |
| 1007 | Set Privilege |
| 1008 | Create / Edit Business Area |
| 1009 | Format Business Area |
| 1010 | Create / Edit Summaries |
| 1012 | Schedule Workbooks |
| 1013 | User is never required to schedule workbooks |
| 1014 | Save Workbooks to Database |
| 1015 | Manage Scheduled Workbooks |
| 1018 | Change Password |
| 1024 | Create Link |

In the results shown here, you can see that the privilege that allows a user to share a workbook has an APP_ID of 1004. We will make use of this shortly.

Now that you know what privileges can be granted, the table that actually holds the granted privileges is called EUL5_ACCESS_PRIVS. This table contains not only information about user grants but also about business area access and workbook sharing.

Running the following simple query will show you what privileges or rights each user has:

```
SELECT * FROM
EUL5_ACCESS_PRIVS;
```

Of particular importance are the following columns:

- **AP_TYPE** is the field that tells you what kind of grant you are looking at. It has three valid values. These are
  - **GP** is the user privilege, and it stands for Grant Privilege.
  - **GD** is the workbook sharing grant, and it stands for Grant Document.
  - **GBA** is the business area sharing grant, and it stands for Grant Business Area.
- **AP_EU_ID** is the user ID of the user to whom the privilege has been granted. This links to the EU_ID in the EUL5_EUL_USERS table, where the EU_USERNAME column will tell you the actual user.
- **GP_APP_ID** is the ID of the privilege itself. This links to the APP_ID in the EUL5_APP_PARAMS table, where the DECODE outlined earlier will tell you the actual privilege. This column is populated only when AP_TYPE = GP.
- **GBA_BA_ID** is the ID of the business area that has been granted. This links to the BA_ID in the EUL5_BAS table, where the BA_NAME column will tell you the actual business area. This column is populated only when AP_TYPE = GBA.
- **GD_DOC_ID** is the ID of the workbook that has been shared. This links to the DOC_ID in the EUL5_DOCUMENTS table, where the DOC_NAME will tell you the actual name of the document. This column is populated only when AP_TYPE = GD.

Now I will answer the original question. To see which users have been granted the ability to share a workbook, you should use the following query:

```
SELECT * FROM
EUL5_ACCESS_PRIVS PRV,
EUL5_EUL_USERS USR
WHERE 1=1
AND PRV.AP_TYPE = 'GP'
AND GP_APP_ID = 1004
AND USR.EU_ID = PRV.AP_EU_ID;
```

**QUESTION:** *I have a Discoverer report that I export to Excel and then run a simple macro. What I want to do is just run this calculation directly in Discoverer. In Excel it looks like this:*

=IF(AND(A>=75,B>=50),"Red",IF(AND(A>=50,B>=20),"Yellow",IF(AND(A>=50,B>=10),"Green", "White")))

*I understand that in Discoverer I will have to use CASE WHEN, but I cannot find anything equivalent to the AND function. Any suggestions would be greatly appreciated.*

**ANSWER:** You can use multiple AND statements in a CASE statement like this:

```
CASE
WHEN A >= 75 AND B >=30 THEN 'Red'
WHEN A >= 50 AND B >=20 THEN 'Yellow'
WHEN A >= 50 AND B >=10 THEN 'Green'
ELSE 'White'
END
```

Please note that you can keep repeating the WHEN clause. It also makes good sense to have an ELSE statement as a catchall at the end, although it is not compulsory. When there are multiple WHEN clauses in use, I refer to this as a WHEN-WHEN solution!

**QUESTION:** *I have read different posts about upgrading from Discoverer 10g to 11g. Can you tell me any general problems that still exist that we should be aware of if we upgrade to 11g?*

**ANSWER:** I do not see any major problems that would stop you from upgrading from 10*g* to 11*g*. The underlying application server changes from OAS to WebLogic, but apart from that you will not see any changes. Certainly Plus and Viewer operate the same way as do Administrator and Desktop. Even the EUL itself is 100 percent compatible between the two.

I recommend using an 11*g* database. The tricky part is installing Discoverer 11*g* and then making sure you have someone who can learn how to manage Discoverer using WebLogic. From an end user perspective, everything will be fine. In fact, in my opinion, Discoverer 11*g* runs much faster than 10*g*, presumably because WebLogic handles the web stuff better than the old OAS.

**QUESTION:** *Do you know where the expressions or calculations that are used to create an item in a folder are stored? I can find the names of the items in the EUL5_Expressions table but not the calculation used to create them.*

**ANSWER:** You are actually looking in the right place because the table EUL5_EXPRESSIONS, or EUL4_EXPRESSIONS if working in 4*i*, contains the calculation. Mind you, at first glance you would never know it.

First, create a filter on this table to show only calculated items. You do this by setting EXP_TYPE = 'CI'. That's *C* for calculated and *I* for item. By the way, the other values are JP for joins, CO for columns, and FIL for admin conditions.

Now that you have done that, look at the column called EXP_FORMULA1. This is the actual calculation. However, it is encrypted, which is why you would not at first glance spot that this is the column containing the calculation.

Taking a closer look at this column, you will see that it contains entries like the following:

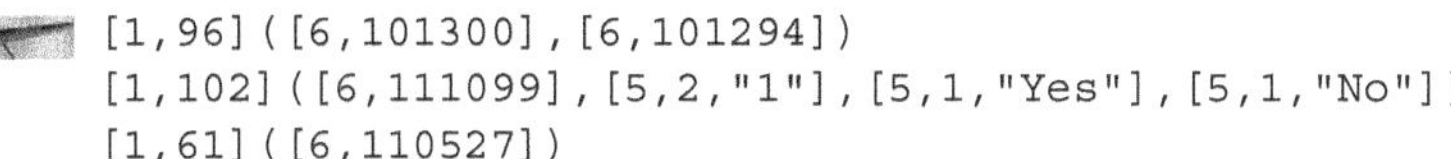

```
[1,96]([6,101300],[6,101294])
[1,102]([6,111099],[5,2,"1"],[5,1,"Yes"],[5,1,"No"])
[1,61]([6,110527])
```

Each set of characters within square brackets is a code, and the important sets are those that begin with 1, 5, or 6. They are

- **1** Functions
- **5** Literal values
- **6** Pointers to other items in the EUL_EXPRESSIONS table

The sets that begin with 1 are functions and take two arguments like [1,96]. In fact, this one is the 96th function in the master list of functions. By the way, the master list of functions can be decoded by looking at the table called EUL5_FUNCTIONS. Search on the column called FUN_ID using the number of the function obtained from the second argument in the set, and then read the column called FUN_NAME. So, for example, when I search FUN_ID using 96, the FUN_ NAME is *, which is the code for multiply. Incidentally, the database functions are in the range 1–99999, while user-defined PL/SQL functions have numbers greater than 99999. The database functions are numbered sequentially, while the user-defined ones come from the master EUL sequence number generator. You will therefore see gaps in the numbers greater than 99999. This is normal; you don't have missing functions.

The sets that begin with 5 have three arguments like [5,1,"Yes"] and [5,2,"1"]. These are literal values. The second argument in the set is the data type, where 1 is a String, 2 is a Number, and 4 is a Date, while the third argument is the actual literal.

The sets that begin with 6 have two values like [6,111099]. These are pointers to other items in the EUL5_EXPRESSIONS table. Use the second number in the EXP_ID column and then read off the EXP_NAME.

So, now that I have given you a lesson on EUL metadata, let me explain what the three earlier examples do.

In the case of [1,96]([6,101300],[6,101294]), because 1 means function and 96 means *, this simply means multiply the item 101300 by the item 101294.

In the case of [1,102]([6,111099],[5,2,"1"],[5,1,"Yes"],[5,1,"No"]), as 1,102 is the decode function, 5,2,"1" means take the numeric literal 1, while 5,1,"Yes" means use the string literal Yes, and 5,1,"No" means use the string literal No. Putting all this together, we get DECODE(item 111099,1,"Yes","No").

This is easy stuff, isn't it?

For [1,61]([6,110527]), because 1,61 is the TO_NUMBER function, this means TO_ NUMBER(the item 110527).

**QUESTION:** *When I look inside the EUL5 tables, I see a column called NOTM. Do you know what this is used for?*

**ANSWER:** This stands for Number of Times Modified.

**QUESTION:** *We have a large number of workbooks and are trying to determine which workbooks use a particular business area. We looked in the EUL5_DOCUMENTS table and thought perhaps we could query the field called DOC_DOCUMENT. Unfortunately, this field is defined as LONG RAW, and we are unable to query from it. Do you know how we can see which workbooks use a particular business area?*

**ANSWER:** You are certainly looking in the right place because the column called DOC_DOCUMENT does indeed contain the inner workings of a workbook. As you have already ascertained, you cannot query this column directly. However, this is a workaround.

First, you need to create a temporary table that converts the LONG RAW column into a LOB. Try the following:

```
CREATE TABLE EUL5_DOCUMENTS_TEMP
AS SELECT
DOC_ID,
DOC_NAME,
DOC_DEVELOPER_KEY,
TO_LOB(DOC_DOCUMENT)  DOC_DOCUMENT
FROM EUL5_DOCUMENTS;
```

With the table created, now it is a simple task to search for all documents containing a certain string. I have a business area called Sales Department, so let's search for it.

```
SELECT DOC_NAME FROM EUL5_DOCUMENTS_TEMP

WHERE DBMS_LOB.INSTR(DOC_DOCUMENT, UTL_RAW.CAST_TO_RAW('Sales Department')) > 0;
```

**QUESTION:** *We are using E-Business Suite and want to know whether you know of a script we can use that will let us check user and responsibility access to business area. The script must tell us the user name or responsibility name and the name of the business area. Can you help?*

**ANSWER:** I certainly can. Take a look at the following script:

```
SELECT
BAS.BA_NAME,
FNDUSRS.USER_NAME USER_OR_RESP_NAME,
'EMPLOYEE'        USER_OR_RESP_TYPE
FROM
EUL_US.EUL5_BAS          BAS,
EUL_US.EUL5_ACCESS_PRIVS PRIVS,
EUL_US.EUL5_EUL_USERS    USRS,
APPLSYS.FND_USER         FNDUSRS
WHERE 1=1
AND PRIVS.GBA_BA_ID = BAS.BA_ID
AND USRS.EU_ID = PRIVS.AP_EU_ID
AND USRS.EU_USERNAME NOT IN ('EUL_US','SYSADMIN')
AND FNDUSRS.USER_NAME NOT IN ('SYSADMIN','REPORT_SCHEDULER')
AND '#' || FNDUSRS.USER_ID = USRS.EU_USERNAME
UNION ALL SELECT
BAS.BA_NAME,
RESP.RESPONSIBILITY_KEY USER_RESP_NAME,
'RESPONSIBILITY'        USER_RESP_TYPE
FROM
EUL_US.EUL5_BAS BAS,
EUL_US.EUL5_ACCESS_PRIVS   PRIVS,
```

```
EUL_US.EUL5_EUL_USERS      USRS,
APPLSYS.FND_RESPONSIBILITY RESP
WHERE 1=1
AND PRIVS.GBA_BA_ID = BAS.BA_ID
AND USRS.EU_ID = PRIVS.AP_EU_ID
AND USRS.EU_USERNAME NOT IN ('EUL_US','SYSADMIN')
AND INSTR(USRS.EU_USERNAME,'#',1,2) > 1
AND APPLICATION_ID = SUBSTR(USRS.EU_USERNAME,INSTR(USRS.EU_USER-
NAME,'#',1,2)+1)
AND RESPONSIBILITY_ID = SUBSTR(USRS.EU_USERNAME,INSTR(USRS.EU_
USERNAME,'#',1,1)+1,INSTR(USRS.EU_USERNAME,'#',1,2)-2)
ORDER BY 1,2;
```

**QUESTION:** *When I create a simple Discoverer worksheet, the default behavior includes the drill icon as part of the column heading. My users can click that drill icon and then "drill to related" items. Is there a way to stop this, in other words, disable or remove the drill icon?*

**ANSWER:** That setting is controlled in the Administrator edition on the Privileges page. Use the following workflow to turn off that privilege:

1. Launch Discoverer Administrator.
2. From the menu bar, select Tools | Privileges.
3. Select the user you want to work with.
4. On the Privileges tab, uncheck Item Drill.
5. Click OK. The drill icon will no longer appear.

If you want to adjust this for all users and you have set up your EUL as a public EUL, you need to edit the privileges for the public role.

**QUESTION:** *We are having a problem with the sessions in Discoverer, and I have a couple of questions. How can I increase the sessions in Discoverer, and how can I prevent this from happening again? Here is the error message we are receiving:*

**Attempt 1. CORBA protocol : Hard limit on number of sessions reached. Please contact your administrator or retry after some time. Hint: An administrator can further diagnose connection problems by running the *check discoverer* script under <ORACLE_HOME>/discoverer/util.**

**ANSWER:** It sounds like a memory issue or that you have a large number of hanging sessions. Stopping and restarting the Discoverer services will probably have little impact because this won't cause the operating system to free up memory. I would reboot the server.

**QUESTION:** *We are running Discoverer Plus. How much memory do you suggest individual PCs should have? We are strictly using Discoverer Plus and Viewer and find the performance to be really slow.*

**ANSWER:** Your question concerning memory on the client is most interesting. Even though Plus and Viewer are web-based applications, the amount of memory available on the client does make a significant difference. I used to say that 512MB was needed, but I have personally come across performance issues at a client whose machines have that amount of memory. My own laptop, which has 8GB of RAM, has no such issues. I will therefore be recommending a minimum of 2GB from now on with an optimum of 4GB. If you can possibly afford it, your new Plus machines should have at least 2GB and be capable of expanding to at least 4GB should the need arise. Of course, if you can get 2GB to begin with, you will have far fewer issues.

**QUESTION:** *We are running Desktop across a T1 line from our branch office to our data center, which is located about 1,000 miles away. Our queries run fine for the selection part of the query but then take what seems like forever to sort. I have a worksheet that takes only ten seconds to select the data, but then takes almost five minutes to complete the sorting. Do you have any idea of what could be wrong?*

**ANSWER:** I do indeed. After connecting to your system and examining the query you refer to, I noticed that the worksheet in question has a large number of complex calculations, using primarily the CASE function. I also noticed that it is using five sorts, three of which are based on these complex calculations. Upon further investigation, I spotted that you are using complex calculated items in your page items.

When you sort using a complex calculation based on a CASE statement every time two data elements are interchanged, their new positions are determined only after the reexecution of the complex functions for both data elements. Even though your final result contains only 400 rows of data, the three sorts based on complex calculated elements are generating thousands and thousands of function comparisons. Therefore, even though you may think your functions are being run once per row, they aren't. In addition, the placement of complex calculated items in the page items is tantamount to running yet more sorts!

Where possible, you should not sort on complex calculated items. If these calculations use complex functions such as CASE and DECODE, I would go further and say that you should never sort by these items. You should also not place these items in your page items. If you really need to use these complex calculations, you ought to consider using a materialized view that precomputes the values in advance. Then you can pull in the data you need and sort it in one go. If you also supply a composite index that matches your conditions, the entire query will execute in no time at all.

I took the liberty of altering your worksheet by removing the page items and as many complex calculations as I could from the sorts. I was able to get the report to run in about 30 seconds. You need to edit your remaining workbooks and do likewise.

**QUESTION:** *I heard that I should disable automatic updates for the Sun Java plug-in. Is this true, and how do I do it?*

**ANSWER:** Yes, this is true. By default, the Sun JRE comes with an automatic update feature that will periodically update the JRE as newer versions become available. This update should be disabled to prevent future problems with Discoverer Plus. To disable the Sun JRE automatic updates, use the following workflow:

1. From the Windows Start menu, select Settings | Control Panel.
2. Click the icon for the Java™ Control Page. It is usually named Java.
3. When the Java Control Panel opens, click the Update tab.
4. Uncheck the Check For Updates Automatically box.
5. Click OK to save and exit.

**NOTE**
*Java 64-bit versions do not ship with an Update tab in the Java Control Panel. For 64-bit versions, you will have to manually disable the jusched.exe job by running msconfig.*

**QUESTION:** *My organization has a very strict policy when it comes to installing software on my PC. For example, I am not allowed to be a local administrator on my machine. When I launch the connection to Plus, it tries to install the Sun JRE, but because I do not have administrative rights, the install fails. Is there a way for my IT department to install the Sun JRE software independently?*

**ANSWER:** Yes, your IT department can install the Sun JRE in advance by following this workflow:

1. Download the latest Sun JRE software from the Sun web site. It can be found at http://java.com/en/download/index.jsp. If you need Java 1.6, it can found at http://java.com/en/download/faq/java_6.xml.
2. On this page, click the Free Java Download button.
3. Look for the 32-bit/64-bit for Windows entry.
4. Alongside this entry are two download links, one for JRE and one for SDK. Click the download link under the heading JRE.
5. On the next page, you will need to read and accept the license agreement.
6. After checking the box Accept License Agreement, download the software labeled Windows Offline Installation, Multi-Language. This file is about 15MB in size.
7. Your IT staff should now connect to your machine as a local administrator and install the software. The application server will recognize that the software has already been installed and will not try to install it again, thus allowing Plus to run.

**NOTE**
*The file that is downloaded is an executable.*

**QUESTION:** *I have created two worksheets, and they are located in different workbooks. One of the worksheets uses a parameter that allows multiple values. However, when I created a hyper-drill from the other worksheet and tried to pass two parameters, the commas were removed, and the destination workbook reported that no data could be found. Are you aware of this, and is there a workaround?*

**ANSWER:** Yes, I am aware of this, and it is very inconvenient. As things stand right now, if I pass two parameters, as 1,2, across a hyper-drill, the parameter in the destination worksheet receives this as 12. For the time being, you will have to make sure you pass single parameters across hyper-drills.

A workaround is to create multiple parameter entries in the destination worksheet and pass a single parameter value to each parameter in turn from the calling worksheet. I recommend you not get carried away, though, and suggest you limit the number of such parameters to three. In the destination worksheet, you will need to allow for the passing of one, two, or three parameter values by creating an appropriate complex Boolean condition.

**NOTE**
*Boolean complex conditions are explained in detail in Chapter 12.*

**QUESTION:** *I am a big user of Discoverer Plus, and I am wondering if there is a way to disable the <All> from displaying as the last item in the page items in a tabular report? I seem to remember that a previous version of Discoverer did not do this.*

**ANSWER:** You are correct in your understanding that earlier versions of Discoverer did not add <All> to the dynamic list of values in page items for a table. You will be delighted to hear that if you follow this workflow, you will be able to suppress this:

1. Edit the pref.txt file located on your mid-tier at one of these locations:
   - Discoverer 10*g*: $ORACLE_HOME/Discoverer/Util
   - Discoverer 11*g*: $ORACLE_HOME/Discoverer/config
2. Locate the section called Database.
3. Locate the property called EnhancedAggregationStrategy.
4. Set this to 0.
5. Save the pref.txt and apply the preferences.
6. Launch Plus and run the tabular worksheet that contains the page items you want to suppress.
7. From the menu bar, select Edit | Worksheet Properties.
8. Click the Aggregation tab.
9. Uncheck the recommended behavior and check either Show Values That Cannot Be Aggregated As or Show The Sum Of The Values In The Contributing Cells.
10. Look at the drop-down list of values alongside your page items. You should notice that the <All> value no longer displays.

**NOTE**
*This works only in a tabular report and only in Plus. However, because this setting is stored with the worksheet, you can apply these on an individual worksheet basis.*

**QUESTION:** *I have some calculations in my worksheet that result in integers. When I have a zero value in these calculations, they display as 00 instead of 0. Do you know why?*

**ANSWER:** Yes, this is caused by your default format, which is probably set to something like 99999990. You need to change this so that there is no zero at the end of the format mask. To correct this, use the following workflow:

1. Right-click in the column that is displaying as 00.
2. From the pop-up list select Format Data.
3. Click the Number tab.
4. Select Custom and from the list select 99999999.
5. Save this setting, and your zero values will display correctly.

**NOTE**
*If this is happening on data items that are pulled directly in from the EUL, your administrator has assigned the wrong default format for that item. Please bring this to their attention and ask them to remove the zero from the end of the format mask.*

**QUESTION:** *When I customize a report in Portal and customize the same report in Viewer, it seems as though I can customize different things. Do you have a list of the things that can be customized from within the two environments?*

**ANSWER:** I do indeed. I am glad you asked because this is a common area of confusion to users of all levels.

As you know, you can customize a Discoverer portlet within Portal. You can format data cells in a table or crosstab, add stoplight formats on cells or items, and even change the display formatting of numbers. For graphs you can choose to change the graph type (change a pie graph to a dual-y bar graph, for example), add or remove 3-D effects, or even add or remove gradients. You can also choose to display the worksheet as a table or crosstab, or graph, or both. You can make all of these changes without having to leave Portal.

This is very similar to the customizations you can do with Discoverer worksheets in Portal. If the portlet has the Analyze link enabled, you can launch the worksheet in Viewer. In there, you can make changes such as drilling, pivoting, slicing, and so on. Just as within Portal, you can also apply stoplight or conditional formats in Viewer, format the data, change the graph types, and so on, and then save these back to Portal as your own customizations.

**QUESTION:** *I am using E-Business Suite and have installed a EUL owned by the user EUL5_US. I am having trouble seeing the Applications check box so that I can access my EUL as SYSADMIN. I am using secure mode for the application. Can you give me the steps for getting access to Discoverer Administrator?*

**ANSWER:** This is an area that troubles many administrators, and I hope the following will help. First you have to enable Discoverer Administrator in Apps mode; it does not do it automatically. To do that, follow this workflow:

1. Connect to Discoverer Admin as EUL5_US.
2. In step 1 of the Load Wizard, click the Cancel button.
3. From the menu bar select Tools | Options and navigate to the Connection tab.
4. Check the button Connect To Both Standard And Application EULs.
5. In the box Gateway User, enter **applsyspub/pub**.
6. In the box Foundation Name, enter **apps**.
7. Click the OK button.
8. From the menu bar select File | Connect.

This time you should see the Oracle Applications User check box.

On your machine you need to also have the DBC file and tnsnames files. Here's how to enable the DBC security:

1. Create a folder under c:\oracle called Secure so that you could have c:\oracle\secure.
2. Obtain the DBC from your database administrator and then place the file in the folder you just created.
3. Launch Control Panel.
4. Select System | Advanced System Settings; this opens the System Properties box.
5. Click the Environment Variables button; this opens the Environment Variables box.

6. In the bottom half of the screen, labeled System variables, click the New button; this opens the New System Variable box.
7. In Variable Name, enter **FND_SECURE**.
8. In Variable Value, enter **c:\oracle\secure**.
9. Click the OK button to close the New Variable box.
10. Click the OK button to close the Environment Variables box.
11. Click the OK button to close the System Properties box.
12. Close Control Panel.

**QUESTION:** *I am using Discoverer against a secure E-Business Suite installation in Apps mode and have just tried Discoverer Plus and Viewer, but I am getting "ORA-01017: invalid username/password; logon denied." We are using Linux. Do you have any ideas?*
**ANSWER:** The most likely answer is that the name of your DBC file is formatted in uppercase. Try renaming it using lowercase. By the way, did you know that for Discoverer Plus and Viewer the DBC setting is found inside the OPMN.XML file? The following may help you:

1. Check OPMN.XML and look for the FND_SECURE setting.
2. Make sure you have a valid DBC file in the location pointed at by the FND_SECURE setting.
3. Double-check your tnsnames file and check the name of the connection and the internal connection information; you can compare this to the settings inside the tnsnames file on Discoverer Administrator.
4. Oracle Note 1074326.1 tells you exactly where the DBC file should be located. Section 4 of this note discusses configuring Discoverer for E-Business Suite. Based on that note, this is where the file is located in my system: $ORACLE_INSTANCE/config/Discoverer/Discoverer_asinst_1.

**QUESTION:** *Is there a log I can check that will tell me which password has expired? I am trying to launch the Admin Console, and it is reporting a password error.*
**ANSWER:** The most likely log is the WLS_DISCO.out log. You will find the previous log in this folder:

```
$MIDDLEWARE_HOME/user_projects/domains/ClassicDomain/servers/WLS_DISCO/logs
```

Look for any line that says the password has expired. This will tell you exactly which account it is. When you have figured out which account it is, all you need to do is have your DBA reset the password. Within 11g there are a couple of database accounts in the repository whose password could have expired. The account will be either DEV_DISCOVERER or DEV_DISCCOVERER_PS. However, please note that the word *DEV* might be *PROD* in your case.

**QUESTION:** *I have a need to modify the tnsnames.ora location for Discoverer 11g. In Discoverer 10g I could set a TNS_ADMIN environment variable. When I tried this for 11g it did not work. Do you know why?*
**ANSWER:** I do indeed. The TNS_ADMIN variable is still used but in 11g it is defined inside OPMN.XML rather than being picked up from an environment variable. You will find OPMN.XML located in the $ORACLE_INSTANCE under your Middleware home.

So, for example, if your Middleware home is located here:

```
/Middleware/
```

and your $ORACLE_INSTANCE is called asinst_1, the full path to your OPMN.XML will therefore be as follows:

```
/Middleware/asinst_1/config/OPMN/opmn
```

In OPMN.XML you should look for the variable_id called TNS_ADMIN. It will currently be pointing at $ORACLE_INSTANCE/config/. After you have updated the variable to point to the new location, you can execute opmnctl reload to make Discoverer pick up the changes in the OPMN.XML file. Alternatively, you can also use opmnctl stopall followed by opmnctl startall.

**NOTE**
*For more information regarding OPMN.XML and the use of opmnctl, please see the section called "Oracle Process and Notification" in Chapter 19.*

# Summary

Well, there you have it. You asked, and I have answered. I hope you have as much fun reading through these answers as I had in putting them together for you.

# APPENDIX B

# SQL Functions

This appendix contains an alphabetic listing of all the SQL functions available within Discoverer. Each function is listed with its correct syntax, an explanation of its purpose or use, and the Discoverer folder in which you will find the function. For most functions, we will give you examples. We also explain in depth how to use the wildcard characters within Discoverer. If you are looking for more information regarding analytic functions, please see Chapter 21.

We will give you a complete listing of all the format masks that can be applied to functions. Finally, we will give you a listing of the standard American Standard Code for Information Interchange (ASCII) character set.

We were complimented many times on this appendix following the publication of the previous editions. The intention was and still is to provide as comprehensive as possible an overview of the functions that are used within Discoverer. One of the amazing discoveries that we uncovered is that not all functions perform the same way they do in standard SQL. This is because Oracle has tried to remove the possibility of crashes by trapping more error situations than you will find in normal SQL.

We are extremely pleased with the way Oracle has implemented functions in Discoverer. If you know SQL, you will know that it can be very unforgiving—demanding that you get the syntax right. With Discoverer, most of the errors you could make have been allowed for and will not cause your query to crash. Instead, the worst that can happen is that the function returns a null value.

This appendix is not designed to teach you all about SQL functions, only to explain in simple terms what each function does. If you want a complete understanding of Oracle's functions, we recommend you look at *Oracle Database 11g: The Complete Reference*, an Oracle Press book by Kevin Loney (McGraw-Hill/Osborne, 2009).

## Standards Used in the Listing

Within the listing of the functions, we refer to data types. Functions usually operate on one data type at a time, although some may be able to use more. The following are the data types referred to in this appendix:

- **Date** This data type represents a date, a date and time combination, or a data item that can be used like a date in an expression or calculation. Format masks can be applied to dates. A full listing of the date and time format masks can be found later in this appendix. Dates are entered within single quotes, for example 'JUL-21-2014'.
- **Character** This data type consists of a single character. Examples of this data type are 'A', 'b', and '1'. Characters are entered into Discoverer surrounded by single quotes, as shown here, and can be in uppercase or lowercase.
- **Integer** This data type represents whole numbers. These numbers can be positive or negative. Examples of this data type are –5, 0, and 50.
- **Number** This data type represents numbers with decimal places. These numbers can be positive or negative. Examples of this data type are –5.15, 0, and 47.775. Format masks can be applied to numbers. A full listing of the numeric format masks can be found in the section "Number Format Masks" later in this appendix.
- **String** This data type represents combinations of characters and is entered into Discoverer surrounded by single quotes. Strings can use any combination of uppercase and lowercase characters. Examples of strings are 'Hello', 'ZIP 55555', and 'CAP'.

# Wildcards

Many of the Discoverer functions will allow you to enter wildcard characters into strings. The wildcard characters used within Discoverer are as follows:

- % The percent symbol is a wildcard character used to represent any number of characters in a string. It can be used in any position and any number of times within the string.
- _ The underscore character is a wildcard character used to represent a single character in a string. It can be used in any position and any number of times within the string.

## Wildcard Examples

The following examples show how to use both of the wildcards in strings:

- **'AB%'** This would constrain the string to values beginning with the uppercase characters *AB*. Valid examples of this are 'AB' and 'ABRACADABRA'.
- **'_b%'** This would constrain the string to values of any length, but where the second character is lowercase *b*. Valid examples of this are 'Abbey' and 'Ebony'.
- **'%m%'** This would constrain the string to values that contain the lowercase character *m* anywhere within the string. Valid examples of this would be 'mountain' and 'America'.
- **'941%'** When used in a condition against U.S. ZIP codes, this will constrain a worksheet to return data only for customers in San Francisco, California.

**NOTE**
*When using the % wildcard character, there does not need to be any characters in the position indicated by the % character. Hence, in the preceding examples, 'AB' is a valid match for the constraint 'AB%', and 'mountain' is a valid match for '%m%'.*

# Folders in Discoverer

When you open a calculation in Discoverer and click the Functions radio button, Discoverer displays a list of folders. If the Discoverer Administrator has registered custom PL/SQL functions, you will see nine folders, including one called Database. If no custom PL/SQL functions are registered, then you will not see a folder called Database. As you can see in Figure B-1, our system has displayed nine folders.

# Alphabetical Listing of Functions

This section lists all of Discoverer's functions in alphabetical order.

**NOTE**
*For completeness, we have included the syntax and basic description of each analytic function in this appendix. For a more complete description and overview of some of Discoverer's most useful analytic functions, please see Chapter 21.*

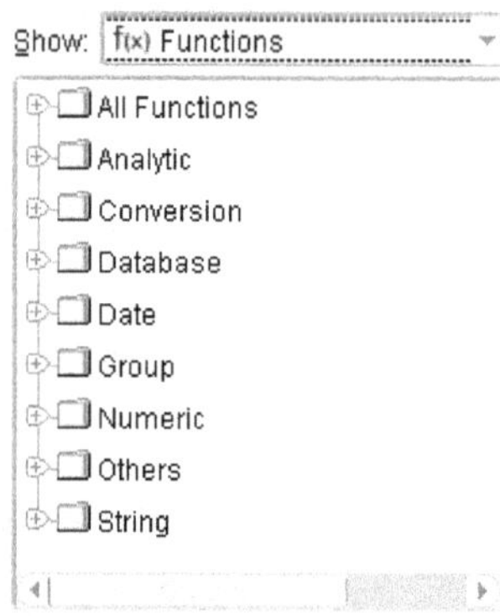


**FIGURE B-1.** *The folders containing functions*

## + (Addition)

**Syntax**: value1 + value2
**Description**: value1 + value2 means add together the two values to produce a new value of the same type. This function can be used with data types of date, integer, and number, and generally you can mix the data types, although you cannot add numbers to dates.
**Folder**: Addition can be found in the Numeric folder, as shown in Figure B-2.
**Examples**:

- **Date** SYSDATE + 1 returns tomorrow's date.
- **Integer** 177 + 192 + 6 returns the answer 375.
- **Number** 10.55 + 8.00 returns the answer 18.55.
- **Mixed** 177 + 10.55 returns the number 187.55.

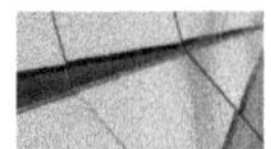

**NOTE**
*Multiple additions can be applied at the same time. In the second example, we added three integers to get the answer we wanted. Generally, you can mix the data types, although you cannot add numbers to dates.*

## – (Subtraction)

**Syntax**: value1 – value2
**Description**: value1 – value2 means subtract the second value from the first value to produce a new value. This function can be used only with data types of date, integer, and number.
**Folder**: Subtraction can be found in the Numeric folder, as shown in Figure B-2.
**Examples**:

- **Date** "5-JUL-2014" – "25-JUN-2014" returns 10.
- **Mixed Date** SYSDATE – 1 returns yesterday's date.

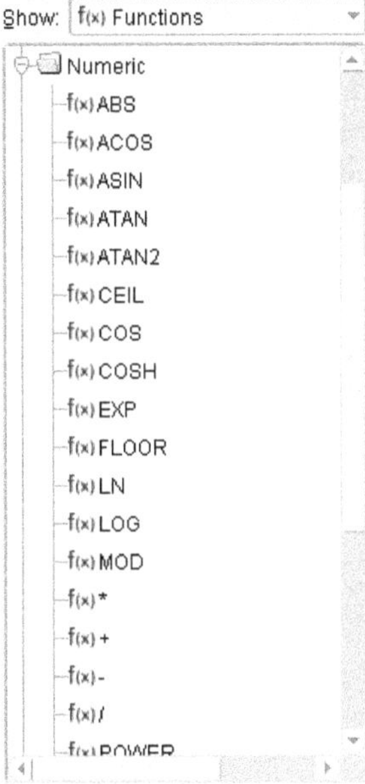


**FIGURE B-2.** *Discoverer's numeric functions*

- **Integer** 200 – 192 – 8 returns the answer 0.
- **Number** 10.55 – 8.00 returns the answer 1.45.
- **Mixed** 200 – 10.55 returns the number 189.45.

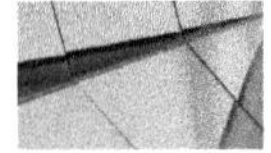

**NOTE**
*Multiple subtractions can be applied at the same time. In the second example, we subtracted three integers to get the answer we wanted. Generally, you can mix the data types, although you cannot subtract numbers from dates.*

# * (Multiplication)

**Syntax**: value1 * value2
**Description**: value1 * value2 means multiply the first value by the second value to produce a new value. This function can be used only with data types of integer and number.
**Folder**: Multiplication can be found in the Numeric folder, as shown in Figure B-2.

## / (Division)

**Syntax**: value1 / value2
**Description**: value1 / value2 means divide the first value by the second value to produce a new value. This function can be used only with data types of integer and number. If either the dividend, which is the number being divided (value1 in the syntax), or the divisor, which is the number being divided into the dividend (value2 in the syntax), is NULL, then the answer will be NULL, even when the divisor is zero. You need to be very careful when using division that you do not finish up dividing by zero; otherwise, Discoverer will return an error. The actual error returned will be ORA-01476: "divisor is equal to zero. "Please see Chapter 13 for tips on how to avoid division-by-zero errors. Discoverer Desktop displays #DIV/0! when it encounters a zero divisor.
**Folder**: Division can be found in the Numeric folder, as shown in Figure B-2.
**Examples**:

- 25 / 5 returns 5.
- NULL / 5 returns NULL.
- 25 / 0 returns error "divisor is equal to zero."
- NULL / 0 returns NULL.

## || (Concatenation)

**Syntax**: value1 || value2
**Description**: value1 || value2 means append or concatenate the character or string with the value of value2 to the end of the character or string in value1. The result is always a string. Concatenating NULL with any string leaves the string unchanged. Concatenating NULL with itself returns NULL. You can use the empty string, signified by placing the left and right quotes side by side, instead of NULL. This function is identical to the CONCAT function described later.
**Folder**: Concatenation can be found in the String folder, as shown in Figure B-3.
**Examples**:

- **Character** 'A' || 'B' returns the string 'AB'.
- **String** 'Apple' || '' || 'Pie' returns 'Apple Pie'.
- **String** 'Moms' || '' || 'Apple' || '' || 'Pie' returns 'Moms Apple Pie'.
- **String** 'Michael' || NULL returns 'Michael'.
- **String** 'Michael' || '' returns 'Michael'; note the empty string.

**NOTE**
*As you can see in the preceding example, you can combine multiple concatenation functions in order to derive more complex strings.*

- SUBSTR(SSN,1,3)||'-'||SUBSTR(SSN,4,2)||'-'||SUBSTR(SSN,6.4) takes a Social Security number (SSN) and converts it into the more typical format used in the United States. For example, if the SSN is 123456789, this example converts this to 123-45-6789.

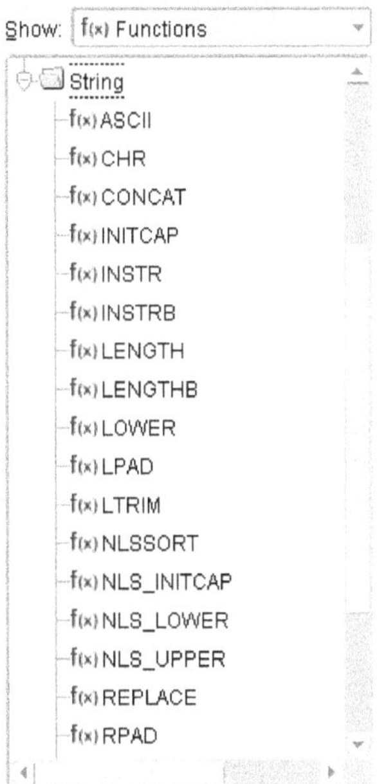


**FIGURE B-3.** *Discoverer's string functions*

- '('||SUBSTR(TEL,1,3)||')'||SUBSTR(TEL,4,3)||'-'||SUBSTR(TEL,7,4) takes a typical ten-digit telephone number and converts it into a more readable format. For example, if the number is 1234567890, this example converts it to (123) 345-7890.

**NOTE**
*The two preceding examples combine multiple concatenation functions with the SUBSTR function.*

# ABS (Absolute Value)

**Syntax**: ABS(value)
**Description**: This function returns the absolute value of the item in parentheses as a positive number, whether the original item is positive or negative. The item must be a number, whether this is a literal number, a string containing only numbers, the name of a column containing a number, or the name of a string column containing only numbers. If the string being evaluated is NULL, the result will be NULL. If the string being evaluated cannot be converted to a number, an error will be generated. You therefore need to be careful when applying the ABS function to a string.
**Folder**: ABS can be found in the Numeric folder, as shown in Figure B-2.

**Examples**:

- ABS(-55) returns the value 55.
- ABS('18') returns the value 18.
- ABS(968.51) returns the value 968.51.
- ABS('') returns NULL.
- ABS('Michael') returns the error "one of the arguments has an incorrect data type."

# ACOS

**Syntax**: ACOS(value)
**Description**: This function returns the arc cosine of a value. The value must be a number between –1 and 1. The function returns a value in the range of 0 to *pi*. The result is expressed in radians.
**Folder**: ACOS can be found in the Numeric folder, as shown in Figure B-2.
**Example**: ACOS(.2) returns 1.37.

# ADD_MONTHS

**Syntax**: ADD_MONTHS(date, integer)
**Description**: This extremely powerful function adds the integer number of months to the date specified, returning a new date that is that number of months in the future or in the past. The date specified must be a valid date. If the date you want to check is not currently a valid date, you must convert it into a valid date first. The second parameter should be an integer. If you provide a negative value, the date returned will be in the past. If you provide a number with decimal places, Discoverer ignores the decimal part. If the date you provide is the null value, then the result will be null.
**Folder**: ADD_MONTHS can be found in the Date folder, as shown in Figure B-4.
**Examples**:

- ADD_MONTHS(SYSDATE, 1) returns the date one month from today.
- ADD_MONTHS(ship date, 2) returns the ship date plus two months.
- ADD_MONTHS(TO_DATE('JULY 21, 2014', 'MONTH DD, YYYY'),2 ) returns the date 21-SEP-2014. This takes the given date as a string, adds two months, and produces a new date. You cannot supply a string directly to ADD_MONTHS, because the date supplied *must* be a valid date in its own right. Hence:
- ADD_MONTHS('JULY 21, 2014',2) returns the error "one of the arguments has an incorrect data type."
- TO_CHAR(ADD_MONTHS(SYSDATE,1),'Month') returns the next month.
- TO_CHAR(ADD_MONTHS(SYSDATE,-1),'Month') returns the previous month.
- ADD_MONTHS(TRUNC(SYSDATE, 'YY'),12)-1 returns the end of the current year.
- ADD_MONTHS(TRUNC(SYSDATE,'Q'),-3) returns the beginning of last quarter.

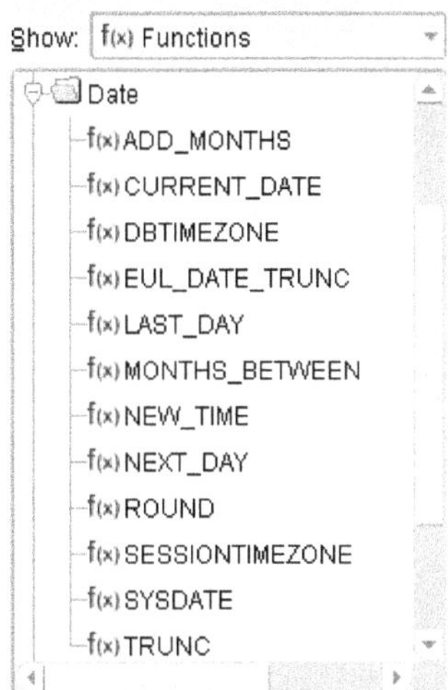


**FIGURE B-4.** *Discoverer's date functions*

# ASCII

**Syntax**: ASCII(string)
**Description**: This function takes a string and returns the American Standard Code for Information Interchange (ASCII) value of the first character. The code is based on a series of numbers from 0 to 254, with 65 representing the character *A*, 66 representing *B*, and so on. The numbers 0 through 9 are represented by the ASCII values 48 through 57. For the table of standard ASCII values, see the "ASCII Character Set" section later in this appendix.

See the function CHR for the opposite function that converts a number to a character.
**Folder**: ASCII can be found in the String folder, as shown in Figure B-3.
**Examples**:

- ASCII('A') returns the value 65.
- ASCII('BANANA') returns the value 66. Only the letter *B* is used in the function.
- ASCII('-15') returns the value 45, because the minus sign is 45 in the ASCII list.

# ASCIISTR

**Syntax**: ASCIISTR(string)
**Description**: You may pass a string from any character set to ASCIISTR, and it will return the string in ASCII. Non-ASCII characters will be converted to the form \xxxx. The xxxx represents a UTF-16 code. For the table of ASCII values, see the "ASCII Character Set" section later in this appendix.
**Folder**: ASCIISTR can be found in the Conversion folder, as shown in Figure B-5.
**Example**: ASCIISTR('ABÄCDE') returns AB\00C4CDE.

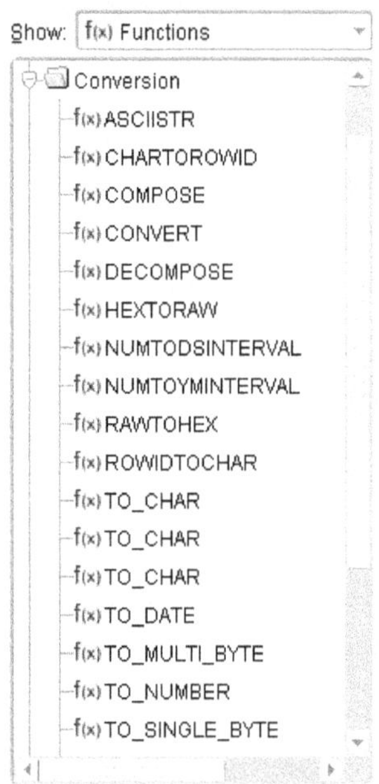


**FIGURE B-5.** *Discoverer's conversion functions*

## ASIN

**Syntax**: ASIN(value)
**Description**: This function returns the arc sin of the value. The value must be a number between –1 and 1. The function returns a value in the range of 0 to *pi*. The result is expressed in radians.
**Folder**: ASIN can be found in the Numeric folder, as shown in Figure B-2.
**Example**: ASIN(.5) returns 0.5236.

## ATAN

**Syntax**: ATAN(x)
**Description**: This function returns the arc tangent of x. The value x can be in an unbounded range and returns a value in the range of –*pi*/2 to *pi*/2. The result is expressed in radians.
**Folder**: ATAN can be found in the Numeric folder, as shown in Figure B-2.
**Example**: ATAN(.4) returns 0.3805.

## ATAN2

**Syntax**: ATAN2(x , y)
**Description**: This function returns the arc tangent of x and y. The value x can be in an unbounded range and returns a value in the range of –*pi* to *pi*. The result depends on the signs of x and y, which are expressed in radians. ATAN2(x,y) is the same as ATAN(n/m).
**Folder**: ATAN2 can be found in the Numeric folder, as shown in Figure B-2.
**Example**: ATAN2(.3, .2) returns 0.9827.

## AVG (Average)

**Syntax**: AVG(value)
**Description**: This function returns the average. The value parameter can be any value, database item, or calculation. Discoverer has this function associated with every datapoint item, so a user using Discoverer Desktop or Discoverer Plus usually does not need to use the AVG function from the New Calculation dialog box. A user creating a new item through Discoverer Administrator or a user interested in using the Analytic features may find AVG quite useful. For details about the analytic clauses, please refer to Chapter 21.
**Folder**: AVG can be found in the Group and Analytic folders, as shown in Figures B-6 and B-7.
**Example**: AVG(Profit SUM) OVER(PARTITION BY Product Name ORDER BY Year) is an analytic function.

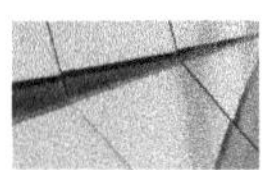

**NOTE**
*Analytic functions are explained in more detail in Chapter 21.*

## AVG_DISTINCT

**Syntax**: AVG_DISTINCT(value)
**Description**: This function returns the distinct average of all the unique items in the list. Please note that null values are ignored by this function, a fact that may affect your results.
**Folder**: AVG_DISTINCT can be found in the Group and Analytic folders, as shown in Figures B-6 and B-7.

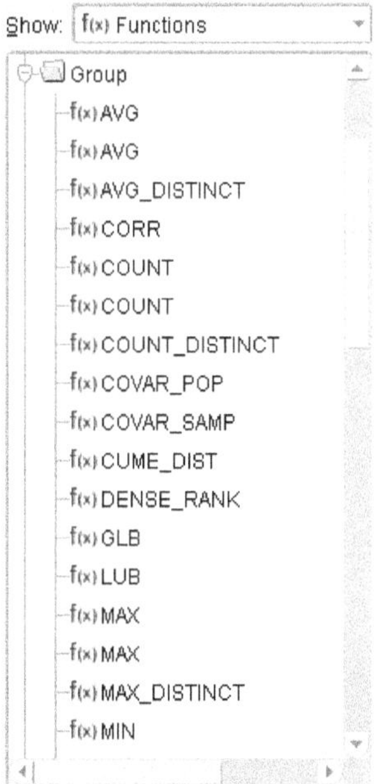


**FIGURE B-6.** *Discoverer's group functions*

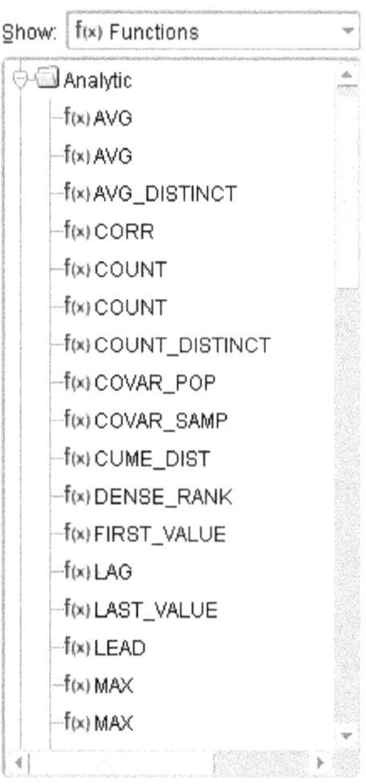


**FIGURE B-7.** *Discoverer's analytic functions*

**Example**:

- In the AVG_DISTINCT(list); function, when the list contains "null, 1, 1, 3, 5, 5, 5, 5, 7, 7, 7", the answer is 4. This is because Discoverer computes the average of the values 1, 3, 5, and 7. If we had used AVG on this same list, the answer would have been 4.6. Which one is correct depends upon your viewpoint and how you want to display the result.

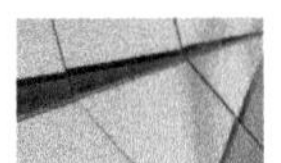

**NOTE**
*Analytic functions are explained in more detail in Chapter 21.*

# CASE

**Syntax**: CASE WHEN x THEN y ELSE z END equates to the following:

IF value = x THEN y ELSE z

**Description**: This expression, like DECODE, is extremely powerful and flexible. After the WHEN clause, you may include any Boolean logic. If the logic after WHEN evaluates to TRUE, the result will be y. If the logic after the WHEN is FALSE, the result will be z. You can also embed CASE statements one within another. If you do this, do not forget that each statement ends with the

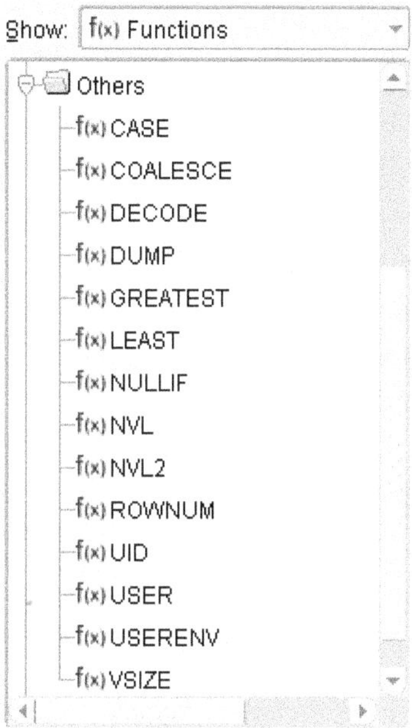


**FIGURE B-8.** *Discoverer's other functions*

word END; otherwise, Discoverer will generate an error. The y and z components must be the same data type.

**Folder**: CASE can be found in the Others folder, as shown in Figure B-8.

**Examples**:

- CASE WHEN 1=2 THEN 'Hello' ELSE 'Goodbye' END returns Goodbye because 1=2 always evaluates to false.
- CASE WHEN ship_date>order_date + 14 THEN 'Delivery Late' ELSE 'Delivery on Time' END returns the phrase *Delivery on Time* if the order was shipped within two weeks of the order date. However, if it took more than two weeks to ship the order, then the phrase *Delivery Late* will be returned.
- CASE WHEN test_value< 0 THEN 'CR' || test_value ELSE test_value END returns a number prefixed by the *CR* characters if the test value is less than zero. This is useful for reports in the banking industry.
- CASE WHEN status = 'SHIPPED' THEN 'Customer has the Goods' ELSE CASE WHEN status = 'CANCELED' THEN 'Customer Canceled' ELSE 'Order is Open' END END returns the string 'Customer has the Goods' if the status of the customer's order is SHIPPED, the string 'Customer Canceled' if the status of the order is CANCELED, or 'Order is Open' in all other cases.

## CEIL

**Syntax**: CEIL(value)
**Description:** This function takes the value given and returns the smallest integer larger than or equal to that value. Refer to FLOOR for the function that returns the highest integer. You cannot use the null value in this function. If you use the null value, the result will be an error.
**Folder**: CEIL can be found in the Number folder, as shown in Figure B-2.
**Examples**:

- CEIL(7) returns the value 7.
- CEIL(–6.75) returns the value –6.
- CEIL(100.55) returns the value 101.

## CHARTOROWID

**Syntax**: CHARTOROWID(string)
**Description:** This function takes a string and makes it act like an internal Oracle row identifier. This function should never be needed for reporting. It apparently is used as a debugging tool yet somehow has made its way into Discoverer.
**Folder**: CHARTOROWID can be found in the Conversion folder, as shown in Figure B-5.

## CHR (Character)

**Syntax**: CHR(integer)
**Description:** This function takes an integer and returns the ASCII character that corresponds to the integer. The code is based on a series of numbers from 0 to 254, with 65 representing the character *A*, 66 representing *B*, and so on. The numbers 0 through 9 are represented by the ASCII values 48 through 57. For the table of ASCII values, see the "ASCII Character Set" section later in this appendix.

See the function ASCII for the opposite function that converts a character into a number.
**Folder**: CHR can be found in the String folder, as shown in Figure B-3.
**Examples**:

- CHR(45) returns the character that is the minus sign.
- CHR(65) returns the character *A*.
- CHR(66) returns the character *B*.

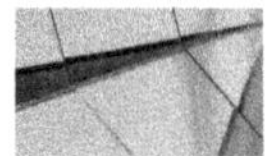

**NOTE**
*Discoverer will convert numbers to ASCII only if the number is less than 128. If you try to use numbers greater than 127, Discoverer returns #NUM!.*

## COALESCE

**Syntax**: COALESCE(value1, value2, value3)
**Description**: This function takes a list of values, scans the list, and then returns the first non-null value in the list. The list is scanned in the order in which you supply the values.

**Folder**: COALESCE can be found in the Others folder, as shown in Figure B-8.
**Examples**:

- COALESCE(NULL, NULL, NULL, NULL, 4004, NULL, NULL) returns 4004.
- COALESCE(manufacturers_suggested_retail_price, wholesale_price * 2, 3000) returns 3000 if both the manufacturer's suggested retail price and the wholesale price are null; otherwise, it returns whichever non-null price is found first.

## CONCAT

**Syntax**: CONCAT(value1, value2)
**Description**: CONCAT(value1, value2) means append or concatenate the character or string with the value of value2 to the end of the character or string in value1. The result is always a string. Concatenating NULL with any string leaves the string unchanged. Concatenating NULL with itself returns NULL. You can use the empty string, signified by placing the left and right quotes side by side, instead of NULL. This function is identical to the || function described earlier, except that when you want to concatenate multiple items, you must use multiple sets of parentheses.
**Folder**: CONCAT can be found in the String folder, as shown in Figure B-3.
**Examples**:

- **Character** CONCAT('A', 'B') returns the string 'AB'.
- **String** CONCAT('Apple', 'Pie') returns 'Apple Pie'.
- **String** CONCAT('Apple', CONCAT('Pie ', CONCAT('is ', 'excellent'))) is an example of using multiple CONCAT statements. This returns the single string 'Apple Pie is excellent'.
- **String** CONCAT ('Michael', NULL) returns 'Michael'.
- **String** CONCAT ('Michael', '') returns 'Michael'; note the empty string.

## CONVERT

**Syntax**: CONVERT(string, destination_set [, source_set ] ] )
**Description**: This function takes a string and converts all the characters from one standard bit representation, or set, to another set. You would normally do this when the characters cannot be properly displayed on your screen or printed. To find out what character set is currently in use on your system, use the USERENV function.
**Folder**: CONVERT can be found in the Conversion folder, as shown in Figure B-5.
**Examples**:

- **F7DEX** Digital's 7-bit ASCII for France
- **US7ASCII** The standard 7-bit ASCII set
- **WE8DEC** Digital's 8-bit ASCII set for Western Europe
- **WE8HP** Hewlett Packard's 8-bit ASCII set for Western Europe
- **WE8ISO8859P1** International Standards Organization's 8859-1 8-bit character set for Western Europe..

## CORR (Correlation)

**Syntax**: CORR(value1, value2)
**Description**: This statistical function returns the coefficient of correlation of value1 and value2. It is known as Pearson's Product Moment (PPM) correlation coefficient, r. Simply, the sample correlation coefficient is a measure of extent to which two values are linearly related. Pearson's r-values can range between –1.00 to +1.00. A correlation coefficient of +1.00 signifies a perfect positive relationship, while –1.00 shows a perfect negative relationship. The smallest correlation is zero.

Smallest correlation also means no correlation; therefore, a correlation of zero signifies that there is no correlation between the two values.
**Folder**: CORR can be found in the Group and Analytic folders, as shown in Figures B-6 and B-7.
**Examples**:

- CORR(list_price, min_price) calculates the coefficient of correlation between the list price and the minimum price.
- CORR (SUM(ship_price), SUM(quantity_shipped)) OVER (ORDER BY ship_month) calculates the cumulative coefficient of monthly sales revenue and monthly units sold.

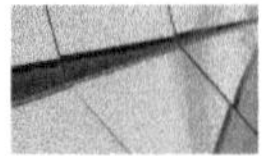

**NOTE**
*Analytic functions are explained in more detail in Chapter 21.*

## COS (Cosine)

**Syntax**: COS(value)
**Description**: This function takes the value given and returns the trigonometric cosine of that value. The function returns an angle expressed in radians.
**Folder**: COS can be found in the Numeric folder, as shown in Figure B-2.
**Examples**:

- COS(–60) returns the value 0.5.
- COS(0) returns the value 1.0.
- COS(180) returns the value –1.0.

## COSH (Hyperbolic Cosine)

**Syntax**: COSH(value)
**Description**: This function returns the hyperbolic cosine of the given value. The function returns an angle expressed in radians.

If you are mathematically oriented, the hyperbolic cosine is defined as $\cosh(x) = (e^x + e^{-x})/2$.
**Folder**: COSH can be found in the Numeric folder, as shown in Figure B-2.
**Examples**:

- COSH(0) returns the value 1.0.
- COSH(0.3) returns the value 1.04534.
- COSH(0.9) returns the value 1.43309.

# COUNT

**Syntax**: COUNT(expression)
**Description**: This function returns a count of the number of non-null items in the given expression.
**Folder**: COUNT can be found in the Group and Analytic folders, as shown in Figures B-6 and B-7.
**Examples**:

- COUNT(Order_Number) returns a count of the number of orders. If you include a condition such as Order Month = 'JULY 2014' and then use the COUNT(Order Number), this will return the number of orders placed in July 2014.
- COUNT(DECODE(age_count, 'over 12', 1, NULL)) ensures that the result of DECODE can be aggregated. If you try adding a total to a calculation such as DECODE(age_count, 'over 12',1, NULL) and any of the rows evaluate to NULL, you will not get a total. However, if you place the COUNT function around the calculation, Discoverer will now be able to compute the total.

**NOTE**
*Analytic functions are explained in more detail in Chapter 21.*

# COUNT_DISTINCT

**Syntax**: COUNT_DISTINCT(expression)
**Description**: This function returns a count of the number of non-null, unique items in the given expression. Please note that null values are ignored by this function, which may affect your results.
**Folder**: COUNT_DISTINCT can be found in the Group and Analytic folders, as shown in Figures B-6 and B-7.
**Example**:

- In the COUNT_DISTINCT(list) function, when the list contains "null, 1, 1, 3 ,5, 5, 5, 5, 7, 7, 7", the answer is 4. This is because Discoverer counts only the items 1, 3, 5, and 7. If we had used COUNT on this same list, the answer would have been 10. Which one is correct depends upon your viewpoint and how you want to display the result.

**NOTE**
*Analytic functions are explained in more detail in Chapter 21.*

# COVAR_POP

**Syntax**: COVAR_POP(value1, value2)
**Description**: This statistical function returns the population covariance of two values. The population covariance of two values is the product of their deviations from their population mean.
**Folder**: COVAR_POP can be found in the Group and Analytic folders, as shown in Figures B-6 and B-7.

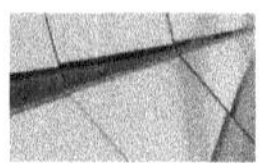

**NOTE**
*Analytic functions are explained in more detail in Chapter 21.*

## COVAR_SAMP

**Syntax**: COVAR_SAMP(value1, value2)
**Description**: This statistical function returns the sample covariance of two values.
**Folder**: COVAR_SAMP can be found in the Group and Analytic folders, as shown in Figures B-6 and B-7.

**NOTE**
*Analytic functions are explained in more detail in Chapter 21.*

## CUME_DIST

**Syntax**: CUME_DIST(value1, value2)
**Description**: This statistical function calculates the cumulative distribution of a single value among a group of values. CUME_DIST will return values that are greater than 0 and less than or equal to 1. When the values are the same, they always evaluate to the same cumulative distribution value.
**Folder**: CUME_DIST can be found in the Group and Analytic folders, as shown in Figures B-6 and B-7.

**NOTE**
*Analytic functions are explained in more detail in Chapter 21.*

## CURRENT_DATE

**Syntax**: CURRENT_DATE
**Description**: This function returns the current date of the user's database session. A traditional alternative is SYSDATE. It is important to understand that SYSDATE is the date of the database server, whereas CURRENT_DATE is sensitive to the location of the user submitting the query. For this function to be useful, the user must submit an ALTER SESSION SET TIME_ZONE = 'number' command upon connecting to the database.
**Folder**: CURRENT_DATE can be found in the Date folder, as shown in Figure B-4.

## DBTIMEZONE

**Syntax**: DBTIMEZONE
**Description**: This function returns the time zone of the database server.
**Folder**: DBTIMEZONE can be found in the Date folder, as shown in Figure B-4.
**Examples**:

- DBTIMEZONE will returns +08:00 if the user is eight hours ahead of GMT.
- DBTIMEZONE will return America/Denver if the DBA has altered the database and set this zone as the server time zone.

**NOTE**
*The command select tzname, tzabbrev from V$TIMEZONE_ NAMES where zabbrev = 'MST' lists all the time zone names within the Mountain standard time zone.*

# DECODE

**Syntax 1**: DECODE(value, x, y, z) equates to the following:

IF value = x THEN y ELSE z

**Syntax 2**: DECODE(value, x1, y1, x2, y2, z) equates to the following:

IF value = x1 THEN y1 ELSE IF value = x2 THEN y2 ELSE z

**NOTE**
*The x and y values in the preceding function are grouped together as a parameter set and can be repeated as many times as are required.*

**Description**: This function is, in our opinion, one of the most powerful and useful of all of Discoverer's functions. Mastery of this function lies at the heart of unlocking the true power of Discoverer.

As stated in the syntax, the basic structure of this function is as follows:

IF value = x (where *value* can be any expression, algorithm, data value, or literal)
THEN y
ELSE z – the default value

The DECODE statement can, and frequently does, check multiple values, culminating eventually with an ELSE, the default expression to be used when all else fails. You can also embed DECODE statements inside one another, which when mixed with other functions makes for very powerful algorithms. If no default expression is specified, the result of DECODE will be the null value.

When using the DECODE statement, you might think you always have to find a value that equates to equality. However, this is not the case, and Discoverer can be made to work with values greater than, equal to, and less than. To do this, though, you will have to create special calculations using the SIGN function. The final example shows this construct. You may use the CASE expression as an alternative to DECODE.

**Folder**: DECODE can be found in the Others folder, as shown in Figure B-8.

**Examples**:

- **DECODE(requested date, SYSDATE, 'Y', 'N')** In this example, if the requested date equals the current date, then the function returns the value 'Y'; otherwise, the value 'N' is returned. This algorithm can be used to work out which orders are due for shipment.

**NOTE**
*You will need to use the TRUNC function in conjunction with the preceding code in cases where your system stores the time as well as the date in the requested date column. The preceding example would then become DECODE(TRUNC(requested date), TRUNC(SYSDATE), 'Y', 'N').*

- **DECODE(code value, 123, 'Classic', 456, 'Old Style', 'New Style')** In this example, if the code value is 123, the function returns the value 'Classic', and if the code value is 456, the function returns the value 'Old Style'. If the code value is neither 123 nor 456, the function returns the value 'New Style'.
- **DECODE(SOB_ID,1,'NON-REGULATED',2,'REGULATED', 'UNKNOWN')** This example looks at the parameter called SOB_ID (which presumably stands for the Sets of Books ID), and if this is 1, it returns the value NON-REGULATED. If the parameter contains 2, the function returns the value REGULATED. Any value other than 1 or 2 will cause the function to return UNKNOWN.
- **DECODE(customer, 'ABC', DECODE(SUM(owed), 0, 5000, 5000 – (SUM(owed) / 2)), 10000)** This more complicated example calculates customer credit limits. If the customer is 'ABC' and the total amount owed is zero, then the credit limit is set to 5000. However, if the total amount owed by 'ABC' is not zero, then we set their credit limit to be 5000 minus half the amount owed. Finally, for all other customers, the credit limit is set to 10000.
- **DECODE(SIGN(SUM(owed) / 15000), -1, 20000, 20000 – SUM(owed))** This is a clever combination of the SIGN and DECODE functions. Because SIGN returns a value of –1 for all numbers less than 1, if the amount owed by the customer is less than 15000, we will allow them to have a credit limit of 20000; otherwise, the credit limit is reduced by the amount owed.
- **DECODE(ITEM,LEAST(ITEM,26),'0-25',DECODE(ITEM,LEAST(ITEM,51),'26-50', DECOD E(ITEM,LEAST(ITEM,76),'51-75','Over 75')))** This example is explained as follows:

  IF ITEM equals the lesser of the ITEM or 26
  THEN include the item in the set called '0-25'
  ELSE IF the ITEM equals the lesser of the ITEM or 51

THEN include the item in the set called '26-50' and so on, which means we are categorizing ITEM into buckets of (0 to 25, 26 to 50, 51 to 75, over 75).

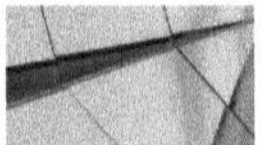

**NOTE**
*The preceding example is a clever way to overcome the fact that DECODE(a,b,c,d) requires a and b to be equal, thus allowing constructs such as these:*
*IF a < b*
*THEN c*
*ELSE d*

## DENSE_RANK

**Syntax**: DENSE_RANK() OVER (PARTITION BY value1 ORDER BY value2)
**Description**: This function computes rank. If it is given a row within an ordered group of rows, it will return the numerical rank starting with 1. When a tie occurs, all numbers within the tie will be given the same ranking. It is dense, as no ranking numbers are skipped. This function is useful to find the top or bottom *n* values. For example, if you wanted to find the ten best sales representatives and half of the sales representatives sold exactly $10,000 and the other half sold exactly $20,000, the first half would all be ranked with 1 and the second half would all be ranked with 2.

**Folder**: DENSE_RANK can be found in the Group and Analytic folders, as shown in Figures B-6 and B-7.
**Example**:

- DENSE_RANK() OVER (ORDER BY salary DESC) could be used alongside a grade to return values like this:

| Grade | Student | Salary |
|---|---|---|
| 1 | abc0 | 5000 |
| 2 | abc1 | 4000 |
| 2 | abc2 | 4000 |
| 3 | abc3 | 3500 |
| 4 | abc4 | 3000 |

**NOTE**
*If you are using page items or group sorts, make sure you include a PARTITION BY clause. Analytic functions are explained in more detail in Chapter 21.*

# DUMP

**Syntax**: DUMP(string [, format [, start [, number_to_dump] ] ] )
**Description**: This function takes a string and displays it in a new format. The function optionally takes a start position and length. If these are provided, Discoverer dumps the string from the start position for the number of characters specified. The format can be 8 for octal, 10 for decimal, 16 for hex, and 17 for character.
**Folder**: DUMP can be found in the Others folder, as shown in Figure B-8.
**Example**:

- DUMP('michael', 16) returns 'Type=96 Len=7: 6d,69,63,68,61,65,6c' where each character of the string was dumped into hex.

# EUL_DATE_TRUNC

**Syntax**: EUL_DATE_TRUNC(date, format)
**Description**: This function takes a date and a format mask and truncates the date based on the format mask. The date specified must be a valid date. If the date you want to check is not currently a valid date, you must convert it into a valid date first. This function is automatically used by Discoverer when the administrator creates a date hierarchy.
**Folder**: EUL_DATE_TRUNC can be found in the Date folder, as shown in Figure B-4.
**Examples**: In the following examples, suppose that the current date is July 21, 2014.

- EUL_DATE_TRUNC(SYSDATE,'YY') returns '01-JAN-14'. Because we specified only the year within our format, Discoverer truncated the current date to the first day of the year.
- EUL_DATE_TRUNC(SYSDATE, 'MM') returns '01-JUL-00'. Because we specified just the month within our format, Discoverer truncated the current date to the first day of the current month.

- EUL_DATE_TRUNC(SYSDATE, 'DD') returns '21-JAN-00'. Because we specified just the day within our format, Discoverer truncated the current date to the earliest day of the year equal to the current day.

**NOTE**
*In the previous two examples, the year was returned as 00. You might think this is the year 2000, but it is in fact 1900. You can prove this yourself by displaying the date in character form, using TO_CHAR, with the format mask of DD-MON-YYYY. So, what happened? MM really returned only the first day of the month in question, July 1, while DD returned only the date, the 1. Because dates need to be displayed with a day, month, and year, Discoverer used January 1, 1900, as a default date to fill in the missing elements.*

## EXP (Exponential)

**Syntax**: EXP(*n*)
**Description:** This function returns e to the *n*th power, where e is the universal constant 2.718281828. It goes on forever repeating the numbers 1828, but for Discoverer usage, the number given here will suffice.

The opposite of EXP(*x*) is the natural logarithm LN(*x*) so that if you compute the exponential of the natural logarithm LN(*x*), you get *x* back. This works either way, as shown in the examples that follow.
**Folder**: EXP can be found in the Numeric folder, as shown in Figure B-2.
**Examples**:

- EXP(1) returns the universal constant, 2.718281828.
- EXP(4) returns the value 54.589150—that is, 2.718281828 to the power 4.
- EXP(LN(8)) returns the number 8.

## FIRST_VALUE

**Syntax**: FIRST_VALUE(expr [IGNORE NULLS]) OVER (PARTITION BY expr1 ORDER BY expr2 RANGE BETWEEN expr3 AND expr4)
**Description:** This function returns the first value in an ordered set of values. If the first value is null, then the function returns null. If you specify IGNORE NULLS, then the function will return the first non-null value within the ordered list, somewhat similar to the COALESCE function.
**Folder**: FIRST_VALUE can be found in the Analytic folder, as shown in Figure B-7.

**NOTE**
*Analytic functions are explained in more detail in Chapter 21.*

## FLOOR

**Syntax**: FLOOR(value)
**Description**: This function takes the value given and returns the highest integer smaller than or equal to that value. Refer to CEIL for the function that returns the largest integer.

**Folder**: FLOOR can be found in the Numeric folder, as shown in Figure B-2.
**Examples**:

- FLOOR(7) returns the value 7.
- FLOOR(-6.75) returns the value –7.
- FLOOR(100.55) returns the value 100.
- TO_CHAR(DECODE(Cost,FLOOR(Cost),FLOOR(Cost),ROUND(Cost,1))) returns an integer if the cost has no decimal places and rounds the original value to one decimal place if the cost has decimal places. For example, if Cost = 1000.00, this function returns 1000, but if the cost is 675.55, it returns 675.6. If the cost is 5.99, it returns 6.

**NOTE**
*The preceding example shows a practical use for combining the TO_CHAR, FLOOR, and ROUND functions.*

## GLB

**Syntax**: GLB(label)
**Description**: This function is an operating system function and would not normally be used within Discoverer. It returns the greatest lower bound of a secure operating system label.
**Folder**: GLB can be found in the Group folder, as shown in Figure B-6.

## GREATEST

**Syntax**: GREATEST(value1, value2, ...)
**Description**: This function returns the value that is the greatest of the given list of values. If one of the arguments in the list is the null value, the result will be null. You can use all of the data types with this function, although some unexpected results may occur if you are not careful. The number 27 is obviously greater than 7, but the string '7' is greater than the string '27'. Strings are compared using their ASCII numbers. You therefore must be careful when comparing strings, especially if those strings contain dates or numbers. If you want to compare dates that are stored as strings, you must use the TO_DATE function. If you want to compare numbers that are stored as strings, you must use the TO_NUMBER function.
**Folder**: GREATEST can be found in the Others folder, as shown in Figure B-8.
**Examples**:

- GREATEST(9, 18, 5, 60) returns the value 60.
- GREATEST('23-JUN-14','14-OCT-14') returns the string '23-JUN-14'.
- GREATEST(TO_DATE('23-JUN-14'), TO_DATE('14-OCT-14')) returns the date 14-OCT-14.
- GREATEST(TO_NUMBER('2'), TO_NUMBER('14')) returns the number 14.

## GREATEST_LB

This function has been dropped from the current version of Discoverer. If you have any workbooks that use this function, you will need to use an alternative function.

## HEXTORAW

**Syntax**: HEXTORAW(hex_string)
**Description**: This function changes a character string of hex numbers into binary.
**Folder**: HEXTORAW can be found in the Conversion folder, as shown in Figure B-5.

## INITCAP (Initial Capitals)

**Syntax**: INITCAP(string)
**Description**: This function takes a string and returns a new string with the first letter of each word capitalized. The function also recognizes the presence of punctuation and uppercases the first letter following any punctuation. The punctuation symbols include the comma, period, colon, semicolon, hyphen, and so on.
**Folder**: INITCAP can be found in the String folder, as shown in Figure B-3.
**Examples**:

- INITCAP('armstrong-smith') returns 'Armstrong-Smith'.
- INITCAP('the cat is on the mat') returns 'The Cat Is On The Mat'.

## INSTR

**Syntax**: INSTR(string1, string2 [, start [, n] ] )
**Description**: This function takes a string and finds the position of a second string in that string. The function will optionally begin the search at a given start position and return the position of the $n^{th}$ set. If you omit the start position, Discoverer will search from the beginning. If you use a negative number for the start, Discoverer begins the search at the end of the string and searches backward. If you use zero for the start position, the answer will be zero.
**Folder**: INSTR can be found in the String folder, as shown in Figure B-3.
**Examples**:

- INSTR('San Francisco', 'an') returns 2.
- INSTR('San Francisco', 'an', 1, 2) returns 7.
- INSTR('San Francisco', 'an', -1, 2) returns 2.

This function is quite useful when nested inside the SUBSTR function.
**More Examples**:

- SUBSTR('Jackson, Arnold', 1 ,INSTR('Jackson, Arnold', ',')-1) returns Jackson.
- SUBSTR('McFly, Marty', 1 ,INSTR('McFly, Marty', ',')-1) returns McFly.

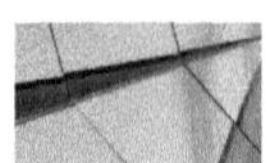

**NOTE**
*As you get used to working with the INSTR function, you will find that you will also be using the SUBSTR function more times than not.*

## INSTRB

**Syntax**: INSTRB(string, set [, start [, occurrence] ] )
**Description**: This function, like INSTR, takes a string and locates the position of a set of characters in that string. However, INSTRB locates the string you are looking for at the byte position. Within Discoverer, we recommend you use INSTR instead of this function.
**Folder**: INSTRB can be found in the String folder, as shown in Figure B-3.

## LAG

**Syntax**: LAG(expr, n) OVER (PARTITION BY expr1 ORDER BY expr2)
**Description**: This function allows you to compare one row in a set of rows to another row in the same set. You may now say good-bye to your slow friend the self-join. In the OVER clause, you specify how to group and sort a set of rows. In the LAG clause, you specify what column's values you want returned and how many rows to lag behind to determine what value to return.
**Folder**: LAG can be found in the Analytic folder, as shown in Figure B-7.

**NOTE**
*Analytic functions are explained in more detail in Chapter 21.*

## LAST_DAY

**Syntax**: LAST_DAY(date)
**Description**: This function returns the date that is the last day of the month for a given date. The date specified must be a valid date. If the date you want to check is not currently a valid date, you must convert it into a valid date first. If you supply a null date, then the result will also be null.
**Folder**: LAST_DAY can be found in the Date folder, as shown in Figure B-4.
**Examples**:

- LAST_DAY(TO_DATE('16-OCT-14')) returns 31-OCT-14.
- LAST_DAY(ship date) returns the last day of the month in which the item shipped. Setting a condition such that ship_date = LAST_DAY(ship_date) will produce a report showing only the shipments that were sent on the last day of the month. You could use this to analyze last-minute shipments.
- LAST_DAY(TO_DATE('')) returns null.

## LAST_VALUE

**Syntax**: LAST_VALUE(expr [IGNORE NULLS]) OVER (PARTITION BY expr1 ORDER BY expr2 RANGE BETWEEN expr3 AND expr4)
**Description**: This function returns the last value in an ordered set of values. If the last value is null, then the function returns null. If you specify IGNORE NULLS, then the function will return the last non-null value within the ordered list.
**Folder**: LAST_VALUE can be found in the Analytic folder, as shown in Figure B-7.

**NOTE**
*Analytic functions are explained in more detail in Chapter 21.*

## LEAD

**Syntax**: LEAD(expr, n) OVER (PARTITION BY expr1 ORDER BY expr2)
**Description**: This function allows you to compare one row in a set of rows to another row in the same set. Like LAG, this function can be used as an alternative to performing a self-join. In the OVER clause, you specify how to group and sort a set of rows. In the LEAD clause, you first specify what column you want returned. The second argument specifies how many rows ahead you want to receive the value from.
**Folder**: LEAD can be found in the Analytic folder, as shown in Figure B-7.

**NOTE**
*Analytic functions are explained in more detail in Chapter 21.*

## LEAST

**Syntax**: LEAST(value1, value2, ...)
**Description**: This function returns the value that is the least of the given list of values. If one of the arguments in the list is the null value, the result will be null. You can use all of the data types with this function, although some unexpected results may occur if you are not careful. The number 7 is obviously less than 27, but the string '7' is greater than the string '27'. The date July 24, 2014, is prior to October 14, 2014, but the string '24-JUL-14' is greater than the string '14-OCT-14'. Strings are compared using their ASCII numbers. You therefore must be careful when comparing strings. If you want to compare dates that are stored as strings, you must use the TO_DATE function. If you want to compare numbers that are stored as strings, you must use the TO_ NUMBER function.
**Folder**: LEAST can be found in the Others folder, as shown in Figure B-8.
**Examples**:

- LEAST(9, 18, 5, 60) returns the value 5.
- LEAST('24-JUL-14','14-OCT-14') returns the string '14-OCT-14'.
- LEAST(TO_DATE('24-JUL-14'), TO_DATE('14-OCT-14')) returns the date 24-JUL-14.
- LEAST(TO_NUMBER('2'), TO_NUMBER('14')) returns the number 2.

**NOTE**
*The LEAST function works very well inside the DECODE statement to handle calculations such as IF a< b. Please look back at the DECODE function in this section for an example.*

## LEAST_UB

This function has been dropped from the current version of Discoverer. If you have any workbooks that use this function, you will need to use an alternative function.

## LENGTH

**Syntax**: LENGTH(string)
**Description**: This function returns the length of a string, number, date, or expression.
**Folder**: LENGTH can be found in the String folder, as shown in Figure B-3.
**Example**: LENGTH('Hien Nguyen') returns 11.

## LENGTHB

**Syntax**: LENGTHB(string)
**Description**: This function takes a string and returns the length as a number of bytes, as opposed to a number of characters. Within Discoverer, we recommend you use LENGTH instead of this function.
**Folder**: LENGTHB can be found in the String folder, as shown in Figure B-3.

## LN (Logarithm)

**Syntax**: LN(number)
**Description**: This function returns the natural, or base *e*, logarithm of a number, where *e* is the universal constant (see EXP for an explanation of *e*). If the number specified is the null value, the result will be null. The number or expression you provide must be positive; otherwise, you will encounter an error.

The opposite of LN(*x*) is EXP(*x*) so that if you compute the natural logarithm of EXP(*x*), you get *x* back. This works either way, as shown in the examples that follow.
**Folder**: LN can be found in the Numeric folder, as shown in Figure B-2.
**Examples**:

- LN(1) returns the value 0.
- LN(8) returns the value 2.079.
- LN(EXP(8)) returns the number 8.
- *x* / LN(*x*-1) returns the approximate number of prime numbers not exceeding the value *x*. This is included just for fun and is something you can experiment with yourself to see the usage of LN.

## LOG

**Syntax**: LOG(base, number)
**Description**: This function returns the power to which a number, called the *base*, must be raised in order to obtain a given positive number. Common logarithms use 10 as the base. Napierian logarithms (named after John Napier, the Scottish inventor of logarithms and, incidentally, the decimal point) use the number *e* (the universal constant) as the base.
**Folder**: LOG can be found in the Numeric folder, as shown in Figure B-2.
**Examples**:

- LOG(10,10) returns the number 1.
- LOG(10, 100) returns the number 2.
- LOG(EXP(1), 3) returns 1.0986, because $^{e}1.0986$ is 3. See the section "EXP" for more details on the universal constant *e*.

## LOWER

**Syntax**: LOWER(string)
**Description**: This function takes a string and returns a new string with every letter in lowercase.
**Folder**: LOWER can be found in the String folder, as shown in Figure B-3.

**Examples**:

- LOWER('Armstrong-Smith') returns the string 'armstrong-smith'.
- DECODE(LOWER(state), 'california', 'CA', 'texas', 'TX', 'US') returns 'CA' when the state is California, 'TX' when the state is Texas, and 'US' in all other cases.

**NOTE**
*By using the LOWER function within a DECODE function, you assure that your search will match uppercase and lowercase data.*

## LPAD (Left Pad)

**Syntax**: LPAD(string, number [, characters] )
**Description**: This function takes a string, a number, and optionally a set of characters, and it pads the string to the length specified by the number. If the current length of the string is less than the number specified, Discoverer inserts as many sets of characters into the beginning of the string as it can, until the length is as required. If the current length of the string is greater than the number specified, Discoverer truncates the string, returning a new string with only that number of characters remaining—counting from the left. When padding, if no character set is specified, Discoverer pads out the string with spaces. If either the specified string or the character set is the null value or the number is not positive, the overall result will be the null value. If the number specified is a decimal, Discoverer ignores the decimal portion, acting on the number before the decimal point.
**Folder**: LPAD can be found in the String folder, as shown in Figure B-3.
**Examples**:

- LPAD('Armstrong', 5) returns 'Armst', containing only the first five characters.
- LPAD('Smith', 15, 'Darlene') returns 'DarleneDarSmith'.
- LPAD('',5,'M') returns a null string because the initial string is empty.
- LPAD('',LENGTH('Luke')+1, '*') returns '****'.

## LTRIM (Left Trim)

**Syntax**: LTRIM(string [, characters] )
**Description**: This function takes a string, and optionally a set of characters, and returns a new string with all occurrences of those characters removed from the beginning of the original string. If no characters are specified, Discoverer removes all leading spaces. If either the specified string or the set of characters is the null value, the result will be the null value.
**Folder**: LTRIM can be found in the String folder, as shown in Figure B-3.
**Examples**:

- LTRIM('  Armstrong') returns 'Armstrong' with all leading spaces removed.
- LTRIM('Armstrong-Smith', 'Armstrong-') returns 'Smith'.
- LTRIM('', 'Jones') returns null.

## LUB

**Syntax**: LUB(label)
**Description**: This function is another of those operating system functions that would not normally be used within Discoverer. It returns the least upper bound of an operating system label.
**Folder**: LUB can be found in the Group folder, as shown in Figure B-6.

## MAX (Maximum)

**Syntax**: MAX(argument)
**Description**: From the argument, column, or set of values specified, this function returns the item that has the largest value. MAX ignores null values.
**Folder**: MAX can be found in the Group and Analytic folders, as shown in Figures B-6 and B-7.
**Examples**:

- MAX(ship date) returns the most recent ship date held on the system.
- MAX(NVL(ship date, SYSDATE)) overcomes null values in the ship date, thus allowing further calculations and aggregations to be applied to this calculation.

**NOTE**
*Analytic functions are explained in more detail in Chapter 21.*

## MAX_DISTINCT

**Syntax**: MAX_DISTINCT(argument)
**Description**: From the argument, column, or set of values specified, this function returns the item that has the largest value. MAX ignores null values. This function is identical to the MAX function.
**Folder**: MAX_DISTINCT can be found in the Group and Analytic folders, as shown in Figures B-6 and B-7.

**NOTE**
*Analytic functions are explained in more detail in Chapter 21.*

## MIN (Minimum)

**Syntax**: MIN(argument)
**Description**: From the argument, column, or set of values specified, this function returns the item that has the lowest value. MIN ignores null values.
**Folder**: MIN can be found in the Group and Analytic folders, as shown in Figures B-6 and B-7.
**Examples**:

- MIN(ship date) returns the oldest ship date held on the system.
- MIN(NVL(ship date, SYSDATE)) overcomes null values in the ship date, thus allowing further calculations and aggregations to be applied to this calculation.

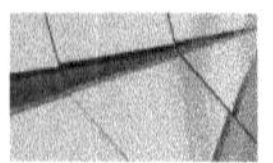

**NOTE**
*Analytic functions are explained in more detail in Chapter 21.*

## MIN_DISTINCT

**Syntax**: MIN_DISTINCT(argument)
**Description**: From the argument, column, or set of values specified, this function returns the item that has the lowest value. MIN_DISTINCT ignores null values. This function is identical to the MIN function.
**Folder**: MIN_DISTINCT can be found in the Group and Analytic folders, as shown in Figures B-6 and B-7.

**NOTE**
*Analytic functions are explained in more detail in Chapter 21.*

## MOD (Modulus)

**Syntax**: MOD(value, divisor)
**Description**: This function divides the given value by the divisor and returns the remainder. Both the value and the divisor can be any real number. If the divisor is zero, Discoverer returns the original value in the result.
**Folder**: MOD can be found in the Numeric folder, as shown in Figure B-2.
**Examples**:

- MOD(7, 8) returns 7.
- MOD(8, 7) returns 1.
- MOD(-8,7) returns –1.
- MOD(8,0) returns 8.

## MONTHS_BETWEEN

**Syntax**: MONTHS_BETWEEN (first_date, second_date)
**Description**: This function returns the number of months between first_date and second_ date. Both dates specified must be valid dates. If either date you want to check is not currently a valid date, you must convert it into a valid date. If first_date precedes second_date, the result will be negative. In most Oracle databases, the result of this function will be a number with decimal places; however, if you are using an Oracle Lite database, the result will be an integer. In some older Oracle databases, not including the 11*g* database, if you want to compare a date prior to January 1, 2000, with a date after this, you must give the complete four-digit year.
**Folder**: MONTHS_BETWEEN can be found in the Date folder, as shown in Figure B-4.
**Examples**:

- MONTHS_BETWEEN(TO_DATE('01-DEC-2013'), TO_DATE('26-MAY-2014')) returns the value –5.80645.
- MONTHS_BETWEEN(TO_DATE('01-DEC-99'), TO_DATE('26-MAY-00')) returns the value –1194.19355 on older databases and returns –5.80645 on newer versions, including 11*g*.

## NEW_TIME

**Syntax**: NEW_TIME(date, this_zone, destination_zone)
**Description**: This function returns the date and time for the destination_zone based on the specified date and time in this_zone. This is a very useful and clever function that can be used to work out the current time in different parts of the world. Both this_zone and destination_zone must be supplied as three-letter abbreviations. A list of the valid time zones used within Discoverer can be found in the section "Time Zones" later in this appendix.

By the clever use of the TO_CHAR function and knowing how many hours ahead or behind you are to other countries, you can work out the time anywhere in the world. To calculate the time in China, for example, we know that China is 15 hours ahead of California. Therefore, we need to add 15/24 to the current time.
**Folder**: NEW_TIME can be found in the Date folder, as shown in Figure B-4.
**Examples**: In the following examples, suppose that the current time zone is Pacific standard time (PST).

- NEW_TIME(SYSDATE, 'PST', 'GMT') returns the date in London.
- TO_CHAR(NEW_TIME(SYSDATE, 'PST', 'GMT'),'HH24:MI') returns the time, based on the 24-hour clock, in London.
- TO_CHAR(NEW_TIME(SYSDATE + (15 / 24), 'PST', 'PST'),'DD-MON-YY HH24:MI') returns the date and time in China.

If you are in a part of the world that does not have a supported time zone, do not despair. The solution is simple. You calculate the time difference between your offices, insert that instead of the word *diff* in the function that follows, and then run the function. Make sure both of the quoted time zones are the same. We inserted GMT, but this works with all supported zones.

- TO_CHAR(NEW_TIME(SYSDATE + (diff / 24), 'GMT', 'GMT'),'DD-MON-YY HH24:MI') returns the date and time of your office.

## NEXT_DAY

**Syntax**: NEXT_DAY(date, string)
**Description**: This function returns the date of the first weekday, named by string, which is later than the date given. The string must contain at least the first three letters of a day of the week.
**Folder**: NEXT_DAY can be found in the Date folder, as shown in Figure B-4.
**Examples**:

- NEXT_DAY(SYSDATE, 'Wednesday') returns the date for next Wednesday.
- NEXT_DAY(ship_date, 'FRI') returns the date for the Friday following the ship date.
- NEXT_DAY(SYSDATE-7, 'Wednesday') returns the preceding Wednesday, or the present day if the function was run on a Wednesday.

## NLSSORT

**Syntax**: NLSSORT(string [, nls_parameters] )
**Description**: This function gives the string of bytes used to sort a string.
**Folder**: NLSSORT can be found in the String folder, as shown in Figure B-3.

**Examples:**

- NLSSORT('DARLENE', 'NLS_SORT = Xdutch') returns the code 2314644B28552800.
- NLSSORT('mike', NLS_SORT = Xswiss) returns the code 503C46280.

**NOTE**
*As you can see, if you look at these two examples, the single quotes around the NLS_SORT = parameter are optional.*

## NLS_INITCAP

**Syntax:** NLS_INITCAP(string [, nls_parameters] )
**Description:** This function is identical to INITCAP, except that it takes an optional National Language Support (NSL) string of parameters. If provided, this string must take the form 'NLS_SORT = option', where option is a linguistic sort sequence. These sequences should be used whenever your Oracle database is not based on the English language. These rules are required in order for Discoverer to work out exactly how to initialize the given string.
**Folder:** NLS_INITCAP can be found in the String folder, as shown in Figure B-3.
**Example:** NLS_INITCAP('ijsland', NLS_SORT = Xdutch) returns 'IJsland'.

## NLS_LOWER

**Syntax:** NLS_LOWER(string [, nls_parameters] )
**Description:** This function is identical to LOWER, except that it takes an optional NLS string of parameters. For an explanation of NLS, see the function NLS_INITCAP.
**Folder:** NLS_LOWER can be found in the String folder, as shown in Figure B-3.

## NLS_UPPER

**Syntax:** NLS_UPPER(string [, nls_parameters] )
**Description:** This function is identical to UPPER, except that it takes an optional NLS string of parameters. For an explanation of NLS, see the function NLS_INITCAP.
**Folder:** NLS_UPPER can be found in the String folder, as shown in Figure B-3.

## NTILE

**Syntax:** NTILE(n) OVER (PARTITION BY expr1 ORDER BY expr2)
**Description:** This function evenly distributes sorted values into different buckets. Based upon ORDER BY, it gives all rows in the first bucket the number 1. The rows at the top are given the number *n*. All rows in between are given an evenly distributed number between 1 and *n*.
**Folder:** NTILE can be found in the Analytic folder, as shown in Figure B-7.
**Example:** NTILE(10) OVER(ORDER BY SUM(Selling Price) ) computes ten equal-sized buckets for Selling Price.

**NOTE**
*Analytic functions are explained in more detail in Chapter 21.*

## NULLIF

**Syntax**: NULLIF(value1, value2)
**Description**: This function compares value1 to value2. If the values are equal, it returns NULL. If they are not equal, it returns value1.
**Folder**: NULLIF can be found in the Others folder, as shown in Figure B-8.
**Examples**:

- NULLIF (10,10) returns NULL.
- NULLIF (10,5) returns 10.

**NOTE**
*The two values must be of the same data type. NULLIF(10,'A') will produce an error, as will NULLIF(NULL,7).*

## NUMTODSINTERVAL

**Syntax**: NUMTODSINTERVAL(value1, [second|minute|hour|day])
**Description**: This function converts the number given as value1 to the INTERVAL DAY TO SECOND data type. The second parameter determines whether value1 is a second, a minute, an hour, or a day.
**Folder**: NUMTODSINTERVAL can be found in the Date folder, as shown in Figure B-4.

**NOTE**
*Oracle requires that, when using the RANGE clause in analytic functions, you submit the RANGE in an INTERVAL data type. Analytic functions are explained in more detail in Chapter 21.*

## NUMTOYMINTERVAL

**Syntax**: NUMTOYMINTERVAL(value1, [year|month])
**Description**: This function converts the number given as value1 to the INTERVAL YEAR TO MONTH data type. The second parameter determines whether value1 is a year or a month.
**Folder**: NUMTOYMINTERVAL can be found in the Date folder, as shown in Figure B-4.

## NVL

**Syntax**: NVL(expr1, expr2)
**Description**: If the first expression is null, Discoverer returns the second expression. If the first expression is not null, Discoverer returns that expression.
**Folder**: NVL can be found in the Others folder, as shown in Figure B-8.
**Examples**:

- NVL(code, 'Y') returns the code if it is not null; otherwise, it returns the value 'Y'.
- NVL(ship quantity, 0) returns the ship quantity if there is one; otherwise, it returns zero.

## NVL2

**Syntax**: NVL2(value1, value2, value3)
**Description**: When using the function, if value1 is not null, then it will return value2. If value1 is null, then it will return value3.
**Folder**: NVL2 can be found in the Others folder, as shown in Figure B-8.
**Examples**:

- NVL2(NULL, 1, 0) returns 0.
- NVL2('X', 'Y', 'Z') returns Y.

## PERCENTILE_CONT (Percentile Continuous)

**Syntax**: PERCENTILE_CONT(value1) WITHIN GROUP (ORDER BY value2 ASC|DESC)
**Description**: This function is an inverse distribution function that depends upon a continuous distribution of values. It receives a percentile, value1, and a sort specification, value2, and returns an interpolated result that would fit into that percentile with attention to the sort specification. To help understand this function, consider that MEDIAN is a specific example of the function where value1 defaults to 0.5.
**Folder**: PERCENTILE_CONT can be found in the Group and Analytic folders, as shown in Figures B-6 and B-7.
**Example**: PERCENTILE_CONT(0.4) WITHIN GROUP (ORDER BY Profit DESC)

**NOTE**
*Analytic functions are explained in more detail in Chapter 21.*

## PERCENTILE_DISC (Percentile Discrete)

**Syntax**: PERCENTILE_DISC(value1) WITHIN GROUP (ORDER BY value2 ASC|DESC)
**Description**: This function is an inverse distribution function that depends upon a discrete distribution of values. It receives a percentile, value1, and a sort specification, value2, and returns a specific value from the set.
**Folder**: PERCENTILE_DISC can be found in the Group and Analytic folders, as shown in Figures B-6 and B-7.
**Example**: PERCENTILE_DISC (0.4) WITHIN GROUP (ORDER BY Profit DESC)

**NOTE**
*Analytic functions are explained in more detail in Chapter 21.*

## PERCENT_RANK

**Syntax**: PERCENT_RANK([value1, value2]) WITHIN GROUP (ORDER BY value3, value4)
**Description**: This function determines a ranking and returns the result as a percentage. value1and value2 are optional and would be used to determine the answer to a what-if question. For example, what if an employee's salary was 25000 and commission was 0.2, then what would the percentage rank be?

**Folder**: PERCENTILE_RANK can be found in the Group and Analytic folders, as shown in Figures B-6 and B-7.
**Example**: PERCENT_RANK(25000, .2) WITHIN GROUP(ORDER BY salary, commission)

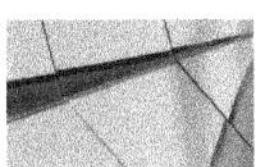

**NOTE**
*Analytic functions are explained in more detail in Chapter 21.*

## POWER

**Syntax**: POWER(base number, *n*)
**Description**: This function raises the base number given to the $n^{th}$ power. The base and the exponent can be any numbers; however, if the base number is negative, the exponent must be an integer. A negative exponent means divide the answer into 1.
**Folder**: POWER can be found in the Numeric folder, as shown in Figure B-2.
**Examples**:

- POWER(2.5, 2) returns 6.25, which is 2.5 squared.
- POWER(2.5, –2) returns 0.16, which is 1 divided by 6.25.
- POWER(–3,–3) returns –0.37037037, and so on, which is 1 divided by –27.

## RANK

**Syntax**: RANK([number, number]) [WITHIN GROUP|OVER] ([PARTITION BY value] ORDER BY value)
**Description**: This function determines a value's rank among a group of numbers. When multiple rows have equal values, they receive the same rank. Ranks might not be consecutive, as Oracle adds the number of rows that have a tie to the ranking of the tied values to compute the next rank.
**Folder**: RANK can be found in the Group and Analytic folders, as shown in Figures B-6 and B-7.
**Examples**:

- RANK() OVER(ORDER BY Ship Qty SUM DESC )
- RANK(5)WITHIN GROUP(ORDER BY Selling Price )
- RANK() OVER (ORDER BY salary DESC) could be used alongside a grade to return values like this:

| Grade | ename | Salary |
|---|---|---|
| 1 | abc0 | 5000 |
| 2 | abc1 | 4000 |
| 2 | abc2 | 4000 |
| 4 | abc3 | 3500 |
| 5 | abc4 | 3000 |

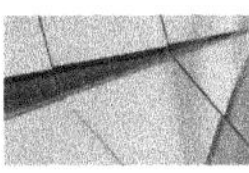

**NOTE**
*Analytic functions are explained in more detail in Chapter 21.*

## RATIO_TO_REPORT

**Syntax**: RATIO_TO_REPORT(value) OVER(PARTITION BY value)
**Description**: This function computes the ratio of a number to the total of a group of numbers.
**Folder**: RATIO_TO_REPORT can be found in the Group and Analytic folders, as shown in Figures B-6 and B-7.
**Example**: RATIO_TO_REPORT(Profit SUM) OVER(PARTITION BY "Year" )

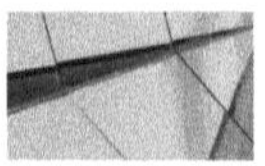

**NOTE**
*Analytic functions are explained in more detail in Chapter 21.*

## RAWTOHEX

**Syntax**: RAWTOHEX(raw)
**Description**: This function takes a raw string of decimal numbers and converts it into a string of hexadecimal numbers.
**Folder**: RAWTOHEX can be found in the Conversion folder, as shown in Figure B-5.

## REGR_xxx (Linear Regression)

**Syntax**: REGR_xxx (value1, value2)
**Description**: Oracle provides a set of linear regression functions. Linear regression is used to make predictions about a single value. Simple linear regression involves discovering the equation for a line that most nearly fits the given data. That linear equation is then used to predict values for the data. For example, if a university wants to predict a student's grade on a freshman college calculus midterm based on their SAT score, then it may apply *linear regression*.
**Folder**: The REGR_xxx functions can be found in the Group and Analytic folders, as shown in Figures B-6 and B-7.

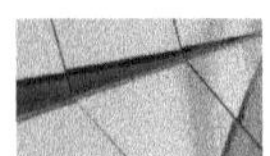

**NOTE**
*Analytic functions are explained in more detail in Chapter 21.*

## REGR_AVGX

**Description**: This function computes the average of the independent variable of the regression line.

## REGR_AVGY

**Description**: This function computes the average of the dependent variable of the regression line.

## REGR_COUNT

**Description**: This function returns the quantity of number pairs used to fit the regression line.

## REGR_INTERCEPT

**Description**: This function returns the y-intercept of the regression line.

## REGR_R2

**Description**: This function returns the coefficient of determination.

## REGR_SLOPE

**Description**: This function returns the slope of a line.

## REPLACE

**Syntax**: REPLACE(string, search_string [, replace_string] )
**Description**: This function takes a string and returns a new string that has had every occurrence of search_string replaced with replace_string. If replace_string is omitted or it is null, all occurrences of search_string are removed. If search_string is null, the original string is returned.
**Folder**: REPLACE can be found in the String folder, as shown in Figure B-3.
**Examples**:

- REPLACE('JACK and 'JUE', J', 'BL') returns 'BLACK and BLUE'.
- REPLACE('The Cat is at the Mat', 'at') returns 'The C is the M'.
- REPLACE('GEORGE', 'GE') returns 'OR'.

## ROUND (for Dates)

**Syntax**: ROUND(date, format)
**Description**: This function rounds a date according to the format specified. When no format is specified, the date is rounded to noon tomorrow if the time is later than midday or to noon today if the time is before midday. In either case, the resulting time is set to noon. For a full list of the formats allowed, see the section "Date Format Masks" later in this appendix.
**Folder**: ROUND can be found in the Date folder, as shown in Figure B-4.
**Examples**: All examples for this function can be found in the section "Date Format Masks" later in this appendix.

## ROUND (for Numbers)

**Syntax**: ROUND(number, places)
**Description**: This function rounds a number to the number of decimal places specified. If the number of places is omitted, Discoverer rounds to zero decimal places. If a negative value is supplied for the number of places, Discoverer rounds the digits to the left of the decimal point.

If any decimals are supplied in the number of places, they are ignored. This function is not the same as TRUNC. We have used the same examples in both functions to show you the difference.
**Folder**: ROUND can be found in the Numeric folder, as shown in Figure B-2.
**Examples**:

- ROUND(578.666, 2) returns 578.67.
- ROUND(578.666, 0) returns 579.00.
- ROUND(578.667, –1) returns 580.00.
- ROUND(578.667, –2) returns 600.00.

## ROWCOUNT

**Syntax**: ROWCOUNT
**Description**: This function returns the total number of rows returned by the query. This total includes duplicates and null values.
**Folder**: ROWCOUNT can be found in the Group folder, as shown in Figure B-6.

## ROWIDTOCHAR

**Syntax**: ROWIDTOCHAR(rowid)
**Description**: This function takes an internal row identifier, or rowid, and converts it into a string. According to the information that we have gathered together, this function should never be needed. It apparently is used as a debugging tool yet somehow has made its way into Discoverer. Your Discoverer administrator will be the one who uses this. There does not seem to be a great use for this function in normal queries, and we advise you not to use it.
**Folder**: ROWIDTOCHAR can be found in the Conversion folder, as shown in Figure B-5.

## ROWNUM

**Syntax**: ROWNUM
**Description**: This function returns a number indicating the order in which the row was selected by the query. The number is assigned before any sorting is done and gives you the true order in which the row was selected.
**Folder**: ROWNUM can be found in the Others folder, as shown in Figure B-8.

## ROW_NUMBER

**Syntax**: ROW_NUMBER(value) OVER (PARTITION BY value1 ORDER BY value2)
**Description**: This highly versatile analytic function assigns a unique consecutive number to each row in a set of rows. The OVER clause allows you to specify the grouping and sorting of the rows you would like numbered. This function is quite useful when used within a from clause query.
**Folder**: ROW_NUMBER can be found in the Analytic folder, as shown in Figure B-7.

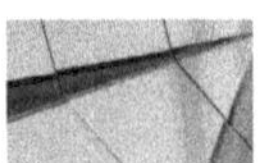

**NOTE**
*Analytic functions are explained in more detail in Chapter 21.*

## RPAD (Right Pad)

**Syntax**: RPAD(string, number [, character] )
**Description**: This function takes a string, a number, and optionally a character and appends the character defined as the third parameter as often as is needed to give the string the length specified in the second parameter. If no character set is specified, Discoverer pads out the string with spaces. If the specified string is the null value, the result will be the null value. If the specified number or character, if supplied, is the null value, Discoverer will report an error. If the length of the original string is already equal to or bigger than the number specified, Discoverer returns the original string.
**Folder**: RPAD can be found in the String folder, as shown in Figure B-3.

**Examples**:

- RPAD('Armstrong', 14) returns a new string 'Armstrong ', now with a length of 14, with five space characters having been appended to the end.
- RPAD('Jones', 7, '-') returns 'Jones—'.

# RTRIM (Right Trim)

**Syntax**: RTRIM(string [, characters] )
**Description**: This function takes a string, and optionally a set of characters, and returns a new string with all occurrences of those characters removed from the end of the original string. If no second string is specified, Discoverer removes all trailing spaces. If either the specified string or the set of characters is the null value, the result will be the null value.
**Folder**: RTRIM can be found in the String folder, as shown in Figure B-3.
**Examples**:

- RTRIM('Armstrong ') returns 'Armstrong' with all trailing spaces removed.
- RTRIM('Armstrong-Smith', '-Smith') returns 'Armstrong'.
- RTRIM('Michael','') returns the null value because the character set is null.

# SESSIONTIMEZONE

**Syntax**: SESSIONTIMEZONE
**Description**: This function returns the number of hours difference between the time zone of the Discoverer user's session and Greenwich mean time (GMT). Discoverer accesses the time zone from the operating system and submits it to the Oracle database upon connecting.
**Folder**: SESSIONTIMEZONE can be found in the Date folder, as shown in Figure B-4.
**Example**: If you are in Mountain time, SESSIONTIMEZONE will return –06:00.

# SIGN

**Syntax**: SIGN(numeric expression)
**Description**: This function returns three possible values: –1, 0, and 1. These values are assigned depending upon whether the numeric expression evaluates to less than zero (–1), zero (0), or greater than zero (1). Using SIGN in conjunction with DECODE produces very effective "if, then" type of expressions.
**Folder**: SIGN can be found in the Numeric folder, as shown in Figure B-2.
**Examples**:

- SIGN(133) returns 1.
- SIGN(-15) returns –1.
- SIGN(0) returns 0.

# SIN (Sine)

**Syntax**: SIN(value)

**Description**: This function takes the value given and returns the sine of that angle. The function returns a result expressed in radians.
**Folder**: SIN can be found in the Numeric folder, as shown in Figure B-2.
**Examples**:

- SIN(30) returns a value of 0.5.
- SIN(90) returns a value of 1.

## SINH (Hyperbolic Sine)

**Syntax**: SINH(value)
**Description**: This function takes the value given and returns the hyperbolic sine of that value. The function returns an angle expressed in radians.
**Folder**: SINH can be found in the Numeric folder, as shown in Figure B-2.

## SOUNDEX

**Syntax**: SOUNDEX(string)
**Description**: This function takes a string and returns the SOUNDEX code for that string. Using SOUNDEX in a parameterized condition can help you or your user find data phonetically. This function is great for bad spellers who want to search for words with similar sounds.
**Folder**: SOUNDEX can be found in the String folder, as shown in Figure B-3.
**Examples**:

- SOUNDEX('m') returns the value M000.
- SOUNDEX('michael') returns the value M240.

## SQRT (Square Root)

**Syntax**: SQRT(number)
**Description**: This function takes a number and returns the square root of that number. You must take care to ensure that the number does not evaluate to a negative number; otherwise, Discoverer will return an error. The square roots of negative numbers are imaginary numbers and cannot be displayed in Discoverer.
**Folder**: SQRT can be found in the Numeric folder, as shown in Figure B-2.
**Examples**:

- SQRT(169) returns the value 13.
- SQRT(-7) returns the value '#NUM!'.

## STDDEV (Standard Deviation)

**Syntax**: STDDEV(value)
**Description**: This function gives the standard deviation from the norm of values in a group of rows. The function is applied to the set of values derived from the argument values by the elimination of null values.
**Folder**: STDDEV can be found in the Group folder, as shown in Figure B-6.

## STDDEV_DISTINCT (Distinct Standard Deviation)

**Syntax**: STDDEV_DISTINCT(value)
**Description**: This function gives the standard deviation from the norm of values in a distinct group of rows. The function is applied to the set of values derived from the argument values by the elimination of null values and duplicates.
**Folder**: STDDEV_DISTINCT can be found in the Group and Analytic folders, as shown in Figures B-6 and B-7.

**NOTE**
*Analytic functions are explained in more detail in Chapter 21.*

## STDDEV_POP

**Syntax**: STDDEV_POP(value1)
**Description**: This function computes the population standard deviation and delivers the square root of the population variance.
**Folder**: STDDEV_POP can be found in the Group and Analytic folders, as shown in Figures B-6 and B-7.

**NOTE**
*Analytic functions are explained in more detail in Chapter 21.*

## STDDEV_SAMP

**Syntax**: STDDEV_SAMP
**Description**: This function computes the cumulative sample standard deviation and delivers the square root of the sample variance.
**Folder**: STDDEV_SAMP can be found in the Group and Analytic folders, as shown in Figures B-6 and B-7.

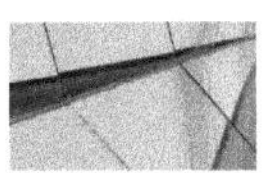

**NOTE**
*Analytic functions are explained in more detail in Chapter 21.*

## SUBSTR (Substring)

**Syntax**: SUBSTR(string, start ['count ] )
**Description**: This function takes a string and returns a portion of that string, beginning at the start position, making the portion count characters long. If you omit the count or provide a count that is bigger than the length of the original string, Discoverer returns a new string with the start number of characters removed. If you provide a start number that is bigger than the length of the original string, the result will be an empty string.
**Folder**: SUBSTR can be found in the String folder, as shown in Figure B-3.
**Examples**:

- SUBSTR('Michael', 5) returns 'ael', with the first five characters of 'Michael' removed.
- SUBSTR('Michael', 2, 3) returns 'ich'.

- SUBSTR(SSN,1,3)||'-'||SUBSTR(SSN,4,2)||'-'||SUBSTR(SSN,6.4) takes a Social Security number and converts it into the more typical format used in the United States. For example, if the SSN is 123456789, this example converts this to 123-45-6789.
- '('||SUBSTR(TEL,1,3)||')'||SUBSTR(TEL,4,3)||'-'||SUBSTR(TEL,7,4) takes a typical ten-digit telephone number and converts it into a more readable format. For example, if the number is 1234567890, this example converts it to (123) 345-7890.

**NOTE**
*The two preceding examples make excellent use of the concatenate function.*

## SUBSTRB

**Syntax**: SUBSTRB(string, start [ count ] )
**Description**: This function takes a string and returns a substring of that string, beginning at the start byte position and going on for count number of bytes.
**Folder**: SUBSTRB can be found in the String folder, as shown in Figure B-3.

## SUM

**Syntax**: SUM(values)
**Description**: This function returns the sum of all the values in the expression or row.
**Folder**: SUM can be found in the Group and Analytic folders, as shown in Figures B-6 and B-7.
**Example**: SUM(ship quantity) returns the total quantity shipped.

**NOTE**
*Analytic functions are explained in more detail in Chapter 21.*

## SUM_DISTINCT

**Syntax**: SUM_DISTINCT(values)
**Description**: This function is similar to the SUM function, except that it returns the sum of all the unique values in the expression or row.
**Folder**: SUM_DISTINCT can be found in the Group and Analytic folders, as shown in Figures B-6 and B-7.

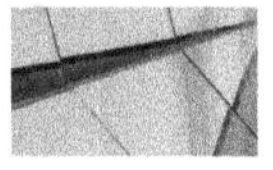

**NOTE**
*Analytic functions are explained in more detail in Chapter 21.*

## SUM_SQUARES

**Syntax**: SUM_SQUARES(number)
**Description**: This function returns the total of the square of the number given. If you select this function and then edit the calculation, you will notice that Discoverer changes the function to SUM(POWER(number, 2)).
**Folder**: SUM_SQUARES can be found in the Group folder, as shown in Figure B-6.
**Example**: SUM_SQUARES(3) returns 9, and Discoverer writes this as SUM(POWER(3,2)).

## SYSDATE (System Date)

**Syntax**: SYSDATE
**Description**: This function returns the current date and time. You can use this date inside many other functions, because it acts exactly like a DATE data type.
**Folder**: SYSDATE can be found in the Date folder, as shown in Figure B-4.
**Examples**:

- TRUNC(SYSDATE –1) returns yesterday's date, minus the time. Most data warehouses store dates in this format, so if you want to look for all shipments that occurred yesterday, you would create this condition: ship_date = TRUNC(SYSDATE-1).
- SYSDATE + (1/288) or SYSDATE + 0.0034722 will add five minutes to the current time.

**NOTE**
*Adding something to SYSDATE, or any other date for that matter, is a simple case of working out the decimal or fraction that needs to be added. Therefore, to add five minutes, once you have worked out that there are 288 five-minute periods in a 24-hour period, the calculation is simple.*

## TAN (Tangent)

**Syntax**: TAN(value)
**Description**: This function takes the value given and returns the trigonometric tangent of that value. The function returns an angle expressed in radians.
**Folder**: TAN can be found in the Numeric folder, as shown in Figure B-2.
**Examples**:

- TAN(–60) returns a value of –1.73205.
- TAN(0) returns a value of 0.
- TAN(30) returns a value of 0.577350.

## TANH (Hyperbolic Tangent)

**Syntax**: TANH(value)
**Description**: This function takes the value given and returns the hyperbolic tangent of that value. The function returns an angle expressed in radians. For those of you who are mathematically oriented, the hyperbolic tangent is defined as $\tan(x) = (e^x - e^{-x}) / (e^x + e^{-x})$.
**Folder**: TANH can be found in the Numeric folder, as shown in Figure B-2.
**Examples**:

- TANH(0) returns a value of 0.
- TANH(0.3) returns a value of 0.291313.
- TANH(0.5) returns a value of 0.462117.

## TO_CHAR (Dates)

**Syntax**: TO_CHAR(date, format [,nls_parameters] )
**Description**: This function converts a date into a string by applying the specified format. The date provided must be a valid date. The function also takes an optional NLS string of parameters. For an explanation of NLS, see the function NLS_INITCAP. For a list of all the date format masks, please refer to the section "Date Format Masks" later in this appendix.
**Folder**: TO_CHAR can be found in the Conversion folder, as shown in Figure B-5.
**Examples**: In the examples that follow, suppose the current date is July 21, 2014, at 3:52 p.m.

- TO_CHAR(SYSDATE, 'fmDay, Month DD, YYYY HH:MI:AM') returns 'Monday, July 21, 2014 3:52 PM'.
- TO_CHAR(SYSDATE, 'MM/DD/YY') returns '07/21/14'.
- TO_CHAR(TO_DATE('21-JUL-14'), 'Month-YYYY') returns the string 'July-2014'.
- TO_CHAR(SYSDATE, 'MON-YYYY') returns JUL-14, which is very useful within E-Business Suite because this function will return the current period.

You need to be very careful when supplying strings directly to TO_CHAR because the date supplied *must* be a valid date in its own right.

## TO_CHAR (Labels)

**Syntax**: TO_CHAR(label, format [,nls_parameters] )
**Description**: This function converts a label into a string by applying the specified format. The function also takes an optional NLS string of parameters. For an explanation of NLS, see the function NLS_INITCAP. This function is for use by administrators only.
**Folder**: TO_CHAR can be found in the Conversion folder, as shown in Figure B-5.

## TO_CHAR (Numbers)

**Syntax**: TO_CHAR(number, [ format [,nls_parameters] ] )
**Description**: This function converts a number into a string by applying the specified optional format. The function also takes an optional NLS string of parameters. For an explanation of NLS, see the function NLS_INITCAP. For a list of all the number format masks, please refer to the section "Number Format Masks" later in this appendix.
**Folder**: TO_CHAR can be found in the Conversion folder, as shown in Figure B-5.
**Examples**:

- TO_CHAR(678) returns the string '678'.
- TO_CHAR(678.7,'999D99') returns the string '678.70'.
- TO_CHAR(678, 'RN') returns the string 'DCLXXVIII'—that is, 678 in roman numerals.

## TO_DATE

**Syntax**: TO_DATE(string, format)
**Description**: This function converts a string in the given format into a standard Oracle date. Only if the string is already in the standard Oracle format of 'DD-MON-YY' can the format option be omitted. For a full listing of the valid format options, please see the section "Date Format Masks" later in this appendix.

**Folder**: TO_DATE can be found in the Conversion folder, as shown in Figure B-5.
**Examples**:

- TO_DATE('14/10/58', 'DD/MM/YY') returns the Oracle date 14-OCT-58.
- TO_DATE('09-09-51', 'MM-DD-YY') returns the Oracle date 09-SEP-51.

# TO_LABEL

This function has been dropped from the current version of Discoverer. If you have any workbooks that use this function, you will need to use an alternative function.

# TO_MULTI_BYTE

**Syntax**: TO_MULTI_BYTE(string)
**Description**: This function converts each of the single-byte characters in the string into their multibyte equivalents. If the character has no multibyte equivalent, the function leaves the character unchanged.
**Folder**: TO_MULTI_BYTE can be found in the Conversion folder, as shown in Figure B-5.

# TO_NUMBER

**Syntax**: TO_NUMBER(string, format [,nls_parameters] )
**Description**: This function converts a string into a number by applying the specified optional format. The function also takes an optional NLS string of parameters. For an explanation of NLS, see the function NLS_INITCAP. For a list of all the number format masks, please refer to the section "Number Format Masks" later in this appendix. Discoverer is good at converting strings into numbers, and we recommend you avoid supplying a format mask.
**Folder**: TO_NUMBER can be found in the Conversion folder, as shown in Figure B-5.
**Examples**:

- See the functions GREATEST and LEAST.
- TO_NUMBER('765.43') returns the number 765.43.
- TO_NUMBER(order_number) will convert the database field called order_number into a number. Care should be taken when doing this that all of the strings being converted are indeed numbers.
- TO_NUMBER('0.5555','990D9999') returns 0.56, 0.556 or 0.5555, depending upon the format you have applied to the column.

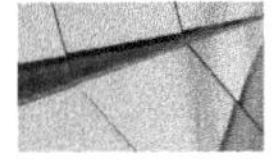

**NOTE**
*Be careful when specifying the optional format mask. If you supply a mask, you must ensure that the mask corresponds exactly to the number within the string. Supplying an incorrect format mask causes Discoverer to error out with an ORA-01722 error. The following function will fail: TO_NUMBER('0.5555','990D99'). It returns an error because the format mask being applied does not match the actual number of decimal places in the string.*

## TO_SINGLE_BYTE

**Syntax**: TO_SINGLE_BYTE(string)
**Description**: This function converts each of the multibyte characters in the string into their single-byte equivalents. If the character has no single-byte equivalent, the function leaves the character unchanged.
**Folder**: TO_SINGLE_BYTE can be found in the Conversion folder, as shown in Figure B-5.

## TRANSLATE

**Syntax**: TRANSLATE(string, search, replace)
**Description**: This function takes the string and looks at each character in the string. It then looks to see whether any of the characters in the search string are in the original string. If any of the search characters are there, Discoverer replaces them with the character in the replace string that is in the same position as the character in the search string.
**Folder**: TRANSLATE can be found in the String folder, as shown in Figure B-3.
**Example**:

- TRANSLATE('MICHAEL SMITH', 'AEI', '123') returns 'M3CH12L SM3TH'. As you can see, Discoverer has replaced each occurrence of *A* with a 1, each *E* with a 2, and each *I* with a 3.

## TRUNC (Dates)

**Syntax**: TRUNC(date, format)
**Description**: This function takes a date and truncates the time component from it, leaving just the date. Refer to the section entitled "Using Formats When Rounding Dates" later in this appendix.
**Folder**: TRUNC can be found in the Date folder, as shown in Figure B-4.
**Examples**:

- TRUNC(SYSDATE) returns the current date minus the time.
- TRUNC(ship date) returns the ship date minus the time. If you have shipped many items in the same day, truncating the date allows you to group all of the items together.

## TRUNC (Numbers)

**Syntax**: TRUNC(number, precision)
**Description**: This function truncates a number according to the precision specified. If the precision is omitted or is zero, Discoverer truncates all of the decimal places. If a negative value is supplied for the precision, Discoverer truncates (makes zero) that number of digits to the left of the decimal point. If any decimals are supplied in the precision, they are ignored. This function is not the same as ROUND. We have used the same examples in both functions to show you the difference.
**Folder**: TRUNC can be found in the Numeric folder, as shown in Figure B-2.
**Examples**:

- TRUNC(578.666, 2) returns 578.66.
- ROUND(578.666, 0) returns 578.00.
- ROUND(578.667, -1) returns 570.00.
- ROUND(578.667, -2) returns 500.00.

# UID

**Syntax**: UID
**Description**: This function returns the user ID of the current user as assigned by Oracle. The number is unique on the current database.
**Folder**: UID can be found in the Others folder, as shown in Figure B-8.

# UPPER

**Syntax**: UPPER(string)
**Description**: This function uppercases every character in the string.
**Folder**: UPPER can be found in the String folder, as shown in Figure B-3.
**Example**:

- UPPER('Darlene') returns 'DARLENE'.

# USER

**Syntax**: USER
**Description**: This function returns the username by which the user is known to the system. Users running Discoverer in Apps mode need to understand that this function will not return the username they have logged in as but rather the database username the application is using to log them in to the database.
**Folder**: USER can be found in the Others folder, as shown in Figure B-8.

# USERENV

**Syntax**: USERENV(option)
**Description**: This function returns information in a string about the current user session. The valid options are 'CLIENT_INFO', 'ENTRYID', 'INSTANCE', 'ISDBA', 'LANG', 'LANGUAGE', 'SESSIONID', and 'TERMINAL'.
**Folder**: USERENV can be found in the Others folder, as shown in Figure B-8.
**Examples**:

- USERENV(TERMINAL) returns the terminal ID you are connected to. If you are using a terminal server, this returns the server name.
- USERENV(ISDBA) returns TRUE if the logged-in user is a DBA; otherwise, it returns FALSE.
- USERENV(LANG) returns the ISO language for the system you are working on. In our system this returns US.
- USERENV(LANGUAGE) returns the language and territory currently used by your session along with the database character set in use. In our system, this function returns AMERICAN_AMERICA WE8ISO8859P1. This tells me the language I am using is American, the territory I am in is America, and the character set I am using is the ISO 8859-1 Western European 8-bit character set.

## VARIANCE

**Syntax**: VARIANCE(number)
**Description**: This function returns the variance for all values, except null values, of a group of rows. The variance is the authorized deviation.
**Folder**: VARIANCE can be found in the Group and Analytic folders, as shown in Figures B-6 and B-7.

**NOTE**
*Analytic functions are explained in more detail in Chapter 21.*

## VARIANCE_DISTINCT

**Syntax**: VARIANCE_DISTINCT(number)
**Description**: This function returns the variance for all unique values, except null values, of a group of rows. The variance is the authorized deviation.
**Folder**: VARIANCE_DISTINCT can be found in the Group and Analytic folders, as shown in Figures B-6 and B-7.

**NOTE**
*Analytic functions are explained in more detail in Chapter 21.*

## VAR_POP (Population Variance)

**Syntax**: VAR_POP(value)
**Description**: This function returns the population variance, except null values, of a group of rows.
**Folder**: VAR_POP can be found in the Group and Analytic folders, as shown in Figures B-6 and B-7.

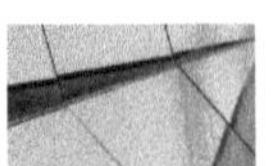

**NOTE**
*Analytic functions are explained in more detail in Chapter 21.*

## VAR_SAMP (Sample Variance)

**Syntax**: VAR_SAMP(value)
**Description**: This function returns the sample variance, except null values, of a group of rows.
**Folder**: VAR_SAMP can be found in the Group and Analytic folders, as shown in Figures B-6 and B-7.

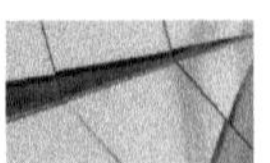

**NOTE**
*Analytic functions are explained in more detail in Chapter 21.*

## VSIZE

**Syntax**: VSIZE(value)
**Description**: This function tells you how much storage space is being taken up by the item concerned. For strings, the size is the same as the length of the string. For numbers, it is usually smaller because less space is needed to store numbers.
**Folder**: VSIZE can be found in the Others folder, as shown in Figure B-8.
**Examples**:

- VSIZE('Michael') returns 7.
- VSIZE(16.8765) returns 4.

## WIDTH_BUCKET

**Syntax**: WIDTH_BUCKET(value1, min_value, max_value, n)
**Description**: This very useful function will evenly distribute a range between your min_value and your max_value. It will then break this range into *n*+2 buckets and place all the values from value1 into one of these buckets. You always receive two more buckets than you request, as it creates an overflow bucket and an underflow bucket. This is used to create equiwidth histograms.
**Folder**: WIDTH_BUCKET can be found in the Group and Analytic folders, as shown in Figures B-6 and B-7.
**Example**:

- WIDTH_BUCKET(Order Qty SUM,0,800000,10) generates ten evenly distributed buckets for the order quantity between 0 and 800,000.

**NOTE**
*Analytic functions are explained in more detail in Chapter 21.*

# Time Zones

The following is a list of the valid time zones that can be used within the Discoverer NEW_TIME date function:

- **'AST', 'ADT'** Atlantic standard or daylight saving time
- **BST', 'BDT'** Bering standard or daylight saving time
- **'CST', 'CDT'** Central standard or daylight saving time
- **'EST', 'EDT'** Eastern standard or daylight saving time
- **'GMT'** Greenwich mean time
- **'HST',' HDT'** Alaska-Hawaii standard or daylight saving time
- **'MST', 'MDT'** Mountain standard or daylight saving time
- **'NST'** Newfoundland standard time
- **'PST', 'PDT'** Pacific standard or daylight saving time
- **'YST', 'YDT'** Yukon standard or daylight saving time

# Using Formats When Rounding Dates

When using the ROUND function on a date, the following is a list of formats available, along with an example of each. All of the examples given assume that the current date is Monday, July 21, 2014, and that the time is 12:35:40 a.m.

- CC, SCC rounds to the first January 1 of the century. It rounds at midnight on the morning of January 1 of 1951, 2001, 2051, and so on.
  - ROUND(SYSDATE, 'CC') rounds to noon on January 1, 2001.
- SYEAR, SYYY, Y, YY, YYY, YYYY, YEAR rounds to January1 of the year. It rounds at midnight on the morning of July 1.
  - ROUND(SYSDATE, 'YEAR') rounds to noon on January 1, 2015.
- Q rounds to the first day of a quarter, and it assumes that the quarters begin with January, April, July, and October. It rounds on the 16$^{th}$day of the second month of the quarter, regardless of how many days there are in the month.
  - ROUND(SYSDATE, 'Q') rounds to noon on July 1, 2014.
- MONTH, MON, MM rounds to the first date of a month. It rounds on the 16$^{th}$ day of the month, regardless of how many days there are in that month.
  - ROUND(SYSDATE, 'MONTH') rounds to noon on August 1, 2014.
- WW rounds to the nearest date that has the same day of the week as the first day of the year.
  - ROUND(SYSDATE, 'WW') rounds to noon on July 23, 2014. This is because January 1, 2014, fell on a Wednesday.
- W rounds to the nearest date that has the same day of the week as the beginning of the current month.
  - ROUND(SYSDATE, 'W') rounds to noon on July 22, 2014. This is because July 1, 2014, fell on a Tuesday.
- DDD, DD, J rounds to noon on the next day or noon on the same day if the time is before noon. This is the same as applying ROUND with no format.
  - ROUND(SYSDATE, 'DD') rounds to noon on July 21, 2014.
- DAY, DY, D rounds to the nearest Sunday, the first day of the week. It rounds at noon on Wednesday.
  - ROUND(SYSDATE, 'D') rounds to noon on July 20, 2014.
- HH, HH12, HH24 rounds to the next whole hour. It rounds at 30 minutes and 30 seconds past the hour.
  - ROUND(SYSDATE, 'HH') rounds to 1:00 a.m. on July 21, 2014.
- MI Rounds to the next whole minute. It rounds to 30 seconds past the minute.
  - ROUND(SYSDATE, 'MI') rounds to 12:36 a.m. on July 21, 2014.

# Date Format Masks

The following sections contain a full list of the format masks that can be used within the TO_ CHAR and TO_DATE functions in Discoverer, along with an example value based on Monday, July 21, 2014.

## Day Format Masks

| Mask | Description | Example |
|---|---|---|
| D | Number of the day of the week | 2 |
| DD | Number of the day of the month | 21 |
| DDD | Number of the day in the year, since January 1st | 202 |
| DY | Three-letter uppercase abbreviation of the day | MON |
| Dy | Three-letter initial-cap abbreviation of the day | Mon |
| Dy | Three-letter lowercase abbreviation of the day | mon |
| DAY | The uppercase full name of the day | MONDAY |
| Day | The initial-cap full name of the day | Monday |
| Day | The lowercase full name of the day | monday |

## Month Format Masks

| Mask | Description | Example |
|---|---|---|
| MM | Number of the month | 07 |
| RM | Roman numeral for the month | VII |
| MON | Three-letter uppercase abbreviation of the month | JUL |
| Mon | Three-letter initial-cap abbreviation of the month | Jul |
| Mon | Three-letter lowercase abbreviation of the month | Jul |
| MONTH | The uppercase full name of the month | JULY |
| Month | The initial-cap full name of the month | July |
| Month | The lowercase full name of the month | july |

## Year Format Masks

| Mask | Description | Example |
|---|---|---|
| Y | Last digit of the year | 4 |
| YY | Last two digits of the year | 14 |
| YYY | Last three digits of the year | 014 |
| YYYY | Full four-digit year | 2014 |
| SYYYY | A signed year if the year is BC, for example | 255 BC |

| Mask | Description | Example |
|---|---|---|
| I | Last digit of the International Organization for Standardization (ISO) year | 4 |
| IY | Last two digits of the ISO year | 14 |
| IYY | Last three digits of the ISO year | 014 |
| IYYY | Full four-digit ISO year | 2014 |
| YEAR | Uppercase year spelled out in full | TWO THOUSAND FOURTEEN |
| Year | The initial-cap year spelled out on full | Two Thousand Fourteen |
| year | Lowercase year spelled out in full | two thousand fourteen |
| RR | Last two digits of the year, possibly in another century | 14 |

## Other Date Masks

| Mask | Description | Example |
|---|---|---|
| Q | Number of the current quarter of the year | 3 |
| WW | Number of the week in the year | 29 |
| W | Number of the week in the month | 4 |
| IW | Week of the year, based on the ISO standard | 30 |
| J | Number of "Julian" days since December 31, 4713 BC | 2456860 |
| AD or BC | Displays AD or BC without periods | AD |
| ad or bc | Displays AD or BC in lowercase without periods | Ad |
| A.D. or B.C. | Displays AD or BC with periods | A.D. |
| a.d. or b.c. | Displays AD or BC in lowercase with periods | a.d. |
| CC | Displays the current century | 21 |
| SCC | Displays the current century and prefixes BC dates with - and AD dates with a space | 21 |

## Time Format Masks

In this section, suppose the current time is 7:02:22 p.m. This is how Discoverer can format that time:

| Mask | Description | Example |
|---|---|---|
| HH or hh | The hour of the day with leading zeros | 07 |
| HH12 or hh12 | The hour of the day with leading zeros | 07 |
| HH24 | The hour of the day in the 24-hour clock | 18 |
| MI or mi | The number of minutes in the hour | 02 |
| SS or ss | The number of seconds in the minute | 22 |
| SSSSS | The number of seconds since midnight | 68542 |

## Special Format Masks

Discoverer allows you to insert special punctuation characters into the TO_CHAR function so that the result is easy to understand. Within the TO_DATE function, you can use the same punctuation to inform Discoverer of the characters that are to be ignored.

| Mask | Description | Example |
|---|---|---|
| / | Inserts or ignores a forward slash character | 21/07/2014 |
| , | Inserts or ignores a comma | 21, July, 2014 |
| - | Inserts or ignores a hyphen | 21-JUL-14 |
| : | Inserts or ignores a colon | 7:02:22 |
| . | Inserts or ignores a period | 19.02.22 |

## Prefixes and Suffixes

Within the TO_CHAR function only, Discoverer allows you to add prefixes and suffixes to some of the standard format masks. These prefixes and suffixes further enhance the functionality of the function. The prefixes and suffixes allowed are as follows:

- **fm** This can be prefixed to both Day and Month, such that the format mask looks like fmDay or fmMonth. Using this mask forces Discoverer to suppress padding of the month or day. Without this prefix, the days of the week and months of the year are padded to make them all display as the same length.
- **TH or th** This can be suffixed to dd and DD to force Discoverer to display the date as $24^{th}$ or $24^{TH}$. The capitalization is applied according to whether you choose dd or DD or a combination like Dd or dD.
- **SP or sp** This can be suffixed to most date numbers and forces Discoverer to spell out the number in full. Using this suffix, you can spell out the date—thus, the twenty-fourth. Again, the capitalization is applied in accordance with the case of the number to be spelled in full.
- **SPTH or THSP** This suffix is a combination of SP and TH. Using this suffix, you can force Discoverer to apply both of the preceding two masks.

# Number Format Masks

The following is a full list of the format masks that can be used within the TO_CHAR function when working with numbers in Discoverer:

- **9999990** The number of nines or zeros determines the maximum number of digits that can be displayed.
- **999,999,999.99** Discoverer inserts commas and the decimal point at the places specified in the pattern. If the value is zero, the result will be blank.
- **999990** This causes Discoverer to display zero if the value is zero.
- **099999** This causes Discoverer to display numbers with leading zeros, such that 678 will display as 000678.
- **$99999** This causes Discoverer to insert the dollar symbol in front of every number.

- **B99999** This causes Discoverer to display a blank field when the value is zero.
- **99999MI** For negative numbers, this causes Discoverer to place the minus sign to the right of the number. Normally, Discoverer places the minus sign to the left.
- **99999S** This is the same as 99999MI.
- **S99999** For negative numbers, this causes Discoverer to place the minus sign to the left of the number.
- **99D99** This causes Discoverer to insert a decimal point in the position specified.
- **C99999** This causes Discoverer to display the ISO currency character in this position, such that 678 will display as USD678.
- **L99999** This causes Discoverer to display the local currency character in this position, such that if your local currency is the U.S. dollar, 678 will display as $678.
- **RN** This causes Discoverer to display the number in Roman numerals.
- **99999PR** For negative numbers, this causes Discoverer to display the number surrounded by the **<** and **>** symbols.
- **9.999EEEE** This causes Discoverer to display the number in scientific notation.
- **999V99** This causes Discoverer to multiply by 10 × *n*, where *n* is the number of digits to the right of the *V* character. For example, 9753 displays as 975300.

# ASCII Character Set

As some of Discoverer's string functions use the American Standard Code for Information Interchange (ASCII, pronounced *ask-ee*) character set, we thought it would be a good idea to give you more background information concerning this well-used character set. The standard ASCII character set uses 7 bits for each character, which means that there are 128 characters in the set. There are many larger character sets that use 8 bits, which gives them an additional 128 characters, making 256 characters altogether. These extra characters are used to represent non-English characters, graphics symbols, and mathematical symbols. Several companies and organizations have proposed extensions for these 128 characters. The DOS operating system uses a superset of ASCII called *extended ASCII* or *high ASCII.*

A more universal standard is the ISO Latin 1 set of characters, which is used by many operating systems, as well as web browsers. Officially named ISO-8859-1, this character set was devised by the Geneva-based International Organization for Standardization (ISO). One of us has the pleasure of having a good friend inside ISO; the name, by the way, is not an acronym but is derived from the Greek word *iso*, which means equal.

Table B-1 contains the standard ASCII character set.

In Table B-1, the first 32 characters (0–31) are considered nonprinting characters. ASCII was originally designed for use with TeleType machines, so today the descriptions, as shown in Table B-2, are somewhat obscure.

You may think that these characters have no use in Discoverer, and generally, you would be correct. However, character 13 is very useful. This is the carriage return character and as such can be concatenated with other strings. To format an address, for printing on labels, for example, so that each line of the address is on a separate line, use a calculation like this:

```
ADDRESS1 || CHR(13) || ADDRESS2 || CHR(13) || CITY || CHR(13) || STATE || ''|| ZIP
```

which will print out as follows:

7531 Smith Road
Suite 17a
Any Town
My State 12345-6789

If you turn on text wrapping, Discoverer will even display your addresses like this in your report:

| 0 | NUL | 16 | DLE | 32 | SPC | 48 | 0 | 64 | @ | 80 | P | 96 | | 112 | p |
|---|---|---|---|---|---|---|---|---|---|---|---|---|---|---|---|
| 1 | SOH | 17 | DC1 | 33 | ! | 49 | 1 | 65 | A | 81 | Q | 97 | a | 113 | q |
| 2 | STX | 18 | DC2 | 34 | " | 50 | 2 | 66 | B | 82 | R | 98 | b | 114 | r |
| 3 | ETX | 19 | DC3 | 35 | # | 51 | 3 | 67 | C | 83 | S | 99 | c | 115 | s |
| 4 | EOT | 20 | DC4 | 36 | $ | 52 | 4 | 68 | D | 84 | T | 100 | d | 116 | t |
| 5 | ENQ | 21 | NAK | 37 | % | 53 | 5 | 69 | E | 85 | U | 101 | e | 117 | u |
| 6 | ACK | 22 | SYN | 38 | & | 54 | 6 | 70 | F | 86 | V | 102 | f | 118 | v |
| 7 | BEL | 23 | ETB | 39 | ' | 55 | 7 | 71 | G | 87 | W | 103 | g | 119 | w |
| 8 | BS | 24 | CAN | 40 | ( | 56 | 8 | 72 | H | 88 | X | 104 | h | 120 | x |
| 9 | TAB | 25 | EM | 41 | ) | 57 | 9 | 73 | I | 89 | Y | 105 | I | 121 | y |
| 10 | LF | 26 | SUB | 42 | * | 58 | : | 74 | J | 90 | X | 106 | j | 122 | z |
| 11 | VT | 27 | ESC | 43 | + | 59 | ; | 75 | K | 91 | [ | 107 | k | 123 | { |
| 12 | FF | 28 | FS | 44 | , | 60 | < | 76 | L | 92 | \ | 108 | l | 124 | \| |
| 13 | CR | 29 | GS | 45 | - | 61 | = | 77 | M | 93 | ] | 109 | m | 125 | } |
| 14 | SO | 30 | RS | 46 | . | 62 | > | 78 | N | 94 | ^ | 110 | n | 126 | ~ |
| 15 | SI | 31 | US | 47 | / | 63 | ? | 79 | O | 95 | _ | 111 | o | 127 | DEL |

**TABLE B-1.** *Standard ASCII Character Set*

| 0 | Null | 8 | Backspace | 16 | Data link escape | 24 | Cancel |
|---|---|---|---|---|---|---|---|
| 1 | Start of heading | 9 | Horizontal tab | 17 | Device control 1 | 25 | End of medium |
| 2 | Start of text | 10 | New line | 18 | Device control 2 | 26 | Substitute |
| 3 | End of text | 11 | Vertical tab | 19 | Device control 3 | 27 | Escape |
| 4 | End of transmission | 12 | Form feed | 20 | Device control 4 | 28 | File separator |
| 5 | Enquiry | 13 | Carriage return | 21 | Negative acknowledge | 29 | Group separator |
| 6 | Acknowledge | 14 | Shift out | 22 | Synchronous idle | 30 | Record separator |
| 7 | Bell | 15 | Shift in | 23 | End of trans block | 31 | Unit separator |

**TABLE B-2.** *Descriptions of First 32 Characters*

## Summary

In this appendix, we listed all of the functions that are used within Discoverer, along with their syntax and many examples. After this, we included a comprehensive listing of the format masks that can be used, along with a table listing the ASCII character set.

# APPENDIX C

# Databases and Views

This appendix explains several database concepts. We begin by explaining the difference between traditional schemas, relational schemas, and star schemas. During the discussion on relational schemas, we introduce the techniques known as *normalization* and *denormalization*. Following this, we will look at the use of Discoverer with the Oracle E-Business Suite. We explain why views are used and introduce you to Oracle's business views. We then take a look at Noetix Corporation's NoetixViews. We close out the chapter by discussing how to create an embedded data warehouse within your E-Business Suite database.

# Database Schemas

You will encounter two basic schemas or types of database structures when working with Discoverer. They are as follows:

- Relational schemas
- Star schemas

## Relational Schemas

A *relational* schema is the traditional type of structure that is used by most databases today. These schemas depend on parent-child relationships, with primary keys and foreign keys. There is also no redundancy in the tables. These schemas are not designed for reporting and can become very complex.

For example, in a typical database of this type, there will be a table of addresses, a table of cities, and a table of countries, with each one appearing in the database once. Therefore, to print a full address, you would have to open several Discoverer folders.

Relational schemas are based on the relational model for database management put forward by Edgar F. Codd, a British computer scientist who devised the model while working for IBM during the 1960s and 1970s. Much to his disappointment, IBM did not fully embrace this new database model until after rivals such as Oracle started to embrace them. You may not be aware of this fact, but Codd also devised the term *online analytical processing* (OLAP) and wrote laws for OLAP.

### The Relational Concept

As defined by Codd in 1985, several rules concisely define what constitutes a relational database. In fact, there are 13 rules, because the rules are numbered rule 0 to rule 12; however, they are commonly known as the *12 rules*.

These 12 rules have become the guideline for the design of all relational databases ever since. However, we must be careful using the term *guideline* because, to date, no commercial relational database system conforms to all 12 rules. We will not discuss all 12 rules here. However, we will mention that, in its simplest form, to be classified as relational, a database must have tables that have primary keys, interlinked to other tables using foreign-key relationships and constraints. The system must also support the concept of having null data and be able to support the use of views to present the data to users in different logical combinations. You will notice that Discoverer obeys all of these rules.

For a full understanding of the 12 rules, we recommend you visit http: //http://en.wikipedia .org/wiki/Codd's_12_rules.

## Normalization and Denormalization

You may have heard of normalization and denormalization. *Normalization* is where the data is stored within the database once and once only. This is the pure relational schema and allows for the quickest method of inserting and updating data in the database. Because the data is stored only once, there is no redundancy of data, but this could make for poor performance when reporting.

The most common level of normalization is called *third normal form,* otherwise known as 3NF. To be classified as third normal form, all of the data in a row of data must be dependent upon the primary key, the whole of the primary key, and nothing but the primary key. In other words, if you have any data in the row that does not have a strict one-to-one relationship with the primary key, you are not strictly adhering to 3NF. Also, if you have calculated items such as totals that can be derived using other items within the row, you are not using a fully normalized structure.

*Denormalization* allows for the data to be stored multiple times when and where required. This allows for faster reporting but slower insertion and updating. A data warehouse uses mainly denormalized data structures. In Discoverer terms, you would use a complex folder to denormalize a schema to make it easier for your users to query from.

Using a classroom setting as an example, the following illustration shows a typical normalized, relational schema:

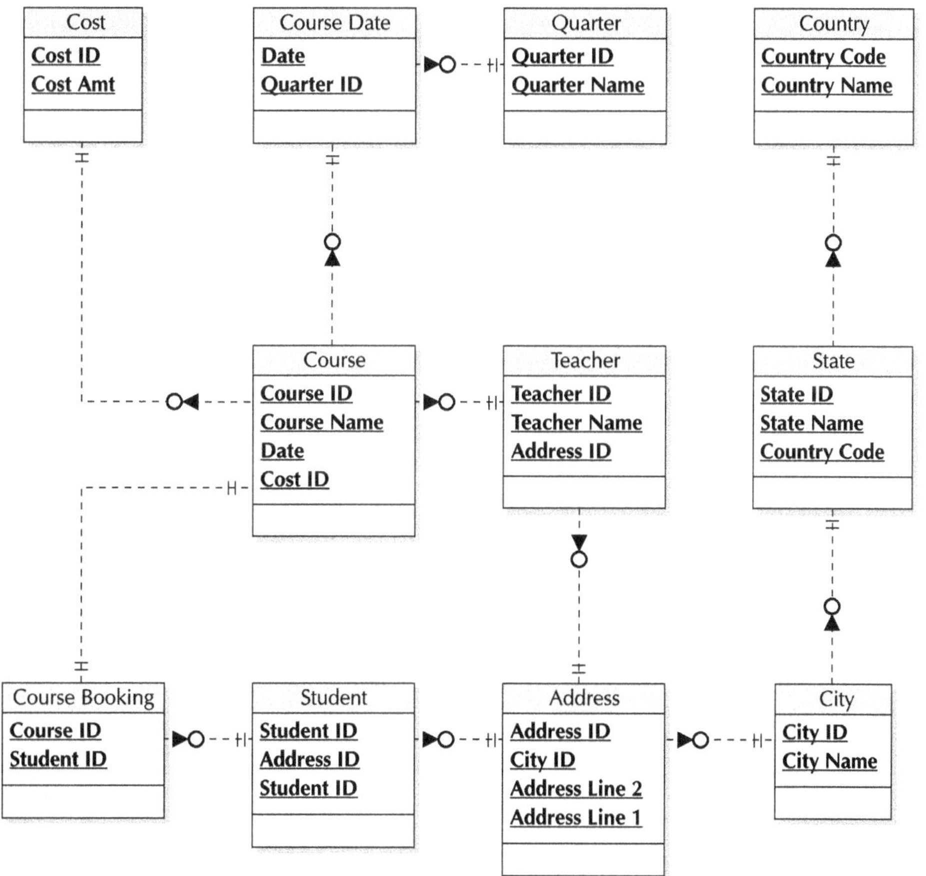

As you can see in the preceding illustration, we have 11 normalized tables. Each table has a unique numeric ID or code, and no data is being duplicated. To find all the students who graduated in a particular quarter and then mail them their certificates, you would need to join nine tables.

## Star Schemas

Otherwise known as a *dimensional* model, a denormalized *star* schema is traditionally used in a data warehouse. There is no attempt to reduce redundant data; instead, data is copied as many times as is needed in order to make querying as efficient and easy as possible. In a star schema, you normally have a central fact table, surrounded by many dimension tables. A pure fact table contains nothing except a foreign key for each of the dimension tables, as well as facts or metrics such as costs, quantities, and so on. Using a star schema with Discoverer, if you select an item from the fact table, all the other tables are available. If you begin selecting from a dimension table, your next selection must come from the fact table.

Using the same classroom setting from our previous example, the following illustration shows the database as a star schema:

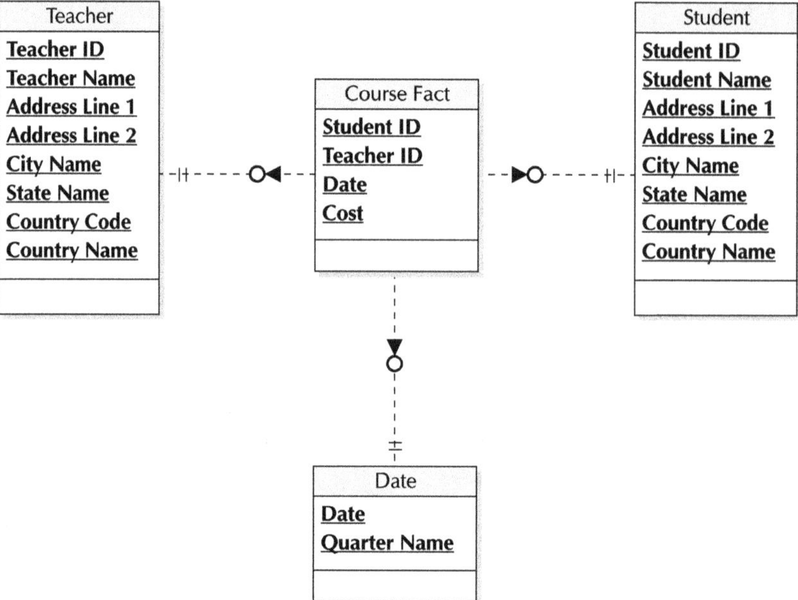


This schema differs from the relational schema as follows:

- The course table has been dropped and has been replaced by a fact table. This fact table contains the foreign-key ID of each of the dimension tables.
- The cost table has been dropped, with the cost of the course added to the fact table.
- The ID of the fact table consists of concatenating all the foreign keys together.
- All of the address information has been denormalized and is now stored in the Student and Teacher tables.
- All of the time information has been denormalized and is in the Date table.

Not all databases have data in a denormalized state, and few databases, other than data warehouses, have anything remotely resembling a star schema. During the section of this book that covers Discoverer administration, we showed the administrator how to create a pseudo star schema using complex folders. Users seem to be able to relate to star schemas better than traditional relational schemas. Discoverer itself works best against a star schema model. Thus, if you can take the time to build either a star schema within the database, perhaps using materialized views and lookup tables, or a star model within Discoverer, your users will thank you for it. Most failed Discoverer implementations are not the fault of the product but the fault of either poor database design or a poor business area design.

# Accessing E-Business Suite Using Discoverer

E-Business Suite provides world-class functionality through transactional power and the ability to support complex business processes. The data stored within its tables is a valuable information asset. Using Discoverer, this data can be leveraged to provide information used across the entire spectrum of decision making. This section explains various mechanisms for how your company could use Discoverer to access E-Business Suite.

Trying to query from E-Business Suite can be daunting. To enjoy the benefit, you have to know the database structures, the field names, and how the tables are joined together. Added to this is the fact that Oracle has made its applications flexible. By flexible, we mean it has provided *flexfields*, fields that you can use to customize your database. The use of these fields causes Oracle Applications to dynamically change the screens you use for data entry. This is perfect for your data entry staff, but just how do you query these fields? You don't know which flexfield is being used, and you certainly won't know the rules or list of values.

In an E-Business Suite application, a flexfield consists of a number of segments. Each segment has an assigned name and a set of valid values. E-Business Suite uses flexfields to capture information about your organization. There are two kinds of flexfields.

- **Key flexfields** These are required within E-Business Suite to record key data elements. They are predefined, with each key flexfield being owned by a specific application but being shared across all the applications. The most well-known is the Accounting flexfield, which is owned by the General Ledger (GL) application and is used to represent an organization's chart of accounts. Even though it is owned by GL, it is used across nearly all of the applications. During setup, your organization will choose how to define the key flexfields by deciding how many segments each field uses. For example, one organization may decide to customize the Accounting flexfield to have three segments called Company, Department, and Account, while another organization may need to use five segments called Company, Cost Center, Account, Sub-Account, and Product. Examples of other key flexfields are the Grade flexfield in Human Resources (HR), the Item Categories flexfield in Oracle Inventory, and the Bank Details Key flexfield in Oracle Payroll.
- **Descriptive flexfields** These are user-defined and are used to store additional, required data elements that are not provided by the standard E-Business Suite functionality. Just about every major table in E-Business Suite has these descriptive flexfields. Using them, you can customize the system to capture additional information without the need for additional programming.

When using query and reporting tools against E-Business Suite, issues arise with concern to flexfields and lookup codes. Out of the box, these tools have no way of knowing the techniques that Oracle has used to add this flexibility. For example, if you have used the Vendor tables in the Purchasing module, you will know that SEGMENT1 is used to store your vendor number, and if you are using Inventory, you will know that SEGMENT1 in the Item Master table contains the item number. However, your query tool does not know this, so when you query the PO_VENDORS table, you have to remember to alias it every time, like this:

```
select vend.segment1 vendor_number,
vend.vendor_name
from apps.po_vendors vend
```

In Appendix A we have provided some further simple SQL scripts you can use against Oracle E-Business Suite.

Given that this situation makes for difficult querying, Oracle provides the ability to create views of the data. A *view* is simply a way to pull together data from related tables into one place in an efficient manner. A view knows how to join the tables together and can change the Oracle field names to make them more meaningful to you. Views do not contain any data, though; they are only pointers to the data, but you can access them in Discoverer just as if they were tables.

Most companies use views of the database. Views simplify querying, and they also ensure that the same joins are being made each time, thereby releasing you from having to worry about linking the Oracle tables. Using a combination of views and an end-user query tool such as Discoverer takes away all of the pain and hardship that writing your own queries creates.

Until the late 1990s there was really only one company, Noetix Corporation, that provided a total set of views against the Oracle E-Business Suite. Its product, NoetixViews, is well known and works very well with Discoverer. Several years ago, Oracle developed its own views, called *business views*. They are being phased out. A third option is for your company to build your own views.

We will give you an overview of all three approaches in the next sections.

## E-Business Suite Business Views

Oracle released a set of preseeded views at the same time that the first *Oracle Discoverer Handbook* was being submitted for publication. These views have been incorporated as standard into every single release of E-Business Suite, including the most recent release, 12. Today they are known as Oracle *business views*.

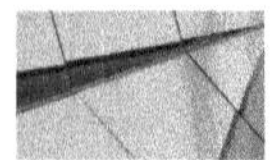

**NOTE**

*Versions 9.2 to 10*g *and 11*g *might cause some column names derived from descriptive flexfields to change when regenerating business views after upgrading the RDBMS to 10*g *or 11*g. *This scenario can also happen when upgrading from Release 11*i *(with the 9.2 RDBMS) to Release 12. While there are no issues with the view content, there may be issues with accessing the views from within Oracle Discoverer folders, custom reports, or custom queries because of changed column names.*

To address the previous issue, a new site-level profile called the Business View Generator Optimizer Mode is used. You can find information on the Web in the Oracle E-Business Suite

Flexfields Guide Release 12.1 at http://docs.oracle.com/cd/E18727_01/doc.121/e12892/T354897T361284.htm.

If you have E-Business Suite, there are nearly 800 Oracle business views, covering virtually all of the modules. Using these views, you can perform ad hoc and custom reporting using Discoverer. Oracle even provides you with prewritten Discoverer business areas and workbooks for use within the business areas. We think this is a wonderful feature.

Oracle business views and Discoverer are two essential components of Oracle's business intelligence offerings. Business views make up a layer of database views relating business entity descriptions for use in ad hoc queries against Oracle Applications data. These views deliver the following three important features:

- The ability to present information at a level that is of interest to business users
- The ability to present information in user-friendly terminology
- The ability to present information with consistency across the various Applications products

Oracle business views come in two flavors: base views and full views. The base views are typically created on a single underlying table or view, perhaps joining two at most. Full views, on the other hand, may point to several underlying tables or views. These full views will, therefore, contain several joins and take slightly longer to query from—as opposed to the base views.

## Security

Another really wonderful feature of business views is that they provide out-of-the-box support for E-Business Suite security, enabling Discoverer to be the only ad hoc query solution on the market with this capability. E-Business Suite has a sophisticated security mechanism, and anyone implementing Discoverer against E-Business Suite using business views can leverage the same security structures. This ensures consistent access control across both the main database and business intelligence systems. All of the user accounts and responsibilities that have been set up in your main E-Business Suite application are available in Discoverer immediately, without any extra setup by your Discoverer administrator.

In particular, you gain the ability to use existing E-Business Suite usernames, passwords, and responsibilities through Discoverer. Oracle Discoverer is fully cognizant of the E-Business Suite security model, and it is capable of returning data that is dependent on the user's user ID and application responsibility combination.

## Cross-Organization Support

Discoverer also provides the same level of multi-organization access control that is available through E-Business Suite. Cross-organization reporting is also supported. With cross-organization reporting support, end users have access to a list of organizations within E-Business Suite, as opposed to a single organization. Discoverer users access the data pertaining to the organizations to which the Applications administrator has granted them access.

E-Business Suite is designed to allow the ability to run reports across multiple organizations captured within your enterprise resource planning (ERP) system. These are distinct operating entities, and up until E-Business Suite release 11 they were implemented via row-level security within most Applications tables and views. Starting with E-Business Suite release 12, Oracle has moved to virtual private database (VPD) technology to secure the views. The concept is the same; however, the operation behind the scenes is different. The new implementation, called Multiple Organizations Access Control (MOAC), is covered in the next section.

Both of these security mechanisms enable E-Business Suite to efficiently store multiple reporting organizations within one set of tables and views.

## Multiple Organizations Access Control

Within E-Business Suite, multiple organizations are managed by the addition of an operating unit column (ORG_ID) to the tables. This column specifies which row in a given table is logically grouped into which organization. The tables that contain multi-org data have the suffix _ALL added to their name with a corresponding secured view created for each table. The Oracle business views in turn then use these secured views.

In E-Business Suite 11 and earlier, whenever an E-Business Suite user logs in with a given user ID and responsibility combination, the system sets up a security mechanism that contains that user's org ID key. Thus, any queries that are run against a secured view will return only a subset of the data in the underlying tables, depending on that user's org ID. If a user wanted to manage data for a different organization, they would need to switch responsibility if working within E-Business Suite or would need to log out and log back in to Discoverer, picking a different responsibility.

If you try and access data from these views using a normal database account you will get no data returned. This is because the security profile is not enabled as part of a standard log in.

When MOAC is enabled and set up, E-Business Suite 12 does not require a user to switch responsibilities as it did in release 11. Instead, the user can use a drop-down to determine which operating unit they are working on. Behind the scenes the user's profile can have multiple allowed Org IDs. If a user has access to more than one operating unit, the user can decide which one should be the default. An operating unit field on the screen will contain a drop-down of the available operating units allowing a user to switch between units without changing responsibilities.

The VPD allows developers to enforce security by attaching a security policy to database tables, views and synonyms. The security adds a predicate function to every SQL statement thereby applying security. For example, if a user only has access to operating unit 5 the following will be added to every SQL statement: AND ORG_ID = 5.

## Oracle Business Views and Discoverer

Oracle business views replace Oracle's Business Intelligence System (BIS), which has been deprecated. The business views make up a performance management system for E-Business Suite, built to work with the proven technology of Oracle Discoverer. When Oracle Discoverer is integrated with the business views, it provides powerful analysis solutions for E-Business Suite. The business views are an integrated set of intelligence modules for financials, purchasing, operations, human resources, and process manufacturing. Each intelligence module comes with prebuilt Discoverer workbooks that provide ad hoc and detailed analysis of critical day-to-day performance measures, calculated from E-Business Suite. Oracle also provides a preseeded E-Business Suite EUL for Discoverer that uses the business views as the underlying objects for reporting.

The E-Business Suite EUL is a complete set of easy-to-understand business definitions that represent E-Business Suite data. The EUL simplifies the entire E-Business Suite database and enables users to quickly create and modify analysis reports in any business area. The Oracle business views are ideal for customers looking for a prepackaged out-of-the-box solution that has comprehensive coverage of almost all the E-Business Suite modules. One big advantage of this solution is that it offers a dramatic time reduction over a "do-it-yourself" approach. Another advantage is that as new releases of E-Business Suite are introduced, the prebuilt, shipped EUL is updated to accommodate these changes, which means less maintenance for you.

For anyone reading this who has Oracle Business Intelligence Enterprise Edition (OBIEE), you will be pleased to know that Oracle Business Intelligence Applications (OBI Apps) is the direct equivalent of the preshipped business views and Discoverer EUL referred to previously.

Many people thought that with the introduction of OBI Apps that Oracle would no longer provide the business views in E-Business Suite 12. This is not the case because the business views and the preseeded Discoverer EUL are both still available for reporting.

### Business Views Performance

We have been asked many times to visit organizations because of poor performance from the business views. Most of them are written really well and perform efficiently; some were not well designed and hence do not perform well. We have noticed that when views use other views that in turn use other views, performance can suffer, particularly when security is being applied at every level.

The way to overcome this, in our opinion, would of course be for Oracle to rewrite the code. However, this is not always possible, and once released the code rarely gets changed unless a bug (in other words, an unwanted, undocumented feature) is encountered. So, what can you do?

Well, we are very pleased that with the onset of E-Business Suite 12*i* that Oracle is beginning to harness VPD security for controlling access. We have seen this done to great effect and have seen performance improve dramatically by hundreds of percentage points at times.

There will also be times when you will want to customize a business view to streamline it to remove links to objects or modules you are not using. We strongly recommend you do not change the original view but rather take a copy of it, customize it, and then give it a new name, preferably using a new schema for your custom code.

**NOTE**

*Oracle will never deliver a table, view, package, function, or schema that begins with the letters XX. We therefore recommend you create a schema using a name like XXCUSTOM and prefix all your custom code with the letters XX. Using prefixes similar to those used by standard Oracle views is dangerous because Oracle could introduce code using the same name as yours, effectively overwriting your code.*

### Flexfield Management

Companies differ from each other in organizational structure and operational procedures. This is obvious through the differences in information systems. To accommodate these different business processes, E-Business Suite is highly customizable and enables customers to set up and configure their OLTP systems in a flexible manner. Descriptive and key flexfields are one of the features of E-Business Suite that provide this type of flexibility. You can set up these flexfields to suit your particular business practices. The architecture of Discoverer supports flexfields. At each customer site, the flexfield customizations are displayed as EUL items within appropriate folders.

Flexfield configuration information is determined once the Discoverer EUL and E-Business Suite business views are installed on your site. Each business view contains placeholders, or tokens, that represent site-specific variable information. These tokens represent the key and descriptive flexfields that you have set up in your system. During the installation and setup process on your site, the Business Views Generator (a new component of the Applications Object Library that is part of Oracle Applications 11*i*) runs, taking as input the "tokenized" views that have been shipped and your specific flexfield configuration.

This program replaces the tokens with columns, derived from the flexfield configuration information, and produces a modified set of views as the output. Discoverer's built-in "refresh" functionality adds the same new columns to the appropriate folders in the EUL. The end result is a complete EUL based on your flexfield customizations, an environment that provides a complete end-user ad hoc query and analysis solution.

### Oracle Help and Guides

Oracle has provided comprehensive information and procedures that are of use to both end users and administrators of Oracle Applications. The guides that are of use to Discoverer users are as follows:

- **BIS 11*i* User Guide Online Help** This guide, in HTML format, is provided as online help from the BIS application and includes information about the various Discoverer workbooks that are available.
- **Oracle Discoverer Administration Guide** This guide provides reference information for your Discoverer administrator. It contains information on how to define security, manage the EUL, create and customize business areas, and manage summary information.
- **Oracle BIS Implementation Guide** This guide contains all information necessary to implement the Oracle Business Intelligence System in your company. It contains an overview of the Discoverer workbooks and worksheets that are provided by the system.

## NoetixViews

NoetixViews converts E-Business Suite data tables into a user-friendly set of business views. Used with Discoverer, NoetixViews delivers a total solution for end-user reporting and ad hoc queries. We have seen NoetixViews in use for several years and can recommend it to anyone considering purchasing a suite of views to use against E-Business Suite 10.7, 11.0, 11*i*,and now 12*i*.

Quoting from Noetix's own documentation, Noetix MetaBuilder technology automatically incorporates the unique configuration of each enterprise application. The software also documents the business metadata of each view and its columns, making search and data understanding faster and easier. It also protects reports from database structural changes inherent with enterprise application upgrades, ensuring established reports remain operational through upgrades and eliminating rework and disruptions by providing metadata consistency across new application releases.

The Noetix MetaBuilder, otherwise known as the Noetix Generator, is available to generate data models not only for Discoverer but also for OBIEE and some of the most popular non-Oracle reporting tools.

Again quoting from Noetix documentation, "As the reporting tool of choice for many business analysts, Oracle Discoverer requires extensive setup of the End User Layer to effectively engage reporting capabilities before users can create and modify reports.

"Noetix Generator significantly reduces the time to implement Oracle Discoverer by automating the process of building and populating Oracle Discoverer with the features and functionality of NoetixViews.

"The extensible End User Layer created by Noetix Generator provides many key reporting benefits, including pre-defined Business Areas, folders, pre-defined joins between folders, item classes, and data drills."

The system uses an autodiscovery process that crawls your specific Oracle E-Business Suite database, generating a set of business views that transforms complex data structures into business intelligence content. Using this technology, Noetix is able to accelerate greatly the deployment of a wide range of BI tools, from custom and ad hoc report development to analytical and dashboard solutions technology.

The Noetix Generator automatically analyzes your application's database looking for customizations that you have made and flexfields that you have set up, creating what Noetix calls a "comprehensive library of metadata." This metadata is presented to you as a series of database views. In these views, Noetix makes data available to you using your business terminology—the terms that you used to set up the system.

For example, let's say you have decided that ATTRIBUTE1 is being used to store the airport name and that ATTRIBUTE2 is being used to store the three-character airport code. NoetixViews will display these fields as Airport_Name and Airport_Code, making it much easier for you to create queries. Another thing that NoetixViews does for you is to remove the complexity of the underlying data structures by making the necessary joins between the base tables for you. Thus, you end up with one view.

The following Oracle E-Business Suite Applications are supported: Financials, Manufacturing, Benefits, Supply Chain, Projects, Human Resources, and Payroll. To identify the business areas or roles, Noetix prefixes the views with a two- or three-letter code indicating which module is being used. For example, BOM indicates Bills of Materials, INV for Inventory, OE for Order Entry, and so on. During the install, NoetixViews examines each set of books, business group, operating unit, or organization and creates a separate role for each. It then appends one or two letters to indicate which organization the view belongs to. Let's say you have three organizations: US for America, EU for Europe, and AF for Africa. Using these codes, BOMUS would be used as the prefix for the Bills of Materials business area for America, while OEAF would be used as the prefix for the Order Entry business area for Africa.

When you open Discoverer, these are the areas that you would look for. Opening one of these business areas displays the folders within. Each folder corresponds to a single view. When you open a folder, you can see the items you need. Noetix uses codes to indicate which items are indexes and which are flexfields. NoetixViews also includes an extensive online help system that is available from both the client and the server. The help system, described later in this section, assists you in finding the right data and how to understand its usefulness.

### Codes Used Within NoetixViews

When you open a folder based on a view that is part of NoetixViews, you will notice the following codes being used:

- **A$** This code is added as a prefix to all columns that are indexed. NoetixViews classifies these columns as Search By columns. You should always select indexed columns when you can and always try to create conditions based on indexed values. Your query will return data much quicker when you do this. Here's an example:
    - A$CUSTOMER is an index based on the customer name.
    - A$SHIP_DATE is an index based on the ship date.

**NOTE**
*Whenever possible, you should always use Search By columns to locate your data. If you do not use these columns, the data will still be located; however, it will take Discoverer much longer. This is because Discoverer has to scan all of the rows in the Oracle table.*

- **$** When you see the dollar symbol embedded inside a column name, this indicates the column is a flexfield. The flexfield can be either an Oracle key flexfield or a descriptive flexfield.

For example, POLIN$Ship_Date is the column associated with the flexfield that you have defined as being the ship date. The word *POLIN* preceding the dollar symbol is a code for the Oracle table that the field is coming from. The word *Ship_Date* following the dollar symbol is the name you have given to one of the flexfields on the purchase order line.

Noetix also provides an excellent help file. The preceding terminology is repeated in the help file so that you can see at a glance the fields in the system.

## NoetixViews Help File

When you install NoetixViews, it builds a context-sensitive help file for you to use. Opening this help file gives you a list of all of the business areas that NoetixViews has created. Clicking a business area allows you to drill down to see a list of the folders that make up that business area. NoetixViews then gives a brief description of each folder and classifies each as being basic, value added, or cross-functional.

These folder types are described as follows:

- **Basic** The folders that are classified as basic draw their information from a single Oracle form or data entry screen. These folders pull their data from a maximum of four tables. Querying from a basic folder is fast.
- **Value added** The folders that are classified as value added draw their information from several forms or data entry screens, but all within the same Oracle module. These folders pull their data from four to eight tables and are slower to query from than basic folders.
- **Cross-functional** The folders that are classified as cross-functional draw their information from forms or entry screens across two or more Oracle modules. These folders pull their data from eight to fourteen tables and are by far the slowest to query from.

Each view contains hints to give you the quickest and most efficient access to your data. These hints tell you how to choose the best columns upon which to apply conditions. Using these hints to build a query is a fast way of getting up and running.

The list of column names uses the same dollar codes outlined earlier in this section. In addition, you may also see columns prefixed by *Z$*. These are joins to other views and indicate what Discoverer folders will be active should you decide to select a column from this view.

## Tips for Using NoetixViews with Discoverer

You can help yourself in a number of ways to write efficient Discoverer queries when using NoetixViews. The following are tips we recommend you follow:

- Have the NoetixViews help file open on your desktop.
- Look at the hints given in the help file for clues on how to build queries. When a hint states that you need to apply a certain condition on an item, you should always do so.
- Try to query from basic folders whenever possible.
- Try to use Search By columns whenever possible.

- Always try to apply conditions on the Search By columns.
- Try not to join to more than four other folders in the same query, and even then try to use only basic folders.

### NoetixViews Customization Certification

To meet the need of custom reporting requirements, it is possible to customize the views. Modifying aspects of a view—for example, by adding columns, tables, and where clauses—requires proper training and certification from Noetix. NoetixViews Customization Certification (NVCC) is an instructor-led training course offered by Noetix. This course provides students with the knowledge and skills necessary to efficiently create customizations. Further, if you are certified to customize the NoetixViews, your customizations will be supported by Noetix. However, if you are not certified, any changes you make to the views will be unsupported, and you could easily make a mess of your whole reporting system. Our recommendation, therefore, is to take the course.

### EUL Generator from Noetix Corporation

The Noetix EUL Generator is a companion tool that can be used to populate the End User Layer of Discoverer, allowing minimal administration of NoetixViews business areas.

The following are the tasks that the EUL Generator takes care of:

- Business area creation
- Security
- Item classes
- Sorts
- Hierarchies

### Why Use NoetixViews?

During the course of our consultations, we are frequently asked why companies should use NoetixViews. We reply, "You mean apart from the fact that they are superbly coded and work out of the box?" We sometimes hear this: "We cannot afford to buy NoetixViews, so what should we do?" To this we answer as follows: "If you have Oracle E-Business Suite and you do not have the means to develop your own, you cannot afford not to use NoetixViews!"

When you install NoetixViews, each Oracle E-Business Suite module comes with between 30 and 50 views. Even if you can replicate the code inside each view, all in one day, it will take you between 30 and 50 workdays to write your own views. This excludes the amount of time and effort required to build a Discoverer business area of these 30 to 50 interlinked views. So, let's allow another two weeks of development effort for each business area, bringing the effort to between 8 and 12 weeks.

What happens if you have ten modules? This will take you 80 to 120 weeks of effort. Would you really want to make your users wait a year or two to get at the data? Of course not, which is why we say that, in many cases, NoetixViews is the only game in town. Here are a few more points for you to consider:

- We are not on commission from Noetix. Our recommendation is based purely upon experience.

- If you are using multiple organizations and multiple currencies, you can double or triple the time estimates just given.
- If you write your own views, you need to retain the services of at least one developer.

## Company-Built Views

Probably the easiest way to get a quick view of the database is to get someone from your IT department to build a SQL script. Most companies use SQL. If you are lucky enough to have experienced IT staff, fluent in the complexities of writing SQL scripts, you probably already have a number of existing queries you use today.

To use these scripts, either you have your IT department run them for you or you log in to the database and run them yourself. The big disadvantage of this approach is that you cannot quickly modify the script, and you can't use it for ad hoc reporting.

However, it takes only a small step further to turn these scripts into views. Then you have your Discoverer administrator create a new folder based on the view and *voilà*! There you have converted a SQL script into a Discoverer folder. Now you, and everyone else who has access to the folder, can create ad hoc queries.

Another thing to consider when it comes to creating your own custom views is database optimization. Even though your Discoverer administrator has the ability to add a database hint to any of the folders that are based on a database object, we have rarely seen this used to good effect. If you are having difficulty with the performance of a complex folder within Discoverer, you ought to give serious consideration to converting these complex folders into database views. You can then insert powerful optimization hints into the view to force the database to pull the data in the most efficient way. The optimization hints that you can provide within a view are far more potent than you could ever provide from within Discoverer. We have seen occurrences of nonoptimized views and Discoverer complex folders taking ten or more minutes to pull the data, with a modified view containing database hints running in only a matter of seconds.

## Embedded Data Warehouse

Continuing from the previous section, you can extend your views by creating new tables within the E-Business Suite database, populating this as needed, and pointing Discoverer at the resulting objects. So, why are we pushing an embedded data warehouse as opposed to a traditional data warehouse? That's a very good question. We will explain.

When we wrote the first editions of the *Discoverer Handbook*, we made no reference to an embedded data warehouse. This was not an omission on our part but a deliberate decision not to encourage you to try it. You see, until relatively recently, adding additional processing to the E-Business Suite database had a negative impact on performance. This is because most of the servers that we saw in production were sized to handle only production E-Business Suite traffic. Anything else would bring the system to its knees, especially running a reporting system like Discoverer.

What changed? Over the last few years we noticed a significant reduction in hardware prices and an even more significant reduction in the cost of memory. Companies are no longer scrimping on servers and memory, and E-Business Suite is being run on much more powerful machines than ever before. Additional memory modules for even the most advanced of servers are now only hundreds of dollars as opposed to a couple of thousand dollars only five years ago.

With this improvement in hardware, the need to have a data warehouse on a separate machine has virtually been done away with for all but the largest volumes of data. Chapter 2 outlines the benefits and drawbacks of having a data warehouse. One of the most important features that an embedded data warehouse must have is to comply with the rule that it does not impact the OLTP production system. The advancements in technology have progressed to the point where we now wholeheartedly encourage customers to go with an embedded data warehouse as opposed to a traditional data warehouse on a separate server.

In a moment, we will list some of the advantages of an embedded data warehouse that are over and above the advantages listed in Chapter 2. However, as a recap, these are the advantages of a data warehouse:

- It is optimized for reporting.
- It contains historical data.
- It does not impact the OLTP system.
- It has meaningful table names.
- It is not subject to change.
- You can perform data mining ("Tell me something I don't already know").
- It contains data from multiple sources, not just your OLTP system.

These are some of the advantages that an embedded data warehouse has in addition to those listed previously:

- There is no need for additional hardware.
- There is no need for a second database license.
- Discoverer can drill directly to the source tables.
- There is no need for any database links.
- You can use objects from the E-Business Suite database within the embedded data warehouse, such as the following:
  - Using EBS base tables to generate lists of values
  - Joining to EBS base tables and views within Discoverer
- You can use the EBS concurrent manager to run your jobs.
- You can use EBS security within the data warehouse, thus preserving data integrity.
- If you are using any of the EBS seeded views or prebuilt Discoverer objects, you can add the embedded data warehouse into the same EUL.

We hope this list encourages you to at least consider using an embedded data warehouse. We have successfully created several of them over the past few years and know for certainty that customers approve. The following are the applications we have personally created embedded data warehouses for so know for sure that they lend themselves well to embedded data warehousing:

- Advanced pricing
- Benefits
- HR and payroll
- Inventory
- Order entry

- Purchasing
- Work in progress

The reason we say that these are ideal candidates is that there are lots of tables in all of these applications, many of which can be hooked in directly.

We are frequently asked about how we go about starting an embedded data warehouse. More often than not, a customer will show us an E-Business Suite screen and tell us that what the users want is a report of the data contained within the screen.

A tip we will pass on to you is to use the E-Business Suite help functionality. Clicking Help followed by Diagnostics and selecting Examine will cause E-Business Suite to prompt for your Oracle password. You will need to get this from your administrator, and generally only the Discoverer administrator or DBA will be given this.

Having entered the Oracle password, you will be presented with the following Examine Field and Variable Values window, as shown here shown at right.

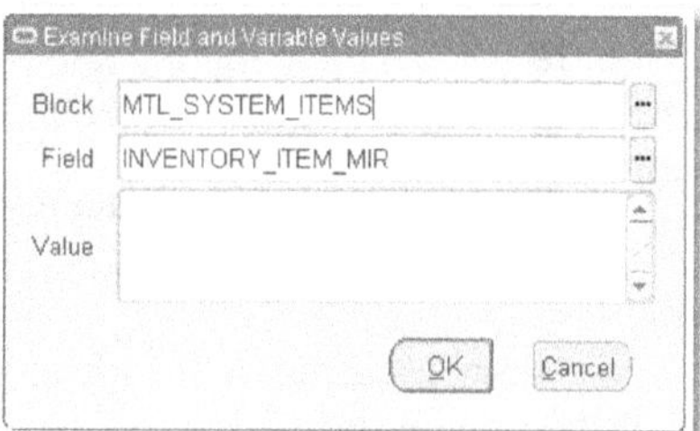


This window has the following three areas:

- Block
- Field
- Value

Rather than try to explain what these do, which is an exercise in itself, we'll just talk about how you go about finding the SQL that was used to generate the data on the form. In the Block field, click the pop-up button. The pop-up button is signified by a small area with three periods. The following Choose a block window will be displayed:

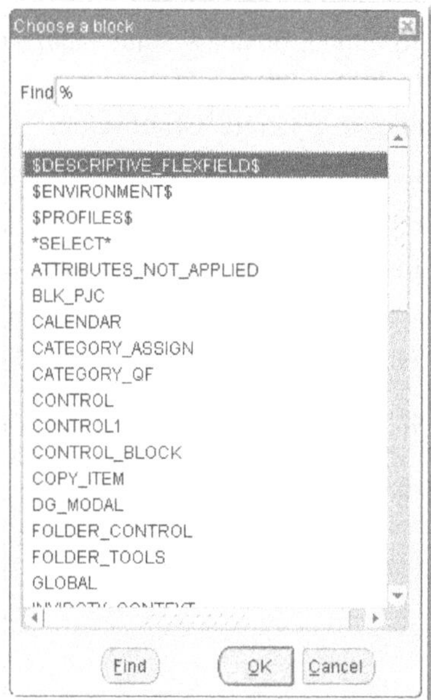

In the Choose a block window, hit the s key. You will either be returned to the Examine Field and Variable Values window with the Block area prefilled with the word *System* or be presented with a list of all the blocks that begin with *S*. In the latter case, you choose System and then click the OK button. The Field and Variable Values window will now look like this:

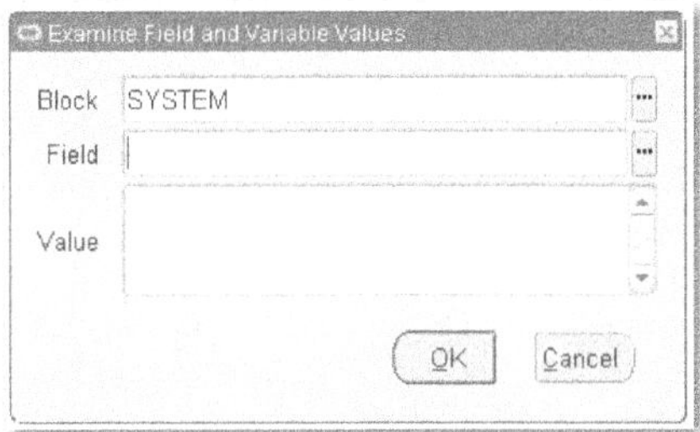


Click the pop-up next to Field. The Choose a field window will be displayed.

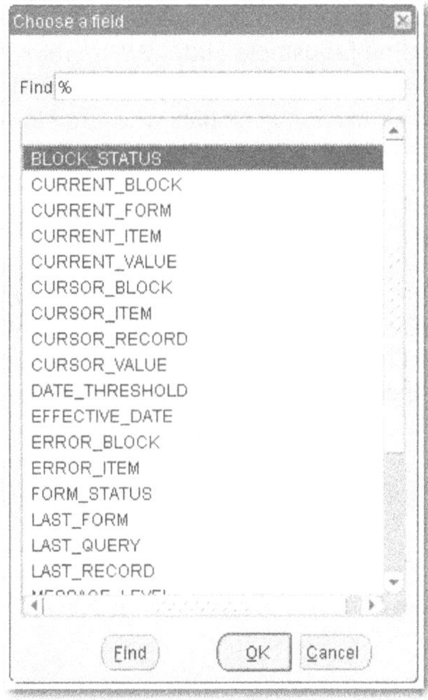

In the Choose a field window, hit the L key. This will generate a list of all the fields that begin with *L*. Choose the option called LAST_QUERY and hit the OK button. The Examine Field and Variable Values window will now look like this:

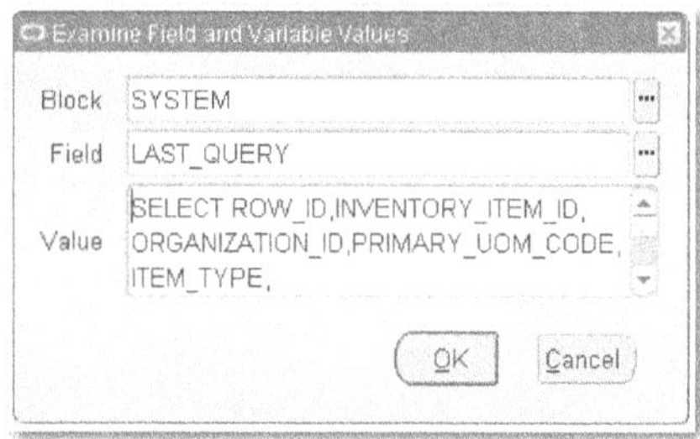


As you can see, Oracle has displayed the SQL that it used to generate the data in the form. You can use this code as the basis for an object in the embedded data warehouse. This is by far the quickest and easiest way to determine how E-Business Suite populated a form.

You will appreciate that this is a Discoverer book and as such is not intended to be a manual for navigating and understanding E-Business Suite. We therefore will not go into great depth about the workings of the system. However, it is safe to say that the tip we have just given you is one of the most widely used tricks known to developers who want to see what code was used to populate an E-Business Suite form.

# Summary

This appendix explained several database concepts. We began by explaining the difference between traditional schemas, relational schemas, and star schemas. Following this, we took an in-depth look at normalization and denormalization. We explained why views are used and introduced you to Oracle's business views. We then took an in-depth look at Noetix Corporation's NoetixViews. Finally, we discussed using an embedded data warehouse within the same database as E-Business Suite and closed by providing a tip that shows you how to find out what SQL Oracle is using to populate an E-Business Suite form.

# APPENDIX D

# Tutorial Database

This appendix contains an entity-relationship diagram (ERD) of the tutorial database used in this book. It also contains all table names, including primary keys, foreign keys, and the majority of the data items. For small tables, we show you all of the values. For the larger tables, such as Sales and Day, we can show you only an extract because of space limitations.

# Entity-Relationship Diagram for the Global Widgets Sales Database

The following is the ERD for the Global Widgets tutorial database:

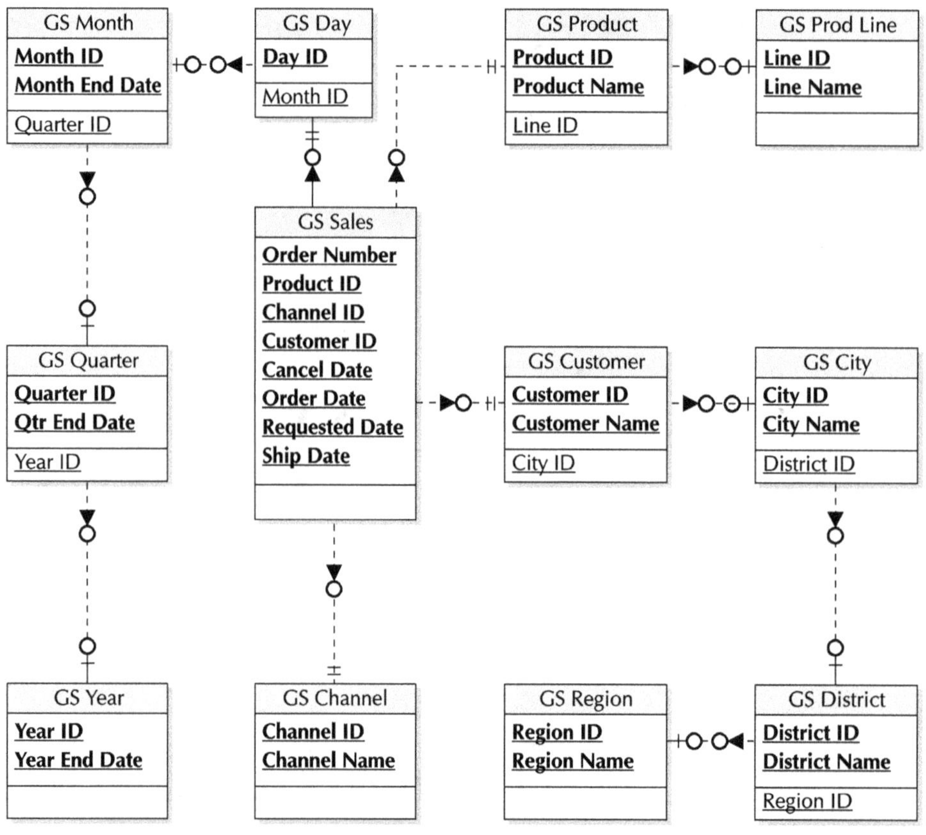

**NOTE**

*If you are familiar with data modeling, you will notice that this is almost a star schema. To convert this model into a star schema, you could move the region, district, and city data into the Customer table; move the product lines into the Product table; and create a new fiscal timetable using the day, month, quarter, and year.*

# The Global Widgets Tables

The following 12 tables are the tables used in the Global Widgets tutorial database:

- **GS Sales** The Sales Fact table
- **GS Channel** Sales Channel
- **GS Products** Products
- **GS Prodline** Product Lines
- **GS Customer** Customer Master
- **GS City** City locations for our customers
- **GS District** Sales Districts
- **GS Region** Sales Regions
- **GS Day** Used for Order Date, Requested Date, Cancelled Date, and Ship Date
- **GS Month** Fiscal months
- **GS Quarter** Fiscal quarters
- **GS Year** Fiscal years

## GS Sales

This is a fact table and is the main table used in the Global Widgets database. All of the aggregations, costs, and quantities are pulled from this table. The Sales Fact table has the following primary key and foreign keys:

- **ORDID** Primary key
- **CUSTID** Foreign key, links to the Customer table
- **PRODID** Foreign key, links to the Product table
- **CHANNELID** Foreign key, links to the Sales Channel table
- **ORDERDATE** Foreign key, links to the Date table
- **REQDATE** Foreign key, links to the Date table
- **CANCELDATE** Foreign key, links to the Date table
- **SHIPDATE** Foreign key, links to the Date table

The following table shows an extract from the Sales table for some orders that were received in June 2013. For clarity the REQDATE is not shown.

| ORDID | CUSTID | PRODID | CHANNELID | ORDER DATE | SHIP DATE | STATUS |
|---|---|---|---|---|---|---|
| 12460 | 13 | 22 | 2 | 6/11/2013 | 6/12/2013 | SHIPPED |
| 12461 | 14 | 23 | 2 | 6/11/2013 | 6/12/2013 | SHIPPED |
| 12462 | 4 | 42 | 2 | 6/11/2013 | 6/12/2013 | SHIPPED |
| 12463 | 7 | 45 | 1 | 6/11/2013 | 6/12/2013 | SHIPPED |

| ORDID | CUSTID | PRODID | CHANNELID | ORDER DATE | SHIP DATE | STATUS |
|---|---|---|---|---|---|---|
| 12464 | 31 | 62 | 2 | 6/11/2013 | 6/12/2013 | SHIPPED |
| 12465 | 1 | 67 | 2 | 6/11/2013 | 6/12/2013 | SHIPPED |
| 12466 | 12 | 21 | 2 | 6/11/2013 | 6/11/2013 | SHIPPED |
| 12467 | 13 | 14 | 1 | 6/12/2013 | 6/17/2013 | SHIPPED |
| 12468 | 17 | 12 | 1 | 6/12/2013 | 6/15/2005 | SHIPPED |
| 12469 | 11 | 22 | 2 | 6/12/2013 | OPEN | |
| 12470 | 15 | 63 | 2 | 6/12/2013 | OPEN | |
| 12471 | 8 | 46 | 2 | 6/12/2013 | OPEN | |
| 12472 | 33 | 21 | 2 | 6/13/2013 | OPEN | |
| 12473 | 38 | 41 | 2 | 6/13/2013 | OPEN | |

## GS Channel

This is the table for the sales channel. It has the following primary key:

- **CHANNELID** Primary key

| CHANNELID | NAME |
|---|---|
| 1 | EXTERNAL |
| 2 | INTERNET |

## GS Products

This is the table for the products. It has the following primary and foreign keys:

- **PRODID** Primary key
- **LINEID** Foreign key, links to the Product Line folder

| PRODID | NAME | PRODSIZE | COST | PRICE | LINEID |
|---|---|---|---|---|---|
| 11 | DS-1200 | MINI | 3.85 | 5.35 | 4 |
| 12 | MS-1200 | MINI | 3.95 | 5.55 | 4 |
| 13 | MS-1300 | MINI | 4.10 | 6.00 | 4 |
| 14 | DS-1300 | MINI | 4.02 | 5.95 | 4 |
| 21 | AB-2000 | SMALL | 7.22 | 13.5 | 1 |
| 22 | AB-2500 | SMALL | 5.99 | 12.75 | 2 |
| 23 | AB-3000 | SMALL | 9.88 | 21.25 | 3 |
| 41 | QB-5000 | MEDIUM | 8.33 | 17.66 | 1 |
| 42 | QB-5500 | MEDIUM | 8.33 | 17.66 | 1 |
| 43 | QB-6000 | MEDIUM | 8.33 | 17.66 | 1 |

| PRODID | NAME | PRODSIZE | COST | PRICE | LINEID |
|---|---|---|---|---|---|
| 44 | CD-100 | MEDIUM | 6.21 | 15.25 | 2 |
| 45 | CD-200 | MEDIUM | 6.21 | 15.25 | 2 |
| 46 | AVR-500 | MEDIUM | 11.48 | 26.95 | 3 |
| 47 | AVR-550 | MEDIUM | 11.48 | 26.95 | 3 |
| 61 | QB-1000 | LARGE | 12.42 | 23.45 | 1 |
| 62 | QB-2000 | LARGE | 12.42 | 23.45 | 1 |
| 63 | QB-3000 | LARGE | 12.42 | 23.45 | 1 |
| 64 | CD-500 | LARGE | 10.62 | 22.18 | 2 |
| 65 | CD-550 | LARGE | 10.62 | 22.18 | 2 |
| 66 | CD-625 | LARGE | 10.62 | 22.18 | 2 |
| 67 | AVR-800 | LARGE | 15.94 | 34.65 | 3 |
| 68 | AVR-900 | LARGE | 15.94 | 34.65 | 3 |

## GS Prodline

This is the table for the product lines. It has the following primary key:

- **LINEID** Primary key

| LINEID | NAME |
|---|---|
| 1 | WONDER-WIDGET |
| 2 | MEGA-WIDGET |
| 3 | SUPER-WIDGET |
| 4 | MINI-WIDGET |

## GS Customer

This is the table for the customers. It has the following primary and foreign keys:

- **CUSTID** Primary key
- **CITYID** Foreign key, links to the City table

The following extract shows the first 12 customers and their associated CITYID:

| CUSTID | NAME | CITYID |
|---|---|---|
| 1 | CEBU WIDGET CO | 1 |
| 2 | WONDER WIDGETS | 2 |
| 3 | WIDGETS ON THE WEB | 8 |
| 4 | WIDGETS DE MEXICO | 13 |
| 5 | MUM'S WIDGET CO | 3 |
| 6 | WIDGETS BY THE BAY | 2 |

| CUSTID | NAME | CITYID |
|---|---|---|
| 7 | CASA DE WIDGETS | 9 |
| 8 | THING'S | 14 |
| 9 | WIDGETS R US | 2 |
| 10 | WIDGET O THE MERSEY | 3 |
| 11 | HONG KONG WIDGETS | 16 |
| 12 | WIDGETS MARKET | 2 |

## GS City

This is the table for the cities. It has the following primary and foreign keys:

- **CITYID** Primary key
- **DISTRICTID** Foreign key, links to the District table

The following extract shows all of the cities and their associated DISTRICTID:

| CITYID | NAME | DISTRICTID | COUNTRYCODE |
|---|---|---|---|
| 1 | MANILA | 6 | PH |
| 2 | SAN FRANCISCO | 1 | US |
| 3 | LIVERPOOL | 3 | GB |
| 4 | LISBON | 4 | PT |
| 5 | RIO DE JANEIRO | 5 | BR |
| 6 | LONDON | 3 | GB |
| 7 | PARIS | 3 | FR |
| 8 | ROME | 4 | IT |
| 9 | MADRID | 4 | ES |
| 10 | DENVER | 1 | US |
| 11 | PHILADELPHIA | 1 | US |
| 12 | QUEBEC | 1 | CA |
| 13 | MEXICO CITY | 2 | MX |
| 14 | SAO PAULO | 5 | BR |
| 15 | TOKYO | 6 | JP |
| 16 | HONG KONG | 6 | HK |
| 17 | SEOUL | 6 | KR |
| 18 | GENEVA | 3 | CH |
| 19 | ATLANTA | 2 | US |
| 20 | DALLAS | 2 | US |
| 21 | NEW YORK | 2 | US |

| CITYID | NAME | DISTRICTID | COUNTRYCODE |
|---|---|---|---|
| 22 | LIMA | 5 | PE |
| 23 | WARSAW | 7 | PL |
| 24 | KANSAS CITY | 2 | US |
| 25 | BOCA RATON | 2 | US |
| 26 | SANTIAGO | 5 | CL |
| 27 | COOKEVILLE | 2 | US |

## GS District

This is the table for the districts. It has the following primary and foreign keys:

- **DISTRICTID** Primary key
- **REGIONID** Foreign key, links to the Region table

| DISTRICTID | NAME | REGIONID |
|---|---|---|
| 1 | NA-NORTH | 1 |
| 2 | NA-SOUTH | 1 |
| 3 | EU-NORTH | 2 |
| 4 | EU-SOUTH | 2 |
| 5 | SA-ALL | 3 |
| 6 | FE-ALL | 4 |
| 7 | EU-EAST | 2 |

## GS Region

This is the table for the regions. It has the following primary key:

- **REGIONID** Primary key

| REGIONID | NAME |
|---|---|
| 1 | NORTH AMERICA |
| 2 | EUROPE |
| 3 | SOUTH AMERICA |
| 4 | FAR EAST |

## Fiscal Time

The tutorial database uses a set of tables to define the fiscal time used by the system. There is one date table, but it is joined to the Sales folder four times, once each for Order, Requested, Cancelled, and Ship Date. The Day table is joined to the Month table, which in turn is joined to the Quarter table, which is finally joined to the Year table. Using these relationships, we are able to build time hierarchies for each of the dates in the Sales folder.

## GS Day

This is the table for the dates. It has the following primary and foreign keys:

- **DAYID** Primary key
- **MONTHID** Foreign key, links to the Month table

In the following extract from the GS Day table, we show the dates used in late August and early September 2013. You will see how the fiscal month changes on August 31.

| DAYID | MONTHID |
|---|---|
| 8/23/2013 | AUG-13 |
| 8/24/2013 | AUG-13 |
| 8/25/2013 | AUG-13 |
| 8/26/2013 | AUG-13 |
| 8/27/2013 | AUG-13 |
| 8/28/2013 | AUG-13 |
| 8/29/2013 | AUG-13 |
| 8/30/2013 | AUG-13 |
| 8/31/2013 | SEP-13 |
| 9/1/2013 | SEP-13 |
| 9/2/2013 | SEP-13 |
| 9/3/2013 | SEP-13 |

## GS Month

This is the table for the months. It has the following primary and foreign keys:

- **MONTHID** Primary key
- **QUARTERID** Foreign key, links to the Quarter table

In the following extract from the GS Month table, we show the months used in calendar year 2012. You will see how the fiscal quarter and month end dates change.

| MONTHID | ENDDATE | SEQUENCENO | QUARTERID |
|---|---|---|---|
| JAN-12 | 1/27/2012 | 76 | 2012-Q2 |
| FEB-12 | 2/24/2012 | 77 | 2012-Q2 |
| MAR-12 | 3/30/2012 | 78 | 2012-Q2 |
| APR-12 | 4/27/2012 | 79 | 2012-Q3 |
| MAY-12 | 5/25/2012 | 80 | 2012-Q3 |
| JUN-12 | 6/29/2012 | 81 | 2012-Q3 |
| JUL-12 | 7/27/2012 | 82 | 2012-Q4 |
| AUG-12 | 8/31/2012 | 83 | 2012-Q4 |

| MONTHID | ENDDATE | SEQUENCENO | QUARTERID |
|---|---|---|---|
| SEP-12 | 9/28/2012 | 84 | 2012-Q4 |
| OCT-12 | 10/26/2012 | 85 | 2013-Q1 |
| NOV-12 | 11/30/2012 | 86 | 2013-Q1 |
| DEC-12 | 12/28/2012 | 87 | 2013-Q1 |

## GS Quarter

This is the table for the quarters. It has the following primary and foreign keys:

- **QUARTERID** Primary key
- **YEARID** Foreign key, links to the Year table

In the following extract from the GS Quarter table, we show the quarter used in fiscal years 2011, 2012, and 2013. You will see how the fiscal year and quarter end dates change.

| QUARTERID | ENDDATE | YEARID |
|---|---|---|
| 2011-Q1 | 12/31/2010 | FY2011 |
| 2011-Q2 | 3/25/2011 | FY2011 |
| 2011-Q3 | 6/24/2011 | FY2011 |
| 2011-Q4 | 9/30/2011 | FY2011 |
| 2012-Q1 | 12/30/2011 | FY2012 |
| 2012-Q2 | 3/30/2012 | FY2012 |
| 2012-Q3 | 6/29/2012 | FY2012 |
| 2012-Q4 | 9/28/2012 | FY2012 |
| 2013-Q1 | 12/28/2012 | FY2013 |
| 2013-Q2 | 3/29/2013 | FY2013 |
| 2013-Q3 | 6/28/2013 | FY2013 |
| 2013-Q4 | 9/27/2013 | FY2013 |

## GS Year

This is the table for the years. It has the following primary key:

- **YEARID** Primary key

In the following extract from the GS Year table, we show the years 2006 to 2013. You will see how the start dates change.

| YEARID | ENDDATE |
|---|---|
| FY2006 | 9/29/2006 |
| FY2007 | 9/28/2007 |
| FY2008 | 9/26/2008 |

| YEARID | ENDDATE |
|---|---|
| FY2009 | 9/25/2009 |
| FY2010 | 9/24/2010 |
| FY2011 | 9/30/2011 |
| FY2012 | 9/28/2012 |
| FY2013 | 9/27/2013 |

# Entity-Relationship Diagram for the Fan Trap

The following is the ERD for the Fan Trap tutorial database.

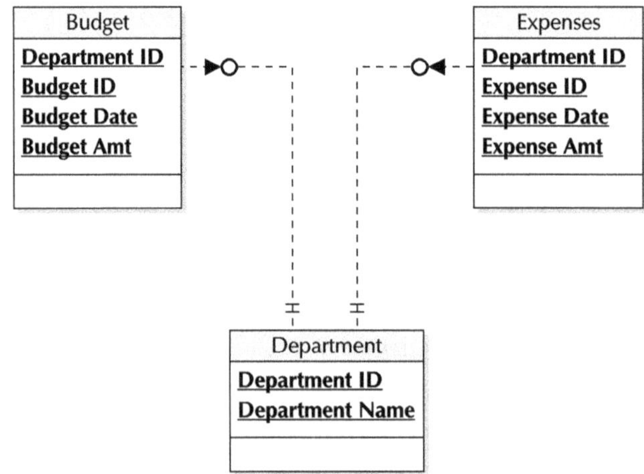


# The Fan Trap Tables

The following three tables are used in the Fan Trap tutorial database:

- **FAN Department** Department Master
- **FAN Expenses** An example table of expense data
- **FAN Budget** An example table of budget data

## FAN Department

This is the table for the departments. It has the following primary key:

- **DEPTNO** Primary key

| DEPTNO | DEPTNAME |
|---|---|
| 10 | SALES |
| 20 | HR |

| DEPTNO | DEPTNAME |
|---|---|
| 30 | MIS |
| 40 | MARKETING |
| 50 | TRAINING |

## FAN Budget

This is the table for the budgets. It has the following primary and foreign keys:

- **BUDGETID** Primary key
- **DEPTNO** Foreign key, links to the Department table

| BUDGETID | DEPTNO | AMOUNT | REASON | BGT_DATE |
|---|---|---|---|---|
| 1 | 10 | 5000 | EQUIPMENT | 3/19/2012 |
| 2 | 20 | 2000 | EQUIPMENT | 3/21/2012 |
| 3 | 30 | 25500 | EQUIPMENT | 4/15/2012 |
| 4 | 40 | 4250 | EQUIPMENT | 2/24/2012 |
| 5 | 50 | 2090 | EQUIPMENT | 2/24/2012 |
| 6 | 10 | 40000 | TRAVEL | 3/20/2012 |
| 7 | 20 | 200 | TRAVEL | 3/21/2012 |
| 8 | 30 | 10000 | TRAVEL | 4/15/2012 |
| 9 | 40 | 25000 | TRAVEL | 2/24/2012 |
| 10 | 50 | 200 | TRAVEL | 2/24/2012 |

## FAN Expenses

This is the table for the expenses. It has the following primary and foreign keys:

- **EXPENSEID** Primary key
- **DEPTNO** Foreign key, links to the Department table

| EXPENSEID | DEPTNO | EXPENSES | EXP_DATE |
|---|---|---|---|
| 1 | 10 | 150 | 2/25/2012 |
| 2 | 10 | 250 | 4/16/2012 |
| 3 | 10 | 1000 | 4/28/2012 |
| 4 | 20 | 1025 | 4/12/2012 |
| 5 | 30 | 12000 | 4/28/2012 |
| 6 | 40 | 2750 | 4/26/2012 |

## Summary

In this appendix, we showed you an entity-relationship diagram of the tutorial database covered in the book. We hope that, using this appendix, you will be able to fully understand our tutorial database and get a "look and feel" for the data. You can find a copy of this tutorial database available for download on our website at http://ascbi.com.

# Index

## B



## C

## D

## E

## G

## H



## I

## J



## K



## L

## M

## N



## O

## P

## Q

## R

## S

## T



## U

## V

## W